GERMAN

ENGLISH-GERMAN
GERMAN-ENGLISH

Stephen Jones

HIPPOCRENE BOOKS, INC.

New York

Trademarks

The symbol® designates entered words that we have reason to believe constitute trademarks. However, neither the presence or absence of such designation should be regarded as affecting the legal status of any trademark.

First Hippocrene Edition, 1983

©Laurence Urdang Associates, 1982.

Revised Hippocrene Edition with larger type, 1995.

Glossary of Menu Terms and special American usage entries ©Hippocrene Books, 1983.

ISBN 0-7818-0355-1

For information, address:
HIPPOCRENE BOOKS, INC.
171 Madison Avenue
New York, NY 10016
Printed in the United States of America.

Abbreviations/Abkürzungen

acc accusative, Akkusativ
adj adjective, Adjektiv
adv adverb, Adverb
anat anatomy, Anatomie
arch architecture, Architektur
art article, Artikel
astrol astrology, Astrologie
astron astronomy, Astronomie
biol biology, Biologie
bot botany, Botanik
chem chemistry, Chemie
coll colloquial,
    umgangssprachlich
comm commerce, Kommerz
dat dative, Dativ
derog derogatory, geringschätzig
elec electricity, Elektrizität
f feminine, Femininum
fig figurative, figürlich
gen genitive, Genetiv
geog geography, Erdkunde
gramm grammar, Grammatik
impol impolite, unhöflich
interj interjection, Ausruf
Jur Jura, Rechtswesen, law
Komm Kommerz, commerce
m masculine, Maskulinum
math mathematics, Mathematik
mech mechanics, machine,
    Mechanik
med medicine, Medizin

mil military, militärisch
mot motoring, Kraftfahrzeuge
n noun, Hauptwort, Substantiv
naut nautical, Schiffahrt
neut neuter, Neutrum
phone telephone, Telefon
phot photography, Photographie
pl plural, Plural
pol politics, Politik
poss possessive, possessiv
prep preposition, Präposition
pron pronoun, Pronomen,
    Fürwort
psychol psychology, Psychologie
rail railways, Eisenbahn
rel religion, Religion
Schiff Schiffahrt, nautical
sing singular, Singular, Einzahl
tech technical, Technik
Telef Telefon, telephone
TV television, Fernsehen
umg. umgangssprachlich,
    colloquial
univ university, Universität
unz. unzählbar, mass noun
US American, Amerikanisch
v verb, Verbum, Zeitwort
V vide (see, siehe)
Wissensch Naturwissenschaft,
    science
zool zoology, Zoologie

German pronunciation

a bald [balt]
a: sagen ['zaːgən]
e Telefon [teleˈfoːn]
e: nehmen ['neːmən]
ɛ Geld [gɛlt]
ɛ: Bär [bɛːr]
i Idee [iˈdeː]
iː bieten ['biːtən]
ɔ Holz [hɔlts]
o Rosette [roˈzɛtə]
oː Mohn [moːn]
u bunt [bunt]
uː Schnur [ʃnuːr]
y fünf [fynf]
yː kühl [kyːl]
ə Butter ['butər]
œ böse ['bœzə]
œː Möbel ['mœbəl]
ai bei [bai]
au Haus [haus]
ɔy Freund [frɔynt]
ã Chance ['ʃãːsə]
ɛ̃ Terrain [tɛˈrɛ̃ː]
ɔ̃ Champignon ['ʃampinjɔ̃]

b Bad [baːt]
d Dank [daŋk]
f Frau [frau]
g gut [guːt]
h halb [halp]
j ja [jaː]
k Kind [kint]
l Lied [liːt]
m Mensch [mɛnʃ]
n neu [nɔy]
p Person [pɛrˈzoːn]
r Rad [raːt]
s falls [fals]
t Gerät [gəˈrɛːt]
v Wein [vain]
z Reise ['raizə]
ç ich [iç]
x Buch [buːx]
ʃ Schuh [ʃuː]
ʒ Garage [gaˈraːʒə]
ŋ lang [laŋ]

The sign ' precedes a syllable having primary stress.

Aussprache auf Englisch

a hat [hat]
e bell [bel]
i big [big]
o dot [dot]
ʌ bun [bʌn]
u book [buk]
ə alone [ə'loun]
a: card [ka:d]
ə: word [wə:d]
i: team [ti:m]
o: torn [to:n]
u: spoon [spu:n]
ai die [dai]
ei ray [rɛi]
oi toy [toi]
au how [hau]
ou road [roud]
eə lair [leə]
iə fear [fiə]
uə poor [puə]

b back [bak]
d dull [dʌl]
f find [faind]
g gaze [geiz]
h hop [hop]
j yell [jel]
k cat [kat]
l life [laif]
m mouse [maus]
n night [nait]
p pick [pik]
r rose [rouz]
s sit [sit]
t toe [tou]
v vest [vest]
w week [wi:k]
z zoo [zu:]
θ think [θiŋk]
ð those [ðouz]
ʃ shoe [ʃu:]
ʒ treasure ['treʒə]
tʃ chalk [tʃo:k]
dʒ jump [dʒʌmp]
ŋ sing [siŋ]

Das Zeichen ' steht vor einer Silbe mit Hauptbetonung.
Das Zeichen , steht vor einer Silbe mit Nebenbetonung.

Guide to the dictionary

English irregular plural forms are shown at the headword and in the text. The following categories of plurals forms are considered regular:

cat	cats
glass	glass**es**
fly	fl**ies**
half	hal**ves**
wife	wi**ves**

German plurals are shown for most words (for example, **Gemälde**) but not for many compounds (for example, **Wandgemälde**). The label *pl -* indicates that the plural does not vary.

Where no gender is shown for a German noun, it may be masculine or feminine, for example **Abgeordnete(r)**. Adjectival nouns are shown by -(**r**) or -(**s**), the final letter being used according to the article, for example: **der Abgeordnete, ein Abgeordneter, die Abgeordnete, eine Abgeordnete, Abgeordnete** (*pl*).

Under a German headword, a sub-entry may be shown preceded by a dash. The full form may be obtained by adding the sub-entry to the nearest preceding full word, less that part after the vertical strokes, if any. Thus, **außerhalb** is shown as follows:

außer‖dem *adv* besides. **-halb** *adv*, *prep* outside.

Irregular verbs listed in the verb tables are marked with an asterisk in the body of the dictionary.

Many English adverbs are not shown in the dictionary if they are regularly formed, that is, by the addition of -(*al*)*ly* to the adjective.

Leitfaden für das Wörterbuch

Englische unregelmäßige Plurale sind bei dem Stichwort und im Text gezeigt. Die folgenden Kategorien von Pluralformen sind als regelmäßig anzusehen:

cat	cats
glass	glasses
fly	flies
half	halves
wife	wives

Deutsche Plurale sind für die meisten Wörter angeführt (z.B. Gemälde), aber nicht für viele zusammengesetzte Wörter (z.B. Wandgemälde). Das Zeichen *pl* - deutet an, daß der Plural mit dem Singular identisch ist.

Wo kein Geschlecht für ein deutsches Hauptwort angegeben ist, kann es sowohl männlich als auch weiblich sein, z.B. **Abgeordnete(r)**. Hauptworte, die aus Adjektiven gebildet sind, sind folgendermaßen gekennzeichnet -(**r**) oder -(**s**), wobei der letzte Buchstabe von dem Artikel abhängt, z.B. **der Abgeordnete, ein Abgeordneter, die Abgeordnete, eine Abgeordnete, Abgeordnete** (*pl*).

Hinter einem deutschen Stichwort, findet man öfter eine weitere Eintragung hinter einem Strich. Das komplette Wort erhält man durch Hinzufügen dieses Wortes an das vorherige Wort ohne den Teil hinter die Vertikalen, wenn nötig. So ist z.B. **außerhalb** wie folgt gezeigt:

außer‖dem *adv* besides. **-halb** *adv*, *prep* outside.

Unregelmäßige Verben, die in der separaten Liste aufgeführt sind, sind mit einem Sternchen (*) bei den Stichwörtern angezeigt.

Viele englische Adverbien sind in dem Wörterbuch nicht aufgeführt, wenn sie aus den Adjektiven regelmäßig durch die Nachsilbe -(*al*)*ly* gebildet sind.

German irregular verbs

Infinitive	Preterite	Past Participle
backen	backte (buk)	gebacken
bedingen	bedang (bedingte)	bedungen
befehlen	befahl	befohlen
beginnen	begann	begonnen
beißen	biß	gebissen
bergen	barg	geborgen
bersten	barst	geborsten
bewegen	bewog	bewogen
biegen	bog	gebogen
bieten	bot	geboten
binden	band	gebunden
bitten	bat	gebeten
blasen	blies	geblasen
bleiben	blieb	geblieben
bleichen	blich	geblichen
braten	briet	gebraten
brauchen	brauchte	gebraucht (brauchen)
brechen	brach	gebrochen
brennen	brannte	gebrannt
bringen	brachte	gebracht
denken	dachte	gedacht
dreschen	drosch	gedroschen
dringen	drang	gedrungen
dürfen	durfte	gedurft
empfehlen	empfahl	empfohlen
erkiesen	erkor	erkoren
erlöschen	erlosch	erloschen
erschrecken	erschrak	erschrocken
essen	aß	gegessen
fahren	fuhr	gefahren
fallen	fiel	gefallen
fangen	fing	gefangen
fechten	focht	gefochten
finden	fand	gefunden
flechten	flocht	geflochten
fliegen	flog	geflogen

Infinitive	Preterite	Past Participle
fliehen	floh	geflohen
fließen	floß	geflossen
fressen	fraß	gefressen
frieren	fror	gefroren
gären	gor	gegoren
gebären	gebar	geboren
geben	gab	gegeben
gedeihen	gedieh	gediehen
gehen	ging	gegangen
gelingen	gelang	gelungen
gelten	galt	gegolten
genesen	genas	genesen
genießen	genoß	genossen
geschehen	geschah	geschehen
gewinnen	gewann	gewonnen
gießen	goß	gegossen
gleichen	glich	geglichen
gleiten	glitt	geglitten
glimmen	glomm	geglommen
graben	grub	gegraben
greifen	griff	gegriffen
haben	hatte	gehabt
halten	hielt	gehalten
hängen	hing	gehangen
hauen	haute (hieb)	gehauen
heben	hob	gehoben
heißen	hieß	geheißen
helfen	half	geholfen
kennen	kannte	gekannt
klimmen	klomm	geklommen
klingen	klang	geklungen
kneifen	kniff	gekniffen
kommen	kam	gekommen
können	konnte	gekonnt
kriechen	kroch	gekrochen
laden	lud	geladen
lassen	ließ	gelassen (lassen)
laufen	lief	gelaufen

Infinitive	Preterite	Past Participle
leiden	litt	gelitten
leihen	lieh	geliehen
lesen	las	gelesen
liegen	lag	gelegen
lügen	log	gelogen
mahlen	mahlte	gemahlen
meiden	mied	gemieden
melken	melkte (molk)	gemolken (gemelkt)
messen	maß	gemessen
mißlingen	mißlang	mißlungen
mögen	mochte	gemocht
müssen	mußte	gemußt
nehmen	nahm	genommen
nennen	nannte	genannt
pfeifen	pfiff	gepfiffen
preisen	pries	gepriesen
quellen	quoll	gequollen
raten	riet	geraten
reiben	rieb	gerieben
reißen	riß	gerissen
reiten	ritt	geritten
rennen	rannte	gerannt
riechen	roch	gerochen
ringen	rang	gerungen
rinnen	rann	geronnen
rufen	rief	gerufen
salzen	salzte	gesalzen (gesalzt)
saufen	soff	gesoffen
saugen	sog	gesogen
schaffen	schuf	geschaffen
schallen	schallte (scholl)	geschallt
scheiden	schied	geschieden
scheinen	schien	geschienen
sheißen	schiß	geschissen
schelten	schalt	gescholten
scheren	schor	geschoren
schieben	schob	geschoben
scheißen	schoß	geschossen
schinden	schund	geschunden

Infinitive	Preterite	Past Participle
schlafen	schlief	geschlafen
schlagen	schlug	geschlagen
schleichen	schlich	geschlichen
schleifen	schliff	geschliffen
schleißen	schliß	geschlissen
schließen	schloß	geschlossen
schlingen	schlang	geschlungen
schmeißen	schmiß	geschmissen
schmelzen	schmolz	geschmolzen
schnauben	schnob	geschnoben
schneiden	schnitt	geschnitten
schreiben	schrieb	geschrieben
schreien	schrie	geschrie(e)n
schreiten	schritt	geschritten
schweigen	schwieg	geschwiegen
schwellen	schwoll	geschwollen
schwimmen	schwamm	geschwommen
schwinden	schwand	geschwunden
schwingen	schwang	geschwungen
schwören	schwor	geschworen
sehen	sah	gesehen
sein	war	gewesen
senden	sandte	gesandt
sieden	sott	gesotten
singen	sang	gesungen
sinken	sank	gesunken
sinnen	sann	gesonnen
sitzen	saß	gesessen
sollen	sollte	gesollt (sollen)
spalten	spaltete	gespalten (gespaltet)
speien	spie	gespie(e)n
spinnen	spann	gesponnen
sprechen	sprach	gesprochen
sprießen	sproß	gesprossen
springen	sprang	gesprungen
stechen	stach	gestochen
stecken	steckte (stak)	gesteckt
stehen	stand	gestanden
stehlen	stahl	gestohlen

Infinitive	Preterite	Past Participle
steigen	stieg	gestiegen
sterben	starb	gestorben
stieben	stob	gestoben
stinken	stank	gestunken
stoßen	stieß	gestoßen
streichen	strich	gestrichen
streiten	stritt	gestritten
tragen	trug	getragen
treffen	traf	getroffen
treiben	trieb	getrieben
treten	trat	getreten
triefen	triefte (troff)	getrieft
trinken	trank	getrunken
trügen	trog	getrogen
tun	tat	getan
verderben	verdarb	verdorben
verdrießen	verdroß	verdrossen
vergessen	vergaß	vergessen
verlieren	verlor	verloren
verschleißen	verschliß	verschlissen
verzeihen	verzieh	verziehen
wachsen	wuchs	gewachsen
wägen	wog (wägte)	gewogen (gewägt)
waschen	wusch	gewaschen
weben	wob	gewoben
weichen	wich	gewichen
weisen	wies	gewiesen
wenden	wandte	gewandt
werben	warb	geworben
werden	wurde	geworden (worden)
werfen	warf	geworfen
wiegen	wog	gewogen
winden	wand	gewunden
wissen	wußte	gewußt
wollen	wollte	gewollt (wollen)
wringen	wrang	gewrungen
zeihen	zieh	geziehen
ziehen	zog	gezogen
zwingen	zwang	gezwungen

Unregelmäßige Verben

Infinitive	Präteritum	Partizip Perfekt
abide	abode	abode
arise	arose	arisen
awake	awoke	awoke
be	was	been
bear	bore	borne *or* born
beat	beat	beaten
become	became	become
begin	began	begun
bend	bent	bent
bet	bet	bet
beware		
bid	bid	bidden *or* bid
bind	bound	bound
bite	bit	bitten
bleed	bled	bled
blow	blew	blown
break	broke	broken
breed	bred	bred
bring	brought	brought
build	built	built
burn	burnt *or* burned	burnt *or* burned
burst	burst	burst
buy	bought	bought
can	could	
cast	cast	cast
catch	caught	caught
choose	chose	chosen
cling	clung	clung
come	came	come
cost	cost	cost
creep	crept	crept
cut	cut	cut
deal	dealt	dealt
dig	dug	dug
do	did	done
draw	drew	drawn
dream	dreamed *or* dreamt	dreamed *or* dreamt

Infinitive	Präteritum	Partizip Perfekt
drink	drank	drunk
drive	drove	driven
dwell	dwelt	dwelt
eat	ate	eaten
fall	fell	fallen
feed	fed	fed
feel	felt	felt
fight	fought	fought
find	found	found
flee	fled	fled
fling	flung	flung
fly	flew	flown
forbid	forbade	forbidden
forget	forgot	forgotten
forgive	forgave	forgiven
forsake	forsook	forsaken
freeze	froze	frozen
get	got	got
give	gave	given
go	went	gone
grind	ground	ground
grow	grew	grown
hang	hung *or* hanged	hung *or* hanged
have	had	had
hear	heard	heard
hide	hid	hidden
hit	hit	hit
hold	held	held
hurt	hurt	hurt
keep	kept	kept
kneel	knelt	knelt
knit	knitted *or* knit	knitted *or* knit
know	knew	known
lay	laid	laid
lead	led	led
lean	leant *or* leaned	leant *or* leaned
leap	leapt *or* leaped	leapt *or* leaped
learn	learnt *or* learned	learnt *or* learned
leave	left	left

Infinitive	Präteritum	Partizip Perfekt
lend	lent	lent
let	let	let
lie	lay	lain
light	lit *or* lighted	lit *or* lighted
lose	lost	lost
make	made	made
may	might	
mean	meant	meant
meet	met	met
mow	mowed	mown
must		
ought		
pay	paid	paid
put	put	put
quit	quitted *or* quit	quitted *or* quit
read	read	read
rid	rid	rid
ride	rode	ridden
ring	rang	rung
rise	rose	risen
run	ran	run
saw	sawed	sawn *or* sawed
say	said	said
see	saw	seen
seek	sought	sought
sell	sold	sold
send	sent	sent
set	set	set
sew	sewed	sewn *or* sewed
shake	shook	shaken
shear	sheared	sheared *or* shorn
shed	shed	shed
shine	shone	shone
shoe	shod	shod
shoot	shot	shot
show	showed	shown
shrink	shrank	shrunk
shut	shut	shut
sing	sang	sung

Infinitive	Präteritum	Partizip Perfekt
sink	sank	sunk
sit	sat	sat
sleep	slept	slept
slide	slid	slid
sling	slung	slung
slink	slunk	slunk
slit	slit	slit
smell	smelt *or* smelled	smelt *or* smelled
sow	sowed	sown *or* sowed
speak	spoke	spoken
speed	sped *or* speeded	sped *or* speeded
spell	spelt *or* spelled	spelt *or* spelled
spend	spent	spent
spill	spilt *or* spilled	spilt *or* spilled
spin	spun	spun
spit	spat	spat
split	split	split
spread	spread	spread
spring	sprang	sprung
stand	stood	stood
steal	stole	stolen
stick	stuck	stuck
sting	stung	stung
stink	stank *or* stunk	stunk
stride	strode	stridden
strike	struck	struck
string	strung	strung
strive	strove	striven
swear	swore	sworn
sweep	swept	swept
swell	swelled	swollen *or* swelled
swim	swam	swum
swing	swung	swung
take	took	taken
teach	taught	taught
tear	tore	torn
tell	told	told
think	thought	thought

Infinitive	Preterite	Past Participle
throw	threw	thrown
thrust	thrust	thrust
tread	trod	trodden
wake	woke	woken
wear	wore	worn
weave	wove	woven
weep	wept	wept
win	won	won
wind	wound	wound
wring	wrung	wrung
write	wrote	written

Glossary of menu terms

There is lots to eat in German-speaking countries: five meals a day are about standard, and there's plenty of scope for snacks — especially nice when traveling with children. **Frühstück** (breakfast) is usually light, perhaps coffee or chocolate and bread; **Zweites Frühstück** (second breakfast) is more serious and will probably feature food that seems like a U.S.-style light lunch. But in the middle of the day comes **Mittagessen** (lunch) which is usually the main meal of the day. In late afternoon, there is **Kaffee mit Kuchen** (coffee and cake and a lot more), and finally **Abendbrot** (supper).

German cuisine is based on the foods the countries produce. Expect to eat simple, hearty food quite fresh from the farm. In Austria, the influence of Hungarian cooking provides some diversion, and in German Switzerland, the French and Italian neighbors have left a pleasing mark. Game is often featured; it is certainly worth trying.

There are many designations in German for establishments which serve food. In large towns, most common is **Restaurant** (the German word is **Gaststätte**); in the country, you will find **Gasthaus** or **Gasthof**. A **Bierstube** or **Weinstube** will serve some food as well as beer or wine, rather like an English pub. Restaurants usually offer full meals, but the menu may not be broken into courses or types of food (appetizers, first courses, meat dishes, fish, etc.). Most restaurants offer one or more **Gedeck** (fixed-priced meal), usually including soup, entrée with one or more vegetable, and a light dessert, no substitutions or additions permitted. These meals are often excellent values. Be sure to tell the waiter that you are having the set meal before you order.

Hotel dining rooms generally offer good **Kaffee mit Kuchen,** but if you are away from your hotel, try a **Café** or **Konditorei.** These places are also good for a light breakfast or a snack at almost any time.

By law, German eating places must list all charges, including service, on the menu in the price of each item. It is still customary, however, to leave a small tip, perhaps 5%, on the table.

Vorspeisen (Hors d'Oeuvre)

Beefsteak Tartar raw ground beef served with raw egg and onion
Bismarckhering pickled herring with onion and spices
Eiersalat egg salad
Froschschenkel frogs' legs
Gänseleber goose liver
Käsebrot open-faced cheese sandwich
Kaviar caviar
Lachsbrot open-faced salmon sandwich
Lachsalm slices of smoked salmon
Ochsenzungesalat salad of sliced tongue
Rollmops bits of smoked herring with mustard, onion, and pickle
Westfälischer Schinken raw cured ham from Westphalia

Würste (Sausages)

Blutwurst blood sausage
Bratwurst grilled pork sausage (spiced)
Knackwurst (or **Knockwurst**) sausage of pork or beef, rather like our hot dog
Leberwurst liver sausage
Wienerwurst Vienna sausage, on the order of small hot dogs
Weisswurst white veal sausage flavored with herbs (a specialty of Munich)

Eierspeisen (Egg Dishes)

Omelette omelette, served plain (**natur**) or with various stuffings (**gefüllt**), e.g.:
mit Champignons with mushrooms;
mit Fines Herbes with herbs, as parsley, tarragon, chives; **mit Geflügelleber**

with chicken livers; **mit Schinken** with ham; **Spanisches** with tomato and onion sauce
Pfannkuchen a sort of egg pancake, also served plain (**natur**) or stuffed (**gefüllt**): **mit Käse** with cheese; **mit Schinken** with ham; **mit Speck** with bacon
Pochierte Eier poached eggs
Rührei scrambled eggs
Spiegeleier (or **Setzeier**) fried eggs
Weichgekochte Eier soft-cooked eggs
Wachsweiche Eier medium-cooked eggs

Fischgerichte (Seafood)

Aal eel
Austern oysters
Dorsch codfish
Forellen trout
Hecht pike
Heilbutt halibut
Hummer lobster
Jacobsmuscheln scallops, coquilles
Krabben shrimp; for the larger shrimp, Germans usually use the Italian word **scampi**
Schellfisch haddock
Seezunge sole; prepared in many different ways in Germany: fried, baked, in various sauces, etc.

Suppen (Soups)

Bauernsuppe "peasant soup": mixed vegetable soup
Biersuppe soup of beer with spices
Bohnensuppe bean soup
Brühe broth: **Fleischbrühe**, meat broth; **Geflügelbrühe**, chicken broth; **Fischbrühe**, fish broth
Champignonrahmsuppe cream of mushroom soup
Kartoffelsuppe potato soup
Leberknödelsuppe dumplings of chopped liver, onion, and spices, in broth
Linsensuppe lentil soup
Nudelsuppe mit Huhn chicken noodle soup
Tomatensuppe tomato soup
Zwiebelsuppe onion soup

Hauptgerichte (Main meat Dishes)

Bauernschmaus "the peasant's delight": platter of bacon, sausages, sauerkraut, mashed potatoes, and dumplings
Burgunderschinken ham cooked in wine sauce with vegetables
Cordon Bleu slices of veal with ham and cheese dipped in batter and fried
Deutsches Beefsteak fried ground beef, with onion rings and potatoes (Note: the term "steak" on German menus often denotes what an American would call Salisbury steak, or hamburger; for something more like the American idea of steak, see **Lendensteak**)
Eisbein pickled ham hocks with sauerkraut and mashed potatoes
Filet Goulasch "Beef Stroganoff": strips of beef cooked in sour cream with onions and mushrooms
Frikadellen fried meat balls
Gulyas (Austria) goulash; spicy stew
Hackrahmsteak ground meat patty in browned cream gravy
Hammelkeule roast leg of lamb
Hammelkotelette lamb chop, grilled
Hasenpfeffer stew of pieces of hare, marinated in wine and spices, then cooked in the marinade with onions and mushrooms
Kalbsbrust Gefüllte mit Geflügelleber breast of veal, rolled and stuffed with chicken livers, ham, etc.
Kalbshirn mit Rührei calf brains with scrambled eggs
Kalbskotelette veal chop, grilled
Kalbsleber mit Zwiebeln calf liver with onions
Kalbsmilch sweetbreads
Kalbsschnitzel veal cutlet; see also **Wienerschnitzel**
Königsberger Klops large meat balls served in a sour cream sauce with capers
Lendensteak tenderloin steak (usually offered with a variety of sauces; if you prefer plain, ask for **"natur"**
Pfeffersteak steak coated with ground

peppercorns and grilled
Rehbraten roast venison; **Rehrücken** saddle of venison
Rostbraten roast beef (Germany); minute steak (Austria)
Roulades thin slices of veal rolled and stuffed with a variety of stuffings and garnishes
Sauerbraten roast beef marinated with wine and spices and vinegar, then pot-roasted with vegetables
Schmorbraten pot roast
Schnitzel usually a thin-sliced pan-fried veal cutlet; but sometimes pork (**Schweineschnitzel**) or other meat; prepared in a number of different ways, associated with different areas, as **Holsteinerschnitzel** (topped with a fried egg), **Schwäbischeschnitzel** (with sour cream sauce), and, the most famous, **Wienerschnitzel** (breaded, with a lemon slice and various other garnishes)
Schweinefüsse pigs' feet
Schweinekotelette pork chop: **natur** (plain) or with a variety of sauces
Schweinslendchen pork tenderloin
Ungarischer Gulasch chunks of meat cooked with paprika, onions, and other vegetables
Wiener Rostbraten beef loin fried in butter with onions

Geflügel und Wild (Fowl and Game)

Backhuhn or **Brathuhn** fried chicken
Damwildkeule roast leg of venison
Fasan im Topf pheasant roasted in casserole
Förstertopf mit Pilzen casserole of venison with mushrooms
Frikassee vom Huhn fricasséed chicken
Gansbraten roast goose
Geflügelleber chicken livers
Geflügelragout chicken stew
Kapaun capon
Puterbraten roast turkey
Rebhuhn partridge
Rehbraten roast venison

Rehrücken saddle of venison
Supreme vom Masthuhn boned breast of chicken
Wiener Backhuhn chicken Vienna style: breaded and deep fried with parsley.
Wildschweinbraten roast of wild boar

Gemüse und Beilagen (Vegetables and Side dishes)

Apfelrotkohl or **-kraut** red cabbage cooked with apples
Artischockenhertzen artichoke hearts
Aubergine eggplant
Beete beets
Blumenkohl cauliflower
Dicke Bohnen broad beans (fava)
Erbsen peas
Grüne Bohnen green beans
Gurkensalat cucumber salad
Karotten carrots
Kartoffeln potatoes, the most common accompaniment to the meat dish in Germany; some of the more common ways they are listed on the menu: **Bratkartoffeln** potatoes boiled, sliced and pan-fried; **Gebackene Kartoffeln** baked potatoes; **Herzoginkartoffeln** ''dutchess'' potatoes: mashed, shaped and browned in oven; **Kartoffelknödel** potato dumplings; **Kartoffelpuffer** potato pancakes; **Pommes Frites** French-fried potatoes; **Würfelkartoffeln** fried diced potatoes
Kartoffelsalat German potato salad, served either hot (**heiss**), sautéed onions and bacon poured over sliced boiled potatoes with vinegar dressing; or cold (**kalt**), with vinegar dressing poured over sliced potatoes and chopped onions
Kohl cabbage
Krautsalat coleslaw
Lattich lettuce
Möhren carrots
Nudeln noodles
Obstsalat fruit salad
Pilzen mushrooms
Rosenkohl Brussel sprouts

Salatplatte salad; may indicate anything from a simple green salad to more elaborate affairs including vegetables, meats, and a variety of dressings
Spätzle short thick noodles often served with meat dishes; preparation varies from area to area
Spinat spinach
Steckrübe turnips
Succini zucchini
Zwiebeln onions

Süssspeisen (Desserts)

Apfelstrudel mixture of apples and spices rolled in very thin pastry and baked
Apfelsinen oranges
Arme Ritter a sort of French toast; bread dipped in batter and fried
Auflauf souffle; the German version may be heavier than the French
Eierschaum whipped custard of egg yolks and sugar, flavored with wine, similar to Italian zabaione
Eis or **Eiskrem** ice cream; may be served in a bowl (**Eisbecher**) with various syrups or fruit toppings; in German Switzerland, **Glace**
Eistorte ice cream cake
Englischer Kuchen pound cake
Erdbeeren strawberries
Haselnussrahm hazelnut cream

Himbeeren raspberries
Käsetorte cheesecake
Königskuchen "King's cake": rum-flavored layer cake with almonds, currants, and raisins
Mohrenkopf "Moor's head": dome-shaped cake filled with custard or whipped cream and topped with chocolate
Pfirsichen peaches
Schokoladencremetorte chocolate layer cake filled with a rich chocolate cream

Getränke (Beverages)

Apfelsinesaft orange juice
Bier beer; **Oktoberbier** is the dark beer enjoyed at the *Oktoberfest*
Himbeersaft raspberry juice; very popular with children
Kaffee coffee; in Austria often served **mit Schlag** or in Germany, **mit Schlagsahne** (whipped cream)
Kirsch brandy distilled from cherries
Kümmel caraway-seed-flavored liqueur
Milch milk
Mineralwasser mineral water
Schnapps brandy
Schokolade chocolate, usually served hot
Tee tea
Wasser water; **Eiswasser** ice water

English—Deutsch

A

a, an [ə, ən] *art* ein *m*, eine *f*, ein *neut*. *once a year* einmal im Jahr. *50 kilometres an hour* 50 Kilometer pro Stunde.
aback [ə'bak] *adv* **taken aback** verblüfft, überrascht.
abandon [ə'bandən] *v* (*leave*) verlassen; (*give up*) aufgeben. *n* **with abandon** ungezwungen. **abandoned** *adj* verfallen.
abashed [ə'baʃt] *adj* verlegen.
abate [ə'beit] *v* abnehmen.
abattoir ['abətwaɪ] *n* Schlachthaus *neut*.
abbey ['abi] *n* *Abtei f*. **abbess** *n* Äbtissin *f*.
abbot *n* Abt *m*.
abbreviate [ə'briɪvieit] *v* (ab)kürzen. **abbreviation** *n* Abkürzung *f*.
abdicate ['abdikeit] *v* abdanken. **abdication** *n* Abdankung *f*.
abdomen ['abdəmən] *n* Bauch *m*, Unterleib *m*. **abdominal** *adj* Leib-, abdominal.
abduct [əb'dʌkt] *v* entführen. **abduction** *n* Entführung *f*.
aberration [abə'reiʃən] *n* Abweichung *f*; (*optics, astron*) Aberration *f*. **mental aberration** Geistesverirrung *f*.
abet [ə'bet] *v* begünstigen, Vorschub leisten (+ *dat*).
abeyance [ə'beiəns] *n* **in abeyance** in der Schwebe.
abhor [əb'hoɪ] *v* hassen, verabscheuen. **abhorrence** *n* Abscheu (vor) *m*. **abhorrent** *adj* abscheulich.
***abide** [ə'baid] *v* bleiben, verweilen; (*tolerate*) ausstehen. **abide by** festhalten an.
ability [ə'biləti] *n* Fähigkeit *f*; (*skill*) Geschicklichkeit *f*. **to the best of one's ability** nach besten Kräften.
abject [abdʒekt] *adj* (*wretched*) elend; (*contemptible*) verächtlich, gemein.

ablaze [ə'bleiz] *adj*, *adv* brennend, in Flammen. **set ablaze** entflammen.
able ['eibl] *adj* fähig; (*talented*) geschickt, begabt. **be able** können, fähig sein; (*be in a position to*) in der Lage sein. **ably** *adv* geschickt.
abnormal [ab'noɪml] *adj* anormal, abnorm; (*unusual*) ungewöhnlich; (*malformed*) mißgestaltet. **abnormality** *n* Abnormität *f*; Mißbildung *f*.
aboard [ə'boɪd] *adj*, *adv* (*ship*) an Bord. **go aboard** an Bord gehen, einsteigen.
abode [ə'boud] *V* **abide**. *n* Wohnsitz *m*.
abolish [ə'boliʃ] *v* abschaffen, beseitigen.
abominable [ə'bominəbl] *adj* scheußlich. **abominate** *v* verabscheuen. **abomination** *n* Abscheu *m*.
aborigine [abə'ridʒini] *n* Ureinwohner *m*. **aboriginal** *adj* Ur-, ursprünglich.
abortion [ə'boɪʃən] *n* (*miscarriage*) Fehlgeburt *f*; (*termination of pregnancy*) Abtreibung *f*. **abortive** *adj* mißlungen.
abound [ə'baund] *v* im Überfluß vorhanden sein. **abound in** reich sein an.
about [ə'baut] *adv* (*approximately*) ungefähr, etwa; (*nearby*) in der Nähe. *prep* (*concerning*) über; (*around*) um ... herum. **be about to do something** eben etwas tun wollen. **walk about** hin- und herlaufen.
above [ə'bʌv] *prep* über. *adv* oben. **above-mentioned** oben erwähnt, obig. **above board** offen, ehrlich.
abrasion [ə'breiʒən] *n* Abschleifen *neut*, Abrieb *m*; (*wound*) Abschürfung *f*. **abrasive** *adj* abschleifend.
abreast [ə'brest] *adv* **keep abreast of** Schritt halten mit.
abridge [ə'bridʒ] *v* (ab)kürzen. **abridgement** *n* Abkürzung *f*.
abroad [ə'broɪd] *adv* (*go*) ins Ausland; (*be*) im Ausland.

abrupt [ə'brʌpt] *adj* (*sudden*) plötzlich; (*brusque*) kurz, unhöflich.

abscess ['abses] *n* Abszeß *m*.

abscond [əb'skond] *v* flüchten.

absent ['absənt] *adj* abwesend. **absent-minded** geistesabwesend. **absentee** *n* Abwesende(r). **absence** *n* Abwesenheit *f*; (*lack*) Mangel *m*.

absolute ['absəluːt] *adj* völlig, vollkommen, absolut; (*unconditional*) bedingungslos; (*pure*) rein. **absolutely** *adv* völlig; (*interj*) gewiß! **absolutism** n Absolutismus *m*.

absolve [əb'zolv] *v* entbinden, freisprechen.

absorb [əb'zoːb] *v* aufsaugen, absorbieren. **absorbed in thought** in Gedanken vertieft. **absorbent** *adj* absorbierend. **absorbent cotton** Watte *f*. **absorbing** *adj* fesselnd.

abstain [əb'stein] *v* (*voting*) seine Stimme enthalten. **abstain from** verzichten auf. **abstinence** *n* Enthaltsamkeit *f*.

abstemious [əb'stiːmiəs] *adj* mäßig, enthaltsam.

abstract ['abstrakt] *adj* abstrakt, theoretisch. **abstraction** *n* Abstraktion *f*.

absurd [əb'səːd] *adj* unsinnig, lächerlich. **absurdity** *n* Unsinn *m*.

abundance [ə'bʌndəns] *n* Überfluß *m*, Reichtum *m*. **abundant** *adj* reichlich. **abundant in** reich an.

abuse [ə'bjuːz; *n* ə'bjuːs] *v* mißbrauchen; (*insult*) beleidigen. *n* Mißbrauch *m*; Beschimpfung *f*. **abusive** *adj* beleidigend.

abyss [ə'bis] *n* Abgrund *m*. **abysmal** *adj* abgrundtief; (*fig*) grenzenlos.

academy [ə'kadəmi] *n* Akademie *f*; (*private school*) Internat *m*. **academic** *adj* akademisch.

accede [ak'siːd] *v* (*agree*) zustimmen (+*dat*), (*join*) beitreten (+*dat*); (*throne*) besteigen.

accelerate [ək'seləreit] *v* (*mot*) gasgeben; (*make quicker*) beschleunigen; (*go faster*) schneller werden. **acceleration** *n* Beschleunigung *f*. **accelerator** *n* Gaspedal *neut*.

accent ['aksənt] *n* Akzent *m*. **accentuate** *v* betonen.

accept [ək'sept] *v* akzeptieren, annehmen; (*agree*) zusagen (+*dat*). **acceptable** *adj* annehmbar. **acceptance** *n* Annahme *f*.

access ['akses] *n* Zutritt *m*, Zugang *m*. **accessible** *adj* erreichbar.

accessory [ak'sesəri] *n* (*mot*) Zubehörteil *m*; (*law*) Mitschuldige(r).

accident ['aksidənt] *n* (*mishap*) Unfall *m*; (*chance*) Zufall *m*. **accidental** *adj* zufällig.

acclaim [ə'kleim] *v* zujubeln (+*dat*). *n* (*also* acclamation) Beifall *m*, Lob *neut*.

acclimatize [ə'klaimətaiz] *v* angewöhnen, akklimatisieren.

accolade ['akəleid] *n* Auszeichnung *f*.

accommodate [ə'komədeit] *n* (*put up*) unterbringen; (*help*) aushelfen. **accommodating** *adj* hilfreich. **accommodation** *n* Unterkunft *f*.

accompany [ə'kʌmpəni] *v* begleiten. **accompaniment** *n* Begleitung *f*. **accompanist** *n* Begleiter(in).

accomplice [ə'kʌmplis] *n* Mittäter *m*.

accomplish [ə'kʌmpliʃ] *v* vollbringen, vollenden. **accomplished** *adj* gebildet, gewandt. **accomplishment** *n* Durchführung, Vollendung *f*.

accord [ə'koːd] *v* übereinstimmen. *n* Übereinstimmung *f*, Einklang *m*. **of one's own accord** freiwillig. **in accordance with** gemäß (+*dat*): *in accordance with the rules* den Regeln gemäß. **accordingly** *adv* dementsprechend, deswegen. **according to** laut (+*gen*).

accordion [ə'koːdiən] *n* Akkordeon *neut*.

accost [ə'kost] *v* ansprechen.

account [ə'kaunt] *n* (*bill*) Rechnung *f*; (*bank, etc*) Konto *neut*; (*report*) Bericht *m*. **accounts** *pl n* Bücher *pl*. **current account** Scheckkonto *neut*. **savings account** Sparkonto *neut*. **on account** auf Konto. **on account of** wegen (+*gen*), auf Grund (+*gen*). **on no account** auf keinen Fall. **take into account** berücksichtigen. *v* **account for** erklären. **accountable** *adj* verantwortlich. **accountant** *n* Buchhalter *m*.

accrue [ə'kruː] *v* auflaufen.

accumulate [ə'kjuːmjuleit] *v* anhäufen, sich häufen. **accumulation** *n* Anhäufung *f*.

accurate ['akjurət] *adj* genau, exakt; (*correct*) richtig. **accuracy** *n* Genauigkeit *f*.

accuse [ə'kjuːz] *v* anklagen. **the accused** der/die Angeklagte(r). **accusation** *n* Anklage *f*. **accusative** *n* Akkusativ *m*.

accustom [ə'kʌstəm] *v* **become accustomed to** sich gewöhnen an. **accustomed** *adj* gewöhnlich, üblich.

ace [eis] *n* (*cards*) As *neut*. *adj* (*coll*) erstklassig.

ache [eik] *n* Schmerz *m. v* schmerzen, weh tun.

achieve [ə'tʃiːv] *v* durchführen, vollbringen; (*reach*) erlangen. **achievement** *n* Vollendung *f*, (*success*) Erfolg *m*.

acid ['asid] *n* Säure *f. adj* sauer.

acknowledge [ək'nolidʒ] *n* anerkennen; (*admit*) zugeben. **acknowledge receipt** Empfang bestätigen. **acknowledgment** *n* Anerkennung *f*.

acne ['akni] *n* Pickel *m*, Akne *f*.

acorn ['eikoːn] *n* Eichel *f*.

acoustic [ə'kuːstik] *adj* akustisch. **acoustics** *pl n* Akustik *f sing*.

acquaint [ə'kweint] *v* bekannt machen. **be acquainted with** kennen (+*acc*). **get acquainted with** kennenlernen (+*acc*). **acquaintance** *n* Bekannte(r).

acquiesce [akwi'es] *v* sich fügen. **acquiescence** *n* Ergebung *f*. **acquiescent** *adj* fügsam.

acquire [ə'kwaiə] *v* erwerben, bekommen. **acquisition** *n* Erwerb *m*. **acquisitive** habsüchtig, gierig.

acquit [ə'kwit] *v* (*law*) freisprechen. **acquittal** *n* Freisprechung *f*.

acrid ['akrid] *adj* scharf, beißend.

acrimony ['akriməni] *n* Bitterkeit *f*. **acrimonious** *adj* bitter, beißend.

acrobat ['akrəbat] *n* Akrobat *m*. **acrobatic** *adj* akrobatisch. **acrobatics** *pl n* Akrobatik *f sing*.

across [ə'kros] *adv* hinüber, herüber. *prep* (quer) über (+*acc*), jenseits (+*gen*), auf der anderen Seite.

act [akt] *v* handeln, tun; (*behave*) sich verhalten; (*theatre*) (eine Rolle) spielen. **act on** wirken auf. *n* Handlung, Tat *f*; (*law*) Gesetz *neut*; (*theatre*) Aufzug *m*. **acting** *adj* amtierend; *n* (*theatre*) Spielen *neut*. **actor** *n* Schauspieler *m*. **actress** *n* Schauspielerin *f*.

action ['akʃən] *n* Handlung *f*; (*deed*) Tat *f*; (*effect*) Wirkung *f*; (*law*) Klage *f*; (*battle*) Gefecht *neut*.

active ['aktiv] *adj* tätig, aktiv. **activate** *v* aktivieren. **activist** *n* Aktivist *m*. **activity** *n* Tätigkeit *f*. **activities** *n* Unternehmungen *pl*.

actual ['aktʃuəl] *adj* wirklich, eigentlich, tatsächlich. **actually** *adv* wirklich, tatsächlich. *interj* eigentlich.

actuate ['aktjueit] *v* in Gang bringen.

acupuncture ['akjupʌŋktʃə] *n* Akupunktur *f*.

acute [ə'kjuːt] *adj* scharf, heftig; (*angle*) spitz; (*person*) scharfsinnig; (*med*) akut.

adamant ['adəmənt] *adj* unnachgiebig.

Adam's apple [adəm'zapl] *n* Adamsapfel *m*.

adapt [ə'dapt] *v* anpassen; verändern. **adapted to** geeignet für. **adaptable** *adj* anpassungsfähig. **adaptation** *n* (*theatre*) Bearbeitung *f*. **adaptor** *n* (*for plug*) Zwischenstecker *m*.

add [ad] *v* (*figures*) addieren; (*word, sentence*) hinzufügen. **add up** addieren. **addition** *n* (*math*) Addition *f*; (*something added*) Zugabe *f*, Zutat *m*. **in addition** außerdem. **in addition to** zusätzlich zu. **additional** *adj* zusätzlich, weiter. **additive** *n* Zusatz *m*.

addendum [ə'dendəm] *n* Zusatz *m*.

adder ['adə] *n* (*snake*) Natter *m*.

addict ['adikt; *v* ə'dikt] *n* Süchtige(r); (*coll*) Fanatiker *m*. **drug addict** Rauschgiftsüchtige(r). **addicted** süchtig. **addiction** *n* Sucht *f*.

address [ə'dres] *v* (*letter*) addressieren; (*person*) anreden. *n* Adresse *f*, Anschrift *f*; (*speech*) Anrede *f*. **address book** Adreßbuch *neut*. **addressee** *n* Empfänger *m*.

adenoids ['adənoidz] *pl n* Polypen *pl*.

adept [ə'dept] *adj* geschickt, erfahren.

adequate ['adikwət] *adj* (*quantity*) ausreichend, genügend; (*quality*) annehmbar.

adhere [əd'hiə] *v* **adhere to** haften *or* kleben an (+*dat*); (*belief, etc.*) festhalten an (+*dat*). **adhesive** *adj* klebrig, haftend. **adhesive tape** Klebeband *neut*. **adherent** *n* Anhänger *m*.

adjacent [ə'dʒeisənt] *adj* angrenzend.

adjective ['adʒiktiv] *n* Adjektiv *neut*, Eigenschaftswort *neut*.

adjoin [ə'dʒoin] *v* angrenzen (an). **adjoining** *adj* angrenzend, anliegend.

adjourn [ə'dʒəːn] *v* vertagen. **adjournment** *n* Vertagung *f*.

adjudicate [ə'dʒuːdikeit] *v* Recht sprechen, entscheiden. **adjudicator** *n* Schiedsrichter *m*.

adjust [ə'dʒʌst] *v* anpassen; berichtigen; (*tech*) einstellen. **adjust to** sich anpassen an. **adjustable** *adj* einstellbar. **adjustment** *n* Anpassung, Einstellung *f*.

ad-lib ['ad'lib] *adv* frei. *v* improvisieren.

administer [əd'ministə] v verwalten.
administer justice Recht sprechen.
administration n Verwaltung f. **administrative** adj Verwaltungs-. **administrator** n Verwalter m.
admiral ['admərəl] n Admiral m.
admire [əd'maiə] v bewundern, hochschätzen. **admirable** adj bewundernswert. **admiration** n Bewunderung f.
admission [əd'miʃən] n Eintritt m; (acknowledgment) Zugeständnis neut.
admit [əd'mit] v (let in) hereinlassen, zulassen; (concede) zugeben. **admittance** n Zutritt, Eintritt m. **no admittance** Zutritt verboten.
adolescence [adə'lesns] Jugend f. **adolescent** adj jugendlich. n Jugendliche(r).
adopt [ə'dopt] v (child) adoptieren; (idea) annehmen, übernehmen. **adoption** n Adoption f; Übernahme f.
adore [ə'doɪ] v lieben; (rel) verehren. **adorable** adj entzückend. **adoration** n Verehrung f.
adorn [ə'doɪn] v schmücken. **adornment** n Schmuck m.
adrenaline [ə'drenəlin] n Adrenalin neut.
adrift [ə'drift] adj, adv (naut) treibend; (fig) hilflos.
adroit [ə'droit] adj gewandt, geschickt.
adulation [adju'leiʃən] n Lobhudelei f.
adult ['adʌlt] n Erwachsene(r). adj erwachsen; (animal, plant) ausgewachsen.
adulterate [ə'dʌltəreit] v verfälschen. **adulteration** n Verfälschung f.
adultery [ə'dʌltəri] n Ehebruch m. **adulterer** n Ehebrecher(in).
advance [əd'vains] v vorwärts gehen, vorrücken; (make progress) Fortschritte machen; (cash) vorschießen; (cause) fördern; (tech) vorstellen. n Vorrücken neut, Fortschritt m; Vorschuß m. **in advance** im voraus. **advancement** n Beförderung f.
advantage [əd'vaintidʒ] n Vorteil m. **take advantage of** ausnutzen (+acc). **advantageous** adj vorteilhaft.
advent ['advənt] n Ankunft f; (rel) Advent m.
adventure [əd'ventʃə] n Abenteuer m. **adventurer** n Abenteurer m. **adventurous** adj gewagt.
adverb ['advɔib] n Adverb neut, Umstandswort neut.
adversary ['advəsəri] n Gegner m.

adverse ['advɔis] adj widrig, ungünstig.
adversity n Mißgeschick neut, Not f.
advertise ['advətaiz] v anzeigen. **advertisement** n Anzeige f. **advertising** n Reklame, Werbung f.
advise [əd'vaiz] v (be)raten, empfehlen; (comm) benachrichtigen. **advisable** adj ratsam. **adviser** n Berater m. **advice** n Rat m, Ratschlag m; (comm) Avis neut.
advocate ['advəkeit] v befürworten.
aerial ['eəriəl] n Antenne f. adj Luft-.
aerodynamics [eərədai'namiks] n Aerodynamik f.
aeronautics [eərə'noitiks] n Aeronautik f, Flugwesen neut.
aeroplane ['eərəplein] n Flugzeug neut.
aerosol ['eərəsol] n Sprühdose f, Spray neut.
aesthetic [iis'θetik] adj ästhetisch.
affair [ə'feə] n Angelegenheit f, Sache f; (love affair) (Liebes) Affäre f.
affect[1] [ə'fekt] v (influence) (ein)wirken auf, beeinflüssen. **affected** adj (moved) bewegt.
affect[2] [ə'fekt] v (pretend) vorgeben. **affectation** n Affektation f. **affected** adj geziert.
affection [ə'fekʃən] n Zuneigung f, Liebe f. **affectionate** adj liebevoll.
affiliated [ə'filieitid] adj angeschlossen. **affiliated company** Tochtergesellschaft f. **affiliation** n Verbindung f, Mitgliedschaft f.
affinity [ə'finəti] n Zuneigung f; (chem) Affinität f.
affirm [ə'fɔim] v behaupten. **affirmation** n Behauptung f. **affirmative** adj bestätigend.
affix [ə'fiks] v befestigen, ankleben (an).
afflict [ə'flikt] v betrüben. **affliction** n Leiden neut.
affluent ['afluənt] adj wohlhabend, reich. **affluence** n Wohlstand m.
afford [ə'foid] v sich leisten (können); (allow) gewähren.
affront [ə'frʌnt] v beleidigen. n Beleidigung f.
afloat [ə'flout] adj, adv schwimmend; (boat) auf dem Meere.
afoot [ə'fut] adv im Gang.
aforesaid [ə'foised] adj vorher erwähnt.
afraid [ə'freid] adj ängstlich, erschrocken, bange. **be afraid of** Angst haben vor. **be afraid to** sich scheuen. I am afraid I must . . . ich muß leider . . .

afresh [ə'freʃ] *adv* von neuem, noch einmal.

Africa ['afrikə] *n* Afrika *neut*. **African** *n* Afrikaner(in). *adj* afrikanisch.

aft [aɪft] *adj* Achter-. *adv* achtern.

after ['aɪftə] *conj* nachdem. *prep* nach, hinter. *adv* später, nachher. *adj* (*naut*) Achter-. **after all** schließlich. **shortly after** kurz danach.

after-effect *n* Nachwirkung *f*.

afterlife ['aɪftəlaif] *n* Leben nach dem Tode *neut*.

aftermath ['aɪftəmaθ] *n* Auswirkung *f*.

afternoon [,aɪftə'nuɪn] *n* Nachmittag *m*. **good afternoon!** guten Tag!

aftershave ['aɪftəʃeiv] *n* Rasierwasser *neut*.

after-taste *n* Nachgeschmack *m*.

afterthought ['aɪftəθoɪt] *n* nachträglicher Einfall *m*.

afterwards ['aɪftəwədz] *adv* nachher, später, danach.

again [ə'gen] *adv* wieder, noch einmal, nochmals; (*moreover*) ferner. **again and again** immer wieder.

against [ə'genst] *prep* gegen. **as against** im Vergleich zu.

age [eidʒ] *n* (*person*) Alter *neut*; (*era*) Zeitalter *neut*. **age group** Altersgruppe *f*. **at the age of ...** im Alter von .... **of age** volljährig. **old age** (hohes) Alter *neut*. *v* alt werden. **aged** *adj* (*elderly*) betagt. **aged five years** fünf Jahre alt. **under age** minderjährig.

agency ['eidʒənsi] *n* Agentur *f*.

agenda [ə'dʒendə] *n* Tagesordnung *f*.

agent ['eidʒənt] *n* Agent *m*, Vermittler *m*; (*chem*) Wirkstoff *m*.

aggravate ['agrəveit] *v* verschlimmern; (*coll*) ärgern. **aggravation** *n* Verschlimmerung *f*; Ärger *m*.

aggregate ['agrigət] *adj* gesamt, ganz. *n* Summe *f*.

aggression [ə'greʃən] *n* Angriff *m*, Aggression *f*. **aggressive** *adj* aggresiv. **aggressor** *n* Angreifer *m*.

aghast [ə'gaɪst] *adj* entsetzt.

agile ['adʒail] *adj* agil, flink. **agility** *n* Flinkheit *f*.

agitate ['adʒiteit] *v* schütteln. **agitated** *adj* beunruhigt. **agitation** *n* Beunruhigung *f*.

agnostic [ag'nostik] *n* Agnostiker *m*. **agnosticism** *n* Agnostizismus *m*.

ago [ə'gou] *adv* vor: *a year ago* vor einem Jahr. **a moment ago** soeben. **a long time ago** schon lange her. **a short time ago** vor kurzem.

agog [ə'gog] *adj* gespannt.

agony ['agəni] *n* Qual *f*, Agonie *f*. **agonize over** sich quälen über.

agree [ə'griɪ] *v* (*concur*) übereinstimmen, einverstanden sein; (*date, etc*.) vereinbaren; (*consent*) zustimmen; (*be in agreement*) einig sein. *eggs do not agree with me* ich kann Eier nicht vertragen. **agreed!** einverstanden! **agreeable** *adj* angenehm. **agreement** *n* Übereinstimmung *f* (*written*) Abkommen *neut*.

agriculture ['agrikʌltʃə] *n* Landwirtschaft *f*. **agricultural** *adj* landwirtschaftlich.

aground [ə'graund] *adv* **run aground** stranden.

ahead [ə'hed] *adv* vorwärts. **straight ahead** gerade aus. **go ahead** fortfahren.

aid [eid] *n* Hilfe *f*. *v* helfen (+ *dat*).

aim [eim] *v* (*gun*) richten; (*intend*) zielen. *n* Ziel *neut*. **aimless** *adj* ziellos.

air [eə] *n* Luft *f*; (*appearance*) Aussehen *neut*; (*music*) Lied *neut*. *v* (*laundry*) trocknen; (*views*) bekanntmachen. **go by air** fliegen. **airy** *adj* luftig.

airbed ['eəbed] *n* Luftmatratze *f*.

airborne ['eəboɪn] *adj* in der Luft; Luft-.

air-conditioned *adj* klimatisiert. **air-conditioning** *n* Klimaanlage *f*.

air-cooled *adj* (*mech*) luftgekühlt.

aircraft ['eəkraɪft] *n* Flugzeug *neut*.

airfield ['eəfiɪld] *n* Flugplatz *m*.

air force *n* Luftwaffe *f*.

air lift *n* Luftbrücke *f*.

airline ['eəlain] *n* Luftverkehrsgesellschaft *f*. **airline passenger** Fluggast *m*.

airmail ['eəmeil] *n* Luftpost *f*. **by airmail** mit Luftpost.

airport ['eəpoɪt] *n* Flughafen *m*.

air-raid *n* Luftangriff *m*.

air steward *n* Steward *m*. **air stewardess** *n* Stewardeß *f*.

airtight ['eətait] *adj* luftdicht.

aisle [ail] *n* Gang *m*.

ajar [ə'dʒaɪ] *adj* halboffen.

akin [ə'kin] *adj* **akin to** ähnlich (+ *dat*).

alabaster ['aləbaɪstə] *n* Alabaster *m*.

à la carte [alaɪ'kaɪt] *adv* nach der Speisekarte, à la carte.

alarm [ə'laɪm] *n* Alarm *m*; (*unrest*) Beunruhigung *f*. *v* beunruhigen. **alarm clock** Wecker *m*.

alas [ə'las] *interj* leider! o weh!
albatross ['albɔtros] *n* Albatros *m*.
albino [al'biːnou] *n* Albino *m*.
album ['albəm] *n* Album *neut*.
alchemy ['alkəmi] *m* Alchimie *f*. alchemist
n Alchimist *m*.
alcohol ['alkəhol] *n* Alkohol *m*. alcoholic
adj alkoholisch. *n* Alkoholiker *m*. alcoholism *n* Alkoholismus *m*. non-alcoholic
adj alkoholfrei.
alcove ['alkouv] *n* Nische *f*.
alderman ['oːldəmən] *n* Ratsherr *m*.
ale [eil] *m* Bier *neut*.
alert [ə'ləːt] *adj* wachsam, munter. *v*
warnen. on the alert auf der Hut.
algebra ['aldʒibrə] *n* Algebra *f*.
alias ['eiliəs] *adv* sonst ... genannt, alias.
n Deckname *m*.
alibi ['alibai] *n* Alibi *neut*.
alien ['eiliən] *n* Fremde(r), Ausländer *m*.
adj fremd. alienate *v* entfremden. alienation *n* Entfremdung *f*.
alight¹ [ə'lait] *v* (*from bus*) aussteigen.
alight² [ə'lait] *adj*, *adv* brennend, in Flammen. set alight entflammen.
align [ə'lain] *v* ausrichten. alignment *n*
Ausrichtung *f*.
alike [ə'laik] *adj*, *adv* gleich.
alimentary canal [ali'mentəri] *m*
Nährungskanal *m*.
alimony ['aliməni] *n* Unterhalt *m*, Alimente *pl*.
alive [ə'laiv] *adj* lebend, am Leben. alive
with wimmelnd von.
alkali ['alkəlai] *n* Alkali *neut*. alkaline *adj*
alkalisch.
all [oːl] *adj* alle, sämtliche *pl*. *pron* alles,
das Ganze. *adv* ganz. all over vorbei. all
gone alle, weg. above all vor allem. all at
once auf einmal. at all überhaupt. all day
den ganzen Tag. all right in Ordnung,
okay.
allay [ə'lei] *v* beruhigen.
allege [ə'ledʒ] *v* angeben, behaupten.
alleged *adj* angeblich. allegation *n*
Behauptung *f*.
allegiance [ə'liːdʒəns] *n* Treue *f*.
allegory ['aligəri] *n* Allegorie *f*. allegorical
adj allegorisch.
allergy ['alədʒi] *n* Allergie *f*. allergic *adj*
allergisch (gegen).
alleviate [ə'liːvieit] *v* erleichtern.
alley ['ali] *n* Gasse *f*. bowling alley
Kegelbahn *f*.

alliance [ə'laiəns] *n* (*pol*) Bündnis *neut*.
form an alliance ein Bündnis schließen.
allied ['alaid] *adj* verbündet, alliiert.
alligator ['aligeitə] *n* Alligator *m*.
alliteration [əlitə'reifən] *n* Alliteration *f*.
alliterative *adj* alliterierend.
allocate ['aləkeit] *v* zuteilen.
allot [ə'lot] *v* (*distribute*) zuteilen; (*assign*)
bestimmen. allotment *n* Zuteilung *f*;
(*garden patch*) Schrebergarten *m*.
allow [ə'lau] *v* erlauben, gestatten. allow
for berücksichtigen. will you allow me
(*to*)? darf ich? allowance *n* Erlaubnis *f*;
(*money*) Rente *f*.
alloy ['aloi; *v* ə'loi] *n* Legierung *f*. *v* legier-
en.
allude [ə'luːd] *v* allude to anspielen auf
(+ *acc*). allusion *n* Anspielung *f*.
allure [ə'ljuə] *n* Reiz *m*. *v* verlocken. allur-
ing *adj* verlockend.
ally ['alai; *v* ə'lai] *n* Verbündete(r); (*pol*)
Alliierte(r). *v* ally oneself with sich
verbünden mit. the Allies die Alliierten.
almanac ['oːlmənak] *n* Jahrbuch *neut*,
Almanach *m*.
almighty [oːl'maiti] *adj* allmächtig; (*coll*)
gewaltig. the Almighty der Allmächtige.
almond ['aːmənd] *n* Mandel *f*.
almost ['oːlmoust] *adv* fast, beinahe.
alms [aːmz] *pl n* Almosen *neut sing*.
aloft [ə'loft] *adv* (*be*) oben; (*go*) nach
oben.
alone [ə'loun] *adj*, *adv* allein. leave alone
bleiben lassen. leave me alone! laß mich
in Ruhe!
along [ə'loŋ] *prep* entlang (+ *acc*): along
the coast die Küste entlang. *adv*
vorwärts, weiter; mit: come along
mitkommen. along with zusammen mit.
get along with someone mit jemandem
gut auskommen. alongside *prep* neben
(+ *acc or dat*); (*ship*) längseits (+ *gen*).
aloof [ə'luːf] *adj* zurückhaltend.
aloud [ə'laud] *adv* laut. read aloud
vorlesen.
alphabet ['alfəbit] *n* Alphabet *neut*. alphabetical *adj* alphabetisch.
Alps [alps] *pl n* Alpen *pl*. alpine *adj*
Alpen-.
already [oːl'redi] *adv* schon, bereits.
Alsatian [al'seifən] *n* (*dog*) Schäferhund
m. *adj* elsässisch.
also ['oːlsou] *adv* auch, ebenfalls; (*moreover*) ferner.

altar ['ɔːltə] *n* Altar *m*.
alter ['ɔːltə] *v* (*modify*) (ab-, ver)ändern; (*become changed*) sich (ver)ändern. **alteration** *n* (Ab-, Ver)Änderung *f*; (*building*) Umbau *m*.
alternate [ɔːl'tɜːnət; *v* 'ɔːltəneit] *adj* abwechselnd. *v* abwechseln.
alternative [ɔːl'tɜːnətiv] *adj* ander. *n* Alternative *f*. *there is no alternative* es gibt keine andere Möglichkeit.
although [ɔːl'ðou] *conj* obwohl, obgleich, wenn auch.
altitude ['altitjuːd] *m* Höhe *f*.
alto ['altou] *n* Alt *m*, Altstimme *f*.
altogether [ɔːltə'geðə] *adv* insgesamt, im ganzen; völlig.
altruistic [altru'istik] *adj* altruistisch.
aluminium [alju'miniəm] *n* Aluminium *neut*.
always ['ɔːlweiz] *adv* immer, stets; schon immer.
am [am] *V* be.
amalgamate [ə'malgəmeit] *v* (*tech*) amalgamieren; (*fig*) vereinigen.
amass [ə'mas] *v* aufhäufen.
amateur ['amətə] *n* Amateur *m*. *adj* Amateur-.
amaze [ə'meiz] *v* erstaunen, verblüffen. *amazed at* erstaunt über. **amazement** *n* Erstaunen *neut*. **amazing** *adj* erstaunlich; (*coll*) sagenhaft.
ambassador [am'basədə] *n* Botschafter *m*.
amber ['ambə] *n* Bernstein *m*. *adj* bernsteinfarb, gelb.
ambidextrous [ambi'dekstrəs] *adj* beidhändig.
ambiguous [am'bigjuəs] *adj* zweideutig; unklar.
ambition [am'biʃən] *n* Ehrgeiz *m*, Ambition *f*. **ambitious** *adj* ehrgeizig, ambitiös.
ambivalence [am'bivələns] *n* Ambivalenz *f*. **ambivalent** *adj* ambivalent.
amble ['ambl] *v* schlendern.
ambulance ['ambjuləns] *n* Krankenwagen *m*.
ambush ['ambuʃ] *n* Hinterhalt *m*. *v* aus dem Hinterhalt überfallen.
ameliorate [ə'miːliəreit] *v* (*make better*) verbessern; (*get better*) besser werden. **amelioration** *n* Verbesserung *f*.
amenable [ə'miːnəbl] *adj* zugänglich; (*accountable*) verantwortlich.
amend [ə'mend] *v* (ab)ändern; ergänzen, richtigstellen. **make amends for**

wiedergutmachen. **amendment** *n* (*to a motion*) Ergänzung *f*.
amenities [ə'miːnətiz] *pl n* Vorzüge *pl*, moderne Einrichtungen *pl*.
America [ə'merikə] *n* Amerika *neut*. **American** *n* Amerikaner(in); *adj* amerikanisch.
amethyst ['aməθist] *n* Amethyst *m*.
amiable ['eimiəbl] *adj* freundlich, liebenswürdig.
amicable ['amikəbl] *adj* freundschaftlich, friedlich.
amid [ə'mid] *prep* mitten unter (+*dat*).
amiss [ə'mis] *adj* verkehrt, nicht richtig. *take amiss* übelnehmen.
ammonia [ə'mouniə] *n* Ammoniak *neut*.
ammunition [amju'niʃən] *n* Munition *f*.
amnesia [am'niːziə] *n* Gedächtnisverlust *m*.
amnesty ['amnəsti] *n* Amnestie *f*.
amoeba [ə'miːbə] *n* Amöbe *f*.
among [ə'mʌŋ] *prep* unter, zwischen (+*dat*); bei (+*dat*). *among other things* unter anderem. **among ourselves/yourselves/themselves** miteinander, untereinander.
amoral [ei'morəl] *adj* amoralisch.
amorous ['amərəs] *adj* verliebt; liebevoll.
amorphous [ə'mɔːfəs] *adj* (*chem*) amorph; formlos.
amount [ə'maunt] *n* (*of money*) Betrag *m*, Summe *f*; (*quantity*) Menge *f*. **amount to** betragen. *it amounts to the same* es läuft auf das gleiche hinaus.
ampere ['ampeə] *n* Ampere *neut*.
amphibian [am'fibiən] *n* Amphibie *f*. **amphibious** *adj* amphibisch; (*vehicle*) Amphibien-.
amphitheatre ['amfiθiətə] *n* Amphitheater *neut*; (*lecture room*) Hörsaal *m*.
ample ['ampl] *adj* ausreichend, reichlich.
amplify ['amplifai] *v* verstärken. **amplification** *n* Verstärkung *f*. **amplifier** *n* Verstärker *m*.
amputate ['ampjuteit] *v* amputieren. **amputation** *n* Amputation *f*.
amuse [ə'mjuːz] *v* belustigen, amüsieren; (*entertain*) unterhalten. **be amused by** *or* **about** lustig finden. **amusing** *adj* lustig, unterhaltend. **amusement** *n* Unterhaltung *f*.
anachronism [ə'nakrənizəm] *n* Anachronismus *m*. **anachronistic** *adj* anachronistisch.

anaemia [ə'niːmiə] *n* Anämie, Blutarmut *f*. **anaemic** *adj* anämisch, blutarm.
anaesthetic [anəs'θetik] *n* Betäubungsmittel *neut*. **under anaesthetic** unter Narkose. **anaesthetize** *v* betäuben.
anagram ['anəgram] *n* Anagramm *neut*.
analogy [ə'nalədʒi] *n* Ähnlichkeit *f*, Analogie *f*. **analogous** *adj* analog, ähnlich.
analysis [ən'aləsis] *n* Analyse *f*. **analyse** *v* analysieren. **analytical** *adj* analytisch.
anarchy ['anəki] *n* Anarchie *f*. **anarchist** Anarchist *m*.
anathema [ə'naθəmə] *n* (*rel*) Kirchenbann *m*. **that is anathema to me** das ist mir ein Greuel.
anatomy [ə'natəmi] *n* Anatomie *f*. **anatomical** *adj* anatomisch.
ancestor ['ansestə] *n* Vorfahr *m*, Ahn *m*.
anchor ['aŋkə] *n* Anker *m*. *v* befestigen. **ride at anchor** vor Anker liegen. **weigh anchor** den Anker lichten.
anchovy ['antʃəvi] *n* Anschovis *f*.
ancient ['einʃənt] *adj* alt, uralt; aus alter Zeit, antik.
ancillary [an'siləri] *adj* zusätzlich, Hilfs-.
and [and] *conj* und.
anecdote ['anikdout] *n* Anekdote *f*.
anemone [ə'neməni] *n* Anemone *f*.
anew [ə'njuː] *adv* von neuem, wieder.
angel ['eindʒəl] *n* Engel *m*. **angelic** *adj* engelhaft.
angelica [an'dʒelikə] *n* Angelika *f*.
anger ['aŋgə] *n* Zorn *m*, Ärger *m*. *v* ärgern. **in anger** im Zorn. **angry** *adj* ärgerlich, zornig. **be angry** sich ärgern, böse sein.
angina [an'dʒainə] *n* Angina *f*.
angle[1] ['aŋgl] *n* Winkel *m*, Ecke *f*; (*coll*) Gesichtspunkt *m*. **be at an angle to** einen Winkel bilden mit.
angle[2] ['aŋgl] *v* angeln (nach). **angler** *n* Angler *m*. **angling** *n* Angeln *neut*.
anguish ['aŋgwiʃ] *n* Qual *f*.
angular ['aŋgjulə] *adj* winkelig, eckig.
animal ['animəl] *n* Tier *neut*. *adj* tierisch, animalisch. **animal fat** Tierfett *neut*. **animal kingdom** Tierreich *neut*.
animate ['animeit] *v* beleben; begeistern. **animated** *adj* lebhaft. **animated cartoon** Zeichentrickfilm *m*.
animosity [ani'mosəti] *n* Feindseligkeit *f*.
aniseed ['anisiːd] *n* Anis *m*.
anisette [,ani'zet] *n* Anisett *m*.
ankle ['aŋkl] *n* (Fuß)Knöchel *m*.
annals ['anlz] *pl n* Annalen *pl*.

annex [ə'neks; *n* 'aneks] *n* (*to building*) Anbau *m*. *v* (*country*) annektieren. **annexation** *n* Annexion *f*.
annihilate [ə'naiəleit] *v* vernichten. **annihilation** *n* Vernichtung *f*.
anniversary [,ani'vəisəri] *n* Jahrestag *m*. **wedding anniversary** Hochzeitstag *m*.
annotate ['anəteit] *v* kommentieren. **annotation** *n* Anmerkung *f*.
announce [ə'nauns] *v* ankündigen, ansagen, anzeigen. **announcement** *n* Ankündigung *f*, Ansage *f*; (*radio*) Durchsage *f*. **announcer** *n* (*radio*) Ansager *m*.
annoy [ə'noi] *v* belästigen, ärgern. **be annoyed at** *or* **with** sich ärgern über (+ *acc*). **annoyance** *n* Belästigung *f*.
annual ['anjuəl] *adj* jährlich; Jahres-. *n* (*book*) Jahrbuch *neut*; (*plant*) einjährige Pflanze *f*.
annul [ə'nʌl] *v* annullieren. **annulment** *n* Annullierung *f*.
anode ['anoud] *n* Anode *f*.
anomaly [ə'noməli] *n* Anomalie *f*.
anonymous [ə'noniməs] *adj* anonym, ungenannt.
anorak ['anərak] *n* Anorak *m*.
another [ə'nʌðə] *pron, adj* (*a different*) ein anderer; (*an additional*) noch ein. **one another** einander, sich.
answer ['ainsə] *n* Antwort *f*; (*solution*) Lösung *f*. *v* antworten, erwidern. **answer back** unverschämt antworten. **answer for** verantwortlich sein für. **answerable** *adj* verantwortlich.
ant [ant] *n* Ameise *f*.
antagonize [an'tagənaiz] *v* reizen, entfremden. **antagonist** *n* Gegner *m*, Feind *m*. **antagonistic** *adj* feindselig.
antecedent [anti'siːdənt] *adj* früher.
antelope ['antəloup] *n* Antilope *f*.
antenatal [anti'neitl] *adj* vor der Geburt. **antenatal care** Schwangerschaftsvorsorge *f*.
antenna [an'tenə] *m* (*insect*) Fühler *m*; (*radio*) Antenne *f*.
anthem ['anθəm] *n* Hymne *f*. **national anthem** Nationalhymne *f*.
anthology [an'θolədʒi] *n* Anthologie *f*.
anthropology [anθrə'polədʒi] *n* Anthropologie *f*. **anthropological** *adj* anthropologisch.
anti-aircraft [anti'eəkraift] *adj* Fliegerabwehr-. **anti-aircraft gun** Fliegerabwehrkanone *f*.

antibiotic [antibai'otik] *n* Antibiotikum *neut. adj* antibiotisch.

antibody ['anti̦bodi] *n* Antikörper *m*.

anticipate [an'tisipeit] *v* (*expect*) erwarten; (*foresee*) voraussehen. **anticipation** *n* Erwartung *f*. **in anticipation of** in Erwartung (+*gen*).

anticlimax [anti'klaimaks] *n* Enttäuschung *f*.

anticlockwise [anti'klokwaiz] *adj*, *adv* dem Uhrzeigersinn entgegen.

antics ['antiks] *pl n* Possen *pl*.

anticyclone [anti'saikloun] *n* Hochdruckgebiet *neut*.

antidote ['antidout] *n* Gegenmittel (gegen) *neut*.

antifreeze ['antifriːz] *n* Frostschutzmittel *neut*.

antipathy [an'tipəθi] *n* Antipathie *f*, Abneigung *f*.

antique [an'tiːk] *adj* antik, altertümlich. *n* Antiquität *f*. **antiquated** *adj* veraltet. **antiquity** *n* Altertum *neut*.

anti-Semitic [antisə'mitik] *adj* antisemitisch.

antiseptic [anti'septik] *n* Antiseptikum *neut. adj* antiseptisch.

antisocial [anti'souʃəl] *adj* gesellschaftsfeindlich; (*person*) unfreundlich.

antithesis [an'tiθəsis] *n* Gegensatz *m*.

antler ['antlə] *n* Geweihsprosse *f*.

antonym ['antənim] *n* Antonym *neut*.

anus ['einəs] *n* After *m*.

anvil ['anvil] *n* Amboß *m*.

anxious ['aŋkʃəs] *adj* (*worried*) beunruhigt, besorgt; (*desirous*) begierig (nach). **be anxious to do something** gespannt sein, etwas zu tun. **anxiety** *n* Angst *f*, Besorgnis *f*.

any ['eni] *pron* irgendein, welche. *adv* etwas. *any faster* schneller, etwas schneller. *any more?* noch mehr? *do you want any?* wollen sie welche? *I haven't any money* ich habe kein Geld. *I can't do it any longer* ich kann es nicht mehr machen. **anybody** *pron* (irgend) jemand; (*everybody*) jeder. **anyhow** *adv* jedenfalls. **anyone** *pron see* **anybody**. **anything** *pron* (irgend) etwas; (*everything*) alles. **anytime** *adv* jederzeit. **anyway** *adv* jedenfalls, sowieso. **anywhere** *adv* irgendwo(hin); (*everywhere*) überall.

apart [ə'paːt] *adv* auseinander, getrennt. **apart from** abgesehen von.

apartheid [ə'paːteit] *n* Apartheid *f*.

apartment [ə'paːtmənt] *n* Wohnung *f*.

apathy ['apəθi] *n* Apathie *f*. **apathetic** *adj* apathisch.

ape [eip] *n* Affe *m*. *v* nachäffen.

aperitive [ə'perətiv] *n* Aperitif *m*.

aperture ['apətjuə] *n* Öffnung *f*; (*phot*) Blende *f*.

apex ['eipeks] *n* Spitze *f*.

aphid ['eifid] *n* Blattlaus *f*.

aphrodisiac [afrə'diziak] *n* Aphrodisiakum *neut*.

apiece [ə'piːs] *adv* (*per person*) pro Person; (*for each article*) pro Stück.

apology [ə'polədʒi] *n* Entschuldigung *f*. **apologetic** *adj* entschuldigend. **apologize** sich entschuldigen.

apoplexy ['apəpleksi] *n* Schlaganfall *m*.

apostle [ə'posl] *n* Apostel *m*.

apostrophe [ə'postrəfi] *n* Apostroph *m*, Auslassungszeichen *neut*.

appal [ə'poːl] *v* entsetzen. **appalling** *adj* entsetzlich.

apparatus [apə'reitəs] *n* Apparat *m*, Gerät *neut*.

apparent [ə'parənt] *adj* (*obvious*) offenbar; (*seeming*) scheinbar. **apparently** allem Anschein nach.

apparition [apə'riʃən] *n* Erscheinung *f*, Geist *m*.

appeal [ə'piːl] *n* Appell *m*, dringende Bitte *f*; (*charm*) Anziehungskraft *f*; (*law*) Berufung *f*. *v* **appeal against** (*law*) Berufung einlegen gegen. **appeal for** dringend bitten um. **appeal to** (*turn to*) appellieren, sich wenden an; (*please*) gefallen (+*dat*). **appealing** *adj* reizvoll.

appear [ə'piə] *v* (*seem*) scheinen; (*become visible, present itself*) erscheinen; (*crop up*) auftauchen. **appearance** *n* Erscheinen *neut*; (*look*) Anschein *m*.

appease [ə'piːz] *v* beruhigen; (*hunger*) stillen. **appeasement** *n* Beruhigung *f*.

appendix [ə'pendiks] *n* (*in book*) Anhang *m*; (*anat*) Blinddarm *m*. **appendicitis** *n* Blinddarmentzündung *f*.

appetite ['apitait] *n* Appetit *m*. **appetizer** *n* Appetitshappen *m*. **appetizing** *adj* appetitlich.

applaud [ə'ploːd] *v* Beifall klatschen (+*dat*); *applaudieren* (+*dat*); (*fig*) loben.

apple ['apl] *n* Apfel *m*. **apple juice** Apfelsaft *m*. **apple tree** Apfelbaum *m*. **apple sauce** Apfelmus *neut*.

appliance [ə'plaiəns] *n* Gerät *neut.*
applicable ['aplikəbl] *adj* zutreffend.
applicant ['aplikənt] *n* Kandidat *m.*
apply [ə'plai] *v* anwenden; (*be valid*) gelten. **apply for** (*job*) sich bewerben um. **apply to** sich wenden an. **apply oneself to** sich bemühen um. **application** *n* Anwendung *f*; (*job*) Bewerbung *f.* **applied** *adj* angewandt.
appoint [ə'point] *v* anstellen, ernennen. **appointed** *adj* vereinbart. **well appointed** gut ausgestattet. **appointment** *n* Anstellung *f*; (*meeting*) Verabredung *f.*
apportion [ə'poːʃən] *v* zuteilen.
appraisal [ə'preizl] *n* Schätzung *f.*
appreciable [ə'priːʃəbl] *adj* merkbar.
appreciate [ə'priːʃieit] *v* schätzen; (*understand*) verstehen; (*be grateful for*) dankbar sein für; (*increase in value*) im Wert steigen. **appreciation** *n* (*gratitude*) Anerkennung *f*; (*in value*) Wertzuwachs *m.* **appreciative** *adj* anerkennend.
apprehend [apri'hend] *v* (*understand*) begreifen; (*seize*) verhaften. **apprehensive** *adj* angstvoll.
apprentice [ə'prentis] *n* Lehrling *m.* **apprenticeship** *n* Lehre *f.*
approach [ə'proutʃ] *v* (*come near*) sich nähern; (*a place*) nähern; (*someone*) sich wenden an. *n* Herankommen *neut*; (*attitude*) Einstellung *f*; (*access*) Zugang *m.* **approachable** *adj* zugänglich.
appropriate [ə'proupriət; *v* ə'prouprieit] *adj* geeignet (+ *dat*). *v* sich aneignen.
approve [ə'pruːv] *v* (*agree*) zustimmen; (*pass, endorse*) billigen, genehmigen. **approve of** billigen. **approved** *adj* bewährt. **approval** *n* Billigung *f*, Genehmigung *f.* **on approval** auf Probe.
approximate [ə'proksimət] *adj* ungefähr. **approximately** *adv* ungefähr, etwa.
apricot ['eiprikot] *n* Aprikose *f.*
April ['eiprəl] *n* April *m.*
apron ['eiprən] *n* Schürze *f.*
apt [apt] *adj* (*remark*) passend. **apt at** geschickt in. **be apt to do something** geneigt sein, etwas zu tun. **aptitude** *n* (*gift*) Begabung *f.*
aqualung ['akwəlʌŋ] *n* Unterwasseratmungsgerät *neut.*
aquarium [ə'kweəriəm] *n* Aquarium *neut.*
Aquarius [ə'kweəriəs] *n* Wassermann *m.*
aquatic [ə'kwatik] *adj* Wasser-.
aqueduct ['akwidʌkt] *n* Aquädukt *m.*
Arab ['arəb] *n* Araber *m.* *adj or* **Arabian,**

Arabic arabisch. **Arabic** *n* arabische Sprache *f.*
arable ['arəbl] *adj* **arable land** Ackerland *neut.*
arbitrary ['aːbitrəri] *adj* willkürlich.
arbitrate ['aːbitreit] *v* entscheiden. **arbitration** *n* Schiedspruch *m.* **arbitrator** *n* Schiedsrichter *m.*
arc [aːk] *n* Bogen *m.*
arcade [aː'keid] *n* Arkade *f.*
arch [aːtʃ] *n* (*architecture*) Bogen *m.* *v* (sich) wölben. *adj* Erz-. **archway** *n* Bogengang *m.*
archaeology [aːki'olədʒi] *n* Archäologie *f.* **archaeological** *adj* archäologisch. **archaeologist** *n* Archäologe *m.*
archaic [aː'keiik] *adj* altertümlich.
archbishop [aːtʃ'biʃəp] *n* Erzbischof *m.*
archduke [aːtʃ'djuːk] *n* Erzherzog *m.*
archer ['aːtʃə] *n* Bogenschütze *m.* **archery** *n* Bogenschießen *neut.*
archetype ['aːkitaip] *n* Vorbild *neut*; (*psychol*) Archetyp *m.*
archipelago [aːki'peləgou] *n* Archipel *m.*
architect ['aːkitekt] *n* Architekt *m.* **architecture** *n* Architektur *f.*
archives ['aːkaivz] *pl n* Archiv *neut sing.*
ardent ['aːdənt] *adj* eifrig, begeistert.
ardour ['aːdə] *n* Eifer *m.*
arduous ['aːdjuəs] *adj* mühsam, anstrengend.
are [aː] *V* be.
area ['eəriə] *n* (*measurement*) Fläche *f*; (*region*) Gebiet *neut.* Zone *f.*
arena [ə'riːnə] *n* Arena *neut.*
argue ['aːguː] *v* streiten; (*case*) diskutieren; (*maintain*) behaupten. **argument** *n* Streit *m*; (*reasoning*) Argument *neut.* **argumentative** *adj* streitlustig.
arid ['arid] *adj* trocken, dürr.
Aries ['eəriːz] *n* Widder *m.*
***arise** [ə'raiz] *v* (*come into being*) entstehen; (*get up*) aufstehen.
arisen [ə'rizn] *V* arise.
aristocracy [ari'stokrəsi] *n* Adel *m*, Aristokratie *f.* **aristocrat** *n* Aristokrat *m.* **aristocratic** *adj* aristokratisch.
arithmetic [ə'riθmətik] *n* Arithmetik *f.* **arithmetical** *adj* arithmetisch.
arm[1] [aːm] *n* Arm *m.* (*of chair*) Seitenlehne *f.* **arm in arm** Arm in Arm. **with open arms** mit offenen Armen.
arm[2] [aːm] *n* (*weapon*) Waffe *f.* *v* bewaffnen. **arms race** Wettrüsten *neut.*

coat of arms Wappen *neut*. **armed forces** Streitkräfte *pl*.

armament ['aːməmənt] *n* Kriegsausrüstung *f*.

armchair ['aːmtʃeə] *n* Sessel, Lehnstuhl *m*.

armistice ['aːmistis] *n* Waffenstillstand *m*.

armour ['aːmə] *n* (*suit of*) Rüstung *f*; (*of ship, tank*) Panzerung *f*. **armoured** *adj* gepanzert.

armpit ['aːmpit] *n* Achselhöhle *f*.

army ['aːmi] *n* Armee *f*, Heer *neut*. **join the army** zum Militär gehen.

aroma [ə'roumə] *n* Aroma *neut*, Duft *m*.

arose [ə'rouz] *V* **arise**.

around [ə'raund] *adv* ringsherum, rundherum; auf allen Seiten; (*nearby*) in der Nähe. *prep* um … herum, rings um; (*approximately*) ungefähr. **look around (for)** sich umsehen (nach). **turn around** sich umdrehen.

arouse [ə'rauz] *v* wecken; (*suspicion*) erregen.

arrange [ə'reindʒ] *v* (*put in order*) anordnen; (*meeting*) verabreden; (*holidays*) festsetzen. (*see to it*) arrangieren, einrichten; (*music*) bearbeiten. **arrangement** *n* Anordnung *f*; (*agreement*) Vereinbarung *f*; (*music*) Bearbeitung *f*. **make arrangements** Vorbereitungen treffen.

array [ə'rei] *n* Aufstellung *f*.

arrears [ə'riəz] *pl n* Rückstände *pl*. **in arrears** im Rückstand *m*.

arrest [ə'rest] *v* (*thief*) verhaften; (*halt*) anhalten; *n* Verhaftung *f*. **under arrest** in Haft, verhaftet. **arresting** *adj* fesselnd.

arrive [ə'raiv] *v* ankommen; (*fig*) gelangen. **arrival** *n* Ankunft *f*. **late arrival** Spätankömmling *m*.

arrogance ['arəgəns] *n* Hochmut *m*. **arrogant** *adj* hochmütig, eingebildet.

arrow ['arou] *n* Pfeil *m*.

arse [aːs] *n* (*vulgar*) Arsch *m*.

arsenal ['aːsənl] *n* Arsenal *neut*.

arsenic ['aːsnik] *n* Arsenik *neut*.

arson ['aːsn] *n* Brandstiftung *f*. **arsonist** *n* Brandstifter *m*.

art [aːt] *n* Kunst *f*. **arts** *pl* Geisteswissenschaften *pl*. **arts and crafts** Kunstgewerbe *neut sing*. **art gallery** Kunstgalerie *f*. **art school** Kunstschule *f*. **work of art** Kunstwerk *neut*.

artefact ['aːtifakt] *n* Artefakt *neut*.

artery ['aːtəri] *n* Arterie *f*.

arthritis [aː'θraitis] *n* Arthritis *f*.

artichoke ['aːtitʃouk] *n* Artischocke *f*.

article ['aːtikl] *n* Artikel *m*; (*newspaper*) Zeitungsartikel *m*, Bericht *m*. **article of clothing** Bekleidungsstück *neut*.

articulate [aː'tikjulət] *adj*. **to be articulate** sich gut ausdrücken.

articulated lorry [aːtikjuleitid] *n* Sattelschlepper *m*.

artifice ['aːtifis] *n* Trick *m*.

artificial [aːti'fiʃəl] *adj* (*manmade*) künstlich, Kunst-; (*affected*) affektiert. **artificial respiration** künstliche Atmung *f*.

artillery [aː'tiləri] *n* Artillerie *f*.

artisan [aːti'zan] *n* Handwerker *m*.

artist ['aːtist] *n* Künstler *m*; (*painter*) Maler *m*. **artiste** *n* Artist(in). **artistic** *adj* künstlerisch.

as [az] *conj, prep* (*while*) als, während; (*in the way that*) wie, sowie; (*since*) da, weil; (*in role of*) als. **as … as** (eben)so … wie. **as far as** soweit. **as if** als ob. **as long as** solange. **as soon as** sobald. **as it were** sozusagen. **as well** auch.

asbestos [az'bestos] *n* Asbest *m*.

ascend [ə'send] *v* aufsteigen. **ascendant** *adj* vorherrschend. **ascent** *n* Aufstieg *m*. **Ascension** *n* Himmelfahrt *f*.

ascertain [asə'tein] *v* feststellen.

ascetic [ə'setik] *adj* askethisch. *n* Asket *m*.

ash¹ [aʃ] *n* (*cinder*) Asche *f*. **ashtray** *n* Aschenbecher *neut*.

ash² [aʃ] *n* (*tree*) Esche *f*.

ashamed [ə'ʃeimd] *adj* **be ashamed** sich schämen.

ashore [ə'ʃoː] *adv* am Ufer. **go ashore** an Land gehen.

Ash Wednesday *n* Aschermittwoch *m*.

Asia ['eiʃə] *n* Asien *neut*. **Asian** *n* Asiat *m*; *adj* asiatisch.

aside [ə'said] *adv* beiseite. **aside from** außer. **step aside** zur Seite treten. **turn aside from** sich wegwenden von.

ask [aːsk] *v* (*to question*) fragen; (*request*) bitten. **ask a question** eine Frage stellen.

askew [ə'skjuː] *adv* verschoben, schief.

asleep [ə'sliːp] *adj, adv* **be asleep** schlafen. **fall asleep** einschlafen.

asparagus [ə'sparəgəs] *n* Spargel *m*.

aspect ['aspekt] *n* (*appearance*) Aussehen *neut*; (*of a problem*) Aspekt *m*.

asphalt ['asfalt] *n* Asphalt *m*.

asphyxiate [əs'fiksieit] *v* ersticken. **asphyxiation** *n* Erstickung *f*.

aspic ['aspik] *n* Aspik *m.*
aspire [ə'spaiə] *v* **aspire to** streben nach.
aspiring *adj* hochstrebend.
aspirin ['aspərin] *n* Aspirin *neut.*
ass [as] *n* Esel *m.*
assail [ə'seil] *v* angreifen. **assailant** *n* Angreifer *m.*
assassin [ə'sasin] *n* Attentäter *m,* Mörder *m.* **assassinate** *v* ermorden. **assassination** *n* Ermordung *f.*
assault [ə'soilt] *v* angreifen, überfallen., *n* Angriff *m.* **indecent assault** Sittlichkeitsverbrechen *neut.*
assemble [ə'sembl] *v* (*congregate*) sich versammeln; (*put together*) montieren, zusammenbauen; (*bring together*) versammeln. **assembly** *n* (*people*) Versammlung *f;* (*tech*) Montage *f.* **assembly hall** Aula *f.* **assembly line** Fließband.
assent [ə'sent] *v* zustimmen (+ *dat*). *n* Zustimmung *f.*
assert [ə'səit] *v* (*insist on*) bestehen auf; (*declare*) erklären. **assertion** *n* Behauptung *f.* (**self-)assertive** *adj* selbstsicher.
assess [ə'ses] *v* (*for tax*) bewerten; (*estimate*) schätzen. **assessment** *n* Bewertung *f.*
asset ['aset] *n* Vorteil *m.* **assets** *pl* Vermögen *neut sing.*
assiduous [ə'sidjuəs] *adj* fleißig.
assign [ə'sain] *v* zuteilen, bestimmen. **assignment** *n* Aufgabe *f.*
assimilate [ə'simileit] *v* aufnehmen. **assimilation** *n* Aufnahme *f.*
assist [ə'sist] *v* helfen (+ *dat*). **assistance** *n* Hilfe *f.* **assistant** *n* Helfer *m.* **sales assistant** *n* Verkäufer *m.*
associate [ə'sousieit; *n* ə'sousiət] *v* verbinden. *n* Kollege *m,* Mitarbeiter *m;* (*comm*) Partner *m.* **association** *n* (*club*) Verein *m,* Verband *m;* (*link*) Verbindung *f.*
assorted [ə'soitid] *adj* verschiedenartig,. gemischt. **assortment** *n* Sortiment *neut.*
assume [ə'sjuim] *v* (*suppose*) annehmen; (*take over*) übernehmen.
assure [ə'ʃuə] *v* (*convince*) versichern (+ *dat*), versprechen; (*ensure*) sicherstellen. **assurance** *n* (*assertion*) Versicherung *f;* (*confidence*) Selbstsicherheit *f.* **life assurance** Lebensversicherung *f.*
asterisk ['astərisk] *n* Sternchen *neut.*
asthma ['asmə] *n* Asthma *neut.*
astonish [ə'stoniʃ] *v* erstaunen, verblüffen.

be astonished (at) erstaunt sein (über), sich wundern (über). **astonishing** *adj* erstaunlich. **astonishment** *n* Erstaunen *neut.*
astound [ə'staund] *v* bestürzen, erstaunen.
astray [ə'strei] *adv* **go astray** in die Irre gehen. **lead astray** vom rechten Weg abführen.
astride [ə'straid] *adv* rittlings. *prep* rittlings auf (+ *dat*).
astringent [ə'strindʒənt] *adj* zusammenziehend.
astrology [ə'strolədʒi] *n* Astrologie *f.* **astrologer** *n* Astrologe *m.* **astrological** *adj* astrologisch.
astronaut ['astrənoit] *n* Astronaut *m.*
astronomy [ə'stronəmi] *n* Astronomie *f.* **astronomer** *n* Astronom *m.* **astronomical** *adj* astronomisch.
astute [ə'stjuit] *adj* scharfsinnig.
asunder [ə'sʌndə] *adv* auseinander.
asylum [ə'sailəm] *n* Asyl *neut.* **lunatic asylum** Irrenanstalt *f.* **political asylum** politisches Asyl *neut.*
at [at] *prep* (*place*) in, zu, bei, an, auf; (*time*) um, zu, in; (*age, speed*) mit; (*price*) zu. **at school** in der Schule. **at four o'clock** um vier Uhr. **at my house** bei mir. **at home** zuhause. **at (age) 65** mit 65. **at Christmas** zu Weihnachten. **at peace** in Frieden.
ate [et] *V* eat.
atheist ['eiθiist] *n* Atheist *m.*
Athens ['aθinz] *n* Athen *neut.*
athlete ['aθliit] *n* Athlet *m.* **athletic** *adj* athletisch. **athletics** *n* (Leicht)Athletik *f.*
Atlantic [ət'lantik] *n* Atlantik *m.*
atlas ['atləs] *n* Atlas *m.*
atmosphere ['atmosfiə] *n* Atmosphäre *f.* **atmospheric** *adj* atmosphärisch, Luft-.
atom ['atəm] *n* Atom *neut.* **atomic** *adj* Atom-. **atomic bomb** Atombombe *f.* **atomic power** Atomkraft *f.* **atomic reactor** Atomreaktor *m.*
atone [ə'toun] *v* **atone for** büßen, wiedergutmachen. **atonement** *n* Buße *f.*
atrocious [ə'trouʃəs] *adj* grausam, brutal; (*coll*) scheußlich. **atrocity** *n* Greueltat *f.*
attach [ə'tatʃ] *v* (*affix*) befestigen, anhängen; (*connect*) anschließen; (*to a letter*) beifügen. **be attached to** mögen, lieb haben. **attach oneself to** sich anschließen an. **attachment** *n* (*liking*) Anhänglichkeit *f;* (*fixture*) Anschluß *m.*

attaché [ə'taʃei] *n* Attaché. **attaché case** Aktentasche *f*.
attack [ə'tak] *v* angreifen; (*criticize*) tadeln, kritisieren. *n* Angriff *m*. **heart attack** Herzanfall *m*.
attain [ə'tein] *v* erreichen, gelangen zu. **attainable** *adj* erreichbar.
attempt [ə'tempt] *v* versuchen, wagen. *n* Versuch *m*.
attend [ə'tend] *v* (*school*) besuchen; (*meeting*) beiwohnen (+*dat*); (*lecture*) hören. **attend to** sich kümmern um. **attendance** *n* Anwesenheit *f*. **good attendance** gute Teilnahme *f*. **attendant** *n* Wächter(in).
attention [ə'tenʃən] *n* Aufmerksamkeit *f*; (*care*) Pflege *f*; (*machine*) Wartung *f*. **pay attention to** aufpassen auf. **stand at attention** Haltung annehmen.
attic ['atik] *n* Dachkammer *f*.
attire [ə'taiə] *n* Kleidung *f*. *v* kleiden.
attitude ['atitjuːd] *n* Einstellung *f*, Verhalten *neut*.
attorney [ə'təːni] *n* (*lawyer*) Rechtsanwalt *m*. **power of attorney** Vollmacht *f*.
attract [ə'trakt] *v* anziehen; (*attention*) erregen. **attraction** *n* Anziehung f; (*charm*) Reiz *m*, Anziehungskraft *f*. **attractive** *adj* attraktiv.
attribute [ə'tribjuːt; *n* 'atribjuːt] *v* zuschreiben (+*dat*). *n* Eigenschaft *f*. **attributable** *adj* zuzuschreiben (+*dat*).
attrition [ə'triʃən] *n* Abnutzung *f*. **war of attrition** Zermürbungskrieg *m*.
aubergine ['oubəʒiːn] *n* Aubergine *f*.
auburn ['oːbən] *adj* kastanienbraun.
auction ['oːkʃən] *n* Auktion *f*, Versteigerung *f*. *v* versteigern. **auctioneer** *n* Versteigerer *m*.
audacious [oː'deiʃəs] *adj* kühn. **audacity** *n* (*boldness*) Wagemut *m*; (*cheek*) Frechheit *f*.
audible ['oːdəbl] *adj* hörbar.
audience ['oːdjəns] *n* (*people*) Publikum *neut*, Zuhörer *pl*; (*interview*) Audienz *f*.
audiovisual [oːdiou'viʒuəl] *adj* audiovisuell.
audit ['oːdit] *v* (Rechnungen) prüfen. *n* Rechnungsprüfung *f*. **auditor** *n* Rechnungsprüfer *m*.
audition [oː'diʃən] *n* (*theatre*) Sprech-, Hörprobe *f*. *v* eine Hörprobe abnehmen.
auditorium [oːdi'toːriəm] *n* Hörsaal *m*.
augment [oːg'ment] *v* vermehren; (*grow*) zunehmen.

August ['oːgəst] *n* August *m*.
aunt [aːnt] *n* Tante *f*.
au pair [ou 'peə] *n* Au-pair-Mädchen *neut*.
aura ['oːrə] *n* Aura *f*; (*med*) Vorgefühl *neut*.
auspicious [oː'spiʃəs] *adj* günstig.
austere [oː'stiə] *adj* (*person*) streng; (*surroundings*) nüchtern. **austerity** *n* Strenge *f*.
Australia [o'streiljə] *n* Australien *neut*. **Australian** *n* Australier(in); *adj* australisch.
Austria ['ostriə] *n* Österreich *neut*. **Austrian** *n* Österreicher(in); *adj* österreichisch.
authentic [oː'θentik] *adj* echt, authentisch. **authenticity** *n* Echtheit *f*.
author ['oːθə] *n* (*writer*) Schriftsteller *m*, Autor *m*; (*of a particular item*) Verfasser *m*.
authority [oː'θorəti] *n* Autorität *f*; (*expert*) Fachmann *m*. **on good authority** aus guter Quelle. **the authorities** die Behörden *pl*. **authoritarian** *adj* autoritär.
authorize ['oːθəraiz] *v* genehmigen, bevollmächtigen. **authorization** *n* Genehmigung *f*.
autobiography [oːtoubai'ogrəfi] *n* Autobiographie *f*.
autocratic [oːtou'kratik] *adj* autokratisch.
autograph ['oːtəgraːf] *n* Autogramm *neut*. *v* unterschreiben.
automatic [oːtə'matik] *adj* automatisch, selbsttätig. **automatic transmission** Automatik *f*.
automobile ['oːtəməbiːl] *n* Wagen *m*, Auto *neut*.
autonomous [oː'tonəməs] *adj* autonom, unabhängig. **autonomy** *n* Autonomie *f*.
autopsy ['oːtopsi] *n* Autopsie *f*.
autumn ['oːtəm] *n* Herbst *m*. **autumnal** *adj* herbstlich, Herbst-.
auxiliary [oːg'ziljəri] *adj* Hilfs-, Zusatz-, zusätzlich. *n* Hilfskraft *f*.
avail [ə'veil] *n* **to no avail** nutzlos. *v* **avail oneself of** Gebrauch machen von, sich bedienen (+*gen*).
available [ə'veiləbl] *adj* (*obtainable*) erhältlich; (*usable*) verfügbar. **be available** zur Verfügung stehen. **availability** *n* Erhältlichkeit *f*.
avalanche ['avəlaːnʃ] *n* Lawine *f*.
avant-garde [avã'gaːd] *adj* avantgardistisch. *n* Avantgarde *f*.

avarice [ˈavəris] *n* Geiz *m*. **avaricious** *adj* geizig.

avenge [əˈvendʒ] *v* rächen. **avenge oneself on** sich rächen an.

avenue [ˈavinjuː] *n* Allee *f*.

average [ˈavəridʒ] *n* Durchschnitt *m*. *adj* durchschnittlich, Durchschnitts-. **on average** im Durchschnitt.

averse [əˈvəːs] *adj* abgeneigt. **aversion** *n* Abneigung *f*.

avert [əˈvəːt] *v* (*gaze*) abwenden; (*danger*) verhindern.

aviary [ˈeiviəri] *n* Vogelhaus *neut*.

aviation [eiviˈeiʃən] *n* Luftfahrt *f*. **aviator** *n* Flieger *m*.

avid [ˈavid] *adj* gierig (auf). **avidity** *n* Begierde *f*.

avocado [avəˈkaːdou] *n* Avocado(birne) *f*.

avoid [əˈvoid] *v* vermeiden; (*person*) aus dem Wege gehen (+ *dat*). **avoidable** *adj* vermeidbar.

await [əˈweit] *v* erwarten.

***awake** [əˈweik] *v* (*wake up*) aufwachen; (*rouse*) wecken; (*arouse*) erwecken. **be awake** wach sein. **wide awake** munter. **awaken** *v* erwecken.

award [əˈwoːd] *v* verleihen. *n* Preis *m*.

aware [əˈweə] *adj* bewußt (+ *gen*). **awareness** *n* Bewußtsein *neut*.

away [əˈwei] *adv* weg, fort. *adj* (*absent*) abwesend. *she is away* sie ist verreist.

awe [oː] *n* Ehrfurcht *f*. **awesome** *adj* (*impressive*) imponierend; (*frightening*) erschreckend.

awful [ˈoːful] *adj* furchtbar.

awhile [əˈwail] *adv* eine Weile, eine Zeitlang.

awkward [ˈoːkwəd] *adj* (*clumsy*) ungeschickt, linkisch; (*embarrassing*) peinlich; (*contrary*) widerspenstig.

awning [ˈoːniŋ] *n* Markise *f*.

awoke [əˈwouk] *V* **awake**.

awoken [əˈwoukn] *V* **awake**.

axe *or US* **ax** [aks] *n* Axt *f*.

axiom [ˈaksiəm] *n* Axiom *neut*.

axis [ˈaksis] *n* Achse *f*.

axle [ˈaksl] *n* Achse *f*.

B

babble [ˈbabl] *v* plappern; (*water*) plätschern.

baboon [bəˈbuːn] *n* Pavian *m*.

baby [ˈbeibi] *n* Baby *neut*, Säugling *m*. **baby carriage** Kinderwagen *m*. **babyish** *adj* kindisch. **babysit** *v* babysitten. **babysitter** *n* Babysitter *m*.

bachelor [ˈbatʃələ] *n* Junggeselle *m*.

back [bak] *n* (*anat*) Rücken *m*; (*rear*) Rückseite *f*; (*football*) Verteidiger *m*. *adj* hinter, Hinter-. *adv* zurück. *v* (*bet on*) wetten auf; (*support*) unterstützen; (*reverse*) rückwärts fahren. **back out** *v* sich zurückziehen.

backache [ˈbakeik] *n* Rückenschmerz *m*.

backbone [ˈbakboun] *n* Rückgrat *neut*, Wirbelsäule *f*.

backdate [ˌbakˈdeit] *v* zurückdatieren.

backer [ˈbakə] *n* Förderer *m*.

backfire [ˌbakˈfaiə] *v* (*car*) fehlzünden; (*plan*) fehlschlagen.

background [ˈbakgraund] *n* Hintergrund *m*.

backhand [ˈbakhand] *n* (*sport*) Rückhandschlag *m*.

backlash [ˈbaklaʃ] *n* (politische) Reaktion *f*.

backlog [ˈbaklog] *n* Rückstand *m*.

backside [ˈbaksaid] *n* Hinterteil *neut*, Hintern *m*.

backstage [ˈbaksteidʒ] *adj, adv* hinter den Kulissen.

backstroke [ˈbakstrouk] *n* Rückenschwimmen *neut*.

backward [ˈbakwəd] *adj* zurückgeblieben.

backwards [ˈbakwədz] *adv* zurück, rückwärts.

backwater [ˈbakwoːtə] *n* Stauwasser *neut*.

backyard [bakˈjaːd] *n* Hinterhof *m*.

bacon [ˈbeikən] *n* (Schinken)Speck *m*.

bacteria [bakˈtiəriə] *pl n* Bakterien *pl*.

bad [bad] *adj* schlecht, schlimm; (*naughty*) böse; (*food*) faul, verfault. **bad-tempered** *adj* mißgelaunt.

bade [bad] *V* **bid**.

badge [badʒ] *n* Abzeichen *neut*.

badger [ˈbadʒə] *n* Dachs *m*. *v* plagen.

badminton [ˈbadmintən] *n* Federballspiel *neut*.

baffle [ˈbafl] *v* verblüffen.

bag [bag] *n* Beutel *m*, Sack *m*; (*paper*) Tüte *f*; (*handbag*) Tasche *f*. **baggage** *n* Gepäck *neut*. **baggy** *adj* bauschig. **bagpipes** *pl n* Dudelsack *m sing*.

bail¹ [beil] *n* (*security*) Kaution *f*. *v* gegen Kaution freilassen.

bail² *or* **bale** [beil] *v* **bail out** (*boat*) ausschöpfen; (*from aeroplane*) abspringen; (*help*) aushelfen.

bailiff ['beilif] *n* Gerichtsvollzieher *m*.

bait [beit] *n* Köder *m*. *v* ködern; (*tease*) quälen.

bake [beik] *v* backen. **baker** *n* Bäcker *m*. **bakery** Bäckerei *f*.

balance ['baləns] *n* Gleichgewicht *neut*; (*scales*) Waage *f*; (*of account*) Saldo *m*; (*amount left*) Rest *m*. *v* ausgleichen. **balance sheet** Bilanz *f*.

balcony ['balkəni] *n* Balkon *m*.

bald [boild] *adj* kahl.

bale¹ [beil] *n* Ballen *m*.

bale² [beil] *V* **bail²**.

ball¹ [boil] *n* (*sport*) Ball *m*; (*sphere*) Kugel *f*.

ball² [boil] *n* (*dance*) Ball *m*.

ballad ['baləd] *n* Ballade *f*.

ballast ['baləst] *n* Ballast *neut*.

ball bearing *n* Kugellager *neut*.

ballet ['balei] *n* Ballett *neut*. **ballet dancer** Balletttänzer(in).

ballistic [bə'listik] *adj* ballistisch.

balloon [bə'luin] *n* Ballon *m*; (*toy*) Luftballon *m*.

ballot ['balət] *n* Abstimmung *f*.

ball-point pen *n* Kugelschreiber *m*.

ballroom ['boilrum] *n* Tanzsaal *m*.

balmy ['baimi] *adj* sanft, lindernd.

bamboo [bam'buі] *n* Bambus *m*.

ban [ban] *v* verbieten. *n* Verbot *neut*.

banal [bə'nail] *adj* banal.

banana [bə'nainə] *n* Banane *f*.

band¹ [band] *n* Gruppe *f*; (*music*) Band *f*, Kapelle *f*; (*criminals*) Bande *f*. *v* **band together** sich vereinen.

band² [band] *n* (*strip*) Band *neut*, Binde *f*.

bandage ['bandidʒ] *n* Bandage *f*, Binde *f*. *v* bandagieren.

bandit ['bandit] *n* Bandit *m*.

bandy ['bandi] *adj* krummbeinig. *v* **bandy words** streiten.

bang [baŋ] *n* Knall *m*. *v* (*sound*) knallen; (*strike*) schlagen; (*door*) zuknallen.

bangle ['baŋgl] *n* (Arm)Spange *f*.

banish ['baniʃ] *v* verbannen.

banister ['banistə] *n* Treppengeländer *neut*.

banjo ['bandʒou] *n* Banjo *neut*.

bank¹ [baŋk] *n* (*river*) Ufer *neut*; (*sand*) Bank *f*.

bank² [baŋk] *n* (*comm*) Bank *f*. *v* (*money*) auf die Bank bringen. **bank on** sich verlassen auf. **bank account** *n* Bankkonto *neut*. **banker** *n* Bankier *m*. **banker's card** Scheckkarte *f*. **bank holiday** *n* Feiertag *m*. **banknote** *n* Banknote *f*.

bankrupt ['baŋkrʌpt] *adj* bankrott. *n* Bankrotteur *m*. **go bankrupt** Bankrott machen. **bankruptcy** Bankrott *m*.

banner ['banə] *n* Banner *neut*.

banquet ['baŋkwit] *n* Bankett *neut*.

banter ['bantə] *v* necken. *n* Neckerei *f*.

baptism ['baptizəm] *n* Taufe *f*. **baptize** *v* taufen.

bar [bai] *n* (*drink*) Bar *f*; (*rod*) Stange *f*, Barre *f*; (*chocolate*) Tafel *f*. *v* (*door*) verriegeln; (*ban*) verbieten.

barbarian [bai'beəriən] *n* Barbar *m*. **barbaric** *adj* barbarisch.

barbecue ['baibikjui] *n* Barbecue *neut*. *v* am Spieß braten.

barbed wire [baibd] *n* Stacheldraht *m*.

barber ['baibə] *n* Barbier *m*, Friseur *m*.

barbiturate [bai'bitjurət] *n* Barbitursäure *f*.

bare [beə] *adj* nackt; (*trees*) kahl; (*empty*) leer; (*mere*) bloß. *v* entblößen. **barefoot** *adj* barfuß. **bare-headed** *adj* mit bloßem Kopf. **barely** *adv* kaum.

bargain ['baigin] *n* (*good buy*) Gelegenheitskauf *m*. (*deal*) Geschäft *neut*. *v* feilschen. **collective bargaining** tarifverhandlungen *pl*. **into the bargain** obendrein.

barge [baidʒ] *n* Lastkahn *m*. *v* **barge in** hereinstürzen.

baritone ['baritoun] *n* Bariton *m*.

bark¹ [baik] *v* (*dog*) bellen. *n* Bellen *neut*.

bark² [baik] *n* (*tree*) Rinde *f*.

barley ['baili] *n* (*crop*) Gerste *f*; (*in soup*) Graupen *pl*.

barmaid ['baimeid] *n* Barmädchen *neut*.

barman ['baiman] *n* Barmann *m*.

barn [bain] *n* Scheune *f*.

barometer [bə'romitə] *n* Barometer *neut*.

baron ['barən] *n* Baron *m*.

baronet ['barənit] *n* Baronet *m*.

baroque [bə'rok] *adj* barock.

barracks ['barəks] *n* Kaserne *f*.

barrage ['barai] *n* (*dam*) Damm *m*; (*mil*) Sperrfeuer *neut*; (*of questions*) Flut *f*.

barrel ['barəl] *n* Faß *neut*.

barren ['barən] *adj* unfruchtbar; (*desolate*) wüst.

barricade [bari'keid] *n* Barrikade *f*. *v* verbarrikadieren.
barrier ['bariə] *n* Schranke *f*.
barrister ['baristə] *n* Rechtsanwalt *m*.
barrow ['barou] *n* Schubkarren *m*.
bartender ['baitendə] *n* Barmann *m*.
barter ['baitə] *n* Tauschhandel *m*. *v* tauschen; (*haggle*) feilschen.
base[1] [beis] *n* (*bottom*) Fuß *m*, Boden *m*; (*basis*) Basis *f*; (*mil*) Stützpunkt *m*; (*chem*) Base *f*. *v* gründen. **be based on** basieren auf (+ *dat*).
base[2] [beis] *adj* (*vile*) gemein.
baseball ['beisboil] *n* Baseball *m*.
basement ['beismənt] *n* Kellergeschoß *neut.*
bash [baʃ] *v* (heftig) schlagen. **have a bash!** versuch's mal!
bashful ['baʃful] *adj* schüchtern.
basic ['beisik] *adj* grundsätzlich, Grund-. **basically** *adv* im Grunde.
basil ['bazl] *n* Basilienkraut *neut.*
basin ['beisin] *n* (*washbasin, river basin*) Becken *neut*; (*dish*) Schale *f*.
basis ['beisis] *n* Basis *f*, Grundlage *f*.
bask [bask] *v* sich sonnen.
basket ['baiskit] *n* Korb *m*. **basketball** *n* Basketball *m*.
bass[1] [beis] *n* (*music*) Baß *m*. **bass guitar** Baßgitarre *f*. **double bass** Kontrabaß *m*.
bass[2] [bas] *n* Seebarsch *m*.
bassoon [bə'suin] *n* Fagott *neut.*
bastard ['baistəd] *n* Bastard *m*; (*derog*) Schweinehund *m*.
baste [beist] *v* (*meat*) mit Fett begießen.
bastion ['bastjən] *n* Bollwerk *neut.*
bat[1] [bat] *n* (*sport*) Schlagholz *neut*. *v* **without batting an eyelid** ohne mit der Wimper zu zucken.
bat[2] [bat] *n* (*zool*) Fledermaus *f*.
batch [batʃ] *n* Stoß *m*.
bath [baiθ] *n* Bad *neut*. *v* baden. **have or take a bath** ein Bad nehmen. **bathroom** *n* Badezimmer *neut*. **bathtub** *n* Badewanne *f*. **baths** *pl n* Schwimmbad *neut sing.*
baton ['batn] *n* (*music*) Taktstock *m*.
battalion [bə'taljən] *n* Bataillon *neut.*
batter[1] ['batə] *v* (*strike*) verprügeln.
batter[2] ['batə] *n* (*cookery*) Schlagteig *m*.
battery ['batəri] *n* Batterie *f*.
battle ['batl] *n* Schlacht *f*; (*fig*) Kampf *m*. *v* kämpfen. **battlefield** *n* Schlachtfeld *neut*. **battleship** Schlachtschiff *neut.*
bawl [boil] *v* brüllen, heulen.
bay[1] [bei] *n* (*coast*) Bai *f*, Bucht *f*.

bay[2] [bei] *n* **keep at bay** abwehren.
bay[3] [bei] *n* (*tree*) Lorbeer *m*. **bay leaf** Lorbeerblatt *neut.*
bayonet ['beiənit] *n* Bajonett *neut*. *v* bajonettieren.
bay window *n* Erkerfenster *neut.*
bazaar [bə'zai] *n* Basar *m*.
***be** [bii] *v* sein; (*be situated*) liegen, stehen. *v aux* (*in passive*) werden. **There is/are** es gibt. *the book is on the table* das Buch liegt auf dem Tisch. *I want to be an engineer* ich will Ingenieur werden. *how much is that car?* wieviel kostet der Wagen
beach [biitʃ] *n* Strand *m*. *v* (*boat*) auf den Strand setzen.
beacon ['biikən] *n* Leuchtfeuer *neut.*
bead [biid] *n* Perle *f*.
beak [biik] *n* Schnabel *m*.
beaker ['biikə] *n* Becher *m*.
beam [biim] *n* (*wood*) Balken *m*; (*light*) Strahl *m*. *v* strahlen.
bean [biin] *n* Bohne *f*.
***bear**[1] [beə] *v* (*carry, yield*) tragen, (*tolerate*) ertragen, leiden; (*child*) gebären. **bring pressure to bear on** Druck ausüben auf. **bear right** sich nach rechts halten.
bear[2] [beə] *n* (*zool*) Bär *m*.
beard [biəd] *n* Bart *m*.
bearing ['beəriŋ] *n* (*posture*) Haltung *f*; (*relation*) Beziehung *f*; (*tech*) Lager *neut*. **bearings** *pl n* Orientierung *f sing.*
beast [biist] *n* Tier *neut*; (*cattle*) Vieh *neut*; (*person*) Bestie *f*. **beastly** *adj* (*coll*) scheußlich.
***beat** [biit] *v* schlagen. *n* (*stroke*) Schlag *m*; (*music*) Rhythmus *m*; (*policeman's*) Revier *neut.*
beaten ['biitn] *V* **beat**.
beautiful ['bjuitəful] *adj* schön. **beautifully** *adv* ausgezeichnet. **beauty** *n* Schönheit *f*.
beaver ['biivə] *n* Biber *m*.
became [bi'keim] *V* **become**.
because [bi'koz] *conj* weil. **because of** wegen (+ *gen*).
***become** [bi'kʌm] *v* werden. **becoming** *adj* passend.
bed [bed] *v* Bett *neut*; (*garden*) Beet *neut*. **river bed** Flußbett *neut*. **seabed** *n* Meeresboden *m*. **bedclothes** *pl n* Bettwäsche *f sing*. **bedridden** *adj* bettlägerig. **bedroom** *n* Schlafzimmer *neut*. **bedsitter** *n* Einzimmerwohnung *f*. **bedspread** *n* Bettdecke *f*. **bedtime** *n* Schlafenszeit *f*.

bee [biː] *n* Biene *f*.
beech [biːtʃ] *n* Buche *f*.
beef [biːf] *n* Rindfleisch *neut*.
beehive ['biːhaiv] *n* Bienenstock *m*.
been [biːn] *V* be.
beer [biə] *n* Bier *neut*.
beetle ['biːtl] *n* Käfer *m*.
beetroot ['biːtruːt] *n* rote Bete *f*.
before [bi'fɔː] *conj* bevor, ehe; *prep* vor; *adv* (*time*) zuvor, früher; (*ahead*) voran. **beforehand** *adv* im voraus.
befriend [bi'frend] *v* befreunden.
beg [beg] *v* (*for money*) betteln; (*beseech*) bitten. **beggar** *n* Bettler *m*.
began [bi'gan] *V* begin.
*begin [bi'gin] *v* beginnen, anfangen. **beginner** *n* Anfänger *m*. **beginning** *n* Anfang *m*, Beginn *m*.
begrudge [bi'grʌdʒ] *v* mißgönnen.
begun [bi'gʌn] *V* begin.
behalf [bi'haːf] *n* on behalf of im Namen von. on my behalf um meinetwillen.
behave [bi'heiv] *v* sich verhalten, sich betragen; (*behave well*) sich gut benehmen. **behave yourself!** benimm dich! **behaviour** *n* Benehmen *neut*, Verhalten *neut*.
behind [bi'haind] *prep* hinter. *adv* (*in the rear*) hinten; (*back*) zurück; (*behind schedule*) im Rückstand. *n* (*coll*) Hinterteil *neut*. **behindhand** *adv* im Rückstand.
*behold [bi'hould] *v* sehen, betrachten. **beholder** *m* Betrachter *m*.
beige [beiʒ] *adj* beige.
being ['biːiŋ] *n* (*existence*) (Da)Sein *neut*; (*creature*) Wesen *neut*, Geschöpf *neut*. **for the time being** einstweilen. **come into being** entstehen. **human being** Mensch *m*.
belated [bi'leitid] *adj* verspätet.
belch [beltʃ] *v* rülpsen; (*fumes*) ausspeien. *n* Rülpsen *neut*.
belfry ['belfri] *n* Glockenturm *m*.
Belgium ['beldʒəm] *n* Belgien *neut*. **Belgian** *n* Belgier(in). *adj* belgisch.
belief [bi'liːf] *n* Glaube *m*; (*conviction*) Überzeugung *f*. **believe** *v* glauben (+ *dat*). **believe in** glauben an (+ *acc*). **believable** *adj* glaublich. **believer** *n* Gläubige(r).
bell [bel] *n* Glocke *f*; (*on door*) Klingel *m*.
belligerent [bi'lidʒərənt] *adj* (*country*) kriegführend; (*person*) aggressiv.
bellow ['belou] *v* brüllen. *n* Gebrüll *neut*.

bellows ['belouz] *n* Blasebalg *m*.
belly ['beli] *n* Bauch *m*.
belong [bi'loŋ] *v* gehören (+ *dat*); (*be a member*) angehören (+ *dat*). **belongings** *pl n* Eigentum *neut sing*; Sachen *pl*.
beloved [bi'lʌvid] *adj* geliebt. *n* Geliebte(r).
below [bi'lou] *prep* unter. *adv* unten.
belt [belt] *n* Gürtel *m*. *v* (*coll*) verprügeln. **belt up!** halt die Klappe!
bemused [bi'mjuːzd] *adj* verwirrt.
bench [bentʃ] *n* Bank *f*; (*work table*) Arbeitstisch *m*.
*bend [bend] *v* biegen; (*be bent*) sich beugen. *n* Kurve *f*.
beneath [bi'niːθ] *prep* unter.
benefactor ['benəfaktə] *n* Wohltäter *m*. **benefactress** *n* Wohltäterin *f*.
beneficent [bi'nefisənt] *adj* wohltätig.
beneficial [benə'fiʃəl] *adj* vorteilhaft, nützlich.
benefit ['benəfit] *n* Nutzen *m*, Gewinn *m*. *v* nützen. **benefit from** Nutzen ziehen aus.
benevolence [bi'nevələns] *n* Wohltätigkeit *f*. **benevolent** *adj* wohltätig.
benign [bi'nain] *adj* gütig; (*tumour*) gutartig.
bent [bent] *V* bend. *adj* krumm, verbogen; (*dishonest*) unehrlich. **be bent on** versessen sein auf (+ *acc*).
bequeath [bi'kwiːð] *v* vermachen.
beret ['berei] *n* Baskenmütze *f*.
berry ['beri] *n* Beere *f*.
berserk [bə'səik] *adj* go berserk wild werden, toben.
berth [bəːθ] *n* (*mooring*) Liegeplatz *m*; (*bunk*) Koje *f*. **give a wide berth to** einen weiten Bogen machen um (+ *acc*).
beside [bi'said] *prep* neben. **be beside oneself with** außer sich sein vor (+ *dat*). **besides** *prep* außer. *adv* außerdem.
besiege [bi'siːdʒ] *v* belagern.
best [best] *adj* best. *adv* am besten, bestens. *n* das Beste. **do one's best** sein Bestes tun. **at best** höchstens. **best man** Trauzeuge *m*.
bestial ['bestjəl] *adj* bestialisch.
bestow [bi'stou] *v* bestow upon schenken (+ *dat*).
bestseller [best'selə] *n* Bestseller *m*.
bet [bet] *v* wetten. *n* Wette *f*.
betray [bi'trei] *v* verraten. **betrayal** *n* Verrat *m*.

better ['betǝ] *adj, adv* besser. *n* das Bessere. *v* verbessern. **get the better of** übertreffen. **better oneself** sich verbessern.

between [bi'twiːn] *prep* zwischen. *adv* dazwischen. **between you and me** unter uns.

beverage ['bevǝridʒ] *n* Getränk *neut*.

***beware** [bi'weǝ] *v* sich hüten vor (+*dat*). **beware of the dog** Vorsicht Vorsicht–bissiger Hund!

bewilder [bi'wildǝ] *v* verwirren, verblüffen.

beyond [bi'jond] *prep* uber ... hinaus, jenseits (+*gen*); mehr als. *adv* jenseits, darüber hinaus. **beyond compare** unvergleichlich. **he is beyond help** ihm ist nicht mehr zu helfen.

bias ['baiǝs] *n* Neigung *f*. **biased** *adj* voreingenommen.

bib [bib] *n* Latz *m*.

Bible ['baibl] *n* Bibel *f*.

bibliography [bibli'ogrǝfi] *n* Bibliographie *f*.

biceps ['baiseps] *n* Bizeps *m*.

bicker ['bikǝ] *v* zanken.

bicycle ['baisikl] *n* Fahrrad *neut*.

***bid** [bid] *v* (*offer*) bieten; (*cards*) reizen. *n* (*offer*) Angebot *neut*; (*attempt*) Versuch *m*. **bid someone welcome** jemanden willkommen heißen. **bidder** *n* Bieter *m*.

bidden ['bidn] *V* bid.

bidet ['biːdei] *n* Bidet *neut*.

biennial [bai'eniǝl] *adj* zweijährig.

big [big] *adj* groß. **big-headed** *adj* eingebildet. **big-hearted** *adj* großherzig.

bigamy ['bigǝmi] *n* Bigamie *f*.

bigot ['bigǝt] *n* Frömmler *m*. **bigotted** *adj* bigott. **bigotry** *n* Bigotterie *f*.

bikini [bi'kiːni] *n* Bikini *m*.

bilateral [bai'latǝrǝl] *adj* bilateral.

bilingual [bai'liŋgwǝl] *adj* zweisprachig.

bill¹ [bil] *n* (*in restaurant*) Rechnung *f*; Banknote *f*; (*comm*) Wechsel *m*; (*pol*) Gesetzentwurf *m*; (*poster*) Plakat *neut*. *v* fakturieren. **billboard** *n* Plakattafel *f*.

bill² [bil] *n* (*beak*) Schnabel *m*.

billiards ['biljǝdz] *n* Billard *neut*.

billion ['biljǝn] *n* Billion *f*; (*US*) Milliarde *f*.

bin [bin] *n* Kiste *f*; (*dustbin*) Mülleimer *m*.

binary ['bainǝri] *adj* binär.

***bind** [baind] *v* (*tie*) binden; (*oblige*)

verpflichten. **binding** *adj* bindend. *n* (*book*) Einband *m*.

binoculars [bi'nokjulǝz] *pl n* Feldstecher *m*.

biography [bai'ogrǝfi] *n* Biographie *f*. **biographer** *n* Biograph *m*. **biographical** *adj* biographisch.

biology [bai'olǝdʒi] *n* Biologie *f*. **biological** *adj* biologisch. **biologist** *n* Biologe *m*.

birch [bǝːtʃ] *n* Birke *f*; (*rod*) Birkenrute *f*.

bird [bǝːd] *n* Vogel *m*.

birth [bǝːθ] *n* Geburt *f*. **date of birth** Geburtsdatum *neut*. **birth certificate** Geburtsurkunde *f*. **birth control** Geburtenregelung *f*. **birthday** Geburtstag *m*. **birthmark** Muttermal *neut*.

biscuit ['biskit] *n* Biskuit *m*, Keks *m*.

bisexual [bai'sekʃuǝl] *adj* bisexuell.

bishop ['biʃǝp] *n* Bischof *m*.

bison ['baisǝn] *n* Bison *m*.

bit¹ [bit] *V* bite. *n* (*morsel*) Bißchen, Stückchen *neut*: **a bit of bread** ein Stückchen Brot. **a bit frightened** ein bißchen ängstlich.

bit² [bit] *n* (*harness*) Gebiß *neut*; (*drill*) Bohreisen *neut*.

bitch [bitʃ] *n* Hündin *f*; (*woman*) Weibsstück *neut*.

***bite** [bait] *v* beißen. *n* (*mouthful*) Bissen *m*; (*wound*) Biß *m*. **bite to eat** Imbiß *m*.

bitten ['bitn] *V* bite.

bitter ['bitǝ] *v* bitter; (*weather*) scharf. **to the bitter end** bis zum bitteren Ende. **bitterness** *n* Bitterkeit *f*.

bizarre [bi'zaː] *adj* bizarr, seltsam.

black ['blak] *adj* schwarz. *n* (*colour*) Schwarz *neut*; (*person*) Schwarze(r).

blackberry ['blakbǝri] *n* Brombeere *f*.

blackbird ['blakbǝːd] *n* Amsel *f*.

blackboard ['blakboːd] *n* Wandtafel *f*.

blackcurrant [blak'kʌrǝnt] *n* schwarze Johannisbeere *f*.

blacken ['blakn] *v* schwarz machen.

black eye *n* blaues Auge *neut*.

blackhead ['blakhed] *n* Mitesser *m*.

blackleg ['blakleg] *n* Streikbrecher *m*.

blackmail ['blakmeil] *n* Erpressung *f*. **blackmailer** *n* Erpresser *m*.

black market *n* schwarzer Markt *m*. **black marketeer** Schwarzhändler *m*.

black out *v* (*darken*) verdunkeln; (*faint*) ohnmächtig werden. **black-out** *n* Verdunkelung *f*; Ohnmachtsanfall *m*; (*elec*) Stromausfall *m*.

black pudding n Blutwurst f.
blacksmith ['blaksmiθ] n Schmied m.
bladder ['bladə] n Blase f.
blade [bleid] n (razor, knife) Klinge f;
(grass) Halm m; (tech) Blatt neut;
(propellor) Flügel m.
blame [bleim] v tadeln, die Schuld geben
(+dat). n Schuld f, Tadel m. I am to
blame for this ich bin daran schuld.
blameless adj untadelig.
blancmange [blə'monʒ] n Pudding m.
bland [bland] adj sanft, mild.
blank [blaŋk] adj leer, unausgefüllt. n
(form) Formular neut; (cartridge)
Platzpatrone f. **blank cheque** Blankoscheck m.
blanket ['blaŋkit] n Decke f. adj Gesamt-,
allgemein.
blare [bleə] v schmettern. n Schmettern
neut.
blaspheme [blas'fiːm] v lästern. **blasphemy**
n Gotteslästerung f.
blast [blaːst] n Explosion f; (of wind)
(heftiger) Windstoß m. v sprengen.
blatant ['bleitənt] adj offenkundig.
blaze [bleiz] n Brand m, Feuer neut. v
lodern.
blazer ['bleizə] n Blazer m.
bleach [bliːtʃ] v bleichen. n Bleichmittel
neut.
bleak [bliːk] adj kahl; (fig) trostlos.
bleat [bliːt] v (sheep) blöken; (goat) meckern. n Blöken neut, Meckern neut.
bled [bled] V **bleed**.
***bleed** [bliːd] v bluten; (brakes, radiators)
entlüften. **bleeding** adj blutend.
blemish ['blemiʃ] n Makel m.
blend [blend] v mischen. n Mischung f.
bless [bles] v segnen. **blessing** n Segen m.
blew [bluː] V **blow¹**.
blind [blaind] adj blind; (corner) unüber-
sichtlich. n (window) Rouleau neut. v
blenden; (fig) verblenden. **blind alley**
Sackgasse f. **blindfold** v die Augen
verbinden (+dat). adv mit verbundenen
Augen.
blink [bliŋk] v blinzeln.
bliss [blis] n Wonne f. **blissful** glückselig.
blister ['blistə] n Blase f.
blizzard ['blizəd] n Schneesturm m.
blob [blob] n Tropfen m.
bloc [blok] n Block m.
block [blok] n (wood) Klotz m; (stone)
Block m; (US) Häuserblock m; (in pipe)
Verstopfung f; (barrier) Sperre f. v

blockieren; verstopfen. **writing block**
Schreibblock m. **blockade** n Blockade f.
blockage n Verstopfung f.
bloke [blouk] n Kerl m.
blond [blond] adj blond. **blonde** n
Blondine f.
blood [blʌd] n Blut neut. **in cold blood**
kaltblütig. **blood clot** Blutgerinnsel neut.
blood pressure Blutdruck m. **blood test**
Blutuntersuchung f. **bloodthirsty** adj
blutdurstig. **blood transfusion** Blutübertragung f. **blood vessel** Blutgefäß neut.
bloody adj blutig; (coll) verdammt.
bloom [bluːm] v blühen. n Blüte f.
blossom ['blosəm] n Blüte f. v blühen.
blot [blot] n Fleck m; (of ink) Tintenklecks m. v (make dirty) beschmieren.
blot out auslöschen.
blotch [blotʃ] n Fleck m; Klecks m.
blotting paper n Löschpapier neut.
blouse [blauz] n Bluse f.
***blow¹** [blou] v blasen; (of wind) wehen;
(fuse) durchbrennen. **blow over**
vorbeigehen. **blow up** (explode) sprengen.
blow the horn (mot) hupen. **blow one's
nose** sich die Nase putzen.
blow² [blou] n Schlag m; (misfortune)
Unglück neut.
blowlamp ['bloulamp] n Lötlampe f.
blown [bloun] V **blow¹**.
blowout ['blouaut] n (mot) geplatzter
Reifen m, Reifenpanne f.
blubber ['blʌbə] n Walfischspeck m.
blue [bluː] adj blau; (depressed)
niedergeschlagen. n Blau neut. **bluebell** n
Glockenblume f. **blueberry** n Heidelber-
ee f. **bluebottle** n Schmeißfliege f. **the
blues** Blues m sing.
bluff [blʌf] v bluffen. n Bluff m.
blunder ['blʌndə] n (dummer) Fehler m,
Schnitzer m. v (stumble) stolpern; (make
mistake) einen Schnitzer machen.
blunt [blʌnt] adj stumpf. v stumpf
machen; (enthusiasm) abstumpfen.
blur [bləː] v verwischen, verschmieren.
blurred adj verschwommen.
blush [blʌʃ] v erröten. n Erröten neut.
boar [boː] n Eber m. **wild boar**
Wildschwein m.
board [boːd] n (wooden) Brett neut;
(comm) Aufsichtsrat m. v (train) einsteigen in (+acc). **board and lodging**
Unterkunft und Verpflegung f. **boarding
house** Pension f. **boarding school**
Internat neut.

boast [boust] v prahlen, angeben. n
Prahlerei f. **boaster** n Prahler m.
boat [bout] n Boot neut. **in the same boat**
in der gleichen Lage.
bob [bob] v sich auf- und abbewegen;
(hair) kurz schneiden.
bobbin ['bobin] n Spule f.
bobsleigh ['bobslei] n Bobsleigh m.
bodice ['bodis] n Mieder neut.
body ['bodi] n Körper, Leib m; (corpse)
Leiche f; (of people) Gruppe f; (car)
Karosserie f. **bodily** adj körperlich.
bog [bog] n Sumpf m. v **get bogged down**
steckenbleiben. **boggy** adj sumpfig.
bogus ['bougəs] adj falsch, unecht.
bohemian [bə'hiːmiən] adj (fig)
zigeunerhaft, ungebunden. n (fig)
Bohemien m.
boil[1] [boil] v kochen. **boiler** n Kessel m.
boiling adj kochend.
boil[2] [boil] n (sore) Furunkel m.
boisterous ['boistərəs] adj ungestüm, laut.
bold [bould] adj kühn, tapfer; (cheeky)
frech. **boldness** n Kühnheit f.
bolster ['boulstə] n Kissen neut. **bolster
up** (fig) unterstützen.
bolt [boult] n (door) Riegel m; (screw)
Bolzen m; (lightning) Blitzstrahl m;
(cloth) Rolle f. v (door) verriegeln; (attach
with bolts) anbolzen; (food)
hinunterschlingen; (dash) (hastig)
fliehen.
bomb [bom] n Bombe f. v bombardieren.
go down a bomb einen Bombenerfolg
haben. **bombard** v bombardieren. **bombardment** n Beschießung f. **bomber** n
(aeroplane) Bombenflugzeug neut. **bombing** n Bombenangriff m.
bond [bond] n (tie) Bindung f; (comm)
Schuldschein m.
bone [boun] n Knochen m, Bein neut;
(fish) Gräte f. v (meat) die Knochen entfernen aus; (fish) entgräten.
bonfire ['bonfaiə] n Gartenfeuer neut.
bonnet ['bonit] n Haube f; (mot)
Motorhaube f.
bonus ['bounəs] n Bonus m.
bony ['bouni] adj knochig.
book [buk] n Buch neut; (notebook) Heft
neut. v (record) buchen; (reserve)
reservieren. **bookcase** n Bücherschrank
m. **booking office** Fahrkartenschalter m.
bookkeeping n Buchhaltung f. **bookmaker** n Buchmacher m. **bookshop** n Buch-
handlung f.

boom [buːm] n (sound) Dröhnen neut;
(econ) Konjunktur f; (naut) Baum m. v
dröhnen.
boost [buːst] v Auftrieb geben (+dat),
(tech) verstärken. n Auftrieb m.
boot [buːt] n Stiefel m; (mot) Kofferraum
m.
booth [buːð] n Bude f. **telephone booth**
Telephonzelle f.
booze [buːz] (coll) v saufen. n
alkoholisches Getränk neut. **boozer** n
Säufer m.
border ['boːdə] n (of country) Grenze f;
(edge) Rand m. v grenzen. **borderline** n
Grenze f. **borderline case** Grenzfall m.
bore[1] [boː] V **bear**[1].
bore[2] [boː] v (drill) bohren; (a hole) aus-
bohren; (cylinder) ausschleifen. n
Kaliber neut.
bore[3] [boː] v (weary) langweilen. n
langweiliger Mensch m. **be bored** sich
langweilen. **boredom** n Langeweile f. **boring** adj langweilig.
born [boːn] adj geboren. **she was born
blind** sie ist von der Geburt blind.
borne [boːn] V **bear**[1].
borough ['bʌrə] n Stadtbezirk m.
borrow ['borou] v borgen, entleihen. **borrower** n Entleiher m.
bosom ['buzəm] n Busen m. **bosom friend**
Busenfreund m.
boss [bos] n Boß, Chef m. v **boss around**
herumkommandieren. **bossy** adj herrisch.
botany ['botəni] n Botanik f. **botanical** adj
botanisch. **botanical gardens** botanischer
Garten m. **botanist** n Botaniker m.
both [bouθ] adj, pron beide(s). **both** (of
the) **dogs** beide Hunde. **both ... and**
sowohl ... als or wie auch.
bother ['boðə] v (disturb) belästigen, stör-
en; (take trouble) sich Mühe geben. n
Belästigung f. **bothersome** adj lästig.
bottle ['botl] n Flasche f. v in Flaschen
füllen. **bottled** adj in Flaschen, Flaschen-
bottleneck n (fig) Engpaß m. **bottle
opener** n Flaschenöffner m.
bottom ['botəm] n Boden m; (coll: anat)
Hintern m. adj **bottom gear** erster Gang
m.
bough [bau] n Ast m.
boulder ['bouldə] n Felsbrocken m.
bounce [bauns] v (of ball) hochspringen;
(of cheque) platzen. **bounce around**
herumhüpfen. **bouncer** n (coll) Rausch-
meißer m.

bought [boɪt] *V* buy.
bound¹ [baund] *V* bind.
bound² [baund] *n* (*leap*) Sprung *m*, Satz *m*. *v* springen.
bound³ [baund] *n* (*limit*) Grenze *f*. out of bounds betreten verboten!
bound⁴ [baund] *adj* bound for unterwegs nach. outward/homeward bound auf der Ausreise/Heimreise.
bound⁵ [baund] *adj* (*obliged*) verpflichtet. He is bound to win er wird bestimmt gewinnen.
boundary ['baundəri] *n* Grenze *f*.
bouquet [buːkei] *n* (*flowers*) Blumenstrauß *m*; (*of wine*) Blume *f*.
bourgeois ['buəʒwaɪ] *adj* bourgeois. *n* Bourgeois *m*. **bourgeoisie** *n* Bourgeoisie *f*.
bout [baut] *n* (*of illness*) Anfall *m*; (*fight*) Kampf *m*.
bow¹ [bau] *v* (*lower head*) sich verbeugen. *n* Verbeugung *f*.
bow² [bou] *n* (*music, archery*) Bogen *m*; (*ribbon*) Schleife *f*.
bow³ [bau] *n* (*naut*) Bug *m*.
bowels ['bauəlz] *pl n* Darm *m* sing; Eingeweide *pl*. open or move one's bowels sich entleeren.
bowl¹ [boul] *n* (*basin*) Schüssel *f*, Schale *f*.
bowl² [boul] *v* (*ball*) werfen. *n* Holzkugel *f*. bowls *n* Kegelspiel *neut*. play bowls kegeln.
box¹ [boks] *n* (*container*) Schachtel *f*, Kasten *m*; (*theatre*) Loge *f*; (*court*) Stand *m*.
box² [boks] *v* (*sport*) boxen. box someone's ears jemanden ohrfeigen. boxer *n* Boxer *m*. boxing *n* Boxen *neut*.
Boxing Day *n* zweiter Weihnachtsfeiertag *m*.
box office *n* (*theatre*) Kasse *f*.
boy [boi] *n* Junge *m*, Knabe *m*. boyfriend *n* Freund *m*. boyhood *n* Jugend *f*. boyish *n* knabenhaft.
boycott ['boikot] *n* Boykott *m*. *v* boykottieren.
bra [braɪ] *n* Büstenhalter *m*, BH *m*.
brace [breis] *n* Paar *neut*; (*tech*) Stütze *f*. *v* stützen. braces *pl n* Hosenträger *pl*.
bracelet ['breislit] *n* Armband *neut*.
bracing ['breisiŋ] *adj* erfrischend.
bracken ['brakən] *n* Farnkraut *neut*.
bracket ['brakit] *n* (*parenthesis*) Klammer *f*; (*support*) Träger *m*.

brag [brag] *v* prahlen, angeben. **braggart** *n* Prahler *m*.
braille [breil] *n* Brailleschrift *f*.
brain [brein] *n* Gehirn *neut*; Verstand *m*; Intelligenz *f*. **brainwashing** *n* Gehirnwäsche *f*. **brainwave** *n* Geistesblitz *m*. **brainy** *adj* klug.
braise [breiz] *v* schmoren.
brake [breik] *n* Bremse *f*. *v* bremsen.
brake pedal Bremspedal *neut*.
bramble ['brambl] *n* (*bush*) Brombeerstrauch *m*; (*berry*) Brombeere *f*.
bran [bran] *n* (Weizen)Kleie *f*.
branch [braɪntʃ] *n* Zweig *m*; (*of bank*) Zweigstelle *f*; (*department*) Abteilung *f*. *v* branch off abzweigen.
brand [brand] *n* (*of goods*) Marke *f*; (*cattle*) Brandzeichen *neut*. *v* (*name*) brandmarken. **brand-new** *adj* nagelneu.
brand name Markenname *m*.
brandish ['brandiʃ] *v* schwingen.
brandy ['brandi] *n* Weinbrand *m*.
brass [braɪs] *n* Messing *neut*; (*music*) Blasinstrumente *pl*. *adj* Messing-.
brassiere ['brasiə] *n* Büstenhalter *m*.
brave [breiv] *adj* mutig, tapfer. *v* trotzen. **bravery** *n* Mut *m*, Tapferkeit *f*.
brawl [broɪl] *n* Rauferei *f*. *v* raufen.
brawn [broɪn] *n* Muskelkraft *f*. (*cookery*) Sülze *f*.
brazen ['breizn] *adj* (*fig*) unverschämt.
breach [briɪtʃ] *n* Bruch *m*; (*mil*) Bresche *f*. *v* durchbrechen; (*law*) übertreten. **breach of contract** Vertragsbruch *m*. **breach of the peace** Friedensbruch *m*.
bread [bred] *n* Brot *neut*. *v* (*cookery*) panieren. **bread and butter** Butterbrot *neut*. **breadwinner** *n* Brotverdiener *m*.
breadth [bredθ] *n* Breite *f*, Weite *f*.
****break** [breik] *v* brechen; (*coll*) kaputt machen; (*law*) übertreten; (*promise*) nicht halten; (*day*) anbrechen. *n* Bruch *m*; (*gap*) Lücke *f*; (*rest*) Pause *f*; (*opportunity*) Chance *f*. break away sich losreißen. break down (*mot*) eine Panne haben; (*person*) zusammenbrechen. break in (*burgle*) einbrechen; (*animal*) abrichten. break out ausbrechen. break up zerbrechen; (*school*) in die Ferien gehen.
breakable ['breikəbl] *adj* zerbrechlich.
breakage ['breikidʒ] *n* Bruchschaden *m*.
breakdown ['breikdaun] *n* (*mot*) Panne *f*. **nervous breakdown** Nervenzusammenbruch *m*.

breakfast ['brekfəst] *n* Frühstück *neut. v* frühstücken.
breakthrough ['breikθruː] *n* Durchbruch *m.*
breast [brest] *n* Brust *f.* Busen *m.* **breastbone** *n* Brustbein *neut.* **breast-stroke** *n* Brustschwimmen *neut.*
breath [breθ] *n* Atem *m.* **out of breath** außer Atem.
breathe [briːð] *v* atmen. **breathe in** einatmen. **breathe out** ausatmen.
bred [bred] *V* **breed.**
*breed [briːd] *v* (*increase*) sich vermehren; (*animals*) züchten; (*fig*) erzeugen. *n* (*of dog*) Rasse *f.* **breeding** *n* Zucht *f;* (*education*) Erziehung *f.*
breeze [briːz] *n* Brise *f.*
brew [bruː] *v* brauen. *n* Bräu *neut.* **brewery** *n* Brauerei *f.*
bribe [braib] *v* bestechen. *n* Bestechungsgeld *neut.* **bribery** *n* Bestechung *f.*
brick [brik] *n* Ziegelstein *m.* **bricklayer** *n* Maurer *m.*
bride [braid] *n* Braut *f.* **bridal** *adj* bräutlich, hochzeitlich. **bridegroom** *n* Bräutigam *m.* **bridesmaid** *n* Brautjungfer *f.*
bridge[1] [bridʒ] *n* Brücke *f;* (*violin*) Steg *m. v* überbrücken.
bridge[2] [bridʒ] *n* (*card game*) Bridge *neut.*
bridle ['braidl] *n* Zaum *m.*
brief [briːf] *adj* kurz. *v* instruieren. **briefcase** *n* Aktentasche *f.* **briefing** *n* Anweisung *f.* **briefly** *adv* kurz. **briefs** *pl n* Slip *m sing.*
brigade [bri'geid] *n* Brigade *f.* **brigadier** *n* Brigadegeneral *m.*
bright [brait] *adj* hell, leuchtend; (*clever*) klug. **brighten** *v* aufheitern. **brightness** *n* Glanz *m* (*tech*) Beleuchtungsstärke *f.*
brilliance ['briljəns] *n* Glanz *m,* Brillanz *f.* **brilliant** *adj* glänzend, brillant; (*clever*) scharfsinnig.
brim [brim] *n* Rand *m;* (*hat*) Krempe *f.*
brine [brain] *n* Salzwasser *neut.* **in brine** eingepökelt, Salz-.
*bring [briŋ] *v* bringen. **bring about** veranlassen. **bring along** mitbringen. **bring down** herunterbringen; (*prices*) herabsetzen. **bring up** (*child*) erziehen; (*vomit*) erbrechen.
brink [briŋk] *n* Rand *m.*
briquette [bri'ket] *n* Brikett *m.*
brisk [brisk] *adj* schnell, lebhaft.
bristle ['brisl] *n* Borste *f.*

Britain ['britn] *n* (*Great Britain*) Großbritannien *neut.* **British** *adj* britisch. **the British** die Briten. **Briton** Brite *m,* Britin *f.*
brittle ['britl] *adj* spröde.
broad [brɔːd] *adj* breit. **broadly** *adv* im allgemeinen.
broadcast ['brɔːdkɑːst] *v* übertragen. *n* Sendung *f.* **broadcasting** *n* Rundfunk *m.* **broadcasting corporation** *n* Rundfunkgesellschaft *f.*
brochure ['brəuʃuə] *n* Broschüre *f.*
broke [brəuk] *V* **break.** *adj* (*coll*) pleite.
broken ['brəukn] *V* **break.**
broker ['brəukə] *n* Makler *m.*
bronchitis [broŋ'kaitis] *n* Bronchitis *f.*
bronze [bronz] *n* Bronze *f. adj* aus Bronze, Bronze-; (*colour*) bronzefarben.
brooch [brəutʃ] *n* Brosche *f.*
brood [bruːd] *n* Brut *f. v* brüten. **broody** *adj* brütig.
brook [bruk] *n* Bach *m.*
broom [bruːm] *n* Besen *m;* (*bot*) Ginster *m.* **broomstick** *n* Besenstiehl *m.*
broth [broθ] *n* Brühe *f.*
brothel ['broθl] *n* Bordell *neut.*
brother ['brʌðə] *n* Bruder *m.* **Smith Bros.** Gebrüder Smith. **brothers and sisters** Geschwister *pl.* **brotherhood** *n* Bruderschaft *f.* **brother-in-law** *n* Schwager *m.* **brotherly** *adj* brüderlich.
brought [brɔːt] *V* **bring.**
brow [brau] *n* (*forehead*) Stirn *f;* (*eyebrow*) Augenbraue *f;* (*of hill*) Bergkuppe *f.*
brown [braun] *adj* braun. *n* Braun *neut. v* bräunen.
browse [brauz] *v* weiden; (*in book*) durchblättern.
bruise [bruːz] *n* blaue Flecke *f,* Quetschung *f. v* quetschen.
brunette [bruː'net] *adj* brünett. *n* Brünette *f.*
brush [brʌʃ] *n* Bürste *f;* (*paintbrush*) Pinsel *m;* (*undergrowth*) Unterholz *neut. v* bürsten. **brush past** vorbeistreichen.
brusque [brusk] *adj* brüsk.
Brussels ['brʌsəlz] *n* Brüssel *neut.* **Brussels sprouts** Rosenkohl *m.*
brute [bruːt] *n* Tier *neut;* (*person*) brutaler Mensch *m.* **brutal** *adj* brutal. **brutality** *n* Brutalität *f.*
bubble ['bʌbl] *n* Blase *f. v* sprudeln. **bubbly** *adj* sprudelnd.

buck¹ [bʌk] *n* Bock *m*; (*US coll*) Dollar *m*.
buck² [bʌk] *v* bocken. **buck up** (*hurry*) sich beeilen; (*cheer up*) munter werden.
bucket ['bʌkit] *n* Eimer *m*. **bucketful** *n* Eimervoll *m*.
buckle ['bʌkl] *n* Schnalle *f*. *v* anschnallen.
bud [bʌd] *n* Knospe *f*. *v* knospen. **nip in the bud** im Keim ersticken. **budding** *adj* angehend.
buddy ['bʌdi] *n* (*coll*) Kumpel *m*.
budge [bʌdʒ] *v* (sich) bewegen.
budgerigar ['bʌdʒəriɡaɪ] *n* Wellensittich *m*.
budget ['bʌdʒit] *n* Budget *neut*. *v* budgetieren.
buffalo ['bʌfəlou] *n* Büffel *m*; (*bison*) Bison *m*.
buffer ['bʌfə] *n* Puffer *m*.
buffet¹ ['bʌfit] *n* (*blow*) Schlag *m*. *v* stoßen.
buffet² ['bufei] *n* (*meal*) Büffett *neut*.
bug [bʌɡ] *n* Wanze *f*. *v* (*coll*) ärgern.
bugle ['bjuɡl] *n* Signalhorn *neut*.
*build [bild] *v* bauen. *n* Körperbau *m*. **build up** aufbauen. **builder** *n* Baumeister *m*. **building** *n* Gebäude *neut*, Haus *neut*. **built-in** *adj* eingebaut.
built [bilt] *V* **build**.
bulb [bʌlb] *n* (*flower*) Zwiebel *f*; (*lamp*) Glühbirne *f*. **bulbous** *adj* zwiebelförmig.
Bulgaria [bʌl'ɡeəriə] *n* Bulgarien *neut*. **Bulgarian** *adj* bulgarisch. *n* Bulgare *m*. Bulgarin *f*.
bulge [bʌldʒ] *v* anschwellen. *n* Schwellung *f*, Ausbauchung *f*.
bulk [bʌlk] *n* Masse *f*; (*greater part*) Hauptteil *m*. **bulky** *adj* umfangreich.
bull [bul] *n* (*cattle*) Stier *m*; (*animal*) Bulle *f*; (*coll: nonsense*) Quatsch *m*. **bulldog** *n* Bulldogge *m*. **bulldozer** *n* Bulldozer *m*. **bullfight** *n* Stierkampf *m*.
bullet ['bulit] *n* (Gewehr)Kugel *f*.
bulletin ['bulətin] *n* Bulletin *neut*.
bullion ['buliən] *n* Gold-, Silberbarren *pl*.
bully ['buli] *v* einschüchtern. *n* Tyrann *m*.
bum [bʌm] *n* (*tramp*) Bummler *m*, Landstreicher *m*.
bump [bʌmp] *v* stoßen (gegen). *n* Stoß *m*; (*on the head*) Beule *f*. **bumper** *n* (*of car*) Stoßstange *f*. *adj* **bumper crop** Rekordernte *f*.
bun [bʌn] *n* (*hair*) Haarknoten *m*; (*cake*) Kuchen *m*; (*bread roll*) Brötchen *neut*.
bunch [bʌntʃ] *n* Bündel *neut*. **bunch of**

flowers Blumenstrauß *m*. **bunch of grapes** Weintraube *f*. **bunch of keys** Schlüsselbund *m*.
bundle ['bʌndl] *n* Bündel *neut*. *v* zusammenbündeln.
bungalow ['bʌnɡəlou] *n* Bungalow *m*.
bungle ['bʌnɡl] *v* verpfuschen. **bungler** *n* Pfuscher.
bunion ['bʌnjən] *n* entzündeter Fußballen *m*.
bunk [bʌnk] *n* Koje *f*.
bunker ['bʌnkə] *n* Bunker *m*; (*golf*) Sandgrube *f*.
buoy [boi] *n* Boje *f*.
burden ['bəɪdn] *n* Last *f*. *v* belasten.
bureau ['bjuərou] *n* Büro *neut*; (*desk*) Schreibtisch *m*.
bureaucracy [bju'rokrəsi] *n* Bürokratie *f*. **bureaucrat** *n* Bürokrat *m*. **bureaucratic** *adj* bürokratisch.
burglar ['bəɪɡlə] *n* Einbrecher *m*. **burglary** *n* Einbruchsdiebstahl *m*.
burial ['beriəl] *n* Beerdigung *f*, Begräbnis *neut*.
*burn [bəɪn] *v* brennen; (*set alight*) verbrennen. *n* Brandwunde *f*. **burn oneself** (*or* **one's fingers**) sich (die Finger) verbrennen.
burnt [bəɪnt] *V* **burn**. *adj* (*food*) angebrannt.
burrow ['bʌrou] *n* (*of rabbit*) Bau *m*. *v* graben.
*burst [bəɪst] *v* platzen. *n* (*of shooting*) Feuerstoß *m*; (*of speed*) Spurt *m*. **burst out laughing/crying** in Lachen/Tränen ausbrechen. **burst tyre** geplatzter Reifen *m*.
bury ['beri] *v* begraben; (*one's hands, face*) vergraben.
bus [bʌs] *n* Bus *m*, Autobus *m*. **bus driver** Busfahrer *m*. **bus conductor** Busschaffner *m*. **bus stop** Bushaltestelle *f*.
bush [buʃ] *n* Busch *m*. **bushy** *adj* buschig.
business ['biznis] *n* Geschäft *neut*. **that's none of your business** das geht dich nichts an. **businessman** *n* Geschäftsmann *m*. **businesswoman** *n* Geschäftsfrau *f*.
bust¹ [bʌst] *n* (*breasts*) Busen *m*; (*sculpture*) Büste *f*.
bust² [bʌst] (*coll*) *adj* (*bankrupt*) pleite; (*broken*) kaputt. *v* zerbrechen, kaputt machen.
bustle ['bʌsl] *n* Aufregung *f*. *v* **bustle about** herumsausen.

busy ['bizi] *n* (*occupied*) beschäftigt; (*hardworking*) fleißig; (*telephone*) besetzt. *v* **busy oneself with** sich beschäftigen mit.
but [bʌt] *conj* aber. *prep* außer. *adv* (*merely*) nur. **not only ... but also** nicht nur ... **sondern auch. nothing but** nichts als. **but for** ohne.
butane ['bjuːtein] *n* Butan *neut*.
butcher [butʃə] *n* Fleischer *m*, Metzger *m*. **butcher's shop** Metzgerei *f*, Fleischerei *f*.
butler ['bʌtlə] *n* Butler *m*.
butt[1] [bʌt] *n* (*thick end*) dickes Ende *neut*; (*of cigarette*) Stummel *m*.
butt[2] [bʌt] *n* (*of jokes*) Zielscheibe *f*.
butt[3] [bʌt] *v* (*with the head*) mit dem Kopf stoßen. *n* Kopfstoß.
butter ['bʌtə] *n* Butter *f*. *v* mit Butter bestreichen.
buttercup ['bʌtəkʌp] *n* Butterblume *f*.
butterfly ['bʌtəflai] *n* Schmetterling *m*.
buttocks ['bʌtəks] *pl n* Gesäß *neut sing*.
button ['bʌtn] *n* Knopf *m*. *v* (zu)knöpfen. **buttonhole** *n* Knopfloch *neut*.
buttress ['bʌtris] *n* Strebepfeiler *m*.
***buy** [bai] *v* kaufen. **buy in** einkaufen. **buyer** *n* Käufer(in).
buzz [bʌz] *v* summen. *n* Summen *neut*. **buzzer** *n* Summer *m*.
by [bai] *prep* (*close to*) bei, neben; (*via*) über; (*past*) an ... vorbei; (*before*) bis; (*written by*) von. *adv* vorbei. **by day** bei tage. **by bus** mit dem Bus. **by that** (*mean, understand*) damit. **by and by** nach und nach. **by-election** Nachwahl *f*. **bypass** *n* Umgehungstraße *f*. **by-product** *n* Nebenprodukt *neut*. **bystander** *n* Zuschauer *m*.

C

cab [kab] *n* (*taxi*) Taxi *neut*; (*horse-drawn*) Droschke *f*; (*in truck*) Fahrerhaus *neut*.
cabaret ['kabərei] *n* Kabarett *neut*.
cabbage ['kabidʒ] *n* Kohl *m*, Kraut *neut*.
cabin ['kabin] *n* Hütte *f*; (*naut*) Kabine *f*.
cabinet ['kabinit] *n* Schrank *m*; (*pol*) Kabinett *neut*. **cabinet-maker** *n* Möbeltischler *m*.
cable ['keibl] *n* (*elec, telegram*) Kabel *neut*; (*rope*) Tau *neut*, Seil *neut*. **cable**

address Telegrammanschrift *f*. **cable railway** Drahtseilbahn *f*.
cackle ['kakl] *v* gackern. *n* Gegacker *neut*.
cactus ['kaktəs] *n* Kaktus *m*.
caddie ['kadi] *n* Golfjunge *m*.
cadence ['keidəns] *n* (*music*) Kadenz *f*. **cadenza** *n* Kadenz *f*.
cadet [kə'det] *n* Kadett *m*.
café ['kafei] *n* Café *neut*.
cafeteria [kafə'tiəriə] *n* Selbstbedienungsrestaurant *neut*.
caffeine ['kafiːn] *n* Koffein *neut*.
cage [keidʒ] *n* Käfig *m*. *v* in einen Käfig sperren.
cake [keik] *n* Kuchen *m*; (*soap*) Tafel *f*. *v* **be caked with mud** vor Schmutz starren.
calamine ['kaləmain] *n* Galmei *m*.
calamity [kə'laməti] *n* Unheil *neut*, Katastrophe *f*.
calcium ['kalsiəm] *n* Kalzium *neut*.
calculate ['kalkjuleit] *v* kalkulieren, berechnen. **calculating** *adj* berechnend. **calculation** *n* Berechnung *f*. **calculator** *n* (*mech*) Rechner *m*.
calendar ['kaləndə] *n* Kalender *m*.
calf[1] [kaːf] *n* (*young cow*) Kalb *neut*. **calfskin** *n* Kalbleder *neut*.
calf[2] [kaːf] *n* (*anat*) Wade *f*. **calf muscle** Wadenmuskel *m*.
calibre ['kalibə] *n* Kaliber *neut*.
call [koːl] *v* rufen; anrufen; (*a doctor*) holen; (*regard as*) halten für. *n* Ruf *m*; (*phone*) Anruf *m*; (*demand*) Aufforderung *f*. **call for** verlangen. **call off** (*cancel*) absagen. **callbox** *n* Telefonzelle *f*. **caller** *n* (*visitor*) Besucher *m*; (*phone*) Anrufer *m*. **calling** *n* Berufung *f*. **call-up** *n* Einberufung *f*.
callous ['kaləs] *adj* gefühllos, herzlos.
calm [kaːm] *adj* ruhig. *n* Ruhe, Stille *f*; (*naut*) Windstille *f*. *v or* **calm down** (sich) *or* beruhigen.
calorie ['kaləri] *n* Kalorie *f*.
came [keim] *V* **come**.
camel ['kaməl] *n* Kamel *neut*. **camelhair** *n* Kamelhaar *neut*.
camera ['kamərə] *n* Kamera *f*, Fotoapparat *m*. **cameraman** *n* Kameramann *m*.
camouflage ['kaməflaːʒ] *n* Tarnung *f*; (*zool*) Schutzfärbung *f*. *v* tarnen.
camp [kamp] *n* Lager *neut*. *v* lagern; (*go camping*) campen, zelten. **camp bed** *n* Feldbett *neut*. **camper** *n* Camper *m*. **camping** *n* Camping *neut*. **camp site** *n* Campingplatz *m*.

campaign [kam'pein] *n* (*mil, pol*) Feldzug *m*; Kampagne *f*. *v* **campaign for** (*fig*) werben um, kämpfen für.
campus ['kampəs] *n* Universitätsgelände *neut*.
camshaft ['kamʃaɪft] *n* Nockenwelle *f*.
***can¹** [kan] *v* (*be able*) können; (*be allowed, may*) dürfen.
can² [kan] *n* (*tin*) Dose *f*, Büchse *f*. *v* konservieren.
Canada ['kanədə] *n* Kanada *neut*. **Canadian** *adj* kanadisch; *n* Kanadier(in).
canal [kə'nal] *n* Kanal *m*.
canary [kə'neəri] *n* Kanarienvogel *m*.
cancel ['kansəl] *v* (*meeting*) absagen; (*arrangement*) aufheben; (*stamp*) entwerten; (*cross out*) durchstreichen.
cancellation *n* Absage *f*; Aufhebung *f*.
cancer ['kansə] *n* (*med*) Krebs *m*. **Cancer** (*astrol*) Krebs *m*. **breast cancer** Brustenkrebs *m*. **lung cancer** Lungenkrebs *m*.
candid ['kandid] *adj* offen, ehrlich.
candidate ['kandidət] *n* Kandidat *m*.
candle ['kandl] *n* Kerze *f*. **candle light** *n* Kerzenlicht *neut*. **candlestick** Leuchter *m*.
candour ['kandə] *n* Offenheit *f*; Ehrlichkeit *f*.
candy ['kandi] *n* Kandiszucker *m*; (*US: sweet*) Bonbon *neut*.
cane [kein] *n* (*walking stick*) Spazierstock *m*. **sugar cane** Zuckerrohr *m*. **cane sugar** Rohrzucker *m*.
canine ['keinain] *adj* Hunde-, Hunds-. **canine tooth** Eckzahn *m*.
canister ['kanistə] *n* Kanister *m*.
cannabis ['kanəbis] *n* Haschisch *neut*.
cannibal ['kanibəl] *n* Kannibale *m*.
cannon ['kanən] *n* Kanone *f*.
canoe [kə'nuɪ] *n* Kanu *neut*. *v* Kanu fahren.
canon ['kanən] *n* Domherr *m*; (*rule*) Kanon *m*.
can opener *n* Büchsenöffner *m*.
canopy ['kanəpi] *n* Baldachin *m*.
canteen [kan'tiɪn] *n* (*restaurant*) Kantine *f*.
canter ['kantə] *n* Handgalopp *m*. *v* Handgalopp reiten.
canton ['kantən] *n* Kanton *m*.
canvas ['kanvəs] *n* Segeltuch *neut*; (*artist's*) Leinwand *f*.
canvass ['kanvəs] *v* werben.
canyon ['kanjən] *n* Cañon *m*, Schlucht *f*.

cap [kap] *n* (*hat*) Kappe *f*, Mütze *f*; (*lid*) Kappe *f*. *v* (*fig*) übertreffen.
capable ['keipəbl] *adj* (*able to do something*) fähig (zu); (*skilled*) begabt. **capability** *n* Fähigkeit *f*.
capacity [kə'pasəti] *n* (*volume*) Inhalt *m*; (*of ship*) Laderaum *m*; (*talent*) Talent *m*. **in the capacity of** als. **filled to capacity** voll (besetzt).
cape¹ [keip] *n* (*cloak*) Cape *neut*, Umhang *m*.
cape² [keip] *n* (*geog*) Kap *neut*.
caper¹ ['keipə] *n* Kapriole *f*. *v* kapriolen.
caper² ['keipə] *n* (*cookery*) Kaper *f*.
capital ['kapitl] *n* (*city*) Hauptstadt *f*; (*comm*) Kapital *neut*. *adj* (*main*) Haupt-; (*comm*) Kapital-; (*splendid*) großartig.
capitalism *n* Kapitalismus *m*. **capitalist** *n* Kapitalist *m*. *adj* kapitalistisch. **capital punishment** Todesstrafe *n*.
capitulate [kə'pitjuleit] *v* kapitulieren (vor).
capricious [kə'priʃəs] *adj* launenhaft.
Capricorn ['kaprikoɪn] *n* Steinbock *m*.
capsize [kap'saiz] *v* kentern.
capsule ['kapsjuɪl] *n* Kapsel *f*.
captain ['kaptin] *n* (*mil*) Hauptmann *m*; (*naut*) Kapitän *m*; (*sport*) Mannschaftsführer *m*. *v* (*sport*) führen.
caption ['kapʃən] *n* (*picture*) Erklärung *f*; (*heading*) Überschrift *f*.
captive ['kaptiv] *n* Gefangene(r). *adj* gefangen. **captivity** *n* Gefangenschaft *f*. **captor** *n* Fänger *m*.
capture ['kaptʃə] *v* gefangennehmen; (*animal*) einfangen. *n* Genangennahme *f*.
car [kaɪ] *n* (*mot*) Wagen *m*, Auto *neut*; (*rail*) Wagen *m*. **by car** mit dem Auto.
caramel ['karəmel] *n* Karamel *m*.
carat ['karət] *n* Karat *neut*.
caravan ['karəvan] *n* (*mot*) Wohnwagen *m*; (*oriental*) Karawane *f*.
caraway ['karəwei] *n* Kümmel *m*.
carbohydrate [kaɪbə'haidreit] *n* Kohlehydrat *neut*.
carbon ['kaɪbən] *n* Kohlenstoff *m*. **carbon copy** Durchschlag *m*. **carbon dioxide** Kohlendioxid *neut*; (*in drinks*) Kohlensäure *f*. **carbon paper** Kohlepapier *neut*.
carburettor ['kaɪbjuretə] **carburetor** *n* Vergaser *m*.
carcass ['kaɪkəs] *n* Kadaver *m*.
card [kaɪd] *n* Karte *f*. **cardboard** *n* Pappe *f*. **cardboard box** Pappschachtel *f*. **card**

game Kartenspiel *neut.* **card index** Kartei *f.*
cardiac ['kaːdiak] *adj* Herz-.
cardigan ['kaːdigən] *n* Wolljacke *f.*
cardinal ['kaːdənl] *n* Kardinal *m. adj* grundsätzlich.
care [keə] *n* (*carefulness*) Sorgfalt *f*; (*looking after*) Pflege *f*; (*worry*) Sorge *f.* **take care** sich hüten; achtgeben. **take care of** (*look after*) pflegen; (*see to*) erledigen. *v* **care about** sich kümmern um. **care for** (*look after*) pflegen; (*see to*) sorgen für; (*like*) mögen. **carefree** *adj* sorgenfrei. **careful** *adj* sorgfältig; (*cautious*) vorsichtig. **carefulness** *n* Sorgfalt *f*; Vorsicht *f.* **careless** *adj* unachtsam, nachlässig. **carelessness** *n* Nachlässigkeit *f.*
career [kə'riə] *n* Laufbahn *f*, Karriere *f.*
caress [kə'res] *v* liebkosen. *n* Liebkosung *f*; Kuß *m.*
cargo ['kaːgou] *n* Fracht *f.* **cargo plane** Transportflugzeug *neut.* **cargo ship** Frachtschiff *neut.*
caricature ['karikətjuə] *n* Karikatur *f. v* karikieren.
carnal ['kaːnl] *adj* fleischlich.
carnation [kaː'neiʃən] *n* Nelke *f.*
carnival ['kaːnivəl] *n* Karneval *m*, Fasching *m.*
carnivorous [kaː'nivərəs] *adj* fleischfressend.
carol ['karəl] *n* Weihnachtslied *neut.*
carpenter ['kaːpəntə] *n* Zimmermann *m*, Tischler *m.* **carpentry** *n* Zimmerhandwerk *neut.*
carpet ['kaːpit] *n* Teppich *m. v* mit einem Teppich belegen.
carriage ['karidʒ] *n* (*rail*) (Eisenbahn) Wagen *m*; (*transport*) Transport *f*; (*posture*) Haltung *f.* **carriageway** Fahrbahn *f.*
carrier ['kariə] *n* Träger *m*; (*med*) Keimträger *m*; (*comm*) Spediteur *m.* **carrier bag** Tragebeutel *m.*
carrot ['karət] *n* Mohrrübe *f*, Möhre *f.*
carry ['kari] *v* tragen; (*transport*) befördern. **carry out** ausführen. **carry cot** Tragbettchen *neut.*
cart [kaːt] *n* Karren *m.*
cartilage ['kaːtəlidʒ] *n* Knorpel *m.*
cartography [kaː'togrəfi] *n* Kartographie *f.*
carton ['kaːtən] *n* Karton *m.*
cartoon [kaː'tuːn] *n* Karikatur *f*; (*film*)

Trickfilm *m.* **cartoonist** *n* Karikaturenzeichner *m.*
cartridge ['kaːtridʒ] *n* Patrone *f.* **cartridge paper** Zeichenpapier *neut.*
carve [kaːv] *v* (*in wood*) schnitzen; (*in stone*) meißeln; (*meat*) vorschneiden. **carving** *n* Schnitzerei *f.*
cascade [kas'keid] *n* Kaskade *f.*
case[1] [keis] *n* (*affair, instance*) Fall *m*; (*law*) Sache *f.* **in case** falls. **in case of** im Falle (+ *gen*). **in any case** auf jeden Fall.
case[2] [keis] *n* (*suitcase*) Koffer *m*; (*for cigarettes, camera*) Etui *neut*; (*tech*) Gehäuse *neut.*
cash [kaʃ] *n* Bargeld *neut. v* einlösen. **cash on delivery** per Nachnahme. **pay cash** bar zahlen. **cash desk** Kasse *f.*
cashier [ka'ʃiə] *n* Kassierer(in).
cashmere [kaʃ'miə] *n* Kaschmir *m.*
casing ['keisiŋ] *n* Gehäuse *neut.*
casino [kə'siːnou] *n* Kasino *neut.*
casket ['kaːskit] *n* Kästchen *neut*; (*coffin*) Sarg *m.*
casserole ['kasəroul] *n* (*vessel*) Kasserolle *f*; (*meal*) Schmorbraten *m. v* schmoren.
cassette [kə'set] *n* Kassette *f.* **cassette recorder** Kassettenrecorder *m.*
cassock ['kasək] *n* Soutane *f.*
***cast** [kaːst] *v* werfen; (*metal*) gießen; (theatre) besetzen. *n* (*theatre*) Besetzung *f.*
caste [kaːst] *n* Kaste *f.*
castle ['kaːsl] *n* Burg *f*, Schloß *neut*; (*chess*) Turm *m. v* (*chess*) rochieren.
castor oil ['kaːstə] *n* Möbelrolle *f.*
castrate [kə'streit] *v* kastrieren. **castration** *n* Kastration *f.*
casual ['kaʒuəl] *adj* beiläufig; (*careless*) nachlässig; (*informal*) leger. **casual labour** Gelegenheitsarbeit *f.*
casualty ['kaʒuəlti] *n* Verletzte(r). **casualties** *pl n* (*mil*) Ausfälle *pl.* **casualty department** Unfallstation *f.*
cat [kat] *n* Katze *f.* **tom cat** Kater *m.*
catalogue ['katəlog] *n* Katalog *m.*
catalyst ['katəlist] *n* Katalysator *m.*
catamaran [katəmə'ran] *n* Katamaran *neut.*
catapult ['katəpʌlt] *n* Katapult *neut.*
cataract ['katərakt] *n* (*med*) grauer Star *m*; Wasserfall *m.*
catarrh [kə'taː] *n* Katarrh *m.*
catastrophe [kə'tastrəfi] *n* Katastrophe *f.* **catastrophic** *adj* katastrophal.

*catch [katʃ] v fangen; (bus, train) nehmen, erreichen; (surprise) ertappen; (illness) sich zuziehen. n Fang m.
category ['katəgəri] n Katagorie f. **categorical** adj kategorisch.
cater ['keitə] v **cater for** versorgen. **catering** n Bewirtung f.
caterpillar ['katəpilə] n Raupe f. **caterpillar track** Gleiskette f.
cathedral [kə'θiːdrəl] n Dom m, Kathedrale f.
cathode ['kaθoud] n Kathode f.
catholic ['kaθəlik] adj (rel) katholisch; universal. n Katholik(in). **Roman Catholic** römisch-katholisch.
catkin ['katkin] n Kätzchen neut.
cattle ['katl] pl n Vieh neut sing, Rindvieh neut sing. **cattle shed** Viehstall m.
catty ['kati] adj (coll) gehässig.
caught [koit] V catch.
cauliflower ['koliflauə] n Blumenkohl m.
cause [coiz] n Ursache f; (reason) Grund m; (interests) Sache f. v verursachen, veranlassen.
causeway ['koizwei] n Damm m.
caustic ['koistik] adj ätzend; (fig) beißend.
caution ['koiʃən] n Vorsicht f. v warnen (vor). **cautious** adj vorsichtig.
cavalry ['kavəlri] n Kavallerie f.
cave [keiv] n Höhle f. v **cave in** einstürzen. **cavern** n Höhle f.
caviar ['kaviaː] n Kaviar m.
cavity ['kavəti] n Hohlraum m; (in tooth) Loch neut.
cease [siːs] v aufhören; (fire) einstellen. **ceasefire** n Feuereinstellung f. **ceaseless** adj unaufhörlich.
cedar ['siːdə] n Zeder f.
ceiling ['siːliŋ] n Decke f; (fig) Höchstgrenze f.
celebrate ['seləbreit] v feiern. **celebrated** adj berühmt. **celebration** n Feier f. **celebrity** n Berühmtheit f.
celery ['seləri] n Sellerie m or f.
celestial [sə'lestiəl] adj himmlisch.
celibacy ['selibəsi] n Zölibat neut or m, Ehelosigkeit f. **celibate** adj ehelos.
cell [sel] n Zelle f.
cellar ['selə] n Keller m.
cello ['tʃelou] n Cello neut.
cellophane ['seləfein] n Zellophan neut.
cellular ['seljulə] adj zellular.
cement [sə'ment] n Zement m. v zementieren; (fig) binden.

cemetery ['semətri] n Friedhof m.
cenotaph ['senətaːf] n Ehrenmal m.
censor ['sensə] n Zensor m. v zensieren. **censorship** n Zensur f.
censure ['senʃə] n Tadel m. v tadeln.
census ['sensəs] n Volkszählung f.
cent [sent] n Cent m. **per cent** Prozent neut.
centenary [sen'tiːnəri] n Hundertjahrfeier f.
centigrade ['sentigreid] adv Celsius.
centimetre ['sentimiːtə] n Zentimeter neut.
centipede ['sentipiːd] n Tausendfuß m.
centre ['sentə] n Zentrum neut, Mittelpunkt m. adj Zentral-. v **centre around** sich drehen um. **centre on** sich konzentrieren auf. **centre forward** (sport) Mittelstürmer m. **centre half** Mittelläufer m. **centre of gravity** Schwerpunkt m. **centrepiece** n Tafelaufsatz m. **central** adj zentral, Zentral-. **Central America** Mittelamerika neut. **central heating** Zentralheizung f. **central station** Hauptbahnhof m.
centrifugal [sen'trifjugəl] adj zentrifugal. **centrifugal force** Zentrifugalkraft f.
century ['sentʃuri] n Jahrhundert neut.
ceramic [sə'ramik] adj keramisch. **ceramics** n Keramik f.
cereal ['siəriəl] n Getreide neut. **breakfast cereal** Getreideflocken pl.
ceremony ['serəməni] n Zeremonie f. **ceremonial** adj zeremoniell. **ceremonious** adj zeremoniös.
certain ['səːtn] adj bestimmt, gewiß; (sure) sicher. **for certain** bestimmt. **certainly** adv sicherlich, gewiß. **certainty** n Sicherheit f.
certificate [sə'tifikət] n Bescheinigung f. **certification** n Bescheinigung f. **certify** v bestätigen.
cervix ['səːviks] n (anat) Gebärmutterhals m.
cesspool ['sespuːl] n Senkgrube f.
chafe [tʃeif] v reiben.
chaffinch ['tʃafintʃ] n Buchfink m.
chain [tʃein] n Kette f. v anketten. **chain reaction** Kettenreaktion f. **chain smoker** Kettenraucher m. **chainstore** n Kettenladen m.
chair [tʃeə] n Stuhl m; (armchair) Sessel m; (at meeting) Vorsitz m. v (meeting) den Vorsitz führen. **chairlift** n Sesselbahn f. **chairman** Vorsitzende(r).

chalet ['ʃalei] *n* Chalet *neut.*
chalk [tʃɔːk] *n* Kreide *f. v* mit Kreide schreiben.
challenge ['tʃalindʒ] *n* Aufforderung *f*; (*objection*) Einwand *m. v* auffordern; (*question*) bestreiten. **challenger** *n* Herausforderer *m.*
chamber ['tʃeimbə] *n* Kammer *f.* **chamber music** Kammermusik *f.* **chamber pot** Nachttopf *m.*
chameleon [kəmiːliən] *n* Chamäleon *neut.*
chamois ['ʃamwaɪ] *n* Gemse *f*; (*leather*) Sämischleder *neut.*
champagne [ʃam'pein] *n* Champagner *m.*
champion ['tʃampiən] *n* (*sport*) Meister *m*, Sieger *m*; (*defender*) Verfechter *m. v* (*cause*) verfechten. **championship** *n* Meisterschaft *f.*
chance [tʃaɪns] *n* Zufall *m*; (*opportunity*) Gelegenheit *f*; (*possibility*) Chance *f*, Möglichkeit *f. v* riskieren. **by chance** zufällig. **stand a chance** Chancen haben. **take a chance** sein Glück versuchen. **no chance!** keine Spur!
chancellor [tʃaɪnsələ] *n* Kanzler *m.*
chandelier [ʃandə'liə] *n* Kronleuchter *m.*
change [tʃeindʒ] *v* (*modify*) (ab-, ver)ändern; (*exchange*) (aus)tauschen; (*become changed*) sich (ver)ändern; (*trains*) umsteigen; (*clothes*) sich umziehen; (*money*) wechseln. **change gear** schalten. **change into** (sich) verwandeln in. **change over to** übergehen zu. *n* (Ab-, Ver)Änderung *f*; (Ver)Wandlung *f*; (*small change*) Kleingeld *neut.* **change of life** Wechseljahre *pl.* **for a change** zur Abwechselung. **changeable** *adj* veränderlich. **changeless** *adj* unveränderlich.
channel ['tʃanl] *n* Kanal *m*; (*fig*) Weg *m. v* lenken. **through official channels** durch die Instanzen. **English Channel** der Ärmelkanal.
chant [tʃaɪnt] *v* intonieren. *n* Gesang *m.*
chaos ['keios] *n* Chaos *neut*; (*mess*) Durcheinander *neut.*
chap¹ [tʃap] *v* (*skin*) rissig machen; (*become chapped*) aufspringen.
chap² [tʃap] *n* (*coll*) Kerl *m.*
chapel ['tʃapəl] *n* Kapelle *f.*
chaperon ['ʃapəroun] *n* Anstandsdame *f. v* begleiten.
chaplain ['tʃaplin] *n* Kaplan *m.*
chapter ['tʃaptə] *n* Kapitel *neut*; (*branch*) Ortsgruppe *f.*

char¹ [tʃaɪ] *v* (*burn*) verkohlen.
char² [tʃaɪ] *n* (*cleaning lady*) Putzfrau *f.*
character ['karəktə] *n* Charakter *m*; (*personality*) Persönlichkeit *f*; (*theatre*) Person *f*; (*reputation*) Ruf *m*; (*letter*) Buchstabe *m.* **characteristic** *n* Kennzeichen *neut*; *adj* charakteristisch. **characterize** *v* charakterisieren.
charcoal ['tʃaɪkoul] *n* Holzkohle *f*; (*for drawing*) Reißkohle *f.*
charge [tʃaɪdʒ] *n* (*cost*) Preis *m*; (*of firearm*) Ladung *f*; (*mil*) Angriff *m*; (*law*) Anklage *f*; (*elec*) Ladung *f. v* (*firearm, battery*) laden; (*price*) verlangen; (*attack*) angreifen. **be in charge of** verantwortlich sein für. **bring a charge against** anklagen.
chariot ['tʃariət] *n* Streitwagen *m.*
charity ['tʃarəti] *n* Nächstenliebe *f*, Wohltätigkeit *f*; (*organization*) Wohlfahrtseinrichtung *f.* **charitable** *adj* wohltätig *f.*
charm [tʃaɪm] *n* (*personal*) Scharm *m*, Reiz *m*; (*magic word*) Zauberwort *neut*; (*trinket*) Amulett *neut. v* entzücken. **charming** entzückend, scharmant.
chart [tʃaɪt] *n* (*naut*) Seekarte *f*; Diagramm *neut.*
charter ['tʃaɪtə] *n* Verfassungsurkunde *f*; (*naut, aero*) Charter *m. v* chartern. *adj* Charter-.
chase [tʃeis] *v* verfolgen, jagen. *n* Verfolgung *f*, Jagd *f.*
chasm ['kazəm] *n* Abgrund *m.*
chassis ['ʃasi] *n* Fahrgestell *neut.*
chaste [tʃeist] *adj* keusch. **chastity** *n* Keuschheit *f.*
chastise [tʃas'taiz] *v* strafen.
chat [tʃat] *v* plaudern, sich unterhalten. *n* Plauderei *f.*
chatter ['tʃatə] *v* schnattern; (*teeth*) klappern. *n* Geschnatter *neut*; Klappern *neut.*
chauffeur ['ʃoufə] *n* Chauffeur *m.*
chauvinism ['ʃouvinizəm] *n* Chauvinismus *m.* **chauvinist** *n* Chauvinist *m.*
cheap [tʃiːp] *adj* billig, preiswert; (*base*) gemein.
cheat [tʃiːt] *v* betrügen. *n* Betrüger *m*, Schwindler *m.*
check [tʃek] *v* (*inspect*) prüfen, kontrollieren; (*hinder*) (ver)hindern; (*look up*) nachsehen; (*tick*) abhaken. **check in** sich anmelden. **check out** (*hotel*) abreisen. *n* Kontrolle *f*; (*bill*) Rechnung; (*check*) Scheck *m*; (*chess*) Schach *m*; (*pattern*) Karo *neut.* **checklist** *n* Kontrolliste *f.*

checkmate *n* Schachmatt *neut*. **checkpoint** Kontrollpunkt *m*. **check-up** *n* (*med*) ärztliche Untersuchung *f*.
cheek [tʃiːk] *n* (*anat*) Wange *f*, Backe *f*; (*impudence*) Frechheit *f*. **cheeky** *adj* frech.
cheer [tʃiə] *v* jubeln; (*applaud*) zujubeln (+ *dat*); (*encourage*) aufmuntern. **cheer up** aufmuntern. *n* Beifallsruf *m*, Hurra *neut*. **cheers!** *interj* prost! **cheerful** *adj* fröhlich. **cheerio!** *interj* tschüs!
cheese [tʃiːz] *n* Käse *f*. **cheesecake** *n* Käsekuchen *m*; **cheesecloth** *n* Musselin *m*.
cheetah ['tʃiːtə] *n* Gepard *m*.
chef [ʃef] *n* Küchenchef *m*.
chemical ['kemikl] *adj* chemisch. **chemicals** *pl n* Chemikalien *pl*.
chemist ['kemist] *n* Chemiker *m*; (*dispensing chemist*) Apotheker *m*. **chemist's shop** Apotheke *f*.
chemistry ['kemistri] *n* Chemie *f*.
cheque [tʃek] *n* Scheck *m*. **chequebook** *n* Scheckbuch *neut*. **cheque card** Scheckkarte *f*.
cherish ['tʃeriʃ] *v* (*feeling*) hegen; (*person*) lieb haben.
cherry ['tʃeri] *n* Kirsche *f*; (*tree*) Kirschbaum *m*.
chess [tʃes] *n* Schach *neut*. **chessboard** *n* Schachbrett *neut*. **chessman** *n* Schachfigur *f*.
chest [tʃest] *n* (*anat*) Brust *f*; (*container*) Kiste *f*; (*trunk*) Truhe *f*. *that's a weight off my chest* da fällt mir ein Stein vom Herzen.
chestnut ['tʃesnʌt] *n* (*sweet chestnut*) (Eß)Kastanie *f*; (*horse chestnut*) (Roß)Kastanie *f*; (*tree*) Kastanienbaum *m*; (*brown horse*) Braune(r) *m*.
chew [tʃuː] *v* kauen. **chewing gum** Kaugummi *m*.
chick [tʃik] *n* Küken *neut*. **chicken** *n* Huhn *neut*; (*for eating*) Hähnchen *neut*. *adj* (*coll*) feige. **chicken soup** Hühnerbrühe *f*.
chicory ['tʃikəri] *n* Zichorie *f*; (*salad plant*) Chicorée *f*.
chief [tʃiːf] *n* (*pl* -s) Chef *m*, Leiter *m*; (*of tribe*) Häuptling *m*. *adj* Haupt-, erster. **chieftain** *m* Häuptling *m*.
chilblain ['tʃilblein] *n* Frostbeule *f*.
child [tʃaild] *n* (*pl* -ren) Kind *neut*. **with child** schwanger. **childbirth** *n* Entbindung

f. **childhood** *n* Kindheit *f*. **childish** *adj* kindisch. **childlike** *adj* kindlich.
Chile ['tʃili] *n* Chile *neut*. **Chilean** *adj* chilenisch. *n* Chilene *m*, Chilenin *f*.
chill [tʃil] *n* Kältegefühl *neut*; (*fever*) Schüttelfrost *m*. **chilled** *adj* (*drink*) gekühlt. **chilly** *adj* fröstelnd.
chilli ['tʃili] *n* Cayennepfeffer *m*.
chime [tʃaim] *v* (*bell*) läuten. *n* Geläut *neut*.
chimney ['tʃimni] *n* Schornstein *m*. **chimney sweep** Schornsteinfeger *m*.
chimpanzee [tʃimpən'ziː] *n* Schimpanse *m*.
chin [tʃin] *n* Kinn *neut*.
china ['tʃainə] *n* Porzellan *neut*. *adj* Porzellan-. **china clay** Kaolin *neut*.
China ['tʃainə] *n* China *neut*. **Chinese** *adj* chinesisch; *n* Chinese *m*, Chinesin *f*.
chink¹ [tʃiŋk] *n* (*fissure*) Ritze *f*, Spalt *m*.
chink² [tʃiŋk] *v* (*sound*) klirren. *n* Klirren *neut*.
chip [tʃip] *n* Splitter *m*. **chips** *pl* Pommes frites *pl*; (*crisps*) Chips *pl*. **chipped** *adj* (*china*) angestoßen.
chiropodist [ki'ropədist] *n* Fußpfleger(in). **chiropody** *n* Fußpflege *f*.
chirp [tʃəːp] *v* zirpen. *n* Gezirp *neut*. **chirpy** *adj* munter.
chisel ['tʃizl] *n* Meißel *m*. *v* meißeln.
chivalrous [ʃivəlrəs] *adj* ritterlich. **chivalry** *n* Ritterlichkeit *f*.
chives [tʃaivz] *pl n* Schnittlauch *m sing*.
chlorine ['klɔːriːn] *n* Chlor *neut*. **chlorinate** *v* chlorieren.
chlorophyll ['klɔrəfil] *n* Chlorophyll *neut*.
chocolate ['tʃokələt] *n* Schokolade *f*. *adj* (*colour*) schokoladenbraun.
choice [tʃois] *n* Wahl *f*; (*selection*) Auswahl *f*. *adj* auserlesen.
choir ['kwaiə] *n* Chor *m*. **choirboy** Chorknabe *m*.
choke [tʃouk] *v* ersticken, würgen; (*throttle*) erwürgen. *n* (*mot*) Starterklappe *f*.
cholera ['kolərə] *n* Cholera *f*.
cholesterol [kə'lestərol] *n* Cholesterin *neut*.
*****choose** [tʃuːz] *v* wählen; (*select*) auswählen; (*prefer*) vorziehen. **choosy** *adj* wählerisch.
chop¹ [tʃop] *v* (*food*) zerhacken; (*wood*) spalten. *n* Kotelett *neut*.
chop² [tʃop] *v* **chop and change** schwanken, wechseln.

chopsticks ['tʃopstiks] *pl n* Eßstäbchen *pl.*
chord [kɔɪd] *n (music)* Akkord *m.*
chore [tʃɔɪ] *n* lästige Pflicht *f.*
choreographer [kori'ogrəfə] *n* Choreograph *m.* **choreography** *n* Choreographie *f.*
chorus ['kɔɪrəs] *n* Chor *m;* *(of song)* Refrain *m.*
chose [tʃouz] *V* **choose.**
chosen ['tʃouzn] *V* **choose.**
Christ [kraist] *n* Christus *m.*
christen ['krisn] *v* taufen. **christening** *n* Taufe *f.*
Christian ['kristʃən] *adj* christlich. *n* Christ *m,* Christin *f.* **Christian name** Vorname *m.* **Christianity** *n* Christentum *neut.*
Christmas ['krisməs] *n* Weihnachten *pl.* **Christmas card** Weihnachtskarte *f.* **Christmas present** Weihnachtsgeschenk *neut.* **Christmas tree** Weihnachtsbaum *m.*
chrome [kroum] *n (plating)* Verchromung *f. adj (yellow)* chromgelb. **chrome-plated** *adj* verchromt.
chromium ['kroumiəm] *n* Chrom *neut.*
chronic ['kronik] *adj (med)* chronisch.
chronicle ['kronikl] *n* Chronik *f.*
chronological [kronə'lodʒikəl] *adj* chronologisch.
chrysalis ['krisəlis] *n* Puppe *f.*
chrysanthemum [kri'sanθəməm] *n* Chrysantheme *f.*
chubby ['tʃʌbi] *adj* pausbäckig.
chuck [tʃʌk] *v (coll)* werfen.
chuckle ['tʃʌkl] *v* glucksen, kichern. *n* Kichern *neut.*
chunk [tʃʌŋk] *n* Klumpen *m,* Stück *neut.*
church [tʃəɪtʃ] *n* Kirche *f.* **church-goer** *n* Kirchgänger *m.* **churchyard** *n* Kirchhof *m.*
churn [tʃəɪn] *n (butter)* Butterfaß *neut;* *(milk)* Milchkanne *f. v (fig)* aufwühlen.
chute [ʃuɪt] *n* Rutsche *f.*
cider ['saidə] *n* Apfelwein *m.*
cigar [si'gaɪ] *n* Zigarre *f.*
cigarette [sigə'ret] *n* Zigarette *f.* **cigarette end** Zigarettenstümmel *m.* **cigarette lighter** *n* Feuerzeug *neut.*
cinder ['sində] *n* Zinder *m.*
cine camera ['sini] *n* Filmkamera *f.*
cinema ['sinəmə] *n* Kino *neut.*
cinnamon ['sinəmən] *n* Zimt *m.*
circle ['səɪkl] *n* Kreis *m;* *(theatre)* Rang *m. v* umkreisen. **circular** *adj* kreisförmig,

rund. **circulate** *v* zirkulieren, umlaufen; *(send round)* in Umlauf setzen. **circulation** *n* Umlauf *m;* *(blood)* Kreislauf *m.*
circuit ['səɪkit] *n* Umlauf *m;* *(elec)* Stromkreis *m.*
circumcise ['səɪkəmsaiz] *n* beschneiden. **circumcision** *n* Beschneidung *f.*
circumference [səɪ'kʌmfərəns] *n* Umfang *m.*
circumscribe ['səɪkəmskraib] *v* umschreiben.
circumstance ['səɪkəmstans] *n* Umstand *m.* **under the circumstances** unter diesen Umständen. **under no circumstances** auf keinen Fall.
circus ['səɪkəs] *n* Zirkus *m.*
cistern ['sistən] *n* Zisterne *f.*
cite [sait] *v* zitieren.
citizen ['sitizn] *n* Bürger(in); *(of country)* Staatsangehörige(r). **citizenship** *n* Staatsangehörigkeit *f.*
citrus ['sitrəs] *adj* **citrus fruit** Zitrusfrucht *f.*
city ['siti] *n* Stadt *f.*
civic ['sivik] *n* städtisch.
civil ['sivl] *adj (polite)* höflich, freundlich; *(not military)* Zivil-. **civility** *n* Höflichkeit *f.* **civil engineer** Bauingenieur *m.* **civil rights** Bürgerrechte *pl.*
civilian [sə'viljən] *adj* Zivil-. *n* Zivilist *m.*
civilization [,sivilai'zeiʃən] *n* Zivilisation *f.* **civilize** *v* zivilisieren. **civilized** *adj* zivilisiert.
clad [klad] *adj* bekleidet; *(tech)* umkleidet.
claim [kleim] *v* verlangen, Anspruch erheben auf. *n* Anspruch *m;* *(right)* Anrecht *neut.* **claimant** *n* Antragsteller *m.*
clairvoyant [kleə'voiənt] *n* Hellseher(in).
clam [klam] *n* Muschel *f.*
clamber ['klambə] *v* klettern.
clammy ['klami] *adj* feucht, klebrig.
clamour ['klamə] *n* Geschrei *neut. v* **clamour for** rufen nach.
clamp [klamp] *n* Klammer *f,* Krampe *f. v* verklammern. **clamp down on** unterdrücken.
clan [klan] *n* Sippe *f.*
clandestine [klan'destin] *adj* heimlich.
clang [klaŋ] *n* Schall *m,* Klirren *neut. v* schallen, klirren.
clank [klaŋk] *n* Gerassel *neut;* Klappern *neut. v* rasseln, klappern.

clap [klap] v (applaud) klatschen, Beifall spenden (+dat); (hit) schlagen, klapsen. n (tap) Klaps m. clapper n (bell) Klöppel m. clapping n Klatschen neut.

claret ['klarət] n Rotwein m, Bordeaux m.

clarify ['klarəfai] v klären. clarification n Klärung f.

clarinet [klarə'net] n Klarinette f. clarinettist n Klarinettist m.

clash [klaʃ] v kollidieren, zusammenprallen; (argue) sich streiten; (colours) nicht zusammenpassen. n Knall m; (conflict) Konflikt m.

clasp [klaːsp] v umklammern; n Haspe f, Klammer f.

class [klaːs] n Klasse f; (lesson) Stunde f. v klassieren. class-conscious adj klassenbewußt. classroom n Klassenzimmer f. classy adj (coll) klasse, erstklassig.

classic ['klasik] adj klassisch. classics pl n die alten Sprachen pl. classical adj klassisch. classicism n Klassik f.

classify ['klasifai] v klassifizieren. classification n Klassifizierung f.

clatter ['klatə] v klappern. n Klappern neut.

clause [kloːz] n (in document) Klausel f.

claustrophobia [kloːstrə'foubiə] n Platzangst f.

claw [kloː] n Kralle f, Klaue f. v zerkratzen.

clay [klei] n Lehm m, Ton m.

clean [kliin] adj rein, sauber; (paper) weiß. adv ganz. v reinigen, putzen, saubermachen. clean up aufräumen. come clean gestehen. cleaner n (woman) Putzfrau f. cleaning n Reinigen neut. cleanness n Sauberkeit f. cleanly adj reinlich. clean-shaven adj glattrasiert.

cleanse [klenz] v reinigen.

clear [kliə] adj klar; (sound, meaning) deutlich, klar; (road, way) frei; (glass) durchsichtig. v räumen; (table) abräumen; (road) freimachen; (forest) roden; (authorize) freigeben. clearance n Räumung f; (authorization) Freigabe f; (tech) Spielraum m. clearcut adj (fig) eindeutig. clearing n Lichtung f. clearly adv offensichtlich.

clef [klef] n Notenschlüssel m.

clench [klentʃ] v (fist) zusammenballen.

clergy ['kləːdʒi] n Klerus m. clergyman n Geistliche(r) m; Kleriker m.

clerical ['klerikəl] adj geistlich. clerical work Büroarbeit f.

clerk [klaːk] n Büroangestellte(r); (sales clerk) Verkäufer(in).

clever ['klevə] adj klug, gescheit; (crafty) raffiniert. cleverness n Klugheit f.

cliché ['kliːʃei] n Klischee neut.

click [klik] n Klicken neut. v klicken.

client ['klaiənt] n Kunde m, Kundin f. clientele n Kundschaft f.

cliff [klif] n Klippe f.

climate ['klaimət] n Klima neut.

climax ['klaimaks] n Höhepunkt m.

climb [klaim] v klettern; (ascend) steigen; (mountain) besteigen. n Aufstieg m. climb up hinaufklettern auf. climb down hinabsteigen. climber n (mountaineer) Bergsteiger m. climbing n (mountaineering) Bergsteigen neut.

*cling [kliŋ] v sich klammern (an); (fig) hängen (an).

clinic ['klinik] n Klinik f. clinical adj klinisch.

clink [kliŋk] n Klirren neut. v klirren.

clip¹ [klip] v (hair) schneiden; (dog) scheren; (ticket) knipsen. clipping n (newspaper) Zeitungsausschnitt m.

clip² [klip] n (fastener) Klammer f, Klemme f. v clip together zusammenklammern.

clitoris ['klitəris] n Kitzler m, Klitoris f.

cloak [klouk] n Umhang m. cloakroom n Garderobe f; (WC) Toilette f.

clock [klok] n Uhr f. clockwise adj, adv im Uhrzeigersinn. clockwork Uhrwerk neut.

clog [klog] n Holzschuh m. v verstopfen.

cloister ['kloistə] n Kreuzgang m.

close¹ [klouz] v zumachen, schließen. n Ende neut; Schluß m. close down eingehen. closed adj (shop) geschlossen; (road) gesperrt.

close² [klous] adj nahe; (intimate) vertraut; (careful) genau; (weather) schwül. adv knapp. close to in der Nähe (+gen or von). close together dicht zusammen. that was close! das war knapp! closely adv genau, gründlich. close-up Nahaufnahme f.

closet ['klozit] n Schrank m.

clot [klot] n Klümpchen neut; (of blood) Blutgerinnsel neut. v gerinnen.

cloth [kloθ] n (material) Stoff m, Tuch neut; (for wiping) Lappen m.

clothe [klouð] v (be)kleiden. clothes pl n Kleider pl. clothes brush Kleiderbürste f.

clothes line Wäscheleine *f.* **clothes peg**
Wäscheklammer *f.* **clothing** *n* Kleidung *f.*
cloud [klaud] *n* Wolke *f.* **cloud over** sich
bewölken.
clove[1] [klouv] *n* (*spice*) Gewürznelke *f.*
clove[2] [klouv] *n* **clove of garlic**
Knoblauchzehe *f.*
clover ['klouvə] *n* Klee *m.*
clown [klaun] *n* Clown *m.*
club [klʌb] *n* (*association*) Klub *m,* Verein
m; (*weapon*) Keule *f*; (*golf*) Golfschläger
m. **clubfoot** *n* Klumpfuß *m.*
clue [kluɪ] *n* Spur *f,* Anhaltspunkt *m. I
haven't a clue* ich habe keine Ahnung *f.*
clump [klʌmp] *n* Klumpen *neut*; (*of
bushes*) Gebüsch *neut.*
clumsy ['klʌmzi] *adj* unbeholfen, linkisch.
clung [klʌŋ] *V* cling.
cluster ['klʌstə] *n* Traube *f.* *v* **cluster
around** schwärmen um.
clutch [klʌtʃ] *n* (*fester*) Griff *m*; (*mot*)
Kupplung *f.* *v* sich festklammern an.
clutch at greifen nach.
clutter ['klʌtə] *n* Unordnung *f,* Durcheinander *neut.* *v* vollstopfen.
coach [koutʃ] *n* Kutsche *f*; (*rail*) Wagen
m; (*sport*) Trainer *m.* *v* eintrainieren.
coagulate [kou'agjuleit] *v* gerinnen.
coal [koul] *n* Kohle *f.* **coal-mine**
Kohlenbergwerk *neut.*
coalition [kouə'liʃən] *n* (*pol*) Koalition *f.*
coarse [koɪs] *adj* grob; (*vulgar*) ordinär.
coast [koust] *n* Küste *f.* **coastal** *adj* Küs-
ten-. **coastline** *n* Küstenlinie *f.*
coat [kout] *n* Mantel *m*; (*of animal*) Fell
neut, Pelz *m*; (*of paint*) Anstrich *m.* *v*
bestreichen. **coated** *adj* überzogen.
coathanger *n* Kleiderbügel *m.* **coating** *n*
Überzug *m.*
coax [kouks] *v* beschwatzen.
cobbler ['koblə] *n* Schuster *m.*
cobra ['koubrə] *n* Kobra *neut.*
cobweb ['kobweb] *n* Spinngewebe *neut.*
cocaine [kə'kein] *n* Kokain *neut.*
cock[1] [kok] *n* (*male chicken*) Hahn *m*;
(*male bird*) (Vogel)Männchen *neut.*
cock[2] [kok] *v* (*gun*) spannen; (*ears*)
spitzen.
cockle ['kokl] *n* (*shellfish*) Herzmuschel *f.*
cockpit ['kokpit] *n* Kanzel *f,* Kabine *f.*
cockroach ['kokroutʃ] *n* Küchenschabe *f.*
cocktail ['kokteil] *n* Cocktail *neut.*
cocoa ['koukou] *n* Kakao *m.*
coconut ['koukənʌt] *n* Kokosnuß *f.*
cocoon [kə'kuɪn] *n* Kokon *m,* Puppe *f.*

cod [kod] *n* Kabeljau *m.*
code [koud] *n* Kode *m.*
codeine ['koudiɪn] *n* Kodein *neut.*
coeducation [kouedju'keiʃən] *n* Gemein-
schaftserziehung *f.*
coerce [kou'əɪs] *v* zwingen. **coercion** *n*
Zwang *m.*
coexist [kouig'zist] *v* koexistieren. **coexistence** *n* Koexistenz *f.*
coffee ['kofi] *n* Kaffee *m.* **coffee bar** Café
neut.
coffin ['kofin] *n* Sarg *m.*
cog [kog] *n* Radzahn *neut.* **cogwheel** Zahnrad *neut.*
cognac ['konjak] *n* Kognak *m.*
cohabit [kou'habit] *v* (*ehelich*) zusam-
menwohnen.
coherent [kou'hiərənt] *adj* zusam-
menhängend.
coil [koil] *n* Rolle *f*; *v* aufwickeln.
coin [koin] *n* Münze *f.* *v* prägen. **coinbox**
n (*phone*) Münzfernsprecher *m.*
coincide [kouin'said] *v* zusammenfallen;
(*agree*) übereinstimmen. **coincidence** *n*
Zufall *m.* **coincidental** zufällig.
colander ['koləndə] *n* Durchschlag *m.*
cold [kould] *adj* kalt. *I am/feel cold* mir
ist kalt. *n* Kälte *f*; (*med*) Erkältung *f.*
catch cold sich erkälten. **in cold blood**
kaltblütig. **coldly** *adv* (*fig*) gefühllos,
unfreundlich. **cold store** Kühlhaus *neut.*
coleslaw ['koulslo] *n* Krautsalat *m.*
colic ['kolik] *n* Kolik *f.*
collaborate [kə'labəreit] *v* zusammenarbeiten. **collaboration** *n* zusammenarbeit *f.* **collaborator** *n* Mitarbeiter
m; (*in war*) Kollaborateur *m.*
collapse [kə'laps] *v* einstürzen; (*person*)
zusammenbrechen. *n* Einsturz *m*; (*fig,
med*) Zusammenbruch *m.* **collapsible** *adj*
zusammenklappbar.
collar ['kolə] *n* Kragen *m*; (*for dog*) Hal-
sband *m.* **collarbone** *n* Schlüsselbein
neut.
colleague ['koliːg] *n* Kollege *m,* Kollegin
f.
collect [kə'lekt] *v* sammeln; (*fetch*)
abholen; (*taxes*) eiؑnehmen; (*come
together*) zusammenkommen. **collect call**
(*phone*) R-Gespräch *neut.* **collected** *adj*
(*calm*) gefaßt. **collection** *n* Sammlung *f*;
(*rel*) Kollekte *f*; (*mail*) Leerung *f.* **collective** *adj* kollektiv. **collective bargaining**
Tarifverhandlungen *pl.* **collector** *n* Sam-
mler *m*; (**of taxes**) Einnehmer *m.*

college ['kolidʒ] *n* Hochschule *f*; (*at Oxford, etc.*) College *neut.* **technical college** Realschule *f*.
collide [kə'laid] *v* kollidieren, zusammenprallen.
colloquial [kə'loukwiəl] *adj* umgangssprachlich.
Cologne [kə'loun] *n* Köln *neut.* **eau de Cologne** Kölnischwasser *neut.*
colon ['koulon] *n* (*anat*) Dickdarm *m*; (*gram*) Doppelpunkt *m*.
colonel ['kəɪnl] *n* Oberst *m*.
colony ['koləni] *n* Kolonie *f*. **colonial** *adj* Kolonial-. **colonialism** Kolonialismus *m*. **colonize** *v* kolonisieren.
colossal [kə'losəl] *adj* kolossal, riesig.
colour ['kʌlə] *n* Farbe *f*; (*fig*) Ton *m*, Charakter *m*. **colours** *pl* Fahne *f sing. v* färben (*also fig*), kolorieren. **colour bar** Rassenschranke *f*. **colour-blind** *adj* farbenblind. **coloured** *adj* farbig. **coloured man/woman** Farbige(r). **colour film** Farbfilm *m*. **colourful** *adj* farbig, bunt. **colour television** Farbfernsehen *neut.*
colt [koult] *n* Fohlen *neut.*
column ['koləm] *n* Säule *f*; (*in newspaper*) Spalte *f*; (*mil*) Kolonne *f*. **columnist** *n* Kolumnist *m*.
coma ['koumə] *n* Koma *f*.
comb [koum] *n* Kamm *m. v* kämmen; (*fig*) durchkämmen.
combat ['kombat] *v* bekämpfen. *n* Kampf *m*, Gefecht *neut.*
combine [kəm'bain; *n* 'kombain] *v* vereinigen, verbinden; (*come together*) sich vereinigen. *n* Konzern *m*. **combine harvester** Mähdrescher *m*.
combustion [kəm'bʌstʃən] *n* Verbrennung *f*. **combustible** *adj* brennbar.
***come** [kʌm] *v* kommen. **come about** geschehen. **come across** stoßen auf. **come back** zurückkommen. **come from** herkommen von stammen aus. **come near** sich nähern. **come on** weiterkommen; (*make progress*) fortschreiten. **come on!** los!; weiter! **come out** herauskommen. **come through** durchkommen. **come to** (*arrive at*) ankommen an, gelangen an; (*amount to*) sich belaufen auf; (*regain consciousness*) zu sich kommen.
comeback *n* Comeback *neut.*
comedy ['komədi] *n* Komödie *f*. **comedian** *n* Komiker *m*.

comet ['komit] *n* Komet *m*.
comfort ['kʌmfət] *n* Bequemlichkeit *f*. Komfort *m*; (*solace*) Trost *m. v* trösten. **comfortable** *adj* bequem; (*room, etc.*) komfortabel.
comic ['komik] *adj* komisch, lustig; (*theatre*) Komödien-. *n* (*person*) Komiker *m*; (*paper*) Comic *neut.* **comical** *adj* komisch.
comma ['komə] *n* Komma *neut.*
command [kə'maind] *n* (*order*) Befehl *m*; (*mil*) Oberbefehl *m*; (*mastery*) Beherrschung *f. v* (*instruct*) befehlen; (*be in charge of*) kommandieren. **commander** *n* Befehlshaber *m*; (*mil*) Kommandant *m*.
commandment *n* Gebot *neut.* **commando** *n* Kommando *neut.*
commemorate [kə'meməreit] *v* gedenken (+ *gen*), feiern. **commemoration** *n* Gedächtnisfeier *f*.
commence [kə'mens] *v* beginnen, anfangen. **commencement** *n* Beginn *m*, Anfang *m*.
commend [kə'mend] *v* (*praise*) loben; (*entrust*) anvertrauen. **commendable** *adj* lobenswert.
comment ['koment] *n* (*remark*) Bemerkung *f*; (*annotation*) Anmerkung *f. v* kommentieren, Bemerkungen machen. **commentary** *n* Reportage *f*. **commentator** *n* Kommentator *m*.
commerce ['komɔɪs] *n* Handel *m*, Kommerz *m*. **commercial** *adj* kommerziell, geschäftlich, Handels-. **commercialize** *v* kommerzialisieren.
commiserate [kə'mizəreit] *v* **commiserate with** bemitleiden.
commission [kə'miʃən] *n* Auftrag *m*; (*committee*) Kommission *f*; (*fee*) Provision *f*; (*mil*) Offizierspatent *neut. v* (*person*) beauftragen; (*thing*) bestellen. **commissioner** *n* Bevollmächtigte(r).
commit [kə'mit] *v* (*offence*) begehen. **commit oneself** sich verpflichten. **commitment** *n* Verpflichtung *f*.
committee [kə'miti] *n* Ausschuß *m*, Kommission *f*.
commodity [kə'modəti] *n* Ware *f*. **commodities** *pl* Grundstoffe *pl*.
common ['komən] *adj* gemein, gemeinsam; (*abundant*) weit verbreitet; (*vulgar*) gemein, ordinär. **Common Market** Gemeinsamer Markt *m*. **commonplace** *adj* alltäglich. **commonsense** *n* gesunder Menschenverstand *m*.

commotion [kə'mouʃən] *n* Erregung *f*. Aufruhr *m*.
commune ['komjuːn] *n* Kommune *f*. Gemeinschaft *f*.
communicate [kə'mjuːnikeit] *v* mitteilen; (*illness*) übertragen. **communicative** *adj* gesprächig. **communication** *n* Kommunikation *f*; (*message*) Mitteilung *f*. **communications** *pl n* Verkehrswege *pl*.
communism ['komjunizəm] *n* Kommunismus *m*. **communist** *adj* kommunistisch. *n* Kommunist(in).
community [kə'mjuːnəti] *n* Gemeinschaft *f*.
commute [kə'mjuːt] *v* (*travel*) pendeln; (*a sentence*) herabsetzen. **commuter** *n* Pendler *m*.
compact¹ [kəm'pakt] *adj* kompakt, dicht.
compact² ['kompakt] *n* (*agreement*) Vertrag *m*, Pakt *m*.
companion [kəm'panjən] *n* Begleiter(in); Genosse *m*, Genossin *f*. **companionable** *adj* gesellig. **companionship** *n* Gesellschaft *f*.
company ['kʌmpəni] *n* Gesellschaft *f*; (*firm*) Gesellschaft *f*, Firma *f*; (*theatre*) Truppe *f*; (*mil*) Kompanie *f*.
compare [kəm'peə] *v* vergleichen; (*match up to*) sich vergleichen lassen. **comparable** *adj* vergleichbar. **comparative** *adj* relativ; (*gram*) steigernd. **comparatively** *adv* verhältnismäßig. **comparison** *n* Vergleich *m*. **in comparison with** im Vergleich zu.
compartment [kəm'paːtmənt] *n* Abteilung *f*.
compass ['kʌmpəs] *n* Kompaß *m*. **pair of compasses** Zirkel *m*.
compassion [kəm'paʃən] *n* Mitleid *neut*. **compassionate** *adj* mitleidig.
compatible [kəm'patəbl] *adj* vereinbar.
compel [kəm'pel] *v* zwingen.
compensate ['kompənseit] *v* (*money*) entschädigen; (*balance out*) ausgleichen. **compensation** *n* Entschädigung *f*; Ausgleich *m*.
compete [kəm'piːt] *v* konkurrieren, sich bewerben; (*take part*) teilnehmen. **competition** *n* Wettbewerb *m*; (*comm*) Konkurrenz *f*. **competitive** *adj* konkurrenzfähig. **competitor** *n* (*sport*) Teilnehmer(in); (*comm*) Konkurrent(in).
compile [kəm'pail] *v* kompilieren.
complacent [kəm'pleisnt] *adj* selbstzufrieden.

complain [kəm'plein] *v* klagen. **complain about/to** sich beschweren über/bei. **complaint** *n* Klage *f*, Beschwerde *f*.
complement ['kompləmənt] *n* Ergänzung *f*. *v* ergänzen; (*go together*) zusammenpassen. **complementary** *adj* komplementär.
complete [kəm'pliːt] *v* vollenden, vervollständigen; (*form*) ausfüllen. *adj* vollständig, vollendet. **completely** *adv* völlig, vollständig, ganz und gar. **completion** *n* Vollendung *f*.
complex ['kompleks] *adj* kompliziert. *n* (*psychol*) Komplex *m*.
complexion [kəm'plekʃən] *n* Teint *m*.
complicate ['komplikeit] *v* verwickeln, komplizieren. **complicated** *adj* kompliziert. **complication** *n* Komplikation *f*, Schwierigkeit *f*.
compliment ['kompləmənt] *n* Kompliment *neut*. *v* komplimentieren. **complimentary** *adj* höflich, artig. **complimentary ticket** Freikarte *f*.
comply [kəm'plai] *v* sich fügen. **comply with** (*rules*) sich halten an; (*request*) erfüllen.
component [kəm'pounənt] *n* Bestandteil *m*.
compose [kəm'pouz] *v* komponieren. **composed** *adj* gefaßt. **be composed of** bestehen aus. **composer** *n* Komponist *m*. **composite** *adj* zusammengesetzt. **composition** *n* Komposition *f*; (*piece of music*) (Musik)Stück *neut*.
compost ['kompost] *n* Kompost *m*.
composure [kəm'pouʒə] *n* Gefaßtheit *f*.
compound ['kompaund] *n* Zusammensetzung *f*; (*chem*) Verbindung *f*; *adj* zusammengesetzt, gemischt.
comprehend [kompri'hend] *v* verstehen, begreifen. **comprehensible** *adj* verständlich. **comprehension** *n* Verständnis.
comprehensive [,kompri'hensiv] *adj* umfassend. **comprehensive school** *n* Gesamtschule *f*.
compress [kəm'pres] *v* verdichten, zusammendrücken. *n* (*med*) Kompresse *f*. **compressed** *adj* zusammengedrückt. **compressed air** Preßluft *f*. **compression** *n* Verdichtung *f*. **compressor** *n* Verdichter *m*.
comprise [kəm'praiz] *v* bestehen aus.
compromise ['komprəmaiz] *n* Kompromiß *m or neut*. *v* einen Kompromiß schließen; (*expose*) kompromittieren.

compulsion [kəm'pʌlʃən] *n* Zwang *m.*
compulsive *adj* Zwangs-. **compulsory** *adj*
Zwangs-.
compunction [kəm'pʌŋkʃən] *n* Gewissensbisse *pl*, Reue *f.*
computer [kəm'pjuːtə] *n* Computer *m.*
comrade ['komrid] *n* Genosse *m,* Genossin *f*; Kamerad(in). **comradeship** *n*
Kameradschaft *f.*
concave [kon'keiv] *adj* konkav, Hohl-.
conceal [kən'siːl] *v* verbergen, verstecken;
(fact, etc.) verschweigen.
concede [kən'siːd] *v* zugeben, einräumen;
(right) bewilligen.
conceit [kən'siːt] *n* Einbildung *f*, Eitelkeit
f. **conceited** *adj* eingebildet.
conceive [kən'siːv] *v* *(plan)* erdenken;
(child) empfangen; *(thoughts)* fassen.
conceive of sich vorstellen (+ *acc*). **conceivable** *adj* denkbar, vorstellbar.
concentrate ['konsəntreit] *v* konzentrier-
en. **concentrate on** sich konzentrieren
auf. **concentrated** *adj* konzentriert. **concentration** *n* Konzentration *f.*
concentric [kən'sentrik] *adj* konzentrisch.
concept ['konsept] *n* Begriff *m,* Idee *f.*
conception *n* Vorstellung *f*; *(of child)*
Empfängnis *f.*
concern [kən'səːn] *v* betreffen, angehen;
(worry) beunruhigen. *n (worry)* Besorgnis
f, Sorge *f*; *(interest)* Interesse *neut*;
(comm) Betrieb *m.* **concern oneself with**
sich befassen mit. **as far as I am concerned** von mir aus. *that's not your concern!* das geht Sie nichts an! **concerning**
adj betreffend.
concert ['konsət] *n* Konzert *neut.*
concerted [kən'səːtid] *adj* konzertiert.
concerto [kən'tʃəːtou] *n* Konzert *neut.*
concession [kən'seʃən] *n* Konzession *f.*
concessionaire *n* Konzessionär *m.*
conciliate [kən'silieit] *v* versöhnen. **concil-
iation** *n* Versöhnung *f.* **conciliatory** *adj*
versöhnlich.
concise [kən'sais] *adj* kurz, knapp.
conclude [kən'kluːd] *v* schließen. **conclude
that** den Schluß ziehen, daß. **conclusive**
adj (evidence) schlüssig.
concoct [kən'kokt] *v* zusammenbrauen.
concrete ['koŋkriːt] *adj* konkret; *(made of
concrete)* Beton-. *n* Beton *m.*
concussion [kən'kʌʃən] *n (med)* Gehirner-
schütterung *f.*
condemn [kən'dem] *v* verurteilen. **condemnation** *n* Verurteilung *f.*

condense [kən'dens] *v* kondensieren. **condensation** *n* Kondensation *f.* **condensed
milk** Kondensmilch *f.*
condescend [kondi'send] *v* sich herablassen. **condescending** *adj* herablassend.
condescension *n* Herablassung *f.*
condition [kən'diʃən] *n (state)* Zustand
m; *(requirement)* Bedingung *f*, Voraussetzung *f.* **conditions** *pl* Umstände *pl.* **on
condition that** unter der Bedingung, daß.
out of condition *(sport)* in schlechter
Form. **conditional** *adj* bedingt.
condolence [kən'douləns] *n* Beileid *neut.*
condom ['kondom] *n* Kondom *neut.*
condone [kən'doun] *v* verzeihen.
conducive [kən'djuːsiv] *adj* förderlich.
conduct [kən'dʌkt; *n* 'kondʌkt]] *v* führen;
(orchestra) dirigieren; *(elec)* leiten. **conduct oneself** sich verhalten. *n* Führung *f*;
(behaviour) Verhalten *neut.*
conductor [kən'dʌktə] *n (music)* Dirigent
m; *(bus)* Schaffner(in).
cone [koun] *n (shape)* Kegel *m*; *(ice
cream)* Waffeltüte *f*; *(bot)* Zapfen *m.*
confectioner [kən'fekʃənə] *n*
Süßwarenhändler *m.* **confectionery** *n*
Süßwaren *pl.*
confederation [kən,fedə'reiʃən] *n* Bund
m.
confer [kən'fəː] *v (bestow)* verleihen; *(discuss)* konferieren. **conference** *n* Konferenz *f.*
confess [kən'fes] *v* bekennen, gestehen;
(rel) beichten. **confession** *n* Geständnis
neut; *(rel)* Beichte *f.* **confessional** *n*
Beichtstuhl *m.*
confetti [kən'feti] *n* Konfetti *pl.*
confide [kən'faid] *v* anvertrauen. **confide
in** vertrauen (+ *dat*). **confidence** *n* Vertrauen *neut*; *(in oneself)* Selbstvertrauen
neut. **confident** *adj* zuversichtlich; selbstsicher. **confidential** *adj* vertraulich.
confine [kən'fain] *v (limit)* beschränken;
(lock up) einsperren. **confinement** *n (in
prison)* Haft *f*; *(childbirth)* Niederkunft *f.*
confirm [kən'fəːm] *v* bestätigen; *(rel)*
konfirmieren. **confirmation** *n* Bestätigung
f; Konfirmation *f.*
confiscate ['konfiskeit] *v* beschlagnahmen.
confiscation *n* Beschlagnahme *f.*
conflict ['konflikt; *v* kən'flikt] *n* Konflikt
m, Streit *m. v* widerstreiten (+ *dat*). **conflict of interests** Interessenkonflikt *m.*
conflicting *adj* widerstreitend.

conform [kən'fɔːm] v (tally) übereinstimmen (mit); (to rules) sich fügen (+dat).
conformist n Konformist.
confound [kən'faund] v (surprise) erstaunen; (mix up) verwechseln. **confound it!** verdammt!
confront [kən'frʌnt] v konfrontieren; (enemy) entgegentreten (+dat). **confrontation** n Konfrontation f.
confuse [kən'fjuːz] v (mix up) verwechseln (mit); (perplex) verwirren. **confused** adj (person) verwirrt; (situation) verworren. **confusion** n Verwirrung f.
congeal [kən'dʒiːl] v gerinnen.
congenial [kən'dʒiːniəl] adj freundlich, gemütlich.
congenital [kən'dʒenitl] adj angeboren.
congested [kən'dʒestid] adj überfüllt. **congestion** n Stauung f; (traffic) Verkehrsstauung f.
conglomeration [kənˌglɒmə'reiʃən] n Anhäufung f, Konglomerat neut.
congratulate [kən'grætjuleit] v beglückwünschen. **congratulations** pl n Glückwünsche pl.
congregate ['kɒŋgrigeit] v sich versammeln. **congregation** n Versammlung f.
congress ['kɒŋgres] n Kongreß m. **congressman/woman** Abgeordnete(r).
conifer ['kɒnifə] n Nadelbaum m. **coniferous** adj Nadel-.
conjecture [kən'dʒektʃə] n Vermutung f.
conjugal ['kɒndʒugəl] adj ehelich.
conjugate ['kɒndʒugeit] v (gramm) konjugieren.
conjunction [kən'dʒʌŋkʃən] n Vereinigung f; (gramm, astrol) Konjunktion f.
conjunctivitis [kənˌdʒʌŋkti'vaitis] n Bindehautentzündung f.
conjure ['kʌndʒə] v **conjure up** heraufbeschwören. **conjurer** n Zauberkünstler m. **conjuring trick** Zauberkunststück neut.
connect [kə'nekt] v verbinden; (phone, etc.) anschließen. **connection** n Verbindung f; (phone, rail) Anschluß m. **in connection with** im Zusammenhang mit.
connoisseur [kɒnə'səː] n Kenner m.
connotation [kɒnə'teiʃən] n Nebenbedeutung f.
conquer ['kɒŋkə] v erobern, besiegen; (fig) überwinden, beherrschen. **conqueror** n Eroberer m. **conquest** n Eroberung f.

conscience ['kɒnʃəns] n Gewissen neut.
conscientious [kɒnʃi'enʃəs] adj pflichtbewußt.
conscious ['kɒnʃəs] adj bewußt. **consciousness** n Bewußtsein neut.
conscript ['kɒnskript] v einziehen. n Wehrpflichtige(r). **conscription** n Wehrpflicht f.
consecrate ['kɒnsikreit] v weihen.
consecutive [kən'sekjutiv] adj aufeinanderfolgend.
consensus [kən'sensəs] n Übereinstimmung f.
consent [kən'sent] v zustimmen (+dat). n Zustimmung f.
consequence ['kɒnsikwəns] n Folge f, Konsequenz f. **of no consequence** unbedeutend. **consequently** adv folglich.
conserve [kən'səːv] v erhalten; (energy) sparen. **conservation** n Schutz m, Erhaltung f. **conservative** adj konservativ; n Konservative(r). **conservatory** n Treibhaus neut; (music) Musikhochschule f.
consider [kən'sidə] n (think about) überlegen; (regard as) halten für. **considerate** adj rücksichtsvoll. **consideration** n (thought) Überlegung f; (thoughtfulness) Rücksicht f. **considering** prep in Anbetracht (+gen).
consign [kən'sain] v versenden. **consignee** n Empfänger m. **consignment** n Sendung f. **consignor** n Absender m.
consist [kən'sist] v **consist of** bestehen aus. **consistency** n (of substance) Dichte f. **consistent** adj konsequent. **consistent with** vereinbar mit.
console [kən'soul] v trösten. **consolation** n Trost m. **consolation prize** Trostpreis m.
consolidate [kən'sɒlideit] v stärken; (comm) konsolidieren. **consolidation** n Stärkung f.
consommé [kən'sɔmei] n Fleischbrühe f.
consonant ['kɒnsənənt] n Konsonant m.
conspicuous [kən'spikjuəs] adj (visible) sichtbar; (striking) auffallend.
conspire [kən'spaiə] v sich verschwören. **conspiracy** n Verschwörung f. **conspirator** n Verschwörer m.
constable ['kʌnstəbl] n Polizist m.
constant ['kɒnstənt] adj beständig, konstant; (continual) dauernd. **constantly** adv ständig.

constellation [konstə'leiʃən] *n* Sternbild *neut.*
constipation [konsti'peiʃən] *n* (Darm)Verstopfung *f.*
constituency [kən'stitjuənsi] *n* Wahlkreis *m.* **constituent** *n* Wähler *m.*
constitute ['konstitjuɪt] *v* bilden, darstellen. **constitution** *n* (*pol*) Grundgesetz *m,* Verfassung *f;* (*of person*) Konstitution *f.*
constrain [kən'strein] *v* zwingen **constraint** *n* Zwang *m,* Druck *m.*
constrict [kən'strikt] *v* zusammendrücken, einengen.
construct [kən'strʌkt] *v* bauen, konstruieren; (*argument*) aufstellen. **construction** *n* Bau *m,* Konstruktion *f.* **constructive** *adj* konstruktiv.
consul ['konsəl] *n* Konsul *m.* **consulate** *n* Konsulat *neut.*
consult [kən'sʌlt] *v* zu Rate ziehen, konsultieren; (*book*) nachsehen in. **consultant** *n* Berater *m.* **consultation** *n* Konsultation *f.* **consulting room** Sprechzimmer *neut.*
consume [kən'sjuɪm] *v* verzehren; (*money, time*) verbrauchen. **consumer** *n* Verbraucher *m.*
contact ['kontakt] *n* Verbindung *f,* Kontakt *m. v* sich in Verbindung setzen mit. **be in contact with** in Verbindung stehen mit.
contagious [kən'teidʒəs] *adj* ansteckend.
contain [kən'tein] *v* enthalten; (*feelings*) beherrschen. **contain oneself** sich beherrschen. **container** *n* Behälter *m*; (*for goods transport*) Container *m.* **container ship** Containerschiff *m.*
contaminate [kən'taməneit] *v* verseuchen. **contamination** *n* Verseuchung *f.*
contemplate ['kontəmpleit] *v* (*observe*) nachdenklich betrachten; (*think about*) nachdenken über; (*doing something*) vorhaben. **contemplation** *n* Betrachtung *f;* Nachdenken *neut.*
contemporary [kən'tempərəri] *adj* zeitgenössisch; (*modern*) modern. *n* Zeitgenosse *m.*
contempt [kən'tempt] *n* Verachtung *f.* **contemptible** *adj* verächtlich. **contemptuous** *adj* voller Verachtung *f.*
contend [kən'tend] *v* kämpfen; (*assert*) behaupten.
content¹ ['kontent] *n* Inhalt *m.* **contents** *pl* Inhalt *m sing.* **table of contents** Inhaltsverzeichnis *neut.*

content² [kən'tent] *adj* zufrieden. **contentment** *n* Zufriedenheit *f.*
contention [kən'tenʃən] *n* Streit *m*; (*assertion*) Behauptung *f.*
contest ['kontest; *v* kən'test] *n* Wettkampf *m. v* bestreiten. **contestant** *n* Bewerber(in).
context ['kontekst] *n* Zusammenhang *m.*
continent ['kontinənt] *n* Festland *neut,* Kontinent *m.* **continental** *adj* Kontinental-.
contingency [kən'tindʒənsi] *n* Eventualität *f.*
continue [kən'tinjuɪ] *v* fortfahren, weitermachen; (*something*) fortsetzen; (*go further*) weitergehen. **continual** *adj* wiederholt. **continually** *adv* immer wieder. **continuation** *n* Fortsetzung *f.* **continuous** *adj* beständig.
contort [kən'toit] *v* verdrehen. **contortion** *n* Verdrehung *f.* **contortionist** *n* Schlangenmensch *m.*
contour ['kontuə] *n* Umrißlinie *f.*
contraband ['kontrəband] *n* Schmuggelware *f.*
contraception [kontrə'sepʃən] *n* Empfängnisverhütung *f.* **contraceptive** *adj* empfängnisverhütend. *n* empfängnisverhütendes Mittel *neut.*
contract ['kontrakt; *v* kən'trakt] *n* Vertrag *m. v* (*become smaller*) sich zusammenziehen; (*illness*) sich zuziehen. **contraction** *n* Zusammenziehung *f.* **contractor** *n* (*building*) Bauunternehmer *m.*
contradict [kontrə'dikt] *v* widersprechen. **contradiction** *n* Widerspruch *m.* **contradictory** *adj* sich widersprechend.
contralto [kən'traltou] *n* (*voice*) Alt *m*; (*singer*) Altistin *f.*
contraption [kən'trapʃən] *n* komisches Ding *neut.*
contrary [kən'trɛəri; (*opposite*) 'kontrəri] *adj* (*person*) widerspenstig; (*opposite*) entgegengesetzt. *n* Gegenteil *m.* **on the contrary** im Gegenteil.
contrast [kən'traist; *n* 'kontraist] *v* (*compare*) vergleichen. **contrast with** kontrastieren mit. *n* Kontrast *m.* **in contrast to** im Gegensatz zu.
contravene [kontrə'viɪn] *v* verstoßen gegen. **contravention** *n* Verstoß *m.*
contribute [kən'tribjut] *v* beitragen; (*money*) spenden. **contribution** *n* Beitrag *m.* **contributor** *n* Beitragende(r); (*to newspaper, etc.*) Mitarbeiter *m.*

contrive [kən'traiv] v (plan) ausdenken. / contrived to meet him es gelang mir, ihn zu treffen.
control [kən'troul] v (curb) zügeln; (machine) steuern. n Leitung f. **controls** pl n Steuerung f. **under/out of control** unter/außer Kontrolle.
controversial [kontrə'vəːʃəl] adj umstritten. **controversy** n Streitfrage f, Kontroverse f.
convalesce [konvə'les] v genesen, gesund werden. **convalescence** n Genesungszeit f.
convection [kən'vekʃən] n Konvektion f.
convenience [kən'viːnjəns] n Bequemlichkeit f; (advantage) Vorteil m. **public convenience** Bedürfnisanstalt f. **convenient** adj (suitable) passend; (time) gelegen; (advantageous) vorteilhaft.
convent ['konvənt] n Kloster neut; (school) Klosterschule f.
convention [kən'venʃən] n (meeting) Tagung f; (agreement) Konvention f; (custom) Brauch m, Konvention f. **conventional** adj konventionell.
converge [kən'vəːdʒ] v konvergieren.
converse [kən'vəːs] v sich unterhalten, sprechen. **conversation** n Unterhaltung f, Gespräch neut.
convert [kən'vəːt; n 'konvəːt] v umwandeln; (rel) bekehren. n Bekehrte(r). **conversion** n Umwandlung f; (rel) Bekehrung f.
convertible [kən'vəːtəbl] adj um-, verwandelbar. n (mot) Kabrio(lett) neut.
convex ['konveks] adj konvex.
convey [kən'vei] v (goods) befördern; (news) übermitteln. **conveyance** n (law) Übertragung f; (vehicle) Fahrzeug neut.
convict [kən'vikt; n 'konvikt] v verurteilen. n Verurteilte(r). **conviction** n (belief) Überzeugung f; (law) Verurteilung f.
convince [kən'vins] v überzeugen. **convincing** adj überzeugend.
convivial [kən'viviəl] adj fröhlich, heiter.
convoy ['konvoi] n (mil) Konvoi m.
convulsion [kən'vʌlʃən] n Zuckung f.
cook [kuk] v kochen; (a meal) zubereiten. n Koch m, Köchin f. **cooker** n Herd m. **cookery** n Küche f. **cookery book** Kochbuch neut. **cooking** n Küche f.
cool [kuːl] adj kühl. v abkühlen. **cooled** adj gekühlt. **coolness** n Kühle.

coop [kuːp] n Hühnerkäfig m. v **coop up** einsperren.
cooperate [kou'opəreit] v zusammenarbeiten. **cooperation** n Zusammenarbeit f, Kooperation f. **cooperative** adj (helpful) hilfsbereit; kooperativ. n Genossenschaft f, Kooperative f.
coordinate [kou'oːdineit] v koordinieren. n (math) Koordinate f. **coordination** n Koordination f.
cope [koup] v **cope with** fertigwerden mit.
copious ['koupiəs] adj reichlich.
copper[1] ['kopə] n (metal) Kupfer neut. adj kupfern; (colour) kupferfarben.
copper[2] ['kopə] n (coll) Polyp m.
copulate ['kopjuleit] v sich paaren. **copulation** n Paarung f.
copy ['kopi] n Kopie f; (book) Exemplar neut; (newspaper) Nummer f. v kopieren.
copyright n Copyright neut.
coral ['korəl] n Koralle f.
cord [koːd] n Schnur f.
cordial ['koːdiəl] adj herzlich.
cordon ['koːdn] n Absperrkette f. v **cordon off** absperren.
corduroy ['koːdəroi] n Kord m.
core [koː] n (apple) Kernhaus neut. v entkernen. **to the core** durch und durch.
cork [koːk] n (material) Kork m; (for bottle) Korken m, Pfropfen m. adj korken. **corkscrew** n Korkenzieher m.
corn[1] [koːn] n Korn neut, Getreide neut; (maize) Mais m; (wheat) Weizen m.
corn[2] [koːn] n (on foot) Hühnerauge neut.
corner ['koːnə] n Ecke f, Winkel m; (mot) Kurve f; (sport) Eckball m. v in die Enge treiben.
cornet ['koːnit] n (music) Kornett neut; (ice cream) Eistüte f.
coronary ['korənəri] adj koronar. **coronary thrombosis** Koronarthrombose f.
coronation [korə'neiʃən] n Krönung f.
coroner ['korənə] n Leichenbeschauer m.
corporal[1] ['koːpərəl] adj körperlich. **corporal punishment** Prügelstrafe f.
corporal[2] ['koːpərəl] n (mil) Obergefreite(r) m.
corporation [koːpə'reiʃən] n Körperschaft f; (city authorities) Gemeinderat m.
corps [koː] n Korps neut.
corpse [koːps] n Leiche f.
correct [kə'rekt] adj richtig; (proper) korrekt. v korrigieren. **correction** n Korrektur f.

correlation [korə'leiʃən] *n* Wechselbeziehung *f*.
correspond [korə'spond] *v* entsprechen (+*dat*); (*write*) korrespondieren. **correspondence** *n* Entsprechung *f*; Korrespondenz *f*. **corresponding** *adj* entsprechend.
corridor ['koridoɪ] *n* Gang *m*.
corrode [kə'roud] *v* zerfressen; (*become corroded*) rosten. **corrosion** *n* Korrosion *f*.
corrupt [kə'rʌpt] *v* bestechen. *adj* bestechlich, korrupt. **corruption** *n* Bestechung *f*, Korruption *f*.
corset ['koɪset] *n* Korsett *neut*.
cosmetic [koz'metik] *adj* kosmetisch. **cosmetic surgery** chirurgische Kosmetik *f*. **cosmetics** *pl n* Schönheitsmittel *pl*.
cosmic ['kozmik] *adj* kosmisch.
cosmopolitan [kozmə'politən] *adj* kosmopolitisch.
*****cost** [kost] *v* kosten. *n* Preis *m*, Kosten *pl*. **costs** Unkosten *pl*. **cost of living** Lebenshaltungskosten *pl*.
costume ['kostjuɪm] *n* Kostüm *neut*.
cosy ['kouzi] *adj* gemütlich.
cot [kot] *n* Kinderbett *neut*.
cottage ['kotidʒ] *n* Hütte *f*, Häuschen *neut*. **cottage cheese** Hüttenkäse *m*.
cotton ['kotn] *n* Baumwolle *f*. *adj* Baumwoll-. **cotton wool** Watte *f*.
couch [kautʃ] *n* Couch *f*.
cough [kof] *n* Husten *m*. *v* husten.
could [kud] *V* can.
council ['kaunsəl] *n* Rat *m*. **councillor** *m* Rat *m*.
counsel ['kaunsəl] *v* beraten. *n* Rat *m*.
count[1] [kaunt] *v* zählen; (*be valid*) gelten. *n* (*number*) (Gesamt)Zahl *f*. **count on** rechnen mit.
count[2] [kaunt] *n* (*noble*) Graf *m*.
counter[1] ['kauntə] *n* (*shop*) Ladentisch *m*, Theke *f*; (*bank*) Schalter *m*; (*game*) Spielmarke *f*.
counter[2] ['kauntə] *adv* entgegen. *adj* entgegengesetzt. *v* entgegnen.
counteract [kauntə'rakt] *v* entgegenwirken (+*dat*).
counterattack ['kauntərə,tak] *n* Gegenangriff *m*.
counter-clockwise *adj*, *adv* dem Uhrzeigersinn entgegen.
counterfeit ['kauntəfit] *adj* gefälscht. *v* fälschen.

counterfoil ['kauntə,foil] *n* Kontrollabschnitt *m*.
counterpart ['kauntə,paɪt] *n* Gegenstück *neut*.
countess ['kauntis] *n* Gräfin *f*.
country ['kʌntri] *n* Land *neut*; (*homeland*) Heimat *f*; (*pol*) Land *neut*, Staat *m*. *adj* Land-. **in the country** auf dem Lande. **country house** Landhaus *neut*. **countryman** *n* Landmann *m*. **fellow countryman** Landsmann *m*. **countryside** Landschaft *f*.
county ['kaunti] *n* Grafschaft *f*.
coup [kuɪ] *n* Coup *m*; (*pol*) Staatsstreich *m*. **coup de grâce** Gnadenstoß *m*.
couple ['kʌpl] *n* Paar *neut*; (*married couple*) Ehepaar *neut*. **a couple of** ein paar.
coupon ['kuɪpon] *n* Coupon *m*, Gutschein *m*.
courage ['kʌridʒ] *n* Mut *m*, Tapferkeit *f*. **courageous** *adj* mutig, tapfer.
courier ['kuriə] *n* Kurier *m*; (*tour guide*) Reiseleiter(in).
course [koɪs] *n* Lauf *m*; (*study*) Kurs(us) *m*; (*race*) Bahn *f*; (*of action*) Richtung *m*. *v* laufen. **of course** natürlich, selbstverständlich. **in the course of** im Laufe (+*gen*).
court [koɪt] *n* (*royal*) Hof *m*; (*law*) Gericht *neut*. *v* (*lover*) werben um. **court martial** Kriegsgericht *neut*. **court-martial** *v* vor ein Kriegsgericht stellen. **courtroom** *n* Gerichtssaal *m*. **courtyard** *n* Hof *m*.
courtesy ['kəɪtəsi] *n* Höflichkeit *f*. **courteous** *adj* höflich.
cousin ['kʌzn] *n* Cousin *m*, Vetter *m*; Kusine *f*, Base *f*.
cove [kouv] *n* Bucht *f*.
cover ['kʌvə] *v* (be)decken; (*extend over*) sich erstrecken über; (*include*) einschließen. *n* (*lid*) Deckel *m*; (*of book*) (Schutz)Umschlag *m*. **covering** *n* (Be)Deckung *f*.
cow [kau] *n* Kuh f. *v* einschüchtern. **cowshed** *n* Kuhstall *m*.
coward ['kauəd] *n* Feigling *m*. **cowardice** *n* Feigheit *f*. **cowardly** *adj* feige.
cower ['kauə] *v* kauern.
coy [koi] *adj* spröde.
crab [krab] *n* Krebs *m*.
crack [krak] *n* (*slit*) Spalt *m*, Riß *m*; (*sound*) Krach *m*. *v* krachen; (*break*) brechen; (*nut*) knacken; (*egg*) aufschlagen; (*joke*) reißen. **crack up** (*coll*) zusammenbrechen. **cracker** *n* (*firework*)

Knallfrosch *m*; (*Christmas*) Knallbonbon *m*; (*biscuit*) Keks *m*.
crackle ['krakl] *v* knistern. *n* Knistern *neut*.
cradle ['kreidl] *n* Wiege *f*. *v* wiegen.
craft [kraift] *n* (*trade*) Handwerk *neut*, Gewerbe *neut*; (*skill*) Kunstfertigkeit *f*; (*ship*) Schiff *neut*. **craftsman** *n* Handwerker *m*, Künstler *m*. **crafty** *adj* schlau, listig.
cram [kram] *v* hineinstopfen; (*study*) pauken.
cramp [kramp] *n* (*med*) Krampf *m*; (*clamp*) Krampe *f*. *v* hemmen.
cranberry ['kranbəri] *n* Preiselbeere *f*.
crane [krein] *n* Kran *m*; (*bird*) Kranich *m*.
crank [kraŋk] *n* Kurbel *f*; (*odd person*) Kauz *m*. *v* ankurbeln. **crankshaft** *n* Kurbelwelle *f*.
crap [krap] *n* (*vulgar*) Scheiße *f*.
crash [kraʃ] *n* (*sound*) Krach *m*; (*mot*) Zusammenstoß *m*; (*aero*) Absturz *m*. *v* stürzen (gegen); (*sound*) krachen. **crash helmet** Sturzhelm *m*.
crate [kreit] *n* Kiste *f*.
crater ['kreitə] *n* Krater *m*.
cravat [krə'vat] *n* Halstuch *neut*, Krawatte *f*.
crave [kreiv] *v* erbitten. **crave for** sehnen nach. **craving** *n* Sehnsucht *f*.
crawl [kroıl] *v* kriechen. *n* Kriechen *neut*; (*swimming*) Kraulstil *m*.
crayfish ['kreifiʃ] *n* Flußkrebs *m*.
crayon ['kreiən] *n* Farbstift *m*.
craze [kreiz] *n* (*coll*) Manie *f*. **crazy** *adj* verrückt.
creak [kriːk] *v* knarren. *n* Knarren *neut*.
cream [kriːm] *n* Sahne *f*, Rahm *m*; (*skin*) Creme *f*. **cream-coloured** *adj* cremefarben. **creamy** *adj* sahnig.
crease [kriːs] *n* Falte *f*, Kniff *m*. *v* falten.
create [kri'eit] *v* erschaffen; (*cause*) verursachen. **creation** *n* Schöpfung *f*; (*product*) Werk *neut*. **creative** *adj* schöpferisch. **creator** *n* Schöpfer *m*. **creature** *n* Lebewesen *neut*, Geschöpf *neut*.
credentials [kri'denʃəlz] *pl n* (*identity papers*) Ausweispapiere *pl*.
credible ['kredəbl] *adj* glaubhaft, glaubwürdig.
credit ['kredit] *n* (*comm*) Guthaben *neut*, Kredit *m*. *v* Glauben schenken (+ *dat*). **on credit** auf Kredit. **take the credit for**

sich als Verdienst anrechnen. **creditable** *adj* rühmlich. **credit card** Kreditkarte *f*. **creditor** *n* Gläubiger *m*.
credulous ['kredjuləs] *adj* leichtgläubig.
creed [kriːd] *n* Bekenntnis *neut*, Kredo *neut*.
*creep [kriːp] *v* kriechen, schleichen. *n* Kriechen *neut*.
cremate [kri'meit] *v* einäschern. **cremation** *n* Einäscherung *f*. **crematorium** *n* Krematorium *neut*.
crept [krept] *V* **creep**.
crescent ['kresnt] *n* Mondsichel *f*.
cress [kres] *n* Kresse *f*.
crest [krest] *n* (*of mountain*) Bergkamm *m*; (*of wave*) Wellenkamm *m*; (*coat of arms*) Wappen *neut*.
crevice ['krevis] *n* Spalte *f*, Sprung *m*.
crew [kruː] *n* Besatzung *f*, Mannschaft *f*.
crib [krib] *n* Kinderbett *neut*.
cricket[1] ['krikit] *n* (*insect*) Grille *f*.
cricket[2] ['krikit] *n* Kricket *neut*.
crime [kraim] *n* Verbrechen *neut*. **criminal** *adj* verbrecherisch, kriminell. *n* Verbrecher(in).
crimson ['krimzn] *n* Karmesinrot *neut*.
cringe [krindʒ] *v* sich ducken.
crinkle ['kriŋkl] *v* kraus machen. *n* Kräuselung *f*. **crinkly** *adj* kraus.
cripple ['kripl] *n* Krüppel *m*. *v* lähmen.
crisis ['kraisis] *n* (*pl* -ses) Krise *f*.
crisp [krisp] *adj* knusprig. **crisps** *pl n* Chips *pl*. **crispy** *adj* knusprig.
criterion [krai'tiəriən] *n* (*pl* -a) Kriterium *neut*.
critic ['kritik] *n* Kritiker *m*. **critical** *adj* kritisch. **criticism** *n* Kritik *f*. **criticize** *v* kritisieren.
croak [krouk] *v* (*person, crow*) krächzen; (*frog*) quaken. *n* Krächzen *neut*; Quaken *neut*.
crochet ['krouʃei] *v* häkeln. **crochet hook** Häkelnadel *f*. **crochet work** Häkelarbeit *f*.
crockery ['krokəri] *n* Geschirr *neut*.
crocodile ['krokə,dail] *n* Krokodil *neut*.
crocus ['kroukəs] *n* Krokus *m*.
crook [kruk] *n* (*shepherd's*) Hirtenstab *m*; (*villain*) Gauner *m*. **crooked** *adj* gekrümmt; (*dishonest*) krumm.
crop [krop] *n* (*harvest*) Ernte *f*; (*whip*) Reitpeitsche *f*. *v* (*cut*) stutzen. **crop up** auftauchen.
croquet ['kroukei] *n* Krocket *neut*.

cross [kros] *n* Kreuz *neut*; (*crossbreed*) Kreuzung *f. adj* Quer-; (*annoyed*) böse, ärgerlich. *v* kreuzen, überqueren. **cross over** hinübergehen. **cross one's mind** einfallen (+*dat*). **crossbow** *n* Armbrust *f.* **crossbreed** *n* Kreuzung *f.* **cross-country** *adj* Gelände-. **cross-examination** *n* Kreuzverhör *m.* **cross-eyed** *adj* schielend. **crossing** *n* Kreuzung *f*; (*rail*) Bahnübergang *m*; (*border*) Überfahrt *f.* **cross-legged** *adj* mit überschlagenen Beinen. **cross-reference** *n* Kreuzverweisung *f.* **crossroads** *n* Straßenkreuzung *f*; (*fig*) Scheideweg *m.* **cross-section** *n* Querschnitt *m.* **crosswind** *n* Seitenwind *m.* **crossword** *n* Kreuzworträtsel *neut.*

crotchet ['krotʃit] *n* (*music*) Viertelnote *f.*

crouch [krautʃ] *v* sich ducken.

crow [krou] *n* Krähe *f. v* krähen. **crow's feet** Krähenfüße *pl.* **crow's nest** (*naut*) Mastkorb *m.*

crowd [kraud] *n* Menge. *v* **crowd around** sich drängen um. **crowded** *adj* gedrängt.

crown [kraun] *n* Krone *f. v* krönen.

crucial ['kruːʃəl] *adj* kritisch, entscheidend.

crucifixion [ˌkruːsi'fikʃən] *n* Kreuzigung *f.* **crucify** *v* kreuzigen.

crude [kruːd] *adj* roh; (*person*) grob. **crude oil** Rohöl *neut.* **crudeness** *n* Roheit *f.*

cruel ['kruːəl] *adj* grausam. **cruelty** *n* Grausamkeit *f.*

cruise [kruːz] *v* (*boat*) kreuzen; (*aircraft*) fliegen. *n* Kreuzfahrt *f.* **cruiser** *n* (*naut*) Kreuzer *m.*

crumb [krʌm] *n* Krume *f*; (*coll*) Brocken *m.*

crumble ['krʌmbl] *v* zerkrümeln. **crumbly** *adj* krümelig.

crumple ['krʌmpl] *v* zerknittern.

crunch [krʌntʃ] *v* knirschen. *n* Knirschen *neut.* **crunchy** *adj* knusprig.

crusade [kruː'seid] *n* Kreuzzug *m.* **crusader** *n* Kreuzfahrer *m.*

crush [krʌʃ] *v* zerdrücken; unterdrücken. *n* Gedränge *neut.* **crushing** *adj* Überwältigend.

crust [krʌst] *n* Kruste *f.*

crustacean [krʌ'steiʃən] *n* Krustentier *neut.*

crutch [krʌtʃ] *n* Krücke *f.*

cry [krai] *v* (*shout*) schreien; (*weep*) weinen. *n* Schrei *m*, Ruf *m.* **cry out** auf-

schreien. **a far cry from** ein weiter Weg von.

crypt [kript] *n* Krypta *f.*

crystal ['kristl] *n* Kristall *m.*

cub [kʌb] *n* Junge(s) *neut*; (*fox, wolf*) Welpe *m*; (*scout*) Wölfling *m.*

cube [kjuːb] *n* Würfel *m*; (*math*) Kubikzahl *f.* **cubic** *adj* würfelförmig. **cubic centimetre** Kubikzentimeter *neut.* **cubic capacity** (*mot*) Hubraum *m.*

cubicle ['kjuːbikl] *n* Kabine *f.*

cuckoo ['kukuː] *n* Kuckuck *m.*

cucumber [kju'kʌmbə] *n* Gurke *f.*

cuddle ['kʌdl] *v* herzen, liebkosen.

cue[1] [kjuː] *n* (*theatre*) Stichwort *neut.*

cue[2] [kjuː] *n* (*billiards*) Billardstock *m.*

cuff[1] [kʌf] *n* (*shirt*) Manschette *f*; (*trousers*) AUfschlag *m.* **cufflink** *n* Manschettenknopf *m.*

cuff[2] [kʌf] *n* Ohrfeige *f*, Klaps *m. v* klapsen.

culinary ['kʌlinəri] *adj* kulinarisch, Küchen-.

culminate ['kʌlmi,neit] *v* kulminieren. **culmination** *n* Höhepunkt *m.*

culprit ['kʌlprit] *n* Täter *m.*

cult [kʌlt] *n* Kult *m.*

cultivate ['kʌlti,veit] *v* bebauen, kultivieren; (*fig*) pflegen. **cultivation** *n* Kultur *f.*

culture ['kʌltʃə] *n* Kultur *f.* **cultural** *adj* kulturell.

cumbersome ['kʌmbəsəm] *adj* sperrig, schwer zu handhaben.

cunning ['kʌniŋ] *adj* schlau, listig. *n* List *f.*

cup [kʌp] *n* Tasse *f*; (*trophy*) Pokal *m.* **cup final** Pokalendspiel *neut.* **cup tie** Pokalspiel *neut.*

cupboard ['kʌbəd] *n* Schrank *m.*

curate ['kjuərət] *n* Unterpfarrer *m.*

curator [kjuə'reitə] *n* Konservator *m.*

curb [kəːb] *v* zügeln. *n* Zaum *m*; (*kerb*) Bordstein *m.*

curdle ['kəːdl] *v* gerinnen.

cure [kjuə] *v* (*illness*) heilen; (*smoke*) räuchern; (*salt*) einsalzen. *n* Heilmittel *neut.*

curfew ['kəːfjuː] *n* Ausgehverbot *m.*

curious ['kjuəriəs] *adj* (*inquisitive*) neugierig; (*odd*) seltsam. **curiosity** *n* Neugier *f.*

curl [kəːl] *n* Locke *f*, Kräuselung *f. v* (sich) kräuseln. **curly** *adj* lockig, kraus.

currant ['kʌrənt] *n* Korinthe *f.*

currency ['kʌrənsi] n (*money*) Währung f.
current ['kʌrənt] adj (*present*) gegenwärtig; (*common*) gebräuchlich, üblich. n Strom m. **current account** Scheckkonto neut. **current events** Zeitgeschehen neut.
currently adv zur Zeit.
curry ['kʌri] n Curry neut. **curry powder** Curry(pulver) neut. **curry sauce** Currysoße f.
curse [kəɪs] v verfluchen; (*swear*) fluchen. n Fluch m.
curt [kəɪt] adj knapp, barsch.
curtail [kərˈteil] v abkürzen. **curtailment** n Abkürzung f; Einschränkung f.
curtain ['kəɪtn] n Gardine f; (*theatre*) Vorhang m.
curtsy ['kəɪtsi] n Knicks m. v knicksen.
curve [kəɪv] n Kurve f. v sich biegen. **curved** adj bogenförmig, gekrümmt.
cushion ['kuʃən] n Kissen neut. v polstern.
custard ['kʌstəd] n Vanillesoße f.
custody ['kʌstədi] n Aufsicht f; (*arrest*) Haft f.
custom ['kʌstəm] n (*habit*) Gewohnheit f; (*tradition*) Brauch m. (*customers*) Kundschaft f. **customary** adj gewöhnlich. **customer** n Kunde m, Kundin f. **customs** n Zoll m. **customs duty** Zoll m. **customs official** Zollbeamte(r) m.
***cut** [kʌt] n Schnitt m; (*wound*) Schnittwunde f; (*in wages*) Kürzung f; (*coll: share*) Anteil m. v schneiden; (*prices*) herabsetzen; (*wages*) kürzen. **cut off** (*phone*) trennen.
cute [kjuɪt] adj (*coll*) niedlich.
cuticle ['kjuɪtikl] n Oberhaut f; (*on nail*) Nagelhaut f.
cutlery ['kʌtləri] n Besteck neut.
cutlet ['kʌtlit] n Kotelett neut.
cycle ['saikl] n Zyklus m; (*bicycle*) Fahrrad neut. v radfahren. **cycling** n Radsport m. **cyclist** n Radfahrer(in).
cyclone ['saikloun] n Zyklon m.
cylinder ['silində] n Zylinder m. **cylinder block** Motorblock m. **cylinder capacity** Hubraum m. **cylinder head** Zylinderkopf m.
cymbals ['simbəlz] pl n Becken neut sing.
cynic ['sinik] n Zyniker(in). **cynical** adj zynisch. **cynicism** Zynismus m.
cypress ['saiprəs] n Zypresse f.
Cyprus ['saiprəs] n Zypern neut. **Cypriot** n Zypriot(in). adj zypriotisch.
cyst [sist] n Zyste f.

Czechoslovakia [ˌtʃekəsləˈvakiə] n die Tschechoslowakei f. **Czechoslovakian** n Tschechoslowake m, Tschechoslowakin f. adj tschechoslowakisch.

D

dab [dab] v betupfen. n Tupfen m.
dabble ['dabl] v plätschern. **he dabbles in art** er beschäftigt sich nebenbei mit Kunst. **dabbler** n Dilettant m.
dad [dad] n Vati m, Papa m.
daffodil ['dafədil] n Narzisse f.
daft [daɪft] adj (*coll*) blöd(e), doof.
dagger ['dagə] n Dolch m.
daily ['deili] adj, adv täglich. **daily paper** Tageszeitung f.
dainty ['deinti] adj (*person*) niedlich; (*food*) lecker.
dairy ['deəri] n Molkerei f. **dairy produce** Milchprodukte pl.
daisy ['deizi] n Gänseblümchen neut.
dam [dam] n Damm m. v eindämmen.
damage ['damidʒ] v beschädigen; verletzen. n Schaden m. **damages** pl n (*compensation*) Schadenersatz m sing.
damn [dam] v verdammen. interj verdammt!
damp [damp] adj feucht. n Feuchtigkeit f. **dampen** v befeuchten.
damson ['damzən] n Pflaume f.
dance [daɪns] n Tanz m. v tanzen. **dancer** n Tänzer(in). **dance hall** Tanzsaal m. **dancing** n Tanz m; Tanzen neut.
dandelion ['dandiˌlaiən] n Löwenzahn m.
dandruff ['dandrəf] n Schuppen pl.
Dane [dein] n Däne m, Dänin f. **Danish** adj dänisch.
danger ['deindʒə] n Gefahr f. **in** (*or* **out of**) **danger** in/außer Gefahr. **dangerous** adj gefährlich.
dangle ['daŋgl] v baumeln; baumeln lassen.
dare [deə] v wagen, riskieren; (*challenge*) herausfordern. **daring** adj wagemutig; (*risky*) gewagt; n Mut m.
dark [daɪk] adj finster; (*esp colour*) dunkel. n Dunkelheit f. **in the dark** im Dunkeln; (*fig*) nicht im Bilde. **darken** v (sich) verdunkeln. **darkness** n Dunkelheit

f. Finsternis *f.* **darkroom** *n* Dunkelkammer *f.*

darling ['da:liŋ] *n* Liebling *m. adj* lieb.

darn [da:n] *v* stopfen. **darning** *n* Stopfen *neut.*

dart [da:t] *v* schießen, sausen; *n* Pfeil *m.* **darts** *pl n* (*game*) (Pfeilwerfen) *neut sing.*

dash [daʃ] *v* (*smash*) zerschlagen; (*rush*) stürzen. *n* (*punctuation*) Gedankenstrich *m;* (*rush*) Stürzen *neut;* (*addition*) Schuß *m.* **dashboard** *n* Armaturenbrett *neut.*

dashing *adj* schneidig.

data ['deitə] *pl n* Daten *pl.* **data processing** Datenverarbeitung *f.*

date[1] [deit] *n* Datum *neut;* (*appointed day*) Termin *m;* (*with someone*) Verabredung *f. v* (*letter*) datieren. **dated** *adj* altmodisch.

date[2] [deit] *n* (*fruit*) Dattel *f.*

dative ['deitiv] *n* Dativ *m.*

daughter ['dɔ:tə] *n* Tochter *f.* **daughter-in-law** *n* Schwiegertochter *f.*

daunt [dɔint] *v* entmutigen.

dawdle ['dɔ:dl] *v* trödeln.

dawn [dɔin] *n* Tagesanbruch *m;* (Morgen)Dämmerung *f;* (*fig*) Anfang *m. v* dämmern (*also fig*).

day [dei] *n* Tag *m.* **daylight** Tageslicht *neut.*

daze [deiz] *v* betäuben. **dazed** *adj* benommen.

dazzle ['dazl] *v* blenden.

dead [ded] *adj* tot. **dead man/woman** Tote(r). **the dead** die Toten *pl.* **deaden** *v* dämpfen. **dead certain** todsicher. **dead end** Sackgasse *f;* (*fig*) totes Geleise *neut.* **deadline** *n* Termin *m.*

deaf [def] *adj* taub. **deaf aid** Hörgerät *neut.* **deaf mute** Taubstumme(r). **deafen** *v* taub machen.

***deal** [di:l] *n* Geschäft *neut. v* handeln; (*cards*) austeilen. **deal with** (*attend to*) sich befassen mit; (*resolve*) erledigen. **a great/good deal of** viel. **dealer** *n* Händler *m;* (*cards*) Kartengeber *m.* **dealings** *pl n* Beziehungen *pl.*

dealt [delt] *V* deal.

dean [di:n] *n* Dekan *m.*

dear [diə] *adj* (*beloved*) lieb; (*expensive*) teuer. (*in letters*) *Dear Mr. Smith* Lieber Herr Smith, Sehr geehrter Herr Smith. *n* Liebling *m.* **dearly** *adv* herzlich.

death [deθ] *n* Tod *m;* (*case of death*) Todesfall *m.* **deathbed** *n* Sterbebett *neut.* **death penalty** Todesstrafe *f.*

debase [di'beis] *v* entwerten.

debate [di'beit] *n* Debatte *f. v* debattieren, diskutieren.

debit ['debit] *n* Soll *neut;* Lastscrift *f. v* belasten.

debris ['deibri:] *n* Schutt *m,* Trümmer *pl.*

debt [det] *n* Schuld *f.* **in debt** verschuldet. **debtor** *n* Schuldner *m.*

decade ['dekeid] *n* Jahrzehnt *neut*

decadence ['dekədəns] *n* Dekadenz *f.* **decadent** *adj* dekadent.

decanter [di'kantə] *n* Karaffe *f.*

decapitate [di'kapi,teit] *v* enthaupten. **decapitation** *n* Enthauptung *f.*

decay [di'kei] *v* verfallen. *n* Verfall *m.* **tooth decay** Karies *f.*

deceased [di'si:st] *adj* verstorben. **the deceased** der/die Verstorbene.

deceit [di'si:t] *n* Täuschung, Betrug *m.* **deceitful** *adj* betrügerisch.

deceive [di'si:v] *v* täuschen.

December [di'sembə] *n* Dezember *m.*

decent ['di:sənt] *adj* (*respectable*) anständig; (*kind*) freundlich. **decency** *n* Anstand *m.*

deceptive [di'septiv] *adj* täuschend.

decibel ['desi,bel] *n* Dezibel *neut.*

decide [di'said] *v* entscheiden; (*make up one's mind*) sich entscheiden. **decided** *adj* entschieden. **decision** *n* Entscheidung *f;* (*of committee*) Beschluß *m.* **make a decision** eine Entscheidung treffen. **decisive** *adj* entscheidend.

deciduous [di'sidjuəs] *adj* (*trees*) Laub-.

decimal ['desiməl] *adj* Dezimal-.

decipher [di'saifə] *v* entziffern.

deck [dek] *n* Deck *neut;* (*of cards*) Pack *neut.* **deckchair** *n* Liegestuhl *m.*

declare [di'kleə] *v* erklären. **declaration** *n* Erklärung *f*

decline [di'klain] *v* ablehnen; (*gram*) deklinieren.

decompose [,di:kəm'pouz] *v* zerfallen.

decor ['deikɔ:] *n* Ausstattung *f.*

decorate ['dekə,reit] *v* schmücken, (*room*) tapezieren; (*mil*) auszeichnen. **decoration** *n* Verzierung *f;* (*of room*) Dekoration *f;* (*mil*) Orden *m.*

decoy ['di:kɔi] *n* Lockvogel *m.*

decrease [di'kri:s] *v* (*make less*) vermindern; (*become less*) abnehmen. *n* Abnahme *f.*

decree [di'kri:] *n* Erlaß *m.*

decrepit

decrepit [di'krepit] *adj* hinfällig.
dedicate ['dedi,keit] *v* widmen; (*rel*) weihen. **dedication** *n* (*book*) Widmung *f*; (*to duty*, *etc.*) Hingabe *f*; (*rel*) Einweihung *f*.
deduce [di'djuːs] *v* schließen (*aus*).
deduct [di'dʌkt] *v* abziehen. **deduction** *n* Abzug *m*.
deed [diːd] *n* Tat *f*; (*document*) Urkunde *f*.
deep [diːp] *adj* tief. **deep freeze** Tiefkühlschrank *m*. **deep-frozen** *adj* tiefgekühlt, Tiefkühl-.
deer [diə] *n* Hirsch *m*.
deface [di'feis] *v* entstellen.
default [di'foːlt] *n* Unterlassung *f*. *v* (*with payments*) in Verzug kommen.
defeat [di'fiːt] *v* schlagen, besiegen. *n* Niederlage *f*.
defect ['diːfekt; *v* di'fekt] *n* Fehler *m*, Defekt *m*. *v* (*pol*) überlaufen. **defective** *adj* fehlerhaft, defektiv.
defence [di'fens] *n* Verteidigung *f*. **defenceless** *adj* schutzlos.
defend [di'fend] *v* verteidigen. **defendant** *n* Angeklagte(r). **defender** *n* Verteidiger *m*. **defensive** *adj* defensiv, Verteidigungs-.
defer [di'fəː] *v* (*postpone*) verschieben. **defer to** (*yield to*) nachgeben (+ *dat*). **deferment** *n* Verschiebung *f*.
defiance [di'faiəns] *n* Trotz *m*. **defiant** *adj* trotzig, unnachgiebig.
deficiency [di'fiʃənsi] *n* Unzulänglichkeit *f*, Mangel *m*. **deficient** *adj* (*defective*) defektiv, mangelhaft; (*inadequate*) unzulänglich.
deficit ['defisit] *n* Defizit *neut*, Fehlbetrag *m*.
define [di'fain] *v* definieren, genau erklären. **(well) defined** *adj* deutlich. **definite** *adj* klar, deutlich. **definitely** *adv* bestimmt. **definition** *n* Erklärung *f*, Definition *f*; (*phot*) Schärfe *f*.
deflate [di'fleit] *v* die Luft ablassen aus. **deflation** (*pol*) Deflation *f*.
deform [di'foːm] *v* deformieren, entstellen. **deformed** *adj* deformiert, verformt. **deformity** *n* Mißbildung *f*.
defraud [di'froːd] *v* betrügen.
defrost [diː'frost] *v* abtauen.
deft [deft] *adj* flink.
defunct [di'fʌŋkt] *adj* verstorben; (*fig*) nicht mehr bestehend.
defy [di'fai] *v* (*resist*) trotzen, (*challenge*) herausfordern

degenerate [di'dʒenə,reit; *adj* di'dʒenərit] *v* degenerieren. *adj* degeneriert.
degrade [di'greid] *v* erniedrigen, entehren. **degradation** *n* Erniedrigung *f*. **degrading** *adj* erniedrigend.
degree [di'griː] *n* Grad *m*. **to a high degree** in hohem Maße.
dehydrate [diː'haidreit] *v* trocknen. **dehydrated** *adj* getrocknet, Trocken-.
deign [dein] *v* sich herablassen.
dejected [di'dʒektid] *adj* niedergeschlagen.
delay [di'lei] *v* (*postpone*) aufschieben. *n* Verzögerung *f*, Aufschub *m*. **be delayed** (*train*, *etc.*) Verspätung haben. **without delay** unverzüglich.
delegate ['deləgeit; 'deləgit] *v* delegieren. *n* Delegierte(r). **delegation** *m* Delegation *f*.
delete [di'liːt] *v* tilgen, streichen.
deliberate [di'libərət; *v* di'libəreit] *adj* (*intentional*) absichtlich. *v* nachdenken. **deliberately** *adv* absichtlich. **deliberation** *n* Überlegung *f*.
delicate ['delikət] *adj* (*fragile*) zart; (*fine*) fein; (*situation*) heikel. **delicacy** *n* Zartheit *f*; (*food*) Delikatesse *f*.
delicious [di'liʃəs] *adj* köstlich.
delight [di'lait] *n* Freude *f*, Vergnügen *neut*. *v* erfreuen. **delighted** *adj* erfreut, entzückt. **delightful** *adj* entzückend.
delinquency [di'liŋkwənsi] *n* Straffälligkeit *f*. **delinquent** *adj* delinquent. *n* Delinquent *m*.
delirious [di'liriəs] *adj* in Delirium. **delirium** *n* Delirium *neut*, Fieberwahn *m*.
deliver [di'livə] *v* (*goods*) (aus)liefern; (*rescue*) befreien; (*a woman in childbirth*) entbinden. **deliverance** *n* Befreiung *f*. **delivery** *n* (Aus)Lieferung *f*; Entbindung *f*.
delta ['deltə] *n* Delta *neut*.
delude [di'luːd] *v* täuschen. **delusion** *n* Täuschung *f*.
deluge ['deljuːdʒ] *n* Flut *f*.
delve [delv] *v* **delve into** erforschen.
demand [di'maɪnd] *v* verlangen. *n* Verlangen *neut*; (*for a commodity*, *etc.*) Nachfrage *f*. **on demand** auf Verlangen. **demanding** *adj* anspruchsvoll.
demented [di'mentid] *adj* wahnsinnig.
democracy [di'mokrəsi] *n* Demokratie *f*. **democrat** *n* Demokrat *m*. **democratic** *adj* demokratisch

demolish [di'molɪʃ] v abbrechen. **demolition** n Abbruch m.

demon ['diːmən] n Teufel m.

demonstrate ['demənˌstreit] v demonstrieren. **demonstration** n Demonstration f.

demoralize [di'morəˌlaiz] v demoralisieren. **demoralization** n Demoralisation f.

demure [di'mjuə] adj bescheiden.

den [den] n Höhle f; (room) Bude f.

denial [di'naiəl] n Leugnung f.

denim ['denim] adj Denim-. **denims** pl n Jeans pl.

Denmark ['denmɑːk] n Dänemark neut.

denomination [diˌnomi'neiʃən] n (rel) Bekenntnis neut; (of banknote) Nennwert m. **denominator** n Nenner m. **common denominator** gemeinsamer Nenner m.

denote [di'nout] v bezeichnen.

denounce [di'nauns] v brandmarken.

dense [dens] adj dicht, dick. **density** n Dichte f.

dent [dent] n Beule f. v einbeulen.

dental ['dentl] adj Zahn-.

dentist ['dentist] n Zahnarzt m. **dentistry** n Zahnheilkunde f.

denture ['dentʃə] n (künstliches) Gebiß neut.

denude [di'njuːd] v entblößen.

denunciation [dinʌnsi'eiʃən] n Denunziation f.

deny [di'nai] v leugnen; (responsibility) ablehnen; (allegation) dementieren. **deny oneself** sich versagen.

deodorant [diː'oudərənt] n Desodorans neut.

depart [di'pɑːt] v abfahren; (fig) abweichen. **departure** n (person) Weggehen neut; (train) Abfahrt f; (aeroplane) Abflug m.

department [di'pɑːtmənt] n Abteilung f; (pol) Ministerium neut. **department store** Warenhaus neut.

depend [di'pend] v **depend on** abhängen von; (rely on) sich verlassen auf. **it (all) depends** es kommt darauf an. **dependable** adj zuverlässig. **dependant** n Familienangehörige(r). **dependent** adj abhängig (+von).

depict [di'pikt] v schildern.

deplete [di'pliːt] v erschöpfen. **depletion** n Erschöpfung f.

deplore [di'plɔː] v bedauern. **deplorable** adj bedauernswert.

deport [di'pɔːt] v deportieren. **deport oneself** sich verhalten. **deportation** n Deportation f. **deportment** n Haltung f.

depose [di'pouz] v absetzen.

deposit [di'pozit] v deponieren. n (surety) Kaution f; (down payment) Anzahlung f; (sediment) Niederschlag m. **deposit account** Sparkonto neut.

depot ['depou] n Depot neut.

depraved [di'preivd] adj lasterhaft, verworfen.

depreciate [di'priːʃiˌeit] v an Wert verlieren. **depreciation** n Wertminderung f.

depress [di'pres] v niederdrücken, deprimieren. **depressed** adj deprimiert. **depressing** adj deprimierend. **depression** n Depression f.

deprive [di'praiv] v berauben.

depth [depθ] n Tiefe f. **in depth** gründlich.

deputy ['depjuti] n Stellvertreter m. adj stellvertretend.

derail [di'reil] v entgleisen. **derailment** n Entgleisen neut.

derelict ['derilikt] adj (building) baufällig.

deride [di'raid] v verspotten. **derision** n Spott m. **derisory** adj spöttisch.

derive [di'raiv] v ableiten; (originate) stammen; (gain) gewinnen. **derivation** n Herkunft f.

derogatory [di'rogətəri] adj geringschätzig.

descend [di'send] v hinabsteigen; (from train) aussteigen. **be descended from** abstammen von. **descendant** n Nachkomme m. **descent** n Abstieg m; Abstammung f.

describe [di'skraib] v beschreiben. **description** n Beschreibung f.

desert[1] ['dezət] n Wüste f.

desert[2] [di'zəːt] n (something deserved) Verdienst neut. **deserts** pl Lohn m sing.

desert[3] [di'zəːt] v verlassen; (mil) desertieren. **deserter** n Deserteur m. **desertion** n Verlassen neut; (mil) Desertion f.

deserve [di'zəːv] v verdienen.

design [di'zain] n Entwurf m; (drawing) Zeichnung f; (pattern) Muster neut. v entwerfen, planen.

designate ['deziɡˌneit] n bezeichnen. **designation** n Bezeichnung f.

desire [di'zaiə] v wünschen, begehren; (ask for) wollen. n Wunsch m; (sexual) Begierde f. **desirous of** begierig nach.

desk 46

desk [desk] *n* Schreibtisch *m*.
desolate ['desələt] *v* wüst, öde; (*person*) trostlos.
despair [di'speə] *v* verzweifeln. *n* Verzweiflung *f*.
desperate ['despərət] *adj* verzweifelt; (*situation*) hoffnungslos.
despicable [di'spikəbl] *adj* verächtlich.
despise [di'spaiz] *v* verachten.
despite [di'spait] *prep* trotz (+*gen*).
despondent [di'spondənt] *adj* mutlos.
despot ['despot] *n* Gewaltherrscher *m*, Despot *m*. **despotism** *n* Despotismus *m*.
dessert [di'zəɪt] *n* Nachtisch *m*. **dessert spoon** Dessertlöffel *m*.
destiny ['destəni] *n* Schicksal *neut*. **destined** *adj* ausersehen, bestimmt. **destination** *n* (*post*) Bestimmungsort *m*; (*travel*) Reiseziel *neut*.
destitute ['destitjuːt] *adj* notleidend, bedürftig.
destroy [di'stroi] *v* zerstören, vernichten. **destroyer** *n* Zerstörer *m*. **destruction** *n* Zerstörung *f*. **destructive** *adj* zerstörerisch.
detach [di'tatʃ] *v* losmachen, abtrennen. **detached** *adj* (*house*) Einzel-; (*fig*) objektiv. **detachment** Objektivität *f*; (*mil*) Abteilung *f*.
detail ['diːteil] *n* Einzelheit *f*, Detail *neut*. **further details** Näheres *neut*; nähere Angaben *pl*. *v* detaillieren **detailed** *adj* eingehend.
detain [di'tein] *v* aufhalten; (*arrest*) verhaften.
detect [di'tekt] *v* entdecken. **detection** *n* Aufdeckung *f*. **detective** *n* Detektiv *m*. **detective story** Kriminalroman *m*.
détente [dei'tãɪnt] *n* Entspannung *f*.
detention [di'tenʃən] *n* (*law*) Haft *m*; (*school*) Nachsitzen *neut*.
deter [di'təɪ] *v* abschrecken.
detergent [di'təɪdʒənt] *n* Reinigungsmittel *neut*.
deteriorate [di'tiəriə,reit] *v* sich verschlechtern. **deterioration** *n* Verschlechterung *f*.
determine [di'təɪmin] *v* bestimmen; (*decide*) sich entschließen. **determined** *adj* entschlossen. **determination** *n* Entschlossenheit *f*.
detest [di'test] *v* hassen, verabscheuen. **detestable** *adj* abscheulich.
detonate ['detə,neit] *v* detonieren.
detour ['diːtuə] *n* Umweg *m*.

detract [di'trakt] *v* **detract from** beeinträchtigen.
detriment ['detrimənt] *n* Schaden *m*, Nachteil *m*. **detrimental (to)** *adj* schädlich (für).
devalue [diː'valjuː] *v* abwerten. **devaluation** *n* Abwertung *f*.
devastate ['devə,steit] *v* verwüsten. **devastating** *adj* vernichtend. **devastation** *n* Verwüstung *f*.
develop [di'veləp] *v* (sich) entwickeln. **developer** *n* Entwickler *m*. **developing** *n* Entwicklungs-. **development** *n* Entwicklung *f*.
deviate ['diːvi,eit] *v* abweichen. **deviation** *n* Abweichung *f*.
device [di'vais] *n* Gerät *neut*, Vorrichtung *f*; (*trick*) Trick *m*.
devil ['devl] *n* Teufel *m*. **talk of the devil** den Teufel an die Wand malen. **devilish** *adj* teuflisch.
devious ['diːviəs] *adj* weitschweifig; (*dishonest*) krumm, unaufrichtig.
devise [di'vaiz] *v* ausdenken, erfinden.
devoid [di'void] *adj* **devoid of** ohne, frei von.
devolution [,diːvə'luːʃən] *n* Dezentralisation *f*.
devote [di'vout] *v* widmen, hingeben. **devoted** *adj* ergeben. **be devoted to someone** sehr an jemandem hängen. **devotee** *n* Anhänger(in). **devotion** *n* Ergebenheit *f*.
devour [di'vauə] *v* verschlingen.
devout [di'vaut] *adj* fromm, andächtig.
dew [djuː] *n* Tau *m*.
dexterous ['dekstrəs] *adj* gewandt, flink. **dexterity** *n* Gewandtheit *f*.
diabetes [,diaə'biːtiːz] *n* Zuckerkrankheit *f*. **diabetic** *adj* zuckerkrank. *n* Diabetiker *m*.
diagnose [,diaəg'nouz] *v* diagnostizieren, erkennen. **diagnosis** *n* Diagnose *f*. **diagnostic** *adj* diagnostisch.
diagonal [dai'agənəl] *adj* diagonal. *n* Diagonale *f*.
diagram ['daiə,gram] *n* Diagramm *neut*, Schaubild *neut*.
dial ['daiəl] *n* (*phone*) Wählscheibe *f*. *v* wählen. **dialling tone** Amtszeichen *neut*.
dialect ['diaəlekt] *n* Dialekt *m*.
dialogue ['daiəlog] *n* Dialog *m*.
diameter [dai'amitə] *n* Durchmesser *m*.
diamond ['daiəmənd] *n* Diamant *m*; (*cards*) Karo *neut*; (*sport*) Spielfeld *neut*. *adj* diamanten.

diaper ['daɪəpə] *n* Windel *f.*
diaphragm ['daɪəˌfram] *n* (*anat*) Zwerchfell *neut*; (*contraceptive*) (Okklusiv)Pessar *neut.*
diarrhoea [ˌdaɪə'rɪə] *n* Durchfall *m.*
diary ['daɪərɪ] *n* Tagebuch *neut.*
dice [daɪs] *pl n* Würfel *pl.* *v* (*cookery*) in Würfel schneiden.
dictate [dɪk'teɪt] *n* diktieren. **dictating machine** Diktiergerät *neut.* **dictation** *n* Diktat *neut.* **dictator** *n* Diktator *m.* **dictatorial** *adj* diktatorisch. **dictatorship** *n.*
dictionary ['dɪkʃənərɪ] *n* Wörterbuch *neut.*
did [dɪd] *V* do.
die [daɪ] *v* sterben. **die away** schwächer werden. **die out** aussterben.
diesel ['diːzəl] *adj* Diesel-. **diesel engine** Dieselmotor *m.*
diet ['daɪət] *n* Kost *f*, Nahrung *f*; (*for weight loss*) Abmagerungskur *f*; (*for convalescence, etc.*) Diät *f*, Schonkost *f.* *v* eine Abmagerungskur machen.
differ ['dɪfə] *v* sich unterscheiden; (*think differently*) anderer Meinung sein. **difference** *n* Unterschied *m.* **different** *adj* verschieden, unterschiedlich; (*another*) ander. **differential** *adj* unterschiedlich. *n* (*mot*) Differentialgetriebe *neut.*
difficult ['dɪfɪkəlt] *adj* schwer, schwierig. **difficulty** *n* Schwierigkeit *f.*
*dig [dɪg] *v* graben. **dig up** ausgraben.
digest [daɪ'dʒest; *n* 'daɪdʒest] *v* verdauen. *n* Auslese *f.* **digestible** *adj* verdaulich. **digestion** *n* Verdauung *f.*
digit ['dɪdʒɪt] *n* (*figure*) Ziffer *f*; (*finger*) Finger *m*; (*toe*) Zehe *f.*
dignified ['dɪgnɪˌfaɪd] *adj* würdevoll.
dignity ['dɪgnətɪ] *n* Würde *f.*
digress [daɪ'gres] *v* abschweifen. **digression** *n* Abschweifung *f.*
digs [dɪgz] *pl n* (*coll*) Bude *f sing.*
dilapidated [dɪ'lapɪˌdeɪtɪd] *adj* baufällig.
dilate [daɪ'leɪt] *v* (sich) weiten.
dilemma [dɪ'lemə] *n* Dilemma *neut.* **be in a dilemma** in der Klemme sitzen.
diligence ['dɪlɪdʒəns] *n* Fleiß *m.* **diligent** *adj* fleißig, gewissenhaft.
dilute [daɪ'luːt] *v* (*with water*) verwässern; verdünnen. *adj* (*also* **diluted**) verwässert.
dim [dɪm] *adj* trübe; (*light, vision*) schwach; (*coll: stupid*) dumm. *v* verdunkeln.
dimension [dɪ'menʃən] *n* Dimension *f.* **dimensions** *pl* Ausmaße *pl.*

diminish [dɪ'mɪnɪʃ] *v* (sich) vermindern. **diminishing** *adj* abnehmend.
diminutive [dɪ'mɪnjutɪv] *adj* winzig.
dimple ['dɪmpl] *n* Grübchen *neut.*
din [dɪn] *n* Lärm *m*, Getöse *neut.*
dine [daɪn] *v* speisen, essen. **diner** *n* (*person*) Tischgast *m*; (*rail*) Speisewagen *m*; (*restaurant*) Speiselokal *neut.* **dining car** Speisewagen *m.* **dining room** Eßzimmer *neut.* **dining table** Eßtisch *n.*
dinghy ['dɪŋgɪ] *n* Dingi *neut*, Beiboot *neut.* **rubber dinghy** Schlauchboot *neut.*
dingy ['dɪndʒɪ] *adj* trübe.
dinner ['dɪnə] *n* Abendessen *neut*; (*at midday*) Mittagessen *neut*; (*public*) Festessen *neut.* **dinner jacket** Smoking *m.* **dinner party** Diner *neut.*
dinosaur ['daɪnəˌsɔɪ] *n* Dinosaurier *m.*
dip [dɪp] *v* (ein)tauchen; (*slope down*) sich senken. **dip one's lights** (*mot*) abblenden. *n* Senkung *f*; (*bathe*) Bad *neut.* **dip switch** Abblendschalter *m.*
diploma [dɪ'pləumə] *n* Diplom *neut.*
diplomacy [dɪ'pləuməsɪ] *n* Diplomatie *f.* **diplomat** *n* Diplomat *m.* **diplomatic** *adj* diplomatisch.
dipstick ['dɪpstɪk] *n* (*mot*) Ölmeßstab *m.*
dire [daɪə] *adj* schrecklich; (*urgent*) dringend.
direct [dɪ'rekt] *adj* direkt. *v* dirigieren, leiten; (*aim*) richten; (*give directions*) den Weg zeigen (+ *dat*); (*order*) anweisen. **direction** *n* Richtung *f*; Leitung *f*; **directions** *pl* (*for use*) Gebrauchsanweisung *f sing*; (*instructions*) Anweisungen *pl.* **directly** *adv* (*immediately*) unmittelbar; (*straight towards*) direkt, gerade. **director** *n* Direktor *m*, Leiter *m*; (*theatre, film*) Regisseur *m.* (**telephone**) **directory** *n* Telefonbuch *neut.*
dirt [dɜɪt] *n* Schmutz *m*, Dreck *m.* **dirt cheap** spottbillig. **dirty** *adj* schmutzig, dreckig.
disability [dɪsə'bɪlətɪ] *n* Körperbehinderung *f.* **disability pension** Invalidenrente *f.*
disadvantage [ˌdɪsəd'vaɪntɪdʒ] *n* Nachteil *m.* **disadvantageous** *adj* ungünstig, unvorteilhaft.
disagree [ˌdɪsə'griː] *v* nicht übereinstimmen; (*argue*) sich streiten. **disagreeable** *adj* unangenehm. **disagreement** *n* Meinungsverschiedenheit *f.*

disappear [ˌdisəˈpiə] v verschwinden. **disappearance** n Verschwinden neut.
disappoint [ˌdisəˈpoint] v enttäuschen. **disappointed** adj enttäuscht. **disappointing** adj enttäuschend. **disappointment** n Enttäuschung f.
disapprove [ˌdisəˈpruːv] v **disapprove of** mißbilligen. **disapproval** n Mißbilligung f.
disarm [disˈaːm] v entwaffnen; (pol) abrüsten. **disarmament** n Abrüstung f. **disarming** adj entwaffnend.
disaster [diˈzaːstə] n Katastrophe f, Unglück neut. **disastrous** adj katastrophal.
disband [disˈband] v (sich) auflösen.
disc or US **disk** [disk] n Scheibe f; (record) Schallplatte f.
discard [disˈkaːd] v ablegen.
disc brake n Scheibenbremse f. **disc jockey** Disk-Jockey m.
discern [diˈsəːn] v (perceive) wahrnehmen; (differentiate) unterscheiden. **discernible** adj wahrnehmbar. **discerning** adj einsichtig.
discharge [disˈtʃaːdʒ] v (dismiss) entlassen; (gun) abschießen; (duty) erfüllen; (ship) entladen; (of wound) eitern. n (med) Ausfluß m.
disciple [diˈsaipl] n Jünger m.
discipline [ˈdisiplin] n Disziplin f. v disziplinieren; (train) schulen.
disclaim [disˈkleim] v ablehnen. **disclaimer** n Dementi neut.
disclose [disˈklouz] v enthüllen. **disclosure** n Bekanntmachung f.
discolour [disˈkʌlə] v (sich) verfärben. **discoloration** n Verfärbung f.
discomfort [disˈkʌmfət] n Unbehagen neut.
disconcert [diskənˈsəːt] v aus der Fassung bringen.
disconnect [diskəˈnekt] v trennen; (elec) abschalten.
disconsolate [disˈkonsələt] adj trostlos.
discontinue [diskənˈtinjuː] v aufhören; (something) einstellen.
discord [ˈdiskoːd] n (disagreement) Zwietracht f; (music) Diskordanz f. **discordant** adj diskordant.
discotheque [ˈdiskətek] n Diskothek f.
discount [ˈdiskaunt] v (ignore) außer Acht lassen. n Rabatt m.
discourage [disˈkʌridʒ] v entmutigen;

(dissuade) abraten. **discouraging** adj entmutigend.
discover [disˈkʌvə] v entdecken. **discoverer** n Entdecker m. **discovery** n Entdeckung f.
discredit [disˈkredit] v in Verruf bringen.
discreet [diˈskriːt] adj diskret, verschwiegen.
discrepancy [diˈskrepənsi] n Widerspruch m, Diskrepanz f.
discretion [diˈskreʃən] n Diskretion f, Takt m. **at your discretion** nach Ihrem Gutdünken.
discriminate [diˈskrimiˌneit] v unterscheiden. **discriminate** (against) diskriminieren. **discriminating** adj anspruchsvoll. **discrimination** n (racial, etc.) Diskriminierung f.
discus [ˈdiskəs] n Diskus m.
discuss [diˈskʌs] v besprechen, diskutieren; (in writing) behandeln. **discussion** n Besprechung f, Diskussion f.
disease [diˈziːz] n Krankheit f. **diseased** adj krank.
disembark [disimˈbaːk] v an Land gehen.
disengage [disinˈgeidʒ] v sich losmachen. **disengage the clutch** auskuppeln.
disfigure [disˈfigə] v entstellen. **disfigurement** n Entstellung f.
disgrace [disˈgreis] n Schande f. v Schande bringen über. **disgraceful** adj schändlich.
disgruntled [disˈgrʌntld] adj mürrisch.
disguise [disˈgaiz] v verkleiden; (voice) verstellen. n Verkleidung f. **in disguise** verkleidet.
disgust [disˈgʌst] n Ekel m (vor). v anekeln. **disgusting** adj ekelhaft, widerlich.
dish [diʃ] n Schüssel f, Schale f; (meal) Gericht neut. **dishes** pl Geschirr neut sing. **wash the dishes** abspülen. **dishcloth** n (for drying) Geschirrtuch neut; (for mopping) Lappen m.
dishearten [disˈhaːtn] v entmutigen.
dishevelled [diˈʃevəld] adj in Unordnung, (hair) zerzaust.
dishonest [disˈonist] adj unehrlich, unaufrichtig. **dishonesty** n Unehrlichkeit f. **dishonour** n Unehre f, Schande f. v schänden. **dishonourable** adj unehrenhaft.
dishwasher [ˈdiʃˌwoʃə] n Geschirrspülmaschine f.

disillusion [disi'luːʒən] v ernüchtern, desillusionieren. **be disillusioned about** die Illusion verloren haben über.
disinfect [disin'fekt] v desinfizieren. **disinfectant** n Desinfektionsmittel neut.
disinherit [disin'herit] v enterben.
disintegrate [dis'intigreit] v (sich) auflösen, (sich) zersetzen. **disintegration** n Auflösung f.
disinterested [dis'intristid] adj unparteiisch.
disjointed [dis'dʒointid] adj unzusammenhängend.
disk V disc.
dislike [dis'laik] v nicht mögen. n Abneigung f (gegen).
dislocate ['disləˌkeit] v verrenken. **dislocation** n Verrenkung f.
dislodge [dis'lodʒ] v verschieben.
disloyal [dis'loiəl] adj untreu. **disloyalty** n Untreue f.
dismal ['dizməl] adj trübe, niederdrückend.
dismantle [dis'mantl] v abmontieren.
dismay [dis'mei] v bestürzen. n Bestürzung f, Angst f.
dismiss [dis'mis] v wegschicken; (employee) entlassen; (idea) ablehnen. **dismissal** n Entlassung f.
dismount [dis'maunt] v absteigen.
disobey [disə'bei] v nicht gehorchen (+dat). **disobedience** n Ungehorsam m. **disobedient** adj ungehorsam.
disorder [dis'oːdə] n Unordnung f; (med) Störung f.
disorganized [dis'oːgənaizd] adj unordentlich.
disown [dis'oun] v ableugnen; (child) verstoßen.
disparage [di'sparidʒ] v herabsetzen. **disparaging** v geringschätzig.
disparity [dis'pariti] n Unterschied m.
dispassionate [dis'paʃənit] adj unparteiisch.
dispatch [di'spatʃ] v absenden; (person) entsenden. n Versand m, Abfertigung f; (report) Meldung f.
dispel [di'spel] v vertreiben.
dispense [di'spens] v ausgeben. **dispense with** verzichten auf. **dispenser** n Verteiler m. **dispensing chemist** Apotheker(in).
disperse [di'spəːs] v zerstreuen.
displace [dis'pleis] v versetzen; (replace) ersetzen; (water) verdrängen. **displacement** n (naut) Wasserverdrängung f.

display [di'splei] v zeigen; (goods, etc.) auslegen. n (goods) Auslage f; (feelings) Zurschaustellung f; (parade) Entfaltung f.
displease [dis'pliːz] v mißfallen (+dat). **displeased** adj ärgerlich. **displeasure** n Mißfallen neut.
dispose [di'spouz] v **dispose of** (get rid of) beseitigen, wegwerfen; (have at disposal) verfügen uber. **disposed** adj geneigt. **disposable** adj zum Wegwerfen; Einweg-. **disposal** n Beseitigung f. **have at one's disposal** zur Verfügung haben. **be at someone's disposal** jemandem zur Verfügung stehen. **disposition** n Natur f, Art f.
disproportion [disprə'poːʃən] n Mißverhältnis neut. **disproportionate** adj unverhältnismäßig.
disprove [dis'pruːv] v widerlegen.
dispute [di'spjuːt] v (contest) bestreiten; (argue) disputieren. n Streit m. **trade dispute** Arbeitsstreitigkeit f.
disqualify [dis'kwoliˌfai] v disqualifizieren, ausschließen. **disqualification** n Disqualifikation f.
disregard [disrə'gaːd] v nicht beachten.
disrepute [disrə'pjuːt] n Verruf m. **bring into disrepute** in Verruf bringen. **disreputable** adj (notorious) verrufen.
disrespect [disrə'spekt] n Respektlosigkeit f. **disrespectful** adj respektlos.
disrupt [dis'rʌpt] v stören, unterbrechen. **disruption** n Störung f.
dissatisfied [di'satisˌfaid] adj unzufrieden.
dissect [di'sekt] v sezieren.
dissent [di'sent] n abweichende Meinung f. v anderer Meinung sein.
dissident ['disidənt] n Dissident m.
dissimilar [di'similə] v unähnlich.
dissociate [di'sousieit] v **dissociate oneself from** sich lossagen von.
dissolve [di'zolv] v (sich) auflösen; (meeting) aufheben.
dissuade [di'sweid] v abraten (+dat).
distance ['distəns] n Ferne f, Entfernung f. (gap) Abstand m. **in the distance** in der Ferne. **keep one's distance** Abstand halten. **distant** adj fern, entfernt.
distaste [dis'teist] n Abneigung f. **distasteful** adj unangenehm.
distended [di'stendid] adj ausgedehnt.
distil [di'stil] v destillieren. **distillery** n Brennerei f.

distinct [di'stiŋkt] *adj* (*different*) verschieden; (*clear*) deutlich, ausgeprägt. **distinction** *n* (*difference*) Unterschied *m*; (*merit*) Würde *f*. **of distinction** von Rang. **gain a distinction** sich auszeichnen. **distinctive** *adj* kennzeichnend.
distinguish [di'stiŋgwiʃ] *v* unterscheiden; (*perceive*) erkennen. **distinguish oneself** sich auszeichnen. **distinguishable** *adj* erkennbar. **distinguished** *adj* hervorragend.
distort [di'stoːt] *v* verdrehen; (*truth*) entstellen. **distortion** *n* Verdrehung *f*.
distract [di'strakt] *v* ablenken. **distracted** *adj* verwirrt, außer sich. **distraction** *n* Ablenkung *f*; (*amusement*) Unterhaltung *f*; (*madness*) Wahnsinn *m*.
distraught [di'stroːt] *adj* verwirrt, bestürzt.
distress [di'stres] *n* Not *f*; (*suffering*) Leid *neut*, Qual *f*. *v* betrüben, quälen. **distress signal** Notsignal *m*.
distribute [di'stribjut] *v* verteilen. **distribution** *n* Verteilung *f*. **distributor** *n* Verteiler *m*.
district ['distrikt] *n* Gebiet *neut*, Gegend *f*; (*of town*) Viertel *neut*; (*administrative*) Bezirk *m*. *adj* Bezirks-. **district attorney** Staatsanwalt *m*.
distrust [dis'trʌst] *v* mißtrauen (+*dat*). *n* Mißtrauen *neut*.
disturb [di'stəːb] *v* stören; (*worry*) beunruhigen. **disturbance** *n* Störung *f*. **disturbances** *pl* (*pol*) Unruhen *pl*. **disturbing** *adj* beunruhigend.
disused [dis'juːzd] *adj* außer Gebrauch.
ditch [ditʃ] *n* Wassergraben *m*. *v* (*coll*) im Stich lassen.
ditto ['ditou] *adv* ebenfalls, dito. **ditto mark** Wiederholungszeichen *neut*.
divan [di'van] *n* Divan *m*, Sofa *neut*.
dive [daiv] *v* tauchen; (*from board*) einen Kopfsprung machen; (*aero*) stürzen. *n* Tauchen *neut*; Kopfsprung *m*; (*aero*) Sturzflug *m*. **diver** *n* Taucher *m*.
diverge [dai'vəːdʒ] *v* auseinandergehen.
diverse [dai'vəːs] *adj* verschieden.
divert [dai'vəːt] *v* ableiten; (*traffic*) umleiten. **diversion** *n* Ablenkung *f*; (*mot*) Umleitung *f*. **diversity** *n* Verschiedenheit *f*.
divide [di'vaid] *v* (sich) teilen.
dividend ['dividend] *n* Dividende *f*.
divine [di'vain] *adj* göttlich. *v* erraten.

division [di'viʒən] *n* Teilung *f*; (*math, mil*) Division *f*; (*comm*) Abteilung *f*.
divorce [di'voːs] *n* (Ehe)Scheidung *f*. *v* scheiden. **divorced** *adj* geschieden. **get divorced** sich scheiden lassen. **divorcee** *n* Geschiedene(r).
divulge [dai'vʌldʒ] *v* preisgeben.
dizzy ['dizi] *adj* schwindlig. **dizziness** *n* Schwindel *m*.
*do [duː] *v* tun, machen. **that will do!** (*that's enough*) das genügt! **that won't do** (*that's no good*) das geht nicht! **How do you do?** Guten Tag! *I could do with the money* ich könnte das Geld gut gebrauchen. **do away with** abschaffen. **do in** (*coll*) umbringen. **do up** (*coll*) überholen. **do without** verzichten auf.
docile ['dousail] *adj* fügsam.
dock[1] [dok] *n* Dock *neut*. **docks** *pl* Hafenanlagen *pl*. *v* (*ship*) docken.
dock[2] [dok] *n* (*law*) **in the dock** auf der Anklagebank *f*.
dock[3] [dok] *v* (*cut*) stutzen; (*pay*) kürzen.
doctor ['doktə] *n* (*of medicine*) Arzt *m*, Ärztin *f*; (*as title*) Doktor *m*.
doctrine ['doktrin] *n* Lehre *f*.
document ['dokjumənt] *n* Urkunde *f*, Dokument *neut*. **documents** *pl* Papiere *pl*. *v* urkundlich belegen. **documentary** *adj* urkundlich. *n* Lehrfilm *m*.
dodge [dodʒ] *v* beiseitespringen; (*avoid*) ausweichen. *n* Knitt *m*.
dog [dog] *n* Hund *m*. **dog-eared** *adj* mit Eselsohren. **dogged** *adj* hartnäckig. **dog kennel** Hundehütte *f*.
dogma ['dogmə] *n* Dogma *neut*. **dogmatic** *adj* dogmatisch.
do-it-yourself [ˌduːitjoː'self] *adj* zum Selbermachen; Bastler-.
dole [doul] *n* Stempelgeld *neut*. **go on the dole** stempeln gehen. *v* **dole out** verteilen.
doll [dol] *n* Puppe *f*.
dollar ['dolə] *n* Dollar *m*.
dolphin ['dolfin] *n* Delphin *m*.
domain [də'mein] *n* Bereich *neut*.
dome [doum] *n* Kuppel *f*.
domestic [də'mestik] *adj* häuslich, Haus-; (*national*) inländisch, Innen-. **domestic animal** Haustier *neut*. **domesticate** *v* (*tame*) zähmen.
dominate ['domiˌneit] *v* beherrschen. **dominant** *adj* (vor)herrschend; (*music, biol*) dominant. **domination** *n* Herrschaft *f*.
domineering [domi'niəriŋ] *adj* herrisch.

dominion [də'minjən] n Herrschaft f;
(country) Dominion neut.
domino ['dominou] n Dominostein m.
dominoes pl Dominospiel neut sing.
don [don] v (clothes) anziehen; (hat) aufsetzen.
donate [də'neit] v stiften, spenden. **donation** n Spende f, Stiftung f. **donor** n
Spender m.
done [dʌn] V do.
donkey ['doŋki] n Esel m.
doom [duːm] n Verhängnis neut. **doomed**
adj verloren.
door [dɔː] n Tür f. **out of doors** draußen.
doorbell Türklingel f. **doorhandle** n Tür-
griff m. **doorway** n Türöffnung f; Torweg
m.
dope [doup] n (coll) Rauschgift neut. v
(sport) dopen.
dormant ['dɔːmənt] adj schlafend.
dormitory ['dɔːmitəri] n Schlafsaal m.
(US: student house) Wohnheim m.
dormouse ['dɔːˌmaus] n Haselmaus f.
dose [dous] n Dosis f. v dosieren.
dot [dot] n Punkt m.
dote [dout] v **dote on** vernarrt sein in.
dotted ['dotid] adj ubersät (mit). **dotted
line** punktierte Linie f.
double ['dʌbl] adj doppelt, Doppel-. adv
doppelt, zweimal. n das Doppelte; (film)
Double neut. **doubles** n (sport) Doppel-
spiel neut. v verdoppeln; (fold) falten.
double-barrelled adj doppelläufig. **double-bass** Kontrabaß m. **double-cross** v
betrügen. **double-decker** Doppeldecker
m. **double meaning** Zweideutigkeit f.
doubt [daut] n Zweifel m. v bezweifeln.
doubt whether zweifeln, ob. **doubtful** adj
zweifelhaft. **doubtless** adv ohne Zweifel,
zweifellos.
dough [dou] n Teig m. **doughnut** n
Krapfen m.
dove [dʌv] n Taube f.
dowdy ['daudi] adj schäbig, schlampig.
down[1] [daun] adv hinab, herab; hinunter,
herunter; unten. I went down the road
ich ging die Straße hinunter. **up and
down** auf und ab.
down[2] [daun] n (feathers) Daunen pl.
downcast ['daunˌkɑːst] adj niedergeschlagen.
downfall ['daunˌfɔːl] n Sturz m.
downhearted [ˌdaun'hɑːtid] adj mutlos.
downhill [ˌdaun'hil] adv bergab.

downpour ['daunˌpɔː] n Wolkenbruch m.
downright ['daunˌrait] adv völlig, höchst.
downstairs [ˌdaun'steəz] adv unten. she
came downstairs sie kam nach unten.
downstream [ˌdaun'striːm] adv
stromabwärts.
downtrodden ['daunˌtrodn] adj
unterworfen.
downward ['daunwəd] adj Abwärts-,
sinkend.
downwards ['daunwədz] adv abwärts.
dowry ['dauəri] n Mitgift f.
doze [douz] v dösen. n Schläfchen neut.
dozen ['dʌzn] n Dutzend neut.
drab [drab] adj eintönig, farblos.
draft [drɑːft] n (plan) Konzept neut,
Entwurf m; (comm) Tratte f; (mil)
Aushebung f. v entwerfen; (mil)
ausheben.
drag [drag] v schleppen, schleifen. n **drag
on** sich in die Länge ziehen.
dragon ['dragən] n Drache m. **dragonfly** n
Libelle f.
drain [drein] n Abfluß m; (fig) Belastung
f. v ablassen; (water) ableiten; (fig)
erschöpfen. **drainage** n Entwässerung f.
drainpipe n Abflußrohr neut.
drama ['drɑːmə] n Drama neut. **dramatic**
adj dramatisch. **dramatize** v dramatisier-
en.
drank [draŋk] V drink.
drape [dreip] v drapieren. n (curtain)
Vorhang m. **draper** n Tuchhändler m.
drastic ['drastik] adj drastisch.
draught or US **draft** [drɑːft] n Zug m;
(naut) Tiefgang m. **draughts** n Damespiel
neut. **draught beer** Bier vom Faß.
draughtsman n Zeichner m. **draughty** adj
zugig.
***draw** [drɔː] v ziehen; (curtain) zuziehen;
(picture) zeichnen; (money) abheben; (water)
(public) anziehen; (water) schöpfen;
(sport) unentschieden spielen. n (lottery)
Ziehung f; (sport) Unentschieden neut.
draw near sich nähern. **draw up** (document) ausstellen. **drawback** n Nachteil m.
drawbridge n Zugbrücke f. **drawer** n
Schublade f. **drawing** n Zeichnung f.
drawing pin n Heftzwecke f. **drawing
room** Salon m.
drawl [drɔːl] v schleppend sprechen.
drawn [drɔːn] V draw.
dread [dred] n Furcht f, Angst f. v Angst
haben vor. **dreadful** adj furchtbar.

*dream [driːm] *n* Traum *m. v* träumen. **dreamer** *n* Träumer *n* **dreamy** *adj* träumerisch.

dreamt [dremt] *V* **dream.**

dreary ['driəri] *adj* trübe, düster.

dredge [dredʒ] *v* (*river*) ausbaggern. **dredger** *n* Bagger *m.*

dregs [dregz] *pl n* Bodensatz *m sing*; (*fig*) Abschaum *m sing.*

drench [drentʃ] *v* durchnässen.

dress [dres] *v* (sich) anziehen; (*wound*) verbinden. *n* (*clothes*) Kleidung *f*; (*woman's*) Kleid *neut.* **dress designer** Modezeichner *m.* **dresser** *n* (*furniture*) Küchenschrank *m.* **dressing** *n* (*salad*) Soße *f*; (*med*) Verband *m.* **dressing gown** Morgenrock *m.* **dressing room** (*theatre*) Garderobe *f.* **dressing table** Toilettentisch *m.* **dressmaking** *n* Damenschneiderei *f.* **dress suit** Gesellschaftsanzug *m.*

drew [druː] *V* **draw.**

dribble ['dribl] *v* tröpfeln; (*football*) dribbeln. *n* Tröpfeln *neut.*

drier ['draiə] *n* Trockner *m.*

drift [drift] *v* treiben; (*coll*) sich treiben lassen. *n* (*snow*) Verwehung *f*; (*tendency*) Tendenz *f.* **drifter** *n* (*person*) Vagabund *m.*

drill [dril] *n* Bohrmaschine *f*; (*training*) Drill *m. v* (*holes*) bohren; (*train*) trainieren, drillen.

*drink [driŋk] *v* trinken; (*animal, coll*) saufen. *n* Getränk *neut*; (*cocktail, etc.*) Drink *m.* **drinker** *n* Trinker *m* (*coll*) Säufer *m.*

drip [drip] *v* tropfen, triefen. *n* Tropfen *m* **drip-dry** *adj* bügelfrei. **dripping** *adj* triefend. *n* Schmalz *neut.*

*drive [draiv] *v* treiben; (*vehicle*) fahren. *n* Fahrt *f*; (*tech*) Antrieb *m*; (*mil*) Kampagne *f.* **drive mad** verrückt machen. **drive-in** (**cinema**) Autokino *neut.*

drivel ['drivl] *v* sabbern, geifern. *n* Quatsch *m.*

driver ['draivə] *n* Fahrer *m*, Chauffeur *m.* **driver's license** Führerschein *m.*

driving ['draiviŋ] *adj* Treib-; (*mot*) Fahr-; (*rain*) heftig. *n* Fahren *neut.* **driving lessons** Fahrunterricht *m.* **driving licence** Führerschein *m.* **driving school** Fahrschule *f.* **driving test** Fahrprüfung *f.*

drizzle ['drizl] *n* Sprühregen *m. v* nieseln.

drone [droun] *v* summen. *n* Drohne *f.*

droop [druːp] *v* (schlaff) herunterhängen; (*flower*) welken.

drop [drop] *n* (*of water*) Tropfen *m*; (*fall*) Fall, Sturz *m. v* (*fall*) fallen; (*let fall*) fallen lassen; (*passenger*) absetzen; (*bomb*) abwerfen. **drop in** vorbeikommen. **drop off** (**to sleep**) einschlafen. **drop-out** *n* Dropout *m.*

drought [draut] *n* Dürre *f.*

drove [drouv] *V* **drive.**

drown [draun] *v* ertrinken. **drown out** ubertönen.

drowsy ['drauzi] *adj* schläfrig.

drudge [drʌdʒ] *n* Packesel *m.* **drudgery** *n* Plackerei *f.*

drug [drʌg] *n* (*medicinal*) Droge *f*; (*narcotic*) Rauschgift *neut. v* betäuben. **drug addict** Rauschgiftsüchtige(r). **drug**

drum [drʌm] *n* Trommel *f. v* trommeln. **drummer** *n* Trommler *m.* **drumstick** *n* Trommelstock *m.*

drunk [drʌŋk] *V* **drink.** *adj* betrunken; (*coll*) besoffen. *n* Betrunkene(r). **get drunk** sich betrinken; (*coll*) besoffen werden. **drunken** *adj* betrunken. **drunkard** *n* Trinker *m*; (*coll*) Säufer. **drunkenness** *n* Betrunkenheit *f.*

dry [drai] *adj* trocken; (*wine*) herb. *v* trocknen. **dry up** austrocknen; (*dishes*) abtrocknen. **dry-clean** chemisch reinigen. **dry cleaner** chemische Reinigung *f.* **dry dock** Trockendock *neut.* **dry land** fester Boden *m.*

dual ['djuəl] *adj* doppelt. **dual-purpose** *adj* Mehrzweck-.

dubbed ['dʌbd] *adj* (*film*) synchronisiert.

dubious ['djuːbiəs] *adj* zweifelhaft, dubiös.

duchess ['dʌtʃis] *n* Herzogin *f.*

duck¹ [dʌk] *n* Ente *f.*

duck² [dʌk] *v* sich ducken; (*under water*) untertauchen.

duct [dʌkt] *n* Kanal *m.*

dud [dʌd] *adj* wertlos. *n* Niete *f*, Versager *m.*

due [djuː] *adj* (*suitable*) gebührend; (*payment*) fällig. *the train is due at 7 o'clock* der Zug soll (planmäßig) um 7 Uhr ankommen. *adv* **due east** genau nach Osten. **due to** infolge (+*gen*). **in due course** zur rechten Zeit. *I am due to* ich muß.

duel ['djuəl] *n* Duell *neut.*

duet [dju'et] *n* Duett *neut.*

dug [dʌg] V **dig.**
duke [djuːk] n Herzog m.
dull [dʌl] adj (colour) matt, düster; (pain) dumpf; (boring) langweilig, uninteressant; (stupid) dumm. **dullness** n Düsterkeit f, Trübe f. v abstumpfen.
duly ['djuːli] adv gebührend, ordnungsgemäß.
dumb [dʌm] adj stumm; (coll: stupid) doof. **deaf and dumb** taubstumm. **dumbfound** v verblüffen.
dummy ['dʌmi] n (baby's) Schnuller m; (tailor's) Schneiderpuppe f; (imitation) Attrappe f.
dump [dʌmp] n Müllhaufen m, Müllkippe f. v abladen.
dumpling ['dʌmpliŋ] n Knödel m, Kloß m.
dunce [dʌns] n Dummkopf m.
dune [djuːn] n Düne f.
dung [dʌŋ] n Mist m.
dungeon ['dʌndʒən] n Kerker m.
duplicate ['djuːplikət; v 'djuːplikeit] n Duplikat neut. v verdoppeln; (make copies) vervielfältigen, kopieren. adj doppelt. **duplication** n Verdoppelung f. **duplicator** n Vervielfältigungsmaschine f.
durable ['djuərəbl] adj dauerhaft.
duration [dju'reiʃən] n Dauer f.
during ['djuəriŋ] prep während (+ gen).
dusk [dʌsk] n (Abend)Dämmerung f. **dusky** adj düster.
dust [dʌst] n Staub m. v abstauben. **dustbin** n Mülleimer m. **dustcart** n Müllwagen m. **duster** n Staubtuch neut. **dustman** n Müllabfuhrmann m. **dusty** adj staubig.
duty ['djuːti] n Pflicht f; (task) Aufgabe f; (tax) Zoll m, Abgabe f. **off/on duty** außer/im Dienst. **duty-free** adj zollfrei. **dutiful** adj pflichtbewußt.
Dutch [dʌtʃ] adj holländisch. **Dutchman** n Holländer m. **Dutchwoman** n Holländerin f.
duvet ['duːvei] n Federbett neut.
dwarf [dwoːf] n Zwerg m. adj zwergenhaft.
*__dwell__** [dwel] n wohnen. **dwell on** bleiben bei. **dwelling** n Wohnung f.
dwelt [dwelt] V **dwell.**
dwindle ['dwindl] v abnehmen.
dye [dai] n Farbstoff m. v färben.
dyke [daik] n Deich m, Damm m.
dynamic [dai'namik] adj dynamisch. **dynamics** n Dynamik f.

dynamite ['dainə‚mait] n Dynamit neut.
dynamo ['dainə‚mou] n Dynamo n.
dynasty ['dinəsti] n Dynastie f.
dysentery ['disəntri] n Ruhr f.
dyslexia [dis'leksiə] n Legasthenie f, Wortblindheit f.
dyspepsia [dis'pepsiə] n Verdauungsstörung f.

E

each [iːtʃ] adj, pron jeder, jede, jedes. adv je. **each other** einander, sich.
eager ['iːgə] adj eifrig. **eagerness** Eifer m.
eagle ['iːgl] n Adler m.
ear[1] [iə] n (anat) Ohr neut; (hearing) Gehör neut. **earache** n Ohrenschmerzen pl. **eardrum** n Trommelfell neut. **earlobe** n Ohrläppchen neut. **earring** n Ohrring m. **earshot** n **within/out of earshot** in/außer Hörweite.
ear[2] [iə] n (of corn) Ähre f.
earl [əːl] n Graf m.
early ['əːli] adj, adv früh; (soon) bald.
earn [əːn] v verdienen. **earnings** pl n Einkommen neut sing.
earnest ['əːnist] adj ernsthaft. n **in earnest** im Ernst.
earth [əːθ] n Erde f. v (elec) erden. **earthly** adj irdisch. **earthenware** n Steingut neut. **earthquake** n Erdbeben neut. **earthworm** n Regenwurm m.
earwig ['iəwig] n Ohrwurm m.
ease [iːz] n Leichtigkeit f; (comfort) Behagen neut. v erleichtern. **at ease** behaglich. **with ease** ohne Mühe.
easel ['iːzl] n Staffelei f.
east [iːst] n Osten m. adj also **easterly** östlich, Ost-. adv also **eastwards** nach Osten; ostwärts. **eastern** adj östlich; orientalisch.
Easter ['iːstə] n Ostern neut.
easy ['iːzi] adj leicht. **easily** adv leicht, mühelos; (by far) bei weitem. **easy-going** adj ungezwungen.
*__eat__** [iːt] v essen; (of animals) fressen.
eaten ['iːtn] V **eat.**
eavesdrop ['iːvzdrop] ι lauschen.
ebb [eb] n Ebbe f; (fig) Tiefstand m. v verebber

ebony ['ebəni] *n* Ebenholz *neut.*
eccentric [ik'sentrik] *adj* exzentrisch. *n* Sonderling *m.*
ecclesiastical [iklizi'astikl] *adj* kirchlich.
echo ['ekou] *n* Echo *neut.* *v* widerhallen.
eclipse [i'klips] *n* Finsternis *f.* *v* verfinstern; (*fig*) in den Schatten stellen.
ecology [i'koladʒi] *n* Ökologie *f.* **ecological** *adj* ökologisch.
economy [i'konəmi] *n* Wirtschaft *f*; (*thrift*) Sparsamkeit *f.* **economic** *adj* ökonomisch, wirtschaftlich, Wirtschafts-. **economical** *adj* sparsam, wirtschaftlich. **economics** *n* Volkswirtschaft *f.* **economist** *n* Volkswirtschaftler *m.* **economize** *v* sparen (an).
ecstasy ['ekstəsi] *n* Ekstase *f.* **ecstatic** *adj* ekstatisch.
eczema ['eksimə] *n* Ekzem *neut.*
edge [edʒ] *n* Rand *m.* **on edge** nervös.
edible ['edəbl] *adj* eßbar.
edit ['edit] *v* redigieren. **edition** *n* Ausgabe *f.* **editor** *n* Redakteur *m.*
editorial [edi'tɔːriəl] *adj* Redaktions-. *n* Leitartikel *m.*
educate ['edjukeit] *n* erziehen, ausbilden. **education** *n* Bildung *f,* Erziehung *f*; (*system*) Schulwesen *neut.* **educational** *adj* pädagogisch.
eel [iːl] *n* Aal *m.*
eerie ['iəri] *adj* unheimlich.
effect [i'fekt] *n* Wirkung *f*; (*impression*) Eindruck *m.* **have an effect on** wirken auf. **in effect** in Wirklichkeit. **effective** *adj* wirksam. **effectiveness** *n* Wirksamkeit *f.*
effeminate [i'feminət] *adj* weibisch.
effervesce [efə'ves] *v* sprudeln. **effervescent** *adj* sprudelnd.
efficiency [i'fiʃənsi] *n* Leistungsfähigkeit *f.* **efficient** *adj* (*person*) tüchtig; (*effective*) wirksam; (*machine*) leistungsfähig.
effigy ['efidʒi] *n* Abbild *neut.*
effort ['efət] *n* Anstrengung *f,* Mühe *f.* **make an effort** sich anstrengen. **make every effort** sich alle Mühe geben. **effortless** *adj* mühelos.
egg [eg] *n* Ei *neut.* *v* **egg on** reizen. **boiled egg** gekochtes Ei *neut.* **fried egg** Spiegelei *neut.* **scrambled egg** Rührei *neut.* **egg cup** Eierbecher *m.* **eggshell** *n* Eierschale *f.*
ego ['iːgou] *pron* Ich *neut.* **egoism** *n* Egoismus *m.* **egoist** *n* Egoist *m.*
Egypt ['iːdʒipt] *n* Ägypten *neut.* **Egyptian** *adj* ägyptisch; *n* Ägypter(in).

eiderdown ['aidədaun] *n* Federbett *neut.*
eight [eit] *adj* acht. *n* Acht *f.* **eighth** *adj* acht; *n* Achtel *neut.*
eighteen [ei'tiːn] *adj* achtzehn. **eighteenth** *adj* achtzehnt.
eighty ['eiti] *adj* achtzig. **eightieth** *adj* achtzigst.
either ['aiðə] *pron* einer (eine, eines) von beiden. **on either side** auf beiden Seiten. **either ... or ...** entweder ... oder ....
ejaculate [i'dʒakjuleit] *v* (*utter*) ausstoßen; ejakulieren.
eject [i'dʒekt] *v* ausstoßen.
eke [iːk] *v* **eke out** (*add to*) ergänzen.
elaborate [i'labərət; *v* i'labəreit] *adj* ausführlich, genau ausgearbeitet. *v* **elaborate on** eingehend erörtern. **elaboration** *n* Ausarbeitung *f.*
elapse [i'laps] *v* vergehen.
elastic [i'lastik] *adj* elastisch. **elastic band** Gummiband *neut.*
elated [i'leitid] *adj* begeistert, froh.
elbow ['elbou] *n* Ellbogen *m.*
elder[1] ['eldə] *adj* älter. *n* Ältere(r).
elder[2] ['eldə] *n* (*tree*) Holunder *m.*
elderly ['eldəli] *adj* älter.
eldest ['eldist] *adj* ältest. *n* Älteste(r).
elect [i'lekt] *v* wählen. **election** *n* Wahl *f.* **elector** *n* Wähler *m.* **electorate** *n* Wählerschaft *f.*
electric [ə'lektrik] *adj also* **electrical** elektrisch. **electrical engineering** Elektrotechnik *f.* **electric blanket** Heizdecke *f.* **electric chair** elektrischer Stuhl *m.* **electric cooker** Elektroherd *neut.* **electrician** *n* Elektriker *m.* **electricity** *n* Strom *m,* Elektrizität *f.*
electrify [ə'lektrifai] *v* elektrifizieren. **electrifying** *adj* (*fig*) elektrisierend.
electronic [elək'tronik] *n* elektronisch. **electronics** *n* Elektronik *f sing.*
elegant ['eligənt] *adj* elegant.
element ['eləmənt] *n* Element *neut.* **elementary** *adj* elementar.
elephant ['elifənt] *n* Elefant *m.*
elevate ['eliveit] *v* heben; (*promote*) erheben. **elevation** *n* Hochheben *neut*; (*promotion*) Erhebung *f.* **elevator** *n* Aufzug *m.*
eleven [i'levn] *adj* elf. **eleventh** *adj* elft.
eligible ['elidʒəbl] *adj* wählbar. **be eligible** in Frage kommen. **be eligible for** berechtigt sein zu. **eligibility** *n* Eignung *f.*

eliminate [i'limineit] *n* beseitigen; (*sport*) ausscheiden. **elimination** *n* Beseitigung *f*; Ausscheidung *f*.

élite [ei'liːt] *n* Elite *f*.

ellipse [i'lips] *n* Ellipse *f*. **elliptical** *adj* elliptisch.

elm [elm] *n* Ulme *f*.

elocution [elə'kjuːʃən] *n* Sprechkunde *f*.

elope [i'loup] *v* entlaufen. **elopement** *n* Entlaufen *neut.*

eloquent ['eləkwənt] *adj* (*person*) redegewandt. **eloquence** *n* Redegewandtheit *f*.

else [els] *adv* sonst. **anyone else?** sonst noch jemand? **someone else** jemand anders. **nothing else** nichts weiter. **elsewhere** *adv* anderswo, woanders.

elucidate [i'luːsideit] *v* aufklären. **elucidation** *n* Aufklärung *f*.

elude [i'luːd] *v* entgehen (*dat*).

emaciated [i'meisieitid] *adj* abgemagert.

emanate ['eməneit] *v* ausströmen (aus); (*fig*) herstammen (von).

emancipate [i'mansipeit] *v* befreien, emanzipieren. **emancipated** *adj* emanzipiert. **emancipation** *n* Befreiung *f*.

embalm [im'baːm] *v* einbalsamieren.

embankment [im'baŋkmənt] *n* Damm *m*; (*road*) Uferstraße *f*.

embargo [im'baːgou] *n* Handelssperre *f*.

embark [im'baːk] *v* sich einschiffen (nach); (*fig*) sich einlassen (in).

embarrass [im'barəs] *v* in Verlegenheit bringen. **be embarrassed** verlegen sein. **embarrassment** *n* Verlegenheit *f*.

embassy ['embəsi] *n* Botschaft *f*.

embellish [im'beliʃ] *v* verzieren.

embers 'embəz] *pl n* Glut *f sing.*

embezzle [im'bezl] *v* unterschlagen. **embezzlement** *n* Unterschlagung *f*.

embitter [im'bitə] *v* verbittern.

emblem ['embləm] *n* Sinnbild *neut.*

embody [im'bodi] *v* verkörpern. **embodiment** *n* Verkörperung *f*.

embossed [im'bost] *adj* erhaben.

embrace [im'breis] *v* umarmen; (*include*) umfassen. *n* Umarmung *f*.

embroider [im'broidə] *v* (be)sticken; (*story*) ausschmücken. **embroidery** *n* Stickerei *f*.

embryo ['embriou] *n* Embryo *m*.

emerald ['emərəld] *n* Smaragd *m*. **emerald green** smaragdgrün.

emerge [i'məːdʒ] *v* (*from water*) auftauchen; (*appear*) hervorkommen. **emergence** *n* Auftauchen *neut.*

emergency [i'məːdʒənsi] *n* Notfall *m. adj* Not-. **emergency exit** Notausgang *m.*

emigrate ['emigreit] *v* auswandern. **emigration** *n* Auswanderung *f*. **emigrant** *n* Auswanderer *m.*

eminent ['eminənt] *adj* hervorragend, erhaben. **eminence** *n* Erhöhung *f*.

emit [i'mit] *v* von sich geben. **emission** *n* Ausstrahlung *f*.

emotion [i'mouʃən] *n* Gefühl *neut.* **emotional** *adj* Gefühls-; (*excitable*) erregbar; (*full of feeling*) gefühlvoll.

empathy ['empəθi] *n* Einfühlung *f*.

emperor ['empərə] *n* Kaiser *m.*

emphasis ['emfəsis] *n* (*pl* -ses) Nachdruck *m.* **emphasize** *v* betonen, unterstreichen. **emphatic** *adj* nachdrücklich.

empire ['empaiə] *n* Reich *neut.*

empirical [im'pirikəl] *adj* empirisch.

employ [im'ploi] *v* (*use*) verwenden; (*appoint*) anstellen. **be employed** beschäftigt *or* tätig sein. **employee** *n* Angestellte(r); (*as opposed to employer*) Arbeitnehmer *m.* **employer** *n* Arbeitgeber *m.* **employment** *n* Arbeit *f*, Beschäftigung *f*.

empower [im'pauə] *v* ermächtigen.

empress ['empris] *n* Kaiserin *f*.

empty ['empti] *adj* leer. *v* leeren. **emptiness** *n* Leere *f*.

emulate ['emjuleit] *v* nacheifern (*dat*).

emulsion [i'mʌlʃən] *n* Emulsion *f*. **emulsify** *v* emulgieren.

enable [i'neibl] *v* ermöglichen.

enact [i'nakt] *v* verordnen; (*law*) erlassen.

enamel [i'naməl] *n* Emaille *f*; (*teeth*) Zahnschmelz *m.* *v* emaillieren.

enamour [i'namə] *v* **be enamoured of** verliebt sein in.

encase [in'keis] *v* umschließen.

enchant [in'tʃaint] *v* entzücken. **enchanting** *adj* entzückend. **enchantment** *n* Zauber *m*, Entzücken *neut.*

encircle [in'səːkl] *v* umringen.

enclose [in'klouz] *v* einschließen; (*in letter*) beifügen. **enclosed** *adj* (*in letter*) beigefügt. **enclosure** *n* Einzäunung *f*; (*in letter*) Anlage *f*.

encore [oŋkoː] *interj* noch einmal! *n* Zugabe *f*.

encounter [in'kauntə] *v* treffen; (*difficulties*) stoßen auf. *n* Begegnung *f*; (*mil*) Gefecht *neut.*

encourage [in'kʌridʒ] *v* ermutigen; (*promote*) fördern. **encouragement** *n* Ermutigung *f*.

encroach [in'krout∫] v eindringen (in). **encroachment** n Eingriff m.
encyclopedia [insaiklə'piːdiə] n Enzyklopädie f.
end [end] n Ende neut; (finish) Schluß m; (purpose) Zweck m. v beend(ig)en; (come to an end) zu Ende gehen. **ending** n Ende neut. **endless** adj unendlich.
endanger [in'deindʒə] v gefährden.
endeavour [in'devə] v sich anstrengen, versuchen. n Versuch m, Bestrebung f.
endemic [en'demik] adj endemisch.
endive ['endiv] n Endivie f.
endorse [in'dɔːs] v indossieren; (approve of) billigen. **endorsement** n Vermerk m; Billigung f.
endow [in'dau] v stiften. **endowed with** begabt mit. **endowment** n Ausstattung f, Stiftung f.
endure [in'djuə] v ertragen. **enduring** adj beständig.
enemy ['enəmi] n Feind m. adj Feind-.
energy ['enədʒi] n Energie f. **energetic** adj energisch.
enforce [in'fɔːs] v durchsetzen. **enforcement** n Durchsetzung f.
engage [in'geidʒ] v (employ) anstellen; (tech) einschalten; (enemy) angreifen. **engaged** adj (to be married) verlobt; (occupied) besetzt. **get engaged** sich verloben. **engagement** n (to marry) Verlobung f; (appointment) Verabredung f.
engine ['endʒin] n Motor m; (rail) Lokomotive f. **engine driver** Lokomotivführer m.
engineer [endʒi'niə] n Ingenieur m. v (fig) organisieren. **engineering** n Technik f.
England ['iŋglənd] n England neut.
English ['iŋgli∫] adj englisch. **(the) English (language)** (das) Englisch(e), die englische Sprache. I am English ich bin Engländer(in). **English Channel** Ärmelkanal m. **Englishman** n Engländer m. **Englishwoman** n Engländerin f.
engrave [in'greiv] v gravieren. **engraving** n Stich m.
engrossed [in'groust] adj vertieft.
engulf [in'gʌlf] v (overcome) überwältigen.
enhance [in'hɑns] v verstärken.
enigma [i'nigmə] n Rätsel neut. **enigmatic** adj rätselhaft.
enjoy [in'dʒoi] v genießen, Freude haben an. **enjoy oneself** sich (gut) unterhalten.

enjoyment n Freude f. **enjoy yourself!** viel spaß/Vergnügen!
enlarge [in'lɑːdʒ] v (sich) vergrößern. **enlargement** n Vergrößerung f.
enlighten [in'laitn] v aufklären. **enlightened** adj aufgeklärt. **enlightenment** n Aufklärung f.
enlist [in'list] v (help) in Anspruch nehmen; (in army) sich melden.
enmity ['enməti] n Feindseligkeit f.
enormous [i'nɔːməs] adj riesig, ungeheuer.
enough [i'nʌf] adv genug. **be enough** genügen. **have enough of something** (be tired of) etwas satt haben.
enquire [in'kwaiə] adv sich erkundigen, fragen. **enquiry** n Nachfrage f.
enrage [in'reidʒ] v wütend machen. **enraged** adj wütend.
enrich [in'rit∫] v bereichern.
enrol [in'roul] v einschreiben; (in club) als Mitglied aufnehmen; (oneself) beitreten (dat). **enrolment** n Aufnahme f.
ensign ['ensain] n (naut) (Schiffs)Flagge f.
enslave [in'sleiv] v versklaven.
ensue [in'sjuː] v (darauf) folgen. **ensuing** adj darauffolgend.
ensure [in'∫uə] v gewährleisten, sichern.
entail [in'teil] v mit sich bringen.
entangle [in'taŋgl] v verstricken. **entangled** adj verstrickt.
enter ['entə] v (go in) eintreten; (a room) hineintreten in; (in book) einschreiben; (sport) sich anmelden.
enterprise ['entə,praiz] n (concern) Unternehmen neut; (initiative) Initiative f. **private enterprise** freie Wirtschaft f. **enterprising** adj unternehmungslustig.
entertain [,entə'tein] v (amuse) unterhalten; (feelings) hegen; (as guests) gastlich bewirten. **entertaining** adj unterhaltsam. **entertainment** n Unterhaltung f.
enthral [in'θrɔːl] v entzücken. **enthralling** adj entzückend.
enthusiasm [in'θuːzi,azəm] n Begeisterung f, Enthusiasmus m. **enthusiastic** adj begeistert, enthusiastisch.
entice [in'tais] v verlocken. **enticement** n Anreiz m. **enticing** adj verlockend.
entire [in'taiə] adj ganz. **entirely** adv ganz, völlig, durchaus. **entirety** n Gesamtheit f.
entitle [in'taitl] v berechtigen (zu).
entity ['entəti] n Wesen neut.

entrails ['entreilz] *pl n* Eingeweide *pl.*
entrance[1] ['entrəns] *n* (*going in, fee*) Eintritt *m*; (*way in*) Eingang *m.*
entrance[2] [in'traːns] *v* entzücken.
entrant ['entrənt] *n* (*sport*) Teilnehmer(in); (*for exam*) Kandidat *m.*
entreat [in'triːt] *v* ernstlich bitten. **entreaty** *n* Bitte *f.*
entrenched [in'trentʃt] *v* **become entrenched** sich festsetzen.
entrepreneur [,ɒntrəprə'nəː] *n* Unternehmer *m.*
entrust [in'trʌst] *v* (*thing*) anvertrauen (*dat*); (*person*) betrauen (mit).
entry ['entri] *n* Eintritt *m*; (*into country*) Einreise *f*; (*comm*) Posten *m*; (*theatre*) Auftritt *m*. **no entry** Eintritt verboten.
entwine [in'twain] *v* umwinden.
enunciate [i'nʌnsiˌeit] *v* aussagen; (*state*) ausdrücken.
envelop [in'veləp] *v* einwickeln; (*fig*) umhüllen.
envelope ['envəˌloup] *n* Umschlag *m.*
enviable ['enviəbl] *adj* beneidenswert.
envious ['enviəs] *adj* neidisch (*of* auf). **be envious of** beneiden.
environment [in'vaiərənmənt] *n* Umgebung *f.* **the environment** Umwelt *f.* **environmental** *adj* Umwelt-.
envisage [in'vizidʒ] *v* sich vorstellen.
envoy ['envoi] *n* Bote *m.*
envy ['envi] *v* beneiden. *n* Neid *m.*
enzyme ['enzaim] *n* Enzym *neut.*
epaulet ['epələt] *n* Epaulette *f.*
ephemeral [i'femərəl] *adj* vergänglich.
epic ['epik] *adj* (*poetry*) episch; heldenhaft. *n* Heldengedicht *neut.*
epicure ['epikjuə] *n* Feinschmecker *m.*
epidemic [epi'demik] *n* Epidemie *f. adj* epidemisch.
epilepsy ['epilepsi] *n* Epilepsie *f.* **epileptic** *adj* epileptisch; *n* Epileptiker(in).
epilogue ['epilog] *n* Epilog *m.*
Epiphany [i'pifəni] *n* Epiphanias *neut.*
episcopal [i'piskəpəl] *adj* bischöflich.
episode ['episoud] *n* Episode *f.*
epitaph ['epiˌtaːf] *n* Grabschrift *f.*
epitome [i'pitəmi] *n* Inbegriff *m.*
epoch ['iːpok] *n* Epoche *f.*
equable ['ekwəbl] *adj* (*person*) gelassen.
equal ['iːkwəl] *adj* gleich (+ *dat*). **be equal to** gleichen (+ *dat*); (*be able*) gewachsen sein (+ *dat*). **equal in size** von gleicher Größe. *n* Gleichgestellte(r). *v* gleichen (+ *dat*), gleich sein (+ *dat*). **equality** *n*

Gleichheit *f*; (*pol*) Gleichberechtigung *f.*
equalize *v* gleichmachen. **equally** *adv* ebenso, in gleichem Maße.
equanimity [ekwə'niməti] *n* Gleichmut *m.*
equate [i'kweit] *v* gleichstellen. **equation** *n* Gleichung *f.*
equator [i'kweitə] *n* Äquator *m.* **equatorial** *adj* äquatorial.
equestrian [i'kwestriən] *adj* Reit-, Reiter-.
equilateral [,iːkwi'latərəl] *adj* gleichseitig.
equilibrium [,iːkwi'libriəm] *n* Gleichgewicht *neut.*
equinox ['ekwinoks] *n* Tagundnachtgleiche *f.*
equip [i'kwip] *v* ausrüsten, ausstatten. **equipment** *n* Ausrüstung *f*, Einrichtung *f.*
equity ['ekwəti] *n* Billigkeit *f*; (*law*) Billigkeitsrecht *f.*
equivalent [i'kwivələnt] *adj* gleichwertig. **be equivalent to** gleichkommen (*dat*). *n* Gegenstück *neut.*
era ['iərə] *n* Epoche *f*, Ära *f.*
eradicate [i'radiˌkeit] *v* ausrotten. **eradication** *n* Ausrottung *f.*
erase [i'reiz] *v* ausradieren, tilgen. **eraser** *n* Radiergummi *m.*
erect [i'rekt] *v* errichten. *adj* aufrecht. **erection** *n* Errichtung *f*; (*anat*) Erektion *f.*
ermine ['əːmin] *n* Hermelin *m.*
erode [i'roud] *v* zerfressen. **erosion** *n* Zerfressung *f.*
erotic [i'rotik] *adj* erotisch. **eroticism** *n* Erotik *f.*
err [əː] *v* sich irren.
errand ['erənd] *n* (Boten)Gang *m.*
erratic [i'ratik] *adj* unberechenbar.
error ['erə] *n* Fehler *m*, Irrtum *m*; (*of compass*) Abweichung *f*; (*oversight*) Versehen *neut.* **erroneous** *adj* irrtümlich.
erudite ['eruːdait] *adj* gelehrt.
erupt [i'rupt] *v* (*volcano*) ausbrechen. **eruption** *n* Ausbruch *m*; (*skin*) Hautausschlag *m.*
escalate ['eskəˌleit] *v* (*a war*) steigern, eskalieren. **escalation** *n* Eskalation *f.* **escalator** *n* Rolltreppe *f.*
escalope ['eskəˌlop] *n* Schnitzel *neut.*
escape [is'keip] *v* entkommen (+ *dat*); (*fig*) entgehen (+ *dat*). *n* Flucht *f*; (*of liquid*) Ausfluß *m.* **have a narrow escape** mit knapper Not entkommen.
escort [i'skoːt; *n* 'eskoːt] *v* begleiten. *n* (*mil*) Eskorte *f.*

esoteric [esə'terik] *adj* esoterisch.
especial [i'speʃəl] *adj* besonder, speziell
especially *adv* besonders.
espionage ['espiə,naɪʒ] *n* Spionage *f*.
esplanade [,esplə'neid] *n* Esplanade *f*.
essay ['esei] *n* (*school*) Aufsatz *m*; (*litera-ry*) Essay *m*.
essence ['esns] *n* Wesen *neut*; (*extract*) Essenz *f*.
essential [i'senʃəl] *adj* wesentlich; (*indispensable*) untentbehrlich, unbedingt notwendig. **essentially** *adv* im wesentlichen.
establish [i'stabliʃ] *v* einrichten, aufstellen; (*a fact*) feststellen; (*found*) gründen.
establishment *n* Gründung *f*; (*comm*) Unternehmen *neut*.
estate [i'steit] *n* (*of deceased*) Nachlaß *m*; (*of noble*) Landsitz *m*. **housing estate** Siedlung *f*. **real estate** Immobilien *pl*. **estate agent** Grundstücksmakler *m*. **estate car** Kombiwagen *m*.
esteem [i'stiːm] *n* Achtung *f*. *v* hochschätzen.
estimate ['esti,meit; *n* 'estimət] *v* schätzen (auf). *n* (Ab)Schätzung. **estimation** *n* Ansicht (*opinion*) *f*.
estuary ['estjuəri] *n* (Fluß)Mündung *f*.
eternal [i'təɪnl] *adj* ewig. **eternity** *n* Ewigkeit *f*.
ether ['iːθə] *n* Äther *m*. **ethereal** *adj* ätherisch.
ethical ['eθikl] *adj* ethisch, sittlich. **ethics** *n* Ethik *f*.
ethnic ['eθnik] *adj* ethnisch, Volks-.
etiquette ['eti,ket] *n* Etikette *f*.
etymology [,eti'molədʒi] *n* Etymologie *f*.
Eucharist ['juːkərist] *n* heilige Messe *f*.
eunuch ['juːnək] *n* Eunuch *m*, Verschnittene(r) *m*.
euphemism ['juːfə,mizəm] *n* Euphemismus *m*. **euphemistic** *adj* beschönigend.
euphoria [ju'fɔɪriə] *n* Wohlbefinden *neut*, Euphorie *f*.
Europe ['juərəp] *n* Europa *neut*. **European** *adj* europäisch; *n* Europäer(in). **European Economic Community (EEC)** Europäische Wirtschaftsgemeinschaft (EWG) *f*. **European Community** Europäische Gemeinschaften (EG) *pl*.
euthanasia [juːθə'neiziə] *n* Euthanasie *f*, Gnadentod *m*.
evacuate [i'vakju,eit] *v* (*depart*) aussiedeln; (*empty*) entleeren; (*people*) evakuieren. **evacuation** *n* Evakuierung *f*.

evade [i'veid] *v* ausweichen, entgehen (+ *dat*); (*tax*) hinterziehen.
evaluate [i'valju,eit] *v* abschätzen. **evaluation** *n* Abschätzung *f*.
evangelical [,iːvan'dʒelikəl] *adj* evangelisch. **evangelism** *n* Evangelismus *m*. **evangelist** *n* Evangelist *m*.
evaporate [i'vapə,reit] *v* verdampfen. **evaporated milk** Kondensmilch *f*. **evaporation** *n* Verdampfung *f*.
evasion [i'veiʒən] *n* Ausweichen *neut*. **tax evasion** Steuerhinterziehung *f*. **evasive** *adj* ausweichend. **evasive action** Ausweichmanöver *neut*.
eve [iːv] *n* Vorabend *m*. **Christmas Eve** Heiliger Abend *m*. **New Year's Eve** Sylvesterabend *m*.
even ['iːvən] *adj* eben, gerade. *adv* sogar. *even bigger* noch größer. **even more** noch mehr. **not even** nicht einmal. **even if** wenn auch. **even-handed** *adj* unparteiisch.
evening ['iːvniŋ] *n* Abend *m*. **in the evening** abends, am Abend. **this evening** heute abend. **evening dress** Gesellschaftsanzug *m*. **evening meal** Abendessen *neut*.
event [i'vent] *n* Ereignis *neut*; (*sport*) Disziplin *f*. **in the event of** im Falle (+ *gen*). **eventful** *adj* ereignisvoll.
ever ['evə] *adv* je(mals); (*always*) immer. *have you ever been to Berlin?* sind Sie schon einmal in Berlin gewesen? **ever so** sehr. **for ever** für immer. **evergreen** *adj* immergrün. **everlasting** *adj* ewig.
every ['evri] *adj* jede; alle *pl*. **every day** jeden Tag. **every one** jeder einzelne. **every other day** jeden zweiten Tag. **every so often** hin und wieder. **everybody/everyone** *pron* jeder. **everything** *pron* alles. **everywhere** *adv* überall.
evict [i'vikt] *n* exmittieren. **eviction** *n* Exmission *f*.
evidence ['evidəns] *v* Zeugnis *neut*; Beweis *m*. **give evidence** Zeugnis ablegen. *v* beweisen.
evil ['iːvl] *adj* übel, böse. *n* Übel *neut*, Böse *neut*.
evoke [i'vouk] *v* hervorrufen.
evolve [i'volv] *v* (sich) entwickeln. **evolution** *n* Entwicklung *f*; (*biol*) Evolution *f*.
ewe [juː] *n* Mutterschaf *neut*.
exacerbate [ig'zasə,beit] *v* verschlimmern.

exact [ig'zakt] *adj* genau, exakt. *v* verlangen; *(payment)* eintreiben. **exacting** *adj* anspruchsvoll. **exactly** *adv* genau.
exaggerate [ig'zadʒəˌreit] *v* übertreiben. **exaggerated** *adj* übertrieben. **exaggeration** *n* Übertreibung *f*.
exalt [ig'zolt] *v* erheben; *(praise)* preisen. **exaltation** *n (joy)* Wonne *f*. **exalted** *adj* erhaben; *(excited)* aufgeregt.
examine [ig'zamin] *v* untersuchen, prüfen; *(law)* verhören. **examination** *n* Prüfung *f*; *(inspection)* Untersuchung *f*. **medical examination** ärztliche Untersuchung *f*.
example [ig'zaːmpl] *n* Beispiel *neut*. **for example** zum Beispiel. **set an example** ein Beispiel geben.
exasperate [ig'zaɪspəˌreit] *v* zum Verzweifeln bringen. **exasperation** *n* Verzweiflung *f*.
excavate ['ekskəˌveit] *v* ausgraben. **excavation** *n* Ausgrabung *f*. **excavator** *n (mech)* Bagger *m*.
exceed [ik'siːd] *v* überschreiten. **exceedingly** *adv* höchst.
excel [ik'sel] *v* sich auszeichnen. **excellence** *n* Vorzüglichkeit *f*. **Excellency** *n* Exzellenz *f*. **excellent** *adj* ausgezeichnet, vorzüglich.
except [ik'sept] *prep* außer. **except for** abgesehen von. *v* ausschließen. **exception** *n* Ausnahme *f*. **take exception to** übelnehmen.
excerpt ['eksəɪpt] *n* Auszug *m*.
excess [ik'ses] *n* Übermaß *neut*, Überfluß *m* (an). *adj* Über-. **excess fare** Zuschlag *m*. **excessive** *adj* übermäßig.
exchange [iks'tʃeindʒ] *v* (aus-, um)tauschen; *(money)* wechseln. *n* Austausch *m*; *(phone)* Zentrale *f*. **foreign exchange** Devisen *pl*. **exchange rate** Wechselkurs *m*.
exchequer [iks'tʃekə] *n* Schatzamt *neut*.
excise ['eksaiz] *v (cut out)* herausschneiden. **excise duty** indirekter Steuer *m*.
excite [ik'sait] *v* erregen, aufregen. **get excited** sich aufregen. **excitement** *n* Aufregung *f*.
exclaim [ik'skleim] *v* ausrufen. **exclamation** *n* Ausruf *m*. **exclamation mark** Ausrufungszeichen *neut*.
exclude [ik'skluːd] *v* ausschließen. **exclusive** *adj* ausschließlich; *(fashionable)* exklusiv. **exclusive of** *also* **excluding** ausschließlich. **exclusion** *n* Ausschluß *m*.

excommunicate [ekskə'mjuːniˌkeit] *v* exkommunizieren. **excommunication** *n* Exkommunikation *f*.
excrement ['ekskrəmənt] *n* Exkrement *neut*, Kot *m*.
excrete [ik'skriːt] *v* ausscheiden. **excretion** *n* Ausscheidung *f*.
excruciating [ik'skruːʃieitiŋ] *adj* peinigend.
excursion [ik'skəɪʃən] *n* Ausflug *m*.
excuse [ik'skjuːz] *n* Ausrede *f*. *v* entschuldigen, verzeihen. **excuse me!** Verzeihung!
execute ['eksiˌkjuːt] *v (carry out)* ausführen; *(person)* hinrichten. **execution** *n* Ausführung *f*; Hinrichtung *f*. **executioner** *n* Henker *m*. **executor** *n* Testamentvollstrecker *m*.
executive [ig'zekjutiv] *adj* vollziehend. *n (comm)* Geschäftsführer *m*.
exemplify [ig'zempliˌfai] *v* als Beispiel dienen für.
exempt [ig'zempt] *v* befreien (von). *adj* **exempt from** frei von.
exercise ['eksəˌsaiz] *n* Übung *f*; *(of duty)* Ausübung *f*. *v* üben; *(wield)* ausüben. **physical exercise** Leibesübung *f*. **exercise book** Schulheft *neut*.
exert [ig'zəɪt] *v* ausüben. **exert oneself** sich anstrengen. **exertion** *n* Anstrengung *f*.
exhale [eks'heil] *v* ausatmen.
exhaust [ig'zoɪst] *v* erschöpfen. **exhausted** *adj* erschöpft. **exhausting** *adj* anstrengend. **exhaustion** *n* Erschöpfung *f*. *n* **exhaust (gases)** Abgase *pl*. **exhaust pipe** Auspuffrohr *neut*.
exhibit [ig'zibit] *v* zeigen; *(goods)* ausstellen. **exhibition** *n* Ausstellung *f*. **exhibitor** *n* Aussteller *m*.
exhilarate [ig'ziləˌreit] *v* erheitern. **exhilarated** *adj* angeregt, heiter. **exhilarating** erheiternd. **exhilaration** *n* Erheiterung *f*.
exile ['eksail] *n* Verbannung *f*; *(person)* Verbannte(r). *v* verbannen.
exist [ig'zist] *v* existieren, sein. **existence** Dasein *neut*, Existenz *f*. **existing** bestehend.
exit ['egzit] *n* Ausgang. *v* abtreten.
exodus ['eksədəs] *n* Auswanderung *f*; *(coll)* allgemeiner Ausbruch *m*.
exonerate [ig'zonəˌreit] *v* freisprechen (von).

exorbitant [ig'zɔːbitənt] *adj* übermäßig.
exorcize ['eksɔːsaiz] *v* austreiben.
exotic [ig'zotik] *adj* exotisch, fremdartig.
expand [ik'spand] *v* (sich) ausdehnen; (*develop*) entwickeln, erweitern. **expanse** *n* Weite *f*, weite Fläche *f*. **expansion** *n* Ausdehnung *f*; (*of firm*) Erweiterung *f*; (*pol*) Expansion *f*.
expatriate [eks'peitrieit; *n* eks'peitriət] *vv* ausbürgern. *n* im Ausland Lebende(r).
expect [ik'spekt] *v* erwarten; (*support*) annehmen. *She is expecting* sie ist in anderen Umständen. **expectation** *n* Erwartung *f*.
expedient [ik'spiːdiənt] *adj* zweckdienlich. *n* Notbehelf *m*.
expedition [ˌekspi'diʃən] *n* Expedition *f*.
expel [ik'spel] *v* ausstoßen; (*from school*) ausschließen.
expenditure [ik'spenditʃə] *n* Ausgabe *f*.
expense [ik'spens] *r* (Geld)Ausgabe *f*. **expenses** *pl* Unkosten *pl*. *at my expense* auf meine Kosten. **at the expense of** zum Schaden von. **expensive** *adj* teuer, kostspielig.
experience [ik'spiəriəns] *n* Erfahrung *f*; (*event*) Erlebnis *neut*. *v* erfahren, erleben. **experienced** *adj* erfahren.
experiment [ik'sperimənt] *m* Experiment *neut*, Probe *f*. *v* experimentieren. **experimental** *adj* Experimental-.
expert ['ekspəːt] *n* Fachmann *m*, Sachkundige(r). *adj* geschickt, gewandt. **expertise** *n* Sachkenntnis *f*.
expire [ik'spaiə] *v* (*breathe out*) ausatmen; (*lapse*) verfallen; (*die*) sterben. **expiry** *n* *also* **expiration** Ablauf *m*.
explain [ik'splein] *v* erklären. **explanation** *n* Erklärung *f*. **explanatory** *adj* erklärend. **be self-explanatory** sich von selbst verstehen.
explicit [ik'splisit] *adj* deutlich, ausdrücklich.
explode [ik'sploud] *v* explodieren. **explosion** *n* Explosion *f*.
exploit[1] ['eksploit] *n* Heldentat *f*, Abenteuer *m*.
exploit[2] [ik'sploit] *v* ausbeuten. **exploitation** *n* Ausbeutung *f*.
explore [ik'splɔː] *v* erforschen. **explorer** *n* (Er)Forscher *m*. **exploration** *n* Erforschung *f*. **exploratory** *adj* forschend, Forschungs-.
exponent [ik'spounənt] *n* (*person*) Verfechter *m*.

export [ik'spɔːt; *n* 'ekspɔːt] *v* exportieren. *n* Export *m*. **exportation** *n* Ausfuhr *f*. **exporter** *n* Exporteur *m*. **export trade** *n* Exporthandel *m*.
expose [ik'spouz] *v* aussetzen; (*phot*) belichten; (*impostor*) aufdecken. **exposed** *adj* (*unprotected*) ungeschützt. **be exposed to** ausgesetzt sein (+ *dat*). **exposure** *n* (*phot*) Belichtung *f* (*med*) Unterkühlung *f*.
express [ik'spres] *v* ausdrücken. *adj* Eil-, Schnell-. **express letter** Eilbrief *m*. **express train** D-zug *m*. **expression** *n* Ausdruck *m*. **expressionism** *n* Expressionismus *m*. **expressionless** *adj* ausdruckslos. **expressive** *adj* ausdrucksvoll. **expressly** *adv* ausdrücklich.
expulsion [ik'spʌlʃən] *n* Ausweisung *f*.
exquisite ['ekswizit] *adj* ausgezeichnet; (*pain*) heftig.
extend [ik'stend] *v* ausdehnen; (*develop*) erweitern; (*hand*) ausstrecken; (*cover area*) sich erstrecken. **extension** *n* Erweiterung *f*; (*comm*) Verlängerung *f*; (*phone*) Nebenanschluß; (*building*) Anbau *m*. **extensive** *adj* ausgedehnt. **extent** *n* Umfang *m*. **to a certain extent** bis zu einem gewissen Grade.
exterior [ik'stiəriə] *adj* äußer, Außen-. *n* das Äußere; (*appearance*) äußeres Ansehen *neut*.
exterminate [ik'stəːmiˌneit] *v* ausrotten. **extermination** *n* Ausrottung *f*.
external [ik'stəːnl] *adj* äußer, äußerlich, Außen-.
extinct [ik'stiŋkt] *adj* ausgestorben; (*volcano*) ausgebrannt. **become extinct** aussterben. **extinction** *n* Aussterben *neut*.
extinguish [ik'stiŋgwiʃ] *v* (aus)löschen. (*fire*) **extinguisher** Feuerlöscher *m*.
extort [ik'stɔːt] *v* erpressen. **extortion** *n* Erpressung *f*. **extortionate** *adj* erpresserisch. **extortionate price** Wucherpreis *m*.
extra ['ekstrə] *adj* zusätzlich, Extra-. *adv* besonders. **extras** *pl n* (*expenses*) Sonderausgaben *pl*; (*accessories*) Sonderzubehörteile *pl*.
extract [ik'strakt; *n* 'ekstrakt] *v* ausziehen; (*tooth*) ziehen; (*numerals*) gewinnen. *n* Auszug *m*. **extraction** *n* Ausziehen *neut*; (*tooth, minerals*) Extraktion *f*.
extradite ['ekstrəˌdait] *v* ausliefern. **extradition** *n* Auslieferung *f*.

extramural [,ekstrə'mjuərəl] *adj* außerplanmäßig.

extraordinary [ik'strɔːdənəri] *adj* außerordentlich, seltsam.

extravagant [ik'strævəgənt] *adj* verschwenderisch; (*exaggerated*) übertrieben.

extreme [ik'striːm] *adj* höchst, letzt; (*fig*) extrem; *n* Extrem *m*, äußerste Grenze *f*. **extremism** *n* Extremismus *m*. **extremist** *n* Extremist *m*.

extricate ['ekstri,keit] *v* herauswickeln.

extrovert ['ekstrəvɜːt] *adj* (*psychol*) extravertiert. *n* Extravertierte(r).

exuberance [ig'zjuːbərəns] *n* Übermut *m*. **exuberant** *adj* übermütig.

exude [ig'zjuːd] *v* ausschlagen; ausstrahlen.

exultation [,egzʌl'teiʃən] *n* Jubel *m*.

eye [ai] *n* Auge *neut*; (*of needle*) Öse *f*. *v* anschauen.

eyeball ['aibɔːl] *n* Augapfel *m*.

eyebrow ['aibrau] *n* Augenbraue *f*.

eye-catching ['aikatʃiŋ] *adj* auffallend.

eyelash ['ailaʃ] *n* Wimper *f*.

eyelid ['ailid] *n* Augenlid *neut*.

eye shadow ['aisait] *m* Lidschatten *m*.

eyesight ['aisait] *m* Sehkraft *f*.

eyewitness ['ai,witnis] *n* Augenzeuge *m*.

F

fable ['feibl] *n* Fabel *f*.

fabric ['fabrik] *n* Stoff *m*, Gewebe *neut*. **fabricate** *v* herstellen; (*fig*) erfinden.

fabulous ['fabjuləs] *adj* fabelhaft, sagenhaft.

façade [fə'saːd] *n* Fassade *f*.

face [feis] *n* Gesicht *neut*; (*of clock*) Zifferblatt *neut*; (*surface*) Oberfläche *f*; (*cheek*) Stirn *f*. **pull faces** Fratzen schneiden. *v* gegenüberstehen; (*fig*) entgegentreten; (*of house, etc.*) liegen nach.

facet ['fasit] *n* Facette *f*; (*fig*) Aspekt *m*.

facetious [fə'siːʃəs] *adj* scherzhaft.

facial ['feiʃəl] *adj* Gesichts-.

facile ['fasail] *adj* (*easy*) leicht; (*superficial*) oberflächlich. **facilitate** *v* erleichtern.

facility *n* Leichtigkeit *f*. **facilities** *pl n* Einrichtungen *pl*.

facing ['feisiŋ] *prep* gegenüber. *n* Verkleidung *f*.

facsimile [fak'siməli] *n* Faksimile *neut*.

fact [fakt] *n* Tatsache *f*; (*reality*) Wirklichkeit *f*. **in fact** in der Tat, tatsächlich.

faction ['fakʃən] *n* Faktion *f*.

factor ['faktə] *n* Faktor *m*; (*comm*) Agent *m*.

factory ['faktəri] *n* Fabrik *f*. **factory worker** Fabrikarbeiter(in).

fad [fad] *n* Mode *f*.

fade [feid] *v* verschießen, verblassen; (*flower*) verwelken; (*sound*) schwinden. **faded** *adj* verschossen.

fag [fag] *n* (*coll: tiresome job*) Plackerei *f*. **fagged** *adj* erschöpft.

fail [feil] *v* fehlschlagen, scheitern; (*to do something*) unterlassen; (*in exam*) durchfallen; (*let down*) im Stich lassen. *n* **without fail** unbedingt.

faint [feint] *adj* (*colour*) blaß; (*sound*) leise; (*memory*) schwach. *v* ohnmächtig werden. *n* Ohnmacht *f*.

fair¹ [feə] *adj* (*hair*) hell, blond; (*beautiful*) schön; (*just*) gerecht, fair. **fair chance** aussichtsreiche Chance *f*. **play fair** fair spielen. **fair and square** offen und ehrlich. **fairly** *adv* (*quite*) ziemlich.

fair² [feə] *n* Messe *f*; (*funfair*) Jahrmarkt *m*. **fairground** Messegelände *neut*; Rummelplatz *m*.

fairy ['feəri] *n* Fee *f*. *adj* feenhaft, Feen-. **fairy tale** Märchen *neut*.

faith [feiθ] *n* Vertrauen *neut*; (*belief*) Glaube *m*. **faithful** *adj* treu; (*accurate*) getreu. **yours faithfully** hochachtungsvoll.

fake [feik] *v* fälschen. *n* Fälschung *f*; (*person*) Schwindler. *adj* vorgetäuscht.

falcon ['fɔːlkən] *n* Falke *m*.

*fall [fɔːl] *n* Sturz *m*, Fall *m*; (*fig*) Untergang *m*. *v* fallen; (*prices*) abnehmen; (*curtain*) niedergehen; (*fortress*) genommen werden. **fall asleep** einschlafen. **fall back** sich zurückziehen. **fall down** (*person*) hinfallen; (*building*) einstürzen. **fall in love with** sich verlieben in. **fall into** geraten in. **fall out with** zanken mit. **fall through** durchfallen.

fallacy ['faləsi] *n* Trugschluß *m*.

fallen ['fɔːlən] *V* fall.

fallible ['faləbl] *adj* fehlbar.

fall-out ['fɔːlaut] *n* Niederschlag *m*.

fallow ['falou] *adj* fahl.

false [fɔːls] *adj* falsch; (*person*) untreu; (*thing*) gefälscht. **false alarm** blinder Alarm *m*. **false start** Fehlstart *m*. **falsehood** *n* Lüge *f*. **falsify** fälschen.

falter ['fɔːltə] *v* stolpern; (*hesitate*) zögern; (*courage*) versagen.

fame [feim] *n* Ruhm *m*, Berühmtheit *f*.

familiar [fə'miljə] *adj* bekannt; (*informal*) ungezwungen. **familiarity** *n* Vertrautheit *f*.

family ['faməli] *n* Familie *f*; (*bot, zool*) Gattung *f*. *adj* Familien-.

famine ['famin] *n* Hungersnot *f*.

famished ['famiʃt] *n* **be famished** großen Hunger haben.

famous ['feiməs] *adj* berühmt. **famously** *adv* (*coll*) glänzend.

fan[1] [fan] *n* (*hand*) Fächer *m*; (*mot, elec*) Ventilator *m*. **fan belt** *n* Keilriemen *m*.

fan[2] [fan] *n* (*admirer*) Fan *m*.

fanatic [fə'natik] *n* Fanatiker(in). **fanatical** *adj* fanatisch.

fancy ['fansi] *n* Neigung *f* (zu); (*fantasy*) Phantasie *f*. **take a fancy to** eingenommen sein für. *v* gern haben *adj* schick. **fancy dress** Maskenkostüm *m*.

fanfare ['fanfeə] *n* Fanfare *f*.

fang [faŋ] *n* Fangzahn *m*; (*of snake*) Giftzahn *m*.

fantastic [fan'tastik] *adj* phantastisch; (*coll*) sagenhaft, toll.

fantasy ['fantəsi] *n* Phantasie *f*.

far [faː] *adj* fern, entfernt. *adv* fern, weit. **as far as** bis (nach). **by far** bei weitem. **far and near** nahe und fern. **far better** viel besser. **far off** weit weg. **on the far side** auf der anderen Seite.

farce [faːs] *n* Posse *f*; (*fig*) Farce *f*.

fare [feə] *n* Fahrpreis *m*; (*food*) Kost *f*. *v* ergehen.

farewell [feə'wel] *interj* lebe wohl! *n* Lebewohl *neut*. *adj* Abschieds-. **bid farewell to** Abschied nehmen von.

far-fetched [,faː'fetʃt] *adj* weit hergeholt.

farm [faːm] *n* Bauernhof *m*. **dairy farm** Meierei *f*. **poultry farm** Geflügelfarm *f*. *v* Landwirtschaft betreiben; (*land*) bebauen. **farm out** (*work*) weitergeben. **farmer** *n* Landwirt *m*, Bauer *m*. **farmhouse** *n* Bauernhaus *neut*. **farming** *n* Landwirtschaft *f*. **farmworker** Landarbeiter(in).

far-sighted [,faː'saitid] *adj* weitsichtig.

fart [faːt] *n* (*vulgar*) Furz *m*. *v* furzen.

farther ['faːðə] *adj, adv* weiter, ferner.

farthest ['faːðist] *adj* fernst, weitest. *adv* am weitesten.

fascinate ['fasi,neit] *v* faszinieren. **fascinating** *adj* fesselnd. faszinierend. **fascination** *n* Bezauberung *f*, Faszination *f*.

fascism ['faʃizəm] *n* Faschismus *m*. **fascist** *adj* faschistisch. *n* Faschist *m*.

fashion ['faʃən] *n* Mode *f*; (*manner*) Art (und Weise) *f*. **in fashion** modisch. **out of fashion** unmodisch. *v* bilden, gestalten. **fashionable** *adj* modisch. **fashion show** Modeschau *f*.

fast[1] [faːst] *adj, adv* (*quick*) schnell, rasch; (*firm*) fest; (*colour*) echt. *my watch is fast* meine Uhr geht vor.

fast[2] [faːst] *v* fasten. *n* Fasten *neut*.

fasten ['faːsn] *v* befestigen, festbinden; (*door*) verriegeln. **fastener** *n* Verschluß *m*.

fastidious [fa'stidiəs] *adj* wählerisch, anspruchsvoll.

fat [fat] *adj* (*person*) dick, fett; (*greasy*) fett, fettig. *n* Fett *neut*.

fatal ['feitl] *adj* tödlich. **fatalistic** *adj* fatalistisch. **fatality** *n* Todesfall *m*.

fate [feit] *n* Schicksal *neut*. **fateful** *adj* verhängnisvoll.

father ['faːðə] *n* Vater *m*. *v* zeugen. **Father Christmas** der Weihnachtsmann. **father-in-law** *n* Schwiegervater *m*. **fatherland** *n* Vaterland *neut*.

fathom ['faðəm] *n* Faden *m*. *v* sondieren; (*fig*) eindringen in.

fatigue [fə'tiːg] *n* Ermüdung *f*. *v* ermüden. **fatiguing** *adj* mühsam, ermüdend.

fatuous ['fatjuəs] *adj* albern.

fault [fɔːlt] *n* Fehler *m*; (*tech*) Störung *f*; (*blame*) Schuld *f*. *It's my fault* es ist meine Schuld. *Whose fault is this?* wer ist daran schuld? **at fault** im Unrecht. **find fault (with)** tadeln.

fauna ['fɔːnə] *n* Fauna *f*.

favour ['feivə] *n* Gunst *f*; (*kindness*) Gefallen *m*. **in favour of** zugunsten von (*or* +*gen*). **be in favour of** einverstanden sein mit. **in his favour** zu seinen Gunsten. **find favour with** Gunst finden bei. *Do me a favour and . . .* Tun sie nur den Gefallen und . . . . **favourable** *adj* günstig.

favourite *adj* Lieblings-; *n* Liebling *m*; (*sport*) Favorit *m*.

fawn [fɔːn] *n* Rehkalb *neut*. *adj* rehfarbig.

fear [fiə] *n* Furcht *f*, Angst *f*. **fears** *pl n* Befürchtungen *pl*. *v* sich fürchten (vor), Angst haben (vor). **fearful** *adj* (*person*)

ängstlich; (*thing*) furchtbar. **fearless** *adj* furchtlos. **fearsome** *adj* schrecklich.
feasible ['fiːzəbl] *adj* möglich. **feasibility** *n* Möglichkeit *f*.
feast [fiːst] *n* Fest *neut*; (*meal*) Festessen *neut*. *v* sich ergötzen (von).
feat [fiːt] *n* Kunststück *neut*.
feather ['feðə] *n* Feder *f*. **featherweight** *n* Federgewicht *neut*.
feature ['fiːtʃə] *n* (*of face*) Gesichtszug *m*; (*characteristic*) Eigenschaft *f*, Kennzeichen *neut*; (*newspaper*) Feature *neut*. *v* darstellen. **feature film** Spielfilm *m*.
February ['februəri] *n* Februar *m*.
fed [fed] *V* **feed**.
federal ['fedərəl] *adj* Bundes-; (*Swiss*) eidgenössisch. **Federal Republic of Germany** Bundesrepublik Deutschland. **federalism** *n* Föderalismus *m*. **federalist** *n* Föderalist *m*. **federation** *n* Bundesstaat *m*; (*organization*) Verband *m*.
fee [fiː] *n* Gebühr *f*. **school fees** Schulgeld *neut sing*.
feeble ['fiːbl] *adj* schwach, kraftlos. **feeble-minded** *adj* schwachsinnig. **feebleness** *n* Schwachheit *f*.
*feed [fiːd] *v* essen; (*of animals*) fressen; (*cattle*) füttern; (*person*) zu essen geben; (*tech*) zuführen. *n* Futter *neut*; (*tech*) Zufuhr *f*. **be fed up with** (*coll*) satt haben, die Nase voll haben. **feedback** *n* Rückkopplung; (*fig*) Rückwirkung. **feeding** *n* Nahrung *f*; (*animals*) Fütterung *f*.
*feel [fiːl] *v* (sich) fühlen; (*detect, sense*) empfinden; (*pulse*) betasten. *I feel cold* mir ist kalt. *I feel better* es geht mir besser. *It feels hard* es fühlt sich hart an. *I don't feel like working* ich habe keine Lust zur Arbeit. *n* (*atmosphere*) Stimmung *f*. **feeler** *n* Fühler *m*. **feeling** *n* Gefühl *neut*. **hurt someone's feelings** jemanden verletzen.
feet [fiːt] *V* **foot**.
feign [fein] *v* simulieren.
feline ['fiːlain] *adj* Katzen-.
fell[1] [fel] *V* **fall**.
fell[2] [fel] *v* (*tree*) fällen.
fellow ['felou] *n* Genosse *m*, Genossin *f*; (*coll*) Kerl *m*. **fellow-countryman** *n* Landsmann *m*. **fellow men** Mitmenschen *pl*. **fellowship** *n* Kameradschaft *f*; Gesellschaft *f*.
felony ['feləni] *n* Schwerverbrechen *neut*.
felon *n* Schwerverbrecher *m*.

felt[1] [felt] *V* **feel**.
felt[2] [felt] *n* Filz *m*.
female ['fiːmeil] *adj* weiblich. *n* Weib *neut*; (*of animals*) Weibchen *neut*.
feminine ['feminin] *adj* weiblich. *n* (*gramm*) Femininum *neut*. **femininity** *n* Weiblichkeit *f*.
feminism ['feminizəm] *n* Frauenrechtlertum *neut*. **feminist** *n* Frauenrechtler(in), Feminist(in).
fence [fens] *n* Zaun *m*. *v* (*sport*) fechten. **fence in** *or* **off** einzäunen.
fend [fend] *v* **fend off** abwehren. **fend for oneself** sich allein durchschlagen.
fender ['fendə] *n* (*US*) Kotflugel *m*. (*fireguard*) Kaminvorsetzer *m*;\
fennel ['fenl] *n* Fenchel *m*.
ferment [fə'ment; *n* 'fəiment] *v* gären (lassen). *n* (*fig*) Unruhe *f*. **fermentation** *n* Gärung *f*.
fern [fəin] *n* Farn *m*.
ferocious [fə'rouʃəs] *adj* wild, grausam; (*dog*) bissig. **ferocity** *n* Wildheit *f*.
ferret ['ferit] *n* Frettchen *neut*. *v* **ferret out** ausforschen. **ferret about** herumsuchen.
ferry ['feri] *n* Fähre *f*. *v* übersetzen.
fertile ['fəitail] *adj* fruchtbar. **fertility** *n* Fruchtbarkeit *f*. **fertilization** *n* Befruchtung *f*; (*of land*) Düngung *f*. **fertilize** *v* befruchten; (*land*) düngen. **fertilizer** *n* Düngemittel *neut*.
fervent ['fəivənt] *adj* glühend, eifrig.
fester ['festə] *v* verfaulen; (*wound*) eitern.
festival ['festəvəl] *n* Fest *neut*.
festive ['festiv] *adj* festlich. **festivity** *n* Fröhlichkeit *f*.
fetch [fetʃ] *v* holen; (*collect*) abholen; (*price*) erzielen. **fetching** *adj* reizend.
fête [feit] *n* Gartenfest *neut*.
fetid ['fiːtid] *adj* übelriechend.
fetish ['fetiʃ] *n* Fetisch *m*.
fetter ['fetə] *v* fesseln. **fetters** *pl n* Fessel *f* *sing*.
feud [fjuːd] *n* Fehde *f*. *v* sich befehden.
feudal ['fjuːdl] *adj* feudal, Lehns-. **feudalism** *n* Feudalismus *m*.
fever ['fiːvə] *n* Fieber *neut*. **feverish** *adj* fiebrig; (*activity*) fieberhaft.
few [fjuː] *adj, pron* wenige. **a few** einige, ein paar.
fiancé [fi'onsei] *n* Verlobte(r) *m*. **fiancée** *n* Verlobte *f*.
fiasco [fi'askou] *n* Fiasko *neut*, Mißerfolg *m*.

fib [fib] *n* Flunkerei *f. v* flunkern. **fibber** *n* Flunkerer *m.*

fibre ['faibə] *n* Faser *f.* **fibreglass** *n* Glasfiber *f.*

fickle ['fikl] *adj* unbeständig. **fickleness** *n* Unbeständigkeit *f.*

fiction ['fikʃən] *n* Erdichtung *f; (as genre)* Erzählungsliteratur *f.* **work of fiction** Roman *m.* **fictitious** *adj* fiktiv. **fictitious character** erfundene Person *f.*

fiddle ['fidl] *v* tändeln, spielen. *n* Schwindel *m; (violin)* Fiedel *f.* **fiddler** *n (violinist)* Fiedler *m.*

fidelity [fi'deləti] *n* Treue *f.*

fidget ['fidʒit] *v* zappeln. **fidgety** *adj* zappelig.

field [fiːld] *n* Feld *neut; (mining)* Flöz *neut; (fig: sphere)* Bereich *m.* **field glasses** Feldstecker *m.* **fieldwork** *n* Feldforschung *f.*

fiend [fiːnd] *n* Teufel *m; (evil person)* Unhold *m.* **fiendish** *adj* teuflisch.

fierce [fiəs] *adj* wild, grausam. **fierceness** *n* Wildheit *f.*

fiery ['faiəri] *adj* feurig.

fifteen [fif'tiːn] *adj* fünfzehn. **fifteenth** *adj* fünfzehnt.

fifth [fifθ] *adj* fünft. *n* Fünftel *neut.*

fifty ['fifti] *adj* fünfzig. **fiftieth** *adj* fünfzigst. **fifty-fifty** *adv* halb und halb.

fig [fig] *n* Feige *f; (tree)* Feigenbaum *m.*

*fight [fait] *v* kämpfen; *(fig)* bekämpfen. **have a fight** sich streiten. *n* Kampf *m; (quarrel)* Streit *m; (brawl)* Schlägerei *f.*

figment ['figmənt] *n* Erzeugnis der Phantasie *neut.*

figure ['figə] *n (number)* Ziffer *f; (of person)* Figur *f; (diagram)* Zeichnung *f,* Diagramm *neut.* **figure of speech** Redewendung *f. v (appear)* auftreten; *(coll: reckon)* meinen. **figure out** ausrechnen.

filament ['filəmənt] *n (elec)* Glühfaden *m.*

file¹ [fail] *n (documents)* Akte *f; (folder)* Mappe *f; (row)* Reihe *f. v (letters)* ablegen; *(suit)* vorlegen; *(mil)* difilieren. **filing cabinet** Aktenschrank *m.* **filing clerk** Registrator *m.*

file² [fail] *n (tool)* Feile *f. v* feilen.

filial ['filiəl] *adj* Kindes-.

fill [fil] *v* (an)füllen; *(with objects)* vollstopfen; *(tooth)* plombieren; *(hole)* zustopfen; *(become full)* sich füllen. **fill up** auffüllen; *(mot)* auftanken.

fillet ['filit] *n* Filet *neut.*

film [film] *n* Film *m. v* filmen. **make a film** einen Film drehen.

filter ['filtə] *n* Filter *m or neut. v* filtrieren. **filter-tip** *n* Filtermundstück *neut.*

filth [filθ] *n* Dreck *m,* Schmutz *m.* **filthy** *adj* dreckig, schmutzig; *(indecent)* unflätig; *(weather)* scheußlich.

fin [fin] *n* Flosse *f.*

final ['fainl] *adj* letzt, End-; *(definitive)* endgültig. *n (sport)* Endspiel *neut.* **finals** *pl n (exams)* Abschlußprüfung *f sing.* **finale** *n* Finale *neut.* **finalist** *n* Endspielteilnehmer(in). **finalize** *v* abschließen. **finally** *adv* schließlich, zum Schluß.

finance [fai'næns] *n* Finanzwesen *neut. v* finanzieren. **finances** *pl n* Finanzen *pl.* **financial** *adj* finanziell, Finanz-.

finch [fintʃ] *n* Fink *m.*

*find [faind] *v* finden. **find guilty** für schuldig erklären. **find oneself** sich befinden. **find out** herausfinden; *(a person)* ertappen. *n* Fund *m.* **findings** *pl n* Beschluß *m sing.*

fine¹ [fain] *adj* fein; *(weather)* schön; *(splendid)* gut, herrlich; *(hair)* dünn; *(point)* spitz; *(clothes)* elegant.

fine² [fain] *n* Geldstrafe *f. v* mit einer Geldstrafe belegen.

finesse [fi'nes] *n* Feinheit *f; (cards)* Schneiden *neut.*

finger ['fingə] *n* Finger *m. v* betasten. **fingernail** *n* Fingernagel *m.* **fingerprint** *n* Fingerabdruck *m.*

finish ['finiʃ] *v* aufhören, zu Ende gehen; beenden; *(complete)* vollenden; *(food)* aufessen; *(drink)* auftrinken. *n* Ende *neut;* Schluß *m.* **finished** *adj* fertig.

finite ['fainait] *adj* endlich.

Finland ['finlənd] *n* Finnland *neut.* **Finn** Finne *m,* Finnin *f.* **Finnish** *adj* finnisch.

fir [fəː] *n* Tannenbaum *m.*

fire ['faiə] *n* Feuer *neut;* Brand *m.* **catch fire** Feuer fangen. **set fire to** in Brand stecken. *v (a gun)* abfeuern; *(with a gun)* schießen; *(mot)* zünden.

fire alarm *n* Feueralarm *m; (device)* Feuermelder *m.*

firearms ['faiəraːmz] *pl n* Schußwaffen *pl.*

fire brigade *n* Feuerwehr *f.*

fire drill *n* Feueralarmübung *f.*

fire engine *n* Feuerwehrauto *neut.*

fire escape *n* Nottreppe *f.*

fire extinguisher n Feuerlöscher m.
fire-guard n Kaminvorsetzer m.
fireman ['faiəmən] n Feuerwehrmann m.
fireplace ['faiə‚pleis] n Kamin m.
fireproof ['faiə‚pruːf] adj feuerfest.
fireside ['faiə‚said] n Kamin m. adj haüslich.
fire station n Feuerwache f.
firewood ['faiə‚wud] n Brennholz m.
firework ['faiə‚wəːk] n Feuerwerkskörper m. **fireworks** pl n Feuerwerk neut sing.
firing squad n Exekutionskommando neut.
firm[1] [fəːm] adj fest, hart; (resolute) entschlossen. **firm friends** enge Freunde pl.
firm[2] [fəːm] n Firma f.
first [fəːst] adj erst. **first name** Vorname m. adv or **firstly** erstens, zuerst, zunächst. **at first** zuerst. **come first** (sport) gewinnen. **first aid** erste Hilfe. **first-class** adj erstklassig.
fiscal ['fiskəl] adj fiskalisch. **fiscal year** Finanzjahr neut.
fish [fiʃ] n Fisch m; v fischen; (in river) angeln. **fishbone** n Gräte f. **fisherman** n Fischer. **fishhook** n Angelhaken m. **fishing** n Fischen neut, Angeln neut. **fishing boat** Fischerboot neut. **fishing rod** Angelrute f. **fishmonger** n Fischhändler m. **fishy** n (coll: suspicious) verdächtig.
fission ['fiʃən] n Spaltung f.
fissure ['fiʃə] n Spalt m.
fist [fist] n Faust f.
fit[1] [fit] adj (suitable) geeignet, angemessen; (healthy) gesund; (sport) fit, in guter Form. n (clothes) Sitz m. v (clothes) sitzen; (insert) einsetzen. **fit in** sich einfügen. **fit into** sich hineinpassen in. **fitness** n Gesundheit f; (sport) Fitneß f. **fitter** n (mech) Monteur m. **fitting** adj passend. **fittings** pl n Zubehör neut sing.
fit[2] [fit] n (med) Anfall m.
five [faiv] adj fünf.
fix [fiks] v befestigen (an); (arrange) bestimmen; (eyes) richten (auf); (repair) reparieren. n (coll) Klemme f; (drugs) Fix m.
fizz [fiz] v zischen, sprudeln. **fizzy** adj sprudelnd, sprudel-.
flabbergast ['flabəgaːst] v verblüffen.
flabby ['flabi] adj schlaff.
flag[1] [flag] n Fahne f; (naut) Flagge f. **flag down** stoppen.

flag[2] [flag] v (wane) nachlassen.
flagrant ['fleigrənt] adj offenkundig.
flair [fleə] n natürliche Begabung f, feine Nase f.
flake [fleik] n (snow, cereals) Flocke f; (thin piece) Schuppe f. v **flake off** sich abschuppen.
flamboyant [flam‚boiənt] adj auffallend.
flame [fleim] n Flamme f. **burst into flames** in Flammen aufgehen. **old flame** alte Flamme f.
flamingo [flə'miŋgou] n Flamingo m.
flan [flan] n Torte f.
flank [flaŋk] n Flanke f. v flankieren.
flannel ['flanl] n (material) Flanell m; (facecloth) Waschlappen m.
flap [flap] n Klappe f; (of skin, etc.) Lappen m. v flattern.
flare [fleə] v flackern; (dress) sich bauschen. **flare up** aufflackern. n (naut) Lichtsignal neut; (of dress) Ausbauchung f.
flash [flaʃ] Blitz m; (phot) Blitzlicht neut. **news flash** Kurznachricht f. v aufblitzen; (fig) sich blitzartig bewegen. **flashback** n Rückblende f. **flashbulb** n Blitzlichtlampe f. **flasher** n (mot) Blinker m. **flashlight** n Taschenlampe f. **flashy** adj auffällig.
flask [flaːsk] n Flasche f; (laboratory) Glaskolben m. **vacuum flask** Warmflasche f.
flat[1] [flat] adj platt, flach; (level) eben; (refusal) glatt. **fall flat** ein glatter Versager sein.
flat[2] [flat] n Wohnung f.
flatter ['flatə] v schmeicheln. **flattering** adj schmeichelnd. **flattery** n Schmeichelei f.
flatulence ['flatjuləns] n Blähsucht f.
flaunt [floːnt] v paradieren mit, prunken mit.
flautist ['floːtist] n Flötist(in)
flavour ['fleivə] n Geschmack m. v würzen. **flavouring** n Würze f.
flaw [floː] n (crack) Sprung m; (defect) Makel m. **flawless** adj tadellos.
flax [flaks] n Flachs m.
flea [fliː] n Floh m.
fleck [flek] n Flecken neut. v tüpfeln.
fled [fled] V flee.
*flee [fliː] v fliehen.
fleece [fliːs] n Vlies neut. v (coll) rupfen. **fleecy** adj flockig.
fleet [fliːt] n Flotte f.
fleeting ['fliːtiŋ] adj flüchtig.

Flemish ['flemiʃ] *adj* flämisch.
flesh [fleʃ] *n* Fleisch *neut.* **flesh-coloured** *adj* fleischfarben. **fleshly** *adj* fleischlich.
fleshy *adj* fleischig.
flew [fluː] *V* **fly¹**.
flex [fleks] *n* Schnur *f.* *v* biegen; (*muscles*) zusammenziehen. **flexibility** *n* Biegsamkeit *f.* **flexible** *adj* biegsam, flexibel.
flick [flik] *v* schnellen, schnippen. *n* Schnippchen *neut.*
flicker ['flikə] *v* flackern. *n* Flackern *neut.*
flight¹ [flait] *n* (*flying*) Flug *m.* **flight of stairs** Treppe *f.* **flighty** *adj* launisch.
flight² [flait] *n* (*fleeing*) Flucht *f.*
flimsy ['flimzi] *adj* dünn, schwach.
flinch [flintʃ] *v* zurückschrecken (vor).
*fling [fliŋ] *v* schleudern, werfen. **fling away** wegwerfen. **fling open** aufreißen.
flint [flint] *n* Feuerstein *m.*
flip [flip] *v* klapsen, schnellen. *n* Klaps *m.*
flippant ['flipənt] *adj* leichtfertig, keck.
flirt [fləːt] *v* flirten. **flirtatious** *adj* kokett.
flit [flit] *v* flitzen.
float [flout] *v* schwimmen, treiben; (*boat*) flott sein. *n* (*angling*) Kokschwimmer *m.* **floating** *adj* schwimmend.
flock [flok] *n* (*sheep*) Herde *f*; (*birds*) Flug *m.* *v* sich scharen.
flog [flog] *v* peitschen, prügeln. **flogging** *adj* Prügelstrafe *f.*
flood [flʌd] *n* Flut *f.* *v* fluten.
floor [floː] *n* (Fuß)Boden *m*; (*storey*) Stock *m.* *v* (*coll*) verblüten.
flop [flop] *v* plumpsen; (*fail*) versagen. *n* (*failure*) Niete *f*, Versager *m.*
flora ['floːrə] *m* Flora *f.* **floral** *adj* Blumen-.
florist ['florist] *n* Blümenhändler *m.*
flounder ['flaundə] *v* herumpflatschen, stolpern.
flour ['flauə] *n* Mehl *neut.* **flour mill** *n* Mühle *f.* **floury** *adj* mehlig.
flourish ['flʌriʃ] *v* (*thrive*) gedeihen. *n* Schnörkel *m.*
flout [flaut] *v* verspotten.
flow [flou] *v* fließen, strömen. *n* Fluß *m*; (*fig*) Strom *m.*
flower ['flauə] *n* (*plant*) Blume *f*; (*bloom*) Blüte *f.* *v* blüten. **flowerbed** *n* Blumenbeet *neut.* **flowerpot** *n* Blumentopf *m.* **flower-seller** *n* Blumenverkäufer(in). **flowery** *adj* blumenreich.
flown [floun] *V* **fly¹**.

flu [fluː] *n* Grippe *f.*
fluctuate ['flʌktjuˌeit] *v* schwanken. **fluctuation** *n* Schwankung *f.*
flue [fluː] *n* Abzugsrohr *neut.*
fluent ['fluənt] *adj* fließend.
fluff [flʌf] *n* Flaum *m*, Federflocke *f.* *v* (*coll*) verpfuschen. **fluffy** *adj* flaumig, flockig.
fluid ['fluid] *n* Flüssigkeit *f.* *adj* flüssig.
fluke [fluːk] *n* (*coll*) Dusel *m.*
flung [flʌŋ] *V* **fling**.
fluorescent [fluə'resnt] *adj* fluoreszierend. **fluorescent light** Leuchtstofflampe *f.*
fluoride ['fluəraid] *n* Fluorid *neut.*
flush¹ [flʌʃ] *v* (*blush*) erröten; (*WC*) spülen. **flush out** ausspülen. *n* Erröten *neut.* **flushed** *adj* erregt.
flush² [flʌʃ] *adj* (*level*) glatt. **be flush** (*coll*) bei Kasse sein.
fluster ['flʌstə] *v* nervös machen, verwirren. **in a fluster** ganz verwirrt.
flute [fluːt] *n* Flöte *f.* **flute-player** *n* Flötenspieler(in).
flutter ['flʌtə] *v* flattern. *n* Flattern *neut.*
flux [flʌks] *n* Fluß *m*; (*tech*) Schmelzmittel *neut.* **in flux** im Fluß.
*fly¹ [flai] *v* fliegen; (*time*) entfliehen; (*flee*) fliehen; (*goods*) im Flugzeug befördern. *n* (*in trousers*) Hosenschlitz *m.* **flyer** *n* (*aero*) Flieger *m.* **flying** *adj* fliegend. **flying visit** Stippvisite *f.* **flyover** *n* Überführung *f.* **flywheel** *n* Schwungrad *neut.*
fly² [flai] *n* (*insect*) Fliege *f.*
foal [foul] *n* Fohlen *neut.*
foam [foum] *n* Schaum *m.* *v* schäumen. **foam rubber** Schaumgummi *m.* **foaming** *adj* schäumend.
focal ['foukəl] *adj* fokal. **focal point** Brennpunkt *m.*
fodder ['fodə] *n* Futter *neut.*
foe [fou] *n* Feind *m.*
fog [fog] *n* Nebel *m.* **foggy** *adj* neblig. **foghorn** *n* Nebelhorn *m.* **foglamp** *n* Nebelscheinwerfer *m.*
foible ['foibl] *n* Schwäche *f.*
foil¹ [foil] *v* vereiteln, verhindern.
foil² [foil] *n* (*metal*) Folie *f.*
foist [foist] *v* **foist something on someone** jemandem etwas andrehen.
fold¹ [fould] *v* (sich) falten; (*paper*) kniffen; (*arms*) kreuzen; (*business*) eingehen. *n* Falte *f*; Kniff *m.* **folder** *n* (*for papers*) Mappe *f.*

fold² [fould] *n* (*for sheep*) Pferch *m*.
foliage ['fouliidʒ] *n* Laub *neut*.
folk [fouk] *n* Leute *pl*. **folks** *pl n* (*relations*) Verwandte *pl*. **folk-dance** *n* Volkstanz *m*. **folklore** *n* Folklore *f*. **folk-song** *n* Volkslied *neut*.
follow ['folou] *v* folgen (+*dat*); (*instructions*) sich halten an; (*profession*) ausüben. **as follows** folgendermaßen. **follow from** sich ergeben aus. **follow up** verfolgen.
folly ['foli] *n* Narrheit *f*.
fond [fond] *adj* zärtlich; (*hopes*) kühn. **be fond of** gern *or* lieb haben. **fondness** *n* Vorliebe *f*.
fondle ['fondl] *v* streicheln.
font [font] *n* Taufbecken *m*.
food [fuːd] *n* Lebensmittel *pl*, Essen *neut*. **food and drink** Essen und Trinken *neut*. **foodstuff** *n* Nahrungsmittel *pl*.
fool [fuːl] *n* Narr *m*, Närrin *f*, Tor *m*. *v* zum Narren halten; betrügen. **fool around** herumalbern. **foolish** *adj* albern, dumm. **foolishness** *n* Torheit *f*.
foot [fut] *n* (*pl* feet) Fuß *m*; (*of bed, page*) Fußende *neut*. **on foot** zu Fuß. **football** *n* (*game*) Fußballspiel *neut*; (*ball*) Fußball *m*. **foothills** *pl n* Vorgebirge *neut sing*. **foothold** *n* Halt *m*. **gain a foothold** Fuß fassen. **footnote** *n* Anmerkung *f*. **footpath** *n* Fußweg *m*. **footprint** *n* (Fuß)Spur *f*. **footstep** *n* Schritt *m*. **footwear** *n* Schuhzeug *neut*.
for [foː] *prep* für. *conj* denn. **leave for London** nach London abreisen. **for fun** aus Spaß. **for joy** vor Freude. **stay for three weeks** drei Wochen bleiben. **what for?** wozu?
forage ['foridʒ] *n* Furage *f*. *v* furagieren.
forbade [foː'bad] *V* **forbid**.
***forbear** [foː'beə] *v* sich enthalten (+*gen*).
***forbid** [foː'bid] *v* verbieten. **forbidden** *adj* verboten. **forbidding** *adj* bedrohlich. **forbidden** [foː'bidn] *V* **forbid**.
force [foːs] *n* Kraft *f*; (*violence*) Gewalt *f*. *v* (*compel*) zwingen; (*a door*) aufbrechen. **by force** gewaltsam. **in force** (*current*) in Kraft. **armed forces** Streitkräfte *pl*. **police force** Polizei *f*. **forced** *adj* gekünstelt. **forceful** *adj* eindringlich. **forcible** *adj* gewaltsam. **forcibly** *adv* zwangsweise.
forceps ['foːseps] *pl n* Zange *f sing*.
ford [foːd] *n* Furt *f*. *v* durchwaten.

fore [foː] *adj* Vorder-. **come to the fore** hervortreten.
forearm ['foːraːm] *n* Unterarm *m*.
forebear ['foːbə] *n* Vorfahr *m*.
foreboding [foː'boudiŋ] *n* Vorahnung *f*.
***forecast** ['foːkaːst] *v* voraussagen. *n* Voraussage *f*. **weather forecast** Wettervorhersage *f*.
forecourt ['foːkoːt] *n* Vorhof *m*.
forefather ['foːfaːðə] *n* Vorfahr *m*.
forefinger ['foːfiŋgə] *n* Zeigefinger *m*.
forefront ['foːfrʌnt] *n* **in the forefront** im Vordergrund.
foreground ['foːgraund] *n* Vordergrund *m*.
forehand ['foːhand] *n* (*sport*) Vorhandschlag *m*.
forehead ['forid] *n* Stirn *f*.
foreign ['forən] *adj* fremd, ausländisch, Auslands-. **foreign body** Fremdkörper *m*. **foreign language** Fremdsprache *f*. **foreign minister** Außenminister *m*. **foreign policy** Außenpolitik *f*. **foreigner** *n* Fremde(r), Ausländer(in).
foreleg ['foːleg] *n* Vorderbein *neut*.
foreman ['foːmən] *n* Vorarbeiter *m*, Aufseher *m*; (*jury*) Sprecher *m*.
foremost ['foːmoust] *adj* vorderst. **first and foremost** zu allererst.
forename ['foːneim] *n* Vorname *m*.
forensic [fə'rensik] *adj* forensisch.
forerunner ['foːrʌnə] *n* Vorgänger *m*.
***foresee** [foː'siː] *v* voraussagen.
foresight ['foːsait] *n* Vorsorge *f*.
foreskin ['foːskin] *n* Vorhaut *f*.
forest ['forist] *n* Forst *m*, Wald *m*. **forest fire** Waldbrand *m*.
forestall [foː'stoːl] *v* zuvorkommen (+*dat*).
foretaste ['foːteist] *n* Vorgeschmack *m*.
***foretell** [foː'tel] *v* vorhersagen.
forethought ['foːθoːt] *n* Vorbedacht *m*.
forever [fo'revə] *adv* immer, ständig.
foreword ['foːwəːd] *n* Vorwort *neut*.
forfeit ['foːfit] *v* verwirken. *n* Verwirkung *f*. *adj* verwirkt.
forgave [fə'geiv] *V* **forgive**.
forge [foːdʒ] *v* (*metal*) schmieden; (*plan*) ersinnen; (*document*) fälschen. *n* Schmiede *f*. **forgery** *n* Fälschung *f*.
***forget** [fə'get] *v* vergessen. **forgetful** *adj* vergeßlich.
***forgive** [fə'giv] *v* verzeihen, vergeben. **forgiveness** *n* Verzeihung *f*. **forgiving** *adj* versöhnlich.

forgiven [fə'gıvn] *V* forgive.
*forgo [foɪ'gou] *v* verzichten auf.
forgot [fə'gɒt] *V* forget.
forgotten [fə'gɒtn] *V* forget.
fork [foɪk] *n* Gabel *f*; (*in road*) Gabelung *f*. *v* fork out (*coll: pay*) blechen.
forlorn [fə'loɪn] *adj* verlassen, hilflos.
form [foɪm] *n* Gestalt *f*, Form *f*; (*to fill out*) Formular *neut*. on form in Form. *v* bilden.
formal ['foɪməl] *adj* formell.
format ['foɪmat] *n* Format *neut*.
formation [foɪ'meıʃən] *n* Bildung *f*; (*geol, mil*) Formation *f*.
former ['foɪmə] *adj* vorig; (*one-time*) ehemalig; (*of two*) jene(r). **formerly** *adv* früher.
formidable ['foɪmidəbl] *adj* furchtbar.
formula ['foɪmjulə] *n* (*pl* -ae) Formel *f*; (*med*) Rezept *neut*. **formulate** *v* formulieren. **formulation** *n* Formulierung *f*.
*forsake [fə'seık] *v* (*person*) verlassen.
forsaken [fə'seıkn] *V* forsake.
forsook [fə'suk] *V* forsake.
fort [foɪt] *n* Festung *f*.
forte ['foɪteı] *adv* (*music*) laut. *n* Stärke *f*.
forth [foɪθ] *adv* (*place*) hervor; (*time*) fort. and so forth und so weiter *or* fort. back and forth hin und her.
fortify ['foɪtiˌfaı] *v* (*mil*) befestigen; (*hearten*) ermutigen; (*food*) anreichern. **fortification** *n* Befestigung *f*; (*fortress*) Festung *f*.
fortitude ['foɪtiˌtjuɪd] *n* Mut *m*.
fortnight ['foɪtnaıt] *n* vierzehn Tage. **fortnightly** *adj* vierzehntägig. *adv* alle vierzehn Tage.
fortress ['foɪtris] *n* Festung *f*.
fortuitous [foɪ'tjuɪitəs] *adj* zufällig.
fortune ['foɪtʃən] *n* Glück *neut*; (*fate*) Schicksal *neut*; (*wealth*) Vermögen *neut*. **fortunate** *adj* glücklich. **fortunately** *adv* glücklicherweise.
forty ['foɪti] *adj* vierzig.
forum ['foɪrəm] *n* Forum *neut*.
forward ['foɪwəd] *adj* vorder, Vorder-; (*impudent*) vorlaut. *adv* vorwärts. *v* (*goods*) spedieren; (*letter*) nachschicken. *n* (*sport*) Stürmer *m*.
fossil ['fɒsl] *n* Fossil *neut*.
foster ['fɒstə] *v* pflegen; (*feelings*) Legen. *adj* Pflege-.
fought [foɪt] *V* fight.
foul [faul] *adj* (*dirty*) schmutzig; (*disgust-*

ing) widerlich; (*weather*) schlecht. *v* verschmutzen. *n* (*sport*) Regelverstoß *m*.
found[1] [faund] *V* find.
found[2] [faund] *v* gründen. be founded on beruhen auf. **foundation** *n* (*of building*) Grundmauer *f*; (*of institute, firm, etc.*) Gründung *f*; (*basis*) Grundlage *f*; (*institute*) Stiftung *f*. **founder** *n* Gründer *m*.
foundry ['faundri] *n* Gießerei *f*.
fountain ['fauntin] *n* Springbrunnen *m*. **fountain pen** Füllfeder *f*.
four [foɪ] *adj* vier. **fourth** *adj* viert; *n* Viertel *neut*.
fourteen [foɪ'tiɪn] *adj* vierzehn.
fowl [faul] *n* Haushuhn *neut*.
fox [fɒks] *n* Fuchs *m*. *v* (*coll*) täuschen.
foyer ['foıeı] *n* Foyer *neut*.
fraction ['frakʃən] *n* Bruchteil *m*; (*math*) Bruch *m*.
fracture ['fraktʃə] *n* (*med*) Knochenbruch *m*. *v* zerbrechen.
fragile ['fradʒaıl] *adj* zerbrechlich.
fragment ['fragmənt] *n* Bruchstück *neut*, Brocken *m*.
fragrance ['freıgrəns] *n* Duft *m*, Aroma *neut*. **fragrant** *adj* duftig, wohlriechend.
frail [freıl] *adj* schwach, gebrechlich. **frailty** *n* Schwäche *f*.
frame [freım] *n* Rahmen *m*. *v* einrahmen. **spectacle frame** Brillengestell *neut*.
France [fraıns] *n* Frankreich *neut*.
franchise ['frantʃaız] *n* (*pol*) Wahlrecht *neut*; (*comm*) Konzession *f*.
frank [fraŋk] *adj* offen, freimütig. **frankly** *adv* frei, offen. **frankness** *n* Freimut *m*.
frantic ['frantik] *adj* wild, rasend.
fraternal [frə'təɪnl] *adj* brüderlich.
fraud [froɪd] *n* Betrug *m*, Unterschlagung *f*; (*person*) Schwindler(in). **fraudulent** *adj* betrügerisch.
fraught [froɪt] *adj* voll. **fraught with danger** gefahrvoll.
fray[1] [freı] *v* (sich) ausfransen.
fray[2] [freı] *n* Rauferei *f*.
freak [friɪk] *n* (*of nature*) Mißbildung *f*; (*event, storm*) Ausnahmeerscheinung *f*. *adj* anormal.
freckle ['frekl] *n* Sommersprosse *f*.
free [friɪ] *adj* frei; kostenlos. *v* befreien, freimachen. **free and easy** ungezwungen. **free speech** Redefreiheit *f*. **free will** freier Wille *m*. **freedom** *n* Freiheit. **freely** *adv* reichlich.
freelance ['friɪlaɪns] *n* freier Schriftsteller *m*. *adj* freiberuflich tätig.

freemason ['friːmeisn] *n* Freimaurer *n*.
*****freeze** [friːz] *v* (*water*) frieren; (*food*) tiefkühlen. **freeze to death** erfrieren. *I'm freezing* ich friere. *n* (*comm*) Stopp *m*. **freezer** *n* Tiefkühltruhe *f*. **freezing point** Gefrierpunkt *m*.
freight [freit] *n* Fracht *f*; (*freight costs*) Frachtgebühr *f*.
French [frentʃ] *adj* französisch. **Frenchman** *n* Franzose *m*. **Frenchwoman** *n* Französin *f*. **French horn** Waldhorn *neut*.
french fries *n pl* Pommes frites *pl*.
frenzy ['frenzi] *n* Raserei *f*.
frequency ['friːkwənsi] *n* Frequenz *f*. **frequent** *adj* häufig, frequent; *v* häufig besuchen. **frequently** *adv* öfters, häufig.
fresco ['freskou] *n* Fresko *neut*.
fresh [freʃ] *adj* frisch; (*water*) süß; (*air*) erfrischend; (*cheeky*) frech. **fresh water** Süßwasser *neut*. **freshen** *v* auffrischen. **freshness** *n* Frische *f*.
fret [fret] *v* sich Sorgen machen.
friar ['fraiə] *n* Mönch *m*.
friction ['frikʃən] *n* Reibung *f*.
Friday ['fraidei] *n* Freitag *m*. **Good Friday** Karfreitag *m*.
fridge [fridʒ] *n* Kühlschrank *m*.
fried [fraid] *adj* gebraten. **fried egg** Spiegelei *neut*. **fried potatoes** Bratkartoffeln.
friend [frend] *n* Freund(in). **make friends with** sich befreunden mit. **friendly** *adj* freundlich, freundschaftlich. **friendship** *n* Freundschaft *f*.
frieze [friːz] *n* Fries *m*.
frigate ['frigit] *n* Fregatte *f*.
fright [frait] *n* Schreck *m* **frighten** *v* erschrecken. **frightening** *adj* erschreckend. **frightened** *adj* erschrocken. **be frightened of** Angst haben vor. **frightful** *adj* schrecklich.
frigid ['fridʒid] *adj* frigid. **frigidity** *n* Frigidität *f*.
frill [fril] *n* Rüsche, Krause *f*. **frilly** *adj* gekräuselt.
fringe [frindʒ] *n* Franse *f*; (*edge*) Randzone *f*; (*hair*) Pony *neut*. **fringe benefits** Nebenbezüge *pl*.
frisk [frisk] *v* herumhüpfen; (*search*) absuchen. **frisky** *adj* munter, lebhaft.
fritter ['fritə] *v* **fritter away** verzetteln.
frivolity [fri'voliti] *n* Leichtfertigkeit *f*. **frivolous** *adj* (*person*) leichtfertig; (*worthless*) nichtig.

frizz [friz] *v* (sich) kräuseln. **frizzy** *adj* kraus.
fro [frou] *adv* **to and fro** auf und ab, hin und her.
frock [frok] *n* Kleid *neut*.
frog [frog] *n* Frosch *m*.
frolic ['frolik] *n* Spaß *m*, Posse *f*. **frolicsome** *adj* lustig, ausgelassen.
from [from] *prep* von; (*place*) aus, von; (*to judge from*) nach. *Where are you from?* wo kommen Sie her?
front [frʌnt] *n* Vorderseite *f*, vorderer Teil *m*; (*mil, pol*) Front *f*; (*fa,cade*) Fassade *f*. *adj* Vor-, Vorder-. **front door** Haustür *f*. **front room** Vorderzimmer *neut*. **in front of** vor.
frontier ['frʌntiə] *n* Grenze *f*.
frost [frost] *n* Frost *m*. *v* (*cookery*) glasieren. **frostbite** *n* Erfrieren *neut*; (*wound*) Frostbeule *f*. **frostbitten** *adj* erfroren. **frosty** *adj* frostig.
froth [froθ] *n* Schaum *m*. **frothy** *adj* schäumig.
frown [fraun] *n* Stirnrunzeln *neut*. *v* die Stirn runzeln. **frown on** mißbilligen.
froze [frouz] *V* **freeze**.
frozen ['frouzn] *V* **freeze**. *adj* gefroren; (*comm*) eingefroren; (*food*) tiefgekühlt. **frozen over** zugefroren.
frugal ['fruːgəl] *adj* sparsam.
fruit [fruːt] *n* Obst *neut*, Früchte *pl*; (*result, yield*) Frucht *f*. **fruitful** *adj* fruchtbar. **fruition** *n* Erfüllung *f*. **fruitless** *adj* fruchtlos. **fruit machine** Spielautomat *neut*. **fruit salad** Obstsalat *m*. **fruit tree** Obstbaum *m*. **fruity** *adj* würzig.
frustrate [frʌ'streit] *v* vereiteln, frustrieren. **frustrated** *adj* vereitelt, frustriert. **frustration** *n* Vereitelung *f*, Frustration *f*.
fry [frai] *v* (in der Pfanne) braten. **frying-pan** *n* Bratpfanne *f*.
fuchsia ['fjuːʃə] *n* Fuchsia *f*.
fudge [fʌdʒ] *n* Karamelle *f*.
fuel ['fjuəl] *n* Brennstoff; (*for engines*) Treibstoff *m*; (*mot*) Benzin *neut*. *v* tanken. **fuel gauge** Treibstoffmesser *m*. **fuel oil** Brennöl *neut*.
fugitive ['fjuːdʒitiv] *adj* flüchtig. *n* Flüchtling *m*.
fulcrum ['fulkrəm] *n* Drehpunkt *m*.
fulfil [ful'fil] *v* erfüllen. **fulfilment** *n* Erfüllung *f*; (*satisfaction*) Befriedigung *f*.
full [ful] *adj* voll; (*after meal*) satt. *adv* direkt, gerade. **pay in full** voll bezahlen. **write out in full** ausschreiben. **full-grown**

adj ausgewachsen. **full moon** Vollmond *m*. **fullness** *n* Fülle *f*. **full stop** Punkt *m*. **full-time** *adj* ganztägig. **fully** *adv* voll, völlig.

fumble ['fʌmbl] *v* umhertasten. **fumble with** herumfummeln an.

fume [fjuːm] *v* dampfen; *(coll)* wütend sein. *n* Dunst *m*, Dampf *m*. **fumigate** *v* ausräuchern.

fun [fʌn] *n* Spaß *m*. **it's fun** es macht Spaß. **for fun** aus Spaß. **in fun** zum Scherz. **have fun** sich amüsieren. **have fun!** viel Spaß/vergnügen! **make fun of** sich lustig machen über.

function ['fʌŋkʃən] *n* Funktion *f*; *(task)* Aufgabe *f*; *(gathering)* Veranstaltung *f*. *v* *(tech)* funktionieren; tätig sein. **functional** *adj* funktionell, zweckmäßig. **functionary** *n* Beamte(r).

fund [fʌnd] *n* Fonds *m*; *(fig)* Vorrat *m*. *v* fundieren.

fundamental [fʌndə'mentl] *adj* grundlegend, grundsätzlich.

funeral ['fjuːnərəl] *n* Begräbnis *neut*.

fungus ['fʌŋgəs] *n* *(pl* -i) Pilz *m*.

funnel ['fʌnl] *n* Trichter *m*; *(ship)* Schornstein *m*.

funny ['fʌni] *adj* *(amusing)* komisch, lustig, spaßhaft; *(strange)* komisch, seltsam. **funny-bone** *n* Musikantenknochen *m*.

fur [fəː] *n* Pelz *m*; *(on tongue)* Belag *m*; *(in boiler)* Kesselstein *m*. **fur coat** Pelzmantel *m*. **furry** *adj* pelzartig, Pelz-; belegt.

furious ['fjuəriəs] *adj* wütend.

furnace ['fəːnis] *n* (Brenn)Ofen *m*.

furnish ['fəːniʃ] *v* *(a room)* möblieren; *(supply)* versehen, ausstatten. **furnishings** *pl n* Möbel *pl*.

furniture ['fəːnitʃə] *n* Möbel *pl*.

furrow ['fʌrou] *n* Furche *f*.

further ['fəːðə] *adj*, *adv* weiter. **until further notice** bis auf weiteres. *v* fördern. **furthermore** *adv* ferner, überdies. **furthest** *adj* weitest; *adv* am weitesten.

furtive ['fəːtiv] *adj* *(person)* hinterlistig; *(action)* verstohlen.

fury ['fjuəri] *n* Wut *f*.

fuse [fjuːz] *n* *(elec)* Sicherung *f*; *(explosives)* Zünder *m*. *v* *(join, melt)* (ver)schmelzen; *(elec)* sichern; *(elec: blow a fuse)* durchbrennen. **fuse box** Sicherungskasten *m*.

fuselage ['fjuːzəlɑːʒ] *n* Rumpf *m*.

fusion ['fjuːʒən] *n* Verschmelzung *f*.

fuss [fʌs] *n* Getue, Theater *neut*. **make a fuss** viel Wesens machen (um). **fussy** *adj* kleinlich.

futile ['fjuːtail] *adj* zwecklos, wertlos. **futility** *n* Zwecklosigkeit *f*.

future ['fjuːtʃə] *n* Zukunft *f*. *adj* künftig. **in future** in Zukunft. **futures** *pl n* *(comm)* Termingeschäfte *pl*. **futuristic** *adj* futuristisch.

fuzz [fʌz] *n* Fussel *f*. **fuzzy** *adj* *(hair)* kraus; *(vision)* verschwommen.

G

gabble ['gabl] *v* schwätzen.

gable ['geibl] *n* Giebel *m*. **gabled** *adj* gegiebelt.

gadget ['gadʒit] *n* Apparat *m*, Gerät *neut*.

gag[1] [gag] *v* knebeln. *n* Knebel *m*.

gag[2] [gag] *(coll: joke)* *n* Witz *m*. *v* einen Witz reißen.

gaiety ['geiəti] *n* Heiterkeit *f*.

gain [gein] *n* Gewinn *m*. *v* gewinnen; *(of clock)* vorgehen. **gain on** einholen. **gains** *pl* *(comm)* Profit *m*.

gait [geit] *n* Gang *m*.

gala ['gɑːlə] *n* Festlichkeit *f*.

galaxy ['galəksi] *n* Sternsystem *neut*; *(ours)* Milchstraße *f*.

gale [geil] *n* heftiger Wind *m*, Sturmwind *m*.

gallant ['galənt] *adj* tapfer; *(courteous)* ritterlich. **gallantry** *n* Tapferkeit *f*; Ritterlichkeit *f*.

gall bladder [gɔːl] *n* Gallenblase *f*.

galleon ['galiən] *n* Galeone *f*.

gallery ['galəri] *n* Galerie *f*.

galley ['gali] *n* Galeere *f*; *(kitchen)* Schiffsküche *f*.

gallon ['galən] *n* Gallone *f*.

gallop ['galəp] *n* Galopp *m*. *v* galoppieren.

gallows ['galouz] *n* Galgen *m*.

gallstone ['gɔːlstoun] *n* Gallenstein *m*.

galore [gə'lɔː] *adv* in Hülle und Fülle.

galvanize ['galvənaiz] *v* galvanisieren, verzinken; *(fig: stimulate)* anspornen (zu).

gamble ['gambl] *v* um Geld spielen. **gamble on** wetten auf. **gamble with** aufs Spiel

setzen. **gambler** *n* Spieler *m.* **gambling** *n*
Spielen (um Geld) *neut. n* Wagnis *neut.*
game [geim] *n* Spiel *neut*; *(hunting)* Wild
neut. **give the game away** den Plan verraten. *adj (leg)* lahm. **be game for** bereit
sein zu. **gamekeeper** *n* Wildhüter *m.*
gammon ['gamən] *n* (geräucherter)
Schinken *m.*
gang [gaŋ] *n (criminals)* Bande *f*; *(workers)* Kolonne *f. v* **gang up** sich zusam-
menrotten. **gangster** *n* Gangster *m.*
gangrene ['gaŋgriːn] *n* Brand *m.*
gangway ['gaŋwei] *n (theatre)* Gang *m*;
(naut) Laufplanke *f.*
gaol [dʒeil] *V* jail.
gap [gap] *n* Lücke *f.*
gape [geip] *v* klaffen; *(person)* gähnen.
garage ['garaɪdʒ] *n* Garage *f*; *(mot: workshop)* Autowerkstatt *f. v* in eine Garage
einstellen *or* unterbringen.
garbage ['gaɪbidʒ] *n* Müll *m.* **garbage can**
Mülkasten *m.*
garble ['gaɪbl] *v* verstümmeln.
garden ['gaɪdn] *n* Garten *m. v* im Garten
arbeiten. **gardening** *n* Gartenbau *m.* **garden party** Gartenfest *neut.*
gargle ['gaɪgl] *v* gurgeln. *n* Mundwasser
neut.
gargoyle ['gaɪgoil] *n (arch)* Wasserspeier
m.
garland ['gaɪlənd] *n* Girlande *f*,
Blumengewinde *neut. v* bekränzen.
garlic ['gaɪlik] *n* Knoblauch *m.*
garment ['gaːmənt] *n* Kleidungsstück
neut.
garnish ['gaɪniʃ] *v (cookery)* garnieren. *n*
Garnierung *f.*
garrison ['garisn] *n* Garnison *f. v (town)*
besetzen; *(troops)* in Garnison legen.
garter ['gaɪtə] *n* Strumpfband *neut.*
gas [gas] *n* Gas *neut*; *(US: petrol)* Benzin
neut. **step on the gas** Gas geben. *v
(poison)* vergasen; *(slang: chatter)*
schwätzen. **gasbag** *n (coll)* Windbeutel *m.*
gas cooker Gasherd *m.* **gas fire**
Gasheizung *f.*
gash [gaʃ] *v* aufschneiden. *n* klaffende
Wunde *f.*
gasket ['gaskit] *n* Dichtung *f.*
gas main *n* Gasleitung *f.*
gas meter *n* Gasmesser *m.*
gasoline ['gasəˌliːn] *n (US)* Benzin *neut.*
gasp [gaɪsp] *v* keuchen. *n* **Keuchen** *neut.*
gas station *n* Tankstelle *f.*
gastric ['gastrik] *adj* gastrisch, Magen-.

gate [geit] *n* Tor *neut.*
gâteau ['gatou] *n* Torte *f.*
gateway ['geitwei] *n* Torweg *m.*
gather ['gaðə] *v* sammeln; *(people)* (sich)
versammeln; *(flowers, etc.)* lesen; *(dress)*
raffen; *(deduce)* schließen (aus). **gathering** *n* Versammlung *f.*
gaudy ['goːdi] *adj (colours)* grell, bunt.
gauge [geidʒ] *v* abmessen; *(judge)*
schätzen. *n* Normalmaß *neut*; *(rail)*
Spurweite *f.* **pressure gauge** Druckmesser
m.
gaunt [goːnt] *adj* mager.
gauze [goɪz] *n* Gaze *f.*
gave [geiv] *V* give.
gay [gei] *adj (colours)* bunt; *(person)*
heiter, lustig; *(slang: homosexual)* warm.
gaze [geiz] *v* starren (auf). *n* (starrer)
Blick *neut.*
gazelle [gə'zel] *n* Gazelle *f.*
gazetteer [gazə'tiə] *n* Namensverzeichnis
neut.
gear [giə] *n (mot)* Gang *m*; *(gear wheel)*
Zahnrad *neut*; *(equipment)* Gerät *neut*,
Ausrüstung *f.* **in gear** eingeschaltet.
change gear *(up or down)* Gang herauf *or*
herab setzen. **gearbox** *n*
Getriebe(gehäuse) *neut.*
geese [giːs] *V* goose.
gelatine ['dʒeləˌtiːn] *n* Gelatine *f*; *(explosive)* Sprenggelatine *f.*
gelignite ['dʒeligˌnait] *n* Gelatinedynamit
neut.
gem [dʒem] *n* Edelstein *m*, Gemme *f.*
Gemini ['dʒemini] *n* Zwillinge *pl.*
gender ['dʒendə] *n* Geschlecht *neut*;
(gramm) Genus *neut.*
gene [dʒiːn] *n* Gen *neut*, Erbeinheit *f.*
genealogy [dʒiːniˌalədʒi] *n* Genealogie *f.*
genealogist *n* Genealoge *m.*
general ['dʒenərəl] *adj* allgemein. *n* General *m.* **in general** im Allgemeinen. **General Assembly** *n* Generalversammlung *f.*
general election allgemeine Wahlen *pl.*
generate ['dʒenəreit] *v* erzeugen, verursachen. **generator** *n* Generator *m*,
Stromerzeuger *m.* **generation** *n* Generation *f*, Zeitalter *m*; *(production)*
Erzeugung *f.*
generic [dʒi'nerik] *adj* allgemein, generell.
generous ['dʒenərəs] *adj* großzügig,
freigebig. **generosity** *n* Großzügigkeit *f.*
genetic [dʒi'netik] *adj* genetisch, Ent-
stehungs-. **genetics** *n* Genetik *f.*

Geneva [dʒi'niːvə] *n* Genf *neut.* **Lake Geneva** der Genfer See *m.*
genial ['dʒiːniəl] *adj* freundlich, herzlich. **geniality** *n* Freundlichkeit *f.*
genital ['dʒenitl] *adj* Geschlechts-. **genitals** *pl n* Geschlechtsteile *pl.*
genitive ['dʒenitiv] *n* Genitiv *m.*
genius ['dʒiːnjəs] *n* Genie *neut;* (*talent*) Begabung *f.*
genocide ['dʒenəsaid] *n* Völkermord *m.*
genteel [dʒen'tiːl] *adj* wohlerzogen, vornehm.
gentle ['dʒentl] *adj* sanft, mild. **gentleman** *n* Herr *m.* **gentleness** *n* Mildheit *f.*
gentry ['dʒentri] *n* Landadel *m.*
gents [dʒents] *n* (*sign*) Herren *pl.*
genuine ['dʒenjuin] *adj* echt, wahr. **genuineness** *n* Wahrheit *f*, Echtheit *f.*
genus ['dʒiːnəs] *n* Gattung *f*, Sorte *f.*
geography [dʒi'ogrəfi] *n* Erdkunde *f*, Geographie *f.* **geographical** *adj* geographisch. **geographer** *n* Geograph(in).
geology [dʒi'olədʒi] *n* Geologie *f.* **geologist** *n* Geologe *m.*
geometry [dʒi'omətri] *n* Geometrie *f.* **geometric** *adj* geometrisch.
geranium [dʒə'reiniəm] *n* Geranie *f.*
geriatric [dʒeri'atrik] *adj* geriatrisch. **geriatrics** *n* Geriatrie *f.*
germ [dʒəːm] *n* Keim *m*, Bakterie *f.*
German measles *n* Röteln *pl.*
Germany ['dʒəːməni] *n* Deutschland *neut.* **German** *adj* deutsch; *n* Deutsche(r); (language) Deutsch *neut.* **Federal Republic of Germany** *n* Bundesrepublik Deutschland (BRD) *f;* **German Democratic Republic** *n* Deutsche Demokratische Republik (DDR) *f.*
germinate ['dʒəːmineit] *v* Keimen. **germination** *n* Keimen *neut.*
gesticulate [dʒe'stikjuˌleit] *v* wilde Gesten machen.
gesture ['dʒestʃə] *n* Geste *f.* *v* eine Geste machen.
***get** [get] *v* (obtain) bekommen, erhalten; (become) werden. **get hold of** bekommen. **get in** einsteigen. **get married** sich verheiraten. **get off** aussteigen. **get ready** vorbereiten.
geyser ['giːzə] *n* Geiser *m.*
ghastly ['gaːstli] *adj* schrecklich, furchtbar.
gherkin ['gəːkin] *n* Essiggurke *f.*
ghetto ['getou] *n* Getto *neut.*

ghost [goust] *n* Gespenst *neut*, Geist *m.* **ghostly** *adj* gespenstisch.
giant ['dʒaiənt] *n* Riese *m.* *adj* riesenhaft.
gibberish ['dʒibəriʃ] *n* Quatsch *m.*
gibe [dʒaib] *v* spotten (über). *n* Spott *m.*
giblets ['dʒiblits] *pl n* Hühnerklein *neut.*
giddy ['gidi] *adj* schwind(e)lig. **giddiness** *n* Schwindel *m.*
gift [gift] *n* Geschenk *neut;* (talent) Begabung *f.* **gifted** *adj* begabt.
gigantic [dʒai'gantik] *adj* riesenhaft, gigantisch.
giggle ['gigl] *v* kichern. *n* Gekicher *neut.*
gill [gil] *n* (fish) Kieme *f.*
gilt [gilt] *adj* vergoldet. *n* Vergoldung *f.*
gimmick ['gimik] *n* Trick *m.*
gin [dʒin] *n* Gin *m*, Wacholderschnapps *m.*
ginger ['dʒindʒə] *n* Ingwer *m.* **gingerbread** *n* Pfefferkuchen *m.* **ginger-haired** *adj* rothaarig.
gingerly ['dʒindʒəli] *adv* vorsichtig.
gipsy ['dʒipsi] *n* Zigeuner(in). *adj* Zigeuner.
giraffe [dʒi'raːf] *n* Giraffe *f.*
***gird** [gəːd] *v* umgürten, umlegen.
girder ['gəːdə] *n* Träger *m*, Tragbalken *m.*
girdle ['gəːdl] *n* Gurt *m.* *v* umgürten.
girl [gəːl] *n* Mädchen *neut.* **girl friend** Freundin *f.* **girlhood** *n* Mädchenjahre *pl.* **girlish** *adj* mädchenhaft.
girt [gəːt] *V* gird.
girth [gəːθ] *n* Umfang *m;* (horse) Gurt *m.*
gist [dʒist] *n* Wesentliche *neut*, Hauptpunkt *m.*
***give** [giv] *v* geben; (gift) schenken (hand over) überreichen. *n* Elastizität *f.* **give away** (betray) verraten. **give back** zurückgeben. **give in** nachgeben. **give up** aufgeben.
given ['givn] *V* give. *adj* (an)gegeben.
glacier ['glasiə] *n* Gletscher *m.*
glad [glad] *adj* froh, fröhlich, glücklich. **gladness** *n* Fröhlichkeit, Glücklichkeit *f.*
glamour [glamə] *n* bezaubernde Schönheit *f.* **glamorous** *adj* bezaubernd.
glance [glaːns] *v* (flüchtig) blicken, einen Blick werfen. *n* flüchtiger Blick *m.*
gland [gland] *n* Drüse *f.* **glandular** *adj* drüsig, Drüsen-. **glandular fever** *n* Drüsenfieber *m.*
glare [gleə] *v* grell leuchten; (stare) starren. **glare at** anstarren. *n* blendendes Licht *neut.*

glass [glɑːs] *n* Glas *neut.* **glasses** *pl* Brille *f sing.* **glassfibre** *n* Glaswolle *f.*

glaze [gleiz] *n* Glasur *f. v* verglasen; (*windows*) mit Glasscheiben versehen. **glazier** *n* Glaser *m.*

gleam [gliːm] *n* Schimmer *m. v* schimmern.

glean [gliːn] *v* (nach)lesen.

glee [gliː] *n* Fröhlichkeit *f.* **gleeful** *adj* fröhlich.

glib [glib] *adj* zungenfertig.

glide [glaid] *v* gleiten. **glider** *n* Segelflugzeug *neut.*

glimmer ['glimə] *n* Schimmer *m. v* schimmern.

glimpse [glimps] *n* flüchtiger Blick. *v* erspähen.

glint [glint] *n* Glitzern *neut. v* glitzern.

glisten ['glisn] *n* Glanz *m. v* glänzen.

glitter ['glitə] *n* Funkeln *neut. v* funkeln.

gloat [glout] *v* sich hämisch freuen über. **gloating** *n* Schadenfreude *f.*

globe [gloub] *n* (Erd)Kugel *f.* **global** *adj* global. **globular** *adj* kugelförmig.

gloom [gluːm] *n* Düsternis *f,* Dunkelheit *f*; (*mood*) Trübsinn *m.* **gloomy** *adj* düster.

glory ['glɔːri] *n* Ruhm *m,* Ehre *f. v* sich freuen. **glorify** *v* verherrlichen. **glorious** *adj* glorreich, herrlich.

gloss [glos] *n* Glanz *m. v* polieren. **gloss paint** Ölfarbe *f.* **gloss over** vertuschen.

glossary ['glosəri] *n* Glossar *neut,* (spezielles) Wortverzeichnis *neut.*

glove [glʌv] *n* Handschuh *m.* **fit like a glove** passen wie angegossen.

glow [glou] *n* Glühen *neut. v* glühen.

glucose ['gluːkous] *n* Traubenzucker *m.*

glue [gluː] *n* Klebstoff *neut. v* kleben.

glum [glʌm] *adj* mürrisch.

glut [glʌt] *n* Überfluß *m*; (*comm*) Überangebot *neut. v* sättigen.

glutton ['glʌtən] *n* Vielfraß *m.* **gluttonous** *adj* gefräßig. **gluttony** *n* Gefräßigkeit *f.*

gnarled [nɑːld] *adj* knorrig.

gnash [naʃ] *v* knirschen.

gnat [nat] *n* Mücke *f.*

gnaw [nɔː] *v* nagen an (+ *dat*).

gnome [noum] *n* Zwerg *m,* Gnom *m.*

*go [gou] *v* gehen; (*travel*) fahren, reisen; (*machine*) funktionieren, in Betrieb sein; (*time*) vergehen; (*coll: become*) werden. **go ahead** fortfahren. **go away** weggehen; (*travel*) verreisen. **go down** hinuntergehen; (*price*) fallen. **go out**

hinausgehen; (*fire*) erlöschen. **go up** hinaufgehen; (*prices*) steigen. **have a go at** einen Versuch machen mit. **it's no go!** es geht nicht!

goad [goud] *n* Stachelstock *m. v* antreiben.

goal [goul] *n* Ziel *neut*; (*sport*) Tor *m.* **goalkeeper** *n* Torwart *m.*

goat [gout] *n* Ziege *f.*

gobble ['gobl] *v* **gobble (down)** (*food*) hinunterschlingen. **gobble up** verschlingen.

goblin ['goblin] *n* Kobold *m.*

god [god] *n* Gott *m.* **thank God!** Gott sei dank! **godchild** *n* Patenkind *neut.* **goddaughter** *n* Patentochter *f.* **goddess** *n* Göttin *f.* **godfather** *n* Pate *m.* **godmother** *n* Patin *f.* **godsend** *n* Glücksfall *m.* **godson** *n* Patensohn *m.*

goggles ['goglz] *pl n* Schutzbrille *f sing.*

gold [gould] *n* Gold *neut.* **golden** *adj* golden. **goldfish** *n* Goldfisch *m.* **gold leaf** *n* Blattgold *neut.* **gold mine** Goldgrube *f.* **gold-plated** *adj* vergoldet. **goldsmith** *n* goldschmied.

golf [golf] *n* Golf(spiel) *neut.* **golfclub** *n* Golfschläger *m.* **golf course** Golfplatz *m.* **golfer** *n* Golfspieler *m.*

gondola ['gondələ] *n* Gondel *f.*

gone [gon] *V* go.

gong [goŋ] *n* Gong *m.*

gonorrhoea [ˌgonə'riə] *n* (*med*) Gonorrhöe *f.*

good [gud] *adj* gut; (*pleasant*) angenehm; (*child*) brav. *n* Gute *neut,* Wohl *neut.* **good afternoon** guten Tag. **goodbye** *interj* auf Wiedersehen. **good evening** guten Abend. **good for nothing** nichts Wert. **good-for-nothing** *n* Taugenichts *m.* **good-looking** *adj* gut aussehend. **good morning** guten Morgen. **good night** gute Nacht. **do (someone) good** (jemanden) wohltun. **it's no good** es nützt nichts. **goodness** *n* Güte *f.* **goods** *pl n* Güter *pl.*

Good Friday *n* Karfreitag *m.*

goose [guːs] *n* (*pl* **geese**) Gans *f.*

gooseberry ['guzbəri] *n* Stachelbeere *f.* **play gooseberry** Anstandswauwau spielen.

gore [gɔː] *n* Blut *neut. v* aufspießen.

gorge [gɔːdʒ] *n* (*geog*) Schlucht *f. v* **gorge oneself** (*coll*) sich vollessen.

gorgeous ['gɔːdʒəs] *adj* Wunderschön, prachtvoll.

gorilla [gə'rilə] *n* Gorilla *m*.
gorse [gɔːs] *n* Stechginster *m*.
gory [gɔːri] *adj* blutig.
gospel ['gɔspəl] *n* Evangelium *neut*.
gossip ['gosip] *n* Geschwätz *neut*; (*person*) Klatschbase *f*. *v* schwätzen.
got [gɔt] *V* get.
Gothic ['goθik] *adj* gotisch.
gotten ['gotn] *V* get.
gouge [gaudʒ] *v* aushöhlen. *n* Hohleisen *neut*.
goulash ['guːlaʃ] *n* Gulasch *neut*.
gourd [guəd] *n* Kürbis *m*.
gourmet ['guəmei] *n* Feinschmecker *m*.
gout [gaut] *n* Gicht *f*. **gouty** gichtkrank, gichtisch.
govern ['gʌvən] *v* (*country*) regieren; (*determine*) bestimmen; (*tech*) regeln. **governess** *n* Gouvernante *f*. **government** *n* Regierung *f*. **governmental** *adj* Regierungs-. **governor** *n* Gouverneur *m*.
gown [gaun] *n* Kleid *neut*.
grab [grab] *v* ergreifen, (an)packen. *n* (plötzlicher) Griff *m*.
grace [greis] *n* Gnade *f*, Güte *f*; (*prayer*) Tischgebet *neut*. *14 days' grace* 14 Tage Aufschub. **Your Grace** Eure Hoheit. **graceful** *adj* anmutig. **gracious** *adj* angenehm, gnädig.
grade [greid] *n* Grad *m*, Stufe *f*; (*comm*) Qualität *f*; (*US*) (Schul)Klasse *f*; (*slope*) Gefälle *neut*. *v* sortieren, einordnen.
gradient ['greidiənt] *n* Gefälle *neut*.
gradual ['gradjuəl] *adj* stufenweise, allmählich.
graduate ['gradjuət; *v* 'gradjueit] *n* Graduierte(r); (*high school*) Absolvent(in). *v* abstufen; (*university*) promovieren. **graduation** *n*. Promovierung *f*; (*high school*) Absolvieren *neut*.
graffiti [grə'fiːtiː] *pl n* Graffiti *neut sing*.
graft¹ [graːft] *n* (*bot*) Pfropfreis *neut*; (*med*) Transplantat *neut*. *v* pfropfen; transplantieren.
graft² [graːft] *n* Korruption *f*.
grain [grein] *n* Getreide *neut*, Korn *neut*; (*sand, etc.*) Körnchen *neut*; (*wood*) *n* Maserung *f*. **grainy** *adj* körnig.
gram [gram] *n* Gramm *neut*.
grammar ['gramə] *n* Grammatik *f*. **grammatical** *adj* grammatisch. **grammar school** Gymnasium *neut*.
gramophone ['graməfoun] *n* Platten-

spieler *m*. **gramophone record** (Schall)Platte *f*.
granary ['granəri] *n* Kornkammer *f*.
grand [grand] *adj* groß, großartig. **grand piano** Flügel *m*. **grandeur** *n* Erhabenheit *f*.
grand-dad *n* also **grandpa** (*coll*) Opa *m*.
grand-daughter *n* Enkelin *f*.
grandfather ['gran,faːðə] *n* Großvater *m*.
grandma ['granmaː] *n* also **granny** (*coll*) Oma *f*.
grandmother ['gran,mʌðə] *n* Großmutter *f*.
grandparents ['gran,peərənts] *pl n* Großeltern *pl*.
grandson ['gransʌn] *n* Enkel *m*.
grandstand ['granstand] *n* Haupttribüne *f*.
grand total *n* Gesamtbetrag *m*.
granite ['granit] *n* Granit *m*.
grant [graːnt] *v* gewähren; (*admit*) zugestehen. *n* (*student*) Stipendium *neut*; (*subsidy*) Subvention *f*, Zuschuß *m*.
granule ['granjuːl] *n* Körnchen *neut*. **granular** *adj* körnig, granuliert.
grape [greip] *n* (Wein)Traube *f*. **grapevine** *n* Rebstock *m*.
grapefruit ['greipfruːt] *n* Grapefruit *neut*, Pampelmuse *f*.
graph [graf] *n* graphische Darstellung *f*, Schaubild *neut*.
grapple ['grapl] *v* sich auseinandersetzen (mit), ringen (mit).
grasp [graːsp] *v* greifen, packen; (*understand*) begreifen. *n* Griff *m*. **grasping** *adj* habgierig.
grass [graːs] *n* Gras *neut*; (*lawn*) Rasen *m*. *v* (*coll*) pfeifen.
grate¹ [greit] *n* (Feuer)Rost *m*, Gitter *neut*.
grate² [greit] *v* (*cookery*) reiben; (*teeth*) knirschen. **grate on one's nerves** auf die Nerven gehen.
grateful ['greitful] *adj* dankbar.
gratify ['grati,fai] *v* befriedigen. **gratification** *n* Befriedigung *f*. **gratitude** *n* Dankbarkeit *f*.
gratuity [grə'tjuəti] *n* Trinkgeld *neut*.
grave¹ [greiv] *n* Grab *neut*. **gravedigger** *n* Totengräber *m*. **gravestone** *n* Grabstein *m*. **graveyard** *n* Friedhof *f*.
grave² [greiv] *adj* ernsthaft, schwerwiegend.
gravel ['gravəl] *n* Kies *m*. **gravelpit** *n* Kiesgrube *f*.

gravity ['gravəti] *n* Schwerkraft *f; (seriousness)* Ernsthaftigkeit *f*, Ernst *m*.
gravy ['greivi] *n* (Braten)Soße *f*.
graze[1] [greiz] *n* (*med*) Abschürfung *f*. *v* abschürfen; (*touch*) leicht berühren.
graze[2] [greiz] *v* (*animal*) (ab)weiden. **grazing** *n* Weide *f*.
grease [griːs] *n* Fett *neut*, Schmalz *neut*; (*tech, mot*) Schmiere *f. v* schmieren.
great [greit] *adj* groß; (*important*) bedeutend; (*coll*) großartig, toll. **greatly** *adv* in hohem Maße. **great-grandparents** *pl n* Urgroßeltern *pl*. **greatness** *n* Größe *f*.
Great Britain *n* Großbritannien *neut*.
Greece [griːs] *n* Griechenland *neut*. **Greek** *adj* griechisch; *n* Grieche *m*, Griechin *f*.
greed [griːd] *n* Gier *f* (nach). **greedy** *adj* gierig.
green [griːn] *adj* grün. *n* Grün *neut*. **greenfly** *n* grüne Blattlaus *f*. **greengage** *n* Reineclaude *f*. **greengrocer's** *n* Obst- und Gemüseladen *m*. **greenhouse** *n* Treibhaus *neut*. **greens** *pl n* (*cookery*) Grünzeug *neut*.
Greenland ['griːnlənd] *n* Grönland *neut*. **Greenlander** *n* Grönlander *m*.
greet [griːt] *v* grüßen, begrüßen. **greeting** *n* Gruß *m*, Begrüßung *f*.
gregarious [gri'geəriəs] *adj* gesellig.
grenade [grə'neid] *n* Granate *f*.
grew [gruː] *V* **grow**.
grey [grei] *adj* grau; (*gloomy*) trübe. *n* Grau *neut*. **greyhound** *n* Windhund *m*.
grid [grid] *n* Gitter *neut*; (*network*) Netz *neut*.
grief [griːf] *n* Trauer *f*. **grievance** *n* Beschwerde *f*. **grieve** *v* trauern.
grill [gril] *v* grillen; (*question*) einem strengen Verhör unterziehen. *n* Bratrost *m*, Grill *m*.
grille [gril] *n* Gitter *neut*.
grim [grim] *adj* (*person*) grimmig, verbissen; (*prospect*) schlimm, hoffnungslos.
grimace [gri'meis] *n* Grimasse *f*. *v* Grimassen schneiden.
grime [graim] *n* Schmutz *m*, Ruß *m*.
grin [grin] *n* Lächeln *neut*, Grinsen *neut*. *v* lächeln, grinsen.
*grind [graind] *v* mahlen; (*knife*) schleifen; (*teeth*) knirschen. *n* (*coll*) Plackerei *f*. **grinder** *n* (*coffee, etc.*) Mühle *f*.
grip [grip] *v* (an)packen, festhalten. *n* Griff *m*.

gripe [graip] *v* zwicken. *n* Kolik *f*; Bauchschmerzen *pl*.
grisly ['grizli] *adj* gräßlich.
gristle ['grisl] *n* Knorpel *m*. **gristly** *adj* knorpelig.
grit [grit] *n* Splitt *m*; (*coll*) Mut *m*, Entschlossenheit *f*. **grit one's teeth** die Zähne zusammenbeißen.
groan [groun] *n* Stöhnen *neut*. *v* stöhnen.
grocer ['grousə] *n* Lebensmittelhändler *m*. **grocer's shop** Lebensmittelgeschäft *neut*. **groceries** *pl n* Lebensmittel *pl*.
groin [groin] *n* (*anat*) Leistengegend *f*.
groom [gruːm] *n* (*of bride*) Bräutigam *m*; (*for horse*) (Pferde)Knecht *m*. *v* pflegen. **well groomed** gepflegt.
groove [gruːv] *n* Rinne *f*, Furche *f*.
grope [group] *v* tasten (nach). **gropingly** *adv* tastend, vorsichtig.
gross [grous] *adj* grob; (*comm*) Brutto-; (*fat*) dick. *n* Gros *neut*. **Gross National Product** (**GNP**) Bruttosozialprodukt *neut*. **gross weight** Bruttogewicht *n*.
grotesque [grə'tesk] *adj* grotesk.
grotto ['grotou] *n* Grotte *f*.
ground[1] [graund] *V* **grind**.
ground[2] [graund] *n* Boden *m*, Erde *f. v* (*aero*) still legen. **ground floor** Erdgeschoß *neut*. **grounds** *pl* (*of house*) Anlagen *pl*; (*coffee*) Bodensatz *m*; (*reason*) Grund *m*.
group [gruːp] *n* Gruppe *f. v* gruppieren.
grouse[1] [graus] *n* Birkhuhn *neut*.
grouse[2] [graus] *v* (*coll: grumble*) meckern. *n* Beschwerde *f*.
grove [grouv] *n* Hain *m*.
grovel ['grovl] *v* kriechen (vor). **grovelling** *adj* kriecherisch.
*grow [grou] *v* wachsen; (*become*) werden; (*plants*) züchten. **grow better** sich bessern. **grow old** alt werden. **grow out of** (*clothes*) herauswachsen aus; (*habit*) entwachsen (+ *dat*); (*arise from*) entstehen aus. **grow up** heranwachsen. **grower** *n* Züchter *m*. **growing** *adj* wachsend.
growth *n* Wachstum *neut*; (*increase*) Zunahme *f*; (*med*) Gewächs *neut*.
grown [groun] *V* **grow**. *adj* erwachsen. **grown-up** Erwachsene(r).
grub [grʌb] *n* Made *f*; (*slang: food*) Futter *neut*. **grubby** *adj* schmutzig, dreckig.
grudge [grʌdʒ] *v* mißgönnen. *n* Mißgunst *f*.

gruelling ['gruəlɪŋ] *adj* mörderisch.
gruesome ['gruːsəm] *adj* grausam.
gruff [grʌf] *adj* barsch.
grumble ['grʌmbl] *v* schimpfen, murren. *n* Murren *neut.*
grumpy ['grʌmpi] *adj* mürrisch.
grunt [grʌnt] *n* Grunzen *neut. v* grunzen.
guarantee [garən'tiː] *n* Garantie *f*, Gewährleistung *f. v* garantieren, gewährleisten. **guarantor** *n* Gewährsmann *m.*
guard [gaːd] *n* Wächter *m*, Wache *f. v* (be)schützen, bewachen. **guard against** sich hüten vor. **on one's guard** auf der Hut. **guard of honour** Ehrenwache *f.*
guerrilla [gə'rɪlə] *n* Guerillakämpfer *m.* **guerilla warfare** Guerillakrieg *m.*
guess [ges] *n* Schätzung *f*, Vermutung *f. v* schätzen, vermuten. **guesswork** *n* Mutmaßung *f.*
guest [gest] *n* Gast *m.* **guest house** Pension *f.* **guestroom** Fremdenzimmer *neut.*
guide [gaɪd] *n* Führer *m*; (*book*) Handbuch *neut. v* führen, leiten. **guide book** Reiseführer *m.*
guild [gɪld] *n* Gilde *f*, Vereinigung *f.*
guillotine ['gɪlətiːn] *n* Guillotine *f*; (*for paper*) Papierschneidemaschine *f. v* guillotinieren.
guilt [gɪlt] *n* Schuld *f*; (*feeling of*) Schuldgefühl *neut.* **guilty** *adj* schuldig. **guilty conscience** schlechtes Gewissen *neut.* **find guilty** für schuldig erklären.
guinea pig ['gɪni] *n* Guinee *f.* **guinea pig** Meerschweinchen *neut*; (*fig: in experiment*) Versuchskaninchen *neut.*
guitar [gɪ'taː] *n* Gitarre *f.* **guitar player** Gitarrenspieler(in).
gulf [gʌlf] *n* Golf *m.*
gull [gʌl] *n* Möwe *f.*
gullet ['gʌlɪt] *n* Schlund *m.*
gullible ['gʌləbl] *adj* naiv, leichtgläubig. **gullibility** *n* Leichtgläubigkeit *f.*
gully ['gʌli] *n* Rinne *f.*
gulp [gʌlp] *v* hinunterschlucken. *n* Schluck *m.*
gum¹ [gʌm] *n* (*glue*) Klebstoff *m*; (*from tree*) Gummi *neut*; (*sweet*) Gummibonbon *neut.* **chewing gum** Kaugummi *neut. v* kleben.
gum² [gʌm] *n* (*in mouth*) Zahnfleisch *neut.*
gun [gʌn] *n* Gewehr *neut*; (*hand gun*) Pistole *f*; (*large*) Kanone *f.* **stick to one's guns** nicht nachgeben. *v* **gun down** erschießen.
gurgle ['gəːgl] *n* Gurgeln *neut. v* gurgeln.

gush [gʌʃ] *v* hervorquellen, entströmen. *n* Strom *m*, Guß *m.* **gushing** *adj* überschwenglich.
gust [gʌst] *n* Bö *neut. v* blasen.
gusto ['gʌstou] *n* Schwung *m.* **with gusto** eifrig.
gut [gʌt] *n* Darm *m.* **guts** *pl* Eingeweide *pl*; (*coll*) Mut *m.*
gutter ['gʌtə] *n* (*roof*) Dachrinne; (*street*) Gosse *f.* **gutter press** Schmutzpresse *f.*
guy¹ [gai] (*coll*) *n* Kerl *m.*
guy² [gai] *n* Halteseil *neut.* **guy-rope** *n* Spannschnur *f.*
gymnasium [dʒim'neiziəm] *n* Turnhalle *f.* **gymnast** *n* Turner(in). **gymnastic** *adj* gymnastisch. **gymnastics** *n* Gymnastik *f.*
gynaecology [gainə'kolədʒi] *n* Frauenheilkunde *f*, Gynäkologie *f.* **gynaecologist** *n* Frauenarzt *m*, Gynäkologe *m.* **gynaecological** *adj* gynäkologisch.
gypsum ['dʒipsəm] *n* Gips *m.*
gyrate [,dʒai'reit] *v* wirbeln.
gyroscope ['dʒairə,skoup] *n* Giroskop *neut.*

H

haberdasher ['habədaʃə] *n* Kurzwarenhändler *m.* **haberdashery** *n* Kurzwaren *pl.*
habit ['habit] *n* Gewohnheit *f.* **be in the habit of** gewöhnt sein. **habitual** *adj* gewohnt, üblich.
habitable ['habitəbl] *adj* bewohnbar. **habitat** *n* Heimat *f.* **habitation** *n* Wohnung *f.* **unfit for human habitation** für Wohnzwecke ungeeignet.
hack¹ [hak] *v* (zer)hacken. **hacksaw** *n* Metallsäge *f.*
hack² [hak] *n* (*horse*) Mietpferd *neut*, Gaul *m*; (*writer*) Lohnschreiber *m.*
hackneyed ['haknid] *adj* abgedroschen, banal.
had [had] *V* **have**.
haddock ['hadək] *n* Schellfisch *m.*
haemorrhage ['heməridʒ] *n* Blutung *f*, Blutsturz *m. v* bluten.
haemorrhoids ['heməroidz] *pl n* Hämorrhoiden *pl.*

haggard ['hagəd] *adj* hager, verstört.
haggle ['hagl] *v* feilschen.
Hague [heig] *n* Den Haag *m.*
hail[1] [heil] *n* Hagel *m. v* hageln. **hailstone** *n* Hagelkorn *neut.* **hailstorm** *n* Hagelschauer *m.*
hail[2] [heil] *v* (*greet*) begrüßen; (*call up*) zurufen. **hail from** herkommen von.
hair [heə] *n* (*single*) Haar *neut*; (*person's*) Haar *neut*, Haare *pl.* **hairy** *adj* behaart, haarig.
hairbrush ['heəbrʌʃ] *n* Haarbürste *f.*
haircut ['heəkʌt] *n* Haarschnitt *m.* **have a haircut** sich die Haare schneiden lassen.
hair-do *n* Frisur *f.*
hairdresser ['heə,dresə] *n* Friseur *m,* Friseuse *f.*
hair-dryer ['heə,draiə] *n* Haartrockner *m.*
hair-net *n* Haarnetz *neut.*
hairpin ['heəpin] *n* Haarnadel *f.*
hair-raising ['heə,reiziŋ] *adj* aufregend.
hake [heik] *n* Seehecht *m.*
half [haːf] *n* Hälfte *f. adj* halb. *adv* halb, zur Hälfte; (*almost*) beinahe. **at half price** zum halben Preis.
half-and-half *adv* halb-und-halb.
half-back ['haːfbak] *n* Läufer *m.*
half-baked [,haːf'beikt] *adj* (*idea*) halbfertig, nicht durchgedacht.
half-breed ['haːfbriːd] *n* Mischling *m.*
half-brother ['haːfbrʌðə] *n* Halbbruder *m.*
half-hearted [,haːf'haːtid] *adj* gleichgültig, lustlos.
half-hour [,haːf'auə] *n* halbe Stunde *f.* **half-hourly** *adv* jede halbe Stunde.
half-mast [,haːf'maːst] *n* **at half-mast** halbmast.
half-sister ['haːfsistə] *n* Halbschwester *f.*
half-term [,haːf'təːm] *n* Semesterhalbzeit *f.*
half-time [,haːf'taim] *n* Halbzeit *f.*
halfway [,haːf'wei] *adv* in der Mitte, halbwegs.
halfwit ['haːfwit] *n* Schwachkopf *m.* **half-witted** *adj* dumm, blöd.
halibut ['halibət] *n* Heilbutt *m.*
hall [hoːl] *n* Halle *f*, Saal *m*; (*entrance*) Diele *f*, Flur *m.* **hall of residence** Studentenheim *neut.* **hall porter** Hotelportier *m.*
hallmark ['hoːlmaːk] *n* Feingehaltsstempel *m*; (*characteristic*) Kennzeichen *neut.*
hallowed ['haloud] *adj* verehrt.
Hallowe'en [halou'iːn] *n* Abend vor Allerheiligen *m.*

hallucinate [hə'luːsineit] *v* halluzinieren. **hallucination** *n* Halluzination *f.*
halo ['heilou] *n* Glorienschein *m.*
halt [hoːlt] *n* Halt *m*, Pause *f*; (*railway*) Haltestelle *f. v* Pause machen; (*put a stop to*) halten lassen.
halter ['hoːltə] *n* Halfter *f.*
halve [haːv] *v* halbieren; (*reduce*) auf die Hälfte reduzieren.
ham [ham] *n* Schinken *m.* (**radio**) **ham** Radio-amateur *m.*
hamburger ['hambəːgə] *n* Frikadelle *f.*
hamlet 'hamlit] *n* Dörfchen *neut.*
hammer ['hamə] *n* Hammer *m. v* hämmern. **hammer and tongs** (*coll*) mit aller Kraft.
hammock ['hamək] *n* Hängematte *f.*
hamper[1] ['hampə] *v* behindern, hemmen.
hamper[2] ['hampə] *n* Packkorb *m*, Eßkorb *m.*
hamster ['hamstə] *n* Hamster *m.*
hamstring ['hamstriŋ] *n* Knieflechse *f. v* (*coll*) lähmen.
hand [hand] *n* Hand *f*; (*of clock*) Zeiger *m. v* (*give*) geben. **at** *or* **to hand** zur Hand. **hand in** einreichen. **hand out** austeilen. **hand over** übergeben. **in hand** im Gange. **on the one hand ... on the other hand ...** einerseits ... andererseits ....
handbag ['handbag] *n* Handtasche *f.*
handbook ['handbuk] *n* Handbuch *neut*; (*travel*) Reiseführer *m.*
handbrake ['handbreik] *n* Handbremse *f.*
handcream ['handkriːm] *n* Handcreme *f.*
handcuff ['handkʌf] *v* Handschellen anlegen (+*dat*). **handcuffs** *pl n* Handschellen *pl.*
handful ['handful] *n* Handvoll *f.*
handicap ['handikap] *n* Behinderung *f*; (*sport*) Handikap *neut. v* (*horse*) extra belasten; (*person*) hemmen, **handicapped** *adj* (*med, etc.*) behindert.
handicraft ['handikraːft] *n* Handwerk *neut.*
handiwork ['handiwəːk] *n* Handarbeit *f.*
handkerchief ['haŋkətʃif] *n* Taschentuch *neut.*
handle ['handl] *n* Griff *m*; (*door*) (Tür)Klinke *f. v* anfassen, handhaben; (*deal with*) behandeln, sich befassen mit. **handlebar** *n* Lenkstange *f.* **handling** *n* Behandlung *f.*
handmade [,hand'meid] *adj* mit der Hand gemacht.

hand-out ['handaut] *n* Almosen *neut*; (*leaflet*) Prospekt *m*, Werbezettel *m*.
hand-pick [hand'pik] *v* (sorgfältig) auswählen.
handrail ['handreil] *n* Geländer *neut*.
handshake ['handʃeik] *n* Händedruck *m*.
handsome ['hansəm] *adj* schön, stattlich.
handstand ['hand‚stand] *n* Handstand *m*.
hand-towel *n* Handtuch *neut*.
handwriting ['hand‚raitiŋ] *n* (Hand)Schrift *f*.
handy ['handi] *adj* greifbar, zur Hand; (*adroit*) geschickt, gewandt.
*hang [haŋ] *v* hängen; (*person*) erhängen. *n* (*of a dress*) Sitz *m*. **to get the hang of** beherrschen, begreifen. **hang on** (*phone*) am Apparat bleiben. **hang up** (*phone*) auflegen; (*picture, coat*) aufhängen.
hangar ['haŋə] *n* Flugzeughalle *f*.
hanger ['haŋə] *n* (*for clothes*) Kleiderbügel *m*.
hangover ['haŋouvə] *n* (*coll*) Kater *m*.
hanker ['haŋkə] *v* sich sehnen (nach). **hankering** *n* Verlangen *neut*.
haphazard [‚hap'hazəd] *adj* zufällig.
happen ['hapən] *v* geschehen, vorkommen. **happen upon** finden. **happen along** erscheinen. **happening** *n* Ereignis *neut*.
happy ['hapi] *adj* glücklich, zufrieden. **happy-go-lucky** *adj* sorglos. **happiness** *n* Glück *neut*, Glückseligkeit *f*.
harass ['harəs] *v* quälen, aufreiben.
harbour ['haɪbə] *n* Hafen *m*. *v* (*protect*) beherbergen.
hard [haɪd] *adj* hart; (*difficult*) schwer, schwierig; (*callous*) gefühllos. **hard-boiled** *adj* hartgekocht; (*coll*) hartnäckig. **hard-pressed** *adj* in schwerer Bedrängnis. **hard up** (*coll*) schlecht bei Kasse. **hard-of-hearing** *adj* schwerhörig.
harden ['haɪdn] *v* härten, hart machen; (*become hard*) hart werden.
hardly ['haɪdli] *adj* kaum. **hardly ever** fast nie.
hardware ['haɪdweə] *n* Eisenwaren *pl*; (*computers*) Hardware *f*.
hardy ['haɪdi] *adj* kräftig, abgehärtet; (*plant*) winterfest.
hare [heə] *n* Hase *m*.
haricot ['harikou] *n* weiße Bohne *f*.
hark [haɪk] *v* horchen. *interj* hör mal!
harm [haɪm] *v* schaden (+ *dat*), verletzen. *n* Schaden *m*, Leid *neut*. **harmful** *adj* schädlich. **harmfulness** *n* Schädlichkeit *f*.

harmless *adj* harmlos. **harmlessness** *n* Harmlosigkeit *f*.
harmonic [haɪ'monik] *adj* harmonisch.
harmonica [haɪ'monikə] *n* Mundharmonika *f*.
harmonious [haɪ'mouniəs] *adj* harmonisch, wohlklingend.
harmonize ['haɪmənaiz] *v* harmonisieren. **harmonization** *n* Harmonisierung *f*.
harmony ['haɪməni] *n* Harmonie *f*; (*agreement*) Einklang *m*, Übereinstimmung *f*.
harness ['haɪnis] *n* (Pferde)Geschirr *neut*. *v* spannen; (*fig*) nutzbar machen.
harp [haɪp] *n* Harfe *f*. *v* **harp on** (*coll*) dauernd reden von.
harpoon [haɪ'puɪn] *n* Harpune *f*. *v* harpunieren.
harpsichord ['haɪpsi‚koɪd] *n* Cembalo *neut*.
harrowing ['harouiŋ] *adj* qualvoll, schrecklich.
harsh [haɪʃ] *adj* hart; (*voice*) rauh; (*strict*) streng. **harshness** *n* Strenge *f*, Härte *f*.
harvest ['haɪvist] *n* Ernte *f*. (*time*) Erntezeit *f*. *v* ernten, einbringen. **harvester** *n* (*mech*) Mähdrescher *f*. **Harvest Festival** Erntedankfest *neut*.
hash [haʃ] *n* Haschee *neut*. **make a hash of** (*coll*) verpfuschen.
hashish ['haʃiːʃ] *n* Haschisch *neut*.
haste [heist] *n* Eile *f*. **make haste** sich beeilen. **hasten** *v* sich beeilen; beschleunigen. **hasty** *adj* eilig; (*rushed*) übereilt. **hastiness** Voreiligkeit *f*.
hat [hat] *n* Hut *m*. **eat one's hat** einen Besen fressen. **keep under one's hat** für sich halten.
hatch[1] [hatʃ] *v* ausbrüten. **hatch a plot** ein Komplott schmieden.
hatch[2] [hatʃ] *n* (*naut*) Luke *f*; (*serving*) Servierfenster *neut*.
hatchet ['hatʃit] *n* Beil *neut*. **bury the hatchet** das Kriegsbeil begraben.
hate [heit] *v* hassen, verabscheuen. *n also* **hatred** Haß *m*, Abscheu *m*. **hateful** *adj* hassenswert.
haughty ['hoɪti] *adj* hochmutig. **haughtiness** *n* Hochmut *m*.
haul [hoɪl] *v* ziehen, schleppen. *n* (*coll: booty*) Fang *m*. **haulage** *n* Transport *m*, Spedition *f*. **haulier** *n* Transportunternehmer *m*, Spediteur *m*.
haunch [hoɪntʃ] *n* Hüfte *f*; (*of animal*) Keule *f*, Lende *f*.

haunt [hɔɪnt] *v* (*ghost*) spuken in. **haunted** *adj* gespenstig.
***have** [hav] *v* haben. *I have to go* ich muß gehen. *I will have it repaired* ich werde es reparieren lassen. *I have got a car* ich habe ein Auto. *he's had it* es ist aus mit ihm. **be had** (*be cheated*) reingelegt sein. **have a tooth out** sich einen Zahn ziehen lassen. **have it out with** sich auseinandersetzen mit.
haven ['heivn] *n* Hafen *m*; (*fig*) Asyl *neut*.
havoc ['havək] *n* Verheerung *f*. **play havoc with** verheeren.
hawk [hɔːk] *n* Habicht *m*, Falke *m*.
hawthorn ['hɔːθɔːn] *n* Hagedorn *m*.
hay [hei] *n* Heu *neut*. **make hay** Heu machen, heuen. **hay fever** Heuschnupfen *m*. **haystack** *n* Heuschober *m*.
haywire ['heiwaiə] *adj* (*coll*) kaputt. **go haywire** kaputtgehen.
hazard ['hazəd] *n* (*danger*) Gefahr *f*; (*risk*) Risiko *neut*; (*chance*) Zufall *m*; (*golf*) Hindernis *neut*. *v* aufs Spiel setzen, wagen. **hazardous** *adj* gefährlich, riskant.
haze [heiz] *n* Dunst *m*, leichter Nebel *m*; (*fig*) Verschwommenheit *f*. **hazy** *adj* dunstig; verschwommen.
hazel ['heizl] *n* Haselstrauch *m*. *adj* (*colour*) nußbraun. **hazelnut** *n* Haselnuß *f*.
he [hiː] *pron* er.
head [hed] *n* Kopf *m*; (*leader*) Leiter *m*; (*top*) Spitze *f*. *v* leiten, führen. **head for** zugehen nach. **head off** umlenken. **per head** pro Kopf. **by a head** um eine Kopflänge *f*.
headache ['hedeik] *n* Kopfweh *neut*, Kopfschmerzen *pl*.
headfirst [ˌhed'fɔɪst] *adj* kopfüber.
heading ['hediŋ] *n* Titel *m*, Überschrift *f*.
headlamp ['hedlamp] *n* Scheinwerfer *m*.
headland ['hedlənd] *n* Landzunge *f*, Landspitze *f*.
headline ['hedlain] *n* Schlagzeile *f*.
headlong ['hedlɒŋ] *adv* kopfüber; ungestüm, blindlings.
headmaster [ˌhed'maɪstə] *n* (Schul)Direktor *n*. **headmistress** *n* Direktorin *f*, Vorsteherin *f*.
head office *n* Hauptsitz *m*.
headphones ['hedfounz] *pl n* Kopfhörer *m sing*.
headquarters [ˌhed'kwɔɪtəz] *n* (*mil*) Hauptquartier *neut*; (*comm*) Hauptsitz *m*.
headrest ['hedrest] *n* Kopfstütze *f*.

headscarf ['hedskaɪf] *n* Kopftuch *neut*.
headstrong ['hedstrɒŋ] *adj* eigensinnig.
head waiter *n* Ober(kellner) *m*.
headway ['hedwei] *n* Fortschritte *pl*. **make headway** vorankommen, Fortschritte machen.
heal [hiːl] *v* heilen. **healer** *n* Heiler *m*.
healing *n* Heilung *f*. *adj* heilend, heilsam.
health [helθ] *n* Gesundheit *f*. **your health!** zum Wohl! **health insurance** Krankenversicherung *f*. **health resort** Kurort *m*. **healthy** *adj* gesund.
heap [hiːp] *n* Haufe(n) *m*. *v* häufen. **heaps better** (*coll*) viel besser. **heap up** anhäufen.
***hear** [hiə] *v* hören; (*listen*) zuhören.
hearing *n* Gehör *neut*; (*law*) Verhör *neut*. **hearing aid** Hörgerät *neut*. **hearsay** *n* Hörensagen *neut*. **preliminary hearing** Voruntersuchung *f*.
heard [hɔɪd] *V* hear.
hearse [hɔɪs] *n* Leichenwagen *m*.
heart [haɪt] *n* Herz *neut*. **change of heart** Gesinningswechsel *m*.
heart attack *n* Herzanfall *m*.
heartbeat ['haɪtbiɪt] *n* Herzschlag *m*.
heart-breaking ['haɪtbreikiŋ] *adj* herzzerbrechend. **heart-broken** *adj* untröstlich.
heartburn ['haɪtbɔɪn] *n* Sodbrennen *neut*.
heart failure *n* Herzschlag *m*.
heartfelt ['haɪtfelt] *adj* tiefempfunden.
hearth [haɪθ] *n* Kamin *m*.
hearty ['haɪti] *adj* herzlich. **heartily** *adv* herzlich, von Herzen.
heat [hiːt] *n* Hitze *f*, Wärme *f*; (*sport*) Vorlauf *m*. **in the heat of passion** (*law*) im Affekt. *v* hitzen. **heated** *adj* (*fig*) erregt. **heating** *n* Heizung *f*. **heatproof** *adj* hitzebeständig. **heat-stroke** *n* Hitzschlag *m*. **heatwave** *n* Hitzewelle *f*.
heath [hiːθ] *n* Heide *f*.
heathen ['hiːðn] *n* Heide *m*. *adj* heidnisch, unzivilisiert.
heather ['heðə] *n* Heidekraut *neut*.
heave [hiːv] *v* hieven; hochheben; (*sigh*) ausstoßen; (*anchor*) lichten. *n* Heben *neut*.
heaven ['hevn] *n* Himmel *m*. **go to heaven** in den Himmel kommen. **to move heaven and earth** (*fig*) Himmel und Erde in Bewegung setzen. **for heaven's sake** um Himmels Willen. **heavenly** *adj* himmlisch. **heavenly body** Himmelskörper *m*.

heavy ['hevi] *adj* schwer, schwerwiegend; (*mood*) träge; (*book*) langweilig. **heaviness** *n* Schwere *f*; (*mood*) Schwerfälligkeit *f*. **heavy-duty** *adj* Hochleistungs-. **heavyweight** *n* (*sport*) Schwergewichtler *m*.

Hebrew ['hiːbruː] *n* Hebräer *m*. *adj* hebräisch.

heckle ['hekl] *v* durch Fragen belästigen. **heckler** *n* Zwischenrufer *m*.

hectare ['hektaː] *n* Hektar *neut*.

hectic ['hektik] *adj* hektisch.

hedge [hedʒ] *n* Hecke *f*, Heckenzaun *m*. **hedgerow** *n* Hecke *f*.

hedgehog ['hedʒhog] *n* Igel *m*.

heed [hiːd] *v* achtgeben auf. *n* Beachtung. **heedful** *adj* achtsam. **heedless** *adj* achtlos.

heel [hiːl] *n* Ferse *f*; (*of shoe*) Absatz *m*. *v* (*shoes*) mit Absätzen versehen. **take to one's heels** die Beine in die Hand nehmen. **down-at-heel** (*fig*) schäbig. **well-heeled** *adj* wohlhabend.

hefty ['hefti] *adj* kräftig.

heifer ['hefə] *n* Färse *f*.

height [hait] *n* Höhe *f*; (*person*) Größe *f*; (*fig*) Höhepunkt *m*. **heighten** *v* verstärken.

heir [eə] *n* Erbe *m*. **heiress** *n* Erbin *f*. **heirloom** *n* Erbstück *neut*.

held [held] *V* **hold**[1]

helicopter ['helikoptə] *n* Hubschrauber *m*.

hell [hel] *n* Hölle *f*. *interj* zum Teufel! **to hell with** zum Teufel mit. **hellish** *adj* höllisch.

hello [hə'lou] *interj* Guten Tag; (*on telephone*) hallo!

helm [helm] *n* Steuer *neut*, Ruder *neut*. **helmsman** *n* Steuermann *m*.

helmet ['helmit] *n* Helm *m*.

help [help] *v* helfen (+ *dat*). *n* Hilfe *f*. **I can't help it** ich kann nichts dafür, ich kann nicht anders. *help yourself* bedienen Sie Sich! **helper** *n* Helfer(in). **helpful** *adj* hilfreich. **helping** *n* Portion *f*. **helpless** *adj* hilflos.

hem [hem] *n* Saum *m*. *v* säumen. **hem in** einengen.

hemisphere ['hemiˌsfiə] *n* Halbkugel *f*, Hemisphäre *f*.

hemp [hemp] *n* Hanf *m*.

hen [hen] *n* Huhn *neut*.

hence [hens] *adv* von hier; (*therefore*) deshalb, daher. *a week hence* in einer Woche. **henceforth** fortan, von jetzt an.

henna ['henə] *n* Henna *f*.

henpecked ['henpekt] *adj* **henpecked husband** Pantoffelheld *m*.

her [həː] *pron* (*acc*) sie; (*dat*) ihr. *poss adj* ihr.

herald ['herəld] *n* Herold *m*. *v* (*fig*) einleiten. **heraldic** *adj* heraldisch, Wappen-. **heraldry** *n* Heraldik *f*, Wappenkunde *f*.

herb [həːb] *n* Kraut *n*. **herbal** *adj* Kräuter-. **herbalist** *n* Kräuterkenner(in).

herd [həːd] *n* Herde *f*. *v* hüten, zusammentreiben.

here [hiə] *adv* hier; (*to here*) hierher. **hereafter** *adv* in Zukunft. **herewith** *adv* hiermit.

hereditary [hi'redətəri] *adj* erblich. **heredity** *n* Vererbung *f*, Erblichkeit *f*.

heresy ['herəsi] *n* Ketzerei *f*. **heretic** *n* Ketzer(in). **heretical** *adj* Ketzerisch.

heritage ['heritidʒ] *n* Erbe *neut*, Erbgut *neut*.

hermit ['həːmit] *n* Eremit *m*. **hermitage** *n* Klause *f*.

hernia ['həːniə] *n* Bruch *m*.

hero ['hiərou] *n* Held *m*. **heroine** *n* Heldin *f*. **heroic** *adj* heroisch, heldenmutig. **heroism** *n* Heldentum *neut*.

heron ['herən] *n* Reiher *m*.

herring ['heriŋ] *n* Hering *m*. **herringbone** *n* (*pattern*) Fischgrätenmuster *neut*. **pickled herring** Rollmops *m*.

hers [həːz] *poss pron* ihrer *m*, ihre *f*, ihres *neut*. **herself** *pron* (*reflexive*) sich; selbst. **by herself** allein.

hesitate ['heziteit] *v* zögern. **hesitant** *adj* zögernd. **hesitation** *n* Zögern *neut*, Bedenken *neut*.

heterosexual [hetərə'sekʃuəl] *adj* heterosexuell.

***hew** [hjuː] *v* hauen.

hewn [hjuːn] *V* **hew**.

hexagon ['heksəgən] *n* Sechseck *neut*.

heyday ['heidei] *n* Höhepunkt *m*, Blütezeit *f*.

hiatus [hai'eitəs] *n* Lücke *f*.

hibernate ['haibəneit] *v* Winterschlafhalten. **hibernation** *n* Winterschlaf *m*.

hiccup ['hikʌp] *n* Schluckauf *m*, Schlucken *m*. *v* den Schluckauf haben.

hid [hid] *V* **hide**[1].

hidden ['hidn] V **hide**[1].
***hide**[1] [haid] v (*conceal*) verstecken, verbergen; (*keep secret*) verheimlichen.
hide[2] [haid] n (*skin*) Fell *neut*, Haut *f*.
hideous ['hidiəs] *adj* abscheulich, schrecklich.
hiding[1] ['haidiŋ] n Versteck *neut*. **be in hiding** sich versteckt halten.
hiding[2] ['haidiŋ] n (*thrashing*) Prügel *neut*.
hierarchy ['haiəraɪki] n Hierarchie *f*, Rangordnung *f*. **hierarchical** *adj* hierarchisch.
high [hai] *adj* hoch; (*wind*) stark.
highbrow ['haibrau] *adj* intellektuell. n Intellektuelle(r).
hi-fi ['haifai] *adj* hi-fi. n Hi-Fi.
high frequency n Hochfrequenz *f*.
high jump n Hochsprung *m*.
highland ['hailənd] n Bergland *neut*.
highlight ['hailait] n Höhepunkt *m*.
highly ['haili] *adv* höchst, in hohem Grad, stark. **highly strung** überempfindlich.
highness ['hainis] n Höhe *f*. **Your Highness** Eure Hoheit.
highpitched [,hai'pitʃt] *adj* hoch.
high point n Höhepunkt *m*.
high-rise building n Hochhaus *neut*.
high-spirited *adj* lebhaft, temperamentvoll.
high street n Hauptstraße *f*.
high tide n Hochwasser *neut*.
highway ['haiwei] n Landstraße *f*.
hijack ['haidʒak] v (*aeroplane*) entführen. n Entführung *f*. **hijacker** n Entführer *m*, Hijacker *m*.
hike [haik] v wandern. n Wanderung *f*. **hiker** n Wanderer *m*.
hilarious [hi'leəriəs] *adj* lustig. **hilarity** n Lustigkeit *f*.
hill [hil] n Hügel *m*, Berg *m*. **hillside** n Hang *m*. **hilltop** n Bergspitze *f*.
him [him] *pron* (*acc*) ihn; (*dat*) ihm. **himself** *pron* (*reflexive*) sich; selbst. **by himself** allein.
hind [haind] *adj* hinter, Hinter-. **hindsight** n **with hindsight** im Rückblick.
hinder ['hində] v (ver)hindern. **hindrance** n Hindernis *neut*, Hinderung *f*.
Hindu [hin'duː] n Hindu *m*. *adj* Hindu-.
hinge [hindʒ] n Scharnier *neut*, Gelenk *neut*. **to hinge on** abhängen (von).
hint [hint] n Wink *m*. v andeuten.
hip [hip] n Hüfte *f*. **hip-bone** n Hüftbein *neut*. **hip-joint** n Hüftgelenk *neut*.

hippopotamus [hipə'potəməs] n Nilpferd *neut*.
hire [haiə] v (ver)mieten; (*staff*) anstellen. n Miete *f*. **hire-car** n Mietwagen *m*. **hire purchase** Ratenkauf *m*. **hire-purchase agreement** Teilzahlungsvertrag *m*.
his [hiz] *poss adj* sein. *poss pron* seiner *m*, seine *f*, seines *neut*.
hiss [his] v zischen. n Zischen *neut*.
history ['histəri] n Geschichte *f*. **history book** Geschichtsbuch *neut*. **historian** n Historiker(in). **historic** *adj* historisch. **historical** *adj* historisch, geschichtlich.
***hit** [hit] v schlagen, stoßen. n Schlag *m*, Stoß *m*; (*record*) Schlager *m*. **make a hit** (*fig*) Erfolg haben. **hard hit** schwer getroffen. **hit upon** zufällig finden.
hitch [hitʃ] v befestigen; (*horse*) anspannen. n (*problem*) Haken *m*. **hitchhike** v per Anhalter fahren.
hitherto [,hiðə'tuː] *adv* bisher.
hive [haiv] n Bienenkorb *m*. v **hive off** abzweigen.
hoard [hoːd] n Schatz *m*, Hort *m*. v sammeln, hamstern.
hoarding ['hoːdiŋ] n Reklamewand *f*.
hoarse [hoːs] *adj* rauh, heiser.
hoax [houks] n Falschmeldung *f*. v zum Besten haben.
hobble ['hobl] v hinken, hoppeln; (*horse*) fesseln.
hobby ['hobi] n Hobby *neut*. **hobby horse** n Steckenpferd *neut*.
hock[1] [hok] n (*joint*) Sprunggelenk *neut*.
hock[2] [hok] n (*wine*) Rheinwein *m*.
hockey ['hoki] n Hockey *neut*.
hoe [hou] n Hacke *f*. v hacken.
hog [hog] n (Schlacht)Schwein *neut*; (*coll*) Vielfraß *m*. **go the whole hog** aufs Ganze gehen.
hoist [hoist] v hochziehen. n Aufzug *m*, Kran *m*.
***hold**[1] [hould] v halten; (*contain*) enthalten. n Halt *m*, Griff *m*; (*fig*) Einfluß *m*. **hold back** zurückhalten. **hold down** (*job*) behalten. **hold up** (*delay*) aufhalten; (*rob*) überfallen. **hold-up** n (*traffic*) Stockung *f*; (*robbery*) Überfall *m*.
hold[2] [hould] n (*naut*) Frachtraum *m*, Schiffsraum *m*.
holder ['houldə] n (*owner*) Inhaber *m*.
holding ['houldiŋ] n (*land*) Grundbesitz *m*, Guthaben *neut*. **holding company** Dachgesellschaft *f*.

hole [houl] *n* Loch *neut.*
holiday ['holədi] *n* Feiertag *m*, Ruhetag *m.* **holidays** *pl* Ferien *pl*, Urlaub *m sing.* **go on holiday** verreisen, in die Ferien gehen, auf Urlaub gehen. **holidaymaker** *n* Feriengast *m*, Urlauber(in).
Holland ['holənd] *n* Holland *neut*, die Niederlände *pl.*
hollow ['holou] *n* Höhle *f*, Loch *neut. adj* hohl, leer. *v* (aus)höhlen. **hollowness** *n* Hohlheit *f*, Leerheit *f.*
holly ['holi] *n* Steckpalme *f.*
holster ['houlstə] *n* Pistolenhalfter *f.*
holy ['houli] *adj* heilig.
homage ['homidʒ] *n* Huldigung *f.* **do or pay homage** huldigen.
home [houm] *n* Heim *neut*, Haus *neut*, Zuhause *neut*; (*institution*) Heim *neut.* **at home** zu Hause. **at home with** vertraut mit. *make yourself at home* mach dich bequem. *go home* nach Hause gehen. **hammer home** (*nail*) fest einschlagen. *adj* häuslich; (*national*) inner, Innen-. **home affairs** innere Angelegenheiten *pl.* **home market** Binnenmarkt *m.* **homecoming** *n* Heimkehr *f.* **homeland** *n* Heimat *f*, Vaterland *neut.* **homeless** *adj* obdachlos. **homely** *adj* heimisch, gemütlich. **be homesick** Heimweh haben. **homesickness** *n* Heimweh *neut.* **homeward** *adj* Heim-; *adv* heimwärts. **homework** *n* Hausaufgaben *pl.*
homicide ['homisaid] *n* Mord *m*; (*person*) Mörder *m.*
homogeneous [homə'dʒiːniəs] *adj* gleichartig, homogen.
homosexual [homə'sekʃuəl] *adj* homosexuell. *n* Homosexuelle(r). **homosexuality** *n* Homosexualität *f.*
honest ['onist] *adj* ehrlich, aufrecht. **honesty** *n* Ehrlichkeit *f*, Aufrichtigkeit *f.*
honey ['hʌni] *n* Honig *m*; (*darling*) Liebling *m*, Schatz *m.* **honey-bee** *n* Honigbiene *f.* **honeycomb** *n* Honigwabe *f.* **honeymoon** *n* Hochzeitsreise *f.*
honeysuckle ['hʌnisʌkl] *n* Geißblatt *neut.*
honour ['onə] *n* Ehre *f*; (*reputation*) guter Ruf *m.* **honours** *pl* Auszeichnungen *pl.* *v* (ver)ehren; (*cheque*) einlösen. **honourable** *adj* ehrenvoll; (*in titles*) ehrenwert.
hood [hud] *n* Kapuze *f*; (*US: on car*) Motorhaube *f*; (*coll*) Gangster *m.* **hoodwink** *v* täuschen.
hoof [huːf] *n* Huf *m.*

hook [huk] *n* Haken *m.* *v* haken **hook up** (*coll*) anschließen.
hooligan ['huːligən] *n* Rowdy *m.* **hooliganism** *n* Rowdytum *neut.*
hoop [huːp] *n* Reif(en) *m.*
hoot [huːt] *v* hupen. *n* Hupen *neut.*
hop¹ [hop] *v* hüpfen. *n* Sprung *m.*
hop² [hop] *n* (*bot*) Hopfen *m.*
hope [houp] *v* hoffen (auf). *n* Hoffnung *f.* **hopeful** *adj* hoffnungsvoll; (*promising*) vielversprechend. **hopefully** *adv* hoffentlich. **hopeless** *adj* hoffnungslos. **hopelessness** *n* Hoffnungslosigkeit *f.*
horde [hoːd] *n* Horde *f.*
horizon [hə'raizn] *n* Horizont *m.* **horizontal** *adj* waagerecht, horizontal.
hormone ['hoːmoun] *n* Hormon *neut.*
horn [hoːn] *n* Horn *neut*; (*mot*) Hupe *f.* **horned** *adj* gehörnt. **hornrimmed spectacles** Hornbrille *f.* **horny** *adj* (*hands*) schwielig.
hornet ['hoːnit] *n* Hornisse *f.*
horoscope ['horəskoup] *n* Horoskop *neut.*
horrible ['horibl] *adj* schrecklich, fürchterlich.
horrid ['horid] *adj* scheußlich, abscheulich.
horrify ['horifai] *v* erschrenken, entsetzen. **horrifying** *adj* entsetzlich.
horror ['horə] *n* Entsetzen *neut*, Grausen *neut.* **horror-stricken** *adj* von Grausen gepackt.
hors d'oeuvre [oː'dəivr] *n* Vorspeise *f.*
horse [hoːs] *n* Pferd *neut*, Roß *neut.* **on horseback** zu Pferd. **horse chestnut** Roßkastanie *f.* **horseman** *n* Reiter *m.* **horsepower** (**hp**) Pferdestärke (PS) *f.* **horse race** *n* Pferderennen *neut.* **horseradish** *n* Meerrettich *m.*
horticulture ['hoːtikʌltʃə] *n* Gartenbau *m.*
hose [houz] *n* (*stockings*) Strümpfe *pl*; (*tech, mot*) Schlauch *m*; (*in garden*) Gartenschlauch *m.*
hosiery ['houziəri] *pl n* Strumpfwaren *pl.*
hospitable [ho'spitəbl] *adj* gastfreundlich.
hospital ['hospitl] *n* Krankenhaus *neut*, Klinik *f.*
hospitality [ˌhospi'taliti] *n* Gastfreundschaft *f.*
host¹ [houst] *n* Gastgeber *m*, Wirt *m.*
host² [houst] *n* (*large number*) Masse *f*, Menge *f.*
hostage ['hostidʒ] *n* Geisel *m, f.*
hostel ['hostəl] *n* Herberge *f.* **student hostel** Studentenheim *neut.* **youth hostel**

          hurry

Jugendherberge *f.* **hostelry** *n* Wirtshaus *neut.*

hostess ['houstis] *n* Gastgeberin *f*, Wirtin *f*; (*air hostess*) Stewardeß *f.*

hostile ['hostail] *adj* feindlich, feindselig (gegen). **hostility** *n* Feindseligkeit *f*, Feindschaft *f.*

hot [hot] *adj* heiß; (*food, drink*) warm. **hotdog** *n* (heißes) Würstchen. **hot meal** warme Mahlzeit. **hot-water bottle** Wärmflasche *f.*

hotel [hou'tel] *n* Hotel *neut*, Gasthof *m.* **hotel register** *n* Fremdenbuch *neut.* **hotelier** *n* Hotelier *m.*

hound [haund] *n* Jagdhund *m.* *v* jagen, verfolgen.

hour ['auə] *n* Stunde *f.* **after hours** nach Geschäftsschluß. **for hours** stundenlang. **hourglass** *n* Sanduhr *f.* **hourly** *adj, adv* stündlich. **hourly wage** Stundenlohn *m.*

house [haus; *v* hauz] *n* Haus *neut*; (*theatre*) Publikum *neut.* **House of Commons** Unterhaus *neut.* **House of Lords** Oberhaus *neut.* **House of Representatives** Abgeordnetenhaus *neut.* *v* unterbringen. **houseboat** ['hausbout] *n* Hausboot *neut.* **household** ['haushould] *n* Haushalt *m.* **housekeeper** ['haus‚ki:pə] *n* Haushälterin *f.* **housekeeping** *n* Haushaltung *f.* **housekeeping money** Haushaltsgeld *neut.* **housemaid** ['hausmeid] *n* Dienstmächen *neut.* **housemaid's knee** (*med*) Kniescheibenentzündung *f.* **house-warming** ['haus‚wo:miŋ] *n* Einzugsfest *neut.* **housewife** ['hauswaif] *n* Hausfrau *f.* **housework** ['hauswə:k] *n* Hausarbeit *f.*

housing ['hauziŋ] *n* Unterbringung *f*, Wohnung *f*; (*tech*) Gehäuse *neut.* **housing estate** Siedlung *f.*

hovel ['hovəl] *n* Schuppen *m.*

hover ['hovə] *v* schweben. **hovercraft** *n* Luftkissenfahrzeug *neut.*

how [hau] *adv* wie. **how do you do?** guten Tag. **how are you?** wie geht es Ihnen? **how much** *or* **how many** wieviel. **however** *adv* aber, jedoch; (*in whatever way*) wie auch immer.

howl [haul] *v* heulen. *n* Heulen *neut.*

hub [hʌb] *n* Nabe *f*; (*fig*) Mittelpunkt *m.* **hub cap** Radkappe *f.*

huddle ['hʌdl] *v* sich zusammendrängen. **huddled** *adj* kauernd.

hue [hju:] *n* Farbe *f*, Färbung *f.*

huff [hʌf] *n* **in a huff** gekränkt, beleidigt.

hug [hʌg] *v* umarmen. *n* Umarmung *f.*

huge [hju:dʒ] *adj* riesig, riesengroß.

hulk [hʌlk] *n* (*naut*) Hulk *m.*

hull [hʌl] *n* (*naut*) Rumpf *m*; (*of seed, etc.*) Hülse *f*, Schale *f.* *v* enthülsen.

hum [hʌm] *v* summen, brummen. *n* Summen *neut*, Brummen *neut.*

human ['hju:mən] *adj* menschlich. **human being** Mensch *m.* **human nature** Menschheit *f*, menschliche Natur *f.* **humane** *adj* human. **humanist** *n* Humanist(in). **humanitarian** *adj* menschenfreundlich. **humanity** *n* Menschheit *f.*

humble ['hʌmbl] *adj* demütig, bescheiden; (*lowly*) niedrig. **humiliate** *v* demütigen. **humiliating** *adj* demütigend. **humility** *n* Demut *f*, Bescheidenheit *f.*

humdrum ['hʌmdrʌm] *adj* langweilig, alltäglich.

humid ['hju:mid] *adj* feucht. **humidity** *n* Feuchtigkeit *f.*

humour ['hju:mə] *n* Humor *m*; (*mood*) Stimmung *f*, Laune *f.* *v* (*person*) nachgeben (+*dat*). **sense of humour** Humor *m.* **humorous** *adj* lustig, humorvoll.

hump [hʌmp] *n* Buckel *m.* *v* (*coll: carry*) schleppen. **humpback** *n* Bucklige(r). **humpbacked** *adj* bucklig.

hunch [hʌntʃ] *n* (*coll*) Vorahnung *f.*

hundred ['hʌndrəd] *adj* hundert. *n* Hundert *neut.* **hundredth** *adj* hundertst; *n* Hundertstel *neut.* **hundredweight** Zentner *m.*

hung [hʌŋ] *V* **hang.**

Hungary ['hʌŋgəri] *n* Ungarn *neut.* **Hungarian** *adj* ungarisch; *n* Ungar(in).

hunger ['hʌŋgə] *n* Hunger *m.* *v* hungern. **hunger for** sehnen nach. **hungry** *adj* hungrig. **be hungry** Hunger haben.

hunt [hʌnt] *n* Jagd *f*, Jagen *neut*; (*for person*) Verfolgung *f.* *v* jagen; verfolgen. **hunter** *n* Jäger *m*; (*horse*) Jagdpferd *neut.* **hunting** *n* Jagd *f.*

hurdle ['hə:dl] *n* Hürde *f*; (*fig*) Hindernis *neut.*

hurl [hə:l] *v* werfen.

hurricane ['hʌrikən] *n* Orkan *m.* **hurricane lamp** Sturmlaterne *f.*

hurry ['hʌri] *v* eilen, sich beeilen; (*something*) beschleunigen. *n* Eile *f*, Hast *f.* **hurry up** mach schnell! **hurried** *adj* eilig, übereilt.

*hurt [hɜːt] *v* (*injure*) verletzen; (*ache*) schmerzen, weh tun; (*offend*) kränken, verletzen. *n* Verletzung *f*; Schmerzen *neut*. **hurtful** *adj* schädlich.
hurtle ['hɜːtl] *v* stürzen, sausen.
husband ['hʌzbənd] *n* (Ehe)Mann *m*. *v* (*resources*) sparsam umgehen mit. **husbandry** *n* Landwirtschaft *f*.
hush [hʌʃ] *n* Stille *f*, Ruhe *f*. *v* beruhigen.
husk [hʌsk] *n* Hülse *f*. *v* enthülsen.
husky ['hʌski] *adj* (*voice*) rauh, heiser.
hussar [hə'zaɪ] *n* Husar *m*.
hustle ['hʌsl] *v* drängen. **hustle and bustle** Gedränge *neut*.
hut [hʌt] *n* Hütte *f*.
hutch [hʌtʃ] *n* Stall *m*.
hyacinth ['haiəsinθ] *n* Hyazinthe *f*.
hybrid ['haibrid] *n* Kreuzung *f*, Mischling *m*. *adj* Misch-.
hydraulic [hai'drɔːlik] *adj* hydraulisch.
hydrocarbon [ˌhaidrou'kaɪbən] *n* Kohlenwasserstoff *m*.
hydro-electric [ˌhaidroui'lektrik] *adj* hydroelektrisch.
hydrogen ['haidrədʒən] *n* Wasserstoff *m*. **hydrogen bomb** Wasserstoffbombe *f*. **hydrogen peroxide** Wasserstoffsuperoxyd *neut*.
hyena [hai'iːnə] *n* Hyäne *f*.
hygiene ['haidʒiːn] *n* Hygiene *f*, Gesundheitspflege *f*. **hygienic** *adj* hygienisch.
hymn [him] *n* Kirchenlied *neut*, Hymne *f*. **hymnbook** *n* Gesangbuch *neut*.
hypersensitive [haipə'sensətiv] *adj* überempfindlich.
hyphen ['haifən] *n* Bindestrich *m*.
hypnosis [hip'nousis] *n* Hypnose *f*. **hypnotic** *adj* hypnotisch. **hypnotist** *n* Hypnotiseur *m*. **hypnotize** *v* hypnotisieren.
hypochondria [haipə'kondriə] *n* Hypochondrie *f*. **hypochondriac** *adj* hypochondrisch. *n* Hypochonder *m*.
hypocrisy [hi'pokrəsi] *n* Heuchelei *f*. **hypocrite** *n* Heuchler(in). **hypocritical** *adj* heuchlerisch.
hypodermic [haipə'dəɪmik] *adj* subkutan. **hypodermic syringe** Spritze *f*.
hypothesis [hai'poθəsis] *n* (*pl* -ses) Hypothese *f*. **hypothetical** *adj* hypothetisch.
hysterectomy [histə'rektəmi] *n* Hysterektomie *f*.

hysteria [his'tiəriə] *n* Hysterie *f*. **hysterical** *adj* hysterisch; (*coll*: *funny*) zum Schreien komisch.

I

I [ai] *pron* ich.
ice [ais] *n* Eis *neut*. *v* (*cookery*) mit Zuckerguß überziehen. **icing** *n* Zuckerguß *m*. **ice age** *n* Eiszeit *f*. **iceberg** *n* Eisberg *m*. **icebox** *n* Kühlschrank *m*. **ice cream** *n* Eis *neut*. **ice cube** *n* Eiswürfel *m*. **icy** *adj* eisig.
Iceland ['aislənd] *n* Island *neut*. **Icelandic** *adj* isländisch. **Icelander** *n* Isländer(in).
icicle ['aisikl] *n* Eiszapfen *m*.
icon ['aikon] *n* Ikone *f*.
idea [ai'diə] *n* Idee *f*; (*concept*) Begriff *m*. **I've no idea** ich habe keine Ahnung.
ideal [ai'diəl] *n* Ideal *neut*. *adj* ideal. **idealism** *n* Idealismus *neut*. **idealist** *n* Idealist *m*. **idealistic** *adj* idealistisch. **ideally** *adv* idealerweise.
identical [ai'dentikəl] *adj* identisch.
identify [ai'dentifai] *v* identifizieren; (*recognize*) erkennen. **identification** *n* Identifizierung *f*; (*pass*) Ausweis *m*.
identity [ai'dentiti] *n* Identität *f*. **identity card** Personalausweis *m*. **identity papers** Ausweispapiere *pl*.
ideology [aidi'olədʒi] *n* Ideologie *f*. **ideological** *adj* ideologisch. **ideologist** *n* Ideologe *m*, Ideologin *f*.
idiom ['idiəm] *n* Mundart *f*, Idiom *neut*. **idiomatic** *adj* idiomatisch.
idiosyncrasy [ˌidiə'siŋkrəsi] *n* Eigenart *f*. **idiosyncratic** *adj* eigenartig.
idiot ['idiət] *n* (*coll*) Idiot *m*, Dummkopf *m*; (*med*) Blödsinnige(r). **idiocy** *n* Blödsinn *m*.
idle ['aidl] *adj* (*person*) faul, untätig; (*words*, *etc*.) eitel, unnütz. **idleness** *n* Faulheit *f*. **idler** *n* Faulenzer *m*.
idol ['aidl] *n* Idol *neut*. **idolize** *v* vergöttern.
idyllic [i'dilik] *adj* idyllisch.
if [if] *conj* wenn, falls; (*whether*) ob. **even if** selbst wenn. **if only** wenn ... nur. **if not** falls nicht. **if so** in dem Fall.
ignite [ig'nait] *v* (ent)zünden.

ignition [ig'niʃən] n Zündung f. **ignition key** Zündschlüssel m.

ignorant ['ignərənt] adj unwissend; (uneducated) ungebildet. **be ignorant of** nicht wissen or kennen. **ignorance** n Unkenntnis f.

ignore [ig'nɔː] v ignorieren, unbeachtet lassen.

ill [il] adj (sick) krank; (bad) schlimm, böse. **fall ill** krank werden. **ill-at-ease** adj unbehaglich. **ill-bred** schlecht erzogen. **ill-disposed** adj bösartig. **ill-fated** adj unselig. **ill-natured** adj boshaft. **illness** n Krankheit f. **ill-treat** v mißhandeln.

illegal [i'liːgəl] adj illegal, gesetzwidrig. **illegality** n Ungesetzlichkeit f.

illegible [i'ledʒəbl] adj unleserlich. **illegibility** n Unleserlichkeit f.

illegitimate [ˌili'dʒitimit] adj (child) unehelich; (unlawful) ungesetzlich.

illicit [i'lisit] adj unzulässig, gesetzwidrig.

illiterate [i'litərit] adj analphabetisch, ungebildet. n Analphabet(in).

illogical [i'lodʒikəl] adj unlogisch.

illuminate [i'luːmiˌneit] v erleuchten. **illuminated** adj beleuchtet. **illumination** n Beleuchtung f.

illusion [i'luːʒən] n Illusion f. **illusory** adj illusorisch.

illustrate ['iləˌstreit] v (book) illustrieren; (idea) erklären. **illustration** n Illustration f, Bild n.

illustrious [i'lʌstriəs] adj berühmt.

image ['imidʒ] n Bild neut, (idea) Vorstellung f; (public) Image neut. **imagery** n Symbolik f.

imagine [i'madʒin] v sich vorstellen or denken. **imaginable** adj denkbar. **imaginary** adj eingebildet, Schein-. **imagination** n Phantasie f. **imaginative** adj phantasiereich.

imbalance [im'baləns] n Unausgeglichenheit f

imbecile ['imbəˌsiːl] n Schwachsinnige(r). adj schwachsinnig.

imitate ['imiˌteit] v nachahmen, imitieren. **imitation** n Nachahmung f; adj künstlich, Kunst-.

immaculate [i'makjulit] adj makellos.

immaterial [ˌimə'tiəriəl] adj belanglos.

immature [ˌimə'tjuə] adj unreif, unentwickelt. **immaturity** n Unreife f.

immediate [i'miːdiət] adj unmittelbar, direkt. **immediately** adv sofort.

immense [i'mens] adj riesig, ungeheuer.

immerse [i'məːs] v versenken, tauchen. **immersion** n Versunkenheit f, Immersion f. **immersion heater** Tauchsieder m.

immigrate ['imiˌgreit] v einwandern. **immigrant** n Einwanderer m, Einwanderin f. **immigration** n Einwanderung f.

imminent ['iminənt] adj drohend.

immobile [i'moubail] adj bewegungslos, unbeweglich. **immobility** n Unbeweglichkeit f. **immobilize** v unbeweglich machen.

immodest [i'modist] adj schamlos.

immoral [i'morəl] adj unsittlich, unmoralisch. **immorality** n Sittenlosigkeit f.

immortal [i'mɔːtl] adj unsterblich, ewig. **immortality** n Unsterblichkeit f.

immovable [i'muːvəbl] adj unbeweglich.

immune [i'mjuːn] adj immun (gegen). **immunity** n Immunität f. **immunization** n Impfung f.

imp [imp] v Kobold m.

impact ['impakt] n Anprall m, Stoß m; (effect) Wirkung f, Einfluß m.

impair [im'peə] v beeinträchtigen. **impairment** n Beeinträchtigung f.

impart [im'paːt] v geben, erteilen.

impartial [im'paːʃəl] adj unparteiisch. **impartiality** n Unparteilichkeit f.

impassable [im'paːsəbl] adj ungangbar, unpassierbar.

impasse [am'paːs] n Sackgasse f.

impassive [im'pasiv] adj ungerührt.

impatient [im'peiʃənt] adj ungeduldig. **impatience** n Ungeduld f.

impeach [im'piːtʃ] v anklagen. **impeachment** n Anklage f.

impeccable [im'pekəbl] adj tadellos. **impeccability** n Tadellosigkeit f.

impede [im'piːd] v (be)hindern. **impediment** n Verhinderung f. **speech impediment** Sprachfehler m.

impel [im'pel] v (an)treiben. **impelled** adj gezwungen.

impending [im'pendiŋ] adj bevorstehend, drohend.

imperative [im'perətiv] adj dringend notwendig. n (gramm) Imperativ m.

imperfect [im'pəːfikt] adj unvollkommen, fehlerhaft. **imperfection** n (blemish) Fehler m.

imperial [im'piəriəl] adj kaiserlich. **imperialism** n Imperialismus m. **imperialist** adj imperialistisch.

imperil [im'perəl] v gefährden.
impermanent [im'pəːmənənt] adj unbeständig.
impersonal [im'pəːsənl] adj unpersönlich. **impersonality** n Unpersönlichkeit f.
impersonate [im'pəːsə,neit] v sich ausgeben als.
impertinent [im'pəːtinənt] adj frech, unverschämt. **impertinence** n Frechheit f, Unverschämtheit f.
impervious [im'pəːviəs] adj undurchdringlich.
impetuous [im'petjuəs] adj ungestüm, impulsiv. **impetuosity** n Ungestüm neut.
impetus ['impətəs] n Antrieb m, Schwung m.
impinge [im'pindʒ] v eingreifen (in), stoßen (an).
implement ['implimənt; v 'impliment] n Werkzeug neut, Gerät neut. v durchführen.
implicate ['implikeit] v hineinziehen. **implication** n Bedeutung f, Konsequenz f.
implicit [im'plisit] adj (tacit) unausgesprochen; (unquestioning) absolut. **implicitly** adv unbedingt.
implore [im'plɔː] v dringend bitten. **imploring** adj flehentlich.
imply [im'plai] v bedeuten.
impolite [impə'lait] adj unhöflich. **impoliteness** n Unhöflichkeit f.
import [im'pɔːt] v einführen, importieren. n Einfuhr f, Import m. **importer** n Importeur m, Einfuhrhändler m. **imports** pl n Importwaren pl.
importance [im'pɔːtəns] n Wichtigkeit f, Bedeutung f. **important** adj wichtig.
impose [im'pouz] v auferlegen. **impose upon** mißbrauchen. **imposing** adj imponierend. **imposition** n Auferlegung f; (unreasonable demand) Zumutung f.
impossible [im'posəbl] adj unmöglich. **impossibility** n Unmöglichkeit f.
impostor [im'postə] n Betrüger(in).
impotent ['impətənt] adj impotent. **impotence** n Impotenz f.
impound [im'paund] v beschlagnahmen.
impoverish [im'povəriʃ] v arm machen. **impoverished** adj verarmt.
impregnate ['impreg,neit] v befruchten, schwanger machen; (fabric, wood, etc.) imprägnieren. **impregnable** adj uneinnehmbar.
impress [im'pres] v beeindrucken. **impres-**

sion n Eindruck m; (book) Auflage f.
impressionism n (painting) Impressionismus m.
imprint [im'print; n 'imprint] v aufdrücken (auf); (fig) einprägen in. n Stempel m; (fig) Eindruck m.
imprison [im'prizn] v einsperren. **imprisonment** n Haft f, Gefangenschaft f.
improbable [im'probəbl] adj unwahrscheinlich. **improbability** n Unwahrscheinlichkeit f.
impromptu [im'promptjuː] adj improvisiert.
improper [im'propə] adj unpassend, unsittlich.
improve [im'pruːv] v verbessern; (become better) sich verbessern, besser werden. **improvement** n Verbesserung f.
improvise ['imprə,vaiz] v improvisieren. **improvisation** n Improvisierung f.
impudent ['impjudənt] adj frech, unverschämt. **impudence** n Unverschämtheit f.
impulse ['impʌls] n Antrieb m, Drang m. **impulsive** adj impulsiv.
impure [im'pjuə] adj unrein. **impurity** n Unreinheit f; (extraneous substance) fremde Bestandteile pl.
in [in] prep (place) in, an auf; (time) in, während. (into) in . . . hinein or herein. **in the street** auf der Straße. **in the evening** abends. **in bad weather** bei schlechtem Wetter. **in three days' time** nach drei Tagen. **in that** insofern als. **be in** (at home) zu Hause sein.
inability [,inə'biləti] n Unfähigkeit f. **inability to pay** Zahlungsunfähigkeit f.
inaccessible [,inak'sesəbl] adj unzugänglich, unerreichbar. **inaccessibility** n Unzugänglichkeit f.
inaccurate [in'akjurit] adj ungenau; (incorrect) falsch. **inaccuracy** n Ungenauigkeit f; Fehler m.
inactive [in'aktiv] adj untätig. **inactivity** n Untätigkeit f.
inadequate [in'adikwit] adj ungenügend, mangelhaft. **inadequacy** n Unzulänglichkeit f, Mangelhaftigkeit f.
inadvertent [,inəd'vəːtənt] adj unabsichtlich, versehentlich.
inane [in'ein] adj leer, albern.
inanimate [in'animit] adj leblos.
inarticulate [,inaː'tikjulit] adj undeutlich. **be inarticulate** sich nicht gut ausdrücken können.

inasmuch [ˌinəz'mʌtʃ] *conj* inasmuch as da.

inaudible [in'ɔːdəbl] *adj* unhörbar.

inaugurate [i'nɔːgjuˌreit] *v* (feierlich) eröffnen. **inauguration** *n* (feierliche) Eröffnung *f*. **inaugural** *adj* Einführungs-.

inborn [ˌin'bɔɪn] *adj* angeboren.

incapable [in'keipəbl] *adj* unfähig. **incapacity** *n* Unfähigkeit *f*.

incendiary [in'sendiəri] *adj* Brand-. **incendiary bomb** Brandbombe *f*.

incense[1] ['insens] *n* Weihrauch *m*.

incense[2] [in'sens] *v* wütend machen.

incentive [in'sentiv] *n* Ansporn *m*; (*bonus*) Leistungsanreiz *m*.

incessant [in'sesənt] *adj* ständig, unaufhörlich.

incest ['insest] *n* Blutschande *f*. **incestuous** *adj* blutschänderisch.

inch [intʃ] *n* Zoll *m*.

incident ['insidənt] *n* Vorfall *m*, Ereignis *neut*.

incinerator [in'sinəˌreitə] *n* Verbrennungsofen *m*. **incinerate** *v* verbrennen. **incineration** *n* Verbrennung *f*.

incite [in'sait] *v* anregen. **incitement** *n* Anregung *f*, Aufreizung *f*.

incline [in'klain] *v* neigen; (*slope*) abfallen. **inclination** *n* Neigung *f*. **inclined** *adj* geneigt.

include [in'kluːd] *v* einschließen. **included** *adj* (*in price*) inbegriffen. **inclusive** *adj* einschließlich. **inclusive of** *also* **including** einschließlich. **inclusion** *n* Einbeziehung *f*.

incognito [ˌinkog'niːtou] *adv* inkognito.

incoherent [ˌinkə'hiərənt] *adj* inkonsequent; (*speech*) unklar.

income ['inkʌm] *n* Einkommen *neut*, Einkünfte *pl*. **income tax** Einkommensteuer *f*. **income tax return** Einkommensteuererklärung *f*.

incompatible [ˌinkəm'patəbl] *adj* unvereinbar. **incompatibility** *n* Unvereinbarkeit *f*.

incompetent [in'kompitənt] *adj* unfähig. **incompetence** *n* Unfähigkeit *f*.

incomplete [ˌinkəm'pliːt] *adj* unvollständig.

incomprehensible [inˌkompri'hensəbl] *adj* unbegreiflich.

inconceivable [ˌinkən'siːvəbl] *adj* unfaßbar. **inconceivability** *n* Unfaßbarkeit *f*.

inconclusive [ˌinkən'kluːsiv] *adj* ohne Beweiskraft.

incongruous [in'kongruəs] *adj* unangemessen.

inconsiderate [ˌinkən'sidərit] *adj* rücksichtslos, besinnungslos.

inconsistent [ˌinkən'sistənt] *adj* inkonsequent; (*person*) unbeständig. **inconsistency** *n* Widerspruch *m*.

inconspicuous [ˌinkən'spikjuəs] *adj* unauffällig.

incontinence [in'kontinəns] *n* (*med*) Inkontinenz *f*.

inconvenient [ˌinkən'viːnjənt] *adj* ungelegen. **inconvenience** *n* Ungelegenheit *f*. *v* stören, lästig sein (+*dat*).

incorporate [in'kɔːpəˌreit] *v* (*combine*) vereinigen; (*comm*) inkorporieren; (*contain, include*) enthalten. **incorporation** *n* (*comm*) Gründung *f*.

incorrect [ˌinkə'rekt] *adj* unrichtig; (*inexact*) ungenau.

increase [in'kriːs] *v* zunehmen; (*in number*) sich vermehren; (*prices*) steigen. *n* Vermehrung *f*, Zunahme *f*; Steigerung *f*; (*wages*) Lohnerhöhung *f*. **increasingly** *adv* immer mehr.

incredible [in'kredəbl] *adj* unglaublich. **incredibility** *n* Unglaublichkeit *f*. **incredibly** *adv* unglaublicherweise; (*coll: extremely*) unglaublich.

incredulous [in'kredjuləs] *adj* skeptisch, ungläubig. **incredulity** *n* Skepsis *f*.

increment ['iŋkrəmənt] *n* Zunahme *f*.

incriminate [in'krimineit] *v* beschuldigen. **incrimination** *n* Beschuldigung *f*.

incubate ['iŋkjuˌbeit] *v* ausbrüten. **incubation** *n* Ausbrütung *f*. **incubator** *n* (*for babies*) Brutkasten *m*.

incur [in'kəɪ] *v* sich zuziehen. **incur debts** Schulden machen. **incur losses** Verluste erleiden.

incurable [in'kjuərəbl] *adj* unheilbar.

indebted [in'detid] *adj* verschuldet.

indecent [in'diːsnt] *adj* unanständig. **indecency** *n* Unanständigkeit *f*.

indeed [in'diːd] *adv* tatsächlich, wirklich.

indefinite [in'definit] *adj* unbestimmt. **indefinitely** *adv* auf unbestimmte Zeit.

indelible [in'deləbl] *adj* unauslöschlich; (*ink*) wasserfest.

indemnify [in'demnifai] *v* entschädigen. **indemnity** *n* Entschädigung *f*.

indent [in'dent] *v* (*type*) einrücken. **indentation** *n* Einrückung *f.*
independence [indi'pendəns] *n* Unabhängigkeit *f,* Selbstständigkeit *f.*
independent *adj* unabhängig, selbstständig; (*pol*) parteilos; *n* (*pol*) Unabhängige(r).
indescribable [indi'skraibəbl] *adj* unbeschreiblich.
indestructible [indi'strʌktəbl] *adj* unzerstörbar.
index ['indeks] *n* (*in book*) Register *neut*; (*file*) Kartei *f;* (*cost of living*) Index *m.* **index finger** Zeigefinger *m.*
India ['indjə] *n* Indien *neut.* **Indian** *adj* indisch; (*American*) indianisch; *n* Inder(in); (*American*) Indianer(in). **Indian ink** chinesische Tusche *f.* **Indian summer** Nachsommer *m.*
indicate ['indikeit] *v* anzeigen; (*hint*) andeuten. **indication** *n* Anzeichen *neut*; (*idea*) Andeutung *f;* (*information*) Angabe; (*med*) Indikation *f.* **indicative** *adj* anzeigend. **indicator** *n* (*sign*) Zeichen *neut*; (*mot*) Richtungsanzeiger *m,* Blinker *m.*
indict [in'dait] *v* anklagen (wegen). **indictment** *n* Anklageschrift *f.*
indifferent [in'difrənt] *adj* gleichgültig; (*poor quality*) mittelmäßig. **indifference** *n* Gleichgültigkeit *f;* Mittelmäßigkeit *f.*
indigenous [in'didʒinəs] *adj* einheimisch.
indigestion [indi'dʒestʃən] *n* Verdauungsstörung *f.* **indigestible** *adj* unverdaulich.
indignant [in'dignənt] *adj* empört. **indignation** *n* Empörung *f.*
indignity [in'dignəti] *n* Demütigung *f.*
indirect [indi'rekt] *adj* indirekt.
indiscreet [indi'skrit] *adj* indiskret, taktlos. **indiscretion** *n* Vertrauensbruch *m,* Indiskretion *f.*
indiscriminate [indi'skriminit] *adj* rücksichtslos. **indiscriminately** *adv* ohne Unterschied.
indispensable [indi'spensəbl] *adj* unerläßlich, unentbehrlich. **indispensability** *n* Unerläßlichkeit *f,* Unentbehrlichkeit *f.*
indisposed [indi'spouzd] *adj* indisponiert, unpäßlich.
indisputable [indi'spjuːtəbl] *adj* unbestreitbar.
indistinct [indi'stiŋkt] *adj* unklar.

individual [indi'vidjuəl] *n* Individuum *neut,* Person *f. adj* einzeln, persönlich, individuell. **individualist** *n* Individualist(in). **individuality** *n* Individualität *f,* Eigenart *f.* **individually** *adv* einzeln.
indoctrinate [in'doktrineit] *v* unterweisen. **indoctrination** *n* Unterweisung *f.*
indolent ['indələnt] *adj* lässig. **indolence** *n* Lässigkeit *f.*
indoor ['indoɪ] *adj* Haus-, Zimmer-. **indoor swimming pool** Hallenbad *neut.* **indoors** *adv* im Haus; (*go*) ins Haus.
induce [in'djuːs] *v* (*cause*) verursachen; (*persuade*) überreden. **inducement** *n* Anreiz *m.*
indulge [in'dʌldʒ] *v* (*a person*) nachgeben (+ *dat*); (*oneself*) verwöhnen. **indulgence** *n* Nachsicht *f;* Verwöhnung *f.* **indulgent** *adj* nachsichtig.
industry ['indəstri] *n* Industrie *f.* **industrial** *adj* industriell. **industrialist** *n* Industrielle(r). **industrious** *adj* fleißig.
inebriated [i'niːbrieitid] *adj* betrunken.
inedible [in'edibl] *adj* nicht eßbar.
inefficient [ini'fiʃnt] *adj* unfähig; (*thing*) unwirksam. **inefficiency** *n* Leistungsunfähigkeit *f.*
inept [i'nept] *adj* albern. **ineptitude** *n* Albernheit *f.*
inequality [ini'kwoləti] *n* Ungleichheit *f.*
inert [i'nəɪt] *adj* inaktiv; (*person*) schlaff. **inertia** *n* Trägheit *f.*
inevitable [in'evitəbl] *adj* unvermeidlich. **inevitability** *n* Unvermeidlichkeit *f.*
inexpensive [inik'spensiv] *adj* billig, preiswert.
inexperienced [inik'spiəriənst] *adj* unerfahren.
infallible [in'faləbl] *adj* unfehlbar. **infallibility** *n* Unfehlbarkeit *f.*
infamous ['infəməs] *adj* schändlich. **infamy** *n* Schande *f.*
infancy ['infənsi] *n* frühe Kindheit *f.* **be still in its infancy** noch in den Kinderschuhen stecken. **infant** (*baby*) Säugling *m*; (*small child*) Kleinkind *neut.* **infantile** *adj* kindisch.
infantry ['infəntri] *n* Infanterie *f.* **infantryman** *n* Infanterist *m.*
infatuated [in'fatjueitid] *adj* vernarrt (in). **infatuation** *n* Vernarrtheit *f.*
infect [in'fekt] *v* infizieren, anstecken. **infection** *n* Infizierung *f,* Ansteckung *f.* **infectious** *adj* ansteckend.

infer [in'fəɪ] v folgern. **inference** n (conclusion) Schlußfolgerung f.
inferior [in'fiəriə] adj minderwertig. **inferiority** n Minderwertigkeit f. **inferiority complex** Minderwertigkeitskomplex m.
infernal [in'fəɪnl] adj höllisch; (coll) verdammt. **inferno** n Inferno neut.
infertile [in'fəɪtail] adj unfruchtbar. **infertility** n Unfruchtbarkeit f.
infest [in'fest] v heimsuchen, plagen. **infestation** n Plage f.
infidelity [ˌinfi'deliti] n Untreue f.
infiltrate [in'filˌtreit] v einsickern in; (pol) unterwandern. **infiltration** n Einsickern neut; Unterwanderung f. **infiltrator** n Unterwanderer m.
infinite ['infinit] adj unendlich. **infinity** n Unendlichkeit f. **infinitesimal** adj winzig.
infinitive [in'finitiv] n (gramm) Infinitiv m, Nennform f.
infirm [in'fəɪm] adj schwach. **infirmary** n Krankenhaus neut. **infirmity** n Krankheit f.
inflame [in'fleim] v entzünden; (fig) erregen. **inflamed** (med) entzündet. **inflammable** adj brennbar. **inflammation** n Entzündung f. **inflammatory** adj (fig) aufrührerisch.
inflate [in'fleit] v aufblasen; (price) übermäßig steigern. **inflatable** adj aufblasbar. **inflated** adj aufgebläht; (fig) aufgeblasen; (price) überhöht. **inflation** n Aufgeblasenheit f; (comm) Inflation f. **inflationary** adj inflationistisch.
inflection [in'flekʃən] n Biegung f; (of voice) Modulation f.
inflict [in'flikt] v (blow) versetzen; (pain) zufügen; (burden) aufbürden. **infliction** n Zufügung f; (burden) Last f.
influence ['influəns] n Einfluß m; (power) Macht f. v beeinflussen, Einfluß ausüben auf. **influential** adj einflußreich.
influenza [ˌinflu'enzə] n Grippe f.
influx ['inflʌks] n Zustrom m.
inform [in'foɪm] v benachrichtigen, unterrichten. **inform against** anzeigen. **informal** [in'foɪml] adj informell. **informality** n Ungezwungenheit f.
information [ˌinfə'meiʃən] n Auskunft f, Information f, Nachricht f; (data) Angaben pl. **information bureau** Auskunftsbüro neut. **informative** adj lehrreich. **informed** adj informiert. **informer** n Angeber(in).
infra-red [ˌinfrə'red] adj infrarot.

infringe [in'frindʒ] v verstoßen gegen; (rights) verletzen. **infringement** n Verletzung f.
infuriate [in'fjuəriˌeit] v wütend machen. **infuriated** adj wütend.
ingenious [in'dʒiːnjəs] adj (person) erfinderisch; (device) raffiniert. **ingenuity** n Erfindungsgabe f.
ingot ['iŋgət] n Barren m.
ingrained [in'greind] adj tief eingewurzelt.
ingredient [in'griːdjənt] n Zutat f.
inhabit [in'habit] v bewohnen. **inhabitable** adj bewohnbar. **inhabitant** n Einwohner(in).
inhale [in'heil] v einatmen. **inhalation** n Einatmung f.
inherent [in'hiərənt] adj angeboren.
inherit [in'herit] v erben. **inheritance** n Erbe neut. **inherited** adj ererbt. **inheritor** n Erbe m, Erbin f.
inhibit [in'hibit] v hemmen; (prevent) hindern. **inhibition** n Hemmung f.
inhospitable [inhə'spitəbl] adj ungastlich.
inhuman [in'hjuːmən] adj unmenschlich. **inhumanity** n Unmenschlichkeit f.
iniquitous [i'nikwətəs] adj (unjust) ungerecht; (sinful) frevelhaft. **iniquity** n Ungerechtigkeit f, (sin) Sünde f.
initial [i'niʃl] adj anfänglich, Anfangs-. n Anfangsbuchstabe m. **initials** pl n Monogramm neut. **initially** adv am Anfang.
initiate [i'niʃiˌeit] v einführen (in); (start) beginnen. n Eingeweihte(r). **initiation** n Einweihung.
initiative [i'niʃiətiv] n Initiative f. **take the initiative** die Initiative ergreifen. **initiator** n Anstifter m.
inject [in'dʒekt] v einspritzen. **injection** n **give/have an injection** eine Spritze geben/bekommen.
injure ['indʒə] v verletzen. **injured party** Geschädigte(r). **injurious** adj schädlich. **injury** n Verletzung f, Wunde f.
injustice [in'dʒʌstis] n Unrecht neut, Ungerechtigkeit f.
ink [iŋk] n Tinte f, Tusche f. **inkblot** n Tintenklecks m. **inkwell** n Tintenfaß neut.
inkling ['iŋkliŋ] n Ahnung f.
inland ['inlənd] adj Binnen-. **Inland Revenue** Steuerbehörde f.
in-laws ['inˌloɪs] pl n angeheiratete Verwandte pl. **daughter-in-law** Schwiegertochter f. **father-in-law**

Schwiegervater *m.* **mother-in-law** Schwiegermutter *f.* **son-in-law** Schwiegersohn *m.*

***inlay** ['inlei] *v* einlegen. *n* eingelegte Arbeit *f*; *(dentistry)* Plombe *f.*

inlet ['inlet] *n* Meeresarm *m.*

inmate ['inmeit] *n* Insasse *m*, Insassin *f.*

inn [in] *n* Gasthof *m*, Wirtshaus *neut.* **innkeeper** *n* Gastwirt(in).

innate [ˌi'neit] *adj* angeboren. **innately** *adv* von Natur.

inner ['inə] *adj* inner, Innen-. **innermost** *adj* innerst.

innocent ['inəsnt] *adj* unschuldig, schuldlos. **innocence** *n* Unschuld *f*, Schuldlosigkeit *f.*

innocuous [i'nokjuəs] *adj* harmlos, unschädlich.

innovation [inə'veiʃən] *n* Neuerung *f.* **innovator** *n* Neuerer *m.*

innuendo [ˌinju'endou] *n* Stichelei *f.*

innumerable [i'njuːmərəbl] *adj* zahllos, unzählig.

inoculate [i'nokjuˌleit] *v* (ein)impfen. **inoculation** *n* Impfung *f.*

inorganic [ˌinoɪ'ganik] *adj* unorganisch.

input ['input] *n* Eingabe *f*, Input *m.*

inquest ['inkwest] *n* gerichtliche Untersuchung *f.*

inquire [in'kwaiə] *v* sich erkundigen (nach). **inquiry** *n* Anfrage *f*; *(examination)* Untersuchung *f*, Prüfung *f.* **inquiry office** Auskunftsbüro *neut.*

inquisition [ˌinkwi'ziʃən] *n* Untersuchung *f*; *(rel)* Ketzergericht *neut.*

inquisitive [in'kwizətiv] *adj* neugierig.

insane [in'sein] *adj* geisteskrank; *(coll)* verrückt. **insanity** *n* Geisteskrankheit *f.*

insatiable [in'seiʃəbl] *adj* unersättlich. **insatiability** *n* Unersättlichkeit *f.*

inscribe [in'skraib] *v* (auf)schreiben. **inscription** *n* Beschriftung *f*; *(in book)* Widmung *f.*

insect ['insekt] *n* Insekt *neut.* **insecticide** *n* Insektizid *neut.*

insecure [ˌinsi'kjuə] *adj* unsicher. **insecurity** *n* Unsicherheit *f.*

inseminate [in'semineit] *v* befruchten. **insemination** *n* Befruchtung *f.*

insensible [in'sensəbl] *adj* gefühllos; *(unconscious)* bewußtlos.

insensitive [in'sensətiv] *adj* unempfindlich. **insensitivity** *n* Unempfindlichkeit *f.*

inseparable [in'sepərəbl] *adj* untrennbar.

insert [in'səɪt; *n* 'insəɪt] *v*˙einfügen, einsetzen. *n* Beilage *f.* **insertion** *n* Einsatz *m.*

inshore [ˌin'ʃoɪ] *adj* Küsten-. *adv* zur Küste hin.

inside [ˌin'said] *adj* inner, Innen-. *adv* *(be)* drinnen; *(go)* nach innen. *prep* in, innerhalb; *(into)* in ... hinein. *n* Innenseite *f*, Innere *neut.* **insides** *(intestines)* Eingeweide *pl.*

insidious [in'sidiəs] *adj* heimtückisch.

insight ['insait] *n* Einblick *m*; *(understanding)* Verständnis *neut.*

insignificant [ˌinsig'nifikənt] *adj* unbedeutend, unwichtig. **insignificance** *n* Bedeutungslosigkeit *f.*

insincere [ˌinsin'siə] *adj* unaufrichtig. **insincerity** *n* Unaufrichtigkeit *f.*

insinuate [in'sinjueit] *v* zu verstehen geben, andeuten. **insinuation** *n* Andeutung *f.*

insipid [in'sipid] *adj* fade.

insist [in'sist] *v* bestehen (auf). **insistence** *n* Bestehen *neut.* **insistent** *adj* beharrlich.

insolent ['insələnt] *adj* unverschämt, frech. **insolence** *n* Unverschämtheit *f*, Frechheit *f.*

insoluble [in'soljubl] *adj* unauflöslich; *(problem)* unlösbar.

insolvent [in'solvənt] *adj* zahlungsunfähig.

insomnia [in'somniə] *n* Schlaflosigkeit *f.*

inspect [in'spekt] *v* untersuchen, besichtigen. **inspection** *n* Untersuchung *f*, Besichtigung *f.* **inspector** *n* Inspektor *m.*

inspire [in'spaiə] *v* inspirieren, begeistern; *(give rise to)* anregen. **inspiration** *n* Inspiration *f*, Anregung *f.* **inspiring** *adj* anregend.

instability [ˌinstə'biləti] *n* Unbeständigkeit *f.*

install [in'stoɪl] *v* einsetzen, einrichten. **installation** *n* Einrichtung *f.*

instalment [in'stoɪlmənt] *n* Rate *f.* **instalment plan** Teilzahlungssystem *neut.*

instance ['instəns] *n* *(case)* Fall *f*; *(example)* Beispiel *neut.* **for instance** zum Beispiel (z.B.).

instant ['instənt] *n* Augenblick *m.* *adj* sofortig. **instant coffee** Pulverkaffee *m.* **instantaneous** *adj* augenblicklich. **instantly** *adv* sofort.

instead [in'sted] *adv* statt dessen. **instead of** (an)statt (+ *gen*).

instep ['instep] n Rist m, Spann m.
instigate ['instigeit] v anstiften. **instigation** n Anstiftung f. **instigator** n Anstifter(in).
instil [in'stil] v (teach) beibringen (+ dat).
instinct ['instiŋkt] n (Natur)Trieb m, Instinkt m. **instinctive** adj instinktiv; (automatic) unwillkürlich.
institute ['institjuːt] n Institut neut. v einführen; (found) gründen. **institution** n Institut neut; (home) Anstalt f; (foundation) Stiftung f.
instruct [in'strʌkt] v unterweisen; (teach) unterrichten. **instruction** n Vorschrift f; (teaching) Unterrichtung f. **instructive** adj lehrreich. **instructor** n Lehrer(in). **instructions for use** Gebrauchsanweisung f.
instrument ['instrəmənt] n Instrument neut; (tool) Werkzeug neut; (means) Mittel neut. **instrumental** adj (helpful) förderlich. **be instrumental in** durchsetzen.
insubordinate [ˌinsə'bɔɪdənət] adj widersetzlich. **insubordination** n Widersetzlichkeit f.
insufficient [ˌinsə'fiʃənt] adj unzureichend. **insufficiency** n Unzulänglichkeit f.
insular ['insjulə] adj insular. **insularity** n Beschränktheit f.
insulate ['insjuleit] v isolieren. **insulation** n Isolierung f. **insulating tape** Isolierband neut.
insulin ['insjulin] n Insulin neut.
insult [in'sʌlt; n 'insʌlt] v beleidigen, beschimpfen. n Beleidigung f. **insulting** adj beleidigend.
insure [in'ʃuə] v versichern. **insurance** n Versicherung f. **insurance broker** Versicherungsmakler m. **insurance policy** Versicherungspolice f. **insurance premium** Versicherungsprämie f.
insurmountable [ˌinsə'mauntəbl] adj unüberwindlich.
insurrection [ˌinsə'rekʃən] n Aufstand m.
intact [in'takt] adj unberührt.
intake ['inteik] n Aufnahme f, Einlaß m.
intangible [in'tandʒəbl] adj unfaßbar.
integral ['intigrəl] adj wesentlich; (math) Integral-.
integrate ['intigreit] v integrieren; (people) eingliedern. **integration** n Integration f; Eingliederung f. **integrity** n Integrität f; (completeness) Vollständigkeit f.
intellect ['intilekt] n Intellekt m. **intellectual** adj intellektuell; n Intellektuelle(r).

intelligent [in'telidʒənt] adj intelligent.
intelligence n Intelligenz f; (information) Information f; (secret service) Geheimdienst m.
intelligible [in'telidʒəbl] adj verständlich, klar.
intend [in'tend] v beabsichtigen, die Absicht haben.
intense [in'tens] adj stark, intensiv; (colour) tief; (person) ernsthaft. **intensely** adv (highly) äußerst. **intensify** v verstärken. **intensity** n Stärke f. **intensive** adj intensiv.
intent[1] [in'tent] n Absicht f, Vorsatz m. **to all intents and purposes** im Grunde.
intent[2] [in'tent] adj intent on versessen auf.
intention [in'tenʃən] n Absicht f; (plan) Vorhaben neut; (aim) Ziel neut; (meaning) Sinn m. **intentional** adj absichtlich.
inter [in'təɪ] v beerdigen. **interment** n Beerdigung f.
interact [ˌintər'akt] v aufeinander wirken. **interaction** n Wechselwirkung f.
intercede [ˌintə'siːd] v sich verwenden (bei). **intercession** n Fürsprache f.
intercept [ˌintə'sept] v abfangen. **interception** n Abfangen neut.
interchange [ˌintə'tʃəindʒ] n Austausch m; (roads) (Autobahn) Kreuz/Dreieck neut. v austauschen.
intercom ['intəˌkom] n Sprechanlage f.
intercourse ['intəkɔɪs] n Verkehr m, Umgang m. **sexual intercourse** Geschlechtsverkehr m.
interest ['intrist] n Interesse neut; (comm) Zinsen pl; (advantage) Vorteil m. **interested** adj interessiert; (biased) beteiligt.
interfere [ˌintə'fiə] v (person) sich einmischen; (adversely affect) stören. **interference** n Einmischung f; Störung f. **interfering** adj lästig, störend.
interim ['intərim] n Zwischenzeit f. adj vorläufig.
interior [in'tiəriə] n Innere neut. adj inner, Binnen-.
interjection [ˌintə'dʒekʃən] n Ausruf m; (gramm) Interjektion f.
interlock [intə'lok] v ineinandergreifen. **interlocking** adj verzahnt.
interlude ['intəluːd] n (interval) Pause f.
intermediate [ˌintə'miːdiət] adj Zwischen-. **intermediary** n Vermittler m.
interminable [in'təɪminəbl] adj endlos.

intermission [,intə'miʃən] *n* Pause *f.* Unterbrechung *f.* **without intermission** pausenlos.
intermittent [,intə'mitənt] *adj* stoßweise, periodisch.
intern [in'tɔin] *v* internieren. *n* Assistentenarzt *m.* **internment** *n* Internierung *f.*
internal [in'tɔinl] *adj* inner; (*domestic*) Innen-, Inlands-; (*within organization*) intern.
international [,intə'naʃənl] *adj* international.
interpose [,intə'pouz] *v* dazwischenstellen. **interposition** *n* Zwischenstellung *f.*
interpret [in'tɔiprit] *v* dolmetschen; (*explain*) auslegen; (*theatre, music*) interpretieren. **interpreter** *n* Dolmetscher(in); Interpret(in). **interpretation** *n* Dolmetschen *neut*; Auslegung *f*; Interpretation *f.*
interrogate [in'terəgeit] *v* verhören. **interrogation** *n* Verhör *neut.* **interrogator** *n* Fragesteller *m.*
interrogative [,intə'rogətiv] *adj* fragend; (*gramm*) Frage-. *n* (*gramm*) Interrogativ *m.*
interrupt [,intə'rʌpt] *v* unterbrechen. **interruption** *n* Unterbrechung *f.*
intersect [,intə'sekt] *v* schneiden. **intersection** *n* Kreuzungspunkt *m*; (*mot*) Kreuzung *f.*
intersperse [,intə'spəis] *v* verstreuen.
interval ['intəvəl] *n* Zwischenraum *m*; (*break*) Pause *f*; (*timespan*) Abstand *m*; (*music*) Tonabstand *m.*
intervene [,intə'viin] *v* (*interfere*) eingreifen; (*come between*) dazwischentreten. **intervention** *n* Intervention *f*, Eingreifen *neut.*
interview ['intəvjui] *n* Interview *neut. v* interviewen. **interviewee** *n* Interviewte(r). **interviewer** *n* Interviewer *m.*
intestine [in'testin] *n* Darm *m.* **intestines** *pl* Eingeweide *pl.* **intestinal** *adj* Darm-.
intimate¹ ['intimət] *adj* vertraut. **intimacy** *n* Vertrautheit *f.*
intimate² ['intimeit] *v* andeuten. **intimation** *n* Andeutung *f*, Wink *m.*
intimidate [in'timideit] *v* einschüchtern. **intimidation** *n* Einschüchterung *f.*
into ['intu] *prep* in (+*acc*) hinein/herein. **be into** (*coll*) sich interessieren für. **get into** (*difficulties, etc.*) geraten in. **look into** (*investigate*) untersuchen.

intolerable [in'tolərəbl] *adj* unerträglich.
intolerant [in'tolərənt] *adj* intolerant. **intolerance** *n* Intoleranz *f.*
intonation [,intə'neiʃən] *n* Intonation *f.* **intone** *v* intonieren.
intoxicate [in'toksikeit] *v* berauschen. **intoxicated** *adj* berauscht; (*drunk*) betrunken. **intoxication** *n* Rausch *m.*
intransitive [in'transitiv] *adj* (*gramm*) intransitiv.
intravenous [,intrə'viinəs] *adj* intravenös.
intrepid [in'trepid] *adj* unerschrocken.
intricate ['intriket] *adj* kompliziert. **intricacy** *n* Kompliziertheit *f.*
intrigue ['intriig; *v* in'triig] *n* Intrige *f. v* faszinieren; (*plot*) intrigieren. **intriguing** *adj* faszinierend.
intrinsic [in'trinsik] *adj* wesentlich.
introduce [,intrə'djuis] *v* einführen; (*person*) vorstellen. **introduction** *n* Einführung *f*; (*in book*) Einleitung *f*, Vorwort *neut*; Vorstellung *f.* **introductory** *adj* einleitend. **letter of introduction** Empfehlungsbrief *m.*
introspective [,intrə'spektiv] *adj* selbstprüfend. **introspection** *n* Selbstprüfung *f.*
introvert ['intrə,vɔit] *n* introvertierter Mensch *m.* **introverted** *adj* introvertiert.
intrude [in'truid] *v* hineindrängen; (*interfere*) sich einmischen. **intruder** *n* Eindringling *m.* **intrusion** *n* Eindrängen *neut*; Einmischung *f.* **intrusive** *adj* zudringlich; (*nuisance*) lästig.
intuition [,intjui'iʃən] *n* Intuition *f.* **intuitive** *adj* intuitiv.
inundate ['inʌndeit] *v* überschwemmen. **inundation** *n* Überschwemmung *f*; Flut *f.*
invade [in'veid] *v* überfallen. **invader** *n* Eindringling *m.* **invasion** *n* Einfall *m*, Invasion *f.*
invalid¹ ['invəlid] *n* Kranke(r), Invalide *m.*
invalid² [in'valid] *adj* ungültig. **invalidate** *v* fürungültig erklären. **invalidation** *n* Ungültigkeitserklärung *f.* **invalidity** *n* Ungültigkeit *f.*
invaluable [in'valjuəbl] *adj* unschätzbar.
invariable [in'veəriəbl] *adj* konstant, unveränderlich. **invariably** *adv* ausnahmslos.
invective [in'vektiv] *n* Beschimpfung *f.*
invent [in'vent] *v* erfinden. **invention** *n* Erfindung *f.* **inventor** *n* Erfinder(in).
inventory ['invəntri] *n* Inventar *neut*, Bestandsverzeichnis *neut*; (*stocktaking*) Bestandsaufnahme *f.*

invert [in'vəit] *v* umkehren. **inversion** *n* Umkehrung *f*.

invertebrate [in'vəitibrət] *adj* wirbellos. *n* wirbelloses Tier *neut*.

invest [in'vest] *v* investieren, anlegen. **investment** *n* Investition *f*, Anlage *f*. **investor** *n* Kapitalanleger *m*.

investigate [in'vestigeit] *v* untersuchen. **investigation** *n* Untersuchung *f*. **investigator** *n* Prüfer(in).

invigorating [in'vigəreitiŋ] *adj* stärkend.

invincible [in'vinsəbl] *adj* unüberwindlich. **invincibility** *n* Unüberwindlichkeit *f*.

invisible [in'vizəbl] *adj* unsichtbar. **invisibility** *n* Unsichtbarkeit *f*.

invite [in'vait] *v* einladen. **invitation** *n* Einladung *f*. **inviting** *adj* verlockend.

invoice ['invois] *n* Rechnung *f*. *v* in Rechnung stellen.

invoke [in'vouk] *v* anrufen. **invocation** *n* Anrufung *f*.

involuntary [in'voləntəri] *adj* unwillkürlich; (*unintentional*) unabsichtlich.

involve [in'volv] *v* (*entail*) mit sich bringen; (*draw into*) hineinziehen. **involved** *adj* verwickelt. **involvement** *n* Verwicklung *f*; Rolle *f*.

inward ['inwəd] *adj* inner. *adv also* **inwards** nach innen. **inwardly** *adv* im Innern.

iodine ['aiədiin] *n* Jod *neut*.

ion ['aiən] *n* Ion *neut*.

irate [ai'reit] *adj* wütend.

Ireland ['aiələnd] *n* Irland *neut*. **Irish** *adj* irisch. **Irishman/woman** *n* Irländer(in), Ire *m*, Irin *f*.

iris ['aiəris] *n* (*eye*) Iris *f*; (*flower*) Schwertlilie *f*.

irk [əik] *v* ärgern. **irksome** *adj* ärgerlich.

iron ['aiən] *n* Eisen *neut*; (*ironing*) Bügeleisen *neut*. *adj* eisern. *v* bügeln. **Iron Curtain** Eiserner Vorhang *m*. **ironing board** *n* Bügelbrett *neut*. **ironmonger** *n* Eisenwarenhändler *m*.

irony ['aiərəni] *n* Ironie *f*. **ironic** *adj* ironisch.

irrational [i'raʃənl] *adj* unlogisch; (*unreasonable*) unvernünftig. **irrationality** *n* Unvernunft *f*.

irredeemable [iri'diiməbl] *adj* untilgbar; (*beyond improvement*) unverbesserlich.

irregular [i'regjulə] *adj* unregelmäßig. **irregularity** *n* Unregelmäßigkeit *f*.

irrelevant [i'reləvənt] *adj* belanglos. **irrelevance** *n* Belanglosigkeit *f*.

irreparable [i'repərəbl] *adj* nicht wiedergutzumachen.

irresistible [iri'zistəbl] *adj* unwiderstehlich.

irrespective [iri'spektiv] *adj* abgesehen (von), ohne Rücksicht (auf).

irresponsible [iri'sponsəbl] *adj* unverantwortlich, verantwortungslos. **irresponsibility** *n* Unverantwortlichkeit *f*, Verantwortungslosigkeit *f*.

irrevocable [i'revəkəbl] *adj* unwiderruflich.

irrigate ['irigeit] *v* bewässern. **irrigation** *n* Bewässerung *f*.

irritate ['iriteit] *v* reizen. **irritable** *adj* reizbar. **irritant** *n* Reizmittel *neut*. **irritation** *n* Reizung *f*.

Islam ['izlaim] *n* Islam *m*. **Islamic** *adj* islamisch.

island ['ailənd] *n* Insel *f*. **islander** *n* Inselbewohner(in).

isolate ['aisəleit] *v* isolieren. **isolated** *adj* abgesondert; (*lonely*) einsam. **isolated case** Einzelfall *m*. **isolation** *n* Isolierung *f*; Einsamkeit *f*. **isolationism** *n* Isolationismus *m*.

issue ['iʃui] *n* Frage *f*; (*newspaper*) Ausgabe *f*; (*offspring*) Nachkommenschaft *f*. *v* ausgeben; (*orders*) erteilen.

isthmus ['isməs] *n* Landenge *f*.

it [it] *pron* (*nom, acc*) es; (*dat*) ihm.

italic [i'talik] *adj* kursiv. **italics** *pl n* Kursivschrift *f sing*. **in italics** kursiv gedruckt.

Italy ['itəli] *n* Italien *neut*. **Italian** *adj* italienisch; *n* Italiener(in).

itch [itʃ] *v* jucken. *n* Jucken *neut*.

item ['aitəm] *n* Gegenstand *m*; (*on agenda*) Punkt *m*; (*in newspaper*) Artikel *m*. **itemize** *v* verzeichnen.

itinerary [ai'tinərəri] *n* Reiseplan *m*.

its [its] *poss adj* sein, ihr. **itself** *pron* sich; selbst. **by itself** von selbst.

ivory ['aivəri] *n* Elfenbein *neut*.

ivy ['aivi] *n* Efeu *m*.

J

jab 94

jab [dʒab] *n* Stoß *m*, Stich *m*; (*coll: injection*) Spritze *f*. *v* Stechen.
jack [dʒak] *n* (*mot*) (Wagen)Heber *m*; (*cards*) Bube *m*. *v* **jack up** aufbocken.
jackal ['dʒakɔːl] *n* Schakal *m*.
jackdaw ['dʒakdɔː] *n* Dohle *f*.
jacket ['dʒakit] *n* Jacke *f*; (*book*) (Schutz)Umschlag *m*.
jack-knife ['dʒaknaif] *n* Klappmesser *neut*.
jackpot ['dʒakpot] *n* Jackpot *m*.
jade [dʒeid] *n* Nephrit *m*, Jade *m*.
jaded ['dʒeidid] *adj* erschöpft, abgemattet.
jagged ['dʒagid] *adj* zackig.
jaguar ['dʒagjuə] *n* Jaguar *m*.
jail [dʒeil] *n* Gefängnis *neut*. *v* ins Gefängnis werfen, einsperren. **jailer** *n* (Gefängnis)Wärter *m*.
jam[1] [dʒam] *v* einklemmen, verstopfen. **jam on the brakes** heftig auf die Bremse treten. **jam-packed** *adj* vollgestopft. *n* Engpaß *m*, Klemme *f*. **traffic jam** (Verkehrs)Stockung *f*.
jam[2] [dʒam] *n* Marmelade *f*.
janitor ['dʒanitə] *n* Hauswart *m*, Pförtner *m*.
January ['dʒanjuəri] *n* Januar *m*.
Japan [dʒə'pan] *n* Japan *neut*. **Japanese** *adj* japanisch; *n* Japaner(in).
jar[1] [dʒɑː] *n* Glass *neut*.
jar[2] [dʒɑː] *v* kreischen. **jar on one's nerves** einem auf die Nerven gehen. **jarring** *adj* mißtönend.
jargon ['dʒɑːgən] *n* Jargon *m*, Kauderwelsch *neut*.
jasmine ['dʒazmin] *n* Jasmin *m*.
jaundice ['dʒɔːndis] *n* Gelbsucht *f*. **jaundiced** *adj* gelbsüchtig; (*fig*) neidisch, voreingenommen.
jaunt [dʒɔːnt] *n* Ausflug *m*. *v* einen Ausflug machen. **jaunty** *adj* lebhaft, flott.
javelin ['dʒavəlin] *n* Speer *m*.
jaw [dʒɔː] *n* Kiefer *m*. **jawbone** *n* Kinnbacken *m*.
jazz [dʒaz] *n* Jazz *m*. **jazz band** Jazzkapelle *f*.
jealous ['dʒeləs] *adj* eifersüchtig. **jealousy** *n* Eifersucht *f*.
jeans [dʒiːns] *pl n* Jeans *pl*.
jeep [dʒiːp] *n* Jeep *m*.
jeer [dʒiə] *v* spotten. **jeer at** verspotten. **jeering** *adj* höhnisch.
jelly ['dʒeli] *n* Gelee *neut*. **jellyfish** *n* Qualle *f*.

jeopardize ['dʒepədaiz] *v* gefährden. **jeopardy** *n* Gefahr *f*.
jerk [dʒəːk] *v* stoßen, rücken. *n* Ruck *m*, Stoß *m*. **jerkily** *adv* stoßweise.
jersey ['dʒəːzi] *n* Pullover *m*; (*fabric*) Jersey *m*.
Jerusalem [dʒə'ruːsələm] *n* Jerusalem *neut*.
jest [dʒest] *n* Scherz *m*. *v* scherzen. **jesting** *adj* scherzhaft. **jestingly** *adv* in Spaß.
jet [dʒet] *n* (*liquid*) Strahl *m*; (*tech*) Düse *f*; (*aero*) Düsenflugzeug *neut*. **jet-black** *adj* rabenschwarz. **jet engine** Düsenmotor *m*. **jet-propelled** *adj* mit Düsenantrieb.
jettison ['dʒetisn] *v* abwerfen; (*discard*) wegwerfen.
jetty ['dʒeti] *n* Landungssteg *m*, Mole *f*.
Jew [dʒuː] *n* Jude *m*, Judin *f*. **Jewish** *adj* jüdisch.
jewel ['dʒuːəl] *n* Edelstein *m*, Juwel *neut*; (*fig*) Perle *f*. **jeweller** *n* Juwelier *m*. **jewellery** *n* Schmuck *m*.
jig [dʒig] *n* Gigue *f*. *v* eine Gigue tanzen.
jigsaw ['dʒigsɔː] *n* Puzzlespiel *neut*, Geduldspiel *neut*.
jilt [dʒilt] *v* sitzenlassen.
jingle ['dʒiŋgl] *n* (*sound*) Geklingel *neut*; (*radio, etc.*) Werbelied *neut*. *v* klingeln.
jinx [dʒiŋks] *n* Unheil *neut*. *v* verhexen.
job [dʒob] *n* Arbeit *f*; (*post*) Stelle *f*; (*task*) Aufgabe *f*. **jobless** *adj* arbeitslos.
jockey ['dʒoki] *n* Jockei *m*.
jocular ['dʒokjulə] *adj* scherzhaft.
jodhpurs ['dʒodpəz] *pl n* Reithose *f*.
jog [dʒog] *v* stoßen; (*run*) trotten. *n* Stoß *m*. **jog trot** *n* Trott *m*.
join [dʒoin] *v* verbinden, vereinigen; (*club, etc.*) beitreten (+ *dat*). (*come together*) zusammenkommen. *n* Verbindungsstelle *f*; (*seam*) Naht *f*. **join in** mitmachen. **joiner** *n* Tischler *m*. **joinery** *n* Tischlerarbeit *f*.
joint [dʒoint] *n* (*anat*) Gelenk *neut*; Verbindung *f*; (*cookery*) Braten *m*; (*slang: place*) Lokal *neut*. *adj* Gesamt-. **jointed** *adj* gegliedert. **jointly** *adv* gemeinsam.
joist [dʒoist] *n* Querbalken *m*, Träger *m*.
joke [dʒouk] *n* Witz *m*, Scherz *m*. *v* scherzen. **joker** *n* Spaßvogel *m*; (*cards*) Joker *m*. **jokingly** *adv* im Spaß.
jolly ['dʒoli] *adj* lustig. **jolliness** *n* Lustigkeit *f*.

jolt [dʒoult] *n* Stoß *m*. *v* stoßen.
jostle ['dʒosl] *v* anstoßen. *n* Stoß *m*.
jot [dʒot] *n* Jota *neut*. *v* **jot down** notieren.
journal ['dʒəːnl] *n* Zeitschrift *f*; (*diary*) Tagebuch *neut*. **journalism** *n* Zeitungswesen *neut*. **journalist** *n* Journalist(in).
journey ['dʒəːni] *n* Reise *f*. *v* (ver)reisen.
jovial ['dʒouviəl] *adj* lustig, jovial. **joviality** *n* Lustigkeit *f*.
joy [dʒoi] *n* Freude *f*, Wonne *f*. **joyful** *adj* erfreut. **joyfulness** *n* Fröhlichkeit *f*.
jubilant ['dʒuːbilənt] *adj* jubelnd, frohlockend. **jubilation** *n* Jubel *m*, Frohlocken *neut*.
jubilee ['dʒuːbiliː] *n* Jubiläum *neut*; (*celebration*) Jubelfest *neut*.
Judaism ['dʒuːdeiˌizəm] *n* Judentum *neut*.
judge [dʒʌdʒ] *n* (*law*) Richter; (*expert*) Kenner *m*. *v* beurteilen; (*value*) (ein)schätzen. **judgment** *n* Beurteilung *f*; (*law*) Urteil *neut*.
judicial [dʒuːˈdiʃəl] *adj* gerichtlich. **judiciary** *n* Gerichtswesen *neut*.
judicious [dʒuːˈdiʃəs] *adj* wohlüberlegt; (*reasonable*) vernünftig.
judo ['dʒuːdou] *n* Judo *neut*.
jug [dʒʌg] *n* Krug *m*, Kanne *f*.
juggernaut ['dʒʌgənɔːt] *n* Moloch *m*; (*mot*) Fernlastwagen *m*.
juggle ['dʒʌgl] *v* jonglieren. **juggler** *n* Jongleur *m*.
jugular ['dʒʌgjulə] *n* Drosselader *f*.
juice [dʒuːs] *n* Saft *m*. **juicy** *adj* saftig.
jukebox ['dʒuːkbɔks] *n* Jukebox *f*.
July [dʒuˈlai] *n* Juli *m*.
jumble ['dʒʌmbl] *n* Durcheinander *neut*. *v* durcheinander bringen. **jumble sale** Basar *m*, Ramschverkauf *m*.
jump [dʒʌmp] *n* Sprung *m*. *v* springen; (*be startled*) zusammenzucken. **jump at the chance** die Gelegenheit ergreifen. **jumpy** *adj* nervös.
jumper ['dʒʌmpə] *n* Pullover *m*.
junction ['dʒʌŋktʃən] *n* (*road*) Kreuzung *f*; (*rail*) Knotenpunkt *m*.
juncture ['dʒʌŋktʃə] *n* Augenblick *m*. **at this juncture** an dieser Stelle.
June [dʒuːn] *n* Juni *m*.
jungle ['dʒʌŋgl] *n* Dschungel *m*.
junior ['dʒuːnjə] *adj* junior, jünger. **junior school** Grundschule *f*.
juniper ['dʒuːnipə] *n* Wacholder *m*.
junk¹ [dʒʌŋk] *n* Trödel *m*. **junk shop** Trödelladen *m*.

junk² [dʒʌŋk] *n* (*naut*) Dschunke *f*.
junta ['dʒʌntə] *n* Junta *f*.
Jupiter ['dʒuːpitə] *n* Jupiter *m*.
jurisdiction [dʒuərisˈdikʃən] *n* Gerichtsbarkeit *f*.
jury ['dʒuəri] *n* die Geschworene *pl*; (*quiz*, *etc.*) Jury *f*. **trial by jury** Schwurgerichtsverhandlung *f*. **juror** *n* Geschworene(r).
just [dʒʌst] *adv* (*recently*) gerade, eben; (*only*) nur; (*exactly*) genau. **just about** so ungefähr. **just as good** ebenso gut. **just a little** ein ganz klein wenig. *adj* gerecht. **justly** *adv* mit Recht, gerecht.
justice ['dʒʌstis] *n* Gerechtigkeit *f*; (*judge*) Richter *m*. **Justice of the Peace** Friedenßrichter *m*.
justify ['dʒʌstifai] *v* rechtfertigen. **justification** *n* Rechtfertigung *f*. **justifiable** *adj* berechtigt.
jut [dʒʌt] *v* **jut out** hervorragen.
jute [dʒuːt] *n* Jute *f*.
juvenile ['dʒuːvənail] *adj* jugendlich. **juvenile court** Jugendgericht *neut*. **juvenile delinquent** jugendlicher Straftäter *m*. **juvenile delinquency** Jugendkriminalität *f*.
juxtapose [ˌdʒʌkstəˈpouz] *v* nebeneinanderstellen.

K

kaleidoscope [kəˈlaidəskoup] *n* Kaleidoskop *neut*.
kangaroo [kaŋgəˈruː] *n* Känguruh *neut*.
karate [kəˈraːti] *n* Karate *neut*.
kebab [kiˈbab] *n* Kebab *m*.
keel [kiːl] *n* Kiel *m*.
keen [kiːn] *adj* (*sharp*) scharf; (*hearing*) fein; (*enthusiastic*) eifrig. **keenness** *n* Eifer *m*.
*keep [kiːp] *v* halten, behalten; haben; (*remain*) bleiben; (*preserve*, *store*) aufbewahren; (*of food*) sich halten; (*support*) versorgen. **keep away** fernhalten. **keep fit** sich gesund erhalten. **keep in mind** im Gedächtnis behalten. **keep on** fortfahren. **keep out!** Eintritt verboten! **keep up with** Schritt halten mit. **keeper** *n* Wächter *m*; (*animals*) Züchter *m*. **be in keeping with** passen zu. **keepsake** *n* Andenken *neut*.

keg 96

keg [keg] *n* Faß *neut.*
kennel ['kenl] *n* Hundehütte *f.*
kept [kept] *V* keep.
kerb [kəɪb] *n* Straßenkante *f.*
kernel ['kəɪnl] *n* Kern *m.*
kerosene ['kerəsiɪn] *n* Petroleum *neut.*
ketchup ['ketʃəp] *n* Ketchup *m.*
kettle ['ketl] *n* Kessel *m.* kettledrum *n* Pauke *f.* a pretty kettle of fish eine schöne Bescherung. a different kettle of fish was ganz anderes.
key [kiɪ] *n* Schlüssel *m*; (*piano, typewriter*) Taste *f*; (*music*) Tonart *f.* keyboard *n* Tastatur *f.* keyring *n* Schlüsselring *m.*
khaki ['kaɪki] *adj* khaki.
kick [kik] *v* mit dem Fuß treten *or* stoßen. *n* Fußtritt *m*; (*football*) Schuß *m*; (*fig*) Schwung *m.* kick-off *n* Anstoß *m.* kick off anstoßen.
kid¹ [kid] *n* (*goat*) Zicklein *neut*; (*leather*) Ziegenleder *neut*; (*child*) Kind *neut.*
kid² [kid] *v* (*coll*) auf den Arm nehmen.
kidnap ['kidnap] *v* entführen. kidnapper *n* Entführer *m*, Kidnapper *m.*
kidney ['kidni] *n* Niere *f.* kidney bean weiße Bohne *f.* kidney stone Nierenstein *m.*
kill [kil] *v* töten, umbringen; (*animals*) schlachten. kill oneself laughing sich totlachen. killer *n* Mörder *m.* killing *n* Tötung *f.* *adj* tötend.
kiln [kiln] *n* Brennofen *m.*
kilo ['kiɪlou] *n* Kilo *neut.*
kilogram ['kiləgram] *n* Kilogramm *neut.*
kilometre ['kiləmiɪtə] *n* Kilometer *m.*
kin [kin] *n* Verwandte *pl.* next of kin nächste(r) Verwandte(r).
kind¹ [kaind] *adj* freundlich, gütig. kindly *adj* gütig. kindness *n* Güte *f.*
kind² [kaind] *n* Sorte *f*, Art *f*; (*species*) Gattung *f.* all kinds of allerlei. in kind in Waren.
kindergarten ['kindəgaɪtn] *n* Kindergarten *m*, Krippe *f.*
kindle ['kindl] *v* entzünden.
kindred ['kindrid] *n* Verwandschaft *f.*
kinetic [kin'etik] *adj* kinetisch. kinetics *n* Kinetik *f.*
king [kiŋ] *n* König *m.* kingdom *n* Königreich *neut.* animal kingdom Tierreich *neut.*
kink [kiŋk] *n* Knick *m.* *v* knicken.
kiosk ['kiɪosk] *n* Kiosk *m.* telephone kiosk Telephonzelle *f.*

kipper ['kipə] *n* Bückling *m*, Räucherhering *m.*
kiss [kis] *n* Kuß *m*, Küßchen *neut.* *v* küssen. kiss goodbye einen Abschiedskuß geben (+*dat*).
kit [kit] *n* Ausrüstung *f*; (*mil*) Gepäck *neut.*
kitchen ['kitʃin] *n* Küche *f.* kitchenette *n* Kochnische *f.*
kite [kait] *n* Drachen *m*; (*bird*) Gabelweihe *f.*
kitten ['kitn] *n* Kätzchen *neut.*
kitty ['kiti] *n* Kasse *f.*
kleptomaniac [kleptə'meiniak] *n* Kleptomane *m.*
knack [nak] *n* Kniff *m*, Trick *m.* get the knack of den Dreh heraushaben (+*gen*).
knapsack ['napsak] *n* Rucksack *m.*
knave [neiv] *n* Schurke *m*; (*cards*) Bube *m.*
knead [niɪd] *v* kneten.
knee [niɪ] *n* Knie *neut.* kneecap *n* Kniescheibe *f.*
*kneel [niɪl] *v* knien.
knelt [nelt] *V* kneel.
knew [njuɪ] *V* know.
knickers ['nikəz] *pl n* Schlüpfer *m sing*; Höschen *neut sing.*
knife [naif] *n* Messer *neut.* *v* (er)stechen.
knight [nait] *n* Ritter *m*; (*chess*) Springer *m.* knighthood Rittertum *neut.* knightly *adj* ritterlich.
*knit [nit] *v* stricken; (*brow*) rünzeln. knitted *adj* Strick-. knitting *n* Strickzeug *neut.* knitting needle Stricknadel *f.* knitwear *n* Strickwaren *pl.*
knob [nob] *n* Knopf *m*, Griff *m.*
knobbly ['nobli] *adj* knorrig.
knock [nok] *v* (*strike*) schlagen; (*on door*) klopfen; (*criticize*) heruntermachen. *n* Schlag *m*; Klopfen *neut.* knock off (*coll: steal*) klauen; (*work*) Feierabend machen. knock out k.o. schlagen.
knot [not] *n* Knoten *m*; (*in wood*) Ast *m.* *v* knoten.
*know [nou] *v* wissen; (*be acquainted with*) kennen; (*know how to*) können; (*understand*) verstehen. know-all Besserwisser *m.* know-how *n* Knowhow *neut.* knowing *adj* geschickt; (*sly*) schlau. knowingly *adv* absichtlich. be in the know Bescheid wissen. known *adj* bekannt.
knowledge ['nolidʒ] *n* Kenntnis *f.* knowledgeable *adj* kenntnisreich.

known [noun] *V* **know.**
knuckle ['nʌkl] *n* Fingerknöchel *m.*
knuckle down eifrig herangehen. **knuckle under** nachgeben.

L

label ['leibl] *n* Zettel *m*; (*sticky*) Klebezettel *neut*; (*luggage*) Anhängezettel *neut*. *v* mit einem Zettel versehen; (*fig*) bezeichnen.
laboratory [lə'borətəri] *n* Labor *neut.* **laboratory assistant** Laborant(in).
labour ['leibə] *n* Arbeit; (*work-force*) Arbeitskräfte *pl*; (*birth*) Wehen *pl. v* (schwer) arbeiten, sich anstrengen. **laboured** *adj* schwerfällig; (*style*) mühsam. **labourer** *n* (ungelernter) Arbeiter *m.*
laburnum [lə'bəːnəm] *n* Goldregen *m.*
labyrinth ['labərinθ] *n* Labyrinth *neut.*
lace [leis] *n* Spitze *f*; (*shoe*) Schnur *f. v* schnüren. **lacy** *adj* Spitzen-.
lacerate ['lasəreit] *v* zerreißen. **laceration** *n* Zerreißung *f.*
lack [lak] *v* mangeln (an). *n* Mangel *m.* **be lacking** fehlen.
lackadaisical [,lakə'deizikəl] *adj* schlapp.
lacquer ['lakə] *n* Lack *m. v* lackieren.
lad [lad] *n* Junge *m*, Bursche *m.*
ladder ['ladə] *n* Leiter *f*; (*stocking*) Laufmasche *f.* **ladder-resistant** *adj* maschenfest.
laden ['leidn] *adj* beladen.
ladle ['leidl] *n* Schöpflöffel *m. v* ausschöpfen.
lady ['leidi] *n* Dame *f.* **Ladies** *n* (*sign*) Damen *pl.* **ladies' man** Frauenheld *m.* **ladybird** Marienkäfer *m.* **lady-in-waiting** *n* Hofdame *f.* **ladylike** *adj* damenhaft.
lag[1] [lag] *v* **lag behind** zurückbleiben. *n* Zeitabstand *m.*
lag[2] [lag] *v* (*cover*) verkleiden.
lager ['laːgə] *n* Lagerbier *neut.*
lagoon [lə'guːn] *n* Lagune *f.*
laid [leid] *V* **lay**[1]**.**
lain [lein] *V* **lie**[2]**.**
lair [leə] *n* Lager *neut.*
laity ['leiəti] *n* Laienstand *m.*
lake [leik] *n* (Binnen)See *m.*
lamb [lam] *n* Lamm *neut*; (*meat*) Lammfleisch *neut.*

lame [leim] *adj* lahm, hinkend; (*excuse*) schwach. *v* lahm machen. **lameness** *n* Lahmheit *f*; Schwäche *f.*
lament [lə'ment] *v* (weh)klagen; (*regret*) bedauern. *n* Klagelied *neut.* **lamentable** *adj* beklagenswert; bedauerlich. **lamentation** *n* Jammer *m.*
laminate ['lamineit] *v* schichten. **laminated** *adj* beschichtet.
lamp [lamp] *n* Lampe *f*; (*street*) Laterne *f.* **lamplight** *n* Lampenlicht *neut.* **lamppost** *n* Laternenpfahl *m.* **lampshade** *n* Lampenschirm *m.*
lance [laːns] *n* Lanze *f. v* (*med*) mit einer Lanzette eröffnen, aufstechen. **lance corporal** *n* Hauptgefreite(r) *m.*
land [land] *n* Land *neut. v* an Land gehen; (*aircraft*) landen; (*goods*) abladen. **landing** *n* Landung *f*; (*stairs*) Treppenabsatz *m.* **landing craft** Landungsboot *neut.* **landing stage** Landesteg *m.*
landlady ['landleidi] *n* Wirtin *f.*
landlord ['landloːd] *n* (Gast-)Wirt *m.*
landmark ['landmaːk] *n* Wahrzeichen *neut*; (*milestone*) Markstein *m.*
landowner ['landounə] *n* Grundbesitzer *m.*
landscape ['landskeip] *n* Landschaft *f.* **landscape gardener** Kunstgärtner *m.* **landscape gardening** Kunstgärtnerei *f.* **landscape painter** Landschaftsmaler(in).
landslide ['landslaid] *n* Erdrutsch *m. adj* (*pol*) überwältigend.
lane [lein] *n* (*country*) (Feld)Weg *m*, Pfad *m*; (*town*) Gasse *f*; (*mot*) Spur *f.* (*sport*) Rennbahn *f.*
language ['laŋgwidʒ] *n* Sprache *f*; (*style*) Stil *m*, Redeweise *f.* **bad language** Schimpfworte *pl.* **foreign language** Fremdsprache *f.*
languish ['laŋgwiʃ] *v* schmachten.
lanky ['laŋki] *adj* schlaksig.
lantern ['lantən] *n* Laterne *f.*
lap[1] [lap] *n* (*anat*) Schoß *m*; (*circuit*) Runde *f.*
lap[2] [lap] *v* (*drink*) auflecken.
lapel [lə'pel] *n* Revers *m or neut.*
lapse [laps] *n* Versehen *neut*; (*mistake*) Irrtum *m*; (*time*) Zeitspanne *f. v* (*time*) vergehen; (*from faith*) abfallen.
larceny ['laːsəni] *n* Diebstahl *m.*
larch [laːtʃ] *n* Lärche *f.*

lard [laɪd] n Schmalz neut. v spicken. **larding needle** Sticknadel f.
larder ['laɪdə] n Speisekammer f.
large [laɪdʒ] adj groß; (considerable) beträchtlich. **at large** auf freiem Fuß m. **large as life** in Lebensgröße. **large-scale** adj Groß-. **largesse** n Freigiebigkeit f. **largely** adv weitgehend. **largeness** n Größe f.
lark¹ [laɪk] n (bird) Lerche f.
lark² [laɪk] n Spaß m. v **lark about** Possen treiben.
larva ['laɪvə] n Larve f. **larval** adj Larven-.
larynx ['lariŋks] n Kehlkopf m. **laryngitis** n Kehlkopfentzündung f.
laser ['leizə] n Laser m. **laser beam** Laserstrahl m.
lash [laʃ] v (whip) peitschen; (tie) festbinden. n Peitschenschnur f; (eyelash) Wimper f. **lash out** ausschlagen.
lass [las] n Mädchen neut, Mädel neut.
lassitude ['lasitjuːd] n Mattigkeit f.
lasso [la'suː] n Lasso m. v mit einem Lasso fangen.
last [laɪst] adj letzt. **at last** endlich, schließlich. **last but not least** nicht zuletzt. **last year** im vorigen Jahr. adv also **lastly** zuletzt. v (time) dauern; (supply) ausreichen; (be preserved) (gut) halten. **lasting** adj anhaltend, dauernd.
latch [latʃ] n Klinke f. v einklinken. **latch onto** (understand) spitzkriegen.
late [leit] adj spät; (tardy) verspätet; (deceased) selig; (former) ehemalig. **be late** Verspätung haben. **lately** adv neuerdings. **lateness** n Verspätung f. **later** adj später. **latest** adj spätest; (newest) neuest. **at the latest** spätestens.
latent ['leitənt] adj latent.
lateral ['latərəl] adj seitlich. **laterally** adv seitwärts.
lathe [leið] n Drehbank f.
lather ['laɪðə] n Seifenschaum m. v schäumen; (beat) verprügeln.
Latin ['latin] adj lateinisch. n Latein neut. **Latin America** n Lateinamerika neut. **Latin-American** adj lateinamerikanisch.
latitude ['latitjuːd] n Breite f; (fig) Spielraum m. **latitudinal** adj Breiten-.
latrine [lə'triːn] n Klosett neut, Latrine f.
latter ['latə] adj letzt. **latterly** adv neuerdings.
lattice ['latis] n Gitter neut; (pattern) Gitterwerk neut.
laugh [laɪf] v lachen. **laugh at** sich lustig

machen über. **laugh off** mit einem Scherz abtun. **laughable** adj lächerlich. n Lachen neut. **laughter** Gelächter neut.
launch [loɪntʃ] n (boat) Barkasse f; (of boat) Stapellauf m; (of rocket) Abschuß m; (start) Start m. v (boat) vom Stapel lassen; (fig) in Gang setzen.
launder ['loɪndə] v waschen. **launderette** n Waschsalon m. **laundry** n Wäscherei f; (washing) Wäsche f.
laurel ['lorəl] n Lorbeer m.
lava ['laɪvə] n Lava f.
lavatory ['lavətəri] n Klosett neut, Toilette f.
lavender ['lavində] n Lavendel m. adj (colour) lavendelfarben.
lavish ['laviʃ] adj verschwenderisch. **lavishness** n Verschwendung f.
law [loɪ] n (single law) Gesetz neut; (system) Recht neut; (study) Jura pl. **lawabiding** adj friedlich. **lawcourt** Gerichtshof m. **lawful** adj rechtmäßig, gesetzlich. **lawless** adj gesetzwidrig. **lawsuit** n Prozeß m. **lawyer** n Rechtsanwalt m.
lawn [loɪn] n Rasen m; (fabric) Batist m. **lawnmower** n Rasenmäher m. **lawn tennis** Tennis neut.
lax [laks] n locker.
laxative ['laksətiv] n Abführmittel neut.
***lay¹** [lei] v legen; (put down) setzen, stellen; (table) decken. **lay down** hinlegen; (law) vorschreiben. **lay off** (dismiss) entlassen.
lay² [lei] adj Laien-. **layman** n Laie m
lay-by ['leibai] n Parkstreifen m.
layer ['leiə] n Schicht f.
lazy ['leizi] adj faul. **laze** v faulenzen. **laziness** n Faulheit f. **lazybones** n Faulpelz m.
***lead¹** [liːd] v leiten, führen. **leader** n Führer m, Leiter m; (in newspaper) Leitartikel m. **leadership** n Führerschaft f. **leading** adj führend, Haupt-. n (dog's) Leine f; (theatre) Hauptrolle f; (cable) Schnur f; (hint) Hinweis m.
lead² [led] n Blei neut; (in pencil) Bleistiftmine f.
leaf [liːf] n Blatt neut. **leaflet** n (pamphlet) Prospekt m. v **leaf through** durchblättern. **leafy** adj belaubt.
league [liːg] n (association) Bund neut; (sport) Liga f.
leak [liːk] n Leck neut; (pol) Durchsickern neut. v lecken; durchsickern. **leakage** n Lecken neut. **leaky** adj leck.

*lean¹ [liːn] v (sich) lehnen. **lean on** sich stützen auf; (*rely on*) sich verlassen auf. **leaning** n Neigung *f*.
lean² [liːn] *adj* mager.
leant [lent] V **lean¹**
*leap [liːp] v hüpfen, springen. n Sprung *m*. **look before you leap** erst wägen, dann wagen. **by leaps and bounds** sprunghaft. **leap frog** Bockspringen *neut*. **leapyear** n Schaltjahr *neut*.
leapt [lept] V **leap**.
*learn [ləɪn] v lernen; (*find out*) erfahren. **learned** *adj* gelehrt. **learner** n Anfänger *m*; (*driver*) Fahrschüler(in). **learning** n Wissen *neut*.
learnt [ləɪnt] V **learn**.
lease [liːs] n Mietvertrag *m*, Pachtvertrag *m*. v (ver)mieten, pachten. **leaseholder** n Pächter(in).
leash [liːʃ] n Leine *f*.
least [liːst] *adj* (*smallest*) kleinst; (*slightest*) geringst. **at least** mindestens. **not in the least** nicht im geringsten.
leather [ˈleðə] n Leder *neut*. *adj* ledern. **leathery** *adj* lederartig.
*leave¹ [liːv] v verlassen, lassen; (*go away*) (ab-, ver)reisen, weggehen. **leave off** aufhören. **leave out** ·auslassen. **left-luggage office** Gepäckaufbewahrung *f*.
leave² [liːv] n (*permission*) Erlaubnis *f*; (*holiday*) Urlaub *m*. **take one's leave of** Abschied nehmen von.
lecherous [ˈletʃərəs] *adj* wollüstig. **lechery** n Wollust *f*.
lectern [ˈlektən] n Lesepult *neut*.
lecture [ˈlektʃə] n Vortrag *m*, Vorlesung *f*. v einen Vortrag halten. **lecturer** n Dozent *m*. **lecture hall** Hörsaal *m*.
led [led] V **lead¹**.
ledge [ledʒ] n Sims *m or neut*.
ledger [ˈledʒə] n Hauptbuch *neut*.
lee [liː] n (*naut*) Leeseite *f*.
leech [liːtʃ] n Blutegel *m*.
leek [liːk] n Porree *m*.
leer [liə] n anzügliches Grinsen. v anzüglich grinsen.
leeway [ˈliːwei] n Abtrift *f*; (*fig*) Spielraum *m*.
left¹ [left] V **leave¹**.
left² [left] *adj* link. *adv* (nach) links. **on the left** links. **left-handed** *adj* linkshändig. **left-wing** *adj* Links-.
leg [leg] n Bein *neut*; (*cookery*) Keule *f*; (*sport*) Lauf *m*. **be on one's last legs** auf

dem letzten Loch pfeifen. **leggy** *adj* langbeinig.
legacy [ˈlegəsi] n Legat *neut*.
legal [ˈliːgəl] *adj* gesetzlich, rechtlich. **legality** n Gesetzlichkeit *f*. **legalize** v legalisieren.
legend [ˈledʒənd] n Sage *f*, Legende *f*. **legendary** *adj* sagenhaft, legendär.
legible [ˈledʒəbl] *adj* leserlich. **legibility** n Leserlichkeit *f*.
legion [ˈliːdʒən] n Legion *f*. **legionary** n Legionär *m*.
legislate [ˈledʒisleit] v Gesetze geben. **legislation** n Gesetzgebung *f*. **legislative** *adj* gesetzgebend. **legislator** n Gesetzgeber *m*.
legitimate [ləˈdʒitimət] *adj* rechtmäßig; (*child*) ehelich; (*justified*) berechtigt. **legitimacy** n Rechtmäßigkeit; Ehelichkeit *f*.
leisure [ˈleʒə] n Freizeit *f*. **leisurely** *adv* ohne Hast.
lemon [ˈlemən] n Zitrone *f*. *adj* zitronengelb. **lemonade** n Zitronenlimonade *f*. **lemon squeezer** Zitronenpresse *f*.
*lend [lend] v (ver)leihen. **lend a hand** helfen. **lending library** Leihbibliothek *f*.
length [leŋθ] n Länge *f*; (*of cloth*) Stück *neut*; (*time*) Dauer *f*. **at length** (*in detail*) ausführlich; (*at last*) schließlich. **lengthen** v (sich) verlängern. **lengthways** *adv* längs. **lengthy** *adj* übermäßig lang.
lenient [ˈliːniənt] *adj* nachsichtig (gegenüber). **leniency** Nachsicht *f*.
lens [lenz] n Linse *f*; (*photographic*) Objektiv *neut*.
lent [lent] V **lend**.
Lent [lent] n Fastenzeit *f*.
lentil [ˈlentil] n Linse *f*.
Leo [ˈliːou] n Löwe *m*. **leonine** *adj* Löwen-.
leopard [ˈlepəd] n Leopard *m*.
leper [ˈlepə] n Leprakranke(r). **leprosy** n Lepra *f*.
lesbian [ˈlezbiən] *adj* lesbisch. n Lesbierin *f*.
less [les] *adv* weniger. *adj* geringer. *prep* minus. **lessen** v (sich) vermindern. **lesser** *adj* kleiner, geringer.
lesson [ˈlesn] n (*in school*) Stunde *f*; (*warning*) Warnung *f*. **lessons** *pl* Unterricht *m sing*.
lest [lest] *conj* damit ... nicht.

*let [let] *v* lassen; (*rooms, etc.*) vermieten.
let's go gehen wir. **let alone** (*not annoy*) in Ruhe lassen; (*much less*) geschweige denn **let down** enttäuschen, im Stich lassen. **let go** gehen lassen. **let go of** loslassen. **let up** (*coll*) nachlassen.
lethal ['liːθəl] *adj* tödlich.
lethargy ['leθədʒi] *n* Lethargie *f*. **lethargic** *adj* lethargisch.
letter ['letə] *n* Brief *m*; (*of alphabet*) Buchstabe *m*. **letter box** Briefkasten *m*.
lettuce ['letis] *n* Kopfsalat *m*.
leukaemia [luːˈkiːmiə] *n* Leukämie *f*.
level ['levl] *adj* gerade, eben; (*equal*) gleich. **level crossing** Bahnübergang *m*. **level-headed** *adj* nüchtern. **draw level with** einholen. *v* ebnen; (*make equal*) gleichmachen. *n* Ebene *f*, Niveau *neut*.
lever ['liːvə] *n* Hebel *m*.
levy ['levi] *n* Abgabe *f*. *v* erheben.
lewd [luːd] *adj* lüstern. **lewdness** *n* Lüsternheit *f*.
liable ['laiəbl] *adj* (*responsible*) verantwortlich. **be liable to** neigen zu. **liability** *n* Verantwortlichkeit. **limited liability** (*comm*) mit beschränkter Haftung. **be liable for** haften für. **liable to prosecution** strafbar.
liaison [liˈeizon] *n* Verbindung *f*; (*love affair*) (Liebes)Verhältnis *neut*.
liar ['laiə] *n* Lügner(in).
libel ['laibəl] *n* Verleumdung *f*. *v* (*schriftlich*) verleumden. **libellous** *adj* verleumderisch.
liberal ['libərəl] *adj* liberal; (*generous*) großzügig. *n* Liberale(r). **liberalize** *v* liberalisieren.
liberate ['libəreit] *v* befreien. **liberation** *n* Befreiung *f*. **liberator** *n* Befreier *m*.
liberty ['libəti] *n* Freiheit *f*. **at liberty** frei.
Libra ['liːbrə] *n* Waage *f*.
library ['laibrəri] *n* Bibliothek *f*, Bücherei *f*. **librarian** *n* Bibliothekar(in).
libretto [liˈbretou] *n* Libretto *neut*, Textbuch *neut*.
lice [lais] *V* louse.
licence ['laisəns] *n* Genehmigung *f*, Lizenz *f*. **driving licence** Führerschein *m*. **marriage licence** Eheerlaubnis *f*. **license** *v* genehmigen. **licensed** *adj* konzessioniert.
lichen ['laikən] *n* Flechte *f*.
lick [lik] *v* lecken; (*coll: defeat*) besiegen; (*flames*) züngeln. *n* Lecken *neut*.
lid [lid] *n* Deckel *m*; (*eyelid*) Lid *neut*.

lie¹ [lai] *n* Lüge. *v* lügen.
*lie² [lai] *v* liegen. **lie down** sich hinlegen. **lie in** (*coll*) sich ausschlafen.
lieutenant [ləfˈtenənt] *n* Leutnant *m*.
life [laif] *n* Leben *neut*. **lifebelt** *n* Rettungsgürtel *m*. **lifeboat** *n* Rettungsboot *neut*. **lifeguard** *n* Bademeister *m*. **life insurance** Lebensversicherung *f*. **life jacket** Schwimmweste *f*. **lifeless** *adj* leblos. **lifelike** *adj* naturgetreu. **lifesize** *adj* lebensgroß. **lifetime** *n* Lebenszeit *f*.
lift [lift] *n* Aufzug *m*, Fahrstuhl *m*. *v* (auf)heben. **give a lift to** (im Auto) mitnehmen.
*light¹ [lait] *n* Licht *neut*; (*lamp*) Lampe *f*. **a light** (*for cigarette*) Feuer *neut*. *v* anzünden.
light² [lait] *adj* leicht; (*colour*) hell.
lighten¹ ['laitn] *v* (*reduce weight*) erleichtern, leichter machen.
lighten² ['laitn] *v* (*brighten*) sich erhellen, heller werden.
lighter ['laitə] *n* (*cigarette*) Feuerzeug *neut*.
lighthouse ['laithaus] *n* Leuchtturm *m*.
lighting ['laitiŋ] *n* Beleuchtung *f*.
lightning ['laitniŋ] *n* Blitz *m*. **lightning conductor** Blitzableiter *m*. **flash of lightning** Blitzschlag *m*.
light ['laitweit]weight *adj* leicht. *n* Leichtgewichtler *m*.
light-year ['laitjiə] *n* Lichtjahr *neut*.
like¹ [laik] *adj* gleich (+ *dat*), ähnlich (+ *dat*). *prep* wie. **what's it like?** wie ist es? **like-minded** *adj* gleichgesinnt. **likewise** *adv* gleichfalls.
like² [laik] *v* gern haben; mögen. **do you like it?** gefällt es Ihnen? (*food*) schmeckt es (Ihnen)? **likeable** *adj* liebenswürdig. **liking** *n* Zuneigung *f*; (*taste*) Geschmack *m*.
likely ['laikli] *adj* wahrscheinlich. **likelihood** *n* Wahrscheinliehkeit *f*.
lilac ['lailək] *n* (*colour*) Lila *neut*. *adj* lilafarben.
lily ['lili] *n* Lilie *f*.
limb [lim] *n* Glied *neut*. **limbs** *pl* Gliedmaßen *pl*.
limbo ['limbou] *n* (*rel*) Vorhölle *f*. **in limbo** (*fig*) in der Schwebe, in Vergessenheit.
lime¹ [laim] *n* (*mineral*) Kalk *neut*.
lime² [laim] *n* (*tree*) Linde *f*, Lindenbaum *m*; (*fruit*) Limonelle *f*.

limit ['limit] *n* Grenze *f*, Schranke *f*. *v* begrenzen, beschränken. **limited** *adj* beschränkt; (*comm*) mit beschränkter Haftung.

limousine ['liməˌziːn] *n* Limousine *f*.

limp[1] [limp] *v* hinken. *n* Hinken *neut*.

limp[2] [limp] *adj* schlaff.

line [lain] *n* Linie *f*, Strich *m*; (*row*) Reihe *f*; (*of print*) Zeile *f*; (*washing*) Leine *f*; (*wrinkle*) Falte *f*. *v* linieren; (*coat, etc.*) füttern. **lineage** *n* Abstammung *f*. **linear** *adj* Linear-.

linen ['linin] *n* Leinen *neut*. **bed linen** Wäsche *f*.

liner ['lainə] *n* (*ship*) Linienschiff *neut*, Überseedampfer *m*.

linesman ['lainzman] *n* Linienrichter *m*.

linger ['liŋgə] *v* verweilen. **lingering** *adj* (*illness*) schleichend.

lingerie ['lãʒəriː] *n* (Damen)Unterwäsche *f*.

linguist ['liŋgwist] *n* Linguist(in). **linguistic** *adj* linguistisch. **linguistics** *n* Linguistik f.

lining ['lainiŋ] *n* Futter *neut*, Fütterung *f*.

link [liŋk] *n* (*of chain*) Glied *neut*; (*connection*) Verbindung *f*. *v* verbinden. **link arms** sich einhaken (bei).

linoleum [li'nouliəm] *n* Linoleum *neut*.

linseed ['linˌsiːd] *n* Leinsamen *m*. **linseed oil** Leinöl *neut*.

lint [lint] *n* Zupfleinen *neut*.

lion ['laiən] *n* Löwe *m*. **lioness** *n* Löwin *f*. **lion's share** Löwenanteil *m*.

lip [lip] *n* Lippe *f*; (*edge*) Rand *m*; (*coll: impudence*) Frechheit *f*. **lip service** Lippendienst *m*. **lipstick** *n* Lippenstift *m*.

liqueur [li'kjuə] *n* Likör *m*.

liquid ['likwid] *n* Flüssigkeit *f*. *adj* flüssig. **liquidate** *v* (*comm*) liquidieren. **liquidation** *n* Liquidierung *f*. **liquidator** *n* Liquidator *m*. **liquidity** *n* Flüssigkeit *f*.

liquor ['likə] *n* alkoholisches Getränk *neut*.

liquorice ['likəris] *n* Lakritze *f*.

lisp [lisp] *n* Lispeln *neut*. *v* lispeln.

list[1] [list] *n* Liste *f*, Verzeichnis *neut*. *v* verzeichnen.

list[2] [list] *n* (*naut*) Schlagseite *f*. *v* Schlagseite haben.

listen ['lisn] *v* hören auf, zuhören (+ *dat*). **listener** *n* Zuhörer *m*. **listening device** Abhörgerät *neut*.

listless ['listlis] *adj* lustlos.

lit [lit] *V* **light**[1].

litany ['litəni] *n* Litanei *f*.

literacy ['litərəsi] *n* die Fähigkeit, lesen und schreiben zu können *f*. **literate** *adj* gelehrt. **be literate** lesen und schreiben können.

literal ['litərəl] *adj* buchstäblich.

literary ['litərəri] *adj* literarisch.

literature ['litrətʃə] *n* Literatur *f*.

lithe [laið] *adj* geschmeidig.

litigation [liti'geiʃən] *n* Prozeß *m*.

litre ['liːtə] *n* Liter *neut*.

litter ['litə] *n* (*rubbish*) Abfall *m*; (*stretcher*) Tragbahre *f*; (*animals*) Wurf *m*. **litter bin** Abfallkorb *m*.

little ['litl] *adj* klein. *adv* wenig. **a little** ein bißchen, ein wenig.

liturgy ['litədʒi] *n* Liturgie *f*.

live[1] [liv] *v* leben; (*reside*) wohnen.

live[2] [laiv] *adj* (*alive*) lebendig; (*radio, etc.*) live; (*electricity*) stromführend. **live broadcast** Livesendung *f*.

livelihood ['laivlihud] *n* Lebensunterhalt *m*.

lively ['laivli] *adj* lebhaft. **liveliness** *n* Lebhaftigkeit *f*.

liver ['livə] *n* Leber *f*.

livestock ['laivstok] *n* Vieh *neut*.

livid ['livid] *adj* (*coll: angry*) wütend.

living ['liviŋ] *adj* lebendig, am Leben. *n* Lebensunterhalt *m*. **make a living** sein Brot verdienen. **living room** Wohnzimmer *neut*.

lizard ['lizəd] *n* Eidechse *f*.

load [loud] *n* Last *f*, Belastung *f*. *v* (be)laden.

loaf[1] [louf] *n* Laib *m*, Brot *neut*.

loaf[2] [louf] *v* **loaf around** faulenzen. **loafer** *n* Bummler *m*, Faulenzer *m*.

loan [loun] *n* Anleihe *f*; (*credit*) Darlehen *neut*. *v* leihen.

loathe [louð] *v* hassen, nicht ausstehen können. **loathing** *n* Abscheu *m*. **loathsome** *adj* abscheulich.

lob [lob] *v* (*sport*) lobben. *n* Lob *m*.

lobby ['lobi] *n* Vorhalle *f*; (*pol*) Interessengruppe *f*.

lobe [loub] *n* Lappen *m*.

lobster ['lobstə] *n* Hummer *m*.

local ['loukəl] *adj* örtlich, Orts-. *n* Ortsbewohner *m*. **local government** Gemeindeverwaltung *f*. **locality** *n* Ort *m*. **localize** *v* lokalisieren.

locate [lə'keit] *v* ausfindig machen. **location** *n* Standort *m*.

lock¹ [lok] *n* Schloß *neut*; (*canal*) Schleuse *f*. *v* verschließen. **lock in** einsperren. **lock out** aussperren. **lock up** verschließen.
lock² [lok] *n* (*of hair*) Locke *f*.
locker ['lokə] *n* Schließfach *neut*.
locket ['lokit] *n* Medaillon *neut*.
locomotive [,loukə'moutiv] *n* Lokomotive *f*.
locust ['loukəst] *n* Heuschrecke *f*.
lodge [lodʒ] *v* (*a person*) unterbringen; (*complaint*) einreichen. *n* (*hunting*) Jagdhütte *f*. **lodger** *n* Untermieter *m*.
lodgings *pl* Wohnung *f sing*, Zimmer *neut sing*.
loft [loft] *n* (Dach)Boden *m*. **lofty** *adj* hoch.
log [log] *n* Klotz *m*; (*naut*) Log *neut*. *v* (*naut*) loggen, ins Logbuch eintragen.
logarithm ['logəriðəm] *n* Logarithmus *m*.
loggerheads ['logəhedz] *pl n* **be at loggerheads with** in den Haaren liegen mit.
logic ['lodʒik] *n* Logik *f*. **logical** *adj* logisch.
loins [loins] *pl n* Lenden *pl*. **loincloth** *n* Lendentuch *neut*.
loiter ['loitə] *v* schlendern. **loiterer** *n* Schlenderer *m*.
lollipop ['loli,pop] *n* Lutscher *m*.
London ['lʌndən] *n* London *neut*.
lonely ['lounli] *adj* einsam. **loneliness** *n* Einsamkeit *f*.
long¹ [loŋ] *adj* lang.
long² [loŋ] *v* sich sehnen (nach).
long-distance *adj* Fern-.
longevity [lon'dʒevəti] *n* Langlebigkeit *f*.
longing ['loŋiŋ] *n* Sehnsucht *f*.
longitude ['londʒitjuːd] *n* Länge *f*. **longitudinal** *adj* Längen-.
long-playing record *n* Langspielplatte *f*.
long-term *adj* langfristig.
long-winded *adj* langatmig.
loo [luː] (*coll*) Klo *neut*.
look [luk] *n* (*glance*) Blick *m*; (*appearance*) Aussehen *neut*; (*expression*) Miene *f*. *v* schauen, blicken, gucken (auf); (*appear*) aussehen. **look after** aufpassen auf; (*care for*) sorgen für. **look for** suchen. **look forward to** sich freuen auf. **look into** untersuchen. **look out!** paß auf!
loom¹ [luːm] *v* **loom up** aufragen.
loom² [luːm] *n* Webstuhl *m*, Webmaschine *f*.
loop [luːp] *n* Schleife *f*, Schlinge *f*. *v* eine Schleife machen.
loophole ['luːphoul] *n* Lücke *f*.
loose [luːs] *adj* schlaff, locker; (*free*) los.

loosen *v* lösen, lockern. **loose change** Kleingeld *neut*. **loose translation** freie Übersetzung *f*.
loot [luːt] *n* Beute *f*. *v* plündern. **looter** *n* Plünderer *m*. **looting** *n* Plünderung *f*.
lop [lop] *v* **lop off** abhacken.
lopsided [,lop'saidid] *adj* schief.
lord [loːd] *n* Herr *m*; (*noble*) Edelmann *m*. **House of Lords** Oberhaus *neut*.
lorry ['lori] *n* Lastkraftwagen (Lkw) *m*.
***lose** [luːz] *v* verlieren; (*clock*) nachgehen. **lose one's way** sich verlieren. **loser** *n* Verlierer(in). **loss** *n* Verlust *m*; (*decrease*) Abnahme *f*. **dead loss** (*coll*) Niete *f*, Versager *m*.
lost [lost] *V* **lose**.
lot [lot] *n* Los *neut*; (*fate*) Schicksal *neut*; (*land*) Bauplatz *m*. **draw lots** Lose ziehen. **a lot of** viel, eine Menge.
lotion ['loufən] *n* Lotion *f*.
lottery ['lotəri] *n* Lotterie *f*.
lotus ['loutəs] *n* Lotos *m*.
loud [laud] *adj* laut; (*colour*) schreiend. **loudmouth** *n* Maulheld *m*. **loudness** *n* Lautstärke *f*. **loudspeaker** *n* Lautsprecher *m*.
lounge [laundʒ] *n* Wohnzimmer *neut*; (*hotel*) Foyer *neut*. *v* faulenzen.
louse [laus] *n* (*pl* **lice**) Laus *f*. **lousy** *adj* (*slang*) saumäßig.
love [lʌv] *n* Liebe *f*; (*person*) Liebling *m*; (*sport*) null. *v* lieben. **love doing something** etwas gern tun. **love affair** Liebesaffäre *f*. **loveless** *adj* lieblos. **love letter** Liebesbrief *m*. **loveliness** *n* Schönheit *f*. **lovely** *adj* lieblich, schön. **lover** *n* Liebhaber(in), Geliebte(r). **lovesick** *adj* liebeskrank. **loving** *adj* liebevoll.
low [lou] *adj* niedrig; (*deep*) tief; (*sad*) niedergeschlagen; (*base*) ordinär. **lowly** *adj* bescheiden. **low tide** Niedrigwasser *neut*.
lower ['louə] *v* senken, niederlassen; (*fig*) erniedrigen.
loyal ['loiəl] *adj* treu. **loyalty** *n* Treue *f*.
lozenge ['lozindʒ] *n* Pastille *f*.
lubricate ['luːbrikeit] *v* schmieren, ölen. **lubricant** *n* Schmiermittel *neut*. **lubrication** *n* Schmierung *f*.
lucid ['luːsid] *adj* deutlich, klar.
luck [lʌk] *n* (*happiness, fortune*) Glück *neut*; (*fate*) Schicksal *neut*; (*chance*) Zufall *m*. **luckily** *adv* glücklicherweise. **lucky** *adj* glücklich.

lucrative ['luːkrətiv] adj gewinnbringend.

ludicrous ['luːdikrəs] adj lächerlich.

lug [lʌg] v (carry, drag) schleppen.

luggage ['lʌgidʒ] n Gepäck neut. **luggage rack** Gepäcknetz neut.

lukewarm ['luːkwoːm] adj lauwarm.

lull [lʌl] n (pause) Pause f; (calm) Stille f.

lullaby ['lʌlə,bai] n Wiegenlied neut.

lumbago [lʌm'beigou] n Hexenschuß m, Lumbago f.

lumber¹ ['lʌmbə] n (timber) Bauholz neut; (junk) Plunder m. **lumber room** Rumpelkammer f.

lumber² ['lʌmbə] v schwerfällig gehen.

luminous ['luːminəs] adj leuchtend.

lump [lʌmp] n Klumpen m, Beule f. **lump sugar** Würfelzucker m. **lump sum** Pauschalsumme f. v **lump together** zusammenfassen. **lumpy** adj klumpig.

lunar ['luːnə] adj Mond-.

lunatic ['luːnətik] n Wahnsinnige(r). **lunacy** n Wahnsinn m.

lunch [lʌntʃ] n Mittagessen neut. v zu Mittag essen. **lunchtime** Mittagspause f.

lung [lʌŋ] n Lunge f. **lung cancer** Lungenkrebs m.

lunge [lʌndʒ] v losstürzen (auf).

lurch¹ [ləːtʃ] v taumeln.

lurch² [ləːtʃ] n **leave in the lurch** im Stich lassen.

lure [luə] v (an)locken. n Köder m.

lurid ['luərid] adj grell.

lurk [ləːk] v lauern.

luscious ['lʌʃəs] adj köstlich, lecker.

lush [lʌʃ] adj saftig.

lust [lʌst] n Wollust f, Begierde f. v **lust after** begehren. **lustful** adj lüstern.

lustre ['lʌstə] n Glanz m. **lustrous** adj strahlend.

lute [luːt] n Laute f.

Luxembourg ['lʌksəm,bəːg] n Luxemburg neut.

luxury ['lʌkʃəri] n Luxus m; (article) Luxusartikel m. **luxuriant** adj üppig. **luxurious** adj luxuriös.

lynch [lintʃ] v lynchen.

lynx [links] n Luchs m.

lyrical ['lirikəl] adj lyrisch.

lyrics ['liriks] pl n Lyrik f sing, Text m sing.

M

mac [mak] n Regenmantel m.

macabre [mə'kaːbr] adj grausig.

macaroni [makə'rouni] n Makkaroni pl.

mace¹ [meis] n Amtsstab m.

mace² [meis] n (cookery) Muskatblüte f.

machine [mə'ʃiːn] n Maschine f. v maschinell herstellen. **machine gun** Maschinengewehr neut. **machinery** n Maschinerie f. **machine tool** Werkzeugmaschine f. **machinist** n Maschinenarbeiter(in).

mackerel ['makrəl] n Makrele f.

mackintosh ['makin,toʃ] n Regenmantel m.

mad [mad] adj wahnsinnig, verrückt; (angry) wütend. **madhouse** n Irrenhaus neut. **madly** adv wie verrückt. **madman** n Verrückte(r) m. **madness** n Wahnsinn m.

madam ['madəm] n gnädige Frau f.

made [meid] V make.

magazine [,magə'ziːn] n (publication) Zeitschrift f, Illustrierte f; (also warehouse, rifle) Magazin neut.

maggot ['magət] n Made f. **maggoty** adj madig.

magic ['madʒik] n Zauberei f. adj also **magical** Zauber-, zauberhaft. **magician** n Zauberer m; (entertainer) Zauberkünstler m.

magistrate ['madʒistreit] n Friedensrichter m.

magnanimous [mag'naniməs] adj großmütig. **magnanimity** n Großmut f.

magnate ['magneit] n Magnat m.

magnet ['magnət] n Magnet m. **magnetic** adj magnetisch. **magnetism** n Magnetismus m; (fig) Anziehungskraft f. **magnetize** v magnetisieren.

magnificent [mag'nifisnt] adj prächtig. **magnificence** n Pracht f.

magnify ['magnifai] v vergrößern. **magnifying glass** Lupe f. **magnification** n Vergrößerung f.

magnitude ['magnitjuːd] n Größe f, Ausmaß neut.

magnolia [mag'nouliə] n Magnolie f.

magpie ['magpai] n Elster f.

mahogany [mə'hogəni] n (wood) Mahagoni neut. adj Mahagoni-.

maid [meid] n Mädchen neut; (servant)

Dienstmädchen *neut*. **old maid** alte Jungfer *f*.
maiden ['meidən] *n* Mädchen *ncut*. **maiden name** Mädchenname *m*. **maiden speech** Jungfernrede *f*.
mail [meil] *n* Post *f*. *v* schicken, absenden. **mailbox** Briefkasten *m*. **mail-order company** Versandhaus *neut*. **mailboat** *n* Paketboot *neut*.
maim [meim] *v* lähmen.
main [mein] *adj* Haupt-, hauptsächlich. **mains** *pl n* (*gas*, *water*) Hauptleitung *f*; (*elec*) Netz *neut sing*. **mainstay** *n* (*fig*) Hauptstütze *f*. **main street** Hauptstraße *f*.
maintain [mein'tein] *v* erhalten; behaupten. **maintenance** *n* Erhaltung *f*; (*tech*, *mot*) Wartung *f*.
maisonette [meizə'net] *n* Wohnung *f*.
maize [meiz] *n* Mais *m*.
majesty ['madʒəsti] *n* Majestät *f*. **His/Her/Your Majesty** Seine/Ihre/Eure Majestät. **majestic** *adj* majestätisch.
major ['meidʒə] *n* (*mil*) Major *m*; (*music*) Dur *neut*. *adj* (*significant*) bedeutend; (*greater*) größer. **majority** *n* Mehrheit *f*; (*law*) Mündigkeit *f*.
***make** [meik] *v* machen; (*produce*) herstellen; (*force*) zwingen; (*build*) bauen; (*reach*) erreichen. *n* (*brand*) Marke *f*; (*type*) Art *f*. **make good** (*succeed*) Erfolg haben. **make out** vergeben. **makeshift** *adj* Behelfs-. **make-up** *n* Schminke *f*.
maladjusted [malə'dʒʌstid] *adj* verhaltensgestört.
malaria [mə'leəriə] *n* Malaria *f*.
male [meil] *n* Mann *m*; (*animals*) Männchen *neut*. *adj* männlich. **male nurse** Krankenpfleger *m*.
malevolent [mə'levələnt] *adj* mißgünstig. **malevolence** *n* Mißgunst *f*.
malfunction [mal'fʌŋkʃən] *n* Funktionsstörung *f*.
malice ['malis] *n* Böswilligkeit. **malicious** *adj* böswillig.
malignant [mə'lignənt] *adj* böswillig; (*med*) bösartig.
malinger [mə'liŋgə] *v* sich krank stellen, simulieren.
mallet ['malit] *n* Schlegel *m*.
malnutrition [malnju'triʃən] *n* Unterernährung *f*.
malt [mɔilt] *n* Malz *neut*.
Malta ['mɔiltə] *n* Malta *neut*. **Maltese** *n* Malteser(in) *adj* maltesisch.

maltreat [mal'tritt] *v* mißhandeln, schlecht behandeln. **maltreatment** *n* schlechte Behandlung *f*.
mammal ['maməl] *n* Säugetier *neut*.
mammoth ['maməθ] *n* Mammut *neut*. *adj* riesig.
man [man] *n* (*pl* **men**) Mann *m*; (*human*) Mensch *m*. *v* bemannen. **manliness** *n* Mannhaftigkeit *f*. **manly** *adj* mannhaft. **manslaughter** *n* Totschlag *m*.
manage ['manidʒ] *v* (*control*) leiten, führen; (*cope*) zurechtkommen, auskommen. **management** *n* Geschäftsleitung *f*, Direktion *f*. **manager** *n* Leiter *m*, Manager *m*.
mandarin ['mandərin] *n* Mandarin *m*; (*fruit*) Mandarine *f*.
mandate ['mandeit] *n* Mandat *neut*. **mandatory** *adj* verbindlich.
mandolin ['mandəlin] *n* Mandoline *f*.
mane [mein] *n* Mähne *f*.
maneuver [mə'nuivə] *n* (*US*) Manöver *neut*. *v* manövrieren.
mange [meindʒ] *n* Räude *f*.
mangle¹ ['maŋgl] *n* (Wäsche)Mangel *f*. *v* mangeln.
mangle² ['maŋgl] *v* (*disfigure*) verstümmeln.
manhandle [man'handl] *v* grob behandeln, mißhandeln.
mania ['meiniə] *n* Manie *f*. **maniac** *n* Wahnsinnige(r). **manic** *adj* manisch.
manicure ['manikjuə] *n* Maniküre *f*. *v* maniküren. **manicurist** *n* Maniküre *f*.
manifest ['manifest] *adj* offenbar. *v* erscheinen. **manifestation** *n* Offenbarung *f*; (*symptom*) Anzeichen *neut*.
manifesto [mani'festou] *n* Manifest *neut*.
manifold ['manifould] *adj* mannigfaltig.
manipulate [mə'nipjuleit] *v* manipulieren. **manipulation** *n* Manipulation *f*.
mankind [,man'kaind] *n* Menschheit *f*.
man-made [,man'meid] *adj* künstlich.
manner ['manə] *n* (*way*) Art *f*, Weise *f*; (*behaviour*) Manier *f*, Benehmen *neut*. **mannered** *adj* manieriert. **mannerism** *n* Manierismus *m*.
manoeuvre [mə'nuivə] *n* Manöver *neut*. *v* manövrieren.
manor ['manə] *n* Herrensitz *m*, Herrenhaus *neut*.
manpower ['man,pauə] *n* Arbeitskräfte *pl*.
mansion ['manʃən] *n* (herrschaftliches) Wohnhaus *neut*.

mantelpiece ['mantlpiːs] *n* Kaminsims *m* or *neut.*
manual ['manjuəl] *adj* manuell, Hand-. *n* Handbuch *neut.*
manufacture [manju'faktʃə] *v* herstellen, erzeugen. *n* Herstellung *f*, Erzeugung *f*.
manufacturer *n* Hersteller *m*, Fabrikant *m*.
manure [mə'njuə] *n* Dünger *m*, Mist *m*. *v* düngen.
manuscript ['manjuskript] *n* Manuskript *neut. adj* handschriftlich.
many ['meni] *adj* viele. **how many?** wieviele? **many times** oft. **a good many** ziemlich viele.
map [map] *n* (Land)Karte *f*; (*of town*) Stadtplan *m. v* eine karte machen von.
maple ['meipl] *n* Ahorn *m*.
mar [maː] *v* verderben, beeinträchtigen.
marathon ['marəθən] *n* Marathonlauf *m. adj* Marathon-.
marble ['maːbl] *n* Marmor *m*; (*toy*) Marmel *f*.
march [maːtʃ] *n* Marsch *m. v* marschieren. **march past** vorbeimarschieren an.
March [maːtʃ] *n* März *m*.
marchioness [,maːʃə'nes] *n* Marquise *f*.
mare [meə] *n* Stute *f*.
margarine [,maːdʒə'riːn] *n* Margarine *f*.
margin ['maːdʒin] *n* Rand *m*; (*limit*) Grenze *f*; (*profit*) Gewinnspanne *f*. **marginal** *adj* Rand-; (*slight*) geringfügig.
marguerite [,maːgə'riːt] *n* Gänseblümchen *neut.*
marigold ['marigould] *n* Ringelblume *f*.
marijuana [mari'waːnə] *n* Marihuana *neut.*
marina [mə'riːnə] *n* Yachthafen *m*.
marinade [,mari'neid] *v* marinieren. *n* Marinade *f*.
marine [mə'riːn] *adj* See-, Meeres-. *n* (*shipping*) Marine *f*; (*mil*) Marineinfanterist *m*. **mariner** *n* Matrose *m*.
marital ['maritl] *adj* ehelich.
maritime ['maritaim] *adj* See-, Schiffahrts-.
marjoram ['maːdʒərəm] *n* Majoran *m*.
mark[1] [maːk] *n* Marke *f*, Zeichen *neut*; (*school*) Note *f*; (*stain*) Fleck *m*; (*distinguishing feature*) Kennzeichen *neut. v* bezeichnen; (*note*) notieren, vermerken. **marked** *adj* markant, ausgeprägt. **markedly** *adv* ausgesprochen.
mark[2] [maːk] *n* (*currency*) Mark *f*.

market ['maːkit] *n* Markt *m. v* auf den Markt bringen. **marketing** *n* Marketing *neut.* **market place** Marktplatz *m*. **market research** Marktforschung *f*.
marmalade ['maːməleid] *n* Orangenmarmelade *f*.
maroon[1] [mə'ruːn] *adj* (*colour*) rotbraun.
maroon[2] [mə'ruːn] *v* (*naut*) aussetzen.
marquee [maː'kiː] *n* großes Zelt *neut.*
marquess ['maːkwis] *n* Marquis *m*.
marriage ['maridʒ] *n* Heirat *f*, Ehe *f*; (*wedding*) Hochzeit *f*; (*ceremony*) Trauung *f*. **marriage certificate** Trauschein *m*.
marrow ['marou] *n* (*of bone*) Mark *neut*; (*vegetable*) Eierkürbis *m*. **marrowbone** *n* Markknochen *m*.
marry ['mari] *v* heiraten; (*get married*) sich verheiraten mit. **married couple** Ehepaar *neut.*
Mars [maːz] *n* Mars *m*. **Martian** *adj* Mars-; *n* Marsbewohner *m*.
marsh [maːʃ] *n* Sumpf *m*. **marshy** *adj* sumpfig.
marshal ['maːʃəl] *n* Marschall *m. v* einordnen; (*troops*) aufstellen.
martial ['maːʃəl] *adj* militärisch, Kriegs-.
martin ['maːtin] *n* Mauerschwalbe *f*.
martyr ['maːtə] *n* Märtyrer(in). **martyrdom** *n* Martyrium *neut.*
marvel ['maːvəl] *n* Wunder *neut. v* staunen (über). **marvellous** *adj* wunderbar.
marzipan [maːzi'pan] *n* Marzipan *neut.*
mascara [ma'skaːrə] *n* Wimperntusche *f*.
mascot ['maskət] *n* Maskottchen *neut.*
masculine ['maskjulin] *adj* männlich; (*manly*) mannhaft; (*of woman*) männisch. *n* (*gramm*) Maskulinum *m*. **masculinity** *n* Männlichkeit *f*, Mannhaftigkeit *f*.
mash [maʃ] *v* zerquetschen. **mashed potatoes** Kartoffelpüree *neut.*
mask [maːsk] *n* Maske *f. v* maskieren.
masochist ['masəkist] *n* Masochist *m*. **masochism** *n* Masochismus *m*.
mason ['meisn] *n* Maurer *m*. **masonic** *adj* Freimaurer-. **masonry** *n* Mauerwerk *neut.*
masquerade [maskə'reid] *n* Maskerade *f. v* sich ausgeben (als).
mass[1] [mas] *n* Masse *f. v* sich ansammeln. *adj* Massen-. **the masses** die breite Masse. **mass meeting** Massenversammlung *f*. **mass-produce** *v* serienmäßig herstellen. **mass production** Massenherstellung *f*.

mass

mass² [mas] *n* (*rel*) Messe *f*.
massacre ['masəkə] *n* Massaker *neut*,
Blutbad *neut*. *v* massakrieren.
massage ['masɑːʒ] *n* Massage *f*. *v* massier-
en. **masseur** *n* Masseur *m*. **masseuse** *n*
Masseuse *f*.
massive ['masiv] *adj* massiv.
mast [maɪst] *n* Mast *m*.
mastectomy [ma'stektəmi] *n* Brus-
tamputation *f*.
master ['maɪstə] *n* Herr *m*; (*school*) Lehrer *m*; (*artist*) Meister m. *v* meistern. **mas-
terful** *adj* meisterhaft. **masterpiece** *n*
Meisterwerk *neut*. **mastery** *n* Beherrschung *f*.
masturbate ['mastəbeit] *v* onanieren. **mas-
turbation** *n* Onanie *f*.
mat [mat] *n* Matte *f*; (*beer*) Untersetzer
m. **matted** *adj* mattiert.
match¹ [matʃ] *n* Streichholz *neut*.
match² [matʃ] *n* (*equal*) Gleiche(r); (*sport*)
Spiel *neut*. *v* anpassen. **meet one's match**
seinen Meister finden. **matchless** *adj*
unvergleichlich.
mate [meit] *n* (*friend*) Kamarad(in);
(*chess*) (Schach)Matt *neut*; (*animal*)
Männchen *neut*, Weibchen *neut*; (*naut*)
Schiffsoffizier *m*. *v* sich paaren; (*chess*)
matt setzen.
material [mə'tiəriəl] *n* Stoff *m*. *adj* mater-
iell; (*important*) wesentlich. **materials** *pl*
Werkstoffe *pl*. **materialist** *n* Materialist
m. **materialistic** *adj* materialistisch.
maternal [mə'təɪnl] *adj* mütterlich;
mütterlicherseits. **maternal grandfather** Großvater. **maternity** *n*
Mutterschaft *f*. **maternity dress**
Umstandskleid *neut*. **maternity home**
Entbindungsheim *neut*.
mathematics [maθə'matiks] *n* Mathmatik
f. **mathematical** *adj* mathematisch. **mathematician** *n* Mathematiker *m*.
matinee ['matinei] *n* Matinee *f*.
matins ['matinz] *n* Frühgottesdienst *m*.
matrimony ['matriməni] *n* Ehestand *m*,
Ehe *f*. **matrimonial** *adj* ehelich, Ehe-.
matrix ['meitriks] *n* Matrix *f*.
matron ['meitrən] *n* (*school*) Hausmutter
f; (*nurse*) Oberin *f*.
matter ['matə] *n* Stoff *m*, Materie *f*;
(*affair*) Sache *f*; (*pus*) Eiter *m*. *v* von
Bedeutung sein. **what's the matter?** was
ist los? **it doesn't matter** es macht nichts.
matter-of-fact *adj* sachlich.
mattress ['matris] *n* Matratze *f*.

mature [mə'tjuə] *adj* reif. *v* reifen. **maturity** *n* Reife *f*.
maudlin ['mɔːdlin] *adj* weinerlich.
maul [mɔːl] *v* zerreißen.
mausoleum [mɔːsə'liəm] *n* Mausoleum
neut, Grabmal *neut*.
mauve [mouv] *adj* malvenfarben.
maxim ['maksim] *n* Grundsatz *m*.
maximum ['maksiməm] *n* Maximum *neut*.
adj Höchst-, Maximal-.
***may** [mei] *v* mögen, können. **may I?** darf
ich? **maybe** *adv* vielleicht.
May [mei] *n* Mai *m*. **mayday** (*SOS*)
Maydaysignal *neut*.
mayonnaise [ˌmeiə'neiz] *n* Mayonnaise *f*.
mayor [meə] *n* Bürgermeister *m*.
mayoress *n* Bürgermeisterin *f*.
maze [meiz] *n* Labyrinth *neut*, Irrgarten
m.
me [miː] *pron* (*acc*) mich; (*dat*) mir.
meadow ['medou] *n* Wiese *f*.
meagre ['miːgə] *adj* mager, dürr.
meal¹ [miːl] *n* Mahlzeit *f*, Essen *neut*.
meal² [miːl] *n* (*flour*) Mehl *neut*.
***mean¹** [miːn] *v* (*word, etc.*) bedeuten;
(*person*) meinen; (*intend*) vorhaben,
beabsichtigen.
mean² [miːn] *adj* (*slight*) gering; (*base*)
gemein; (*tight-fisted*) geizig. **meanness** *n*
Gemeinheit *f*.
mean³ [miːn] *n* Durchschnitt *m*. *adj* mittler, Durschnitts-.
meander [mi'andə] *v* sich winden. *n*
Windung *f*.
meaning ['miːniŋ] *n* (*significance*)
Bedeutung *f*; (*sense*) Sinn *m*. **meaningful**
adj bedeutsam. **meaningless** *adj* sinnlos.
means [miːnz] *n* Mittel *neut*. **by means of**
durch, mittels. **by no means** auf keinen
Fall. **by all means** selbstverständlich.
meant [ment] *V* **mean¹**.
meanwhile ['miːnwail] *adv* mittlerweile.
measles ['miːzlz] *n* Masern *pl*. **German
measles** Röteln *pl*.
measure ['meʒə] *v* messen. *n* Maß *neut*.
measurement *n* Messung *f*, Maß *neut*.
meat [miːt] *n* Fleisch *neut*. **meatball** *n*
Fleischklößchen. **meaty** *adj* fleischig.
mechanic [mi'kanik] *n* Mechaniker *m*.
mechanical *adj* mechanisch. **mechanics** *n*
Mechanik *f*. **mechanism** *n* Mechanismus
m. **mechanize** *v* mechanisieren.
medal ['medl] *n* Medaille *f*, Orden *m*.
medallion *n* Schaumünze *f*.

meddle ['medl] v sich (ein)mischen (in). **meddlesome** adj zudringlich.

media ['miːdiə] pl n Medien pl. **mass media** Massenmedien pl.

mediate ['miːdieit] v vermitteln. **mediation** n Vermittlung f. **mediator** n Vermittler m.

medical ['medikəl] adj medizinisch, ärztlich. **medical certificate** Krankenschein m. **medical student** Medizinstudent m.

medicament n Arzneimittel neut. **medicinal** adj heilkräftig. **medicine** n Arznei f, Arzneimittel neut; (science) Medizin f.

medieval [medi'iːvəl] adj mittelalterlich.

mediocre [miːdi'oukə] adj mittelmäßig. **mediocrity** n Mittelmäßigkeit f.

meditate ['mediteit] v meditieren; (reflect) nachdenken (über). **meditation** n (rel) Meditation f; Nachdenken neut.

Mediterranean [meditə'reiniən] n Mittelmeer neut. adj Mittelmeer-.

medium ['miːdiəm] adj mittler, Mittel-. n Mitte f; (spiritualist) Medium neut. **medium-sized** adj mittelgroß.

medley ['medli] n Gemisch neut; (music) Potpourri neut.

meek [miːk] adj mild, sanft. **meekness** n Milde f, Sanftmut f.

meet [miːt] v treffen, begegnen (+ dat); (by appointment) sich treffen (mit); (requirements) erfüllen; (call for) abholen. **meeting** n Treffen neut; (session) Versammlung f, Sitzung f.

megaphone ['megəfoun] n Megaphon neut.

melancholy ['melənkəli] n Melancholie f, Trübsinn m. **melancholic** adj melancholisch.

mellow ['melou] adj reif; (person) freundlich, heiter.

melodrama ['melədraimə] n Melodrama neut. **melodramatic** adj melodramatisch.

melody ['melədi] n Melodie f. **melodious** adj wohlklingend.

melon ['melən] n Melone f.

melt [melt] v schmelzen. **melt away** zergehen. **melting point** Schmelzpunkt m.

member ['membə] n Mitglied m. **membership** n Mitgliedschaft f.

membrane ['membrein] n Membrane f.

memento [mə'mentou] n Andenken neut.

memo ['memou] n (note) Notiz f; (message) Mitteilung f.

memoirs ['memwaiz] pl n Memoiren pl.

memorable ['memərəbl] adj denkwürdig.

memorandum [memə'randəm] n (note) Notiz f; (message) Mitteilung f.

memorial [mi'moiriəl] n Denkmal neut. adj **memorial service** Gedenkgottesdienst m.

memory ['meməri] n (power of) Gedächtnis neut; (of something) Erinnerung f. **memorize** v auswendig lernen.

men [men] V **man**.

menace ['menis] n Drohung f. v bedrohen. **menacing** adj drohend.

menagerie [mi'nadʒəri] n Menagerie f.

mend [mend] v reparieren; (clothes) flicken; (socks, etc.) stopfen. n ausgebesserte Stelle f. **on the mend** (coll) auf dem Wege der Besserung.

menial ['miːniəl] adj niedrig.

menopause ['menəpoiz] n Wechseljahre pl, Menopause f.

menstrual ['menstruəl] adj Menstruations-. **menstruate** v die Regel haben, menstruieren. **menstruation** n Menstruation f, Monatsblutung f.

mental ['mentl] adj geistig, Geistes-; (slang) verrückt. **mental deficiency** Schwachsinn m. **mental hospital** Nervenheilanstalt f. **mental illness** Geisteskrankheit f. **mentality** n Mentalität f, Gesinnung f. **mentally ill** geisteskrank.

menthol ['menθəl] n Menthol neut.

mention ['menʃən] v erwähnen. n Erwähnung f. **don't mention it!** bitte sehr!

menu ['menjui] n Speisekarte f, Menü neut.

mercantile ['məikən,tail] adj kaufmännisch, Handels-.

mercenary ['məisinəri] adj gewinnsüchtig, geldgierig. n Söldner m.

merchandise ['məitʃəndaiz] n Waren pl, Handelsgüter pl. v verkaufen.

merchant ['məitʃənt] n Kaufmann m; (wholesaler) Großhändler m. **merchant navy** Handelsflotte f.

mercury ['məikjuri] n Quecksilber neut. **Mercury** n Merkur m.

mercy ['məisi] n Erbarmen neut, Gnade f. **merciful** adj barmherzig. **merciless** adj erbarmungslos.

mere [miə] adj bloß, rein.

merge [məidʒ] v verschmelzen; (comm) fusionieren. **merger** n Fusion f.

meridian [mə'ridiən] n Meridian m.

meringue **meringue** 10

meringue [mə'raŋ] *n* Meringe *f*, Baiser *neut*.

merit ['merit] *n* Verdienst *neut*; (*value*) Wert *m*. *v* verdienen.

mermaid ['məɪmeid] *n* Seejungfrau *f*.

merry ['meri] *adj* lustig, fröhlich. **make merry** feiern. **merry-go-round** *n* Karussell *neut*. **merriment** *n* Lustigkeit *f*.

mesh [meʃ] *n* Masche *f*. *v* ineinandergreifen. **meshed** *adj* maschig.

mesmerize ['mezməraiz] *n* hypnotisieren; (*fig*) faszinieren.

mess [mes] *n* Durcheinander *neut*, Unordnung *f*; (*mil*) Messe *f*. *v* beschmutzen. **mess about** herumpfuschen. **mess up** verderben, verpfuschen. **messy** *adj* unordentlich.

message ['mesidʒ] *n* Mitteilung *f*; (*news*) Nachricht *f*. **messenger** *n* Bote *m*.

met [met] *V* **meet**.

metabolism [mi'tabəlizm] *n* Stoffwechsel *m*. **metabolic** *adj* metabolisch.

metal ['metl] *n* Metall *neut*. **metallic** *adj* metallisch. **metallurgy** *n* Metallurgie *f*.

metamorphosis [metə'moɪfəsis] *n* Metamorphose *f*, Verwandlung *f*. **metamorphose** *v* verwandeln.

metaphor ['metəfə] *n* Metapher *f*. **metaphorical** *adj* metaphorisch.

metaphysics [,metə'fiziks] *n* Metaphysik *f*. **metaphysical** *adj* metaphysisch.

meteor ['miɪtiə] *n* Meteor *m*. **meteoric** *adj* meteorartig, plötzlich.

meteorology [,miɪtiə'rolədʒi] *n* Meteorologie *f*, Wetterkunde *f*. **meteorological** *adj* meteorologisch, Wetter-.

meter ['miɪtə] *n* Messer *m*. **gas meter** Gasuhr *f*. **parking meter** Parkuhr *f*.

methane ['miɪθein] *n* Methan *neut*.

method ['meθəd] *n* Methode *f*; (*procedure*) Verfahren *neut*. **methodical** *adj* methodisch.

methylated spirits ['meθileitid] *n* Brennspiritus *m*.

meticulous [mi'tikjuləs] *adj* übergenau, peinlich genau.

metre ['miɪtə] *n* Meter *m or neut*. **metric** *adj* metrisch.

metronome ['metrənoum] *n* Metronom *neut*, Taktmesser *m*.

metropolis [mə'tropəlis] *n* Metropole *f*, Hauptstadt *f*.

mice [mais] *V* **mouse**.

microbe ['maikroub] *n* Mikrobe *f*.

microfilm ['maikrə,film] *n* Mikrofilm *m*.

microphone ['maikrəfoun] *n* Mikrophon *neut*.

microscope ['maikrəskoup] *n* Mikroscop *neut*. **microscopic** *adj* mikroscopisch. (*tiny*) verschwindend klein.

mid [mid] *adj* mittler, Mittel-. **in mid air** mitten in der Luft. **midday** *n* Mittag *m*.

middle ['midl] *n* Mitte *f*. *adj* mittler, Mittel-. **middle-aged** *adj* im mittleren Alter. **middle-class** *adj* bürgerlich, bourgeois. **middle classes** Mittelstand *m*.

Middle Ages *pl n* Mittelalter *neut*.

Middle East *n* Naher Osten *m*.

midge [midʒ] *n* Mücke *f*.

midget ['midʒit] *n* Zwerg *m*.

midnight ['midnait] *n* Mitternacht *f*.

midsummer ['mid,sʌmə] *n* Hochsomme *m*.

midst [midst] *n* Mitte *f*. **in the midst o** mitten unter (+ *dat*).

midwife ['midwaif] *n* Hebamme *f*. **midwifery** *n* Geburtshilfe *f*.

might[1] [mait] *V* **may**.

might[2] [mait] *n* Macht *f*; (*force*) Gewalt *f*. **mighty** ['maiti] *adj* mächtig. *adv* sehr.

migraine ['miɪgrein] *n* Migräne *f*.

migrate [mai'greit] *v* abwandern. **migrant** *adj* Wander-; *n* Umsiedler *m*. **migration** *n* Wanderung *f*.

mike [maik] *n* (*coll*) Mikrophon *neut*.

mild [maild] *adj* mild, sanft. **to put i mildly** gelinde gesagt. **mildness** *f* Sanftheit *f*.

mildew ['mildjuɪ] *n* Mehltau *m*, Moder *m*.

mile [mail] *n* Meile *f*. **mileage** *f* Meilenzahl *f*. **milestone** *n* (*fig*) Markstein *m*.

militant ['militənt] *adj* militant, kämpferisch. *n* (*pol*) Radikale(r).

military ['militəri] *adj* militärisch, Militär-, Kriegs-.

milk [milk] *n* Milch *f*. *v* melken. **milk tooth** *n* Milchzahn *m*. **milky** *adj* milchig. **Milky Way** Milchstraße *f*.

mill [mil] *n* Mühle *f*; (*works*) Fabrik *f*. *v* mahlen. **run-of-the-mill** *adj* mittelmäßig. **miller** *n* Müller *m*.

millennium [mi'leniəm] *n* Jahrtausend *neut*.

milligram ['mili,gram] *n* Milligramm *neut*.

millilitre ['mili,liɪtə] *n* Milliliter *neut*.

millimetre ['mili,miɪtə] *n* Millimeter *neut*.

millinery ['milinəri] *n* Müte *pl*.

million ['miljən] n Million f. **millionaire** n Millionär n. **millionairess** n Millionärin f.
milometer [mai'lomitə] n Meilenzähler m, Kilometerzähler m.
mime [maim] n (actor) Mime m. v mimen.
mimic ['mimik] v nachäffen. **mimicry** n Nachäffung f.
mince [mins] v zerhacken. n (mincemeat) Hackfleisch neut. **mincer** n Fleischwolf m. **mince about** geziert gehen. **mincing** adj geziert, affektiert. **not mince one's words** kein Blatt vor den Mund nehmen.
mind [maind] n Geist m, Verstand m; (opinion) Meinung f. v etwas dagegen haben; (look after) aufpassen auf. **frame of mind** Gesinnung f, Stimmung f. **make up one's mind** sich entschließen. **mind out!** paß auf! Achtung! **Never mind!** macht nichts! **I don't mind** ist mir egal.
mine[1] [main] poss pron meiner m, meine f, meines neut; der, die, das meine or meinige. **a friend of mine** ein Freund von mir. **it's mine** es gehört mir.
mine[2] [main] n (coal, etc.) Bergwerk neut; (mil) Mine f. v minieren. **miner** n Bergarbeiter m. **minefield** n Minenfeld. **mining** n Bergbau m. **minesweeper** n Minensuchboot neut.
mineral ['minərəl] n Mineral neut. adj mineralisch. **mineral water** Mineralwasser neut.
mingle ['miŋgl] v (sich) vermischen.
miniature ['minitʃə] n Miniatur f. adj Klein-.
minimum ['miniməm] n Minimum neut. **minimal** adj Mindest-, Minimal-.
minister ['ministə] n (pol) Minister m; (rel) Pfarrer m. **ministry** n (pol) Ministerium neut.
mink [miŋk] n Nerz m.
minor ['mainə] adj kleiner, geringer; (trivial) geringfügig. n (under age) Minderjährige(r); (music) Moll neut. **minority** n Minderheit f; (under age) Minderjährigkeit f.
minstrel ['minstrəl] n Minnesänger m.
mint[1] [mint] n (cookery) Minze f.
mint[2] [mint] n (money) Münzanstalt f. v münzen.
minuet [minju'et] n Menuett neut.
minus ['mainəs] prep weniger, minus. **it's minus 20 degrees** wir haben 20 Grad Kälte.

minute[1] ['minit] n Minute f. **just a minute!** Moment mal!
minute[2] [mai'njuit] adj winzig.
miracle ['mirəkl] n Wunder neut, Wundertat f. **miraculous** adj wunderbar. **miraculously** adv durch ein Wunder.
mirage ['miraɪʒ] n Luftspiegelung f.
mirror ['mirə] n Spiegel m. v widerspiegeln.
mirth [məɪθ] n Fröhlichkeit f, Lustigkeit f.
misadventure [misəd'ventʃə] n Unfall m, Unglück neut.
misanthropist [miz'anθrəpist] n Menschenfeind m. **misanthropic** adj menschenfeindlich.
misapprehension [misapri'henʃən] n Mißverständnis neut.
misbehave [misbi'heiv] v sich schlecht benehmen. **misbehaviour** n schlechtes Benehmen neut.
miscalculate [mis'kalkjuleit] v sich verrechnen.
miscarriage [mis'karidʒ] n Fehlgeburt f. **miscarriage of justice** Fehlspruch m, Rechtsbeugung f. **miscarry** v eine Fehlgeburt haben; (go wrong) mißlingen.
miscellaneous [misə'leiniəs] adj vermischt. n Verschiedenes neut. **miscellany** n Gemisch neut.
mischance [mis'tʃains] n Unfall m.
mischief ['mistʃif] n Unfug m. **mischievous** adj schelmisch, durchtrieben. **mischief-maker** n Störenfried m.
misconception [miskən'sepʃən] n Mißverständnis neut.
misconduct [mis'kondʌkt] n schlechtes Benehmen neut.
misconstrue [miskən'struɪ] v mißdeuten.
misdeed [mis'diɪd] n Untat f, Verbrechen neut.
misdemeanour [misdi'miɪnə] n Vergehen neut.
miser ['maizə] n Geizhals m. **miserly** adj geizig. **miserliness** n Geiz m.
miserable ['mizərəbl] adj (unhappy) unglücklich; (wretched) elend.
misery ['mizəri] n Elend neut, Not f.
misfire [mis'faiə] v versagen; (mot) fehlzünden. n Versager m; Fehlzündung f.
misfit ['misfit] n Einzelgänger m.
misfortune [mis'foɪtʃən] n Unglück neut.
misgiving [mis'giviŋ] n Zweifel m.

misguided [mis'gaidid] *adj* (*erroneous*) irrig.
mishap ['mishap] *n* Unglück *neut*.
***mishcar** [mis'liiə] *v* sich verhören.
misinterpret [misin'təɪprit] *v* mißdeuten.
***mislay** [mis'lei] *v* verlegen.
***mislead** [mis'liid] *v* irreführen. **misleading** *adj* irreführend.
misnomer [mis'noumə] *n* falsche Bezeichnung *f*.
misplace [mis'pleis] *v* verlegen. **misplaced** *adj* (*inappropriate*) unangebracht.
misprint ['misprint] *n* Druckfehler *m*.
miss[1] [mis] *v* (*shot*) verfehlen; (*train, opportunity*) verpassen, versäumen; (*absent friend*) vermissen. *n* Fehlschuß *m*. **missing** *adj* fehlend; (*person*) vermißt.
miss[2] [mis] *n* (*title*) Fräulein *neut*.
missile ['misail] *n* Rakete *f*, Geschoß *neut*. **guided missile** Fernlenkrakete *f*.
mission ['miʃən] *n* Mission *f*; (*task*) Auftrag *m*; (*pol*) Gesandschaft *f*. **missionary** *n* Missionar(in).
mist [mist] *n* (feuchter) Dunst *m*, Nebel *m*.
***mistake** [mi'steik] *n* Fehler *m*, Irrtum *m*. *v* verwechseln. **be mistaken** im Irrtum sein.
mister ['mistə] *n* Herr *m*.
mistletoe ['misltou] *n* Mistel *f*.
mistress ['mistris] *n* (*lover*) Mätresse *f*; (*school*) Lehrerin *f*; (*of house or animal*) Herrin *f*.
mistrust [mis'trʌst] *v* mißtrauen. *n* Mißtrauen *neut*, Argwohn *m*. **mistrustful** *adj* mißtrauisch.
***misunderstand** [misʌndə'stand] *v* mißverstehen. **misunderstanding** *n* Mißverständnis *neut*.
misuse [mis'juːs; *v* mis'juːz] *v* mißbrauchen. *n* Mißbrauch *m*.
mitigate ['mitigeit] *v* mildern. **mitigating circumstances** strafmildernde Umstände *pl*.
mitre ['maitə] *n* Bischofsmütze *f*.
mitten ['mitn] *n* Fausthandschuh *m*.
mix [miks] *v* (ver)mischen. *n* Mischung *f*. **mix up** verwechseln. **mixer** *n* Mixer *m*. **mixture** *n* Mischung *f*; (*med*) Mixtur *f*.
moan [moun] *n* Stöhnen *neut*. *v* stöhnen.
mob [mob] *n* Pöbel *m*, Gesindel *neut*.
mobile ['moubail] *adj* beweglich; (*motorized*) motorisiert. *n* Mobile *neut*. **mobility** *n* Beweglichkeit *f*. **mobilization** *n* Mobilisierung *f*. **mobilize** *v* mobilisieren.

moccasin ['mokəsin] *n* Mokassin *m*.
mock [mok] *v* verhöhnen, verspotten. *ac* Schein-. **mock trial** Scheinprozeß *n* **mockery** *n* Verhöhnung *f*. (*travesty* Zerrbild *neut*. **mocking** *adj* spöttisch.
mode [moud] *n* Weise *f*, Methode *f*.
model ['modl] *n* Modell *neut*; (*pattern* Muster *neut*, Vorbild *neut*; (*fashion* Mannequin *neut*. *adj* vorbildlich, mus terhaft. *v* modellieren; (*clothes* vorführen.
moderate ['modərət; *v* 'modəreit] *ac* gemäßigt, mäßig. *v* mäßigen. **moderatio** *n* Mäßigung *f*. **in moderation** mit Maß
modern ['modən] *adj* modern. **modernit** *n* Modernität *f*. **modernize** modernisieren. **modernization** Modernisierung *f*.
modest ['modist] *adj* bescheiden; (*reason able*) vernünftig. **modesty** Bescheidenheit *f*.
modify ['modifai] *v* abändern, modifizie en. **modification** *n* Abänderung *f* Modifikation *f*.
modulate ['modjuleit] *v* modulieren.
mohair ['mouheə] *n* Mohair *m*.
moist [moist] *adj* feucht. **moisture** Feuchtigkeit *f*.
molar ['moulə] *n* Backenzahn *m*.
molasses [mə'lasiz] *n* Melasse *f*.
mold (*US*) *V* **mould**.
mole[1] [moul] *n* (*birthmark*) Mutterma neut, Leberfleck *m*.
mole[2] [moul] *n* (*zool*) Maulwurf *m*.
molecule ['molikjuːl] *n* Molekül *neu* **molecular** *adj* molekular.
molest [mə'lest] *v* belästigen.
mollusc ['moləsk] *n* Weichtier *neut*.
molt (*US*) *V* **moult**.
molten ['moultən] *adj* geschmolzen flüssig.
moment ['moumənt] *n* Moment *m* Augenblick *m*. **momentary** *aa* momentan, augenblicklich.
monarch ['monək] *n* Monarch(in). **monar chy** *n* Monarchie *f*.
monastery ['monəstəri] *n* Kloster *neu* **monastic** *adj* kloster-.
Monday ['mʌndi] *n* Montag *m*.
money ['mʌni] *n* Geld *neut*. **money bo** Sparbüchse *f*. **money order** Zahlung sanweisung *f*. **monetary** *adj* Währungs-
mongolism ['moŋgəlizm] *n* Mongolismu *m*.

mongrel ['mʌŋgrəl] *n* Mischling *m*, Kreuzung *f*.

monitor ['monitə] *n* (*TV*) Monitor *m*. *v* überwachen, kontrollieren.

monk [mʌŋk] *n* Mönch *m*. **monkish** *adj* mönchisch.

monkey ['mʌŋki] *n* Affe *m*. *v* **monkey around** herumalbern.

monogamy [mə'nogəmi] *n* Monogamie *f*. **monogamous** *adj* monogam.

monogram ['monəgram] *n* Monogramm *neut*.

monologue ['monəlog] *n* Monolog *m*.

monopolize [mə'nopəlaiz] *v* monopolisieren. **monopoly** *n* Monopol *neut*.

monosyllable ['monəsiləbl] *n* einsilbiges Wort *neut*.

monotonous [mə'notənəs] *adj* monoton. **monotony** *n* Monotonie *f*.

monsoon [mon'suɪn] *n* Monsun *m*.

monster ['monstə] *n* Ungeheuer *neut*; (*malformation*) Mißbildung *f*. **monstrous** *adj* ungeheuer.

month [mʌnθ] *n* Monat *m*. **monthly** *adj* monatlich; *n* (*magazine*) Monatsschrift *f*.

monument ['monjument] *n* Denkmal *neut*. **monumental** *adj* kolossal.

mood [muɪd] *n* Laune *f*, Stimmung *f*. **be in a good/bad mood** guter/schlechter Laune sein. **moody** *adj* launisch.

moon [muɪn] *n* Mond *m*. **full moon** Vollmond *m*. **moonlight** *n* Mondschein *m*.

moor¹ [muə] *n* Heide *f*, Moor *neut*.

moor² [muə] *v* (*boat*) vertäuen. **mooring** *n* Liegeplatz *m*.

mop [mop] *n* Mop *m*. *v* aufwischen.

mope [moup] *v* traurig sein, (*coll*) Trübsal blasen.

moped ['mouped] *n* Moped *neut*.

moral ['morəl] *adj* moralisch. *n* (*of story*) Lehre *f*. **morals** *pl* Moral *f* *sing*, Sitten *pl*. **morale** *n* Morale *f*. **morality** *n* Sittlichkeit *f*. **mores** *pl* *n* Sitten *pl*.

morbid ['moɪbid] *adj* (*fig*) schauerlich.

more [moɪ] *adj* mehr; (*in number*) weitere, mehr. *adv* mehr, weiter. **more rapid** schneller. **more and more** immer mehr. **more or less** mehr oder weniger. **once more** noch einmal. **moreover** *adv* überdies, fernerhin.

morgue [moɪg] *n* Leichenhaus *neut*.

morning ['moɪniŋ] *n* Morgen *m*, Vormittag *m*. **in the mornings** morgens. **this morning** heute früh.

moron ['moɪron] *n* Schwachsinnige(r). **moronic** *adj* schwachsinnig.

morose [mə'rous] *adj* mürrisch.

morphine ['moɪfiɪn] *n* Morphium *neut*.

morse code [moɪs] *n* Morsealphabet *neut*.

morsel ['moɪsəl] *n* Bissen *m*, Stückchen *neut*.

mortal ['moɪtl] *adj* sterblich; (*wound*) tödlich. **mortality** *n* Sterblichkeit *f*.

mortar ['moɪtə] *n* (*for bricks*) Mörtel *m*; (*mil*) Granatwerfer *m*.

mortgage ['moɪgidʒ] *n* Hypothek *f*.

mortify ['moɪtifai] *v* demütigen. **mortification** *n* Demütigung *f*.

mortuary ['moɪtʃuəri] *n* Leichenhaus *neut*.

mosaic [mə'zeiik] *n* Mosaik *neut*.

mosque [mosk] *n* Moschee *f*.

mosquito [mə'skiɪtou] *n* Moskito *m*.

moss [mos] *n* Moos *neut*. **mossy** *adj* bemoost.

most [moust] *adj* die meisten. *adv* äußerst, höchst; am meisten. *n* das Meiste. **most people** die meisten Leute. **at most** höchstens. **mostly** *adv* meistens, größtenteils.

motel [mou'tel] *n* Motel *neut*.

moth [moθ] *n* Motte *f*. **mothball** *n* Mottenkugel *f*.

mother ['mʌθə] *n* Mutter *f*. *v* bemuttern **on one's mother's side** mütterlicherseits. **mother country** Mutterland *neut*. **motherhood** *n* Mutterschaft *f*. **mother-in-law** Schwiegermutter *f*. **motherless** *adj* mutterlos. **motherly** *adj* mütterlich. **mother-of-pearl** *n* Perlmutt *neut*.

motion ['mouʃən] *n* Bewegung *f*; (*pol*) Antrag *m*. *v* zuwinken. **set in motion** in Gang setzen.

motivate ['moutiveit] *v* motivieren. **motivation** *n* Motivierung *f*.

motif [mou'tiɪf] *n* Motiv *m*.

motive ['moutiv] *n* Beweggrund *m*.

motor ['moutə] *n* Motor *m*. **motor accident** Autounfall *m*. **motorcar** *n* Wagen *m*, Auto *neut*. **motor cycle** *n* Mottorrad *neut*. **motorist** *n* Autofahrer *m*.

mottled ['motld] *adj* gefleckt.

motto ['motou] *n* Motto *neut*.

mould¹ [mould] *or US* **mold** *n* (*tech*) Form *f*; (*type*) Art *f*. *v* bilden, formen; (*tech*) gießen.

mould² [mould] *or US* **mold** *n* (*mildew*) Schimmel *m*. **mouldy** *adj* schimmelig.

moult [moult] *or US* **molt** *v* sich mausern.
mound [maund] *n* (Erd)Hügel *m*.
mount[1] [maunt] *v* (*horse*) besteigen. *n*
(*framc*) Gestell *neut*; (*horse*) Reittier
neut.
mount[2] [maunt] *n* Berg *m*, Hügel *m*.
mountain ['mauntən] *n* Berg *m*. **moun-**
taineer *n* Bergsteiger *m*.
mourn [moin] *v* trauern (um). **mourning** *n*
Trauer *f*. **go into mourning** Trauer
anlegen.
mouse [maus] *n* (*pl* **mice**) Maus *f*. **mouse-**
trap *n* Mausefalle *f*.
mousse [muis] *n* Kremeis *neut*.
moustache [mə'staiʃ] *or US* **mustache** *n*
Schnurrbart *m*.
mouth [mauθ] *n* Mund *m*; (*opening*)
Öffnung *f*; (*river*) Mündung *f*; (*animal*)
Maul *neut*. **mouthful** *n* Mundvoll *m*.
mouthpiece *n* Mundstück *neut*.
mouthwash *n* Mundwasser *neut*.
move [muiv] *v* (sich) bewegen; (*emotion-*
ally) rühren; (*house*) umziehen. **movable**
adj beweglich. **movement** *n* Bewegung *f*.
moving *adj* rührend. **moving staircase**
Rolltreppe *f*.
movie [muivi] *n* Film *m*. **go to the movies**
ins Kino gehen.
***mow** [mou] *v* mähen. **mower** *n*
(Rasen)Mäher *m*.
mown [moun] *V* **mow**.
Mr ['mistə] *n* Herr *m*.
Mrs ['misiz] *n* Frau *f*.
much [mʌtʃ] *adj, adv* viel. **how much?**
wieviel?
muck [mʌk] *n* (*dung*) Mist *m*; (*dirt*)
Dreck *m*. **mucky** *adj* schmutzig, dreckig.
mucus ['mjuikəs] *n* Schleim *m*.
mud [mʌd] *n* Schlamm *m*. **muddy** *adj*
schlammig. **mudguard** *n* Kotflügel *m*.
mudslinger *n* Verleumder(in).
muddle ['mʌdl] *n* Durcheinander *neut*,
Wirrwarr *m*. *v* **muddle through** sich
durchwursteln. **muddled** *adj* konfus.
muff [mʌf] *n* Muff *m*.
muffle ['mʌfl] *v* (*noise*) dämpfen. **muffler** *n*
Schal *m*; (*mot*) Schalldämpfer *m*.
mug [mʌg] *n* Krug *m*, Becher *m*. *v* (*rob*)
überfallen. **muggy** *adj* (*weather*) schwül.
mulberry ['mʌlbəri] *n* Maulbeere *f*.
mule [mjuil] *n* Maulesel *m*. **mulish** *adj*
störrisch.
multicoloured [ˌmʌlti'kʌləd] *adj* bunt,
vielfarbig.

multiple ['mʌltipl] *adj* mehrfach, vielfach.
multiply ['mʌltiplai] *v* (sich) vermehren;
(*math*) multiplizieren. **multiplication** *v*
Vermehrung; (*math*) Multiplikation *f*.
multiplicity *n* Vielfalt *f*.
multiracial [ˌmʌlti'reiʃəl] *adj* gemischtras-
sig.
multitude ['mʌltitjuid] *n* Menge *f*. **multi-**
tudinous *adj* zahlreich.
mumble ['mʌmbl] *v* murmeln. *n*
Gemurmel *neut*.
mummy[1] ['mʌmi] *n* (*embalmed*) Mumie *f*.
mummy[2] ['mʌmi] *n* (*coll*) Mutti *f*.
mumps [mʌmps] *n* Ziegenpeter *m*.
munch [mʌntʃ] *v* schmetzend kauen.
mundane [mʌn'dein] *adj* alltäglich, banal.
municipal [mju'nisipəl] *adj* städtisch,
Stadt-. **municipality** *n* Stadt *f*,
Stadtbezirk *m*.
mural ['mjuərəl] *n* Wandgemälde *neut*.
murder ['məidə] *n* Mord *m*, Ermordung *f*.
v (er)morden. **murderer** *n* Mörder *m*.
murderous *adj* mörderisch, tödlich.
murmur ['məimə] *v* murmeln. *n* Murmeln
neut.
muscle ['mʌsl] *n* Muskel *m*. **muscular** *adj*
(*person*) muskulös.
muse [mjuiz] *n* Muse *f*. *v* (nach)denken.
museum [mju'ziəm] *n* Museum *neut*.
mushroom ['mʌʃrum] *n* Pilz *m*, Champignon *m*. *v* (*coll*) sich ausbreiten.
music ['mjuizik] *n* Musik *f*. **musical** *adj*
musikalisch. **musician** *n* Musiker *m*.
music stand Notenständer *m*.
musk [mʌsk] *n* Moschus *m*.
musket ['mʌskit] *n* Flinte *f*, Muskete *f*.
musketeer *n* Musketier *m*.
Muslim ['mʌzlim] *n* Mohammedaner(in).
adj mohammedanisch.
muslin ['mʌzlin] *n* Musselin *m*.
mussel ['mʌsl] *n* Muschel *f*.
***must**[1] [mʌst] *v* müssen.
must[2] [mʌst] *n* Most *m*. **musty** *adj* muffig,
schimmelig.
mustard ['mʌstəd] *n* Senf *m*.
muster ['mʌstə] *v* antreten lassen. **muster**
one's courage sich zusammennehmen. *n*
pass muster Zustimmung finden.
mutation [mju'teiʃən] *n* Veränderung *f*;
(*biol*) Mutation *f*.
mute [mjuit] *adj* stumm. *n* Stumme(r);
(*music*) Sordine *f*.
mutilate ['mjuitileit] *v* verstümmeln. **muti-**
lation *n* Verstümmelung *f*.

mutiny ['mjuːtini] *n* Meuterei *f*. *v* meutern. **mutineer** *n* Meuterer *m*. **mutinous** *adj* meuterisch.

mutter ['mʌtə] *v* murmeln.

mutton ['mʌtn] *n* Hammelfleisch *neut*.

mutual ['mjuːtʃuəl] *adj* gegenseitig.

muzzle ['mʌzl] *n* Maul *neut*; (*protection*) Maulkorb *m*.

my [mai] *poss adj* mein, meine, mein. **myself** *pron* mich (selbst). **by myself** allein.

mystery ['mistəri] *n* Rätsel *neut*, Geheimnis *neut*. **mysterious** *adj* geheimnisvoll, mysteriös. **mystic** *n* Mystiker(in). *adj* mystisch. **mysticism** *n* Mystizismus *m*. **mystify** *v* täuschen, verblüffen.

myth [miθ] *n* Mythos *m*. **mythical** *adj* mythisch. **mythological** *adj* mythologisch. **mythology** *n* Mythologie *f*.

N

nag [nag] *v* herumnörgeln an. *n* Gaul *m*.

nail [neil] *n* Nagel *m*. *v* (an)nageln. **nail down** zunageln. **nailbrush** *n* Nagelbürste *f*. **nail-file** *n* Nagelfeile *f*. **nail polish** Nagellack *m*. **nail scissors** Nagelschere *f sing*.

naive [nai'iːv] *adj* naiv. **naïveté** *n* Naivität *f*.

naked ['neikid] *adj* nackt. **nakedness** *n* Nacktheit *f*.

name [neim] *n* Name *m*; (*reputation*) Ruf *m*. **by name** namentlich. **by the name of** namens. *what's your name?* wie heißen Sie? *v* nennen; (*mention*) erwähnen. **namely** *adv* nämlich.

nanny ['nani] *n* Kindermädchen *neut*.

nap [nap] *n* Nickerchen *neut*.

napkin ['napkin] *n* (*table*) Serviette *f*.

nappy ['napi] *n* Windel *f*.

narcotic [naːˈkotic] *n* Narkotikum *neut*. *adj* narkotisch.

narrate [nə'reit] *v* erzählen. **narration** *n* *also* **narrative** Erzählung *f*. **narrative** *adj* Erzählungs-. **narrator** *n* Erzähler(in).

narrow ['narou] *adj* eng, schmal; (*fig*) beschränkt. *v* sich verengen. **narrowly** *adv* (*just*) mit Mühe. **narrow-minded** *adj* engstirnig.

nasal ['neizəl] *adj* Nasen-; (*voice*) nasal.

nasturtium [nə'stəːʃəm] *n* Kapuzinerkresse *f*.

nasty ['naːsti] *adj* ekelhaft, widerlich; (*serious*) ernst, schlimm; (*person*) gemein, böse.

nation ['neiʃən] *n* Nation *f*, Volk *neut*. **national** *adj* national, Volks-. **nationalism** *n* Nationalismus *m*. **nationality** *n* Staatsangehörigkeit *f*. **nationalization** *n* Verstaatlichung *f*. **nationalize** *v* verstaatlichen. **national anthem** Nationalhymne *f*. **National Insurance** Sozialversicherung *f*.

native ['neitiv] *adj* eingeboren. *n* Eingeborene(r).

nativity [nə'tivəti] *n* Geburt *f*. **nativity play** Krippenspiel *neut*.

natural ['natʃərəl] *adj* natürlich, Natur-. **natural resources** Naturschätze *pl*. **naturalist** *n* Naturforscher *m*. **naturalize** *v* einbürgern.

nature ['neitʃə] *n* Natur *f*.

naughty ['noːti] *adj* unartig, ungezogen. **naughtiness** *n* Ungezogenheit *f*.

nausea ['noːziə] *n* Übelkeit *f*, Brechreiz *m*; (*seasickness*) Seekrankheit *f*. **nauseating** *adj* widerlich.

nautical ['noːtikəl] *adj* nautisch, Schiffs-. **nautical mile** Seemeile *f*.

naval ['neivəl] *adj* Flotten-, See-. **naval battle** Seeschlacht *f*.

navel ['neivəl] *n* Nabel *m*.

navigate ['navigeit] *v* navigieren. **navigable** *adj* schiffbar. **navigation** *n* Navigation *f*. **navigator** *n* Navigator *m*.

navy ['neivi] *n* Flotte *f*, Kriegsmarine *f*. **navy-blue** *adj* marineblau.

near [niə] *adj* nahe. *adv* nahe, in der Nähe. *prep* in der Nähe (von *or* +*gen*), nahe an. **nearby** *adv* in der Nähe; *adj* nahe gelegen. **nearly** *adv* fast, beinahe.

neat [niːt] *adj* ordentlich; (*alcohol*) rein, unverdünnt. **neatness** *n* Ordentlichkeit *f*.

necessary ['nesisəri] *adj* nötig, erforderlich. **necessarily** *adv* notwendigerweise. **necessitate** *v* erfordern. **necessity** *n* Notwendigkeit *f*. **necessities** *pl* Bedarfsartikel *pl*.

neck [nek] *n* Hals *m*. **neckerchief** *n* Halstuch *neut*. **necklace** *n* Halskette *f*. **necktie** *n* Krawatte *f*.

nectar ['nektə] *n* Nektar *m*.

née [nei] *adj* geborene.
need [niːd] *v* Bedürfnis *neut*, Bedarf *m*; (*necessity*) Notwendigkeit *f*. **if need arise** im Notfall. **needful** *adj* nötig. **neediness** Armut *f*. **needless** *adj* unnötig. **needy** *adj* arm.
needle ['niːdl] *n* Nadel *f*; (*indicator*) Zeiger *m*. *v* (*coll*) reizen. **needlework** *n* Handarbeit *f*.
negate [ni'geit] *v* annullieren, verneinen. **negation** *n* Annullierung *f*, Verneinung *f*. **negative** *adj* negativ; (*answer*) ablehnend. *n* (*phot*) Negativ *neut*.
neglect [ni'glekt] *v* vernachlässigen. *n* Vernachlässigung *f*.
negligée ['negliʒei] *n* Negligé *neut*.
negligence ['neglidʒəns] *n* Nachlässigkeit *f*. **negligent** *adj* nachlässig. **negligible** *adj* geringfügig.
negotiate [ni'gouʃieit] *v* verhandeln. **negotiation** *n* Verhandlung *f*. **negotiator** Vermittler *m*.
Negro ['niːgrou] *n* Neger *m*. *adj* Neger-. **Negress** *n* Negerin *f*.
neigh [nei] *v* wiehern. *n* Wiehern *neut*.
neighbour ['neibə] *n* Nachbar(in). **neighbourhood** *n* Nachbarschaft *f*. **neighbourly** *adj* freundlich.
neither ['naiðə] *adj, pron* kein (von beiden). **neither ... nor ...** weder ... noch ... .
neon ['niːon] *n* Neon *neut*.
nephew ['nefjuː] *n* Neffe *m*.
nepotism ['nepətizəm] *n* Vetternwirtschaft *f*.
nerve [nəːv] *n* Nerv *m*; (*cheek*) Frechheit *f*. **nerves** *pl* Nervosität *f sing*. **nervous** *adj* Nerven-; (*on edge*) nervös. **nervousness** *n* Nervosität *f*. **nervy** *adj* nervös. **nerve-racking** nervenaufreibend.
nest [nest] *n* Nest *neut*. *v* nisten.
nestle ['nesl] *v* sich anschmiegen.
net[1] [net] *n* Netz *neut*; (*fabric*) Tüll *m*. *v* fangen.
net[2] [net] *adj* (*comm*) netto, Netto-. **net amount** Nettobetrag *m*. **net price** Nettopreis *m*. **net profit** Reingewinn *m*.
Netherlands ['neðələndz] *pl n* Niederlände *pl*.
nettle ['netl] *n* Nessel *f*. *v* ärgern. **nettle rash** Nesselausschlag *m*. **grasp the nettle** die Schwierigkeit anpacken.
neurosis [nju'rousis] *n* Neurose *f*. **neurotic** *adj* neurotisch; *n* Neurotiker(in).

neuter ['njuːtə] *adj* (*gramm*) sächlich. *n* Neutrum *neut*. *v* (*male*) kastrieren; (*female*) sterilisieren.
neutral ['njuːtrəl] *adj* neutral. *n* (*mot*) Leerlauf *m*. **neutrality** *n* Neutralität *f*. **neutralize** *v* neutralisieren.
never ['nevə] *adv* nie, niemals. **never-ending** *adj* endlos. **never-failing** *adj* unfehlbar. **nevermore** *adv* nimmermehr. **nevertheless** *adv* nichtsdestoweniger.
new [njuː] *adj* neu; (*strange*) unbekannt. **newborn** *adj* neugeboren. **newcomer** *n* Neuankömmling *m*. **new-fangled** *adj* neumodisch. **newish** *adj* ziemlich neu. **newly** *adv* neulich. **newly-wed** *adj* jungvermählt. **newness** *n* Neuheit *f*. **news** *pl n* Nachrichten *pl*. **newspaper** *n* Zeitung *f*. **newsagent** Zeitungshändler *m*. **news flash** Kurznachricht *f*. **newsstand** *n* Zeitungskiosk *m* **newsworthy** *adj* aktuell.
newt [njuːt] *n* Wassermolch *m*.
New Testament *n* Neujahr *neut*. **New Year's Day** Neujahr *neut*. **New Year's Eve** Sylvester *neut*.
next [nekst] *adj* nächst, nächstfolgend; *adv* gleich daran, nächstens. *prep* neben, bei. **next door** nebenan.
nib [nib] *n* (Füllfeder)Spitze *f*.
nibble ['nibl] *v* nagen, knabbern (an). *n* Nagen *neut*, Knabbern *neut*; (*morsel*) Happen *m*.
nice [nais] *adj* nett; (*kind*) freundlich. **nicely** *adv* nett. **nicety** *n* Feinheit *f*.
niche [nitʃ] *n* Nische *f*.
nick [nik] *v* einkerben; (*coll: catch*) erwischen. *n* Kerbe *f*; (*coll*) Gefängnis *neut*; Polizeiwache *f*.
nickel ['nikl] *n* Nickel *neut*; (*US*) Fünfcentstück *neut*. *adj* Nickel-. **nickel-plated** *adj* vernickelt.
nickname ['nikneim] *n* Spitzname *m*.
nicotine ['nikətiːn] *n* Nikotin *neut*.
niece [niːs] *n* Nichte *f*.
niggle ['nigl] *v* trödeln.
night [nait] *n* Nacht *f*; (*evening*) Abend *m*. **all night** die ganze Nacht. **goodnight** gute Nacht. **nightclub** *n* Nachtlokal *neut*. **nightdress** *n* Nachthemd *neut*. **nightly** *adj* nächtlich. **nightmare** *n* Alptraum *m*. **nighttime** *n* Nacht *f*.
nightingale ['naitiŋgeil] *n* Nachtigall *f*.
nil [nil] *n* Null *f*.
nimble ['nimbl] *adj* flink. **nimbleness** *n* Gewandtheit *f*.

nine [nain] *adj* neun. *n* Neun *f.* **ninth** *adj* neunt; *n* Neuntel *neut.*
nineteen [nain'tiːn] *adj* neunzehn. *n* Neunzehn *f.* **nineteenth** *adj* neunzehnt.
ninety ['nainti] *adj* neunzig. *n* Neunzig *f.* **ninetieth** *adj* neunzigst.
nip [nip] *v* kneifen, zwicken. **nip in the bud** im Keim ersticken.
nipple ['nipl] *n* Brustwarze *f*; (*baby's bottle*) Lutscher *m*; (*tech*) Nippel *m.*
nit [nit] *n* Niß *f*, Nisse *f.*
nitrogen ['naitrədʒən] *n* Stickstoff *m.*
no [nou] *adv* nein. *adj* kein. **on no account** auf keinen Fall. **in no way** keineswegs. **no more** nicht mehr. **no smoking** Rauchen verboten. **no-smoking compartment** Nichtraucher *m.*
noble ['noubl] *adj* edel, adlig. **nobility** *n* Adel *m*, Adelsstand, *m.* **nobleman** *n* Edelmann *m.*
nobody ['noubodi] *pron* niemand, keiner.
nocturnal [nok'təːnəl] *adj* nächtlich, Nacht-.
nod [nod] *v* nicken. *n* Nicken *neut.* **nod off** einschlafen.
noise [noiz] *n* Lärm *m*, Geräusch *neut.* **noiseless** *adj* geräuschlos. **noisy** *adj* laut.
nomad ['noumad] *n* Nomade *m*, Nomadin *f.* **nomadic** *adj* nomadisch.
nominal ['nominl] *adj* nominell, Nenn-.
nominate ['nomineit] *v* ernennen. **nomination** *n* Ernennung *f.*
nominative ['nominətiv] *n* (*gramm*) Nominativ *m.*
nonchalant ['nonʃələnt] *adj* unbekümmert. **nonchalance** *n* Gleichgültigkeit *f.*
nondescript ['nondiskript] *adj* nichtssagend.
none [nʌn] *pron* kein; (*person*) niemand. *adv* keineswegs.
nonentity [non'entəti] *n* Unding *neut*; (*coll: person*) Null *f.*
nonetheless [ˌnʌnðə'les] *adv* nichtsdestoweniger.
nonsense ['nonsəns] *n* Unsinn *m.* *interj* Unsinn! Quatsch! **nonsensical** *adj* sinnlos. **stand no nonsense** sich nichts gefallen lassen.
non-smoker [non'smoukə] *n* Nichtraucher(in). **non-smoking compartment** Nichtraucher(abteil) *m.*
non-stop [non'stop] *adj* pausenlos; (*train*) durchgehend.
noodles ['nuːdlz] *pl n* Nudeln *pl.*

noon [nuːn] *n* Mittag *m.* **at noon** zu Mittag.
no-one ['nouwʌn] *pron* keiner, niemand.
noose [nuːs] *n* Schlinge *f.*
nor [noː] *adj* noch. **nor do I** ich auch nicht.
norm [noːm] *n* Norm *f.* **normal** *adj* normal. **normality** *n* Normalität *f.* **normalize** *v* normalisieren. **normally** *adv* normalerweise.
north [noːθ] *n* Norden *m.* *adj also* **northerly, northern** nördlich, Nord-. *adv also* **northwards** nach Norden, nordwärts. **North America** Nordamerika *neut.* **north-east** *n* Nordosten *m.* **North Pole** Nordpol *m.* **north-west** *n* Nordwesten *m.*
Norway ['noːwei] *n* Norwegen *neut.* **Norwegian** *adj* norwegisch; *n* Norweger(in).
nose [nouz] *n* Nase *f.* **nosy** *adj* (*coll*) neugierig.
nostalgia [no'staldʒə] *n* Nostalgie *f.* **nostalgic** *adj* wehmütig.
nostril ['nostrəl] *n* Nasenloch *neut.*
not [not] *adv* nicht. **not a** kein. **is it not?** *or* **isn't it?** nicht wahr?
notch [notʃ] *n* Kerbe *f.* *v* einkerben.
note [nout] *n* Vermerk *m*, Notiz *f*; (*letter*) Zettel *m*; (*music*) Note *f*; (*money*) Schein *m*; (*importance*) Bedeutung *f.* *v* merken. **take notes** Notizen machen.
nothing ['nʌθiŋ] *pron* nichts. *n* Nichts *neut.* **nothing but** nichts als.
notice ['noutis] *n* Notiz *f*; (*law*) Kündigung *f.* *v* bemerken. **period of notice** Kündigungsfrist *f.* **take notice (of)** achtgeben (auf). **give notice** kündigen. **until further notice** bis auf weiteres. **noticeable** *adj* bemerkenswert. **noticeboard** *n* Anschlagtafel *f.*
notify ['noutifai] *v* melden, benachrichtigen. **notification** *n* Meldung *f*; Benachrichtigung *f.*
notion ['nouʃən] *n* Begriff *m.* **have no notion** keine Ahnung haben.
notorious [nou'toːriəs] *adj* notorisch.
notwithstanding [notwið'standiŋ] *prep* trotz (+ *gen*).
nougat ['nuːgaː] *n* Nugat *m.*
nought [noːt] *n* Null *f.* **come/bring to nought** zunichte kommen/bringen.
noun [naun] *n* Hauptwort *neut.*
nourish ['nʌriʃ] *v* (er)nähren. **nourishing** *adj* nahrhaft. **nourishment** *n* Ernährung *f.*

novel ['novəl] *adj* neu, neuartig. *n* Roman *m*. **novelist** *n* Romanschriftsteller(in). **novelty** *n* Neuheit *f*.
November [nə'vembə] *n* November *m*.
novice ['novis] *n* Anfänger(in); (*rel*) Novize *m*, *f*.
now [nau] *adv* jetzt, nun; (*straightaway*) sofort. **now and again** ab und zu, hin und wieder. **nowadays** *adv* heutzutage.
nowhere ['nouweə] *adv* nirgends, nirgendwo. **from nowhere** aus dem Nichts.
noxious ['nokʃəs] *adj* schädlich.
nozzle ['nozl] *n* Schnauze *f*, Ausguß *m*.
nuance ['njuːɑ̃s] *n* Nuance *f*, Schattierung *f*.
nuclear ['njuːkliə] *adj* Kern-. **nuclear energy** Atomkraft *f*. **nuclear reactor** Kernreaktor *m*.
nucleus ['njuːkliəs] *n* Kern *m*.
nude ['njuːd] *adj* nackt. **nudist** *n* Nudist(in). **nudity** *n* Nacktheit *f*.
nudge [nʌdʒ] *n* Rippenstoß *m*. *v* leicht anstoßen.
nugget ['nʌgit] *n* Goldklumpen *m*.
nuisance ['njuːsns] *n* Ärgernis *neut*.
null [nʌl] *adj* nichtig, ungültig. **null and void** null und nichtig.
numb [nʌm] *adj* starr, erstarrt. *v* taub machen.
number ['nʌmbə] *n* Nummer *f*; (*amount*) Anzahl *f*; (*figure*) Ziffer *f*. *v* numerieren. **number-plate** *n* Nummernschild *neut*. **numeral** *n* Ziffer *f*. **numerous** *adj* zahlreich.
nun [nʌn] *n* Nonne *f*.
nurse [nəːs] *n* Krankenschwester *f*, Krankenpfleger(in). *v* pflegen; (*feed baby*) stillen. **nursemaid** *n* Kindermädchen *neut*. **nursing** *n* Krankenpflege *f*. **nursing home** Privatklinik *f*.
nursery ['nəːsəri] *n* (*in house*) Kinderzimmer *neut*; (*institution*) Krippe *f*, Kindertagesstätte *f*; (*bot*) Gärtnerei *f*. **nurseryman** *n* Pflanzenzüchter *m*. **nursery rhyme** *n* Kinderlied *neut*, Kinderreim *m*. **nursery school** *n* Kindergarten *m*.
nurture ['nəːtʃə] *v* erziehen.
nut [nʌt] *n* Nuß *f*; (*for bolt*) Mutter *f*. **nutcracker** Nußknacker *m*. **nuts** *adj* (*coll*) verrückt. **nutmeg** *n* Muskatnuß *f*.
nutrient ['njuːtriənt] *n* Nährstoff *m*. *adj* nährend. **nutrition** *n* Ernährung *f*. **nutritious** *adj* nahrhaft.

nuzzle ['nʌzl] *v* sich schmiegen (an).
nylon ['nailon] *n* Nylon *neut*. **nylons** *pl* Strümpfe *pl*.
nymph [nimf] *n* Nymphe *f*.

O

oak [ouk] *n* Eiche *f*, (*wood*) Eichenholz *neut*. **oaken** *adj* eichen.
oar [oː] *n* Ruder *neut*, Riemen *m*. **oarsman** *n* Ruderer *m*.
oasis [ou'eisis] *n* (*pl* **-ses**) Oase *f*.
oath [ouθ] *n* Eid *m*; (*swear word*) Fluch *m*.
oats [outs] *pl n* Hafer *m sing*. **oatmeal** *n* Hafermehl *neut*.
obedient [ə'biːdiənt] *adj* gehorsam. **obedience** *n* Gehorsam *m*.
obese [ə'biːs] *adj* fettleibig. **obesity** *n* Fettleibigkeit *f*.
obey [ə'bei] *v* gehorchen (+*dat*); (*an order*) befolgen.
obituary [ə'bitjuəri] *n* Todesanzeige *f*.
object ['obʒikt; *v* əb'ʒekt] *n* Gegenstand *m*; (*aim*) Ziel *neut*; (*gramm*) Objekt *neut*. **money is no object** Geld spielt keine Rolle. **objective** *adj* objektiv. *v* einwenden (gegen). **objection** *n* Einwand *m*, Einspruch *m*. **objectionable** *adj* unangenehm.
oblige [ə'blaidʒ] *v* (*coerce*) zwingen. **be obliged to do something** etwas tun müssen. **much obliged!** besten Dank! **obligation** *n* Verpflichtung *f*. **obligatory** *adj* verbindlich.
oblique [ə'bliːk] *adj* schräg.
obliterate [ə'blitəreit] *v* auslöschen, tilgen. **obliteration** *n* Auslöschung *f*, Vertilgung *f*.
oblivion [ə'bliviən] *n* Vergessenheit *f*. **oblivious (to)** *adj* blind (gegen).
oblong ['oblon] *n* Rechteck *neut*. *adj* rechteckig.
obnoxious [əb'nokʃəs] *adj* gehässig.
oboe ['oubou] *n* Oboe *f*. **oboist** *n* Oboist(in).
obscene [əb'siːn] *adj* obszön. **obscenity** *n* Obszönität *f*, Unzüchtigkeit *f*.
obscure [əb'skjuə] *adj* (*dark*) dunkel, düster; (*meaning, etc.*) obskur, udeutlich.

obscurity n Dunkelheit f; Undeutlichkeit f.

observe [əb'zəɪv] v beobachten; (remark) bemerken. **observer** n Beobachter m. **observation** n Beobachtung f; Bemerkung f.

obsess [əb'ses] v quälen, heimsuchen. **obsessed** adj besessen. **obsession** n Besessenheit f.

obsolescent [obsə'lesnt] adj veraltend. **obsolescence** n Veralten neut.

obsolete ['obsəliːt] adj überholt, veraltet.

obstacle ['obstəkl] n Hindernis neut.

obstetrics [ob'stetriks] n Geburtshilfe f. **obstetrician** n Geburtshelfer(in).

obstinate ['obstinət] adj hartnäckig. **obstinacy** n Hartnäckigkeit f.

obstruct [əb'strʌkt] v versperren, blockieren; (hinder) hemmen. **obstruction** n Versperrung f; Hemmung f; (obstacle) Hindernis neut.

obtain [əb'tein] v erhalten, bekommen. **obtainable** adj erhältlich.

obtrusive [əb'truːsiv] adj aufdringlich.

obtuse [əb'tjuːs] adj stumpf.

obvious ['obviəs] adj offensichtlich.

occasion [ə'keiʒən] n Gelegenheit f; (possibility) Möglichkeit f; (cause) Anlaß m. **occasional** adj gelegentlich.

occult ['okʌlt] adj okkult. **the occult** okkulte Wissenschaften pl.

occupy ['okjupai] v (person) beschäftigen; (house) bewohnen; (mil) besetzen. **occupied** adj (phone booth, etc.) besetzt. **occupant** n Bewohner(in). **occupation** n Beschäftigung f; (profession) Beruf m; (mil) Besatzung f. **occupational** adj beruflich.

occur [ə'kəɪ] v vorkommen. **it occurs to me** es fällt mir ein. **occurrence** n Ereignis neut.

ocean ['ouʃən] n Ozean m, Meer neut. **oceanic** adj ozeanisch. **ocean-going** adj Hochsee-.

ochre ['oukə] adj ockerfarbig.

octagon ['oktəgən] n Achteck neut. **octagonal** adj achteckig.

octave ['oktiv] n Oktave f.

October [ok'toubə] n Oktober m.

octopus ['oktəpəs] n Tintenfisch m.

oculist ['okjulist] n Augenarzt m.

odd [od] adj (strange) seltsam; (numbers) ungerade. **oddity** n Seltsamkeit f. **oddly (enough)** seltsamerweise. **oddments** pl n Reste pl. **oddness** n Seltsamkeit f. **odds** pl n (Gewinn)Chancen pl. **at odds with** uneins mit. **odds and ends** Krimskrams m.

ode [oud] n Ode f.

odious ['oudiəs] adj verhaßt.

odour ['oudə] n Geruch m. **odourless** adj geruchlos.

oesophagus [iː'sofəgəs] n Speiseröhre f.

of [ov] prep von or gen.

off [of] prep fort, weg. adv weg, entfernt; ab. adj (food) verdorben, nicht mehr frisch. **go off** weggehen; (food) verderben. **take off** (clothes) ausziehen; (holiday) frei nehmen. **switch off** ausschalten. **off and on** ab und zu. **off duty** dienstfrei.

offal ['ofəl] n Innereien pl.

offend [ə'fend] v kränken, beleidigen. **offender** n Missetäter(in). **offence** n Vergehen neut, Verstoß m. **take offence (at)** Anstoß nehmen (an). **offensive** adj widerwärtig; n (mil) Angriff m.

offer ['ofə] v (an)bieten. n Angebot neut. **offering** n (gift) Spende f.

offhand [of'hand] adj lässig.

office ['ofis] n Büro neut; (official position or department) Amt neut. **officer** n (mil) Offizier. **take office** das Amt antreten. **office staff** Büropersonal neut.

official [ə'fiʃəl] n Beamte(r). adj amtlich; (report, function) offiziell. **officially** adj offiziell.

officious [ə'fiʃəs] adj aufdringlich.

offing ['ofiŋ] n **in the offing** in Sicht, drohend.

off-licence ['oflaisns] n Wein- und Spirituosenhandlung f.

off-peak [of'piːk] adj außerhalb der Hauptverkehrszeit.

off-putting ['ofputiŋ] adj abstoßend.

off-season [of'siːzn] n stille Saison f.

offset [of'set, n 'ofset] v ausgleichen. n (printing) offsetdruck m.

offshore ['ofʃoɪ] adj Küsten-. adv von der Küste entfernt, auf dem Meere.

offside [of'said] adj abseits.

offspring ['ofspriŋ] n Nachkommenschaft f.

offstage ['ofsteidʒ] adv hinter den Kulissen.

often ['ofn] adv oft, häufig.

ogre ['ougə] n Ungeheuer neut, Riese m.

oil [oil] n Öl n; (petroleum) Erdöl neut. v ölen. **oilfield** Ölfeld neut. **oil-paint** n

Ölfarbe *f.* **oil-painting** *n* Ölgemalde *neut.*
oily *adj* fettig.
ointment ['ointmənt] *n* Salbe *f.*
old [ould] *adj* alt. **grow old** alt werden.
five years old fünf Jahre alt. **old age** Alter
neut. **old-fashioned** *adj* altmodisch.
olive ['oliv] *n* Olive *f.* **olive-green** *adj* oliv-
grün. **olive branch** *n* Ölzweig *m.* **olive oil**
Olivenöl *neut.* **olive tree** Ölbaum *m.*
Olympics [ə'limpiks] *pl n* Olympische
Spiele *pl,* Olympiade *f.*
omelette ['omlit] *n* Omelett *neut.*
omen ['oumən] *n* Vorzeichen *neut.* **omi-
nous** *adj* verhängnisvoll, drohend.
omit [ou'mit] *v* auslassen; (*to do something*) unterlassen. **omission** *n* Unterlassung *f.*
omnipotent [om'nipətənt] *adj* allmächtig.
omnipotence *n* Allmacht *f.*
on [on] *prep* (*position*) an, auf; (*concerning*) über. *adv* (*forward*) fort, weiter. **have
on one** bei sich haben. **on fire** in Brand.
on foot zu Fuß. **on time** pünktlich. **put
on** (*clothes*) anziehen; (*manner*) affektier-
en. **switch on** einschalten.
once [wʌns] *adv, conj* einmal. **at once**
sofort. **once and for all** ein für allemal.
all at once auf einmal, plötzlich.
one [wʌn] *adj* ein, eine, ein. *n* Eins *f.* *pron*
man. **oneself** *pron* sich (selbst). **by oneself** allein. **one-piece** *adj* einteilig. **one-
way street** Einbahnstraße *f.*
onion ['ʌnjən] *n* Zwiebel *f.*
onlooker ['onlukə] *n* Zuschauer(in).
only ['ounli] *adj* einzig. *adv* nur; (*with
times*) erst. *conj* jedoch. **only just** gerade.
not only ... but also ... nicht nur ...
sondern auch ... .
onset ['onset] *n* Anfang *m.*
onslaught ['onsloɪt] *n* Angriff *m.*
onus ['ounəs] *n* Last *f,* Verpflichtung *f.*
onward ['onwəd] *adv* vorwärts, weiter.
ooze [uɪz] *v* (aus)sickern.
opal ['oupəl] *n* Opal *m.*
opaque [ə'paik] *adj* undurchsichtig.
open ['oupən] *v* öffnen, aufmachen;
(*book*) aufschlagen; (*event, shop*)
eröffnen; (*begin*) anfangen. *adj* offen,
auf. **open-air** *adj* Freiluft-. **in the open air**
im Freien. **with open arms** herzlich.
open-handed *adj* freigiebig. **opening** *n*
Öffnung *f.* (*shop*) Eröffnung *f.* **open-
minded** *adj* aufgeschlossen.
opera ['opərə] *n* Oper *f.* **opera house** Oper

f, Opernhaus *neut.* **opera singer** Opern-
sänger(in). **operatic** *adj* Opern-.
operate ['opəreit] *v* funktionieren, laufen;
(*med, tech, comm*) operieren. **operation** *n*
Arbeitslauf *m,* Betrieb *m;* Operation *f.*
operative *adj* tätig, wirksam; *n* Arbeiter
m.
ophthalmic [of'θalmik] *adj* Augen-. **ophthalmologist** *n* Augenarzt *m.* **ophthalmol-
ogy** *n* Ophthalmologie *f.*
opinion [ə'pinjən] *n* Meinung *f,* Ansicht *f.*
in my opinion meines Erachtens. **opinion
poll** Meinungsumfrage *f.*
opium ['oupiəm] *n* Opium *neut.*
opponent [ə'pounənt] *n* Gegner(in).
opportune [opə'tjuːn] *adj* rechtzeitig.
opportunist *n* Opportunist(in).
opportunity [opə'tjuːnəti] *n* Gelegenheit
f; (*possibility*) Möglichkeit *f.* **take the
opportunity** die Gelegenheit ergreifen.
oppose [ə'pouz] *v* bekämpfen, sich widersetzen (+ *dat*). **opposed** *adj* feindlich
(gegen). **as opposed to** im Vergleich zu.
opposing *adj* (*ideas*) widerstreitend.
opposition *n* Widerstand *m;* (*pol*) Opposition *f.*
opposite ['opəzit] *adj* gegenüberliegend. *n*
Gegenteil *neut.*
oppress [ə'pres] *v* unterdrücken. **oppres-
sion** *n* Unterdrückung *f.* **oppressive** *adj*
bedrückend; (*weather*) schwül.
opt [opt] *v* sich entscheiden (für).
optical ['optikl] *adj* optisch. **optician** *n*
Optiker *m.* **optics** *n* Optik *f.*
optimism ['optimizəm] *n* Optimismus *m.*
optimist *n* Optimist(in). **optimistic** *adj*
optimistisch.
optimum ['optiməm] *n* Optimum *neut. adj*
optimal.
option ['opʃən] *n* Wahl *f;* (*comm*) Option
f. **have no option (but to)** keine andere
Möglichkeit haben (, als zu). **optional** *adj*
wahlfrei.
opulent ['opjulənt] *adj* opulent, üppig.
opulence *n* Opulenz *f,* Üppigkeit *f.*
or [oɪ] *conj* oder. **or else** sonst.
oracle ['orəkl] *n* Orakel *neut.*
oral ['oɪrəl] *adj* mündlich; (*med*) oral. *n*
mündliche Prüfung *f.*
orange ['orindʒ] *n* Apfelsine *f,* Orange *f.*
adj orange.
orator ['orətə] *n* Redner *m.* **oration** *n*
Rede *f.* **oratory** *n* Redekunst *f.*
orbit ['oɪbit] *n* Umlaufbahn *f.* *v*
umkreisen.

orchard ['ɔːtʃəd] *n* Obstgarten *m*.
orchestra ['ɔːkəstrə] *n* Orchester *neut*.
orchestral *adj* Orchester-, orchestral.
orchid ['ɔːkid] *n* Orchidee *f*.
ordain [ɔː'dein] *v* ordinieren, weihen; (*decree*) anordnen.
ordeal [ɔː'diːl] *n* schwere Prüfung *f*.
order ['ɔːdə] *n* Ordnung *f*; (*series*) Reihenfolge *f*; (*comm*) Bestellung *f*, Auftrag *m*; (*command*) Befehl *m*; (*rel*) Orden *m*. *v* (*comm*) bestellen; (*command*) befehlen. **put in order** ordnen. **in order to** ... um ... zu .... .
orderly ['ɔːdəli] *adj* ordentlich. *n* (*med*) Sanitäter *m*.
ordinal ['ɔːdinl] *adj* Ordinal-.
ordinary ['ɔːdənəri] *adj* gewöhnlich, normal. **out-of-the-ordinary** außerordentlich. **ordinarily** *adv* normalerweise.
ore [ɔː] *n* Erz *neut*.
oregano [ori'gɑːnou] *n* Origanum *neut*.
organ ['ɔːgən] *n* Organ *neut*; (*music*) Orgel *f*. **organist** *n* Organist(in).
organic [ɔː'ganik] *adj* organisch.
organism ['ɔːgənizəm] *n* Organismus *m*.
organize ['ɔːgənaiz] *v* organisieren. **organization** *n* Organisation *f*; (*association*) Verband *m*. **organizer** *n* Organisator *m*.
orgasm ['ɔːgazəm] *n* Orgasmus *m*.
orgy ['ɔːdʒi] *n* Orgie *f*.
orient ['ɔːriənt] *v* orientieren. **the Orient** Morgenland *neut*, Orient *m*. **oriental** *adj* orientalisch; *n* Orientale *m*, Orientalin *f*.
orientate ['ɔːriənteit] *v* orientieren. **orientation** *n* Orientierung *f*.
origin ['ɔridʒin] *n* Ursprung *f*; Herkunft *f*, Entstehung *f*. **original** *adj* ursprünglich; (*unusual*) originell; *n* Original *neut*. **originality** *n* Originalität *f*. **originate** *v* entstehen.
ornament ['ɔːnəmənt] *n* Ornament *neut*. *v* verzieren, schmücken. **ornamental** *adj* ornamental.
ornate [ɔː'neit] *adj* reich verziert.
ornithology [ɔːni'θolədʒi] *n* Ornithologie *f*, Vogelkunde *f*. **ornithologist** *n* Ornithologe *m*, Ornithologin *f*.
orphan ['ɔːfən] *n* Waise *f*, Waisenkind *neut*. *v* verwaisen. **orphanage** *n* Waisenhaus *neut*.
orthodox ['ɔːθədoks] *adj* orthodox.
orthopaedic [ɔːθə'piːdik] *adj* orthopädisch. **orthopaedics** *n* Orthopädie *f*.

oscillate ['osileit] *v* oszillieren, schwingen. **oscillation** *n* Schwingung *f*.
ostensible [o'stensəbl] *adj* scheinbar.
ostentatious [osten'teiʃəs] *adj* großtuerisch. **ostentation** *n* Prahlerei *f*.
osteopath ['ostiəpaθ] *n* Osteopath(in).
ostracize ['ostrəsaiz] *v* verbannen.
ostrich ['ostritʃ] *n* Strauß *m*.
other ['ʌðə] *adj, pron* ander. **other than** anders als. **each other** einander. **somebody or other** irgend jemand. **one after the other** einer/eine/eins nach dem/der andern.
otherwise ['ʌðəwaiz] *adv* sonst.
otter ['otə] *n* Otter *m*.
***ought** [ɔːt] *v* sollen. *you ought to do it* Sie sollten es tun.
ounce [auns] *n* Unze *f*.
our [auə] *adj* unser. **Our Father** Vaterunser *neut*. **ours** *poss pron* unsere. **ourselves** uns (selbst).
oust [aust] *v* vertreiben.
out [aut] *adv* aus, hinaus, heraus; (*outside*) draußen. **come out** herauskommen; (*book, etc.*) erscheinen. **go out** hinausgehen. **out of the question** ausgeschlossen. **out-of-date** *adj* veraltet.
outboard ['autbɔːd] *adj* Außenbord-. *n* Außenbordmotor *m*.
outbreak ['autbreik] *n* Ausbruch *m*.
outbuilding ['autbildiŋ] *n* Nebengebäude *neut*.
outburst ['autbəːst] *n* Ausbruch *m*.
outcast ['autkɑːst] *n* Ausgestoßene(r).
outcome ['autkʌm] *n* Ergebnis *neut*.
outcry ['autkrai] *n* Aufschrei *m*.
***outdo** [aut'duː] *v* übertreffen.
outdoor ['autdɔː] *adj* Außen-. **outdoor swimming pool** Freibad *neut*. **outdoors** *adv* draußen.
outer ['autə] *adj* äußer, Außen-. **outer garments** Oberkleidung *f*. **outer space** Weltraum *m*.
outfit ['autfit] *n* Ausstattung *f*; (*coll: team*) Mannschaft *f*. **outfitter** *n* (Herren)Ausstatter *m*.
outgoing ['autgouiŋ] *adj* (*pol*) abtretend; (*friendly*) gesellig.
***outgrow** [aut'grou] *v* hinauswachsen über; (*clothes*) herauswachsen aus.
outhouse ['authaus] *n* Anbau *m*, Nebengebäude *neut*.
outing ['autiŋ] *n* Ausflug *m*.
outlandish [aut'landiʃ] *adj* seltsam, grotesk.

outlaw ['autlɔɪ] *n* Vogelfreie(r). *v* ächten.
outlay ['autlei] *n* Auslage *f*, Ausgabe *f*.
outlet ['autlit] *n* Auslaß *m*.
outline ['autlain] *n* Umriß *m*. *v* umreißen.
outlive [aut'liv] *v* überleben.
outlook ['autluk] *n* Aussicht *f*; (*attitude*) Auffassung *f*.
outlying ['autlaiiŋ] *adj* entlegen.
outnumber [aut'nʌmbə] *v* (zahlenmäßig) überlegen sein (+ *dat*).
outpatient ['autpeiʃənt] *n* ambulanter Patient *m*.
outpost ['autpoust] *n* Vorposten *m*.
output ['autput] *n* Leistung *f*, Output *m*.
outrage ['autreidʒ] *n* Schande *f*. **outraged** *adj* beleidigt, schockiert. **outrageous** *adj* frevelhaft.
outright ['autrait; *adv* aut'rait] *adj*, *adv* ganz, völlig; (*immediately*) sogleich, auf der Stelle.
outside [aut'said; *adj* 'autsaid] *n* Äußere *neut*; Außenseite *f*. *adj* äußer, Außen-. *prep* außerhalb (+ *gen*). *adv* (*go*) hinaus; (*be*) draußen. **outsider** *n* Außenseiter(in).
outsize ['autsaiz] *adj* übergroß. *n* Übergröße *f*.
outskirts ['autskɔɪtz] *pl n* Umgebung *f sing*, Staatrand *m sing*.
outspoken [aut'spoukən] *adj* freimütig.
outstanding [aut'standiŋ] *adj* hervorragend; (*not settled*) unerledigt.
outstrip [aut'strip] *v* überholen.
outward ['autwəd] *adj* äußer. *adv also* **outwards** nach Außen. **outward-bound** *adj* auf der Ausreise. **outwardly** *adv* äußerlich.
outweigh [aut'wei] *v* überwiegen.
outwit [aut'wit] *v* überlisten.
oval ['ouvəl] *n* Oval *neut*. *adj* oval.
ovary ['ouvəri] *n* Eierstock *m*.
ovation [ou'veiʃən] *n* Ovation *f*, Beifallssturm *m*.
oven ['ʌvn] *n* (*cookery*) Backofen *m*; (*industrial, etc.*) Ofen *m*.
over ['ouvə] *adv* über, hinüber, herüber; (*finished*) zu Ende; (*during*) während; (*too much*) allzu. *prep* über; (*more than*) mehr als. **over and over again** immer wieder. **over there** drüben. **all over England** in ganz England. **it's all over** es ist aus.
overall ['ouvərɔɪl] *adj* gesamt. *adv* insgesamt. *n also* **overalls** *pl* Overall *m*, Schutzanzug *m*.
overbalance [ouvə'baləns] *v* umkippen.

overbearing [ouvə'beəriŋ] *adj* anmaßend, arrogant.
overboard ['ouvəbɔɪd] *adv* über Bord.
overcast [ouvə'kaɪst] *adj* bedeckt, bewölkt.
overcharge [ouvə'tʃaɪdʒ] *v* zuviel verlangen von.
overcoat ['ouvəkout] *n* Mantel *m*.
***overcome** [ouvə'kʌm] *v* überwinden. *adj* (*with emotion*) tief bewegt.
overcrowded [ouvə'kraudid] *adj* überfüllt.
***overdo** [ouvə'duɪ] *v* übertreiben. **overdo it** zu weit gehen. **overdone** *adj* (*cookery*) übergar.
overdose ['ouvədous] *n* Überdosis *f*.
***overdraw** [ouvə'drɔɪ] *v* überziehen. **overdraft** *n* (Konto)Überziehung *f*.
overdrive ['ouvədraiv] *n* Schongang *m*.
overdue [ouvə'djuɪ] *adj* überfällig; (*train*) verspätet.
overestimate [ouvə'estimeit] *v* überschätzen.
overexpose [ouvəik'spouz] *v* (*phot*) überbelichten.
overfill [ouvə'fil] *v* überfüllen.
overflow [ouvə'flou; *n* 'ouvəflou] *v* überlaufen. *n* Überlauf *m*.
overgrown [ouvə'groun] *adj* überwachsen.
***overhang** [ouvə'haŋ; *n* 'ouvəhaŋ] *v* überhängen. *n* Überhang *m*.
overhaul [ouvə'hɔɪl] *v* überholen. *n* Überholung *f*.
overhead [ouvə'hed] *adj* obenliegend. **overheads** *pl n* allgemeine Unkosten *pl*.
***overhear** [ouvə'hiə] *v* (*zufällig*) hören.
overheat [ouvə'hiɪt] *v* überheizen; (*mot*) heißlaufen.
overjoyed [ouvə'dʒoid] *adj* entzückt, außer sich vor Freude.
overland [ouvə'land] *adj* Überland-.
overlap [ouvə'lap; *n* 'ouvəlap] *v* sich überschneiden (mit). *n* Überscheiden *neut*, Übergreifen *neut*.
***overlay** [ouvə'lei; *n* 'ouvəlei] *v* bedecken, belegen. *n* Auflage *f*, Bedeckung *f*.
overleaf [ouvə'liɪf] *adv* umseitig, umstehend.
overload [ouvə'loud; *n* 'ouvəloud] *v* überbelasten. *n* Überbelastung *f*.
overlook [ouvə'luk] *v* (*room, etc.*) überblicken; (*let pass*) nicht beachten.
overnight [ouvə'nait] *adv* über Nacht. **stay overnight** übernachten. *adj* Nacht-. **overnight case** Handkoffer *m*.

overpower [ouvə'pauə] *v* überwältigen.
overrate [ouvə'reit] *v* überschätzen.
overrule [ouvə'ruːl] *v* zurückweisen; (*person*) überstimmen.
*overrun [ouvə'rʌn] *v* überschwemmen, überlaufen.
overseas [ouvə'siːz] *adv* in Übersee. *adj* überseeisch, Übersee-.
overseer [ouvə'siə] *n* Vorarbeiter *m.*
overshadow [ouvə'ʃadou] *v* überschatten.
*overshoot [ouvə'ʃuːt] *v* hinausschießen über.
oversight ['ouvəsait] *n* Versehen *neut.*
*oversleep [ouvə'sliːp] *v* sich verschlafen.
overspill ['ouvəspil] *n* Überschuß *m.*
overt [ou'vəːt] *adj* offenkundig.
*overtake [ouvə'teik] *v* überholen.
*overthrow [ouvə'θrou; *n* 'ouvəθrou] *v* (um)stürzen. *n* Umsturz *m.*
overtime ['ouvətaim] *n* Überstunden *pl.* **work overtime** Überstunden machen.
overtone ['ouvətoun] *n* Nuance *f.*
overture ['ouvətjuə] *n* (*music*) Ouvertüre *f.*
overturn [ouvə'təːn] *v* umkippen.
overweight [ouvə'weit] *adj* (zu) dick, fettleibig.
overwhelm [ouvə'welm] *v* überwältigen. **overwhelming** *adj* überwältigend.
overwork [ouvə'wəːk] *v* (sich) überanstrengen.
overwrought [ouvə'rɔːt] *adj* nervös, überreizt.
ovulate ['ovjuleit] *v* ovulieren. **ovulation** *n* Ovulation *f.* **ovum** *n* Ei *neut,* Eizelle *f.*
owe [ou] *v* schulden; (*have debts*) Schulden haben. **owing** *adj* zu zahlen. **owing to** infolge *or* wegen (+gen).
owl [aul] *n* Eule *f.*
own [oun] *adj* eigen. *v* besitzen; (*admit*) zugeben. **own up** gestehen. **owner** *n* Inhaber(in) *n* Besitz *m.* **ownership** *n* Besitz *m.*
ox [oks] *n* (*pl* **oxen**) Ochse *m,* Rind *neut.* **oxtail** Ochsenschwanz *m.*
oxygen ['oksidʒən] *n* Sauerstoff *m.*
oyster ['oistə] *n* Auster *f.*

P

pace [peis] *n* (*step*) Schritt *m;* (*speed*) Geschwindigkeit *f,* Tempo *neut. v* schreiten. **keep pace with** Schritt halten mit. **pacemaker** *n* Schrittmacher *m.*
Pacific [pə'sifik] *n* Pazifik *m.*
pacify ['pasifai] *v* befrieden. **pacifier** *n* (*for baby*) Schnuller *m.* **pacifism** *n* Pazifismus *m.* **pacifist** *n* Pazifist(in).
pack [pak] *n* Pack *m,* Packung *f;* (*cards*) Spiel *neut;* (*dogs*) Meute *f. v* einpacken; (*stuff*) vollstopfen. **package** *n* Paket *neut.* **packaging** *n* Verpackung *f.* **packet** *n* Packung *f,* Päckchen *neut.* **packhorse** *n* Lastpferd *neut.*
pact [pakt] *n* Pakt *m,* Vertrag *m.*
pad¹ [pad] *n* Polster *neut;* (*paper*) Block *m;* (*sport*) Schützer *m;* (*ink*) Stempelkissen *neut.* **padding** *n* Polsterung *f.*
pad² [pad] *v* trotten.
paddle¹ ['padl] *n* Paddel *neut. v* paddeln. **paddle-steamer** *n* Raddampfer *m.*
paddle² ['padl] *v* (*wade*) planschen, herumpaddeln.
paddock ['padək] *n* Pferdekoppel *f;* (*on racecourse*) Sattelplatz *m.*
paddyfield ['padifiːld] *n* Reisfeld *neut.*
padlock ['padlok] *n* Vorhängeschloß *neut.* *v* (mit einem Vorhängeschloß) verschließen.
paediatric [piːdi'atrik] *adj* pädiatrisch. **paediatrician** *n* Kinderarzt *m,* Kinderärztin *f.* **paediatrics** *n* Kinderheilkunde *f.*
pagan ['peigən] *adj* heidnisch. *n* Heide *m,* Heidin *f.*
page¹ [peidʒ] *n* (*book*) Seite *f.*
page² [peidʒ] *n* (*boy*) Page *m.*
pageant ['padʒənt] *n* Festzug *m.* **pageantry** *n* Prunk *m.*
paid [peid] *V* **pay.**
pail [peil] *n* Eimer *m.*
pain [pein] *n* Schmerz *m,* Schmerzen *pl;* (*suffering*) Leid *neut. v* peinigen. **take pains** sich Mühe geben. **on pain of** bei Strafe von. **painful** *adj* schmerzhaft. **painkiller** *n* schmerzstillendes Mittel *neut.* **painless** *adj* schmerzlos. **painstaking** *adj* sorgfältig.
paint [peint] *n* Farbe *f,* Lack *m. v* anstreichen; (*pictures*) malen. **paintbrush** *n* Pinsel *m.* **painted** *adj* bemalt. **painter** *n* Maler(in). **painting** *n* Gemälde *neut.*
pair [peə] *n* Paar *neut;* (*animals*) Pärchen *neut;* (*married couple*) Ehepaar *neut.* **pair off** paarweise anordnen. **a pair of trousers** eine Hose.

pal [pal] *n* (*coll*) Kamerad *m*, Kumpel *m*.
palace ['palǝs] *n* Palast *m*.
palate ['palit] *n* (Vorder)Gaumen *m*; (*taste*) Geschmack *m*. **palatable** *adj* schmackhaft.
pale [peil] *adj* blaß, bleich. *v* blaßwerden. **pale ale** helles Bier *neut*. **paleness** *n* Blässe *f*.
palette ['palit] *n* Palette *f*.
pall¹ [poɪl] *v* (*become boring*) jeden Reiz verlieren.
pall² [poɪl] *n* (*for coffin*) Leichentuch *neut*; (*fig*) Hülle *f*. **pall-bearer** *n* Sargträger *m*.
palm¹ [paɪm] *n* (*of hand*) Handfläche *f*. **palmist** *n* Handwahrsager(in). **palmistry** *n* Handlesekunst *f*.
palm² [paɪm] *n* (*tree*) Palme *f*.
palpitate ['palpiteit] *v* (*heart*) unregelmäßigschlagen; (*tremble*) beben, zittern.
pamper ['pampǝ] *v* verwöhnen.
pamphlet ['pamflit] *n* Broschüre *f*.
pan [pan] *n* Pfanne *f*.
pancreas ['paŋkriǝs] *n* Bauchspeicheldrüse *f*.
panda ['pandǝ] *n* Panda *m*.
pander ['pandǝ] *v* nachgeben (+*dat*).
pane [pein] *n* (Fenster)Scheibe *f*.
panel ['panl] *n* Tafel *f*; (*door*) Füllung *f*; (*dress*) Einsatzstück *m*; (*instrument*) Armaturenbrett *neut*. *v* täfeln. **panelling** *n* Täfelung *f*.
pang [paŋ] *n* (*of remorse*) Gewissensbisse *pl*.
panic ['panik] *n* Panik *f*. *v* hinreißen (zu). **panic-stricken** *adj* von panischer Angst erfüllt. **panicky** *adj* uberängstlich.
pannier ['paniǝ] *n* (Trag)Korb *m*; (*motorcycle*) Satteltasche *f*.
panorama [,panǝ'raɪmǝ] *n* Panorama *neut*, Rundblick *m*. **panoramic** *adj* panoramisch.
pansy ['panzi] *n* Stiefmütterchen *neut*.
pant [pant] *v* keuchen, schnaufen.
panther ['panθǝ] *n* Panther *m*.
panties ['pantiz] *pl n* (*coll*) Schlüpfer *m sing*, Höschen *neut sing*.
pantomime ['pantǝmaim] *n* Pantomime *f*.
pantry ['pantri] *n* Speiseschrank *m*.
pants [pants] *pl n* (*trousers*) Hose *f sing*; (*underpants*) Unterhose *f sing*. **pantyhose** Strumpfhose *f*.
papal ['peipl] *adj* päpstlich.
paper ['peipǝ] *n* Papier *neut*; (*newspaper*) Zeitung *f*; (*scientific*) Abhandlung *f*. *v* (a

room) tapezieren. **paperback** *n* Taschenbuch *neut*. **paper bag** Tüte *f*. **paperclip** *n* Büroklammer *f*. **paper-thin** *adj* hauchdünn. **paperweight** *n* Briefbeschwerer *m*. **paperwork** *n* Büroarbeit *f*.
paprika ['paprikǝ] *n* Paprika *m*.
par [paɪ] *n* Nennwert *m*, (*golf*) Par *neut*. **on a par with** gleich (+*dat*).
parable ['parǝbl] *n* Parabel *f*.
parachute ['parǝʃuɪt] *n* Fallschirm *m*. *v* mit dem Fallschirm abspringen.
parade [pǝ'reid] *n* Parade *f*. *v* (*march past*) vorbeimarschieren. **parade ground** Paradeplatz *m*.
paradise ['parǝdais] *n* Paradies *neut*.
paradox ['parǝdoks] *n* Paradox *neut*. **paradoxical** *adj* paradox.
paraffin ['parǝfin] *n* Paraffin *neut*.
paragraph ['parǝgraɪf] *n* Absatz *m*.
parallel ['parǝlel] *n* Parallele *f*. *adj* parallel. *v* entsprechen (+*dat*).
paralyse ['parǝlaiz] *v* paralysieren. **paralysed** *adj* gelähmt. **paralysis** *n* (*pl -ses*) Lähmung *f*, Paralyse *f*. **paralytic** *adj* paralytisch; (*coll*) besoffen.
paramilitary [,parǝ'militǝri] *adj* paramilitärisch.
paramount ['parǝmaunt] *adj* äußerst wichtig, überragend.
paranoia [,parǝ'noiǝ] *n* Paranoia *f*. **paranoid** *adj* paranoid.
parapet ['parǝpit] *n* Brüstung *f*.
paraphernalia [,parǝfǝ'neiliǝ] *n* Zubehör *neut*.
paraphrase ['parǝfreiz] *n* Umschreibung *f*, Paraphrase *f*. *v* umschreiben.
paraplegia [parǝ'pliɪdʒǝ] *n* Paraplegie *f*. **paraplegic** *adj* paraplegisch.
parasite ['parǝsait] *n* Parasit *m*, Schmarotzer *m*. **parasitic** *adj* parasitisch.
parasol ['parǝsol] *n* Sonnenschirm *m*.
paratrooper ['parǝ,truɪpǝ] *n* Fallschirmjäger *m*.
parcel ['paɪsǝl] *n* Paket *neut*, Päckchen *neut*; (*of land*) Parzelle *f*. **parcel post** Paketpost *f*. **parcels office** Gepäckabfertigung *f*. *v* **parcel out** austeilen.
parch [paɪtʃ] *v* dörren. **parched** *adj* ausgetrocknet; (*coll*) sehr durstig.
parchment ['paɪtʃmǝnt] *n* Pergament *neut*.
pardon ['paɪdn] *n* Verzeihung *f*. *v* verzeihen (+*dat*); (*law*) begnadigen. **I beg your pardon** *or* **pardon me** Verzeihung! **pardonable** *adj* verzeihlich.

pare [peə] v schälen; (prices, costs, etc.)
herabsetzen, beschneiden.
parent ['peərənt] n Vater m, Mutter f.
parents pl Eltern pl. **parentage** n Abkunft
f. **parental** adj elterlich.
parenthesis [pə'renθəsis] n (pl -ses)
Parenthese f.
parish ['pariʃ] n (Kirchen)gemeinde f. adj
Gemeinde-.
parity ['pariti] n Parität f.
park [paɪk] n Park m. v (mot) parken. **car
park** Parkplatz m. **no parking** Parken
verboten. **parking place** or **lot** Parkplatz
m. **parking light** Standlicht neut. **parking
meter** Parkuhr f.
parliament ['paɪləmənt] n Parlament neut.
member of parliament Abgeordnete(r),
Parlamentarier m. **parliamentary** adj
parlamentarisch, Parlaments-.
parlour ['paɪlə] n Wohnzimmer neut. **ice-
cream parlour** Eisdiele f.
parochial [pə'roukiəl] adj Gemeinde-;
(fig) engstirnig.
parody ['parədi] n Parodie f. v parodier-
en.
parole [pə'roul] n Bewährung f. **release
on parole** auf Bewährung entlassen.
paroxysm ['parəksizəm] n Anfall m.
parrot ['parət] n Papagei m.
parsley ['paɪsli] n Petersilie f.
parsnip ['paɪsnip] n Pastinake f.
parson ['paɪsn] n Pfarrer m. **parsonage** n
Pfarrhaus neut.
part [paɪt] n Teil m; (theatre) Rolle f. adj
Teil-. v trennen; (people) sich trennen;
(hair) scheiteln. **for my part** meinerseits.
in part teilweise. **take part (in)**
teilnehmen (an).
*partake [paɪteik] v **partake of** (eat) zu
sich nehmen.
partial ['paɪʃəl] adj Teil-; (biased) eingenommen. **be partial to** (coll) eine Vorliebe haben für. **partially** adv teilweise.
participate [paɪ'tisipeit] v teilnehmen (an).
participant n Teilnehmer(in). **participation** n Teilnahme f.
participle ['paɪtisipl] n Partizip neut.
particle ['paɪtikl] n Teilchen neut.
particular [pə'tikjulə] adj besonder,
speziell; (fussy) wählerisch. **particulars** pl
n Einzelheiten pl. **particularly** adv
besonders.
parting ['paɪtiŋ] n Abschied neut; (hair)
Scheitel m.

partisan [paɪti'zan] n Anhänger m.
partition [paɪ'tiʃən] n Aufteilung f, Trennung f; (wall, etc.) Scheidewand f.
partly ['paɪtli] adv zum Teil, teils.
partner ['paɪtnə] n Partner(in). **partnership** n Partnerschaft f.
partridge ['paɪtridʒ] n Rebhuhn neut.
party ['paɪti] n (pol, law) Partei f; (social
gathering) Party f. **be a party to** beteiligt
sein an.
pass [paɪs] v (go past) vorbeigehen(an);
(go beyond) überschreiten, übertreffen;
(exam) bestehen; (of time) vergehen;
(time) vertreiben; (hand) überreichen;
(approve) billigen; (sport) zuspielen. n
(travel document) Zeitkarte f. **pass away**
sterben. **pass off (as)** ausgeben (als). **pass
out** (coll) ohmächtig werden. **pass up**
verzichten auf.
passage ['pasidʒ] n Durchfahrt f, Reise f;
(in book) Stelle f; (corridor) Gang m; (of
time) Verlauf m.
passenger ['pasindʒə] n Fahrgast m,
Reisende(r); (aeroplane) Fluggast m.
passion ['paʃən] n Leidenschaft f; (anger)
Zorn m; (rel) Passion f. **passionate** adj
leidenschaftlich.
passive ['pasiv] adj passiv. **passivity** n
Passivität f.
Passover ['paɪsouvə] n Passahfest neut.
passport ['paɪspoɪt] n (Reise)Paß m.
password ['paɪswoɪd] n Kennwort neut.
past [paɪst] n Vergangenheit f. adj vergangen. prep nach, über; (in front of) an
... vorbei. **ten past six** zehn (Minuten)
nach sechs. **half past six** halb sieben. **in
the past** früher.
pasta ['pastə] n Teigwaren pl.
paste [peist] n Paste f; (glue) Klebstoff m.
v kleben.
pastel ['pastəl] adj **pastel colour** Pastellfarbe f.
pasteurize ['pastʃəraiz] v pasteurisieren.
pastime ['paɪstaim] n Zeitvertreib m.
pastor ['paɪstə] n Pfarrer m, Pastor m.
pastoral adj (poetry) Hirten-; (rel) pastoral.
pastry ['peistri] n Teig m; (cake)
Tortengebäck neut.
pasture ['paɪstʃə] n Weide f, Grasland
neut.
pasty¹ ['peisti] adj teigig; (complexion)
bleich.
pasty² ['pasti] n Pastete f.

pat [pat] *n* (leichter) Schlag *m. v* klopfen, patschen. **pat on the back** (*v*) beglückwünschen.

patch [patʃ] *n* Flicken *m*, Lappen *m*; (*on eye*) Augenbinde *f. v* flicken. **patchwork** *n* Flickwerk *neut.* **patchy** *adj* ungleichmäßig.

pâté ['patei] *n* Pastete *f.*

patent ['peitənt] *n* Patent *neut. adj* patentiert, Patent-; (*obvious*) offenkundig. *v* patentieren.

paternal [pə'təɪnl] *adj* väterlich. **paternal grandfather** Großvater väterlicherseits. **paternity** *n* Vaterschaft *f.*

path [paɪθ] *n* Weg *m*, Pfad *m*. **pathway** *n* Weg *m*, Bahn *f.*

pathetic [pə'θetik] *adj* (*moving*) rührend; (*pitiable*) kläglich.

pathology [pə'θolədʒi] *n* Pathologie *f.* **pathological** *adj* pathologisch. **pathologist** *n* Pathologe *m*, Pathologin *f.*

patience ['peiʃəns] *n* Geduld *f.* **patient** *adj* geduldig, duldsam. *n* Patient(in).

patio ['patiou] *n* Patio *m.*

patriarchal ['peitriaɪkəl] *adj* patriarchalisch.

patriot ['patriət] *n* Patriot(in). **patriotic** *adj* patriotisch. **patriotism** *n* Patriotismus *m.*

patrol [pə'troul] *n* Patrouille *f. v* durchstreifen. **patrol car** Streifenwagen *m.* **patrolman** *n* Streifenpolizist *m.*

patron ['peitrən] *n* Patron *m*, Gönner *m.* **patronage** *n* Gönnerschaft *f.* **patronize** *v* (*theatre, restaurant*) besuchen; (*person*) gönnerhaft behandeln. **patronizing** *adj* gönnerhaft.

patter[1] ['patə] *n* (*rain*) Prasseln *neut. v* prasseln.

patter[2] ['patə] *n* (*speech*) Geplapper *neut*, Rotwelsch *neut. v* plappern.

pattern ['patən] *n* Muster *neut.*

paunch [pɔintʃ] *n* Wanst *m.* **paunchy** *adj* dickbäuchig.

pauper ['pɔipə] *n* Arme(r).

pause [pɔiz] *n* Pause *f. v* anhalten, zögern.

pave [peiv] *v* pflastern. **pave the way** den Weg bahnen. **pavement** *n* Bürgersteig *m.*

pavilion [pə'viljən] *n* Pavillon *m.*

paw [pɔi] *n* Pfote *f*, Tatze *f. v* (*ground*) stampfen auf.

pawn[1] [pɔin] *n* (*chess*) Bauer *m.*

pawn[2] [pɔin] *v* verpfänden. **pawnbroker** *n* Pfandleiher *m.*

*pay [pei] *n* Lohn *m*, Gehalt *neut. v* zahlen; (*bill*) bezahlen; (*be worthwhile*) sich lohnen; (*visit, compliment*) machen. **pay attention** achtgeben (auf). **pay homage** huldigen (+ *dat*). **pay for** bezahlen. **payable** *adj* fällig. **payday** *n* Zahltag *m.* **paying guest** zahlender Gast *m.* **payload** *n* Nutzlast *f.* **payment** *n* (Be)Zahlung *f*; (*cheque*) Einlösung *f.*

pea [piɪ] *n* Erbse *f.*

peace [piɪs] *n* Frieden *m*; (*quiet*) Ruhe *f.* **make one's peace with** sich aussöhnen mit. **leave in peace** in Ruhe lassen. **peace of mind** Seelenruhe *f.* **peace treaty** Friedensvertrag *m.* **peaceable** *adj* friedlich. **peaceful** *adj* ruhig.

peach [piɪtʃ] *n* Pfirsich *m.*

peacock ['piɪkok] *n* Pfau *m.*

peak [piɪk] *n* Spitze *f*, Gipfel *m. adj* Höchst-, Spitzen-. **peaked** *adj* spitz.

peal [piɪl] *v* (*bells*) läuten. *n* Geläute *neut.* **peal of thunder** Donnerschlag *m.*

peanut ['piɪnʌt] *n* Erdnuß *f.*

pear [peə] *n* Birne *f.* **pear-shaped** *adj* birnenförmig.

pearl [pəɪl] *n* Perle *f. adj* Perlen-.

peasant ['peznt] *n* Bauer *m. adj* bäuerlich.

peat [piɪt] *n* Torf *m.*

pebble ['pebl] *n* Kieselstein *m.*

peck [pek] *v* picken, hacken. *n* Picken *neut*; (*kiss*) (flüchtiger) Kuß *m.* **peckish** *adj* (*coll*) hungrig.

peculiar [pi'kjuɪljə] *adj* (*strange*) seltsam. **peculiar to** eigentümlich (+ *dat*). **peculiarity** *n* Eigentümlichkeit *f.*

pedal ['pedl] *n* Pedal *neut*, Fußhebel *m. v* (*a bicycle*) fahren.

pedantic [pi'dantik] *adj* pedantisch.

peddle ['pedl] *v* hausieren. **peddler** *n* Hausierer *m.*

pedestal ['pedistl] *n* Sockel *m.* **put on a pedestal** vergöttern.

pedestrian [pi'destriən] *n* Fußgänger(in). *adj* Fußgänger-; (*humdrum*) langweilig, banal. **pedestrian crossing** Fußgängerüberweg *m.* **pedestrian precinct** Fußgängerzone *f.*

pedigree ['pedigriɪ] *n* Stammbaum *m.*

pedlar ['pedlə] *n* Hausierer *m.*

peel [piɪl] *n* Schale *f. v* schälen. **peeler** *n* Schäler *m.*

peep [piɪp] *v* gucken, verstohlen blicken. *n* verstohlener Blick *m.* **peephole** *n* Guckloch *neut.*

peer¹ [piə] v (*look*) spähen, gucken.
peer² [piə] n (*equal*) Ebenbürtige(r); (*noble*) Peer m. **peerage** n Peerwürde f. **peerless** adj unvergleichlich.
peevish ['piːviʃ] adj verdrießlich.
peg [peg] n Pflock m; (*coathook*) Haken m; (*clothes*) Klammer f. v anpflöcken; (*prices*) festlegen. **off the peg** von der Stange.
pejorative [pə'dʒorətiv] adj herabsetzend.
pelican ['pelikən] n Pelikan m.
pellet ['pelit] n Kügelchen neut; (*shot*) Schrotkorn neut.
pelmet ['pelmit] n Falbel f.
pelt¹ [pelt] v (*throw*) bewerfen.
pelt² [pelt] n (*skin*) Fell neut, Pelz m.
pelvis ['pelvis] n (*anat*) Becken neut.
pen¹ [pen] n (*writing*) (Schreib)Feder f, Federhalter m.
pen² [pen] n (*animals*) Pferch m, Hürde f. v einpferchen.
penal ['piːnl] adj Straf-. **penalize** v bestrafen. **penalty** n (gesetzliche) Strafe f. **penalty kick** Elfmeterstoß m.
penance ['penəns] n Buße f.
pencil ['pensl] n Bleistift m. v **pencil in** (*a date*) vorläufig festsetzen. **pencil-sharpener** n Bleistiftspitzer m.
pendant ['pendənt] n Anhänger m.
pending ['pendiŋ] adj (noch) unentschieden. prep bis.
pendulum ['pendjuləm] n Pendel neut.
penetrate ['penitreit] v durchdringen, eindringen (in). **penetrating** adj durchdringend. **penetration** n Durchdringen neut.
penguin ['peŋgwin] n Pinguin m.
penicillin [peni'silin] n Penizillin neut.
peninsula [pə'ninsjulə] n Halbinsel f. **peninsular** adj Halbinsel-.
penis ['piːnis] n Penis m.
penitent ['penitənt] adj bußfertig. n Büßer(in). **penitence** n Buße f.
penknife ['nennaif] n Taschenmesser neut.
pen-name n Pseudonym neut.
pennant ['penənt] n Wimpel m.
penny ['peni] n Penny m, Pfennig m. **penniless** adj mittellos.
pension ['penʃən] n Rente f. **pensioner** n Rentner(in).
pensive ['pensiv] adj gedankenvoll.
pent [pent] adj **pent up** (*feelings*) angestaut, zurückgehalten.
pentagon ['pentəgən] n Fünfeck neut.

Pentagon (*US*) Pentagon neut. **pentagonal** adj fünfeckig.
penthouse ['penthaus] n Dachwohnung f.
penultimate [pi'nʌltimit] adj vorletzt.
people ['piːpl] pl n Leute pl, Menschen pl; sing (*nation*) Volk neut.
pepper ['pepə] n Pfeffer m. **peppercorn** n Pfefferkorn neut. **peppermint** n Pfefferminze f. **peppery** adj pfefferig, scharf.
per [pəː] prep pro. **per capita** pro Kopf.
perceive [pə'siːv] v wahrnehmen; (*understand*) begreifen. **perceptible** adj spürbar. **perception** n Wahrnehmung f. **perceptive** adj (*person*) scharfsinnig.
per cent adv, n Prozent neut. **sixty per cent** sechzig Prozent. **percentage** n Prozentsatz m.
perch [pəːtʃ] n Sitzstange f; (*fish*) Barsch m. v sitzen.
percolate ['pəːkəleit] v durchsickern. **percolator** n Kaffeemaschine f.
percussion [pə'kʌʃən] n (*music*) Schlaginstrumente pl.
perennial [pə'reniəl] adj beständig; (*plant*) perennierend. n perennierende Pflanze f.
perfect ['pəːfikt; v pə'fekt] adj vollkommen, vollendet, perfekt. v vervollkommnen. **perfection** n Vollkommenheit f. **perfectionist** n Perfektionist(in). **perfectly** adv (*coll*) ganz, völlig.
perforate ['pəːfəreit] v perforieren. **perforation** n Perforation f.
perform [pə'fɔːm] n machen, ausführen; (*music, play*) aufführen, spielen. n (*work, output*) Leistung f; (*music, theatre*) Aufführung f. **performer** n Artist(in).
perfume ['pəːfjuːm] n (*fragrance*) Duft m; (*woman's*) Parfüm neut. v parfümieren.
perhaps [pə'haps] adv vielleicht.
peril ['peril] n Gefahr f. **perilous** adj gefährlich.
perimeter [pə'rimitə] n Umkreis ; (*outer area*) Peripherie f.
period ['piəriəd] n Periode f, Frist f; (*lesson*) Stunde f; (*menstrual*) Regel f, Periode f; (*full stop*) Punkt m. **periodic** adj periodisch. **periodical** n Zeitschrift f. **periodically** adv periodisch, von Zeit zu Zeit.
peripheral [pə'rifərəl] adj peripherisch, Rand-. **periphery** n Peripherie f.
periscope ['periskoup] n Periskop neut.
perish ['periʃ] v umkommen, sterben;

(*materials*) verwelken. **perishable** *adj* leicht verderblich.

perjure ['pɜːdʒə] *v* **perjure oneself** meineidig werden. **perjurer** *n* Meineidige(r). **perjury** *n* Meineid *m*.

perk¹ [pɜːk] *v* **perk up** munter werden. **perky** *adj* munter.

perk² [pɜːk] *n* (*coll: of job*) Vorteil *m*, Vergünstigung *f*.

perm [pɜːm] *n* Dauerwelle *f*.

permanent ['pɜːmənənt] *adj* dauernd, ständig, permanent. **permanence** *n* Permanenz *f*, Ständigkeit *f*.

permeate ['pɜːmieit] *v* durchdringen. **permeable** *adj* durchlässig.

permit [pə'mit; *n* 'pɜːmit] *v* erlauben, gestatten; (*officially*) zulassen, genehmigen. *n* Genehmigung *f*; (*certificate*) Zulassungsschein *m*. **permissible** *adj* zulässig. **permission** *n* Erlaubnis *f*, Genehmigung *f*. **permissive** *adj* freizügig.

permutation [pɜːmju'teiʃən] *n* Permutation *f*.

pernicious [pə'niʃəs] *adj* bösartig.

perpendicular [,pɜːpen'dikjulə] *adj* senkrecht. *n* Senkrechte *f*.

perpetrate ['pɜːpitreit] *v* begehen. **perpetration** *n* Begehung *f*. **perpetrator** *n* Täter *m*.

perpetual [pə'petʃuəl] *adj* beständig, ewig. **perpetuate** [pə'petʃueit] *v* verewigen, fortsetzen.

perplex [pə'pleks] *v* verwirren, verblüffen. **perplexed** *adj* perplex, verwirrt.

persecute ['pɜːsikjuːt] *v* verfolgen. **persecution** *n* Verfolgung *f*. **persecutor** *n* Verfolger(in).

persevere [,pɜːsi'viə] *v* beharren, nicht aufgeben. **perseverance** *n* Beharrlichkeit *f*. **persevering** *adj* beharrlich.

persist [pə'sist] *v* (*person*) beharren (bei); (*thing*) fortdauern. **persistence** *n* Beharren *neut*, Hartnäckigkeit *f*. **persistent** *adj* (*person*) hartnäckig; (*questions, etc.*) anhaltend.

person ['pɜːsn] *n* Person *f*. **personal** *adj* persönlich. **personal matter** Privatsache *f*. **personality** *n* Personalität *f*; (*personage*) Persönlichkeit *f*.

personnel [pɜːsə'nel] *n* Personal *neut*, Belegschaft *f*. **personnel department** Personalabteilung *f*. **personnel manager** Personalchef *m*.

perspective [pə'spektiv] *n* Perspektive *f*.

perspire [pə'spaiə] *v* schwitzen, transpirieren. **perspiration** *n* Schweiß *m*.

persuade [pə'sweid] *v* überreden; (*convince*) überzeugen. **persuasion** *n* Überredung *f*; Überzeugung *f*. **persuasive** *adj* überredend; überzeugend.

pert [pɜːt] *adj* keck.

pertain [pə'tein] *v* betreffen. **pertaining to** betreffend. **pertinacious** *adj* hartnäckig. **pertinent** *adj* angemessen.

perturb [pə'tɜːb] *v* beunruhigen.

peruse [pə'ruːz] *v* durchlesen.

pervade [pə'veid] *v* erfüllen, durchdringen. **pervasive** *adj* durchdringend.

perverse [pə'vɜːs] *adj* pervers, widernatürlich. **perversion** *n* Perversion *f*, Verdrehung *f*. **perversion of justice** Rechtsbeugung *f*. **pervert** *v* verdrehen. *n* perverser Mensch *m*.

pest [pest] *n* Schädling *m*; (*coll: person*) lästiger Mensch *m*. **pesticide** *n* Pestizid *neut*.

pester ['pestə] *v* quälen, plagen.

pet [pet] *n* Haustier *neut*; (*darling*) Schätzchen *neut*. *adj* Lieblings-. *v* liebkosen. **pet name** Kosename *m*.

petal ['petl] *n* Blumenblatt *neut*.

petition [pə'tiʃən] *n* Bittschrift *f*.

petrify ['petrifai] *v* versteinern. **petrified** *adj* (*coll*) starr, bestürzt.

petrol ['petrəl] *n* Benzin *neut*. **petrol station** Tankstelle *f*. **petroleum** *n* Erdöl *neut*.

petticoat ['petikout] *n* Unterrock *m*.

petty ['peti] *adj* (*unimportant*) unbedeutend; (*mean*) kleinlich. **petty cash** Kleinkasse *f*.

petulant ['petjulənt] *adj* verdrießlich.

pew [pjuː] *n* Kirchensitz *m*.

pewter ['pjuːtə] *n* Hartzinn *neut*.

phantom ['fantəm] *n* Phantom *neut*, Gespenst *neut*. *adj* Schein-.

pharmacy ['faːməsi] *n* Apotheke *f*. **pharmacist** *n* Apotheker(in).

pharynx ['fariŋks] *n* Schlundkopf *m*.

phase [feiz] *n* (*tech*) Phase *f*; (*stage*) Stadium *neut*, Etappe *f*.

pheasant ['feznt] *n* Fasan *m*.

phenomenon [fə'nomənən] *n* (*pl* **-a**) Phänomen *neut*. **phenomenal** *adj* phänomenal.

phial ['faiəl] *n* Ampulle *f*.

philanthropy [fi'lanθrəpi] *n* Philanthropie *f*. **philanthropic** *adj* philanthropisch, menschenfreundlich. **philanthropist** *n* Philanthrop, Menschenfreund *m*.

philately [fi'latəli] *n* Briefmarkensammeln *neut*. **philatelist** *n* Briefmarkensammler(in).

philosophy [fi'losəfi] *n* Philosophie *f*. **philosopher** *n* Philosoph *m*. **philosophical** *adj* philosophisch.

phlegm [flem] *n* Schleim *m*, Phlegma *neut*. **phlegmatic** *adj* phlegmatisch.

phobia ['foubiə] *n* Phobie *f*.

phone [foun] *n* (*coll*) Fernsprecher *m*. *v* anrufen. **phone booth** *or* **box** Telefonzelle *f*.

phonetic [fə'netik] *adj* phonetisch. **phonetics** *n* Phonetik *f*.

phoney ['founi] *adj* (*coll*) falsch, fingiert. *n* Schwindler *m*.

phosphate ['fosfeit] *n* Phosphat *neut*.

phosphorescence [fosfə'resəns] *n* Phosphoreszenz *f*. **phosphorescent** *adj* phosphoreszierend.

phosphorus ['fosfərəs] *n* Phosphor *m*.

photo ['foutou] *n* Foto *neut*.

photocopy ['foutou,kopi] *n* Fotokopie *f*. *v* fotokopieren.

photogenic [,foutou'dʒenik] *adj* fotogen.

photograph ['foutəgraːf] *n* Lichtbild *neut*, Foto *neut*. *v* aufnehmen, fotografieren. **photographer** *n* Fotograf *m*. **photographic** *adj* fotografisch. **photography** *n* Fotografie *f*.

phrase [freiz] *n* (*expression*) Ausdruck *m*, Redewendung *f*; (*music*) Phrase *f*. *v* fassen.

physical ['fizikəl] *adj* physisch, körperlich. **physical education** Leibeserziehung *f*.

physician [fi'ziʃən] *n* Arzt *m*, Ärztin *f*.

physics ['fiziks] *n* Physik *f*. **physicist** *n* Physiker *m*.

physiology [,fizi'olədʒi] *n* Physiologie *f*. **physiological** *adj* physiologisch.

physiotherapy [,fiziou'θerəpi] *n* Physiotherapie *f*.

physique [fi'ziːk] *n* Körperbau *m*.

piano [pi'anou] *n* Klavier *neut*. **pianist** *n* Klavierspieler(in).

pick¹ [pik] *v* (*choose*) auswählen, (*fruit*) pflücken; (*lock*) knacken. *n* **pick of the bunch** (*coll*) das Beste (von allen).

pick² [pik] *or* **pickaxe** *n* Spitzhacke *f*.

picket ['pikit] *n* Pfahl *m*; (*strike*) Streikposten *m*. *v* (*factory, etc.*) Streikposten aufstellen vor.

pickle ['pikl] *n* Pökel *m*. *v* einpökeln.

pickled *adj* gepökelt; (*coll: drunk*) blau.

pickles *pl n* Eingepökeltes *neut sing*.

picnic ['piknik] *n* Picknick *neut*.

pictorial [pik'toːriəl] *adj* Bilder-.

picture ['piktʃə] *n* Bild *neut*; (*painting*) Gemälde *neut*; (*film*) Film *m*. *v* (*imagine*) sich vorstellen. **pictures** *pl* Kino *neut sing*. **picture book** Bilderbuch *neut*. **picture postcard** Ansichtskarte *f*.

picturesque [piktʃə'resk] *adj* pittoresk.

pidgin ['pidʒən] *n* Mischsprache *f*.

pie [pai] *n* (*meat*) Pastete *f*; (*fruit*) Torte *f*.

piece [piːs] *n* Stück *neut*; (*part*) Teil *m*; (*paper*) Blatt *neut*. **piece of advice** Ratschlag *m*. **fall to pieces** in Stücke gehen, zerfallen. **go to pieces** zusammenbrechen. *v* **piece together** zusammenstellen. **piecemeal** *adv* stückweise.

piecework *n* Akkordarbeit *f*.

pier [piə] *n* Pier *m*, Kai *m*.

pierce [piəs] *v* durchbohren, durchstechen. **piercing** *adj* durchdringend.

piety ['paiəti] *n* Frömmigkeit *f*.

pig [pig] *n* Schwein *m*. **pigheaded** *adj* störrisch. **piglet** *n* Schweinchen *neut*. **pigskin** *n* Schweinsleder *neut*. **pigsty** *n* Schweinestall *m*. **pigtail** *n* Zopf *m*.

pigment ['pigmənt] *n* Pigment *neut*, Farbstoff *m*. **pigmentation** *n* Pigmentation *f*.

pike [paik] *n* (*fish*) Hecht *m*; (*weapon*) Pike *f*, Spieß *m*.

pilchard ['piltʃəd] *n* Sardine *f*.

pile¹ [pail] *n* (*heap*) Haufen *m*, Stapel *m*. *v* (an)häufen, stapeln. **pile-up** *n* (*mot*) (Massen)Karambolage *f*.

pile² [pail] *n* (*post*) Pfahl *m*, Joch *neut*.

pile³ [pail] *n* (*of carpet*) Flor *m*.

piles [pailz] *pl n* Hämorrhoiden *pl*.

pilfer ['pilfə] *v* klauen. **pilferage** *n* Dieberei *f*.

pilgrim ['pilgrim] *n* Pilger(in). **pilgrimage** *n* Pilgerfahrt *f*, Wallfahrt *f*.

pill [pil] *n* Pille *f*, Tablette *f*. **the pill** (*contraceptive*) die Pille.

pillage ['pilidʒ] *v* (aus)plündern. *n* Plünderung *f*.

pillar ['pilə] *n* Pfeiler *m*, Säule *f*. **pillarbox** *n* Briefkasten *m*.

pillion ['piljən] *n* Soziussitz *m*. **ride pillion** auf dem Sozius fahren.

pillow ['pilou] *n* Kopfkissen *neut*. **pillow case** *n* Kissenbezug *m*.

pilot ['pailət] *n* Pilot *m*. *v* steuern, lenken. **pilot light** Zündflamme *f*.

pimento [pi'mentou] *n* Piment *m or neut.*
pimp [pimp] *n* Zuhälter *m.*
pimple ['pimpl] *n* Pustel *f*, Pickel *m.* **pimply** *adj* pickelig.
pin [pin] *n* Stecknadel *f. v* befestigen. **pin down** festnageln. **pincushion** *n* Nadelkissen *neut.*
pinafore ['pinəfoɪ] *n* Schürze *f.* **pinafore dress** Kleiderrock *m.*
pincers ['pinsəz] *pl n* Zange *f sing*; (*crab's*) Krebsschere *f sing.*
pinch [pintʃ] *v* zwicken, kneifen; (*coll*) klauen. *n* Kneifen *neut*, Zwicken *neut*; (*salt, etc.*) Prise *f.*
pine¹ [pain] *n* Kiefer *f*, Pinie *f.* **pine cone** *n* Kiefernzapfen *m.*
pine² [pain] *v* sich sehnen (nach). **pine away** verschmachten.
pineapple ['painapl] *n* Ananas *f.*
ping-pong ['piŋpoŋ] *n* (*coll*) Tischtennis *neut.*
pinion ['pinjən] *n* (*tech*) Ritzel *m. v* fesseln.
pink [piŋk] *adj* rosa, blaßrot. *n* (*flower*) Nelke *f. v* (*mot*) klopfen. **in the pink** kerngesund.
pinnacle ['pinəkl] *n* Spitzturm *m*; (*fig*) Gipfel *m.*
pinpoint ['pinpoint] *v* ins Auge fassen, hervorheben.
pint [paint] *n* Pinte *f.*
pioneer [ˌpaiə'niə] *n* Pionier *m*, Bahnbrecher *m. v* den Weg bahnen für. **pioneering** *adj* bahnbrechend.
pious ['paiəs] *adj* fromm.
pip¹ [pip] *n* (*fruit*) (Obst)Kern *m.*
pip² [pip] *n* (*sound*) Ton *m*; (*mil*) Stern *m*; (*on card*) Auge *neut*; (*on dice*) Punkt *m.*
pipe [paip] *n* Rohr *neut*, Röhre *f*; (*tobacco, music*) Pfeife *f*; (*sound*) Pfeifen *neut. v* (*liquid*) durch Röhren leiten; (*play pipes, etc.*) pfeifen; (*cookery*) spritzen. **pipedream** *n* Luftschloß *neut.* **pipeline** *n* Rohrleitung *f.*
piquant ['piːkənt] *adj* pikant.
pique [piːk] *n* Groll *m.*
pirate ['paiərət] *n* Seeräuber *m.* **piracy** *n* Seeräuberei *f.*
pirouette [piru'et] *n* Pirouette *f. v* pirouettieren.
Pisces ['paisiːz] *n* Fische *pl.*
piss [pis] *v* (*vulgar*) pissen. *n* Pisse *f.*
pistachio [pi'staɪʃiou] *n* Pistazie *f.*
pistol ['pistl] *n* Pistole *f.*

piston ['pistən] *n* Kolben *m.*
pit [pit] *n* Grube *f*; (*mining*) Zeche *f*, Bergwerk *neut.* **pitted** *adj* vernarbt; (*corroded*) zerfressen.
pitch¹ [pitʃ] *v* werfen; (*tent*) aufschlagen. *n* Wurf *m*; (*sport*) Feld *neut*; (*music*) Tonhöhe *f*; (*level*) Grad *m.* **pitcher** *n* Werfer *m*; (*jug*) Krug *m.* **pitchfork** *n* Mistgabel *f.*
pitch² [pitʃ] *n* (*tar*) Pech *neut.*
pitfall ['pitfoɪl] *n* Fallgrube *f*, Falle *f.*
pith [piθ] *n* Mark *neut.* **pithy** *adj* markig.
pittance ['pitəns] *n* Hungerlohn *m.*
pituitary [pi'tjuːitəri] *n* Hirnanhangdrüse *f*, Hypophyse *f.*
pity ['piti] *n* Mitleid *neut. v* bemitleiden. **it's a pity** es ist schade, es ist ein Jammer *m.*
pivot ['pivət] *n* Drehpunkt *m. v* sich drehen.
placard ['plakaɪd] *n* Plakat *neut.*
placate [plə'keit] *v* beschwichtigen.
place [pleis] *n* Platz *m*; (*town, locality*) Ort *m*; (*spot*) Stelle *f.* **go places** (*coll*) es weit bringen. **out-of-place** *adj* (*remark*) unangebracht. **placename** *n* Ortsname *m.* **place of interest** Sehenswürdigkeit *f.* **take place** stattfinden. *v* stellen, legen, setzen; (*identify*) identifizieren, erkennen.
placenta [plə'sentə] *n* Plazenta *f.*
placid ['plasid] *adj* ruhig, gelassen.
plagiarize ['pleidʒəraiz] *v* plagiieren. **plagiarism** *n* Plagiat *neut.*
plague [pleig] *n* Seuche *f*, Pest *f. v* plagen, quälen.
plaice [pleis] *n* Scholle *f.*
plain [plein] *adj* einfach, schlicht; (*obvious*) klar; (*not pretty*) unansehnlich. *adv* einfach. *n* Ebene *f.* **plainly** *adv* offensichtlich. **speak plainly** offen reden.
plaintiff ['pleintif] *n* Kläger(in).
plaintive ['pleintiv] *adj* traurig, wehmütig.
plait [plat] *n* Zopf *m*, Flechte *f. v* flechten.
plan [plan] *n* Plan *m*; (*drawing*) Entwurf *m*, Zeichnung *f. v* planen; (*intend*) vorhaben. **according to plan** planmäßig.
plane¹ [plein] *adj* flach, eben. *n* Ebene *f*; (*aeroplane*) Flugzeug *neut.*
plane² [plein] *n* (*tool*) Hobel *m. v* (ab)hobeln.
planet ['planit] *n* Planet *m.*
plank [plaŋk] *n* Planke *f*, Diele *f.*
plankton ['plaŋktən] *n* Plankton *neut.*

planning ['planiŋ] *n* Planung *f*.
plant [plɑːnt] *n* Pflanze *f*; *(factory)* Betrieb *m*, Fabrik *f*. *v* pflanzen. **plantation** *n* Pflanzung *f*.
plaque [plɑːk] *n* Gedenktafel *f*.
plasma ['plazmə] *n* Plasma *neut*.
plaster ['plɑːstə] *n* *(med)* Pflaster *neut*; *(of Paris)* Gips *m*. *v* bepflastern. **adhesive plaster** Heftpflaster *neut*. **plaster cast** Gipsabdruck *m*; *(med)* Gipsverband *m*.
plastic ['plastik] *n* Kunststoff *m*. *adj* Kunststoff-.
plate [pleit] *n* *(for food)* Teller *m*; *(tech)* Platte *f*, Scheibe *f*. *v* *(metal)* plattieren. **gold-plated** *adj* vergoldet.
plateau ['platou] *n* Hochebene *f*, Plateau *neut*.
platform ['platfoːm] *n* *(rail)* Bahnsteig *m*; *(speaker's)* Tribüne *f*; *(fig: pol)* Parteiprogramm *neut*.
platinum ['platinəm] *n* Platin *neut*.
platonic [plə'tonik] *adj* platonisch.
platoon [plə'tuːn] *n* *(mil)* Zug *m*.
plausible ['ploːzəbl] *adj* glaubhaft.
play [plei] *n* Spiel *neut*; *(theatre)* Schauspiel *neut*, Stück *neut*; *(tech)* Spielraum *m*. *v* spielen. **play safe** kein Risiko eingehen. **playboy** *n* Playboy *m*. **player** *n* Spieler(in); *(actor)* Schauspieler(in). **playful** *adj* scherzhaft. **playground** *n* Spielplatz *m*; *(school)* Schulhof *m*. **playing card** Spielkarte *f*. **playing field** Sportplatz *m*. **playmate** *n* Spielkamerad(in). **plaything** *n* Spielzeug *neut*. **playwright** *n* Dramatiker *m*.
plea [pliː] *n* dringende Bitte *f*; *(law)* Plädoyer *neut*.
plead [pliːd] *v* *(law)* plädieren. **plead for** flehen um.
please [pliːz] *v* gefallen (+ *dat*), Freude machen (+ *dat*). *adv* bitte! **pleasant** angenehm; *(person)* freundlich, nett. **pleased** *adj* zufrieden. **pleasing** *adj* angenehm. **pleasurable** *adj* vergnüglich. **pleasure** *n* Vernügen *neut*.
pleat [pliːt] *n* Falte *f*. *v* in Falten legen.
plebiscite ['plebisait] *n* Volksabstimmung *f*, Plebiszit *neut*.
pledge [pledʒ] *n* Pfand *neut*; *(promise)* Versprechen *neut*. *v* versprechen.
plenty ['plenti] *n* Fülle *f*, Reichtum *m*. **plenty of** eine Menge, viel.
pleurisy ['pluərisi] *n* Rippenfellentzündung *f*.

pliable ['plaiəbl] *adj* biegsam. **pliability** *n* Biegsamkeit *f*.
pliers ['plaiəz] *pl n* Zange *f* *sing*.
plight [plait] *n* Notlage *f*.
plimsoll ['plimsəl] *n* Turnschuh *m*.
plod [plod] *v* sich hinschleppen, schwerfällig gehen.
plonk[1] [ploŋk] *v* **plonk down** hinschmeißen.
plonk[2] [ploŋk] *n* *(coll)* billiger Wein.
plot[1] [plot] *n* Komplott *neut*; *(in novel)* Handlung *f*. *v* sich verschwören; *(on map)* einzeichnen. **plotter** *n* Verschwörer(in).
plot[2] [plot] *n* *(land)* Parzelle *f*, Grundstück *neut*.
plough [plau] *n* Pflug *m*; *(astron)* Großer Bär *m*. *v* (um)pflügen. **ploughman** *n* Pflüger *m*.
pluck [plʌk] *v* pflücken; *(poultry)* rupfen; *(music)* zupfen. *n* *(courage)* Mut *m*. **plucky** *adj* mutig. **pluck up courage** Mut fassen.
plug [plʌg] *n* *(elec)* Stecker *m*; *(stopper)* Stöpsel *m*. *v* verstopfen; *(coll)* befürworten. **plug in** anschließen, einstecken.
plum [plʌm] *n* Pflaume *f*, Zwetschge *f*.
plumage ['pluːmidʒ] *n* Gefieder *neut*.
plumb [plʌm] *n* Senkblei *neut*. *adj* senkrecht. *v* *(sound)* sondieren. **plumber** *n* Klempner *m*. **plumbing** *n* Klempnerarbeit *f*; *(pipes)* Rohrleitungen *pl f*.
plume [pluːm] *n* Feder *f*; *(of smoke)* Streifen *m*.
plummet ['plʌmit] *v* abstürzen.
plump[1] [plʌmp] *adj* *(fat)* rundlich, mollig. **plumpness** *n* Rundlichkeit *f*.
plump[2] [plʌmp] *v* *(fall)* plumpsen. **plump for** sich entscheiden für.
plunder ['plʌndə] *v* plündern *n* *(spoils)* Beute *f*.
plunge [plʌndʒ] *v* tauchen; *(fall)* stürzen. *n* Sturz *m*.
pluperfect [pluːˈpəfikt] *n* *(gramm)* Vorvergangenheit *f*.
plural ['pluərəl] *adj* Plural-. *n* Plural *m*, Mehrzahl *f*.
plus [plʌs] *prep* plus. *adj* Plus-. *n* Plus *neut*.
plush [plʌʃ] *adj* *(fig)* luxuriös.
Pluto ['pluːtou] *n* Pluto *m*.
ply[1] [plai] *v* *(trade)* ausüben; *(travel)* verkehren.

ply² [plai] *n* (*of yarn*) Strähne *f.* **plywood** *n* Sperrholz *neut.*
pneumatic [nju'matik] *adj* pneumatisch. **pneumatic tyre** *n* Luftreifen *m.* **pneumatic drill** Preßluftbohrer *m.*
pneumonia [nju'mouniə] *n* Lungenentzündung *f.*
poach¹ [poutʃ] *v* (*cookery*) pochieren. **poached egg** verlorenes Ei *neut.*
poach² [poutʃ] *v* wildern. **poacher** *n* Wilddieb *m.*
pocket ['pokit] *n* Tasche *f. adj* Taschen-. *v* in die Tasche stecken, einstecken. **to be in pocket** gut bei Kasse sein. **pocketknife** *n* Taschenmesser *neut.* **pocket-money** Taschengeld *neut.*
pod [pod] *n* Schote *f.*
podgy ['podʒi] *adj* (*coll*) mollig, dick.
poem ['pouim] *n* Gedicht *neut.* **poet** *n* Dichter *m.* **poetess** *n* Dichterin *f.* **poetic** *adj* poetisch, dichterisch. **poetry** *n* Dichtkunst *f;* (*poems*) Gedichte *f.*
poignant ['poinjənt] *adj* schmerzlich; (*wit*) scharf; (*grief*) bitter.
point [point] *n* (*tip*) Spitze *f;* (*place, spot*) Punkt *m;* (*in time*) Zeitpunkt *m;* (*main thing*) Hauptsache *f.* **be on the point of doing** eben tun wollen. **point of view** Standpunkt *m.* **points** *pl n* (*rail*) Weichen *pl.* **that's the point!** das is es ja! **there's no point in** es hat keinen Zweck, zu. *v* spitzen; (*indicate*) (mit dem Finger) zeigen. **point out** hinweisen auf. **pointed** *adj* zugespitzt; (*remark*) treffend, beißend. **pointless** *adj* sinnlos.
poise [poiz] *n* Haltung *f;* (*calmness*) Gelassenheit *f.*
poison ['poizən] *n* Gift *neut. v* vergiften. **poisoner** *n* Giftmörder(in). **poisonous** *adj* giftig.
poke [pouk] *n* Stoß *m*, Puff *m. v* stoßen; (*fire*) schüren.
poker¹ ['poukə] *n* (*for fire*) Feuerhaken *m.*
poker² ['poukə] *n* (*gambling*) Poker(spiel) *neut.*
Poland ['poulənd] *n* Polen *neut.* **Pole** *n* Pole *m*, Polin *f.* **Polish** *adj* polnisch.
polar ['poulə] *adj* polar. **polar bear** Eisbär *m.*
pole¹ [poul] *n* (*geog*) Pol *m.* **pole star** *n* Polarstern *m.*
pole² [poul] *n* Pfosten *m*, Pfahl *m;* (*telegraph, etc.*) Stange *f.* **pole-vault** *n* Stabhochsprung *m.*

police [pə'liːs] *n* Polizei *f. n* (polizeilich) überwachen. *adj* polizeilich, Polizei-. **police force** Polizei *f.* **policeman** *n* Polizist *m*, Schutzmann *m.* **police station** Polizeiwache *f*, Polizeirevier *neut.*
policy¹ ['poləsi] *n* Politik *f;* (*personal*) Methode *f.*
policy² ['poləsi] *n* (*insurance*) Police *f.*
polio ['pouliou] *n* Kinderlähmung *f.*
polish ['poliʃ] *n* Politur *f;* (*floors, furniture*) Bohnerwachs *neut;* (*shoes*) Schuhcreme *f. v* polieren; (*furniture*) bohnern; (*shoes*) wichsen. **polished** *adj* poliert; (*fig*) fein, elegant. **polisher** *n* Polierer *m.*
polite [pə'lait] *adj* höflich. **politeness** *n* Höflichkeit *f.*
politics ['politiks] *n* Politik *f.* **political** *adj* politisch. **politician** *n* Politiker *m.*
polka ['polkə] *n* Polka *f.*
poll [poul] *n* (*voting*) Abstimmung *f;* (*opinion poll*) Meinungsumfrage *f.*
pollen ['polən] *n* Pollen *m*, Blütenstaub *m.* **pollinate** *v* befruchten.
pollute [pə'luːt] *v* verschmutzen, verunreinigen. **pollution** *n* (*environmental*) Umweltverschmutzung *f.*
polo ['poulou] *n* Polo *neut.* **polo-neck** *n* Rollkragen *m.*
polygamy [pə'ligəmi] *n* Polygamie *f.* **polygamous** *adj* polygam.
polygon ['poligən] *n* Polygon *neut.*
polytechnic [,poli'teknik] *n* Polytechnikum *neut.*
polythene ['poliθiːn] *n* Polyäthylen *neut. adj* **polythene bag** Plastiktüte *f.*
pomegranate ['pomigranit] *n* Granatapfel *m.*
pomp [pomp] *n* Prunk *m*, Pracht *f.* **pomposity** *n* Bombast *m.* **pompous** *adj* bombastisch.
pond [pond] *n* Teich *m.*
ponder ['pondə] *v* nachdenken (über).
ponderous *adj* schwer; (*movement*) schwerfällig.
pony ['pouni] *n* Pony *neut*, Pferdchen *neut.* **pony-tail** Pferdeschwanz *m.*
poodle ['puːdl] *n* Pudel *m.*
poof [puːf] *n* (*derog*) Schwule(r) *m.*
pool¹ [puːl] *n* (*pond*) Teich *m;* (*blood, etc.*) Lache *f;* (*swimming*) (Schwimm)Bad *neut.*
pool² [puːl] *n* (*game*) Pool *m;* (*fund*) Kasse *f. v* (*resources*) vereinigen. **football pools** Fußballtoto *m.*

poor [puə] *adj* arm, bedürftig; (*earth*) dürr; (*bad*) schlecht. **the poor** die Armen *pl*. **poorly** *adj* (*coll*) krank, unwohl.
pop[1] [pop] *n* Knall *m*, Puff *m*; (*drink*) Limonade *f*. *v* knallen; (*burst*) platzen. **pop in** schnell vorbeikommen. **pop up** (*appear*) auftauchen.
pop[2] [pop] *adj* **pop music** Popmusik *f*. **pop song** Schlager *m*.
pope [poup] *n* Papst *m*.
poplar ['poplə] *n* Pappel *f*.
poppy ['popi] *n* Mohn *m*.
popular ['popjulə] *adj* populär; (*well-liked*) beliebt; (*of the people*) Volks-. **popularity** *n* Popularität *f*.
population [,popju'leifən] *n* Bevölkerung *f*. **populate** *v* bevölkern. **populous** *adj* volkreich.
porcelain ['poːslin] *n* Porzellan *neut*. *adj* Porzellan-.
porch [poːtʃ] *n* Vorhalle *neut*.
porcupine ['poːkjupain] *n* Stachelschwein *neut*.
pore[1] [poː] *n* Pore *f*.
pore[2] [poː] *v* **pore over** eifrig studieren, brüten über.
pork [poːk] *n* Schweinefleisch *neut*. **pork butcher** Schweineschlächter *m*. **pork chop** Schweinskotelett *neut*. **roast pork** Schweinebraten *m*.
pornography [poː'nogrəfi] *n* Pornographie *f*. **pornographic** *adj* pornographisch; (*film, book*) Porno-.
porous ['poːrəs] *adj* porös.
porpoise ['poːpəs] *n* Tümmler *m*.
porridge ['poridʒ] *n* Haferflockenbrei *m*. **porridge oats** Haferflocken *pl*.
port[1] [poːt] *n* (*harbour*) Hafen *m*; (*town*) Hafenstadt *f*.
port[2] [poːt] *n* (*naut*) Backbord *neut*. *adj* Backbord-.
port[3] [poːt] *n* (*wine*) Portwein *m*.
portly ['poːtli] *adj* wohlbeleibt.
portable ['poːtəbl] *adj* tragbar. **portable radio** Kofferradio *neut*.
portent ['poːtent] *n* Omen *neut*, Vorzeichen *f*. **portentous** *adj* ominös.
porter ['poːtə] *n* (*rail, etc.*) Gepäckträger *m*.
portfolio [poːt'fouliou] *n* Mappe *f*; (*pol*) Portefeuille *neut*. **minister without portfolio** Minister ohne Geschäftsbereich *m*.
porthole ['poːthoul] *n* Luke *f*.
portion ['poːʃən] *n* (*food*) Portion *f*; (*share*) (An)Teil *m*.

portrait ['poːtrət] *n* Porträt *neut*. **portray** *v* malen; (*fig*) schildern. **portrayal** *n* Porträt *neut*, Schilderung *f*.
Portugal ['poːtʃugəl] *n* Portugal *neut*. **Portuguese** *adj* portugiesisch; *n* Portugiese *m*, Portugiesin *f*.
pose [pouz] *n* Pose *f*. *v* sitzen, posieren; (*problem*) stellen. **pose as** sich ausgeben als. **poseur** *n* Poseur *m*.
posh [poʃ] *adj* vornehm.
position [pə'ziʃən] *n* Position *f*, Stellung *f*; (*situation*) Lage *f*; (*attitude*) Standpunkt *m*; (*standing*) Rang *m*. *v* stellen.
positive ['pozətiv] *adj* positiv.
possess [pə'zes] *v* besitzen. **possessed** *adj* besessen. **possession** *n* Besitz *m*. **take possession of** in Besitz nehmen. **possessive** *adj* (*person*) besitzgierig. **possessor** *n* Inhaber(in).
possible ['posəbl] *adj* möglich; (*imaginable*) eventuell. **possibility** *n* Möglichkeit *f*. **possibly** *adv* möglicherweise.
post[1] [poust] *n* (*pole*) Pfahl *m*, Pfosten *m*. **deaf as a post** stocktaub.
post[2] [poust] *n* (*mil*) Posten *m*; (*job*) Stelle *f*. *v* aufstellen.
post[3] [poust] *n* (*mail*) Post *f*. **by post** per Post. **postage stamp** Briefmarke *f*. **postcard** *n* Postkarte *f*. **postman** *n* Briefträger *m*. **post office** Postamt *neut*. *v* zur Post bringen; (*send*) (mit der Post) schicken. **keep someone posted** jemanden auf dem laufenden halten. **postage** *n* Porto *neut*, Postgebühr *f*. **postal** *adj* Post-.
poste restante [poust'testãt] *adv* postlagernd.
poster ['poustə] *n* Plakat *neut*.
posterior [po'stiəriə] *adj* später, hinter. *n* Hintern *m*.
posterity [po'sterəti] *n* Nachwelt *f*.
postgraduate [poust'gradjuit] *n* Doktorand(in).
post-haste *adv* schnellstens.
posthumous ['postjuməs] *adj* postum.
post-mortem [poust'moːtəm] *n* Autopsie *f*.
post-natal [pous'neitl] *adj* postnatal.
postpone [pous'poun] *v* verschieben. **postponement** *n* Verschiebung *f*.
postscript ['pousskript] *n* Postskriptum *neut*.
postulate ['postjuleit] *v* voraussetzen, annehmen.

posture ['postʃə] *n* (Körper)Haltung *f.*
post-war *adj* Nachkriegs-.
pot [pot] *n* Topf *m*; (*tea, coffee*) Kanne *f.*
v (*coll*) schießen. **go to pot** vor die
Hunde gehen. **pot-bellied** *adj*
dickbauchig.
potassium [pə'tasjəm] *n* Kalium *neut.*
potato [pə'teitou] *n* Kartoffel *f.* **boiled
potatoes** Salzkartoffeln *pl.* **chipped** *or*
french-fried potatoes Pommes frites *pl.*
roast *or* **fried potatoes** Bratkartoffeln *pl.*
potent ['poutənt] *adj* stark; (*sexually*)
potent. **potency** *n* Stärke *f*; Potenz *f.*
potential [pə'tenʃəl] *adj* möglich, potential. *n* Potential *neut.*
pothole ['pothoul] *n* Höhle *f.*
potion ['pouʃən] *n* Arzneitrank *m.* **love
potion** Liebestrank *m.*
potluck [pot'lʌk] *n* **take potluck with** (*coll*)
probieren, es riskieren mit/bei.
potted ['potid] *adj* (*meat*) eingemacht;
(*plant*) Topf-; (*version*) gekürzt.
potter ['potə] *v* **potter around**
herumhantieren, herumbasteln.
pottery ['potəri] *n* Töpferwaren *pl*, Steingut *neut.*
potty ['poti] *n* Töpfchen *neut.*
pouch [pautʃ] *n* Beutel *m.*
poultice ['poultis] *n* Breiumschlag *m.*
poultry ['poultri] *n* Geflügel *neut.*
pounce [pauns] *v* springen, sich stürzen.
n Sprung *m*, Satz *m.*
pound¹ [paund] *v* zerstampfen; (*hit*) hämmern, klopfen.
pound² [paund] *n* (*currency, weight*)
Pfund *neut.*
pour [poɪ] *v* gießen. **pour out** (*a liquid*)
ausgießen; (*drink*) einschenken; (*come
out*) herausströmen.
pout [paut] *v* schmollen, maulen.
poverty ['povəti] *n* Armut *f.* **poverty-
stricken** *adj* verarmt.
powder ['paudə] *n* Pulver *neut*; (*face*)
Puder *m. v* (*face*) pudern. **powder room**
Damentoilette *f.* **powdery** *adj* pulverig.
power ['pauə] *n* Macht *f*; (*tech*) Kraft *f*;
(*elec*) Strom *m. v* betreiben, antreiben.
great power (*pol*) Großmacht *f.* **powerful**
adj mächtig. **powerless** *adj* machtlos.
power station Kraftwerk *neut.*
practicable ['praktikəbl] *adj*
durchführbar.
practical ['praktikəl] *adj* praktisch.
practice ['praktis] *n* Praxis *f*; (*exercise*)

Übung *f*; (*custom*) Brauch *m*; (*procedure*)
Verfahren *neut. v see* **practise.**
practise ['praktis] *v* üben; (*profession*)
ausüben; (*med, law*) praktizieren. **practised** *adj* geübt.
practitioner [prak'tiʃənə] *n* Praktiker *m.*
medical practitioner praktischer Arzt *m.*
pragmatic [prag'matik] *adj* pragmatisch.
pragmatism *n* Pragmatismus *m.* **pragmatist** *n* Pragmatiker *m.*
Prague [praɪg] *n* Prag *neut.*
prairie ['preəri] *n* Prärie *f.*
praise [preiz] *v* loben. *v* Lob *neut.* **praise-
worthy** *adj* lobenswert.
pram [pram] *n* Kinderwagen *m.*
prance [prains] *v* tänzeln.
prank [praŋk] *n* Streich *m*, Possen *m.*
prattle ['pratl] *v* plappern, schwatzen. *n*
Geplapper *neut*, Geschwätz *neut.*
prawn [proɪn] *n* Garnele *f.*
pray [prei] *v* beten; (*ask*) bitten. **prayer** *n*
Gebet *neut.* **prayerbook** Gebetbuch *neut.*
preach [priɪtʃ] *v* predigen. **preacher** *n*
Prediger(in). **preaching** *n* Lehre *f.*
precarious [pri'keəriəs] *adj* unsicher,
gefährlich.
precaution [pri'koɪʃən] *n* Vorkehrung *f.*
precautionary *adj* vorbeugend.
precede [pri'siɪd] *v* vorhergehen. **precedence** *n* Vorrang *m.* **precedent** *n*
Präzedenzfall *m.* **order of precedence**
Rangordnung *f.* **preceding** *adj*
vorhergehend.
precinct ['priɪsiŋkt] *n* Bezirk *m.* **precincts**
pl Umgebung *f.*
precious ['preʃəs] *adj* kostbar, wertvoll;
(*jewels*) edel. *adv* (*coll*) äußerst.
precipice ['presipis] *n* Abgrund *m.*
precipitate [pri'sipiteit] *v* (*bring about*)
herbeiführen; (*chem*) fällen. **precipitation**
n (*haste*) Hast *f*; (*chem*) Fällung *f*; (*rain,
etc.*) Niederschlag *m.*
précis ['preisi] *n* Zusammenfassung *f. v*
zusammenfassen.
precise [pri'sais] *adj* präzis, genau. **precisely** *adv* genau. **precision** *n* Genauigkeit
f; (*tech*) Präzision.
preclude [pri'kluɪd] *v* ausschließen; (*prevent*) vorbeugen.
precocious [pri'kouʃəs] *adj* frühreif. **pre-
cociousness** *n* Frühreife *f.*
preconceive [,priɪkən'siɪv] *v* vorher ausdenken. **preconception** *n* Vorurteil *neut.*
precondition [,priɪkən'diʃən] *n* Voraussetzung *f.*

precursor [ˌpriːˈkɜːsə] *n* Vorläufer(in).
precursory *adj* vorausgehend.
predatory [ˈpredətəri] *adj* räuberisch.
predator *n* Raubtier *neut.*
predecessor [ˈpriːdisesə] *n* Vorgänger(in).
predestine [priˈdestin] *v* prädestinieren.
predestination *n* Vorbestimmung *f*, Prädestination *f.*
predicament [priˈdikəmənt] *n* schwierige Lage *f.*
predicate [ˈpredikət] *n* (*gramm*) Prädikat *neut. v* aussagen.
predict [priˈdikt] *v* voraussagen. **predictable** *adj* voraussagbar. **prediction** *n* Voraussage *f.*
predominate [priˈdomineit] *v* vorwiegen. **predominance** *n* Vorherrschaft *f.* **predominant** *adj* vorwiegend.
pre-eminent [priːˈeminənt] *adj* hervorragend. **pre-eminence** *n* Überlegenheit *f.*
preen [priːn] *v* (sich) putzen.
prefabricate [priːˈfabrikeit] *v* vorfabrizieren. **prefabricated** *adj* Fertig-.
preface [ˈprefis] *n* Vorwort *neut. v* einleiten.
prefect [ˈpriːfekt] *n* (*pol*) Präfekt *m*; (*school*) Aufsichtsschüler(in).
prefer [priˈfɜː] *v* vorziehen, lieber haben. **preferable** *adj* vorzuziehen. **preferably** *adv* am besten. **preference** *n* Vorzug *m.* **preferential** *adj* bevorzugt.
prefix [ˈpriːfiks] *n* Präfix *neut*, Vorsilbe *f.*
pregnant [ˈpregnənt] *adj* schwanger; (*animals*) trächtig; (*fig*) bedeutend, vielsagend. **pregnancy** *n* Schwangerschaft *f.*
prehistoric [ˌpriːhiˈstorik] *adj* vorgeschichtlich. **prehistory** *n* Vorgeschichte *f.*
prejudice [ˈpredʒədis] *n* Vorurteil *neut. v* beeinträchtigen; (*person*) beeinflussen. **prejudiced** *adj* voreingenommen. **prejudicial** *adj* nachteilig, schädlich.
preliminary [priˈliminəri] *adj* vorläufig, Vor-.
prelude [ˈpreljuːd] *n* Vorspiel *neut*, Präludium *neut.*
premarital [priːˈmaritl] *adj* vorehelich.
premature [preməˈtʃuə] *adj* frühzeitig. **premature birth** Frühgeburt *f.* **prematurity** *n* Frühzeitigkeit *f.*
premeditate [priːˈmediteit] *v* vorher überlegen. **premeditated** *adj* (*crime*) vorsätzlich. **premeditation** *n* Vorbedacht *m.*
premier [ˈpremiə] *adj* erst. *n* Premierminister *m.*

premiere [ˈpremieə] *n* Erstaufführung *f*, Premiere *f.*
premise [ˈpremis] *n* Voraussetzung *f*, Prämisse *f.*
premises [ˈpremisis] *pl n* Gelände *neut sing.* **business premises** Büro *neut*, Geschäftsräume *pl.* **on the premises** im Hause.
premium [ˈpriːmiəm] *n* Prämie *f.*
premonition [ˌpreməˈniʃən] *n* Vorahnung *f.*
prenatal [priːˈneitl] *adj* prenatal, vor der Geburt.
preoccupied [priːˈokjupaid] *adj* vertieft (in).
prepare [priˈpeə] *v* vorbereiten; (*food*) zubereiten; (*produce*) herstellen. **prepare for** sich vorbereiten auf. **preparation** *n* Vorbereitung *f*; (*med*) Präparat *neut*; (*homework*) Hausaufgaben *pl.* **preparatory** *adj* vorbereitend. **prepared** *adj* bereit.
preposition [ˌprepəˈziʃən] *n* Präposition *f.*
preposterous [priˈpostərəs] *adj* absurd, lächerlich.
prerogative [priˈrogətiv] *n* Vorrecht *neut.*
prescribe [priˈskraib] *v* vorschreiben, anordnen; (*med*) verordnen. **prescription** *n* Verordnung *f.*
present[1] [ˈpreznt] *adj* (*time*) gegenwärtig; (*people*) anwesend; (*things*) vorhanden. *n* Gegenwart *f.* **at the present time** im Moment, zur Zeit. **be present at** Beiwohnen (+ *dat*). **presently** *adv* gleich. **presence** *n* (*people*) Anwesenheit *f*, Beisein *neut*; (*things*) Vorhandensein *neut.* **presence of mind** Geistesgegenwart *f.*
present[2] [ˈpreznt; *v* priˈzent] *n* Geschenk *neut. v* vorlegen; (*gift*) schenken; (*person*) vorstellen; (*play*) vorführen. **presentation** *n* Vorlegung *f*, Schenkung *f*, Übergabe *f*, Vorführung *f.*
preserve [priˈzɜːv] *v* bewahren; (*food*) einmachen. *n* Konserve *f.*
preside [priˈzaid] *v* den Vorsitz führen. **preside over** (*meeting*) leiten.
president [ˈprezidənt] *n* Präsident *m*; (*comm*) Generaldirektor *m.* **presidency** *n* (*pol*) Präsidentschaft *f*; (*meeting*) Vorsitz *m.* **presidential** *adj* Präsidenten-.
press [pres] *v* drücken; (*iron*) bügeln. *n* Presse *f.* **press conference** Pressekonferenz *f.* **press stud** Druckknopf *m.* **press-up** *n* Liegestütz *m.* **pressing** *adj* dringend.

pressure ['preʃə] *n* Druck *m*. **pressure cooker** Schnellkochtopf *m*. **pressure gauge** Druckmesser *m*. **pressure group** Interessengruppe *f*. **pressurize** (*aircraft*) auf Normaldruck halten; (*person*) unter Druck setzen.

prestige [pre'stiːʒ] *n* Prestige *neut*. **prestigious** *adj* Prestige-.

presume [pri'zjuːm] *v* annehmen; (*dare to*) sich erlauben. **presumably** *adv* vermutlich. **presumption** *n* Vermutung *f*; (*cheek*) Unverschämtheit *f*. **presumptuous** *adj* unverschämt.

pretend [pri'tend] *v* vorgeben. **pretend to** so tun, als ob; (*claim*) Anspruch erheben (auf). **pretence** *n* Vorwand *m*, Anschein *m*. **under false pretences** unter Vorspiegelung falscher Tatsachen. **pretentious** *adj* ammaßend. **pretentiousness** *n* Anmaßung *f*.

pretext ['priːtekst] *n* Vorwand *m*, Ausrede *f*.

pretty ['priti] *adj* hübsch, niedlich. *adv* (*coll*) ziemlich. **prettify** *v* hübsch machen. **prettiness** *n* Schönheit *f*.

prevail [pri'veil] *v* (*win*) siegen (über); (*be prevalent*) vorwiegen, vorherrschen. **prevailing** *adj* vorherrschend; (*opinion*) allgemein. **prevalence** *n* Herrschen *neut*. **prevalent** *adj* (vor)herrschend.

prevent [pri'vent] *v* verhindern, verhüten. **prevention** *n* Verhütung *f*. **preventive** *adj* vorbeugend. **preventive measure** Vorsichtsmaßnahme *f*.

preview ['priːvjuː] *n* Vorschau *f*, Probeaufführung *f*.

previous ['priːviəs] *adj* vorhergehend, früher. **previously** *adv* vorher.

prey [prei] *n* Opfer *neut*. *v* **prey on** erbeuten.

price [prais] *n* Preis *m*, Kosten *pl*. *v* den Preis festsetzen für; (*evaluate*) bewerten. **priceless** *adj* unschätzbar. **price-tag** *n* Preiszettel *m*.

prick [prik] *n* Stich *m*. *v* stechen.

prickle ['prikl] *n* Stachel *m*, Dorn *m*. *v* prickeln, kribbeln. **prickly** *adj* stachelig; (*person*) reizbar, übellaunig.

pride [praid] *n* Stolz *m*; (*arrogance*) Hochmut *m*; (*lions*) Rudel *neut*. *v* **pride oneself on** stolz sein auf.

priest [priːst] *n* Priester *m*. **priestess** *n* Priesterin *f*. **priesthood** *n* Priesterschaft *f*. **priestly** *adj* priesterlich.

prim [prim] *adj* steif, affektiert. **primness** *n* Steifheit *f*.

primary ['praiməri] *adj* erst, ursprünglich; (*main*) primär, Haupt-; (*basic*) grundlegend. **primary school** Grundschule *f*. **primarily** *adv* hauptsächlich.

primate ['praimət] *n* (*biol*) Primat *m*.

prime [praim] *adj* erst; (*main*) Haupt-; (*number*) unteilbar; (*best*) erstklassig. **prime minister** Premierminister(in). *n* Blüte *f*. *v* (*gun*) laden; (*paint*) grundieren; (*fig*) vorbereiten. **primer** *n* (*paint*) Grundierfarbe *f*; (*book*) Elementarbuch *neut*. **priming** *n* Vorbereitung *f*.

primeval [prai'miːvəl] *adj* urzeitlich.

primitive ['primitiv] *adj* (*early*) urzeitlich, Ur-; (*crude*, *unrefined*) primitiv. **primitiveness** *n* Primitivität *f*.

primrose ['primrouz] *n* Primel *f*.

prince [prins] *n* (*ruler*) Fürst *m*; (*king's son*) Prinz *m*. **princely** *adj* fürstlich. **princess** *n* Fürstin *f*, Prinzessin *f*. **principality** *n* Fürstentum *neut*.

principal ['prinsəpəl] *adj* erst, Haupt-. *n* Vorsteher(in); (*comm*) Kapital *neut*. **principally** *adv* hauptsächlich.

principle ['prinsəpəl] *n* Prinzip *neut*, Grundsatz *m*; (*basis*) Grundlage *f*. **principled** *adj* mit hohen Grundsätzen.

print [print] *v* drucken. **printed matter** Drucksache *f*. **printer** *n* Drucker *m*. **printing** *n* Druck *m*. **printing press** Druckerei *f*. *n* Druck *m*; (*of photograph*) Abzug *m*, Kopie *f*.

prior ['praiə] *adj* früher. *adv* **prior to** vor.

priority *n* Priorität *f*; (*precedence*) Vorrang *m*.

prise [praiz] *v* **prise open** aufbrechen.

prism ['prizm] *n* Prisma *neut*.

prison ['prizn] *n* Gefängnis *neut*. **prisoner** *n* Gefangene(r), Häftling *m*.

private ['praivət] *adj* privat; (*personal*) persönlich. *n* gemeiner Soldat *m*. **privacy** *n* Privatleben *neut*, Ruhe *f*.

privet ['privət] *n* Liguster *m*.

privilege ['privəlidʒ] *n* Privilegium *neut*, Sonderrecht *neut*; (*honour*) Ehre *f*. **privileged** *adj* bevorrechtet. **be privileged to** die Ehre haben, zu.

privy ['privi] *n* Abort *m*. *adj* **be privy to** eingeweiht sein in. **privy council** Geheimer Rat *m*.

prize [praiz] *n* Preis *m*; (*lottery*) Los *neut*. *adj* Preis-. *v* hochschätzen.

probable ['probəbl] *adj* wahrscheinlich.
probability *n* Wahrscheinlichkeit *f.*
probation [prə'beiʃən] *n* Probezeit *f;* (*law*) bedingte Freilassung *f.* **probationary** *adj* Probe-.
probe [proub] *n* (*tech*) Sonde *f;* (*enquiry*) Untersuchung *f. v* **probe into** eindringen in, erforschen.
problem ['probləm] *n* Problem *neut.* **problematical** *adj* problematisch.
proceed [prə'siːd] *v* weitergehen; (*continue*) fortfahren; (*begin*) beginnen. **procedure** *n* Vorgehen *neut.* **proceedings** *pl n* (*law*) Verfahren *neut sing.* **proceeds** *pl n* Erlös *m sing,* Ertrag *m sing.*
process ['prouses] *v* bearbeiten, verarbeiten. *n* Verfahren *neut,* Prozeß *m.* **processing** *n* Verarbeitung *f.*
procession [prə'seʃən] *n* Prozession *f,* Zug *m.*
proclaim [prə'kleim] *v* proklamieren, verkünden. **proclamation** *n* Proklamation *f.*
procreate ['proukrieit] *v* erzeugen. **procreation** *n* Zeugung *f.*
procure [prə'kjuə] *v* beschaffen, besorgen.
prod [prod] *v* stechen, stoßen; (*coll: induce*) anspornen (zu). *n* Stich *m,* Stoß *m.*
prodigy ['prodidʒi] *n* Wunder *neut;* (*child*) Wunderkind *neut.* **prodigious** *adj* riesig, erstaunlich.
produce [prə'djuːs; *n* 'prodjuːs] *v* (*goods*) erzeugen, herstellen; (*submit*) vorlegen; (*cause, call forth*) hervorrufen; (*theatre*) aufführen; (*films*) herausbringen. *n* Erzeugnis *neut,* Produkte *pl.* **producer** *n* Hersteller; (*theatre, film*) Regisseur *m.*
product *n* Produkt *neut,* Erzeugnis *neut;* (*result*) Ergebnis *neut.* **production** *n* Herstellung *f,* Produktion *f;* (*theatre*) Aufführung *f;* (*film*) Regie *f.* **production line** Fließband *neut.* **productive** *adj* fruchtbar, leistungsfähig. **productivity** *n* Leistungsfähigkeit *f,* Produktivität *f.*
profane [prə'fein] *adj* profan. **profanity** *n* Fluchen *neut.*
profess [prə'fes] *v* erklären. **profession** *n* (*occupation*) Beruf *m;* (*assertion*) Beteuerung *f.* **professional** *adj* Berufs-, beruflich; (*education*) fachlich, Fach-.
professor [prə'fesə] *n* Professor(in). **professorship** *n* Lehrstuhl *m.*
proficient [prə'fiʃənt] *adj* erfahren. **proficiency** *n* Erfahrenheit *f.*

profile ['proufail] *n* Profil *neut. v* profilieren.
profit ['profit] *n* (*comm*) Gewinn *m,* Profit *m;* (*advantage*) Vorteil *m. v* **profit from** Nutzen ziehen aus. **profitable** *adj* rentabel; (*advantageous*) vorteilhaft. **profiteer** *n* Profitmacher *m; v* sich bereichern.
program ['prougram] *n* (*computer*) Programm *neut. v* programmieren. **programmer** *n* Programmierer(in).
programme ['prougram] *n* Programm *neut;* (*TV, radio: broadcast*) Sendung *f. v* planen.
progress ['prougres] *n* Fortschritt *m;* (*development*) Entwicklung *f. v* fortschreiten, sich entwickeln. **in progress** im Gange. **progression** *n* Fortbewegung *f.* **progressive** *adj* fortschrittlich.
prohibit [prə'hibit] *v* verbieten. **prohibition** *n* Verbot *neut;* (*of drinking*) Alkoholverbot *neut.* **prohibitive** *adj* verbietend; (*excessively high*) untragbar.
project ['prodʒekt; *v* prə'dʒekt] *n* Projekt *neut,* Plan *m;* (*school*) Planaufgabe *f. v* (*film, etc.*) projizieren; (*plan*) planen. **projection** *n* Projektion *f.* **projector** *n* Projektionsapparat *m.*
proletariat [proulə'teəriət] *n* Proletariat *neut.* **proletarian** *adj* proletarisch. *n* Proletarier(in).
proliferate [prə'lifəreit] *v* sich vermehren, wuchern. **proliferation** *n* Wucherung *f.*
prolific [prə'lifik] *adj* fruchtbar.
prologue ['proulog] *n* Prolog *m.*
prolong [prə'loŋ] *v* verlängern. **prolonged** *adj* anhaltend. **prolongation** *n* Verlängerung *f.*
promenade [promə'naːd] *n* Promenade *f;* (*walk*) Spaziergang *m. v* promenieren, spazieren.
prominent ['prominənt] *adj* (*person*) prominent, maßgebend. **prominence** *n* Prominenz *f,* hervorragende Bedeutung *f.*
promiscuous [prə'miskjuəs] *adj* promiskuitiv. **promiscuity** *n* Promiskuität *f.*
promise ['promis] *n* Versprechen *neut. v* versprechen. **promising** *adj* vielversprechend.
promontory ['proməntəri] *n* Landspitze *f.*
promote [prə'mout] *v* (*person*) befördern; (*encourage, support*) fördern, Vorschub leisten (+ *dat*); (*comm*) Reklame machen für. **promoter** *n* (*sport*) Promoter *m.* **pro-**

motion *n* Beförderung; (*publicity*) Werbung *f.*, Reklame *f.*
prompt [prompt] *adj* sofortig, prompt. *v* (*theatre*) soufflieren; (*cause*) hervorrufen. **promptness** *n* Pünktlichkeit *f.*
prone [proun] *adj* hingestreckt. **prone to** geneigt zu.
prong [proŋ] *n* Zinke *f.* **pronged** *adj* gezinkt.
pronoun ['prounaun] *n* Pronomen *neut.*
pronounce [prə'nauns] *v* aussprechen. **pronouncement** *n* Ausspruch *m.* **pronunciation** *n* Aussprache *f.*
proof [pruːf] *n* Beweis *m*, Nachweis *m*; (*printing*) Korrekturabzug *m.* *adj* undurchlässig, fest. **proof against** sicher vor. **proof-reader** *n* Korrektor(in).
prop[1] [prop] *n* Stütze *f.* *v* **prop up** stützen.
prop[2] [prop] *n* (*theatre*) Requisit *neut.*
propaganda [propə'gandə] *n* Propaganda *f.* **propagandist** *n* Propagandist(in).
propagate ['propəgeit] *v* fortpflanzen. **propagation** *n* Fortpflanzung *f.*
propel [prə'pel] *v* (an)treiben. **propellant** *n* Treibstoff *m.* **propeller** *n* Propeller *m.*
proper ['propə] *adj* (*fitting*) richtig, passend, geeignet; (*thorough*) ordentlich. **properly** *adv* richtig, wie es sich gehört.
property ['propəti] *n* Eigentum *neut*; (*characteristic*) Eigenschaft *f*; (*real estate*) Immobilien *pl.*
prophecy ['profəsi] *n* Weissagung *f.* **prophesy** *v* prophezeien. **prophet** *n* Prophet *m.* **prophetic** *adj* prophetisch.
proportion [prə'poːʃən] *n* Verhältnis *neut*; (*part*) Anteil *m*; (*measurement*) Ausmaß *neut.* **in proportion to** im Verhältnis zu. **be out of proportion to** in keinem Verhältnis stehen zu. **well-proportioned** *adj* wohlgestaltet. **proportional** *adj* verhältnismäßig, proportional.
propose [prə'pouz] *v* vorschlagen; (*a motion*) beantragen; (*marriage*) einen Heiratsantrag machen (+ *dat*). **proposal** *n* Vorschlag *m*; (*offer*) Angebot *neut*; (*marriage*) Heiratsantrag *m.* **proposer** *n* Antragsteller *n.* **proposition** *n* Vorschlag *m*; (*project*) Projekt *neut*, Plan *m.*
proprietor [prə'praiətə] *n* Besitzer(in), Inhaber(in).
propriety [prə'praiəti] *n* Schicklichkeit *f*, Anstand *m.*
propulsion [prə'pʌlʃən] *n* Antrieb *m.*
prose [prouz] *n* Prosa *f.* *adj* Prosa-.

prosecute ['prosikjuːt] *v* (*law*) gerichtlich verfolgen. **prosecution** *n* Verfolgung *f*; (*law*) Anklage *f.*
prospect ['prospekt; *v* prə'spekt] *n* Aussicht *f.* *v* **prospect for** (*gold, etc.*) graben nach. **prospective** *adj* künftig, voraussichtlich.
prospectus [prə'spektəs] *n* (Werbe)-Prospekt *m.*
prosper ['prospə] *v* gedeihen. **prosperity** *n* Wohlstand *m.* **prosperous** *adj* erfolgreich, wohlhabend.
prostitute ['prostitjuːt] *n* Prostituierte *f.* *v* prostituieren. **prostitution** *n* Prostitution *f.*
prostrate ['prostreit; *v* pro'streit] *adj* hingestreckt. *v* zu Boden werfen. **prostrate oneself** sich demütigen (vor).
protagonist [prou'tagənist] *n* Hauptfigur *f.*
protect [prə'tekt] *v* (be)schützen. **protection** *n* Schutz *m.* **protectionism** *n* Schutzzollpolitik *f.* **protective** *adj* (be)schützend. **protector** *n* Beschützer *m.*
protectorate *n* Schutzgebiet *neut.*
protégé ['protəʒei] *n* Schützling *m.*
protein ['proutiːn] *n* Protein *neut*, Eiweiß *neut.*
protest ['proutest; *v* prə'test] *n* Protest *m*, Einspruch *m.* *v* protestieren, Einspruch erheben (auf).
Protestant ['protistənt] *n* Protestant(in). *adj* protestantisch. **Protestantism** *n* Protestantismus *m.*
protocol ['proutəkol] *n* Protokoll *neut.*
prototype ['proutətaip] *n* Prototyp *m.*
protractor [prə'traktə] *n* Winkelmesser *m.*
protrude [prə'truːd] *v* herausstehen, hervorstehen.
proud [praud] *adj* stolz (auf); (*arrogant*) hochmütig.
prove [pruːv] *v* beweisen. **prove to be** sich erweisen als.
proverb ['provəːb] *n* Sprichwort *neut.* **proverbial** *adj* sprichwörtlich.
provide [prə'vaid] *v* versehen, versorgen. **provide for** sorgen für. **provided** *conj* vorausgesetzt.
provident ['providənt] *adj* fürsorglich. **providence** *n* Vorsehung *f.* **providential** *adj* glücklich.
province ['provins] *n* Provinz *f.* **provincial** *adj* Provinz-, provinzial; (*limited, narrow*) provinziell.

provision [prə'viʒən] *n* Vorrichtung *f*; (*regulation*) Vorschrift *f*. **provisions** *pl* Vorrat *m*. **provisional** *adj* vorläufig, provisorisch.
proviso [prə'vaizou] *n* Vorbehalt *m*, Klausel *f*.
provoke [prə'vouk] *v* (*cause*) veranlassen; (*person*) provozieren; (*annoy*) ärgern. **provocation** *n* Provokation *f*; (*challenge*) Herausforderung *f*.
prow [prau] *n* Bug *m*.
prowess ['prauis] *n* Tüchtigkeit *f*.
prowl [praul] *v* herumstreichen. **prowler** *n* Herumtreiber *m*.
proximity [prok'siməti] *n* Nähe *f*.
proxy ['proksi] *n* Vollmacht *f*; (*person*) Bevollmächtigte(r).
prude [pruːd] *n* prüder Mensch *m*. **prudery** *n* Prüderie *f*. **prudish** *adj* prüde.
prudent ['pruːdənt] *adj* vernünftig, umsichtig. **prudence** *n* Klugheit *f*.
prune¹ [pruːn] *n* Backpflaume *f*.
prune² [pruːn] *v* (*tree*) beschneiden.
pry [prai] *v* herumschnüffeln. **pry into** die Nase stecken in. **prying** *adj* neugierig.
psalm [saːm] *n* Psalm *m*.
pseudonym ['sjuːdənim] *n* Pseudonym *neut*, Deckname *m*.
psychedelic [ˌsaikə'delik] *adj* psychedelisch.
psychiatry [sai'kaiətri] *n* Psychiatrie *f*. **psychiatric** *adj* psychiatrisch. **psychiatrist** *m* Psychiater(in).
psychic ['saikik] *adj* psychisch.
psychoanalysis [ˌsaikouə'naləsis] *n* Psychoanalyse *f*. **psychoanalyst** *n* Psychoanalytiker(in).
psychology [sai'kolədʒi] *n* Psychologie *f*. **psychological** *adj* psychologisch. **psychologist** *n* Psycholog(in).
psychopath ['saikəpaθ] *n* Psychopath(in)
psychosomatic [ˌsaikəsə'matik] *adj* psychosomatisch.
pub [pʌb] *n* (*coll*) Kneipe *f*.
puberty ['pjuːbəti] *n* Pubertät *f*, Geschlechtsreife *f*.
pubic ['pjuːbik] *adj* Scham-.
public ['pʌblik] *adj* öffentlich; (*national*) Volks-, national. *n* Öffentlichkeit *f*, Publikum *neut*. **public house** *n* Wirtshaus *neut*. **public school** Privatschule *f*. **public-spirited** *adj* gemeinsinnig. **publication** *n* Veröffentlichung *f*, Publikation *f*. **publicity** *n* Reklame *f*, Werbung *f*. **publicize** *v* veröffentlichen.

publish ['pʌbliʃ] *v* (*publicize*) veröffentlichen; (*book*) herausbringen. **publisher** *n* Verleger(in), Herausgeber(in); (*firm*) Verlag *m*. **publishing** *n* Verlagswesen *neut*.
pucker ['pʌkə] *v* runzeln; (*mouth*) spitzen.
pudding ['pudiŋ] *n* Pudding *m*. **black pudding** *n* Blutwurst *f*.
puddle ['pʌdl] *n* Pfütze *f*, Lache *f*.
puerile ['pjuərail] *adj* pueril.
puff [pʌf] *n* Hauch *m*; (*on cigar, etc.*) Zug *m*. *v* blasen, pusten. **powder puff** Puderquaste *f*. **puffed-up** *adj* (*coll*) aufgeblasen. **puff pastry** Blätterteig *m*. **puffy** *adj* angeschwollen.
pull [pul] *v* ziehen; (*tug*) zerren; (*rip*) reißen. *n* Zug *m*. **pull through** (*survive*) durchkommen.
pulley ['puli] *n* Rolle *f*.
pullover ['pulˌouvə] *n* Pullover *m*.
pulp [pʌlp] *n* Brei *m*; (*fruit*) Fruchtfleisch *neut*; (*paper*) Pulpe *f*. **pulpy** *adj* breiig, weich.
pulpit ['pulpit] *n* Kanzel *f*.
pulsate [pʌl'seit] *v* pulsieren. **pulsation** *n* Pulsieren *neut*.
pulse [pʌls] *n* Puls *m*, Pulsschlag *m*. *v* pulsieren.
pulverize ['pʌlvəraiz] *v* pulverisieren, zermahlen. **pulverization** *n* Pulverisierung *f*.
pump [pʌmp] *n* Pumpe *f*. *v* pumpen.
pumpkin ['pʌmpkin] *n* Kürbis *m*.
pun [pʌn] *n* Wortspiel *neut*.
punch¹ [pʌntʃ] *n* (*blow*) (Faust)Schlag *m*. *v* (mit der Faust) schlagen.
punch² [pʌntʃ] *n* (*drink*) Punsch *m*. **punchbowl** *n* Punschbowle *f*.
punch³ [pʌntʃ] *n* (*tool*) Locher *m*, Lochzange *f*. *v* lochen; (*tickets*) knipsen. **punchcard** *n* Lochkarte *f*.
punctual ['pʌŋktʃuəl] *adj* pünktlich. **punctuality** *n* Pünktlichkeit *f*.
punctuate ['pʌŋktʃueit] *v* interpunktieren; (*fig*) unterbrechen. **punctuation** *n* Interpunktion *f*.
puncture ['pʌŋktʃə] *v* durchstechen, perforieren; (*tyre*) platzen. *n* Loch *neut*; (*tyre*) Reifenpanne *f*.
pungent ['pʌndʒənt] *adj* scharf.
punish ['pʌniʃ] *v* (be)strafen. **punishment** *n* Strafe *f*.
puny ['pjuːni] *adj* schwächlich.

pupil¹ ['pjuːpl] *n* Schüler(in).
pupil² ['pjuːpl] *n* (*eye*) Pupille *f*.
puppet ['pʌpit] *n* Marionette *f*. **puppet show** Puppenspiel *neut*, Marionettentheater *neut*.
puppy ['pʌpi] *n* junger Hund *m*, Welpe *m*.
purchase ['pəːtʃəs] *n* Einkauf *m*. *v* (ein)kaufen. **purchaser** *n* Käufer(in).
pure ['pjuə] *adj* rein. **purebred** *adj* reinrassig. **purify** *v* reinigen; (*tech*) klären. **purification** *n* Reinigung *f*; Klärung *f*. **purity** *n* Reinheit *f*.
purée ['pjuərei] *n* Purée *neut*.
purgatory ['pəːgətəri] *n* Fegefeuer *neut*.
purge [pəːdʒ] *v* reinigen, säubern. *n* Reinigung *f*; (*pol*) Säuberung *f*.
puritan ['pjuəritən] *n* Puritaner(in). **puritanical** *adj* puritanisch. **puritanism** *n* Puritanismus *m*.
purl [pəːl] *n* Linksstricken *neut*. *v* linksstricken.
purple ['pəːpl] *adj* purpurn, purpurrot. *n* Purpur *m*.
purpose ['pəːpəs] *n* Zweck *m*, Ziel *neut*. **for the purpose of** zwecks (+ *gen*). **on purpose** absichtlich. **purposeful** *adj* zielbewußt. **purposeless** *adj* zwecklos. **purposely** *adv* absichtlich.
purr [pəː] *v* schnurren, summen. *n* Schnurren *neut*.
purse [pəːs] *n* Portemonnaie *neut*, Geldbeutel *m*; Handtasche *f*; (*prize*) Börse *f*. *v* (*lips*) spitzen.
purser ['pəːsə] *n* Zahlmeister *m*.
pursue [pə'sjuː] *v* verfolgen; (*studies*) betreiben; (*continue*) fortfahren in. **pursuit** *n* Verfolgung *f*; (*activity*) Beschäftigung *f*; (*of happiness, etc*.) Jagd *f*, Suche *f*.
pus [pʌs] *n* Eiter *m*.
push [puʃ] *n* Stoß *m*, Schub *m*. **get the push** (*coll*) entlassen werden. *v* stoßen, schieben; (*button*) drücken; (*in crowd*) drängen. **be pushed for time** keine zeit haben. **push aside** beiseite schieben. **push open/to** (*door*) auf/zuschieben. **push off** (*coll*) abhauen. **push through** durchsetzen. **pushbike** *m* (*coll*) Rad *neut*. **pushbutton** *n* Druckknopf *m*. **pushchair** *n* Kinderwagen *m*. **pusher** *n* (*drugs*) Pusher *m*. **pushing** *adj* aufdringlich.
pussy ['pusi] *n* (*coll*) Mieze *f*.
*put [put] *v* stellen, setzen, legen; (*express*) ausdrücken; (*shot*) werfen. **put away** weglegen. **put back** (*clock*) nach-

stellen; (*postpone*) aufschieben. **put by** aufsparen. **put down** hinlegen; (*revolt*) unterdrücken; (*animal*) töten. **put off** verschieben; (*discourage*) davon abraten (+ *dat*). **put through** durchführen; (*phone*) verbinden. **put up** (*coll*) unterbringen. **put up with** dulden, ausstehen.
putrid ['pjuːtrid] *adj* verfault.
putt [pʌt] *v* putten.
putty ['pʌti] *n* Kitt *m*.
puzzle ['pʌzl] *n* Rätsel *neut*; (*jigsaw*) Puzzlespiel *neut*. *v* verwirren. **puzzlement** *n* Verwirrung *f*. **puzzling** *adj* rätselhaft.
pyjamas [pə'dʒaiməz] *n* Schlafanzug *m*.
pylon ['pailən] *n* (*elec*) Leitungsmast *m*.
pyramid ['pirəmid] *n* Pyramide *f*.
python ['paiθən] *n* Pythonschlange *f*.

Q

quack¹ [kwak] *n* (*duck*) Quaken *neut*. *v* quaken.
quack² [kwak] *n* (*doctor*) Quacksalber *m*. *adj* quacksalberisch.
quadrangle ['kwodraŋgl] *n* Viereck *neut*; Hof *m*. **quadrangular** *adj* viereckig.
quadrant ['kwodrənt] *n* Quadrant *m*.
quadrilateral [kwodrə'latərəl] *adj* vierseitig.
quadruped ['kwodruped] *n* Vierfüßer *m*.
quadruple [kwod'ruːpl] *adj* vierfach, vierfältig. *v* vervierfachen.
quagmire ['kwagmaiə] *n* Morast *m*.
quail¹ [kweil] *n* (*bird*) Wachtel *f*.
quail² [kweil] *v* verzagen, den Mut verlieren.
quaint [kweint] *adj* kurios, merkwürdig.
quake [kweik] *v* beben. *n* Erdbeben *neut*.
qualify ['kwolifai] *v* (sich) qualifizieren; (*limit*) einschränken. **qualification** *n* Qualifikation *f*; Einschränkung *f*. **qualified** *adj* qualifiziert, geeignet; eingeschränkt.
quality ['kwoləti] *n* Qualität *f*; (*property*) Eigenschaft *f*; (*type*) Sorte *f*. *adj* erstklassig, guter Qualität *f*.
qualm [kwaːm] *n* Skrupel *m*.
quandary ['kwondəri] *n* Verlegenheit *f*.
quantify ['kwontifai] *v* messen, (quantitativ) bestimmen.

quantity ['kwontəti] *n* Quantität *f*, Menge *f*.

quarantine ['kworəntiɪn] *n* Quarantäne *f*. *v* unter Quarantäne stellen.

quarrel ['kworəl] *n* Streit *m*, Zank *m*. *v* (sich) streiten, (sich) zanken. **quarrelsome** *adj* streitsüchtig, zankig.

quarry[1] ['kwori] *n* (*hunting*) Jagdbeute *f*; (*fig*) Opfer *neut*.

quarry[2] ['kwori] *n* Steinbruch *m*. *v* brechen, hauen.

quart [kwoɪt] *n* Quart *neut*.

quarter ['kwoɪtə] *n* (*fourth, of town, etc.*) Viertel *neut*; (*of year*) Quartal *neut*, Vierteljahr *neut*. *v* vierteln; (*to house*) unterbringen. **quarter of an hour** Viertelstunde *f*. **quarter to/past** Viertel vor/nach. **quarterdeck** *n* Achterdeck *neut*. **quarter-final** *n* Viertelfinale *neut*. **quarterly** *adj* vierteljährlich.

quartet [kwoɪ'tet] *n* Quartett *neut*.

quartz [kwoɪts] *n* Quartz *m*.

quash [kwoʃ] *v* annullieren; (*resistance, etc.*) unterdrücken.

quaver ['kweivə] *v* zittern. *n* (*music*) Achtelnote *f*.

quay [kiɪ] *n* Kai *m*.

queasy ['kwiɪzi] *adj* übel. *I feel queasy* mir ist übel.

queen [kwiɪn] *n* Königin *f*; (*cards, chess*) Dame *f*. **queen bee** Bienenkönigin *f*. **queen mother** Königinmutter *f*.

queer [kwiə] *adj* seltsam, sonderbar; (*odd*) komisch; (*coll: homosexual*) schwul. *n* (*coll*) Homo *m*, Schwule(r).

quell [kwel] *v* unterdrücken.

quench [kwentʃ] *v* löschen.

query ['kwiəri] *n* Frage *f*, Erkundigung *f*. *v* in Frage stellen.

quest [kwest] *n* Suche *f* (nach).

question ['kwestʃən] *n* Frage *f*. *v* (be)fragen. **put** *or* **ask a question** eine Frage stellen. **out of the question** ausgeschlossen. **the question is** es handelt sich darum. **questionable** *adj* fragwürdig. **questioning** *adj* fragend. *n* Befragung *f*. **questionnaire** *n* Fragebogen *m*.

queue [kjuɪ] *n* Schlange *f*. *v* Schlange stehen, sich anstellen.

quibble ['kwibl] *v* Haare spalten, spitzfindig sein.

quick [kwik] *adj* schnell; (*nimble*) flink; (*temper*) hitzig; (*ear, eye*) scharf. **quicken** *v* beschleunigen. **quickness** *n* Schnel-

ligkeit *f*. **quicksand** *n* Treibsand *m*. **quicksilver** *n* Quecksilber *neut*. **quick-tempered** *adj* hitzig, reizbar. **quick-witted** *adj* scharfsinnig.

quid [kwid] *n* (*coll*) Pfund *neut*.

quiet ['kwaiət] *adj* ruhig, still. **quieten** *v* beruhigen. **quietness** *n* Ruhe *f*, Stille *f*.

quill [kwil] *n* Feder *f*.

quilt [kwilt] *n* Steppdecke *f*.

quinine [kwi'niɪn] *n* Chinin *neut*.

quinsy ['kwinzi] *n* Mandelentzündung *f*.

quintet [kwin'tet] *n* Quintett *neut*.

quirk [kwəɪk] *n* Eigenart *f*.

*quit [kwit] *v* (*stop*) aufhören; (*leave*) verlassen; (*job*) aufgeben. **notice to quit** Kündigung *f*. **quits** *adj* (*coll*) quitt.

quite [kwait] *adv* (*fairly*) ziemlich; (*wholly*) ganz, durchaus.

quiver[1] ['kwivə] *v* zittern.

quiver[2] ['kwivə] *n* (*arrows*) Köcher *m*.

quiz [kwiz] *n* Quiz *neut*. *v* (aus)fragen.

quizzical ['kwizikl] *adj* spöttisch.

quota ['kwoutə] *n* Quote *f*, Anteil *m*.

quote [kwout] *v* zitieren. **quotation** *n* Zitat *f*; (*comm*) Preisangabe *f*. **quotation marks** Anführungszeichen *pl*.

R

rabbi ['rabai] *n* Rabbiner *m*.

rabbit ['rabit] *n* Kaninchen *neut*. **rabbit hutch** Kaninchenstall *m*.

rabble ['rabl] *n* Pöbel *m*.

rabies ['reibiɪz] *n* Tollwut *f*. **rabid** *adj* tollwütig; (*coll: angry*) wütend.

race[1] [reis] *n* Rennen *neut*, Wettlauf *m*. *v* um die Wette laufen (mit), rennen. **the races** Pferderennen *pl*. **racecourse** *n* Rennbahn *f*. **racehorse** *n* Rennpferd *neut*. **racing** *n* Pferderennen *neut*; *adj* Renn-. **racing driver** Rennfahrer *m*.

race[2] [reis] *n* (*group*) Rasse *f*. **racial** *adj* rassisch, Rassen-. **racialism** *or* **racism** *n* Rassismus *m*. **racialist** *or* **racist** *n* Rassist(in); *adj* rassistisch.

rack [rak] *n* Gestell *neut*; (*luggage*) Gepäcknetz *neut*. *v* **rack one's brains** sich den Kopf zerbrechen.

racket[1] ['rakit] *n* (*sport*) Rakett *neut*, Schläger *m*.

racket² ['rakıt] n (noise) Krach m, Trübel m; (coll: swindle) Schwindel m. **racketeer** n Schwindler m, Gangster m.

radar ['reidɑ:] n Radar m or neut.

radial ['reidiəl] adj radial. n (tyre) Gürtelreifen m.

radiant ['reidiənt] adj strahlend. **radiance** n Strahlung f.

radiate ['reidieit] v ausstrahlen. **radiation** n Strahlung f. **radiator** n (house) Heizkörper m; (mot) Kühler m.

radical ['radikəl] adj radikal. n Radikale(r). **radicalism** n Radikalismus m.

radio ['reidiou] n (set) Radio neut; (network) Rundfunk m. v senden, durchgeben. **radio ham** (coll) Funkamateur m. **radio station** Sender m, Funkstation f. **radio wave** Radiowelle f.

radioactive [reidiou'aktiv] adj radioaktiv. **radioactivity** n Radioaktivität f.

radiology [reidi'olədʒi] n Radiologie f, Röntgenlehre f. **radiologist** n Radiologe m.

radiotherapy [reidiou'θerəpi] n Radiotherapie f, Strahlenbehandlung f.

radish ['radiʃ] n Radieschen neut.

radium ['reidiəm] n Radium neut.

radius ['reidiəs] n Radius m.

raffia ['rafiə] n Raffiabast m.

raffle ['rafl] n Tombola f. v verlosen.

raft [rɑ:ft] n Floß neut.

rafter ['rɑ:ftə] n Dachsparren m.

rag¹ [rag] n Fetzen m, Lumpen m; (coll: newspaper) Blatt neut. **rag doll** Stoffpuppe f. **ragged** adj zerfetzt.

rag² [rag] v (coll: tease) necken, piesacken.

rage [reidʒ] n Wut f. v wüten. **in a rage** wütend. **be all the rage** die große Mode sein.

raid [reid] n Angriff m, Überfall m; (police) Razzia f. v überfallen; eine Razzia machen auf.

rail [reil] n Riegel m, Schiene f. **by rail** mit der Bahn. **railing** n Geländer neut. **railway** or **railroad** n Eisenbahn f. **railway station** Bahnhof m.

rain [rein] n Regen m. v regnen. **rainbow** n Regenbogen m. **raincoat** n Regenmantel m. **rainfall** n Niederschlag m. **rainproof** adj wasserdicht. **rainstorm** n Regenguß. **rainy** adj regnerisch.

raise [reiz] v erheben, aufrichten; (provoke) hervorrufen; (money) beschaffen. n (in pay) Erhöhung f. **raised** adj erhöht.

raisin ['reizən] n Rosine f.

rake [reik] n Rechen m. v rechen.

rally ['rali] n (meeting) (Massen)Versammlung f; (mot) Sternfahrt f, Rallye f. v (wieder) sammeln; (spirits) sich erholen. **rally round** sich scharen um.

ram [ram] n (zool) Widder m; (tech) Ramme f. v rammen.

ramble ['rambl] v wandern; (speech) drauflos reden. n Wanderung f, Bummel m. **rambler** n Wanderer m; (rose) Kletterrose f. **rambling** adj wandernd; (speech) unzusammenhängend, weitschweifig.

ramp [ramp] n Rampe f.

rampage [ram'peidʒ] v (herum)toben.

rampant ['rampənt] adj üppig, wuchernd.

rampart ['rampɑ:t] n Festungswall m.

ramshackle ['ramʃakl] adj wackelig.

ran [ran] V **run.**

ranch [rɑ:ntʃ] n Ranch f.

rancid ['ransid] adj ranzig.

rancour ['raŋkə] n Erbitterung f, Böswilligkeit f.

random ['randəm] adj zufällig. n **at random** wahllos, aufs Geratewohl.

randy ['randi] adj (coll) geil, wollüstig.

rang [raŋ] V **ring².**

range [reindʒ] n Reihe f; (mountains) Kette f; (reach) Tragweite f. v anordnen; (vary) variieren, schwanken; (rove) wandern.

rank¹ [raŋk] n (status) Rang m; (row) Reihe f. v **rank with** zählen zu. **the rank** (mil) die Mannschaften pl.

rank² [raŋk] adj (plants) üppig; (offensive) widerlich; (coarse) grob.

rankle ['raŋkl] v nagen.

ransack ['ransak] v plündern, durchwühlen.

ransom ['ransəm] n Lösegeld neut. v loskaufen.

rap [rap] n Klopfen neut. v klopfen.

rape [reip] n Vergewaltigung f. v vergewaltigen. **rapist** n Vergewaltiger m.

rapid ['rapid] adj schnell, rasch. **rapidity** n Schnelligkeit f. **rapids** pl n Stromschnelle f.

rapier ['reipiə] n Rapier neut.

rapture ['raptʃə] n Verzückung f, Begeisterung f. **rapturous** adj hingerissen.

rare[1] ['reə] *adj* selten, rar; (*air*) dünn. **rarely** *adv* selten. **rarity** *n* Seltenheit *f*.
rare[2] ['reə] *adj* (*cookery*) nicht durchgebraten, englisch.
rascal ['raɪskəl] *n* Schurke *m*. **rascally** *adj* schurkisch.
rash[1] [raʃ] *n* (*on skin*) Hautausschlag *m*.
rash[2] [raʃ] *adj* hastig, übereilt. **rashness** *n* Hast *f*.
rasher ['raʃə] *n* (Schinken)Schnitte *f*.
raspberry ['raɪzbəri] *n* Himbeere *f*.
rat [rat] *n* Ratte *f*. *v* rat on (*coll*) verraten.
rate [reit] *n* (*comm*) Satz *m*, Kurs *m*; (*charge*) Gebühr *f*; (*speed*) Geschwindigkeit *f*. *v* schätzen. **rates** *pl* Gemeindesteuer *f*. **birth rate** Geburtenziffer *f*. **at any rate** auf jeden Fall. **first-rate** *adj* erstklassig. **second-rate**, **third-rate**, *etc. adj* minderwertig.
rather ['raɪðə] *adv* (*quite*) ziemlich, etwas; (*preferably*) lieber, eher. *I would rather* ich möchte lieber.
ratify ['ratifai] *v* ratifizieren. **ratification** *n* Ratifizierung *f*.
ratio ['reiʃiou] *n* Verhältnis *neut*.
ration ['raʃən] *n* Ration *f*. *v* rationieren. **rations** *pl* Verpflegung *f sing*.
rational ['raʃənl] *adj* rational, vernünftig. **rationale** *n* Grundprinzip *neut*. **rationalization** *n* Rationalisierung *f*. **rationalize** *v* rationalisieren.
rattle ['ratl] *v* klappern, rasseln. *n* Gerassel *neut*, Klappern *neut*. **rattlesnake** *n* Klapperschlange *f*.
raucous ['rɔɪkəs] *adj* rauh, heiser.
ravage ['ravidʒ] *v* verwüstern. *n* Verwüstung. **ravages of time** Zahn der Zeit *m*.
rave [reiv] *v* irre reden, toben. **rave about** (*coll*) schwärmen von. **raving** *adj* delirierend. **ravings** *pl n* Fieberwahn *m*, Delirien *pl*.
raven ['reivən] *n* Rabe *m*.
ravenous ['ravənəs] *adj* heißhungrig.
ravine [rə'viɪn] *n* Schlucht *f*.
ravish ['raviʃ] *v* (*delight*) hinreißen; (*rape*) vergewaltigen. **ravishing** *adj* entzückend.
raw [rɔɪ] *adj* roh; (*voice*) rauh; (*sore*) wund. **rawhide** *n* Rohleder *neut*. **rawness** *n* Rohzustand *m*.
ray [rei] *n* Strahl *m*. **ray of light** Lichtstrahl *m*.
rayon ['reion] *n* Kunstseide *f*.
razor ['reizə] *n* Rasiermesser *neut*. **electric razor** Elektrorasierer *m*. **razor blade**

Rasierklinge *f*. **razor-sharp** *adj* messerscharf.
reach [riɪtʃ] *v* (*arrive at*) erreichen; (*stretch to*) sich erstrecken (bis). *n* Reichweite *f*. **reach (out) for** reichen *or* greifen nach.
react [ri'akt] *v* reagieren. **reaction** *n* Reaktion *f*. **reactionary** *adj* reaktionär; *n* Reaktionär(in).
*read [riɪd] *v* lesen; (*interpret*) auslegen, deuten. **read aloud** vorlesen. **read through** durchlesen. **readable** *adj* leserlich; (*worth reading*) lesenswert. **reader** *n* Leser(in); (*university*) Dozent *m*. **readership** *n* Leserkreis *m*. **reading** *n* Lesen *neut*; (*public*) Vorlesung *f*. **reading matter** Lektüre *f*.
readjust [riːə'dʒʌst] *v* wieder in Ordnung bringen; (*tech*) wieder einstellen; (*person*) (sich) wieder anpassen (an). **readjustment** *n* Wiederanpassung *f*.
ready ['redi] *adj* bereit, fertig; (*quick*) prompt. **get** *or* **make ready** sich vorbereiten; (*thing*) fertig machen. **readiness** *n* Bereitschaft *f*. **ready-made** *adj* Fertig-. **ready-reckoner** *n* Rechentabelle *f*. **readily** *adv* ohne weiteres.
real [riəl] *adj* wirklich, wahr; (*genuine*) echt. **real estate** Immobilien *pl*. **realism** n Realismus *m*. **realist** *n* Realist(in). **realistic** *adj* realistisch. **reality** *n* Wirklichkeit *f*, Realität *f*. **really** *adv* tatsächlich, in der Tat; (*very, actually*) wirklich.
realize ['riəlaiz] *v* begreifen, erkennen; (*bring about*) verwirklichen. **realizable** *adj* durchführbar. **realization** *n* Erkenntnis *f*; Verwirklichung *f*.
realm [relm] *n* Königreich *neut*; (*sphere*) Gebiet *neut*.
reap [riɪp] *v* ernten, mähen. **reaper** *n* Mäher(in).
reappear [riːə'piə] *v* wieder erscheinen. **reappearance** *n* Wiedererscheinen *neut*.
rear[1] [riə] *adj* hinter, Hinter-. *n* Hinterseite *f*, Rückseite *f*. **rear lamp** Schlußlicht *neut*. **rear wheel** Hinterrad *neut*.
rear[2] [riə] *v* (*child*) erziehen; (*animals*) züchten.
rearrange [riːə'reindʒ] *v* neu ordnen, umordnen; (*date, etc.*) ändern. **rearrangement** *n* Neuordnung *f*; Änderung *f*.
reason ['riːzn] *n* Grund *m*; (*good sense*) Vernunft *f*. *v* folgern. **for this reason** aus diesem Grund. **by reason of** wegen (+*gen*). **reason with** zu überzeugen ver-

suchen. **reasonable** *adj* vernünftig. **reasonableness** *n* Vernünftigkeit. **reasonably** *adv* vernünftigerweise; (*fairly*) ziemlich. **reasoning** *n* Schlußfolgerung *f*, Argument *neut*. **reassure** [riə'ʃuə] *v* beruhigen. **reassurance** *n* Beruhigung *f*.

rebate ['riːbeit] *n* Rabatt *m*. **rebel** ['rebl] *n* Rebell(in), Aufrührer(in). *adj* aufrührerisch. *v* rebellieren. **rebellion** *n* Aufstand *m*. **rebellious** *adj* aufrührerisch.

rebound [ri'baund; *n* 'riːbaund] *v* zurückprallen. *n* Rückprall *m*.

rebuff [ri'bʌf] *v* abweisen. *n* Abweisung *f*.

*rebuild [riː'bild] *v* wiederaufbauen.

rebuke [ri'bjuːk] *v* zurechtweisen, rüffeln. *n* Rüffel *m*.

recall [ri'koːl] *v* (*call back*) zurückrufen; (*remember*) sich erinnern an. *n* Rückruf *m*; Erinnerung *f*.

recap ['riːkap] *v* kurz zusammenfassen. *n* Zusammenfassung *f*.

recede [ri'siːd] *v* zurückgehen, zurückweichen.

receipt [rə'siːt] *n* (*of letter*) Empfang *m*; (*of goods*) Annahme *f*; (*bill*) Quittung *f*. **receipts** *pl* Einnahmen *pl*. **acknowledge receipt** Empfang bestätigen.

receive [rə'siːv] *v* empfangen, bekommen. **receiver** *n* (*phone*) Hörer *m*; (*comm*) Konkursverwalter *m*; (*radio*) Empfänger *m*. **receivership** *n* Konkursverwaltung *f*.

recent ['riːsnt] *adj* neu, modern, neulich entstanden. **recently** *adv* neulich, vor kurzem.

receptacle [rə'septəkl] *n* Behälter *m*, Gefäß *neut*.

reception [rə'sepʃən] *n* Empfang *m*. **receptionist** *n* Empfangsdame *f*. **reception room** Empfangszimmer *neut*.

recess [ri'ses] *n* Pause *f*, Unterbrechung *f*; (*holiday*) Ferien *pl*; (*niche*) Nische *f*.

recession [rə'seʃən] *n* (*comm*) Rezession *f*.

recharge [riː'tʃaidʒ] *v* (*battery*) wieder aufladen.

recipe ['resəpi] *n* Rezept *neut*.

recipient [rə'sipiənt] *n* Empfänger(in).

reciprocate [rə'siprəkeit] *v* erwidern. **reciprocal** *adj* gegenseitig. **reciprocation** *n* Erwiderung *f*.

recite [rə'sait] *v* vortragen, rezitieren. **piano/song recital** Klavier-/Liederabend *m*.

reckless ['rekləs] *adj* rücksichtslos. **recklessness** *n* Rücksichtslosigkeit *f*.

reckon ['rekən] *v* rechnen, zählen (*believe*) meinen. **reckon on** sich verlassen auf. **reckon with** rechnen mit. **reckoning** *n* Abrechnung *f*.

reclaim [ri'kleim] *v* (*ask for back*) zurückfordern; (*land from sea*) gewinnen.

recline [rə'klain] *v* sich zurücklehnen (an).

recluse [rə'kluːs] *n* Einsiedler(in).

recognize ['rekəgnaiz] *v* (*wieder*) erkennen; (*acknowledge*) anerkennen; (*concede*) zugeben. **recognition** *n* (Wieder)Erkennen *neut*; Anerkennung *f*. **recognizable** *adj* erkennbar.

recoil [rə'koil; *n* 'riːkoil] *v* zurückprallen (*in fear*) zurückschrecken. *n* Rückprall *m*.

recollect [rekə'lekt] *n* sich erinnern an. **recollection** *n* Erinnerung *f*.

recommence [riːkə'mens] *v* wieder beginnen.

recommend [rekə'mend] *v* empfehlen. **to be recommended** empfehlenswert. **recommendation** *n* Empfehlung *f*; (*suggestion*) Vorschlag *m*.

recompense ['rekəmpens] *n* Belohnung *f* *v* belohnen.

reconcile ['rekənsail] *v* versöhnen. **reconcile oneself to** sich abfinden mit. **reconcilable** *adj* vereinbar (mit). **reconciliation** *n* Versöhnung *f*.

reconstruct [riːkən'strʌkt] *v* wieder aufbauen; (*events*) rekonstruieren. **reconstruction** *n* Wiederaufbau *m*; Rekonstruktion *f*.

record [rə'koːd; *n* 'rekoːd] *v* (*film, tape*) aufnehmen; (*write down*) aufschreiben eintragen. *n* (*disc*) Schallplatte *f*; (*of proceedings, etc.*) Protokoll *neut*, Bericht *m* (*sport*) Rekord *m*. **break the record** den Rekord brechen. **off the record** inoffiziell **recorder** *n* (*music*) Blockflöte *f*. **recording** *n* Aufnahme *f*. **record-player** *n* Plattenspieler *m*.

recount [ri'kaunt] *v* (*narrate*) erzählen.

recoup [ri'kuːp] *v* (*loss*) wieder einholen

recover [rə'kʌvə] *v* zurückgewinnen; (*get better*) sich erholen. **recovery** *n* Zurückgewinnung *f*; Erholung *f*.

recreation [rekri'eifən] *n* Erholung *f*, Entspannung *f*. **recreation ground** *n* Spielplatz *neut*.

recrimination [riˌkrimi'neiʃən] *n* Gegenbeschuldigung *f*.
recruit [rə'kruːt] *n* Rekrut *m*. *v* rekrutieren. **recruitment** *n* Rekrutierung *f*.
rectangle ['rektaŋgl] *n* Rechteck *neut*. **rectangular** *adj* rechteckig.
rectify ['rektifai] *v* richtigstellen, korrigieren; (*elec*) gleichrichten. **rectification** *n* Richtigstellung *f*, Korrektur *f*.
rectum ['rektəm] *n* Mastdarm *m*. **rectal** *adj* rektal.
recuperate [rə'kjuːpəreit] *v* sich erholen. **recuperation** *n* Erholung *f*.
recur [ri'kəi] *v* wieder auftreten, sich wiederholen. **recurrence** *n* Wiederauftreten *neut*. **recurrent** *adj* wiederkehrend.
red [red] *adj* rot. *n* Rot *neut*. **red tape** Amtsschimmel *m*. **redden** *v* erröten, rot werden. **redness** *n* Röte *f*. **red-handed** *adj* auf frischer Tat.
redeem [rə'diːm] *v* (*pledge*) einlösen; (*prisoner*) loskaufen; (*promise*) einhalten. **redemption** *n* Ablösung *f*; Rückkauf *m*.
redevelop [ˌriːdi'veləp] *v* neu entwickeln; (*town*) umbauen.
redress [rə'dres] *n* (*legal*) Rechtshilfe *f*; (*compensation*) Wiedergutmachung *f*. *v* wiedergutmachen. **redress the balance** das Gleichgewicht wiederherstellen.
reduce [rə'djuːs] *v* vermindern, verringern; (*prices*) herabsetzen; (*tech*) reduzieren; (*slim*) eine Abmagerungskur machen. **in reduced circumstances** verarmt. **reduction** *n* Verminderung *f*; Herabsetzung *f*; (*tech*) Reduktion *f*.
redundant [rə'dʌndənt] *adj* überflüssig; (*jobless*) arbeitslos. **be made redundant** entlassen werden. **'redundancy** *n* Überflüssigkeit *f*; (*worker*) Entlassung *f*.
reed [riːd] *n* Rohr *neut*; (*music*) (Rohr)Blatt *neut*. **reedy** *adj* (*voice*) piepsig.
reef [riːf] *n* (Felsen)Riff *neut*.
reek [riːk] *v* stinken (nach). *n* Gestank *m*.
reel¹ [riːl] *n* Spule *f*; (*cotton*) Rolle *f*.
reel² [riːl] *v* taumeln, schwanken.
refectory [rə'fektəri] *n* Speisesaal *m*; (*university*) Mensa *f*.
refer [rə'fəi] *v* **refer to** hinweisen auf, sich beziehen auf; (*mention*) erwähnen; (*a book*) nachschlagen in. **reference** *n* Bezug *m*, Hinweis *m*; Erwähnung *f*; (*in book*) Verweis *m*. **with reference to** in Bezug auf, hinsichtlich (+*gen*). **reference book** Nachschlagewerk *neut*.

referee [refə'riː] *n* Schiedsrichter *m*.
referendum [refə'rendəm] *n* Volksentscheid *m*.
refill [riː'fil; *n* 'riːfil] *v* nachfüllen. *n* (*for pen*) Ersatzmine *f*.
refine [rə'fain] *v* (*tech*) raffinieren; (*improve*) verfeinern. **refined** *adj* raffiniert; (*person, etc.*) kultiviert **refinement** *n* Verfeinerung *f*; (*good breeding*) Kultiviertheit *f*. **refinery** *n* Raffinerie *f*.
reflation [rə'fleiʃn] *n* Wirtschaftsbelebung *f*.
reflect [rə'flekt] *v* widerspiegeln; (*consider*) nachdenken. **reflection** *n* Widerspiegelung *f*. (*thought*) Überlegung *f*; (*remark*) Bemerkung *f*. **reflective** *adj* zurückstrahlend; (*thoughtful*) nachdenklich. **reflector** *n* (*mot*) Rückstrahler *m*.
reflex ['riːfleks] *n* Reflex *m*.
reform [rə'foɪm] *n* Reform *f*, Verbesserung *f*. *v* reformieren, (ver)bessern. **reformation** *n* Verbesserung *f*; (*history*) Reformation *f*. **reformatory** *n* Besserungsanstalt *f*. **reformed** *adj* verbessert. **reformer** *n* Reformer(in).
refract [rə'frakt] *v* brechen.
refrain¹ [rə'frein] *v* **refrain from** sich enthalten (+*gen*).
refrain² [rə'frein] *n* Refrain *m*.
refresh [rə'freʃ] *v* erfrischen; (*memory*) auffrischen. **refresher course** Wiederholungskurs *m*. **refreshing** *adj* erfrischend. **refreshment** *n* Erfrischung *f*. **refreshments** *pl* Imbiß *m sing*.
refrigerator [rə'fridʒəreitə] *n* Kühlschrank *m*. **refrigerate** *v* kühlen. **refrigeration** *n* Kühlung *f*.
refuel [riː'fjuːəl] *v* tanken.
refuge ['refjuːdʒ] *n* Zuflucht *f*, Schutz *m*. **refugee** *n* Flüchtling *m*.
refund ['riːfʌnd; *v* ri'fʌnd] *n* Rückvergütung *f*. *v* zurückzahlen.
refuse¹ [rə'fjuːz] *v* ablehnen, verweigern. **refusal** *n* Verweigerung *f*, Ablehnung *f*.
refuse² ['refjuːs] *n* Abfall *m*, Müll *m*. **refuse collection** Müllabfuhr *f*.
refute [ri'fjuːt] *v* widerlegen.
regain [ri'gein] *v* wiedergewinnen.
regal ['riːgəl] *adj* königlich.
regard [rə'gaɪd] *v* ansehen, betrachten. *n* (*esteem*) (Hoch)Achtung *f*; (*consideration*) Rücksicht *f*, Hinblick *m*. **in this regard** in dieser Hinsicht. **with regard to** in bezug auf. **as regards** was ... betrifft.
regarding *prep* hinsichtlich (+*gen*),

bezüglich (+*gen*). **regardless** *adj* ohne Rücksicht (auf).
regatta [rə'gatə] *n* Regatta *f.*
regent ['riːdʒənt] *n* Regent(in).
regime [rei'ʒiːm] *n* Regime *f.*
regiment ['redʒimənt] *n* Regiment *neut.*
region ['riːdʒən] *n* Gebiet *neut*, Gegend *f.* **in the region of** etwa, ungefähr. **regional** *adj* regional, örtlich.
register ['redʒistə] *v* registrieren; (*report*) sich eintragen lassen. *n* Register *neut.* **registered** *adj* eingetragen. **registered letter** Einschreibebrief *m.* **send by registered post** per Einschreiben schicken. **registrar** *n* (*births,* *etc.*) Standesbeamte(r); (*hospital,* *etc.*) Direktor *m.* **registration** *n* Registrierung *f.* **registration number** (*mot*) polizeiliches Kennzeichen *neut.* **registry office** Standesamt *neut.*
regress [ri'gres] *v* zurückgehen. **regression** *n* Regression *f.* **regressive** *adj* rückläufig.
regret [rə'gret] *v* bedauern. *n* Reue *f,* Bedauern *neut.* **regrettable** *adj* bedauerlich.
regular ['regjulə] *adj* regelmäßig; (*normal*) gewöhnlich; (*correct*) ordnungsgemäß. **regular (customer)** Stammgast *m.* **regularity** *n* Regelmäßigkeit *f.*
regulate ['regjuleit] *v* regeln, ordnen. **regulation** *n* (*rule*) Vorschrift *f*; (*tech*) Regelung *f.* **regulator** *n* Regler *m.*
rehabilitate [riːhə'biliteit] *n* rehabilitieren. **rehabilitation** *n* Rehabilitation *f.*
rehearse [rə'həːs] *v* proben. **rehearsal** *n* Probe *f.*
reign [rein] *n* Regierung(szeit) *f.* *v* regieren, herrschen.
reimburse [riːim'bəːs] *v* (*person*) entschädigen. **reimbursement** *n* Entschädigung *f.*
rein [rein] *n* Zügel *m.*
reincarnation [riːinkaː'neiʃən] *n* Reinkarnation *f,* Wiederverkörperung *f.*
reindeer ['reindiə] *n* Ren(tier) *neut.*
reinforce [riːin'fɔːs] *v* verstärken; (*concrete*) armieren. **reinforcement** *n* Verstärkung *f.*
reinstate [ˌriːin'steit] *v* wiedereinsetzen. **reinstatement** *n* Wiedereinsetzung *f.*
reinvest [riːin'vest] *v* wiederinvestieren.
reissue [riː'iʃuː] *v* neu herausgeben. *n* Neuausgabe *f.*
reject [rə'dʒekt; *n* 'riːdʒekt] *v* ablehnen,

verwerfen. **rejection** *n* Ablehnung *f,* Verwerfung *f.* *n* Ausschußartikel *m.*
rejoice [rə'dʒois] *v* sich freuen. **rejoicing** *adj* froh; *n* Freude *f.*
rejoin [rə'dʒoin] *v* sich wieder anschließen; (*reply*) erwidern. **rejoinder** *n* Erwiderung *f.*
rejuvenate [rə'dʒuːvəneit] *v* verjüngen. **rejuvenation** *n* Verjüngung *f.*
relapse [rə'laps] *v* zurückfallen; (*med*) einen Rückfall bekommen. *n* Rückfall *m.*
relate [rə'leit] *v* (*tell*) erzählen; (*link*) verbinden. **related** *adj* verwandt. **relating to** in bezug auf.
relation [rə'leiʃn] *n* Verhältnis *neut*; (*business*) Beziehung *f*; (*person*) Verwandte(r). **relationship** *n* Verhältnis *neut*; (*family*) Verwandtschaft *f.*
relative ['relətiv] *n* Verwandte(r). *adj* relativ, verhältnismäßig. **relatively** *adv* verhältnismäßig. **relativity** *n* Relativität *f.*
relax [rə'laks] *v* entspannen. **relaxation** *n* Entspannung *f.*
relay ['riːlei; *v* ri'lei] *n* (*race*) Staffellauf *m*; (*tech*) Relais *neut.* *v* weitergeben.
release [rə'liːs] *v* freilassen, entlassen; (*film, etc.*) freigeben; (*news*) bekanntgeben; (*let go*) loslassen. *n* Entlassung *f*; Freigabe *f.*
relent [rə'lent] *v* nachgiebig werden. **relentless** *adj* unbarmherzig.
relevant ['reləvənt] *adj* erheblich, relevant; (*appropriate*) entsprechend. **relevance** *n* Relevanz *f.*
reliable [ri'laiəbl] *adj* zuverlässig. **reliability** *n* Zuverlässigkeit *f.* **reliance** *n* Vertrauen *neut.*
relic ['relik] *n* Überbleibsel *neut*; (*rel*) Reliquie *f.*
relief [rə'liːf] *n* Erleichterung *f*; (*mil*) Ablösung *f*; (*help*) Hilfe *f*; (*geog*) Relief *neut.* **tax relief** Steuerbegünstigung *f.*
relieve [rə'liːv] *v* erleichtern; (*from burden*) entlasten; (*person*) ablösen; (*reassure*) beruhigen.
religion [rə'lidʒən] *n* Religion *f.* **religious** *adj* religiös.
relinquish [rə'liŋkwiʃ] *v* aufgeben, verzichten auf.
relish ['reliʃ] *v* sich erfreuen an. *n* (*fig*) Vergnügen *neut*; (*sauce*) Soße *f.*
reluctant [rə'lʌktənt] *adj* widerwillig. **be reluctant to do** ungern tun. **reluctance** *n* Widerstreben *neut.* **reluctantly** *adv* ungern.

rely [rə'lai] v sich verlassen (auf).
remain [rə'mein] v bleiben; *(be left over)* übrigbleiben. **remains** *pl n* Überreste *pl*; *(person)* die sterblichen Überreste *pl*. **remainder** *n* Rest *m*, Restbestand *m*. **remaining** *adj* übriggeblieben.
remand [rə'maind] v in Untersuchungshaft zurückschicken.
remark [rə'maik] *n* Bemerkung *f*. v bemerken. **remarkable** *adj* bemerkenswert.
remarry [rii'mari] v wieder heiraten.
remedy ['remədi] *n* Gegenmittel *neut*; *(med)* Heilmittel *neut*. v berichtigen.
remember [ri'membə] v sich erinnern an. *remember me to your mother* grüße deine Mutter von mir. **remembrance** *n* Erinnerung *f*.
remind [rə'maind] v erinnern (an); *(someone to do something)* mahnen. **reminder** *n* Mahnung *f*.
reminiscence [remə'nisens] *n* Erinnerung *f*. **be reminiscent of** erinnern an.
remiss [rə'mis] *adj* nachlässig.
remit [rə'mit] v überweisen. **remittance** *n* Überweisung *f*.
remnant ['remnənt] *n* (Über)Rest *m*, Überbleibsel *neut*.
remorse [rə'mois] *n* Gewissensbisse *pl*, Reue *f*. **remorseful** *n* reumütig. **remorseless** *adj* unbarmherzig.
remote [rə'mout] *adj* fern, entfernt. **remote control** Fernsteuerung *f*. **remoteness** *n* Ferne *f*.
remove [rə'muiv] v beseitigen, entfernen; *(move house)* umziehen. **removal** *n* Beseitigung *f*; Umzug *m*. **remover** *n* (Möbel)Spediteur *m*.
remunerate [rə'mjuinəreit] v belohnen. **remuneration** *n* Lohn *m*, Vergütung *f*.
renaissance [rə'neisəns] *n* Renaissance *f*.
rename [rii'neim] v umbenennen.
render ['rendə] v *(make)* machen; *(give back)* wiedergeben; *(service)* leisten.
rendezvous ['rondivui] *n* Verabredung *f*, Stelldichein *neut*.
renegade ['renigeid] *n* Abtrünnige(r). *adj* abtrünnig.
renew [rə'njui] v erneuern; *(contract)* verlängern. **renewal** *n* Erneuerung *f*.
renounce [ri'nauns] v verzichten auf; *(person)* verleugnen; *(beliefs)* abschwören.
renovate ['renəveit] v erneuern, renovier-

en. **renovation** *n* Renovierung *f*, Erneuerung *f*.
renown [rə'naun] *n* Ruhm *m*, Berühmtheit *f*. **renowned** *adj* berühmt.
rent [rent] *n* Miete *f*. v mieten; *(let)* vermieten. **rental** *n* Mietbetrag *m*.
renunciation [ri,nʌnsi'eifən] *n* *(rejection)* Ablehnung *f*.
reopen [rii'oupən] v wieder öffnen; *(shop, etc.)* wiedereröffnen.
reorganize [rii'oigənaiz] v reorganisieren, neugestalten. **reorganization** *n* Reorganisation *f*.
rep [rep] *n* *(coll: representative)* Vertreter(in).
repair [ri'peə] v reparieren, ausbessern; *(clothes)* flicken. *n* Reparatur *f*. **in good repair** in gutem Zustand. **in need of repair** reparaturbedürftig. **repair kit** Flickzeug *neut*. **reparation** *n* Wiedergutmachung *f*.
repartee [repai'tii] *n* Schlagabtausch *m*.
repatriate [rii'patrieit] v repatriieren. **repatriation** *n* Repatriierung *f*.
***repay** [ri'pei] v zurückzahlen; *(kindness)* erwidern. **repayable** *adj* rückzahlbar. **repayment** *n* Rückzahlung *f*.
repeal [rə'piil] v aufheben, widerrufen. *n* Aufhebung *f*.
repeat [rə'piit] v wiederholen. *n* Wiederholung *f*. **repeated** *adj* wiederholt.
repel [rə'pel] v abweisen. **repellent** *adj* abstoßend, widerlich.
repent [rə'pent] v bereuen. **repentance** *n* Reue *f*. **repentant** *adj* bußfertig.
repercussions [riipə'kʌfənz] *pl n* Rückwirkungen *pl*.
repertoire ['repətwai] *n* Repertoire *neut*.
repetition [repə'tifn] *n* Wiederholung *f*. **repetitive** *adj* sich wiederholend.
replace [rə'pleis] v ersetzen. **replacement** *n* Ersatz *m*. **replacement part** Ersatzteil *neut*.
replay ['riiplei] *n* *(sport)* Wiederholungsspiel *neut*; *(tape)* Wiedergabe *f*.
replenish [rə'plenif] v ergänzen.
replica ['replikə] *n* Kopie *f*.
reply [rə'plai] v antworten, erwidern. *n* Antwort *f*, Erwiderung *f*. **reply to** *(person)* antworten (+ *dat*); *(question, letter)* antworten auf. **in reply to** in Erwiderung auf.
report [rə'poit] *n* Bericht *m*; *(factual statement)* Meldung *f*. v berichten;

(*denounce*) melden; (*present oneself*) sich melden. **reporter** *n* Reporter *m*.
repose [rə'pouz] *n* Ruhe *f*. *v* ruhen.
represent [reprə'zent] *v* darstellen; (*act as representative*) vertreten. **representation** *n* Darstellung *f*; Vertretung *f*. **representative** *n* Vertreter(in). *adj* (*typical*) typisch.
repress [rə'pres] *v* unterdrücken; (*psychol*) verdrängen. **repression** *n* Unterdrückung *f*; Verdrängung *f*.
reprieve [rə'priːv] *v* begnadigen. *n* Strafaufschub *m*; (*fig*) Gnadenfrist *f*.
reprimand ['reprimaɪnd] *v* rügen. *n* Rüge *f*, Verweis *m*.
reprint [riː'print; *n* 'riːprint] *v* neu drucken. *n* Neudruck *m*.
reprisal [rə'praizəl] *n* Repressalie *f*.
reproach [rə'proutʃ] *n* Vorwurf *m*, Tadel *m*. *v* Vorwürfe machen (+ *dat*). **reproachful** *adj* vorwurfsvoll.
reproduce [riːprə'djuːs] *v* (sich) fortpflanzen; (*copy*) kopieren. **reproduction** *n* Fortpflanzung *f*; (*copy*) Reproduktion *f*.
reproof [rə'pruːf] *n* Verweis *m*, Rüge *f*. **reprove** *v* rügen.
reptile ['reptail] *n* Reptil *neut*, Kriechtier *neut*.
republic [rə'pʌblik] *n* Republik *f*. **republican** *adj* republikanisch; *n* Republikaner(in).
repudiate [rə'pjuːdieit] *v* zurückweisen, nicht anerkennen. *n* Nichtanerkennung *f*.
repugnant [rə'pʌgnənt] *adj* widerlich, widerwärtig.
repulsion [rə'pʌlʃn] *n* Abscheu *m*. **repulsive** *adj* widerwärtig, abscheulich.
repute [rə'pjuːt] *n* Ruf *m*. **reputation** *n* Ruf *m*. **reputed** *adj* angeblich. **be reputed** betrachtet sein (als).
request [ri'kwest] *n* Bitte *f*. *v* bitten (um). **on request** auf Wunsch.
requiem ['rekwiəm] *n* Requiem *neut*.
require [rə'kwaiə] *v* (*need*) brauchen; (*person*) verlangen (von); (*call for*) erfordern. **be required** erforderlich sein. **requirement** *n* Anforderung *f*; (*need*) Bedürfnis *neut*.
requisite ['rekwizit] *adj* erforderlich, notwendig.
re-route [ˌriː'ruːt] *v* umleiten.
resale [riː'seil] *n* Weiterverkauf *m*.
rescue ['reskjuː] *v* retten, befreien. *n* Rettung *f*. **come to the rescue of** zur Hilfe kommen (+ *dat*). **rescuer** *n* Retter *m*.

research [ri'səːtʃ] *n* Forschung *f*. *v* forschen. **researcher** *n* Forscher *m*.
resemble [rə'zembl] *v* ähnlich sein (+ *dat*). **resemblance** *n* Ähnlichkeit *f*.
resent [ri'zent] *v* übelnehmen. **resentful** *adj* ärgerlich (auf). **resentment** *n* Groll *m*, Unwille *m*.
reserve [rə'zəːv] *v* reservieren (lassen). *n* Reserve *f*; (*for animals*) Schutzgebiet *neut*; (*sport*) Ersatzmann *m*. **reserved** *adj* reserviert. **reservation** *n* Vorbehalt *m*; Reservierung *f*.
reservoir ['rezəvwai] *n* Reservoir *neut*.
reside [rə'zaid] *v* wohnen. **residence** *n* Wohnung *f*; (*domicile*) Wohnsitz *m*. **resident** *adj* wohnhaft. **residential** *adj* Wohn-.
residue ['rezidjuː] *n* Rest *m*, Rückstand *m*. **residual** *adj* übrig, Rest-.
resign [rə'zain] *v* zurücktreten. **resign oneself** to sich abfinden mit. **resignation** *n* Rücktritt *m*; (*mood*) Resignation *f*. **hand in one's resignation** seinen Rücktritt einreichen. **resigned** *adj* resigniert, ergeben.
resilient [rə'ziliənt] *adj* elastisch; (*person*) unverwüstlich.
resin ['rezin] *n* Harz *neut*.
resist [rə'zist] *v* widerstehen. **resistance** *n* Widerstand *m*. **resistant** *adj* widerstehend, beständig.
*resit [riː'sit] *v* (*exam*) wiederholen.
resolute ['rezəluːt] *adj* entschlossen. **resolution** *n* (*determination*) Entschlossenheit *f*; (*decision*) Beschluß *m*.
resolve [rə'zolv] *v* (*problem*) lösen; (*tech*) auflösen; (*decide*) beschließen. *n* (*determination*) Entschlossenheit *f*. **resolved** *adj* entschlossen.
resonant ['rezənənt] *adj* widerhallend; (*voice*) volltönend. **resonance** *n* Resonanz *f*.
resort [rə'zoːt] *n* (*hope*) Ausweg *m*; (*place*) Ferienort *m*; (*use*) Anwendung *f*. **seaside resort** Seebad *neut*. *v* **resort to** zurückgreifen auf.
resound [rə'zaund] *v* widerhallen.
resource [rə'zoːs] *n* Mittel *neut*. **natural resources** Bodenschätze *pl*. **resourceful** *adj* findig.
respect [rə'spekt] *v* (hoch)achten; (*take account of*) berücksichtigen. *n* (*for person*) Hochachtung *f*, Respekt *m*; Rücksicht *f*. **in this respect** in dieser Hinsicht. **respectable** *adj* ansehnlich, respektabel.

respectful *adj* achtvoll. **respective** *adj* entsprechend. **respectively** *adv* beziehungsweise.

respiration [respə'reiʃn] *n* Atmung *f*.

respite ['respait] *n* **without respite** ohne Unterlaß.

respond [rə'spond] *v* **respond to** (*question*) antworten (auf); (*react*) reagieren (auf). **response** *n* Antwort *f*; Reaktion *f*. **responsible** [rə'sponsəbl] *adj* verantwortlich. **responsibility** *n* Verantwortung *f*; (*commitment*) Verpflichtung *f*.

rest[1] [rest] *n* Ruhe *f*. **day of rest** Ruhetag *m*. **have a rest** sich ausruhen. **without rest** unaufhörlich. *v* ruhen. **rested** *adj* ausgeruht. **restful** *adj* ruhig. **restive** *adj* unruhig. **restless** *adj* ruhelos. **restlessness** *n* Unruhe *f*.

rest[2] [rest] *n* (*remainder*) Rest *m*.

restaurant ['restront] *n* Restaurant *neut*, Gaststätte *f*. **restaurant car** Speisewagen *m*.

restore [rə'stoɪ] *v* wiederherstellen. **restoration** *n* Wiederherstellung *f*; (*of painting, etc.*) Restauration *f*.

restrain [rə'strein] *v* zurückhalten. **restrained** *adj* zurückhaltend. **restraint** *n* Zurückhaltung *f*; (*limitation*) Einschränkung *f*.

restrict [rə'strikt] *v* einschränken, beschränken. **restricted** *adj* eingeschränkt, beschränkt. **restriction** *n* Einschränkung *f*, Beschränkung *f*. **restrictive** *adj* einschränkend.

result [rə'zʌlt] *n* Ergebnis *neut*, Resultat *neut*; (*consequence*) Folge *f*. *v* sich ergeben. **result in** enden mit. **resultant** *adj* daraus entstehend.

resume [rə'zjuɪm] *v* wieder beginnen; (*work*) wieder aufnehmen. **resumption** *n* Wiederaufnahme *f*.

résumé ['reizumei] *n* Resümee *neut*.

resurgence [ri'səɪdʒəns] *n* Wiederaufstieg *m*.

resurrect [rezə'rekt] *v* (*thing*) ausgraben, wieder einführen. **resurrection** *n* Auferstehung *f*.

resuscitate [rə'sʌsəteit] *v* wiederbeleben. **resuscitation** *n* Wiederbelebung *f*.

retail ['riɪteil] *n* Einzelhandel *m*. *adj* Einzelhandels-. **retail price** Ladenpreis *m*. **retail shop** Einzelhandelsgeschäft *neut*. *v* im Einzelhandel verkaufen. **retailer** *n* Einzelhändler(in).

retain [rə'tein] *v* behalten. **retention** *n* Beibehaltung *f*.

retaliate [rə'talieit] *v* sich rächen. **retaliation** *n* Vergeltung *f*. **relaliatory** *adj* Vergeltungs-.

retard [rə'taɪd] *v* hindern. **retarded** *adj* zurückgeblieben.

reticent ['retisənt] *adj* schweigsam. **reticence** *n* Schweigsamkeit *f*, Zurückhaltung *f*.

retina ['retinə] *n* Netzhaut *f*.

retinue ['retinjuɪ] *n* Gefolge *neut*.

retire [rə'taiə] *v* sich zurückziehen; (*from work*) in den Ruhestand treten. **retired** *adj* pensioniert. **retirement** *n* Ruhestand *m*; (*resignation*) Rucktritt *m*. **retiring** *adj* zurückhaltend.

retort[1] [rə'toɪt] *v* (scharf) erwidern. *n* (schlagfertige) Antwort *f*.

retort[2] [rə'toɪt] *n* (*vessel*) Retorte *f*.

retrace [ri'treis] *v* zurückverfolgen.

retract [rə'trakt] *v* (*draw in*) einziehen; (*take back*) zurücknehmen, widerrufen. **retractable** *adj* einziehbar.

retreat [rə'triɪt] *v* sich zurückziehen. *n* Rückzug *m*; (*place*) Zufluchtsort *m*.

retrieve [rə'triɪv] *v* wiederfinden, herausholen. **retriever** *n* Apporthund *m*.

retrograde ['retrəgreid] *adj* rückläufig.

retrospect ['retrəspekt] *n* Rückblick *m*. **in retrospect** rückschauend. **retrospective** *adj* rückwirkend.

return [rə'təɪn] *v* zurückkommen, wiederkehren; (*give back*) zurückgeben; (*answer*) erwidern. *n* Rückkehr *f*; (*ticket*) Rückfahrkarte *f*; (*comm*) Ertrag *m*. **tax return** Steuererklärung *f*. **many happy returns** herzlichen Glückwunsch.

reunite [riɪju'nait] *v* wiedervereinigen. **reunion** *n* Wiedervereinigung *f*; (*meeting*) Treffen *neut*.

rev [rev] *v* (*coll: mot*) auf Touren bringen. **revs** *pl n* Drehzahl *f sing*.

reveal [rə'viɪl] *v* enthüllen, offenbaren; (*display*) zeigen. **revealing** *adj* aufschlußreich. **revelation** *n* Enthüllung *f*, Offenbarung *f*.

revel ['revl] *v* feiern. **revel in** schwelgen in. **reveller** *n* Feiernde(r). **revelry** *n* Festlichkeit *f*.

revenge [rə'vendʒ] *n* Rache *f*. *v* rächen. **take revenge on** sich rächen an.

revenue ['revinjuɪ] *n* Einnahmen *pl*.

reverberate [rə'vəɪbəreit] *v* (*sound*)

widerhallen. **reverberation** *n* Widerhall *m*.

reverence ['revərəns] *n* Verehrung *f*, Ehrfurcht *f*. **revere** *v* (ver)ehren. **reverend** *adj* ehrwürdig. **reverent** *adj* ehrerbietig.

reverse [rə'vəɪs] *v* umkehren; (*mot*) rückwarts fahren. *n* (*opposite*) Gegenteil *neut*; (*of coin, etc.*) Rückseite *f*; (*mot*) Rückwärtsgang *m*. **reverse-charge call** R-Gespräch *neut*. **reversible** *adj* (*coat*) wendbar; (*law*) umstoßbar.

revert [rə'vəɪt] *v* zurückkehren.

review [rə'vjuɪ] *n* Nachprüfung *f*; (*magazine*) Rundschau *f*; (*troops*) Parade *f*. *v* nachprüfen. **reviewer** *n* Kritiker *m*.

revise [rə'vaiz] *v* revidieren; (*book*) überarbeiten. **revision** *n* Revision *f*; Überarbeitung *f*.

revive [rə'vaiv] *v* wiederbeleben. **revival** *n* Wiederbelebung *f*; (*play*) Wiederaufführung *f*.

revoke [rə'vouk] *n* widerrufen. **revocable** *adj* widerruflich. **revocation** *n* Widerruf *m*.

revolt [rə'voult] *n* Aufruhr *m*, Aufstand *m*. *v* revoltieren, sich empören; (*disgust*) abstoßen. **revolting** *adj* abstoßend.

revolution [revə'luɪʃən] *n* (*pol*) Revolution *f*; (*turning*) Umdrehung *f*, Rotation *f*. **revolutions per minute** Drehzahl *f*. **revolutionary** *adj* revolutionär; *n* Revolutionär(in).

revolve [rə'volv] *v* (sich) drehen. **revolver** *n* Revolver *m*. **revolving** *adj* drehbar.

revue [rə'vjuɪ] *n* Revue *f*.

revulsion [rə'vʌlʃən] *n* Ekel *m*.

reward [rə'woɪd] *n* Belohnung *f*; *v* belohnen. **rewarding** *adj* lohnend.

rhetoric ['retərik] *n* Rhetorik *f*; (*empty*) Redeschwall *m*. **rhetorical** *adj* rhetorisch.

rheumatism ['ruɪmətizəm] *n* Rheumatismus *m*. **rheumatic** *adj* rheumatisch.

rhinoceros [rai'nosərəs] *n* Nashorn *neut*.

rhododendron [roudə'dendrən] *n* Rhododendron *m or neut*.

rhubarb ['ruɪbaɪb] *n* Rhabarber *m*.

rhyme [raim] *n* Reim *m v* reimen. **nursery rhyme** Kinderreim *m*.

rhythm ['riðəm] *n* Rhythmus *m*. **rhythmic** *adj* rhythmisch.

rib [rib] *n* Rippe *f*. **ribbed** *adj* (*material*) gerippt.

ribbon ['ribən] *n* Band *neut*; (*typewriter*) Farbband *neut*. **ribbons** *pl* (*rags*) Fetzen *pl*. **ribboned** *adj* gestreift.

rice [rais] *n* Reis *m*.

rich [ritʃ] *adj* reich, wohlhabend; (*earth*) fruchtbar; (*food*) schwer. **rich man/woman** Reiche(r). **the rich** die Reichen. **riches** *pl n* Reichtum *m*. **richness** *n* Reichtum *m*; (*food*) Schwere *f*; (*finery*) Pracht *f*.

rickety ['rikəti] *adj* (*wobbly*) wackelig.

***rid** [rid] *v* befreien, frei machen. **be rid of** los sein (+ *acc*). **get rid of** loswerden (+ *acc*). **good riddance to him!** Gott sei Dank ist man ihn los!

ridden ['ridn] *V* ride.

riddle ['ridl] *n* Rätsel *neut*.

riddled ['ridld] *adj* durchlöchert.

***ride** [raid] *v* reiten; (*bicycle, motor cycle*) fahren. **riding whip** Reitpeitsche *f*. *n* Ritt *m*; Fahrt *f*. **take for a ride** (*coll*) übers Ohr hauen. **rider** *n* Reiter(in); (*cycle*) Fahrer(in). **riding** *n* Reitsport *m*.

ridge [ridʒ] *n* Kamm *m*, Grat *m*; (*roof*) First *m*.

ridicule ['ridikjuɪl] *n* Spott *m*. *v* verspotten, lächerlich machen. **ridiculous** *adj* lächerlich.

rife [raif] *adj* **be rife** vorherrschen, grassieren. **rife with** voll von.

rifle[1] ['raifl] *n* (*gun*) Gewehr *neut*. **rifle-range** *n* Schießstand *m*.

rifle[2] ['raifl] *v* ausplündern.

rift [rift] *n* Spalte *f*, Riß *m*.

rig [rig] *n* Takelung *f*; (*coll*) Vorrichtung *f*, Anlage *f*. *v* auftakeln. **rig out** (*coll*) ausstatten. **rigging** *n* Takelwerk *neut*.

right [rait] *adj* (*correct*) recht, richtig; (*proper*) angemessen; (*right-hand*) recht. **all right** in Ordhung. **be right** (*thing*) recht sein; (*person*) recht haben. **feel all right** sich wohl befinden. **right-handed** *adj* rechtshändig. **right-wing** *adj* Rechts-. *adv* (*correctly*) recht, richtig; (*completely*) ganz; (*to the right*) (nach) rechts. **right away** sofort. *n* Recht *neut*. **right of way** (*mot*) Vorfahrt *f*. *v* berichtigen. **rightly** *adv* mit Recht.

righteous ['raitʃəs] *adj* rechtschaffen, gerecht.

rigid ['ridʒid] *adj* starr, steif; (*person*) streng, unbeugsam. **rigidity** *n* Starrheit *f*.

rigmarole ['rigməroul] *n* (*coll*) Theater *neut*.

rigour ['rigə] *n* Strenge *f*, Härte *f*. **rigorous** *adj* streng.

rim [rim] *n* Rand *m*.
rind [raind] *n* (*cheese*) Rinde *f*; (*bacon*) Schwarte *f*.
ring[1] [riŋ] *n* Ring *m*; (*comm*) Kartell *neut*. **wedding ring** *n* Trauring *m*. **ringleader** *n* Rädelsführer *m*.
***ring**[2] [riŋ] *v* (*sound*) läuten, klingeln; (*echo*) widerhallen. *n* (Glocken)Klang *m*, Klingeln *neut*. **there's a ring at the door** es klingelt. **ring (up)** (*coll*: *phone*) anrufen. **ringing** *n* Läuten *neut*.
rink [riŋk] *n* (*ice*) Eisbahn *f*.
rinse [rins] *v* ausspülen. *n* Spülung *f*.
riot ['raiət] *n* Aufruhr *m*, Tumult *m*. *v* randalieren. **rioter** *n* Aufrührer(in). **riotous** *adj* aufrührerisch; (*laughter*) zügellos.
rip [rip] *v* reißen, zerreißen. *n* Riß *m*. **ripcord** *n* Reißleine *f*.
ripe [raip] *adj* reif. **ripen** *v* reifen, reif werden.
ripple ['ripl] *n* Kräuselung *f*; (*noise*) Platschern *neut*. *v* (sich) kräuseln.
***rise** [raiz] *v* sich erheben; (*get up*) aufstehen; (*meeting*) vertagen; (*prices*) steigen. *n* Aufstieg *m*; (*prices*) Steigen *neut*; (*increase*) Zuwachs *m*; (*pay*) Erhöhung *f*. **give rise to** hervorrufen, veranlassen. **rising** *adj* steigend.
risen ['rizn] *V* rise.
risk [risk] *n* Risiko *neut*; (*danger*) Gefahr *f*. *v* riskieren. **take a risk** ein Risiko eingehen. **risky** *adj* riskant.
rissole ['risoul] *n* Boulette *f*, Frikadelle *f*.
rite [rait] *n* Ritus *m*, Zeremonie *f*.
ritual ['ritʃuəl] *n* Ritual *neut*. *adj* rituell.
rival ['raivəl] *n* Rivale *m*, Rivalin *f*. *adj* rivalisierend. *v* rivalisieren *or* wetteifern mit. **rivalry** *n* Rivalität *f*.
river ['rivə] *n* Fluß *m*. **down river** stromabwärts. **up river** stromaufwärts. **riverside** *n* Flußufer *neut*; *adj* Ufer-.
rivet ['rivit] *n* Niet *m*. *v* vernieten; (*captivate*) fesseln.
road [roud] *n* Straße *f*; (*esp. fig*) Weg *m*. **main road** Landstraße *f*. **on the road to** auf dem Wege zu. **road accident** Verkehrsunfall *m*. **road block** Straßensperre *f*. **road sign** Straßenschild *neut*. **roadworks** *pl n* Straßenbauarbeiten *pl*.
roam [roum] *v* (umher)wandern.
roar [rɔː] *v* brüllen; (*person*) laut schreien; (*wind*) toben. *n* Gebrüll *neut*. **roaring** *adj* (*coll*) enorm, famos.

roast [roust] *v* braten, rösten. *n* Braten *m*.
rob [rob] *v* rauben. **robber** *n* Räuber *m*. **robbery** *n* Raub *m*.
robe [roub] *n* Talar *m*. **bathrobe** Bademantel *m*. *v* kleiden.
robin ['robin] *n* Rotkehlchen *neut*.
robot ['roubot] *n* Roboter *m*.
robust [rə'bʌst] *adj* robust, kräftig. **robustness** *n* Robustheit *f*.
rock[1] [rok] *n* (*stone*) Fels *m*, Felsen *m*; (*naut*) Klippe *f*. **steady as a rock** felsenfest. **on the rocks** (*fig*) gescheitert; (*drink*) mit Eis. **rockery** *n* Steingarten *m*. **rocky** *adj* felsig.
rock[2] [rok] *v* schaukeln; (*baby*) wiegen. **rocking-horse** *n* Schaukelpferd *neut*. **rock 'n' roll** *n* Rock and Roll *m*.
rocket ['rokit] *n* Rakete *f*. *v* hochschießen.
rod [rod] *n* Rute *f*.
rode [roud] *V* ride.
rodent ['roudənt] *n* Nagetier *neut*.
roe [rou] *n* Rogen *m*.
rogue [roug] *n* Schurke *m*. **roguish** *adj* schurkisch.
role [roul] *n* Rolle *f*.
roll [roul] *v* rollen. **roll out** ausrollen. **roll over** sich herumdrehen. **roll up** aufwickeln, aufrollen. **roller** *n* Walze *f*. **roller blind** Rouleau *neut*. **roller-skate** *n* Rollschuh *m*. **rolling-pin** *n* Nudelholz *neut*. **roll-neck** *n* Rollkragen *m*. *n* Rolle *f*; (*bread*) Brötchen *neut*; (*meat*) Roulade *f*. **roll-call** *n* Namensaufruf *m*.
romance [rou'mans] *n* Romanze *f*. **romantic** romantisch; *n* Romantiker(in).
Rome [roum] *n* Rom *neut*. **Roman** *adj* römisch. *n* Römer(in). **Roman Catholic** römisch-katholisch.
romp [romp] *v* sich herumbalgen. **romp through** leicht hindurchkommen.
roof [ruːf] *n* (*pl* -s) Dach *neut*. *v* bedachen. **roofing** *n* Dachwerk *neut*.
rook[1] [ruk] *n* Saatkrähe *f*. *v* (*coll*) schwindeln, betrügen.
rook[2] [ruk] *n* (*chess*) Turm *m*.
room [ruːm] *n* (*house*) Zimmer *neut*; (*space*) Raum *m*, Platz *m*. *v* logieren (bei). **rooms** *pl* Wohnung *f*. **room-mate** *n* Zimmergenosse *m*, -genossin *f*. **roomy** *adj* geräumig.
roost [ruːst] *n* Hühnerstall *m*. *v* (*bird*) auf der Stange sitzen, schlafen. **rooster** *n* Hahn *m*.

root¹ [ruːt] *n* Würzel *f*; (*source*) Quelle *f*. **take root** Wurzel schlagen. **rooted** *adj* eingewürzelt. **rootless** *adj* wurzellos. **root**² [ruːt] *v* **root for** (*pigs*) wühlen nach. **root out** ausgraben.

rope [roup] *n* Seil *neut*; (*naut*) Tau *neut*. *v* festbinden. **know the ropes** sich auskennen. **ropeladder** *n* Strickleiter *f*. **ropy** *adj* (*coll*) kläglich, schäbig.

rosary ['rouzəri] *n* Rosenkranz *m*.

rose¹ [rouz] *V* **rise**.

rose² [rouz] *n* Rose *f*. **rosebush** *n* Rosenstrauch *m*. **rose-coloured** *adj* rosenrot. **through rose-coloured spectacles** durch eine rosarote Brille. **rosette** *n* Rosette *f*. **rosy** *adj* rosig.

rosemary ['rouzməri] *n* Rosmarin *m*.

rot [rot] *v* verfaulen. *n* Fäulnis *f*; (*nonsense*) Quatsch *m*. **rotten** *adj* faul, verfault; (*corrupt*) morsch, faul. **rottenness** *n* Fäule *f*. **rotter** *n* (*coll*) Schweinehund *m*.

rota ['routə] *n* Turnus *m*.

rotate [rou'teit] *v* sich drehen, rotieren; (*crops*) wechseln lassen. **rotary** *adj* rotierend, kreisend. **rotation** *n* Umdrehung *f*, Rotation *f*; (*crops, etc.*) Abwechselung *f*. **rotor** *n* Rotor *m*.

rouge [ruːʒ] *n* (*make-up*) Rouge *neut*.

rough [rʌf] *adj* rauh; (*sea*) stürmisch; (*hair*) struppig; (*person*) grob, roh; (*approximate*) ungefähr. **roughage** *n* Ballaststoffe *pl*. **roughen** *v* aufrauhen. **roughly** *adv* ungefähr. **roughness** *n* Rauhheit *f*.

roulette [ruːˈlet] *n* Roulette *f*.

round [raund] *adj* rund. *adv* rundherum. *n* Runde *f*. *v* runden; (*corner*) (herum)fahren um. **round off** abrunden. **round up** (*cattle*) zusammentreiben; (*criminals*) ausheben. **round trip** (Hinund) Rückfahrt *f*. **roundabout** *n* Karussell *neut*; (*mot*) Kreisverkehr *m*; *adj* weitschweifig. **roundly** *adv* gründlich. **roundness** *n* Rundheit *f*.

route [ruːt] *n* Weg *m*, Route *f*.

routine [ruːˈtiːn] *n* Routine *f*. *adj* üblich.

rove [rouv] *v* herumwandern. **rover** *n* Wanderer *m*.

row¹ [rou] *n* Reihe *f*. **in rows** reihenweise.

row² [rou] *v* (*boat*) rudern. **rowing** *n* Rudern *neut*; (*sport*) Rudersport *m*. **rowing boat** Ruderboot *neut*.

row³ [rau] *n* (*quarrel*) Streit *m*; (*noise*) Krach *m*. *v* sich streiten, zanken.

rowdy ['raudi] *adj* lärmend, flegelhaft. *n* Rowdy *m*.

royal ['roiəl] *adj* königlich. **royalist** *n* Royalist *m*. **royalty** *n* Königtum *neut*. **royalties** *pl* Tantieme *f*.

rub [rʌb] *v* reiben. **rub off** abreiben. **rub out** (*erase*) ausradieren. *n* Reiben *neut*.

rubber ['rʌbə] *n* Gummi *m*; (*eraser*) Radiergummi *m*. **rubber band** Gummiband *neut*. **rubber stamp** Gummistempel *m*.

rubbish ['rʌbiʃ] *n* Abfall *m*, Müll *m*; (*nonsense*) Quatsch *m*. **rubbishy** *adj* wertlos.

rubble ['rʌbl] *n* Trümmer *pl*, Schutt *m*.

ruby ['ruːbi] *n* Rubin *m*. *adj* (*colour*) rubinrot.

rucksack ['rʌksak] *n* Rucksack *m*.

rudder ['rʌdə] *n* Ruder *neut*.

rude [ruːd] *adj* grob, unverschämt; (*rough*) roh, wild. **rudeness** *n* Grobheit *f*, Roheit *f*.

rudiment ['ruːdimənt] *n* Rudiment *neut*. **rudiments** *pl* Grundlagen *pl*.

rueful ['ruːfəl] *adj* kläglich, traurig. **ruefulness** *n* Traurigkeit *f*.

ruff [rʌf] *n* Krause *f*; (*bird's*) Halskrause *f*.

ruffian ['rʌfiən] *n* Schurke *m*, Raufbold *m*.

ruffle ['rʌfl] *v* kräuseln. *n* Krause *f*.

rug [rʌg] *n* (*floor*) Vorleger *m*; (*blanket*) Wolldecke *f*.

rugby ['rʌgbi] *n* Rugby *neut*.

rugged ['rʌgid] *adj* wild, rauh; (*face*) runzelig. **ruggedness** *n* Rauheit *f*.

ruin ['ruːin] *n* Verfall *m*, Vernichtung *f*; (*building*) Ruine *f*. *v* vernichten, ruinieren. **ruins** *pl* Trümmer *pl*. **ruinous** *adj* ruinierend.

rule [ruːl] *n* Regel *f*; (*pol*) Regierung *f*; (*drawing*) Lineal *neut*. **rule of thumb** Faustregel *f*. *v* (*govern*) regieren; (*decide*) entscheiden. **ruler** *n* (*pol*) Herrscher(in); (*drawing*) Lineal *neut*. **ruling** *adj* herrschend; *n* Entscheidung *f*.

rum [rʌm] *n* Rum *m*.

Rumania [ruːˈmainjə] *n* Rumänien *neut*. **Rumanian** *n* Rumäne *m*, Rumänin *f*; *adj* rumänisch.

rumble ['rʌmbl] *v* poltern, knurren. *n* Dröhnen *neut*, Gepolter *neut*.

rummage ['rʌmidʒ] *v* **rummage through** durchsuchen, herumwühlen in.

rumour ['ruːmə] *n* Gerücht *neut*.

rump [rʌmp] *n* Hinterteil *neut.* **rump steak** Rumpsteak *neut.*
***run** [rʌn] *v* rennen, laufen; (*river*) fließen; (*machine*) laufen, in Gang sein; (*nose*) laufen. **run away** weglaufen. **run down** (*person*) heruntermachen. **run-down** *adj* erschöpft. **run out** zu Ende laufen. **run out of** knapp werden mit. **run over** (flüchtig) durchsehen. **runway** *n* Rollbahn *f. n* Lauf *m,* Rennen *neut.* **in the long run** auf die Dauer. **on the run** auf der Flucht. **runner** *n* Läufer(in). **running** *adj* laufend; (*water*) fließend.
rung¹ [rʌŋ] *V* ring².
rung² [rʌŋ] *n* Sprosse *f.*
rupture ['rʌptʃə] *n* Bruch *m. v* brechen, zerreißen.
rural ['ruərəl] *adj* ländlich, Land-.
rush¹ [rʌʃ] *v* stürzen, rasen. *n* Stürzen *neut.* **be in a rush** es eilig haben. **rush hour** Hauptverkehrszeit *f.*
rush² [rʌʃ] *n* (*bot*) Binse *f.*
rusk [rʌsk] *n* Zwieback *m.*
Russia ['rʌʃə] *n* Rußland *neut.* **Russian** *adj* russisch; *n* Russe *m,* Russin *f.*
rust [rʌst] *n* Rost *m. v* rosten, rostig werden. **rust-coloured** *adj* rostfarben. **rustproof** *adj* rostfrei. **rusty** *adj* rostig.
rustic ['rʌstik] *adj* ländlich, bäuerlich. *n* Bauer *m.*
rustle ['rʌsl] *v* rascheln, rauschen. *n* Rascheln *neut.*
rut [rʌt] *n* Furche *f.* **be stuck in a rut** beim alten Schlendrian verbleiben.
ruthless ['ruːθlis] *adj* unbarmherzig, rücksichtslos. **ruthlessness** *n* Unbarmherzigkeit *f.*
rye [rai] *n* Roggen *m.*

S

Sabbath ['sabəθ] *n* Sabbat *m.*
sabbatical [sə'batikəl] *adj* **sabbatical year** Urlaubsjahr *neut.*
sable ['seibl] *n* Zobel *m*; (fur) Zobelpelz *m. adj* Zobel-.
sabotage ['sabətɑːʒ] *n* Sabotage *f. v* sabotieren. **saboteur** *n* Saboteur *m.*
sabre ['seibə] *n* Säbel *m.*
saccharin ['sakərin] *n* Saccharin *neut.*

sachet ['saʃei] *n* Kissen *neut,* Täschchen *neut.*
sack [sak] *n* Sack *m. v* entlassen. **get the sack** (*coll*) entlassen werden.
sacrament ['sakrəmənt] *n* Sakrament *neut.* **sacramental** *adj* sakramental.
sacred ['seikrid] *adj* heilig.
sacrifice ['sakrifais] *v* opfern. *n* Opfer *neut.* **sacrificial** *adj* Opfer-.
sacrilege ['sakrəlidʒ] *n* Sakrileg *neut.* **sacrilegious** *adj* gotteslästerlich.
sad [sad] *adj* traurig. **sadden** *v* traurig machen. **sadness** *n* Traurigkeit *f.*
saddle ['sadl] *n* Sattel *m,* (*meat*) Rücken *m. v* satteln; (*with task*) belasten. **saddlebag** *n* Satteltasche *f.* **saddler** *n* Sattler *m.*
sadism ['seidizəm] *n* Sadismus *m.* **sadist** *n* Sadist(in). **sadistic** *adj* sadistisch.
safe [seif] *adj* (*secure*) sicher; (*not dangerous*) ungefährlich; (*careful*) vorsichtig; (*dependable*) verläßlich. *n* Safe *m,* Geldschrank *m.* **safe and sound** gesund und munter. **safe conduct** Geleitbrief *m.* **safeguard** *n* Sicherung *f,* Vorsichtsmaßnahme *f.* **safety** *n* Sicherheit *f.* **safety belt** Sicherheitsgurt *m.* **safety pin** Sicherheitsnadel *f.*
saffron ['safrən] *n* Safran *m. adj* safrangelb.
sag [sag] *v* absacken, herabhängen.
saga ['sɑːgə] *n* Saga *f.*
sage¹ [seidʒ] *adj* weise. *n* Weise(r). **sagacious** *adj* scharfsinnig, klug. **sagacity** *n* Klugheit *f.*
sage² [seidʒ] *n* (*bot*) Salbei *f.*
Sagittarius [sadʒi'teəriəs] *n* Schütze *m.*
sago ['seigou] *n* Sago *m.*
said [sed] *V* say.
sail [seil] *n* Segel *neut. v* segeln; (*depart*) fahren. **sailing** *n* Segelsport *m.* **sailing boat** *n* Segelboot *neut.* **sailor** *n* Matrose *m.*
saint [seint] *n* Heilige(r). **saintliness** *n* Heiligkeit *f.* **saintly** *adj* fromm.
sake [seik] *n* **for the sake of** wegen (+*gen*), um . . . (+*gen*) willen. **for heaven's sake** um Himmels willen. **for my sake** um meinetwillen.
salad ['saləd] *n* Salat *m.* **salad dressing** Salatsoße *f.*
salami [sə'lɑːmi] *n* Salami *f.*
salary ['saləri] *n* Gehalt *neut.* **salaried employee** Gehaltsempfänger(in). **salary increase** Gehaltserhöhung *f.*

sale [seil] *n* Verkauf *m*; (*end of season*) Schlußverkauf *m*. **on** *or* **for sale** zu verkaufen. **sales** *pl* Absatz *m*, Umsatz *m*. **sales department** Verkaufsabteilung *f*. **salesgirl** *or* **saleswoman** *n* Verkäuferin. **salesman** *n* Verkäufer *m*; (*travelling*) Geschäftsreisende(r).

saline ['seilain] *adj* salzig. **salinity** *n* Salzigkeit *f*.

saliva [sə'laivə] *n* Speichel *m*. **salivary** *adj* Speichel-.

sallow ['salou] *adj* bläßlich.

salmon ['samən] *n* Lachs *m*. *adj* (*colour*) lachsrot.

salon ['salon] *n* Salon *m*.

saloon [sə'luɪn] *n* Saal *m*, Salon *m*; (*bar*) Kneipe *f*, Ausschank *m*.

salt [soɪlt] *n* Salz *neut*. *v* salzen; (*pickle*) einsalzen. **salt beef** gepökeltes Rindfleisch *neut*. **salt cellar** Salzfäßchen *neut*. **salted** *adj* gesalzen. **saltiness** *n* Salzigkeit *f*. **salt water** Salzwasser *neut*. **salty** *adj* salzig.

salute [sə'luɪt] *v* grüßen. *n* Gruß *m*; (*of guns*) Salut *m*.

salvage ['salvidʒ] *n* Bergung *f*, Rettung *f*. *v* bergen, retten.

salvation [sal'veiʃən] *n* Rettung *f*, Heil *neut*. **Salvation Army** Heilsarmee *f*.

same [seim] *pron*, *adj* derselbe, dieselbe, dasselbe; der/die/das gleiche. **all the same** trotzdem. **it's all the same to me** es ist mir gleich *or* egal. **the same old story** die alte Leier *f*. **sameness** *n* Gleichheit *f*; (*monotony*) Eintönigkeit *f*.

sample ['saɪmpl] *n* Muster *neut*, Probe *f*. *v* probieren.

sanatorium [sanə'toɪriəm] *n* Sanatorium *neut*.

sanction ['saŋkʃən] *n* Sanktion *f*. *v* billigen.

sanctity ['saŋktəti] *n* Heiligkeit *f*.

sanctuary ['saŋktʃuəri] *n* Heiligtum *neut*; (*place of safety*) Asyl *neut*.

sand [sand] *n* Sand *m*. *v* **sand down** abschmirgeln. **sandbag** *n* Sandsack *m*. **sandbank** *n* Sandbank *f*. **sandpaper** *n* Sandpapier *neut*. **sand-pit** *n* Sandgrube *f*. **sandy** *adj* sandig.

sandal ['sandl] *n* Sandale *f*.

sandwich ['sanwidʒ] *n* Sandwich *neut*.

sane [sein] *adj* geistig gesund. **sanity** *n* geistige Gesundheit *f*.

sang [saŋ] *V* sing.

sanitary ['sanitəri] *adj* hygienisch. **sanita-ry towel** Damenbinde *f*. **sanitation** *n* Sanierung *f*, sanitäre Einrichtungen *pl*.

sank [saŋk] *V* sink.

sap [sap] *n* Saft *m*. **sapling** *n* junger Baum *m*.

sapphire ['safaiə] *n* Saphir *m*.

sarcasm ['saɪkazəm] *n* Sarkasmus *m*. **sarcastic** *adj* sarkastisch, höhnisch.

sardine [saɪ'diɪn] *n* Sardine *f*.

sardonic [saɪ'donik] *adj* sardonisch, zynisch.

sash[1] [saʃ] *n* (*garment*) Schärpe *f*.

sash[2] [saʃ] *n* (*window*) Fensterrahmen *m*. **sash window** Fallfenster *neut*.

sat [sat] *V* sit.

satchel ['satʃəl] *n* Schulmappe *f*.

satellite ['satəlait] *n* Satellit *m*; (*pol*) Satellitenstaat *m*.

satin ['satin] *n* Satin *m*. *adj* Satin-.

satire ['sataiə] *n* Satire *f*. **satirical** *adj* satirisch. **satirist** *n* Satiriker(in).

satisfy ['satisfai] *v* befriedigen. **satisfaction** *n* Befriedigung *f*; (*contentment*) Zufriedenheit *f*. **satisfactory** *adj* befriedigend. **satisfied** *adj* zufrieden.

saturate ['satʃəreit] *v* sättigen. **saturation** *n* Sättigung *f*.

Saturday ['satədi] *n* Sonnabend *m*, Samstag *m*.

Saturn ['satən] *n* Saturn *m*. **saturnine** *adj* (*person*) stillschweigend, verdrießlich.

sauce [soɪs] *n* Soße *f*; (*cheek*) Frechheit *f*. **sauce-boat** *n* Soßenschüssel *f*.

saucepan ['soɪspən] *n* Kochtopf *m*, Kasserolle *f*.

saucer ['soɪsə] *n* Untertasse *f*. **flying saucer** fliegende Untertasse *f*.

saucy ['soɪsi] *adj* frech, keck.

sauna [soɪnə] *n* Sauna *f*.

saunter [soɪntə] *v* schlendern.

sausage ['sosidʒ] *n* Wurst *f*.

savage ['savidʒ] *adj* (*animal*) wild; (*tribe, etc.*) primitiv, barbarisch; (*behaviour*) brutal, roh. *n* Wilde(r). **savageness** *n* Wildheit *f*. **savagery** *n* Unzivilisiertheit *f*.

save[1] [seiv] *v* (*rescue*) (er)retten; (*money*) sparen; (*avoid*) ersparen; (*time*) gewinnen; (*protect*) schützen. *n* (*football*) Abwehr *f*. **saving** *n* Ersparnis *f*. **savings** *pl* Ersparnisse *pl*. **savings account** Sparkonto *neut*. **savings bank** Sparkasse *f*. **savings book** Sparbuch *neut*.

save[2] [seiv] *prep*, *conj* außer (+ *dat*), mit Ausnahme von (+ *dat*).

saviour ['seivjə] *n* Retter *m*.
savoir-faire [savwaːˈfeə] *n* Gewandtheit *f*, Feingefühl *neut*.
savoury ['seivəri] *adj* wohlschmeckend, würzig. *n* (*piquant*) Vorspeise *f*.
saw[1] [soː] *V* **see**[1].
***saw**[2] [soː] *n* Säge *f*. *v* sägen. **sawdust** *n* Sägemehl *neut*. **sawmill** *n* Sägewerk *neut*.
sawn [soːn] *V* **saw**[2].
saxophone ['saksəfoun] *n* Saxophon *neut*.
saxophonist *n* Saxophonist(in).
***say** [sei] *v* sagen; (*maintain*) behaupten. **saying** *n* Sprichwort *neut*. **have one's say** seine Meinung äußern. **it goes without saying** selbstverständlich.
scab [skab] *n* Schorf *m*; (*strike-breaker*) Streikbrecher *m*.
scaffold ['skafəld] *n* (*execution*) Schafott *m*. **scaffolding** *n* Baugerüst *neut*, Gestell *neut*.
scald [skoːld] *v* verbrühen. *n* Verbrühung *f*. **scalding** *adj* brühheiß.
scale[1] [skeil] *n* (*fish, etc.*) Schuppe *f*; (*kettle*) Kesselstein *m*. *v* schuppen. **scaly** *adj* schuppig.
scale[2] [skeil] *n* also **scales** *pl* Waage *f*.
scale[3] [skeil] *n* (*gradation*) Skala *f*; (*music*) Tonleiter *f*; (*proportion*) Maßstab *m*. *v* (*climb*) erklettern. **to scale** maßstabgetreu. **scale model** maßstabgetreues Modell *neut*.
scallop ['skaləp] *n* Kammuschel *f*.
scalp [skalp] *n* Kopfhaut *f*; (*as trophy*) Skalp *m*. *v* skalpieren.
scalpel ['skalpəl] *n* Skalpell *neut*.
scampi ['skampi] *pl n* Scampi *pl*.
scan [skan] *v* (*carefully*) prüfen, genau untersuchen; (*briefly*) (flüchtig) überblicken.
scandal ['skandl] *n* Skandal *m*. **scandalize** *v* schockieren. **scandalous** *adj* skandalös. **scandalmonger** *n* Lästermaul *neut*.
scant [skant] *adj* knapp, spärlich. **scanty** *adj* knapp; (*insufficient*) unzulänglich.
scapegoat ['skeipgout] *n* Sündenbock *m*.
scar [skaɪ] *n* Narbe *f*. *v* vernarben.
scarce [skeəs] *adj* knapp, selten. **scarcely** *adv* kaum. **scarcity** *n* Mangel *m*.
scare [skeə] *v* erschrecken, in Schrecken versetzen. *n* Schreck *m*. **scarecrow** *n* Vogelscheue *f*. **scary** *adj* erschreckend.
scarf [skaɪf] *n* Halstuch *neut*, Schal *m*.
scarlet ['skaːlit] *adj* scharlachrot. **scarlet fever** Scharlachfieber *neut*.

scathing ['skeiðiŋ] *adj* (*fig*) verletzend, beißend.
scatter ['skatə] *v* (ver)streuen; bestreuen (mit). **scatterbrain** *n* Wirrkopf *n*.
scavenge ['skavindʒ] *v* durchsuchen, herumwühlen (in). **scavenger** *n* (*zool*) Aasfresser *m*.
scene [siːn] *n* Szene *f*; (*situation*) Ort *m*. **scenery** *n* Landschaft *f*; (*theatre*) Bühnenbild *neut*. **scenic** *adj* malerisch.
scent [sent] *n* Duft *m*; (*perfume*) Parfüm *neut*. *v* (*smell*) riechen; (*perfume*) parfümieren. **scented** *adj* parfümiert.
sceptic ['skeptik] *n* Skeptiker(in). **sceptical** *adj* skeptisch. **scepticism** *n* Skeptizismus *m*.
sceptre ['septə] *n* Zepter *neut*.
schedule ['ʃedjuːl] *n* Plan *m*; (*list*) Verzeichnis *neut*; (*trains*) Fahrplan *m*. *v* planen.
scheme [skiːm] *n* Schema *neut*; (*plan*) Plan *m*, Programm *neut*. *v* (*coll*) intrigieren. **schemer** *n* Ränkeschmied *m*.
schizophrenia [ˌskitsəˈfriːniə] *n* Schizophrenie *f*. **schizophrenic** *adj* schizophren; *n* Schizophrene(r).
scholar ['skolə] *n* Gelehrte(r); (*pupil*) Schüler(in). **scholarly** *adj* gelehrt. **scholarship** *n* Gelehrsamkeit *f*; (*grant*) Stipendium *neut*.
scholastic [skəˈlastik] *adj* akademisch.
school[1] [skuːl] *n* Schule *f*. *v* schulen. **schoolboy** *n* Schüler *m*. **schoolgirl** *n* Schülerin *f*. **schooling** *n* Unterricht *m*. **schoolteacher** *n* Lehrer(in).
school[2] [skuːl] *n* (*fish*) Zug *m*; (*whales*) Schar *f*.
schooner ['skuːnə] *n* Schoner *m*; (*glass*) Humpen *m*.
sciatica [saiˈatikə] *n* Ischias *m or neut*.
science ['saiəns] *n* Wissenschaft *f*; (*natural science*) Naturwissenschaft *f*. **scientific** *adj* wissenschaftlich. **scientist** *n* Wissenschaftler(in).
scissors ['sizəz] *pl n* Schere *f sing*.
scoff[1] [skof] *v* spotten (über). *n* Spott *m*, Hohn *m*.
scoff[2] [skof] *v* (*coll: eat*) fressen, hinunterschlingen.
scold [skould] *v* schimpfen. **give a scolding** ausschelten (+ *acc*).
scone [skon] *n* Teegebäck *neut*.
scoop [skuːp] *n* Schaufel *f*, Schöpfer *m*; (*newspaper*) (sensationelle) Erstmeldung *f*. *v* schöpfen.

scooter ['skuːtə] *n* Roller *m*.
scope [skoup] *n* Umfang *m*, Gebiet *neut*.
scorch [skoːtʃ] *v* verbrennen. **scorching** *adj* (*weather*) brennend.
score [skoː] *n* (*score*) Punktzahl *f*, Spielergebnis *neut*; (*20*) zwanzig (Stück); (*music*) Partitur *f*. *v* (*points*) zählen, machen. **know the score** (*coll*) Bescheid wissen. **scoreboard** *n* Anzeigetafel *f*.
scorn [skoin] *n* Verachtung *f*, Spott *m*. *v* verachten. **scornful** *adj* verächtlich.
scorpion ['skoːpiən] *n* Skorpion *m*.
Scotland ['skotlənd] *n* Schottland *neut*. **Scotch** *n* (schottischer) Whisky *m*. **Scotsman** *n* Schotte *m*. **Scotswoman** *n* Schottin *f*. **Scottish** *adj* schottisch.
scoundrel ['skaundrəl] *n* Schurke *m*, Schuft *m*.
scour[1] [skauə] *v* (*clean*) scheuern, schrubben. **scourer** *n* Scheuerlappen *m*.
scour[2] [skauə] *v* (*search*) durchsuchen.
scout [skaut] *n* (*mil*) Späher *m*; (*boy scout*) Pfadfinder *m*.
scowl [skaul] *v* finster (an)blicken. *n* finsterer Blick *m*.
scramble ['skrambl] *v* krabbeln, klettern; (*eggs*) rühren. **scramble for** balgen um. **scrambled egg(s)** Rührei *neut*.
scrap [skrap] *n* (*piece*) Stück *neut*, Fetzen *m*; (*metal*) Schrott *m*; (*fight*) Prügelei *f*. *v* (*metal*) verschrotten; (*plan*) verwerfen. **scrapbook** *n* Sammelalbum *neut*, Einklebebuch *neut*.
scrape [skreip] *v* schaben, kratzen. *n* Kratzen *neut*; (*coll*) Klemme *f*.
scratch [skratʃ] *v* (zer)kratzen. *n* Kratzstelle *f*, Riß *m*; (*wound*) Schramme *f*. **scratchy** *adj* kratzend.
scrawl [skroil] *v* kritzeln. *n* Gekritzel *neut*.
scream [skriːm] *n* Schrei *m*. *v* schreien. **it's a scream** es ist zum Schreien.
screech [skriːtʃ] *n* Gekreisch *neut*; (*cry*) (durchdringender) Schrei *m*. *v* kreischen.
screen [skriːn] *n* (Schutz)Schirm *m*, (Schutz)Wand *f*; (*film*) Leinwand *f*; (*TV*) Bildschirm *m*. *v* abschirmen. **screenplay** *n* Drehbuch *neut*.
screw [skruː] *n* Schraube *f*. *v* schrauben. **screwdriver** *n* Schraubenzieher *m*.
scribble ['skribl] *n* Gekritzel *neut*. *v* kritzeln. **scribbler** *n* Kritzler *m*.
script [skript] *n* Schrift *f*; (*handwriting*) Handschrift *f*; (*film*) Drehbuch *neut*.
scripture ['skriptʃə] *n* Heilige Schrift *f*.

scroll [skroul] *n* Schriftrolle *f*; (*decoration*) Schnörkel *m*.
scrounge [skraundʒ] *v* (*coll*) schmarotzen, schnorren. **scrounger** *n* Schmarotzer *m*.
scrub[1] [skrʌb] *v* schrubben, scheuern. *n* Schrubben *neut*. **scrubbing brush** *n* Scheuerbürste *f*.
scrub[2] [skrʌb] *n* (*bush*) Gestrüpp *neut*, Busch *m*.
scruffy ['skrʌfi] *adj* schäbig.
scruple ['skruːpl] *n* Skrupel *m*. **scrupulous** *adj* peinlich, voller.
scrutiny ['skruːtəni] *n* (genaue) Untersuchung *f*. **scrutinize** *v* genau untersuchen.
scuffle ['skʌfl] *n* Rauferei *f*. *v* sich raufen.
sculpt [skʌlpt] *v* formen, schnitzen. **sculptor** *n* Bildhauer *m*. **sculpture** *n* Skulptur *f*.
scum [skʌm] *n* Abschaum *m*.
scurf [skəːf] *n* Schorf *m*; (*dandruff*) Schuppen *pl*.
scurvy ['skəːvi] *n* Skorbut *m*.
scuttle ['skʌtl] *n* Kohleneimer *m*.
scythe [saið] *n* Sense *f*. *v* (ab)mähen.
sea [siː] *n* See *f*, Meer *neut*. **at sea** auf See. **all at sea** (*coll*) perplex, im Dunkeln. **on the high seas** auf hoher see. **go to sea** zur See gehen.
seabed ['siːbed] *n* Meeresgrund *m*.
sea front *n* Strandpromenade *f*.
seagoing ['siːgouiŋ] *adj* Hochsee-.
seagull ['siːgʌl] *n* Möwe *f*.
seahorse ['siːhoːs] *n* Seepferdchen *neut*.
seal[1] [siːl] *n* Siegel *neut*. *v* besiegeln. **seal up** versiegeln. **sealing wax** Siegellack *m*.
seal[2] [siːl] *n* (*zool*) Robbe *f*, Seehund *m*. **sealskin** *n* Seehundsfell *neut*.
sea-level *n* Meeresspiegel *m*.
sea-lion *n* Seelöwe *m*.
seam [siːm] *n* Saum *m*, Naht *f*; (*minerals*) Flöz *neut*. *v* säumen.
seaman ['siːmən] *n* Seemann *m*, Matrose *m*. **seamanlike** *adj* seemännisch. **seamanship** *n* Seemannskunst *f*.
search [səːtʃ] *v* suchen, forschen (nach); (*for criminal*) fahnden (nach); (*person, place*) durchsuchen (nach). **searchlight** Scheinwerfer *m*. **search party** Suchtrupp *m*. **search warrant** Haussuchungsbefehl *m*. *n* Suche *f*; Untersuchung *f*. **searcher** *n* Sucher *m*, Forscher *m*. **searching** *adj* (*enquiry*) gründlich.
sea-shore *n* Seeküste *f*.

seasick ['siːsik] *adj* seekrank. **seasickness** *n* Seekrankheit *f*.

seaside ['siːsaid] *n* See *f*. **at the seaside** an der See. **to the seaside** an die See. **seaside town** Küstenstadt *f*.

season ['siːzn] *n* Jahreszeit *f*; (*comm*) Saison *f*. *v* (*cookery*) würzen; (*wood*) ablagern. **seasonal** *adj* saisonbedingt. **seasoning** *n* Würze *f*. **season-ticket** *n* Zeitkarte *f*; (*theatre*) Abonnement *neut*.

seat [siːt] *n* Sitz *m*; (*train, theatre*) Platz *m*; (*residence*) Wohnsitz *m*. *v* setzen. *please be seated!* bitte setzen Sie sich! **seating** *n* Sitzgelegenheit *f*.

seaweed ['siːwiːd] *n* Tang *m*, Alge *f*.

seaworthy ['siːwəːði] *adj* seetüchtig.

secluded [si'kluːdid] *adj* abgelegen. **seclusion** *n* Zurückgezogenheit *f*.

second¹ ['sekənd] *n* (*time*) Sekunde *f*. *wait a second!* moment mal!

second² ['sekənd] *adj* zweit; (*next*) nächst, folgend. *adv* an zweiter Stelle. *n* Zweite(r). **for the second time** zum zweiten Mal. **on second thoughts** bei näherer Überlegung. **play second fiddle** die Nebenrolle spielen. **secondary** *adj* nebensächlich, sekundär. **secondary school** Sekundarschule *f*. **second-best** *adj* zweitbest. **second-class** *adj* zweitrangig. **second-hand** *adj* gebraucht, Gebraucht-. **secondly** *adv* zweitens. **second-rate** *adj* minderwertig.

secret ['siːkrit] *adj* geheim, heimlich. **keep secret** geheimhalten. *n* Geheimnis *neut*. **in secret** *or* **secretly** *adv* heimlich. **secrecy** *n* Verborgenheit *f*, Heimlichkeit *f*. **secretive** *adj* verschlossen. **secretiveness** *n* Verschlossenheit *f*.

secretary ['sekrətəri] *n* Sekretär(in). **secretarial** *adj* Sekretär-. **secretary general** Generalsekretär *m*.

secrete [si'kriːt] *v* absondern. **secretion** *n* Absonderung *f*.

sect [sekt] *n* Sekte *f*. **sectarian** *adj* sektiererisch.

section ['sekʃən] *n* (*part*) Teil *m*; (*of firm*) Abteilung *f*; (*of book, document*) Abschnitt *m*. *v* **section off** abteilen.

sector ['sektə] *n* Sektor *m*.

secular ['sekjulə] *adj* weltlich. **secularism** *n* Säkularismus *f*.

secure [si'kjuə] *adj* sicher. *v* sichern; (*affix*) festmachen (an); (*procure*) sich beschaffen. **security** *n* Sicherheit *f*; (*bond*) Bürgschaft *f*. **securities** *pl* (*comm*) Wertpapiere *pl*.

sedate [si'deit] *adj* ruhig, gelassen. **sedateness** *n* Gelassenheit *f*. **sedative** *n* Beruhigungsmittel *neut*. **sedation** *n* (Nerven)Beruhigung *f*.

sediment ['sedimənt] *n* Sediment *neut*. **sedimentation** *n* Sedimentation *n*.

seduce [si'djuːs] *v* verführen. **seducer** *n* Verführer *m*. **seduction** *n* Verführung *f*. **seductive** *adj* verlockend.

*see¹ [siː] *v* sehen; (*understand*) einsehen, verstehen; (*consult*) konsultieren, besuchen. **see home** (*person*) nach Hause begleiten. **seeing that** da. **see through** (*understand*) durchschauen; (*finish*) zu Ende führen. **see to** sich kümmern um. **see to it that** darauf achten, daß. **wait and see** abwarten.

see² [siː] *n* Bistum *neut*.

seed [siːd] *n* Same *m*; (*pip*) Kern *m*. **seedy** *adj* schäbig.

*seek [siːk] *v* suchen. **seeker** *n* Sucher(in).

seem [siːm] *v* scheinen. **seeming** *adj* scheinbar. **seemly** *adj* schicklich.

seen [siːn] *V* see¹.

seep [siːp] *v* (durch)sickern.

seesaw ['siːsoː] *n* Wippe *f*. *v* schaukeln.

seethe [siːð] *v* sieden. **seething** *adj* (*coll*) wütend.

segment ['segmənt] *n* Abschnitt *m*, Segment *neut*.

segregate ['segrigeit] *v* trennen, absondern. **segregation** *n* Absonderung *f*; (*racial*) Rassentrennung *f*.

seize [siːz] *v* ergreifen. **seize up** festfahren. **seizure** *n* Ergreifung *f*; (*med*) Anfall *m*.

seldom ['seldəm] *adv* selten.

select [sə'lekt] *v* auswählen, auslesen. *adj* exklusiv. **selected** *adj* ausgewählt. **selection** *n* Auswahl *f*. **selective** *adj* auswählend.

self [self] *n* Selbst *neut*, Ich *neut*.

self-assured *adj* selbstsicher. **self-assurance** *n* Selbstsicherheit *f*.

self-centred *adj* ichbezogen.

self-confident *adj* selbstbewußt, selbstsicher. **self-confidence** *n* Selbstbewußtsein *neut*.

self-conscious *adj* gehemmt, befangen. **self-consciousness** *n* Befangenheit *f*.

self-contained *adj* (*flat*) separat; (*person*) zurückhaltend.

self-control *n* Selbstbeherrschung *f.*
self-defence *n* Selbstverteidigung *f.*
self-denial *n* Selbstverleugnung *f.*
self-discipline *n* Selbstdisziplin *f.*
self-employed *adj* selbständig.
self-esteem *n* Selbstachtung *f.*
self-evident *adj* selbstverständlich.
self-important *adj* wichtigtuerisch.
self-indulgent *adj* selbstgefällig.
self-interest *n* Eigennutz *m.* **self-interested** *adj* eigennützig.
selfish ['selfiʃ] *adj* selbstisch, selbstsüchtig. **selfishness** *n* Egoismus *m.*
selfless ['selflis] *adj* selbstlos.
self-made *adj* **self-made man** Emporkömmling *m.*
self-pity *n* Selbstmitleid *neut.*
self-portrait *n* Selbstporträt *neut.*
self-respect *n* Selbstachtung *f.*
self-righteous *adj* selbstgerecht.
self-sacrifice *n* Selbstaufopferung *f.* **self-sacrificing** *adj* aufopferungsvoll.
selfsame ['selfseim] *adj* ebenderselbe, ebendieselbe, ebendasselbe.
self-satisfied *adj* selbstzufrieden.
self-service *adj* Selbstbedienung *f. adj* Selbstbedienungs-.
self-sufficient *adj* unabhängig; *(person)* selbstgenügsam.
self-will *n* Eigensinn *m.* **self-willed** *adj* eigensinnig.
*sell [sel] *v* verkaufen. **seller** *n* Verkäufer(in). **sell out** *(betray)* verraten. **sold out** ausverkauft.
Sellotape ® ['seləteip] *n* Tesa-Film *m.*
semantic [sə'mantik] *adj* semantisch. **semantics** *n* Semantik *f.*
semaphore ['seməfoɪ] *n* Semaphor *m.*
semen ['siːmən] *n* Samen *m,* Sperma *neut.*
semicircle ['semisɜɪkl] *n* Halbkreis *m.* **semicircular** *adj* halbkreisförmig.
semicolon [,semi'koulən] *n* Strichpunkt *m.*
semi-detached (house) *adj* halbfreistehend.
semifinal [semi'fainl] *n* Vorschlußrunde *f;* Halbfinale *neut.*
seminal ['seminl] *adj* Samen-; *(influential)* einflußreich, wichtig.
seminar ['seminaɪ] *n* Seminar *neut.*
semiprecious [semi'preʃəs] *adj* halbedel.
semolina [,semə'liːnə] *n* Grieß *m;* *(pudding)* Grießbrei *m.*
senate ['senit] *n* Senat *m.* **senator** *n* Senator *m.* **senatorial** *adj* senatorisch.

*send [send] *v* schicken, senden. **send away** fortschicken. **send for** *(person)* schicken nach. **send off** *(letter)* absenden. **send-off** *n* Abschiedsfeier *f.* **sender** *n* Absender(in).
senile ['siːnail] *adj* senil. **senility** *n* Senilität *f.*
senior ['siːnjə] *adj* älter; *(school)* Ober-. *n* Ältere(r).
sensation [sen'seiʃən] *n* Gefühl *neut,* Empfindung *f;* *(excitement)* Sensation *f.* **sensational** *adj* sensationell. **sensationalism** *n* Effekthascherei *f.*
sense [sens] *n* Sinn *m;* *(feeling)* Gefühl *neut.* **common sense** Vernunft *f.* **make sense** sinnvoll sein. **sense of humour** Sinn für Humor *m.* *v* empfinden, spüren. **senseless** *adj* sinnlos.
sensible ['sensəbl] *adj* vernünftig. **sensibility** *n* Sensibilität *f.* **sensibleness** *n* Vernünftigkeit *f.*
sensitive ['sensitiv] *adj* empfindlich *(gegen).* **sensitivity** *n* Empfindlichkeit *f;* *(appreciativeness)* Sensibilität *f.* Feingefühl *neut.*
sensual ['sensjuəl] *adj* sinnlich. **sensuality** *n* Sinnlichkeit *f.*
sensuous ['sensjuəs] *adj* sinnlich. **sensuousness** *n* Sinnlichkeit *f.*
sent [sent] *V* **send.**
sentence ['sentəns] *n* Satz *m;* *(punishment)* Strafe *f,* Urteil *neut.* *v* verurteilen.
sentiment ['sentimənt] *n* Empfindsamkeit *f;* *(feeling)* Gefühl *neut.* **sentiments** *pl* Meinungen *pl,* Gesinnung *f sing.* **sentimental** *adj* sentimental. **sentimentality** *n* Sentimentalität *f.*
sentry ['sentri] *n* Wachposten *m.*
separate ['sepərət; *v* 'sepəreit] *adj* getrennt. *v* trennen; *(couple)* sich trennen. **separable** *adj* trennbar. **separateness** *n* Getrenntheit *f.* **separation** *n* Trennung *f.*
September [sep'tembə] *n* September *m.*
septic ['septik] *adj* septisch.
sequel ['siːkwəl] *n* *(novel, etc.)* Fortsetzung *f;* *(consequence)* Folge *f.*
sequence ['siːkwəns] *n* (Reihen)Folge *f.* Reihe *f;* *(film)* Szene *f.* **sequential** *adj* (aufeinander)folgend.
sequin ['siːkwin] *n* Paillette *f.*
serenade [serə'neid] *n* Serenade *f.*
serene [sə'riːn] *adj* heiter, gelassen. **serenity** *n* Heiterkeit *f.*

serf [sɔːf] *n* Leibeigene(r). **serfdom** *n* Leibeigenschaft *f.*
sergeant ['saːdʒənt] *n* (*mil*) Feldwebel *m*; (*police*) Wachtmeister *m.*
serial ['sɪərɪəl] *n* (*book*) Fortsetzungsroman *m*; (*TV, radio*) Sendereihe *f. adj* Fortsetzungs-. **serial number** Seriennummer *f.*
series ['sɪəriːz] *n* Serie *f.*
serious ['sɪərɪəs] *adj* ernst(haft); (*illness*) gefährlich. **seriously** *adv* ernstlich, im Ernst; (*injured*) schwer. **seriousness** *n* Ernst *m.*
sermon ['sɔːmən] *n* Predigt *f.*
serpent ['sɔːpənt] *n* Schlange *f.*
servant ['sɔːvənt] *n* Diener(in). **domestic servant** Hausangestellte(r). **public servant** *n* Beamte(r), Beamtin *f.*
serve [sɔːv] *v* dienen (+*dat*); (*customer*) bedienen; (*food*) servieren; (*tennis*) aufschlagen. **serve no purpose** nichts nützen. *it serves him right* es geschieht ihm recht.
service ['sɔːvis] *n* Dienst *m*; (*shop, restaurant*) Bedienung *f*; (*after-sales*) Kundendienst *m*; (*mot*) Inspektion; (*favour*) Gefallen *m*; (*church*) Gottesdienst *m.* **military service** Wehrdienst *m.* **service station** Tankstelle *f. v* (*mot*) warten, überholen. **serviceable** *adj* brauchbar.
serviette [ˌsɔːviˈet] *n* Serviette *f.*
servile ['sɔːvail] *adj* servil. **servility** *n* Unterwürfigkeit *f.*
session ['seʃən] *n* Sitzung *f*; (*university*) Semester *neut.*
*****set** [set] *v* setzen, stellen; (*date, etc.*) festsetzen; (*table*) decken; (*sun*) untergehen; (*become solid*) gerinnen. **set aside** aufheben. **setback** *n* Rückschlag *m.* **set fire to** in Brand stecken. **set off** (*on journey*) sich auf den Weg machen, aufbrechen. **set one's heart on** sein Herz hängen an. **set to** darangehen. **setting** *n* Hintergrund *m. n* Satz *m*; (*crockery*) Service *f*; (*radio*) Apparat *m*; (*clique*) Kreis *m*, Clique *f.*
settee [seˈtiː] *n* Sofa *neut.*
settle ['setl] *v* (*arrange*) festsetzen; (*dispute*) schlichten; (*debt*) bezahlen; (*come to rest*) sich niederlassen; (*subside*) sich senken; (*in place*) sich ansiedeln. **settle down** (*calm down*) sich beruhigen; (*in place*) sich niederlassen. **settle for** (*coll*)

annehmen. **settle in** sich einleben. **settle up** bezahlen. **settled** *adj* abgemacht, erledigt. **settlement** *n* (*place*) Siedlung *f*; (*agreement*) Übereinkommen *neut.* **settler** *n* Siedler(in).
seven ['sevn] *adj* sieben. *n* Sieben *f.* **seventh** *adj* siebt, siebent; *n* Siebtel *neut.*
seventeen [sevnˈtiːn] *adj* siebzehn. *n* Siebzehn *f.* **seventeenth** *adj* siebzehnt.
seventy ['sevnti] *adj* siebzig. *n* Siebzig *f.*
sever ['sevə] *v* trennen. **severance** *n* Trennung *f.* **severance pay** Abfindungsentschädigung *f.*
several ['sevrəl] *adj* mehrere; (*separate*) getrennt. **severally** *adv* getrennt.
severe [səˈviə] *adj* streng, hart; (*weather*) rauh; (*difficult*) schwierig. **severity** *n* Strenge *f*; Härte *f*; (*seriousness*) Ernst *m.*
*****sew** [sou] *v* nähen. **sewing** *n* Näharbeit *f.* **sewing machine** Nähmaschine *f.*
sewage ['sjuːdʒ] *n* Abwasser *neut.* **sewer** *n* Abwasserkanal *m.* **sewerage** *n* Kanalisation *f.*
sewn [soun] *V* sew.
sex [seks] *n* Geschlecht *neut*, Sex *m. adj* Geschlechts-, sexual. **sexual** *adj* sexual. **sexual intercourse** Geschlechtsverkehr *m.* **sexuality** *n* Sexualität *f.* **sexy** *adj* sexy.
sextet [seksˈtet] *n* Sextett *neut.*
shabby ['ʃabi] *adj* schäbig.
shack [ʃak] *n* Hütte *f.*
shackle ['ʃakl] *v* fesseln. **shackles** *pl n* Fesseln *pl.*
shade [ʃeid] *n* Schatten *m. v* beschatten; (*protect*) schützen; (*drawing*) schattieren. **shading** *n* Schattierung *f.* **shady** *adj* schattig; (*dubious*) fragwürdig.
shadow ['ʃadou] *n* Schatten *m.* **without a shadow of doubt** ohne den geringsten Zweifel. **shadow cabinet** Schattenkabinett *neut.* **shadowy** *adj* schattig.
shaft [ʃaːft] *n* (*handle*) Schaft *m*; (*lift*) Schacht *m*; (*tech*) Welle *f.*
shaggy ['ʃagi] *adj* zottig.
*****shake** [ʃeik] *v* schütteln; (*shock*) erschüttern; (*tremble*) zittern; (*hand*) drücken. **shake hands with** die Hand geben (+*dat*). **shake off** (*coll*) loswerden. *n* Schütteln *neut.* **shaky** *adj* wackelig.
shall [ʃal] *v* (*to form future*) werden; (*implying permission*) sollen, dürfen. *I shall go* ich werde gehen. *shall I go?* soll ich gehen?
shallot [ʃəˈlot] *n* Schalotte *f.*

shallow ['ʃalou] adj flach, seicht; (superficial) oberflächlich, seicht. **shallows** pl n Untiefe f. **shallowness** n Seichtheit f.
sham [ʃam] n Betrug m; (person) Schwindler m. adj falsch.
shambles ['ʃamblz] n Durcheinander neut.
shame [ʃeim] n Scham f, Schamgefühl neut; (scandal) Schande f. **it's a shame that ...** schade, daß ... **shame-faced** adj verschämt. **shamefacedness** n Verschämtheit f. **what a shame!** (wie) shade! v schämen. **shameful** adj schändlich. **shamefulness** n Schändlichkeit f. **shameless** adj schamlos. **shamelessness** n Schamlosigkeit f.
shampoo [ʃam'puː] n Shampoo neut, Haarwaschmittel neut. v shampooieren.
shamrock ['ʃamrok] n Kleeblatt neut.
shanty[1] ['ʃanti] n (hut) Hütte f. **shanty town** Elendsviertel neut.
shanty[2] ['ʃanti] n (song) Matrosenlied neut.
shape [ʃeip] n Gestalt f, Form f. v gestalten, formen. **shaped** adj geformt. **shapeless** adj formlos. **shapelessness** n Formlosigkeit f. **shapely** adj wohlgeformt.
share [ʃeə] n (An)Teil m; (comm) Aktie f. v teilen. **shareholder** n Aktionär m.
shark [ʃaːk] n Hai(fisch) m.
sharp [ʃaːp] adj scharf; (pointed) spitz; (outline) deutlich. adv (coll) pünktlich. **look sharp!** mach schnell! **sharpen** v (knife) schleifen; (pencil) spitzen. **sharp-eyed** adj scharfsichtig. **sharpness** n Schärfe f. **sharpshooter** n Scharfschütze m. **sharp-witted** adj scharfsinnig.
shatter ['ʃatə] v zerschmettern; (glass) zersplittern. **shattered** adj (coll) erschüttert.
shave [ʃeiv] v (sich) rasieren. **clean-shaven** adj glattrasiert. **shaving brush** Rasierpinsel m. **shaving soap** Rasierseife f. **shaving foam** Rasierschaum m. n Rasur f. **shaver** n Rasierapparat m.
shawl [ʃoːl] n Schal m.
she [ʃiː] pron sie.
sheaf [ʃiːf] n (pl sheaves) Garbe f.
***shear** [ʃiə] v scheren. **shears** pl n Schere f sing. **shearer** n Scherer m. **shearing** n Schur f.
sheath [ʃiːθ] n Scheide f. **sheathe** v (sword) in die Scheide stecken. **sheathed** adj (tech) verkleidet.
***shed**[1] [ʃed] v (tears, blood) vergießen; (leaves) abwerfen.

shed[2] [ʃed] n (hut) Schuppen m; (cows) Stall m.
sheen [ʃiːn] n Glanz m, Schimmer m.
sheep [ʃiːp] n (pl sheep) Schaf neut. **sheepdog** n Schäferhund. **sheepskin** n Schaffell neut. **sheepish** adj einfältig, verlegen.
sheer [ʃiə] adj (pure) bloß; (steep) steil.
sheet [ʃiːt] n (bed) Bettuch neut. (Bett)Laken neut; (paper, metal) Blatt neut.
shelf [ʃelf] n (pl shelves) Regal neut, Fach neut. **on the shelf** sitzengeblieben.
shell [ʃel] n Schale f; (snail) Schneckenhaus neut; (mil) Granate f. **shellfish** n Schalentier neut. **shell-shock** n Kriegsneurose f. v (egg) schälen; (nuts) enthülsen. **shelling** n (mil) Artilleriefeuer neut.
shelter ['ʃeltə] n Obdach neut; (little hut) Schutzhütte f. v beschützen; (take shelter) Schutz suchen.
shelve [ʃelv] v (plan) auf die lange Bank schieben, aufschieben.
shepherd ['ʃepəd] n Schäfer m, Hirt m. **shepherdess** n Schäferin f, Hirtin f.
sheriff ['ʃerif] n Sheriff m.
sherry ['ʃeri] n Sherry m.
shield [ʃiːld] n Schild m; (fig) Schutz m. v beschirmen.
shift [ʃift] v (sich) verschieben; (get rid of) beseitigen; (coll: move fast) schnell fahren; (gear) schalten. n Verschiebung f; (work) Schicht f. **shifty** adj schlau.
shimmer ['ʃimə] n Schimmer m. v schimmern.
shin [ʃin] n Schienbein neut. v **shin up** hinaufklettern.
***shine** [ʃain] v scheinen, leuchten; (shoes) putzen. n Glanz m. **shiny** adj glänzend, strahlend.
shingle ['ʃingl] n (on beach) Strandkies m.
shingles ['ʃinglz] n (med) Gürtelrose f.
ship [ʃip] n Schiff neut. **shipowner** n Reeder m. **shipwreck** n Schiffbruch m. **be shipwrecked** Schiffbruch erleiden. **shipyard** n Werft f. v verschiffen, spedieren. **shipment** n Verladung f. **shipper** n Spediteur m.
shirk [ʃəːk] v sich drücken (vor). **shirker** n Drückeberger(in).
shirt [ʃəːt] n Hemd neut. **shirty** adj (coll) verdrießlich.
shit [ʃit] n (vulgar) Scheiße f. v scheißen. **shitty** adj beschissen.

shiver ['ʃɪvə] v zittern. n Zittern neut.
shoal [ʃoul] n Schwarm m, Zug m.
shock [ʃok] v (impact) Stoß m, Anprall m; (fright) Schreck m, Schock m; (med) Nervenschock m; (elec) Schlag m. v schockieren, entsetzen. **shocked** adj schockiert. **shocking** adj schockierend.
shod [ʃod] V shoe.
shoddy ['ʃodi] adj schäbig.
***shoe** [ʃuː] n Schuh m; (horse) Hufeisen neut. **shoe-horn** n Schuhlöffel m. **shoelace** n Schnürsenkel m. v beschuhen. **shoemaker** n Schuhmacher m.
shone [ʃon] V shine.
shook [ʃuk] V shake.
***shoot** [ʃuːt] v schießen; (hit) anschießen; (kill) erschießen; (film) drehen. **shoot down** (aeroplane) abschießen. **shooting** n (game, etc.) Jagd f. **shooting star** Sternschnuppe f.
shop [ʃop] n Laden m, Geschäft neut; (factory) Werkstatt f. **shop assistant** Verkäufer(in). **shopkeeper** n Ladenbesitzer m. **shop-lifting** n Ladendiebstahl m. **shop-steward** n Betriebsrat m. **shop-window** n Schaufenster neut. v (also go shopping) einkaufen gehen. **shopper** n Einkäufer(in). **shopping** n Einkäufe pl.
shore [ʃoː] n Küste f, Strand m.
shorn [ʃoːn] V shear.
short [ʃoːt] adj kurz; (person) klein. adv plötzlich. **short of** knapp an.
shortage ['ʃoːtidʒ] n Mangel m, Knappheit f.
shortbread ['ʃoːtbred] n Mürbekuchen m.
short-circuit n Kurzschluß m. v kurzschließen.
shortcoming ['ʃoːtkʌmiŋ] n Fehler m, Unzulänglichkeit f.
short cut n Abkürzung f.
shorthand ['ʃoːthand] n Kurzschrift f. **shorthand typist** Stenotypist(in).
short list v in die engere Wahl ziehen.
short-lived adj kurzlebig.
shortly ['ʃoːtli] adv bald, in kurzer Zeit.
short-sighted adj kurzsichtig. **short-sightedness** n Kurzsichtigkeit f.
shorts [ʃoːts] pl n kurze Hose f sing.
short-tempered adj reizbar.
short-term adj kurzfristig.
short-time adj **short-time work** Kurzarbeit f.
short-wave adj Kurzwellen-.
shot [ʃot] V shoot. n Schuß m; (pellets)

Schrot m; (sport) Kugel f; (films) Aufnahme f; (injection) Spritze f. adj (coll) erschüttert. **have a shot** (coll) versuchen. **shotgun** n Schrotflinte f. **shot put** Kugelstoß m.
should [ʃud] v sollen. I should go ich sollte gehen. I should like (to) Ich möchte.
shoulder ['ʃouldə] n Schulter f, Achsel f. **shoulder-blade** n Schulterblatt neut.
shout [ʃaut] v rufen, schreien. n Schrei m, Ruf m. **shouting** n Geschrei neut.
shove [ʃʌv] v schieben, stoßen. n Stoß m, Schub m.
***show** v zeigen; (goods, etc.) ausstellen. **showcase** n Schaukasten m. **showman** n Schausteller m. **show off** angeben, sich großtun. **show-off** n Angeber m, Großtuer m. **showpiece** n Paradestück neut. **showroom** n Ausstellungsraum m. n Ausstellung f; (theatre) Vorstellung f. **mere show** leerer Schein m.
shower ['ʃauə] n (rain) Schauer m; (bath) Dusche f. v sich duschen.
shown [ʃoun] V show.
shred [ʃred] n Fetzen m. v zerfetzen. **not a shred of** keine Spur von.
shrew [ʃruː] n Spitzmaus f; (woman) zankisches Weib neut.
shrewd [ʃruːd] adj scharfsinnig, schlau. **shrewdness** n Scharfsinn m.
shriek [ʃriːk] n Schrei m, Gekreisch neut. v schreien, kreischen.
shrill [ʃril] adj schrill, gellend.
shrimp [ʃrimp] n Garnele f.
shrine [ʃrain] n Schrein m.
***shrink** [ʃriŋk] v einschrumpfen. **shrink from** zurückweichen von. **shrinkage** n Schrumpfung f.
shrivel ['ʃrivl] v runzelig werden, schrumpfen.
shroud [ʃraud] n Leichentuch neut. v (fig) umhüllen.
Shrove Tuesday [ʃrouv] n Fastnachtsdienstag m.
shrub [ʃrʌb] n Strauch m, Busch m. **shrubbery** n Gebüsch neut.
shrug [ʃrʌg] v zucken. n (Achsel)Zucken neut.
shrunk [ʃrʌŋk] V shrink.
shudder ['ʃʌdə] v schaudern. n Schauder m.
shuffle ['ʃʌfl] v (mit den Füßen) scharren, schlurfen; (cards) mischen. n Schlurfen neut; (cards) (Karten)Mischen neut.

shun [ʃʌn] *v* vermeiden.
shunt [ʃʌnt] *v* (*rail*) rangieren.
*shut [ʃʌt] *v* schließen, zumachen; (*book*) zuklappen. **shut down** stillegen. **shut off** abstellen. **shut out** aussperren. **shut up** (*be silent*) den Mund halten. *adj* geschlossen, zu.
shutter ['ʃʌtə] *n* Fensterladen *m*; (*phot*) Verschluß *m*.
shuttle ['ʃʌtl] *n* Pendelverkehr *m*.
shuttlecock ['ʃʌtlkok] *n* Federball *m*.
shy [ʃai] *adj* schüchtern. *v* (*horse*) scheuen. **shy away from** zurückschrecken vor. **shyness** *n* Schüchternheit *f*.
sick [sik] *adj* krank. *I feel sick* mir ist übel. **sick humour** schwarzer Humor *m*.
sicken *v* erkranken; (*disgust*) anekeln. **sickening** *adj* ekelhaft. **sick leave** Krankheitsurlaub *m*. **sickly** *adj* kränklich. **sickness** *n* Krankheit *f*; (*vomiting*) Erbrechen *neut*.
sickle [sikl] *n* Sichel *f*.
side [said] *n* Seite *f*; (*edge*) Rand *m*; (*team*) Mannschaft *f*. *adj* seitlich, Seiten-. **sideboard** *n* Buffet *neut*. **sideboards** or **sideburns** *pl n* Koteletten *pl*. **sidelight** *n* (*mot*) Standlicht *neut*. **sideline** *n* Nebenbeschäftigung *f*. **sidelong** *adj* seitlich. **sideshow** *n* Jahrmarktsbude *f*. **siding** *n* Nebengleis *neut*.
sidle ['saidl] *v* sich schlängeln. **sidle up to** heranschleichen an.
siege [siːdʒ] *n* Belagerung *f*. **lay siege to** belagern.
sieve [siv] *n* Sieb *neut*. *v* (durch)sieben.
sift [sift] *v* (durch)sieben; (*evidence, etc*.) sorgfältig überprüfen.
sigh [sai] *v* seufzen. *n* Seufzer *m*.
sight [sait] *n* (*power of*) Sehvermögen *neut*; (*instance of seeing*) Anblick *m*; (*range of vision*) Sicht *f*; (*of gun*) Visier *neut*; (*place of interest*) Sehenswürdigkeit *f*. **at sight** (*comm*) bei Sicht. **at first sight** beim ersten Anblick. **sighted** *adj* sichtig. **sightless** *adj* blind. **go sightseeing** die Sehenswürdigkeiten besichtigen.
sign [sain] *n* Zeichen *neut*; (*noticeboard, etc*.) Schild *neut*. *v* unterschreiben. **signwriter** *n* Schriftmaler *m*. **signpost** *n* Wegweiser *m*.
signal ['signəl] *n* Signal *neut*. *v* signalisieren.
signature ['signətʃə] *n* Unterschrift *f*. **signature tune** Kennmelodie *f*. **signatory** *n* Unterzeichner *m*; (*pol*) Signatar *m*.

signify ['signifai] *v* bedeuten. **significance** *n* Bedeutung *f*. **significant** *adj* wichtig.
silence ['sailəns] *n* Ruhe *f*, Stille *f*; (*absence of talking, etc*.) Schweigen *neut*. *v* zum Schweigen bringen.
silent ['sailənt] *adj* still, ruhig; stillschweigend. **be** or **fall silent** schweigen. **silent film** Stummfilm *m*.
silhouette [silu'et] *n* Silhouette *f*.
silk [silk] *n* Seide *f*. *adj* Seiden-.
sill [sil] *n* Fensterbrett *neut*; (*door*) Schwelle *f*.
silly ['sili] *adj* dumm, albern. **silly season** Sauregurkenzeit *f*.
silt [silt] *n* Schlamm *m*. *v* **silt up** verschlammen.
silver ['silvə] *n* Silber *neut*. *adj* silbern, Silber-. **silver plate** Tafelsilber *neut*. **silver-plated** *adj* versilbert.
similar ['similə] *adj* ähnlich (+*dat*). **similarity** *n* Ähnlichkeit *f*. **similarly** *adv* gleichermaßen.
simile ['siməli] *n* Gleichnis *neut*.
simmer ['simə] *v* leicht kochen (lassen).
simple ['simpl] *adj* einfach. **simple-minded** *adj* einfältig. **simpleton** *n* Einfaltspinsel *m*. **simplicity** *n* Einfachheit *f*. **simplify** *v* vereinfachen. **simply** *adv* einfach.
simulate ['simjuleit] *v* simulieren. **simulation** *n* Simulation *f*. **simulator** *n* Simulator *m*.
simultaneous [siməl'teinjəs] *adj* gleichzeitig.
sin [sin] *n* Sünde *f*. *v* sündigen. **sinful** *adj* sündig. **sinner** *n* Sünder(in).
since [sins] *prep* seit. *I've been living here since 1960* ich wohne hier seit 1960. *conj* (*time*) seit(dem); (*because*) da. *adv* seitdem, seither; (*in the meantime*) inzwischen.
sincere [sin'siə] *adj* aufrichtig, ehrlich. **yours sincerely** mit freundlichen Grüßen. **sincerity** *n* Aufrichtigkeit *f*.
sinew ['sinjuː] *n* Sehne *f*. **sinewy** *adj* sehnig.
*sing [siŋ] *v* singen. **singer** *n* Sänger(in). **singing** *n* Singen *neut*, Gesang *m*.
singe [sindʒ] *v* (ver)sengen.
single ['siŋgl] *adj* einzig; (*individual*) einzeln; (*room, bed, etc*.) Einzel-; (*unmarried*) ledig. *v* **single out** auslesen. **single ticket** einfache Fahrkarte *f*. **single-handed** *adj* eigenhändig. **single-minded** *adj* zielstrebig. **singly** *adv* einzeln, allein.

singular ['siŋgjulə] *adj* einzigartig; (*gramm*) im Singular. *n* (*gramm*) Singular *m.*

sinister ['sinistə] *adj* drohend, unheilvoll.

***sink** [siŋk] *v* sinken; (*cause to sink*) senken. *n* Spülbecken *neut.*

sinuous ['sinjuəs] *adj* gewunden, sich windend.

sinus ['sainəs] *n* (Nasen) Nebenhöhle *f.* **sinusitis** *n* Nebenhöhlenentzündung *f.*

sip [sip] *v* nippen an, schlürfen. *n* Schlückchen *neut.*

siphon ['saifən] *n* Heber *m;* (*soda*) Siphon *m. v* aushebern.

sir [səi] *n* (mein) Herr. **Dear Sir** (*in letters*) sehr geehrter Herr!

siren ['saiərən] *n* Sirene *f.*

sirloin ['səiloin] *n* Lendenstück *neut.*

sister ['sistə] *n* Schwester *f;* (*nurse*) Oberschwester *f.* **sister-in-law** *n* Schwägerin *f. adj* Schwester-. **sisterly** *adj* schwesterlich.

***sit** [sit] *v* sitzen; (*exam*) machen; (*hen*) brüten. **sit down** sich (hin)setzen. **sitting** *n* Sitzung *f.* **sitting duck** leichtes Opfer *neut.* **sitting-room** *n* Wohnzimmer *neut.*

site [sait] *n* Stelle *f.* **building site** Baustelle *f. v* placieren.

situation [sitju'eifən] *n* Lage *f;* (*state of affairs*) Situation *f,* (Sach)Lage *f;* (*job*) Stelle *f.* Posten *m.* **situated** *adj* gelegen.

six [siks] *adj* sechs. *n* Sechs *f.* **sixth** *adj* sechst; *n* Sechstel *neut.* **sixth form** Prima *f.*

sixteen [siks'tiːn] *adj* sechzehn. *n* Sechzehn *f.*

sixty ['siksti] *adj* sechzig. *n* Sechzig *f.*

size [saiz] *n* Größe *f. v* **size up** (*coll*) abschätzen.

sizzle ['sizl] *v* zischen.

skate¹ [skeit] *n* (*ice*) Schlittschuh *m;* (*roller*) Rollschuh *m. v* Schlittschuh/Rollschuh laufen. **skater** *n* Eisläufer(in); Rollschuhläufer(in).

skate² [skeit] *n* (*fish*) Rochen *m.*

skeleton ['skelitn] *n* Skelett *neut,* Knochengerüst *neut.* **skeleton key** Dietrich *m.*

sketch [sketʃ] *n* Skizze *f;* (*theatre*) Sketch *m. v* skizzieren. **sketchy** *adj* oberflächlich.

skewer ['skjuə] *n* Fleischspieß *m. v* spießen.

ski [skiː] *n* Ski *m. v* Ski laufen. **skier** *n* Skiläufer(in), Skifahrer(in). **skiing** *n* Skilaufen *neut,* Skifahren *neut.*

skid [skid] *v* schleudern. *n* Schleudern *neut.*

skill [skil] *n* (*skilfulness*) Geschicklichkeit *f,* Gewandtheit *f;* (*expertise*) Fachkenntnis *f.* **skilled** *adj* geschickt. **skilled worker** Facharbeiter *m.* **skilful** *adj* geschickt.

skim [skim] *v* abschöpfen; (*milk*) entrahmen. **skim through** (*read*) überfliegen. **skim milk** Magermilch *f.*

skimp [skimp] *v* geizen (mit); (*work*) nachlässig machen.

skin [skin] *n* Haut *f;* (*animal*) Fell *neut,* Pelz *m;* (*fruit*) Schale *f,* Rinde *f.* **skin-deep** *adj* oberflächlich. **skin-diving** *n* Schwimmtauchen *neut.* **skinflint** *n* Geizhals *m.* **skin-tight** *adj* hauteng. *v* enthäuten. **skinny** *adj* mager.

skip [skip] *v* hüpfen; (*with rope*) seilspringen; (*miss*) auslassen. **skip through** (*read*) überfliegen. *n* Sprung *m.* **skipping-rope** *n* Hüpfseil *neut.*

skipper ['skipə] *n* (*coll: naut*) Kapitän *m.*

skirmish ['skəimiʃ] *n* Gefecht *neut.*

skirt [skəit] *n* Rock *m. v* (*go around*) herumgehen um. **skirting board** Wandleiste *f.*

skittle ['skitl] *n* Kegel *m.* **play skittles** kegeln. **skittle alley** Kegelbahn *f.*

skull [skʌl] *n* Schädel *m.* **skull-cap** *n* Käppchen *neut.*

skunk [skʌŋk] *n* Skunk *m,* Stinktier *neut.*

sky [skai] *n* Himmel *m.* **sky-blue** *adj* himmelblau. **sky-high** *adj, adv* himmelhoch. **skylark** *n* Lerche *f.* **skylight** *n* Dachfenster *neut.* **skyscraper** *n* Hochhaus *neut,* Wolkenkratzer *m.*

slab [slab] *n* (*stone*) (Stein)Platte *f;* (*chocolate*) Tafel *f.*

slack [slak] *adj* schlaff, locker; (*person*) nachlässig; (*trade*) flau. **slacken** *v* lockern, entspannen; (*pace, etc.*) vermindern. **slackness** *n* Schlaffheit *f.*

slacks [slaks] *pl n* Hose *f sing.*

slag [slag] *n* Schlacke *f.* **slagheap** *n* Halde *f.*

slalom ['slaıləm] *n* Slalom *m.*

slam [slam] *v* (*door*) zuknallen. *n* Knall *m.*

slander ['slaındə] *n* Verleumdung *f. v* verleumden. **slanderer** *n* Verleumder *m.* **slanderous** *adj* verleumderisch.

slang [slaŋ] *n* Jargon *m. v* beschimpfen.

slant [slaınt] *n* Schräge *f;* (*attitude*) Einstellung *f. v* schräg liegen. **slant-eyed** *adj*

mit schräggestellten Augen. **slanting** *adj* schräg.
slap [slap] *v* klapsen, schlagen. *n* Klaps *m*, Schlag *m*. **slapdash** *adj* schlampig.
slash [slaʃ] *v* schlitzen, zerfetzen. *n* Schnitt *m*, Schlitz *m*.
slat [slat] *n* Latte *f*, Leiste *f*.
slate [sleit] *n* Schiefer *m*; (*writing*) Schiefertafel *f*; (*on roof*) Dachschiefer *m*. *v* (*coll*) heftig tadeln, kritisieren.
slaughter [ˈslɔːtə] *v* schlachten. *n* Schlachten *neut*. **slaughterhouse** *n* Schlachthaus *neut*. **slaughterer** *n* Schlächter *m*.
slave [sleiv] *n* Sklave *m*, Sklavin *f*. **slave-driver** *n* Leuteschinder *m*. *v* **slave away** schuften. **slavery** *n* Sklaverei *f*. **slavish** *adj* sklavisch.
sledge [sledʒ] *n* Schlitten *m*.
sledgehammer [ˈsledʒˌhamə] *n* Schmiedehammer *m*, Schlägel *m*.
sleek [sliːk] *adj* glatt. **sleekness** *n* Glätte *f*.
*sleep [sliːp] *v* schlafen; (*spend the night*) übernachten. *n* Schlaf *m*. **go to sleep** einschlafen. **sleeper** *n* Schläfer(in); (*railway*) Schwelle *f*. **sleeping bag** Schlafsack *m*. **sleeping car** Schlafwagen *m*. **sleepless** *adj* schlaflos. **sleeplessness** *n* Schlaflosigkeit *f*. **sleepwalker** *n* Nachtwandler *m*. **sleepy** *adj* schläfrig, müde.
sleet [sliːt] *n* Schneeregen *m*.
sleeve [sliːv] *n* Ärmel *m*. **sleeved** *adj* mit Ärmeln. **sleeveless** *adj* ärmellos.
sleigh [slei] *n* Schlitten *m*.
slender [ˈslendə] *adj* schlank, schmal. **slenderness** *n* Schlankheit *f*.
slept [slept] *V* **sleep**.
slice [slais] *n* Scheibe *f*, Schnitte *f*. *v* aufschneiden. **sliced** *adj* geschnitten, in Scheiben. **slicer** *n* Schneidemaschine *f*.
slick [slik] *adj* glatt; (*person*) raffiniert. **slicker** *n* Gauner *m*.
slid [slid] *V* **slide**.
*slide [slaid] *v* gleiten, rutschen. **slide rule** Rechenschieber *m*. **sliding door** Schiebetür *f*. **sliding scale** gleitende Skala *f*. *n* (*phot*) Dia(positiv) *neut*; (*playground*) Schlitterbahn *f*.
slight [slait] *adj* gering, unbedeutend, klein; (*person*) schmächtig, dünn. **not in the slightest** nicht im geringsten. *v* (*person*) kränken. *n* Beleidigung *f*. **slightly** *adv* leicht, ein bißchen.

slim [slim] *adj* schlank, dünn; (*chance, etc.*) gering. *v* eine Schlankheitskur machen, abnehmen. **slimness** *n* Schlankheit *f*.
slime [slaim] *n* Schleim *m*. **slimy** *adj* schleimig.
*sling [sliŋ] *n* (*weapon*) Schleuder *m*; (*arm*) Schlinge *f*. *v* schleudern.
*slink [sliŋk] *v* schleichen.
slip [slip] *n* Fehltritt *m*; (*underskirt*) Unterrock *m*. *v* gleiten, rutschen. **slip away** sich davonmachen. **slip off** (*clothes*) ausziehen. **slip on** (*clothes*) anziehen. **slip up** sich irren, sich vertun. **slipknot** *n* Laufknoten *m*. **slipshod** *adj* schlampig.
slipper [ˈslipə] *n* Pantoffel *m*.
slippery [ˈslipəri] *adj* schlüpfrig, glitschig; (*person*) aalglatt.
*slit [slit] *n* Schlitz *m*. *v* aufschlitzen. **slit-eyed** *adj* schlitzäugig.
slither [ˈsliðə] *v* rutschen, schlittern. **slithery** *adj* schlüpfrig.
slobber [ˈslobə] *v* sabbern, geifern. *n* Geifer *m*. **slobbery** *adj* sabbernd.
sloe [slou] *n* Schlehe *f*.
slog [slog] *v* hart schlagen; (*work hard*) schuften. *n* (harter) Schlag *m*.
slogan [ˈslougən] *n* Slogan *m*, Schlagwort *neut*.
slop [slop] *v* verschütten. *n* Pfütze *f*. **slops** *pl n* Abwasser *neut*.
slope [sloup] *n* Abhang *m*. *v* abfallen. **sloping** *adj* schräg.
sloppy [ˈslopi] *adj* matschig; (*slapdash*) schlampig. **sloppiness** *n* Matschigkeit *f*, Schlampigkeit *f*.
slot [slot] *n* Schlitz *m*; (*for coin*) Münzeinwurf *m*.
slouch [slautʃ] *v* latschen. **slouching** *adj* latschig.
slovenly [ˈslʌvnli] *adj* schlampig.
slow [slou] *adj* langsam; (*boring*) langweilig. *v also* **slow down** *or* **up** (sich) verlangsamen. **slow-down** *n* Verlangsamung *f*. **slow motion** Zeitlupentempo *neut*. **slowness** *n* Langsamkeit *f*; (*wits*) Schwerfälligkeit *f*.
sludge [slʌdʒ] *n* Schlamm *m*.
slug [slʌg] *n* Schnecke *f*.
sluggish [ˈslʌgiʃ] *adj* träge, schwerfällig; (*river*) langsam fließend. **sluggishness** *n* Schwerfälligkeit *f*.
sluice [sluːs] *n* Schleuse *f*. *v* ausspülen.

slums [slʌmz] *pl n* Elendsviertel *neut.*
slumber ['slʌmbə] *v* schlummern. *n* Schlummer *m.*
slump [slʌmp] *v* hinplumpsen; (*prices*) stürzen. *n* (*comm*) Geschäftsrückgang *m*, Wirtschaftskrise *f.*
slung [slʌŋ] *V* sling.
slunk [slʌŋk] *V* slink.
slur [sləɪ] *v* (*words*) verschlucken, undeutlich aussprechen. *n* Vorwurf *m.*
slush [slʌʃ] *n* Matsch *m*; (*snow*) Schneematsch *m*; (*sentimentality*) Schmalz *m.* **slushy** *adj* matschig; schmalzig.
slut [slʌt] *n* Schlampe *f.* **sluttish** *adj* schlampig.
sly [slai] *adj* schlau, hinterhältig. **slyness** *n* Schlauheit *f.*
smack¹ [smak] *n* Klaps *m*, Klatsch *m.* *v* schlagen, einen Klaps geben (+ *dat*).
smack² [smak] *n* (*flavour*) Geschmack *m.* *v* schmecken (nach).
small [smoɪl] *adj* klein; (*number, extent*) gering. **small change** Kleingeld *neut.* **small talk** Geplauder *neut.* **smallness** *n* Kleinheit *f.*
smallpox ['smoɪlpoks] *n* Pocken *pl.*
smart [smaɪt] *adj* schick, gepflegt; (*coll: clever*) gescheit, raffiniert. **smart aleck** (*coll*) Naseweis *m.* *v* (*suffer*) leiden. **smarten up** zurechtmachen.
smash [smaʃ] *v* zerschmettern, zerschlagen; (*enemy, etc.*) vernichten. *n* (*mot*) Zusammenstoß *m.* **smash hit** Bombenerfolg *m.* **smashing** *adj* (*coll*) toll, sagenhaft.
smear [smiə] *v* (be)schmieren. *n* (Schmutz) Fleck *m*; (*med*) Abstrich *m.* **smear campaign** Verleumdungskampagne *f.*
*smell [smel] *n* Geruch *m*; (*pleasant*) Duft *m.* *v* riechen. **smell of** riechen nach. **smelly** *adj* übelriechend.
smelt [smelt] *V* smell.
smile [smail] *v* lächeln. *n* Lächeln *neut.* **smiling** *adj* lächelnd.
smirk [sməɪk] *v* schmunzeln.
smock [smok] *n* Kittel *m.*
smog [smog] *n* Smog *m*, Rauchnebel *m.*
smoke [smouk] *v* rauchen; (*meat, fish*) räuchern. *n* Rauch *m.* **smokescreen** *n* Nebelvorhang *m.* **smokestack** *n* Schornstein *m.* **smoker** *n* Raucher(in); (*train*) Raucherabteil *m.* **smoking** *n* Rauchen *neut.* **no smoking** Rauchen verboten.

smooth [smuɪð] *adj* glatt. **smoothness** *n* Glätte *f.* **smooth-tongued** *adj* schmeichlerisch. *v* glätten.
smother ['smʌðə] *v* ersticken; (*with gifts, etc.*) überhäufen.
smoulder ['smouldə] *v* schwelen.
smudge [smʌdʒ] *n* Schmutzfleck *m*, Klecks *m.* *v* beschmutzen.
smug [smʌg] *adj* selbstgefällig.
smuggle ['smʌgl] *v* schmuggeln. **smuggler** *n* Schmuggler *m.* **smuggling** *n* Schmuggel *m.*
snack [snak] *n* Imbiß *m.* **snack bar** Imbißstube *f.*
snag [snag] *n* (*difficulty*) Haken *m.*
snail [sneil] *n* Schnecke *f.* **at a snail's pace** im Schneckentempo.
snake [sneik] *n* Schlange *f.*
snap [snap] *v* (*break*) (zer)brechen; (*dog*) schnappen; (*noise*) knacken; (*phot*) knipsen. **snap at** (*person*) anschnauzen. **snapdragon** *n* Löwenmaul *neut.* **snap-fastener** *n* Druckknopf *m.* **snapshot** *n* Schnappschuß *m.* **snappy** *adj* (*coll*) schnell, lebhaft.
snare [sneə] *n* Schlinge *f.* *v* fangen. **snare drum** *n* Schnarrtrommel *f.*
snarl [snaɪl] *n* Knurren *neut.* *v* knurren.
snatch [snatʃ] *v* schnell ergreifen. **snatch at** greifen nach.
sneak [sniɪk] *v* schleichen; (*tell tales*) petzen. *n* Petzer *m.* **sneakers** *pl n* Turnschuhe *pl.* **sneaking** *adj* heimlich. **sneaky** *adj* heimtückisch.
sneer [sniə] *v* spötteln (über). *v* höhnisch lächeln. *n* Hohnlächeln *neut.*
sneeze [sniɪz] *v* niesen. *n* Niesen *neut.*
sniff [snif] *v* schnüffeln. *n* Schnüffeln *neut.*
snigger ['snigə] *v* kichern. *n* Kichern *neut.*
snip [snip] *v* schneiden. *n*, Schnitt *m.*
snipe [snaip] *n* Schnepfe *f.* *v* aus dem Hinterhalt schießen. **sniper** *n* Heckenschütze *m.*
snivel ['snivl] *v* wimmern. **snivelling** *adj* weinerlich.
snob [snob] *n* Snob *m.* **snobbery** *n* Snobismus *m.* **snobbish** *adj* snobistisch.
snooker ['snuɪkə] *n* Snooker *neut.*
snoop [snuɪp] *v* herumschnüffeln. *n* Schnüffler *m.*
snooty ['snuɪti] *adj* hochnäsig.
snooze [snuɪz] *n* Nickerchen *neut.* *v* ein Nickerchen machen.

snore [snoː] *v* schnarchen. *n* Schnarchen *neut.*
snorkel ['snoːkəl] *n* Schnorchel *m.*
snort [snoːt] *n* Schnauben *neut. v* schnauben.
snout [snaut] *n* Schnauze *f.*
snow [snou] *n* Schnee *m.* **snowball** *n* Schneeball *m; v* (*develop*) lawinenartig anwachsen. **snowdrift** *n.* Schneewehe *f.* **snowdrop** *n* Schneeglöckchen *neut. v* schneien.
snub [snʌb] *n* Rüffel *m,* Verweis *m. v* rüffeln. *adj* stumpf.
snuff [snʌf] *n* Schnupftabak *m.* **take snuff** schnupfen.
snug [snʌg] *adj* gemütlich, bequem.
snuggle ['snʌgl] *v* sich schmiegen (an).
so [sou] *adv* so; (*very*) sehr. *conj* also, daher. **so that** damit. *so am/do I* ich auch. **so what?** na und? *I think so* ich glaube schon.
soak [souk] *v* durchtränken; (*washing*) einweichen. **soaking wet** triefend naß.
soap [soup] *n* Seife *f. v* (ein)seifen. **soapy** *adj* seifig. **soapy water** Seifenwasser *neut.*
soar [soː] *v* (*fly up*) hochfliegen; (*rise*) hoch aufsteigen.
sob [sob] *v* schluchzen. *n* Schluchzen *neut.*
sober ['soubə] *adj* nüchtern. *v* **sober up** nüchtern werden. **sobriety** *n* Nüchternheit *f.*
sociable ['souʃəbl] *adj* gesellig. **sociability** *n* Geselligkeit *f.*
social ['souʃəl] *adj* (*animals*) gesellig; (*gathering*) gesellschaftlich, gesellig; (*of society*) Gesellschafts-, Sozial-, gesellschaftlich. **social security** Sozialversicherung *f.* **social services** soziale Einrichtungen *pl.* **social worker** Sozialarbeiter(in). **socialism** *n* Sozialismus *m.* **socialist** *n* Sozialist(in).
society [sə'saiəti] *n* Gesellschaft *f.*
sociology [sousi'olədʒi] *n* Soziologie *f.* **sociological** *adj* soziologisch. **sociologist** *n* Soziologe *m.*
sock [sok] *n* Socke *f.*
socket ['sokit] *n* (*elec*) Steckdose *f*; (*eye*) Höhle *f*; (*bone*) Gelenkpfanne *f.*
soda ['soudə] *n* Soda; *also* **soda water** Soda(wasser) *neut.*
sodden ['sodn] *adj* durchnäßt.
sofa ['soufə] *n* Sofa *neut.*
soft [soft] *adj* weich; (*voice, etc.*) leise; (*gentle*) sanft, mild. **soften** *v* weich

machen *or* werden; (*water*) enthärten.
soft-hearted *adj* weichherzig.
soggy ['sogi] *adj* feucht.
soil¹ [soil] *n* Boden *m,* Erde *f.*
soil² [soil] *n* (*dirt*) Schmutz *m. v* beschmutzen.
solar ['soulə] *adj* Sonnen-.
sold [sould] *V* sell.
solder ['soldə] *v* löten. *n* Lot *neut.* **soldering iron** Lötkolben *m.*
soldier ['souldʒə] *n* Soldat *m.*
sole¹ [soul] *adj* (*only*) einzig, alleinig.
sole² [soul] *n* (*of shoe*) Sohle *f. v* besohlen.
sole³ [soul] *n* (*fish*) Seezunge *f.*
solemn ['soləm] *adj* feierlich; (*person*) ernst. **solemnity** *n* Feierlichkeit *f.*
solicitor [sə'lisitə] *n* (*law*) Anwalt *m.*
solicitous [sə'lisitəs] *adj* fürsorglich; (*eager*) eifrig.
solid ['solid] *adj* (*not liquid*) fest; (*pure*) massiv. **solidarity** *n* Solidarität *f.* **solidify** *v* fest werden.
solitary ['solitəri] *adj* (*person*) einsam; (*single*) einzeln.
solitude ['solitjuːd] *n* Einsamkeit *f.*
solo ['soulou] *n* Solo *neut. adj* Solo-, Allein-. *adv* allein. **soloist** *n* Solist(in).
solstice ['solstis] *n* Sonnenwende *f.*
solve [solv] *v* lösen. **soluble** *adj* löslich; (*problem*) lösbar. **solution** *n* Lösung *f.*
solvent *n* Lösungsmittel *neut; adj* (*comm*) zahlungsfähig.
sombre ['sombə] *adj* düster.
some [sʌm] *adj* (*several*) einige; (*a little*) etwas; (*some ... or other*) (irgend)ein; (*approx.*) ungefähr. **somebody** *or* **someone** *pron* jemand. **some day** eines Tages. **something** *pron* etwas. **sometime** *adv* irgendwann. **sometimes** *adv* manchmal. **somewhat** *adv* ziemlich. **somewhere** *adv* irgendwo(hin).
somersault ['sʌməsoːlt] *n* Purzelbaum *m. v* (*person*) einen Purzelbaum schlagen; (*thing*) sich überschlagen.
son [sʌn] *n* Sohn *m.* **son-in-law** *n* Schwiegersohn *m.*
sonata [sə'naːtə] *n* Sonate *f.*
song [soŋ] *n* Lied *neut,* Gesang *m.* **songbird** *n* Singvogel *m.*
sonic ['sonik] *adj* Schall-. **sonic barrier** Schallgrenze *f.*
sonnet ['sonit] *n* Sonett *neut.*
soon [suːn] *adv* bald. **as soon as** sobald. **as soon as possible** so bald wie möglich. **sooner** *adv* früher.

soot [sut] *n* Ruß *m*. **sooty** *adj* rußig.
soothe [su:ð] *v* beruhigen; (*pain*) lindern.
soothing *adj* lindernd, besänftigend.
sophisticated [sə'fistikeitid] *adj* (*person*) kultiviert; (*machinery, etc*.) kompliziert, hochentwickelt. **sophistication** *n* Kultiviertheit *f*.
sopping ['sopiŋ] *adj* patschnaß.
soprano [sə'pra:nou] *n* Sopranistin *f*; (*voice*) Sopran *m*. *adj* Sopran-.
sordid ['so:did] *adj* schmutzig, gemein.
sore [so:] *adj* wund; (*inflamed*) entzündet; (*coll: annoyed*) verärgert. *n* Wunde *f*. **sorely** *adv* äußerst. **soreness** *n* Empfindlichkeit *f*.
sorrow ['sorou] *n* Kummer *m*, Leid *neut*; (*regret*) Reue *f*. **sorrowful** *adj* betrübt, traurig.
sorry ['sori] *adj* traurig, betrübt; (*sight, etc*.) jämmerlich, traurig. *interj* Verzeihung! *I am sorry* es tut mir leid. *I am/feel sorry for you* Sie tun mir leid.
sort [so:t] *n* Sorte *f*, Art *f*; (*brand*) Marke *f*. **all sorts of** allerlei. **a sort of** eine Art. **sort of** (*coll*) gewissermaßen. **that sort of thing** so etwas. *v* sortieren.
soufflé ['su:flei] *n* Auflauf *m*.
sought [so:t] *V* **seek**. **sought-after** *adj* gesucht.
soul [soul] *n* Seele *f*. **not a soul** kein Mensch. **soul-destroying** *adj* seelentötend. **soulful** *adj* seelenvoll. **soulless** *adj* seelenlos.
sound[1] [saund] *n* Schall *m*; (*noise*) Geräusch *neut*, Klang *m*. **soundproof** *adj* schalldicht. **sound wave** Schallwelle *f*. *v* klingen. **sound the alarm** den Alarm schlagen. **sound the horn** hupen. **soundless** *adj* geräuschlos.
sound[2] [saund] *adj* (*healthy*) gesund; (*safe*) sicher; (*reasoning*) stichhaltig.
sound[3] [saund] *v* loten, sondieren.
soup [su:p] *n* Suppe *f*, Brühe *f*.
sour [sauə] *adj* sauer.
source [so:s] *n* Quelle *f*.
south [sauθ] *n* Süden *m*. *adj also* **southerly, southern** südlich, Süd-. *adv also* **southwards** nach Süden, südwärts. **South America** Sudamerika *neut*. **south-east** *n* Südosten. **South Pole** Südpol *m*. **southwest** *n* Südwesten *m*.
souvenir [su:və'niə] *n* Andenken *neut*.
sovereign ['sovrin] *n* Souverän *m*. *adj* souverän. **sovereignty** *n* Souveränität *f*.
Soviet Union ['souviət] *n* Sowjetunion *f*.

*sow[1] [sou] *v* säen; (*field*) besäen. **sower** *n* Säer *m*.
sow[2] [sau] *n* Sau *f*.
sown [soun] *V* **sow**[1].
soya ['soiə] *n* Sojabohne *f*.
spa [spa:] *n* Badekurort *m*.
space [speis] *n* Raum *m*; (*gap*) Zwischenraum *m*, Abstand *m*; (*astron*) Weltraum *m*. **space flight** Raumflug *m*. **spaceship** *n* Raumschiff *neut*. *v* (räumlich) einteilen. **spacious** *adj* geräumig.
spade[1] [speid] *n* Spaten *m*. **spadework** *n* (*fig*) Vorabeit *f*.
spade[2] [speid] *n* (*cards*) Pik *neut*.
Spain [spein] *n* Spanien *neut*. **Spaniard** *n* Spanier(in). **Spanish** *adj* spanisch.
span [span] *n* (*arch*) Spannweite *f*; (*time*) Zeitspanne *f*.
spaniel ['spanjəl] *n* Spaniel *m*.
spank [spaŋk] *v* verhauen, prügeln.
spanner ['spanə] *n* Schraubenschlüssel *m*.
spare [speə] *adj* Ersatz-; (*over*) übrig; (*thin*) hager, dürr. **spare time** Freizeit *f*. **spare tyre** Ersatzreifen *m*. **spare rib** Rippenspeer *m*. *v* (*pains, expense*) scheuen; (*give*) übrig haben (für); (*feelings, etc*.) verschonen. **sparing** *adj* sparsam. *n also* **spare part** Ersatzteil *m*.
spark [spa:k] *n* Funke *m*. *v* funkeln. **spark** *or* **sparking plug** Zündkerze *f*.
sparkle ['spa:kl] *v* funkeln, glänzen. *n* Funkeln *neut*, Glanz *m*. **sparkler** *n* Wunderkerze *f*. **sparkling** *adj* funkelnd; (*wine*) schäumend.
sparrow ['sparou] *n* Spatz *m*, Sperling *m*.
sparse [spa:s] *adj* spärlich, dünn. **sparseness** *n* Spärlichkeit *f*.
spasm ['spazəm] *n* (*med*) Krampf *m*; (*fig*) Anfall *m*. **spasmodic** *adj* (*fig*) sprunghaft.
spastic ['spastik] *adj* spastisch. *n* Spastiker(in).
spat [spat] *V* **spit**[1].
spatial ['speiʃl] *adj* räumlich.
spatula ['spatjulə] *n* Spachtel *m*.
spawn [spo:n] *n* Laich *m*. *v* (*eggs*) ablegen; (*fig*) hervorbringen.
*speak [spi:k] *v* sprechen, reden. **speak out** frei herausreden. **speak to** reden mit. **speak up** laut sprechen. **speak up for** sich einsetzen für. **speaker** *n* Redner *m*.
spear [spiə] *n* Speer *m*. *v* aufspießen.
special ['speʃəl] *adj* besonder, speziell; (*train, case*) Sonder-. **specialist** *n* Fachmann *m*. **speciality** *n* Spezialität *f*. **specialization** *n* Spezialisierung *f*. **special-**

ize v spezialisieren. **specially** adv besonders.

species ['spi:ʃi:z] n Art f; (biol) Spezies f. **specify** ['spesifai] v spezifizieren, im einzeln angeben. **specific** adj spezifisch. **specifications** n pl· (tech) technische Daten pl.

specimen ['spesimin] n Muster neut, Probe f.

speck [spek] n Fleck m. **speckle** v flecken.

spectacle ['spektəkl] n Schauspiel neut. **spectacles** pl Brille f sing. **spectacular** adj sensationell.

spectator [spek'teitə] n Zuschauer(in).

spectrum ['spektrəm] n Spektrum neut.

speculate ['spekjuleit] v nachdenken; (comm) spekulieren. **speculation** n Mutmaßung f, Annahme f; (comm) Spekulation f. **speculative** adj spekulativ. **speculator** n Spekulant m.

sped [sped] V **speed**.

speech [spi:tʃ] n Sprache f; (a talk) Rede f. **make a speech** eine Rede halten.

*speed [spi:d] n Geschwindigkeit f, Tempo neut. v rasen, eilen; (exceed limit) (zu) schnell fahren. **speed up** beschleunigen. **speed limit** Geschwindigkeitsbegrenzung f. **speedboat** n Schnellboot neut. **speedometer** n Tachometer m. **speedy** adj schnell.

*spell¹ [spel] v (name the letters in) buchstabieren; (signify) bedeuten. how do you spell ...? wie schreibt man ...? **spell out** (fig) deutlich erklären. **spelling** n Rechtschreibung f.

spell² [spel] n (magic) Zauber m, Zauberspruch m. **cast a spell on** bezaubern. **spellbound** adj fasziniert.

spell³ [spel] n (period) Periode f, Weile f.

spelt [spelt] V **spell¹**.

*spend [spend] v (money) ausgeben; (time) verbringen. **spending money** Taschengeld neut. **spendthrift** n Verschwender(in); adj verschwenderisch.

spent [spent] V **spend**.

sperm [spəim] n Sperma neut.

sperm whale n Pottwal m.

spew [spjuː] v (vulgar) sich erbrechen, kotzen. **spew out** ausspeien.

sphere [sfiə] n Kugel f; (fig) Bereich m. **spherical** adj kugelförmig.

spice [spais] n Gewürz neut. v würzen. **spiced** adj gewürzt. **spicy** adj pikant, scharf.

spider ['spaidə] n Spinne f. **spider's web** Spinngewebe neut. **spidery** adj spinnenartig.

spike [spaik] n Spitze f, Dorn m.

*spill [spil] v verschütten; (blood) vergießen. n (coll) Sturz, Fall m.

spilt [spilt] V **spill**.

*spin [spin] v (thread, web) spinnen; (turn) (herum)wirbeln, spinnen; (washing) schleudern. n (coll: in car, etc.) Spazierfahrt f. **spin-dryer** n Wäscheschleuder f. **spinning wheel** Spinnrad neut.

spinach ['spinidʒ] n Spinat m.

spindle ['spindl] n Spindel f. **spindly** adj spindeldürr.

spine [spain] n (thorn, etc.) Stachel m; (anat) Rückgrat neut, Wirbelsäule f. **spiny** adj stachelig.

spinster ['spinstə] n unverheiratete Frau f; (elderly) alte Jungfer f.

spiral ['spaiərəl] adj schraubenförmig, spiral. **spiral staircase** Wendeltreppe f. n Spirale f.

spire ['spaiə] n Turmspitze f.

spirit ['spirit] n Geist m. **spirits** pl (drinks) Spirituosen pl, Alkohol m. **high spirits** Frohsinn m, gehobene Stimmung f. v **spirit away** hinwegzaubern. **spirited** adj lebhaft. **spiritual** adj geistig, geistlich.

*spit¹ [spit] n (saliva) Spucke f, Speichel m. v spucken.

spit² [spit] n (roasting) (Brat)Spieß m; (geog) Landzunge f.

spite [spait] n Boshaftigkeit f. **in spite of** trotz (+ gen). **spiteful** adj boshaft.

splash [splaʃ] v (be)spritzen. n Spritzen neut; (mark) Fleck m.

spleen [spliːn] n Milz f.

splendid ['splendid] adj prächtig, herrlich. **splendour** n Pracht f.

splice [splais] v (ropes) spleißen; (tapes, films) zusammenfügen.

splint [splint] n Schiene f. **splinter** n Splitter m. v zersplittern. **splinter group** Splittergruppe f.

*split [split] v (zer)spalten, sich spalten. **split up** sich trennen. **split hairs** Haarspalterei treiben. **splitting headache** rasende Kopfschmerzen pl. n Spalt m, Riß m. adj gespalten.

splutter ['splʌtə] v stottern.

*spoil [spoil] v verderben; (child) verwöhnen. **spoils** pl n Beute f. **spoilsport** n Spielverderber(in).

spoke¹ [spouk] *V* **speak.**
spoke² [spouk] *n* (*wheel*) Speiche *f.*
spoken ['spoukn] *V* **speak.**
spokesman ['spouksmən] *n* Sprecher *m.*
sponge [spʌndʒ] *n* Schwamm *m.* *v* **sponge down** (mit einem Schwamm) abwaschen.
sponge-cake *n* Sandtorte *f.* **sponger** *n* (*coll*) Schmarotzer *m.* **spongy** *adj* schwammig.
sponsor ['sponsə] *n* Förderer *m,* Schirmherr *m;* (*radio, TV*) Sponsor *m.* *v* unterstützen, fördern. **sponsorship** *n* Schirmherrschaft *f.*
spontaneous [spon'teinjəs] *adj* spontan. **spontaneity** *n* Freiwilligkeit *f,* Spontaneität *f.*
spool [spuːl] *n* Spule *f.*
spoon [spuːn] *n* Löffel *m.* *v* **spoon out** auslöffeln. **spoon-feed** *v* verhätscheln. **spoonful** *n* Löffelvoll *m.*
sporadic [spə'radik] *adj* verstreut, sporadisch.
sport [spoːt] *n* Sport *m;* (*fun*) Spaß *m.* **play sports** Sport treiben. **sportscar** *n* Sportwagen *m.* **sportsman** *n* Sportler *m.* **sportswoman** *n* Sportlerin *f.* *v* scherzen; (*wear*) tragen. **sporting** *adj* sportlich.
spot [spot] *n* (*mark*) Fleck *m;* (*place*) Stelle *f;* (*pimple*) Pickel *m.* **spot check** Stichprobe *f.* **spotlight** *n* Scheinwerfer *m.* **spotless** *adj* fleckenlos. *v* beflecken; (*notice*) entdecken, erspähen. **spotted** *adj* fleckig. **spotty** *adj* pickelig.
spouse [spaus] *n* Gatte *m,* Gattin *f,* Gemahl(in).
spout [spaut] *n* Tülle *f,* Schnauze *f.* *v* (*coll*) deklamieren.
sprain [sprein] *n* Verrenkung *f.* *v* verrenken.
sprang [spraŋ] *V* **spring.**
sprawl [sproːl] *v* (*person*) sich rekeln; (*town*) sich ausbreiten.
spray¹ [sprei] *v* (be)sprühen. *n* (*aerosol, etc.*) Sprühdose *f,* Spray *m;* (*sea*) Schaum *m.*
spray² [sprei] *n* (*of flowers*) Blütenzweig *m.*
*spread [spred] *v* ausbreiten; (*butter, etc.*) streichen; (*rumour*) (sich) verbreiten. *n* Ausbreitung *f;* (*extent*) Umfang *m,* Spanne *f;* (*for bread*) Aufstrich *m.*
spree [spriː] *n* (*shopping*) Einkaufsbummel *m.*
sprig [sprig] *n* Schößling *m.*

sprightly ['spraitli] *adj* lebhaft, munter.
*spring [spriŋ] *n* (*season*) Frühling *m;* (*tech*) Feder *f;* (*water*) Brunnen *m,* Quelle *f.* **springboard** *n* Sprungbrett *neut.* *v* springen. **spring a leak** ein Leck bekommen. **springing** *n* Federung *f.* **springy** *adj* elastisch.
sprinkle ['spriŋkl] *v* sprenkeln. **sprinkler** *n* Brause *f.* **a sprinkling of** ein bißchen.
sprint [sprint] *n* Sprint *m.* *v* sprinten. **sprinter** *n* Sprinter *m.*
sprout [spraut] *v* sprießen. *n* Sprößling *m.* (**Brussels**) **sprouts** Rosenkohl *m sing.*
spruce [spruːs] *n* (*tree*) Fichte *f.*
sprung [sprʌŋ] *V* **spring.**
spur [spəː] *n* Sporn *m;* (*fig*) Ansporn *m.* *v* (*horse*) die Sporen geben (+*dat*); (*fig*) anspornen.
spurious ['spjuəriəs] *adj* falsch, unecht.
spurn [spəːn] *v* zurückweisen.
spurt [spəːt] *v* (*water*) hervorspritzen. *n* (*sport*) Spurt *m.*
spy [spai] *v* (*espy*) erspähen; (*pol*) spionieren. *n* Spion(in). **spy-glass** *n* Fernglas *neut.* **spying** *n* Spionage *f.*
squabble ['skwobl] *v* sich zanken. *n* Kabbelei *f,* Zank *m.*
squad [skwod] *n* Gruppe *f;* (*mil*) Zug *m;* (*police*) Kommando *neut.* **flying squad** Überfallkommando *neut.* **squad car** Streifenwagen *m.*
squadron ['skwodrən] *n* (*naut*) Geschwader *neut;* (*aero*) Staffel *f.* **squadron leader** Major *m.*
squalid ['skwolid] *adj* schmutzig. **squalor** *n* Schmutz *m.*
squall [skwoːl] *n* heftiger Windstoß *m;* (*storm*) Gewitter *neut.*
squander ['skwondə] *v* verschwenden, vergeuden.
square [skweə] *n* Quadrat *neut,* Viereck *neut;* (*in town*) Platz *m.* *adj* viereckig, quadratisch.
squash [skwoʃ] *n* (*people*) Gedränge *neut;* (*game*) Squash *neut.* *v* zerquetschen. **fruit squash** Fruchtsaft *m.*
squat [skwot] *v* hocken; (*ein Haus*) unberechtigt besetzen. *adj* gedrungen. **squatter** *n* Squatter *m.*
squawk [skwoːk] *n* Kreischen *neut.* *v* kreischen.
squeak [skwiːk] *v* (*wheel, etc.*) quietschen; (*mouse, etc.*) piepsen. *n* Quietschen *neut;* Piepsen *neut.* **squeaky** *adj* quietschend.

squeal [skwiːl] v schreien, quieken; (criminal) pfeifen. n Schrei m, Quieken neut.
squeamish ['skwiːmiʃ] adj überempfindlich. **squeamishness** n Überempfindlichkeit f.
squeeze [skwiːz] v drücken; (fruit) auspressen, ausquetschen. n Druck m. **credit squeeze** Kreditbeschränkung f. **squeezer** n Presse f.
squid [skwid] n Tintenfisch m.
squiggle ['skwigl] n Kritzelei f.
squint [skwint] n Schielen neut. v schielen. **squint-eyed** adj schielend.
squire ['skwaiə] n Junker m, Gutsherr m.
squirm [skwəːm] v sich winden.
squirrel ['skwirəl] n Eichhörnchen neut.
squirt [skwəːt] v spritzen. n Spritze f.
stab [stab] v (kill) erstechen. n Stich m. **stab wound** Stichwunde f. **make a stab at** versuchen.
stabilize ['steibilaiz] v stabilisieren. **stability** n Stabilität f. **stabilization** n Stabilisierung f.
stable[1] ['steibl] n Stall m. v einstallen. **stable-lad/man** n Stallknecht m.
stable[2] ['steibl] adj stabil.
staccato [stə'kaːtou] adj, adv staccato.
stack [stak] n Schober m; (wood, etc.) Stapel m. v aufschobern.
stadium ['steidiəm] n Stadion neut.
staff [staːf] n (stick) Stock m; (work force) Personal neut; (mil) Stab m. adj Personal-; stabs-.
stag [stag] n Rothirsch m. **stag party** Herrengesellschaft f.
stage [steidʒ] n (of development, etc.) Stufe f, Stadium neut; (theatre) Bühne. **stage fright** Lampenfieber neut. **stagemanager** n Inspizient m. v (play) aufführen; (fig) veranstalten.
stagger ['stagə] v schwanken, taumeln; (amaze) verblüffen. **staggering** adj taumelnd; phantastisch.
stagnant ['stagnənt] adj stillstehend, stagnierend. **stagnate** v stagnieren. **stagnation** n Stagnation f.
staid [steid] adj gesetzt, seriös.
stain [stein] adj Fleck m; (for wood, etc.) Färbung f. v beflecken; färben. **stainless** adj (steel) rostfrei.
stair [steə] n Treppenstufe f. **(flight of) stairs** Treppe f. **stair-carpet** n Treppenläufer m.
stake[1] [steik] n (post) Pfahl m, Pfosten m.

stake a claim (to) Anspruch erheben (auf).
stake[2] [steik] n (betting) Einsatz m; (share) Anteil m. v (money) setzen. **put at stake** aufs Spiel setzen.
stale [steil] adj (bread) alt, altbacken; (beer, etc.) abgestanden; (thing) abgedroschen.
stalemate ['steilmeit] n (chess) Patt neut; (fig) Stillstand m. v pattsetzen.
stalk[1] [stɔːk] n (bot) Stiel m.
stalk[2] [stɔːk] v sich anpirschen an.
stall[1] [stɔːl] n (stable) Stand m; (market) Bude f. **stalls** pl (theatre) Parkett neut sing. v (engine) aussetzen; (car) stehenbleiben.
stall[2] [stɔːl] v (delay) ausweichen, Ausflüchte machen.
stallion ['staljən] n Hengst m.
stamina ['staminə] n Durchhaltevermögen neut, Ausdauer f.
stammer ['stamə] v stottern, stammeln. n Stottern neut, Gestammel neut. **stammerer** n Stotterer m. **stammering** adj stotternd.
stamp [stamp] v (with foot) stampfen; (rubber stamp) stempeln; (letters) frankieren. n Stempel m; (letter) Briefmarke f. **stamp album** Briefmarkenalbum neut. **stamp collector** Briefmarkensammler m.
stampede [stam'piːd] n wilde Flucht f.
***stand** [stand] n (sales, etc.) Bude f, Stand m; (attitude) Standpunkt m; (for spectators) (Zuschauer)Tribüne f; (resistance) Widerstand m. v stehen. I can't stand him ich kann ihn nicht ausstehen. I can't stand it ich kann es nicht aushalten. **as things stand** unter den Umständen. **my offer stands** mein Angebot gilt noch. **stand aside** beiseite treten. **stand back** zurücktreten. **stand by** (be loyal to) treu bleiben (+dat). **stand for** (mean) bedeuten, stehen für; (tolerate) sich gefallen lassen; (parliament) kandidieren. **stand in for** einspringen für. **stand up** aufstehen. **stand up to** sich verteidigen gegen. **standby** n Stütze f; (alert) Alarmbereitschaft f. **standing** n Stand m, Rang m. **standing order** (bank) Dauerauftrag m. **stand-offish** adj hochmütig.
standard ['standəd] n Standard m, Norm f. (flag) Standarte f. adj Normal-; (usual) gewöhnlich, normal. **standardize** v

normen, standardisieren. **standardization**
n Normung *f.*
stank [staŋk] *V* stink.
stanza ['stanzə] *n* Strophe *f,* Stanza *f.*
staple[1] [steipl] *n* Heftklammer *f. v* heften.
stapler *n* Heftmaschine *f.*
staple[2] [steipl] *adj* Haupt-.
star [staɪ] *n* Stern *m;* (*films, etc.*) Star *m.*
starlight *n* Sternenlicht *neut. v* die Hauptrolle spielen. **starring** in der Hauptrolle.
starry *adj* (*sky*) Sternen-; (*night*)
sternhell.
starboard ['staɪbəd] *n* Steuerbord *neut.*
adj Steuerbord-.
starch [staɪtʃ] *n* (Wäsche)Stärke *f. v*
stärken. **starched** *adj* gestärkt. **starchy**
adj (*person*) steif, förmlich.
stare [steə] *n* starrer Blick *m,* Starrblick
m. v starren. **stare at** anstarren.
stark [staɪk] *adj* kahl, öde. *adv* **stark**
naked splitternackt. **stark-staring mad**
total verrückt.
starling ['staɪliŋ] *n* Star *m.*
start [staɪt] *v* anfangen, beginnen; (*leave*)
abfahren; (*arise*) entstehen; (*sport*)
starten (lassen); (*engine*) anlassen;
(*jump*) hochschrecken. *n* Anfang *m,*
Beginn *m;* (*sport*) Start *m;* (*journey*)
Abreise *f.* **from the start** vom Anfang an.
starter *n* (*sport*) Starter *m.* **starter motor**
Anlaßmotor *m.*
startle ['staɪtl] *v* erschrecken, überraschen.
startling *adj* erschreckend.
starve [staɪv] *v* verhungern. **starvation** *n*
Hungern *neut,* Verhungern *neut.*
state [steit] *n* (*pol*) Staat *m;* (*condition*)
Zustand *m;* (*situation*) Lage *f. v* erklären,
behaupten. *adj* Staats-, staatlich. **stated**
adj angegeben. **stateless** *adj* staatenlos.
stately *adj* stattlich. **statement** *n*
Erklärung *f.* **statement of account**
Kontoauszug *m.* **statesman** *n* Staatsmann
m. **statesmanship** *n* Staatskunst *f.*
static ['statik] *adj* statisch. *n* statische
Elekrizität *f.*
station ['steiʃən] *n* Platz *m,* Posten *m;*
(*rail*) Bahnhof *m;* (*standing*) Stand *m.*
station master Bahnhofsvorsteher *m.* **sta-**
tion wagon Kombi(wagen) *m. v* station-
ieren.
stationary ['steiʃənəri] *adj* stillstehend,
stationär.
stationer ['steiʃənə] *n* Schreibwarenhänd-
ler *m.* **stationery** *n* Schreibwaren *pl;*
(*office*) Büromaterial *neut.*

statistics [stə'tistiks] *n* Statistik *f.* **statisti-**
cal *adj* statistisch.
statue ['statjuː] *n* Standbild *neut,* Statue *f.*
stature ['statʃə] *n* Körpergröße *f,* Statur *f;*
(*moral, etc.*) Kaliber *neut.*
status ['steitəs] *n* Status *m;* (*rank*) Stand
m, Rang *m.* **status quo** Status quo *m.*
status symbol Statussymbol *neut.*
statute ['statjuːt] *n* Gesetz *neut.* **statutory**
adj gesetzlich (vorgeschrieben).
staunch [stoɪntʃ] *adj* getreu, zuverlässig.
stay [stei] *v* bleiben; (*in hotel*) logieren,
unterkommen; (*with friends, etc.*) zu
Besuch sein (bei). **stay the night**
übernachten. **stay behind** zurückbleiben.
stay in zu Hause bleiben. *n* Aufenthalt
m; Besuch *m.*
steadfast ['stedfaɪst] *adj* fest, treu.
steady ['stedi] *adj* sicher, fest, stabil; (*reg-*
ular) regelmäßig, gleichmäßig; (*cautious*)
vorsichtig. *v* festigen. **steady on!** langsam!, vorsichtig! **steadiness** *n* Festigkeit
f, Sicherheit *f.*
steak [steik] *n* Steak *neut.*
*****steal** [stiːl] *v* stehlen. **steal away** sich
davonstehlen.
stealthy ['stelθi] *adj* heimlich. **stealth** *n*
Heimlichkeit *f.*
steam [stiːm] *n* Dampf *m. v* dampfen;
(*food*) dünsten. **steam-boiler** *n*
Dampfkessel *m.* **steamer** *n* (*naut*)
Dampfer *m,* Dampfschiff *neut;* (*cookery*)
Dampfkochtopf *m.* **steam-roller** *n*
Dampfwalze *f;* *v* (*opposition*)
niederwalzen. **steamy** *adj* dampfig.
steel [stiːl] *n* Stahl *m. adj* stählern, Stahl-.
steelworks *pl* Stahlwerk *neut sing.*
steely hart.
steep[1] [stiːp] *adj* steil, jäh; (*coll: improba-*
ble) unwahrscheinlich; (*prices*) gepfeffert.
steep[2] [stiːp] *v* (*soak*) einweichen.
steeple ['stiːpl] *n* Kirchturm *m,* Spitzturm
m.
steeplechase ['stiːpltʃeis] *n* Steeplechase *f.*
steeplejack *n* Turmarbeiter *m.*
steer [stiə] *v* steuern, lenken. **steering col-**
umn Lenksäule *f.* **steering lock** Len-
kradschloß *m.* **steering wheel** Lenkrad
neut, Steuer *neut.*
stem[1] [stem] *n* (*stalk*) Stiel *m;* (*line of*
descent) Stamm *m. v* **stem from** stammen
von, zurückgehen auf.
stem[2] [stem] *v* eindämmen; (*blood*) stillen.

stench [stentʃ] *n* Gestank *m.*
stencil ['stensl] *n* Schablone *f. v* schablonieren.
step [step] *v* treten, schreiten. *n* Schritt *m;* (*measure*) Maßnahme *f;* (*stage, gradation*) Stufe *f.* **step by step** Schritt für Schritt. **step on it** (*coll*) Gas geben. **step aside** zur seite treten. **step-ladder** *n* Trittleiter *f.* **stepping-stone** *n* Trittstein *m;* (*fig*) Sprungbrett *neut.*
stepbrother ['stepbrʌðə] *n* Stiefbruder *m.*
stepdaughter ['stepdɔːtə] *n* Stieftochter *f.*
stepfather ['stepfaːðə] *n* Stiefvater *m.*
stepmother ['stepmʌðə] *n* Stiefmutter *f.*
stepsister ['stepsistə] *n* Stiefschwester *f.*
stepson ['stepsʌn] *n* Stiefsohn *m.*
stereo ['steriou] *n* Stereoanlage *f. adj* Stereo-. **stereophonic** *adj* stereophonisch.
stereotyped ['steriətaipt] *adj* stereotyp.
sterile ['sterail] *adj* steril. **sterility** *n* Sterilität *f.*
sterling ['stəːliŋ] *n* Sterling *m.*
stern[1] [stəːn] *adj* streng, hart. **sternness** *n* Strenge *f.* Härte *f.*
stern[2] [stəːn] *n* (*naut*) Heck *neut.*
stethoscope ['steθəskoup] *n* Stethoskop *neut.*
stew [stjuː] *n* Eintopfgericht *neut. v* schmoren. **stewed** *adj* geschmort.
steward ['stjuəd] *n* (*ship, aeroplane*) Steward *m;* (*race, etc.*) Ordner *m.* **stewardess** *n* Stewardeß *f.*
stick[1] [stik] *n* (*wood*) Stock *m;* (*hockey*) Schläger *m.*
***stick**[2] [stik] *v* (*with glue, etc.*) kleben *or* heften (an); (*pointed instrument*) stecken; **stick out** (*tongue*) herausstrecken; (*protrude*) hervorstehen. **stick to** (*remain with*) bleiben bei. **stick up for** sich einsetzen für. **be stuck** steckenbleiben. **stuck-up** *adj* hochnäsig. **sticking plaster** Heftpflaster *neut.* **sticky** *adj* klebrig.
stiff [stif] *adj* steif, starr; (*drink*) stark; (*difficult*) schwierig. *n* (*coll*) Leiche *f.* **stiffen** *v* (ver)steifen, (ver)stärken. **stiff-necked** *adj* halsstarrig. **stiffness** *n* Steife *f,* Starrheit *f.*
stifle ['staifl] *v* ersticken. **stifling** *adj* zum Ersticken.
stigma ['stigmə] *n* Brandmal *neut,* Stigma *neut.*
stile [stail] *n* Zauntritt *m.*
still[1] [stil] *adj* still. *adv* (immer)noch. *conj* und doch, dennoch. *v* beruhigen. **still-**

birth Totgeburt *f.* **stillborn** *adj* totgeboren. **stillness** *n* Stille *f.*
still[2] [stil] *n* (*for spirits*) Brennerei *f.*
stilt [stilt] *n* Stelze *f.* **stilted** *adj* gespreizt.
stimulus ['stimjuləs] *n* (*pl* -i) Stimulus *m.* **stimulant** *n* Reizmittel *neut.* **stimulate** *v* anregen. **stimulating** *adj* anregend. **stimulation** *n* Anreiz *m.*
***sting** [stiŋ] *v* (*insect*) stechen; (*be painful*) brennen; (*remark*) kränken. *n* Stich *m.* **stinging** *adj* brennend; schmerzend. **stinging nettle** Brennessel *f.*
stingy ['stindʒi] *adj* geizig.
***stink** [stiŋk] *v* stinken, übel riechen. *n* Gestank *m;* (*coll: scandal*) Skandal *m.*
stint [stint] *v* knausern mit. *n* (*of work*) Schicht *f.*
stipulate ['stipjuleit] *v* festsetzen; (*insist on*) bestehen auf. **stipulation** Bedingung *f.*
stir [stəː] *v* (*liquids*) (an)rühren; (*move*) sich rühren *or* bewegen; (*excite*) aufrühren, bewegen. *n* Rühren *neut;* (*sensation*) Sensation *f.* **stirring** *adj* aufregend.
stirrup ['stirəp] *n* Steigbügel *m.*
stitch [stitʃ] *n* Stich *m;* (*knitting*) Masche *f;* (*pain*) Stechen *m. v* nähen. **stitch up** vernähen. **stitching** *n* Näherei *f.*
stoat [stout] *n* Hermelin *neut.*
stock [stok] *n* (*of goods*) Vorrat *m,* Lager *neut;* (*cookery*) Brühe; (*descent*) Stamm *m.* **stocks** *pl* (*comm*) Aktien *pl.* **stockbroker** *n* Börsenmakler *m.* **stock exchange** Börse *f.* **stockpile** *v* aufstapeln. **stock-still** *adj* bewegungslos. **stocktaking** *n* Bestandaufnahme *f. v* (*goods*) führen, vorrätig haben.
stocking ['stokiŋ] *n* Strumpf *m.*
stocky ['stoki] *adj* stämmig, untersetzt.
stodge [stodʒ] *n* schwerverdauliches Zeug *neut.* **stodgy** *adj* schwer(verdaulich).
stoical ['stouikl] *adj* stoisch.
stoke [stouk] *v* schüren. **stoker** *n* Heizer *m.*
stole[1] [stoul] *V* steal.
stole[2] [stoul] *n* Stola *f.*
stolen ['stoulən] *V* steal.
stomach ['stʌmək] *n* Magen *m;* (*coll: abdomen*) Bauch *m;* (*taste for*) Appetit (zu) *f. v* ertragen. **stomach-ache** *n* Magenschmerzen *pl.*
stone [stoun] *n* Stein *m;* (*fruit*) Kern *m. adj* steinern, Stein-. *v* (*fruit*) entkernen; (*to death*) steinigen. **stone age** Steinzeit *f.*

stoned adj (coll) besoffen. **stone-deaf** adj stocktaub. **stonemason** n Steinmetz m. **stony** adj steinig.
stood [stud] V **stand.**
stool [stuːl] n Hocker m, Stuhl m; (med) Stuhlgang m.
stoop [stuːp] v sich bücken; (posture) gebeugt gehen. n Beugen neut, krumme Haltung f.
stop [stop] v (activity) aufhören; (motion) anhalten, stoppen; (clock) stehenbleiben; (put a stop to) einstellen; (bus, train) anhalten; (pipe, etc.) verstopfen. n Halt m, Stillstand m; (break) Pause f; (bus) Haltestelle f. **stoppage** n Stillstand m. **stopper** n Stöpsel m. **stop-watch** n Stoppuhr f.
store [stoː] v aufbewahren. n Vorrat m, Lager neut; (shop) Laden m. **storage** n Lagerung f. **storekeeper** n (shop) Ladenbesitzer m.
storey ['stoːri] n Stockwerk neut. **four-storied** adj vierstöckig.
stork [stoːk] n Storch m.
storm [stoːm] n Sturm m, Unwetter neut; (thunderstorm) Gewitter neut. **storm-tossed** adj sturmgepeitscht. v stürmen. **storm-troops** Sturmtruppen pl. **stormy** adj stürmisch.
story ['stoːri] n Geschichte f, Erzählung f. **to cut a long story short** um es ganz kurz zu sagen. **story-book** n Märchenbuch neut. **story-teller** n Erzähler(in).
stout [staut] adj dick, beleibt; (strong) kräftig. n dunkles Bier neut, Malzbier neut.
stove [stouv] n Ofen m; (cooking) Kochherd m. **stove-pipe** Ofenrohr neut.
stow [stou] v verstauen. **stowaway** blinder Passagier m.
straddle ['stradl] v (sitting) rittlings sitzen auf.
straggle ['stragl] v umherstreifen. **straggle behind** nachhinken. **straggler** n Nachzügler m.
straight [streit] adj gerade; (hair) glatt; (candid) offen, freimütig. adv gerade, direkt. **get straight** (clarify) klarstellen. **think straight** logisch denken. **straight on** or **ahead** gerade aus. **straightaway** adv sofort. **straighten** v gerademachen. **straighten out** (put in order) in Ordnung bringen. **straightforward** adj (thing) einfach, schlicht; (person) offen, aufrichtig. n (sport) Gerade f.

strain[1] [strein] v spannen; (muscle) zerren; (tech) verzerren; (filter) sieben, filtern. **strain oneself** sich (über)anstrengen. n Überanstrengung f; (emotional) Streß m, Anspannung f; (med) Zerrung. **strained** adj (relations, etc.) gespannt.
strain[2] [strein] n (race) Abstammung f, Rasse f.
straits [streits] pl n Straße f, Meerenge f. **dire straits** Notlage f. **strait-jacket** n Zwangsjacke f.
strand[1] [strand] n (rope) Strang m; (hair) Strähne f; (thought) Faden m.
strand[2] [strand] n (shore) Strand m, Ufer neut. v stranden. **stranded** adj gestrandet.
strange [streindʒ] adj (odd) seltsam, sonderbar; (alien) fremd. **strangeness** n Seltsamkeit f; Fremdartigkeit f. **stranger** n Fremde(r). **be a stranger to** nicht vertraut sein mit. **strangely** adv seltsamerweise.
strangle ['strangl] v erwürgen, erdrosseln. **stranglehold** n Würgegriff m.
strap [strap] n Riemen m; (dress) Träger m. v festschnallen. **strapless** adj trägerlos. **strapping** adj stramm.
strategy ['stratədʒi] n Strategie f. **strategic** adj strategisch.
stratum ['straitəm] n (pl -a) Schicht f.
straw [stroː] n Stroh neut; (single) Strohhalm m; (drinking) Trinkhalm m. adj Stroh-. **straw hat** Strohhut m.
strawberry ['stroːbəri] n Erdbeere f.
stray [strei] v sich verirren; (from path, etc.) abgehen (von); (attention) wandern. adj verirrt. n verirrtes Tier neut.
streak [striːk] n Streifen neut; (in character) Einschlag m. **streak of lightning** Blitzstrahl m. v streifen; (race, fly) rasen, sausen. **streaked** adj gestreift.
stream [striːm] n Bach m; (current) Strom m, Strömung f. v strömen. **streamer** n (party) Papierschlange f. **streamline** v (fig) rationalisieren. **streamlined** adj windschnittig.
street [striːt] n Straße f. **streetcar** n Straßenbahn f. **street lamp** Straßenlaterne f. **street-walker** n Straßendirne f.
strength [streŋθ] n Stärke f, Kraft f, Kräfte pl; (liquids) Stärke f; (mil) Macht f, Schlagkraft f. **strengthen** v (ver)stärken. **strengthening** n Verstärkung f.

strenuous ['strenjuəs] *adj* anstrengend.
stress [stres] *n* (*emphasis*) Nachdruck *m*; (*psychological*) Streß *m*; (*pronunciation*) Akzent *m*. *v* betonen. **stressful** *adj* belastend.
stretch [stretʃ] *v* (aus)strecken, ausdehnen; (*person*) sich strecken; (*e.g. land, town*) sich erstrecken. *n* (*time*) Zeitspanne *f*; (*place*) Strecke *f*. **stretcher** *n* Tragbahre *f*. **stretchy** *adj* dehnbar.
stricken ['strikən] *adj* (*sickness*) befallen (von); (*emotion*) ergriffen (von).
strict [strikt] *adj* streng. **strictness** *n* Strenge *f*.
stridden ['stridn] *V* **stride**.
***stride** [straid] *v* schreiten. *n* Schritt *m*. **make great strides** Fortschritte machen. **get into one's stride** in Schwung kommen.
strident ['straidənt] *adj* grell.
strife [straif] *n* Kampf *m*.
***strike** [straik] *v* schlagen; (*target*) treffen; (*workers*) streiken; (*match*) entzünden. **it strikes me** es fällt mir ein. **strike off** streichen von. *n* Schlag *m*, Stoß *m*; (*labour*) Streik *m*. **striking** *adj* auffallend.
***string** [striŋ] *n* Schnur *f*, Bindfaden *m*; (*instrument*) Saite *f*. **strings** *pl* (*mus*) Streicher *pl*. *v* (*instrument*) besaiten. **string together** verknüpfen. **stringed instrument** Streichinstrument *neut*.
stringent ['strindʒənt] *adj* streng. **stringency** *n* Strenge *f*.
strip¹ [strip] *v* abziehen; (*clothes*) ausziehen.
strip² [strip] *n* (*narrow piece*) (schmaler) Streifen *m*.
stripe [straip] *n* Streifen *m*, Strich *m*. *v* streifen. **striped** *adj* gestreift.
***strive** [straiv] *v* (*for*) streben (nach); (*to do*) sich anstrengen (zu).
striven ['strivn] *V* **strive**.
strode [stroud] *V* **stride**.
stroke¹ [strouk] *n* (*blow*) Schlag *m*; (*pen*) Strich *m*; (*med*) Schlaganfall *m*.
stroke² [strouk] *v* streicheln.
stroll [stroul] *v* schlendern. *n* Bummel *m*, Spaziergang *m*.
strong [stroŋ] *adj* (*person, thing*) stark; (*person*) kräftig; (*flavour, etc.*) scharf. **be going strong** wohlauf sein. **strong-room** *n* Tresor *m*. **strong-willed** *adj* willensstark. **strongly** *adv* kräftig.

strove [strouv] *V* **strive**.
struck [strʌk] *V* **strike**.
structure ['strʌktʃə] *n* Struktur *f*. **structural** *adj* strukturell.
struggle ['strʌgl] *v* kämpfen, ringen. *n* Kampf *m*.
strum [strʌm] *v* klimpern (auf).
strung [strʌŋ] *V* **string**.
strut¹ [strʌt] *v* (herum)stolzieren. **strutting** *adj* prahlerisch.
strut² [strʌt] *n* Stütze *f*, Spreize *f*.
stub [stʌb] *n* Stumpf *m*; (*cheque*) Kontrollabschnitt *m*, Talon *m*; (*cigarette*) (Zigaretten)Stummel *m*. *v* **stub out** ausdrücken.
stubble ['stʌbl] *n* Stoppel *f*; (*beard*) Stoppeln *pl*. **stubbly** *adj* stoppelig.
stubborn ['stʌbən] *adj* hartnäckig, eigensinnig. **stubbornness** *n* Hartnäckigkeit *f*.
stuck [stʌk] *V* **stick²**.
stud¹ [stʌd] *n* Beschlagnagel *m*; (*button*) Knopf *m*.
stud² [stʌd] *n* (*farm*) Gestüt *neut*; (*horse*) Zuchthengst *m*.
student ['stju:dənt] *n* Student(in); (*at school, also fig*) Schüler(in).
studio ['stju:diou] *n* Studio *neut*.
study ['stʌdi] *n* Studium *neut*; (*piece of research, etc.*) Studie *f*, Untersuchung *f*; (*room*) Studierzimmer *neut*. *v* studieren.
stuff [stʌf] *n* Stoff *m*; (*coll*) Zeug *neut*, Kram *m*. *v* vollstopfen; (*taxidermy*) ausstopfen; (*cookery*) füllen. **stuffing** *n* Füllung *f*.
stuffy ['stʌfi] *adj* (*air*) dumpf, schwül; (*thing*) langweilig; (*person*) pedantisch; (*nose*) verstopft.
stumble ['stʌmbl] *v* stolpern. **stumblingblock** *n* Hindernis *neut*.
stump [stʌmp] *n* Stumpf *m*. *v* (*coll*) verblüffen. **stumpy** *adj* stumpfartig.
stun [stʌn] *v* betäuben; (*fig*) bestürzen. **stunning** *adj* (*coll*) phantastisch.
stung [stʌŋ] *V* **sting**.
stunk [stʌŋk] *V* **stink**.
stunt¹ [stʌnt] *v* (*growth*) hindern, hemmen. **stunted** *adj* verkümmert.
stunt² [stʌnt] *n* (*feat*) Kunststück *neut*.
stupid ['stju:pid] *adj* dumm, blöd. **stupidity** *n* Dummheit *f*.
stupor ['stju:pə] *n* Erstarrung *f*; (*dullness*) Stumpfsinn *m*.
sturdy ['stə:di] *adj* robust, kräftig.
sturgeon ['stə:dʒən] *n* Stör *m*.

stutter ['stʌtə] *n* Stottern *neut.* *v* stottern.
stutterer *n* Stotterer *m.*
sty [stai] *n* Schweinestall *m.*
style [stail] *n* Stil *m.* *v* (*name*) benennen; (*shape*) formen. **latest style** neueste Mode *f.* **hairstyle** *n* Frisur *f.* **stylish** *adj* elegant.
stylus ['stailəs] *n* Griffel *m*; (*record-player*) Nadel *f.*
suave [swaɪv] *adj* weltmännisch, zuvorkommend.
subconscious [sʌb'kɔnʃəs] *adj* unterbewußt. *n* das Unterbewußte *neut.*
subcontract [sʌbkən'trakt] *n* Nebenvertrag *m.* **subcontractor** *n* Unterkontrahent *m.*
subdue [səb'djuɪ] *v* unterwerfen. **subdued** *adj* (*person*) zurückhaltend; (*lights*) gedämpft.
subject ['sʌbdʒikt; *v* səb'dʒekt] *n* (*school, etc.*) Fach *neut*; (*theme*) Thema *neut*, Gegenstand *m*; (*gramm*) Subjekt *neut*; (*citizen*) Staatsangehörige(r). *adj* (*to ruler*) untertan (+*dat*); (*liable*) geneigt (zu); (*exposed*) ausgesetzt (+*dat*). *v* unterwerfen; (*expose*) aussetzen (+*dat*). **subjection** *n* Unterwerfung *f.* **subjective** *adj* subjektiv.
subjunctive [səb'dʒʌŋktiv] *n* Konjunktiv *m.*
*****sublet** [,sʌb'let] *n* untervermieten.
sublime [sə'blaim] *adj* sublim, erhaben.
submarine ['sʌbməriɪn] *n* Unterseeboot (U-Boot) *neut.* *adj* Untersee-.
submerge [səb'məɪdʒ] *v* (ein)tauchen. **submerged** *adj* untergetaucht.
submit [səb'mit] *v* sich unterwerfen; (*maintain*) behaupten; (*hand in*) einreichen, vorlegen. **submission** *n* Unterwerfung *f*; (*documents*) Vorlage *f.* **submissive** *adj* gehorsam.
subnormal [sʌb'nɔɪməl] *adj* (*child, etc.*) minderbegabt.
subordinate [sə'bɔɪdinət] *v* unterordnen. *adj* untergeordnet. *n* Untergebene(r).
subscribe [səb'skraib] *v* (*money*) zeichnen. **subscribe to** (*newspaper*) abonnieren auf; (*view, etc.*) billigen. **subscriber** *n* Abonnent(in); (*phone*) Teilnehmer(in). **subscription** *n* Abonnement *neut.*
subsequent ['sʌbsikwənt] *adj* (nach)folgend. **subsequently** *adv* nachher, hinterher.
subservient [səb'səɪviənt] *adj* unterwürfig. **subservience** *n* Unterwürfigkeit *f.*

subside [səb'said] *v* (*noise, etc.*) nachlassen, abnehmen; (*sink*) sich senken. **subsidence** *n* (Boden)Senkung *f.*
subsidiary [səb'sidiəri] *adj* Hilfs-, Neben-. *n* (*company*) Tochtergesellschaft.
subsidize ['sʌbsidaiz] *v* subventionieren. **subsidy** *n* Subvention *f.*
subsist [səb'sist] *v* existieren. **subsist on** sich ernähren von. **subsistence** *n* Existenz *f.*
substance ['sʌbstəns] *n* Substanz *f*, Stoff *m*; (*of argument, etc.*) Gehalt *neut*, Kern *m.* **substantial** *adj* beträchtlich. **substantiate** *v* begründen.
substitute ['sʌbstitjuɪt] *n* Ersatz *m*; (*sport*) Ersatzspieler(in). *adj* Ersatz-. *v* ersetzen. **substitution** *n* Einsetzung *f.*
subtitle ['sʌbtaitl] *n* Untertitel *m.*
subtle ['sʌtl] *adj* fein, subtil. **subtlety** *n* Feinheit *f.*
subtract [səb'trakt] *v* abziehen. **subtraction** *n* Abziehen *neut*; (*thing subtracted*) Abzug *m.*
suburb ['sʌbəɪb] *n* Vorort *m.* **suburban** *adj* Vororts-; (*coll: provincial*) kleinstädtisch.
subvert [səb'vəɪt] *v* (*government*) stürzen; (*morals*) untergraben. **subversion** *n* Sturz *m*; Untergrabung *f.* **subversive** *adj* umstürzlerisch.
subway ['sʌbwei] *n* (*in UK*) Fußgängerunterführung *f*; (*in US*) U-Bahn *f.*
succeed [sək'siɪd] *v* (*follow*) folgen auf, nachfolgen (+*dat*); (**be successful**) Erfolg haben, erfolgreich sein; gelingen (*impers*). *I succeeded in doing it* es gelang mir, es zu tun. **success** *n* Erfolg *m.* **successful** *adj* erfolgreich. **succession** *n* Reihenfolge *f*, Folge *f.* **successive** *adj* (aufeinander)folgend. **successor** *n* Nachfolger(in).
succinct [sək'siŋkt] *adj* kurz(gefaßt).
succulent ['sʌkjulənt] *adj* saftig. *n* (*bot*) Sukkulente *f.* **succulence** *n* Saftigkeit *f.*
succumb [sə'kʌm] *v* nachgeben (+*dat*).
such [sʌtʃ] *adj* solch, derartig. *such a big house* ein so großes Haus. **no such thing** nichts dergleichen. **such as** wie zum Beispiel. **as such** an sich. **such is life** so ist das Leben.
suck [sʌk] *v* saugen; (*sweet, thumb*) lutschen. **sucker** *n* (*coll*) Gimpel *m*; (*bot*) Wurzelschößling *m.* **sucking pig** *n* Spanferkel *neut.* **suckle** *v* stillen. **suckling** *n* Säugling *m.*

suction ['sʌkʃən] *v* Saugwirkung *f*. Sog *m*.
sudden ['sʌdən] *adj* plötzlich. **suddenness**
n Plötzlichkeit *f*.
suds [sʌdz] *n* Seifenlauge *f*.
sue [suɪ] *v* verklagen (auf).
suede [sweid] *n* Wildleder *neut.*
suet ['suɪit] *n* Nierenfett *neut*, Talg *m*.
suffer ['sʌfə] *v* leiden (an). **sufferer** *n*
Leidende(r). **suffering** *n* Leiden *neut*; *adj*
leidend (an).
sufficient [sə'fiʃənt] *adj* genügend, ausreichend.
suffocate ['sʌfəkeit] *v* ersticken. **suffocating** *adj* erstickend. **suffocation** *n* Erstick-
en *neut.*
sugar ['ʃugə] *n* Zucker *m*. *v* zuckern;
süßen. **sugar cane** *n* Zuckerrohr *neut.*
sugared *adj* gezuckert. **sugary** *adj*
süßlich; (*fig*) zuckersüß.
suggest [sə'dʒest] *v* vorschlagen; (*maintain*) behaupten; (*indicate*) hindeuten
auf. **suggestion** *n* Vorschlag *m*; (*trace*)
Spur *f*. **suggestive** *adj* anzüglich,
zweideutig. **be suggestive of** deuten auf.
suicide ['suɪisaid] *n* Selbstmord *m*. **suicid-
al** *adj* selbstmörderisch.
suit [suɪt] *n* (*man's*) Anzug *m*; (*woman's*)
Kostüm *neut*; (*cards*) Farbe *f*; (*law*)
Klage *f*. **follow suit** dasselbe tun. **suitcase**
n Handkoffer *m*. *v* (an)passen; (*clothes*)
(gut) stehen (+ *dat*); (*food*) bekommen
(+ *dat*). **suitable** *adj* geeignet, passend.
suite [swiːt] *n* (*furniture*) Garnitur *f*;
(*rooms*) Zimmerflucht *f*.
sulk [sʌlk] *v* schmollen, trotzen. **sulky** *adj*
mürrisch, schmollend.
sullen ['sʌlən] *adj* mürrisch.
sulphur ['sʌlfə] *n* Schwefel *m*. **sulphurous**
adj schwefelig; (*fig*) hitzig.
sultan ['sʌltən] *n* Sultan *m*.
sultana [sʌl'tɑːnə] *n* (*dried fruit*) Sultanine
f.
sultry ['sʌltri] *adj* schwül. **sultriness** *n*
Schwüle *f*.
sum [sʌm] *n* Summe *f*; (*money*) Betrag *m*;
(*calculation*) Rechenaufgabe *f*. *v* **sum up**
zusammenfassen.
summarize ['sʌməraiz] *v* zusammenfassen. **summary** *n* Zusammenfassung *f*.
summer ['sʌmə] *n* Sommer *m*. *adj* som-
merlich, Sommer-. **summerhouse** *n*
Gartenhaus *neut*. **summery** *adj* sommer-
lich.
summit ['sʌmit] *n* Gipfel *m*. **summit conference** Gipfelkonferenz *f*.

summon ['sʌmən] *v* aufrufen, kommen
lassen; (*meeting*) einberufen; (*courage*)
fassen. **summons** *n* Berufung *f*; (*law*)
(Vor)Ladung *f*. **take out a summons
against** vorladen lassen.
sump [sʌmp] *n* Ölwanne *f*.
sumptuous ['sʌmptʃuəs] *adj* prächtig,
kostspielig.
sun [sʌn] *n* Sonne *f*. *v* **sun oneself** sich
sonnen.
sunbathe ['sʌnbeið] *v* ein Sonnenbad
nehmen, sich sonnen.
sunbeam ['sʌnbiːm] *n* Sonnenstrahl *m*.
sunburn ['sʌnbəːn] *n* Sonnenbrand *m*.
sunburnt *adj* sonnenverbrannt.
sundae ['sʌndei] *n* Eisbecher *m*.
Sunday ['sʌndi] *n* Sonntag *m*. **Sunday
best** Sonntagskleider *pl*.
sundial ['sʌndaiəl] *n* Sonnenuhr *f*.
sundry ['sʌndri] *pl adj* verschiedene,
diverse. **sundries** *pl n* Verschiedenes *neut*
sing.
sunflower ['sʌn,flauə] *n* Sonnenblume *f*.
sung [sʌŋ] *V* **sing.**
sun-glasses *pl n* Sonnenbrille *f sing.*
sunk [sʌŋk] *V* **sink.**
sunlight ['sʌnlait] *n* Sonnenlicht *neut.*
sunny ['sʌni] *adj* sonnig.
sunrise ['sʌnraiz] *n* Sonnenaufgang *m*.
sunset ['sʌnset] *n* Sonnenuntergang *m*.
sunshine ['sʌnʃain] *n* Sonnenschein *m*.
sunstroke ['sʌnstrouk] *n* Sonnenstich *m*.
sun-tan *n* (Sonnen)Bräune *f*.
super ['suɪpə] *adj* (*coll*) prima.
superannuation [,suɪpərənju'eiʃən] *n* (*contribution*) Altersversicherungsbeitrag *m*;
(*pension*) Pension *f*. **superannuated** *adj*
pensioniert.
superb [suɪ'pəːb] *adj* herrlich, prächtig.
supercilious [,suɪpə'siliəs] *adj* herablassend, hochmütig.
superficial [,suɪpə'fiʃəl] *adj* oberflächlich.
superfluous [suɪ'pəːfluəs] *adj* überflüssig.
superhuman [,suɪpə'hjuɪmən] *adj*
übermenschlich.
superimpose [,suɪpərim'pouz] *v* legen
(auf); (*add*) hinzufügen (zu). **superim-
posed** *adj* darübergelegt.
superintendent [,suɪpərin'tendənt] *n*
Inspektor *m*, Vorsteher *m*.
superior [suɪ'piəriə] *adj* überlegen;
(*higher*) höherliegend; (*quality*) hervorragend, erlesen. *n* Überlegene(r). **mother
superior** Oberin *f*. **superiority** *n*
Überlegenheit *f*.

superlative [su'pəːlətiv] *adj* unübertref-
flich, hervorragend. *n* Superlativ *m*.
supermarket ['suːpə,maːkit] *n* Supermarkt
m.
supernatural [,suːpə'natʃərəl] *adj*
übernatürlich. *n* das Übernatürliche
neut.
supersede [,suːpə'siːd] *v* ersetzen.
supersonic [,suːpə'sonik] *adj* Überschall-.
superstition [suːpə'stiʃən] *n* Aberglaube
m. **superstitious** *adj* abergläubig.
supervise ['suːpəvaiz] *v* beaufsichtigen,
kontrollieren. **supervision** *n* Beaufsichtigung *f*, Kontrolle *f*. **supervisor** *n* Aufseher *m*, Kontrolleur *m*. **supervisory** *adj*
Aufsichts-.
supper ['sʌpə] *n* Abendessen *neut*.
supple ['sʌpl] *adj* geschmeidig, biegsam.
suppleness *n* Geschmeidigkeit *f*.
supplement ['sʌpləmənt] *n* Ergänzung *f*;
(*newspaper*) Beilage *f*. **supplementary** *adj*
ergänzend, Zusatz-.
supply [sə'plai] *v* liefern, versorgen; (*a
need*) decken. *n* Lieferung *f*. (*stock*) Vorrat *m*; (*water, electricity, etc.*) Versorgung
f. **supply and demand** Angebot und
Nachfrage. **supplies** *pl n* Zufuhren *pl*.
supplier *n* Lieferant *m*.
support [sə'poːt] *v* tragen, stützen; (*withstand*) ertragen; (*family*) unterhalten;
(*cause*) befürworten. *n* (*tech*) Stütze *f*;
Unterstützung *f*. **supporter** *n* Anhänger
m.
suppose [sə'pouz] *v* annehmen, sich vorstellen; (*believe, think*) meinen. **supposed**
adj angenommen. **be supposed to** sollen.
supposition *n* Vermutung *f*, Annahme *f*.
suppository [sə'pozitri] *n* (Darm-)
Zäpfchen *neut*.
suppress [sə'pres] *v* unterdrücken; (*truth*)
verheimlichen. **suppression** *n* Unterdrückung *f*; Verheimlichung *f*.
supreme [su'priːm] *adj* oberst, höchst.
supremacy *n* Obergewalt *neut*.
surcharge ['səːtʃaːdʒ] *n* Zuschlag *m*.
sure [ʃuə] *adj* sicher, gewiß. *adv* (*coll*)
sicherlich. **for sure** gewiß. **make sure** sich
vergewissern. *you can be sure* du kannst
dich darauf verlassen. **sure-fire** *adj* todsicher. **surely** *adv* sicherlich. **sureness** *n*
Sicherheit *f*. **surety** *n* Bürge *f*.
surf [səːf] *n* Brandung *f*. *v* wellenreiten.
surfboard *n* Wellenreiterbrett *neut*. **surfer**
n Wellenreiter(in).
surface ['səːfis] *n* Oberfläche *f*. *adj* ober-

flächlich. *v* auftauchen. **surface mail**
gewöhnliche Post *f*.
surfeit ['səːfit] *n* Übermaß *neut*. *v* übersät-
tigen.
surge [səːdʒ] *n* (*water*) Woge *f*; (*emotion*)
Aufwallung *f*. *v* (*waves*) branden; (*crowd*)
(vorwärts)drängen.
surgeon ['səːdʒən] *n* Chirurg *m*. **surgery** *n*
Chirurgie *f*; (*consulting room*)
Sprechzimmer *neut*. **surgical** *adj*
chirurgisch.
surly ['səːli] *adj* verdrießlich, mürrisch.
surliness *n* Verdrießlichkeit *f*.
surmount [sə'maunt] *v* überwinden. **sur-
mountable** *adj* überwindlich.
surname ['səːneim] *n* Familienname *m*,
Zuname *m*.
surpass [sə'paːs] *v* übertreffen. **surpass
oneself** sich selbst übertreffen.
surplus ['səːpləs] *n* Überschuß *m*. *adj*
überschüssig.
surprise [sə'praiz] *v* überraschen. *n* Über-
raschung *f*. *adj* unerwartet. **surprised** *adj*
überrascht. **surprising** *adj* erstaunlich.
surrealism [sə'riəlizəm] *n* Surrealismus *m*.
surrealist *n* Surrealist(in). **surrealistic** *adj*
surrealistisch.
surrender [sə'rendə] *v* sich ergeben, kapitulieren; (*office*) aufgeben; (*prisoner*) ausliefern. *n* Kapitulation *f*; Auslieferung *f*.
surreptitious [,sʌrəp'tiʃəs] *adj* erschlichen;
(*stealthy*) heimlich.
surround [sə'raund] *v* umgeben, umringen. *n* Einfassung *f*. **surrounding** *adj*
umgebend. **surroundings** *pl n* Umgebung
f.
survey ['səːvei; *v* sə'vei] *n* Überblick *m*;
(*land, house, etc.*) Vermessung *f*; (*questionnaire*) Umfrage *f*. *v* überblicken;
vermessen. **surveyor** *n* Landmesser *m*.
survive [sə'vaiv] *v* (*outlive*) überleben;
(*continue to exist*) weiterleben,
weiterbestehen. **survival** *n* Überleben
neut. **survivor** *n* Überlebende(r).
susceptible [sə'septəbl] *adj* anfällig,
empfänglich (für). **susceptibility** *n* Anfäl-
ligkeit *f*, Empfänglichkeit *f*.
suspect [sə'spekt; *n* 'sʌspekt] *v* verdäch-
tigen; (*believe*) vermuten. *n* Verdachtsperson *f*. *adj* verdächtig.
suspend [sə'spend] *v* aufhängen; (*person*)
suspendieren; (*regulation*) (zeitweilig)
aufheben. **suspended** *adj* ausgesetzt, verschoben. **suspender** *n* Strumpfhalter *m*.
suspenders *pl n* (*for trousers*) Hosenträger

pl. **suspense** *n* Spannung *f.* **suspension** *n* (*mot*) Federung *f*; (*person*) Suspension *f.* **suspension bridge** Hängebrücke *f.* **suspension railway** Schwebebahn *f.*
suspicion [sə'spiʃən] *n* Verdacht *m*; (*mistrust*) Mißtrauen *neut*; (*trace*) Spur *f.* **suspicious** *adj* mißtrauisch; (*behaviour*) verdächtig. **suspiciousness** *n* Mißtrauen *neut.*
sustain [sə'stein] *v* (*suffer*) erleiden; (*family*) ernähren. **sustained** *adj* anhaltend. **sustenance** *n* Ernährung *f.*
suture ['suːtʃə] *n* Naht *f. v* vernähen.
swab [swob] *n* (*med*) Abstrich *m.*
swagger ['swagə] *v* (herum)stolzieren. **swaggering** *adj* stolzierend.
swallow¹ ['swolou] *v* schlucken. *n* Schluck *m.*
swallow² ['swolou] *n* (*bird*) Schwalbe *f.*
swam [swam] *V* swim.
swamp [swomp] *n* Sumpf *m*, Moor *neut. v* überschwemmen. **swampy** *adj* sumpfig.
swan [swon] *n* Schwan *m.*
swank [swaŋk] *v* protzen, prahlen. **swanky** *adj* protzig.
swap [swop] *v* (aus)tauschen. *n* Tausch *m.*
swarm [swoːm] *n* Schwarm *m. v* schwärmen.
swarthy ['swoːði] *adj* dunkelhäutig, schwärzlich.
swat [swot] *v* zerquetschen.
sway [swei] *v* schwanken, schaukeln. *n* Schwanken *neut*; (*power*) Macht *f*, Einfluß *m.*
*swear [sweə] *v* schwören; (*bad language*) fluchen. **swearword** *n* Fluch *m*, Fluchwort *neut.*
sweat [swet] *n* Schweiß *m. v* schwitzen. **sweater** *n* Pullover *m.* **sweaty** *adj* verschwitzt.
swede [swiːd] *n* Kohlrübe *f.*
Sweden ['swiːdn] *n* Schweden *neut.* **Swede** *n* Schwede *m*, Schwedin *f.* **Swedish** *adj* schwedisch.
*sweep [swiːp] *v* kehren, fegen; (*mines*) suchen. **sweep aside** beiseite schieben, abtun. **sweepstake** *n* Toto *neut. n* Schornsteinfeger *m.* **make a clean sweep** reinen Tisch machen. **sweeper** *n* Kehrer *m.* **sweeping** *adj* radikal, weitreichend. **sweepings** *pl* Kehricht *m sing.*
sweet [swiːt] *adj* süß; (*kind*) nett. **sweet corn** Mais *m.* **sweeten** *v* süßen. **sweetheart** *n* Schatz *m.* **sweet-tempered** *adj*

gutmütig. *n* Bonbon *m*; (*dessert*) Nachspeise *f.* **sweetshop** *n* Süßwarengeschäft *neut.* **sweetness** *n* Süßigkeit *f*; (*person*) Lieblichkeit *f.*
*swell [swel] *v* (auf)schwellen. *n* (*sea*) Wellengang *m. adj* (*coll*) prima. **swelling** *n* (*med*) Schwellung *f.*
swelter ['sweltə] *v* vor Hitze kochen. **sweltering** *adj* schwül.
swept [swept] *V* sweep.
swerve [swəːv] *v* ausscheren.
swift [swift] *n* (*zool*) Segler *m. adj* schnell, rasch. **swift-footed** *adj* schnellfüßig. **swiftness** *n* Schnelligkeit *f.*
swill [swil] *n* Schweinefutter *neut. v* spülen.
*swim [swim] *v* schwimmen. **my head is swimming** mir ist schwindlig. *n* Schwimmen *neut*, Bad *neut.* **in the swim** auf dem laufenden. **swimmer** *n* Schwimmer(in). **swimming** *n* Schwimmen *neut.* **swimming pool** Schwimmbad *neut.*
swindle ['swindl] *v* betrügen. *n* Schwindel *m*, Betrug *m.* **swindler** *n* Schwindler(in).
swine [swain] *n* (*pl* swine) Schwein *neut.*
*swing [swiŋ] *v* schwingen. *n* (*child's*) Schaukel *f.* **swing a door open/shut** eine Tür auf/zustoßen.
swipe [swaip] *v* hauen; (*coll: steal*) klauen. *n* Hieb *m.*
swirl [swəːl] *v* wirbeln. *n* Wirbel *m.*
swish [swiʃ] *v* rascheln. *n* Rascheln *neut.*
Swiss [swis] *n* Schweizer(in). *adj* schweizerisch. **Swiss German** Schweizerdeutsch *neut.*
switch [switʃ] *n* Schalter *m*; (*change*) Wechsel *m*; (*whip*) Rute *f.* **on/off-switch** *n* Ein/Ausschalter *m. v* (*change*) wechseln. **switchboard** *n* (*phone*) Vermittlung *f.* **switch on** einschalten. **switch off** ausschalten. **switch over to** übergehen zu.
Switzerland ['switsələnd] *n* die Schweiz *f.*
swivel ['swivl] *v* (sich) drehen.
swollen ['swoulən] *V* swell. *adj* geschwollen. **swollen-headed** *adj* eingebildet, aufgeblasen.
swoop [swuːp] *v* niederschießen, sich stürzen (auf).
swop [swop] *V* swap.
sword [soːd] *n* Schwert *neut.* **swordfish** *n* Schwertfisch *m.* **swordsman** *n* Fechter *m.*
swore [swoː] *V* swear.
sworn [swoːn] *V* swear. *adj* vereidigt; (*enemy*) geschworen.

swot [swot] *v* (*coll*) büffeln, pauken. *n* Büffler *m*.

swum [swʌm] *V* swim.

swung [swʌŋ] *V* swing.

sycamore ['sikəmɔɪ] *n* Sykamore *f*.

syllable ['siləbl] *n* Silbe *f*.

syllabus ['siləbəs] *n* Lehrplan *m*.

symbol ['simbl] *n* Sinnbild *neut*, Symbol *neut*. **symbolic** *adj* sinnbildlich, symbolisch (für). **symbolism** *n* Symbolik *f*. **symbolize** *v* symbolisieren.

symmetry ['simitri] *n* Symmetrie *f*. **symmetrical** *adj* symmetrisch.

sympathy ['simpəθi] *n* Mitleid *neut*, Mitgefühl *neut*. **sympathetic** *adj* mitleidend.

symphony ['simfəni] *n* Sinfonie *f*. **symphonic** *adj* sinfonisch.

symposium [sim'pouziəm] *n* Symposion *neut*.

symptom ['simptəm] *n* Symptom *neut*. **symptomatic** *adj* symptomatisch.

synagogue ['sinəgog] *n* Synagoge *f*.

synchromesh ['siŋkroumeʃ] *n* Synchrongetriebe *neut*.

synchronize ['siŋkrənaiz] *v* synchronisieren.

syndicate ['sindikit] *n* Syndikat *neut*. **syndication** *n* Syndikatsbildung *f*.

syndrome ['sindroum] *n* (*med*) Syndrom *neut*.

synonym ['sinənim] *n* Synonym *neut*. **synonymous** *adj* synonym.

synopsis [si'nopsis] *n* (*pl* -ses) Synopse *f*, Zusammenfassung *f*. **synoptic** *adj* synoptisch.

syntax ['sintaks] *n* Syntax *f*. **syntactic** *adj* syntaktisch.

synthesis ['sinθisis] *n* (*pl* -ses) Synthese *f*. **synthetic** *adj* synthetisch, Kunst-.

syphilis ['sifilis] *n* Syphilis *f*.

syringe [si'rindʒ] *n* Spritze *f*.

syrup ['sirəp] *n* Sirup *m*, Zuckersaft *m*. **syrupy** *adj* sirupartig.

system ['sistəm] *n* System *neut*; (*geol*) Formation *f*. **systematic** *adj* systematisch.

T

tab [tab] *n* (*in garment*) Aufhänger *m*; (*label*) Etikett *neut*; (*coll: bill*) Rechnung *f*.

table ['teibl] *n* Tisch *m*; (*math, etc.*) Tabelle *f*. **table of contents** Inhaltsverzeichnis *neut*. **table-cloth** *n* Tischtuch *neut*. **table-spoon** *n* Eßlöffel *m*.

table d'hôte [taɪblə'dout] *n* Table d'hôte *f*.

tablet ['tablit] *n* Tablette *f*; (*stone*) Tafel *f*.

taboo [ta'buɪ] *adj* tabu. *n* Tabu *neut*.

tacit ['tasit] *adj* stillschweigend. **taciturn** *adj* schweigsam.

tack [tak] *n* Reißnagel *m*; (*naut*) Lavieren *neut*; (*sewing*) Heftstich *m*. *v* lavieren; heften. **tacky** *adj* klebrig.

tackle ['takl] *n* (*naut*) Takel *neut*; (*equipment, etc.*) Zeug *neut*, Ausrüstung *f*. *v* (*sport*) angreifen; (*person*) angehen; (*problem*) anpacken.

tact [tàkt] *n* Takt *m*. **tactful** *adj* taktvoll. **tactless** *adj* taktlos.

tactics ['taktiks] *pl n* Taktik *f*. **tactical** *adj* taktisch.

tadpole ['tadpoul] *n* Kaulquappe *f*.

taffeta ['tafitə] *n* Taft *m*.

tag [tag] *n* (*loop*) Anhänger *m*, (*label*) Etikett *neut*. **price-tag** Preiszettel *m*.

tail [teil] *n* Schwanz *m*. *v* (*coll: follow*) beschatten. **tail end** Schluß *m*. **tailcoat** *n* Frack *m*. **tail-lamp** *n* Schlußlicht *neut*.

tailor ['teilə] *n* Schneider *m*. *v* schneidern. **tailor-made** *adj* nach Maß angefertigt.

taint [teint] *n* Fleck *m*, Makel *m*. *v* verderben.

*take [teik] *v* nehmen; (*something somewhere*) bringen; (*prisoner*) fassen; (*photo, exam*) machen. *how long does it take?* wie lange dauert es? wie lange braucht man? **take aback** verblüffen. **take along** mitnehmen. **take away** wegnehmen; (*subtract*) abziehen. **take back** (*retract*) zurücknehmen. **take down** (*on paper*) aufschreiben. **take off** (*clothes*) ausziehen; (*mimic*) nachäffen. **take over** übernehmen. **take up** aufnehmen.

taken ['teikn] *V* take.

talcum powder ['talkəm] *n* Talkumpuder *m*.

tale [teil] *n* Erzählung *f*. **old wives' tale** Ammenmärchen *neut*.

talent ['talənt] *n* Talent *neut*, Begabung *f*. **talented** *adj* begabt.

talk [tɔːk] *n* Rede *neut*; (*conversation*) Gespräch *neut*; (*chat*) Unterhaltung *f*; (*lecture*) Vortrag *m*. *v* reden, sprechen. **talk over** besprechen. **talkative** *adj* geschwätzig.

tall [tɔːl] *adj* groß, hoch. **tallness** *n* Größe, Höhe *f*. **tall story** unglaubliche Geschichte *f*.

tally ['tali] *v* (*coll*) übereinstimmen (mit), entsprechen (+ *dat*).

talon ['talən] *n* Klaue *f*.

tambourine [tambə'riːn] *n* Tamburin *neut*.

tame [teim] *adj* zahm, gezähmt. *v* zähmen.

tamper ['tampə] *v* herumpfuschen (an), sich einmishcen (in).

tampon ['tampon] *n* Tampon *m*.

tan [tan] *v* gerben; (*skin*) sich braünen. *n* (*colour*) Gelbbraun *neut*; (*skin*) Sonnenbräunung *f*.

tandem ['tandəm] *n* Tandem *neut*.

tangent ['tandʒənt] *n* Tangente *f*.

tangerine [tandʒə'riːn] *n* Mandarine *f*.

tangible ['tandʒəbl] *adj* greifbar.

tangle ['taŋgl] *n* Gewirr *neut*. *v* verwickeln.

tank [taŋk] *n* Tank *m*, Behälter *m*; (*mil*) Panzer *m*. **tanker** *n* (*ship*) Tanker *m*.

tankard ['taŋkəd] *n* Krug *m*.

tantalize ['tantəlaiz] *v* quälen.

tantamount ['tantəmaunt] *adj* **be tantamount to** gleichkommen (+ *dat*).

tantrum ['tantrəm] *n* Wutanfall *m*.

tap¹ [tap] *v* leicht schlagen, klopfen. *n* leichter Schlag *m*. **tap-dance** *n* Steptanz *m*.

tap² [tap] *n* Hahn *m*. *v* anzapfen. **taproom** *n* Schankstube *f*.

tape [teip] *n* Band *neut*, Streifen *m*; (*recording*) Tonband *neut*; (*sport*) Zielband *m*. *v* heften. **adhesive tape** Klebestreifen. **tape measure** *n* Metermaß *m*. **tape-recorder** *n* Tonbandgerät *neut*. **tape-recording** *n* Bandaufnahme *f*.

taper ['teipə] *n* (dünne) Wachskerze *f*. *v* spitz zulaufen. **tapered** *adj* spitz (zulaufend).

tapestry ['tapəstri] *n* Wandteppich *m*.

tapioca [tapi'oukə] *n* Tapioka *f*.

tar [taɪ] *n* Teer *m*.

tarantula [tə'rantjulə] *n* Tarantel *f*.

target ['taɪgit] *n* (*sport*) Zielscheibe *f*; (*ambition*) Ziel *neut*.

tariff ['tarif] *n* (*imports*) Zolltarif *m*; (*price list*) Preisverzeichnis *neut*.

tarmac ® ['taɪmak] *n* Asphalt *m*; (*runway*) Rollbahn *f*.

tarnish ['taɪniʃ] *v* (*metal*) anlaufen; (*reputation*) beflecken.

tarpaulin [taɪ'pɔːlin] *n* Persenning *f*.

tarragon ['tarəgən] *n* Estragon *m*.

tart¹ [taɪt] *n* Torte *f*; (*prostitute*) Dirne *f*.

tart² [taɪt] *adj* sauer, herb.

tartan ['taɪtən] *n* Tartan *m*, Schottenmuster *neut*.

tartar ['taɪtə] *n* Weinstein *m*; (*teeth*) Zahnstein *m*.

task [taɪsk] *n* Aufgabe *f*. **take to task** zur Rede stellen.

tassel ['tasəl] *n* Quaste *f*.

taste [teist] *n* Geschmack *neut*; (*sample*) Kostprobe *f*; (*liking*) Neigung *f*. *v* schmecken. **tasteful** *adj* geschmackvoll. **tasteless** *adj* geschmacklos. **tasty** *adj* schmackhaft.

tattered ['tatəd] *adj* zerrissen.

tattoo [tə'tuɪ] *n* Tätowierung *f*. *v* tätowieren.

taught [tɔːt] *V* **teach**.

taunt [tɔːnt] *v* sticheln, verspotten. *n* Stichelei *f*.

Taurus ['tɔːrəs] *n* Stier *m*.

taut [tɔːt] *adj* stramm, straff.

tavern ['tavən] *n* Taverne *f*, Kneipe *f*.

tax [taks] *n* Steuer *f*. **tax-free** *adj* steuerfrei. **taxpayer** *n* Steuerzahler(in). **tax return** *n* Steuererklärung *f*. *v* besteuern; (*test*) anstrengen. **taxable** *adj* steuerpflichtig.

taxi ['taksi] *n* Taxi *neut*. **taxi-driver** *n* Taxifahrer *m*.

tea [tiɪ] *n* Tee *m*; (*meal*) Abendbrot *neut*. **tea-cloth** *n* Geschirrtuch *neut*. **teacup** *n* Teetasse *f*. **teapot** *n* Teekanne *f*. **teaspoon** *n* Teelöffel *m*.

*teach [tiɪtʃ] *v* lehren; (*animals*) dressieren. **teacher** *n* Lehrer(in). **teaching** *n* Unterricht *m*. **teachings** *pl* Lehre *f sing*.

teak [tiɪk] *n* Teakholz *neut*.

team [tiɪm] *n* (*sport*) Mannschaft *f*; (*horses*) Gespann *neut*. *v* **team up** sich zusammentun (mit). **teamwork** *n* Zusammenarbeit *f*.

*tear¹ [teə] *v* reißen, zerreißen. *n* Riß *m*. **tear away** wegreißen. **tear oneself away** sich losreißen.

tear² [tiə] *n* Träne *f*. **tear gas** *n* Tränengas *neut*. **tearful** *adj* weinerlich.

tease [tiːz] v necken.
teat [tiːt] n (bottle) Sauger m; (anat) Brustwarze f; (zool) Zitze f.
technical ['teknikəl] adj technisch. **technician** n Techniker m. **technique** n Technik f. **technological** adj technologisch. **technology** n Technologie f.
tedious ['tiːdiəs] adj langweilig. **tedium** n Langeweile f.
tee [tiː] n (golf) Abschlagstelle f.
teem [tiːm] v wimmeln (von).
teenage ['tiːneidʒ] adj Jugend-. **teenager** n Teenager m.
teeth [tiːθ] V tooth.
teethe [tiːð] v zahnen. **teething troubles** (fig) Kinderkrankheiten pl.
teetotal [tiː'toutl] adj abstinent. **teetotaller** n Abstinenzler(in).
telecommunications [ˌtelikəmjuːni-'keiʃənz] pl n Fernmeldewesen neut sing.
telegram ['teligram] n Telegramm neut. **by telegram** telegraphisch.
telegraph ['teligraɪf] n Telegraph m. v telegraphieren. **telegraphic** adj telegraphisch.
telepathy [tə'lepəθi] n Telepathie f, Gedankenübertragung f. **telepathic** adj telepathisch.
telephone ['telifoun] n Fernsprecher m, Telefon neut. v anrufen, telefonieren. **by telephone** telefonisch. **telephone booth** Telefonzelle f. **telephone call** Telefongespräch neut, Anruf m. **telephone directory** Telefonbuch neut. **telephone exchange** (Telefon)Zentrale f. **telephonist** n Telefonist(in).
telescope ['teliskoup] n Fernrohr neut, Teleskop neut. **telescopic** adj teleskopisch.
television ['teliviʒən] n Fernsehen neut. **televize** v (im Fernsehen) übertragen. **on television** im Fernsehen.
telex ['teleks] n Fernschreiber m, Telex neut. v (durch Telex) übertragen.
***tell** [tel] v sagen; (story) erzählen; (recognize) erkennen. **telltale** n Klatschbase f. **tell the truth** die Wahrheit sagen. **teller** n Kassierer m. **telling** adj wirkungsvoll.
temper ['tempə] n Wut f, Zorn m; (mood) Laune f. **lose one's temper** in Wut geraten. v mildern; (steel) härten. **temperament** n Temperament neut. **temperamental** adj temperamentvoll. **temperance** n

Mäßigkeit f. **temperate** adj maßvoll; (climate) gemäßigt. **tempered** adj gehärtet.
temperature ['temprətʃə] n Temperatur f. **have a temperature** Fieber haben. **take (a person's) temperature** die Temperatur messen (+ dat).
tempestuous [tem'pestjuəs] adj stürmisch.
temple¹ ['templ] n (arch) Tempel m.
temple² ['templ] n (anat) Schläfe f.
tempo ['tempou] n Tempo neut.
temporary ['tempərəri] adj provisorisch, vorläufig.
tempt [tempt] v verlocken. **temptation** n Verlockung f. **tempting** adj verlockend; (food) appetitanregend.
ten [ten] adj zehn. n Zehn f. **tenth** adj zehnt; n Zehntel neut.
tenable ['tenəbl] adj haltbar.
tenacious [tə'neiʃəs] adj zäh. **tenacity** n Zähigkeit f.
tenant ['tenənt] n Mieter m. **tenancy** n Mietverhältnis neut.
tend¹ [tend] v (be inclined) neigen (zu), eine Tendenz haben (zu).
tend² [tend] v (care for) bedienen, sich kümmern um.
tendency ['tendənsi] n Tendenz f.
tender¹ ['tendə] adj zart; (affectionate) zärtlich. **tender-hearted** adj weichherzig. **tenderloin** n Filet neut. **tenderness** n Zartheit f; Zärtlichkeit f.
tender² ['tendə] v anbieten; (comm) ein Angebot machen. n Angebot neut.
tendon ['tendən] n Sehne f.
tendril ['tendril] n Ranke f.
tenement ['tenəmənt] n Mietshaus neut.
tennis ['tenis] n Tennis neut. **tennis ball** Tennisball m. **tennis court** Tennisplatz m. **tennis racket** (Tennis)Schläger m.
tenor ['tenə] n Tenor m. adj Tenor-.
tense¹ [tens] adj gespannt. v (sich) straffen. **tensile** adj dehnbar. **tension** n Spannung f.
tense² [tens] n (gramm) Zeitform f, Tempus neut.
tent [tent] n Zelt neut.
tentacle ['tentəkl] n Tentakel m, Fühler m; (octupus) Fangarm m.
tentative ['tentətiv] adj versuchend, Versuchs-; (temporary) vorläufig. **tentatively** adv versuchsweise.
tenterhooks ['tentəhuks] n **be on tenterhooks** wie auf heißen Kohlen sitzen.
tenuous ['tenjuəs] adj dünn; (argument) schwach.

tepid ['tepid] *adj* lauwarm. **tepidness** *n* Lauheit *f.*
term [təːm] *n* (*expression*) Ausdruck *m*; (*period of time*) Frist *f*; (*academic, two per year*) Semester *neut*; (*academic, three per year*) Trimester *neut*. **end of term** (*school*) Schulschluß *m.* **terms** *pl* Bedingungen *pl.* **be on good terms with** gut auskommen mit. **come to terms with** sich abfinden mit.
terminal ['təːminəl] *adj* End-, Schluß-; (*med*) unheilbar. *n* Terminal *neut.*
terminate ['təːmineit] *v* beendigen; (*contract*) kündigen. **termination** *n* Ende *neut*, Schluß *m.*
terminology [təːmi'nolədʒi] *n* Terminologie *f.*
terminus ['təːminəs] *n* Endstation *f.*
terrace ['terəs] *n* Terrasse *f*; (*houses*) Häuserreihe *f.*
terrain [tə'rein] *n* Terrain *neut*, Gelände *neut.*
terrestrial [tə'restriəl] *adj* irdisch.
terrible ['terəbl] *adj* schrecklich, furchtbar. **terribleness** *n* Schrecklichkeit *f*, Fürchterlichkeit *f.*
terrier ['teriə] *n* Terrier *m.*
terrify ['terifai] *v* erschrecken. **terrific** *adj* (*coll*) klasse, unwahrscheinlich. **terrified** *adj* erschrocken. **be terrified of** sich fürchten vor.
territory ['teritəri] *n* Gebiet *neut*, Territorium *neut*; (*pol*) Staatsgebiet *neut.* **territorial waters** Hoheitsgewässer *pl.*
terror ['terə] *n* Schrecken *m*, Entsetzen *neut*; (*pol*) Terror *m.* **terrorism** *n* Terrorismus *m.* **terrorist** *n* Terrorist(in); *adj* terroristisch.
test [test] *n* Versuch *m*, Probe *f*; (*examination*) Prüfung *f*. *v* prüfen, erproben. **test-case** *n* Präzedensfall *m.*
testament ['testəmənt] *n* Testament *neut.*
testicle ['testikl] *n* Hoden *m.*
testify ['testifai] *v* bezeugen.
testimony ['testiməni] *n* Zeugnis *neut.*
testimonial *n* Zeugnis *neut*, Empfehlungsschreiben *m.*
tetanus ['tetənəs] *n* Wundstarrkrampf *m*, Tetanus *m.*
tether ['teðə] *n* Haltestrick *m.* **be at the end of one's tether** mit seiner Geduld am Ende sein. *v* anbinden.
text [tekst] *n* Text *m.* **textbook** *n* Lehrbuch *neut.* **textual** *adj* textlich.

textile ['tekstail] *n* Gewebe *neut*, Faserstoff *m.* **textiles** *pl* Textilien *pl.*
texture ['tekstjuə] *n* Textur *f.*
than [ðən] *conj* als.
thank [θaŋk] *v* danken (+ *dat*), sich bedanken bei. **thanks** *pl n* Dank *m sing. interj* danke! **thankful** *adj* dankbar. **thankless** *adj* undankbar. **thank you!** danke! **many thanks!** dankeschön! **thank goodness!** Gott sei Dank!
that [ðat] *adj* der, die, das; jener, jene, jenes. *pron* das; (*who, which*) der, die, das, welch. **that is** (i.e.) das heißt (d.h.). **that's it!** so ist es! **like that** so. **that which** das, was. **the man that I saw** der Mann, den ich sah. **in order that** damit. *conj* daß. *adv* (*coll*) so, dermaßen.
thatch [θatʃ] *n* Dachstroh *neut.* **thatched roof** Strohdach *neut.*
thaw [θoi] *v* tauen. *n* Tauwetter *neut.*
the [ðə] *art* der, die, das *sing*; die *pl.*
theatre ['θiətə] *n* Theater *neut*; (*operating*) Operationssaal *m.* **theatre-goer** *n* Theaterbesucher(in). **theatrical** *adj* theatralisch.
theft [θeft] *n* Diebstahl *m.*
their [ðeə] *poss adj* ihr, ihre, ihr. **theirs** *pron* der/die/das ihrige. **a friend of theirs** ein Freund von ihnen.
them [ðem] *pron* (*acc*) sie; (*dat*) ihnen.
theme [θiːm] *n* Thema *neut.*
then [ðen] *adv* (*at that time*) damals; (*next*) dann, darauf. *conj* also. *adj* damalig.
theology [θi'olədʒi] *n* Theologie *f.* **theologian** *n* Theologe *m.* **theological** *adj* theologisch.
theorem ['θiərəm] *n* Theorem *m.*
theory ['θiəri] *n* Theorie *f.* **theoretical** *adj* theoretisch. **theorist** *n* Theoretiker(in). **theorize** *v* theoretisieren.
therapy ['θerəpi] *n* Therapie *f*, Behandlung *f.* **therapeutic** *adj* therapeutisch. **therapist** *n* Therapeut(in).
there [ðeə] *adv* dort, da; (*to that place*) dahin, dorthin. **here and there** hier und da. **over there** da drüben. **thereabouts** *adv* so ungefähr. **thereafter** *adv* danach. **there and back** hin und zurück. **there are** es sind, es gibt. **there is** es ist, es gibt. **up there** da oben. *interj* na!
thermal ['θəːməl] *adj* thermal, Wärme-. *n* (*aero*) Thermik *f.*
thermodynamics [θəːmoudai'namiks] *n* Thermodynamik *f.*

thermometer [θə'mɒmɪtə] n Thermometer neut.

thermonuclear [θɜːmou'njuklɪə] adj thermonuklear.

thermos ® ['θɜːməs] n Thermosflasche f.

thermostat ['θɜːməstat] n Thermostat m.

these [ðiːz] pl adj, pron diese. **one of these days** eines Tages. **these are** dies sind.

thesis ['θiːsɪs] n (pl -ses) These f, Satz m; (university) Dissertation f.

they [ðei] pl pron sie. **they say** man sagt.

thick [θik] adj dick; (hair, woods) dicht; (coll: stupid) dumm. **thicken** v dick machen or werden, (sich) verdicken; (cookery) legieren. **thickness** n Dicke f, Stärke f. **thick-skinned** adj (fig) dickfellig.

thief [θiːf] n (pl thieves) Dieb(in). **thieve** v stehlen. **thievish** adj diebisch.

thigh [θai] n (Ober)Schenkel m. **thighbone** n Schenkelknochen m.

thimble ['θimbl] n Fingerhut m.

thin [θin] adj dünn; (person) mager; (weak) schwach. v dünn machen or werden; (cookery) verdünnen. **thinner** n Verdünner m. **thinness** n Dünne f, Magerkeit f. **thin-skinned** adj empfindlich.

thing [θiŋ] n Ding neut. **things** pl Sachen pl, Zeug neut sing. **how are things?** wie geht es?

*think [θiŋk] v denken; (hold opinion) denken, meinen. **think about** denken an; (consider) überlegen, nachdenken über. **think of** (doing) daran denken, vorhaben. **what do you think of it?** was halten sie davon? **I think so** ich glaube schon. **thinker** n Denker(in). **thinking** n (opinion) Meinung f.

third [θɜːd] adj dritt. n Drittel neut. **third party** Dritte(r). **third-party insurance** Haftpflichtversicherung f. **third-rate** adj (coll) minderwertig.

thirst [θɜːst] n Durst (nach) m. **die of thirst** verdursten. v dursten. **thirsty** adj durstig. **be thirsty** Durst haben.

thirteen [θɜː'tiːn] adj dreizehn. n Dreizehn f. **thirteenth** adj dreizehnt.

thirty ['θɜːti] adj dreißig. n Dreißig f. **thirtieth** adj dreißigst.

this [ðis] adj (pl these) dieser, diese, dieses. pron dies, das. **like this** so, folgendermaßen. **this morning** heute früh. **this year** dieses Jahr.

thistle ['θisl] n Distel f.

thorn [θɔːn] n Dorn m. **thorny** adj dornig.

thorough ['θʌrə] adj gründlich; (person) genau, sorgfältig. **thoroughbred** n Vollblut neut. adj Vollblut-. **thoroughfare** n Durchgangsstraße f. **thoroughness** n Gründlichkeit f.

those [ðouz] pl adj, pron jene.

though [ðou] conj obwohl, obgleich. adv aber, dennoch, jedoch. **as though** als ob. **even though** wenn ... auch.

thought [θɔːt] V think. n Gedanke m; (thinking) Denken neut; (reflection) Überlegung f. **thoughtful** adj gedankenvoll; (considerate) rücksichtsvoll. **thoughtless** adj gedankenlos; rücksichtslos.

thousand ['θauzənd] adj tausend. n Tausend neut. **thousandth** adj tausendst; n Tausendstel neut.

thrash [θraʃ] v verdreschen; (defeat) heftig schlagen. **thrash about** hin und her schlagen. **thrashing** n Prügel pl, Dresche f.

thread [θred] n Faden m; (screw) Gewinde neut. **threadbare** adj fadenscheinig. v (needle) einfädeln; (beads) einreihen. **thread one's way through** sich winden durch.

threat [θret] n Drohung f; (danger) Gefahr f, Bedrohung f. **threaten** v bedrohen; (endanger) gefährden. **threatening** adj drohend.

three [θriː] adj drei. n Drei f. **three-cornered** dreieckig. **three-dimensional** adj dreidimensional. **threefold** adv, adj dreifach. **three-ply** adj dreifach. **three-quarters of an hour** eine Dreiviertelstunde f.

thresh [θreʃ] v dreschen.

threshold ['θreʃould] n (Tür)Schwelle f.

threw [θruː] V throw.

thrift [θrift] n Sparsamkeit f. **thrifty** adj sparsam.

thrill [θril] v erregen, begeistern. n Zittern neut, Erregung f. **thriller** n Reißer m. **thrilling** adj sensationell.

thrive [θraiv] v gedeihen. **thriving** adj blühend.

throat [θrout] n Kehle f, Rachen m; (neck) Hals m. **throaty** adj rauh.

throb [θrob] v pulsieren, klopfen. n Pulsieren neut.

thrombosis [θrom'bousis] n Thrombose f.

throne [θroun] *n* Thron *m.*
throng [θroŋ] *n* Gedränge *neut. v* sich
scharen.
throttle ['θrotl] *v* erwürgen. *n* (*tech*) Dros-
selklappe *f.* **open the throttle** (*mot*) Gas
geben.
through [θruː] *prep, adv* durch. **fall
through** (*coll*) ins Wasser fallen. **get
through** fertig sein mit; (*exam*) bestehen.
go through with zu Ende führen. **wet
through** durchnäßt. **throughout** *adv*
(*place*) überall in. **throughout the night**
die ganze Nacht hindurch. *adj* (*ticket,
train*) durchgehend.
***throw** [θrou] *v* werfen. **throw away**
wegwerfen; (*chance*) verpassen. **throw-
back** *n* Rückkehr *f.* **throw up** (*coll*) kotz-
en. **throw-in** (*sport*) Einwurf *m. n* Wurf
m.
thrush [θrʌʃ] *n* Drossel *f.*
***thrust** [θrʌst] *v* stecken, schieben. *n* Stoß
m, Hieb *m;* (*tech*) Schubkraft *f.*
thud [θʌd] *n* (dumpfer) Schlag *m. v*
dumpf schlagen.
thumb [θʌm] *n* Daumen *m. v* **thumb
through** durchblättern. **thumb a lift** per
Anhalter fahren. **thumbtack** Reißnagel
m.
thump [θʌmp] *n* Puff *m,* Schlag *m. v* puffen.
thunder ['θʌndə] *n* Donner *m. v* donnern.
thunderbolt *n* Blitz *m.* **thunderclap** *n*
Donnerschlag *m.* **thunderstorm** *n* Gewitter *neut.* **thunderstruck** *adj* wie vom Blitz
getroffen.
Thursday ['θəːzdi] *n* Donnerstag *m.* **on
Thursdays** donnerstags.
thus [ðʌs] *adv* so, folgendermaßen. **thus
far** bis jetzt, soweit.
thwart [θwoːt] *v* (*person*) entgegenarbeiten
(+ *dat*); (*plan*) vereiteln.
thyme [taim] *n* Thymian *m.*
thyroid ['θairoid] *n* Schilddrüse *f. adj*
Schilddrüsen-.
tiara [ti'aːrə] *n* Tiara *f.*
tick¹ [tik] *v* (*clock*) ticken; (*with pen*)
abhaken. **tick over** (*mot*) im Leerlauf
sein. *n* Ticken *neut;* Häkchen *neut.*
tick² [tik] *n* (*parasite*) Zecke *f.*
ticket ['tikit] *n* (*label*) Etikett *neut,* Zettel
m; (*travel*) Fahrkarte *f,* Fahrschein *m;*
(*theatre*) Karte *f.* **ticket-collector** *n*
Schaffner *m.* **ticket-office** *n* Fahrkartenschalter *m.*

tickle ['tikl] *v* kitzeln; (*fig*) amüsieren. *n*
Kitzel *m,* Juckreiz *m.* **ticklish** *adj* kitzlig.
tide [taid] *n* Gezeiten *pl,* Ebbe und Flut *f.*
high tide Flut *f,* Hochwasser *neut.* **low
tide** Ebbe *f,* Niedrigwasser *neut.* **tidal** *adj*
Gezeiten-, Flut-.
tidy ['taidi] *adj* ordentlich, sauber. *v* in
Ordnung bringen. **tidy up** aufräumen.
tie [tai] *v* (an)binden, festbinden; (*knot*)
machen; (*necktie*) binden. **tie in with**
übereinstimmen mit. **tie up** verbinden.
be tied up nicht abkömmlich sein. *n*
(*necktie*) Schlips *m,* Krawatte *m;* (*sport*)
Unentschieden *neut;* (*obligation*) Verpflichtung *f,* Last *f.*
tier [tiə] *n* Reihe *f,* Rang *m.*
tiger ['taigə] *n* Tiger *m.* **tigress** *n* Tigerin
f.
tight [tait] *v* fest, stramm; (*clothes*) eng,
knapp; (*watertight, etc.*) dicht; (*in short
supply*) knapp; (*coll: mean*) geizig. **tight-
en** *v* festziehen, straffen. **tight-fisted** *adj*
geizig. **tights** *pl n* Strumpfhose *f sing. adv*
hold tight festhalten. **sit tight** sitzen-
bleiben.
tile [tail] *n* (*roof*) (Dach)Ziegel *m;* (*wall*)
Fliese *f.*
till¹ [til] *V* until.
till² [til] *n* (*in shop*) Kasse *f.*
till³ [til] *v* (*land*) bebauen, pflügen.
tiller ['tilə] *n* (*naut*) (Ruder)Pinne *f.*
tilt [tilt] *v* kippen, (sich) neigen. *n*
Neigung *f,* Schräglage *f.* **tilt over** umkippen.
timber ['timbə] *n* (Bau)Holz *neut.* **timber
forest** Hochwald *m.*
time [taim] *n* Zeit *f;* (*occasion*) Mal *neut;*
(*era*) Zeitalter *neut,* (*music*) Takt *m.* **at all
times** stets. **at this time** zu dieser Zeit.
behind the times rückständig. **have a
good time** sich gut unterhalten. **in good
time** rechtzeitig. **time limit** *n* Frist *f.*
timepiece *n* Uhr *f.* **timetable** *n* (*bus, train*)
Fahrplan *m;* (*school*) Stundenplan *m.*
what time is it? wieviel Uhr ist es? *or* wie
spät ist es? *v* (mit der Uhr) messen, zeitlich abstimmen. **timeless** *adj* ewig. **timely**
adj rechtzeitig.
timid ['timid] *adj* ängstlich, schüchtern.
timidity *n* Ängstlichkeit *f,* Schüchternheit
f.
tin [tin] *n* Zinn *neut;* (*can*) Dose *f,*
Büchse *f. adj* zinnern, Zinn-. **tin can**
Blechdose *f.* **tin foil** *n* Stanniol *neut.* **tin-
opener** *n* Dosenöffner *m.*

tool

tinge [tindʒ] *v* (leicht) färben. *n* Färbung *f*; (*fig*) Anstrich *m*.

tingle ['tiŋgl] *v* prickeln, kribbeln. *n* Prickeln *neut*.

tinker ['tiŋkə] *n* Kesselflicker *m*. *v* **tinker with** herumbasteln an.

tinkle ['tiŋkl] *v* klingeln. *n* Klingeln *neut*, Geklingel *neut*.

tinsel ['tinsəl] *n* Lametta *neut*.

tint [tint] *n* Farbton *m*. *v* tönen, leicht färben.

tiny ['taini] *adj* winzig.

tip¹ [tip] *n* (*sharp end*) Spitze *f*; (*summit*) Gipfel *m*. **tipped** *adj* (*cigarette*) Filter-. **on tiptoe** auf den Zehenspitzen.

tip² [tip] *n* (*for rubbish*) (Müll)Abladeplatz *m*. *v* kippen. **tip over** umkippen.

tip³ [tip] *n* (*gratuity*) Trinkgeld *neut*; (*hint*) Wink *m*, Tip *m*. *v* ein Trinkgeld geben (+ *dat*); einen Tip geben (+ *dat*). **tip off** *n* rechtzeitiger Wink *m*.

tipsy ['tipsi] *adj* (*coll*) beschwipst.

tire¹ ['taiə] *v* ermüden; (*become tired*) müde werden. **tire out** erschöpfen. **tired** *adj* müde. **tiredness** *n* Müdigkeit *f*. **tireless** *adj* unermüdlich. **tiresome** *adj* lästig.

tire² ['taiə] (*US*) *V* tyre.

tissue ['tiʃuɪ] *n* Gewebe *neut*; (*paper handkerchief*) Papiertaschentuch *neut*. **tissue paper** *n* Seidenpapier *neut*.

tit [tit] *n* (*bird*) Meise *f*.

title ['taitl] *n* Titel *m*; (*right*) Rechtstitel *m*. **titled** *adj* betitelt. **title-deed** Eigentumsurkunde *f*. **title-holder** *n* (*sport*) Titelverteidiger(in). **title-role** Titelrolle *f*.

to [tu] *prep* zu; (*motion, travel*) nach; (*time of day*) vor; (*in order to*) um zu. *adv* (*shut*) zu, geschlossen. **to and fro** auf und ab. *fix to the wall* an die Wand befestigen. *go to bed/the movies/school* ins Bett/ins Kino/in die Schule gehen. *go to Berlin* nach Berlin fahren. *I gave it to him* ich gab es ihm. *ten to one* (*o'clock*) zehn vor eins; (*odds*) zehn gegen eins. **to-do** *n* Getue *neut*.

toad [toud] *n* Kröte *f*. **toadstool** *n* Pilz *m*.

toast [toust] *n* Toast *m*; (*drink*) Trinkspruch *m*, Toast *m*. *v* toasten. **toaster** *n* Toaster *m*. **toastmaster** *n* Toastmeister *m*.

tobacco [tə'bakou] *n* Tabak *m*. **tobacconist** *n* Tabakhändler *m*.

toboggan [tə'bogən] *n* Schlitten *m*, Rodel(schlitten) *m*. *v* rodeln.

today [tə'dei] *n, adv* heute. **today's** *or* **of**

today heutig, von heute; (*of nowadays*) der heutigen Zeit.

toddler ['todlə] *n* Kleinkind *neut*.

toe [tou] *n* Zehe *f*. **on one's toes** auf Draht. **toe-cap** *n* Kappe *f*. **toe-nail** *n* Zehennagel *m*.

toffee ['tofi] *n* Karamelle *f*.

together [tə'geðə] *adv* zusammen; (*at the same time*) gleichzeitig. **get together** (*coll*) sich treffen.

toil [toil] *n* Mühe *f*, schwere Arbeit *f*. *v* mühselig arbeiten, schuften (an).

toilet ['toilit] *n* (*all senses*) Toilette *f*; (*WC*) Klosett *neut*. **toilet-paper** Klosettpapier *neut*. **toilet soap** Toilettenseife *f*.

token ['toukən] *n* Zeichen *neut*, Beweis *m*; (*voucher*) Gutschein *m*, Bon *m*. *adj* nominell.

told [tould] *V* tell.

tolerate ['toləreit] *v* dulden, tolerieren. **tolerable** *adj* erträglich. **tolerance** *n* Toleranz *f*. **tolerant** *adj* duldsam, tolerant.

toll¹ [toul] *n* Zoll *m*.

toll² [toul] *v* (*bell*) läuten.

tomato [tə'maɪtou] *n* (*pl* **tomatoes**) Tomate *f*.

tomb [tuɪm] *n* Grabmal *neut*, Grab *neut*. **tombstone** *n* Grabstein *m*.

tomorrow [tə'morou] *n, adv* morgen. **tomorrow morning** morgen früh. **tomorrow's** *or* **of tomorrow** morgig, von morgen. **the day after tomorrow** übermorgen.

ton [tʌn] *n* Tonne *f*.

tone [toun] *n* Ton *m*; (*muscle*) Tonus *m*. **tone down** *v* mildern. **tonal** *adj* tonal.

tongs [toŋz] *pl n* Zange *f sing*.

tongue [tʌŋ] *n* Zunge *f*; (*language*) Sprache *f*. **tongue-tied** *adj* zungenlahm. **tongue twister** *n* Zungenbrecher *m*.

tonic ['tonik] *adj* tonisch, Ton-. **tonic water** Tonic *neut*. *n* Tonikum *neut*.

tonight [tə'nait] *adv* heute abend, heute nacht.

tonsil ['tonsil] *n* Mandel *f*. **tonsillectomy** *n* Mandelentfernung *f*. **tonsillitis** *n* Mandelentzündung *f*.

too [tuɪ] *adv* (*excessively*) zu, allzu; (*as well*) auch, ebenfalls.

took [tuk] *V* take.

tool [tuɪl] *n* Werkzeug *neut*. **toolbox** *n* Werkzeugkasten *m*. **tooling** *n* Bearbeitung *f*.

tooth 184

tooth [tuːθ] n (pl **teeth**) Zahn m. **toothache** n Zahnweh neut. **toothbrush** n Zahnbürste f. **toothless** adj zahnlos. **toothpaste** n Zahnpasta f. **toothpick** n Zahnstocher m.

top[1] [top] n oberes Ende neut, obere Seite f; (hill) Gipfel m; (lid) Deckel m; (page) Kopf m. **on top of** oben auf; (besides) über. **top hat** Zylinder m. **top-heavy** adj kopflastig. **topsoil** n Ackerkrume f. adj oberst, höchst; (chief) Haupt-. v krönen.

top[2] [top] n (toy) Kreisel m.

topaz ['toupaz] n Topas m.

topic ['topik] n Thema neut, Gegenstand m. **topical** adj aktuell.

topography [tə'pogrəfi] n Topographie f.

topple ['topl] v (um)kippen.

topsy-turvy [topsi'təːvi] adv durcheinander, in Unordnung.

torch [toːtʃ] n Fackel f; (elec) Taschenlampe f.

tore [toː] V tear[1].

torment [toː'ment; n 'toːment] v quälen. n Qual f. **tormentor** n Quälgeist m.

torn [toːn] V tear[1]. adj zerrissen.

tornado [toː'neidou] n Tornado m, Wirbelsturm m.

torpedo [toː'piːdou] n Torpedo m.

torrent ['torənt] n Wildbach m; (of abuse, etc.) Strom m, Ausbruch m. **torrential** adj strömend. **torrential rain** Wolkenbruch m.

torso ['toːsou] n Torso m.

tortoise ['toːtəs] n Schildkröte f. **tortoiseshell** n Schildpatt m.

tortuous ['toːtʃuəs] adj gekrümmt.

torture ['toːtʃə] n Folter f, Folterung f; Tortur f. v foltern. **torturer** n Folterer m.

toss [tos] v (hoch)werfen; (coin) hochwerfen; tossed about by the waves von den Wellen hin und her geworfen.

tot[1] [tot] n (whisky, etc.) Schlückchen neut; (child) Knirps m.

tot[2] [tot] v **tot up** zusammenzählen.

total ['toutəl] adj total, ganz, Gesamt-. n Summe f, Gesamtbetrag m. **in total** als Ganzes. **totalitarian** adj totalitär. **totalisator** n Totalisator m. v sich belaufen auf; (person) zusammenzählen. **totality** n Gesamtheit f. **totally** adv völlig, total.

totter ['totə] v taumeln, wanken. **tottering** adj wackelig.

touch [tʌtʃ] v anrühren, anfassen; (feel) betasten; (border on) grenzen an; (emotionally) berühren. **touch down** landen.

touching adj rührend. **touchline** n Marklinie f. **touchstone** n Prüfstein m. n Berührung f, Anrühren neut; (sense) Tastsinn m, (trace) Spur f. **be/keep in touch with** in Verbindung stehen/bleiben mit. **touchy** adj empfindlich, reizbar.

tough [tʌf] adj zäh; (person) zäh, robust; (difficult) schwierig, sauer. **toughen** v zäher machen or werden. **toughness** n Zähigkeit f, Härte f.

toupee ['tuːpei] n Toupet neut.

tour [tuə] n Tour f, Rundreise f, (of inspection) Rundgang m; (theatre) Tournee f. v bereisen. **touring** adj Touren-. **tourism** n Tourismus m. **tourist** n Tourist(in).

tournament ['tuənəmənt] n Turnier neut.

tow [tou] v bugsieren, schleppen. n Schlepptau neut. **have in tow** im Schlepptau haben. **towline** or **towrope** n Schlepptau neut.

towards [tə'woːdz] prep (place) auf ... zu, nach ... hin; (behaviour, attitude) gegen(über). **towards midday** gegen Mittag.

towel ['tauəl] n Handtuch neut. **towelling** n Handtuchstoff m.

tower ['tauə] n Turm m. v (hoch)ragen.

town [taun] n Stadt f. adj Stadt-. **town council** Stadtrat m. **town hall** Rathaus neut. **town planning** Stadtplanung f.

toxic ['toksik] adj giftig, toxisch. **toxin** n Toxin neut.

toy [toi] n Spielzeug neut. **toys** pl Spielwaren pl. v **toy with** spielen mit.

trace [treis] n Spur f. v nachspüren, verfolgen; (draw) pausen, durchzeichnen. **tracing** n Pause f. **tracing paper** Pauspapier neut.

track [trak] n Spur f, Fährte f; (rail) Gleis neut; (road) Weg m, Pfad m; (sport) Bahn f. **track suit** Trainingsanzug m.

tract[1] [trakt] n (land) Strecke f. **digestive tract** Verdauungssystem neut.

tract[2] [trakt] n (treatise) Traktat neut.

tractor ['traktə] n Traktor m.

trade [treid] n Handel m; (job, skill) Gewerbe neut. **trade balance** n Handelsbilanz f. **trade fair** Messe f. **trademark** n Warenzeichen neut. **tradesman** n Lieferant m. **trade union** n Gewerkschaft f. **trade-unionist** n Gewerkschaftler(in). v handeln; (exchange) eintauschen. **trader** n Händler m.

tradition [trə'diʃən] *n* Tradition *f*. **traditional** *adj* traditionell.
traffic ['trafik] *n* Verkehr *m*. **traffic jam** Verkehrsstockung *f*. **trafficker** *n* Händler *m*. **traffic lights** Verkehrsampel *f sing*.
tragedy ['tradʒədi] *n* (*theatre*) Tragödie *f*; (*fig*) Unglück *neut*. **tragic** *adj* tragisch.
trail [treil] *n* Spur *f*, Fährte *f*. *v* schleifen, (nach)schleppen; (*follow*) verfolgen; (*lag behind*) nachhinken.
train [trein] *n* Zug *m*; (*of dress*) Schleppe *f*. *v* (*person for job, etc.*) ausbilden; (*sport*) trainieren; (*child*) schulen; (*animal*) dressieren. **trainee** *n* Lehrling *m*. **trainer** *n* (*sport*) Trainer *m*. **training** *n* Ausbildung *f*; (*sport*) Training *neut*.
trait [treit] *n* Zug *m*, Merkmal *neut*.
traitor ['treitə] *n* Verräter(in). **traitorous** *adj* verräterisch.
tram [tram] *n* Straßenbahn *f*.
tramp [tramp] *n* Landstreicher *m*. *v* stampfen.
trample ['trampl] *v* trampeln.
trampoline ['trampəliːn] *n* Trampoline *f*.
trance [trains] *n* Trance *f*.
tranquil ['traŋkwil] *adj* ruhig, friedlich. **tranquillity** *n* Ruhe *f*. **tranquillizer** *n* Beruhigungsmittel *neut*.
transact [tran'zakt] *v* durchführen. **transaction** *n* Geschäft *neut*, Transaktion *f*.
transcend [tran'send] *v* überschreiten. **transcendental** *adj* transzendental.
transcribe [tran'skraib] *v* abschreiben. **transcription** *n* Abschrift *f*.
transept ['transept] *n* Querschiff *neut*.
transfer [trans'fəː; *n* 'transfəː] *v* übertragen; (*money*) überweisen; (*trains*) umsteigen. *n* Übertragung *f*; Überweisung *f*; Umsteigen *neut*; (*design*) Abziehbild *neut*. **transferable** *adj* übertragbar. **transferred-charge call** R-Gespräch *neut*.
transform [trans'fɔːm] *v* umwandeln. **transformation** *n* Umwandlung *f*. **transformer** *n* (*elec*) Transformator *m*.
transfuse [trans'fjuːz] *v* (*blood*) übertragen. **transfusion** *n* (*blood*) Blutübertragung *f*.
transient ['tranziənt] *adj* vorübergehend.
transistor [tran'zistə] *n* Transistor *m*.
transit ['transit] *n* Durchfahrt *f*; (*of goods*) Transport *f*. *adj* Durchgangs-. **in transit** unterwegs.
transition [tran'ziʃən] *n* Übergang *m*. **transitional** *adj* Übergangs-.

transitive ['transitiv] *adj* transitiv.
translate [trans'leit] *v* übersetzen. **translation** *n* Übersetzung *f*. **translator** *n* Übersetzer(in).
translucent [trans'luːsnt] *adj* lichtdurchlässig.
transmit [tranz'mit] *v* übersenden; (*radio, TV*) senden. **transmitter** *n* (*radio, TV*) Sender *m*. **transmission** *n* (*mot*) Getriebe *neut*; (*radio, TV*) Sendung *f*.
transparent [trans'peərənt] *adj* durchsichtig, transparent; (*fig*) offensichtlich. **transparency** *n* Durchsichtigkeit *f*; (*phot*) (Dia)Positiv *neut*.
transplant [trans'plaint; *n* 'transplaint] *v* verpflanzen; (*med*) transplantieren. *n* (*operation*) Transplantation *f*; (*actual organ*) Transplantat *neut*. **transplantation** *n* Verpflanzung *f*.
transport [trans'pɔːt; *n* 'transpɔːt] *v* befördern, transportieren. *n* Beförderung *f*, Transport *m*. **transportable** *adj* transportierbar. **transportation** *n* Transport *m*.
transpose [trans'pouz] *v* umstellen, versetzen.
transverse ['tranzvəːs] *adj* quer, Quer-.
trap [trap] *n* Falle *f*. **lay a trap** eine Falle stellen. **shut your trap!** (*impol*) halt die Klappe! **trapdoor** *n* Falltür *f*. *v* fangen. **trapper** *n* Trapper *m*.
trapeze [trə'piːz] *n* Trapez *neut*.
trash [traʃ] *n* Abfall *m*; (*film, book, etc.*) Kitsch *m*. **trash-can** *n* Abfalleimer *m*. **trashy** *adj* wertlos.
trauma ['trɔːmə] *n* Trauma *neut*. **traumatic** *adj* traumatisch.
travel ['travl] *v* reisen. *n* Reisen *neut*. **travel agency** Reisebüro *neut*. **traveller** Reisende(r). **travelling** *adj* Reise-. **travelling expenses** Reisespesen *pl*.
travesty ['travəsti] *n* Travestie *f*.
trawl [trɔːl] *n* Grundschleppnetz *neut*, Trawl *neut*. **trawler** *n* Trawler *m*.
treachery ['tretʃəri] *n* Verrat *m*. **treacherous** *adj* verräterich; (*dangerous*) gefährlich.
treacle ['triːkl] *n* Sirup *m*, Melasse *f*.
*****tread** [tred] *n* Tritt *m*, Schritt *m*; (*tyre*) Profil *neut*; (*ladder*) Sprosse *f*. *v* treten. **treadmill** *n* Tretmühle *f*.
treason ['triːzn] *n* Verrat *m*.
treasure ['treʒə] *n* Schatz *m*. *v* hochschätzen. **treasurer** *n* Schatzmeister(in); (*club*) Kassenwart *m*. **treasury** *n*

Schatzkammer *f.* **Treasury** *n* (*pol*) Finanzministerium *neut.*
treat [triːt] *v* behandeln. **treat someone to something** jemandem zu etwas einladen. *n* (*coll*) Genuß *m*, Vergnügen *neut.* **treatment** *n* Behandlung *f.*
treatise ['triːtiz] *n* Abhandlung *f.*
treaty ['triːti] *n* Vertrag *m*, Pakt *m.*
treble ['trebl] *adj* dreifach; (*music*) Diskant-. *v* (sich) verdreifachen.
tree [triː] *n* Baum *m.* **family tree** Stammbaum *m.*
trek [trek] *n* Treck *m. v* trecken.
trellis ['trelis] *n* Gitter *neut*, Gitterwerk *neut.*
tremble ['trembl] *v* zittern. *n* Zittern *neut.*
tremendous [trə'mendəs] *adj* enorm, kolossal; (*coll: excellent*) ausgezeichnet.
tremor ['tremə] *n* Beben *neut.*
trench [trentʃ] *n* Graben *m*; (*mil*) Schützengraben *m.* **trench coat** *n* Trenchcoat *m.*
trend [trend] *n* Tendenz *f*, Trend *m.* **trendy** *adj* (neu)modisch.
trespass ['trespəs] *v* unbefugt betreten. **trespasser** *n* Unbefugte(r). **trespassers will be prosecuted** Eintritt bei Strafe verboten.
trestle ['tresl] *n* Gestell *m.*
trial ['traiəl] *n* Probe *f*, Versuch *m*; (*legal*) Prozeß *m. adj* Probe-. **on trial** vor Gericht.
triangle ['traiaŋgl] *n* Dreieck *neut*; (*music*) Triangel *m.* **triangular** *adj* dreieckig.
tribe [traib] *n* Stamm *m.* **tribal** *adj* Stammes-. **tribesman** *n* Stammesangehörige(r).
tribunal [trai'bjuːnl] *n* Gerichtshof *m*, Tribunal *neut.*
tributary ['tribjutəri] *n* Nebenfluß *m.*
tribute ['tribjuːt] *n* Tribut *m.* **pay tribute** (*fig*) Anerkennung zollen.
trick [trik] *n* Trick *m*, Kniff *m*; (*practical joke*) Streich *m*; (*cards*) Stich *m. adj* Trick-. *v* betrügen. **trickery** *n* Betrügerei *f.* **trickster** *n* Schwindler(in). **tricky** *adj* knifflig.
trickle ['trikl] *v* tröpfeln, sickern. *n* Tröpfeln *neut.*
tricycle ['traisikl] *n* Dreirad *neut.*
tried [traid] *adj* erprobt, bewährt.
trifle ['traifl] *n* Kleinigkeit *f*; (*cookery*) Trifle *m*, (süßer) Auflauf *m.* **a trifle** ein bißchen. *v* spielen. **trifling** *adj* belanglos.
trigger ['trigə] *n* Abzug *m.* **pull the trigger** abdrücken. *v* **trigger off** auslösen.

trigonometry [trigə'nomətri] *n* Trigonometrie *f.*
trilby ['trilbi] *n* weicher Filzhut *m.*
trim [trim] *adj* gepflegt, nett; (*slim*) schlank. *v* zurechtmachen; (*hair, etc.*) ausputzen, beschneiden. **trimming** *n* Verzierung *f.*
trinket ['triŋkit] *n* Schmuckstück *neut.*
trio ['triːou] *n* Trio *neut.*
trip [trip] *n* Reise *f*, Ausflug *m*; (*stumble*) Fehltritt *m*, Stolpern *neut. v* stolpern; (*dance*) tänzeln, trippeln. **trip up** (*someone else*) ein Bein stellen (+ *dat*). **tripper** *n* Ausflügler(in).
tripe [traip] *n* Kaldaunen *pl*; (*coll: nonsense*) Quatsch *m.*
triple ['tripl] *adj* dreifach, Drei-. *v* verdreifachen. **triplet** *n* Drilling *m.* **triplex glass** Sicherheitsglas *neut.*
tripod ['traipod] *n* Dreifuß *m*; (*phot*) Stativ *neut.*
trite [trait] *adj* platt, banal.
triumph ['traiʌmf] *n* Triumph *m*; Sieg *m. v* triumphieren. **triumphal** *adj* Triumph-, Sieger-. **triumphant** *adj* triumphierend, siegreich.
trivial ['triviəl] *adj* geringfügig, trivial. **triviality** *n* Trivialität *f.*
trod [trod] *V* **tread.**
trodden ['trodn] *V* **tread.**
trolley ['troli] *n* (*supermarket*) Einkaufswagen *m*; (*tea*) Servierwagen *m*; (*airport, etc.*) Kofferkuli *m*; (*tram*) Straßenbahn *f.* **trolleybus** *n* O-Bus *m.*
trombone [trom'boun] *n* Posaune *f.* **trombonist** *n* Posaunist(in).
troop [truːp] *n* Trupp *m.* **troops** *pl* Truppen *pl.* **trooping the colour** Fahnenparade *f.*
trophy ['troufi] *n* (*sport*) Preis *m*; (*mil, hunting*) Trophäe *f.*
tropic ['tropik] *n* Wendekreis *m.* **tropics** *pl* Tropen *pl.* **tropical** *adj* tropisch.
trot [trot] *n* Trott *m*, Trab *m. v* trotten, traben.
trouble ['trʌbl] *n* Schwierigkeiten *pl*; (*effort*) Mühe *f*; (*burden*) Belästigung *f*; (*tech*) Störung *f. v* beunruhigen, stören. **troubles** *pl* (*pol*) Unruhe *f*, Aufruhr *f.* **be in trouble** Schwierigkeiten haben. **be troubled** bekümmert sein. **get into trouble** Ärger bringen (+ *dat*) *or* bekommen. **take (the) trouble** sich die Mühe ge'·n. **trouble-maker** *n* Unruhestifter(in). **trou·**

ble-shooter n Störungssucher(in). **troublesome** adj lästig.
trough [trof] n Trog m.
trousers ['trauzəz] pl n Hose f sing.
trout [traut] n Forelle f.
trowel ['trauəl] n Kelle f; (gardening) Pflanzenheber m.
truant ['truːənt] n Schwänzer(in). **play truant** (die Schule) schwänzen. **truancy** n Schwänzerei f.
truce [truːs] n Waffenstillstand m.
truck [trʌk] n (road) Lastkraftwagen (Lkw) m; (rail) Güterwagen m. **truckdriver** n Lastwagenfahrer m.
trudge [trʌdʒ] v sich mühsam schleppen.
true [truː] adj wahr; (genuine) echt; (loyal) treu; (rightful) rechtmäßig. **truism** n Binsenwahrheit f. **truly** adv wirklich, in der Tat. **yours truly** hochachtungsvoll.
truffle ['trʌfl] n Trüffel f.
trump [trʌmp] n Trumpf m. **trump card** Trumpfkarte f. v (über)trumpfen. **trumped up** falsch, erdichtet.
trumpet ['trʌmpit] n Trompete f. v trompeten. **trumpeter** n Trompeter m.
truncheon ['trʌntʃən] n Knüppel m.
trunk [trʌŋk] n (tree) Baumstamm m; (anat) Leib m; (case) Schankkoffer m. (mot) n Kofferraum m. **trunks** pl Badehose f sing. **trunk-call** Ferngespräch neut. **trunk-road** Fernstraße f.
truss [trʌs] n (med) Bruchband neut. v zusammenbinden; (cookery) dressieren.
trust [trʌst] v trauen (+dat); (hope) hoffen. n Vertrauen neut; (expectation) Erwartung f; (comm) Trust m. **hold in trust** als Treuhänder verwalten. **trustee** n Treuhänder m. **trusting** adj vertrauensvoll. **trustworthy** adj vertrauenswürdig. **trusty** adj treu.
truth [truːθ] n Wahrheit f. **truthful** adj wahr, wahrhaftig. **truthfulness** n Wahrhaftigkeit f.
try [trai] v (attempt) versuchen; (test, sample) probieren; (law) vor Gericht stellen, verhandeln gegen (wegen). **try on** (clothes) anprobieren. **try out** probieren. n Versuch m. **trying** adj peinlich, schwierig; (person) belästigend.
tsar [zaː] n Zar m.
T-shirt ['tiːʃəːt] n T-Shirt neut.
tub [tʌb] n (Bade)Wanne f; (barrel) Faß neut, Tonne f. **tubby** adj (coll) rundlich.
tuba ['tjuːbə] n Tuba f.
tube [tjuːb] n Rohr neut, Röhre f; (of

tyre) (Luft)Schlauch m; (coll: underground railway) U-Bahn f.
tuber ['tjuːbə] n Knolle f.
tuberculosis [tjubəːkjuˈlousis] n Tuberkulose f.
tuck [tʌk] n Einschlag m. v **tuck in** (shirt) einstecken; (food) einhauen, zugreifen; (sheet) feststecken; (person) warm zudecken.
Tuesday ['tjuːzdi] n Dienstag m. **on Tuesdays** dienstags.
tuft [tʌft] n Büschel neut, Schopf m.
tug [tʌg] v ziehen, zerren; (boat) schleppen. n Zerren neut, Zug m; (boat) Schlepper m, Bugsierdampfer m.
tuition [tjuˈiʃən] n Unterricht m.
tulip ['tjuːlip] n Tulpe f.
tumble ['tʌmbl] v hinfallen, umstürzen. **tumbledown** adj baufällig. **tumble-dryer** (Wäsche)Trockner m. n Fall m, Sturz m. **tumbler** n Glas neut.
tummy ['tʌmi] n (coll) Bauch m, Bäuchlein neut. **tummy-ache** n Bauchweh neut.
tumour ['tjuːmə] n Geschwulst f, Tumor m.
tumult ['tjuːmʌlt] n Tumult m, Lärm m. **tumultuous** adj stürmisch.
tuna ['tjuːnə] n Thunfisch m.
tune [tjuːn] n Melodie f. **in/out of tune** gestimmt/verstimmt. **to the tune of** (coll) im Ausmaß von. v (ab)stimmen. **tune in to** einstellen auf. **tuneful** adj melodisch, wohlklingend. **tuner** n (pianos, etc.) Stimmer m.
tunic ['tjuːnik] n (school) Kittel m. (mil) Uniformrock m.
tunnel ['tʌnl] n Tunnel m, Unterführung f. v **tunnel through** einen Tunnel bauen durch.
tunny ['tʌni] V tuna.
turban ['təːbən] n Turban m.
turbine ['təːbain] n Turbine f.
turbot ['təːbət] n Steinbutt m.
turbulent ['təːbjulənt] adj unruhig, stürmisch. **turbulence** n Turbulenz f.
tureen [tjuˈriːn] n Terrine f.
turf [təːf] n Rasen m; (sport) Turf m, Rennbahn f. v **turf out** (coll) hinausschmeißen.
turkey ['təːki] n (cock) Truthahn m; (hen) Truthenne f.
Turkey ['təːki] n die Türkei f. **Turk** n Türke m, Türkin f. **Turkish** adj türkisch.

turmeric ['təɪmərik] n Gelbwurz f.

turmoil ['təɪmoil] n Aufruhr m.

turn [təɪn] v (sich) drehen; (become) werden. **turn around** or **round** (person) sich umdrehen; (thing) herumdrehen. **turn back** umkehren. **turn down** (offer) ablehnen; (radio) leiser stellen. **turning** n (mot) Abzweigung f. **turning point** Wendepunkt m. **turn left/right** links/rechts abbiegen. **turn loose** freilassen. **turn off** (light) ausschalten; (radio) abstellen; (mot) abbiegen. **turn on** einschalten. **turn out** (expel) ausweisen; (produce) herstellen. **turn-out** n (spectators) Teilnahme f. **turn over** (sich) umdrehen. **turnover** n (comm) Umsatz m. **turnstile** n Drehkreuz neut. **turntable** n (records) Plattenteller m. **turn up** (appear) auftauchen; (radio) lauter stellen. **turn-up** n (trousers) Umschlag m. n Umdrehung f; (change of direction) Wendung f. **it's my turn** ich bin an der Reihe. **do someone a good turn** jemandem einen Gefallen tun.

turnip ['təɪnip] n (weiße) Rübe f.

turpentine ['təɪpəntain] n Terpentin neut.

turquoise ['təɪkwoiz] n Türkis m. adj (colour) türkisblau.

turret ['tʌrit] n Türmchen neut; (gun) Geschützturm m, Panzerturm m.

turtle ['təɪtl] n Schildkröte f. **turtle dove** Turteltaube f.

tusk [tʌsk] n Stoßzahn m.

tussle ['tʌsl] n Balgerei f, Ringen neut. v sich balgen, kämpfen.

tutor ['tjuɪtə] n Privatlehrer m; (university) Tutor m.

tuxedo [tʌk'siɪdou] n Smoking m.

tweed [twiɪd] n Tweed m.

tweezers ['twiɪzəz] pl n Pinzette f sing.

twelve [twelv] adj zwölf. n Zwölf f. **twelfth** adj zwölft.

twenty ['twenti] adj zwanzig. n Zwanzig f. **twentieth** adj zwanzigst.

twice [twais] adv zweimal. **twice as much** zweimal so viel. **think twice about** sich gründlich überlegen.

twiddle ['twidl] v herumdrehen, spielen mit.

twig [twig] n Zweig m.

twilight ['twailait] n (Abend)Dämmerung f, Zwielicht neut. adj Zwielicht-.

twin [twin] n Zwilling m. adj Zwillings-. **twin-cylinder engine** Zweizylindermotor m.

twine [twain] n Bindfaden m, Schnur f. v (threads) zusammendrehen. **twine around** winden um.

twinge [twindʒ] n Stich m, Stechen neut. **twinge of conscience** Gewissensbiß m. v zwicken, kneifen.

twinkle ['twiŋkl] v glitzern, funkeln; (eyes) blinzeln. n Glitzern neut; Blinzeln neut. **in a twinkle** im Nu.

twirl [twəɪl] v wirbeln. n Wirbel m.

twist [twist] v (sich) drehen, (sich) winden; (meaning) verdrehen; (features) verzerren. **twist one's ankle** sich den Fuß verrenken. **twisted** adj (person) verschroben. **twisting** adj sich windend. n Drehung f, Windung f; (in story) Wendung f.

twit [twit] n (coll) Dummkopf m.

twitch [twitʃ] v zucken. n Zucken neut.

twitter ['twitə] v zwitschern. n Gezwitscher neut, Zwitschern neut.

two [tuɪ] adj zwei. **two-faced** adj heuchlerisch. **twofold** adj zweifach. **two-stroke engine** Zweitaktomotor m. n Zwei f; (pair) Paar neut.

tycoon [tai'kuɪn] n Industriemagnat m.

type [taip] n Typ m, Sorte f, Klasse f; (person) Typ m; (print) Druck m, Druckschrift f. v (mit der Maschine) schreiben, tippen. **typed** adj maschinengeschrieben. **typewriter** n Schreibmaschine f. **typing error** Tippfehler m. **typist** n Typist(in).

typhoid ['taifoid] n Typhus m.

typhoon [tai'fuɪn] n Taifun m.

typical ['tipikəl] adj typisch. **typify** v verkörpern.

tyrant ['tairənt] n Tyrann(in). **tyrannical** adj tyrannisch. **tyrannize** v tyrannisieren. **tyranny** n Tyrannei f.

tyre ['taiə] or US **tire** n Reifen m.

U

ubiquitous [ju'bikwitəs] adj überall zu finden(d).

udder ['ʌdə] n Euter neut.

ugly ['ʌgli] adj häßlich. **ugliness** n Häßlichkeit f.

ulcer ['ʌlsə] n Geschwür neut.

ulterior [ʌl'tiəriə] *adj* **ulterior motives** Hintergedanken *pl.*
ultimate ['ʌltimət] *adj* allerletzt; *(conclusive)* endgültig, entscheidend. **ultimately** *adv* schließlich. **ultimatum** *n* Ultimatum *neut.*
ultraviolet [ʌltrə'vaiələt] *adj* ultraviolett.
umbilical [ʌm'bilikəl] *n* Nabelschnur *f.*
umbrella [ʌm'brelə] *n* Regenschirm *m.*
umlaut ['umlaut] *n* Umlaut *m.*
umpire ['ʌmpaiə] *n* Schiedsrichter *m.*
umpteen [ʌmp'tiːn] *adj* zahllos. **umpteen times** x-mal.
unable [ʌn'eibl] *adj* unfähig. **be unable** nicht können.
unacceptable [ʌnək'septəbl] *adj* unannehmbar.
unaccompanied [ʌnə'kumpənid] *adj* unbegleitet; *(music)* ohne Begleitung.
unanimous [ju'naniməs] *adj* einstimmig. **unanimity** *n* Einstimmigkeit *f.*
unannounced [ʌnə'naunst] *adj* unangekündigt.
unarmed [ʌn'aimd] *adj* unbewaffnet.
unassuming [ʌnə'sjuːmiŋ] *adj* bescheiden.
unattractive [ʌnə'traktiv] *adj* reizlos, nicht anziehend.
unauthorized [ʌn'oiθəraizd] *adj* unbefugt.
unavoidable [ʌnə'voidəbl] *adj* unvermeidlich.
unaware [ʌnə'weə] *adj* **be unaware of** sich nicht bewußt sein (+ *gen*). **unawares** *adv* **take unawares** überraschen.
unbalanced [ʌn'balənst] *adj* unausgeglichen; *(mentally disturbed)* geistesgestört.
unbearable [ʌn'beərəbl] *adj* unerträglich.
unbelievable [ʌnbi'liːvəbl] *adj* unglaublich. **unbeliever** *n* Ungläubige(r). **unbelieving** *adj* ungläubig.
***unbend** [ʌn'bend] *v (person)* freundlicher werden. **unbending** *adj* unbeugsam.
unbounded [ʌn'baundid] *adj* unbegrenzt, grenzenlos.
unbreakable [ʌn'breikəbl] *adj* unzerbrechlich.
unbridled [ʌn'braidld] *adj* zügellos.
unbroken [ʌn'broukn] *adj (continuous)* ununterbrochen.
uncalled-for [ʌn'koɪldfoɪ] *adj* unangebracht.
uncanny [ʌn'kani] *adj* unheimlich.
uncertain [ʌn'səitn] *adj* unsicher, ungewiß. **uncertainty** *n* Unsicherheit *f,* Ungewißheit *f.*

uncle ['ʌŋkl] *n* Onkel *m.*
unclean [ʌn'kliːn] *adj* unrein.
uncomfortable [ʌn'kʌmfətəbl] *adj* unbequem; *(fact, etc.)* beunruhigend.
uncommon [ʌn'komən] *adj* ungewöhnlich, selten. **uncommonly** *adv (extremely)* außerordentlich.
unconditional [ʌnkən'diʃənl] *adj* bedingungslos, uneingeschränkt.
unconfirme [ʌnkən'fəimd]d *adj* unbestätigt.
unconscious [ʌn'konʃəs] *adj (unknowing)* unbewußt; *(med)* bewußtlos. **unconsciousness** *n* Bewußtlosigkeit *f.*
uncontrollable [ʌnkən'trouləbl] *adj* unbeherrscht, unkontrollierbar.
unconventional [ʌnkən'venʃənl] *adj* unkonventionell.
unconvinced [ʌnkən'vinst] *adj* nicht überzeugt. **unconvincing** *adj* nicht überzeugend.
uncooked [ʌn'kukt] *adj* roh, ungekocht.
uncork [ʌn'koːk] *v* entkorken.
uncouth [ʌn'kuːθ] *adj* ungehobelt, unfein.
uncover [ʌn'kʌvə] *v* aufdecken.
uncut [ʌn'kʌt] *adj (gem)* ungeschliffen; *(grass)* ungemäht; *(book)* unabgekürzt.
undecided [ʌndi'saidid] *adj (thing)* unentschieden; *(person)* unentschlossen.
undeniable [ʌndi'naiəbl] *adj* unbestreitbar.
under ['ʌndə] *prep* unter; *(less than)* weniger als. **under age** minderjährig. **under construction** im Bau. **under cover of** im Schutz (+ *gen*). *adv* unten. **go under** zugrunde gehen. *adj* Unter-.
undercharge [ʌndə'tʃaidʒ] *v* zu wenig berechnen.
underclothes ['ʌndəklouðz] *pl n* Unterwäsche *f sing.*
undercoat ['ʌndəkout] *n* Grundierung *f,* Grundanstrich *m.*
undercover [ʌndə'kʌvə] *adj* Geheim-.
***undercut** [ʌndə'kʌt] *v (comm)* unterbieten.
underdeveloped [ʌndədi'veləpt] *adj* unterentwickelt. **underdeveloped country** Entwicklungsland *neut.*
underdone [ʌndə'dʌn] *adj (meat)* nicht durchgebraten.
underestimate [ʌndə'estimeit] *adj* unterschätzen.
underexpose [ʌndərik'spouz] *v* unterbelichten. **underexposure** *n* Unterbelichtung *f.*

underfoot [ʌndə'fut] *adv* am Boden.

***undergo** [ʌndə'gou] *v* erleben; *(operation)* sich unterziehen (+*dat*).

undergraduate [ʌndə'grædjuət] *n* Student(in).

underground ['ʌndəgraund; *adv* ʌndə'graund] *adj* unterirdisch, Untergrund-; *(pol)* geheim, Untergrund-. *n* *(rail)* Untergrundbahn *f*, *(coll)* U-Bahn *f*. *adv* unter der Erde. **go underground** *(hide)* untertauchen.

undergrowth ['ʌndəgrouθ] *n* Unterholz *neut*.

underhand [ʌndə'hænd] *adj* heimlich, hinterlistig.

***underlie** [ʌndə'lai] *v* zugrunde liegen (+*dat*).

underline [ʌndə'lain] *v* unterstreichen; *(stress)* betonen.

undermine [ʌndə'main] *v* unterminieren, untergraben.

underneath [ʌndə'niːθ] *prep* unter, unterhalb. *adv* unten, darunter.

underpants ['ʌndəpænts] *pl n* Unterhose *f* *sing*.

underpass ['ʌndəpaɪs] *n* Unterführung *f*.

underprivileged [ʌndə'prɪvɪlidʒd] *adj* benachteiligt.

underrate [ʌndə'reit] *v* unterschätzen.

***understand** [ʌndə'stænd] *v* verstehen. **understandable** *adj* verständlich. **understanding** *n* Verständnis *neut*; *(agreement)* Verständigung *f*; *adj* verständnisvoll.

understate [ʌndə'steit] *v* untertreiben. **understatement** *n* Untertreibung *f*.

understudy ['ʌndəstʌdi] *n* Ersatzschauspieler(in).

***undertake** [ʌndə'teik] *v* übernehmen. **undertaker** *n* Leichenbestatter *m*. **undertaking** *n* Unternehmen *neut*; *(promise)* Versprechen *neut*.

undertone ['ʌndətoun] *n* Unterton *m*.

underwear ['ʌndəweə] *n* Unterwäsche *f*.

underweight [ʌndə'weit] *adj* untergewichtig.

underworld ['ʌndəwɔːld] *n* Unterwelt *f*.

***underwrite** [ʌndə'rait] *v* unterzeichnen, versichern. **underwriter** *n* Versicherer *m*.

undesirable [ʌndi'zaiərəbl] *adj* nicht wünschenswert, unerwünscht.

***undo** [ʌn'duː] *v* *(package)* öffnen, aufmachen; *(coat, knot)* aufknöpfen; *(work)* zunichte machen. **undoing** *n* Ruin *m*, Vernichtung *f*.

undoubted [ʌn'dautid] *adj* unbestritten. **undoubtedly** *adv* ohne Zweifel.

undress [ʌn'dres] *v* (sich) ausziehen. **undressed** *adj* unbekleidet.

undue [ʌn'djuː] *adj* übermäßig, übertrieben; *(improper)* unschicklich. **unduly** *adv* übertrieben.

undulate ['ʌndjuleit] *v* wogen, wallen. **undulation** *n* Wallen *neut*.

unearth [ʌn'əːθ] *v* ausgraben; *(fig)* ans Tageslicht bringen.

uneasy [ʌn'iːzi] *adj* *(person)* beunruhigt, ängstlich; *(feeling)* unbehaglich.

uneducated [ʌn'edjukeitid] *adj* ungebildet.

unemployed [ʌnem'ploid] *adj* arbeitslos. **unemployment** *n* Arbeitslosigkeit *f*.

unending [ʌn'endiŋ] *adj* endlos.

unequal [ʌn'iːkwəl] *adj* ungleich. **unequalled** *adj* unübertroffen.

uneven [ʌn'iːvn] *adj* uneben. **unevenness** *n* Unebenheit *f*.

uneventful [ʌni'ventfəl] *adj* ereignislos.

unexpected [ʌneks'pektid] *adj* unerwartet.

unfailing [ʌn'feiliŋ] *adj* unfehlbar.

unfair [ʌn'feə] *adj* ungerecht, unfair. **unfairness** *n* Unbilligkeit *f*.

unfaithful [ʌn'feiθfəl] *adj* untreu. **unfaithfulness** *n* Untreue *f*.

unfamiliar [ʌnfə'miljə] *adj* unbekannt.

unfasten [ʌn'faisn] *v* aufmachen, losbinden.

unfit [ʌn'fit] *adj* ungeeignet; *(sport)* nicht fit.

unfold [ʌn'fould] *v* (sich) entfalten.

unforeseen [ʌnfɔː'siːn] *adj* unvorhergesehen.

unforgettable [ʌnfə'getəbl] *adj* unvergeßlich.

unfortunate [ʌn'fɔːtʃənət] *adj* unglücklich; *(regrettable)* bedauerlich. *n* Unglückliche(r). **unfortunately** *adv* unglücklicherweise, leider.

unfurnished [ʌn'fəːniʃd] *adj* unmöbliert.

ungrateful [ʌn'greitfəl] *adj* undankbar.

unhappy [ʌn'hapi] *adj* unglücklich; *(with something)* unzufrieden. **unhappily** *adv* leider. **unhappiness** *n* Unglück *neut*.

unhealthy [ʌn'helθi] *adj* *(person)* ungesund; *(damaging to health)* gesundheitsschädlich.

unhurt [ʌn'həːt] *adj* unverletzt.

unicorn ['juːnikɔːn] *n* Einhorn *m*.

uniform ['juːnifɔːm] *n* Uniform *f*, Dienstkleidung *f*. *adj* einförmig, gleichförmig.
uniformity *n* Gleichheit *f*.
unify ['juːnifai] *v* vereinigen. **unification** *n* Vereinigung *f*.
unilateral [juːni'lætərəl] *adj* einseitig.
uninhabited [ʌnin'habitid] *adj* unbewohnt. **uninhabitable** *adj* unbewohnbar.
unintelligible [ʌnin'telidʒəbl] *adj* unverständlich.
uninterested [ʌn'intristid] *adj* uninteressiert. **uninteresting** *adj* uninteressant.
union ['juːnjən] *n* Vereinigung *f*; (*pol*) Staatenbund *m*; (*agreement*) Eintracht *f*; (*trade union*) Gewerkschaft *f*. **unionize** *v* gewerkschaftlich organisieren.
unique [juː'niːk] *adj* einzigartig; (*only*) einzig.
unison ['juːnisn] *n* Einklang *m*.
unit ['juːnit] *n* Einheit *f*.
unite [juː'nait] *v* (sich) vereinigen. **united** *adj* vereint, vereinigt. **unity** *n* Einheit *f*; (*accord*) Einigkeit *f*.
United Kingdom *n* Vereinigtes Königreich.
United Nations *pl n* Vereinte Nationen.
United States of America *n* Vereinigte Staaten von Amerika.
universe ('juːnivəːs] *n* Weltall *neut*, Universum *neut*. **universal** *adj* universal.
university [juːni'vəːsəti] *n* Universität *f*, Hochschule *f*. *adj* Universitäts-, Hochschul-.
unjust [ʌn'dʒʌst] *adj* ungerecht.
unkempt [ʌn'kempt] *adj* ungepflegt.
unkind [ʌn'kaind] *adj* unfreundlich. **unkindness** *n* Unfreundlichkeit *f*.
unknown [ʌn'noun] *adj* unbekannt. *n* das Unbekannte.
unlawful [ʌn'lɔːfəl] *adj* rechtswidrig, unzulässig.
unless [ʌn'les] *conj* wenn ... nicht, es sei denn.
unlike [ʌn'laik] *adj, prep* unähnlich, (*in contrast to*) im Gegensatz zu. **unlikely** *adv* unwahrscheinlich.
unload [ʌn'loud] *v* (*goods*) abladen; (*truck, etc.*) entladen.
unlock [ʌn'lok] *v* aufschließen, öffnen. **unlocked** *adj* unverschlossen.
unlucky [ʌn'lʌki] *adj* unglücklich.
unmarried [ʌn'marid] *adj* ledig, unverheiratet.
unnatural [ʌn'natʃərəl] *adj* unnatürlich.

unnecessary [ʌn'nesəsəri] *adj* unnötig, nicht notwendig.
unobtainable [ʌnəb'teinəbl] *adj* unerhältlich.
unoccupied [ʌn'okjupaid] *adj* unbesetzt; (*house*) unbewohnt; (*person*) unbeschäftigt.
unofficial [ʌnə'fiʃəl] *adj* inoffiziell.
unorthodox [ʌn'ɔːθədoks] *adj* unorthodox.
unpack [ʌn'pak] *v* auspacken.
unpleasant [ʌn'pleznt] *adj* unangenehm. **unpleasantness** *n* Unannehmlichkeit *f*.
unpopular [ʌn'popjulə] *adj* unbeliebt.
unprecedented [ʌn'presidentid] *adj* unerhört.
unpretentious [ʌnpri'tenʃəs] *adj* anspruchslos.
unravel [ʌn'ravəl] *v* auftrennen; (*fig*) enträtseln.
unreal [ʌn'riəl] *adj* unwirklich. **unrealistic** *adj* unrealistisch.
unreasonable [ʌn'riːzənəbl] *adj* übertrieben, übermäßig; (*person*) unvernünftig.
unrelenting [ʌnri'lentiŋ] *adj* unerbittlich.
unreliable [ʌnri'laiəbl] *adj* unzuverlässig. **unreliability** *n* Unzuverlässigkeit *f*.
unrest [ʌn'rest] *n* Unruhe *f*.
unruly [ʌn'ruːli] *adj* unlenksam.
unsafe [ʌn'seif] *adj* unsicher, gefährlich.
unsatisfactory [ʌnsatis'faktəri] *adj* unbefriedigend. **unsatisifed** *adj* unzufrieden.
unscrew [ʌn'skruː] *v* aufschrauben.
unsettle [ʌn'setl] *v* beunruhigen. **unsettled** *adj* unruhig.
unsightly [ʌn'saitli] *adj* unansehnlich.
unskilled [ʌn'skild] *adj* ungelernt.
unsound [ʌn'saund] *adj* (*advice, etc.*) unzuverlässig. **of unsound mind** geistesgestört.
unspeakable [ʌn'spiːkəbl] *adj* unbeschreiblich; (*horrible*) scheußlich, entsetzlich.
unstable [ʌn'steibl] *adj* nicht fest, schwankend; (*person*) labil.
unsteady [ʌn'stedi] *adj* wackelig, unsicher.
unsuccessful [ʌnsək'sesfəl] *adj* erfolglos.
unsuitable [ʌn'suːtəbl] *adj* ungeeignet.
untangle [ʌn'taŋgl] *v* entwirren.
untidy [ʌn'taidi] *adj* unordentlich. **untidiness** *n* Unordentlichkeit *f*.

untie [ʌn'tai] v losbinden.
until [ən'til] prep, conj bis. **not until** erst.
untoward [ʌntə'wɔːd] adj ungünstig.
untrue [ʌn'truː] adj unwahr, falsch; (friend) untreu. **untruth** n Unwahrheit f, Falschheit f. **untruthful** adj unwahr, unaufrichtig.
unusual [ʌn'juːʒuəl] adj ungewöhnlich, außergewöhnlich.
unwell [ʌn'wel] adj unwohl.
unwieldy [ʌn'wiːldi] adj unhandlich.
*unwind [ʌn'waind] v loswickeln, abspulen; (rest) sich entspannen, (sich) ausruhen.
unworthy [ʌn'wəːði] adj unwürdig.
unwrap [ʌn'rap] v auswickeln.
up [ʌp] prep auf, hinauf. adv auf, hoch; hinauf, herauf; (out of bed) auf; (sun) aufgegangen. **it's up to me** es liegt an mir. **up to now** bis jetzt. **up for trial** vor Gericht. **what's up?** was ist los?
upbringing ['ʌpbriŋiŋ] n Erziehung f.
update [ʌp'deit] v modernisieren; (book) neu bearbeiten.
upheaval [ʌp'hiːvl] n Umwälzung f.
uphill [ʌp'hil] adv bergauf. adj (fig) mühsam.
*uphold [ʌp'hould] v unterstützen, billigen.
upholster [ʌp'houlstə] v (auf)polstern. **upholsterer** n Polsterer m. **upholstery** n Polsterung f.
upkeep ['ʌpkiːp] n Instandhaltung f; (cost) Unterhaltskosten pl.
uplift [ʌp'lift] v erbauen.
upon [ə'pon] prep auf. **once upon a time** es war einmal.
upper ['ʌpə] adj ober, höher. **uppermost** adj oberst, höchst. n (shoe) Oberleder neut.
upright ['ʌprait] adj, adv gerade, aufrecht; (honest) aufrecht, aufrichtig.
uprising ['ʌpraiziŋ] n Aufstand m.
uproar ['ʌprɔː] n Aufruhr m, Tumult m.
uproot [ʌp'ruːt] v ausreißen, entwurzeln.
*upset [ʌp'set; n 'ʌpset] v (person) bestürzen, beunruhigen; (plan) vereiteln; (tip over) umkippen. adj bestürzt, außer Fassung; (stomach) verstimmt. n (stomach) Verstimmung f.
upshot ['ʌpʃot] n Ergebnis neut.
upside down [ʌpsai'daun] adv verkehrt herum, mit dem Kopf nach unten. **turn upside down** sich auf den Kopf stellen.
upstairs [ʌp'steəz] adv (go) nach oben, die

Treppe hinauf; (be) oben. adj (room) obere(r).
upstream [ʌp'striːm] adv stromaufwärts.
uptight ['ʌptait] adj (coll) nervös, aufgeregt.
up-to-date [ʌptə'deit] adj modern, aktuell.
upward ['ʌpwəd] adj nach oben (gerichtet). **upward glance** Blick nach oben m. adv also **upwards** aufwärts, nach oben.
uranium [ju'reiniəm] n Uran neut.
Uranus [juə'reinəs] n Uranus m.
urban ['əːbən] adj städtisch, Stadt-. **urbanization** n Verstädterung f. **urbanize** v verstädtern.
urchin ['əːtʃin] n (boy) Bengel m.
urge [əːdʒ] v (implore) (dringend) bitten, raten (+dat); (insist on) betonen, bestehen auf. **urge on** antreiben. n Drang m, (An)Trieb m.
urgent ['əːdʒənt] adj dringend. **urgency** n Dringlichkeit f.
urine ['juːrin] n Urin m, Harn m. **urinal** n Urinbecken neut, Pissoir neut. **urinary** adj Urin-. **urinate** v urinieren.
urn [əːn] n Urne f.
us [ʌs] pron uns. **both of us** wir beide. **all of us** wir alle.
usage ['juːzidʒ] n Brauch m, Gebrauch m.
use [juːz; n juːs] v benutzen, gebrauchen; (apply) anwenden; (coll: exploit) ausbeuten. n Gebrauch m, Verwendung f. **be of use** von Nutzen sein, helfen. **for the use of** zum Nutzen von. **it's no use** es hilft nichts. **make use of** Gebrauch machen von. **use up** verbrauchen. I used to live here ich wohnte (früher) hier. she used to say sie hat immer gesagt, sie pflegte zu sagen. **useful** adj nützlich, brauchbar. **usefulness** n Nützlichkeit f. **useless** adj nutzlos, unnütz. **user** Benutzer(in). **uselessness** n Nutzlosigkeit f.
usher ['ʌʃə] n Platzanweiser(in). v **usher in** (fig) einleiten.
usual ['juːzuəl] adj üblich, gewöhnlich. **usually** adv gewöhnlich, normalerweise.
usurp [ju'zəːp] v gewaltsam nehmen, usurpieren. **usurpation** n Usurpation f. **usurper** n Usurpator m.
utensil [ju'tensl] n Gerät neut, Werkzeug neut; (pl) Utensilien pl.
uterus ['juːtərəs] n Gebärmutter f, Uterus m. **uterine** adj Gebärmutter-.

utility [ju'tilǝti] *n* Nutzen *m*. **public utility** *n* öffentlicher Versorgungsbetrieb *m*.
utilize ['juːtilaiz] *v* verwenden. **utilization** *n* Verwendung *f*.
utmost ['ʌtmoust] *adj* äußerst. **do one's utmost** sein möglichstes tun.
utter¹ ['ʌtǝ] *v* äußern, aussprechen. **utterance** *n* Äußerung *f*.
utter² ['ʌtǝ] *adj* rein, bloß, höchst.
U-turn ['juːtǝːn] *n* Wende *f*; (*pol*) Kehrtwendung *f*.

V

vacant ['veikǝnt] *adj* leer. **vacancy** *n* Leere *f*; (*job*) freie Stelle. **vacate** *v* verlassen; (*seat*) freimachen. **vacation** *n* Urlaub *m*.
vaccine ['vaksiːn] *n* Impfstoff *m*. **vaccinate** *v* impfen. **vaccination** *n* Impfung *f*.
vacillate ['vasileit] *v* schwanken. **vacillation** *n* Schwanken *neut*.
vacuum ['vakjum] *n* Vakuum *neut*. **vacuum-cleaner** *n* Staubsauger *m*. *v* (*coll*) mit dem Staubsauger reinigen. **vacuous** *adj* leer.
vagina [vǝ'dʒainǝ] *n* Scheide *f*, Vagina *f*.
vagrant ['veigrǝnt] *n* Vagabund *m*, Landstreicher *m*.
vague [veig] *adj* vage, undeutlich; (*person*) zerstreut. **vagueness** *n* Verschwommenheit *f*.
vain [vein] *adj* (*person*) eitel, eingebildet; (*thing*) eitel, leer; (*effort*) vergeblich. **in vain** umsonst, vergeblich.
valiant ['valiǝnt] *adj* tapfer, heroisch.
valid ['valid] *adj* gültig. **validate** *v* für gültig erklären. **validity** *n* Gültigkeit *f*.
valley ['vali] *n* Tal *neut*.
value ['valjuː] *n* Wert *neut*. **value-added tax** (**VAT**) Mehrwertsteuer (Mwst) *f*. *v* (*establish value of*) einschätzen; (*treasure*) bewerten. **valuable** *adj* wertvoll, kostbar. **valuables** *pl n* Wertsachen *pl*. **valuation** *n* Schätzung *f*. **valued** *adj* hochgeschätzt. **valueless** *adj* wertlos.
valve [valv] *n* Ventil *neut*; (*anat*) Klappe *f*; (*elec*) Röhre *f*.
vampire ['vampaiǝ] *n* Vampir *m*.
van [van] *n* Lastwagen *m*, Lieferwagen *m*. **luggage van** Gepäckwagen *m*.

vandal ['vandl] *n* Vandale *m*, Vandalin *f*. **vandalism** *n* Vandalismus *m*.
vanilla [vǝ'nilǝ] *n* Vanille *f*.
vanish ['vaniʃ] *v* verschwinden. **vanishing cream** Tagescreme *f*.
vanity ['vanǝti] *n* Eitelkeit *f*. **vanity bag** Kosmetiktasche *f*.
vapour ['veipǝ] *n* Dampf *m*. **vaporize** *v* verdampfen.
varicose veins ['varikous] *pl n* Krampfadern *pl*.
varnish ['vaːniʃ] *n* Lack *m*, Firnis *m*. *v* lackieren.
vary ['veǝri] *v* (*modify*) (ab)ändern, variieren; (*become changed*) sich ändern, variieren. **variable** *adj* veränderlich. **variation** *n* Veränderung; (*music, biology*) Variation *f*. **varied** *adj* verschiedenartig, abwechslungsvoll. **variety** *n* Verschiedenheit, Mannigfaltigkeit *f*; (*species*) Art *f*, Varietät *f*. **variety show** Variété *neut*. **various** *adj* verschieden; (*several*) mehrere. **varying** *adj* wechselnd, unterschiedlich.
vase [vaːz] *n* Vase *f*.
vasectomy [vǝ'sektǝmi] *n* Vasektomie *f*.
vast [vaːst] *adj* ungeheuer, riesig; (*wide*) weit, ausgedehnt. **vast majority** überwiegende Mehrheit *f*. **vast numbers of** zahllos(e). **vastly** *n* gewaltig. **vastness** *n* Weite *f*.
vat [vat] *n* großes Faß *neut*.
vault¹ [voːlt] *n* (*ceiling*) Gewölbe *neut*; (*cellar*) Keller *m*; (*safe*) Stahlkammer *f*.
vault² [voːlt] *v* (*jump*) springen (über). *n* Sprung *m*. **vaulting-horse** *n* Sprungpferd *neut*.
veal [viːl] *n* Kalbfleisch *neut*.
veer [viǝ] *v* sich drehen; (*mot*) ausscheren.
vegetable ['vedʒtǝbl] *n* Gemüse *neut*. *adj* pflanzlich. **vegetarian** *n* Vegetarier(in); *adj* vegetarisch. **vegetation** *n* Pflanzenwuchs *m*, Vegetation *f*.
vehement ['viːǝmǝnt] *adj* heftig, gewaltig.
vehicle ['viǝkl] *n* Fahrzeug *neut*; (*medium*) Mittel *neut*, Vehikel *neut*.
veil [veil] *n* Schleier *m*. *v* verschleiern. **veiled** *adj* verschleiert.
vein [vein] *n* Vene *f*; (*mood*) Stimmung *f*; (*in rock*) Ader *f*. **veined** *adj* geädert.
velocity [vǝ'losǝti] *n* Geschwindigkeit *f*.
velvet ['velvit] *n* Samt *m*. *adj* Samt-. **velvety** *adj* samtweich, samtartig.

vending machine ['vendiŋ] *n* (Verkaufs)Automat *m.*
veneer [vəˈniə] *n* Furnier *neut;* (*fig*) Anstrich *m. v* furnieren.
venerate ['venəreit] *v* verehren, bewundern. **venerable** *adj* ehrwürdig. **veneration** *n* Verehrung *f.*
venereal disease [vəˈniəriəl] *n* Geschlechtskrankheit *f.*
Venetian blind [vəˈniːʃən] *n* Jalousie *f.*
vengeance ['vendʒəns] *n* Rache *f.* **take vengeance on** sich rächen an. **vengeful** *adj* rachsüchtig.
venison ['venisn] *n* Reh *neut,* Wildbret *neut.*
venom ['venəm] *n* (Tier)Gift *neut.* **venomous** *adj* giftig.
vent [vent] *n* Öffnung *f,* Luftloch *neut;* (*in jacket*) Schlitz *m. v* lüften; (*feelings*) freien Lauf lassen (+*dat*), äußern.
ventilate ['ventileit] *v* ventilieren, lüften. **ventilation** *n* Ventilation *f,* Lüftung *f.* **ventilator** *n* Ventilator *m,* Lüftungsanlage *f.*
venture ['ventʃə] *n* (*risk*) Risiko *neut,* Wagnis *neut;* (*undertaking*) Unternehmen *neut. v* wagen.
venue ['venjuː] *n* Schauplatz *m;* (*meeting place*) Treffpunkt *m.*
Venus ['viːnəs] *n* Venus *f.*
verb [vəːb] *n* Verbum *neut,* Zeitwort *neut.* **verbal** *adj* mündlich. **verbalize** *v* formulieren. **verbatim** *adv* wortwörtlich. **verbose** *adj* wortreich.
verdict ['vəːdikt] *n* Urteil *neut.*
verge [vəːdʒ] *n* Rand *m,* Grenze *f;* (*grass*) Grasstreifen *m.* **verge on** grenzen an.
verify ['verifai] *v* beweisen, bestätigen, beglaubigen. **verification** *n* Beglaubigung *f.*
vermin ['vəːmin] *pl n* Schädlinge *pl.*
vermouth ['vəːməθ] *n* Wermut *m.*
vernacular [vəˈnakjulə] *n* Volkssprache *f.*
versatile ['vəːsətail] *adj* (*person*) vielseitig. **versatility** *n* Vielseitigkeit *f.*
verse [vəːs] *n* (*stanza*) Strophe *f;* (*line*) Vers *m;* (*poetry*) Poesie *f,* Dichtung *f.* **versed** *adj* versiert.
version ['vəːʃən] *n* Fassung *f,* Version *f;* (*Bible, etc.*) Übersetzung *f.*
versus ['vəːsəs] *prep* gegen.
vertebra ['vəːtibrə] *n* (*pl* -ae) Wirbel *m.* **vertebral column** Wirbelsäule *f.* **vertebrate** *n* Wirbeltier *neut.*

vertical ['vəːtikl] *adj* senkrecht, lotrecht. *n* Senkrechte *f.*
vertigo ['vəːtigou] *n* Schwindelgefühl *neut.*
very ['veri] *adj* sehr. *very best* allerbest. *adj that very day* an ebendemselben Tag. *at the very beginning* gerade am Anfang.
vessel ['vesl] *n* Gefäß *neut;* (*ship*) Schiff *neut.*
vest [vest] *n* (*undershirt*) Unterhemd *neut;* (*waistcoat*) Weste *f.*
vestige ['vestidʒ] *n* Spur *f.*
vestments ['vestmənts] *pl n* (*rel*) Amtstracht *f.*
vestry ['vestri] *n* Sakristei *f.*
vet [vet] *n* (*animals*) Tierarzt *m. v* prüfen, überholen.
veteran ['vetərən] *n* Veteran *m.*
veterinary ['vetərinəri] *n* Tierarzt *m.*
veto ['viːtou] *n* Veto *neut,* Einspruch *m. v* Veto einlegen gegen.
vex [veks] *v* ärgern, belästigen. **vexation** *n* Ärger *m.* **vexed** *adj* ärgerlich; (*question*) strittig.
via [vaiə] *prep* über.
viable ['vaiəbl] *adj* lebensfähig; (*practicable*) durchführbar.
viaduct ['vaiədʌkt] *n* Viadukt *m.*
vibrate [vaiˈbreit] *v* vibrieren. **vibration** *n* Vibrieren *neut,* Vibration *f.*
vicar ['vikə] *n* Pfarrer *m.* **vicarage** *n* Pfarrhaus *neut.*
vicarious [viˈkeəriəs] *adj* aus zweiter Hand.
vice[1] [vais] *n* (*evil*) Laster *neut,* Untugend *f.*
vice[2] [vais] *n* (*tool*) Schraubstock *m,* Zwinge *f.*
vice-chancellor [vaisˈtʃaːnsələ] *n* (*university*) Rektor *m.*
vice-president [vaisˈprezidənt] *n* Vizepräsident *m.*
vice versa [vaisiˈvəːsə] *adv* umgekehrt.
vicinity [viˈsinəti] *n* Nähe *f,* Nachbarschaft *f.*
vicious ['viʃəs] *adj* bösartig, gemein; (*blow, etc*) heftig, gewaltig. **vicious circle** Teufelskreis *m.* **viciousness** *n* Gemeinheit *f.*
victim ['viktim] *n* Opfer *neut.* **victimize** *v* ungerecht behandeln.
victor ['viktə] *n* Sieger(in). **victorious** *adj* siegreich. **victory** *n* Sieg *m.*
video-tape ['vidiouteip] *n* Magnetbildband *neut.*

view [vjuɪ] *n* Ausblick *m*, Aussicht *f*; *(picture, opinion)* Ansicht *f*. **in view** in Sicht. **viewfinder** *n* Sucher *m*. **viewpoint** *n* Gesichtspunkt *m*, Standpunkt *m*. **with a view to** mit der Absicht, zu. *v* ansehen, betrachten. **viewer** *n* *(TV)* Zuschauer(in).

vigil ['vidʒil] *n* Wachen *neut*. **keep vigil** wachen. **vigilance** *n* Wachsamkeit *f*. **vigilant** *adj* wachsam.

vigour ['vigə] *n* Kraft *f*, Vitalität *f*. **vigorous** *adj* kräftig, energisch.

vile [vail] *adj* gemein, ekelerregend, widerlich.

villa ['vilə] *n* Villa *f*.

village ['vilidʒ] *n* Dorf *neut*. *adj* dörflich, Dorf-. **villager** *n* Dorfbewohner(in).

villain ['vilən] *n* Schurke *m*; *(coll)* Schelm *m*. **villainous** *adj* schurkisch. **villainy** *n* Schurkerei *f*.

vindictive [vin'diktiv] *adj* rachsüchtig. **vindictiveness** *n* Rachsucht *f*.

vine [vain] *n* Rebe *f*, Weinstock *m*. **vineleaf** *n* Weinblatt *m*. **vineyard** *n* Weinberg *m*. **viniculture** *n* Weinbau *m*.

vinegar ['vinigə] *n* Essig *m*. **vinegary** *adj* sauer.

vintage ['vintidʒ] *n* Weinernte *f*; *(particular year)* Jahrgang *m*.

vinyl ['vainil] *n* Vinyl *neut*. *adj* Vinyl-.

viola [vi'oulə] *n* Viola *f*.

violate ['vaiəleit] *v* *(law)* übertreten; *(woman)* vergewaltigen. **violation** *n* Übertretung *f*.

violence ['vaiələns] *n* Gewalt *f*, Gewalttätigkeit *f*. **violent** *adj* *(blow)* heftig, gewaltig; *(person, action)* gewaltsam.

violet ['vaiəlit] *n* Veilchen *neut*. *adj* violett.

violin [vaiə'lin] *n* Geige *f*, Violine *f*. **violinist** *n* Geiger(in).

viper ['vaipə] *n* Vıper *f*, Natter *f*.

virgin ['vəɪdʒin] *n* Jungfrau *f*. *adj* jungfräulich; *(soil)* unbebaut. **virginity** *n* Jungfernschaft *f*.

Virgo ['vəɪgou] *n* Jungfrau *f*.

virile ['virail] *adj* männlich, kräftig. **virility** *n* Männlichkeit *f*.

virtual ['vəɪtʃuəl] *adj* eigentlich; *(coll)* praktisch. **virtually** *adv* praktisch.

virtue ['vəɪtʃuɪ] *n* Tugend *f*. **by virtue of** wegen (+ *gen*). **virtuous** *adj* tugendhaft, rechtschaffen.

virtuoso [,vəɪtju'ouzou] *n* Virtuose *m*, Virtuosin *f*. **virtuosity** *n* Virtuosität *f*.

virus ['vaiərəs] *n* Virus *neut*.

visa ['viɪzə] *n* Visum *neut*.

viscount ['vaikaunt] *n* Vicomte *m*.

viscous ['viskəs] *adj* zähflüssig. **viscosity** *n* Viskosität *f*.

visible ['vizəbl] *adj* sichtbar. **visibility** *n* Sichtbarkeit *f*. **visibly** *adv* offenbar.

vision ['viʒən] *n* *(power of sight)* Sehvermögen *neut*; *(insight)* Einsicht *f*; *(mystical, etc.)* Vision *f*. **field of vision** Blickfeld *neut*. **visionary** *adj* phantastisch; *n* Hellseher(in).

visit ['vizit] *v* besuchen. *n* Besuch *m*. **visitation** *n* Besuchen *neut*. **visiting** *adj* Besuchs-. **visitor** *n* Besucher(in). **visitor's book** Gästebuch *neut*.

visor ['vaizə] *n* Visier *neut*; *(peak)* Schirm *m*.

visual ['viʒuəl] *adj* visuell. **visual aids** Anschauungsmaterial *neut*. **visualize** *v* vergegenwärtigen.

vital ['vaitl] *adj* lebenswichtig. **vitality** *n* Lebenskraft *f*.

vitamin ['vitəmin] *n* Vitamin *neut*.

vivacious [vi'veiʃəs] *adj* lebhaft, munter. **vivacity** *n* Lebhaftigkeit *f*.

vivid ['vivid] *adj* *(description)* lebendig; *(colour)* leuchtend; *(imagination)* lebhaft.

vixen ['viksn] *n* Füchsin *f*.

vocabulary [və'kabjuləri] *n* Wortschatz *m*; *(glossary)* Wörterverzeichnis *neut*.

vocal ['voukəl] *adj* stimmlich; *(music)* Vokal-. **vocal cords** *pl* Stimmbänder *pl*. **vocalist** *n* Sänger(in).

vocation [vou'keiʃən] *n* *(rel)* Berufung *f*; *(occupation)* Beruf *m*. **vocational** *adj* Berufs-.

vociferous [və'sifərəs] *adj* brüllend, lärmend.

vodka ['vodkə] *n* Wodka *m*.

voice [vois] *n* Stimme *f*. *v* ausdrücken, äußern.

void [void] *adj* leer; *(invalid)* nichtig, ungültig.

volatile ['volətail] *adj* flüchtig; *(person)* wankelmütig, sprunghaft.

volcano [vol'keinou] *n* Vulkan *m*. **volcanic** *adj* vulkanisch. **volcanic eruption** Vulkanausbruch *m*.

volley ['voli] *n* *(mil)* Salve *f*; *(tennis)* Flugschlag *m*.

volt [voult] *n* Volt *neut*. **voltage** *n* Spannung *f*.

volume ['voljum] *n* Volumen *neut*, Inhalt *m*; *(book)* Band *m*; *(noise level)* Lautstärke *f*.

voluntary ['vɔləntri] *adj* freiwillig.
volunteer [vɔlən'tiə] *n* Freiwillige(r). *adj* Freiwilligen-. *v* sich freiwillig melden.
voluptuous [və'lʌptʃuəs] *adj* wollüstig. **voluptuousness** *n* Wollust *f*.
vomit ['vɔmit] *v* (sich) erbrechen.
voodoo ['vuːduː] *n* Wodu *m*.
voracious [və'reiʃəs] *adj* gierig.
vote [vout] *n* (*individual*) Stimme *f*; (*right to vote*) Stimmrecht *neut*; (*election*) Abstimmung *f*, Wahl *f*. **vote of no confidence** Mißtrauensvotum *neut*. *v* abstimmen. **vote for** stimmen für. **voter** *n* Wähler(in).
vouch [vautʃ] *v* (sich) bürgen für. **voucher** *n* Gutschein *m*. **vouchsafe** *v* gewähren.
vow [vau] *n* Gelübde *neut*. *v* schwören, geloben.
vowel ['vauəl] *n* Vokal *m*. *adj* vokalisch.
voyage ['vɔiidʒ] *n* Reise *f*. *v* reisen. **voyager** *n* Reisende(r).
vulgar ['vʌlgə] *adj* vulgär, ordinär. **vulgarity** *n* Ungezogenheit *f*.
vulnerable ['vʌlnərəbl] *adj* verwundbar.
vulture ['vʌltʃə] *n* Geier *m*.

W

wad [wɔd] *n* Bausch *m*; (*money*) Rolle *f*.
waddle ['wɔdl] *v* watscheln.
wade [weid] *v* waten.
wafer ['weifə] *n* Waffel *f*; (*rel*) Hostie *f*. **wafer-thin** *adj* hauchdünn.
waffle ['wɔfl] *n* Waffel *f*.
waft [wɔft] *v* wehen.
wag [wag] *v* **wag one's head** mit dem Kopf wackeln. **wag one's tail** wedeln.
wage [weidʒ] *n* *also* **wages** Lohn *m*. **wage agreement** Tarifvertrag *m*. **wage-earner** *n* Lohnempfänger(in). **wage freeze** *n* Lohnstopp *m*. **wage-packet** *n* Lohntüte *f*. *v* (*war*) führen.
waggle ['wagl] *v* wackeln (mit).
wagon ['wagən] *n* Wagen *m*; (*rail*) Waggon *m*.
waif [weif] *n* verwahrlostes Kind *neut*.
wail [weil] *v* jammern, wehklagen. **wailing** *n* Jammern *neut*.
waist [weist] *n* Taille *f*. **waistband** n Bund *m*. **waistcoat** *n* Weste *f*.
wait [weit] *v* warten. **no waiting** Parken

verboten. **wait and see** abwarten. **wait for** warten auf. **waiting-room** *n* Wartesaal *m*. **wait on** bedienen. *n* Wartezeit *f*. **waiter** *n* Kellner *m*. **waitress** *n* Kellnerin *f*.
waive [weiv] *v* verzichten auf.
***wake** [weik] *v* *also* **waken** *or* **wake up** aufwachen, erwachen; (*awaken*) (auf)wecken, erwecken. **wakeful** *adj* wachsam. **waking** *adj* wach.
walk [wɔːk] *v* laufen, (zu Fuß) gehen. **walk out** streiken. **walk out on** im Stich lassen. **walk-over** *n* leichter Sieg *m*, Spaziergang *m*. *n* Spaziergang *m*; (*path*) Weg *m*. **go for a walk** einen Spaziergang machen, spazierengehen. **walk of life** Lebensstellung *f*.
wall [wɔːl] *n* Mauer *f*; (*internal*) Wand *f*. **wallpaper** *n* Tapete *f*; *v* tapezieren.
wallet ['wɔlit] *n* Brieftasche *f*, Geldtasche *f*.
wallop ['wɔləp] *v* prügeln. *n* (heftiger) Schlag *m*.
wallow ['wɔlou] *v* sich wälzen.
walnut ['wɔːlnʌt] *n* Walnuß *f*.
walrus ['wɔːlrəs] *n* Walroß *neut*.
waltz [wɔːlts] *n* Walzer *m*. *v* Walzer tanzen, walzen.
wand [wɔnd] *n* Rute *f*; (*magic*) Zauberstab *m*.
wander ['wɔndə] *v* wandern. **wander about** umherwandern. **wanderlust** *n* Wanderlust *f*. **wanderer** *n* Wanderer *m*. **wandering** *n* Wandern *neut*. *adj* wandernd.
wane [wein] *v* abnehmen.
wangle ['waŋgl] *v* organisieren, (hintenherum) beschaffen. **wangler** *n* Schieber *m*.
want [wɔnt] *v* wollen; (*need*) benötigen; (*wish*) wünschen. **wants** *pl n* Bedürfnisse *pl*. **wanted** *adj* gesucht. **be found wanting** den Erwartungen nicht entsprechen.
wanton ['wɔntən] *adj* lüstern; (*cruelty, etc.*) rücksichtslos.
war [wɔː] *n* Krieg *m*. **be at war with** Kriegführen mit. **prisoner-of-war** Kriegsgefangene(r). **war crime** *n* Kriegsverbrechen *neut*. **warfare** *n* Kriegführung *f*. **warlike** *adj* kriegerisch. **war memorial** Kriegerdenkmal *neut*.
warble ['wɔːbl] *v* trillern.
ward [wɔːd] *n* (*town*) Bezirk *n*; (*hospital*) Station *f*; (*of court*) Mündel *neut*. *v* **ward off** abwehren. **warden** *n* Vorsteher *m*. **warder** *n* Gefängniswärter *m*.

wardrobe ['woɪdroub] *n* Kleiderschrank *m*; (*clothes*) Garderobe *f*.
wares [weəz] *pl n* Waren *pl*.
warehouse ['weəhaus] *n* Lager(haus) *neut*.
warm [woɪm] *adj* warm. **warm-blooded** *adj* warmblütig. **warm-hearted** *adj* warmherzig. *v* (auf)wärmen. **warm up** *v* (*become warm*) warm werden; (*engine*) warmlaufen (lassen). **warmish** *adj* lauwarm. **warmth** *n* Wärme *f*.
warn [woɪn] *v* warnen. **warn off** verwarnen. **warning** *n* Warnung *f*. *adj* warnend. **warning light** Warnlicht *neut*.
warp [woɪp] *v* sich verziehen, krumm werden. **warped** *adj* verzogen.
warrant ['worənt] *n* Vollmacht *f*, Berechtigung *f*. **warrant of arrest** Haftbefehl *m*.
warren ['worən] *n* Kaninchengehege *neut*.
warrior ['woriə] *n* Krieger *m*.
wart [woɪt] *n* Warze *f*.
wary ['weəri] *adj* vorsichtig, behutsam. **wary of** auf der Hut vor.
was [woz] *V* be.
wash [woʃ] *v* waschen; (*oneself*) sich waschen; (*dishes*) spülen. **washbasin** *n* Waschbecken *neut*. **wash down** abwaschen. **washed-out** *adj* verblaßt; (*coll*) ermüdet. **washed-up** *adj* (*coll*) ruiniert, fertig. **washing** *n* (*laundry*) Wäsche *f*. **washing machine** Waschmaschine *f*. **washing powder** Waschmittel *neut*. **wash up** (ab)spülen, abwaschen. *n* Waschen *neut*, Wäsche *f*. **washable** *adj* waschecht. **washer** *n* (*tech*) Scheibe *f*, Dichtungsring *m*.
wasp [wosp] *n* Wespe *f*. **waspish** *adj* reizbar.
waste [weist] *v* verschwenden, vergeuden. **waste away** abnehmen, verfallen. *n* Verschwendung *f*; (*rubbish*) Abfall *m*. **waste of time** Zeitverschwendung *f*. *adj* (*land*) wüst; Abfall-. **lay waste** verwüsten. **waste-bin** *n* Abfalleimer *m*. **waste-paper basket** *n* Papierkorb *neut*. **wasteful** *adj* verschwenderisch.
watch [wotʃ] *v* (*guard*) bewachen; (*observe*) zusehen, beobachten; (*pay attention to*) achtgeben auf. **watch out!** paß auf! **watch out for** auf der Hut sein vor. **watch television** fernsehen. *n* Wache *f*; (*wristwatch*) Armbanduhr *f*. **keep watch** Wache halten. **watchdog** *n* Wachhund *m*. **watchman** *n* Wächter *m*. **watchful** *adj* wachsam.

water ['woɪtə] *n* Wasser *neut*. *v* wässern. **water down** verwässern.
water-closet *n* (Wasser)Klosett *neut*, WC *neut*.
water-colour *n* Aquarell *neut*. *adj* Aquarell-.
watercress ['woɪtəkres] *n* Brunnenkresse *f*.
waterfall ['woɪtəfoɪl] *n* Wasserfall *m*.
watering-can *n* Gießkanne *f*.
water-lily *n* Seerose *f*, Wasserlilie *f*.
waterlogged ['woɪtəlogd] *adj* vollgesogen.
watermark ['woɪtəmaɪk] *n* (*in paper*) Wasserzeichen *neut*.
water-melon *n* Wassermelone *f*.
water-mill *n* Wassermühle *f*.
waterproof ['woɪtəpruɪf] *adj* wasserdicht. *n* Regenmantel *m*. *v* imprägnieren.
watershed ['woɪtəʃed] *n* Wasserscheide *f*.
water-ski *n* Wasserski *m*. *v* Wasserski fahren.
watertight ['woɪtətait] *adj* wasserdicht; (*argument*) unanfechtbar.
water-way *n* Wasserstraße *f*.
waterworks ['woɪtəwəɪks] *pl n* Wasserwerk *neut sing*.
watery ['woɪtəri] *adj* wässerig; (*eyes*) tränend.
watt [wot] *n* Watt *neut*. **wattage** *n* Wattleistung *f*.
wave [weiv] *n* Welle *f*; (*gesture*) Wink *m*. **waveband** *n* Wellenband *neut*. **wavelength** *n* Wellenlänge *f*. *v* winken; (*hair*) in Wellen legen. **wavy** *adj* wellig; (*hair*) gewellt.
waver ['weivə] *v* schwanken.
wax¹ [waks] *n* Wachs *neut*. *v* (*floor*) bohnern. **waxen** *adj* wächsern. **waxwork** *n* Wachsfigur *f*.
wax² [waks] *v* (*increase*) wachsen; (*become*) werden.
way [wei] *n* Weg *m*; (*direction*) Richtung *f*; (*method*) Art *f*, Weise *f*; (*respect*) Hinsicht *f*, Beziehung *f*. **by the way** übrigens. **on the way** unterwegs. **out-of-the-way** *adj* abgelegen; (*odd*) ungewöhnlich.
***waylay** [wei'lei] *v* auflauern (+ *dat*).
wayward ['weiwəd] *adj* eigensinnig. **waywardness** *n* Eigensinn *m*.
we [wiɪ] *pl pron* wir.
weak [wiɪk] *adj* schwach; (*liquids*) dünn. **weak-minded** *adj* charakterschwach. **weaken** *v* schwächen. *n* Schwächling *m*. **weakly** *adj*, *adv* schwächlich. **weakness** *n* Schwäche *f*; (*disadvantage*) Nachteil *m*; (*liking*) Vorliebe *f*.

wealth [welθ] *n* Reichtum *m*; (*fortune*) Vermögen *neut*. **wealthy** *adj* reich, wohlhabend.
wean [wiːn] *v* entwöhnen.
weapon ['wepən] *n* Waffe *f*.
*****wear** [weə] *v* tragen; (*wear out*) abnutzen; (*become worn*) abgenutzt werden; *n* Tragen *neut*; (*wear and tear*) Abnutzung *f*, Verschleiß *m*. **wear off** (*fig*) sich verlieren. **wear out** (*person*) ermüden.
weary ['wiəri] *adj* müde; (*task*) lästig. *v* ermüden; (*become tired of*) müde werden (+ *gen*). **weariness** *n* Müdigkeit *f*. **wearisome** *adj* ermüdend, langweilig.
weasel ['wiːzl] *n* Wiesel *neut*.
weather ['weðə] *n* Wetter *neut*. **weatherbeaten** *adj* verwittert. **weathercock** *n* Wetterhahn *m*. **weather forecast** Wettervorhersage *f*. **weatherman** *n* (*coll*) Meteorologe *m*. **weather-proof** *adj* wetterfest.
*****weave** [wiːv] *v* weben. **weave into** einflechten in. **weaving** *n* Weberei *f*; *adj* Web-.
web [web] *n* (*spider's*) Spinngewebe *neut*. **webbed foot** Schwimmfuß *m*. **webbing** *n* Gewebe *neut*. **web-footed** *adj* schwimmfüßig.
wedding ['wediŋ] *n* Hochzeit *f*. **wedding cake** Hochzeitskuchen *m*. **wedding day** Hochzeitstag *m*. **wedding ring** Trauring *m*.
wedge [wedʒ] *n* Keil *m*; (*of cheese*) Ecke *f*. **wedge-shaped** *adj* keilförmig. *v* einkeilen.
Wednesday ['wenzdi] *n* Mittwoch *m*. **on Wednesdays** mittwochs.
weed [wiːd] *n* Unkraut *neut*. *v* (Unkraut) jäten. **weedy** *adj* (*coll*) schmächtig.
week [wiːk] *n* Woche *f*. **weekday** *n* Wochentag *m*. **weekend** *n* Wochenende *neut*. **weekly** *adj* wöchentlich; *n* (*magazine*) Wochenzeitschrift *f*.
*****weep** [wiːp] *v* weinen. **weeping** *adj* weinend; *n* Weinen *neut*. **weeping willow** Trauerweide *f*.
weigh [wei] *v* wiegen. **weigh one's words** seine Worte abwägen. **weigh up** abschätzen. **weight** *n* Gewicht *neut*. **carry weight with** viel gelten bei. **lose weight** abnehmen. **put on weight** zunehmen. **weight-lifting** *n* Gewichtheben *neut*. **weighty** *adj* schwerwiegend.
weir [wiə] *n* Wehr *neut*.

weird [wiəd] *adj* unheimlich.
welcome ['welkəm] *n* Willkommen *neut*. *adj, interj* willkommen. **you're welcome** (*coll*) bitte, nichts zu danken. *v* willkommen heißen; (*fig*) begrüßen.
weld [weld] *v* (ver)schweißen. *n* Schweißstelle *f*, Schweißnaht *f*. **welder** *n* Schweißer *m*. **welding** *n* Schweißen *neut*.
welfare ['welfeə] *n* Wohlfahrt *f*. **welfare state** Wohlfahrtsstaat *m*.
well¹ [wel] *n* (*for water*) Brunnen *m*, Quelle *f*.
well² [wel] *adv* gut. **as well** auch. **as well as** sowohl ... als auch. **you may well ask** du kannst wohl fragen. *adj* (*healthy*) wohl, gesund. **feel well** sich wohl fühlen. **I'm not well** mir ist nicht wohl. *interj* na, schön.
well-being *n* Wohlergehen *neut*.
well-behaved *adj* artig.
well-bred *adj* wohlerzogen.
well-built *adj* gut gebaut; (*person*) kräftig gebaut.
well-done *adj* (*meat*) gut durchgebraten.
wellingtons ['weliŋtənz] *pl n* Gummistiefel *pl*.
well-known *adj* (wohl)bekannt.
well-meaning *adj* wohlmeinend.
well-off *adj* wohlhabend.
well-paid *adj* gut bezahlt.
well-spoken *adj* höflich.
well-to-do *adj* wohlhabend.
well-worn *adj* abgenutzt; (*phrase*) abgedroschen.
went [went] *V* go.
wept [wept] *V* weep.
west [west] *n* Westen *m*. *adj also* **westerly** westlich, West-. *adv also* **westwards** nach Westen; westwärts. **western** *adj* westlich; *n* Wildwestfilm *m*.
wet [wet] *adj* naß. **wet through** durchnäßt. **wet weather** Regenwetter *neut*. *n* Nässe *f*. *v* anfeuchten, naßmachen. **wetness** *n* Nässe *f*.
whack [wak] *v* schlagen, verhauen. *n* Schlag *m*.
whale [weil] *n* Wal *m*, Walfisch *m*. **whaler** *n* Walfänger *m*. **whaling** *n* Walfang *m*.
wharf [woːf] *n* Kai *m*.
what [wot] *pron* was. **so what?** na und? **what about ... ?** wie wäre es mit ... ? **whatever** *pron* was auch immer. **nothing whatever** überhaupt nichts. **what for?** wozu? **what's up?** was ist los? **what's your**

name? wie heißt du? or (polite) wie ist Ihr Name? adj was für ein, welch.

wheat [wi:t] n Weizen m.

wheel [wi:l] n Rad neut; (steering) Lenkrad neut. **at the wheel** am Steuer. v rollen. **wheelbarrow** n Schubkarren m. **wheelchair** n Rollstuhl m.

wheeze [wi:z] n Keuchen neut; (coll) Plan m. v keuchen, schnaufen.

whelk [welk] n Wellhornschnecke f.

when [wen] adv (question) wann. conj (with past tense) als; (with present tense) wenn. **whenever** conj wann auch immer.

where [weə] adv, conj wo; (motion) wohin. **where from?** woher? **where to?** wohin? where do you come from? wo kommen Sie her? where are you going? wo gehen Sie hin? **whereabouts** adv wo; n Verbleib m. **whereas** conj wohingegen, während. **whereby** adv wodurch, womit. **whereupon** adv woraufhin. **wherever** adv wo auch immer.

whether ['weðə] conj ob.

which [witʃ] pron (question) welch; (the one that) welch, der/die/das.

whiff [wif] n Hauch m.

while [wail] conj während; (whereas) wogegen. n Weile f. **a long while ago** schon lange her. **for a while** eine Zeitlang. **in a while** bald. v **while away the time** sich die Zeit vertreiben.

whim [wim] n Laune f, Einfall m.

whimper ['wimpə] n Wimmer neut. v wimmern.

whimsical ['wimzikl] adj launenhaft.

whine [wain] n Gewinsel neut. v winseln. **whining** adj weinerlich.

whip [wip] n Peitsche f. v peitschen; (cream) schlagen. **whipped cream** Schlagsahne f. **whipping** n Peitschen neut. **whip-round** n (coll) Geldsammlung f.

whippet ['wipit] n Whippet m.

whirl [wə:l] n Wirbel m. v wirbeln. **whirlwind** n Wirbelwind m.

whisk [wisk] n Schneebesen m. v schlagen. **whisk away/off** v wegzaubern.

whiskers ['wiskəz] pl n (animals) Schnurrhaare pl; (man's) Barthaare pl.

whisky ['wiski] n Whisky m.

whisper ['wispə] v flüstern. n Flüstern m.

whist [wist] n Whist neut.

whistle ['wisl] v pfeifen. n Pfiff m; (instrument) Pfeife f.

white [wait] adj weiß; (pale) blaß. **white bread** Weißbrot neut. **white lie** Notlüge f. **white man** Weiße(r) m. **whitewash** v tünchen. **white wine** Weißwein m. n Weiß neut; (person) Weiße(r). **whiten** v weiß machen; (bleach) bleichen. **whiteness** n Weiße f.

whiting ['waitiŋ] n Weißfisch m.

Whitsun ['witsn] n Pfingsten neut sing.

whiz [wiz] v zischen.

who [hu:] pron (question) wer; (the one which, that) wer, welch, der/die/das. **whoever** pron wer auch immer.

whole [houl] adj ganz; (undamaged) heil, unverletzt. n das Ganze neut; (collective) Gesamtheit f. **on the whole** im großen und ganzen.

whole-hearted adj rückhaltlos.

wholemeal ['houlmi:l] adj Vollkorn-.

wholesale ['houlseil] adv en gros; (fig) unterschiedslos. adj Großhandels-. n Großhandel m. **wholesaler** n Großhändler m.

wholesome ['houlsəm] adj bekömmlich, gesund.

whom [hu:m] pron (question) (acc) wen, (dat) wem; (that, the one whom) den, dem.

whooping cough ['hu:piŋ] n Keuchhusten m.

whore [ho:] n Hure f. v huren.

whose [hu:z] pron (question) wessen; (of whom) dessen, deren. whose is this? wem gehört dies?

why [wai] adv warum. interj nun, ja. **that is why** deshalb. **the reason why** der Grund, weshalb.

wick [wik] n Docht m.

wicked ['wikid] adj böse. **wickedness** n Bosheit f.

wicker ['wikə] adj Weiden-, Korb-. **wickerwork** n Korbwaren pl.

wicket ['wikit] n (gate) Pförtchen neut.

wide [waid] adj breit. adv weit. **far and wide** weit und breit. **wide awake** hellwach. **widespread** adj weitverbreitet. **widely** adv weit. **widely known** allgemein bekannt. **widen** v breiter machen or werden. **wideness** n Breite f.

widow ['widou] n Witwe f. **widowed** adj verwitwet. **widower** n Witwer m. **widowhood** n Witwenstand m.

width [widθ] n Breite f, Weite f.

wield [wi:ld] v (weapon) handhaben; (influence) ausüben.

wife [waif] *n* (*pl* **wives**) Frau *f*.
wig [wig] *n* Perücke *f*.
wiggle ['wigl] *v* wackeln. *n* Wackeln *neut*.
wild [waild] *adj* wild; (*coll*: *angry*) wütend. **be wild about** (*coll*) schwärmen für. **wildcat strike** wilder Streik *m*. **wild flower** Feldblume *f*. **Wildness** *n* Wildheit *f*.
wilderness ['wildənəs] *n* Wüste *f*.
wilful ['wilfəl] *adj* eigensinnig. **wilfulness** *n* Eigensinn *m*.
will[1] [wil] *v* (*to form future*) werden; (*expressing wish or determination*) wollen.
will[2] [wil] *n* Wille *m*; (*testament*) Testament *neut*. **will-power** *n* Willenskraft *f*.
willing ['wiliŋ] *adj* bereit. **willingly** *adv* bereitwillig. **willingness** *n* Bereitschaft *f*.
willow ['wilou] *n* Weide *f*.
wilt [wilt] *v* verwelken.
wily ['waili] *adj* schlau, listig.
*****win** [win] *v* gewinnen; (*mil*) siegen. *n* Seig *m*.
wince [wins] *v* zusammenzucken. *n* (Zusammen)Zucken *neut*.
winch [wintʃ] *n* Winde *f*.
wind[1] [wind] *n* Wind *m*. **wind instrument** Blasinstrument *neut*.
*****wind**[2] [waind] *v* (sich) winden; (*yarn*) aufwickeln; (*clock*) aufziehen. **wind up** (*come to a close*) Schluß machen. (*business*) auflösen. **winder** *n* Winde *f*. **winding** *adj* sich windend, schlängelnd.
windlass ['windləs] *n* Winde *f*.
windmill ['wind,mil] *n* Windmühle *f*.
windpipe ['windpaip] *n* Luftröhre *f*.
window ['windou] *n* Fenster *neut*; (*ticket office, etc.*) Schalter *m*; (*shop*) Schaufenster *neut*. **window-box** *n* Blumenkasten *m*. **window-frame** *n* Fensterrahmen *m*. **window-pane** *n* Fensterscheibe *f*. **window-shopping** *n* Schaufensterbummel *m*. **window-sill** Fensterbrett *neut*.
windshield ['windʃiːld] *n* Windschutzscheibe *f*. **windshield-wiper** Scheibenwischer *m*.
windy ['windi] *adj* windig.
wine [wain] *n* Wein *m*. **wine bar** Weinstube *f*. **wineglass** *n* Weinglas *neut*.
wing [wiŋ] *n* Flügel *m*; (*theatre*) Kulisse *f*; (*mot*) Kotflügel *m*. **on the wing** im Fluge. **winged** *adj* geflügelt. **winger** *n* (*sport*) Außenstürmer *m*. **wing-nut** *n* Flügelmutter *f*.
wink [wiŋk] *n* Zwinkern *neut*. *v* **wink at** zuzwinkern (+ *dat*).

winkle ['wiŋkl] *n* Strandschnecke *f*.
winner ['winə] *n* Sieger(in), Gewinner(in).
winnings *pl n* Gewinn *m sing*.
winter ['wintə] *n* Winter *m*. *v* überwintern. **wintry** *adj* winterlich.
wipe [waip] *v* wischen. **wipe out** (*destroy*) ausrotten. **wipe up** (*dishes*) abtrocknen. **wiper** *n* Wischer *m*.
wire [waiə] *n* Draht *m*; (*telegram*) Telegramm *neut*. **wire netting** Maschendraht *m*. *v* (*house, etc.*) Leitungen legen in. **wireless** *n* Radio *neut*. **wiring** *n* Leitungsnetz *neut*.
wiry ['waiəri] *adj* (*person*) sehnig, zäh, (*hair*) borstig.
wisdom ['wizdəm] *n* Weisheit *f*. **wisdom tooth** *n* Weisheitszahn *m*.
wise [waiz] *adj* weise, klug. **wise guy** (*coll*) Besserwisser *m*. **wise man/woman** Weise(r).
wish [wiʃ] *v* wünschen. **wish for** sich wünschen. *I wish to know* ich möchte wissen. **wished-for** *adj* erwünscht. *n* Wunsch *m*.
wisp [wisp] *n* (*hair*) Strähne *f*. **wispy** *adj* (*hair*) wuschelig.
wistful ['wistfəl] *adj* sehnsüchtig. **wistfulness** *n* Sehnsucht *f*.
wit [wit] *n* Witz *m*, Esprit *m*. **wits** *pl* Verstand *m*.
witch [witʃ] *n* Hexe *f*. **witchcraft** *n* Hexerei *f*. **witch-doctor** *n* Medizinmann *m*.
with [wið] *prep* mit; (*among people*) bei. **weep with joy** vor Freude weinen. **stay with** bleiben bei.
*****withdraw** [wið'drɔː] *v* (sich) zurückziehen; (*remark*) zurücknehmen; (*money*) abheben. **withdrawal** *n* Zurückziehung *f*; Zurücknahme *f*; Abhebung *f*. **withdrawn** *adj* zurückgezogen.
wither ['wiðə] *v* verdorren, verwelken. **withered** *adj* welk.
*****withhold** [wið'hould] *v* zurückhalten.
within [wi'ðin] *prep* innerhalb (+ *gen*). *adv* darin, innen. **within a short time** binnen kurzem.
without [wi'ðaut] *prep* ohne (+ *acc*).
*****withstand** [wið'stand] *v* widerstehen (+ *dat*).
witness ['witnis] *n* Zeuge *m*, Zeugin *f*. **bear witness to** Zeuge ablegen von. **witness-box** *n* Zeugenstand *m*. *v* bezeugen; (*be present at*) erleben, sehen.

witty ['witi] *adj* witzig. **witticism** *n* Witz *m*.

wizard ['wizəd] *n* Zauberer *m*. **wizardry** *n* Zauberei *f*.

wobble ['wobl] *v* wackeln, schwanken. *n* Wackeln *neut*. **wobbly** *adj* wackelig.

woke [wouk] *V* wake.

woken ['woukn] *V* wake.

wolf [wulf] *n* (*pl* wolves) Wolf *m*. *v* (*gobble*) verschlingen. **she-wolf** *n* Wölfin *f*.

woman ['wumən] *n* (*pl* women) Frau *f*. **woman doctor** Ärztin *f*. **womanly** *adj* weiblich, fraulich.

womb [wuːm] *n* Gebärmutter *f*.

won [wʌn] *V* win.

wonder ['wʌndə] *n* (*marvel*) Wunder *neut*; (*astonishment*) Erstaunen *neut*, Verwunderung *f*. **no wonder** kein Wunder. *v* (*be surprised*) sich wundern; (*ask oneself, muse*) sich fragen, gespannt sein. **wonderful** *adj* wunderbar. **wondrous** *adj* erstaunlich.

wonky ['woŋki] *adj* wackelig.

wood [wud] *n* Holz *neut*; (*forest*) Wald *m*. **wooden** *adj* hölzern, Holz-.

woodcock ['wudkok] *n* Waldschnepfe *f*.

woodpecker ['wudpekə] *n* Specht *m*.

wood-pigeon *n* Ringeltaube *f*.

woodwind ['wudwind] *n* Holzblasinstrument *neut*; Holzbläser *m*.

woodwork ['wudwəːk] *n* Holzarbeit *f*, Tischlerei *f*.

woodworm ['wudwəːm] *n* Holzwurm *m*.

woody ['wudi] *adj* Holz-, holzig; (*countryside*) Wald-, waldig.

wool [wul] *n* Wolle *f*. **woollen** *adj* wollen, Woll-. **woolly** *adj* wollig.

word [wəːd] *n* Wort *neut*. **break/keep one's word** sein Wort brechen/halten. **wording** *n* Fassung *f*. **wordy** *adj* wortreich, langatmig.

wore [woː] *V* wear.

work [wəːk] *n* Arbeit *f*; (*piece of work, art, music, etc.*) Werk *neut*. **works** *pl* Werk *neut*. *v* arbeiten; (*of machine*) laufen, funktionieren; (*succeed*) klappen; (*land*) bebauen; (*metal*) schmieden; (*operate (machine)*) bedienen. **work off** (*debt*) abarbeiten; (*feelings*) abreagieren. **work out** ausrechnen. **out of work** arbeitslos. **worked-up** *adj* aufgeregt, aufgebracht. **worker** *n* Arbeiter(in). **working** *adj* Arbeits-; (*person*) berufstätig. **working class** Arbeiterklasse *f*; *adj* Arbeiter-. **in working order** betriebsfähig.

working party Arbeitsgruppe *f*. **workman** *n* Handwerker *m*. **work-to-rule** *n* Bummelstreik *m*.

world [wəːld] *n* Welt *f*. **not for all the world** nicht um alles in der Welt. **the world to come** das Jenseits *neut*. **world champion** Weltmeister(in). **world-famous** *adj* weltberühmt. **worldly-wise** *adj* weltklug. **world-wide** *adj* weitverbreitet. **worldly** *adj* irdisch.

worm [wəːm] *n* Wurm *m*.

worn [woːn] *v* wear. *adj* (*worn out*) abgenutzt. **worn out** *adj* (*thing*) abgenutzt; (*person*) todmüde.

worry ['wʌri] *v* (*bother*) beunruhigen; (*be worried*) sich Sorgen machen, sich beunruhigen. *n* Sorge *f*, Besorgnis *f*. **worrying** *adj* beunruhigend. **worried** *adj* beunruhigt, besorgt.

worse [wəːs] *adj, adv* schlimmer, schlechter. **worse and worse** immer schlechter. **worsen** *v* (sich) verschlechtern *or* verschlimmern.

worship ['wəːʃip] *n* Anbetung *f*, Verehrung *f*; (*in church*) Gottesdienst *m*. *v* anbeten, verehren. **worshipful** *adj* ehrwürdig. **worshipper** *n* Anbeter(in).

worst [wəːst] *adj* schlechtest, schlimmst. *adv* am schlechtesten *or* schlimmsten. **at the worst** im schlimmsten Falle.

worsted ['wustid] *n* Kammgarn *neut*.

worth [wəːθ] *n* Wert *m*. *adj* wert. **it's worth ten marks** es ist zehn Mark wert. **it's not worth it** es lohnt sich nicht. **worthless** *adj* wertlos. **worthwhile** *adj* der Mühe wert. **worthy** *adj* würdig, wert.

would [wud] *v* (*to form conditional*) würde, würdest, etc. (*used to*) pflegte, pflegtest, etc; (*expressing desire, volition*) wollte, wolltest, etc. **he would go** (*if*) er würde gehen(wenn). *I* **would like** ich möchte. **he would come in the summer** er pflegte im Sommer zu kommen. **he would not come** er wollte durchaus nicht kommen.

wound¹ [waund] *V* wind².

wound² [wuːnd] *n* Wunde *f*. *v* verwunden. **wounded** *adj* verletzt.

wove [wouv] *V* weave.

woven ['wouvn] *V* weave.

wrangle ['raŋgl] *v* zanken, streiten. *n* Zank *m*, Streit *m*.

wrap [rap] *v* wickeln. **wrap up** einwickeln. *n* Schal *m*. **wrapper** *n* Umschlag *m*. **wrap-**

ping *n* Verpackung *f.* **wrapping paper** Einwickelpapier *neut.*
wreath [riːθ] *n* Kranz *m.*
wreck [rek] *n* wrack *neut*; (*naut*) Schiffbruch *m. v* zerstören. **wreckage** *n* Trümmer *pl.*
wren [ren] *n* Zaunkönig *m.*
wrench [rentʃ] *v* zerren, ziehen. *n* (*tool*) Schraubenschlüssel *m.*
wrestle ['resl] *v* ringen. **wrestler** *n* Ringer *m.* **wrestling** *n* Ringkampf *m*, Ringen *neut.*
wretch [retʃ] *n* Elende(r), armes Wesen *neut.* **wretched** *adj* unglücklich, elend.
wriggle ['rigl] *v* sich schlängeln. *n* Schlängeln *neut.*
*wring [riŋ] *v* (*hands*) ringen; (*clothes*) auswringen. **wringer** *n* Wringermaschine *f.* **wringing wet** triefend naß.
wrinkle ['riŋkl] *n* (*face, brow*) Runzel *f*, Falte *f*; (*paper*) Knitter *m.* **wrinkled** *adj* runzlig.
wrist [rist] *n* Handgelenk *neut.* **wristwatch** *n* Armbanduhr *f.*
writ [rit] *n* (*law*) (Vor)Ladung *f.* **Holy Writ** Heilige Schrift *f.*
*write [rait] *v* schreiben. **write down** aufschreiben. **write off** abschreiben. **write out** (*cheque*) ausstellen. **writer** *n* Schriftsteller(in). **writing** *n* Schreiben *neut.* **in writing** schriftlich. **writing-paper** *n* Schreibpapier *neut.*
written ['ritn] *V* write. *adj* schriftlich.
writhe [raið] *v* sich winden.
wrong [roŋ] *adj* (*incorrect*) falsch; (*bad, immoral*) unrecht. **be wrong** sich irren, unrecht haben. **what's wrong with ... ?** was ist los mit ... ? **that was wrong of you** das war unrecht von dir. **go wrong** (*mech*) kaputtgehen; (*plan*) schiefgehen. **get it wrong** es ganz falsch verstehen. **wrongdoer** *n* Missetäter(in). **wrongdoing** *n* Missetat *f.* **wrongly** *adv* mit Unrecht.
wrote [rout] *V* write.
wrought iron [ˌrɔit'aiən] *n* Schweißeisen *neut.*
wrung [rʌŋ] *V* wring.
wry [rai] *adj* verschroben.

X

xenophobia [ˌzenə'foubiə] *n* Fremdenfeindlichkeit *f.*
Xerox ® ['ziəroks] *n* Fotokopiergerät *neut. v* fotokopieren.
X-ray [eks'rei] *n* Röntgenstrahl *m*; (*picture*) Röntgenbild *neut. v* röntgen. *adj* Röntgen-.
xylophone ['zailəfoun] *n* Xylophon *neut.*

Y

yacht [jot] *n* Jacht *f.* **yachting** *n* Segeln *neut.*
yank [jaŋk] *v* (*coll*) heftig ziehen (an). *n* Ruck *m.*
yap [jap] *v* kläffen; (*coll*) schwätzen. *n* Kläffen *neut.*
yard¹ [jaid] *n* (*measure*) Yard *neut.* **yardstick** *n* Maßstab *m.*
yard² [jaid] *n* Hof *m.*
yarn [jain] *n* Garn *neut*; (*story*) Geschichte *f.*
yawn [join] *n* Gähnen *neut. v* gähnen.
year [jiə] *n* Jahr *neut.* **5 years old** fünf Jahre alt. **for years** jahrelang. **yearbook** *n* Jahrbuch *neut.* **yearly** *adj* jährlich.
yearn [jəin] *v* sich sehnen (nach). **yearning** *n* Sehnsucht *f.*
yeast [jiist] *n* Hefe *f.*
yell [jel] *v* (gellend) aufschreien. *n* Schrei *m.*
yellow ['jelou] *adj* gelb. *n* Gelb *neut.*
yelp [jelp] *v* jaulen. *n* Jaulen *neut.*
yes [jes] *adv* ja, jawohl. **yes-man** *n* Jasager *m.*
yesterday ['jestədi] *n, adv* gestern. **yesterday morning** gestern früh. **yesterday's** *or* **of yesterday** gestrig, von gestern. **the day before yesterday** vorgestern.
yet [jət] *adv* noch, immer noch. *conj* aber.
yew [jui] *n* Eibe *f.*
yield [jiild] *n* Ertrag *m.* **yielding** *adj* ergiebig.
yoga ['jougə] *n* Joga *m.*
yoghurt ['jogət] *n* Joghurt *m.*
yoke [jouk] *n* Joch *m. v* verbinden.
yolk [jouk] *n* Eidotter *m*, Eigelb *neut.*
yonder ['jondə] *adv* da, dort drüben. *adj* jene(r).

you [juː] *pron* (*fam sing*) du; (*fam pl*) ihr; (*polite sing or pl*) Sie; (*impers, one*) man. *acc*: dich; euch; Sie; einen. *dat*: dir; euch; Ihnen; einem.
young [jʌŋ] *adj* jung. *n* (Tier)Junge *pl*.
young children kleine Kinder *pl*.
your [jɔː] *adj* (*fam sing*) dein; (*fam pl*) euer; (*polite sing or pl*) Ihr; (*impers, one's*) sein. **yours** (der/die/das) deine *or* eure *or* Ihre *or* seine. *a friend of yours* ein Freund von dir.
youth [juːθ] *n* Jugend *f*; (*lad*) Jüngling *m*. *adj* Jugend-. **youth hostel** Jugendherberge *f*. **youthful** *adj* jugendlich, jung.
Yugoslavia [juːgouˈslaːvjə] *n* Jugoslawien *neut*. **Yugoslav** *n* Jugoslawe *m*, Jugoslawin *f*. *adj* jugoslawisch.

Z

zeal [ziːl] *n* Eifer *m*. **zealous** *adj* eifrig.
zebra [ˈzebrə] *n* Zebra *neut*. **zebra crossing** *n* Zebrastreifen *m*.
zero [ˈziərou] *n* Null *f*.
zest [zest] *n* Lust *f*, Begeisterung *f*.
zigzag [ˈzigzag] *adj* Zickzack-. *n* Zickzack *m*.
zinc [ziŋk] *n* Zink *neut*.
zip [zip] *n also* **zipper** Reißverschluß *m*. **zip code** Postleitzahl *f*.
zodiac [ˈzoudiak] *n* Tierkreis *m*. **signs of the zodiac** Tierkreiszeichen *pl*.
zone [zoun] *n* Zone *f*.
zoo [zuː] *n* Zoo *m*. **zoological** *adj* zoologisch. **zoologist** *n* Zoologe *m*. **zoology** *n* Zoologie *f*, Tierkunde *f*.
zoom [zuːm] *v* summen, brummen; (*coll: rush*) sausen; (*prices*) Hochschnellen. **zoom lens** *n* Zoom (objektiv) *neut*.

German—Englisch

A

Aal [aːl] *m* (*pl* -e) eel.
ab [ap] *adv* off; *prep* (*abwärts, nach unten*) from; (*weg, fort*) from. **ab und zu** now and again, from time to time. **auf und ab** up and down, to and fro.
abänderlich ['apɛndərliç] *adj* variable. **abändern** *v* change, modify. **Abänderung** *f* modification; (*Pol*) amendment.
abarbeiten ['aparbaitən] (*Schuld*) work off; (*Werkzeug*) wear out. **sich die Finger abarbeiten** work one's fingers to the bone.
Abbau ['apbau] *m* (*unz.*) demolition; (*Personal*) reduction of staff, staff-cut. **abbauen** *v* demolish; (*Personal*) cut.
abbestellen ['apbəʃtɛlən] *v* cancel.
*****abbiegen** ['apbiːɡən] *v* deflect, turn aside; (*Straße*) bend; (*Mot*) turn off.
Abbild ['apbilt] *neut* image, likeness. **abbilden** *v* illustrate, depict. **Abbildung** *f* illustration, drawing.
abblenden ['apblɛndən] *v* (*Mot*) dip one's headlights.
*****abbrechen** ['apbrɛçən] *v* break off; (*Blumen, Obst*) pick; (*abbauen*) demolish; (*Lager*) break.
*****abbringen** ['apbriŋən] *v* dissuade, put off; (*entfernen*) remove.
Abbruch ['apbrux] *m* (*unz.*) (*Haus*) demolition; (*Einstellung*) stop, cessation.
abdanken ['apdaŋkən] *v* (*König*) abdicate; (*Beamter*) resign. **Abdankung** *f* (*pl* -en) abdication; resignation.
abdecken ['apdɛkən] *v* uncover; (*Tisch*)

clear; (*schützen*) shield, cover; (*Verlust*) make good.
abdichten ['apdiçtən] *v* seal up; (*wasserdicht machen*) make watertight.
Abdomen [ap'doːmən] *neut* abdomen. **abdominal** *adj* abdominal.
abdrehen ['apdreːən] *v* unscrew, twist off; (*Hals*) wring.
Abdruck ['apdruk] *m* reprint, new impression; (*Finger-*) print. **abdrucken** *v* print.
abdrücken ['apdrykən] *v* (*Pistole*) fire.
Abend ['aːbənt] *m* (*pl* -e) evening. **gestern abend** yesterday evening, last night. **–brot** *or* **–essen** *neut* supper, dinner. **–land** *neut* West, Occident. **–mahl** *neut* Holy Communion. **abends** *adv* in the evening(s).
Abenteuer ['aːbəntɔyər] *neut* (pl -) adventure. **abenteuerlich** *adj* adventurous. **Abenteurer** *m* adventurer.
aber ['aːbər] *conj* but; (*jedoch*) however. *das ist aber schrecklich!* that's just awful!
Aberglaube ['aːbərɡlaubə] *m* superstition. **abergläubisch** *adj* superstitious.
aberkennen ['apɛrkɛnən] *v* deprive, dispossess.
abermals ['aːbərmals] *adv* again, once more.
*****abfahren** ['apfaːrən] *v* set off, depart; (*Mot*) drive off. **Abfahrt** *f* departure; (*Ski*) descent, downhill run.
Abfall ['apfal] **1** (*unz.*) falling off, decline; (*Neigung*) slope. **2** *m* waste, rubbish. **–eimer** *m* dustbin. **abfallen** *v* fall off, decline. **abfällig** *adj* disparaging.
abfassen ['apfasən] *v* compose, draw up, formulate. **Abfassung** *f* wording.
abfertigen ['apfɛrtiɡən] *v* (*Güter*) (prepare for) dispatch; (*Fahrzeug*) check over, prepare (for departure); (*Kundschaft*) see to.

abfinden ['apfɪndən] v pay off. **sich abfinden mit** come to terms with (*auch fig*) **Abfindung** f (*pl* -en) settlement, agreement.
*****abfliegen** ['apfliːgən] fly away; (*Flugzeug*) take off.
*****abfließen** ['apfliːsən] flow away, drain off.
Abflug ['apfluːk] m (*Flugzeug*) take-off.
Abfluß ['apflus] m outflow, draining off. **-rohr** *neut* waste-pipe.
Abfuhr ['apfuːr] m removal. **abführen** v lead away. **Abführmittel** n laxative.
Abgabe ['apgaːbə] f delivery, handing over; (*Steuer*) tax, duty. **Abgaben** pl (*Verkauf*) sales. **abgabenfrei** adj tax-free, duty-free.
Abgang ['apgaŋ] m (*Zug, usw.*) departure; (*Abtreten*) retirement; (*Verlust*) loss, depreciation.
Abgas ['apgaːs] neut exhaust gas.
*****abgeben** ['apgeːbən] v give up, hand over; (*Stimme*) cast.
abgedroschen ['apgədrɔʃən] adj commonplace, hackneyed.
abgegriffen ['apgəgrifən] adj (*Münze*) worn; (*Buch*) dog-eared, well-thumbed.
*****abgehen** ['apgeːən] v go away, depart; (*Straße*) branch off; (*Knopf, usw.*) come off.
abgemacht ['apgəmaxt] adj agreed.
Abgeordnete(r) ['apgəɔrdnətə(r)] delegate; (*Parlament*) Member of Parliament; (*US*) congressman. **Abgeordnetenhaus** neut parliament; (*GB*) House of Commons.
abgesehen ['apgəzeːən] prep **abgesehen von** apart from, except for.
abgestanden ['apgəʃtandən] adj stale; (*Bier, usw.*) flat.
abgestorben ['apgəʃtɔrbən] adj numb.
Abgott ['apgɔt] m idol.
abgrenzen ['apgrɛntsən] v (*Gebiete*) limit, mark off. **Abgrenzung** f demarcation, definition.
Abgrund ['apgrunt] m abyss.
abhalten ['aphaltən] v keep away; (*hindern*) hinder, stop; (*Versammlung, usw.*) hold.
Abhandlung ['aphandluŋ] f essay, written report.
Abhang ['aphaŋ] m slope.
abhauen ['aphauən] v cut off; (*umg.*) go away, (*umg.*) buzz off.
abhelfen ['aphɛlfən] v remedy, correct.

abholen ['aphoːlən] v call for, pick up.
abhören ['aphœːrən] v (*Platte*) listen to; (*Gespräch*) eavesdrop on; (*Telef*) monitor, listen in, tap; (*Zeugen*) question. **Abhörgerät** neut (electronic) listening device, bug.
Abitur [abi'tuːr] neut school-leaving exam, 'A'-levels.
abkanzeln ['apkantsəln] v scold, reprimand.
abkehren ['apkeːrən] v sweep up. **sich abkehren** turn away.
abknöpfen ['apknœpfən] v unbutton.
Abkommen ['apkɔmən] neut (*pl* -) agreement, settlement.
abkühlen ['apkyːlən] v cool, cool off.
Abkunft ['apkunft] f descent, lineage.
abkürzen ['apkyrtsən] v shorten; (*Wort*) abbreviate. **Abkürzung** f abbreviation; (*Weg*) short cut.
*****abladen** ['aplaːdən] v unload.
Ablauf ['aplauf] m (*Abfluß*) outlet, drain; (*Verlauf*) sequence of events; (*Ende*) expiry, end. **ablaufen** v drain, flow off; (*Zeit*) elapse; (*Schuhe*) wear out.
ablegen ['apleːgən] v put down; (*Kleider*) take off; (*Gewohnheiten*) give up.
ablehnen ['apleːnən] v reject, refuse; (*Einladung*) decline. **Ablehnung** f (*pl* -en) refusal.
ableiten ['aplaitən] v divert, lead away; (*Flüssigkeit*) draw off. **Ableitung** f diversion.
ablenken ['aplɛŋkən] v turn away, divert.
abliefern ['apliːfərn] v deliver. **Ablieferung** f delivery.
ablösen ['aplœːzən] v (*Person*) relieve, replace; (*Schuld*) settle; (*loslösen*) loosen, free. **Ablösung** f relief; loosening.
abmachen ['apmaxən] v detach; (*Geschäft*) arrange, agree about. **Abmachung** f (*pl* -en) arrangement, agreement.
abmelden ['apmɛldən] v **sich abmelden** v give notice (of one's departure).
*****abmessen** ['apmɛsən] v measure off; (*Grundstück*) survey; (*Worte*) weigh. **Abmessung** f measurement, dimension.
Abnahme ['apnaːmə] f (*pl* -n) reduction, decrease; (*Entfernung*) removal.
*****abnehmen** ['apneːmən] v take off, take away; (*sich vermindern*) decrease; (*schlanker werden*) lose weight, grow slim. **Abnehmer** m (*pl* -) customer, consumer.

Abneigung ['apnaiguŋ] *f* dislike, aversion.
abnorm [ap'nɔrm] *adj* abnormal.
Abnormität *f* (*pl* -en) abnormality.
abnutzen ['apnutsən] *v* wear out.
Abnutzung *f* wear (and tear).
Abonnement [abɔn'mã] *neut* (*pl* -s) subscription. **Abonnent** *m* (*pl* -en) subscriber. **abonnieren** *v* subscribe.
Abort [a'bɔrt] *m* (*pl* -e) lavatory.
abquälen ['apkvɛːlən] *v* **sich abquälen** take great pains.
abraten ['apraitən] *v* advise against, dissuade from.
abräumen ['aprɔymən] *v* clear away.
abrechnen ['apreçnən] *v* settle; (*abziehen*) deduct. **abrechnen mit** settle up with.
Abrede ['apreɪdə] *f* agreement. **in Abrede stellen** deny. **abreden** *v* agree.
abreiben ['apraibən] *v* rub off; (*trocknen*) rub down.
Abreise ['apraizə] *f* departure. **abreisen** *v* depart, leave.
***abreißen** ['apraisən] *v* tear off; (*Haus*) demolish, tear down; (*sich ablösen*) break off.
Abrieb ['apriːp] *m* abrasion, wear.
***abrufen** ['apruɪfən] *v* cancel, call off; (*Person*) recall.
abrüsten ['aprystən] *v* disarm. **Abrüstung** *f* disarmament.
Absage ['apza:gə] *f* (*pl* -n) refusal. **absagen** *v* cancel, call off; (*Einladung*) decline, refuse.
Absatz ['apzats] **1** *m* (*Pause*) stop, break; (*Schuh*) heel; paragraph. **2** *m* (*unz.*) (*Waren*) sales (*pl*), turnover.
abschaffen ['apʃafən] *v* abolish, do away with. **Abschaffung** *f* abolition.
abschalten ['apʃaltən] *v* switch off.
abschätzen ['apʃɛtsən] *v* estimate, appraise. **Abschätzung** *f* estimate, assessment.
Abscheu ['apʃɔy] *m or f* horror, revulsion. **abscheulich** *adj* horrible, revolting.
abschicken ['apʃikən] *v* send off *or* away.
Abschied ['apʃiːt] *m* (*pl* -e) departure, leaving. **Abschied nehmen von** say goodbye to, take one's leave of.
***abschießen** ['apʃiːsən] *v* (*Gewehr*) fire; (*Flugzeug*) shoot down.
Abschlag ['apʃlaːk] *m* reduction, rebate. **abschlagen** *v* strike off; (*ablehnen*) refuse.
***abschließen** ['apʃliːsən] *v* lock up; (*Geschäft, Vertrag*) conclude, settle; end, close.

Abschluß ['apʃlus] *m* conclusion; (*Geschäft, Vertrag*) settlement. **-prüfung** *f* final exam(s), finals.
abschnallen ['apʃnalən] *v* unbuckle.
***abschneiden** ['apʃnaidən] *v* cut off.
Abschnitt ['apʃnit] *m* section, part; (*Kontroll-*) counterfoil.
abschrauben ['apʃraubən] *v* unscrew.
abschrecken ['apʃrɛkən] *v* scare off, deter. **-d** *adj* deterrent. **Abschreckung** *f* deterrence. **-smittel** *neut* deterrent.
***abschreiben** ['apʃraibən] *v* copy out, write out; (*Verlust, usw.*) abschreiben; (*plagieren*) plagiarize.
Abschrift ['apʃrift] *f* copy.
Abschuß ['apʃus] *m* (*Gewehr*) firing; (*Flugzeug*) shooting down.
***absehen** ['apzɛːən] *v* see, perceive; (*voraussehen*) foresee. **absehbar** *adj* within sight; (*Zeit*) foreseeable.
abseits ['apzaits] *adv* aside.
***absenden** ['apzɛndən] *v* send (off). **Absender** *m* sender.
absetzen ['apzɛtsən] *v* set down; (*verkaufen*) sell; (*entlassen*) dismiss; (*aussteigen lassen*) drop off.
Absicht ['apziçt] *f* (*pl* -en) intention, purpose. **absicht‖lich** *adj* deliberate; *adv* on purpose, deliberately. **-slos** *adj* unintentional.
absolut [apzo'luːt] *adj* absolute.
absondern ['apzɔndərn] *v* isolate, cut off, separate; (*Med, Bot*) secrete. **Absonderung** *f* (*pl* -en) isolation.
absorbieren [apzɔr'biːrən] *v* absorb. **Absorption** *f* absorption.
absperren ['apʃpɛrən] *v* block off; (*Gas, Strom*) cut off; (*Straße*) block, cordon off.
abspielen ['apʃpiːlən] *v* (*Schallplatte, usw.*) play; (*Musik*) sight-read; (*Ball*) pass.
***abspringen** ['apʃpriŋən] *v* jump down (from), jump off; (*Flugzeug*) bale out; (*Splitter*) chip *or* break off; (*Farbe*) flake off.
abspülen ['apʃpyːlən] *v* wash, wash up. **Abspülwasser** *neut* dishwater.
abstammen ['apʃtamən] *v* be descended from. **Abstammung** *f* descent, lineage.
Abstand ['apʃtant] *m* distance. **Abstand halten** keep one's distance.
abstatten ['apʃtatən] *v* (*Besuch*) pay; (*Dank*) give.

*absteigen ['apʃtaigən] v climb down, descend; (vom Pferd) dismount.

abstellen ['apʃtɛlən] v (Gerät, Licht) turn off; (niederlegen) put down; (Mot) park.

Abstieg ['apʃtiːk] m (pl -e) descent.

abstimmen ['apʃtimən] v vote, (Instrument, Radio) tune. **sich abstimmen** agree. **aufeinander abstimmen** collate, coordinate. **Abstimmung** f vote, poll.

Abstinenz [apsti'nɛnts] f abstinence; (Alkohol) teetotalism. **–ler** m (pl -) abstainer; teetotaller.

abstoßend ['apʃtoːsənt] adj repulsive, repellent.

abstrakt [ap'strakt] adj abstract.

Absturz ['apʃturts] m fall; (Flugzeug) crash; (Abgrund) precipice. **abstürzen** v fall, plummet; (Flugzeug) crash.

absurd [ap'zurt] adj absurd.

Abszeß [aps'tsɛs] m (pl **Abszesse**) abcess.

Abt [apt] m (pl **Äbte**) abbott. **Abtei** f (pl -en) abbey.

Abteil [ap'tail] neut (pl -e) compartment. **abteilen** v separate, divide off. **Abteilung** f (auch Mil) division; (einer Firma) department. **–sleiter** m head of department.

Äbtissin [ɛp'tisin] f (pl -nen) abbess.

*abtreiben ['aptraibən] v drive away; (Med) abort. **Abtreibung** f (pl -en) (induced) abortion.

Abtritt ['aptrit] m departure; (Theater) exit.

abtrocknen ['aptrɔknən] v wipe dry; (Geschirr) wipe up, dry.

abtrünnig ['aptryniç] adj disloyal, rebellious.

*abtun ['aptuːn] put aside; (Kleider) take off; (erledigen) close, settle; (Tier) put down.

abwandeln ['apvandəln] v vary. **Abwandlung** f variation.

abwarten ['apvartən] v wait for, expect; wait and see.

abwärts ['apvɛrts] adv downwards, down.

abwaschen ['apvaʃən] v wash off; (Geschirr) wash up.

Abwasser ['apvasər] neut waste water, effluent.

abwechseln ['apvɛksəln] v take turns; (wechseln) change, vary. **–d** adj alternating. adv alternately, in turns. **Abwechslung** f change.

Abwehr ['apveːr] f defence; (Widerstand) resistance. **abwehren** v ward off; (Feind) repel.

*abweichen ['apvaiçən] v deviate. **–d** adj discrepant, anomalous; (Meinung) dissenting.

*abweisen ['apvaisən] v turn away, refuse; (Bewerber) turn down. **–d** adj unfriendly, dismissive.

*abwenden ['apvɛndən] v turn away or aside; (Gefahr) avert, prevent.

*abwerfen ['apvɛrfən] v throw off; (Bomben) drop; (Zinsen) yield.

abwerten ['apvɛrtən] v devalue. **Abwertung** f devaluation.

abwesend ['apveːzənt] adj absent; (zerstreut) absent-minded. **Abwesenheit** f absence.

abzahlen ['aptsaːlən] v pay off.

abzählen ['aptsɛːlən] v count; (Geld) count out.

abzäunen ['aptsɔynən] v fence off.

Abzeichen ['aptsaiçən] neut badge; (Kennzeichen) mark.

*abziehen ['aptsiːən] v draw off, remove; (Math) subtract; (fortgehen) go away, withdraw.

Abzug ['aptsuːk] m departure; (Geld) deduction; (Foto) print; (Abdruck) copy.

abzweigen ['aptsvaigən] v branch off. **Abzweigung** f (pl -en) branch; (Mot) turning.

ach! [ax] interj oh! ah!

Achse ['aksə] f (pl -n) (Rad) axle; (Math, Pol) axis.

Achsel ['aksəl] f (pl -n) shoulder. **–bein** neut shoulder-blade. **–höhle** f armpit. **–zucken** neut (pl -) shrug (of the shoulders).

acht [axt] adj eight. **(heute) vor acht Tagen** a week ago (today).

Acht [axt] f (unz.) attention. **außer acht lassen** ignore, disregard. **sich in acht nehmen** be careful, take care. **acht‖en** v esteem. **–en auf** pay attention to, heed. **–geben** v pay attention. **–los** adj careless. **–sam** adj attentive. **Achtung** f attention; (Wertschätzung) esteem; interj watch out! look out!

achtzig ['axtsiç] adj eighty.

ächzen ['ɛçtsən] v groan.

Acker ['akər] m (pl **Äcker**) field. **–bau** m agriculture, farming.

addieren [a'diːrən] v add (up). **Addiermaschine** f adding machine.

Adel ['aɪdəl] *m* nobility, aristocracy.
ad(e)lig *adj* noble, aristocratic.
Ad(e)lige(r) noble(man), aristocrat.
Ader ['aɪdər] *f* (*pl* -n) blood vessel; vein, artery.
Adjektiv ['atjɛktiːf] *neut* (*pl* -e) adjective.
Adler ['aɪdlər] *m* (*pl* -) eagle.
Admiral [atmi'raːl] *m* (*pl* -e) admiral. **–ität** *f* admiralty.
adoptieren [adɔp'tiːrən] *v* adopt. **Adoptiv-** adopted, adoptive.
Adrenalin [adrena'liːn] *neut* adrenaline.
Adresse [a'drɛsə] *f* (*pl* -n) address. **Adreßbuch** *neut* address book, directory. **adressieren** *v* address.
Advokat [atvo'kaɪt] *m* (*pl* -en) lawyer.
Affäre [a'fɛːrə] *f* (*pl* -n) affair; (*Liebes-*) (love) affair.
Affe ['afə] *m* (*pl* -n) ape, monkey.
affektiert [afɛk'tiːrt] *adj* affected, conceited.
äffen ['ɛfən] *v* ape, imitate.
Afrika ['aɪfrika] *neut* Africa. **Afrikaner** *m* African. **afrikanisch** *adj* African.
After ['aftər] *m* (*pl* -) anus.
Agent [a'gɛnt] *m* (*pl* -en) agent. **–ur** *f* (*pl* -en) agency.
Agnostiker [a'gnɔstikər] *m* (*pl* -) agnostic. **agnostisch** *adj* agnostic.
Ägypten [ɛ'gyptən] *neut* Egypt. **Ägypter** *m* (*pl* -) Egyptian. **ägyptisch** *adj* Egyptian.
Ahn [aɪn] *m* (*pl* -en) ancestor.
ähneln ['ɛɪnəln] *v* look like, resemble.
ahnen ['aɪnən] *v* suspect, guess.
ähnlich ['ɛɪnliç] *adj* like, similar (to). **Ähnlichkeit** *f* (*pl* -en) likeness, similarity.
Ahorn ['aɪhɔrn] *m* (*pl* -e) maple.
Ähre ['ɛɪrə] *f* (*pl* -n) ear (of corn).
Akadem||ie [akade'miː] *f* (*pl* -n) academy; (*Hochschule, Fachschule*) college. **–iker** *m* (*pl* -) university graduate. **akademisch** *adj* academic.
Akkord [a'kɔrt] *m* (*pl* -e) agreement; (*Musik*) chord. **–arbeit** *f* piece-work.
Akrobat [akro'baɪt] *m* (*pl* -en) acrobat. **akrobatisch** *adj* acrobatic.
Akt [akt] *m* (*pl* -e) act, action, deed; document; (*Kunst*) nude.
Akte ['aktə] *f* (*pl* -n) file, dossier. **zu den Akten legen** file (away). **Akten||schrank** *m* filing cabinet. **–tasche** *f* briefcase.
Aktie ['aktsiə] *f* (*pl* -n) share. **Aktien||gesellschaft** *f* joint-stock company. **–makler** *m* stockbroker.

Aktionär [aktsio'nɛɪr] *m* (*pl* -e) shareholder.
aktiv [ak'tiːf] *adj* active. **–ieren** *v* activate.
aktuell [aktu'ɛl] *adj* current, contemporary, up-to-date.
Akzent [ak'tsɛnt] *m* (*pl* -e) accent.
akzeptieren [aktsɛp'tiːrən] *v* accept.
Alarm [a'larm] *m* (*pl* -e) alarm. **alarm||bereit** *adj* standing by, on the alert. **–ieren** *v* alarm.
albern ['albərn] *adj* silly, foolish.
Album ['album] *neut* (*pl* **Alben**) album.
Alge ['algə] *f* (*pl* -n) seaweed.
Algebra ['algebra] *f* algebra.
Alimente [ali'mɛntə] *pl* alimony *sing.*
Alkohol [alko'hoːl] *m* (*pl* -e) alcohol. **alkoholfrei** *adj* non-alcoholic. **Alkoholiker** *m* alcoholic. **alkoholisch** *adj* alcoholic.
all [al] *pron, adj* all. **All** *neut* universe. **alle** *pl* all; everybody *sing.* **alle beide** both. **wir alle** we all, all of us. **die Milch ist alle** the milk is all gone. **alle zwei Tage** every other day. **alles** everything. **alledem** *pron* **trotz alledem** nevertheless.
Allee [a'leɪ] *f* (*pl* -n) avenue.
Allegorie [alego'riː] (*pl* -n) allegory. **allegorisch** *adj* allegorical.
allein [a'lain] *adj, adv* alone; (*ohne Hilfer*) (by) oneself. *conj* but. **alleinstehend** *adj* (*Haus*) detached; (*Person*) single.
allemal ['aləmal] *adv* always. **ein für allemal** once and for all.
allenfalls ['alənfals] *adv* if need be; (*höchstens*) at most.
aller||best ['alərbɛst] *adj* very best, best of all. **–dings** *adv* certainly, surely, indeed. **–erst** *adj* first of all, very first. **–höchst** *adj* supreme, highest of all. **–lei** *adj* (*undeklinierbar*) various, all kinds of. **–liebst** *adj* (most) delightful, dearest. **–wenigst** *adj* very least.
allezeit ['aləsait] *adv* always, at any time.
allgemein ['algəmain] *adj* common, general. **im allgemeinen** in general.
Alliierte(r) [ali'iːrtə(r)] *m* ally.
alljährlich ['aljɛːrliç] *adj* annual.
allmächtig [al'mɛçtiç] *adj* all-powerful, almighty.
allmählich [al'mɛːliç] *adj* gradual.
allseitig ['alzaitiç] *adj* universal, comprehensive.
alltäglich ['altɛːkliç] *adj* everyday. *adv* every day.

allzu ['altsuɪ] *adv* much too, all too.
Almanach ['almanax] *m* (*pl* -e) almanac.
Alpen ['alpən] *pl* Alps *pl.*
Alphabet [alfa'beɪt] *neut* (*pl* -e) alphabet.
alphabetisch *adj* alphabetical.
Alptraum ['alptraum] *m* nightmare.
als [als] *conj* as; (*da, zu der Zeit*) when; (*nach Komparativen*) than. **als ob** as if. **nichts als** nothing but. *als dein Freund möchte ich sagen* ... as your friend, I would like to say ... *als ich noch ein Kind war* when I was a child.
also ['alzo] *conj* so, therefore.
alt [alt] *adj* old.
Alt [alt] *m* (*unz.*) alto (voice).
Altar [al'taɪr] *m* (*pl* **Altäre**) altar.
Alter ['altər] *neut* (*unz.*) age; (*hohes Alter*) old age. **–heim** *neut* old people's home. **Alters‖fürsorge** *f* care of the aged. **altersschwach** *adj* (*Person*) senile, feeble. **Altertum** *neut* (*unz.*) antiquity. **altertümlich** *adj* ancient, archaic.
Aluminium [alu'miɪnium] *neut* aluminium.
am [am] *prep* + *art* an dem.
Amboß ['ambɔs] *m* (*pl* **Ambosse**) anvil.
Ameise ['aɪmaɪzə] *f* (*pl* -n) ant.
Amerika [a'meɪrika] *neut* America. **Amerikaner** *m* American. **amerikanisch** *adj* American.
Ampel ['ampəl] *f* (*pl* -n) (*Verkehrs-*) traffic light; (*Hängelampe*) hanging lamp.
Amsel ['amzəl] *f* (*pl* -n) blackbird.
Amt [amt] *neut* (*pl* **Ämter**) office; (*Stellung*) official position, post; (*Telef*) exchange. **das Auswärtige Amt** the Foreign Office. **das Amt antreten** take office. **amtieren** *v* officiate. **amtlich** *adj* official. **Amts‖geheimnis** *neut* offical secret. **–gericht** *neut* district court. **–zeichen** *neut* dial tone.
amüsant [amy'zant] *adj* amusing. **amüsieren** *v* amuse. **sich amüsieren** amuse *or* enjoy oneself.
an [an] *prep* at; (*nahe*) near; (*auf*) on. *adv* on. *an diesem Tag* on this day. *an diesem Ort* at this place. *der Ort, an dem* the place where. *an der Wand* on the wall. *an die Tür klopfen* knock at *or* on the door. *von heute an* from today. *von jetzt an* from now on. *sie hat nichts an* she has nothing on.
analog [ana'loɪk] *adj* analagous. **Analogie** *f* analogy. **analogisch** *adj* analogous.

Analphabet [analfa'beɪt] *m* (*pl* -en) illiterate.
Analyse [ana'lyɪzə] *f* (*pl* -n) analysis. **analysieren** *v* analyse. **Analytiker** *m* analyst. **analytisch** *adj* analytical.
Ananas ['ananas] *f* (*pl* -se) pineapple.
Anarchie [anar'çiɪ] *f* (*pl* -n) anarchy. **Anarchist** *m* (*pl* -en) anarchist.
Anatomie [anato'miɪ] *f* (*pl* -n) anatomy. **anatomisch** *adj* anatomical.
Anbau ['anbau] **1** *m* (*unz.*) cultivation, tillage. **2** *m* extension, annexe.
***anbeißen** ['anbaisən] *v* bite into; (*Fisch*) bite, take the bait.
anbelangen ['anbəlaŋən] *v* concern, relate to. *was mich anbelangt* as to me, as far as I am concerned.
anbeten ['anbeɪtən] *v* worship, adore.
***anbieten** ['anbiɪtən] *v* offer.
Anblick ['anblik] *m* sight, view; (*Aussehen*) appearance. **anblicken** *v* look at, gaze at.
***anbrechen** ['anbrɛçən] *v* (*Essen, Vorrat*) break into, begin; (*Tag*) dawn, break; (*Nacht*) fall.
***anbrennen** ['anbrɛnən] (*Speisen*) burn; (*Zigarette, Lampe*) light.
***anbringen** ['anbriŋən] *v* bring, place; (*befestigen*) attach; (*Klage*) lodge, bring.
Anbruch ['anbrux] *m* (*unz.*) beginning. *bei Anbruch der Nacht* at nightfall.
Andacht ['andaxt] *f* (*pl* -en) devotion.
Andenken ['andɛŋkən] *neut* (*pl* -) memory, remembrance; (*Erinnerungstück*) souvenir.
ander ['andər] *adj, pron* other, different. *ein andermal adv* another time.
ändern ['ɛndərn] *v* alter, change. **Änderung** *f* (*pl* -en) alteration, change.
ander‖thalb ['andərthalp] *adj* one-and-a-half. **–nfalls** *adv* otherwise, else. **–s** *adv* differently. **–seits** *adv* on the other hand. **–swo** *adv* elsewhere.
andeuten ['andɔytən] *v* indicate, point to; (*anspielen*) imply, suggest, allude to. **Andeutung** *f* indication; suggestion, allusion.
andrehen ['andreɪən] *v* turn on, switch on; (*Mot*) start up; (*umg.*) wangle, fix up.
andrer ['andrər] *pron* anderer. *V* **ander.**
aneignen ['anaignən] *v* **sich aneignen** appropriate; (*Kenntnisse*) acquire. **Aneignung** *f* (*pl* -en) appropriation; acquisition.

aneinander [anain'andər] *adv* to *or* against one another, together. **–liegend** *adj* neighbouring, adjacent. **–schließen** *v* join together.

*anerkennen ['anɛrkɛnən] *v* recognize, acknowledge. **Anerkennung** *f* recognition, approval.

*anfahren ['anfaːrən] *v* begin (to move); (*bringen*) convey, carry; (*ankommen*) arrive; (*zusammenstoßen*) drive into. **Anfahrt** *f* arrival; (*Zufahrtsstraße*) drive.

Anfall ['anfal] *m* attack.

Anfang ['anfaŋ] *m* beginning, start. **anfangen** *v* begin, start. **Anfänger** *m* (*pl* -) beginner. **anfangs** *adv* at first, initially. **Anfangsbuchstabe** *m* (*pl* -n) initial letter.

anfassen ['anfasən] *v* touch; (*ergreifen*) hold, grasp; (*Aufgabe*) set *or* go about.

*anfecht‖en ['anfɛçtən] *v* contest, dispute; (*beunruhigen*) trouble; (*Versuchung*) tempt. **–bar** *adj* questionable, contestable.

Anforderung ['anfɔrdəruŋ] *f* demand, claim; (*Bedürfnis*) requirement.

Anfrage ['anfraːgə] *f* inquiry.

anfühlen ['anfyːlən] *v* touch, feel. **sich anfühlen** feel (to the touch).

anführen ['anfyːrən] *v* lead, command; (*Worte*) quote, state; (*täuschen*) trick, deceive. **Anführungszeichen** *pl* quotation marks.

anfüllen ['anfylən] *v* fill (up).

Angabe ['angaːbə] *f* declaration, statement. **–n** *pl* specifications, data. **nähere Angaben** details, particulars.

*angeben ['angeːbən] *v* state, declare; (*anzeigen*) inform against; (*vorgeben*) pretend; (*prahlen*) brag, boast, show off. **Angeber** *m* (*pl* -) informer; (*Prahler*) show off, boaster. **angeblich** *adj* supposed, alleged.

angeboren ['angəboːrən] *adj* innate, inherent.

Angebot ['angəboːt] *neut* (*pl* -e) offer. **Angebot und Nachfrage** supply and demand.

*angehen ['angeːən] *v* begin; (*angreifen*) attack; (*betreffen*) concern. *das geht mich nichts an* that is none of my business.

angehören ['angəhœːrən] *v* belong (to). **Angehörige(r)** member.

Angeklagte(r) ['angəklaːktə(r)] (*Jur*) (the) accused, defendant.

Angelegenheit ['angəleːgənhait] *f* matter, concern, business.

angeln ['aŋəln] *v* fish, angle. **Angeln** *neut* angling, fishing. **Angelrute** *f* fishing rod. **Angelsachse** ['aŋəlzaksə] *m* Anglo-Saxon. **angelsächsisch** *adj* Anglo-Saxon.

angemessen ['angəmɛsən] *adj* proper, suitable.

angenehm ['angəneːm] *adj* pleasant, agreeable.

angenommen ['angənɔmən] *adj* supposing, assuming.

angesehen ['angəzeːən] *adj* respected.

Angesicht ['angəziçt] *neut* face, countenance. **angesichts** *prep* considering, in view of.

Angestellte(r) ['angəʃtɛltə(r)] employee, office worker.

angewandt ['angəvant] *adj* applied, practical.

angewöhnen ['angəvœːnən] *v* accustom. **sich angewöhnen** get used to, make a habit of. **Angewohnheit** *f* habit, custom.

Angler ['aŋlər] *m* (*pl* -) angler, fisherman.

*angreifen ['angraifən] *v* (*anfassen*) take hold of; (*feindlich*) attack; (*unternehmen*) set about. **Angreifer** *m* (*pl* -) aggressor, attacker.

angrenzen ['angrɛntsən] *v* border on, adjoin.

Angriff ['angrif] *m* attack. **angriffslustig** *adj* aggressive.

Angst [aŋst] *f* (*pl* Ängste) fear, anxiety. **Angst haben vor** be afraid of.

ängst‖igen ['ɛŋstigən] *v* frighten. **–lich** *adj* fearful, timid; (*peinlich*) scrupulous, (over-)careful.

*anhaben ['anhaːbən] *v* wear, have on.

Anhalt ['anhalt] *m* support, prop; (*fig*) clue. **anhalten** *v* stop; (*andauern*) continue, last. **Anhalter** *m* hitchhiker. **per Anhalter fahren** hitchhike.

Anhang ['anhaŋ] *m* appendix, supplement. **anhängen** *v* hang on, attach; (*hinzufügen*) add. **Anhänger** *m* follower; (*Fußball*) supporter; (*Mot*) trailer. **Anhängeschloß** *neut* padlock. **anhänglich** *adj* affectionate.

Anhöhe ['anhœːə] *f* (low) hill.

anhören ['anhœːrən] *v* listen (to).

Ankauf ['ankauf] *m* purchase. **ankaufen** *v* purchase, buy.

Anker ['aŋkər] *m* (*pl* -) anchor. **den Anker lichten/werfen** weigh/cast anchor. **ankern** *v* anchor.

Anklage ['anklaːgə] *f* accusation, charge. **–bank** *f* dock. **anklagen** *v* accuse.
Ankläger *m* plaintiff.
Anklang ['anklaŋ] *m* approval, recognition; (*Spur*) touch, echo.
anknüpfen ['anknypfən] *v* fasten (on), tie (on); (*fig*) take up, establish.
***ankommen** ['ankɔmən] *v* arrive; (*abhängen*) depend (on). *es kommt darauf an* it depends.
ankündigen ['ankyndigən] *v* announce, publicize. **Ankündigung** *f* announcement.
Ankunft ['ankunft] *f* (*pl* **Ankünfte**) arrival.
Anlage ['anlaːgə] *f* installation; (*Entwurf*) plan, layout; park, gardens *pl*; (*Brief*) enclosure; (*Begabung*) talent; (*Neigung*) tendency, susceptibility; (*Komm*) investment; (*Fabrik*) plant, works.
anlangen ['anlaŋən] *v* (*ankommen*) arrive; (*betreffen*) concern.
Anlaß ['anlas] *m* (*pl* **Anlässe**) occasion, cause. **Anlaß geben** cause, give rise to.
anlassen *v* leave on; (*Mot*) start. **anläßlich** *prep* on the occasion of. **Anlasser** *m* (*pl* -) (*Mot*) starter-motor.
Anlauf ['anlauf] *m* start; (*kurzer Lauf*) run, dash. **anlaufen** *v* run at, rush at; (*Hafen*) put into; (*wachsen*) rise, increase.
anlegen ['anleːgən] *v* put on *or* against; (*Gewehr*) aim at; (*gründen*) found; (*Geld*) invest; (*Schiff*) lie alongside.
Anleihe ['anlaiə] *f* (*pl* -n) loan.
Anleitung ['anlaituŋ] *f* instruction.
***anliegen** ['anliːgən] *v* (*Schiff*) lie beside; (*Kleidung*) fit well. **Anliegen** *neut* (*pl* -) request. **anliegend** *adj* adjoining.
anlocken ['anlɔkən] *v* entice, attract.
anmachen ['anmaxən] *v* attach; (*Speisen*) prepare; (*Feuer*) kindle; (*Licht*) turn on.
Anmarsch ['anmarʃ] *m* advance, approach. **anmarschieren** *v* advance on, march on.
anmaßen ['anmaːsən] *v* **sich anmaßen, zu** presume to, take it upon oneself to. **Anmaßung** *f* presumptuousness.
anmelden ['anmɛldən] *v* announce, report. **sich anmelden** *v* report; (*polizeilich*) register (with the police). **Anmeldung** *f* announcement; (*polizeilich*) registration.
anmerken ['anmɛrkən] *v* note, observe. **Anmerkung** *f* note, observation.
Anmut ['anmuːt] *f* grace, charm, elegance. **anmutig** *adj* graceful.

annähern ['annɛːərn] *v* bring closer; (*ähnlich machen*) make similar. **sich annähern** approach. **annähernd** *adj* approaching. *adv* almost, close to.
Annahme ['annaːmə] *f* (*pl* -n) acceptance; (*Vermutung*) assumption.
***annehm‖en** ['anneːmən] *v* accept, take; (*vermuten*) assume, suppose. **–bar** *adj* acceptable.
anonym [ano'nyːm] *adj* anonymous. **Anonymität** *f* anonymity.
anordnen ['anɔrdnən] *v* put in order, arrange; (*befehlen*) direct, command. **Anordnung** *f* arrangement; (*Befehl*) order, instruction.
anpacken ['anpakən] *v* grasp, seize.
anpassen ['anpasən] *v* fit, adapt. **sich anpassen** *v* adapt, adjust. **Anpassung** *f* adaptation, adjustment. **anpassungsfähig** *adj* adaptable. **Anpassungsfähigkeit** *f* adaptability.
anrechnen ['anrɛçnən] *v* charge; (*hochschätzen*) value, esteem highly.
Anrede ['anreːdə] *f* speech, address. **anreden** *v* address, speak to.
anregen ['anreːgən] *v* stimulate, incite; (*geistig*) excite, inspire. **–d** *adj* exciting. **Anregung** *f* excitement.
anrichten ['anriçtən] *v* (*Schaden*) cause, do; (*Essen*) prepare.
Anruf ['anruːf] *m* call, shout; (*Telef*) call. **anrufen** *v* call, hail; (*Telef*) ring up, call.
anrühren ['anryːrən] *v* touch, handle; (*Küche*) stir.
ans [ans] *prep* + *art* **an das**.
Ansage ['anzaːgə] *f* announcement; (*Kartenspiel*) bidding. **ansagen** *v* announce, declare; bid. **Ansager** *m* (*pl* -) announcer.
ansammeln ['anzaməln] *v* collect. **sich ansammeln** gather. **Ansammlung** *f* collection, accumulation; (*Menge*) crowd, gathering.
Ansatz ['anzats] *m* (*Anfang*) start, beginning; (*Zusatzstück*) (added) piece, fitting. **–punkt** *m* starting point.
anschaffen ['anʃafən] *v* procure, obtain.
anschalten ['anʃaltən] *v* switch, turn on.
anschau‖en ['anʃauən] *v* look at, view. **–lich** *adj* obvious, evident.
Anschein ['anʃain] *m* (*unz.*) (outer) appearance. **allem Anschein nach** to all appearances.

Anschlag ['anʃlaɪk] *m* (*Med*) stroke, attack; (*Plakat*) poster; (*Kosten-*) estimate; (*Angriff*) (criminal) attack, outrage.

*anschließen ['anʃliːsən] *v* connect; (*anketten*) chain up. **-d** *adj* subsequent.

Anschluß ['anʃlus] *m* connection; (*pol*) annexation.

anschnallen ['anʃnalən] *v* fasten, buckle.

Anschove [an'ʃoɪvə] *f* (*pl* -n), **Anschovis** *f* (*pl* -) anchovy.

Anschrift ['anʃrift] *f* address.

anschuldigen ['ənʃuldigən] *v* accuse (of), charge (with).

*ansehen ['anzeɪən] *v* look at, consider. **Ansehen** *neut* appearance; (*Hochachtung*) respect, esteem. **ansehnlich** *adj* notable.

ansetzen ['anzɛtsən] *v* put on, attach; (*Gewicht*) put on; (*anfangen*) begin; (*versuchen*) try.

Ansicht ['anziçt] *f* view, sight; (*Meinung*) opinion.

Anspiel ['anʃpiːl] *neut* (*Tennis*) service; (*Fußball*) kick-off. **anspielen** *v* play first; (*Tennis*) serve; (*Fußball*) kick off. **anspielen auf** hint at, allude to. **Anspielung** *f* (*pl* -en) allusion.

ansprechen ['anʃprɛçən] speak to, address; (*auf der Straße, usw.*) accost.

Anspruch ['anʃprux] *m* claim. **Anspruch haben auf** have a right to. **in Anspruch nehmen** lay claim to, claim; (*Zeit*) take up. **Ansprüche stellen** make demands. **anspruchsvoll** *adj* demanding.

Anstalt ['anʃtalt] *f* (*pl* -en) (*Heim*) institution; (*Schule*) institute; (*Vorbereitung*) arrangement.

Anstand ['anʃtant] *m* (*unz.*) decency. **anständig** *adj* decent, proper. **Anstandsdame** *f* chaperone.

anstatt ['anʃtat] *prep* instead of. **anstatt daß** rather than.

anstecken ['anʃtɛkən] *v* pin on (to); (*Ring*) put on; (*Med*) infect; (*Feuer*) light. **-d** *adj* infectious. **Ansteckung** *f* infection.

anstellen ['anʃtɛlən] *v* carry out, do; (*Person*) appoint, employ; (*Mot*) start, (*Radio*) switch on. **Anstellung** *f* appointment.

anstiften ['anʃtiftən] *v* cause, instigate.

Anstoß ['anʃtoɪs] *m* impulse; (*Sport*) kick-off. **Anstoß geben/nehmen** give/take offence (*US* offense). **anstoßen** *v* knock against; (*Haus, usw.*) adjoin.

anstrengen ['anʃtrɛŋən] *v* strain, exert; (*Prozeß*) bring in. **sich anstrengen** strain *or* exert oneself; make an effort.

Antarktika [an'tarktika] *f* Antarctica. **Antarktis** *f* Antarctic. **antarktisch** *adj* antarctic.

antasten ['antastən] *v* touch, handle; (*Thema*) touch on; (*Recht, usw.*) injure.

Anteil ['antail] *m* share, portion; (*Mitgefühl*) sympathy. **-nahme** *f* sympathy.

Antenne [an'tɛnə] *f* (*pl* -n) aerial.

Antibiotikum [antibi'oɪtikum] *neut* (*pl* -biotika) antibiotic.

antik [an'tiɪk] *adj* ancient, classical.

Antikörper ['antikœrpər] *m* antibody.

Antiquität [antikvi'tɛɪt] *f* (*pl* -en) antique. **-enhändler** *m* antique dealer.

antisemitisch [antize'miɪtiʃ] *adj* antisemitic.

Antiseptikum [anti'sɛptikum] *m* (*pl* -septika) antiseptic. **antiseptisch** *adj* antiseptic.

Antrag ['antraik] *m* (*pl* Anträge) offer, proposal; (*Pol*) motion. **einen Antrag stellen** propose a motion. **Antragsteller** *m* applicant; (*Pol*) mover (of a motion).

*antreffen ['antrɛfən] *v* encounter.

*antreiben ['antraibən] *v* drive, propel; (*Person*) urge; (*ans Ufer*) drift ashore.

*antreten ['antreɪtən] *v* (*Amt*) enter, take over; (*Reise*) set out on.

Antrieb ['antriɪp] *m* drive, impulse; (*Tech*) drive. **aus eigenem Antrieb** of one's own free will.

Antritt ['antrit] *m* beginning; (*Amt*) entrance.

*antun ['antuɪn] *v* (*Kleidung*) put on; (*Verletzung*) do, inflict.

Antwort ['antvort] *f* (*pl* -en) answer, reply. **antworten** *v* answer, reply (to).

anvertrauen ['anfɛrtrauən] *v* entrust.

Anwalt ['anvalt] *m* (*pl* Anwälte) (defending) lawyer, solicitor.

anwärmen ['anvɛrmən] *v* warm (up).

*anweisen ['anvaisən] *v* (*zuweisen*) assign; (*anleiten*) direct, show; (*Geld*) transfer. **Anweisung** *f* instruction, order; (*Geld*) remittance, transfer.

*anwend‖en ['anvɛndən] *v* employ, use; (*Gewalt, Methode, Wissenschaft, usw.*) apply. **-bar** *adj* applicable. **Anwendung** *f*. application.

anwesend ['anveɪzənt] *adj* present.
Anwesenheit *f* presence.
Anzahl ['antsaɪl] *f* number. **Anzahlung** *f* deposit, down payment.
Anzeichen ['antsaiçən] *neut* mark, sign.
Anzeige ['antsaigə] *f* (*pl* -n) announcement; (*Inserat*) advertisement; (*bei der Polizei*) report. −**blatt** *neut* advertiser, advertising journal. **anzeig‖en** *v* announce; (*person*) inform against, report (to the police). −**epflichtig** *adj* notifiable.
*anziehen ['antsiɪən] *v* (*Kleider*) put on; (*Schraube*) tighten; (*Person*) dress; (*heranlocken*) attract. **sich anziehen** get dressed. **anziehend** *adj* attractive. **Anziehung** *f* attraction. −**skraft** *f* power of attraction; (*Person*) attractiveness.
Anzug ['antsuɪk] **1** *m* (*unz.*) approach. **2** *m* suit.
anzünden ['antsyndən] *v* light, ignite.
Apfel ['apfəl] *m* (*pl* **Äpfel**) apple. −**baum** *m* apple tree. −**garten** *m* apple orchard. −**kuchen** *m* apple cake. −**mus** *neut* apple sauce. −**saft** *m* apple juice. −**sine** *f* orange. −**wein** *m* cider.
Apostel [a'pɔstəl] *m* (*pl* -) apostle. −**geschichte** *f* Acts of the Apostles.
Apostroph [apo'stroɪf] *m* (*pl* -e) apostrophe.
Apotheke [apo'teɪkə] *f* (*pl* -n) chemist's (shop), pharmacy. −**r** *m* (*pl* -) chemist, pharmacist. −**rkunst** *f* pharmacy, pharmaceutics.
Apparat [apa'raɪt] *m* (*pl* -e) apparatus; (*Vorrichtung*) appliance, device; (*Foto*) camera; (*Telef*) telephone, handset. **am Apparat!** speaking! **am Apparat bleiben** hold the line.
appellieren [apɛ'liɪrən] *v* appeal.
Appetit [ape'tiɪt] *m* (*pl* -e) appetite.
Aprikose [apri'koɪzə] *f* (*pl* -n) apricot.
April [a'pril] *m* (*pl* -e) April. **der erste April** April Fools' Day.
Aquarell [akva'rɛl] *neut* (*pl* -e) water-colour.
Aquarium [a'kvaɪrium] *neut* (*pl* **Aquarien**) aquarium.
Äquator [ɛ'kvaɪtər] *m* equator. **äquatorial** *adj* equatorial.
Arab‖er ['arabər] *m* (*pl* -) Arab. −**ien** *neut* Arabia. **arabisch** *adj* Arab, Arabian.
Arbeit ['arbait] *f* (*pl* -en) work; (*Beschäftigung*) job. **arbeiten** *v* work. **Arbeiter** *m*

worker, workman. −**klasse** *f* working class. **Arbeitgeber** *m* employer. **Arbeits‖amt** *neut* employment office. −**erlaubris** *f* work permit. **arbeits‖fähig** *adj* able to work. −**los** *adj* unemployed. −**losenunterstützung** *f.* unemployment benefit. −**losigkeit** *f* unemployment.
Archäolog‖ie [arçɛolo'giɪ] *f* archaeology. −**e** *m* archaeologist. **archäologisch** *adj* archaeological.
Architekt [arçi'tɛkt] *m* (*pl* -en) architect. −**ur** *f* (*pl* -en) architecture.
Archiv [ar'çiɪf] *neut* (*pl* -e) archives *pl*, records *pl.*
arg [ark] *adj* bad, evil; (*ernst*) serious.
Ärger ['ɛrgər] *m* (*unz.*) (*Verdruß*) annoyance, irritation; (*Zorn*) anger. **ärgerlich** *adj* (*Person*) angry, annoyed; (*Sache*) annoying. **ärgern** *v* annoy, irritate. **sich ärgern über** be angry about.
Argument [argu'mɛnt] *neut* (*pl* -e) argument, reasoning.
Argwohn ['arkvoɪn] *m* (*unz.*) distrust, suspicion. **argwöhnisch** *adj* suspicious, mistrustful.
Aristokrat [aristo'kraɪt] *m* (*pl* -en) aristocrat. −**ie** *f* aristocracy. **aristokratisch** *adj* aristocratic.
Arithmetik [arit'meɪtik] *f* arithmetic. **arithmetisch** *adj* arithmetical.
Arktis ['arktis] *f* Arctic. **arktisch** *adj* arctic.
arm [arm] *adj* poor. −**arm** *adj* poor in . . . . **nikotinarm** *adj* low-nicotine.
Arm [arm] *m* (*pl* -e) arm; (*Fluß*) branch, tributary.
Armaturenbrett [arma'tuɪrənbrɛt] *neut* dashboard, instrument panel.
Armband ['armbant] *neut* bracelet. −**uhr** *f* (wrist)watch.
Armee [ar'meɪ] *f* (*pl* -n) army.
Ärmel ['ɛrməl] *m* (*pl* -) sleeve. −**kanal** *m* English Channel.
ärmlich ['ɛrmliç] *adj* poor, miserable.
armselig ['armzɛɪliç] *adj* wretched, miserable.
Arm‖sessel *m* armchair. −**stuhl** *m* armchair.
Armut ['armuɪt] *f* poverty.
Arrest [a'rɛst] *m* (*pl* -e) arrest, detention.
Arsch [arʃ] *m* (*pl* **Ärsche**) (*vulgär*) arse.
Art [art] *f* (*pl* -en) type, kind, sort; (*Weise*) way, method; (*Biol*) species; (*Brauch*) habit.

artig ['artiç] *adj* (*Kind*) good, well-behaved.
-artig [-artiç] *adj* -like.
Artikel [ar'tiːkəl] *m* (*pl* -) article.
Artillerie [artilə'riː] *f* (*pl* -n) artillery.
Artischocke [arti'ʃɔkə] *f* (*pl* -n) artichoke.
Artist [ar'tist] *m* (*pl* -en) artiste.
Arznei [arts'nai] *f* (*pl* -en) medicine, medicament, drug. **-mittel** *neut* medicine.
Arzt [artst] *m* (*pl* **Ärzte**) doctor, physician.
Ärztin ['ɛrtstin] *f* (*pl* -nen) (woman) doctor. **ärztlich** *adj* medical.
As [as] *neut* (*pl* -se) ace.
Asbest [as'bɛst] *m* asbestos.
Asche ['aʃə] *f* (*pl* -n) ash. **-nbecher** *m* ashtray.
Aspekt [as'pɛkt] *m* (*pl* -e) aspect.
Asphalt [as'falt] *m* asphalt, tarmac.
Assistent [asis'tɛnt] *m* (*pl* -en) assistant.
Ast [ast] *m* (*pl* **Äste**) bough, branch.
ästhetisch [ɛs'teːtiʃ] *adj* aesthetic.
Astronaut [astro'naut] *m* (*pl* -en) astronaut. **-ik** *f* astronautics. **astronautisch** *adj* astronautical.
Astronom [astro'noːm] *m* (*pl* -en) astronomer. **-ie** *f* astronomy. **astronomisch** *adj* astronomical.
Asyl [a'zyːl] *neut* (*pl* -e) asylum.
Atelier [atə'ljeː] *neut* (*pl* -s) studio.
Atem ['aːtəm] *m* (*pl* -) breath. **Atem holen** take breath.
Atheis‖mus [ate'ismus] *m* atheism. **-t** *m* (*pl* -en) atheist.
Äther ['ɛːtər] *m* ether. **ätherisch** *adj* ethereal.
Athlet [at'leːt] *m* (*pl* -en) athlete. **-ik** *f* athletics. **athletisch** *adj* athletic.
Atlantik [at'lantik] *m* Atlantic (Ocean).
Atlas¹ ['atlas] *m* (*pl* **Atlanten**) (*Buch*) atlas.
Atlas² *m* (*pl* -se) (*Stoff*) satin.
atmen ['aːtmən] *v* breathe.
Atmosphäre [atmos'fɛːrə] *f* (*pl* -n) atmosphere.
Atmung ['aːtmuŋ] *f* respiration, breathing. **-sapparat** *m* respirator.
Atom [a'toːm] *neut* (*pl* -e) atom. **-abfall** *m* atomic waste. **-antrieb** *m* nuclear propulsion. **-bombe** *f* atom bomb. **-kraft** *f* nuclear power. **-kraftwerk** *f* nuclear power station.
Attentat [atɛn'taːt] *neut* (*pl* -e) assassination (attempt). **Attentäter** *m* assassin, assailant.

ätzen ['ɛtsən] *v* corrode; (*Med*) cauterize; (*Kupferstich*) etch. **-d** *adj* corrosive, caustic.
Aubergine [obɛr'ʒiːnə] *f* (*pl* -n) aubergine.
auch [aux] *conj* also, too; (*sogar*) even; (*tatsächlich*) indeed, but. **nicht nur ... sondern auch ...** not only ... but also .... **sowohl ... als auch ...** both ... and .... **auch wenn** even if, (even) though. **ich auch!** me too! **ich auch nicht** nor me, me neither. **was er auch sagen mag** whatever he may say. **wer auch immer** whoever.
Audienz [audi'ɛnts] *f* (*pl* -en) audience, interview.
auf [auf] *prep* on. *adv* up; (*offenstehend*) open. **auf und ab** up and down. *auf den Tisch stellen* put on the table. *auf dem Tisch finden* find on the table. *auf die Schule gehen* go to school. *auf der Schule sein* be at school. *auf deutsch* in German. **auf einmal** at once.
Aufbau ['aufbau] *m* (*unz.*) building, construction; structure.
aufbessern ['aufbɛsərn] *v* improve; (*Gehalt*) increase. **Aufbesserung** *f* improvement; (*Gehalt*) increase, rise.
aufbewahren ['aufbəvaːrən] *v* store (up), keep. **Aufbewahrung** *f* storage, safe-keeping.
***aufblasen** ['aufblaːzən] *v* blow up, inflate.
aufblicken ['aufblikən] *v* look up.
aufbrauchen ['aufbrauxən] *v* use up.
***aufbrechen** ['aufbrɛçən] *v* break open; (*Knospen, Wunden*) open; (*abreisen*) set off.
***aufbringen** ['aufbriŋən] *v* bring up, raise; (*ärgern*) imitate, provoke.
Aufbruch ['aufbrux] *m* departure, start.
aufdecken ['aufdɛkən] *v* uncover, reveal; (*Tisch*) spread. **Aufdeckung** *f* revealing, unveiling.
aufdrehen ['aufdreːən] *v* switch *or* turn on; (*Schraube*) unscrew.
aufdringlich ['aufdriŋliç] *adj* intrusive, importunate.
aufeinander [aufain'andər] *adv* (one) after another; (*gegeneinander*) one against the other. **-folgen** *v* follow (one after another). **-folgend** *adj* successive. **-stoßen** *v* (*Mot*) collide; (*Meinungen*) clash. **-treffen** *v* meet.

Aufenthalt ['aufənthalt] *m* (*pl* -e) (*kurze Wartezeit*) delay, stop; (*längerer Besuch usw.*) stay. **–serlaubnis** *f* residence permit.

auferlegen ['aufɛrleːgən] *v* impose.

***auferstehen** ['aufɛrʃteːən] *v* rise from the dead. **Auferstehung** *f* resurrection.

***auffahren** ['auffaːrən] *v* rise, go up; (*herauffahren*) draw up; (*aufspringen*) start, jump; (*zornig werden*) flare up; (*wagen*) collide. **Auffahrt** *f* ascent; (*in den Himmel*) Ascension; (*Zufahrtsweg*) drive.

***auffallen** ['auffalən] *v* strike, come to one's attention. **es fiel mir ein** it struck me, I realized. **auffallend** *or* **auffällig** *adj* striking, remarkable.

auffassen ['auffasən] *v* pick up; (*begreifen*) understand; (*deuten*) interpret. **Auffassung** *f* comprehension; (*Auslegung*) interpretation; (*Meinung*) opinion.

***auffliegen** ['auffliːgən] *v* fly up; (*Flugzeug*) take off; (*Tür*) fly open; (*explodieren*) explode.

auffordern ['auffɔrdərn] *v* challenge; (*einladen*) ask, invite. **Aufforderung** *f* challenge; (*Recht*) summons; (*Einladung*) invitation, request.

***auffressen** ['auffrɛsən] *v* devour.

auffrischen ['auffriʃən] *v* freshen up; (*Kenntnisse*) refresh.

aufführen ['auffyːrən] *v* (*Theater*) put on, perform; (*Film*) show; (*Konzert*) give; (*zitieren*) cite; (*aufbauen*) erect. **Aufführung** *f* performance; (*Film*) showing; (*Benehmen*) behaviour.

Aufgabe ['aufgaːbə] *f* task, duty; (*Übergabe*) handing in.

Aufgang ['aufgaŋ] *m* rise, ascent.

***aufgeben** [aufgeːbən] *v* give up; (*Gepäck*) check in.

aufgeblasen ['aufgəblaːzən] *adj* arrogant, conceited.

aufgeklärt ['aufgəklɛrt] *adj* enlightened.

aufgelegt ['aufgəleːkt] *adj* inclined, in the mood. **gut/schlecht aufgelegt** in a good/bad mood.

aufgeregt ['aufgərɛːkt] *adj* excited.

aufgeschlossen ['aufgəʃlɔsən] *adj* enlightened, open-minded.

***aufhalten** ['aufhaltən] *adj* keep open; (*anhalten*) stop; (*hinhalten*) delay. **sich aufhalten** stay.

***aufhängen** ['aufhɛŋən] *v* hang up.

***aufheben** ['aufheːbən] *v* lift, raise; (*aufbewahren*) store, keep; (*abschaffen*) abolish, cancel. **Aufhebung** *f* raising, abolition.

aufheitern ['aufhaitərn] *v* cheer up. **sich aufheitern** (*Wetter*) brighten up.

aufhören ['aufhœːrən] *v* stop, cease.

aufklären ['aufklɛːrən] *v* (*Person*) enlighten; (*Sache*) clarify, explain. **Aufklärung** *f* clarification; (the) Enlightenment.

aufkleben ['aufkleːbən] *v* stick on, paste on.

aufknöpfen ['aufknœpfən] *v* unbutton.

***aufkommen** ['aufkɔmən] *v* arise. **aufkommen für** take responsibility for.

***aufladen** ['auflaːdən] *v* load.

Auflage ['auflaːgə] *f* (*Buch*) edition; (*Zeitung*) circulation.

***auflassen** ['auflasən] *v* leave open.

Auflauf ['auflauf] *m* riot; (*Speise*) trifle, soufflé. **auflaufen** *v* run up; (*Schiff*) run aground; (*Geld*) increase.

auflegen ['aufleːgən] *v* put on; (*Buch*) print, publish; (*Telef*) hang up.

auflösbar ['auflœːzbaːr] *adj* soluble. **auflösen** *v* (*Knoten*) loosen; (*in Wasser, usw.*) dissolve; (*Rätsel*) solve; (*Vertrag*) cancel; (*Geschäft*) close down; (*Ehe*) break up. **Auflösung** *f* loosening; solution; cancellation; closure; break-up.

***aufmachen** ['aufmaxən] *v* open; (*Knoten, Knöpfe*) undo. **sich aufmachen** set off. **Aufmachung** *f* outward appearance.

aufmerksam ['aufmɛrkzam] *adj* attentive. **jemanden auf etwas aufmerksam machen** draw something to someone's attention. **Aufmerksamkeit** *f* attentiveness, attention.

aufmuntern ['aufmuntərn] *v* encourage, cheer up.

Aufnahme ['aufnaːmə] *f* (*pl* -n) taking up; (*Foto*) shot, picture; (*Tonband, usw.*) recording; (*Zulassung*) admission; (*Empfang*) reception. **aufnahmefähig** *adj* receptive. **Aufnahmeprüfung** *f* entrance exam.

***aufnehmen** ['aufneːmən] *v* take up; (*zulassen*) admit; (*empfangen*) receive; (*Radio*) pick up; (*Foto*) photograph; (*Protokoll, Tonband*) record.

aufopfern ['aufɔpfərn] *v* sacrifice.

aufpassen ['aufpasən] *v* pay attention; (*vorsichtig sein*) take care. **aufpassen auf** take care of, look after.

Aufprall ['aufpral] *m* (*pl* -e) impact, collision. **aufprallen** *v* strike, collide.
aufputzen ['aufputsən] *v* dress up, adorn; (*reinigen*) clean up.
aufräumen ['aufrɔymən] *v* tidy up, clean up; (*wegschaffen*) clear away. **Aufräumung** *f* cleaning up.
aufrecht ['aufrɛçt] *adj* upright, erect; (*fig*) upright, honest. **-erhalten** *v* maintain, keep up.
aufregen ['aufreɪgən] *v* excite, upset. **sich aufregen** get excited *or* upset. **Aufregung** *f* excitement, agitation.
aufrichten ['aufriçtən] *v* erect, set up; (*trösten*) console.
aufrichtig ['aufriçtiç] sincere, honest. **Aufrichtigkeit** *f* sincerity, honesty.
aufrücken ['aufrykən] *v* move up; (*Dienstgrad*) be promoted.
Aufruf ['aufruːf] *m* call, appeal. **aufrufen** *v* call out.
Aufruhr ['aufruːr] *m* (*pl* -e) tumult; (*Erhebung*) revolt. **aufrühren** *v* stir up; (*Erhebung*) incite to revolt. **Aufrührer** *m* (*pl* -) agitator, rebel. **aufrührerisch** *adj* rebellious, riotous.
aufrüsten ['aufrystən] *v* (re)arm. **Aufrüstung** *f* (re)armament.
aufs [aufs] *prep* + *art* auf das.
aufsagen ['aufzagən] *v* recite, repeat.
Aufsatz ['aufzats] *m* essay; (*Tech*) top (piece); (*Tafel-*) centre-piece.
***aufsaugen** ['aufzaugən] *v* suck up. **-d** *adj* absorbent.
***aufschieben** ['aufʃiːbən] *v* push open; (*fig*) put off, delay. **Aufschiebung** *f* postponement, delay.
Aufschlag ['aufʃlaɪk] *m* surcharge, extra charge; (*Hose*) turn-up; (*Jacke*) lapel; (*Auftreffen*) impact; (*Tennis*) service. **aufschlagen** *v* (*Preis*) raise; (*Stoff*) turn up; (*auftreffen*) hit; (*Buch*) open, consult; (*Tennis*) serve.
***aufschließen** ['aufʃliːsən] *v* open up, unlock; (*erklären*) explain.
Aufschluß ['aufʃlus] *m* unlocking; (*Erklärung*) explanation. **aufschlußreich** *adj* informative.
***aufschneiden** ['aufʃnaidən] *v* cut open; (*Fleisch*) carve.
Aufschnitt ['aufʃnit] *m* (cold) sliced meat.
Aufschrei ['aufʃrai] *m* scream, shriek; (*fig*) outcry.
***aufschreiben** ['aufʃraibən] *v* write down, note.

Aufschrift ['aufʃrit] *f* (*Briefumschlag*) address; (*Etikett*) labelling, information; (*Inschrift*) inscription.
Aufschub ['aufʃuːp] *m* delay, deferment.
Aufschwung ['aufʃvuŋ] *m* swinging up, rising up; (*Komm*) boom, upturn (in economy).
***aufsehen** ['aufzeɪən] *v* look up. **Aufsehen** *neut* (*unz.*) stir, sensation. **Aufseher** *m* (*pl* -) overseer, inspector.
aufsetzen ['aufzɛtsən] *v* put on; (*Schriftliches*) draft, draw up.
Aufsicht ['aufziçt] *f* supervision, control; (*Verantwortung*) charge, care. **-srat** *m* board of directors.
***aufspringen** ['aufʃpriŋən] *v* spring up; (*Tür*) fly open; (*Riß*) crack, open.
Aufstand ['aufʃtant] *m* revolt, rebellion.
aufstapeln ['aufʃtaɪpəln] *v* stack up, pile up.
aufstauen ['aufʃtauən] *v* dam (up).
***aufstehen** ['aufʃteɪən] *v* stand up; (*morgens, usw.*) get up, rise; (*revoltieren*) revolt; (*offenstehen*) stand open.
***aufsteigen** ['aufʃtaigən] *v* climb up, ascend, rise; (*Pferd*) mount.
aufstellen ['aufʃtɛlən] *v* set up; (*Kandidat*) nominate; (*Mil*) draw up; (*Theorie, usw.*) propose, advance.
Aufstieg ['aufʃtiːk] *m* ascent, rise.
aufsuchen ['aufzuːxən] *v* (*Arzt, Gasthaus*) visit; (*Person*) visit, look up.
auftanken ['auftaŋkən] *v* refuel.
auftauchen ['auftauxən] *v* (*aus Wasser*) emerge; (*fig*) turn up, crop up.
auftauen ['auftauən] *v* thaw (out), melt.
aufteilen ['auftailən] *v* divide up; (*verteilen*) share out.
Auftrag ['auftraɪk] *m* (*pl* Aufträge) (*Komm*) order; (*Aufgabe*) task. **auftragen** *v* (*Farbe*) apply; (*Essen*) serve. **Auftrag‖geber** *m* customer, purchaser. **-nehmer** *m* contractor, supplier.
***auftreiben** ['auftraibən] *v* (*auffinden*) hunt out, find; (*Staub*) stir up; (*Geld*) raise.
***auftreten** ['auftrɛtən] *v* come forward, appear.
Auftritt ['auftrit] *m* (*Szene*) scene; (*Schauspieler*) appearance, entrance.
***auftun** ['auftuːn] *v* open.
aufwachen ['aufvaxən] *v* wake up.
***aufwachsen** ['aufvaksən] grow up.

Aufwand ['aufvant] *m* (*unz.*) expenditure.
aufwärmen ['aufvɛrmən] *v* (*Sport*) warm up; (*speisen*) heat up.
aufwärts ['aufvɛrts] *adv* up(wards).
aufwecken ['aufvɛkən] *v* wake up.
***aufwend‖en** ['augvɛndən] *v* (*Geld*) spend; (*Zeit*) devote; (*Energie*) expend. **–ig** *adj* expensive. **Aufwendung** *f* expenditure.
***aufwerfen** ['aufvɛrfən] *v* throw up.
aufwerten ['aufvɛrtən] *v* raise the value of, revalue. **Aufwertung** *f* revaluation.
***aufwinden** ['aufvindən] *v* wind up; (*mit der Winde*) winch up.
aufwirbeln ['aufvirbəln] *v* whirl up.
aufwischen ['aufviʃən] *v* wipe up.
aufwühlen ['aufvyɪlən] *v* root up; (*fig*) stir up, agitate.
aufzählen ['auftsɛɪlən] *v* count out.
aufzeichnen ['auftsaiçnən] *v* sketch; (*niederschreiben*) write down.
***aufziehen** ['auftsiɪən] *v* (*Kind, Tier, Flagge*) raise; (*Vorhang*) open; (*Pflanze*) grow; (*necken*) tease.
Aufzug ['auftsuɪk] *m* lift, (*US*) elevator; (*Festzug*) procession, parade; (*Theater*) act.
Augapfel ['aukapfəl] *m* eyeball.
Auge ['augə] *neut* (*pl* -n) eye. **unter vier Augen** in private. **ins Auge fallen** be conspicuous, catch the eye. **Augen‖arzt** *m* oculist, ophthalmologist. **–blick** *m* moment, instant. **–braue** *f* eyebrow. **–lid** *neut* eyelid. **–loch** *neut* eye socket.
August [au'gust] *m* (*pl* -e) August.
Aula ['aula] *f* (*pl* **Aulen**) (great) hall.
Au-pair-Mädchen [o'pɛɪrmɛɪtçən] *neut* au-pair girl.
aus [aus] *prep* from. *adv* out; (*vorbei*) over, finished. *aus London* from London. *aus dem Fenster* out of the window. *aus Liebe zu* for love of. *aus Holz* (made) of wood, wooden. *von mir aus* as far as I'm concerned. *es ist aus* it's over.
ausarbeiten ['ausarbaitən] *v* work out; (*vervollkommnen*) perfect, finish off. **Ausarbeitung** *f* working out; finishing off, completion.
ausarten ['ausaɪrtən] *v* degenerate.
ausatmen ['ausaɪtmən] *v* exhale, breathe out.
ausbaggern ['ausbagərn] *v* dredge.
Ausbau ['ausbau] *m* (*pl* -ten) extension; (*Fertigstellung*) completion.

ausbauchen ['ausbauxən] *v* bulge. **Ausbauchung** *f* bulge.
ausbessern ['ausbɛsərn] *v* repair, mend.
Ausbeute ['ausbɔytə] *f* profit, gain; (*Ernte*) crop, yield. **ausbeuten** *v* exploit. **Ausbeut‖er** *m* exploiter. **–ung** *f* exploitation.
ausbilden ['ausbildən] *v* educate; (*Lehrling*) train; (*gestalten*) develop, shape. **Ausbildung** *f* education; training; (*Gestaltung*) development, shaping.
***ausbleiben** ['ausblaibən] *v* stay away; (*aufhören*) stop.
Ausblick ['ausblik] *m* view; (*fig*) prospect, outlook.
***ausbrechen** ['ausbrɛçən] *v* break out.
ausbreiten ['ausbraitən] *v* spread (out), stretch (out), extend.
Ausbruch ['ausbrux] *m* outbreak; (*vom Gefängnis*) escape, break-out; (*Zorn, Vulkan*) eruption.
ausbrüten ['ausbryɪtən] *v* hatch.
Ausdauer ['ausdauər] *f* endurance, perseverance. **ausdauern** *v* persevere, endure.
ausdehnen ['ausdeɪnən] *v* extend; (*Metall*) expand. **Ausdehnung** *f* extension; expansion.
***ausdenken** ['ausdɛŋkən] *v* invent, think out; (*sich vorstellen*) imagine.
ausdrehen ['ausdreɪən] *v* turn off, switch off; (*Gelenk*) dislocate.
Ausdruck ['ausdruk] *m* expression; phrase. **ausdrück‖en** *f* express; (*auspressen*) squeeze out. **–lich** *adj* express, explicit. **ausdrucks‖los** *adj* expressionless, vacant. **–voll** *adj* expressive.
auseinander [ausain'andər] *adv* apart. **–bauen** *v* take apart, dismantle. **–fallen** *v* fall to pieces. **–gehen** *v* break up; (*sich trennen*) part. **–nehmen** *v* take apart. **–setzen** *v* explain. **Auseinandersetzung** *f* (vigorous) discussion; (*Streit*) argument.
auserlesen ['ausɛrleɪzən] *adj* selected.
ausersehen ['ausɛrzeɪən] *v* choose, select.
auserwählen ['ausɛrvɛɪlən] *v* choose, select.
***ausfahren** ['ausfaɪrən] *v* drive out; (*Person*) take for a drive *or* walk. **Ausfahrt** *f* exit; (*Ausflug*) excursion; (*Ausfahren*) departure.
Ausfall ['ausfal] *m* loss; (*Fehlbetrag*) deficiency, deficit; (*Ergebnis*) result; (*Mil*) attack, sally. **ausfallen** *v* fall out; (*unterbleiben*) fail, be wanting; attack.

ausfertigen ['ausfɛrtigən] v (*Schriftliches*) draw up; (*ausstellen*) issue.

ausfindig ['ausfindiç] adj **ausfindig machen** find out.

Ausflug ['ausfluːk] m excursion, outing.

ausfragen [ausfraːgən] v question, interrogate.

Ausfuhr ['ausfuːr] f (pl -en) export.

ausführ‖en ['ausfyːrən] v carry out, perform; (*Waren*) export; (*erklären*) explain, set out (in detail). **–bar** adj feasible. **–lich** adj detailed, extensive; adv in full. **Ausführung** f execution, performance; (*Darstellung*) explanation.

ausfüllen ['ausfylən] v fill; (*Formular*) fill out.

Ausgabe ['ausgaɪbə] f expenditure, expense; (*Buch*) edition.

Ausgang ['ausgaŋ] m going out; (*Tür*) way out, exit; (*Ergebnis*) result, issue; (*freier Tag*) day off.

*ausgeben ['ausgeːbən] v (*Geld*) spend; (*herausgeben*) distribute; (*Karten*) deal. **sich ausgeben für** pose as.

ausgeglichen ['ausgəgliçən] adj (well-)balanced.

*ausgehen ['ausgeːən] v go out; (*enden*) come to an end; (*Vorrat*) run out. **Ausgehverbot** neut curfew.

ausgelassen ['ausgəlasən] adj wild, unrestrained, boisterous.

ausgemacht ['ausgəmaxt] adj agreed, settled.

ausgenommen ['ausgənomən] prep except for.

ausgeprägt ['ausgəprɛikt] adj marked, distinct.

ausgerechnet ['ausgərɛçnət] adv precisely, just.

ausgeschlossen ['ausgəflɔsən] adj impossible, out of the question.

ausgesprochen ['ausgəfprɔxən] adj pronounced, distinct. adv distinctly, very.

ausgewachsen ['ausgəvaksən] adj full-grown.

ausgezeichnet ['ausgətsaiçnət] adj excellent.

*ausgießen ['ausgiːsən] v pour out.

Ausgleich ['ausglaiç] m (pl -e) settlement; (*Entschädigung*) compensation; (*Sport*) equalizer. **ausgleichen** v equalize, make even; (*Verlust*) compensate; (*Konto*) balance.

Ausguß ['ausgus] m outlet; (*Kanne*) spout.

*aushalten ['aushaltən] v bear, endure; (*durchhalten*) persevere.

*ausheben ['ausheɪbən] v pull out, lift out; (*Truppen*) enlist. **Aushebung** f enlistment; (*Wehrdienst*) conscription.

*aushelfen ['aushɛlfən] v help (out), assist.

Aushilfe ['aushilfə] f (temporary) help, assistance.

aushöhlen ['aushœːlən] v hollow out, excavate.

*auskennen ['auskɛnən] v **sich auskennen** (*umg.*) know what's what; (*in einer Sache*) know well.

auskleiden ['ausklaidən] v line. **sich auskleiden** undress.

*auskommen ['auskɔmən] v (*mit etwas*) manage or cope with; (*mit einer Person*) get on well with.

Auskunft ['auskunft] f (pl **Auskünfte**) information.

auslachen ['auslaxən] v laugh at.

*ausladen ['auslaɪdən] v unload.

Auslage ['auslaɪgə] f display; (*Schaufenster*) shop window. **–n** pl expenses pl.

Ausland ['auslant] neut foreign country or countries. **ins** or **im Ausland** abroad.

Ausländer m (pl -), **Ausländerin** f (pl -nen) foreigner. **ausländisch** adj foreign.

*auslassen ['auslasən] v omit, leave out; (*Butter*) melt; (*Kleider*) let down. **Auslassung** f omission; (*Äußerung*) utterance. **–szeichen** neut apostrophe.

Auslauf ['auslauf] m outflow; (*Schiff*) sailing, departure; (*Bewegungsfreiheit*) room to move. **auslaufen** v run out; (*Schiff*) put to sea.

ausleeren ['ausleːrən] v empty. **Ausleerung** f emptying, draining.

auslegen ['ausleːgən] v lay out; (*Geld*) spend; (*erklären*) explain, interpret. **Auslegung** f display; (*Erklärung*) interpretation.

Auslese ['ausleːzə] f (pl -n) selection; (*Wein*) choice wine. **auslesen** v select; (*Buch*) read to the end.

ausliefern ['ausliːfərn] v deliver; (*Verbrecher*) extradite. **Auslieferung** f delivery; extradition.

auslösen ['auslœːzən] v loosen; (*Gefangene*) ransom; (*veranlassen*) cause, spark off.

ausmachen ['ausmaxən] v (*Feuer, Licht*) put out; (*betragen*) amount to; (*ver-*

abreden) agree, fix. **das macht nichts aus** that doesn't matter.
Ausmaß ['ausmaɪs] *neut* scale, extent.
Ausnahme ['ausnaɪmə] *f* (*pl* -n) exception. **mit Ausnahme von** excepting, with the exception of. **-fall** *m* exception, special case. **-zustand** *m* (*Pol*) state of emergency. **ausnahms‖los** *adj* without exception. **-weise** *adv* by way of exception, just for once.
*ausnehmen ['ausneɪmən] *v* take out; (*ausschließen*) exclude, make an exception of.
ausnutzen ['ausnutsən] *v* take advantage of.
auspacken ['auspakən] *v* unpack.
ausprobieren ['ausprobiːrən] *v* try (out), test.
Auspuff ['auspuf] *m* (*pl* -e) exhaust. **-rohr** *neut* exhaust pipe. **-topf** *m* silencer.
ausradieren ['ausradiːrən] *v* erase, rub out.
ausräumen ['ausrɔymən] *v* clear out, clean out.
ausrechnen ['ausreçnən] *v* calculate, work out. **Ausrechnung** *f* calculation.
Ausrede ['ausreɪdə] *f* excuse.
ausreichen ['ausraiçən] *v* be enough *or* sufficient. **-d** *adj* sufficient, enough.
Ausreise ['ausraizə] *f* outward journey; (*Grenzübertritt*) departure, exit. **ausreisen** *v* depart.
ausrichten ['ausriçtən] *v* adjust, align; (*durchsetzen*) accomplish, do; (*Botschaft*) convey.
ausrotten ['ausrɔtən] *v* stamp out, root out.
Ausruf ['ausruːf] *m* cry, exclamation; (*Bekanntmachung*) proclamation. **ausrufen** *v* cry out, exclaim; (*Namen*) call out. **Ausrufung** *f* exclamation. **-zeichen** *neut* exclamation mark.
ausruhen ['ausruːən] *v* rest.
ausrüsten ['ausrystən] *v* equip; (*Mil*) arm. **Ausrüstung** *f* equipment; (*Mil*) armament.
Aussage ['auszaɪgə] *f* (*pl* -n) statement, declaration; (*Jur*) evidence, testimony. **aussagen** *v* declare, state; (*Jur*) give evidence, make a statement, testify.
ausschalten ['ausʃaltən] *v* switch off; (*fig*) exclude.
Ausschank ['ausʃaŋk] *m* (*Ausgabe*) service

(of alcoholic drinks); (*Kneipe*) bar, pub.
Ausschank über die Straße off-sales, off-licence.
*ausscheiden ['ausʃaidən] *v* withdraw, retire; (*absondern*) separate. **Ausscheidung** *f* withdrawal; separation.
ausschicken ['ausʃikən] *v* send out.
ausschiffen ['ausʃifən] *v* disembark, land. **Ausschiffung** *f* disembarkation.
ausschimpfen ['ausʃimpfən] *v* scold, abuse.
*ausschlafen ['ausʃlaːfən] *v* lie in, sleep until completely rested.
Ausschlag ['ausʃlaːk] *m* (*Med*) rash; (*Bot*) shoot; (*Zeiger*) deflection. **ausschlagen** *v* knock out; (*ablehnen*) refuse; (*Pferd*) kick out.
*ausschließen ['ausʃliːsən] *v* shut out, lock out; (*fig*) exclude. **ausschließlich** *adj* exclusive; *prep* excluding, exclusive of. **Ausschließung** *f* exclusion; (*Arbeiter*) lock-out.
*ausschneiden ['ausʃnaidən] *v* cut out.
Ausschnitt ['ausʃnit] *m* (*Teil*) section; (*Zeitung*) press cutting; (*Kleid*) low neckline.
ausschöpfen ['ausʃœpfən] *v* (*Wasser*) scoop out; (*Boot*) bail out; (*Möglichkeiten*) exhaust.
*ausschreiben ['ausʃraibən] *v* write out, copy out; (*Formular*) fill out; (*ankündigen*) announce.
Ausschreitung ['ausʃraituŋ] *f* excess, transgression.
Ausschuß ['ausʃus] **1** *m* committee, board. **2** *m* (*unz.*) (*Abfall*) refuse, rejects *pl*.
ausschweifen ['ausʃwaifən] *v* (*moralisch*) lead a dissolute life; (*von Thema*) digress. **Ausschweifung** *f* debauchery, immorality; digression.
*aussehen ['ausseɪən] *v* appear, look. **sie sieht hübsch aus** she looks pretty. **es sieht nach Regen aus** it looks like rain.
außen ['ausən] *adv* (to the) outside, outwards. **Außenbordmotor** *m* outboard motor.
*aussenden ['ausszendən] *v* send out; (*Strahlen*) emit; (*Radio*) transmit.
Außen‖handel *m* foreign trade. **-läufer** *m* wing-half. **-minister** *m* foreign minister. **-politik** *f* foreign policy; (*allgemein*) foreign affairs. **-seite** *f* outside. **-seiter** *m* outsider. **-stürmer** *m* wing (forward).

außer ['ausər] *prep* (*räumlich*) out of, outside; (*ausgenommen*) except. **außer Betrieb** out of order.

äußer ['ɔysər] *adj* external, exterior, outer.

außer‖dem *adv* besides. –**halb** *adv*, *prep* outside.

äußerlich ['ɔysərliç] *adj* external.

äußern ['ɔysərn] *v* express, utter; (*zeigen*) manifest, reveal.

außerordentlich [ausər'ɔrdəntliç] *adj* extraordinary.

äußerst ['ɔysərst] *adj* the utmost.

aussetzen ['auszɛtzən] *v* (*Pflanze*) plant out; (*Kind*) abandon; (*Tier*) set free; (*Geld*) offer; (*einer Gefahr, dem Spott, usw.*) expose (to); (*aufhören*) stop; (*Mot*) stall.

Aussicht ['auszіçt] *f* outlook, prospect; (*Blick*) view. **aussichts‖los** *adj* unpromising, hopeless. –**voll** *adj* promising.

aussondern ['auszɔndərn] (*auswählen*) select; excrete. **Aussonderung** *f* separation; selection; excretion.

ausspeien ['ausʃpaiən] *v* spit out; (*Rauch*) belch out.

Aussprache ['ausʃpraıxə] *f* pronunciation.

*****aussprechen** ['ausʃprɛçən] *v* pronounce.

Ausspruch ['ausʃprux] *m* remark, saying; (*Jur*) verdict.

ausspülen ['ausʃpyːlən] *v* wash out, rinse.

Ausstand ['ausʃtant] *m* strike.

ausstatten ['ausʃtatən] *v* equip, furnish; (*Tochter*) provide with a dowry. **Ausstattung** *f* (*pl* -en) equipment, outfit; dowry.

*****ausstehen** ['ausʃteːən] *v* be missing; (*Geld*) be owed; (*ertragen*) endure, bear. *ich kann ihn nicht ausstehen* I can't stand him.

*****aussteigen** ['ausʃtaigən] *v* get off, alight.

ausstellen ['ausʃtɛlən] *v* display, exhibit; (*Paß, Urkunde*) issue; (*Quittung*) write out. **Aussteller** *m* (*pl* -) exhibiter. **Ausstellung** *f* exhibition; issue; writing out.

*****aussterben** ['ausʃtɛrbən] *v* die out.

Ausstieg ['ausʃtiːg] *m* (*pl* -e) exit door.

*****ausstoßen** ['ausʃtoːsən] *v* push out, thrust out; (*Schrei*) give.

ausstrahlen ['ausʃtraːlən] *v* radiate.

ausstrecken ['ausʃtrɛkən] *v* stretch out, extend.

*****ausstreichen** ['ausʃtraiçən] *v* (*Wort*) strike out, cross out; (*Teig*) roll out.

ausströmen ['ausʃtrœːmən] *v* (*Flüssigkeit*) pour out; (*Gas*) escape.

aussuchen ['auszuːxən] *v* search (out), select.

Austausch ['austauʃ] *m* exchange. **austauschen** *v* exchange.

austeilen ['austailən] *v* distribute, share out.

Auster ['austər] *f* (*pl* -n) oyster.

Austrag ['austraık] *m* (*pl* **Austräge**) decision, end, result. **austragen** *v* carry out; (*Kampf*) decide; (*Post*) deliver.

Australi‖en [au'straːliən] *neut* Australia. –**er** *m* (*pl* -), –**erin** *f* (*pl* -nen) Australian. **australisch** *adj* Australian.

*****austreiben** ['austraibən] *v* expel.

*****austreten** ['austreːtən] *v* leave, withdraw (from); (*Schuhe, usw.*) wear out.

*****austrinken** ['austriŋkən] *v* drain, drink off.

Austritt ['austrit] *m* leaving, departure.

ausüben ['ausyːbən] *v* practise; (*Druck, Einfluß*) exert; (*Macht*) wield. –**d** *adj* practising. **Ausübung** *f* practice, exercise.

Ausverkauf ['ausfɛrkauf] *m* (clearance) sale. **ausverkauft** *adj* sold out.

Auswahl ['ausvaıl] *f* choice, selection.

Auswanderer ['ausvandərər] *m* emigrant. **auswandern** *v* emigrate. **Auswanderung** *f* emigration.

auswärtig ['ausvɛrtiç] *adj* foreign. **das Auswärtige Amt** the Foreign Office.

auswärts ['ausvɛrts] *adv* outwards; (*nach draußen*) outside.

auswechseln ['ausvɛksəln] *v* change (for), exchange.

Ausweg ['ausveık] *m* way out.

*****ausweichen** ['ausvaiçən] *v* make way; (*Frage*) evade, dodge. –**d** *adj* evasive, elusive. **Ausweichung** *f* evasion.

Ausweis ['ausvais] *m* (*pl* -e) identity card *or* papers; (*Paß*) passport. **ausweisen** *v* expel, turn out. **Ausweisung** *f* expulsion.

auswendig ['ausvɛndiç] *adj* external. **auswendig lernen** learn by heart.

*****auswerfen** ['ausvɛrfən] *v* throw out; (*Anker*) cast.

auswirken ['ausvirkən] *v* obtain. **sich auswirken auf** have an effect on. **Auswirkung** *f* effect.

auswischen ['ausviʃən] *v* wipe out.

Auswuchs ['ausvuks] *m* growth; (*Nebenerscheinung*) (unwelcome) product, side-effect.

auszahlen ['austsailən] *v* pay out. **Auszahlung** *f* payment.

auszeichnen ['austsaiçnən] *v* (*Ware*) label; (*ehren*) honour; (*hervorheben*) distinguish, mark out. **sich auszeichnen** distinguish oneself. **Auszeichnung** *f* distinction, honour, award.

***ausziehen** ['austsiːən] *v* pull out, extract; (*Person*) undress; (*aus einer Wohnung*) move out. **sich ausziehen** undress.

Auszug ['austsuːk] *m* removal; (*Abmarsch*) departure; (*Exzerpt*) excerpt.

authentisch [au'tɛntiʃ] *adj* authentic.

Auto ['auto] *neut* (*pl* -s) car, automobile. **–ausstellung** *f* motor show. **–bahn** *f* motorway. **–fahrer** *m* driver, motorist.

Autogramm [auto'gram] *neut* (*pl* -e) autograph.

Automat [auto'mait] *m* (*pl* -en) vending machine. **automatisch** *adj* automatic. **automatisieren** *v* automate.

autonom [auto'noːm] *adj* autonomous.

Autor ['autor] *m* (*pl* -en) author.

autoritär [autori'tɛir] *adj* authoritarian. **Autorität** *f* authority.

Auto‖unfall *m* road accident. **–vermietung** *f* car hire.

avantgardistisch [avãgar'distiʃ] *adj* avantgarde.

Axt [akst] *f* (*pl* **Äxte**) axe.

B

Baby ['beɪbi] *neut* (*pl* -s) baby.

Bach [bax] *m* (*pl* **Bäche**) stream, brook.

Backbord ['bakbɔrt] *neut* (*naut*) port (side).

Backe ['bakə] *f* (*pl* -n) cheek.

backen ['bakən] *v* bake.

Bäcker ['bɛkər] *m* (*pl* -) baker. **–ei** *f* (*pl* -en) bakery.

Back‖ofen *m* oven. **–pulver** *neut* baking powder. **–stein** *m* brick.

Bad [baɪt] *neut* (*pl* **Bäder**) bath; (*Badeort*) spa. **Bade‖anstalt** *f* baths, swimming pool. **–anzug** *m* bathing costume. **–hose** *f* bathing trunks *pl*. **baden** *v* bathe. **Bade‖wanne** *f* bath tub. **–zimmer** *neut* bathroom.

Bagger ['bagər] *m* (*pl* -) dredger, excavator. **baggern** *v* dredge, excavate.

Bahn [baɪn] *f* (*pl* -en) railway; (*Weg*) path. **–brecher** *m* pioneer. **bahnen** *v* **den Weg bahnen** pave the way (for).

Bahn‖hof *m* (railway) station. **–steig** *m* (railway) platform.

Bahre ['baɪrə] *f* (*pl* -n) stretcher; (*Toten-*) bier.

Bai [bai] *f* (*pl* -en) (*Bucht*) bay.

Bajonett [bajo'nɛt] *neut* (*pl* -e) bayonet.

Bakterium [bak'teɪrium] *neut* (*pl* **Bakterien**) bacterium (*pl* -a).

balancieren [balã'siːrən] *v* balance.

bald [balt] *adv* soon. **–ig** *adj* early, quick. **–möglichst** *adv* as soon as possible.

Balken ['balkən] *m* (*pl* -) beam.

Balkon [bal'koː] *m* (*pl* -e) balcony.

Ball[1] [bal] *m* (*pl* **Bälle**) ball.

Ball[2] *m* (*pl* **Bälle**) (*Tanz*) dance, ball.

Ballade [ba'laɪdə] *f* (*pl* -n) ballad.

ballen ['balən] *v* (*Faust*) clench. **sich ballen** cluster, clump together.

Ballen ['balən] *m* (*pl* -) bale, bundle; (*Anat*) palm. **–entzündung** *f* bunion.

Ballett [ba'lɛt] *neut* (*pl* -e) ballet. **Balletttänzer** *m* (*pl* -), **–tänzerin** *f* (*pl* -nen) ballet dancer. **Balletteuse** *f* (*pl* -n) ballerina.

Ballistik [ba'listik] *f* (*unz.*) ballistics. **ballistisch** *adj* ballistic.

Ballon [ba'loː] *m* (*pl* -e) balloon.

Balsam ['balzaɪm] *m* (*pl* -e) balsam; (*fig*) balm. **balsamieren** *v* embalm.

baltisch ['baltiʃ] *adj* Baltic.

Bambus ['bambus] *m* (*pl* -se) bamboo.

Banane [ba'naɪnə] *f* (*pl* -n) banana.

Band[1] [bant] **1** *neut* (*pl* **Bänder**) tape; (*Haar*) ribbon; (*Anat*) ligament; (*Radio*) waveband. **2** *neut* (*pl* -e) bond, tie.

Band[2] *m* (*pl* **Bände**) (*Buch*) volume.

Band[3] [bɛnt] *f* (*pl* -s) (*Jazz*) band.

Bandage [ban'daɪʒə] *f* (*pl* -n) bandage. **bandagieren** *v* bandage.

Bandaufnahme ['bantaufnaɪmə] *f* tape recording.

Bande ['bandə] *f* (*pl* -n) gang, band.

bändigen ['bɛndigən] *v* tame, subdue; (*Wut*) control.

Bandit [ban'diɪt] *m* (*pl* -en) bandit.

Bandscheibe ['bantʃaibə] *f* (*Anat*) disc. **–nverfall** *m* slipped disc.

bang(e) ['baŋ(ə)] *adj* afraid, anxious. **bangen** *v* be afraid *or* anxious.

Bank[1] [baŋk] *f* (*pl* **Bänke**) (*zum Sitzen*) bench, seat.

Bank[2] *f* (*pl* -en) (*Komm*) bank.

Bankett [baŋ'kɛt] *neut* (*pl* -e) banquet.

bankrott [baŋ'rɔt] *adj* bankrupt. **Bankrott** *m* (*pl* -e) bankruptcy. **Bankrott machen**

go bankrupt. **Bankrotteur** *m* (*pl* -e) bankrupt.

Bank∥konto *neut* bank account. **–note** *f* banknote.

Bann [ban] *m* (*pl* -e) ban; (*Kirche*) excommunication; (*Zauber*) spell.

bar [baɪr] *adj* bare; (*Geld*) ready, in cash. **für bare Münze nehmen** accept, take at face value.

Bar [baɪr] *f* (*pl* -s) bar, tavern.

Bär [bɛɪr] *m* (*pl* -en) bear.

Barbar [bar'baɪr] *m* (*pl* -en) barbarian. **Barbarei** *f* (*pl* -en) barbarism. **barbarisch** *adj* barbarian.

barfuß ['baɪrfuɪs] *adv* barefoot. **barfüßig** *adj* barefoot.

Bargeld ['baɪrgɛlt] *neut* cash.

Bariton ['bariton] *m* (*pl* -e) baritone.

Barmädchen ['baɪrmɛtçən] *neut* barmaid.

barmherzig [barm'hɛrtsiç] *adj* merciful, compassionate. **Barmherzigkeit** *f* mercifulness, mercy.

Barock [ba'rɔk] *neut or m* baroque. **barock** *adj* baroque.

Barometer [ba'romɛtər] *neut* barometer.

Baron [ba'roɪn] *m* (*pl* -e) baron. **–in** *f* (*pl* -nen) baroness.

Barre ['barə] *f* (*pl* -n) bar; (*Gold*) ingot.

Barriere [bari'ɛɪrə] *f* (*pl* -n) barrier, gate.

barsch [barʃ] *adj* rude, brusque.

Bart [baɪrt] *m* (*pl* **Bärte**) beard. **bärtig** ['bɛɪrtiç] *adj* bearded.

Base[1] ['baɪzə] f (*pl* -n) (female) cousin.

Base[2] *f* (*pl* -n) alkali, base.

Basel ['baɪzəl] *neut* Basle, Bâle.

basieren [ba'ziɪrən] *v* be based (on). **Basis** *f* (*pl* **Basen**) basis (*pl* -ses), base.

Baß [bas] *m* (*pl* **Bässe**) bass. **–geige** *f* double-bass.

Bassist [ba'sist] *m* (*pl* -en) (*Sänger*) bass (singer); (*Baßgeigenspieler*) double-bass (player).

Bastard ['bastart] *m* (*pl* -e) bastard.

basteln ['bastəln] *v* put together, rig up; (*umg.*) do-it-yourself. *er bastelt gern* he loves to tinker around. **Bastler** *m* (*pl* -) handyman, tinkerer.

Bataillon [batai'ljoɪn] *neut* (*pl* -e) battalion.

Batterie [batə'riɪ] *f* (*pl* -n) battery.

Bau [bau] **1** *m* (*unz.*) building, construction; (*Getreide, usw.*) cultivation, growing. **2** *m* (*pl* -e) (*Bergwerk*) mine; (*Tiere*) burrow. **3** *m* (*pl* -ten) building. **–arbeiter** *m* construction worker.

Bauch [baux] *m* (*pl* **Bäuche**) belly, abdomen. **bauchig** *adj* bellied, bulging, convex. **Bauchweh** *neut or* **Bauschmerzen** *pl* stomach-ache.

bauen ['bauən] build; (*Bot*) grow, cultivate.

Bauer ['bauər] *m* (*pl* -n) (small) farmer, peasant; (*Schach*) pawn.

Bäuerin ['bɔyərin] *f* (*pl* -nen) farmer's wife, peasant woman. **bäuerlich** *adj* rustic, rural.

Bauern∥haus *neut* farmhouse. **–hof** *m* farm(yard).

baufällig ['baufɛliç] *adj* dilapidated. **Bau∥genossenschaft** *f* building society. **–ingenieur** *m* structural or civil engineer. **–stelle** *f* building site.

Baum [baum] *m* (*pl* **Bäume**) tree; (*Schiff*) boom. **–garten** *m* orchard. **–wolle** *f* cotton.

Bayer ['baiər] *m* (*pl* -) Bavarian. **–n** *neut* Bavaria. **bay(e)risch** *adj* Bavarian.

beabsichtigen [bə'apziçtigən] *v* intend, propose.

beachten [bə'axtən] *v* pay attention to. **beachtungswert** *adj* noteworthy. **Beachtung** *f* attention, notice.

Beamte(r) [bə'amtə(r)] *m*, **Beamtin** *f* (*Staats-*) civil servant, official; (*Privat-*) officer, representative.

beängstigen [bə'ɛŋstigən] *v* worry, frighten.

beanspruchen [bə'anʃpruxən] *v* claim, demand; (*Person*) make demands on. **Beanspruchung** *f* claim; (*Belastung*) strain, load.

***beantragen** [bə'antraɪgən] *v* propose.

beantworten [bə'antvɔrtən] *v* answer, reply to.

bearbeiten [bə'arbaitən] *v* work on; (*Metall, Holz, Land*) work; (*Buch*) edit, revise; (*Musik*) arrange; (*Theaterstück*) adapt. **Bearbeiter** *m* editor, reviser; arranger. **Bearbeitung** *f* working; (*Verbesserung*) revision, adaptation; (*Musik*) arrangement.

beaufsichtigen [bə'aufziçtigən] *v* supervise, control. **Beaufsichtigung** *f* supervision, control.

***beauftragen** [bə'auftraɪgən] *v* commission, authorize. **Beauftragte(r)** *m* deputy, agent.

bebauen [bə'bauən] *v* (*Gelände*) build on; (*Land*) cultivate. **bebaute Fläche** *f* built-up area.

beben ['beɪbən] *v* tremble, shake.
Becher ['bɛçər] *m* (*pl* -) tumbler, glass.
–glas *neut* (laboratory) beaker.
Becken ['bɛkən] *neut* (*pl* -) basin; (*Anat*) pelvis; (*Musik*) cymbal.
bedacht [bə'daxt] *adj* thoughtful, mindful. **Bedacht** *m* consideration; (*Überlegung*) deliberation. **bedächtig** *adj* thoughtful, careful.
Bedarf [bə'darf] *m* (*unz.*) need; (*Nachfrage*) demand.
bedauerlich [bə'dauərliç] *adj* regrettable, unfortunate. **bedauern** *v* (*Sache*) regret, deplore; (*Person*) be *or* feel sorry for.
bedecken [bə'dɛkən] *v* cover. **bedeckt** *adj* (*Himmel*) overcast. **Bedeckung** *f* (*pl* -en) cover(ing).
*bedenken [bə'dɛŋkən] *v* consider, think over. **sich bedenken** deliberate, weigh the consequences (of).
bedeuten [bə'dɔytən] *v* mean, signify. **–d** *adj* important. **Bedeutung** *f* meaning; (*Wichtigkeit*) significance, importance. **bedeutungs‖los** *adj* meaningless. **–voll** *adj* significant.
bedienen [bə'diːnən] *v* serve, wait on; (*Maschine*) operate, work. **Bedienung** *f* service; (*Maschine*) operation; (*Diener*) staff, servants *pl*.
bedingt [bə'dɪŋkt] *adj* conditional, limited. **Bedingung** *f* (*pl* -en) condition.
Bedrängnis [bə'drɛŋnis] *f* (*pl* -se) distress, trouble.
bedrohen [bə'droɪən] *v* threaten. **Bedrohung** *f* (*pl* -en) threat.
*bedürfen [bə'dryfən] *v* need, require. **Bedürfnis** *neut* (*pl* -se) need, requirement. **Bedürfnisanstalt** *f* public toilet.
beeilen [bə'ailən] *v* **sich beeilen** hurry.
beeindrucken [bə'aindrukən] *v* impress.
beeinflussen [bə'ainflusən] *v* influence, have an influence *or* effect on.
beeinträchtigen [bə'aintrɛçtigən] *v* reduce, inhibit, be detrimental to.
beendigen [bə'ɛndigən] *v* end, finish. **Beendigung** *f* end, termination.
Beerdigung [bə'eɪrdiguŋ] *f* burial, funeral.
Beere ['beɪrə] *f* (*pl* -n) berry.
Beet [beɪt] *neut* (*pl* -e) bed; (*Blumen-*) flowerbed; (*Gemüse*) vegetable patch.
befähigen [bə'fɛɪigən] *v* enable, make fit. **befähigt** *adj* able, qualified. **Befähigung** *f* (*pl* -en) capacity, fitness.

befahrbar [bə'faɪrbaɪr] *adj* passable, usable. **befahren** *v* travel *or* drive on.
*befallen [bə'falən] *v* befall; (*Krankheit*) attack, strike.
befangen [bə'faŋən] *adj* shy, self-conscious; (*parteiisch*) biased.
befassen [bə'fasən] *v* **sich befassen mit** engage in, occupy oneself with.
*befehlen [bə'feɪlən] *v* command, order. **Befehl** *m* (*pl* -e) command, order. **Befehlshaber** *m* (*pl* -) commander, commanding officer.
befestigen [bə'fɛstigən] *v* fasten; (*stärken*) strengthen; (*Mil*) fortify. **Befestigung** *f* (*pl* -en) fastening; strengthening; (*Mil*) fortification.
*befinden [bə'findən] *v* find. **sich befinden** be, be situated; (*Person*) be, find oneself. **sich wohl befinden** feel well. **befindlich** *adj* present, to be found.
beflecken [bə'flɛkən] *v* stain, soil.
befolgen [bə'fɔlgən] *v* obey, follow.
befördern [bə'fœdərn] *v* convey, dispatch; (*Rang*) promote. **Beförderung** *f* (*pl* -en) transport, conveyance; promotion.
befragen [bə'fraɪgən] *v* question. **sich befragen** enquire, inquire.
befreien [bə'fraiən] *v* liberate, free. **Befreier** *m* (*pl* -) liberator. **Befreiung** *f* (*pl* -en) liberation; (*Entlastung*) exemption.
befreunden [bə'frɔyndən] *v* **sich befreunden mit** make friends with. **befreundet** *adj* friendly (with); intimate. **eng befreundet sein mit** be a close friend of.
befriedigen [bə'friːdigən] *v* satisfy. **–d** *adj* satisfactory. **Befriedigung** *f* (*pl* -en) satisfaction.
befruchten [bə'fruxtən] *v* fertilize; (*anregen*) stimulate. **Befruchtung** *f* (*pl* -en) fertilization.
befugen [bə'fuɪgən] *v* authorize, empower. **Befugnis** *f* (*pl* -se) authority, right.
befürchten [bə'fyrçtən] *v* fear; (*vermuten*) suspect. **Befürchtung** *f* (*pl* -en) fear, apprehension.
befürworten [bə'fyrvortən] *v* recommend, advocate.
begabt [bə'gaɪpt] *adj* talented, gifted. **Begabung** *f* talent, gift.
begatten [bə'gatən] *v* **sich begatten** mate, copulate. **Begattung** *f* (*pl* -en) mating, copulation.
*begeben [bə'geɪbən] *v* **sich begeben** go, proceed; (*verzichten*) renounce, give up.

beide

begegnen [bə'geɪgnən] v meet, encounter.
Begegnung f (pl -en) meeting, encounter.
*begehen [bə'geɪən] (Unrecht) commit, do; (gehen auf) walk on.
begehren [bə'geɪrən] v desire, covet.
begeistern [bə'gaistərn] v inspire, fill with enthusiasm. begeistert adj inspired, enthusiastic. Begeisterung f enthusiasm.
Begier [bə'giːr], f (unz.), also Begierde f (pl -n) desire, craving. begierig adj desirous, covetous.
begießen [bə'giːsən] v water, sprinkle; (Braten) baste.
Beginn [bə'gin] m (unz.) beginning. beginnen v begin.
beglaubigen [bə'glaubigən] v certify, attest. Beglaubigung f (pl -en) certification.
begleiten [bə'glaitən] v accompany. Begleit‖er m (pl -) attendant; (Musik) accompanist. –schreiben neut covering letter. –ung f (pl -en) attendants pl, escort; (Musik) accompaniment.
beglücken [bə'glykən] v make happy. beglückwünschen v congratulate. Beglückwünschung f (pl -en) congratulations pl.
begnadigen [bə'gnaɪdigən] v pardon.
begnügen [bə'gnyːgən] v sich begnügen mit content oneself with, be satisfied with.
*begraben [bə'graːbən] v bury. Begräbnis neut (pl -se) burial, funeral.
*begreifen [bə'graifən] v understand, grasp, apprehend. begreiflich adj comprehensible.
begrenzt [bə'grɛntst] adj restricted, limited.
Begriff [bə'grif] m (pl -e) concept, idea. Begriffsvermögen neut comprehension.
begründen [bə'gryndən] v found, establish, (Behauptung) substantiate. Begründer m founder.
begrüßen [bə'gryːsən] v greet, welcome.
begünstigen [bə'gynstigən] v (vorziehen) favour; (fördern) promote, further.
begütert [bə'gyːtərt] adj wealthy, well-to-do.
begütigen [bə'gyːtigən] v placate, appease.
behäbig [bə'hɛːbiç] adj (beleibt) portly, corpulent; (bequem, langsam) comfortable.
behagen [bə'haɪgən] v please, suit. Behagen neut (pl -) ease, comfort. behaglich adj comfortable, at ease.

*behalten [bə'haltən] v keep, retain; (im Gedächtnis) remember. Behälter m (pl -) container; (Flüssigkeiten) tank.
behandeln [bə'handəln] v treat, handle. Behandlung f treatment, handling; (Med) treatment, therapy.
beharren [bə'harən] v persist. beharrlich adj persistent, pertinacious.
behaupten [bə'hauptən] v maintain, asset, state. Behauptung f (pl -eu) statement, assertion.
behend(e) [bə'hɛnt, bə'hɛndə] adj, also behendig nimble, agile. Behendigkeit f agility.
beherbergen [bə'hɛrbɛrgən] v rule, govern.
beherrschen [bə'hɛrʃən] v (Zorn, usw.) control; (meistern, können) master. sich beherrschen control oneself. Beherrschung f rule, control; mastery.
beherzigen [bə'hɛrtsigən] v take to heart.
behilflich [bə'hilfliç] adj helpful.
behindern [bə'hindərn] v hinder, obstruct. Behinderung f (pl -en) hindrance.
Behörde [bə'hoeirdə] f (pl -n) authority, authorities pl.
behüten [bə'hyːtən] v guard, protect. Behüter m (pl -) protector, guard.
bei [bai] prep at; (neben) near. bei mir at (my) home; (in der Tasche) on me. bei Herrn Schmidt at Herr Schmidt's (house). bei der Post arbeiten work for the Post Office. bei der Hand nehmen take by the hand. beim Aussteigen while or when getting out. bei Nacht at night. bei Tag during the day. bei der Arbeit at work. bei weitem by far. bei Shakespeare in Shakespeare.
*beibehalten ['baibəhaltən] v retain; keep.
*beibringen ['baibriŋən] v bring forward; (Verlust, Wunde) inflict; (lehren) teach.
Beichte ['baiçtə] f (pl -n) (Rel) confession. beichten v confess. Beichtvater m confessor.
beide ['baidə] adj, pron both. alle beide both. einer von beiden either of two. in beiden Fällen in either case. wir beide both of us. zu beiden Seiten on both sides. beider‖lei adj of both sorts. –seitig adj mutual, reciprocal. –seits adv mutually. beidhändig adj ambidextrous.

Beifahrer ['baifaɪrər] *m* (*pl* -) passenger.
Beifall ['baifal] *m* (*unz.*) applause; (*Billigung*) approval. **Beifall klatschen** applaud.
beifügen ['baifyɪgən] *v* enclose, attach.
***beigeben** ['baigeɪbən] *v* add. **klein beigeben** draw in one's horns, yield.
Beigeschmack ['baigəʃmak] *m* (after)taste; (*fig*) tinge.
Beihilfe ['baihilfə] *f* financial aid, subsidy; (*Jur*) aiding and abetting.
***beikommen** ['baikɔmən] *v* get at, get near, reach.
Beil [bail] *neut* (*pl* -e) (*Holz*) hatchet; (*Fleisch*) cleaver.
Beilage ['bailaɪgə] *f* enclosure, insert; (*Zeitung*) supplement.
beiläufig ['bailɔyfiç] *adj* incidental. *adv* incidentally, by the way.
beilegen ['baileɪgən] *v* add; (*zuschreiben*) attribute, ascribe; (*schlichten*) settle.
Beileid ['bailait] *neut* (*unz.*) condolence.
beiliegend ['bailiːgənt] *adj* enclosed.
beim [baim] *prep* + *art* **bei dem**.
***beimessen** ['baimɛsən] *v* attribute, credit with.
Bein [bain] *neut* (*pl* -e) leg; (*Knochen*) bone.
beinah(e) ['bainaɪ(ə)] *adv* almost, nearly.
Beiname ['bainaɪmə] *m* nickname. **mit dem Beinamen . . .** known as . . . , called . . . .
beirren [bə'irən] *v* **sicht nicht beirren lassen** stick to one's opinions, not be misled.
beisammen [bai'zamən] *adv* together.
Beischlaf ['baiʃlaɪf] *m* (sexual) intercourse.
beiseite [bai'zaitə] *adv* to one side, aside. **–legen** *v* put aside *or* by.
Beispiel ['baiʃpiːl] *neut* (*pl* -e) example. **zum Beispiel** for example *or* instance. **beispielsweise** *adv* for instance, as an example.
***beißen** ['baisən] *v* bite. **beißend** *adj* biting; (*Säure*) caustic. **Beiß‖zahn** *m* incisor. **–zange** *f* pincers.
Beistand ['baiʃtant] *m* help, assistance.
***beistehen** ['baiʃteɪən] *v* help, assist.
beistimmen ['baiʃtimən] *v* agree, consent. **Bestimmung** *f* agreement, consent.
Beitrag ['baitraɪk] *m* (*pl* **Beiträge**) contribution; (*Klub*) subscription. **beitragen** *v* contribute. **Beiträger** *m* (*pl* -) contributor.

***beitreten** ['baitreɪtən] *v* join; (*Meinung*) agree to, accept.
Beiwagen ['baivaɪgən] *m* sidecar.
beiwohnen ['baivoɪnən] *v* be present at, attend; (*beischlafen*) have sex with.
beizeiten [bai'tsaitən] *adv* early.
beizen ['baitsən] *v* (*Holz*) stain; (*Metall*) etch; (*Fleisch*) salt, pickle.
bejahen [bə'jaɪən] *v* affirm, agree to.
bejahrt [bə'jaɪrt] *adj* aged.
bekämpfen [bə'kɛmpfən] *v* fight (against), combat.
bekannt [bə'kant] *adj* known. **bekannt werden mit** become acquainted with. **sich bekanntmachen mit** acquaint oneself with. **Bekannt‖e(r)** acquaintance. **–gabe** *f* announcement, notification. **bekannt‖geben** *v* make known, disclose. **–lich** *adv* as is well known. **Bekanntschaft** *f* acquaintance.
bekehren [bə'keɪrən] *v* convert. **Bekehr‖te(r)** convert. **–ung** *f* conversion.
***bekennen** [bə'kɛnən] *v* acknowledge, confess. **Bekenntnis** *neut* (*pl* -se) confession; (*Glaube*) faith, creed.
beklagen [bə'klaɪgən] *v* lament, deplore. **–swert** *adj* lamentable. **Baklagte(r)** *m* accused, defendant.
bekleiden [bə'klaidən] *v* clothe; (*beziehen*) coat; (*Amt*) occupy. **Bekleidung** *f* clothing; (*Material*) coating.
***beklemmen** [bə'klɛmən] *v* oppress, frighten; (*ersticken*) stifle. **Angst beklemmt mich** I am seized by fear.
***bekommen** [bə'kɔmən] *v* obtain, get, receive; (*Zug*) catch; (*Krankheit*) catch, get. **bekömmlich** *adj* wholesome, beneficial.
bekräftigen [bə'krɛftigən] *v* confirm, strengthen.
bekreuzigen [bə'krɔytsigən] *v* **sich bekreuzigen** cross oneself.
bekümmern [bə'kymərn] *v* trouble, distress. **bekümmert sein** be anxious *or* troubled.
bekunden [bə'kundən] *v* state; (*zeigen*) show, manifest.
***beladen** [bə'laidən] *v* load.
Belag [bə'laik] *m* (*pl* **Beläge**) covering, coating; (*Aufstrich*) spread. **Butterbrot mit Belag** sandwich.
belagern [bə'laigərn] *v* besiege. **Belagerung** *f* siege.

belangen [bə'laŋən] v concern; (Jur) prosecute. **belanglos** adj unimportant.

belasten [bə'lastən] v burden; (Konto) debit, charge; (Jur) accuse.

belästigen [bə'lɛstigən] v pester, bother; (umg.) bug. **Belästigung** f bother, annoyance.

Belastung [bə'lastuŋ] f (pl -en) load; (Konto) debit, charge.

*****belaufen** [bə'laufən] v **sich belaufen auf** amount to, total.

belauschen [bə'lauʃən] v eavesdrop on, listen to (secretly).

beleben ·[bə'leɪbən] v animate; (Med) revive. **belebt** adj animated, lively; (Ort) crowded, bustling. **Beleb‖theit** f liveliness. **–ung** f animation; revival.

Beleg [bə'leɪk] m (pl -e) proof, evidence; (Urkunde) voucher. **belegen** v cover; (Platz) reserve; (Kursus) enrol for; (Brot) spread. **belegtes Brötchen** filled roll, sandwich. **Belegschaft** f personnel, staff.

belehren [bə'leɪrən] v instruct, teach.

beleibt [bə'laipt] adj portly, stout.

beleidigen [bə'laidigən] v insult. **beleidigend** adj insulting, offensive. **Beleidigung** f (pl -en) insult.

beleuchten [bə'lɔyçtən] v illuminate, light (up). **Beleuchtung** f lighting, illumination.

Belgien ['bɛlgiən] neut Belgium. **Belgier** m (pl -), **Belgierin** f (pl -nen) Belgian. **belgisch** adj Belgian.

belichten [bə'liçtən] v (Foto) expose. **Belichtung** f (pl -en) exposure. **Belichtungsmesser** m light meter.

belieben [bə'liːbən] v (gefallen) please; (wünschen) like, wish. **Belieben** neut pleasure, will. **nach Belieben** at will, as you like. **beliebig** adj any (you like), whatever. **beliebt** adj loved, popular.

bellen ['bɛlən] v bark.

belohnen [bə'loːnən] v reward, recompense. **Belohnung** f reward, recompense.

belüften [bə'lyftən] v ventilate. **Belüftung** f ventilation.

belustigen [bə'lustigən] v amuse. **Belustigung** f amusement.

bemächtigen [bə'mɛçtigən] v **sich bemächtigen** seize, take possession of.

bemerkbar [bə'mɛrkbaɪr] adj noticeable, observable. **bemerken** v notice; (sagen) remark. **–swert** adj remarkable, noteworthy. **Bemerkung** f (pl -en) remark.

*****bemessen** [bə'mɛsən] v measure. adj restricted.

bemitleiden [bə'mitlaidən] v pity, feel sorry for.

bemühen [bə'myːən] v trouble (oneself), take pains. **Bemühen** neut or **Bemühung** f (pl -en) effort, exertion.

benachbart [bə'naxbaɪrt] adj neighbouring.

benachrichtigen [bə'naxriçtigən] v inform. **Benachrichtigung** f report.

benannt [bə'nant] adj named.

*****benehmen** [bə'neːmən] v **sich benehmen** behave. **Benehmen** neut behaviour.

beneiden [bə'naidən] v envy.

*****benennen** [bə'nɛnən] v name, call. **Benennung** f (pl -en) name, title.

Bengel ['bɛŋəl] m (pl -) brat, little rascal.

benommen [bə'nɔmən] adj confused.

benötigen [bə'nœːtigən] v need, require.

benutzen [bə'nutsən] v use, make use of. **Benutzung** f use, employment.

Benzin [bɛn'tsiːn] neut petrol, (US) gasoline. **–uhr** f petrol or fuel gauge. **–verbrauch** m fuel consumption.

beobachten [bə'oːbaxtən] v observe, watch; (bemerken) notice. **Beobach‖ter** m (pl -) observer, onlooker. **–tung** f (pl -en) observation.

bepflanzen [bə'pflantsən] v plant.

bequem [bə'kveːm] adj comfortable; (mühelos) convenient. **bequemlich** adj lazy, comfort-loving.

*****beraten** [bə'raːtən] v advise. **sich beraten** confer. **beratend** adj advisory. **Berater** m adviser, counsellor. **Beratung** f consultation.

berauben [bə'raubən] v rob or deprive of.

berauschen [bə'rauʃən] v intoxicate.

berechenbar [bə'rɛçənbaɪr] adj calculable. **berechnen** v calculate, evaluate. **berechnend** adj (Person) selfish, calculating. **Berechnung** f calculation, evaluation.

berechtigen [bə'rɛçtigən] v entitle, authorize. **berechtigt** adj entitled. **Berechtigung** f authorization, entitlement.

bereden [bə'reːdən] v persuade. **beredsam** adj eloquent.

Bereich [bə'raiç] m (pl -e) region, domain; (fig) field, sphere, realm.

bereichern [bə'raiçərn] v enrich. **sich bereichern** acquire wealth, get rich.

bereit [bə'rait] adj ready, prepared. **bereiten** v prepare, make ready. **bereit‖halten** v keep in readiness. **–machen**

v make ready. **Bereitschaft** *f* readiness. **bereit‖stehen** *v* be ready. –**stellen** *v* make ready, prepare. **Bereitung** *f* (*pl* -en) preparation. **bereitwillig** *adj* ready.
bereuen [bə'rɔyən] *v* regret, repent.
Berg [bɛrk] *m* (*pl* -e) mountain. **bergab** *adv* downhill. **Bergarbeiter** *m* miner. **bergauf** *adv* uphill. **Bergbau** *m* mining.
***bergen** ['bɛrgən] *v* conceal; (*schützen*) protect; (*Güter*) recover.
Bergführer ['bɛrkfyrər] *m* mountain guide.
bergig ['bɛrgiç] *adj* mountainous, hilly. **Berg‖leute** *pl* miners. –**mann** *m* miner. **bergmännisch** *adj* mining. **Berg‖rutsch** *m* landslide. –**steigen** *neut* mountain climbing. –**steiger** *m* (mountain) climber, mountaineer.
Bergung ['bɛrguŋ] *f* (*pl* -en) rescue; (*Schiff*) salvage. –**sarbeiten** *f pl* salvage or rescue operations.
Bergwerk ['bɛrkvɛrk] *neut* mine, pit.
Bericht [bə'riçt] *m* (*pl* -e) report, account. **berichten** *v* report, give an account. **Berichterstatter** *m* (*pl* -) reporter; (*Radio*) commentator, correspondent.
berichtigen [bə'riçtigən] *v* correct, amend; (*Schulden*) pay. **Berichtigung** *f* correction; (*Schulden*) settlement.
beritten [bə'ritən] *adj* mounted.
Bernstein ['bɛrnʃtain] *m* amber.
berüchtigt [bə'ryçtiçt] *adj* notorious, infamous.
berücksichtigen [bə'rykziçtigən] *v* keep in mind, consider, take account of. **Berücksichtigung** *f* consideration.
Beruf [bə'ruːf] *m* (*pl* -e) occupation, job, profession; (*Gewerbe*) trade. **beruf‖en** *v* appoint; (*kommen lassen*) summon, send for. –**lich** *adj* professional, vocational. **Berufs‖ausbildung** *f* vocational training. –**krankheit** *f* occupational disease. –**schule** *f* vocational school, technical college. **berufstätig** *adj* employed. **Berufstätigkeit** *f* employment, professional activity. **Berufung** *f* (*pl* -en) appointment; (*Jur*) appeal.
beruhen [bə'ruːən] *v* rest (on), be founded (on).
beruhigen [bə'ruːigən] *v* pacify, calm. **beruhigend** *adj* calming. **Beruhigung** *f* calming, pacification. **Beruhigungsmittel** *neut* sedative.
berühmt [bə'ryːmt] *adj* famous, celebrat-

ed. **Berühmtheit** *f* fame; (*Person*) celebrity.
berühren [bə'ryːrən] *v* touch, handle; (*angrenzen*) border; (*angehen*) concern; (*erwähnen*) touch on.
besäen [bə'zɛːən] *v* sow.
besänftigen [bə'zɛnftigən] *v* soothe, calm (down).
Besatzung [bə'zatsuŋ] *f* (*Mil*) garrison; (*Schiff, Flugzeug*) crew; (*Pol*) occupation. –**szone** *f* occupied area (of a country).
beschädigen [bə'ʃɛːdigən] *v* damage. **Beschädigung** *f* damage.
beschaffen [bə'ʃafən] *v* get, procure. *adj* constituted.
beschäftigen [bə'ʃɛftigən] *v* employ; (*zu tun geben*) occupy, keep busy. **beschäftigt** *adj* employed; occupied, busy. **Beschäftigung** *f* (*pl* -en) employment, occupation.
beschämen [bə'ʃɛːmən] *v* shame.
beschatten [bə'ʃatən] *v* shade; (*verfolgen*) shadow.
beschauen [bə'ʃauən] *v* look at; (*prüfen*) examine, look over. **Beschauer** *m* (*pl* -) spectator, inspector. **beschaulich** *adj* contemplative.
Bescheid [bə'ʃait] *m* (*pl* -e) information; (*Entscheidung*) decision, ruling. **Bescheid geben/sagen** give information, inform. **Bescheid wissen** know the situation, be well informed.
bescheinigen [bə'ʃainigən] *v* certify, attest. **Bescheinigung** *f* (*pl* -en) certificate; (*Quittung*) receipt.
beschenken [bə'ʃɛnkən] *v* give a present to, present (with).
bescheren [bə'ʃeːrən] *v* give presents. **Bescherung** *f* giving (of presents). **eine schöne Bescherung** a fine mess.
***beschießen** [bə'ʃiːsən] *v* fire on, shell. **Beschießung** *f* shelling, bombardment.
beschimpfen [bə'ʃimpfən] *v* insult.
Beschlag [bə'ʃlaik] *m* (*pl* **Beschläge**) clasp, catch; (*Jur*) seizure. **in Beschlag nehmen** seize, confiscate. **beschlagen** *v* cover, fit; (*Pferd*) shoe. **Beschlagnahme** *f* (*pl* -n) confiscation, seizure. **beschlagnahmen** *v* seize, confiscate.
beschleunigen [bə'ʃlɔynigən] *v* accelerate. **Beschleunigung** *f* acceleration.
***beschließen** [bə'ʃliːsən] *v* decide, resolve; (*beendigen*) terminate, end.

bestehen

Beschluß [bə'ʃlus] *m (pl* **Beschlüsse)** decision, resolution; (*Ende*) end, close.
beschmutzen [bə'ʃmutsən] *v* dirty, soil.
***beschneiden** [bə'ʃnaidən] *v* cut, prune, clip; (*Kind*) circumcize. **Beschneidung** *f* circumcision.
beschränken [bə'ʃrɛnkən] *v* restrict, limit. **beschränkt** *adj* limited, confined. **Beschränkung** *f* limitation.
***beschreiben** [bə'ʃraibən] *v* describe. **Beschreibung** *f* description.
beschuldigen [bə'ʃuldigən] *v* accuse. **Beschuldigte(r)** *m* accused, defendant. **Beschuldigung** *f* accusation.
beschützen [bə'ʃytsən] *v* protect.
Beschwerde [bə'ʃveirdə] *f (pl* **-n)** complaint. **beschweren** *v* burden. **sich beschweren über** complain about.
beschwerlich *adj* troublesome; (*mühselig*) tedious.
beschwichtigen [bə'ʃviçtigən] *v* appease, pacify. **Beschwichtigung** *f* allaying, appeasement.
beschwipst [bə'ʃvipst] *adj* (*umg.*) tipsy.
***beschwören** [bə'ʃvœ:rən] *v* swear (on oath); (*Person*) implore, beg; (*Erinnerungen, Geister*) conjure up.
***besehen** [bə'zeiən] *v* look at, inspect.
beseitigen [bə'zaitigən] *v* remove, get rid of, eliminate; (*Schwierigkeiten*) overcome. **Beseitigung** *f* removal, elimination.
Besen ['beizən] *m (pl* **-)** broom.
besessen [bə'zɛsən] *adj* possessed.
besetzen [bə'zɛtsən] *v* (*Platz*) occupy, take; (*Mil*) occupy; (*Kleid*) trim, decorate; (*Posten*) fill. **besetzt** *adj* (*Theater*) full; (*Platz*) taken; (*WC*) occupied, engaged; (*Telef*) engaged. **Besetzung** *f* occupation; (*Theater*) casting.
besichtigen [bə'ziçtigən] *v* inspect, view. **Besichtigung** *f* inspection; (*Sehenswürdigkeiten*) sightseeing.
besiedeln [bə'ziidəln] *v* colonize.
besiegen [bə'ziigən] *v* conquer.
***besinnen** [bə'zinən] *v* **sich besinnen** remember, recollect. **Besinnen** *neut* reflection, consideration. **Besinnung** *f* contemplation; (*Bewußtsein*) consciousness. **besinnunglos** *adj* unconscious, senseless.
Besitz [bə'zits] *m (pl* **-e)** possession. **besitzen** *v* possess, own. **Besitzer** *m (pl* **-)** owner.
besoffen [bə'zɔfən] *adj* (*vulgär*) drunk.

Besoldung [bə'zɔlduŋ] *f (pl* **-en)** salary, wages *pl.*
besonder [bə'zɔndər] *adj* special, particular. **besonders** *adv* especially, particularly. **nichts Besonderes** nothing special, not up to much.
besonnen [bə'zɔnən] *adj* sensible, prudent. **Besonnenheit** *f* prudence.
besorgen [bə'zɔrgən] *v* take care of, see to; (*beschaffen*) obtain. **Besorgnis** *f (pl* **-se)** apprehension, anxiety. **besorgniserregend** *adj* giving cause for worry. **besorgt** *adj* anxious, worried. **Besorgung** *f (pl* **-en)** management; (*Einkauf*) purchase.
bespannen [bə'ʃpanən] *v* (*verkleiden*) cover; (*Fahrzeug*) harness; (*Musik*) string. **Bespannung** *f (pl* **-en)** covering; (*Pferde*) team (of horses).
***besprechen** [bə'ʃprɛçən] *v* discuss; (*Buch, Film*) review. **Besprechung** *f* discussion; (*Buch, Film*) review.
besser ['bɛsər] *adj* better. **desto besser** so much the better. **um so besser** all the better. **er ist besser dran** he is better off. **bessern** *v* improve, make better. **Besserung** *f (pl* **-en)** improvement.
best [bɛst] *adj* best. **am besten** *adv* best. **aufs Beste** in the best possible way. **besten Dank!** many thanks!
Bestand [bə'ʃtant] *m (pl* **Bestände)** continuance, duration; (*Vorrat*) stock, supply.
beständig [bə'ʃtɛndiç] *adj* constant, lasting.
Bestandteil [bə'ʃtanttail] *m* component, part.
bestärken [bə'ʃtɛrkən] *v* strengthen; (*bestätigen*) confirm. **Bestärkung** *f* strengthening; confirmation.
bestätigen [bə'ʃtɛitigən] *v* confirm, verify. **bestätigend** *adj* confirmatory. **Bestätigung** *f (pl* **-en)** confirmation.
bestatten [bə'ʃtatən] *v* bury. **Bestattung** *f (pl* **-en)** funeral, burial.
***bestechen** [bə'ʃtɛçən] *v* bribe, corrupt. **bestechlich** *adj* corrupt, bribable. **Bestechung** *f* bribery, corruption.
Besteck [bə'ʃtɛk] *neut (pl* **-e)** cutlery; knife, fork, and spoon; (*Med*) (medical) instruments *pl.*
***bestehen** [bə'ʃteiən] *v* exist, be; (*überstehen*) undergo; (*Examen*) pass; (*fortdauern*) endure, survive. **bestehen auf** insist on. **bestehen aus** consist of.

*besteigen [bə'ʃtaigən] v climb, ascend; (*Pferd*) mount. **Besteigung** f ascent; mounting.
bestellen [bə'ʃtɛlən] v (*Waren*) order; (*Zimmer*) reserve; (*Boden*) cultivate. **Bestellung** f order; reservation; cultivation.
bestenfalls ['bɛstənfals] adv at best.
bestens adv in the best manner.
besteuern [bə'ʃtɔyərn] v tax. **Besteuerung** f taxation.
Bestie ['bɛstiə] f (pl -n) beast.
bestimmen [bə'ʃtimən] v determine, fix; (*ernennen*) appoint. **bestimmt** adj definite, certain. **Bestimmung** f determination; (*Vorschrift*) regulation; (*Ernennung*) appointment.
bestrafen [bə'ʃtraifən] v punish. **Bestrafung** f punishment.
Bestrahlung [bə'ʃtrailuŋ] f radiation; (*Med*) radiotherapy.
bestreben [bə'ʃtreibən] v **sich bestreben** strive, endeavour. **Bestreben** neut or **Bestrebung** f endeavour, exertion.
*bestreiten [bə'ʃtraitən] v dispute, contest.
bestürmen [bə'ʃtyrmən] v assault, storm.
bestürzen [bə'ʃtyrtsən] v startle, disconcert. **bestürzt** adj taken aback, dismayed.
Besuch [bə'zuːx] m (pl -e) visit, call. **Besuch haben** have visitors. **ich bin zu Besuch hier** I am visiting, I am a visitor. **besuchen** v visit, see; (*Schule*) go to, attend. **Besucher** m (pl -) visitor, caller; (*Gast*) guest.
betagt [bə'taikt] adj aged, elderly.
betasten [bə'tastən] v finger, touch.
betätigen [bə'tɛitigən] v put into action; (*Maschine*) operate; (*Bremse*) apply. **sich betätigen** occupy oneself, work; (*activ sein*) be active, participate. **Betätigung** f operation; (*Teilnahme*) participation.
betäuben [bə'tɔybən] v stun; (*narkotisieren*) anaesthetize. **Betäubung** f anaesthesia. **Betäubungsmittel** neut anaesthetic.
Bete ['beitə] f beet, beetroot.
beteiligen [bə'tailigən] v give a share to. **sich beteiligen** participate in. **beteiligt sein an** be involved in. **Beteiligung** f (pl -en) participation; (*Anteil*) share.
beten ['beitən] v pray.
beteuern [bə'tɔyərn] v affirm, declare; (*Unschuld*) protest. **Beteuerung** f (pl -en) affirmation, declaration.

Beton [be'tõ] m concrete.
betonen [bə'tonən] v stress, emphasize. **Betonung** f stress, emphasis.
Betracht [bə'traxt] m (*unz.*) consideration. **außer Betracht lassen** leave aside, not consider. **in Betracht ziehen** take into consideration. **betrachten** v look at; (*ansehen als*) consider. **beträchtlich** adj considerable. **Betrachtung** f consideration.
Betrag [bə'traik] m (pl **Beträge**) amount. **betragen** v amount to. **sich betragen** behave. **Betragen** neut behaviour.
betrauen [bə'trauən] v entrust.
Betreff [bə'trɛf] m (*unz.*) in Betreff with regard to, concerning. **betreff||en** v concern; (*befallen*) befall; (*erwischen*) surprise. **–end** adj in question. prep concerning. **–s** prep concerning.
*betreiben [bə'traibən] v carry on, follow; (*Studien*) pursue; (*Maschine*) operate.
*betreten [bə'treitən] v tread on; (*eintreten*) enter. adj surprised, disconcerted.
Betrieb [bə'triːp] m (pl -e) firm, concern, business; (*Wirken*) running; (*Verkehr*) bustle, activity. **außer Betrieb** out of order. **in Betrieb** in operation, working, in use. **in Betrieb setzen** put into operation. **Betriebs||anlage** f industrial plant, works. **–anweisung** f operating instructions pl. **–führer** m works manager. **–kosten** pl operating costs. **–rat** m works council. **–unfall** m industrial accident.
*betrinken [bə'triŋkən] v **sich betrinken** get drunk.
betroffen [bə'trɔfən] adj perplexed, disconcerted.
betrüben [bə'tryːbən] v grieve, depress. **betrübt** adj sad.
Betrug [bə'truːk] m (*unz.*) fraud, swindle, deception. **betrügen** v cheat, deceive. **Betrüger** m (pl -) cheat, swindler. **betrügerisch** adj deceitful.
betrunken [bə'truŋkən] adj drunk. **Betrunkenheit** f drunkenness.
Bett [bɛt] neut (pl -en) bed. **ins Bett gehen** go to bed. **–decke** f bedspread.
betteln ['bɛtəln] v beg.
bettlägerig ['bɛtlɛigəriç] adj bedridden.
Bettler ['bɛtlər] m (pl -) beggar.
Bett||wäsche f bed linen. **–zeug** neut bedding.

beugen ['bɔygən] *v* bend; (*Gramm*) inflect. **sich beugen** bow; (*sich fügen*) submit. **Beugung** *f* bow, bend(ing).

Beule ['bɔylə] *f* (*pl* -n) swelling, lump; (*Metall*) dent.

beunruhigen [bə'unruːigən] *v* disturb, make anxious. **beunruhigt sein** be anxious *or* alarmed. **Beunruhigung** *f* agitation, uneasiness.

beurkunden [bə'uːrkundən] *v* certify, attest. **Beurkundung** *f* certification.

beurlauben [bə'uːrilaubən] *v* grant leave to, send on holiday.

beurteilen [bə'uːrtailən] *v* judge. **Beurteilung** *f* judgment.

Beute ['bɔytə] *f* (*unz.*) booty, loot.

Beutel ['bɔytəl] *m* (*pl* -) bag; (*Geld*) purse; (*Zool*) pouch. **beuteln** *v* be baggy, bulge. **Beuteltier** *neut* marsupial.

bevölkern [bə'fœlkərn] *v* populate. **dicht/spärlich bevölkert** densely/sparsely populated. **Bevölkerung** *f* population.

bevollmächtigen [bə'fɔlmɛçtigən] *v* authorize. **bevollmächtigt** *adj* authorized. **Bevollmächtigte(r)** *m* authorized agent *or* representative; (*Jur*) attorney.

bevor [bə'foːr] *conj* before.

***bevorstehen** [bə'foːrʃteiən] *v* be imminent, be at hand.

bevorzugen [bə'foːrtsuːgən] *v* favour, prefer.

bewachen [bə'vaxən] *v* guard.

bewaffnen [bə'vafnən] *v* arm. **bewaffnet** *adj* armed. **Bewaffnung** *f* armament.

bewahren [bə'vaːrən] *v* keep, preserve.

bewähren [bə'vɛːrən] *v* **sich bewähren** prove true. **bewährt** *adj* tried, proved.

Bewahrung [bə'vaːruŋ] *f* (*pl* -en) preservation.

Bewährung [bə'vɛːruŋ] *f* trial, test; (*Jur*) probation. **–sfrist** *f* probation (period).

bewaltigen [bə'vɛltigən] *v* overpower; (*Schwierigkeit*) master, overcome.

bewässern [bə'vɛsərn] *v* irrigate. **Bewässerung** *f* irrigation.

***bewegen** [bə'veːgən] *v* move; (*rühren*) move, touch; (*überreden*) persuade. **sich bewegen** move. **Beweggrund** *m* motive. **beweglich** *adj* movable, mobile. **bewegt** *adj* excited; (*gerührt*) touched, moved. **Bewegung** *f* (*pl* -en) motion, movement; (*Rührung*) emotion. **in Bewegung setzen** set in motion.

Beweis [bə'vais] *m* (*pl* -e) proof, evidence. **beweisen** *v* prove, demonstrate.

Beweis‖führung *f* reasoning, demonstration. **–stück** *neut* (piece of) evidence, exhibit.

bewerben [bə'vɛrbən] *v* **sich bewerben um** apply for. **Bewerber** *m* applicant, candidate. **Bewerbung** *f* application, candidacy.

bewerkstelligen [bə'vɛrkʃtɛligən] *v* accomplish, achieve.

bewerten [bə'veːrtən] *v* value, rate.

bewilligen [bə'viligən] *v* allow, grant. **Bewilligung** *f* (*pl* -en) grant, permission.

bewirken [bə'virkən] *v* bring about, cause.

bewirten [bə'virtən] *v* entertain. **bewirtschaften** *v* manage, administer. **Bewirtung** *f* hospitality.

bewohnbar [bə'voːnbaːr] *adj* inhabitable. **bewohnen** *v* live in, inhabit. **Bewohner** *m* (*pl* -) inhabitant, resident.

bewölken [bə'vœlkən] *v* **sich bewölken** (*Himmel*) become cloudy. **bewölkt** *adj* overcast, cloudy.

Bewunderer [bə'vundərər] *m* (*pl* -) admirer. **bewundern** *v* admire. **bewundernswert** *adj* admirable. **Bewunderung** *f* admiration.

bewußt [bə'vust] *adj* conscious, deliberate; (*klar*) aware, conscious. **ich bin mir meines Fehlers bewußt** I am aware of my mistake. **Bewußtheit** *f* awareness. **bewußtlos** *adj* unconscious. **Bewußt‖losigkeit** *f* unconsciousness. **–sein** *neut* consciousness. **zu Bewußtsein kommen** regain consciousness.

bezahlen [bə'tsailən] *v* pay for; (*Rechnung*) pay. **Bezahlung** *f* payment, settlement.

bezaubern [bə'tsaubərn] *v* enchant, charm, bewitch. **Bezauberung** *f* spell.

bezeichnen [bə'tsaiçnən] *v* designate; (*Zeichen*) mark. **Bezeichnung** *f* (*Beschreibung*) description; (*Name*) designation; (*Zeichen*) mark.

bezeugen [bə'tsɔygən] *v* testify (to), provide evidence of.

***beziehen** [bə'tsiːən] *v* cover; (*Geige*) string; (*Wohnung*) move into; (*Posten*) take up; (*Gehalt*) draw; (*erhalten, kaufen*) procure. **das Bett frisch beziehen** change the sheets. **sich beziehen auf** refer to, relate to. **Beziehung** *f* relation(ship). **in Beziehung auf** with regard *or* respect to. **beziehungsweise** *adv* respectively, or.

Bezirk [bə'tsirk] *m* (*pl* -e) district, area.
Bezug [bə'tsuːk] *m* (*pl* **Bezüge**) covering; (*Kopfkissen*) pillow-case; (*Waren*) supply, purchase. **bezüglich** *prep* concerning, relating to.
bezweifeln [bə'tsvaifəln] *v* doubt.
***bezwingen** [bə'tsviŋən] *v* conquer, overcome. **sich bezwingen** control *or* restrain oneself.
Bibel ['biːbəl] *f* (*pl* -n) Bible. **–stelle** *f* (biblical) text *or* passage.
Biber ['biːbər] *m* (*pl* -) beaver.
Bibliographie [bibliogra'fiː] *f* (*pl* -n) bibliography. **bibliographisch** *adj* bibliographic.
Bibliothek [biblio'teːk] *f* (*pl* -en) library. **–ar** *m* (*pl* -e) librarian.
biblisch ['bibliʃ] *adj* biblical.
bieder ['biːdər] *adj* honest, upright, respectable. **Biedermann** *m* honest man *or* fellow.
***biegen** ['biːgən] *v* bend; (*beim Fahren, usw.*) turn. **biegsam** *adj* supple; (*f* –ügsam) yielding. **Biegung** *f* (*pl* -en) bend; curve.
Biene ['biːnə] *f* (*pl* -n) bee. **Bienen‖stich** *m* bee sting; (*Kuchen*) almond pastry. **–stock** *m* beehive. **–wabe** *f* honeycomb. **–zucht** *f* beekeeping. **–züchter** *m* beekeeper.
Bier [biːr] *neut* (*pl* -e) beer. **–faß** *neut* beer barrel, cask. **–garten** *m* beer garden.
Biest [biːst] *neut* (*pl* -er) beast; (*fig*) brute.
***bieten** ['biːtən] *v* offer; (*Versteigerung*) bid.
Bigamie [biga'miː] *f* bigamy. **bigamisch** *adj* bigamous.
bigott [bi'gɔt] *adj* bigoted.
Bikini [bi'kiːniː] *m* (*pl* -s) bikini.
Bilanz [bi'lants] *f* (*pl* -en) balance (sheet), annual accounts.
Bild [bilt] *neut* (*pl* -er) picture; (*Buch*) illustration; (*Vorstellung*) idea.
bilden ['bildən] *v* form, shape; (*erziehen*) educate; (*darstellen*) constitute.
Bilder‖buch *neut* picture book. **–galerie** *f* (picture) gallery. **Bild‖feld** *neut* field of vision. **–hauer** *m* sculptor. **bildhübsch** *adj* very pretty, lovely. **Bildnis** *neut* (*pl* -se) image, likeness. **bildsam** *adj* plastic, flexible; (*fig*) docile. **Bildsäule** *f* statue.
Bildung ['bilduŋ] *f* (*pl* -en) formation; (*Erziehung*) education.

Billard ['biljart] *neut* (*pl* -e) billiards; (*Tisch*) billiard table. **–stock** *m* cue.
Billett [bil'jɛt] *neut* (*pl* -s *or* -e) ticket; (*Zettel*) note.
billig ['biliç] *adj* cheap, inexpensive; (*gerecht*) fair. **–en** *v* approve. **Billig‖keit** *f* cheapness, fairness. **–ung** *f* approval.
Billion [bil'joːn] *f* (*pl* -en) billion, (*US*) trillion.
Bimsstein ['bimsʃtain] *m* pumice stone.
binär [bi'nɛːr] *adj* binary.
Binde ['bində] *f* (*pl* -n) bandage; (*Arm*) sling. **–haut** *f* conjunctiva.
***binden** ['bindən] *v* bind, tie. **Bind‖estrich** *m* hyphen. **–faden** *m* string. **–ung** *f* binding; (*Verpflichtung*) obligation.
binnen ['binən] *prep* within. **Binnenhandel** *m* internal trade.
Biograph [bio'graːf] *m* (*pl* -en) biographer. **–ie** *f* biography. **biographisch** *adj* biographical.
Biologe [bio'loːgə] *m* (*pl* -n) biologist. **Biologie** *f* biology. **biologisch** *adj* biological.
Birke ['birkə] *f* (*pl* -n) birch.
Birne ['birnə] *f* (*pl* -n) pear; (*Glühbirne*) light-bulb.
bis [bis] *prep* (*räumlich*) as far as, (up) to; (*zeitlich*) until, till, to. *conj* until, till. **bis an, bis nach,** *or* **bis zu** up to, as far as. **bis jetzt** until now. **bis morgen** by tomorrow; (*Gruß*) see you tomorrow.
Bischof ['biʃɔf] *m* (*pl* **Bischöfe**) bishop. **bischöflich** *adj* episcopal.
bisher [bis'heːr] *adv* until now, hitherto. **–ig** *adj* until now, previous.
Biß [bis] *m* (*pl* **Bisse**) bite. **ein bißchen** a bit, a little.
bisweilen [bis'vailən] *adv* occasionally, sometimes.
bitte ['bitə] *interj* please. **Bitte** *f* request. **bitten** *v* request, ask; (*anflehen*) beg, implore.
bitter ['bitər] *adj* bitter. **Bitter‖keit** *f* bitterness. **–salz** *neut* Epsom salts. **bittersüß** *adj* bittersweet.
Bizeps ['biːtsɛps] *m* (*pl* -e) biceps.
Blamage [bla'maːʒə] *f* (*pl* -n) disgrace. **blamieren** *v* disgrace, compromise.
blank [blaŋk] *adj* bright, polished; (*rein*) clean; (*bloß*) bare.
blanko ['blaŋko] *adj* blank. **Blankoscheck** *m* blank cheque.

Blase ['blaːzə] f (pl -n) bubble; (Haut) blister; (Harn) bladder. **blasen** v blow.
blasiert [blaˈziːrt] adj blasé, conceited.
Blasinstrument ['blaːzinstrumɛnt] neut wind instrument.
blaß [blas] adj pale. **Blässe** f paleness, pallor. **bläßlich** adj pale, palish.
Blatt [blat] neut (pl **Blätter**) leaf; (Papier) sheet; (Zeitung) newspaper; (Klinge) blade. **blätterabwerfend** adj deciduous. **blättern** v (Buch) leaf through. **Blätterteig** m puff pastry. **Blatt‖grün** neut chlorophyll. **–laus** f greenfly, aphid.
blau [blau] adj blue; (umg.) drunk. **blaues Auge** black eye. **Blau** neut blue.
Blech [blɛç] neut (pl -e) sheet metal, tin. **–bläser** pl (Musik) brass (section). **–dose** f tin-can.
blecken ['blɛkən] show, bare (teeth).
Blei [blai] neut (pl -e) lead.
*bleiben ['blaibən] v remain, stay. **bleiben bei** keep or stick to.
bleich [blaiç] adj pale, faded. **Bleiche** f paleness. **bleichen** v black; (farblos werden) grow pale, fade. **Bleich‖mittel** neut bleach(ing agent). **–sucht** f anaemia. **bleichsüchtig** adj anaemic.
Bleistift ['blaiʃtift] m (pl -e) pencil.
Blende ['blɛndə] f (pl -n) blind, shutter; (Foto) shutter. **blenden** v blind, dazzle. **–d** adj dazzling, brilliant.
Blick [blik] m (pl -e) glance, look; (Aussicht) view. **blicken** v look.
blind [blint] adj blind. **Blind‖darm** m (Anat) appendix. **–darmentzündung** f appendicitis. **–e(r)** m blind man. **–enhund** m guide dog. **–enschrift** f braille. **–gänger** m dud (bomb or shell). **–heit** f blindness. **blindlings** adv blindly.
blinken ['bliŋkən] v sparkle, twinkle, glitter. **Blinker** m (Mot) indicator. **Blinklicht** neut flashing light.
blinzeln ['blintsəln] v blink, wink.
Blitz [blits] m (pl -e) lightning. **blitzen** v flash, emit flashes. **Blitzlicht** neut (Foto) flash, flashlight. **blitz‖sauber** adj spruce, very clean. **–schnell** adj quick as lightning. **Blitzschlag** m flash of lightning.
Block [blok] m (pl **Blöcke**) block; (Papier) pad. **–ade** f blockade. **–flöte** f (Musik) recorder. **blockieren** v blockade, block. **Blockschrift** f block letters.
blöd(e) [blœːt, 'blœːdə] adj silly, daft. **Blöd‖heit** f stupidity, silliness. **–sinn** m idiocy. **blödsinnig** adj idiotic, silly.

blöken ['blœːkən] v bleat.
blond [blont] adj blond, fair-haired. **Blondine** f blonde.
bloß [bloːs] adj bare, simple. adv only, merely.
Blöße ['blœːsə] f nakedness; (fig) weakness.
bloßlegen ['bloːsleːgən] v reveal, expose.
blühen ['blyːən] v bloom, flower. **blühend** adj blooming; (fig) flourishing.
Blume ['bluːmə] f (pl -n) flower; (Wein) bouquet. **Blumen‖beet** neut flowerbed. **–blatt** neut petal. **–kohl** m cauliflower. **–muster** neut floral pattern. **–strauß** m bunch of flowers, bouquet. **–topf** m flowerpot. **–zwiebel** f bulb.
Bluse ['bluːzə] f (pl -n) blouse.
Blut [bluːt] neut blood. **–druck** m blood pressure. **blutdurstig** adj bloodthirsty.
Blüte ['blyːtə] f (pl -n) blossom, bloom.
bluten ['bluːtən] v bleed. **Blut‖gefäß** neut blood vessel. **–gerinnsel** neut blood clot. **–gruppe** f blood group. **blutig** adj bloody. **Blut‖übertragung** f blood transfusion. **–untersuchung** f blood test.
Bö [bœː] f (pl -en) squall, gust of wind.
Bock [bok] m (pl **Böcke**) (Schaf-) ram; (Ziegen-, Reh-) buck; (Sport) horse. **bockig** adj obstinate. **Bockwurst** f saveloy, large Frankfurter.
Boden ['boːdən] m (pl **Böden**) (Erde) ground; (Fuß-) floor; (Dach-) loft; (Fluß-, Meeres-) bottom, bed. **bodenlos** adj bottomless.
Bogen ['boːgən] m (pl -) curve, arch; (Waffe, auch für Geige) bow. **–schießen** neut archery. **–schütze** m archer.
Bohne ['boːnə] f (pl -n) bean.
bohren ['boːrən] v bore, drill. **Bohrer** m (pl -) borer, drill. **Bohrmaschine** f drill.
Boje ['boːjə] f (pl -n) buoy.
Bollwerk ['bolvɛrk] neut (pl -e) bulwark.
Bolzen ['boltsən] m (pl -) peg; (Tech) bolt; (Pfeil) arrow, bolt.
bombardieren [bombarˈdiːrən] v bombard.
Bombe ['bombə] f (pl -n) bomb. **Bomben‖angriff** m bombing raid. **–anschlag** m (terrorist) bombing. **–flugzeug** neut bomber.
Bonbon [bõˈbõ] neut (pl -s) sweet, (US) candy.
Boot [boːt] neut (pl -e) boat.

Bord¹ [bɔrt] *neut* (*pl* -e) board.
Bord² *m* (*pl* -e) edge, rim. **an Bord gehen** go aboard, board.
Bordell [bɔr'dɛl] *neut* (*pl* -e) brothel.
borgen ['bɔrgən] *v* (*entleihen*) borrow; (*verleihen*) lend. **Borger** *m* (*pl* -) (*Entleiher*) borrower; (*Verleiher*) lender.
Borke ['bɔrkə] *f* (*pl* -n) bark.
Börse ['bœɪrzə] *f* (*pl* -n) stock exchange; (*Beutel*) purse. **–nmakler** *m* stockbroker.
Borste ['bɔrstə] *f* (*pl* -n) bristle.
bös(e) ['bœɪz(ə)] *adj* bad; (*Mensch*) wicked; (*Geist*) evil; (*Kind*) naughty; (*wütend*) cross. **bösartig** *adj* malicious; (*Med*) malignant. **Böse** *neut* mischief; *m* evil person, devil.
boshaft ['bɔɪshaft] *adj* malicious, spiteful.
Boß [bɔs] *m* (*pl* **Bosse**) boss.
böswillig ['bœɪzvɪliç] *adj* malicious, malevolent. **Böswilligkeit** *f* malice.
Botanik [bo'taɪnik] *f* botany. **–er** *m* (*pl* -) botanist. **botanisch** *adj* botanical.
Bote ['boɪtə] *m* (*pl* -n) messenger. **Bot‖engang** *m* errand. **–schaft** *f* message; (*Gesandschaft*) embassy. **-schafter** *m* ambassador.
Bottich ['bɔtiç] *m* (*pl* -e) tub, vat.
Bowle ['boɪlə] *f* (*pl* -n) (*Getränk*) punch, fruit cup; (*Gefäß*) punchbowl.
boxen ['bɔksən] *v* box. **Boxer** *m* (*pl* -) boxer. **Boxkampf** *m* boxing match.
brach [braɪx] *adj* fallow, untilled.
Branche ['brãʃə] *f* (*pl* -n) (*Geschäftszweig*) line of business, trade; (*Abteilung*) department.
Brand [brant] *m* (*pl* **Brände**) fire, blaze; (*Med*) gangrene; (*Bot*) mildew. **–bombe** *f* incendiary bomb. **brandmarken** *v* brand, stigmatize. **Brand‖stifter** *m* arsonist, fire-raiser. **–stiftung** *f* arson.
Brandung ['brandʊŋ] *f* (*pl* -en) surf, breakers *pl*.
Branntwein ['brantvain] *m* brandy.
*braten ['braɪtən] *v* roast; (*in der Pfanne*) fry; (*auf dem Rost*) grill. **Braten** *m* roast (meat), joint. **Brat‖fisch** *m* fried fish. **–hähnchen** *neut* roast chicken. **–kartoffeln** *pl* fried potatoes. **–pfanne** *f* frying pan. **–wurst** *f* fried sausage.
Bräu [brɔy] *neut* brew; (*Brauerei*) brewery.
Brauch [braux] *m* (*pl* **Bräuche**) custom, usage. **brauchbar** *adj* serviceable; usable; (*nützlich*) useful. **brauchen** *v* need, require; (*gebrauchen*) use.

brauen ['brauən] *v* brew. **Brauerei** *f* brewery.
braun [braun] *adj* brown. **Braun** *neut* brown.
Braunschweig ['braunʃvaik] *neut* Brunswick.
Brause ['brauzə] *f* (*pl* -n) (*Dusche*) shower; (*Gießkanne*) rose; (*Limonade*) lemonade, pop. **–bad** *neut* shower.
Braut [braut] *f* (*pl* **Bräute**) (*am Hochzeitstag*) bride; (*Verlobte*) fiancée.
Bräutigam [brɔytigam] *m* bridegroom.
Braut‖jungfer *f* bridesmaid. **–kleid** *neut* wedding dress.
bräutlich [brɔytliç] *adj* bridal.
brav [braɪf] *adj* honest, worthy; (*tapfer*) brave; (*artig*) good, well-behaved.
*brechen ['brɛçən] *v* break; (*Marmor*) quarry. **Bahn brechen** (*fig*) blaze a trail. **Brech‖bohne** *f* French bean. **–mittel** *neut* emetic.
Brei [brai] *m* (*pl* -e) paste, pulp.
breit [brait] *adj* broad, wide. **Breite** *f* breadth, width; (*Geog*) latitude.
Bremse¹ ['brɛmzə] *f* (*pl* -n) brake. **bremsen** *v* brake. **Brems‖licht** *f* brake light, stop light. **–pedal** *neut* brake pedal.
Bremse² *f* (*pl* -n) horse-fly.
brennbar ['brɛnbaɪr] *adj* combustible, inflammable. **brennen** *v* burn; (*Branntwein*) distill. **Brenn‖erei** *f* distillery. **–nessel** *f* stinging nettle. **–punkt** *m* focus. **–stoff** *m* fuel.
Brett [brɛt] *neut* (*pl* -er) board; (*Regal*) shelf.
Brezel ['breitsəl] *f* (*pl* -n) pretzel.
Brief [briɪf] *m* (*pl* -e) letter. **–kasten** *m* letterbox. **–kopf** *m* letterhead. **brieflich** *adj* written. **Brief‖marke** *f* (postage) stamp. **–tasche** *f* wallet, pocket book. **–träger** *m* postman.
Brigade [bri'gaɪdə] *f* (*pl* -n) brigade.
brillant [bril'jant] *adj* brilliant.
Brille ['brilə] *f* (*pl* -n) spectacles, glasses; (*Schutz*) goggles.
*bringen ['briŋən] *v* bring; (*mitnehmen, begleiten*) take; (*Zeitung*) print, publish; (*Theater*) present, put on. **es weit bringen** do well, go far. **ans Licht bringen** bring to light.
Brite ['briɪtə] *m* (*pl* -n), **Britin** *f* (*pl* -nen) Briton.
bröckelig ['brœkəliç] *adj* crumbly. **bröckeln** *v* crumble.

Brocken ['brɔkən] *m* (*pl* -) crumb; (*pl*) scraps, bits and pieces.

Brombeere ['brɔmbeɪrə] *f* blackberry. **Brombeerstrauch** *m* blackberry bush, bramble.

Bronze ['brõsə] *f* (*pl* -n) bronze. **bronzefarben** *adj* bronze(-coloured).

Brosche ['brɔʃə] *f* (*pl* -n) brooch.

Broschüre [brɔ'ʃyɪrə] *f* (*pl* -n) brochure.

Brot [broːt] *neut* (*pl* -e) bread; (*Laib*) loaf.

Brötchen [brœːtçən] *neut* bread roll.

Brot‖schnitte *f* slice (of bread). **–verdiener** *m* bread-winner.

Bruch [brux] *m* (*pl* **Brüche**) break; (*Knochen*) fracture; (*Math*) fraction; (*Versprechen*, *Vertrag*) breech; (*Gesetz*) violation, breech. **bruchfest** *adj* unbreakable.

brüchig [bryçiç] *adj* brittle.

Bruch‖landung *f* crash landing. **–stück** *neut* fragment. **–teil** *m* fraction.

Brücke ['brykə] *f* (*pl* -n) bridge.

Bruder ['bruːdər] *m* (*pl* **Brüder**) brother. **brüderlich** ['brydəarliç] *adj* brotherly. **Brüderschaft** *f* brotherhood.

Brühe ['bryːə] *f* (*pl* -n) broth; (*Suppengrundlage*) stock. **brühen** *v* scald. **brühheiß** *adj* boiling hot.

brüllen ['brylən] *v* bellow; (*Sturm*, *Raubtier*) roar. **Brüllfrosch** *m* bullfrog.

brummen ['brumən] growl; (*Insekten*) buzz, hum; (*mürrisch sein*) grumble; (*umg.*) go to prison, do time.

brünett [bry'nɛt] *adj* brunette, dark brown. **Brünette** *f* brunette.

Brunnen ['brunən] *m* (*pl* -) well; (*Quelle*) spring.

Brunst [brunst] *f* (*pl* **Brünste**) lust, ardour; (*Tier*) heat. **brünstig** *adj* lusty; (*Tier*) in heat.

Brüssel ['brysəl] *neut* Brussels.

Brust [brust] *f* (*pl* **Brüste**) breast, chest; (*Frauen*) breast. **–kasten** *m* chest. **–krebs** *m* breast cancer. **–schwimmen** *neut* breaststroke. **–warze** *f* nipple.

brutal [bru'taːl] *adj* brutal.

brüten ['brytən] *v* brood.

brutto ['bruto] *adj* gross. **Bruttogewicht** *neut* gross weight. **Bruttosozialprodukt** *neut* gross national product.

Bube ['buːbə] *m* (*pl* -n) boy, lad; (*Karten*) jack, knave.

Buch [buːx] *neut* (*pl* **Bücher**) book.

Buche ['buːxə] *f* (*pl* -n) beech (tree).

buchen ['buːçən] *v* record, enter (in a book).

Bücherei ['byçərai] *f* (*pl* -en) library. **Bücherschrank** *m* bookcase.

Buchfink [buːçfiŋk] *m* chaffinch.

Buch‖halter *m* book-keeper. **–haltung** *f* book-keeping; accounts department. **–händler** *m* bookseller. **–handlung** *f* bookshop. **–macher** *m* bookmaker.

Büchse ['byksə] *f* (*pl* -n) box; (*Blechdose*) tin, can; (*Gewehr*) rifle.

Buchstabe ['buːxʃtaːbə] *f* (*pl* -n) letter (of the alphabet). **buchstabieren** *v* spell. **Buchstabierung** *f* spelling. **buchstäblich** *adj* literal.

Bucht [buxt] *f* (*pl* -en) bay.

Buckel ['bukəl] *m* (*pl* -) hump, mound; (*am Rücken*) humpback. **buckelig** *adj* hunchbacked.

bücken ['bykən] *v* **sich bücken** stoop, bow.

Bude ['buːdə] *f* (*pl* -n) booth; (*Markt*) stall; (*umg.*) lodgings, digs, room(s).

Budget [by'dʒɛı] *neut* (*pl* -s) budget.

Büfett [by'fɛt] *neut* (*pl* -s) sideboard, dresser. **kaltes Büfett** cold buffet.

Büffel ['byfəl] *m* (*pl* -) buffalo.

Bug [buːk] *m* (*pl* -e) (*Schiff*) bow; (*Flugzeug*) nose; (*Pferd*) shoulder.

Bügel ['byːgəl] *m* (*pl* -) hoop, handle; (*Kleider-*) hanger; (*Steig-*) stirrup. **–brett** *neut* ironing board. **–eisen** *neut* iron. **bügelt** *adj* permanent press, non-iron. **bügeln** *v* iron.

bugsieren ['bugziːrən] *v* tow. **Bugsierer** *m* tugboat.

Bühne ['byːnə] *f* (*pl* -n) stage. **Bühnen‖bild** *neut* set, scenery. **–dichter** *m* playwright. **–deutsch** *neut* high German, standard German.

Bulgare [bul'gaːrə] *m* (*pl* -n), **Bulgarin** *f* (*pl* -nen) Bulgarian. **Bulgarien** *neut* Bulgaria. **bulgarisch** *adj* Bulgarian.

Bulle ['bulə] *m* (*pl* -n) bull; (*umg.*) cop.

Bummel ['buməl] *m* (*pl* -) stroll. **bummeln** *v* stroll; (*nichts tun*) loaf, loiter. **Bummel‖streik** *m* work-to-rule, go-slow. **–zug** *m* slow train, local (train).

Bund[1] [bunt] *neut* (*pl* -e) bundle; (*Schlüssel*, *Radieschen*, *usw.*) bunch.

Bund[2] *m* (*pl* **Bünde**) band; (*Verein*) association, league; (*Staat*) federation.

Bündel ['byndəl] *neut* (*pl* -) bundle, bunch. **bündeln** bundle (up).

Bundes‖bahn *f* federal railway, West German railway. **–haus** parliament buildings. **–präsident** *m* federal (West German) president. **–rat** *m* (*BRD, Österreich*) upper house (of parliament); (*Schweiz*) (Swiss) government. **–republik Deutschland (BRD)** *f* Federal Republic of Germany, West Germany. **–tag** *m* West German parliament, federal parliament. **–staat** *m* federal state.

Bündnis ['byntnis] *neut* (*pl* **-se**) alliance.

Bunker ['bunkər] *m* (*pl* **-**) bunker.

bunt [bunt] *adj* brightly coloured, gay.

Bürde ['byrdə] *f* (*pl* **-n**) burden.

Burg [burk] *f* (*pl* **-en**) castle; (*Festung*) fort.

Bürge ['byrgə] *m* (*pl* **-n**) surety, guarantor. **bürgen** *v* guarantee, vouch for; (*Jur*) stand bail for.

Bürger ['byrgər] *m* (*pl* **-**) citizen; (*Stadt*) townsman; bourgeois. **–krieg** *m* civil war. **bürgerlich** *adj* bourgeois, middle-class; (*Küche*) simple, plain; (*zivil*) civilian. **Bürger‖meister** *m* mayor. **–recht** *neut* civil rights. **–schaft** *f* citizenry, citizens. **–stand** *m* middle class(es). **–steig** *m* pavement, (*US*) sidewalk.

Bürgschaft ['byrgʃaft] *f* (*pl* **-en**) surety, bond.

Büro [by'roː] *neut* (*pl* **-s**) office. **–klammer** *f* paperclip. **–krat** *m* (*pl* **-en**) bureaucrat. **–kratie** *f* bureaucracy. **bürokratisch** *adj* bureaucratic.

Bursche ['burʃə] *m* (*pl* **-n**) lad, fellow.

Bürste ['byrstə] *f* (*pl* **-n**) brush. **bürsten** *v* brush.

Busch [buʃ] *m* (*pl* **Büsche**) bush, shrub.

Büschel ['byʃəl] *neut* (*pl* **-**) bunch; (*Haare*) tuft.

buschig ['buʃiç] *adj* bushy.

Busen ['buːzən] *m* (*pl* **-**) breast. **–freund** *m* bosom friend.

Buße ['buːsə] *f* (*pl* **-n**) penance; (*Geld*) fine.

büßen ['byːsən] *v* do penance (for).

Büste ['bystə] *f* (*pl* **-n**) bust. **–nhälter** *m* brassière.

Butter ['butər] *f* (*unz.*) butter. **–blume** *f* buttercup. **–brot** *neut* (slice of) bread and butter. **–brotpapier** *neut* greaseproof paper.

C

Café [ka'feː] *neut* (*pl* **-s**) café, coffee house.

campen ['kɛmpən] *v* camp. **Camper** *m* camper. **Camping** *neut* camping. **–platz** *m* camp(ing) site.

Caravan ['karavaɪn] *m* (*pl* **-s**) caravan; (*Kombiwagen*) estate car.

Cellist [tʃɛ'list] *m* (*pl* **-en**), **Cellistin** *f* (*pl* **-nen**) cellist. **Cello** *neut* cello.

Cembalo ['tʃɛmbalo] *neut* (*pl* **-s**) harpsichord.

Champagner [ʃam'panjər] *m* (*pl* **-**) champagne.

Champignon ['ʃampinjɔ̃] *m* (*pl* **-s**) mushroom.

Chance ['ʃɑ̃ːsə] *f* (*pl* **-n**) chance. **Chancengleichheit** *f* equality of opportunity.

Chaos ['kaɪɔs] *neut* (*unz.*) chaos. **chaotisch** *adj* chaotic.

Charakter ['karaktər] *m* (*pl* **-e**) character. **charakterisieren** *v* characterize. **charakteristisch** *adj* characteristic.

Chauffeur [ʃɔ'fœɪr] *m* (*pl* **-e**) driver, chauffeur.

Chaussee [ʃo'seː] *f* (*pl* **-n**) highway, main road.

Chef [ʃɛf] *m* (*pl* **-s**) boss, head; (*Arbeitgeber*) employer.

Chemie [çe'miː] *f* (*unz.*) chemistry. **Chemikalien** *f pl* chemicals. **Chemiker** *m* (*pl* **-**) (industrial *or* research) chemist. **chemisch** *adj* chemical. **–e Reinigung** *f* dry cleaning.

China ['çiɪna] *neut* China. **Chinese** *m* (*pl* **-n**), **Chinesin** *f* (*pl* **-nen**) Chinese (person). **chinesisch** *adj* Chinese.

Chirurg [çi'rurk] *m* (*pl* **-en**) surgeon. **–ie** *f* surgery. **chirurgisch** *adj* surgical.

Chlor [kloɪr] *neut* (*unz.*) chlorine. **Chloroform** *neut* chloroform. **Chlorophyll** *neut* chlorophyll. **Chlorwasser** *neut* chlorinated water.

Cholera ['kolera] *f* (*unz.*) cholera.

Chor [koɪr] *m* (*pl* **Chöre**) choir; (*Gesang*) chorus. **–direktor** *m* choirmaster.

Christ [krist] *m* (*pl* **-en**) Christian. **christlich** *adj* Christian. **Christ‖nacht** *f* Christmas Eve. **–us** *m* Christ.

Chrom [kroɪm] *neut* (*unz.*) chromium; (*Verchromung*) chrome, chrome-plating. **chromiert** *adj* chrome-plated.

Chronik ['kroɪnik] *f* (*pl* **-en**) chronicle. **chronisch** *adj* chronic.

Computer [kɔm'pjuːtər] *m* (*pl* -) computer.

Coupé [ku'peɪ] *neut* (*pl* -s) railway carriage.

Cousin [ku'zɛ̃] *m* (*pl* -s) (male) cousin. **–e** *f* (female) cousin.

Creme [kreɪm] *f* (*pl* -s) cream; (*Süßspeise*) cream pudding; (*Hautsalbe*) handcream, skincream.

D

da [da] *adv* (*örtlich*) there; (*zeitlich*) then. *conj* because, since. **da draußen/drinnen** out/in there. **da sein** be present. **da bin ich** here I am. **da siehst Du!** see! **da hingegen** whereas.

dabei [da'bai] *adv* close (by), near; (*bei diesem*) thereby; (*außerdem*) moreover. **dabei sein** be present. **es bleibt dabei** that is *or* remains settled. **was ist dabei?** what does it matter? **dabei sein, es zu tun** be on the point of doing it. **dabei bleiben** stick to one's opinion.

Dach [dax] *neut* (*pl* Dächer) roof. **–boden** *m* attic. **–fenster** *neut* skylight. **–gesellschaft** *f* holding company. **–kammer** *f* attic, garret. **–rinne** *f* gutter.

Dachs [daks] *m* (*pl* -e) badger. **–hund** *m* dachshund.

Dachziegel ['daxtsiːɡəl] *m* roof tile.

dadurch [da'durç] *adv* for this reason, in this way. **dadurch daß** because, since.

dafür [da'fyːr] *adv* for that; (*Gegenleistung*) in return. **dafür sein** be in favour (of it). **er kann nichts dafür** he can't help it.

dagegen [da'ɡeɪɡən] *adv* against it; (*Vergleich*) in comparison. *conj* on the contrary, however. *ich habe nichts dagegen* I have no objections. *er stimmt dagegen* he is voting against it.

daher [da'heɪr] *adv* from there. *conj* hence, accordingly. **daher kommt es** hence it follows. **daher, daß** since, because.

dahin [da'hin] *adv* there, to that place.

dahinten [da'hintən] *adv* back there.

dahinter [da'hintər] *adv* behind it *or* that. **–kommen** *v* find out (about it), get to the bottom of it. **–stecken** *v* lie behind, be the cause.

damals ['daːmaɪls] *adv* then, at that time.

Dame ['daːmə] *f* (*pl* -n) lady; (*Karten*) queen. **–brett** *neut* draughtboard, (*US*) checker-board. **Damen‖binde** *f* sanitary towel. **–toilette** *f* ladies' lavatory. **–wäsche** *f* lingerie. **Dame‖spiel** *neut* draughts. **–stein** *m* draughtsman, (*US*) checker.

Damm [dam] *m* (*pl* Dämme) dam; dike; (*Bahn-, Straßen-*) embankment.

dämmen ['dɛmən] *v* dam (up).

dämmern ['dɛmərn] *v* (*morgens*) dawn, grow light; (*abends*) grow dark. **es dämmert** dawn is breaking. **Dämmerung** *f* (*pl* -en) (*morgens*) dawn; (*abends*) twilight, dusk.

Dampf [dampf] *m* (*pl* Dämpfe) steam, vapour. **dampfen** *v* steam; (*Rauch*) smoke, fume.

dämpfen ['dɛmpfən] *v* (*Ofen*) damp down; (*Schall*) muffle; (*Licht*) soften; (*Küche*) steam.

Dampf‖er ['dampfər] *m* (*pl* -) steamer, steamship. **–kessel** *m* boiler. **–kochtopf** *m* pressure cooker. **–maschine** *f* steam engine. **–schiff** *neut* steamship, steamer.

danach [da'naːx] *adv* after it; (*darauf*) afterwards; (*entsprechend*) accordingly.

Däne ['dɛːnə] *m* (*pl* -n), **Dänin** (-nen) Dane. **Dänemark** *neut* Denmark. **dänisch** *adj* Danish.

daneben [da'neɪbən] *adv* beside (it); (*außerdem*) besides.

Dank [daŋk] *m* (*unz.*) thanks. **dankbar** *adj* grateful, thankful. **Dankbarkeit** *f* gratitude. **danken** *v* thank.

dann [dan] *adv* then.

daran [da'ran] *adv* on *or* at *or* by it. **nahe daran sein zu** be on the point of. **nahe daran** close by. **gut daran sein** be well off.

darauf [da'rauf] *adv* on it; (*nachher*) afterwards. **es kommt darauf an** (**ob**) it depends (whether). *wie kommt er darauf?* why does he think so?

daraus [da'raus] *adv* out of it, from it. *es ist nichts daraus geworden* nothing has come of that.

*darbieten ['daɪrbiːtən] *v* offer, present.

darein [da'rain] *adv* in(to) it; (*hierin*) therein.

darin [da'rin] *adv* in it, within; (*hierin*) therein.

darlegen ['daɪrleɪɡən] *v* explain, expound. **Darlegung** *f* explanation.

Darlehen ['daɪrleɪən] *neut* (*pl* -) loan.
Darm [darm] *m* (*pl* **Därme**) intestines *pl.*
-verstopfung *f* constipation.
darstellen ['daɪrʃtɛlən] *v* represent. **Darsteller** *m* (*Theater*) actor, performer.
Darstellung *f* exhibition.
darüber [da'ryɪbər] *adv* over it; (*davon*) about it; (*hinüber*) across. **darüber hinaus** over and above that, furthermore.
darum [da'rum] *adv* around *or* about it, for it. *conj* therefore.
darunter [da'runtər] *adv* under *or* beneath it; (*dazwischen*) among them; (*weniger*) less.
das [das] *art* the. *pron* which, that.
Dasein ['daɪzain] *neut* (*unz.*) existence, being; (*Vorhandensein*) presence. **Daseinskampf** *m* struggle for existence.
daß [das] *conj* that.
Daten ['daɪtən] *neut pl* data *pl.* **-verarbeitung** *f* data processing.
datieren [da'tiɪrən] *v* date.
Datum ['daɪtum] *neut* (*pl* **Daten**) date; (*Tatsache*) datum, fact.
Dauer ['dauər] *f* (*unz.*) period (of time), duration. **-auftrag** *m* (*Bank*) standing order. **dauerhaft** *adj* lasting, durable. **Dauerkarte** *f* season ticket. **dauern** *v* last, continue. **-d** *adj* lasting, permanent. **Dauerwelle** *f* perm, permanent wave.
Daumen ['daumən] *m* (*pl* -) thumb.
Daunendecke ['daunəndɛkə] *f* eiderdown, continental quilt.
davon [da'fɔn] *adv* of *or* from it; (*weg*) away; (*darüber*) about it. **-kommen** *v* escape. **sich davonmachen** *v* (*umg.*) make one's escape, slide off.
davor [da'foɪr] *adv* (*örtlich*) before it, in front of it; (*zeitlich*) before that *or* then. **Angst haben davor** be afraid of it. **eine Stunde davor** an hour earlier.
dawider [da'viɪdər] *adv* against it.
dazu [da'tsuɪ] *adv* to it; (*Zweck*) for this (purpose), to that end; (*überdies*) in addition.
dazwischen [da'tsviʃən] *adv* between *or* among them. **-treten** *v* intervene.
Debatte [de'batə] *f* (*pl* -n) debate. **debattieren** *v* debate.
Debet ['deɪbɛt] *neut* (*pl* -s) debit.
Debüt [de'byɪ] *neut* (*pl* -s) début.
Deck [dɛk] *neut* (*pl* -e) deck.
Decke ['dɛkə] *f* (*pl* -n) cover(ing); (*Bett*) blanket; (*Zimmer*) ceiling. **-l** *m* lid.
decken *v* cover; set (the table).

Deck||mantel *m* pretext. **-name** *m* pseudonym. **-ung** *f* cover(ing); (*Verteidigung*) protection.
definieren [defi'niɪrən] *v* define. **definitiv** *adj* definite.
Defizit ['deɪfitsit] *neut* (*pl* -e) deficit.
degenerieren [degene'riɪrən] *v* degenerate.
dehnbar ['deɪnbaɪr] *adj* elastic, malleable; (*Begriff*) loose, vague. **Dehnbarkeit** *f* elasticity, malleability. **dehnen** *v* stretch. **Dehnung** *f* stretching, expansion.
Deich [daiç] *m* (*pl* -e) dike.
Deichsel ['daiksəl] *f* (*pl* -n) shaft, pole. **deichseln** *v* (*umg.*) wangle.
dein [dain] *adj* your. *pron* yours. **deinerseits** *adv* on *or* for your part. **deinesgleichen** *pron* your likes, people like you. **deinethalben, deinetwegen,** *or* **deinetwillen** *adv* for your sake. **deinige** *pron* **der die, das deinige** yours.
dekadent [deka'dɛnt] *adj* decadent. **Dekadenz** *f* decadence.
Dekan [de'kain] *m* (*pl* -e) dean.
deklamieren [dekla'miɪrən] *v* declaim.
deklarieren [dekla'riɪrən] *v* declare.
Deklination [deklinatsi'oɪn] *f* (*pl* -en) declension. **deklinieren** *v* decline.
Dekor [de'koɪr] *m* (*pl* -s) decoration(s). **dekorieren** *v* decorate.
Dekret [de'kreɪt] *neut* (*pl* -e) decree.
delegieren [dele'giɪrən] *v* delegate. **Delegierte(r)** *m* delegate.
delikat [deli'kaɪt] *adj* (*Person, Angelegenheit*) delicate; (*Speise*) delicious. **Delikatesse** *f* (*pl* -n) delicacy.
Delikt [de'likt] *neut* (*pl* -e) crime.
Delphin [dɛl'fiɪn] *m* (*pl* -e) dolphin.
dem [deɪm] *art* to the. *pron* to this *or* that (one); (*wem*) to whom, to which.
Dementi [de'mɛnti] *neut* (*pl* -s) (official) denial. **dementieren** *v* deny.
demgemäß ['deɪmgəmɛɪs] *adv* accordingly.
Demission [demisi'oɪn] *f* (*pl* -en) resignation. **demissionieren** *v* resign.
demnach [deɪmnaɪx] *adv* accordingly.
demnächst ['deɪmnɛɪçst] *adv* shortly, soon.
Demokrat [demo'kraɪt] *m* (*pl* -en) democrat. **-ie** *f* democracy. **demokratisch** *adj* democratic.
demolieren [demo'liɪrən] *v* demolish.
Demonstrant [demɔn'strant] *m* (*pl* -en) demonstrator. **Demonstration** *f* (*pl* -en)

demonstration. **demonstrieren** v demonstrate. **demonstrativ** adj demonstrative.
Demut ['deɪmuɪt] f (unz.) humility. **demütig** adj humble. **–en** v humiliate, humble.
Demütigung f (pl **-en**) humiliation.
demzufolge ['deɪmtsufɔlgə] adv accordingly. pron according to which.
den [deɪn] art the. pl to the. pron whom, which. pl to these. **denen** pron to whom or which.
Denkart ['dɛŋkaɪrt] f way of thinking. **denk‖bar** adj conceivable, thinkable. **–en** v think. **Denk‖en** neut thinking, thought. **–er** m (pl -) thinker. **–freiheit** f freedom of thought. **–mal** neut monument. **denkwürdig** adj memorable. **Denkzettel** m lesson, punishment.
dennoch ['dennɔx] conj nevertheless.
Denunziant [denuntsi'ant] m (pl **-en**) informer. **denunzieren** v denounce, inform against.
Depesche [de'pɛʃə] f (pl **-n**) telegram, dispatch.
deponieren [depo'niɪrən] v deposit.
Depot [de'poɪ] neut (pl **-s**) warehouse, storehouse, depot.
Depression [depresi'oɪn] f (pl **-en**) depression. **depressiv** adj depressed.
deprimieren [depri'miɪrən] v depress. **–d** adj depressing.
der [deɪr] art the; (to) the; pl of the. pron who, which; (to) whom or which.
derart ['deɪraɪrt] adv in such a way, so. **–ig** adj of such a type, such, of that kind.
derb [dɛrp] adj crude, coarse; (Person) rough, tough. **Derbheit** f crudeness; (Person) roughness.
deren ['deɪrən] pron whose, of which. **derenthalben, derentwegen,** or **derentwillen** adv on whose account, for whose sake.
dergleichen [deɪr'glaiçən] adv suchlike, of the kind.
derjenige ['deɪrjeɪnigə] **diejenige, dasjenige** pron he who, she who, that which.
dermaßen ['deɪrmaɪsən] adv to such a degree, in such a way.
derselbe [deɪr'zɛlbə] pron **dieselbe, dasselbe** the same.
derzeitig ['deɪrtsaitiç] adj present; (damalig) of that time.
des [dɛs] art of the.
desgleichen [dɛs'glaiçən] adv likewise.
deshalb ['dɛshalp] adv therefore.

Desillusion [dɛziluzi'oɪn] f disillusionment.
Desinfektion [dɛzinfɛktsi'oɪn] f disinfection. **–smittel** neut disinfectant. **desinfizieren** v disinfect.
dessen ['dɛsən] pron whose, of which.
destillieren [dɛsti'liɪrən] v distil.
desto ['dɛsto] adv the, all the, so much. **je … desto …** the … the ….
deswegen ['dɛsveɪgən], **deswillen** adv therefore.
Detail [de'tai] neut (pl **-s**) detail, item. **–geschäft** neut retail firm or business. **–handel** m retail trade. **detaillieren** v detail, particularize.
deuten ['dɔytən] v explain, interpret. **deuten auf** point to, indicate, suggest. **deutlich** adj clear, plain. **Deutlichkeit** f clearness, distinctness.
deutsch [dɔytʃ] adj German. **Deutsch** neut German (language). **Deutsche(r)** German man. **Deutschland** neut Germany.
Devise [de'viɪzə] f (pl **-n**) motto; pl foreign currency or exchange. **Devisenkurs** m rate of exchange.
Dezember [de'tsɛmbər] m (pl **-**) December.
dezimal [detsi'maɪl] adj decimal.
Dia ['diɪa] neut (pl **-s**), also **Diapositiv** slide, transparency.
Dialekt [dia'lɛkt] m (pl **-e**) dialect.
Dialog [dia'loɪk] m (pl **-e**) dialogue.
Diamant [dia'mant] m (pl **-en**) diamond. **diamanten** adj diamond.
Diät [di'ɛɪt] f (pl **-en**) diet.
dich [diç] pron sing you.
dicht [diçt] adj dense; (Wald, Nebel, Stoff) thick; (nahe) close (by); (wasserdicht) watertight.
dichten¹ ['diçtən] v seal, make watertight or airtight.
dichten² v write (poetry); (erträumen) invent. **Dichter** m (pl **-**), **Dichterin** f (pl **-nen**) poet. **dichterisch** adj poetic.
Dichtheit ['diçthait] or **Dichtigkeit** f density.
Dichtung ['diçtuŋ] f poetry, literature.
dick [dik] adj think; (Person) fat. **Dick‖darm** m large intestine. **–e** f fatness, thickness. **–icht** neut thicket.
die [diɪ] art the; pron who, which.
Dieb [diɪp] m (pl **-e**) thief. **diebisch** adj thieving. **Diebstahl** m theft.
Diele ['diɪlə] f (pl **-n**) board, plank; (Vor-

raum) hall, vestibule; (*Eis-*) ice-cream parlour. **Dielenbrett** *neut* floorboard.
dienen ['diːnən] *v* serve. **Diener** *m* (*pl* -), **Dienerin** *f* (*pl* -nen) servant. **Dienerschaft** *f* servants *pl*, domestics *pl*. **Dienst** *f* (*pl* -e) service; (*Amt*) duty.
Dienstag ['diːnstaːk] *m* Tuesday. **Dienst‖entlassung** *f* dismissal. –**grad** *m* rank. –**leistung** *f* service. **dienstlich** *adj*, *adv* official(ly). **Dienst‖mädchen** *neut* (serving) maid. –**pflicht** *f* conscription. –**stunden** *f pl* working hours. –**wohnung** *f* official residence.
dieser ['diːzər] **diese, dieses** *pron*, *adj* this. **dies‖jährig** *adj* this year's. –**mal** *adv* this time. –**seits** *adv* on this side.
Dietrich ['diːtriç] *m* (*pl* -e) skeleton key.
diffizil [difi'tsiːl] *adj* difficult, awkward.
Diktat [dik'taːt] *neut* (*pl* -e) dictation. **Diktator** *m* (*pl* -en) dictator. **diktatorisch** *adj* dictatorial. **Diktatur** *f* (*pl* -en) dictatorship. **diktieren** *v* dictate. **Diktiergerät** *neut* dictaphone, dictating machine.
Diner [di'neɪ] *neut* (*pl* -s) dinner, dinnerparty.
Ding [diŋ] *neut* (*pl* -e) thing. **vor allen Dingen** above all. **Dingelchen** *neut* (pretty) little thing. **Dingsbums** *neut* (*umg.*) what's-it's-name, what's-his-name.
Diplom [di'ploːm] *neut* (*pl* -e) diploma. –**at** *m* (*pl* -en) diplomat. –**atie** *f* diplomacy. **diplomatisch** *adj* diplomatic. **Diplomingenieur** *m* graduate engineer.
dir [diːr] *pron sing* to you.
Dirigent [diri'gɛnt] *m* (*pl* -en) (*Musik*) conductor. **dirigieren** *v* conduct.
Dirne ['dirnə] *f* (*pl* -n) prostitute, whore; wench.
diskontieren [diskɔn'tiːrən] *v* discount. **Diskontsatz** *m* bank-rate.
Diskothek [diskoɪ'teːk] *f* (*pl* -en) disco(theque).
diskriminieren [diskrimi'niːrən] *v* discriminate (against). **Diskriminierung** *f* discrimination.
Diskussion [diskusi'oɪn] *f* (*pl* -en) discussion. **diskutieren** *v* discuss.
disponieren [dispo'niːrən] *v* arrange, dispose (of). **disponieren über** have at one's disposal.
Dissident [disi'dɛnt] *m* (*pl* -en) dissident, dissenter.
Distel ['distəl] *f* (*pl* -n) thistle.
Disziplin [distsi'pliːn] *f* (*pl* -en) discipline.

disziplinarisch *adj* disciplinary. **Disziplinarverfahren** *neut* disciplinary action.
D-Mark ['deɪmark] *f* (*pl* -) (West) German mark.
doch [dɔx] *conj* nevertheless, yet, but; *adv* indeed, oh yes.
Docht [dɔxt] *m* (*pl* -e) wick.
Dock [dɔk] *neut* (*pl* -e) dock. –**arbeiter** *m* docker, (*US*) longshoreman.
Dogge ['dɔgə] *f* (*pl* -n) Great Dane; bulldog.
Dogma ['dɔgma] *f* (*pl* **Dogmen**) Dogma. **dogmatisch** *adj* dogmatic.
Doktor ['dɔktɔr] *m* (*pl* -en) doctor. –**arbeit** *f* doctoral *or* PhD thesis. –**at** *neut* doctorate, PhD.
Dolch [dɔlç] *m* (*pl* -e) dagger.
dolmetschen ['dɔlmɛtʃən] *v* interpret. **Dolmetscher** *m* interpreter.
Dom [doɪm] *m* (*pl* -e) cathedral. –**herr** *m* canon. –**pfaff** (*Zool*) *m* bullfinch.
Domino ['doɪmino] *neut* (*pl* -s) dominoes. –**stein** *m* domino.
Donau ['doɪnau] *f* Danube.
Donner ['dɔnər] *m* (*pl* -) thunder. **donnern** *v* thunder.
Donnerstag ['dɔnərstaːk] *m* Thursday. **Donnerwetter** ['dɔnərvɛtər] *neut* thunderstorm. *interj* damn!
doof [doɪf] *adj* (*umg.*) daft, dumb, stupid.
Doppel ['dɔpəl] *neut* (*pl* -) duplicate. **Doppel-** *adj* double-. **Doppel‖bett** *neut* double bed. –**ehe** *f* bigamy. –**gänger** *m* ghostly double; doppelgänger **doppeln** *v* double. **Doppel‖punkt** *m* colon. –**sinn** *m* ambiguity. **doppelt** *adj* double(d).
Dorf [dɔrf] *neut* (*pl* **Dörfer**) village. –**bewohner** *m* villager.
Dorn [dɔrn] *m* (*pl* -en) thorn. –**röschen** *neut* Sleeping Beauty.
Dorsch [dɔrʃ] *m* (*pl* -e) cod.
dort [dɔrt] *adv* there. –**her** *adv* (from) there. –**herum** *adv* around there. –**hin** (to) there. –**ig** *adj* of that place.
Dose ['doɪzə] *f* (*pl* -n) tin, box; (*Konserven-*) tin, can. **Dosenöffner** *m* tin-opener, can-opener.
dosieren [do'ziːrən] *v* measure out (a dose of). **Dosis** *f* (*pl* **Dosen**) dose.
Dotter ['dɔtə] *m* (*pl* -) (egg) yolk.
Dozent [do'tsɛnt] *m* (*pl* -en) university *or* college lecturer.
Drache ['draxə] *m* (*pl* -n) dragon.

Drachen ['draxən] *m* (*pl* -) kite.
Draht [draɪt] *m* (*pl* **Drähte**) wire, (*Kabel*) cable. **–anschrift** *f* telegraphic address. **–seil** *neut* cable. **–seilbahn** *f* cable car, funicular.
Drama ['draɪma] *neut* (*pl* **Dramen**) drama. **–tiker** *m* (*pl* -) dramatist. **dramatisch** *adj* dramatic.
dran [dran] *V* **daran.**
Drang [draŋ] *m* (*pl* **Dränge**) drive, urge; (*Druck*) pressure.
drängeln ['drɛŋəln] *v* jostle, shove.
drängen ['drɛŋən] *v* press, urge.
drapieren [dra'piːrən] *v* drape.
drastisch ['drastiʃ] *adj* drastic.
drauf [drauf] *V* **darauf.**
draußen ['drausən] *adv* outside, out of doors.
Dreck [drɛk] *m* (*unz.*) filth, dirt; (*Kot*) excrement; (*Kleinigkeit*) trifle. **dreckig** *adj* filthy, dirty.
Dreh [dreɪ] *m* (*pl* -e) turn. **den Dreh heraushaben** get the hang *or* knack of it. **–bank** *f* lathe. **–buch** *neut* film-script, scenario. **drehen** *v* turn, rotate. **Dreh||punkt** *m* pivot. **–ung** *f* (*pl* -en) turn, rotation, revolution. **–zahl** *f* revolutions per minute, rpm.
drei [drai] *adj* three. **Dreieck** *neut* triangle. **dreieckig** *adj* triangular. **dreifach** *adj* triple, treble. **Dreifuß** *m* tripod. **dreimal** *adv* three times. **Dreirad** *neut* tricycle. **dreißig** ['draisiç] *adj* thirty.
dreist [draist] *adj* cheeky, impudent.
dreiviertel ['draifɪrtəl] *adj* three-quarter. *adv* three-quarters. **Dreiviertelstunde** *f* three-quarters of an hour.
dreizehn ['draitseɪn] *adj* thirteen.
***dreschen** ['drɛʃən] *v* thresh.
dressieren [drɛ'siːrən] *v* train.
Drillich ['driliç] *m* (*pl* -e) (*Stoff*) drill, canvas.
Drilling ['driliŋ] *m* (*pl* -e) triplet.
drin [drin] *V* **darin.**
***dringen** ['driŋən] *v* penetrate. **dringen auf** insist on. **dringen in** implore, urge.
dritte ['dritə] *adj* third. **Drittel** *neut* (*pl* -) third.
Droge ['droɪgə] *f* (*pl* -n) drug. **Drogerie** *f* (*pl* -n) chemist's (shop), pharmacy. **Drogist** *m* (*pl* -en) pharmacist, chemist.
drohen ['droɪən] *v* threaten. **–d** *adj* threatening; (*Gefahr, usw.*) impending, imminent.
Drohne ['droɪnə] *f* (*pl* -n) drone.

dröhnen ['drœɪnən] *v* roar; (*Kanone*) boom; (*Donner*) rumble.
Drohung ['droɪuŋ] *f* (*pl* -en) threat.
Droschke ['drɔʃkə] *f* (*pl* -n) taxi; (*Pferde-*) cab.
Drossel ['drɔsəl] *f* (*pl* -n) (*Vogel*) thrush; (*Mot*) throttle. **–ader** *f* jugular vein. **drosseln** *v* throttle.
drüben ['dryːbən] *adv* over there.
Druck[1] [druk] *m* (*pl* **Drücke**) pressure.
Druck[2] *m* (*pl* -e) print; (*Auflage*) impression. **drucken** *v* print.
drücken ['drykən] *v* press, push; (*Hand*) shake; (*bedrücken*) oppress. **sich drücken** get out of, avoid.
Druck||er ['drukər] *m* (*pl* -) printer. **–erei** *f* (*pl* -en) printing plant, press. **–fehler** *m* misprint. **–knopf** *m* push button; (*Kleidung*) snap fastener. **–luft** *f* compressed air. **–messer** *m* pressure gauge. **–sache** *f* printed matter. **–schrift** *f* publication; (*Buchstaben*) block letter.
drum [drum] *V* **darum.**
drunter ['druntər] *V* **darunter.**
Drüse ['dryːzə] *f* (*pl* -n) gland.
Dschungel ['dʒuŋəl] *m* (*pl* -) jungle.
du [duː] *pron* you.
Dübel ['dyːbəl] *m* (*pl* -) dowel, wall-plug.
ducken ['dukən] *v* humble, humiliate. **sich ducken** duck; (*fig*) cower.
Dudelsack ['duːdəlzak] *m* bagpipes *pl*.
Duell [du'ɛl] *neut* (*pl* -e) duel. **–ant** *m* duellist.
Duett [du'ɛt] *neut* (*pl* -e) duet.
Duft [duft] *m* (*pl* **Düfte**) fragrance, aroma; (*Blumen*) scent. **dufte** *adj* (*umg.*) splendid, fine. **duften** *v* smell (sweet), be fragrant. **–d** *adj* fragrant, aromatic.
dulden ['duldən] *v* endure; (*erlauben*) tolerate, allow. **duldsam** *adj* tolerant, patient.
dumm [dum] *adj* stupid. **–helt** *f* stupidity; (*Tat*) foolish action, blunder. **–kopf** *m* idiot, fool.
dumpf [dumpf] *adj* (*Klang*) dull, hollow, muffled; (*schwül*) close, sultry; (*muffig*) musty.
Düne ['dyːnə] *f* (*pl* -n) dune.
Düngemittel ['dyːnəmitəl] *neut* fertilizer. **düngen** *v* fertilize, manure. **Dünger** *m* manure.
dunkel ['dyŋkəl] *adj* dark; (*düster*) gloomy, dim; (*ungewiß*) obscure. **Dunkel||heit** *f* darkness, obscurity.

-kammer *f* (*Foto*) darkroom. **dunkeln** *v* **es dunkelt** it is growing dark.
Dünkel ['dyŋkəl] *m* arrogance.
dünn [dyn] *adj* thin. **Dünn‖darm** *m* small intestine.
Dunst [dunst] *m* (*pl* **Dünste**) haze, mist.
dunsten *v* steam.
dünsten ['dynstən] *v* steam; (*Küche*) stew.
Dur [duːr] *neut* (*Musik*) major (key).
durch [durç] *prep* through; (*mittels*) by, through; (*Zeit*) during. *adv* through(out). **durch Zufall** by chance. **durch und durch** thoroughly.
durchaus [durç'aus] *adv* completely, thoroughly.
durchblättern [durç'blɛtərn] *v* leaf through, skim through.
durchbohren ['durçboːrən] *v* pierce, bore through.
***durchbrechen** ['durçbrɛçən] *v* break through. **Durchbruch** *m* break-through; (*Öffnung*) breach.
***durchdringen** ['durçdriŋən] *v* penetrate; ['driŋən] (*durchsickern*) permeate.
durcheinander [durçain'andər] *adv* in confusion, in disorder, in a mess. **Durcheinander** *neut* muddle. **durcheinanderbringen** *v* muddle up; (*aufregen*) upset, excite.
Durchfahrt ['durçfaːrt] *f* passage; (*Tor*) gate. **keine Durchfahrt** no thoroughfare.
Durchfall ['durçfal] *m* failure; (*Med*) diarrhoea. **durchfallen** *v* fall through; (*Prüfung*) fail.
durchführen ['durçfyːrən] *v* carry out, perform; (*begleiten*) lead through. **Durchführung** *f* implementation, execution.
Durchgabe ['durçgaːbə] *f* transmission.
Durchgang ['durçgaŋ] *m* passage.
durchgeben ['durçgeːbən] *v* transmit, pass on.
durchgehen ['durçgeːən] *v* walk *or* go through, (*fliehen*) run away; (*durchdringen*) penetrate. **-d** *adj* continuous; (*Zug*) through.
***durchkommen** ['durçkɔmən] *v* come *or* pass through.
***durchlaufen** ['durçlaufən] *v* run through.
durchleuchten [durç'lɔyçtən] *v* (*Med*) x-ray.
durchmachen ['durçmaxən] *v* endure, live through.
Durchmesser ['durçmɛsər] *m* diameter.

Durchreise ['durçraizə] *f* journey through, passage, transit.
durchs [durçs] *prep + art* **durch das**.
Durchsage ['durçzaːgə] *f* announcement. **durchsagen** *v* announce.
Durchschlag ['durçʃlaːk] *m* carbon (copy); (*Sieb*) strainer, sieve. **-papier** *neut* carbon paper.
Durchschnitt ['durçʃnit] *m* cutting through; (*Querschnitt*) cross-section; (*Mittelwert*) mean, average. **durchschnittlich** *adj* average. **Durchschnittsmensch** *m* average person, man in the street.
Durchschrift ['durçʃrift] *f* (carbon) copy.
***durchsehen** ['durçzeːən] *v* look *or* see through; (*prüfen*) look through *or* over.
Durchsicht ['durçziçt] *f* (*pl* **-en**) perusal, inspection. **durchsichtig** *adj* transparent.
durchsuchen ['durçzuːxən] *v* search.
durchtrieben [durç'triːbən] *adj* cunning, sly.
***durchwinden** ['durçvindən] *v* **sich durchwinden** struggle through.
***durchziehen** ['durçtsiːən] *v* pass through; (*etwas durch etwas*) pull *or* draw through; [-'tsiːən] traverse; (*durchdringen*) fill, permeate.
***dürfen** ['dyrfən] *v* be allowed *or* permitted to, may. **darf ich?** may I? **wenn ich bitten darf** if you please. **du darfst nicht** you may *or* must not.
dürftig ['dyrftiç] *adj* needy, poor. **Dürftigkeit** *f* poverty.
dürr [dyr] *adj* arid, dry; (*hager*) lean. **Dürre** *f* drought; (*Magerkeit*) leanness.
Durst [durst] *m* thirst. **durst‖en** *v* be thirsty. **-ig** *adj* thirsty. **-stillend** *adj* thirst-quenching.
Dusche ['duʃə] *f* (*pl* **-n**) shower. **duschen** *v* shower, have *or* take a shower.
Düse ['dyzə] *f* (*pl* **-n**) jet, nozzle. **Düsen‖antrieb** *m* jet propulsion. **-flugzeug** *neut* jet (plane).
düster ['dystər] *adj* dark; (*fig*) gloomy.
Dutzend ['dutsənt] *neut* (*pl* **-e**) dozen.
duzen ['duːtsən] *v* address familiarly (using du), be on first-name terms with.
Dynamik [dy'naimik] *f* dynamics. **dynamisch** *adj* dynamic.
Dynamit [dyna'miːt] *neut* (*unz.*) dynamite.
Dynamo [dy'naimo] *m* (*pl* **-s**) dynamo.
Dynastie [dynas'tiː] *f* (*pl* **-n**) dynasty.
D-Zug ['deːtsuk] *m* (*pl* **D-Züge**) express train.

E

Ebbe ['ɛbə] f (pl **-n**) ebb; (Niedrigwasser) low tide. **ebben** v ebb.
eben ['eɪbən] adj level, even. adv just. ich war eben abgereist I had just left. **eben deswegen** for that very reason. **Ebenbild** neut image. **ebenbürtig** adj equal (in rank). **Ebene** f (pl **-n**) plain; (Math) plane. **ebenfalls** adv likewise. **Eben‖heit** f evenness, smoothness. **–holz** neut ebony. **ebenso** adv just so. **–gut** adv just as well. **–viel** adv just as much.
Eber ['eɪbər] m (pl **-**) boar.
ebnen ['eɪbnən] v level, smooth.
Echo ['ɛçoɪ] neut (pl **-s**) echo.
echt [ɛçt] adj genuine, real. **Echtheit** f genuineness, authenticity.
Eck [ɛk] neut (pl **-e**) corner. **–ball** m corner (kick). **–e** f corner, angle. **eckig** adj angular. **Eckzahn** m eyetooth.
edel ['eɪdəl] adj noble. **Edel‖mann** m nobleman. **–metall** neut precious metal. **–stein** m precious stone, gemstone.
Edikt [e'dikt] neut (pl **-e**) edict.
Efeu ['eɪfɔy] m ivy.
Effekten [ɛ'fɛktən] pl effects, personal belongings; (Komm) bonds, shares. **Effekthascherei** f sensationalism. **effekt‖iv** adj effective, actual. **–voll** adj effective.
egal [e'gaɪl] adj equal, (all) the same. das ist mir ganz egal it's all the same to me.
Egoismus [ego'ismus] m (pl **Egoismen**) selfishness, egotism. **Egoist** m egotist. **egoistisch** adj egotistic, selfish.
ehe ['eɪə] conj, adv before. **–malig** adj former.
Ehe ['eɪə] f (pl **-n**) marriage. **–brecher** m adulterer. **–brecherin** f adulteress. **ehebrecherisch** adj adulterous. **Ehe‖bruch** m adultery. **–frau** f wife, married woman. **ehe‖lich** adj matrimonial, conjugal. **–los** adj unmarried, single. **Ehe‖mann** m husband. **–paar** neut married couple.
eher ['eɪər] adv sooner; (lieber) rather.
Ehre ['eɪrə] f (pl **-n**) honour. **ehren** v honour. **–haft** adj honourable. **Ehrenmal** neut war memorial. **ehrenvoll** adj honourable.
Ehrfurcht ['eɪrfurçt] f awe. **ehrfürchtig** adj full of awe or reverence.
Ehr‖gefühl neut sense of honour, self-

respect. **–geiz** m ambition. **ehrgeizig** adj ambitious.
ehrlich ['eɪrliç] adj honest, sincere. **Ehrlichkeit** f honesty. **ehrlos** adj dishonourable. **Ehrung** f (pl **-en**) honour, award. **ehrwürdig** adj venerable.
Ei [ai] neut (pl **-er**) egg. **–abstoßung** f ovulation. **–dotter** m yolk.
Eiche ['aiçə] f (pl **-n**) oak. **Eich‖el** f acorn. **–hörnchen** neut squirrel.
Eid [ait] m (pl **-e**) oath. **einen Eid ablegen** swear an oath.
Eidechse ['aidɛksə] f (pl **-n**) lizard.
Eidgenosse m confederate. **–nschaft** f confederacy; (Schweiz) Switzerland. **eidgenössisch** adj confederate; (schweizerisch) Swiss.
Eier‖becher ['aiərbɛçər] m eggcup. **–kuchen** m omelette. **–schale** f eggshell. **–stock** m ovary.
Eifer ['aifər] m (unz.) fervour, zeal. **–sucht** f jealousy. **eifersüchtig** adj jealous. **eifrig** adj eager, zealous. **Eifrigkeit** f zeal.
Eigelb ['aigɛlp] neut (pl **-e**) (egg) yolk.
eigen ['aigən] adj own; (eigentümlich) particular; (eigenartig) peculiar. **sich etwas zu eigen machen** get or acquire something. **etwas auf eigene Faust unternehmen** do something of one's own accord.
Eigenart f (pl **-en**) peculiarity. **eigenartig** adj peculiar.
eigen‖händig adj by oneself. **–mächtig** adj arbitrary.
Eigen‖name m proper name. **–nutz** m self-interest.
Eigenschaft f (pl **-en**) quality, attribute, trait. **–swort** neut adjective.
Eigensinn m obstinacy. **eigensinnig** adj obstinate, headstrong.
eigen‖ständig adj independent. **–süchtig** adj egoistic.
eigentlich ['aigəntliç] adv actually, really. adj real, actual.
Eigentum ['aigəntuɪm] neut (pl **Eigentümer**) property. **Eigentümer** m owner. **eigentümlich** adj peculiar.
eignen ['aignən] v **sich eignen für** or **zu** be suited for.
Eil‖bote ['ailboɪtə] m (pl **-n**) courier, express messenger. **–brief** m express letter.
Eile ['ailə] f haste, hurry. **eilen** v hurry, hasten. **eilig** adj hasty, fast. **Eil‖sendung** f

(*Post*) special delivery. **–zug** *m* fast train, limited-stop train.
Eimer ['aimər] *m* (*pl* -) bucket, pail.
ein [ain], **eine, ein** *art* a, an. *pron, adj* one.
einander [ain'andər] *pron* each other, one another.
einatmen ['ainaːtmən] *v* inhale, breathe in. **Einatmung** *f* inhalation.
Einbahnstraße ['ainbaːnʃtraːsə] *f* one-way street.
einbalsamieren [ainbaːlza'miːrən] *v* embalm.
Einband ['ainbant] *m* binding, cover (of book).
Einbau ['ainbau] *m* installation. **einbauen** *v* install, build in; (*fig*) incorporate (into).
*einbegreifen ['ainbəgraifən] *v* include, comprise. **mit einbegriffen** included.
*einbiegen ['ainbiːgən] *v* bend in; (*Straße*) turn into.
einbilden ['ainbildən] *v* **sich einbilden** imagine. **Einbildung** *f* imagination; (*Dünkel*) conceit. **–svermögen** *neut* (power of) imagination.
Einblick ['ainblik] *m* insight.
*einbrechen ['ainbreçən] *v* break open; (*Haus*) break into, burgle. **Einbrecher** *m* burglar. **Einbruch** *m* break-in, burglary; (*Mil*) invasion. **–sdiebstahl** *m* burglary.
einbürgern ['ainbyrgən] *v* naturalize. **sich einbürgen** become naturalized; (*Wort, usw.*) come into use, gain acceptance. **Einbürgerung** *f* naturalization.
eindeutig ['aindɔytiç] *adj* unequivocal, clear.
*eindringen ['aindriŋən] *v* enter by force; (*Mil*) invade. **eindringlich** *adj* urgent.
Eindruck ['aindruk] *m* impression. **eindrücken** *v* press in. **sich eindrücken** leave an impression. **eindrucksvoll** *adj* impressive.
einerlei ['ainərlai] *adj* of one kind. **est ist einerlei** it makes no difference.
einerseits ['ainərzaits] *adv* on (the) one hand.
einfach ['ainfax] *adj* simple; (*nicht doppelt*) single. **Einfachheit** *f* simplicity.
*einfahren ['ainfaːrən] *v* drive in; (*Mot*) run in; (*einbringen*) bring in. **Einfahrt** *f* entrance, way in; (*Hineinfahren*) arrival, entrance.
Einfall ['ainfal] *m* idea, inspiration; (*Mil*) invasion, assault. **einfallen** *v* fall in;

(*idee*) occur (to). **es fällt mir ein** it strikes me.
einfältig ['ainfɛltiç] *adj* naive, artless. **Einfältigkeit** *f* naivety, artlessness.
einfetten ['ainfɛtən] *v* grease, lubricate.
*einfinden ['ainfindən] *v* **sich einfinden** appear, turn up.
*einflechten ['ainfleçtən] *v* interweave; (*Wort*) put in.
Einflug ['ainfluːk] *m* incursion; (*Aero*) approach.
Einfluß ['ainflus] *m* influence. **einflußreich** *adj* influential.
einförmig ['ainfœrmiç] *adj* monotonous, uniform.
einfügen ['ainfyːgən] *v* fit in.
einfühlen ['ainfyːlən] *v* **sich einfühlen in** sympathize with, get into the spirit of. **Einfühlung** *f* sympathizing, sympathy.
Einfuhr ['ainfuːr] *f* (*pl* -en) import. **einführen** *v* bring in; (*Waren*) import; (*Gebrauch*) introduce. **Einfuhrhandel** *m* import trade. **Einführung** *f* introduction. **Einfuhrverbot** *neut* import ban.
Eingang ['aingaŋ] *m* way in; (*Ankunft*) arrival; (*Einleitung*) introduction.
eingebildet ['aingəbildət] *adj* conceited; (*erfunden*) imaginary.
eingeboren ['aingəboːrən] *adj* native; (*angeboren*) innate. **Eingeborene(r)** *m* native.
Eingebung ['aingeːbuŋ] *f* (*pl* -en) inspiration.
*eingehen ['aingeːən] *v* go *or* enter into; (*aufhören*) stop; (*welken*) decay; (*Risiko*) run; (*zustimmen*) agree. **–d** *adj* thorough, detailed.
eingemacht ['aingəmaxt] *adj* bottled; canned; (*Fleisch*) potted.
eingenommen ['aingenɔmən] *adj* biased (in favour of).
Eingeweide ['aingəvaidə] *neut* (*pl* -) intestines *pl*, entrails *pl*.
Eingeweihte(r) ['aingəvaitə(r)] *m* (*pl* -) initiate.
eingewöhnen ['aingəvœːnən] *v* accustom. **sich eingewöhnen** become accustomed (to).
*eingießen ['aingiːsən] *v* pour in *or* out.
eingliedern ['aingliːdərn] *v* incorporate; (*einordnen*) classify. **Eingliederung** *f* incorporation; classification.
*eingreifen ['aingraifən] *v* catch (hold of); (*einmischen*) interfere. **Eingriff** *m*

catch; interference; (*Übergriff*) encroachment.
*einhalten ['ainhaltən] *v* restrain, check; observe; stop.
einhändig ['ainhɛndig] *adj* with one hand. **–en** *v* hand in.
einheimisch ['ainhaimiʃ] *adj* native, indigenous.
Einheit ['ainhait] *f* (*pl* -en) unit; (*Pol*) unity. **einheitlich** *adj* uniform.
einholen ['ainhoilən] *v* collect; (*einkaufen*) shop, buy; (*erreichen*) catch up with.
einig ['ainiç] *adj* united, at one. **einig sein** be in agreement. **–en** *v* unite. **sich einigen** agree.
einiger ['ainigər], **einige, einiges** *pron* some, any. **einigermaßen** *adv* to some extent.
Einigkeit *f* (*unz.*) unity; (*Eintracht*) agreement. **Einigung** *f* unification; agreement.
einjährig ['ainjɛiriç] *adj* one-year-old; (*Bot*) annual.
einkassieren ['ainkasiirən] *v* cash (in).
Einkauf ['ainkauf] *m* (*pl* **Einkäufe**) purchase. **einkaufen** *v* buy, purchase. **einkaufen gehen** go shopping.
einkehren ['ainkeirən] *v* call in (at).
Einklang ['ainklaŋ] *m* (*pl* **Einklänge**) harmony.
*einkommen ['ainkɔmən] *v* come in, arrive. **Einkommen** *neut* income.
einkreisen ['ainkraisən] *v* encircle.
Einkünfte ['ainkynftə] *pl* revenue, income *sing*.
*einladen ['ainlaidən] *v* invite. **Einladung** *f* (*pl* -en) invitation.
Einlage ['ainlaigə] *f* (*pl* -n) lining, filler; (*Brief*) enclosure; (*Geld*) deposit.
Einlaß ['ainlas] *m* (*pl* **Einlässe**) admission; (*Öffnung*) inlet. **einlassen** *v* let in, admit.
*einlaufen ['ainlaufən] *v* arrive; (*Wasser*) run in.
einleben ['ainleibən] *v* **sich einleben in** accustom oneself to.
einlegen ['ainleigən] *v* enclose, insert; (*Beschwerde*) file; (*Fleisch*) salt, pickle.
einleiten ['ainlaitən] *v* introduce, initiate; (*beginnen*) start. **Einleitung** *f* introduction.
einlösen ['ainlœizən] *v* redeem. **Einlösung** *f* payment, redemption.
einmachen ['ainmaxən] *v* (*Obst*) preserve, bottle.

einmal ['ainmal] *adv* once. **auf einmal** all at once. **noch einmal** (once) again. **nicht einmal** not even. **–ig** *adj* unique.
Einmarsch ['ainmarʃ] *m* (*pl* **Einmärsche**) marching in, entry. **einmarschieren** *v* enter, march in (to).
einmischen ['ainmiʃən] *v* **sich einmischen in** interfere *or* meddle in.
einmünden ['ainmyndən] *v* run *or* flow (into), join.
Einnahme ['ainnaimə] *f* (*pl* -n) receipts *pl*, takings *pl*, revenue.
*einnehmen ['ainneimən] *v* take (in); (*Geld*) receive.
Einöde ['ainœidə] *f* (*pl* -n) desert, wasteland.
einölen ['ainœilən] *v* oil.
einordnen ['ainɔrdnən] *v* order, arrange; (*Mot*) get in lane.
einpacken ['ainpakən] *v* pack, wrap up.
einpökeln ['ainpœikəln] *v* pickle.
einprägen ['ainprɛigən] *v* imprint. **jemandem etwas einprägen** impress something on somebody.
einrahmen ['ainraimən] *v* frame.
einräumen ['ainrɔymən] *v* tidy up, put away; (*zugeben*) concede; (*einrichten*) furnish; (*Platz*) vacate, give up.
Einrede ['ainreidə] *f* (*pl* -n) objection. **einreden** *v* persuade; (*widersprechen*) contradict.
einreichen ['ainraiçən] *v* hand over *or* in.
Einreise ['ainraisə] *f* (*pl* -n) entry.
einrichten ['ainriçtən] *v* arrange, set up; (*gründen*) establish; (*Zimmer*) furnish. **Einrichtung** *f* establishment; arrangement; (*Anstalt*) institution; (*Zimmer*) fittings *pl*, furnishings *pl*.
einrücken ['ainrykən] *v* enter.
eins [ains] *pron* one.
einsam ['ainzaim] *adj* lonely, solitary. **Einsamkeit** *f* loneliness.
Einsatz ['ainzats] *m* (*pl* **Einsätze**) insertion; insert, filling; (*Spiel*) stake; (*Mil*) mission, operation.
einschalten ['ainʃaltən] *v* switch on; (*einfügen*) insert, put in. **Einschaltung** *f* switching on; insertion.
einschiffen ['ainʃifən] *v* bring on board, load (into a ship). **sich einschiffen** go on board, embark.
*einschlafen ['ainʃlaifən] *v* go to sleep, fall asleep.

Einschlag ['ainʃlaik] *m* (*pl* **Einschläge**) impact; (*Umschlag*) wrapper. **einschlagen** *v* drive in, break; (*einwickeln*) wrap; (*Weg*) take, follow; (*Hände*) shake hands; (*zustimmen*) agree.

*einschließen ['ainʃliisən] *v* lock up *or* in; (*umfassen*) comprise, include; (*umzingeln*) encircle. **einschließlich** *adj* inclusive; *prep* including, inclusive of. **Einschluß** *m* (*pl* **Einschlüsse**) inclusion.

einschmeicheln ['ainʃmaiçəln] *v* **sich einschmeicheln bei** ingratiate oneself with.

einschränken ['ainʃrɛnkən] *v* restrict, limit. **Einschränkung** *f* restriction, limitation.

Einschreibebrief ['ainʃraibəbriif] *m* registered letter. **einschreiben** *v* register; (*eintragen*) inscribe, write in. **per Einschreiben** *adv* (by) registered mail. **Einschreibung** *f* registration.

einschüchtern ['ainʃyçtərn] *v* intimidate.

*einsehen ['ainzeiən] *v* inspect, look over; (*prüfen*) examine; (*begreifen*) realize.

einseitig ['ainzaitiç] *adj* one-sided; (*Pol*) unilateral.

einsenden ['ainzɛndən] *v* send in.

einsetzen ['ainzɛtsən] *v* set in, put in; (*Amt*) install; begin; (*Geld*) deposit.

Einsicht ['ainziçt] *f* (*pl* **-en**) insight; (*Verständnis*) understanding. **einsichtsvoll** *adj* judicious, sensible.

Einsiedler ['ainziidlər] *m* (*pl* **-**) hermit.

einspannen ['ainʃpanən] *v* (*Pferd*) harness; (*mit Rahmen*) stretch.

einsperren ['ainʃpɛrən] *v* lock in *or* up; (*Gefängnis*) imprison, jail.

einspritzen ['ainʃpritsən] *v* inject.

Einspruch ['ainʃprux] *m* (*pl* **Einsprüche**) objection, protest. **Einspruch erheben gegen** raise an objection against.

einst [ainst] *adv* (*Vergangenheit*) once, at one time; (*Zukunft*) some day, one day.

einstecken ['ainʃtɛkən] *v* put in; (*in die Tasche*) pocket.

*einsteigen ['ainʃtaigən] *v* (*Auto, Schiff, usw.*) get in, get on, board.

einstellen ['ainʃtɛlən] *v* cease, stop; (*tech*) adjust; (*phot*) focus; (*radio, usw.*) tune. **-bar** *adj* adjustable. **Einstellung** *f* stop, suspension; adjustment; (*Ansicht*) attitude.

einstig ['ainstiç] *adj* former.

einstimmen ['ainʃtimən] *v* agree; join (in). **einstimmig** *adj* unanimous.

einstmalig ['ainstmailiç] *adj* former.

einstöckig ['ainʃtœkiç] *adj* one-storeyed.

*einstoßen ['ainʃtoisən] *v* push *or* drive in(to); (*Tür*) knock *or* break down.

einströmen ['ainʃtrœimən] *v* flow *or* stream in(to).

einstufen ['ainʃtuifən] *v* classify, grade.

einstürmen ['ainʃtyrmən] *v* rush in; (*angreifen*) attack.

Einsturz ['ainʃturts] *m* (*pl* **Einstürze**) downfall, collapse. **einstürzen** *v* collapse; (*niederreißen*) knock down, demolish.

einstweilen ['ainstvailən] *adv* meanwhile, for the time being. **einstweilig** *adj* temporary, provisional.

eintägig ['aintɛigiç] *adj* one-day.

Eintausch ['aintauʃ] *m* exchange. **eintauschen** *v* exchange, trade.

einteilen ['aintailən] *v* divide up, classify; (*Skala*) graduate; (*Arbeit*) plan out.

eintönig ['aintœiniç] *adj* monotonous.

Eintopf ['aintɔpf] *m* stew, casserole.

Eintracht ['aintraxt] *f* (*unz.*) harmony, unity.

Eintrag ['aintraik] *m* (*pl* **Einträge**) (*Komm*) entry; (*Schaden*) damage. **eintragen** *v* carry in; (*einschreiben*) enter; (*einbringen*) yield. **einträglich** *adj* profitable. **Eintragung** *f* entry.

*eintreten ['aintreitən] *v* come in; (*eindrücken*) kick in; (*beitreten*) join; (*geschehen*) occur.

Eintritt ['aintrit] *m* entrance; (*Anfang*) beginning. **-skarte** *f* admission ticket.

einverleiben ['ainfɛrlaibən] *v* incorporate.

einverstanden ['ainfɛrʃtandən] *adj* in agreement. **einverstanden sein mit** agree with, approve of.

Einwand ['ainvant] *m* (*pl* **Einwände**) objection. **einwandfrei** *adj* perfect, faultless.

Einwanderer ['ainvandərər] *m* (*pl* **-**) immigrant. **einwandern** *v* immigrate. **Einwanderung** *f* immigration.

einwärts ['ainvɛrts] *adv* inwards.

einwechseln ['ainvɛksəln] *v* change; exchange.

Einwegflasche ['ainveikflaʃə] *f* non-returnable bottle.

einweichen ['ainvaiçən] *v* soak, steep.

einweihen ['ainvaiən] *v* inaugurate; (*Person*) initiate; (*Kirche*) consecrate. **Einweihung** *f* inauguration; initiation; consecration.

Einwendung ['ainvɛnduŋ] *f* (*pl* -en) objection.
einwickeln ['ainvikəln] *v* wrap (up).
einwilligen ['ainviligən] *v* consent, agree. **Einwilligung** *f* consent.
einwirken ['ainvirkən] *v* **einwirken auf** influence, affect. **Einwirkung** *f* influence.
Einwohner ['ainvoɪnər] *m* (*pl* -) inhabitant.
Einzahl ['aintsaɪl] *f* (*unz.*) (*Gramm*) singular.
einzahlen ['aintsaɪlən] *v* pay in, deposit.
Einzel‖erscheinung ['aintsəlɛrʃainuŋ] *f* (isolated) phenomenon. **–fall** *m* individual case. **–handel** *m* retail trade. **–handelsgeschäft** *neut* retail shop. **–händler** *m* retailer. **–haus** *neut* detached house. **–heit** *f* detail. **–kind** *neut* only child. **einzeln** *adj* single; (*getrennt*) isolated; (*alleinstehend*) detached. **einzelnstehend** *adj* detached. **Einzelzimmer** *neut* single room.
einziehen ['aintsiɪən] *v* pull *or* draw in; (*einkassieren*) collect; (*beschlagnahmen*) confiscate; (*Rekruten*) draft; (*Wohnung*) move in.
einzig ['aintsiç] *adj* only, single.
Einzug ['aintsuɪk] *m* entry, entrance; (*Wohnung*) moving in.
Eis [ais] *neut* (*unz.*) ice; (*Speise*) ice-cream. **–bahn** *f* ice/skating rink. **–bär** *m* polar bear. **–bein** *neut* knuckle of pork. **–berg** *m* iceberg.
Eischale ['aiʃaɪlə] *f* eggshell.
Eisen ['aizən] *neut* (*pl* -) iron. **–bahn** *f* railway. **–händler** *m* ironmonger. **–waren** *f pl* ironmongery.
eisern ['aizərn] *adj* iron.
eisig ['aiziç] *adj* icy. **eiskalt** *adj* ice-cold.
Eis‖lauf *m* skating. **–läufer** *m* (*pl* -) skater. **–laufbahn** *f* skating rink. **–meer** *neut* polar sea. **–regen** *m* freezing rain. **–tüte** *f* ice-cream cone/cornet. **–vogel** *m* kingfisher. **–würfel** *m* ice cube. **–zapfen** *m* icicle.
eitel ['aitəl] *adj* vain. **Eitelkeit** *f* vanity.
Eiter ['aitər] *m* (*unz.*) pus. **eitern** *v* fester, suppurate.
Eiweiß ['aivais] *neut* (*pl* -e) egg-white; protein; albumen. **–stoff** *m* protein.
Ekel ['eɪkəl] *m* (*unz.*) disgust, repugnance. **ekelhaft** *adj* loathsome, disgusting. **sich ekeln** be disgusted by.
Ekzem [ɛk'tseɪm] *neut* (*pl* -e) eczema.

elastisch [e'lastiʃ] *adj* elastic.
Elefant [ele'fant] *m* (*pl* -en) elephant.
elegant [ele'gant] *adj* elegant. **Eleganz** *f* elegance.
elektrifizieren [elɛktrifi'tsiɪrən] *v also* **elektrisieren** electrify. **Elektriker** *m* electrician. **elektrisch** *adj* electric(al). **Elektrizität** *f* electricity.
Elektro‖gerät [e'lɛktrogərɛit] *neut* electric appliance. **–installateur** *m* electrician. **–motor** *m* electric motor.
Elektronik [elɛk'troɪnik] *f* electronics. **elektronisch** *adj* electronic.
Elektrotechnik [elɛktro'tɛçnik] *f* electrical engineering.
Element [ele'mɛnt] *neut* (*pl* -e) element; (*Zelle*) battery. **elementar** *adj* elementary.
elend ['eɪlɛnt] *adj* miserable. **Elend** *neut* misery. **–sviertel** *neut* slums *pl*.
elf [ɛlf] *pron, adj* eleven.
Elf [ɛlf] *m* (*pl* -en) elf, fairy.
Elfenbein ['ɛlfənbain] *neut* (*unz.*) ivory.
elfte [ɛlftə] *adj* eleventh.
Elite [e'liɪtə] *f* (*pl* -n) elite.
Ellbogen ['ɛlboɪgən] *m* (*pl* -) elbow.
Ellipse ['ɛlipsə] *f* (*pl* -n) ellipse. **elliptisch** *adj* elliptical.
Elsaß ['ɛlsas] *neut* Alsace. **Elsässer** *m* (*pl* -), **Elsässerin** *f* (*pl* -nen) Alsatian. **elsässisch** *adj* Alsatian.
Elster ['ɛlstər] *f* (*pl* -n) magpie.
Eltern ['ɛltərn] *pl* parents. **elterlich** *adj* parental.
Email [e'maɪj] *neut* (*pl* -s) enamel.
emanzipieren [emantsi'piɪrən] *v* emancipate. **Emanzipation** *f* emancipation.
Empfang [ɛm'pfaŋ] *m* (*pl* **Empfänge**) welcome, reception. **empfangen** *v* welcome, receive; (*Kind*) conceive. **Empfänger** *m* receiver. **empfänglich** *adj* susceptible. **Empfängnis** *f* conception. **–verhütung** *f* contraception.
*empfehlen [ɛm'pfeɪlən] *v* recommend. **–swert** *adj* to be recommended. **Empfehlung** *f* recommendation. **–sschreiben** letter of recommendation.
empfinden [ɛm'pfindən] *v* feel. **empfindlich** *adj* sensitive; (*reizbar*) touchy. **Empfindung** *f* feeling; (*Wahrnehmung*) perception.
empor [ɛm'poɪr] *adv* up(wards). **–ragen** *v* tower (up/over). **–streben** *v* struggle up(wards).

empören [ɛm'pœɪrən] v shock, revolt; (erregen) stir up. **sich empören** rebel.
emsig ['ɛmzɪç] adj diligent, industrious.
Ende ['ɛndə] neut (pl -n) end.
endemisch [ɛn'deɪmɪʃ] adj endemic.
enden ['ɛndən] v finish, end. **end‖gültig** adj final. –**lich** adv finally, at last; adj final; (beschränkt) finite. –**los** adj endless, infinite.
End‖punkt m end (point). –**spiel** neut (Sport) final. –**station** f terminus. –**zweck** m (ultimate) goal or purpose.
Energie [enɛr'giː] f (pl -n) energy. –**krise** energy crisis. **energisch** adj energetic.
eng [ɛŋ] adj narrow; (dicht) tight, close; (Freund) close. **Enge** f narrowness; tightness; (Klemme) difficulty.
Engel ['ɛŋəl] m (pl -) angel. **engelhaft** adj angelic.
England ['ɛŋlant] neut England. **Engländer** m (pl -) Englishman. **Engländerin** f (pl -nen) Englishwoman. ich bin Engländer(in) I am English. **englisch** adj English.
Engpaß ['ɛŋpas] m narrow pass; (verkehr) bottleneck; (Klemme) difficulty, tight spot.
engros [ā'groɪ] adv wholesale.
engstirnig ['ɛŋʃtirnɪç] adj narrow-minded.
Enkel ['ɛŋkəl] m (pl -) grandson. –**in** f granddaughter. –**kind** neut grandchild.
enorm [e'nɔrm] adj enormous.
entarten [ɛnt'aɪrtən] v degenerate. **Entartung** f degeneracy, degeneration.
entbehrlich [ɛnt'beɪrlɪç] adj dispensable, (to) spare.
*entbinden [ɛnt'bindən] v release, set free; (eine Frau) deliver. **Entbindung** f release, setting free; (Geburt) delivery.
entblößen [ɛnt'blœɪsən] v uncover; (berauben) deprive, rob.
entdecken [ɛnt'dɛkən] v discover. **Entdecker** m discoverer. **Entdeckung** f discovery.
Ente ['ɛntə] f (pl -n) duck; (Falschmeldung, Lüge) hoax, canard.
entehren [ɛnt'eɪrən] v dishonour, disgrace.
enteignen [ɛnt'aignən] v expropriate, dispossess. **Enteignung** f expropriation; seizure.
enterben [ɛnt'ɛrbən] v disinherit.
*entfallen [ɛnt'falən] v fall or slip from; (Gedächtnis) slip, escape.
entfalten [ɛnt'faltən] v unfold; (zeigen) display. (Mil) deploy; **Entfaltung** f unfolding; display; deployment; development.
entfernen [ɛnt'fɛrnən] v remove. **sich entfernen** go away, withdraw. **Entfernung** f distance; (Wegbringen) removal.
entflammen [ɛnt'flamən] v inflame, kindle.
*entfliehen [ɛnt'fliɪən] v flee from.
entfremden [ɛnt'frɛmdən] v alienate, estrange. **Entfremdung** f alienation, estrangement.
entführen [ɛnt'fyɪrən] v abduct; (Flugzeug) hijack. **Entführer** m abductor, kidnapper; hijacker. **Entführung** f abduction, kidnapping; hijacking.
entgegen [ɛnt'geɪgən] prep against, contrary to; (hinzu) towards. adv towards. –**kommen** v meet; (Kompromiß) make concessions. –**sehen** v look forward to. –**treten** v move towards; (widerstehen) oppose. –**wirken** v work against.
entgegnen [ɛnt'geɪgnən] v retort, answer back.
*entgehen [ɛnt'geɪən] v escape from.
Entgelt [ɛnt'gɛlt] neut (unz.) compensation.
entgiften [ɛnt'giftən] v decontaminate.
entgleisen [ɛnt'glaizən] v be or become derailed. **Entgleisung** f derailment.
entgräten [ɛnt'grɛɪtən] v bone; fillet (fish).
enthaaren [ɛnt'haɪrən] v remove hair from, depilate.
*enthalten [ɛnt'haltən] v hold, contain. **sich enthalten** refrain (from). **enthaltsam** adj abstemious. **Enthaltung** f abstention.
enthaupten [ɛnt'hauptən] v behead, decapitate.
enthüllen [ɛnt'hylən] v uncover, reveal.
Enthusiasmus [ɛntuzi'asmus] m (unz.) enthusiasm. **enthusiastisch** adj enthusiastic.
entkernen [ɛnt'kɛrnən] v (Obst) stone.
entkleiden [ɛnt'klaidən] v (Person) undress, strip; (wegnehmen) divest. **sich entkleiden** undress.
*entkommen [ɛnt'kɔmən] v escape.
entkuppeln [ɛnt'kupəln] v disconnect; (Mot) declutch.
entladen [ɛnt'laɪdən] v unload; (Gewehr, Batterie) discharge.
entlang [ɛnt'laŋ] prep, adv along. –**fahren** v travel along. –**gehen** walk along.
*entlassen [ɛnt'lasən] v dismiss, discharge, (umg.) fire, sack; (Gefangene) release. **entlassen werden** be dismissed,

(*coll*) get the sack. **Entlassung** *f* dismissal, discharge; release.
entlasten [ɛnt'lastən] *v* unburden; (*erleichtern*) relieve; (*Bank*) credit; (*Verdachtsperson*) clear, exonerate.
entleeren [ɛnt'leırən] *v* empty. **sich entleeren** relieve oneself.
entlegen [ɛnt'leıgən] *adj* remote.
entmilitarisieren [ɛntmilitari'ziırən] *v* demilitarize.
entmutigen [ɛnt'muıtigən] *v* discourage. **Entmutigung** *f* discouragement.
Entnahme [ɛnt'naımə] *f* (*unz.*) taking *or* drawing out; (*Geld*) withdrawal; (*Strom*) use.
entnazifizieren [ɛntnatsifi'tsiırən] *v* denazify.
***entnehmen** [ɛnt'neımən] *v* take away *or* out; (*folgern*) conclude, infer; (*Geld*) withdraw; (*Strom*) use. **Entnehmer** *m* (*Komm*) drawer (of bills); (*Strom*) user.
entrahmen [ɛnt'raımən] *v* skim (milk).
entrüsten [ɛnt'rystən] *v* irritate, anger. **Entrüstung** *f* indignation, anger.
entsagen [ɛnt'zaıgən] *v* renounce, give up.
entschädigen [ɛnt'ʃɛıdigən] *v* compensate. **Entschädigung** *f* compensation.
Entscheid [ɛnt'ʃait] *m* (*pl* -e) decision.
entscheiden *v* decide. **sich entscheiden** decide, resolve, make up one's mind. **entscheidend** *adj* decisive. **Entscheidung** *f* decision; (*Urteil*) sentence.
entschieden [ɛnt'ʃiıdən] *adj* determined, resolute. *adv* decidedly. **Entschiedenheit** *f* determination.
***entschließen** [ɛnt'ʃliısən] *v* **sich entschließen** decide, determine.
entschlossen [ɛnt'ʃlɔsən] *adj* determined, resolute.
Entschluß [ɛnt'ʃlus] *m* (*pl* **Entschlüsse**) decision. **-kraft** *f* power of decision, decisiveness.
entschuldigen [ɛnt'ʃuldigən] *v* excuse, pardon. **sich entschuldigen** apologize, excuse oneself. **entschuldigen Sie!** excuse me! **Entschuldigung** *f* apology; *interj* I'm sorry! pardon me!
entsetzen [ɛnt'zɛtsən] *v* horrify, appal; (*von einem Posten*) dismiss; (*Mil*) relieve. **Entsetzen** *neut* horror. **entsetzlich** *adj* dreadful, horrible. **entsetzt** *adj* horrified, shocked.
entspannen [ɛnt'ʃpanən] *v* relax, release. **sich entspannen** relax, calm down. **Entspannung** *f* relaxation; (*Pol*) détente.

***entsprechen** [ɛnt'ʃprɛçən] *v* correspond (to); (*Anforderung*) comply with. **entsprechend** *adj* corresponding, appropriate.
***entspringen** [ɛnt'ʃpriŋən] *v* escape from, run away from.
entstammen [ɛnt'ʃtamən] *v* descend (from).
***entstehen** [ɛnt'ʃteıən] *v* arise, originate. **Entstehung** *f* origin.
enttäuschen [ɛnt'tɔyʃən] *v* disappoint. **enttäuscht** *adj* disappointed. **Enttäuschung** *f* disappointment.
entvölkern [ɛnt'fœlkərn] *v* depopulate.
***entwachsen** [ɛnt'vaksən] *v* grow out of.
entwaffnen [ɛnt'vafnən] *v* disarm.
entwässern [ɛnt'vɛsərn] *v* drain; (*austrocknen*) dehydrate. **Entwässerung** *f* drainage; dehydration.
entweder [ɛnt'veıdər] *conj* either.
***entweichen** [ɛnt'vaiçən] *v* escape.
entweihen [ɛnt'vaiən] *v* desecrate, profane.
***entwerfen** [ɛnt'vɛrfən] *v* design, plan; (*skizzieren*) sketch; (*Fassung*) draft, draw up.
entwerten [ɛnt'vɛrtən] *v* devalue; (*Briefmarke*) cancel. **Entwertung** *f* devaluation; cancellation.
entwickeln [ɛnt'vikəln] *v* develop. **sich entwickeln** develop. **Entwicklung** *f* development. **Entwicklungs∥land** *neut* developing country. **-lehre** *f* theory of evolution.
entwirren [ɛnt'virən] *v* disentangle.
entwischen [ɛnt'viʃən] *v* slip *or* steal away from.
entwürdigen [ɛnt'vyrdigən] *v* degrade, debase.
Entwurf [ɛnt'vurf] *m* (*pl* **Entwürfe**) design, plan; (*Skizze*) sketch; (*Fassung*) draft.
entwurzeln [ɛnt'vurtsəln] *v* uproot; (*vernichten*) eradicate.
***entziehen** [ɛnt'tsiıən] *v* take away, withdraw; (*rauben*) deprive.
entziffern [ɛnt'tsifərn] *v* decipher, make out.
entzücken [ɛnt'tsykən] *v* delight, enchant. **Entzücken** *neut* delight, enchantment. **entzückt** *adj* delighted, enchanted. **entzückend** *adj* delightful, enchanting.
entzündbar [ɛnt'tsyntbair] *adj* inflammable. **entzünden** *adj* kindle, light. **sich entzünden** catch fire. **Entzündung** *f* ignition; (*med*) inflammation.

entzwei [ɛnt'tsvai] *adv* in two, asunder. –brechen *v* break in two.

Enzyklopädie [ɛntsyklopɛ'diː] *f* (*pl* -n) encyclopedia.

Epidemie [epide'miː] *f* (*pl* -n) epidemic. epidemisch *adj* epidemic.

Epilepsie [epilɛp'siː] *f* (*unz.*) epilepsy. Epileptiker *m* epileptic. epileptisch *adj* epileptic.

Episode [epi'zoːdə] *f* (*pl* -n) episode.

er [ɛr] *pron* he.

erachten [ɛr'axtən] *v* think, consider. Erachten *neut* opinion, judgment. meines Erachtens in my opinion.

Erbarmen [ɛr'barmən] *neut* (*unz.*) pity, compassion. erbärmlich *adj* pitiful, pitiable. erbarmungs‖los *adj* merciless, pitiless. –voll *adj* compassionate, merciful.

erbauen [ɛr'bauən] *v* build, erect.

Erbe ['ɛrbə] *m* (*pl* -n) heir; *neut* (*unz.*) inheritance. Erbeinheit *f* gene. erben *v* inherit. Erb‖fehler *m* hereditary defect. –feind *m* traditional enemy. –gut *neut* inheritance; (*Erbhof*) ancestral estate. erblich *adj* hereditary.

erbittern [ɛr'bitərn] *v* embitter. erbittert *adj* embittered, bitter.

erblassen [ɛr'blasən] *v* grow pale.

erblicken [ɛr'blikən] *v* glimpse, catch sight of.

erblinden [ɛr'blindən] *v* blind.

*erbrechen [ɛr'brɛçən] *v* sich erbrechen vomit.

Erbschaft ['ɛrpʃaft] *v* (*pl* -en) legacy, inheritance.

Erbse ['ɛrpsə] *f* (*pl* -n) pea.

Erd‖beben ['ɛːrtbeːbən] *neut* (*pl* -) earthquake. –beere *f* strawberry. –boden *m* earth, soil.

Erde ['eːrdə] *v* (*pl* -n) earth. erden *v* (*Strom*) earth.

*erdenken [ɛr'dɛŋkən] *v* think of, think out; (*erfinden*) invent.

Erdgas *neut* natural gas.

erdichten [ɛr'diçtən] *v* fabricate, invent. Erdichtung *f* fabrication, invention.

Erd‖kreis *m* globe, earth. –kunde *f* geography. erdkundlich *adj* geographic(al). Erd‖nuß *f* peanut. –öl *neut* oil, petroleum.

erdrosseln [ɛr'drɔsəln] *v* strangle.

erdulden [ɛr'duldən] *v* endure.

ereignen [ɛr'aignən] *v* sich ereignen happen. Ereignis *neut* event, occurrence.

*erfahren [ɛr'faːrən] *v* experience; (*hören, lernen*) learn, hear of. *adj* experienced, proficient. Erfahrung *f* experience.

erfassen [ɛr'fasən] *v* seize; (*einschließen*) include; (*begreifen*) understand, grasp.

*erfinden [ɛr'findən] *v* invent. Erfinder *m* inventor. erfinderisch *adj* inventive. Erfindung *f* invention.

Erfolg [ɛr'fɔlk] *m* (*pl* -e) success; (*Ergebnis*) result, outcome. Erfolg haben achieve success, succeed. erfolgen *v* result, follow. erfolg‖los *adj* unsuccessful. –reich *adj* successful.

erforderlich [ɛr'fɔrdərliç] *adj* necessary. erfordern *v* require, need; (*verlangen*) demand. Erfordernis *neut* necessity; (*Voraussetzung*) requirement.

erforschen [ɛr'fɔrʃən] *v* investigate. Erforsch‖er *m* investigator. –ung *f* investigation.

erfreuen [ɛr'frɔyən] *v* delight. sich erfreuen an enjoy, take delight in. erfreulich *adj* gratifying. erfreut *adj* gratified.

*erfrieren [ɛr'friːrən] *v* freeze to death. Erfrierung *f* frostbite.

erfrischen [ɛr'friʃən] *v* refresh. –d *adj* refreshing. Erfrischung *f* refreshment.

erfüllen [ɛr'fylən] *v* fill; (*Aufgabe*) carry out; (*Bitte, Forderung*) comply with, fulfil. Erfüllung *f* accomplishment, fulfilment.

ergänzen [ɛr'gɛntsən] *v* supplement, add to; (*vervollständigen*) complete. Ergänzung *f* supplement; completion.

*ergeben [ɛr'geːbən] *v* yield. sich ergeben surrender; (*folgen*) result. Ergebenheit *f* devotion; (*Fügsamkeit*) submissiveness. Ergebnis *neut* result.

*ergehen [ɛr'geːən] *v* (*Gesetz*) be promulgated, come out.

ergiebig [ɛr'giːbiç] *adj* productive, profitable.

*ergreifen [ɛr'graifən] *v* grasp, seize; (*rühren*) touch, move (deeply). –d *adj* touching, affecting. Ergreifung *f* seizure.

erhaben [ɛr'haːbən] *adj* exalted, sublime.

*erhalten [ɛr'haltən] *v* receive, obtain; (*bewahren*) preserve, maintain. erhältlich *adj* available, obtainable. Erhaltung *f* preservation, maintenance.

*erheben [ɛr'heːbən] *v* lift up; (*Einspruch*) raise. sich erheben rise (up). Anspruch erheben auf lay claim to. erheblich *adj* considerable. Erhebung *f* uprising.

erheitern [ɛr'haitərn] *v* cheer up; (*unterhalten*) amuse. **sich erheitern** (*Himmel*) brighten, clear up.

erhitzen [ɛr'hitsən] *v* heat (up); (*Person*) inflame.

erhöhen [ɛr'høːən] *v* raise, heighten. **Erhöhung** *f* raising, heightening.

erholen [ɛr'hoːlən] *v* **sich erholen** recover, get better; (*sich ausruhen*) rest. **Erholung** *f* recovery; rest; (*Unterhaltung*) recreation.

erinnern [ɛr'inərn] *v* remind. **sich erinnern an** remember. **Erinnerung** *f* (*pl* -en) memory, remembrance.

erkälten [ɛr'kɛltən] *v* cool. **sich erkälten** catch (a) cold. **Erkältung** *f* (*pl* -en) (*Med*) cold.

erkennbar [ɛr'kɛnbair] *adj* recognizable.

erkennen *v* recognize; (*Fehler*) acknowledge; (*merken*) perceive.

Erkenntnis¹ [ɛr'kɛntnis] *neut* (*pl* -se) judgment, sentence.

Erkenntnis² *f* (*pl* -se) recognition; (*Einsicht*) understanding.

Erkenn‖ung [ɛr'kɛnuŋ] *f* (*pl* -en) recognition. **-ungswort** *neut* password. **-ungszeichen** *neut* distinguishing mark.

Erkerfenster ['ɛrkərfɛnstər] *neut* bay window.

erklären [ɛr'klɛːrən] *v* explain; (*aussprechen*) declare. **sich erklären** declare oneself. **Erklärung** *f* explanation; declaration.

erkranken [ɛr'kraŋkən] *v* fall ill, become sick.

erkundigen [ɛr'kundigən] *v* **sich erkundigen** (nach) inquire (about). **Erkundigung** *f* inquiry.

erlangen [ɛr'laŋən] *v* obtain, acquire; (*erreichen*) get to, reach.

Erlaß [ɛr'las] *m* (*pl* Erlässe) decree, edict.

*erlassen [ɛr'lasən] *v* issue; (*befreien*) release, absolve.

erlauben [ɛr'laubən] *v* permit. **Erlaubnis** *f* permission.

erläutern [ɛr'lɔytərn] *v* explain, elucidate. **Erläuterung** *f* explanation; *pl* commentary, notes.

erleben [ɛr'leːbən] *v* live through, experience. **Erlebnis** *neut* (*pl* -se) experience.

erledigen [ɛr'leːdigən] *v* take care of, deal with; (*beenden*) finish (off). **erledigt** *adj* settled; (*erschöpft*) exhausted. **Erledigung** *f* (*pl* -en) carrying out, execution.

erlegen [ɛr'leːgən] *v* kill.

erleichtern [ɛr'laiçtərn] *v* ease, aid, lighten. **Erleichterung** *f* (*pl* -en) relief.

*erleiden [ɛr'laidən] *v* suffer, undergo.

erlernen [ɛr'lɛrnən] *v* learn, acquire.

Erlös [ɛr'løːs] *m* (*pl* -e) proceeds *pl*.

*erlöschen [ɛr'løːʃən] *v* go *or* die out.

ermächtigen [ɛr'mɛçtigən] *v* authorize, empower.

ermahnen [ɛr'maːnən] *v* admonish.

Ermangelung [ɛr'maŋəluŋ] *f* (*pl* -) **in Ermangelung** in the absence *or* default (of).

ermäßigen [ɛr'mɛːsigən] *v* reduce, lower. **Ermäßigung** *f* reduction.

ermitteln [ɛr'mitəln] *v* ascertain, find out.

ermöglichen [ɛr'møːkliçən] *v* enable, render possible.

ermorden [ɛr'mɔrdən] *v* murder, assassinate.

ermüden [ɛr'myːdən] *v* tire out; grow tired.

ermuntern [ɛr'muntərn] *v* encourage, cheer up.

ermutigen [ɛr'muːtigən] *v* encourage. **Ermutigung** *f* encouragement.

ernähren [ɛr'nɛːrən] *v* feed, nourish. **sich ernähren** support oneself. **Ernährer** *m* breadwinner. **Ernährung** *f* nourishment.

*ernennen [ɛr'nɛnən] *v* appoint, designate. **Ernennung** *f* appointment.

erneuern [ɛr'nɔyərn] *v* renew; renovate, restore. **Erneuerung** *f* renewal; renovation. **erneut** *adj* repeated; *adv* again.

erniedrigen [ɛr'niːdrigən] *v* lower; (*degradieren*) degrade, humble.

ernst [ɛrnst] *adj* serious, grave. **Ernst** *m* seriousness, gravity. **im Ernst** in earnest. **ernsthaft** *adj* earnest, serious. **-lich** *adj* serious.

Ernte ['ɛrntə] *f* (*pl* -n) harvest; (*Wein*) vintage. **ernten** *v* harvest, reap.

ernüchtern [ɛr'nyçtərn] *v* disillusion, disenchant; (*vom Rausch*) sober (up). **sich ernüchtern** sober up. **Ernüchterung** *f* disillusionment; sobering up.

Eroberer [ɛr'oɪbərər] *m* (*pl* -) conqueror. **erobern** *v* conquer. **Eroberung** *f* conquest.

eröffnen [ɛr'œfnən] *v* open; (*anfangen*) open, begin. **Eröffnung** *f* opening, beginning.

erörtern [ɛr'œrtərn] *v* discuss. **Erörterung** *f* discussion.

Erotik [e'roːtik] *f* (*unz.*) eroticism.
erotisch *adj* erotic.
erpressen [ɛr'prɛsən] *v* (*Sache*) extort;
(*Person*) blackmail. **Erpresser** *m* blackmailer. **erpresserisch** *adj* extortionate.
Erpressung *f* blackmail, extortion.
erproben [ɛr'proːbən] *v* try (out), test.
Erprobung *f* trial, test.
*****erraten** [ɛr'raːtən] *v* guess.
errechnen [ɛr'rɛçnən] *v* calculate.
erregen [ɛr'reːgən] *v* excite; (*hervorrufen*)
create, produce. **erregbar** *adj* excitable.
erregend *adj* exciting. **erregt** *adj* excited.
Erregung *f* excitement.
erreichen [ɛr'raiçən] *v* attain, reach.
erreichbar *adj* attainable. **Erreichung** *f*
attainment.
errichten [ɛr'riçtən] *v* erect, build;
(*gründen*) set up, establish.
erröten [ɛr'rœːtən] *v* blush.
Errungenschaft [ɛr'ruŋənʃaft] *f* (*pl* -en)
achievement.
Ersatz [ɛr'zats] *m* (*unz.*) substitute;
(*Wiedergutmachung*) compensation;
(*Nachschub*) reinforcements *pl*. –**kaffee**
m coffee substitute. –**rad** *neut* spare
wheel. –**spieler** *m* (*Sport*) substitute.
–**teil** *neut* spare part.
*****erschaffen** [ɛr'ʃafən] *v* create. **Erschaffer**
m creator. **Erschaffung** *f* creation.
*****erscheinen** [ɛr'ʃainən] *v* appear.
Erscheinung *f* phenomenon; (*Aussehen*)
appearance.
*****erschießen** [ɛr'ʃiːsən] *v* shoot (dead).
Erschießungskommando *neut* firing
squad.
*****erschließen** [ɛr'ʃliːsən] *v* open up; (*folgern*) infer, deduce.
erschöpfen [ɛr'ʃœpfən] *v* exhaust, use up;
(*Person*) exhaust, tire out. **erschöpft** *adj*
exhausted. **Erschöpfung** *f* exhaustion.
*****erschrecken** [ɛr'ʃrɛkən] *v* scare, frighten;
be frightened *or* scared. **Erschrecken**
neut fright. **erschreckend** *adj* frightening.
erschrocken [ɛr'ʃrɔkən] *adj* frightened,
terrified. **Erschrockenheit** *f* fright, terror.
erschüttern [ɛr'ʃytərn] *v* shake; (*Person*)
shake, disturb, shock. **Erschütterung** *f*
shock.
erschweren [ɛr'ʃveːrən] *v* make (more)
difficult, aggravate.
*****ersehen** [ɛr'zeːən] *v* perceive, see.
ersetzen [ɛr'zɛtsən] *v* replace; (*Schaden*)
make good. **ersetzlich** *adj* replaceable,
renewable.

ersichtlich [ɛr'ziçtliç] *adj* evident.
*****ersinnen** [ɛr'zinən] *v* contrive, devise.
ersparen [ɛr'ʃpaːrən] *v* save.
erst [eːrst] *adj* first. *adv* at first; (*nur*)
only, just.
erstarren [ɛr'ʃtarən] *v* stiffen, become rigid; (*Flüssigkeit*) congeal, solidify. **Erstarrung** *f* stiffness.
erstatten [ɛr'ʃtatən] *v* restore; (*ersetzen*)
replace. **Bericht erstatten** report, make a
report. **Erstattung** *f* restitution.
Erstaufführung ['eːrstauffyːruŋ] *f* (*pl* -en)
première, first performance.
erstaunen [ɛr'ʃtaunən] *v* astonish; be
astonished. **Erstaunen** *neut* astonishment, amazement. **erstaunlich** *adj* astonishing.
erste(r) ['eːrstə(r)], **erste, erste(s)** *adj* first.
erstens ['eːrstəns] *adv* first(ly).
ersticken [ɛr'ʃtikən] *v* suffocate; (*fig*) stifle. **erstickend** *adj* suffocating. **Erstickung**
f suffocation; stifling.
erst‖klassig *adj* first-class. –**malig** *adj* for
the first time, first-time.
erstrecken [ɛr'ʃtrɛkən] *v* **sich erstrecken**
stretch, extend.
ertappen [ɛr'tapən] *v* catch, surprise. **auf
frischer Tat ertappen** catch red-handed.
Ertrag [ɛr'traːk] *m* (*pl* **Erträge**) profit;
(*Boden*) yield. **ertragen** *v* bear, stand.
erträglich *adj* bearable, tolerable.
ertränken [ɛr'trɛŋkən] *v* (cause to) drown.
*****ertrinken** [ɛr'triŋkən] *v* drown, be
drowned.
erwachen [ɛr'vaxən] *v* awake, wake up.
*****erwachsen** [ɛr'vaksən] *v* grow up.
Erwachsene(r) *m* adult.
*****erwägen** [ɛr'vɛːgən] *v* consider, weigh.
Erwägung *f* consideration.
erwähnen [ɛr'vɛːnən] *v* mention.
Erwähnung *f* mention.
erwärmen [ɛr'vɛrmən] *v* warm, heat.
erwarten [ɛr'vartən] *v* expect. **über
Erwarten** better than expectation. **wider
Erwarten** contrary to expectation. **Erwartung** *f* (*pl* -en) expectation.
erwecken [ɛr'vɛkən] *v* awaken; (*erregen*)
arouse, rouse.
*****erweisen** [ɛr'vaizən] *v* prove; (*Dienst*)
render, do; (*Ehrung*) pay. **sich erweisen
als** prove to be.
erweitern [ɛr'vaitərn] *v* enlarge, widen,
extend. **Erweiterung** *f* (*pl* -en) extension,
enlargement.

Erwerb [ɛr'vɛrp] *m* (*pl* **-e**) acquisition; (*Lohn*) earnings. **erwerben** *v* acquire; (*Verdienen*) earn. **erwerbstätig** *adj* (gainfully) employed. **Erwerbung** *f* acquisition.

erwidern [ɛr'viːdərn] *v* reply; (*vergelten*) retaliate. **Erwiderung** *f* reply.

erwischen [ɛr'viʃən] *v* (*Person*) catch.

erwünscht [ɛr'vynʃt] *adj* desired, wishedfor.

erwürgen [ɛr'vyrgən] *v* strangle.

Erz [ɛrts] *neut* (*pl* **-e**) ore.

erzählen [ɛr'tsɛːlən] *v* tell, relate. **Erzähler** *m* narrator; story-teller. **erzählerisch** *adj* narrative. **Erzählung** *f* story.

Erz‖bischof *n* archbishop. **–engel** *m* archangel.

erzeugen [ɛr'tsɔygən] *v* (*herstellen*) produce; (*Strom*) generate; (*Kinder*) procreate. **Erzeuger** *m* producer; father, procreator. **Erzeugnis** *neut* product(ion); (*Boden*) produce.

Erz‖feind *m* arch-enemy. **–herzog** *m* archduke. **–herzogin** *f* archduchess.

*erziehen [ɛr'tsiːən] *v* (*Tiere, Menschen*) bring up; (*Bildung*) educate. **Erzieher** *m* educator. **erzieherisch** *adj* educational. **Erziehung** *f* upbringing; (*Bildung*) education.

erzogen [ɛr'tsoːgən] *adj* **gut/schlecht erzogen** well/badly brought up.

es [ɛs] *pron* it.

Esche ['ɛʃə] *f* (*pl* **-n**) ash (tree).

Esel ['eɪzəl] *m* (*pl* **-**) donkey, ass. **eselhaft** *adj* asinine. **Eselsohr** *neut* dog's-ear (on page).

esoterisch [ezo'teːriʃ] *adj* esoteric.

Essay ['ɛse] *m, neut* (*pl* **-s**) essay.

eßbar ['ɛsbar] *adj* edible.

essen ['ɛsən] *v* eat. **zu Mittag essen** lunch, have lunch. **zu Abend essen** dine, have supper. **Essen** *neut* food; (*Mahlzeit*) meal.

Essig ['ɛsiç] *m* (*pl* **-e**) vinegar. **–gurke** *f* pickled cucumber, gherkin.

Eß‖kastanie *f* sweet chestnut. **–löffel** *m* tablespoon. **–tisch** *m* dinner table. **–zimmer** *neut* dining room.

etablieren [eta'bliːrən] *v* establish.

Etage [e'taːʒə] *f* (*pl* **-n**) storey, floor. **–nwohnung** *f* flat, (*US*) apartment.

Etat [e'taː] *m* (*pl* **-s**) budget; (*Komm*) balance-sheet.

Ethik ['eːtik] *f* (*unz.*) ethics. **ethisch** *adj* ethical.

ethnisch ['eɪtniʃ] *adj* ethnic.

Etikett [eti'kɛt] *neut* (*pl* **-e**) tag, label. **Etikette** [eti'kɛtə] *f* (*pl* **-n**) etiquette.

etliche ['ɛtliçə] *pron pl* some, several.

Etui [ɛt'viː] *neut* (*pl* **-s**) (small) case; (*Zigaretten*) cigarette-case; (*Brillen*) spectacles-case.

etwa ['ɛtva] *adv* about, around; (*vielleicht*) perhaps.

etwas ['ɛtvas] *pron* something, anything. *adj* some, any, a little.

Etymologie [etymolo'giː] *f* (*pl* **-n**) etymology.

euch [ɔyç] *pron* you; (to) you.

euer ['ɔyər] *pl adj* your. *pron* yours.

Eule ['ɔylə] *f* (*pl* **-n**) owl.

Eunuch [ɔy'nuːx] *m* (*pl* **-en**) eunuch.

Europa [ɔy'roːpa] *neut* Europe. **Europäer** *m* European. **europäisch** *adj* European. **Europäische Gemeinschaften (EG)** European Community. **Europäische Wirtschaftsgemeinschaft (EWG)** European Economic Community (EEC).

evakuieren [evaku'iːrən] *v* evacuate.

evangelisch [evan'geːliʃ] *adj* Protestant. **Evangelium** *neut* gospel.

eventuell [evɛntu'ɛl] *adj* possible. *adv* possibly, if necessary.

ewig ['eɪviç] *adj* eternal, everlasting. **auf ewig** for ever. **Ewigkeit** *f* eternity.

exakt [ɛ'ksakt] *adj* exact, accurate.

Examen [ɛ'ksaɪmən] *neut* (*pl* **-**, *or* **Examina**) exam(ination).

Exempel [ɛ'ksɛmpəl] *neut* (*pl* **-**) example. **Exemplar** [ɛksɛm'plaɪr] *neut* (*pl* **-e**) specimen; (*Buch*) copy.

Exil [e'ksiːl] *neut* (*pl* **-e**) exile.

Existenz [ɛksis'tɛnts] *f* (*pl* **-en**) existence; (*Unterhalt*) livelihood. **existieren** *v* exist.

exklusiv [ɛksklu'ziːf] *adj* exclusive.

exkommunizieren [ɛkskɔmuni'tsiːrən] *v* excommunicate.

exotisch [ɛ'ksoːtiʃ] *adj* exotic.

Expedition [ɛkspeditsi'oɪn] *f* (*pl* **-en**) expedition; (*Versendung*) dispatching.

Experiment [ɛksperi'mɛnt] *neut* (*pl* **-e**) experiment. **experimentell** *adj* experimental. **experimentieren** *v* experiment.

explodieren [ɛksplo'diːrən] *v* explode. **Explosion** *f* explosion. **explosiv** *adj* explosive.

Export [ɛks'pɔrt] *m* (*pl* **-e**) export. **–eur** *m* exporter. **–handel** *m* export trade. **exportieren** *v* export.

extrem [εks'treɪm] *adj* extreme.
Extrem‖ismus *m* extremism. **–ist(in)**
extremist.
Exzentriker [εk'tsεntrikər] *m* (*pl* -) eccentric. **exzentrisch** *adj* eccentric.

F

Fabel ['faɪbəl] *f* (*pl* -n) fable; (*Handlungsablauf*) plot. **fabelhaft** *adj* fabulous, marvellous.
Fabrik [fa'briːk] *f* (*pl* -en) factory. **–ant** *m* (*pl* -en) manufacturer. **–arbeiter(in)** factory worker. **–at** *neut* (*pl* -e) manufacture. **fabrizieren** *v* manufacture.
Fach [fax] *neut* (*pl* **Fächer**) (*Abteil*) compartment, pigeonhole; (*Wissensgebiet*) subject; speciality. **–arbeiter** *m* skilled worker. **–arzt** *m* medical specialist.
fächeln ['fεçəln] *v* fan. **Fächer** *m* (*pl* -) fan.
Fach‖mann *m* specialist. **–schule** *f* technical college *or* school. **–sprache** *f* technical language, jargon. **–wort** *neut* technical term. **–zeitschrift** *f* technical journal.
Fackel ['fakəl] *f* (*pl* -n) torch.
fade ['faɪdə] *adj* insipid, boring; (*Essen*) tasteless.
Faden ['faɪdən] *m* (*pl* **Fäden**) thread.
Fagott [fa'gɔt] *neut* (*pl* -e) bassoon.
fähig ['fεːiç] *adj* capable, able. **Fähigkeit** *f* (*pl* -en) ability.
fahl [faːl] *adj* pale, sallow.
Fahne ['faːnə] *f* (*pl* -n) flag, standard; (*mil*) colours. **Fahnen‖flucht** *f* desertion. **–flüchtige(r)** *m* deserter. **–stock** *m* flagstaff.
Fahrbahn ['faːrbaɪn] *f* (*Mot*) lane. **fahrbar** *adj* passable; (*Wasser*) navigable; (*beweglich*) mobile.
Fähre ['fεːrə] *f* (*pl* -n) ferry.
***fahren** ['faɪrən] *v* go, travel; (*Mot, Zug*) drive; (*Rad, Motorrad*) ride. **Fahrer** *m* driver.
Fahr‖gast *m* passenger. **–geld** *neut* fare. **–gestell** *neut* (*Mot*) chassis; (*Flugzeug*) undercarriage. **–karte** *f* ticket. **–kartenschalter** *m* ticket office.
fahrlässig ['faːrlεsiç] *adj* careless, negligent.
Fahr‖plan *m* timetable. **–preis** *m* fare.

–prüfung *f* driving test. **–rad** *neut* bicycle. **–schein** *m* ticket. **–schule** *f* driving school. **–stuhl** *m* lift, (*US*) elevator.
Fahrt [faɪrt] *f* (*pl* en) drive, journey.
Fährte ['fεːrtə] *f* (*pl* -n) track, trail.
Fahrzeug ['faɪrtsɔyk] *neut* vehicle.
Faktur [fak'tuːr] *f* (*pl* -en) *also* **Faktura** invoice. **fakturieren** *v* invoice.
Fakultät [fakul'tεːt] *f* (*pl* -en) faculty.
Falke ['falkə] *m* (*pl* -n) hawk, falcon.
Fall [fal] *m* (*pl* **Fälle**) (*Sturz*) fall; (*Angelegenheit*) case. **–beil** *neut* guillotine. **–brücke** *f* drawbridge.
Falle ['falə] *f* (*pl* -n) trap, snare; (*umg.*) bed. **in die Falle gehen** go to bed.
***fallen** ['falən] *v* fall. **Fallen** *neut* fall, decline.
fällen ['fεlən] *v* cut down; (*Urteil*) pass; (*Chem*) precipitate.
fällig ['fεliç] *adj* due.
falls [fals] *conj* if, in case.
Fall‖schirm *m* (*pl* -e) parachute. **–schirmjäger** *m* paratrooper. **–sucht** *f* epilepsy. **–tür** *f* trapdoor.
falsch [falʃ] *adj* false.
fälschen ['fεlʃən] *v* falsify, fake; (*Geld*) counterfeit. **Fälscher** *m* (*pl* -) counterfeiter, forger.
Falschheit ['falʃhait] *f* (*pl* -en) falsehood.
Fälschung ['fεʃuŋ] *f* (*pl* -en) falsification; (*Geld*) forgery, counterfeiting.
Falte ['faltə] *f* (*pl* -n) crease, fold. **falten** *v* crease; (*zusammenlegen*) fold.
familiär [famil'jεːr] *adj* familiar.
Familie [fa'miːliə] *f* (*pl* -n) family. **–stand** *m* personal *or* marital status. **–zulage** *f* family allowance. **Familien‖name** *m* surname.
famos [fa'moːs] *adj* splendid, excellent.
Fanatiker [fa'naːtikər] *m* (*pl* -) fanatic. **fanatisch** *adj* fanatical
Fanfare [fan'faːrə] *f* (*pl* -n) fanfare.
Fang [faŋ] *m* (*pl* **Fänge**) catch. **fangen** *v* catch.
Farbe ['farbə] *f* (*pl* -n) colour. **Farbe bekennen** show one's colours; (*Karten*) follow suit.
färben ['fεrbən] *v* colour, tint; (*Stoff*) dye.
farbenblind ['farbanblint] *adj* colour blind. **Farb‖fernsehen** *neut* colour television. **–film** *m* colour film. **–stoff** *m* dye.
farbig *adj* coloured. **Farbiger(r)** *m* coloured (man). **farblos** *adj* colourless.
Fasan [fa'zaɪn] *m* (*pl* -e) pheasant.

Fasching ['faʃɪŋ] *m* (*pl* -e) carnival.
Faschismus [fa'ʃɪsmus] *m* (*unz.*) fascism.
Faschist *m* (*pl* -en) fascist. **faschistisch** *adj* fascist.
Faser ['faːzər] *f* (*pl* -n) fibre; (*fein*) filament. −**stoff** *m* synthetic fibre, man-made material.
Faß [fas] *neut* (*pl* **Fässer**) barrel, cask, vat. −**bier** *neut* draught beer.
Fassade [fa'saːdə] *f* (*pl* -n) façade.
fassen ['fasən] *v* grasp, seize; (*begreifen*) understand. **sich fassen** pull oneself together; (*ausdrücken*) express oneself.
Fassung *f* (*Kleinod*) mounting; (*Gemütsruhe*) composure; (*Wortlaut*) wording; (*Verständnis*) comprehension. −**skraft** *f* (power of) comprehension.
fast [fast] *adv* almost, nearly.
fasten ['fastən] *v* fast. **Fasten** *neut* fasting. −**zeit** *f* Lent. **Fastnacht** *f* Shrove Tuesday.
fatal [fa'taːl] *adj* disastrous; (*peinlich*) awkward.
faul [faul] *adj* rotten; (*person*) lazy. −**en** *v* rot. −**enzen** *v* idle, be lazy. **Faul‖enzer** *m* loafer. −**heit** *f* laziness, sloth.
Fäulnis ['fɔylnɪs] *f* rottenness, putrefaction.
Faust [faust] *f* (*pl* **Fäuste**) fist. −**handschuh** *m* mitten.
Februar ['feːbruaːr] *m* (*pl* -e) February.
*****fechten** ['fɛçtən] *v* fence, fight (with swords).
Feder ['feːdər] *f* (*pl* -n) feather; (*tech*) spring; (*schreiben*) pen. −**bett** *neut* featherbed. −**gewicht** *neut* featherweight.
federleicht *adj* light as a feather.
Federung *f* suspension, springs *pl*.
Fee [feː] *f* (*pl* -n) fairy.
fegen ['feːgən] *v* sweep.
Fehde ['feːdə] *f* (*pl* -n) feud.
fehlbar ['feːlbaːr] *adj* fallible. **Fehl‖betrag** *m* deficit. −**druck** *m* misprint; (*Briefmarken*) error. **fehlen** *v* (*mangeln*) be missing or lacking; (*abwesend*) be absent; (*irren*) make a mistake. −**d** *adj* missing, absent.
Fehler ['feːlər] *m* (*pl* -) mistake; (*Schwäche*) weakness; (*Mangel*) defect. **fehler‖frei** *adj* flawless. −**haft** *adj* faulty, defective.
Fehlgeburt ['feːlgəburt] *f* miscarriage.
fehlschlagen *v* fail, not succeed.
Fehl‖tritt *m* false move *or* step, slip. −**zündung** *f* (*Mot*) misfire.

Feier ['faiər] *f* (*pl* -n) festival. **Feierabend** *m* evening leisure time, free time. **Feierabend machen** finish work (for the day). **feierlich** *adj* solemn, ceremonial. **feiern** *v* celebrate. **Feiertag** *m* holiday; (*Festtag*) festival.
feige ['faigə] *adj* cowardly.
Feige ['faigə] *f* (*pl* -n) fig.
Feig‖heit *f* (*unz.*) cowardice. −**ling** *m* coward.
feil [fail] *adj* for sale; (*bestechlich*) venal, corrupt.
Feile ['failə] *f* (*pl* -n) file. **feilen** *v* file.
feilschen ['failʃən] *v* haggle.
fein [fain] *adj* fine.
Feind [faint] *m* (*pl* -e) enemy. **feindlich** *adj* hostile. **Feindschaft** *f* enmity, hostility. **feind/schaftlich** *adj* inimical. −**selig** *adj* hostile.
Fein‖gehaltsstempel *m* hallmark (stamp). −**heit** *f* fineness. −**schmecker** *m* gourmet.
Feld [fɛlt] *neut* (*pl* -er) field; (*Schach*) square. −**bau** *m* agriculture. −**blume** *f* wild flower. −**früchte** *f pl* crops. −**herr** *m* commander(-in-chief). −**messer** *m* surveyor. −**zug** *m* campaign.
Fell [fɛl] *neut* (*pl* -e) skin, hide.
Fels [fɛls] *m* (*pl* -en) rock, boulder. −**enklippe** *f* cliff. −**sturz** *m* rockfall.
Femininum [fɛmi'niːnum] *neut* (*pl* **Feminina**) (*Gramm*) feminine (gender).
Fenster ['fɛnstər] *neut* (*pl* -) window.
Ferien ['feːrjən] *neut pl* holiday. **in die Ferien gehen** go on holiday. −**kolonie** *f* holiday-camp. −**ort** *m* holiday resort.
Ferkel ['fɛrkəl] *neut* (*pl* -) piglet.
Ferment [fɛr'mɛnt] *neut* (*pl* -e) enzyme, ferment.
fern [fɛrn] *adj* far(away), distant. −**bleiben** *v* stay away. **Ferne** *f* distance. **ferner** *adj* farther; *adv* further; *conj* in addition. −**hin** *adv* in future.
Fern‖gespräch *neut* (*phone*) long-distance call. −**glas** *neut* telescope. −**laster** *m* long-distance lorry. −**lenkung** *f* remote control. −**meldedienst** *m* telecommunications. −**rohr** *neut* telescope. −**schreiber** *m* teletype machine; Telex. −**sehapparat** *m* television (set). −**sehen** *neut* television. *v* watch television. −**sprecher** *m* telephone. −**straße** *f* trunkroad. −**zug** *m* long-distance train.
Ferse ['fɛrzə] *f* (*pl* -n) heel.

fertig ['fɛrtiç] *adj* (*bereit*) ready; (*beendet*) finished. **−en** *v* produce. **Fertigkeit** *f* (*pl* **-en**) skill, proficiency. **fertigmachen** *v* finish; (*umg.*) beat (into submission).
Fessel ['fɛsəl] *f* (*pl* **-n**) fetter, chain. **fesseln** *v* fetter, chain. **−d** *adj* fascinating; (*bezaubernd*) enchanting.
fest [fɛst] *adj* firm, secure; (*dicht*) solid.
Fest [fɛst] *neut* (*pl* **-e**) festival. **−essen** *neut* banquet.
*****festhalten** ['fɛsthaltən] *v* hold (tight); (*Bild, Buch*) portray; (*anpacken*) seize. **festigen** *v* make firm *or* secure. **Festland** *neut* continent. **festlegen** *v* lay down, fix. **sich festlegen** commit oneself.
festlich ['fɛstliç] *adj* festive. **Festlichkeit** *f* festivity.
fest‖machen *v* fasten; (*vereinbaren*) agree, arrange. **−nehmen** *v* arrest, capture. **−setzen** *v* settle, fix. **Festsetzung** *f* settling, establishment. **fest‖stehen** *v* stand fast. **−stellen** *v* settle; (*herausfinden*) establish, ascertain. **Feststellung** *f* establishment, ascertaining.
Festtag ['fɛsttaik] *m* holiday.
Festung ['fɛstuŋ] *f* (*pl* **-en**) fortress.
Festzug ['fɛsttsuːk] *m* procession.
fett [fɛt] *adj* fat; (*schmierig*) greasy. **Fett** *neut* (*pl* **-e**) fat; grease. **fettig** *adj* fatty; greasy.
Fetzen ['fɛtsən] *m* (*pl* **-**) rag, shred.
feucht [fɔyçt] *adj* damp, moist. **−en** *v* dampen, moisten. **Feuchtigkeit** *f* dampness, moisture.
Feuer ['fɔyər] *neut* (*pl* **-**) fire. **−alarm** *m* fire alarm. **feuer‖beständig** *or* **−fest** *adj* fireproof. **−gefährlich** *adj* inflammable. **Feuerlöscher** *m* fire extinguisher. **feuern** *v* fire. **Feuer‖schaden** *m* fire damage. **−spritze** *f* fire engine. **−stein** *m* flint. **−waffe** *f* gun. **−wehr** *f* fire brigade, (*US*) fire department. **−wehrmann** *m* fireman. **−zeug** *neut* (cigarette) lighter.
Feuilleton ['fœjətɔ̃] *neut* (*pl* **-s**) newspaper supplement, review section.
feurig ['fɔyriç] *adj* fiery.
Fiber ['fiːbər] *f* (*pl* **-n**) fibre.
Fichte ['fiçtə] *f* (*pl* **-n**) fir, spruce (tree).
Fieber ['fiːbər] *neut* (*pl* **-**) fever. **fieberartig** *adj* feverish. **fieberhaft** *adj* feverish.
Fiedel ['fiːdəl] *f* (*pl* **-n**) fiddle, violin. **fiedeln** *v* (play the) fiddle.
Figur [fi'guːr] *f* (*pl* **-en**) figure; (*Schach*) piece, chessman.

fiktiv [fik'tiːf] *adj* fictitious.
Filiale [fili'aːlə] *f* (*pl* **-n**) (*Komm*) branch.
Film [film] *m* (*pl* **-e**) film.
Filter ['filtər] *m* (*pl* **-**) filter. **filtrieren** *v* filter.
Filz [filts] *m* (*pl* **-e**) felt; (*Geizhals*) miser.
Finanz [fi'nants] *f* (*pl* **-en**) finance. **−amt** *neut* tax office, Inland Revenue. **finanziell** *adj* financial. **Finanzier** *m* (*pl* **-s**) financier. **finanzieren** *v* finance. **Finanz‖jahr** *m* financial year. **−minister** *m* finance minister.
*****finden** ['findən] *v* find; (*glauben*) think, believe. **Finder** *m* (*pl* **-**) finder. **findig** *adj* clever, resourceful.
Finger ['fiŋər] *m* (*pl* **-**) finger. **−abdruck** *m* fingerprint. **−hut** *m* thimble; (*Bot*) foxglove. **−nagel** *m* fingernail. **−spitze** *f* fingertip.
Fink [fiŋk] *m* (*pl* **-en**) finch.
Finne ['finə] *m* (*pl* **-**), **Finnin** *f* (*pl* **-nen**) Finn. **finnisch** *adj* Finnish. **Finnland** *neut* Finland. **Finnländer(in)** *f* Finn.
finster ['finstər] *adj* dark; (*düster*) gloomy; (*drohend*) foreboding. **Finsternis** *f* darkness; gloom.
Firma ['firmə] *f* (*pl* **Firmen**) firm, business.
Firnis ['firnis] *m* (*pl* **-se**) varnish.
Fisch [fiʃ] *m* (*pl* **-e**) fish. **Fische** *pl* (*Astrol*) Pisces. **fischen** *v* fish. **Fischer** *m* (*pl* **-**) fisherman. **−boot** *neut* fishing boat. **−ei** *f* fishing. **−korb** *m* creel. **−otter** *m or f* otter. **−reiher** *m* heron. **−zeug** *neut* (*fishing*) tackle.
fix [fiks] *adj* firm; (*fig*) quick.
flach [flax] *adj* flat, even; (*nicht tief*) shallow; (*uninteressant*) dull.
Fläche ['flɛçə] *f* (*pl* **-n**) flatness; (*Gebiet*) area; (*Oberfläche*) surface. **−ninhalt** *m* surface area.
Flachs [flaks] *m* (*unz.*) flax.
flackerig ['flakəriç] *adj* flickering. **flackern** *v* flicker, flare.
Flagge ['flagə] *f* (*pl* **-n**) flag.
Flamme ['flamə] *f* (*pl* **-n**) flame. **flammen** *v* flame, blaze.
Flanell [fla'nɛl] *m* (*pl* **-e**) flannel.
Flanke ['flaŋkə] *f* (*pl* **-n**) flank. **flankieren** *v* (out)flank.
Flasche ['flaʃə] *f* (*pl* **-n**) bottle. **Flaschen‖** *adj* cylindrical. **Flaschenöffner** *m* bottle-opener.
flattern ['flatərn] *v* flutter.

flau [flau] *adj* weak; (*Getränke*) flat; (*Komm*) slack, dull.

Flaum [flaum] *m* (*unz.*) down. **flaumig** *adj* downy.

Flaute ['flautə] *f* (*pl* -n) lull, calm; (*Wirtschaft*) recession.

Flechte ['flɛçtə] *f* (*pl* -n) braid; (*Bot*) lichen; (*Med*) ringworm, herpes. **flechten** *v* braid, interweave; (*Korb*) weave. **Flechtkorb** *m* wicker basket.

Fleck [flɛk] *m* (*pl* -e) stain, spot; (*Makel*) blemish, flaw. **flecken** *v* stain.

Fledermaus ['fleːdərmaus] *f* bat.

flehen ['fleːən] *v* implore, entreat (for). −**tlich** *adj* imploring.

Fleisch [flaiʃ] *neut* (*unz.*) meat. −**brühe** *f* (meat) stock. **Fleischer** *m* (*pl* -) butcher. −**ei** *f* (*pl* -en) butcher's (shop). **fleisch‖farbig** *adj* flesh-coloured. −**fressend** *adj* carnivorous. −**ig** *adj* fleshy. −**lich** *adj* carnal. **Fleisch‖topf** *m* meat saucepan; (*fig*) fleshpot. −**werdung** *f* (*Rel*) Incarnation. −**wolf** *m* mincer.

Fleiß [flais] *m* (*unz.*) diligence, industry. **fleißig** *adj* industrious, hard-working.

Flick [flik] *m* (*pl* -en) patch. −**arbeit** *f* patching; (*Pfuscherei*) botch. **flicken** *v* mend, patch.

Fliege ['fliːgə] *f* (*pl* -n) fly. **fliegen** *v* fly. **Flieger** *m* (*pl* -) aviator, flier. −**abwehr** *f* anti-aircraft defence.

***fliehen** ['fliːən] *v* flee.

Fließband ['fliːsbant] *neut* conveyor belt, assembly line. **fließen** *v* flow. **fließend** *adj* flowing, running.

flimmern ['flimərn] *v* glimmer, twinkle.

flink [fliŋk] *adj* nimble, agile.

Flinte ['flintə] *f* (*pl* -n) musket; (*Schrot*) shotgun.

flirten ['flirtən] *v* flirt.

Flitterwochen ['flitərvɔxən] *f pl* honeymoon *sing*.

Flocke ['flɔkə] *f* (*pl* -n) flake; (*Wolle, Haar*) flock, tuft. **flocken** *v* fall in flakes. **flockig** *adj* flaky; (*Haar, usw.*) fluffy.

Floh [floː] *m* (*pl* Flöhe) flea. −**stich** *m* fleabite.

Floskel ['flɔskəl] *f* (*pl* -n) flowery *or* fine phrase.

Floß [floːs] *neut* (*pl* Flöße) raft.

Flosse ['flɔsə] *f* (*pl* -n) fin.

Flöte ['fløːtə] *f* (*pl* -n) flute. **flöten** *v* play the flute. **Flötist(in)** flautist.

flott [flɔt] *adj* brisk; (*Schnell*) fast;

(*schick*) smart; (*schwimmend*) afloat. **Flotte** *f* fleet, navy.

Flöz [fløːts] *neut* (*pl* -e) (*Mineralien*) seam.

Fluch [fluːx] *m* (*pl* Flüche) curse; (*Fluchwort*) swear-word. **fluchen** *v* swear, curse.

Flucht [fluxt] *f* (*pl* -en) flight, escape; (*Reihe*) row.

flüchtig ['flyçtiç] *adj* fleeting, cursory. **Flüchtling** *m* (*pl* -e) refugee.

Flug [fluːk] *m* (*pl* Flüge) flight, flying; (*Vögel*) flock. −**bahn** *f* trajectory. −**blatt** *neut* handbill, pamphlet.

Flügel ['flyːgəl] *m* (*pl* -) wing; (*Klavier*) grand piano. −**fenster** *neut* French window.

Flug‖gast *m* air passenger. −**hafen** *m* airport. −**post** *f* air-mail. −**schiff** *m* flyingboat. −**schrift** *f* pamphlet. −**wesen** *neut* aviation, flying. −**zeug** *neut* aeroplane. −**zeug-halle** *f* hangar. −**zeug-träger** *m* aircraft-carrier.

flunkern ['fluŋkərn] *v* fib, lie; (*übertreiben*) exaggerate, brag.

Flur [fluːr] *m* (*pl* -e) floor; (entrance) hall.

Fluß [flus] *m* (*pl* Flüsse) river. **fluß‖abwärts** *adv* downstream. −**aufwärts** *adv* upstream. **Flussfisch** *m* fresh-water fish.

flüssig ['flysiç] *adj* liquid. **Flüssigkeit** *f* liquid.

flüstern ['flystərn] *v* whisper.

Flut [fluːt] *f* (*pl* -en) flood; (*Hochwasser*) (high) tide. **Ebbe und Flut** ebb and flow. **fluten** *v* flood.

Fohlen ['foːlən] *neut* (*pl* -) foal.

Föhn [føːn] *m* (*pl* -e) (warm) south wind.

Folge ['fɔlgə] *f* (*pl* -n) succession; (*Wirkung*) consequence. **folgen** *v* follow; (*gehorchen*) obey. **folgend** *adj* (the) following. −**ermaßen** *adv* as follows. **folgerichtig** *adj* consistent, logical. **folgern** *v* conclude, infer. **Folgerung** *f* (*pl* -en) conclusion, inference. **folgewidrig** *adj* inconsistent, illogical. **folglich** *adv* consequently.

Folter ['fɔltər] *f* (*pl* -n) torture; (*Gerät*) rack. **foltern** *v* torture. **Folterung** *f* torture, torturing.

Fön [føːn] *m* (*pl* -e) hairdrier.

Fonds [fɔ̃] *m* (*pl* -) fund.

Förderer ['fœrdərər] *m* (*pl* -) promoter, sponsor. **förderlich** *adj* useful, beneficial.

fordern ['fɔrdərn] v demand; (*beanspruchen*) *claim*.

fördern ['fœɪrdərn] v further, promote.

Forderung ['fɔrdəruŋ] f (pl -en) demand.

Förderung ['fœɪrdəruŋ] f (pl -en) furtherance, advancement; (*Komm*) promotion; (*Kohle*) mining.

Forelle [fo'rɛlə] f (pl -n) trout.

Form [fɔrm] f (pl -en) form; (tech, Kuchen) mould. **in Form** (*sport*) fit, on form. **Formel** f (pl -n) formula. **form‖ell** adj formal. -en v form, shape. -los adj shapeless, formless. **Formular** neut (pl -e) (question) form, (*US*) blank. **formulieren** v formulate.

forschen ['fɔrʃən] v investigate; (*fragen*) inquire; (*Wissenschaft*) do research. **forschend** adj searching. **Forscher** m (pl -) investigator, enquirer; researcher. **Forschung** f (pl -en) investigation; research.

Forst [fɔrst] m (pl -e) forest.

Förster ['fœɪrstər] m (pl -) forester.

Forstwirtschaft ['fɔrstvɪrtʃaft] f forestry.

fort [fɔrt] adv away; (*vorwärts*) forward(s); (*weiter*) on.

fortan [fɔrt'an] adv from now on.

***fortbestehen** ['fɔrtbəʃteɪən] v continue (to exist), live on, survive.

Fortbildung ['fɔrtbɪlduŋ] f further education.

***fortbleiben** ['fɔrtblaɪbən] v remain away.

fortdauern ['fɔrtdauərn] v last, continue. -d adj continual, incessant.

***fortfahren** ['fɔrtfaɪrən] v drive away, depart; (*weitermachen*) proceed, continue.

***fortgehen** ['fɔrtgeɪən] v go away.

fortgeschritten ['fɔrtgəʃrɪtən] adj advanced.

***fortkommen** ['fɔrtkɔmən] v escape; (*fig*) prosper, make progress.

***fortlaufen** ['fɔrtlaufən] v run away; (*fortkommen*) escape; (*weiterlaufen*) continue. -d adj continuous.

fortleben ['fɔrtleɪbən] v survive. **Fortleben** neut survival; (*nach dem Tode*) afterlife.

fortpflanzen ['fɔrtpflantsən] v **sich fortpflanzen** reproduce, multiply; (*Krankheit*) spread.

***fortschreiten** ['fɔrtʃraɪtən] v go forward, proceed.

Fortschritt ['fɔrtʃrɪt] m (pl -e) progress. **fortschrittlich** adj progressive.

fortsetzen ['fɔrtzɛtsən] v continue. **Fortsetzung** f continuation.

fortwährend ['fɔrtvɛɪrənt] adj continuous, incessant.

Fossil [fɔ'siɪl] neut (pl -ien) fossil.

Foto ['foɪto] neut (pl -s) (*umg.*) photo.

Fötus ['fœtus] m (pl -se) foetus.

Fracht [fraxt] f (pl -en) freight. -brief m consignment or dispatch note. -gut neut cargo, goods. -schiff neut merchantman.

Frack [frak] m (pl Fräcke) dresscoat, tails. -hemd neut dress shirt. -zwang m obligatory evening dress, formal dress.

Frage ['fraɪgə] f (pl -n) question. -bogen m questionnaire. **fragen** v ask. **Fragezeichen** neut question mark. **frag‖lich** adj in question, doubtful. -los adj unquestionable.

Fragment [frag'mɛnt] neut (pl -e) fragment.

fragwürdig ['fraɪkvurdiç] adj questionable.

Fraktion [fraktsi'oɪn] f (pl -en) (*Pol*) parliamentary party, faction.

Fraktur [frak'tuɪr] f (pl -en) fracture; (*Druck*) Gothic type or script.

frankieren [fraŋ'kiɪrən] v (*Brief*) stamp; (*Päckchen*) pre-pay. **franko** adv post paid.

Frankreich ['fraŋkraiç] neut France.

Franse ['franzə] f (pl -n) fringe. **fransig** adj fringed; (*ausgefasert*) frayed.

Franzose [fran'tsoɪzə] m (pl -n) Frenchman. **Französin** f (pl -nen) Frenchwoman. **französich** adj French.

Fratze ['fratsə] f (pl -n) grimace. **Fratzen schneiden** make or pull faces.

Frau [frau] f (pl -en) woman; (*Ehefrau*) wife; (*Titel*) Mrs. **Frauen‖arzt** m gynaecologist. -befreiung f women's liberation. **frauenhaft** adj womanly. **Frauen‖rechtlerin** f (pl -nen) feminist. -welt f womankind, women pl.

Fräulein ['frɔylain] neut (pl -) young lady; (*Titel*) Miss.

frech [frɛç] adj cheeky, insolent. **Frechheit** f cheek, insolence.

frei [frai] adj free; (*nicht besetzt*) vacant, unoccupied; (*offen*) candid.

Freibad ['fraibat] neut outdoor swimming pool.

freiberuflich ['fraibəruflɪç] adj freelance, self-employed, professional.

Freibrief ['fraibriɪf] m charter.

Freie ['fraiə] neut (unz.) outdoors, open air. **im Freien** in the open air.

Freigabe ['fraiga:bə] *f* release.
*freigeben ['fraige:bən] *v* set free;
(Straße, usw.) open; (Waren, Arznei)
pass, approve, decontrol. **freigebig** *adj*
generous.
Freihandel ['fraihandəl] *m* free-trade.
Freiheit ['fraihait] *f* (*pl* -en) freedom, liberty. **freiheitlich** *adj* liberal.
Freiherr ['fraihɛr] *m* (*pl* -) baron. **–in** *f*
(*pl* -nen) baroness.
Freikarte ['fraika:rtə] *f* complimentary
ticket.
*freilassen ['frailasən] *v* set free.
freilich ['frailiç] *adv* certainly, indeed, of
course.
freimachen ['fraimaxən] *v* deliver (from
captivity), release.
Freimaurer ['fraimaurər] *m* (*pl* -) freemason.
Freimut ['fraimu:t] *m* (*unz.*) candour,
frankness. **freimütig** *adj* candid, frank.
*freisprechen ['fraiʃprɛçən] *v* acquit, discharge.
Freitag ['fraita:k] *m* Friday.
freiwillig ['fraiviliç] *adj* voluntary.
Freizeit ['fraitsait] *f* leisure time, spare
time.
fremd [frɛmt] *adj* strange; (ausländisch)
foreign. **Fremde(r)** stranger; foreigner.
Fremd‖enzimmer *neut* guest room. **–heit**
f strangeness. **–körper** *m* foreign body.
–sprache *f* foreign language. **–wort** *neut*
foreign word, loan word.
Frequenz [fre'kvɛnts] *f* (*pl* -en) frequency.
*fressen ['frɛsən] *v* eat, devour.
Freude ['frɔydə] *f* (*pl* -n) joy; (Vergnügen)
delight. **–ntag** *m* red-letter day. **freudig**
adj joyful, joyous.
freuen ['frɔyən] *v* give pleasure to. **es freut
mich** I am glad *or* pleased. **sich freuen** be
glad, rejoice. **sich freuen auf** look forward to.
Freund [frɔynt] *m* (*pl* -e) friend;
(Liebhaber) boyfriend. **–in** *f* (*pl* -nen)
(girl) friend. **freundlich** *adj* friendly;
(liebenswürdig) kind. **Freund‖lichkeit** *f*
friendliness. **–schaft** *f* friendship. **freundschaftlich** *adj* friendly.
Frevel ['fre:fəl] *m* (*pl* -) sacrilege.
frevelhaft *adj* sacrilegious.
Friede(n) ['fri:də(n)] *m* (*pl* -) peace.
Friedens‖bruch *m* breach of the peace.
–stifter *m* peacemaker. **–vertrag** *m*
peace (treaty). **Friedhof** *m* cemetary.
friedlich *adj* peaceful.

*frieren ['fri:rən] *v* freeze.
Frikadelle [frika'dɛlə] *f* (*pl* -n) rissole.
frisch [friʃ] *adj* fresh; (lebhaft) lively.
Frische *f* freshness; liveliness.
Friseur [fri'zœːr] *m*, (*pl* -e) **Friseuse** *f* (*pl*
-n) hairdresser; (nur für Herren) barber.
frisieren *v* cut *or* style hair; (Bücher)
cook, falsify; (Mot) soup up. **Frisiersalon**
m hairdressing salon.
Frist [frist] *f* (*pl* -en) period, time;
(Termin) time limit, deadline.
Frisur [fri'zu:r] *f* (*pl* en) hairstyle; (umg.)
hairdo.
froh [fro:] *adj* glad, cheerful, happy.
fröhlich ['frœliç] *adj* cheerful, joyous.
Fröhlichkeit *f* cheerfulness.
frohlocken ['fro:lɔkən] *v* rejoice. **Frohsinn**
m gaiety.
fromm [frɔm] *adj* pious, religious.
frömmelnd ['frœməlnd] *adj* religiose, hypocritical. **Frömmler** *m* hypocritic.
Fronleichnam [fro:n'laiçna:m] *m* Corpus
Christi Day.
Front [frɔnt] *f* (*pl* -en) front, face; (Pol)
front. **–antrieb** *m* front-wheel drive.
Frosch [frɔʃ] *m* (*pl* Frösche) frog;
(Feuerwerk) squib, banger.
Frost [frɔst] *m* (*pl* Fröste) frost; (Kälte)
coldness, chill. **–beule** *f* chilblain. **frostig**
adj chilly, frosty. **Frostschutzmittel** *neut*
antifreeze.
Frucht [fruxt] *f* (*pl* Früchte) fruit.
fruchtbar *adj* fertile. **Fruchtbarkeit** *f* fertility. **fruchtlos** *adj* fruitless. **Fruchtsaft** *m*
fruit juice.
früh [fry:] *adj* early. **Frühe** *f* early hour,
early morning. **früher** *adj* earlier;
(ehemalig) former. **frühestens** *adv* earliest.
Früh‖geburt *f* premature birth. **–jahr**
neut spring. **–ling** *m* spring. **–reife** *f* pre-
cocity. **–stück** *neut* breakfast.
früh‖stücken *v* breakfast. **–zeitig** *adj*
premature, untimely; (rechtzeitig) early,
in good time.
Fuchs [fuks] *m* (*pl* Füchse) fox.
Füchsin ['fyçsin] *f* (*pl* -nen) vixen.
Fuge ['fu:gə] *f* (*pl* -n) joint; (Musik)
fugue.
fügen ['fy:gən] *v* join together; (ordnen)
dispose. **sich fügen** submit. **fügsam** *adj*
submissive, obedient.
fühlen ['fy:lən] *v* touch, feel. **sich fühlen**
feel. **sich glücklich fühlen** feel *or* be hap-

py. **Fühlen** *neut* feeling. **Fühler** *m* feeler. **Fühlung** *f* touch.

führen ['fyːrən] *v* lead, direct; (*Waren*) stock, carry; (*Bücher*) keep. **-d** *adj* prominent, leading. **Führer** *m* leader, guide. **-haus** *neut* (*Zug*) driver's cab. **-schaft** *f* leadership. **-schein** *m* driving licence, (*US*) driver's license. **-sitz** *m* driver's *or* pilot's seat. **Führung** *f* command, management.

Fülle ['fylə] *f* (*pl* -n) abundance, plenty. **Hülle und Fülle** plentiful, in plenty. **füllen** *v* fill (up). **Füll‖feder** *f* fountain-pen. **-ung** *f* (*pl* -en) filling.

Fundament [funda'mɛnt] *neut* (*pl* -e) foundation, base.

fünf [fynf] *adj* five. **fünft** *adj* fifth. **Fünftel** *neut* fifth. **fünf‖zehn** *pron, adj* fifteen.

fungieren [fuŋ'giːrən] *v* function (as), act (as).

Funk [funk] *m* (*unz.*) radio, wireless. **-e** *m* (*pl* -n) spark. **funkeln** *v* sparkle. **Funksendung** *f* (*Radio*) programme transmission.

Funktion [funktsi'oːn] *f* (*pl* -en) function. **-är** *m* (*pl* -e) functionary. **funktionieren** *v* function.

für [fyːr] *prep* for.

Furche ['furçə] *f* (*pl* -n) furrow; (*Runzel*) wrinkle. **furchen** *v* furrow.

Furcht [furçt] *f* (*unz.*) fear. **furchtbar** *adj* frightful.

fürchten ['fyrçtən] *v* fear. **sich fürchten vor** be afraid of. **fürchterlich** *adj* terrible, dreadful.

Furnier [fur'niːr] *neut* (*pl* -e) veneer.

Fürsorge ['fyːrzɔrgə] *f* care; (*Hilfstätigkeit*) welfare work; (*Geld*) social security. **-arbeit** *f* social work.

Fürsprecher ['fyːrʃprɛçər] *m* advocate. **fürsprechen** *v* intercede.

Fürst [fyrst] *m* (*pl* -en) prince. **-in** *f* (*pl* -nen) princess. **fürstlich** *adj* princely.

Furz [furts] *m* (*pl* **Fürze**) (*vulgär*) fart. **furzen** *v* fart.

Fuß [fuːs] *m* (*pl* **Füße**) foot. **-ball** *m* football. **-boden** *m* floor. **-bremse** *f* footbrake. **-gänger** *m* pedestrian. **-pflege** *f* chiropody. **-steig** *m* pavement, (*US*) sidewalk. **-tritt** *m* kick; (*Gang*) step. **-volk** *neut* infantry. **-weg** *m* footpath.

Futter ['futər] *neut* (*pl* -) feed, fodder; (*Kleider*) lining.

füttern ['fytərn] *v* feed; line. **Fütterung** *f* feeding, fodder; lining.

G

Gabe ['gaːbə] *f* (*pl* -n) gift.

Gabel ['gaːbəl] *f* (*pl* -n) fork. **gabeln** *v* fork. **Gabelung** *f* fork, branching.

gackern ['gakərn] *v* cackle.

gähnen ['gɛːnən] *v* yawn.

galant [ga'lant] *adj* polite, gallant.

Galeere [ga'leːrə] *f* (*pl* -n) galley.

Galerie [galə'riː] *f* (*pl* -n) gallery.

Galgen ['galgən] *m* (*pl* -) gallows *pl*.

Galle ['galə] *f* (*pl* -n) gall, bile; (*fig*) rancour.

Gallen‖blase ['galənˌblaːzə] *f* gallbladder. **-stein** *m* gallstone.

Galopp [ga'lɔp] *m* (*pl* -e) gallop. **galoppieren** *v* gallop.

galvanisieren [galvani'ziːrən] *v* galvanize.

Gang [gaŋ] *m* (*pl* **Gänge**) walk; (*Gangart*) gait; (*Flur*) corridor; (*Essen*) course; (*Mot*) gear. **im Gang** in motion. **Gang‖art** *f* gait. **-schalter** *m* gear lever.

Gans [gans] *f* (*pl* **Gänse**) goose.

Gänse‖blume ['gɛnzəˌbluːmə] *f* daisy. **-braten** *m* roast goose. **-füßchen** *pl* quotation marks. **-rich** *m* gander.

ganz [gants] *adj* whole, all; (*vollständig*) complete. *adv* quite; (*vollends*) fully. **Ganze** *neut* whole.

gar [gaːr] *adj* (*Kochen*) done, cooked. *adv* very. **gar nicht** not at all. **gar keiner** none whatever.

Garantie [garan'tiː] *f* (*pl* -n) guarantee.

Garde ['gardə] *f* (*pl* -n) guard.

Garderobe [gardə'roːbə] *f* (*pl* -n) cloakroom; (*Kleider*) wardrobe.

Gardine [gar'diːnə] *f* (*pl* -n) curtain.

*gären ['gɛːrən] *v* ferment.

garnieren [gar'niːrən] *v* garnish; (*Kleidung*) trim.

Garnison [garni'zoːn] *f* (*pl* -en) garrison.

Garnitur [garni'tuːr] *f* (*pl* -en) (*Verzierung*) trimming; (*Satz*) set; (*Ausrüstung*) equipment.

Garten ['gartən] *m* (*pl* **Gärten**) garden. **-bau** *m* horticulture. **-haus** *neut* summer house. **-laube** *f* arbour.

Gärtner ['gɛrtnər] *m* (*pl* -) gardener. **-ei** *f* (*pl* -en) nursery.

Gärung ['gɛɪruŋ] *f* (*pl* -en) fermentation.
Gas [gaɪs] *neut* (*pl* -e) gas. –**flasche** *f* gas cylinder *or* bottle. -**hebel** *m* accelerator. -**hahn** *m* gas cock. -**herd** *m* gas cooker.
Gasse ['gasə] *f* (*pl* -n) alley, lane.
Gast [gast] *m* (*pl* Gäste) guest. **gastfreundlich** *adj* hospitable. **Gast‖freundschaft** *f* hospitality. –**geber** *m* (*pl* -) host. –**geberin** *f* (*pl* -nen) hostess. –**hof** *m* hotel, inn. –**mahl** *neut* banquet. –**stätte** *f* restaurant, café. –**wirt** *m* landlord, innkeeper.
Gatte ['gatə] *m* (*pl* -n) spouse, husband. **gatten** *v* match. **Gattin** *f* (*pl* -nen) spouse, wife.
Gattung ['gatuŋ] *f* (*pl* -en) sort, kind; (*Biol*) species.
gaukeln ['gaukəln] *v* perform tricks, juggle.
Gaul [gaul] *m* (*pl* Gäule) nag.
Gaumen ['gaumən] *m* (*pl* -) palate.
Gauner ['gaunər] *m* (*pl* -) swindler, trickster.
Gaze ['gaɪzə] *f* (*pl* -n) gauze.
Gazelle [ga'tsɛlə] *f* (*pl* -n) gazelle.
geartet [gə'aɪrtət] *adj* constituted, composed.
Gebäck [gə'bɛk] *neut* (*pl* -e) pastry, cakes; (*Keks*) biscuit.
Gebärde [gə'bɛɪrdə] *f* (*pl* -n) gesture.
***gebären** [gə'bɛɪrən] *v* give birth to, bear. **Gebärmutter** *f* womb.
Gebäude [gə'bɔydə] *neut* (*pl* -) building.
***geben** ['geɪbən] *v* give. **sich geben** relent, abate. **es gibt** there is/are. **was gibt es?** what is the matter? **sich zufrieden geben** be content. **das gibt's nicht!** that's impossible! **Geben** *neut* giving. **Geber** *m* (*pl* -), **Geberin** *f* (*pl* -nen) giver, donor.
Gebet [gə'beɪt] *neut* (*pl* -e) prayer. –**buch** *neut* prayerbook.
Gebiet [gə'biɪt] *neut* (*pl* -e) (*Staats-*) territory; (*Gegend*) area, district; (*fig*) field, sphere.
Gebilde [gə'bildə] *neut* (*pl* -) (*Erzeugnis*) product; (*Form*) structure, shape.
gebildet [gə'bildət] *adj* educated, cultured.
Gebirge [gə'birgə] *neut* (*pl* -) mountain range, mountains *pl*.
Gebiß [gə'bis] *neut* (*pl* Gebisse) (set of) teeth; (*Zaum*) bit; (*künstlich*) denture.
Gebläse [gə'blɛɪzə] *neut* (*pl* -) blower, bellows *pl*; (*Mot*) supercharger.
geboren [gə'bɔɪrən] *adj* born. *geborener*

Hamburger native of Hamburg. *Frau Maria Müller, geborene (geb.) Schmidt* Mrs. Maria Müller, nee Schmidt.
Gebot [gə'boɪt] *neut* (*pl* -e) order. **die zehn Gebote** the Ten Commandments.
Gebrauch [gə'braux] *neut* (*pl* Gebräuche) custom; (*Benutzen*) use. **gebrauchen** *v* use. **gebräuchlich** *adj* customary. **Gebrauchs‖anweisung** *f or* –**anleitung** *f* instructions (for use). **Gebrauchtwagen** *m* second-hand car.
gebrechlich [gə'brɛçliç] *adj* (*Gegenstand*) fragile; (*Person*) frail.
Gebrüder [gə'brydər] *m pl* brothers. **Gebrüder Schmidt** Schmidt Bros.
Gebrüll [gə'bryl] *neut* (*unz.*) roar, roaring.
Gebühr [gə'byɪr] **1** *f* (*pl* -en) fee, charge. **2** *f* (*unz.*) decency, propriety. **nach Gebühr** duly. **gebühren** *v* be due. **sich gebühren** be fitting *or* decent. **gebührend** *adj* seemly, proper.
gebunden [gə'bundən] *adj* bound.
Geburt [gə'burt] *f* (*pl* -en) birth. **Geburten‖beschränkung** *f or* –**regelung** *f* birth control. **gebürtig** *adj* born (in). **Geburts‖fehler** *m* congenital defect. –**helfer** *m* obstetrician. –**helferin** *f* midwife; (*Ärztin*) obstetrician. –**hilfe** *f* obstetrics. –**mal** *neut* mole. –**ort** *m* birthplace. –**schein** *m* birth certificate. –**tag** *m* birthday.
Gebüsch [gə'byʃ] *neut* (*pl* -e) (clump of) bushes.
Gedächtnis [gə'dɛçtnis] *neut* (*pl* -se) memory. –**feier** *f* commemoration. –**schwund** *m* loss of memory, amnesia.
Gedanke [gə'daŋkə] *m* (*pl* -n) thought. **sich Gedanken machen über** worry about. **gedankenlos** *adj* thoughtless. **gedanklich** *adj* mental.
Gedeck [gə'dɛk] *neut* (*pl* -e) cover, place-setting; menu.
***gedeihen** [gə'daiən] *v* flourish, thrive.
***gedenken** [gə'dɛŋkən] *v* think (of); (*vorhaben*) intend. **Gendenkfeier** *f* commemoration.
Gedicht [gə'diçt] *neut* (*pl* -e) poem. –**sammlung** *f* anthology (of verse).
gediegen [gə'diɪgən] *adj* (*echt*) genuine; (*rein*) pure; (*solide*) solid; (*sorgfältig*) thorough.
Gedränge [gə'drɛŋə] *neut* (*unz.*) crowd, press; (*Notlage*) difficulty. **gedrängt** *adj* narrow, close; (*Stil*) terse, concise.

gedruckt [gə'drukt] *adj* printed.
gedrückt [gə'drykt] *adj* depressed.
Geduld [gə'dult] *f* patience. **geduldig** *adj* patient. **Geduldspiel** *neut* puzzle.
geehrt [gə'eɪrt] *adj* honoured. **sehr geehrter Herr (Smith)** Dear Sir (Dear Mr Smith).
geeignet [gə'aignət] *adj* suitable, adapted (to).
Gefahr [gə'faɪr] *f* (*pl* -en) danger. **gefährden** *v* endanger, jeopardize. **gefährlich** *adj* dangerous. **gefahr‖los** *adj* safe, without risk. **-voll** *adj* dangerous.
Gefährte [gə'fɛɪrtə] *m* (*pl* -n), **Gefährtin** *f* (*pl* -nen) companion.
***gefallen** [gə'falən] *v* please. **es gefällt mir** I like it. **sich nicht gefallen lassen** not put up with.
Gefallen¹ [gə'falən] *neut* (*unz.*) pleasure.
Gefallen² *m* (*pl* -) favour. **tun Sie mir den Gefallen und . . .** Do me the favour of . . . .
gefällig [gə'fɛlɪç] *adj* pleasing; obliging.
gefangen [gə'faŋən] *adj* captive. **Gefangene(r)** *m* prisoner, captive. **Gefangenschaft** *f* captivity.
Gefängnis [gə'fɛŋnɪs] *neut* (*pl* -se) prison. **-wärter** *m* warder, prison officer.
Gefäß [gə'fɛɪs] *neut* (*pl* -e) container, vessel.
gefaßt [gə'fast] *adj* collected, calm, (*bereit*) ready.
Gefecht [gə'fɛçt] *neut* (*pl* -e) fight, combat.
Gefieder [gə'fiɪdər] *neut* (*unz.*) feathers *pl*, plumage.
Geflügel [gə'flyɪgəl] *neut* (*unz.*) poultry.
Gefolge [gə'fɔlgə] *neut* (*pl* -) followers *pl*, entourage.
gefräßig [gə'frɛɪsɪç] *adj* voracious, gluttonous.
Gefrier‖punkt [gə'friɪrpuŋkt] *m* freezing point. **-schutzmittel** *neut* antifreeze.
gefügig [gə'fyɪgɪç] *adj* pliant, submissive.
Gefühl [gə'fyɪl] *neut* (*pl* -e) feeling. **gefühllos** *adj* unfeeling. **Gefühlssinn** *m* sense of touch. **gefühlvoll** *adj* full of feeling, emotional.
gegebenenfalls [gə'geɪbənənfals] *adv* if need be, should the need arise.
Gegebenheit *f* (*pl* -en) reality.
gegen ['geɪgən] *prep* against; (*in Richtung*) towards; (*ungefähr*) about; compared with; (*Tausch*) in exchange for.

Gegen‖angriff *m* counterattack. **-besuch** *m* return visit. **-bild** *neut* counterpart.
Gegend ['geɪgənt] *f* (*pl* -en) district, area.
gegeneinander ['geɪgənainandər] *adv* against one another. **-stoßen** *v* collide.
Gegen‖gift *neut* antidote. **-leistung** *f* return (service). **-mittel** *neut* remedy. **-satz** *m* opposite, contrary. **gegen‖sätzlich** *adj* opposite, contrary. **-seitig** *adj* reciprocal, mutual. **Gegen‖stand** *m* object; (*Thema*) subject. **-stück** *neut* counterpart. **-teil** *neut* opposite, contrary. **im Gegenteil zu** contrary to, in contrast to.
gegenüber ['geɪgənybər] *adv, prep* opposite. **-liegend** *adj* opposite. **-stehen** *v* stand opposite. **Gegenüberstellung** *f* confrontation; antithesis.
Gegenwart ['geɪgənvaɪrt] *f* (*unz.*) present; (*Anwesenheit*) presence. **gegenwärtig** *adj* present, current.
Gegner ['geɪgnər] *m* (*pl* -) opponent, enemy. **gegnerisch** *adj* antagonistic, hostile.
Gehalt¹ [gə'halt] *m* (*unz.*) contents *pl*; (*Wert*) worth, value.
Gehalt² *neut* (*pl* Gehälter) salary, pay. **Gehalts‖empfänger** *m* salaried employee. **-erhöhung** *f* rise (in salary).
gehässig [gə'hɛsɪç] *adj* spiteful, malicious.
Gehäuse [gə'hɔyzə] *neut* (*pl* -) case, box; (*Tech*) casing.
geheim [gə'haim] *adj* secret. **Geheim‖agent** *m* secret agent. **-dienst** *m* secret *or* intelligence service. **geheimhalten** *v* keep secret. **Geheimnis** *neut* (*pl* -se) secret; (*unerklärbar*) mystery. **geheimnisvoll** *adj* mysterious. **Geheim‖polizei** *f* secret police. **-schrift** *f* code, cipher. **geheimtuerisch** *adj* secretive.
***gehen** ['geɪən] *v* walk, go (on foot); (*Maschine*) go, work. **wie geht es Ihnen?** how are you? **es geht** it's all right. **es geht nicht** it can't be done, that's no good. **sie geht mit ihm** she is going out with him. **an die Arbeit gehen** set to work.
Gehilfe [gə'hilfə] *m* (*pl* -n) assistant, help.
Gehirn [gə'hirn] *neut* (*pl* -e) brain. **-erschütterung** *f* concussion. **-schlag** *m* cerebral apoplexy. **-wäsche** *f* brainwashing.
gehoben [gə'hoɪbən] *adj* high, elevated.
Gehör [gə'hœɪr] *neut* (*unz.*) hearing; (*Musik*) ear.

gehorchen [gə'hɔrçən] *v* obey.
gehören [gə'hœːrən] *v* belong (to). **es gehört sich** it is proper *or* fitting. **gehörig** *adj* fit, proper.
gehorsam [gə'hoːrzaɪm] *adj* obedient. **Gehorsam** *m* obedience. **–sverweigerung** *f* insubordination.
Geh‖steig ['geːʃtaik] *m* (*pl* -e) pavement. **–werk** *neut* movement, works.
Geier ['gaiər] *m* (*pl* -) vulture.
Geifer ['gaifər] *m* (*unz.*) spittle, slaver; (*fig*) venom. **geifern** *v* slaver; (*fig*) rave, foam with rage.
Geige [gaigə] *f* (*pl* -n) violin, fiddle. **–r** *m* violinist.
Geisel ['gaizəl] *m* (*pl* -) hostage.
Geist [gaist] **1** *m* (*unz.*) mind; (*Witzigkeit*) wit; (*nichtmaterielle Eigenschaften*) spirit. **2** *m* (*pl* -er) (*Genius*) genius; (*Gespenst*) ghost, spirit. **geistesabwesend** *adj* absent-minded. **Geistes‖blitz** *m* brainwave. **–freiheit** *f* freedom of thought. **geisteskrank** *adj* mentally ill, insane. **Geisteskranke(r)** *m* mental patient. **geist‖ig** *adj* intellectual; (*nicht körperlich*) spiritual; (*Getränke*) alcoholic. **–lich** *adj* spiritual, religious; (*kirchlich*) clerical. **Geistliche(r)** *m* cleric, clergyman. **geistreich** *adj* clever, ingenious.
Geiz [gaits] *m* (*unz.*) avarice, miserliness. **geizig** *adj* miserly, avaricious.
Gekicher [gə'kiçər] *neut* (*unz.*) giggling.
Geklapper [ge'klapər] *neut* (*unz.*) clatter(ing).
Geklimper [gə'klimpər] *neut* (*unz.*) jingling, chinking; (*Instrument*) strumming.
Geklingel [gə'kliŋəl] *neut* (*unz.*) tinkling, ringing.
gekünstelt [gə'kynstəlt] *adj* artificial, affected.
Gelächter [gə'lɛçtər] *neut* (*pl* -) laughter.
geladen [gə'laɪdən] *adj* loaded; (*Batterie*) charged.
Gelände [gə'lɛndə] *neut* (*pl* -) tract of land, area; (*Bau-*) site; (*Sport-*) grounds *pl*. **–lauf** *m* cross-country (running).
Geländer [gə'lɛndər] *neut* (*pl* -) railing, banister.
gelangen [gə'laŋən] *v* reach, arrive at; (*Ziel*) attain.
gelassen [gə'lasən] *adj* calm, composed.
geläufig [gə'lɔyfiç] *adj* familiar; (*Sprache*) fluent.
gelaunt [gə'launt] *adj* disposed. **gut**

gelaunt sweet-tempered. **schlecht** *or* **übel gelaunt** bad-tempered.
gelb [gɛlp] *adj* yellow. **Gelb** *neut* yellow. **–sucht** *f* jaundice. **gelbsüchtig** *adj* (*Med*) jaundiced.
Geld [gɛlt] *neut* (*pl* -er) money. **–ausgabe** *f* expenditure. **–beutel** *m* purse. **–geber** *m* financial backer. **geldlich** *adj* pecuniary. **Geld‖nehmer** *m* borrower. **–strafe** *f* fine. **–stück** *neut* coin. **–sucht** *f* avarice.
Gelee [ʒe'leː] *neut* (*pl* -s) jelly.
gelegen [gə'leːgən] *adj* situated; (*günstig*) convenient, opportune. **Gelegenheit** *f* (*pl* -en) opportunity, occasion. **Gelegenheits‖arbeit** *f* casual work. **–kauf** *m* bargain. **gelegentlich** *adj* occasional.
gelehrig [gə'leːriç] *adj* eager to learn; (*klug*) intelligent. **gelehrt** *adj* learned. **Gelehrte(r)** *m* scholar.
Geleit [gə'lait] *neut* (*pl* -) escort, entourage. **–brief** *m* (letter of) safe conduct. **geleiten** *v* escort, accompany.
Gelenk [gə'lɛnk] *neut* (*pl* -e) joint. **–entzündung** *f* arthritis.
gelernt [gə'lɛrnt] *adj* skilled, trained.
Geliebte(r) [gə'liːptə] *m* beloved, sweetheart.
gelinde [gə'lində] *adj* gentle, mild.
gelingen [gə'liŋən] *v* succeed, be successful. **es gelingt mir, zu ...** I am able to ....
geloben [gə'loːbən] *v* vow, promise solemnly.
*gelten [gɛltən] *v* be worth, cost; (*gültig sein*) be valid; (*betreffen*) concern. **–d** *adj* valid. **geltend machen** urge, insist (on).
Gelübde [gə'lypdə] *neut* (*pl* -) vow.
Gemach [gə'max] *neut* (*pl* Gemächer) room, chamber.
Gemahl [gə'maːl] *m* (*pl* -e) husband. **–in** *f* (*pl* -nen) wife.
Gemälde [gə'mɛɪldə] *neut* (*pl* -) painting, picture. **–galerie** *f* picture gallery.
gemäß [gə'mɛɪs] *prep* in accordance with. *adj* suitable.
gemein [gə'main] *adj* common; (*öffentlich*) public; vulgar, low; (*böse*) nasty, mean.
Gemeinde [gə'maində] *f* (*pl* -n) community; (*Kommune*) municipality, town; (*Kirche*) congregation. **–rat** *m* local council; (*Person*) councillor. **–schule** *f* village school. **–steuer** *f* rates *pl*.

Gemeine(r) [gə'mainə(r)] *m* (*Mil*) private.
Gemeinheit *f* meanness, nastiness; (*Tat*) mean trick, piece of spite. **gemein‖nützig** *adj* charitable. **–sam** *adj* joint, common.
Gemeinschaft *f* community; (*Komm*) partnership. **–serziehung** *f* coeducation. **–sschule** *f* coeducational school.
Gemenge [gə'mɛŋə] *neut* (*pl* -n) mixture; (*Gewühl*) scuffle.
gemessen [gə'mɛsən] *adj* measured, sedate.
Gemisch [gə'miʃ] *neut* (*pl* -e) mixture. **gemischt** *adj* mixed.
Gemurmel [gə'murməl] *neut* (*unz.*) murmuring.
Gemüse [gə'myːzə] *neut* (*pl* -) vegetable(s). **–gärtner** *m* market gardener. **–händler** *m* greengrocer.
Gemüt [gə'myːt] *neut* (*pl* -er) disposition, temperament, heart. **gemütlich** *adj* comfortable, cosy; (*leutselig*) good-natured. **Gemütlichkeit** *f* cosiness, comfortableness; good-nature.
Gen [gɛn] *neut* (*pl* -e) gene.
genannt [gə'nant] *adj* named, called.
genau [gə'nau] *adj* precise, exact. **Genauigkeit** *f* precision, exactness.
genehmigen [gə'neːmigən] *v* authorize, permit. **Genehmigung** *f* (*pl* -en) authorization, permission.
geneigt [gə'naikt] *adj* disposed, inclined.
General [gene'raːl] *m* (*pl* -e) general. **–police** *f* comprehensive insurance policy. **–probe** *f* dress rehearsal. **–sekretär** *m* secretary-general. **–versammlung** *f* general meeting.
Generation [generatsi'oːn] *f* (*pl* -en) generation.
*****genesen** [gə'neːzən] *v* recover, convalesce, get better. **Genesung** *f* recovery. **–sheim** *neut* convalescent home.
Genetik [ge'neːtik] *f* genetics. **genetisch** *adj* genetic.
Genf [gɛnf] *neut* Geneva.
genial [geni'aːl] *adj* (*Person*) brilliant, gifted; (*Sache*) ingenious, inspired.
Genick [gə'nik] *neut* (*pl* -e) (nape of the) neck.
Genie [ʒe'niː] *neut* (*pl* -s) genius.
genieren [ʒe'niːrən] *v* bother, trouble. **sich genieren** be embarrassed.
genießbar [gə'niːsbaːr] *adj* enjoyable; (*Essen, Trinken*) palatable. **genießen** *v* enjoy; eat; drink. **Genießer** *m* (*pl* -) epicure, gourmet.

Genitalien [geni'taːliən] *pl* genitals.
Genosse [gə'nɔsə] *m* (*pl* -n), **Genossin** *f* (*pl* -nen) comrade; (*Kollege*) colleague. **Genossenschaft** *f* cooperative (society). **genossenschaftlich** *adj* cooperative.
genug [gə'nuːk] *adv*, *adj* enough, sufficient(ly). **genügen** *v* be enough, suffice. **–d** *adj* sufficient, enough. **genügsam** *adj* easily satisfied. **Genugtuung** *f* satisfaction.
Genuß [gə'nus] *m* (*pl* **Genüsse**) pleasure, enjoyment.
Geograph [geo'graːf] *m* (*pl* -en) geographer. **–ie** *f* geography. **geographisch** *adj* geographical.
Geologe [geo'loːgə] *m* (*pl* -n) geologist. **Geologie** *f* geology. **geologisch** *adj* geological.
Geometrie [geome'triː] *f* (*pl* -n) geometry. **geometrish** *adj* geometrical.
Gepäck [gə'pɛk] *neut* (*unz.*) baggage, luggage. **–aufbewahrung** *f* left-luggage office. **–netz** *neut* luggage rack. **–träger** *m* porter.
gepflegt [gə'pfleːkt] *adj* well-tended; (*Person*) well-groomed, well-dressed.
gepanzert [gə'pantsərt] *adj* armoured.
Gepflogenheit [gə'pfloːgənhait] *f* (*pl* -en) habit, custom.
Geplapper [gə'plapər] *neut* (*unz.*) chatter.
Geplauder [gə'plaudər] *neut* (*unz.*) chat, small talk.
Gepräge [gə'prɛːgə] *neut* (*pl* -) stamp; (*Münze*) coinage; (*Eigenart*) character.
Geprassel [gə'prasəl] *neut* (*unz.*) clatter.
gerade [gə'raːdə] *adj* straight; (*direkt*) direct; (*Haltung*) erect; (*Zahl*) even. *adv* just; (*genau*) exactly, precisely; (*direkt*) straight, directly. **–aus** *adv* straight on *or* ahead. **–so** *adv* just so, just the same. **–stehen** *v* stand erect, stand up straight. **–swegs** *adv* immediately; (*ohne Umwege*) directly. **–zu** *adv* directly; (*freimütig*) plainly, flatly; (*durchaus*) sheer, downright. **Geradheit** *f* straightness; (*Ehrlichkeit*) honesty. **gerad‖läufig** *adj* straight. **–zahlig** *adj* even(-numbered).
Geranie [ge'raːniə] *f* (*pl* -n) geranium.
Gerassel [gə'rasəl] *neut* (*unz.*) clatter, rattle.
Gerät [gə'rɛːt] *neut* (*pl* -e) tool, implement; (*kompliziert*) instrument; (*Maschine*) device, appliance; (*Radio, TV*) set; (*Ausrüstung*) equipment.

*geraten [gə'raɪtən] *v* come upon; (*gelingen*) turn out well; (*gedeihen*) thrive. **in Schwierigkeiten geraten** get into difficulties. **in Zorn geraten** fly into a rage. **über etwas geraten** come across, stumble upon something.
Geratewohl [gə'raɪtəvoɪl] *neut* **aufs Geratewohl** at random.
geräumig [gə'rɔymiç] *adj* roomy, spacious.
Geräusch [gə'rɔyʃ] *neut* (*pl* -e) noise.
gerben ['gɛrbən] *v* tan. **Gerber** *m* (*pl* -) tanner. **Gerberei** *f* (*pl* -en) tannery.
gerecht [gə'rɛçt] *adj* just, fair; (*geeignet*) suitable. **-fertigt** *adj* justified; (*legitim*) legitimate. **Gerechtigheit** *f* justice; (*Rechtschaffenheit*) righteousness.
Gerede [gə'reɪdə] *neut* (*unz.*) gossip.
Gericht¹ [gə'riçt] *neut* (*pl* -e) (*Essen*) dish; (*Gang*) course.
Gericht² *neut* (*pl* -e) law-court; (*fig*) justice, judgment. **gerichtlich** *adj* judicial, legal. **Gerichts‖hof** *m* (law) court. **-kosten** *pl* (legal) costs. **-medizin** *f* forensic medicine. **-saal** *m* courtroom. **-schreiber** *m* clerk (of the court). **-verfahren** *neut* legal proceedings *pl*. **-vollzieher** *m* bailiff.
gerieben [gə'riːbən] *adj* grated.
gering [gə'riŋ] *adj* small; (*Vorrat*) short; (*Preis*) low; (*unbedeutend*) unimportant, insignificant. **-fügig** *adj* trivial, insignificant. **-schätzen** *v* think little of, despise. **-schätzig** *adj* disdainful.
gerinnen [gə'rinən] *v* congeal; (*Blut*) clot. **Gerinnsel** *neut* clot.
Gerippe [gə'ripə] *neut* (*pl* -) skeleton.
Germane [gɛr'maɪnə] *m* (*pl* -n), **Germanin** *f* (*pl* -nen) German; *pl* Germanic (tribes or peoples). **germanisch** *adj* Germanic.
gern(e) ['gɛrn(ə)] *adv* willingly, gladly, readily. **gern haben** *or* **mögen** be fond of, like. **gern tun** like to do. *ich möchte gern* ... I should like ... . **gut und gern** easily.
Gerste ['gɛrstə] *f* barley.
Geruch [gə'ruːx] *m* (*pl* Gerüche) smell, odour. **-ssinn** *m* (sense of) smell.
Gerücht [gə'ryçt] *neut* (*pl* -e) rumour.
Gerümpel [gə'rympəl] *neut* junk, trash.
Gerüst [gə'ryst] *neut* (*pl* -e) scaffolding.
gesamt [gə'zamt] *adj* whole, entire. **Gesamt‖betrag** *m* total (amount). **-heit** *f* whole, totality. **-schule** comprehensive

school. **-übersicht** *f* overall view. **-versicherung** *f* comprehsive insurance. **-zahl** *f* total (number).
Gesandte(r) [gə'zantə] *m* (*pl* -n) ambassador. **Gesandtschaft** *f* embassy.
Gesang [gə'zaŋ] *m* (*pl* Gesänge) song; (*Singen*) singing. **-buch** *neut* songbook; (*Kirche*) hymnbook.
Gesäß [gə'zeɪs] *neut* (*pl* -e) seat, bottom.
Geschäft [gə'ʃɛft] *neut* (*pl* -e) business; (*Laden*) shop; (*Handel*) deal. **das Geschäft blüht** business is booming. **ein unsauberes Geschäft** a dirty business. **ein gutes Geschäft machen** get a bargain. **geschäftlich** *adj* commercial, business. **Geschäfts‖freund** *m* business associate, customer. **-führer** *m* manager; (*Verein*) secretary. **-haus** *neut* firm. **-jahr** *neut* business year. **-mann** *m* businessman. **-raum** *m or* **-räume** *pl* office(s). **geschäftsmäßig** *adj* businesslike. **Geschäfts‖reisende(r)** *m* commercial traveller, representative. **-schluß** *m* closing time. **-stunden** *pl* office hours.
*geschehen [gə'ʃeɪən] *v* happen.
gescheit [gə'ʃaɪt] *adj* clever, smart.
Geschenk [gə'ʃɛŋk] *neut* (*pl* -e) present, gift.
Geschichte [gə'ʃiçtə] *f* (*pl* -n) (*Erzählung*) story; (*Vergangenheit*) history; (*Angelegenheit*) affair. **Geschichtenbuch** *neut* story book. **geschichtlich** *adj* historical. **Geschichts‖buch** *neut* history book. **-fo-- cher** *m* (research) historian. **-s‖ iber** *m* historian.
Geschick [gə'ʃik] *neut* (*pl* -e) aptitude; (*Schicksal*) fate. **-lichkeit** *f* skill. **geschickt** *adj* able, skilful.
geschieden [gə'ʃiːdən] *adj* divorced.
Geschirr [gə'ʃir] *neut* (*pl* -e) crockery, dishes; (*Pferde*) harness. **-tuch** *neut* dishcloth. **-spülmaschine** *f* dishwasher.
Geschlecht [gə'ʃlɛçt] *neut* (*pl* -er) sex; (*Art*) kind, sort; (*Familie*) family, house; (*Gramm*) gender. **geschlechtlich** *adj* sexual. **Geschlechts‖krankheit** *f* venereal disease. **-reife** *f* puberty. **-teile** *pl* genitals. **-verkehr** *m* sexual intercourse.
geschlossen [gə'ʃlɔsən] *adj* closed.
Geschmack [gə'ʃmak] *m* (*pl* Geschmäcke) taste. **geschmacklos** *adj* tasteless. **Geschmacks‖sache** *f* matter of taste. **-sinn** *m* sense of taste. **geschmackvoll** *adj* tasteful.

Geschnatter [gəˈʃnatər] *neut* (*unz.*) cackling.
Geschöpf [gəˈʃœpf] *neut* (*pl* -e) creature.
Geschoß [gəˈʃɔs] *neut* (*pl* Geschosse) projectile, missile; (*Kanone*) shell; (*Stockwerk*) floor, storey.
Geschrei [gəˈʃrai] *neut* (*pl* -e) cry, shouting, crying; (*fig*) fuss, noise.
Geschütz [gəˈʃyts] *neut* (*pl* -e) gun, cannon.
Geschwätz [gəˈʃvɛts] *neut* idle talk, prattle. **geschwätzig** *adj* talkative.
geschweige [gəˈʃvaigə] *conj* **geschweige denn** let alone, to say nothing of.
geschwind [gəˈʃvint] *adj* quick, fast. **Geschwindigkeit** *f* speed, velocity. **Geschwindigheits‖grenze** *f* speed limit. **–messer** *m* speedometer.
Geschwister [gəˈʃvistər] *pl* brother(s) and sister(s); siblings. *haben Sie Geschwister?* have you any brothers and sisters?
Geschworene(r) [gəˈʃvoːrənə] *m* (*pl* -n) juror. **Geschworenengericht** *neut* (trial by) jury.
Geschwür [gəˈʃvyːr] *neut* (*pl* -e) ulcer, sore.
Geselle [gəˈzɛlə] *m* (*pl* -n) comrade, companion; (*Bursche*) lad, fellow; (*gelehrter Handwerker*) journeyman. **gesellig** *adj* sociable. **Gesellschaft** *f* society; (*Firma*) company; (*Verein*) society, association; (*Abend-, usw.*) party, social gathering; (*Begleitung*) company. **gesellschaftlich** *adj* social. **Gesellschaftsanzug** *m* evening dress. **gesellschaftsfeindlich** *adj* antisocial. **Gesellschafts‖kleid** *neut* party dress. **–steuer** *f* corporation tax. **–tanz** *m* society dance, ball.
Gesetz [gəˈzɛts] *neut* (*pl* -e) law. **–buch** *neut* statute book, law code. **–entwurf** *m* bill. **gesetzgebend** *adj* legislative. **Gesetzgebung** *f* legislation. **gesetz‖lich** *adj* legal, lawful. **–los** *adj* lawless. **–mäßig** *adj* legal, lawful.
gesetzt [gəˈzɛtst] *adj* sedate, quiet.
gesetzwidrig [gəˈzɛtsviːdriç] *adj* illegal, unlawful.
Gesicht [gəˈziçt] *neut* (*pl* -er) face; (*Miene*) expression. **Gesichts‖ausdruck** *m* (facial) expression. **–farbe** *f* complexion. **–feld** *neut* field of vision. **–punkt** *m* viewpoint.
gesinnt [gəˈzint] *adj* disposed, minded.
Gesinnung *f* opinion, mind, conviction.
gesinnungslos *adj* unprincipled.

Gespann [gəˈʃpan] *neut* (*pl* -e) (*Pferden*) (team of) horses.
gespannt [gəˈʃpant] *adj* tense; (*Verhältnis*) strained. **gespannt sein** be eager *or* anxious.
Gespenst [gəˈʃpɛnst] *neut* (*pl* -er) ghost. **gespenstig** *adj* ghostly.
Gespräch [gəˈʃprɛːç] *neut* (*pl* -e) conversation, talk. **Gespräche** *pl* talks, discussion *sing.* **gesprächig** *adj* talkative.
Gestalt [gəˈʃtalt] *f* (*pl* -en) form, shape; (*Körper-*) figure, build; (*Literatur*) character. **gestalt‖en** *v* form, shape. **–et** *adj* formed, shaped. **–los** *adj* shapeless. **Gestaltung** *f* (*unz.*) shaping, formation.
Geständnis [gəˈʃtɛntnis] *neut* (*pl* -se) confession.
Gestank [gəˈʃtaŋk] *m* stink, stench.
gestatten [gəˈʃtatən] *v* permit, allow.
Geste [ˈɡɛstə] *f* (*pl* -n) gesture.
*gestehen [gəˈʃteːən] *v* confess.
Gestell [gəˈʃtɛl] *neut* (*pl* -e) (*Rahmen*) frame, stand; (*Bock*) trestle; (*Regal*) shelf; (*Bett-*) bedstead.
gestern [ˈɡɛstərn] *adv* yesterday.
Gesträuch [gəˈʃtrɔyç] *neut* (*unz.*) shrubbery, bushes *pl.*
gestrichen [gəˈʃtriçən] *adj* painted. **frisch gestrichen** newly painted; wet paint.
gestrig [ˈɡɛstriç] *adj* yesterday's.
Gestrüpp [gəˈʃtryp] *neut* undergrowth, scrub.
Gesuch [gəˈzuːx] *neut* (*pl* -e) petition. **gesucht** *adj* in demand; (*Person*) wanted.
gesund [gəˈzunt] *adj* healthy, well. **Gesundheit** *f* health. *interj* bless you! **gesundheitlich** *adj* sanitary. **gesundheitsförderlich** *adj* wholesome, healthy. **Gesundheitslehre** *f* hygiene. **gesundheitsschädlich** *adj* insanitary, unhealthy.
Getränk [gəˈtrɛŋk] *neut* (*pl* -e) drink.
Getreide [gəˈtraidə] *neut* (*pl* -) grain, cereals *pl*
getreu [gəˈtrɔy] *adj* loyal, faithful.
Getriebe [gəˈtriːbə] *neut* (*pl* -) commotion, bustle; (*Tech*) transmission, gears *pl.* **–gehäuse** *neut* gearbox.
getrost [gəˈtroːst] *adj* confident. *adv* without hesitation.
Getto [ˈɡetoː] *neut* (*pl* -s) ghetto.
geübt [gəˈypt] *adj* practised, skilful.
Gewächs [gəˈvɛks] *neut* (*pl* -e) plant; (*Med*) growth.

gewachsen [gə'vaksən] *adj* grown.
gewachsen sein be equal (to), be up (to).
gewagt [gə'vaːkt] *adj* bold, daring.
gewählt [gə'vɛːlt] *adj* select(ed), choice.
Gewähr [gə'vɛːr] *f* (*unz.*) guarantee, surety. **gewähren** *v* allow, grant. **gewährleisten** *v* guarantee, vouch for.
Gewalt [gə'valt] *f* (*pl* -en) force; (*Macht*) power; (*Obrigkeit*) authority; (*Gewalttätigkeit*) violence. **-herrscher** *m* tyrant. **gewalt‖ig** *adj* forceful, powerful; enormous; (*gewalttätig*) violent. **-los** *adj* powerless. **-sam** *adj* violent; *adv* by force. **-tätig** *adj* violent.
Gewand [gə'vant] *neut* (*pl* **Gewänder**) garment, robe.
gewandt [gə'vant] *adj* skilled, skilful. **Gewandtheit** *f* dexterity, skill.
Gewässer [gə'vɛsər] *neut* (*pl* -) water(s).
Gewebe [gə'veːbə] *neut* (*pl* -) material, textile; (*Biol*) tissue; (*Lügen, usw.*) web, network.
geweckt [gə'vɛkt] *adj* bright, lively.
Gewehr [gə'veːr] *neut* (*pl* -e) rifle, gun. **-kugel** *f* (rifle) bullet.
Geweih [gə'vai] *neut* (*pl* -e) antlers *pl.*
Gewerbe [gə'vɛrbə] *neut* (*pl* -) trade. **-schule** *f* technical school. **gewerb‖lich** *adj* industrial. **-smäßig** *adj* professional.
Gewerkschaft [gə'vɛrkʃaft] *f* (*pl* -en) (trade) union. **-ler** *m* (trade) unionist. **gewerkschaftlich** *adj* trade-union.
Gewicht [gə'viçt] *neut* (*pl* -e) weight; (*fig*) importance. **-heben** *neut* weight-lifting. **gewichtig** *adj* heavy; (*fig*) important.
Gewimmel [gə'vimǝl] *neut* (*pl* -) crowd, swarm.
Gewinde [gə'vində] *neut* (*pl* -) (*Schraube*) thread.
Gewinn [gə'vin] *m* (*pl* -e) profit; (*Ertrag*) yield, returns; (*Preis*) prize; (*Erwerben*) gaining. **-beteiligung** *f* profit-sharing. **gewinn‖bringend** *adj* profitable. **-en** *v* (*Preis*) win; (*erwerben*) gain, acquire; (*siegen*) win. **-süchtig** *adj* acquisitive.
Gewirr [gə'vir] *neut* (*pl* -e) confusion, tangle.
gewiß [gə'vis] *adj* certain, sure. *adv* certainly. *ein gewisser Herr Schmidt* a certain Mr Schmidt. *ein gewisses Etwas* a certain something.
Gewissen [gə'visən] *neut* (*unz.*) conscience. **gewissen‖haft** *adj* conscientious. **-los** *adj* unscrupulous. **Gewissens‖bisse**

pl pangs of conscience. **-konflikt** *m* conflict of conscience.
gewissermaßen [gə'visərmaisən] *adv* to some extent.
Gewißheit [gə'vishait] *f* (*unz.*) certainty.
Gewitter [gə'vitər] *neut* (*pl* -) thunderstorm. **gewitterhaft** *adj* stormy.
gewogen [gə'voigən] *adj* well disposed, favourably inclined.
gewöhnen [gə'vœnən] *v* accustom. **sich gewöhnen an** become accustomed to, get used to. **Gewohnheit** *f* (*pl* -en) habit; (*Brauch*) custom. **gewohnheitsmäßig** *adj* customary. **gewöhnlich** *adj* usual, ordinary; (*unfein*) vulgar. *adv* usually. **gewohnt** *adj* used (to).
Gewölbe [gə'vœlbə] *neut* (*pl* -) vault. **gewölbt** *adj* arched, vaulted.
Gewühl [gə'vyːl] *neut* (*unz.*) crowd, tumult.
Gewürz [gə'vyrts] *neut* (*pl* -e) spice, seasoning. **gewürzig** *adj* spicy. **gewürzt** *adj* spiced, seasoned.
gezackt [gə'tsakt] *adj* serrated; (*Fels*) jagged.
geziemend [gə'tsiːmənt] *or* **geziemlich** *adj* seemly.
geziert [gə'tsiːrt] *adj* affected.
gezwungen [gə'tsvuŋən] *adj* forced; (*steif*) formal, stiff.
Gicht [giçt] *f* (*unz.*) gout.
Giebel ['giːbəl] *m* (*pl* -) gable. **-dach** *neut* gabled roof.
Gier [giːr] *f* greed; (*nach etwas*) craving, burning desire (for). **gierig** *adj* greedy.
*gießen ['giːsən] *v* pour; (*Pflanzen*) water; (*schmelzen*) cast. **Gieß‖erei** *f* (*pl* -en) foundry. **-kanne** *f* watering can.
Gift [gift] *neut* (*pl* -e) poison. **-gas** *neut* poison gas. **giftig** *adj* poisonous. **Giftschlange** *f* poisonous snake.
Ginster ['ginstər] *m* (*pl* -) (*Bot*) broom.
Gipfel ['gipfəl] *m* (*pl* -) peak, summit. **-gespräche** *pl* summit talks. **-leistung** *f* record.
Gips [gips] *m* (*pl* -e) gypsum; (*erhitzt*) plaster (of Paris). **-verband** *m* plaster cast.
Giraffe [gi'rafə] *f* (*pl* -n) giraffe.
Giro ['dʒiːroi] *neut* (*pl* -s) giro. **-konto** *neut* current account.
Gitarre [gi'tarə] *f* (*pl* -n) guitar.
Gitter ['gitər] *neut* (*pl* -) grille, grating; (*Fenster*) bars; (*Spalier*) trellis.

Glanz [glants] *m* (*unz.*) shine, brilliance, brightness; (*fig*) splendour.
glänzen ['glɛntsən] *v* gleam, shine; (*fig*) excel, shine. **–d** *adj* brilliant.
Glas [glaːs] *neut* (*pl* **Gläser**) glass. **–haus** *neut* greenhouse, hothouse. **–perle** *f* bead. **–scheibe** *f* (window) pane. **glasieren** *v* glaze; (*Kuchen*) ice. **Glasur** *f* glaze; (*Kuchen*) icing.
glatt [glat] *adj* smooth; (*glitschig*) slippery. **Glatteis** *neut* (*Mot*) black ice. **glattrasiert** *adj* clean-shaven.
Glaube ['glaubə] *m* (*unz.*) belief; (*Rel*) faith. **glauben** *v* believe; (*vermuten*) think, suppose; (*vertrauen*) trust. **glaubhaft** *adj* credible.
gläubig ['glɔybiç] *adj* believing; (*fromm*) pious. **Gläubige(r)** *m* believer; (*Komm*) creditor.
glaublich ['glauplɪç] *adj* credible. **glaubwürdig** *adj* (*Person*) trustworthy; (*Sache*) credible.
gleich [glaɪç] *adj* (the) same, equal; (*eben*) level. *adv* equally; (*sofort*) at once; (*schon*) just. **von gleichem Alter** of the same age. **das ist mir gleich** it makes no difference to me. **das gleiche gilt für Dich** the same goes for you. **Ich komme gleich** I'm just coming. **gleich viel** just as much. **gleich‖artig** *adj* similar. **–bedeutend** *adj* synonymous. **–berechtigt** *adj* having equal rights.
*****gleichen** ['glaɪçən] *v* equal; (*ähnlich sein*) resemble.
gleichermaßen ['glaɪçərmasən] *or* **gleicherweise** *adv* likewise.
gleich‖falls *adv* also, likewise. **–gesinnt** *adj* like-minded.
Gleichgewicht ['glaɪçgəviçt] *neut* equilibrium, balance.
gleichgültig ['glaɪçgyltɪç] *adj* unconcerned, indifferent. **Gleichgültigkeit** *f* indifference.
Gleich‖heit *f* equality. **–maß** *neut* proportion, symmetry. **–mut** *m* equanimity. **–nis** *neut* (*pl* **-se**) simile; (*Erzählung*) parable.
gleichschalten ['glaɪçʃaltən] *v* coordinate; (*Tech*) synchronize.
Gleichschritt ['glaɪçʃrit] *m* **Gleichschritt halten** keep step.
Gleich‖strom *m* direct current. **–ung** *f* (*pl* **-en**) equation.
gleich‖viel *adv* no matter. **–wertig** *adj*

equivalent, of the same value. **–wohl** *adv* nonetheless. **–zeitig** *adj* simultaneous.
Gleis [glaɪs] *neut* (*pl* **-e**) track, platform.
*****gleiten** ['glaɪtən] *v* slide, slip. **Gleitflugzeug** *neut* glider, sailplane.
Gletscher ['glɛtʃər] *m* (*pl* **-**) glacier. **Gletscherspalte** *f* crevasse.
Glied [gliːt] *neut* (*pl* **-er**) limb; (*Kette*) link. **gliedern** *v* organize, arrange; divide into. **Gliederung** *f* (*pl* **-en**) organization, arrangement.
Glocke ['glɔkə] *f* (*pl* **-n**) bell. **Glocken‖blume** *f* bluebell. **–turm** *m* belltower.
glorreich ['glɔrraɪç] *adj* glorious.
Glossar [glɔˈsaːr] *neut* (*pl* **-e**, **-ien**) glossary. **Glosse** *f* (*pl* **-n**) comment.
glotzen ['glɔtsən] *v* stare.
Glück [glyk] *neut* luck; (*Geschick*) fortune; (*Freude*) happiness. **glück‖lich** *adj* happy, fortunate. **–licherweise** *adv* fortunately, luckily. **–selig** *adj* blissful. **Glücks‖fall** *m* lucky chance. **–spiel** *neut* game of chance.
glühen ['glyːən] *v* glow. **Glüh‖hitze** *f* white heat. **–wein** *m* mulled wine.
Glut [gluːt] *f* (*pl* **-en**) glow. **–asche** *f* embers *pl*.
Gnade ['gnaːdə] *f* (*pl* **-n**) grace, mercy. **Gnaden‖frist** *f* reprieve, period of grace. **–stoß** *m* coup de grâce.
gnädig ['gnɛːdiç] *adj* gracious; kind. **gnädige Frau** Madam.
Gold [gɔlt] *neut* (*unz.*) gold. **–barren** *m* gold bar or ingot. **gold‖en** *adj* golden. **–ig** *adj* sweet, lovely.
Golf¹ [gɔlf] *m* (*pl* **-e**) gulf.
Golf² *neut* (*unz.*) (*Sport*) golf.
gönnen ['gœnən] *v* not begrudge; grant, allow.
Gönner *m* (*pl* **-**) patron, sponsor. **gönnerhaft** *adj* patronizing; condescending.
Gosse ['gɔsə] *f* (*pl* **-n**) gutter.
Gott [gɔt] *m* God; (*pl* **Götter**) god. **grüß Gott!** greetings! God be with you! **Gott sei dank!** thank God! **um Gottes willen!** for God's sake! **Gottes‖dienst** *m* (church) service. **–lästerung** *f* blasphemy. **Gottheit** *f* godhead, divinity.
Göttin ['gœtin] *f* (*pl* **-nen**) goddess. **göttlich** *adj* divine.
Götze ['gœtsə] *m* (*pl* **-n**) idol, false god.
Grab [graːp] *neut* (*pl* **Gräber**) grave. **graben** *v* dig. **Graben** *m* ditch, trench. **Grab‖schrift** *f* epitaph. **–stätte** *f* grave. **–stein** *m* tombstone.

Grad [graɪt] *m* (*pl* -e) degree; (*Rang*) rank, grade. –**messer** *m* (*fig*) indication, sign.
graduieren [gradu'iːrən] *v* graduate. **Graduierte(r)** *m* graduate.
Graf [graɪf] *m* (*pl* -en) count.
Gräfin ['grɛɪfin] *f* (*pl* -en) countess.
Grafschaft ['graɪfʃaft] *f* (*pl* -en) county.
Gram [graɪm] *m* (*unz.*) grief.
Gramm [gram] *neut* (*pl* -e) gram(me).
Grammatik [gra'matik] *f* (*pl* -en) grammar.
Granatapfel [gra'naɪtapfəl] *m* (*pl* Granatäpfel) pomegranate.
Granate [gra'naɪtə] *f* (*pl* -n) shell, grenade.
Granit [gra'niːt] *m* (*pl* -e) granite.
Graphik ['graɪfik] *f* (*unz.*) graphics. -**er** *m* (*pl* -) designer, commercial artist. **graphisch** *adj* graphic. **graphische Darstellung** graph.
Gras [graɪs] *neut* (*pl* Gräser) grass. **grasen** *v* graze.
gräßlich ['grɛsliç] *adj* horrible, ghastly.
Grat [graɪt] *m* (*pl* -e) ridge, edge.
Gräte ['grɛɪtə] *f* (*pl* -n) fishbone. –**nmuster** *neut* herringbone pattern.
gratulieren [gratu'liːrən] *v* congratulate.
grau [grau] *adj* grey. **Graubrot** *neut* ryebread.
grauen ['grauən] *v* be horrible. *es graut mir vor* I have a horror of. –**haft** *adj* dreadful, horrible.
Graupe ['graupə] *f* (*pl* -n) groats *pl*, pearl barley.
graupeln ['graupəln] *pl* sleet *sing*.
grausam ['grauzaɪm] *adj* cruel. **Grausamkeit** *f* cruelty. **grausig** *adj* fearful, dreadful.
gravieren [gra'viːrən] *v* engrave.
greif‖en ['graifən] *v* seize, grasp. –**bar** *adj* (*Waren*) available, at hand; (*fig*) tangible. **greifen an** touch. **greifen in** dip into.
Greis [grais] *m* (*pl* -e) old man.
grell [grɛl] *adj* (*Ton*) shrill, harsh; (*Farbe*) glaring.
Grenze ['grɛntsə] *f* (*pl* -n) (*eines Staates*) border, frontier; (*einer Stadt, Zone*) boundary; (*fig*) limit. **grenzen** border (on). **Grenz‖fall** *m* borderline case. –**übergang** *m* crossing (of a frontier).
Greuel ['grɔyəl] *m* (*pl* -) (*Abscheu*) horror; (*Scheußlichkeit*) atrocity, abomination.

Grieche ['griːçə] *m* (*pl* -n) Greek (man). **Griechenland** *neut* Greece. **Griechin** *f* (*pl* -nen) Greek (woman). **griechisch** *adj* Greek.
Grieß [griːs] *m* (*unz.*) (*Essen*) semolina; (*Kies*) gravel. –**pudding** *m* semolina pudding.
Griff [grif] *m* (*pl* -e) (*Henkel, Knopf, usw.*) handle; (*Greifen*) hold, grip.
Grille ['grilə] *f* (*pl* -n) (*Insekt*) cricket; (*Laune*) whim.
Grimasse [gri'masə] *f* (*pl* -n) grimace.
grimmig ['grimiç] *adj* furious.
grinsen ['grinzən] *v* grin.
Grippe ['gripə] *f* (*pl* -n) influenza.
grob [groɪp] *adj* coarse; (*Benehmen*) coarse, rude; (*Scherz*) crude, coarse; (*Fehler*) gross, serious. **Grobheit** *f* coarseness, rudeness.
Groll [grɔl] *m* animosity, rancour. **grollen** *v* be resentful, be angry.
gros [groɪ] **en gros** wholesale.
Gros¹ [groɪ] *neut* (*pl* -) (*Armee*) main body.
Gros² [grɔs] *neut* (*pl* -e) gross, twelve dozen.
Groschen ['grɔʃən] *m* (*pl* -) (*Österreich*) Groschen; (*BRD*) ten-pfennig piece; (*fig*) penny.
groß [groɪs] *adj* big, large; (*wichtig*) great, grand; (*hoch*) tall. *im großen und ganzen* on the whole. –**artig** *adj* splendid, grand.
Großbritannien [groɪsbri'taniən] *neut* Great Britain.
Großbuchstabe ['groɪsbuxʃtaɪbə] *m* capital (letter).
Großeltern ['groɪseltərn] *pl* grandparents.
großenteils ['groɪsentails] *adv* mostly, for the most part.
Groß‖handel *m* wholesale trade. –**händler** *m* wholesaler.
großherzig ['groɪshɛrtsiç] *adj* magnanimous.
Groß‖industrie *f* large-scale industry. –**macht** *f* great power. –**maul** *neut* braggart, big-mouth. –**mutter** *f* grandmother. –**stadt** *f* large town, city.
größtenteils ['grœɪstəntails] *adv* mostly, largely.
Groß‖teil *m* bulk. –**tuer** *m* show-off, big-head. –**vater** *m* grandfather.
großzügig ['groɪstsyɪgiç] *adj* generous; (*weittragend*) large-scale. **Großzügigkeit** *f* generosity; largeness.

grotesk [gro'tɛsk] *adj* grotesque.
Grübchen ['gryːpçən] *neut* (*pl* -) dimple.
Grube ['gruːbə] *f* (*pl* -n) pit, hole; (*Bergbau*) mine, pit; (*Höhle, Bau*) hole, burrow; (*Falle*) snare.
grübeln ['gryːbəln] *v* brood, ponder.
grün [gryːn] *adj* green. **Grün** *neut* green. **–anlage** *f* public park, open space.
Grund [grunt] *m* (*pl* Gründe) (*Erdboden*) ground, soil; (*Veranlassung*) reason, grounds *pl*; (*Grundlage*) basis, base; (*Grundbesitz*) land; (*eines Meeres*) bottom. **–bau** *m* foundation. **–besitz** *m* landed property, real estate. **im Grunde (genommen)** basically.
gründen ['gryndən] *v* found, establish. **sich gründen auf** be based on. **Gründer** *m* (*pl* -) founder.
Grund‖gesetz *neut* basic law; (*Verfassung*) constitution. **–lage** *f* basis, foundation.
gründlich ['gryntliç] *adj* thorough.
grundlos ['gruntloːs] *adj* unfounded, baseless.
Grund‖maß *neut* standard of measurement. **–riß** *m* outline, design. **–satz** *m* principle, axiom. **grundsätzlich** *adj* fundamental.
Grund‖schule *f* primary school. **–stoff** *m* raw material; (*Chem*) element. **–stück** *neut* lot of land.
Gründung ['grynduŋ] *f* (*pl* -en) establishment, foundation.
Grund‖unterschied *m* basic difference. **–zahl** *f* cardinal number. **–zug** *m* characteristic, feature.
Grünkohl ['gryːnkoːl] *m* kale.
grunzen ['gruntsən] *v* grunt.
Grünzeug ['gryːntsɔyk] *neut* greens *pl*, green vegetables *pl*.
Gruppe ['grupə] *f* (*pl* -n) group. **–nführer** *m* section leader. **gruppieren** *v* group.
gruselig ['gruːzəliç] *adj* gruesome; (*umg.*) creepy.
Gruß [gruːs] *m* (*pl* Grüße) greeting; (*Mil*) salute. **herzliche Grüße** kind regards, best wishes.
grüßen ['gryːsən] *v* greet; (*Mil*) salute.
gucken ['gukən] *v* (take a) look, peep.
Gulasch ['guːlaʃ] *neut, m* (*pl* -e) goulash.
gültig ['gyltiç] *adj* valid; (*Gesetz*) in force. **Gültigkeit** *f* validity, currency. **–sdauer** *f* (period of) validity.
Gummi ['gumi] *neut* (*pl* -s) rubber; (*Kleb-*

stoff) gum; (*Kau-*) (chewing) gum. **–band** *neut* rubber band. **gummiert** *adj* (*Briefmarke, usw.*) gummed.
Gunst [gunst] *f* (*unz.*) favour.
günstig ['gynstiç] *adj* favourable, advantageous.
gurgeln ['gurgəln] *v* gargle. **Gurgelwasser** *neut* gargle.
Gurke ['gurkə] *f* (*pl* -n) cucumber; (*saure*) gherkin.
Gurt [gurt] *m* (*pl* -e) belt; (*Pferd*) girth.
Gürtel ['gyrtəl] *m* (*pl* -) belt; (*Geog*) zone. **–reifen** *m* radial-ply tyre, (*umg.*) radial.
Guß [gus] *m* (*pl* Güsse) (*Regen*) downpour, gush; (*Metall*) casting, founding.
gut [guːt] *adj* good. *adv* well. **gut sein mit** be on good terms with. **es wird schon alles gut werden** everything will be all right. **das tut mir gut** that does me good. **schon gut!** that's all right. **gut aussehen** look good; (*gesund*) look well. **Gut** *neut* (*pl* Güter) possession; (*Land*) landed estate; (*Ware*) commodity. **gutartig** *adj* good-natured. **Gutdünken** *neut* discretion. **nach (Ihrem) Gutdünken** at your discretion.
Güte ['gyːtə] *f* (*unz.*) kindness, goodness; (*Qualität*) quality.
Güter‖flugzeug *neut* cargo plane. **–zug** *m* freight train.
gut‖gelaun *adj* good-humoured. **–gesinnt** *adj* friendly, well-disposed. **–gläubig** *adj* acting in good faith, bona-fide; *adv* in good faith.
Guthaben ['guːthaːbən] *neut* credit (balance).
*gut‖heißen *v* approve. **–herzig** *adj* kind-hearted.
gütig ['gyːtiç] *adj* kind.
gutmachen ['guːtmaxən] *v* **wieder gutmachen** make amends for, make good.
gutmütig ['guːtmyːtiç] *adj* good-natured.
Gutschein ['guːtʃain] *m* (*pl* -e) voucher, credit-note.
Gymnasium [gym'naːzium] *neut* (*pl* Gymnasien) grammar school.
Gymnastik [gym'nastik] *f* gymnastics. **gymnastisch** *adj* gymnastic.

H

Haag, Den [deɪnˈhaɪk] *m* The Hague.
Haar [haɪr] *neut* (*pl* -e) hair. **sich die Haare schneiden lassen** have a haircut.
haarig *adj* hairy. **Haar∥nadelkurve** *f* hairpin bend. **–schnitt** *m* haircut. **haarsträubend** *adj* hair-raising.
Habe [ˈhaɪbə] *f* (*unz.*) property, possessions *pl*. **haben** *v* have. **habsüchtig** *adj* greedy, (*umg.*) grasping.
Hackbrett [ˈhakbrɛt] *neut* chopping board. **hacken** *v* chop, hack; (*Fleisch*) mince. **Hackfleisch** *neut* mince, minced meat.
Hafen [ˈhaɪfən] *m* (*pl* **Häfen**) port, harbour. **–arbeiter** *m* docker. **–damm** *m* pier, mole. **–sperre** *f* embargo. **–stadt** *f* port.
Hafer [ˈhaɪfər] *m* (*pl* -) oats *pl*. **–flocken** *f pl* rolled oats, oat-flakes.
Haft [haft] *f* arrest, detention, custody. **haften** *v* adhere, cling. **haften für** be liable for, answer for. **Haftpflichtversicherung** *f* (compulsory) third-party insurance.
Hagel [ˈhaɪgəl] *m* (*pl* -) hail. **–korn** *neut* hailstone. **hageln** *v* **es hagelt** it is hailing.
hager [ˈhaɪgər] *adj* lean, haggard.
Hahn [haɪn] *m* (*pl* **Hähne**) cock; (*Wasser-, usw.*) tap. **Hahnenkamm** *m* cockscomb.
Hähnchen [ˈhɛnçən] *neut* (*pl* -) cock; (*Wasser-, usw.*) tap.
Hai [hai] *m* (*pl* -e) *or* **Haifisch** *m* shark.
Hain [hain] *m* (*pl* -e) grove.
Häkelarbeit [ˈhɛɪkəlaɪrbait] *f* crochet work. **häkeln** *v* crochet.
haken [ˈhaɪkən] *v* hook. **sich haken an** catch on, get caught on. **Haken** *m* (*pl* -) hook; (*fig*) snag. **–kreuz** *neut* swastika.
halb [halp] *adj* half. **um halb drei** at half past two. **eine halbe Stunde** half an hour. **–jährlich** *adj* half-yearly. **Halb∥kreis** *m* semicircle. **–kugel** *f* hemisphere. **–messer** *m* radius. **–starke(r)** *m* hooligan. **halbwegs** *adv* halfway. **Halbzeit** *f* half-time.
Hälfte [ˈhɛlftə] *f* (*pl* -n) half.
Halfter [ˈhalftər] *f or neut* (*pl* -n) halter.
Hall [hal] *m* (*pl* -e) sound, peal.
Halle [ˈhalə] *f* (*pl* -n) hall; (*Hotel*) lobby; (*Flugzeug-*) hangar.
hallen [ˈhalən] *v* sound, resound.
Hallenbad [ˈhalənbait] *neut* indoor swimming-pool *or* baths.
Halm [halm] *m* (*pl* -e) stalk; (*Gras*) blade.

Hals [hals] *m* (*pl* **Hälse**) neck; (*innerer Hals, Kehle*) throat. **–band** *neut* (*Hund*) collar; (*Frauen*) necklace, choker. **–binde** *f* tie. **–kette** *f* necklace. **–weh** *neut* sore throat.
Halt [halt] *m* (*pl* -e) (*Anhalten*) stop, halt; (*Stütze*) hold, support; (*Standhaftigkeit*) steadiness, firmness. **haltbar** *adj* durable, lasting. **haltbar bis ...** (*Speisen*) use by .... **halten** *v* hold; (*bewahren*) keep; (*dauern*) last, keep; (*Gebot, usw.*) observe; (*anhalten*) stop. **viel halten von** think highly of. **halten für** consider (to be), think of as. **Halte∥stelle** *f* (*Bus*) busstop. **–tau** *neut* guy-rope. **haltmachen** *v* stop. **Haltung** *f* (*pl* -en) attitude; (*Körper-*) bearing, posture.
hämisch [ˈhɛɪmɪʃ] *adj* spiteful, sardonic.
Hammelfleisch [ˈhaməlflaiʃ] *neut* mutton.
Hammer [ˈhamər] *m* (*pl* **Hämmer**) hammer.
hämmern [ˈhɛmərn] *v* hammer.
Hämorrhoiden {hɛmoroˈiɪdən] *pl* piles, haemorrhoids *pl*.
Hamster [ˈhamstər] *m* (*pl* -) hamster. **hamstern** *v* hoard.
Hand [hant] *f* (*pl* **Hände**) hand. **an Hand von** with the aid of. **bei der Hand** ready, at hand. **mit der Hand** by hand. **von Hand gemacht** hand-made. **zur linken/rechten Hand** on the left/right hand side. **Hand∥arbeit** *f* handiwork; (*Nadelarbeit*) needlework. **–becken** *neut* hand basin. **–bremse** *f* handbrake. **–buch** *neut* manual, handbook.
Händedruck [ˈhɛndədruk] *m* handshake.
Handel [ˈhandəl] *m* trade, commerce; (*Geschäft*) transaction, deal. **handeln** *v* act. **handeln mit** (*Person*) trade *or* deal with; (*Waren*) trade *or* deal in. **handeln von** treat, deal with. **Handels∥beziehungen** *pl* trade relations. **–bilanz** *f* balance of trade. **–schule** *f* business *or* commercial school. **–sperre** *f* (trade) embargo.
handfest [ˈhantfest] *adj* sturdy, strong.
Hand∥fläche *f* palm. **–gebrauch** *m* everyday use. **–gelenk** *neut* wrist. **–gepäck** *neut* hand luggage.
handhaben [ˈhanthaɪbən] *v* (*gebrauchen*) use, employ; (*fig*) handle.
Händler [ˈhɛntlər] *m* (*pl* -) trader, dealer.
handlich [ˈhantlɪç] *adj* handy.

Handlung ['hantluŋ] f (pl -en) deed, act; (Roman, usw.) plot; (Geschäft) business, firm; (Laden) shop.
Hand‖schellen pl handcuffs pl. **–schuh** m glove. **–tasche** f handbag. **–tuch** neut towel. **–werk** neut craft, trade. **–werker** m craftsman, workman.
Hang [haŋ] m (pl Hänge) slope; (Neigung) tendency.
Hängematte ['hɛŋəmatə] f hammock.
***hängen¹** [hɛŋən] v be suspended, hang; (sich neigen) slope; (unentschieden) be pending, remain undecided; (abhängen) depend.
hängen² v hang, suspend; (hinrichten) hang.
Hannover [ha'nɔɪfər] neut Hanover.
hantieren [han'tiːrən] v busy oneself, potter around.
Happen ['hapən] m (pl -) mouthful, bite.
Harfe ['harfə] f (pl -n) harp.
harmlos ['harmloɪs] adj harmless.
Harmonie [harmɔ'niɪ] f (pl -n) harmony. **harmonisch** adj harmonic. **harmonisieren** v harmonize.
Harn [harn] m urine. **–blase** f (Anat) bladder.
Harnisch ['harniʃ] m (pl -e) armour; harness.
Harpune [har'puːnə] f (pl -n) harpoon.
harren ['harən] v wait for, await.
hart [hart] adj hard; (fig) harsh, rough.
Härte ['hɛɪrtə] f (pl -n) hardness; (Strenge) severity; (Grausamkeit) cruelty.
härten v harden; (Metall) temper.
hart‖gekocht adj hard-boiled. **–näckig** adj stubborn.
Harz [harts] neut (pl -e) resin.
Haschisch ['haʃiʃ] neut hashish.
Hase ['haɪzə] m (pl -n) hare.
Haselnuß ['haɪzəlnus] f hazelnut.
Haspe ['haspə] f (pl -n) hinge.
Haß [has] m hate.
hassen ['hasən] v hate. **–swert** adj hateful, odious.
häßlich ['hɛsliç] adj ugly; (fig) wicked, nasty. **Häßlichkeit** f ugliness; (fig) wickedness.
Hast [hast] f haste. **hasten** v hasten. **hastig** adj hasty.
hätscheln ['hɛɪtʃəln] v (liebkosen) caress, fondle; (verwöhnen) pamper.
Haube ['haubə] f (pl -n) bonnet, cap; (Mot) bonnet, (US) hood.

Hauch [haux] m (pl -e) breath; (fig) touch, trace.
Haue ['hauə] f (pl -n) pick; (umg.) beating, spanking. **hauen** v hew; (zerhacken) chop up; (umg.) beat, belt.
Haufen ['haufən] m (pl -) heap, pile; (umg.) heaps of, lots of.
häufen ['hɔyfən] v heap (up), accumulate.
häufig ['hɔyfiç] adj frequent, numerous. adv frequently.
Haupt [haupt] neut (pl Häupter) head; (Führer) leader, chief. **–bahnhof** m main railway station, central station. **–buch** neut ledger. **–film** m feature film, main film. **–leitung** f (Gas, Strom) mains pl. **–mann** m (Mil) captain. **–rolle** f (Theater) leading part or role.
Hauptsache ['hauptzaxə] f main thing or point. **hauptsächlich** adj essential. adv principally, mainly.
Haupt‖sitz m head office. **–stadt** f capital (city). **–straße** f main street. **–wort** neut noun.
Haus [haus] neut (pl Häuser) house; (Heim) home. **zu Hause** at home. **–arbeit** f housework; (Schule) homework. **–aufgaben** pl (Schule) homework sing.
Häuschen ['hɔsçən] neut (pl -) cottage, small house.
Haus‖frau f housewife. **–halt** m household; (Budget) budget. **–hälterin** f housekeeper. **–haltsplan** m budget.
hausieren [hau'ziːrən] v peddle, hawk.
häuslich ['hɔysliç] adj domestic.
Haus‖mädchen neut housemaid. **–meister** m caretaker. **–tür** f front door. **–wart** m caretaker. **–wirt** m landlord. **–wirtin** f landlady. **–wirtschaft** f housekeeping.
Haut [haut] f (pl Häute) skin; (Tier) hide, pelt. **–ausschlag** m rash. **–krem** m skin cream.
Hebamme ['heɪpamə] f (pl -n) midwife.
Hebel ['heɪbəl] m (pl -) lever.
***heben** ['heɪbən] v lift, raise; (Steuer) raise, levy. **sich heben** rise. **Hebung** f raising; (Beseitigung) removal.
Hecht [hɛçt] m (pl -e) pike.
Heck [hɛk] neut (pl -e) stern; (eines Autos) rear. **–klappe** f (Mot) hatchback, tailgate.
Hecke ['hɛkə] f (pl -n) hedge; (Brut) brood, hatch. **–nschütze** m sniper.

Heer [heɪr] *neut (pl* -e) army.
Hefe ['heɪfə] *f* yeast.
Heft [hɛft] *neut (pl* -e) notebook, exercise book; (*Zeitschrift*) issue; (*Griff*) handle, haft.
heftig ['hɛftiç] *adj* violent; (*leidenschaftlich*) passionate, vehement.
hegen ['heɪgən] *v* (*hätscheln*) cherish; (*schützen*) protect; (*Gedanken*) nurture.
Heide[1] ['haɪdə] *m (pl* -n) heathen, pagan.
Heide[2] *f (pl* -n) heath, moor. **-kraut** *neut* heather.
Heidelbeere ['haɪdəlbeɪrə] *f* bilberry.
heidnisch ['haɪtniʃ] *adj* heathen, pagan.
heikel ['haɪkəl] *adj* delicate, awkward.
heil [haɪl] *adj* safe, uninjured; (*geheilt*) healed; (*ganz*) whole. **Heil** *neut* welfare; (*Kirche*) salvation. **-and** *m* saviour. **heil‖bringend** *adj* salutary. **-en** *v* heal, cure.
heilig ['haɪliç] *adj* holy, sacred. **Heiliger Abend** Christmas Eve. **Heilige(r)** *m* saint. **Heiligenschein** *m* halo.
Heil‖kunde *f* medicine, medical science. **-mittel** *neut* remedy, cure.
heim [haɪm] *adv* home(ward). **Heim** *neut (pl* -e) home.
Heimat ['haɪmaːt] *f (unz.)* home(land), native place. **-land** *neut* homeland. **heimatlos** *adj* homeless. **Heimatstadt** *f* home town.
Heimfahrt [haɪmfaːrt] *f* return journey. **heimisch** *adj* domestic; (*heimatlich*) native. **Heimkehr** *f* return (home).
heim‖lich *adj* secret. **-suchen** *v* plague, afflict. **-tückisch** *adj* malicious, insidious.
Heimweh ['haɪmveɪ] *neut* homesickness. **Heimweh haben** be homesick.
Heirat ['haɪraɪt] *f (pl* -en) marriage. **heiraten** *v* marry.
heiser ['haɪzər] *adj* hoarse.
heiß [haɪs] *adj* hot.
***heißen** ['haɪsən] *v* be called *or* named; (*bedeuten*) mean. **wie heißt Du?** what's your name? **das heißt (d.h.)** that is (i.e.).
heiter ['haɪtər] *adj* (*Person*) serene; (*Erählung*) happy; (*Wetter*) bright, clear. **Heiterkeit** *f* serenity.
Heiz‖apparat ['haɪtsaparaɪt] *m (pl* -e) heater. **-decke** *f* electric blanket. **heizen** *v* heat. **Heiz‖ung** *f* heating. **-material** *neut* fuel.
Hektar [hɛk'taɪr] *neut (pl* -e) hectare.

Held [hɛlt] *m (pl* -en) hero. **Helden‖mut** *m* heroism. **-tat** *f* heroic deed, exploit. **Heldin** *f (pl* -nen) heroine.
helfen ['hɛlfən] *v* help, assist; (*nützen*) help, do good. **Helfer** *m (pl* -), **Helferin** *f (pl* -nen) helper, assistant.
hell [hɛl] *adj* (*Licht*) bright; (*Farbe*) light; (*Klang*) clear. **hellblau** *adj* light blue. **Hellseher** *m (pl* -), **Hellseherin** *f (pl* -nen) clairvoyant.
Helm [hɛlm] *m (pl* -e) helmet; (*Naut*) rudder; (*Kuppel*) dome.
Hemd [hɛmt] *neut (pl* -en) shirt. **-särmel** *m* shirtsleeve.
hemmen ['hɛmən] *v* restrain, hinder, inhibit; (*Psychol*) inhibit. **Hemmung** *f (pl* -en) hindrance, stoppage; (*Psychol*) inhibition. **hemmungslos** *adj* unrestrained.
Hengst [hɛnst] *m (pl* -e) stallion.
Henkel ['hɛnkəl] *m (pl* -) handle.
Henker ['hɛnkər] *m (pl*-) hangman.
her [heɪr] *adv* (to) here; (*zeitlich*) ago, since; (*von*) from. **hin und her** to and fro, back and forth. **komm her!** come here! **wo kommen Sie her?** where do you come from? **schon lange her** a long time ago. **von weit her** from afar.
herab [hɛ'rap] *adv* down(wards). **-hängen** *v* hang down. **-lassen** *v* lower. **sich herablassen** condescend. **herab‖lassend** *adj* patronizing. **-setzen** *v* reduce; (*Person*) degrade. **-setzend** *adj* contemptuous. **-würdigen** *v* debase, degrade.
heran [hɛ'ran] *adv* near, up to; (*hierher*) (to) here. **-gehen** *v* go up to, approach. **-kommen** *v* approach, draw near.
herauf [hɛ'rauf] *adv* (up) here; (*hinauf*) upwards. **-beschwören** *v* conjure up. **-ziehen** *v* pull up.
heraus [hɛ'raus] *adv* out; (*draußen, aus dem Hause*) outside. **-fordern** *v* challenge. **Herausforderung** *f* challenge. **herausgeben** *v* give out; (*Buch, usw.*) publish. **Herausgeber** *m* publisher. **herauswachsen aus** *v* grow out of.
herb [hɛrp] *adj* sharp, tart; (*Wein*) dry; (*fig*) harsh.
herbei [hɛr'bai] *adv* (to) here, this way. **-führen** *v* cause.
Herberge ['hɛrbɛrgə] *f (pl* -n) hostel.
Herbst [hɛrpst] *m (pl* -e) autumn, (*US*) fall. **herbstlich** *adj* autumnal.
Herd [heɪrt] *m (pl* -e) cooker, stove.
Herde ['heɪrdə] *f (pl* -n) herd.

herein [hɛ'rain] *adv* in, inside, in here.
–führen *v* usher in. **–treten** *v* enter.
*hergeben ['heɪrgeɪbən] *v* hand over.
hergebracht ['heɪrgəbraxt] *adj* traditional, customary.
Hering ['hɛriŋ] *m* (*pl* -e) herring.
*herkommen ['heɪrkɔmən] *v* come here; (*abstammen*) come from. **herkommen von** be caused by, be due to. **herkömmlich** *adj* customary, traditional.
Herkunft ['hɛrkunft] *f* (*unz*) origin; (*Person*) birth, descent.
herleiten ['heɪrlaitən] *v* lead here; (*fig*) derive, deduce. **Herleitung** *f* derivation.
Hermelin [hɛrmə'liɪn] *neut* (*pl* -e) ermine.
hernach [hɛr'naɪx] *adv* afterwards, after this.
Heroin [hero'iɪn] *neut* heroin.
Herr [hɛr] *m* (*pl* -en) (*Anrede*) Mr; (*Herrscher*) master, lord. **der Herr Gott** Lord God. **dieser Herr** this gentleman. **Herren‖artikel** *pl* men's clothing. **–haus** *neut* manor house. **–toilette** *f* men's lavatory.
herrichten ['hɛriçtən] *v* prepare, arrange.
Herrin ['hɛrin] *f* (*pl* -nen) lady, mistress.
herr‖isch *adj* overbearing, domineering. **–lich** *adj* splendid, magnificent. **Herr‖lichkeit** *f* splendour, magnificence. **–schaft** *f* power, rule; (*fig*) mastery.
herrschen *v* rule, govern; (*vorhanden sein*) prevail. **Herrscher** *m* (*pl* -) ruler.
her‖rühren *v* originate (from). **–stammen** *v* descend (from). **–stellen** *v* manufacture, make; (*reparieren*) repair. **Hersteller** *m* manufacturer, maker. **Herstellung** *f* manufacture.
herüber [hɛ'ryɪbər] *adv* across, over here.
herum [hɛ'rum] *adv* (a)round, about. **–fahren** *v* drive around. **–pfuschen** *v* tinker, mess around (with). **–streichen** *v* roam about, wander around.
herunter [hɛ'runtər] *adv* downwards, down (here). **–kommen** *v* come down; (*sinken*) decline.
hervor [hɛr'foɪr] *adv* forth, out. **–bringen** *v* produce; (*Worte*) utter. **–heben** *v* make prominent, bring out. **–ragen** *v* stand out, jut out. **–ragend** *adj* outstanding. **–rufen** *v* arouse; (*verursachen*) cause. **–treten** *v* come forward.
Herz [hɛrts] *neut* (*pl* -en) heart. **–anfall** *m* heart attack. **herz‖erfreuend** *adj* heartening, cheering. **–erschütternd** *adj* appalling. **–haft** *adj* stout-hearted. **–ig** *adj*

lovely. **–lich** *adj* hearty. **–los** *adj* heartless.
Herzog ['hɛrtsoɪk] *m* (*pl* **Herzöge**) duke. **–in** *f* (*pl* -nen) duchess. **Herzogtum** *neut* duchy, dukedom.
herzu [hɛr'tsuɪ] *adv* (to) here, towards.
Hessen ['hɛsən] *neut* Hesse.
Hetze [hɛtsə] *f* (*pl* -n) hounding, baiting; (*Eile*) mad rush, dash; (*Jagd*) hunt. **hetzen** *v* hound; rush, dash; hunt.
Heu [hɔy] *neut* hay. **Heu‖fieber** *neut* hay fever. **–gabel** *f* pitchfork. **–schober** *m* haystack. **–schrecke** *f* grasshopper, locust.
Heuchelei [hɔyçə'lai] *f* (*pl* -en) hypocrisy. **heucheln** *v* be hypocritical. **Heuchler** *m* (*pl* -), **Heuchlerin** *f* (*pl* -nen) hypocrite. **heuchlerisch** *adj* hypocritical.
heulen ['hɔylən] *v* cry, howl.
heute ['hɔytə] *adv* today. **heutig** *adj* today's; (*gegenwärtig*) present, current. **heutzutage** *adv* nowadays, these days.
Hexe ['hɛksə] *f* (*pl* -n) witch.
Hieb [hiɪp] *m* (*pl* -e) blow, stroke; (*Schnitt*) cut, slash.
hier [hiɪr] *adv* here. **hier und da** now and then. **hier und dort** here and there. **hier‖auf** *adv* then, upon this. **–aus** *adv* from this. **–bei** *adv* hereby, herewith; (*Brief*) enclosed. **–für** *adv* for this.
hi-fi ['haifai] *adj* hi-fi.
Hilfe ['hilfə] *f* (*pl* -n) help, assistance. **–ruf** *m* cry for help. **hilf‖los** *adj* helpless. **–reich** *adj* helpful. **–sbereit** *adj* eager to help. **Hilfs‖lehrer** *m* assistant teacher. **–mittel** *neut* remedy, aid.
Himbeere ['himbeɪrə] *f* raspberry.
Himmel ['himəl] *m* (*pl* -) sky; (*Paradies*) heaven. **–fahrt** *f* Ascension. **–reich** *neut* heaven. **–skörper** *m* celestial body. **himmlisch** ['himliʃ] *adj* celestial, heavenly.
hin [hin] *adv* (to) there, from here, towards. **hin und her** to and fro, back and forth. **hin und wieder** now and again. **hin und zurück** there and back. **vor sich hin** to oneself. **es ist noch lange hin** there's a long time to go.
hinab [hi'nap] *adv* down(wards). **–lassen** *v* lower, let down. **–steigen** *v* descend.
hinan [hi'nan] *adv* up (to), upwards.
hinauf [hi'nauf] *adv* up (there), upwards. **die Treppe hinauf** up the stairs. **–setzen** *v* put up. **–ziehen** *v* pull up, (*umziehen*) move up.

hinaus [hi'naus] *adv* out, forth. **-gehen** *v* go out. **hinausgehen über** surpass, exceed. **hinaus‖kommen** *v* come out. **-werfen** *v* throw out.

Hinblick ['hinblik] *m* **im Hinblick auf** with regard to.

hinderlich ['hindərliç] *adj* restrictive, hindering. **hindern** *v* hinder; (*verhindern*) prevent. **Hindernis** *neut* (*pl* -se) obstacle, hindrance.

hindeuten ['hindɔytən] *v* point (at); (*fig*) hint (at).

hindurch [hin'durç] *adv* through, across; (*zeitlich*) throughout.

hinein [hi'nain] *adv* in(to). **sich hineindrängen** *v* force one's way in. **hineinziehen** *v* draw in; (*fig: verwickeln*) involve; (*umziehen*) move to.

hinfahren ['hinfairən] *v* drive there; (*hinbringen*) take there. **Hinfahrt** *f* outward journey, way there.

*****hinfallen** ['hinfalən] *v* fall down. **hinfällig** *adj* feeble, frail; (*Meinung*) untenable, invalid.

Hingabe ['hingaibə] *f* devotion.

*****hingeben** ['hingeibən] *v* give up. **sich hingeben** devote oneself (to).

hingegen ['hingeigən] *conj* on the other hand, whereas.

*****hingehen** ['hingeiən] *v* go there; (*Zeit*) pass, elapse. **etwas hingehen lassen** let something pass.

hinken ['hiŋkən] *v* limp.

hin‖kommen *v* arrive, get there; (*umg.*) manage. **-langen** *v* reach. **-länglich** *adj* sufficient. **-legen** *v* put down. **sich hinlegen** lie down. **hin‖nehmen** *v* put up with, bear. **-reichend** *adj* sufficient.

Hinreise ['hinraizə] *f* outward journey, way there.

hinreißen ['hinraisən] *v* carry along; (*entzücken*) charm, transport. **-d** *adj* charming, enchanting.

hinrichten ['hinriçtən] *v* (*Person*) execute. **Hinrichtung** *f* execution.

*****hinschreiben** ['hinʃraibən] *v* write down.

Hinsicht ['hinziçt] *f* **in Hinsicht auf** with regard to. **in dieser Hinsicht** in this regard. **hinsichtlich** *adv* with regard to.

hinten ['hintən] *adv* behind, at the back. **nach hinten** to the back, backwards. **von hinten** from behind.

hinter ['hintər] *prep* behind, after. *adj* rear, back. **Hinter‖achse** *f* rear axle. **-bein** *neut* hind leg. **Hintere(r)** *m* back

part; (*Körper*) bottom, backside.

hintergehen *v* deceive, fool.

Hinter‖grund *m* background. **-halt** *m* ambush. **aus dem Hinterhalt überfallen** ambush. **Hinterhof** *m* rear court, back yard.

hinter‖lassen *v* leave (behind). **-legen** *v* deposit.

Hintern ['hintərn] *m* (*pl* -) bottom, backside.

Hinter‖schiff *neut* stern. **-teil** *m* back part. **-tür** *f* back door.

hinterziehen [hintər'tsiːən] *v* (*Steuern*) evade. **Hinterziehung** *f* (tax) evasion.

hinüber [hi'nyːbər] *adv* over, across, to the other side. **-gehen** *v* cross (over).

hinunter [hi'nuntər] *adv* downwards, down (there). **die Treppe hinunter** downstairs.

hinweg [hin'vɛk] *adv* away (from here), off. **Hinweg** *m* outward journey. **hinwegkommen über** get over.

Hinweis ['hinvais] *m* (*pl* -e) indication, hint. **hinweisen** *v* point out, show; (*Person*) direct; (*anspielen*) refer, allude.

*****hinziehen** ['hintsiːən] *v* draw, attract; (*verzögern*) drag out.

hinzu [hin'tsuː] *adv* in addition, as well. **-fügen** *v* add. **-kommen** *v* be added. **-kommend** *adj* additional. **-ziehen** *v* draw *or* bring in; (*Fachmann*) consult.

Hirn [hirn] *neut* (*pl* -e) brain.

Hirsch [hirʃ] *m* (*pl* -e) stag. **-fleisch** *neut* venison. **-kalb** *neut* fawn. **-kuh** *f* doe, hind.

Hirt [hirt] *m* (*pl* -en) shepherd, herdsman. **-in** *f* (*pl* -nen) shepherdess.

hissen ['hisən] *v* hoist.

Historiker [hi'stoːrikər] *m* (*pl* -) historian. **historisch** *adj* historical; (*bedeutend*) historic.

Hitze ['hitsə] *f* (*unz.*) heat; (*Leidenschaft*) passion. **hitzebeständig** *adj* heat-resistant. **hitzig** *adj* hot; (*fig*) fiery, passionate. **Hitz‖kopf** *m* hothead. **-schlag** *m* heat-stroke.

hoch [hoːx] (**hoher, hohe, hohes, höher, höchst**) *adj* high; (*Baum*) tall; (*Alter*) old, advanced. *adv* highly, greatly. **hohe Blüte** full bloom. **hohe See** high *or* open sea. **10 hoch 4** 10 to the power of 4. **Hoch** *neut* (*pl* -s) cheer; (*Hochdruckgebiet*) high-pressure area. **Dreimal hoch** three cheers.

Hochachtung ['hoːxaxtuŋ] *f* respect, esteem. **hochachtungsvoll** respectfully, yours faithfully.
hochdeutsch ['hoxdɔytʃ] *adj* high German, standard German.
Hoch‖druck *m* high pressure. −**ebene** *f* plateau. −**flut** *f* high tide. −**frequenz** *f* high frequency.
*****hochhalten** ['hoːxhaltən] *v* think highly of, esteem.
Hoch‖haus *neut* tall building, high-rise block. −**konjunktur** *f* boom. −**land** *neut* highland(s). −**leistung-** *adj* heavy-duty. −**mut** *m* pride, arrogance. **hochmütig** *adj* proud, arrogant.
Hoch‖ruf *m* cheer. −**schätzung** *f* (high) esteem. −**schule** *f* college, university; (*technische*) polytechnic. −**spannung** *f* high tension, high voltage. −**sprung** *m* high jump. −**verrat** *m* high treason. −**wasser** *neut* high tide, high water; (*Überschwemmung*) flooding. **Hochzeit** *f* wedding. **hochzeitlich** *adj* nuptial, bridal. **Hochzeitskleid** *neut* wedding dress.
höchst [hœːxst] *adj* highest, greatest. *adv* very (much), greatly, highly.
hochstehend ['hoxʃteːənt] *adj* high-ranking, eminent.
höchstens [hœxstəns] *adv* at most, at best.
Höchst‖geschwindigkeit *f* maximum speed. −**preis** *m* maximum price.
hocken ['hɔkən] *v* squat, crouch. **Hocker** *m* (*pl* -) stool.
Hode ['hoːdə] *f* (*pl* -n) *or* **Hoden** *m* (*pl* -) testicle.
Hof [hoːf] *m* (*pl* **Höfe**) (court)yard; (*Landwirtschaft*) farm; (*fürstlich*) court.
hoffen ['hɔfən] *v* hope. **hoffentlich** *adv* I hope (so); let us hope (that). **Hoffnung** *f* (*pl* -en) hope. **hoffnungs‖los** *adj* hopeless. −**voll** *adj* hopeful.
höflich ['hœfliç] *adj* polite, courteous. **Höflichkeit** *f* courtesy, politeness.
hohe(r) ['hoːə(r)] *V* hoch.
Höhe ['hœːə] *f* (*pl* -n) height; (*Gipfel*) top; (*Geog*) latitude; (*Hügel*) hill.
Hoheit ['hoːhait] *f* (*unz.*) grandeur, greatness; (*Titel*) Highness. −**sgewässer** *pl* territorial waters.
Höhepunkt ['hœːəpuŋkt] *m* climax.
höher ['hœːər] *V* hoch.
hohl [hoːl] *adj* hollow, (*Linse*) concave.
Höhle ['hœːlə] *f* (*pl* -n) cave; (*Loch*) hole;

(*eines Tiers*) burrow, hole. **höhlen** *v* hollow (out).
höhnen ['hœːnən] *v* mock, taunt. **höhnisch** *adj* mocking, scornful.
hold [hɔlt] *adj* charming, gracious. −**selig** *adj* most charming, most gracious.
holen ['hoːlən] *v* fetch. **Atem holen** draw breath. **sich Rat holen bei** ask for advice.
Holländer ['hɔləndər] *m* (*pl* -) Dutchman. −**in** *f* (*pl* -nen) Dutchwoman. **holländisch** *adj* Dutch.
Hölle ['hœlə] *f* (*pl* -n) hell.
Holunder [ho'lundər] *m* (*pl* -) elder (tree). −**beere** *f* elderberry.
Holz [hɔlts] *neut* (*pl* **Hölzer**) wood. −**blasinstrument** *neut* woodwind instrument.
hölzern ['hœltsərn] *adj* wooden; (*fig*) stiff, awkward, clumsy.
holzig ['hɔltsiç] *adj* woody.
Holz‖klotz *m* wooden block. −**kohle** *f* charcoal. −**schnitt** *m* woodcut. −**weg** *m* **auf dem Holzwege sein** be on the wrong track. **Holzwurm** *m* woodworm.
Homosexualität [homozɛksuali'tɛit] *f* homosexuality. **homosexuell** *adj* homosexual. **Homosexuelle(r)** *m* homosexual.
Honig ['hoːniç] *m* honey. −**biene** *f* honeybee.
Honorar [hono'raːr] *neut* (*pl* -e) fee, honorarium; (*eines Autors*) royalties *pl*.
Hopfen ['hɔpfən] *m* (*pl* -) hops *pl*.
hörbar ['hœːrbaːr] *adj* audible.
horchen ['hɔrçən] *v* listen (to); (*heimlich*) eavesdrop.
Horde ['hɔrdə] *f* (*pl* -n) horde.
hören ['hœːrən] *v* hear; (*Radio*) listen to. **Hören** *neut* (sense of) hearing. −**sagen** *neut* hearsay. **Hörer** *m* hearer; (*Radio*) listener; (*Telef*) receiver; (*pl*) audience. −**schaft** *f* audience. **Hörgerät** *neut* hearing aid.
Horizont [hɔri'tsɔnt] *m* (*pl* -e) horizon. **horizontal** *adj* horizontal.
Hormon [hɔr'moːn] *neut* (*pl* -e) hormone.
Horn [hɔrn] *neut* (*pl* **Hörner**) horn. −**brille** *f* horn-rimmed spectacles. −**haut** *f* (*Anat*) cornea.
Horoskop [horo'skoːp] *neut* (*pl* -e) horoscope.
Hör‖probe *f* audition. −**saal** *m* lecture hall. −**spiel** *neut* radio play.
Hose ['hoːzə] *f* (*pl* -n) trousers. **Hosen‖schlitz** *m* flies, (*US*) fly. −**träger** *pl* braces, (*US*) suspenders.

Höschen ['hœɪsçən] *neut* (*pl* -) knickers *pl*; panties *pl*.
Hotel [ho'tɛl] *neut* (*pl* -s) hotel.
Hub [huɪp] *m* (*pl* **Hübe**) lift; (*Mot*) stroke. **–raum** *m* cylinder capacity.
hübsch [hypʃ] *adj* pretty, nice; (*Mann*) good-looking.
Hubschrauber ['hupʃraubər] *m* (*pl* -) helicopter.
Huf [huɪf] *m* (*pl* -e) hoof. **–eisen** *neut* horseshoe.
Hüftbein ['hyftbain] *neut* hipbone. **Hüfte** *f* hip.
Hügel ['hyɪgəl] *m* (*pl* -) hill. **hügelig** *adj* hilly.
Huhn [huɪn] *neut* (*pl* **Hühner**) hen; (*Küche*) chicken.
Hühner‖auge *neut* (*Med*) corn. **–braten** *m* roast chicken. **–brühe** *f* chicken broth. **–ei** *neut* hen's egg. **–stall** *m* henhouse.
huldigen ['huldigən] *v* pay homage to; (*Ansicht*) hold, subscribe to. **Huldigung** *f* homage.
Hülle ['hylə] *f* covering, wrapping; (*Umschlag*) envelope; (*Buch*) jacket, cover. **in Hülle und Fülle** in abundance. **hüllen** *v* wrap, cover.
Hülse ['hylzə] *f* (*pl* -n) husk, shell; (*Erbse*) pod; (*aus Papier, usw.*) case, casing.
human [hu'maɪn] *adj* humane. **Humanist** *m* (*pl* -en) humanist. **humanitär** *adj* humanitarian.
Hummel ['huməl] *f* (*pl* -n) bumblebee.
Hummer ['humər] *m* (*pl* -) lobster.
Humor [hu'moɪr] *m* (sense of) humour. **humorvoll** *adj* humorous.
humpeln ['humpəln] *v* hobble, limp.
Hund [hunt] *m* (*pl* -e) dog. **Hunde‖hütte** *f* kennel. **–leine** *f* leash.
hundert ['hundərt] *adj*, *pron* hundred. **Hundert‖füßler** *m* centipede. **–jahrfeier** *f* centenary. **hundert‖mal** *adv* a hundred times. **–prozentig** *adj* one-hundred-percent, complete.
Hündin ['hyndin] *f* (*pl* -nen) bitch.
Hunger ['huŋər] *m* hunger. **Hunger haben** be hungry. **–lohn** *m* starvation wages *pl*; pittance. **hungern** *v* starve; be hungry. **Hungersnot** *f* famine. **Hungerstreik** *m* hungerstrike. **hungrig** *adj* hungry.
Hupe ['huɪpə] *f* (*pl* -n) (*Mot*) horn. **hupen** *v* sound the horn, beep.
hüpfen ['hypfən] *v* hop, skip.
Hürde ['hyrdə] *f* (*pl* -n) hurdle; (*Schafe*) fold, pen.

Hure ['huɪrə] *f* (*pl* -n) whore.
hurra [hu'raɪ] *interj* hurrah!
husten ['huɪstən] *v* cough. **Husten** *m* (*pl* -) cough.
Hut¹ [huɪt] *m* (*pl* **Hüte**) hat.
Hut² *f* (*unz.*) (*Schutz*) protection; (*Vorsicht*) care; (*Aufsicht*) guard. **auf der Hut sein** (**vor**) be on one's guard (against).
hüten ['hyɪtən] *v* guard. **sich hüten** (**vor**) be careful *or* wary (of).
Hütte ['hyɪtə] *f* (*pl* -n) hut, cabin; (*Metall*) foundry, ironworks. **–nkäse** *m* cottage cheese.
Hyäne [hy'ɛɪnə] *f* (*pl* -n) hyena.
Hydraulik [hy'draulik] *f* hydraulics. **hydraulisch** *adj* hydraulic.
Hygiene [hygi'eɪnə] *f* hygiene. **hygienisch** *adj* hygienic.
Hymne ['hymnə] *f* (*pl* -n) hymn.
Hypnose [hyp'noɪzə] *f* (*pl* -n) hypnosis. **hypno‖tisch** *adj* hypnotic. **–tisieren** *v* hypnotize.
Hypothek [hypo'teɪk] *f* (*pl* -en) mortgage.
Hypothese [hypo'teɪzə] *f* (*pl* -n) hypothesis. **hypothetisch** *adj* hypothetical.
Hysterie [hyste'riɪ] *f* hysteria. **hysterisch** *adj* hysterical. **hysterische Anfälle** *pl* hysterics.

I

ich [iç] *pron* I. **Ich** *neut* self, ego. **ichbezogen** *adj* egocentric.
ideal [ide'aɪl] *adj* ideal. **Ideal** *neut* (*pl* -e) ideal. **Idealismus** *m* idealism.
Idee [i'deɪ] *f* (*pl* -n) idea.
identifizieren [iːdɛntifi'tsiːrən] *v* identify. **identisch** *adj* identical. **Identität** *f* identity.
Idiot [idi'oɪt] *m* (*pl* -en) idiot. **idiotisch** *adj* idiotic.
Igel ['iɪgəl] *m* (*pl* -) hedgehog.
ignorieren [igno'riːrən] *v* ignore.
ihm [iɪm] *pron* (*Person*) (to) him; (*Sache*) (to) it.
ihn [iɪn] *pron* (*Person*) him; (Sache) it.
ihnen ['iɪnən] *pron* (to) them. **Ihnen** *pron* (to) you.
ihr [iɪr] *pron* you; (*Dat*) (to) her. *pron, adj* (*Person*) her; its; their. **Ihr** *pron, adj* your. **ihrer, ihre, ihres** *pron* hers; its; theirs. **Ihrer, Ihre, Ihres** yours. **ihrseits** *adv* for your part. **ihr‖esgleichen** *adv* like

her (it, them). **−etwegen** *or* **−etwillen** on her (its, their) account. **der, die, das ihrige** *pron* hers; its; theirs.

Illusion [iluzi'oɪn] *f* (*pl* -en) illusion. **illusorisch** *adj* illusory.

illustrieren [ilu'striːrən] *v* illustrate. **Illustrierte** *f* (illustrated) magazine.

im [im] *prep* + *art* in dem.

Imbiß ['imbis] *m* (*pl* **Imbisse**) snack. **−stube** *f* snack bar.

Immatrikulation [imatrikulatsi'oɪn] *f* (*pl* -en) matriculation, registration.

immer ['imər] *adv* always. **immer mehr** more and more. **immer noch** still. **immer wieder** again and again. **wenn auch immer** although. **auf immer** forever. **−fort** *adv* constantly. **−grün** *adj* evergreen. **−hin** *adv* nevertheless. **−zu** *adv* all the time.

Immigrant [imi'grant] *m* (*pl* -en) immigrant.

Immobilien [imo'biːliən] *pl* real estate *sing.*

Imperialismus [imperia'lismus] *m* imperialism. **Imperialist** *m* (*pl* -en) imperialist.

impfen ['impfən] *v* inoculate, vaccinate. **Impfung** *f* (*pl* -en) inoculation, vaccination.

imponieren [impo'niːrən] *v* impress. **−d** *adj* impressive.

Import [im'pɔrt] *m* (*pl* -e) import(ation); (*Ware*) import. **−eur** *m* (*pl* -e) importer. **−handel** *m* import trade. **importieren** *v* import.

impotent ['impotɛnt] *adj* impotent.

imprägnieren [impreg'niːrən] *v* impregnate, saturate.

improvisieren [improvi'ziːrən] *v* improvise. **improvisiert** *adj* improvized, ad-lib.

imstande [im'ʃtandə] *adv* **imstande sein** be able *or* capable.

in [in] *prep* (+ *Dat*) in; (+ *Acc*) into, in; (*Zeit*) (with)in.

Inanspruchnahme [in'anʃpruxnaimə] *f* demands *pl.*

Inbegriff ['inbəgrif] *m* essence, epitome. **mit Inbegriff von** inclusive of. **inbegriffen** *adj, adv* (*Steuer*) included, inclusive(ly).

Inbrunst ['inbrunst] *f* ardour, fervour.

indem [in'deɪm] *conj* (*dadurch daß*) in that, by; (*während*) while.

Inder [in'dər] *m* (*pl* -) (Asian) Indian.

indessen [in'dɛsən] *conj* (*inzwischen*) meanwhile, in the meantime; (*immerhin*) however, nevertheless.

Indianer [indi'aɪnər] *m* (*pl* -) (American) Indian. **indianisch** *adj* (American) Indian.

Indien ['indiən] *neut* India.

indirekt ['indirɛkt] *adj* indirect.

indisch ['indiʃ] *adj* (Asian) Indian.

indiskret ['indiskreɪt] *adj* indiscreet, tactless.

Individualist [individua'list] *m* (*pl* -en) individualist. **individualistisch** *adj* individualist(ic). **individuell** *adj* individual. **Individuum** *neut* (*pl* -duen) individual.

industrialisieren [industriali'ziːrən] *v* industrialize. **Industrie** *f* (*pl* -n) industry. **−gebiet** *neut* industrial region. **industriell** *adj* industrial. **Industrielle(r)** *m* industrialist.

ineinander [inain'andər] *adv* in(to) each other. **−greifen** *v* (*Tech*) engage; (*fig*) overlap.

Infanterie [infantə'riː] *f* infantry. **Infanterist** *m* (*pl* -en) infantryman.

infiltrieren [infil'triːrən] *v* infiltrate.

infizieren [infi'tsiːrən] *v* infect. **sich infizieren** become infected, catch a disease.

Inflation [inflatsi'oɪn] *f* (*Komm*) inflation. **inflationär, inflationistisch** *adj* inflationary.

infolge [in'fɔlgə] *prep* on account of, owing to. **−dessen** *adv* consequently.

Information [infɔrmatsi'oɪn] *f* (*pl* -en) information. **eine Information** a piece of information.

informell ['infɔrmɛl] *adj* informal.

informieren [infɔr'miːrən] *v* inform, instruct. **sich informieren über** find out about, gather information about.

Ingenieur [inʒe'njœɪr] *m* (*pl* -e) engineer. **−schule** *f* engineering college. **−wesen** *neut* engineering.

Ingwer ['iŋvɛɪr] *m* ginger.

Inhaber ['inhaɪbər] *m* (*pl* -) owner; (*Titel, Paß, Patent*) holder.

inhalieren [inha'liːrən] *v* inhale.

Inhalt ['inhalt] *m* (*pl* -e) contents *pl*; (*Bedeutung*) meaning, content. **−sverzeichnis** *neut* table of contents.

Initiative [initsia'tiːvə] *f* (*unz.*) initiative. **die Initiative ergreifen** take the initiative.

inklusive [inklu'ziːvə] *prep* including, inclusive of.

inkonsequent ['inkɔnzekvɛnt] *adj* inconsistent.

Inkontinenz ['inkɔntinɛnts] *f* incontinence.

inkorporieren [inkɔrpɔ'riːrən] *v* incorporate.

Inkrafttreten [in'kraftreɪtən] *neut* coming into effect.

Inland ['inlant] *neut* inland, interior.

inmitten [in'mitən] *prep* in the midst of, among.

inne ['inə] *adv* within.

innen ['inən] *adv* within, inside. **nach innen** inwards. **Innen‖ausstattung** *f* interior decoration, decor. **–minister** *m* Home Secretary, Minister of the Interior. **–politik** *f* domestic policy. **innenpolitisch** *adj* (relating to) internal affairs. **Innenraum** *m* interior.

inner ['inər] *adj* internal, inner. **Innereien** *pl* offal. **Innere(s)** *neut* (*pl* -(e)n) interior. **inner‖halb** *prep* within. **–lich** *adj* inward, internal. **innerst** *adj* innermost.

innewohnen ['inəvoːnən] *v* be inherent (in).

innig ['iniç] *adj* (*Gefühle*) sincere; (*Freunde*) intimate.

ins [ins] *prep + art* in das.

Insasse ['inzasə] *m* (*pl* -n) inmate.

insbesondere [insbə'zɔndərə] *adv* particularly.

Inschrift ['infrift] *f* inscription.

Insekt [in'zɛkt] *neut* (*pl* -en) insect. **–enpulver** *neut* insect powder. **–izid** *neut* insecticide.

Insel ['inzəl] *f* (*pl* -n) island.

Inserat [inze'raɪt] *neut* (*pl* -e) (newspaper) advertisement.

insgesamt [insgə'zamt] *adv* altogether.

insofern [inzo'fɛrn] *conj* so far as; [in'zofɛrn] (*bis zu diesem Punkt*) to that extent. **insofern als** inasmuch as.

insoweit [inzo'vait] *adv* to that extent.

Inspektor [inspɛk'tɔr] *m* (*pl* -en) inspector.

instand halten [in'ftant haltən] *v* maintain (in good order). **instand setzen** *v* repair, overhaul; (*Person*) enable. **Instandhaltung** *f* unkeep, maintenance.

Instanz [in'ftants] *f* (*pl* -en) authority. **durch die Instanzen** through official channels.

instinktiv [instiŋk'tiːf] *adj* instinctive.

Institut [insti'tuːt] *neut* (*pl* -e) institute.

Instrument [instru'mɛnt] *neut* (*pl* -e) instrument.

inszenieren [instse'niːrən] *v* (*Film,* *Schauspiel*) produce; (*fig*) create, engineer.

integrieren [inte'griːrən] *v* integrate. **Integration** *f* integration.

intellektuell [intɛlɛktu'ɛl] *adj* intellectual.

intelligent [intɛli'gɛnt] *adj* intelligent, clever.

interessant [intərɛ'sant] *adj* interesting. **Interesse** *neut* interest. **interessieren** *v* interest. **sich interessieren für** take an interest in, be interested in.

intern [in'tɛrn] *adj* internal.

Internat [intər'nait] *neut* (*pl* -e) boarding school.

international [intɛrnatsio'naɪl] *adj* international.

Interview [intər'vjuɪ] *neut* (*pl* -s) interview. **interviewen** *v* interview. **Interviewer** *m* interviewer. **Interviewte(r)** interviewee.

intim [in'tiːm] *adj* intimate.

Intrige [in'triːgə] *f* (*pl* -n) intrigue. **intrigieren** *v* plot, scheme.

Invalide(r) [inva'liːdə(r)] *m* invalid. **Invaliden‖heim** *neut* home for the disabled. **–rente** *f* disability pension. **invalid** *adj* invalid.

Inventar [invɛn'taɪr] *neut* (*pl* -e) inventory.

Inventur [invɛn'tuːr] *f* (*pl* -en) stock-taking.

inwendig ['invɛndiç] *adj* inner.

inwiefern [invi'fɛrn] *conj* to what extent, how far.

inzwischen [in'tsvifən] *adv* meanwhile.

irdisch ['irdif] *adj* earthly, worldly.

Ire ['iɪrə] *m* (*pl* -n) Irishman. **Irin** *f* (*pl* -nen) Irishwoman.

irgend ['irgənt] *adv* perhaps, ever. *pron* some, any. **irgend etwas** something, anything. **irgend jemand** someone, anyone. **irgend‖ein** *adj* some, any. **–wann** *adv* (at) sometime (or other). **–was** *pron* something, anything. **–wie** *adv* somehow, anyhow. **–wo** *adv* somewhere, anywhere.

Iris ['iɪris] *f* (*pl* -) (*Anat*) iris.

irisch ['iɪrif] *adj* Irish.

Irland ['irlant] *neut* Ireland. **Irländer** *m* (*pl* -) Irishman. **Irländerin** *f* (*pl* -nen) Irishwoman. **irländisch** *adj* Irish.

Ironie [iro'niː] *f* (*pl* -n) irony. **ironisch** *adj* ironic; (*spöttisch*) ironical.

irre ['irə] *adj* (*geistesgestört*) insane, mad; (*verwirrt*) confused. *adv* (*von Ziel weg*) astray. **irr werden** go insane. **irren** *v* err.

Irre(r) madman/woman). **irreführen** v lead astray; (täuschen) mislead. **Irrenanstalt** f mental home. **Irrglaube** m heresy. **irrig** adj erroneous. **Irrsinn** m insanity, madness. **irrsinnig** adj insane. **Irrtum** m (pl **Irrtümer**) error. **irrtümlich** adj erroneous, wrong.
Isolierband [izo'liːrbant] neut insulating tape; **isolieren** v isolate; (Elek) insulate. **Isolierung** f isolation; insulation.
Italien [i'taːliən] neut Italy. **Italiener** m (pl -), **Italienerin** f (pl -nen) Italian. **italienisch** adj Italian.

J

ja [ja] adv yes. **ja doch** to be sure, but yes. **ja freilich** yes indeed. **wenn ja** if so.
Jacht [jaxt] f (pl -en) yacht.
Jacke ['jakə] f (pl -n) jacket.
Jagd [jaɪkt] f (pl -en) hunt; (Jagen) hunting. **–flugzeug** neut fighter plane. **–hund** m hound. **–schloß** neut hunting lodge.
jagen ['jaɪgən] v hunt; (treiben) drive (away); (verfolgen) pursue; (eilen) rush, race.
Jäger ['jɛːgər] m (pl -) hunter; (Flugzeug) fighter.
jäh [jɛː] adj steep; (plötzlich) sudden.
Jahr [jaɪr] neut (pl -e) year. **–buch** neut yearbook. **jahrelang** adv for years. **Jahres‖einkommen** neut annual income. **–ende** neut end of the year. **–tag** m anniversary. **–viertel** neut quarter. **–wende** f New Year, turn of the year. **–zeit** f season. **jahreszeitlich** adj seasonal. **Jahrhundert** neut century.
jährig ['jɛːriç] adj lasting a year. **dreijährig** adj three-year-old.
jährlich ['jɛːrliç] adj yearly, annual.
Jahr‖markt m fair. **–zehnt** neut decade.
Jalousie [ʒalu'ziː] f (pl -n) venetian blind.
Jammer ['jamər] m (unz.) wailing; (Elend) misery; (Verzweiflung) despair.
jämmerlich ['jɛmərliç] adj pitiable.
jammern ['jamərn] v wail; (klagen) complain.
Januar ['januaːr] m (pl -e) January.
Japan ['jaːpan] neut Japan. **–er** m (pl -), **Japanerin** f (pl -nen) Japanese. **japanisch** adj Japanese.
jauchzen ['jauxtsən] v shout joyfully, rejoice.

jawohl [ja'voːl] adv, interj yes indeed, certainly.
Jazz [dʒɛs] m jazz.
je [jeː] adv ever. **je und je** always. **je zwei** two each. conj **je mehr, desto besser** the more, the better. **je nachdem** that depends.
jedenfalls ['jeːdənfals] adv in any case.
jeder ['jeːdər], **jede, jedes** pron, adj each, every. **jedermann** pron everybody. **jederzeit** adv always, (at) any time.
jedesmal ['jeːdəsmaːl] adv each time.
jedoch [je'dɔx] adv however, yet.
jemals ['jeːmaːls] adv ever, at any time.
jemand ['jeːmant] pron someone; (Fragen) anyone.
jener ['jeːnər], **jene, jenes** pron, adj that, pl those; (zuerst erwähnt) the former.
jenseits adv on the other side. prep on the other side of, across.
jetzig ['jɛtsiç] adj current, present. **jetzt** adv now, at present.
jeweilig ['jeːvailiç] adj at the time; (Vergangenheit) at that time, then. **jeweils** adv at a(ny) given time.
Jiddisch ['jidiʃ] neut Yiddish (language).
Joch [jɔx] neut (pl -e) yoke.
Jockei ['dʒɔki] m (pl -s) jockey.
Jod [joːt] neut iodine.
jodeln ['joːdəln] v yodel.
Joghurt ['joːgurt] neut (pl -s) yoghurt.
Johannisbeere [jo'hanisbeɪrə] f redcurrant. **schwarze Johannisbeere** blackcurrant.
Journalismus [ʒurna'lismus] m journalism. **Journalist** m (pl -en) journalist. **journalistisch** adj journalistic.
Jubel ['juːbəl] m rejoicing, jubilation. **jubeln** v rejoice. **Jubiläum** neut (pl -äen) anniversary, jubilee.
jucken ['jukən] v itch. **Jucken** neut itch.
Jude ['juːdə] m (pl -n), **Jüdin** f (pl -nen) Jew. **jüdisch** adj Jewish.
Judo ['juːdo] neut judo.
Jugend ['juːgənt] f (unz.) youth. **–gericht** neut juvenile court. **–herberge** f youth hostel. **–kriminalität** f juvenile delinquency. **jugendlich** adj youthful, young, juvenile. **jugendlicher Verbrecher** m juvenile delinquent. **Jugendliche(r)** m youth, juvenile.
Jugoslawe [jugo'slaːvə] m, **Jugoslawin** f Yugoslav. **Jugoslawien** neut Yugoslavia. **jugoslawisch** adj Yugoslav.

Juli ['juːli] *m* (*pl* -s) July.
jung [juŋ] *adj* young. **Junge** *m* (*pl* -n) boy; (*Lehrling*) apprentice; (*Karten*) jack. **jungenhaft** *adj* boyish.
jünger ['jyŋər] *adj* younger, junior. **Jünger** *m* (*pl* -) disciple.
Junges ['juŋəs] *neut* (*pl* **Jungen**) young (animal), offspring.
Jung‖fer *f* (*pl* -n) virgin; (*Mädchen*) girl. **alte Jungfer** old maid, spinster. −**frau** *f* virgin. **jungfräulich** *adj* maidenly, chaste. **Junggeselle** *m* bachelor.
Jüngling ['jyŋliŋ] *m* (*pl* -e) youth, young man. −**salter** *neut* youth, adolescence.
jüngst [jyŋst] *adj* youngest; (*letzt*) latest. **das jüngste Gericht** the Last Judgment.
Juni ['juːni] *m* (*pl* -s) June.
Junker ['juŋkər] *m* (*pl* -) squire; (*jung*) young aristocrat.
Jura¹ ['juːra] *f* law *sing*. **Jura studieren** study law.
Jura² *m* (*pl* -s) the Jura, Jura Mountains.
Jurist [ju'rist] *m* (*pl* -en) lawyer.
just [just] *adv* just, exactly.
Justiz [jus'tiːts] *f* (*unz.*) justice, administration of the law. −**irrtum** *m* miscarriage of justice. −**wesen** *neut* legal affairs, the law.
Juwel [ju'veːl] *neut* (*pl* -en) jewel. −**ier** *m* (*pl* -e) jeweller.
Jux [juks] *m* (*pl* -e) joke, prank. **aus Jux** as a joke, for fun.

K

Kabarett [kaba'rɛt] *neut* (*pl* -e) cabaret.
Kabel ['kaːbəl] *neut* (*pl* -) cable.
Kabeljau ['kaːbəljau] *m* (*pl* -e) cod.
kabeln ['kaːbəln] *v* cable, wire.
Kabine [ka'biːnə] *f* (*pl* -n) (*Schiff*) cabin; (*Umkleide-*) cubicle; (*Seilbahn*) cable-car.
Kabinett [kabi'nɛt] *neut* (*pl* -e) (*Pol*) cabinet; (*Zimmer*) closet.
Kadaver [ka'daːvər] *m* (*pl* -) carcass.
Kadett [ka'dɛt] *m* (*pl* -en) cadet.
Käfer ['kɛːfər] *m* (*pl* -) beetle.
Kaffee [ka'feː] *m* (*pl* -s) coffee. −**bohne** *f* coffee bean. −**kanne** *f* coffee-pot. −**mühle** *f* coffee-grinder. −**satz** *m* coffee grounds *pl*.
Käfig ['kɛːfɪç] *m* (*pl* -e) cage.
kahl [kaːl] *adj* bald; (*Landschaft*) bare,

barren. **Kahlheit** *f* baldness. **kahlköpfig** *adj* bald-headed.
Kahn [kaːn] *m* (*pl* **Kähne**) small boat, punt; (*Last-*) barge.
Kai [kai] *m* (*pl* -e) quay, wharf.
Kaiser ['kaizər] *m* (*pl* -) emperor. −**in** *f* empress. **kaiserlich** *adj* imperial. **Kaiserreich** *neut* empire.
Kakao [ka'kao] *m* cocoa.
Kaktee [kak'teː] *f*, **Kaktus** *m* (*pl* **Kakteen**) cactus.
Kalb [kalp] *neut* (*pl* **Kälber**) calf. −**fleisch** *neut* veal. −**sbraten** *m* roast veal.
Kalender [ka'lɛndər] *m* (*pl* -) calendar.
Kaliber [ka'liːbər] *neut* (*pl* -) calibre.
Kalk [kalk] *m* (*pl* -e) lime. −**stein** *m* limestone.
Kalorie [kalo'riː] *f* (*pl* -n) calorie.
kalt [kalt] *adj* cold. −**blütig** *adj* cold-blooded.
Kälte ['kɛltə] *f* (*unz.*) cold(ness).
Kamel [ka'meːl] *neut* (*pl* -e) camel.
Kamera ['kamera] *f* (*pl* -s) camera. −**mann** *m* cameraman.
Kamerad [kame'raːt] *m* (*pl* -en) companion, comrade. −**schaft** *f* companionship, comradeship.
Kamin [ka'miːn] *m* (*pl* -e) (*Feuerstelle*) hearth, fireplace; (*Schornstein*) chimney. −**feger** *m* chimneysweep. −**gesims** *neut* mantelpiece. −**vorsatz** *m* fireguard, fender.
Kamm [kam] *m* (*pl* **Kämme**) comb; (*Vogel*) crest; (*Berg*) ridge, crest.
kämmen ['kɛmən] *v* comb. **sich kämmen** comb one's hair.
Kammer ['kamər] *f* (*pl* -n) small room, chamber; (*Mil, Pol*) chamber. −**frau** *f* chambermaid. −**herr** *m* chamberlain. −**musik** *f* chamber music.
Kampf [kampf] *m* (*pl* **Kämpfe**) fight, struggle; (*Schlacht*) battle.
kämpfen ['kɛmpfən] *v* fight, struggle. **Kämpfer** *m* (*pl* -) fighter. **Kampf‖handlung** *f* (*Mil*) engagement; action. −**platz** *m* battlefield. −**wagen** *m* (*Mil*) tank.
Kanada ['kanada] *neut* Canada. **Kanadier** *m* (*pl* -), **Kanadierin** *f* (*pl* -nen) Canadian. **kanadisch** *adj* Canadian.
Kanal [ka'naːl] *m* (*pl* **Kanäle**) canal; (*natürlicher, auch Radio, fig*) channel; (*Abwasser*) drain, sewer. −**inseln** *pl* Channel Islands.

Kanarienvogel [ka'naːriənfoɪɡəl] *m* canary.

Kandidat [kandi'daɪt] *m* (*pl* -en) candidate. **kandidieren** *v* (*Wahl*) stand (for election); (*Posten*) apply (for).

Känguruh [kɛŋɡu'ruː] *neut* (*pl* -s) kangaroo.

Kaninchen [ka'niːnçən] *neut* (*pl* -) rabbit. **-stall** *m* rabbit hutch.

Kanne ['kanə] *n* (*pl* -n) can; (*Kaffee, Tee*) pot; (*Krug*) jug, pitcher.

Kannibale [kani'baːlə] *m* (*pl* -n) cannibal. **kannibalisch** *adj* cannibal.

Kanon ['kanon] *m* (*pl* -s) canon.

Kanone [ka'noːnə] *f* (*pl* -n) cannon, gun. **Kanonen‖feuer** *neut* bombardment. **-kugel** *f* cannonball.

Kante ['kantə] *f* (*pl* -n) edge.

Kantine [kan'tiːnə] *f* (*pl* -n) canteen.

Kanton [kan'toɪn] *m* (*pl* -e) canton.

Kanzel ['kantsəl] *f* (*pl* -n) pulpit. **-rede** *f* sermon.

Kanzlei [kants'lai] *f* (*pl* -en) (*Büro*) office; (*Behörde*) chancellery. **-papier** *neut* foolscap.

Kanzler ['kantslər] *m* (*pl* -) chancellor.

Kap [kap] *neut* (*pl* -s) cape, headland.

Kapazität [kapatsi'tɛɪt] **1** *f* (*unz.*) capacity. **2** *f* (*pl* -en) (*Könner*) authority, expert.

Kapelle [ka'pɛlə] *f* (*pl* -n) chapel; (*Musik*) band.

Kaper ['kaɪpər] *f* (*pl* -n) (*Gewürz*) caper.

kapieren [ka'piːrən] *v* (*umg.*) understand, catch on, (*umg.*) get.

Kapital [kapi'taɪl] *neut* (*Komm*) capital. **-ismus** *m* capitalism. **-ist** *m* capitalist. **kapitalistisch** *adj* capitalist.

Kapitän [kapi'tɛɪn] *m* (*pl* -e) (ship's) captain.

Kapitel [ka'pitəl] *neut* (*pl* -) chapter.

kapitulieren [kapitu'liːrən] *v* capitulate, surrender. **Kapitulation** *f* (*pl* -en) capitulation, surrender.

Kaplan [ka'plan] *m* (*pl* **Kapläne**) chaplain.

Kappe ['kapə] *f* (*pl* -n) cap; (*Deckel*) top; (*Arch*) dome; (*Schuh*) toecap.

Kapriole [kapri'oɪlə] *f* (*pl* -n) caper, cartwheel.

kaputt [ka'put] *adj* broken, (*umg.*) bust; (*erschöpft*) exhausted, (*umg.*) shattered. **-machen** *v* break, ruin.

Kapuze [ka'puɪtsə] *f* (*pl* -n) hood.

Karaffe [ka'rafə] *f* (*pl* -n) carafe.

Karamelle [kara'mɛlə] *f* (*pl* -n) toffee.

Karat [ka'raɪt] *neut* (*pl* -e) carat.

Karate [ka'raɪtə] *neut* karate.

Karawane [kara'vaɪnə] *f* (*pl* -n) caravan.

Kardinal [kardi'naɪl] *m* (*pl* **Kardinäle**) cardinal.

Karfreitag [kaɪr'fraitak] *m* Good Friday.

karg [kark] *adj* meagre, poor; (*geizig*) miserly.

kärglich ['kɛrkliç] *adj* scanty, poor.

kariert [ka'riərt] *adj* chequered, checked.

Karies ['kaɪriɛs] *f* (*Med*) caries.

Karikatur [karika'tuɪr] *f* (*pl* -en) caricature.

karmesin [karmɛ'ziɪn] *adj* crimson.

Karneval ['karnɛval] *m* (*pl* -s) (Shrovetide) carnival.

Karo ['kaɪro] *neut* (*pl* -s) square; (*Karten*) diamonds.

Karosserie [karɔsə'riɪ] *f* (*pl* -n) body, coachwork.

Karotte [ka'rɔtə] *f* (*pl* -n) carrot.

Karpfen ['karpfən] *m* (*pl* -) carp.

Karre ['karə] *f* (*pl* -n), **Karren** *m* (*pl* -) cart.

Karriere [kari'ɛɪrə] *f* (*pl* -n) rise, (successful) career; (*Pferd*) full gallop.

Karte ['kartə] *f* (*pl* -n) (*Blatt*) card; (*Land-*) map; (*Eintritt, Reise*) ticket.

Kartei [kar'tai] *f* (*pl* -en) card file, card index.

Kartell [kar'tɛl] *neut* (*pl* -e) cartel, combine.

Karten‖ausgabe *f* ticket office. **-spiel** *neut* card game.

Kartoffel [kar'tɔfəl] *f* (*pl* -n) potato. **-chips** *pl* potato crisps (*US* chips). **-püree** *neut* mashed potatoes *pl*. **-puffer** *m* potato pancake. **-salat** *m* potato salad.

Karton [kar'tɔ̃] *m* (*pl* -s) cardboard; (*Schachtel*) cardboard box, carton; (*Skizze*) cartoon.

Kartusche [kar'tuʃə] *f* (*pl* -n) cartridge.

Karussell [karu'sɛl] *neut* (*pl* -s) roundabout, merry-go-round.

Kaschmir [kaʃ'miɪr] *neut* cashmere.

Käse [kɛɪzə] *m* (*pl* -) cheese.

Kaserne [ka'zɛrnə] *f* (*pl* -n) barracks *pl*.

Kasino [ka'ziɪno] *neut* (*pl* -s) casino; (*Mil*) (officers') mess; (*Gesellschaftshaus*) club.

Kasse ['kasə] *f* (*pl* -n) cash box, till; (*Laden, Supermarkt*) cash-desk; (*Kino, Theater*) box office; (*Bank*) cashier's window, counter. **gut/schlecht bei Kasse sein** be flush/hard up. **Kassen‖buch** *neut* cash book. **-wart** *m* treasurer.

Kassette [ka'sɛtə] *f (pl* -n) small box, cas-
ket; *(Geld)* strong-box; *(Tonband)* cas-
sette. **-nrecorder** *m* cassette recorder.
kassieren [ka'siːrən] *v (Geld)* receive;
(Scheck) cash; *(Urteil)* annul, reverse;
(Mil) cashier, dismiss. **Kassierer** *m* cash-
ier.
Kastanie [ka'staːniə] *f (pl* -n) chestnut.
kastanienbraun *adj* chestnut, auburn.
Kasten ['kastən] *m (pl* **Kästen)** box, chest;
(Schrank) cupboard.
kastrieren [ka'striːrən] castrate.
Kasus ['kaːzus] *m (pl* -n) *(Gramm)* case.
Katalog [kata'loːg] *m (pl* -e) catalogue.
Katarakt¹ [kata'rakt] *m (pl* -e) rapids,
waterfall.
Katarakt² *f (pl* -e) *(Med)* cataract.
Katarrh [ka'tar] *m (pl* -e) catarrh.
katastrophal [katastro'faːl] *adj* cata-
strophic. **Katastrophe** *f (pl* -n) catastro-
phe.
Kategorie [katego'riː] *f (pl* -n) category.
kategorisch *adj* categorical.
Kater ['kaːtər] *m (pl* -) tom cat;
(Katzenjammer) hangover.
Kathedrale [kate'draːlə] *f (pl* -n) cathedral.
Katholik(in) [kato'liːk(in)] Catholic.
katholisch *adj* Catholic. **Katholizismus** *m*
Catholicism.
Kätzchen ['kɛtsçən] *neut* kitten.
Katze ['katsə] *f (pl* -n) cat. **katzenartig** *adj*
feline, cat-like. **Katzen‖auge** *neut (Rückstrahler)* rear reflector. **-jammer** *m* hangover.
Kauderwelsch ['kaudərvɛlʃ] *neut* gibberish.
kauen ['kauən] *v* chew.
kauern ['kauərn] *v* cower.
Kauf [kauf] *m (pl* **Käufe)** purchase. **einen
guten Kauf machen** make a good buy,
get a bargain. **kaufen** *v* buy, purchase.
Käufer ['kɔyfər] *m (pl* -) buyer.
Kauf‖haus *neut* department store. **-kraft**
f purchasing power.
käuflich ['kɔyfliç] *adj* saleable,
purchasable; *(bestechlich)* corrupt, venal.
Kaufmann *m* businessman; *(Kleinhandel)*
shopkeeper; *(Großhandel)* merchant.
kaufmännisch *adj* commercial, mercantile. **Kaufpreis** *m* purchase price.
kaum [kaum] *adv* hardly, scarcely.
Kaution [kau'tsioːn] *f (pl* -en) security,
deposit. **gegen Kaution freilassen** release
on bail.

Kauz [kauts] *m (pl* **Käuze)** screech owl;
(fig) odd fellow.
Kavaller‖ie [kavalə'riː] *f (pl* -n) cavalry.
-ist *m* cavalryman.
Kaviar ['kaːviar] *m (pl* -e) caviar.
keck [kɛk] *adj* pert, cheeky.
Kegel ['keːgəl] *m (pl* -) cone; *(Spiel)* skittle. **-bahn** *f* bowling alley. **kegel‖förmig**
adj conical. **-n** *v* play skittles, go bowling. **Kegelspiel** *neut* skittles, bowling.
Kehle ['keːlə] *f (pl* -n) throat. **Kehlkopf** *m*
larynx. **-entzündung** *f* laryngitis.
kehren¹ [keːrən] *v* sweep, brush.
kehren² *v* turn. **sich kehren** turn (round).
sich kehren an pay attention to.
Kehricht ['keːriçt] *m (unz.)* sweepings *pl.*
Kehr‖reim *m* refrain. **-seite** *f* reverse,
other side.
Keil [kail] *m (pl* -e) wedge; *(Arch)* key-
stone. **keilen** *v* wedge; *(werben)* win over.
sich keilen scuffle.
Keiler ['kailər] *m (pl* -) (wild) boar.
Keilriemen ['kailriːmən] *m (Mot)* fan-
belt.
Keim [kaim] *m (pl* -e) germ; *(Bot)* bud;
embryo; *(Anfang)* origin. **keimen** *v* germinate; bud. **Keim‖träger** *m* carrier.
-ung *f* germination.
kein [kain] **keine, kein** *pron, m, f* no one,
nobody; *neut* nothing, none. *adj* no, not
any. **kein anderer als** none other than.
keine Ahnung! (I've) no idea! **keiner von
beiden** neither (of the two). **keinerlei** *adj*
of no sort. **keines‖falls** *adv* on no
account. **-wegs** *adv* not at all.
Keks [keːks] *m (pl* -e) biscuit.
Keller ['kɛlər] *m (pl* -) cellar. **-ei** *f* wine
cellar. **-geschoß** *neut* basement.
Kellner ['kɛlnər] *m (pl* -) waiter. **-in**
waitress.
***kennen** ['kɛnən] *v* know. **-lernen** *v* get
to know, become acquainted with. **Kenner** *m (Wein, Kunst)* connoisseur;
(Fachmann) expert. **kenntlich** *adj* distinguishable, distinct. **Kenntnis** *f*
knowledge. **kenntnisreich** *adj* experienced. **Kennwort** *neut* password.
kennzeichnen *v (fig)* characterize, distinguish. **-d** *adj* characteristic. **Kennziffer** *f*
reference *or* code number; *(Math)* index.
kentern ['kɛntərn] *v* capsize.
Kerbe ['kɛrbə] *f (pl* -n) notch.
Kerker ['kɛrkər] *m (pl* -) dungeon.

Kerl [kɛrl] *m* (*pl* -e) fellow.
Kern [kɛrn] *m* (*pl* -e) kernel; (*Obst*) stone, pit; (*Atom*) nucleus; (*fig*) core, essence. **kerngesund** *adj* thoroughly healthy. **Kern‖haus** *neut* core. **–reaktion** *f* nuclear reaction. **–waffe** *f* nuclear weapon. **–kraftwerk** *neut* nuclear power station.
Kerze ['kɛrtsə] *f* (*pl* -n) candle. **Kerzen‖leuchter** *neut* candlestick. **–licht** *neut* candlelight.
Kessel ['kɛsəl] *m* (*pl* -) kettle; (*Tech*) boiler; (*Geog*) depression, hollow.
Kette ['kɛtə] *f* (*pl* -n) chain. **ketten** *v* chain, link. **Ketten‖gebirge** *neut* mountain range. **–geschäft** *neut* chain store. **–raucher** *m* chain smoker. **–reaktion** *f* chain reaction.
Ketzer ['kɛtsər] *m* (*pl* -) heretic. **–ei** *f* (*pl* -en) heresy. **ketzerisch** *adj* heretical.
keuchen ['kɔyçən] *v* gasp, pant. **Keuchhusten** *m* whooping cough.
Keule ['kɔylə] *f* (*pl* -n) club, bludgeon; (*Fleisch*) leg.
keusch [kɔyʃ] *adj* chaste, modest. **Keuschheit** *f* chastity.
kichern ['kiçərn] *v* giggle.
Kiefer¹ ['kiːfər] *m* (*pl* -) (*Anat*) jaw.
Kiefer² *f* (*pl* -n) (*Bot*) pine.
Kieferknochen ['kiːfərknoxən] *m* jawbone.
Kiefern‖holz *neut* pinewood. **–wald** *m* pine forest.
Kiel [kiːl] *m* (*pl* -e) keel.
Kieme ['kiːmə] *f* (*pl* -n) gill.
Kies [kiːs] *m* (*pl* -e) gravel. **Kiesel** *m* (*pl* -) pebble, flint. **–stein** *m* pebble. **Kiesgrube** *f* gravelpit.
Kilo ['kiːlo] *neut* (*pl* -) kilo, kilogram(me). **–gramm** *neut* (*pl* -) kilogram(me). **Kilometer** *neut* kilometre. **–zähler** *m* milometer, odometer.
Kind [kint] *neut* (*pl* -er) child. **ein Kind bekommen/erwarten** have/expect a baby.
Kinder‖arzt *m* paediatrician. **–bett** *neut* cot, crib. **–buch** *neut* children's book. **–heilkunde** *f* paediatrics. **–jahre** *pl* childhood *sing*. **–lähmung** *f* polio. **–spiel** *neut* children's game; (*fig*) child's play. **–wagen** *m* pram, (*US*) baby carriage.
Kindheit *f* childhood. **kindisch** *adj* childish. **kindlich** *adj* childlike.
Kinn [kin] *neut* (*pl* -e) chin.
Kino ['kiːno] *neut* (*pl* -s) cinema.

Kiosk ['kiːɔsk] *m* (*pl* -e) kiosk.
kippen ['kipən] *v* tip, tilt. **Kippwagen** *m* tipper, tip cart.
Kirche ['kirçə] *f* (*pl* -n) church. **Kirchen‖gemeinde** *f* parish. **–lied** *neut* hymn. **–schändung** *f* desecration, profanation. **Kirch‖gänger** *m* church-goer. **–hof** *m* churchyard. **kirchlich** *adj* ecclesiastical, church.
Kirsch [kirʃ] *m* kirsch, cherry brandy. **–e** *f* (*pl* -n) cherry.
Kissen ['kisən] *neut* (*pl* -) cushion; (*Kopf-*) pillow; (*pl*) bedding.
Kiste ['kistə] *f* (*pl* -n) chest, case, box.
Kitsch [kitʃ] *m* (tasteless) trash, kitsch. **kitschig** *adj* trashy.
Kittel ['kitəl] *m* (*pl* -) smock.
Kitzel ['kitsəl] *m* (*pl* -) tickle. **kitzeln** *v* tickle. **kitzlig** *adj* ticklish.
klaffen ['klafən] *v* gape, yawn. **–d** *adj* gaping.
Klage ['klaːgə] *f* (*pl* -n) complaint, grievance; (*Jur*) action, lawsuit. **klagen** *v* complain, (*Jur*) bring an action. **Klagende(r)** plaintiff.
kläglich ['klɛːkliç] *adj* miserable, pitiful.
Klammer ['klamər] *f* (*pl* -n) clamp; (*kleine*) clip; (*Wäsche*) peg. **klammern** *v* clamp; (*befestigen*) fasten. **sich klammern an** cling to.
Klamotten [kla'mɔtən] *pl* (*umg.*) gear *sing*, clothes *pl*.
Klang [klaŋ] *m* (*pl* Klänge) sound.
klapp‖en ['klapən] flap, clap; (*umg.*) work out, be all right. **–bar** *adj* collapsible, folding. **Klappe** *f* flap; (*umg.*) mouth, trap. **halt die Klappe!** (*vulgär*) shut up!
Klapper ['klapər] *f* (*pl* -n) rattle. **klapperig** *adj* clattering, rattling. **klappern** *v* rattle, clatter.
Klapp‖messer *neut* jack-knife. **–stuhl** *m* folding chair. **–tür** *f* trapdoor.
klar [klaːr] *adj* clear.
klären ['klɛːrən] *v* clarify.
Klarheit ['klaːrhait] *f* clarity, clearness.
Klarinette [klari'nɛtə] *f* (*pl* -n) clarinet. **Klarinettist** *m* clarinettist.
klarlegen ['klaːrleːgən] *v* clear up.
Klärung ['klɛːruŋ] *f* clarification.
klarwerden ['klaːrveːrdən] *v* become clear.
klasse ['klasə] *adj* (*umg.*) marvellous, splendid. **Klasse** *f* class. *ein Musiker von Klasse* an excellent musician. *ein Restaurant erster Klasse* a first-class restaurant.

klassenbewußt adj class-conscious. **Klassenzimmer** neut classroom.
Klassik ['klasik] f classical era; (*Literatur, Musik*) classicism. **–er** m classicist. **klassisch** adj classical.
Klatsch [klatʃ] m (pl -e) slap, smack; (*Gerede*) gossip, chatter. **–base** f gossip, chatterbox. **klatschen** v clap; (*reden*) gossip, chatter.
Klaue ['klauə] f (pl -n) claw; (*Raubvogel*) talon. **klauen** v (*umg.*) steal, pinch.
Klausel ['klauzəl] f (pl -n) clause.
Klavier [klaviːr] neut (pl -e) piano. **–spieler(in)** pianist.
Klebeband ['kleɪbəbant] neut (adhesive) tape. **kleben** v glue, paste; (*anhaften*) stick. **klebrig** adj sticky. **Klebstoff** m glue.
Klecks [klɛks] m (pl -e) blot, spot.
Klee [kleɪ] m clover. **–blatt** neut cloverleaf.
Kleid [klait] neut (pl -er) garment; (*Frau*) dress; (*pl*) clothes. **kleiden** v clothe.
Kleider‖bügel m coat-hanger. **–bürste** f clothes brush. **–schrank** m wardrobe.
Kleidung f clothing, clothes. **–sstück** neut article of clothing, garment.
klein [klain] adj small, little. **der kleine Mann** the ordinary man. **klein stellen** turn down, put on low. **im kleinen** in miniature; (*Komm*) retail.
Klein‖anzeige f classified advertisement. **–asien** neut Asia Minor. **–bürger** m petty bourgeois. **–geld** neut (small) change. **–handel** m retail trade. **Kleinigkeit** f (pl -en) trifle, trivial matter. **Klein‖kind** neut infant. **–lebewesen** neut microorganism. **klein‖lich** adj petty. **–mütig** adj faint-hearted, cowardly.
Kleinod ['klainoːt] neut (pl -ien) jewel, gem.
Kleister ['klaistər] m (pl -) paste, gum.
Klemme ['klɛmə] f (pl -n) clamp; (*Haar*) grip; (*Klammer*) clip. **in der Klemme sitzen** be in a dilemma or tight corner. **klemmen** v squeeze, pinch.
Klempner ['klɛmpnər] m (pl -) plumber; (*Metall*) metalworker. **–ei** f plumbing. **klempnern** v do plumbing.
Kleriker ['kleɪrikər] m (pl -) cleric, clergyman. **Klerus** m (*unz.*) clergy.
Kletterer ['klɛtərər] m (pl -) climber. **klettern** v climb. **Kletterpflanze** f climbing plant, creeper.
Klima ['kliːma] f (pl -te) climate. **–anlage**

f air-conditioning (equipment). **klimatisch** adj climatic.
Klinge ['klɪŋə] f (pl -n) blade.
Klingel ['klɪŋəl] f (pl -n) (door)bell. **klingeln** v ring the bell, ring.
klingen ['klɪŋən] v sound; ring.
Klinik ['kliːnik] f (pl -en) clinic, hospital. **klinisch** adj clinical.
Klinke ['klɪŋkə] f (pl -n) doorhandle, latch.
Klippe ['klɪpə] f (pl -n) cliff; (*im Meer*) rocks pl, reef.
klirren ['klɪrən] v tinkle, jangle.
Klischee [kli'ʃeɪ] neut (pl -s) (*fig*) cliché.
Klo [kloː] neut (pl -s) (*umg.*) toilet, loo.
Kloake [klo'aɪkə] f (pl -n) sewer.
klopfen ['klɔpfən] v (*Tür*) knock; (*Herz*) beat; (*Schulter*) tap, pat. **Klopfen** neut knocking; beating.
Klosett [klo'zɛt] neut (pl -s) toilet. **–papier** neut toilet paper.
Kloß [kloːs] m (pl Klöße) dumpling; (*Fleisch*) meatball.
Kloster ['kloːstər] neut (pl Klöster) monastery, abbey, convent. **–gang** m cloister.
Klotz [klɔts] m (pl Klötze) block, log.
Klub [klup] m (pl -s) club, association.
Kluft [kluft] m (pl Klüfte) cleft; (*Abgrund*) chasm, abyss; (*fig*) rift.
klug [kluːk] adj clever; (*Ansicht, Rat*) sensible, prudent. **Klugheit** f cleverness, intelligence.
Klumpen ['klumpən] m (pl -) lump; (*Gold*) nugget.
knabbern ['knabərn] v nibble.
Knabe ['knaɪbə] m (pl -n) boy. **–nalter** neut boyhood, youth. **knabenhaft** adj boyish.
Knäckebrot ['knɛkəbroɪt] neut crispbread.
knacken ['knakən] v crack.
Knall [knal] m (pl -e) bang; explosion. **–bonbon** m cracker. **knallen** v crack, bang; explode. **Knallfrosch** m banger, jumping jack.
knapp [knap] adj scant, insufficient; (*Kleidung*) tight. **knapp sein** be in short supply. **knapp werden** be running short or out. **knapp bei Kasse sein** be hard up. *knapp drei Meter* just under (or barely) three metres.
knarren ['knarən] v creak.
knattern ['knatərn] v crackle, rattle.
Knebel ['kneɪbəl] m (pl -) gag. **knebeln** v gag.

Knecht [knɛçt] *m* (*pl* -e) (farm) worker; (*Diener*) servant.
***kneifen** ['knaifən] *v* pinch, nip.
Kneifzange *f* pincers.
Kneipe ['knaipə] *f* (*pl* -n) pub, bar.
kneipen *v* go boozing.
kneten ['kneitən] *v* knead; (*Körper*) massage.
Knick ['knik] *m* (*pl* -e) crack; (*Kniff*) crease; (*Kurve*) sharp bend. **knicken** *v* break, crack; fold, crease.
Knicks [kniks] *m* (*pl* -e) curtsey.
Knie [kniː] *neut* (*pl* -) knee. **knien** *v* kneel. **-d** *adj* kneeling, on one's knees. **Kniescheibe** *f* kneecap.
Kniff [knif] *m* (*pl* -e) pinch; (*Falte*) crease; trick. **den Kniff heraushaben** get the hang of it.
knipsen ['knipsən] *v* punch, clip; (*Foto*) snap.
knirschen ['knirʃən] *v* gnash.
Knitter ['knitər] *m* (*pl* -) crease. **knitter‖frei** *adj* crease-resistant. **-n** *v* crease.
Knoblauch ['knoːplaux] *m* garlic.
Knöchel ['knœçəl] *m* (*pl* -) (*Finger*) knuckle; (*Bein*) ankle.
Knochen ['knɔxən] *m* (*pl* -) bone. **-bruch** *m* fracture. **-gerüst** *neut* skeleton. **-mark** *neut* (bone) marrow. **knochig** *adj* bony.
Knödel ['knœidəl] *m* (*pl* -) dumpling.
Knolle ['knɔlə] *f* (*pl* -n) tuber; (*Zwiebel, Tulpe*) bulb.
Knopf [knɔpf] *m* (*pl* **Knöpfe**) button.
knöpfen ['knœpfən] *v* button.
Knorpel ['knɔrpəl] *m* (*pl* -) cartilage; (*bei gekochtem Fleisch*) gristle.
Knospe ['knɔspə] *f* (*pl* -n) bud. **knospen** *v* bud.
Knoten ['knoːtən] *m* (*pl* -) knot; (*Tech*) node. **knoten** *v* knot. **Knotenpunkt** *m* junction.
knüpfen ['knypfən] *v* join, tie.
knusprig ['knusprɪç] *adj* crisp.
Koalition [koali'tsioːn] *f* (*pl* -en) coalition.
Kobold ['koːbɔlt] *m* (*pl* -e) goblin.
Koch [kɔx] *m* (*pl* **Köche**) cook. **-buch** *neut* cookery book. **kochen** *v* cook; (*sieden*) boil. **-d** boiling. **Kocher** *m* cooker. **Kochherd** *m* kitchen range.
Köchin ['kœçin] *f* (*pl* -nen) (female) cook.
Koch‖platte *f* hotplate, ring. **-topf** *m* saucepan, pot.
Köder ['kœidər] *m* (*pl* -) bait. **ködern** *v* lure, entice.

Koexistenz [koːɛksi'stɛnts] *f* coexistence. **koexistieren** *v* coexist.
Koffer ['kɔfər] *m* (*pl* -) suitcase; (*Schrankkoffer*) trunk. **-kuli** *m* (luggage) trolley. **-raum** *m* (*Mot*) trunk.
Kohl [koːl] *m* (*pl* -e) cabbage.
Kohle ['koːlə] *f* (*pl* -n) coal; (*Holzkohle*) charcoal. **Kohlen‖bergwerk** *neut* coal mine, pit. **-säure** *f* carbonic acid; (*in Getränken*) carbon dioxide. **-hydrat** *neut* carbohydrate. **-stoff** *m* carbon. **Kohle‖papier** *neut* carbon paper. **-stift** *m* charcoal crayon.
Kohl‖rabi [koːl'rabi] *m* (*pl* -s) kohlrabi. **-rübe** *f* swede.
Koje ['koːjə] *f* (*pl* -n) bunk, berth; (*Zimmer*) cabin.
kokett [ko'kɛt] *adj* coquettish. **-ieren** *v* flirt.
Kokosnuß ['koːkɔsnus] *f* coconut.
Koks ['koːks] *m* (*pl* -e) coke.
Kolben ['kɔlbən] *m* (*pl* -) club; (*Gewehr*) butt; (*Zylinder*) piston.
Kollege [kɔ'leigə] *m* (*pl* -n) **Kollegin** *f* (*pl* -nen) colleague.
kollektiv [kɔlɛk'tiːf] *adj* collective.
Köln [kœln] *neut* Cologne. **-ischwasser** *neut* eau de Cologne.
Kolon ['koːlɔn] *neut* (*pl* -s) colon.
kolonial [kɔlo'niaːl] *adj* colonial. **Kolonialwaren** *pl* groceries. **-händler** *m* grocer.
Kolonne [kɔ'lɔnə] *f* (*pl* -n) column.
Kombi ['kɔmbi] *m* (*pl* -s) estate car.
Kombination [kɔmbina'tsioːn] *f* (*pl* -en) combination; (*Sport*) teamwork; (*Unterkleidung*) combinations *pl*; (*Schützkleidung*) one-piece suit; (*Ideen*) conjecture. **kombinieren** *v* combine.
Komet [ko'meːt] *m* (*pl* -en) comet.
Komfort [kɔm'foːr] *m* (*unz.*) comfort. **komfortabel** *adj* comfortable.
Komiker ['koːmikər] *m* (*pl* -) comedian, comic. **komisch** *adj* funny; (*seltsam*) strange.
Komitee [kɔmi'teː] *neut* (*pl* -s) committee.
Komma ['kɔma] *neut* (*pl* -s) comma.
Kommandant [kɔman'dant] *m* (*pl* -en) commander. **kommandieren** *v* command.
Kommanditgesellschaft (**KG**) [kɔman'dɪtɡəzɛlʃaft (ka'ɡeː)] *f* limited-liability company.
Kommando [kɔ'mandoː] *neut* (*pl* -s) order, command; (*Abteilung*) squad, detachment, detail. **-truppe** *f* commando (unit).

*kommen ['kɔmən] v come. **kommen lassen** send for. **um etwas kommen** lose something. **hinter etwas kommen** get to the bottom of something. **Kommen** neut arrival, coming. **kommend** adj coming.
Kommentar [kɔmɛn'taɪr] m (pl -e) commentary. **kommentieren** v comment on.
Kommerz [kɔ'mɛrts] m commerce. **komerziell** adj commercial.
Kommisar [kɔmi'saɪr] m (pl -e) commissioner; (Polizei) inspector. **Kommission** f commission.
kommun [kɔ'muɪn] adj common. **–al** adj municipal. **Kommune** f (pl -n) commune; (Gemeinde) municipality.
Kommunikation [komunika'tsioɪn] f (pl -en) communication.
Kommuniqué [kɔmyni'keɪ] neut (pl -s) communiqué.
Kommunismus [kɔmu'nizmus] m communism. **Kommunist(in)** communist. **kommunistisch** adj communist.
Komödie [kɔ'mœɪdiə] f (pl -n) comedy; (Ereignis) farce.
Kompaß ['kɔmpas] m (pl **Kompasse**) compass. **–strich** m: point of the compass.
kompetent [kɔmpɛ'tɛnt] adj competent.
Komplex [kɔm'plɛks] m (pl -e) complex.
Kompliment [kɔmpli'mɛnt] neut (pl -e) compliment.
komplizieren [kɔmpli'tsiɪrən] v complicate. **kompliziert** adj complicated, complex.
Komplott [kɔm'plɔt] neut (pl --e) plot, conspiracy.
komponieren [kɔmpo'niɪrən] v compose. **Komponist** m (pl -en) composer.
Kompott [kɔm'pɔt] neut (pl -e) stewed fruit, compote.
Kompresse [kɔm'prɛsə] f (pl -n) compress.
Kompromiß [kɔmpro'mis] m (pl **Kompromisse**) compromise. **kompromittieren** v compromise.
kondensieren [kɔndɛn'siɪrən] v condense. **Kondensmilch** f condensed milk.
Konditorei [kɔndito'rai] (pl -en) patisserie, cake shop. **–waren** pl pastries, cakes.
Kondom [kɔn'dɔɪm] m (pl -e) condom.
Konferenz [kɔnfɛ'rɛnts] f (pl -en) conference.
Konfession [kɔnfɛ'sioɪn] f (pl -en) confession, creed, faith.
Konflikt [kɔn'flikt] m (pl -e) conflict.

konform [kɔn'fɔrm] adj in agreement, in accordance.
Konfrontation [kɔnfrɔnta'tsioɪn] f (pl -en) confrontation. **konfrontieren** v confront.
konfus [kɔn'fuɪs] adj confused, muddled. **Konfusion** f confusion.
Kongreß [kɔŋ'grɛs] m (pl **Kongresse**) congress.
König ['kœɪniç] m (pl -e) king. **–in** f (pl -nen) queen. **–inmutter** m queen mother. **königlich** adj royal, regal. **Königreich** neut kingdom, realm.
Konjunktur [kɔnjuŋk'tuɪr] f (pl -en) (state of the) economy, economic trends pl; (Aufschwung) boom.
Konkurrent [kɔnku'rɛnt] m (pl -en) competitor. **Konkurrenz** f (unz.) competition. **konkurrenzfähig** adj competitive. **konkurrieren** v compete.
Konkurs [kɔn'kurs] m (pl -e) bankruptcy, insolvency. **in Konkurs gehen** become bankrupt.
*können ['kœnən] v can, be able (to); (dürfen) may, be allowed (to); (gelernt haben) know. **tun können** know how to do. **eine Sprache können** speak a language. Ich kann nicht mehr! I can't go on. **das kann sein** it may be so. er kann nichts dafür it's not his fault, he can't help it. **Können** neut ability.
konsequent [kɔnzɛ'kvɛnt] adj consistent.
Konsequenz f consistency; (Folge) consequence. **die Konsequenzen tragen** bear the consequences. **Konsequenzen ziehen** draw conclusions.
konservativ [kɔnzɛrva'tiɪf] adj conservative. **Konservative(r)** conservative.
Konserve [kɔn'zɛrvə] f (pl -n) preserve, tinned or bottled food. **Konservenbüchse** f tin (of preserves). **konservieren** v preserve.
konsolidieren [kɔnzɔli'diɪrən] v consolidate.
Konsonant [kɔnzo'nant] m (pl -en) consonant.
konstant [kɔn'stant] adj constant.
konstruieren [kɔnstru'iɪrən] v construct. **Konstruktion** f (pl -en) construction; (Entwurf) design.
Konsul [kɔn'zuɪl] m (pl -n) consul. **–at** neut (pl -e) consulate.
Konsum [kɔn'zuɪm] m consumption. **–gesellschaft** f consumer society. **konsumieren** v consume. **Konsumverein** m co-operative society.

Kontakt [kɔn'takt] *m* (*pl* -e) contact.
Kontinent [kɔnti'nɛnt] *m* (*pl* -e) continent.
Konto ['kɔnto] *neut* (*pl* **Konten**) account. **–auszug** *m* (bank) statement. **–buch** *neut* passbook. **–inhaber** *m* accountholder.
Kontrabaß ['kɔntrabas] *m* double bass.
konträr [kɔn'trɛɪ] *adj* adverse.
Kontrast [kɔn'trast] *m* (*pl* -e) contrast. **kontrastieren** *v* contrast.
Kontrolle [kɔn'trɔlə] *f* (*pl* -n) control, supervision. **–abschnitt** *m* counterfoil. **–eur** *m* controller. **kontrollieren** *v* control, supervise. **Kontrollpunkt** *m* checkpoint. **unter Kontrolle** under control.
konventionell [kɔnvɛntsio'nɛl] *adj* conventional.
Konversation [kɔnvɛrza'tsioɪn] *f* (*pl* -en) conversation. **–slexikon** *neut* encyclopedia.
konvertieren [kɔnvɛr'tiɪrən] *v* convert.
konvex [kɔn'vɛks] *adj* convex.
Konzentrat [kɔntsən'traɪt] *neut* (*pl* -e) concentrate. **–ion** *f* (*pl* -en) concentration. **–ionslager** *neut* concentration camp. **konzentrieren** *v* concentrate.
Konzept [kɔn'tsɛpt] *neut* (*pl* -e) rough draft.
Konzert [kɔn'tsɛrt] *neut* (*pl* -e) concert; (*Stück*) concerto.
Kopf [kɔpf] *m* (*pl* **Köpfe**) head. **auf den Kopf stellen** turn upside down. **pro Kopf** per capita, each. **im Kopf haben** be preoccupied with. **–ball** *m* (*Sport*) header.
köpfen ['kœpfən] *v* behead, decapitate.
Kopf‖haut *f* scalp. **–hörer** *m* headphone. **–kissen** *neut* pillow. **–putz** *m* headdress. **–salat** *m* lettuce. **–schmerzen** *pl* headache *sing*. **–sprung** *m* header. **–stand** *m* headstand. **kopfüber** *adv* headlong, head first.
Kopie [ko'piɪ] *f* (*pl* -n) copy. **kopieren** *v* copy.
Kopulation [kɔpula'tsioɪn] *f* (*pl* -en) copulation. **kopulieren** *v* copulate; (*Bäume*) graft.
Koralle [ko'ralə] *f* (*pl* -n) coral. **–nriff** *neut* coral reef.
Korb [kɔrp] *m* (*pl* **Körbe**) basket. **–ball** *m* basketball. **–geflecht** *neut* basketwork.
Kord [kɔrt] *or* **Kordsamt** *m* cord(uroy). **Kordhose** *f* corduroy trousers; (*umg.*) cords.

Korinthe [ko'rintə] *f* (*pl* -n) currant.
Kork [kɔrk] *m* (*pl* -e) cork. **–enzieher** *m* corkscrew.
Korn [kɔrn] *neut* (*pl* **Körner**) grain, corn. **Körnchen** ['kœrnçən] *neut* (*pl* -) granule.
Koronarthrombose [kɔro'naɪrtrɔmboɪzə] *f* (*pl* -n) coronary thrombosis.
Körper [kœrpər] *m* (*pl* -) body. **–bau** *m* physique, build. **körperbehindert** *adj* physically handicapped. **Körper‖bildung** *f* body-building. **–geruch** *m* body odour. **–gewicht** *neut* weight. **–haltung** *f* posture.
körperlich ['kœrpərliç] *adj* bodily, physical; (*Strafe*) corporal.
Körper‖maß *neut* cubic measure. **–pflege** *f* hygiene. **–schaft** *f* (*pl* -en) corporation.
Korporal [kɔrpo'raɪl] *m* (*pl* -e) corporal.
korrekt [ko'rɛkt] *adj* correct. **Korrektur** *f* (*pl* -en) correction; (*Druck*) proof.
Korrespondent [kɔrɛspɔn'dɛnt] *m* (*pl* -en) correspondent. **Korrespondenz** *f* correspondence.
korrigieren [kɔri'giɪrən] *v* correct; (*gedrucktes*) proofread.
Kosename ['koɪzənaɪmə] *m* pet name.
Kosmetik [kɔz'mɛɪtik] *f* (*unz.*) cosmetics *pl*. **kosmetisch** *adj* cosmetic.
Kosmos ['kɔsmɔs] *m* (*pl* **Kosmen**) cosmos, universe. **kosmisch** *adj* cosmic.
Kost [kɔst] *f* (*unz.*) food, fare. **Kost und Wohnung** board and lodging. **kräftige Kost** rich diet.
kostbar ['kɔstbaɪr] *adj* expensive; (*sehr wertvoll*) precious.
kosten¹ ['kɔstən] *v* (*probieren*) taste, try, sample.
kosten² *v* cost. **Kosten** *pl* costs. **auf meine Kosten** at my expense. **kostenlos** *adj* free (of charge).
köstlich ['kœstliç] *adj* delicious; (*reizend*) charming; (*wertvoll*) precious.
kostspielig ['kɔstʃpiɪliç] *adj* expensive.
Kostüm [kɔs'tyɪm] *neut* (*pl* -e) costume; (*Damen-*) suit. **–ball** *m* fancy-dress ball. **–probe** *f* dress rehearsal.
Kot [koɪt] *m* dung, droppings *pl*; (*Schmutz*) dirt, mud.
Kotelett [kɔtə'lɛt] *neut* (*pl* -e) chop, cutlet. **–en** *pl* sideburns, mutton-chop whiskers.
Kotflügel ['koɪtflyɪgəl] *m* mudguard; fender.

kotzen ['kɔtsən] v (*vulgär*) puke, be sick. **zum Kotzen** enough to make you sick.
Krabbe ['krabə] f (*pl* **-n**) shrimp.
krabbeln ['krabəln] v scuttle, scurry.
Krach [krax] m (*pl* **-e**) noise; (*Streit*) quarrel, row; (*Knall*) crash.
krächzen ['krɛçtsən] v croak.
kraft [kraft] *prep* on the strength of, by virtue of. **Kraft** f (*pl* **Kräfte**) strength; (*Macht*) power. **–fahrer** m driver. **–fahrzeug** *neut* motor vehicle.
kräftig ['krɛftiç] *adj* strong; (*mächtig*) powerful; (*Essen*) substantial. **–en** v strengthen. **–end** *adj* invigorating.
kraftlos *adj* powerless. **Kraft‖probe** f trial of strength. **–rad** *neut* motorcycle. **–stoff** m fuel. **–wagen** m motor vehicle. **–werk** *neut* power station.
Kragen ['kraɪgən] m (*pl* **-**) collar.
Krähe ['krɛːə] f (*pl* **-n**) crow. **krähen** v crow.
Kralle ['kralə] f (*pl* **-n**) claw. **krallen** v claw. **sich krallen an** clutch.
Kram [kraɪm] m stuff, trash; (*umg.*) things, stuff.
Krampf [krampf] m (*pl* **Krämpfe**) cramp, spasm. **krampfhaft** *adj* convulsive; (*heftig*) frenzied, frantic.
Kran [kraɪn] m (*pl* **Kräne**) (*Mech*) crane.
Kranich ['kraɪniç] m (*pl* **-e**) (*Zool*) crane.
krank [kraŋk] *adj* sick, ill, unwell. **Kranke(r)** patient.
kränken ['krɛŋkən] v vex, annoy.
Kranken‖haus *neut* hospital. **–kasse** f health insurance (company). **–schein** m medical certificate. **–schwester** f nurse. **–versicherung** f health insurance. **–wagen** m ambulance. **krankhaft** *adj* diseased, unhealthy. **Krankheit** f (*pl* **-en**) disease, illness.
Kranz [krants] m (*pl* **Kränze**) wreath, garland.
Krapfen ['krapfən] m (*pl* **-**) fritter; doughnut.
kraß [kras] *adj* crass, gross.
kratzen ['kratsən] v scratch. **Kratzwunde** f scratch.
kraulen ['kraulən] *or* **kraulschwimmen** v swim the crawl. **Kraulstil** m crawl.
kraus [kraus] *adj* curly, crinkled.
Kraut [kraut] *neut* (*pl* **Kräuter**) herb; (*Kohl*) cabbage; (*grüne Pflanzen*) vegetation.
Kräuter‖buch ['krɔytərbuːx] *neut* herbal. **–tee** m herb tea.

Krawall [kra'val] m (*pl* **-e**) brawl.
Krawatte [kra'vatə] f (*pl* **-n**) (neck)tie.
Krebs [kreːps] m (*pl* **-e**) crab; (*Med*) cancer; (*Astrol*) Cancer.
Kredit [kre'diːt] m (*pl* **-e**) (*Komm*) credit. **–brief** m letter of credit. **kreditieren** v credit.
Kreide ['kraidə] f (*pl* **-n**) chalk. **–fels** m chalk cliff.
Kreis ['krais] m (*pl* **-e**) circle; (*Gebiet*) district, area. **–bahn** f orbit. **–bewegung** f rotation, revolution. **–bogen** m arc (of a circle).
kreischen ['kraiʃən] v screech, shriek.
Kreisel ['kraizəl] m (*pl* **-**) (spinning) top. **kreiseln** v spin (like a top).
kreis‖en v revolve, rotate. **–förmig** *adj* circular. **Kreis‖lauf** m circulation. **–säge** f circular saw. **–umfang** m circumference.
Krem [kreim] f (*pl* **-s**) cream.
Krematorium [krema'toːrium] *neut* (*pl* **Krematorien**) crematorium.
Kreml ['kreməl] m Kremlin.
Krempel ['krempəl] m junk, rubbish.
krepieren [kre'piːrən] v burst; (*umg.*) die.
Kresse ['kresə] f (*pl* **-n**) cress.
Kreuz [krɔyts] *neut* (*pl* **-e**) cross; (*Karten*) club(s); (*Anat*) small of the back. **kreuz und quer** in all directions. **kreuzen** v cross; (*Schiff*) cruise. **sich kreuzen** intersect. **Kreuzer** m (*pl* **-**) cruiser. **Kreuz‖fahrer** m crusader. **–fahrt** f (*Schiff*) cruise; (*Kreuzzug*) crusade.
kreuzigen ['krɔytsigən] v crucify. **Kreuzigung** f (*pl* **-en**) crucifixion.
Kreuzung ['krɔytsuŋ] f (*pl* **-en**) crossing.
Kreuz‖verhör *neut* cross-examination. **–verweis** m cross-reference. **–weg** m crossroads. **–worträtsel** *neut* crossword puzzle. **–zug** m crusade.
*kriechen ['kriːçən] v creep, crawl; (*fig*) cringe, grovel. **kriecherisch** *adj* cringing, servile.
Krieg [kriːk] m (*pl* **-e**) war. **den Krieg erklären/führen** declare/wage war. **Krieger** m (*pl* **-**) warrior. **kriegführend** *adj* belligerent. **Kriegs‖dienstverweigerer** m conscientious objector. **–gefangene(r)** prisoner of war. **–gericht** *neut* court-martial. **–hetzer** m warmonger. **–verbrecher** m war criminal. **–zeit** f wartime.
Krimi ['krimi] *neut* (*pl* **-s**) detective novel, thriller.

kriminal [krimiˈnaɪl] *adj* criminal.
Kriminal‖polizei *f* detective force, CID.
–roman *m* detective novel, thriller.
Krippe [ˈkrɪpə] *f* (*pl* -n) crib; (*Kinder-*)
crèche.
Krise [ˈkriːzə] *f* (*pl* -n) crisis.
Kristall [krɪˈstal] *m* (*pl* -e) crystal. **kristal-
lisieren** *v* crystallize.
Kritik [kriˈtiːk] *f* (*pl* -en) criticism. **–er** *m*
critic. **kritisch** *adj* critical. **kritisieren** *v*
criticize; (*Buch, Film*) review.
Krokodil [krɔkoˈdiːl] *neut* (*pl* -e) croco-
dile.
Krone [ˈkroːnə] *f* (*pl* -n) crown.
krönen [ˈkrœɪnən] *v* crown. **Krönung** *f*
coronation.
Kröte [ˈkrœɪtə] *f* (*pl* -n) toad.
Krücke [ˈkrykə] *f* (*pl* -n) crutch.
Krug [kruːk] *m* (*pl* **Krüge**) jug; (*Becher*)
mug.
Krume [ˈkruːmə] *f* (*pl* -n) crumb.
Krümel [ˈkryməl] *m* (*pl* -) crumb.
krümelig [ˈkryməlɪç] *adj* crumbly.
krumm [krum] *adj* crooked. **–beinig** *adj*
bow-legged.
Krumme [ˈkrumə] *f* (*pl* -n) sickle.
Krümmung [ˈkrymuŋ] *f* curve, bend.
Krüppel [ˈkrypəl] *m* (*pl* -) cripple.
Kruste [ˈkrustə] *f* (*pl* -n) crust. **–ntier**
neut crustacean.
Kruzifix [kruːtsiˈfiks] *neut* (*pl* -e) crucifix.
Kubikinhalt [kuˈbiːkinhalt] *m* volume.
Küche [ˈkyçə] *f* (*pl* -n) kitchen; cookery,
cuisine.
Kuchen [ˈkuːxən] *m* (*pl* -) cake.
Küchen‖schabe *f* cockroach. **–schrank**
m kitchen cupboard.
Kuckuck [ˈkukuk] *m* (*pl* -e) cuckoo.
Kugel [ˈkuːgəl] *f* (*pl* -n) ball; (*Gewehr*)
bullet; (*Math*) sphere. **kugel‖fest** *adj* bul-
let-proof. **–förmig** *adj* spherical.
Kugel‖lager *neut* ball-bearing. **–schrei-
ber** *m* ball(point) pen.
Kuh [kuː] *f* (*pl* **Kühe**) cow.
kühl [kyːl] *adj* cool. **Kühle** *f* coolness.
kühlen *v* cool. **Kühl‖schrank** *m* refrigerator. **–ung** *f* cooling.
kühn [kyːn] *adj* daring, bold, audacious.
Kühnheit *f* daring, boldness, audacity.
Kuhstall [ˈkuːʃtal] *m* cowshed.
Kulissen [kuˈlisən] *pl* (*Theater*) scenery
sing. **hinter den Kulissen** (*fig*) behind the
scenes.
Kult [kult] *m* (*pl* -e) cult; (*Verehrung*)
worship.

kultivieren [kultiˈviːrən] *v* cultivate.
Kultur [kulˈtuːr] *f* (*pl* -en) culture;
(*Boden*) cultivation; (*Bakterien*) culture.
kulturell *adj* cultural.
Kümmel [ˈkyməl] *m* caraway (seed).
Kummer [ˈkumər] *m* (*unz.*) sorrow, distress.
kümmerlich [ˈkymərlɪç] *adj* miserable,
poor. **kümmern** *v* grieve; (*angehen*) concern. **sich kümmern um** take care of,
look after.
Kumpel [ˈkumpəl] *m* (*pl* -s) (*umg.*) mate,
buddy; (*Bergmann*) miner.
kund [kunt] *adj* (generally) known.
Kunde[1] [ˈkundə] *f* information,
(*Nachrichten*) news.
Kunde[2] *m*, **Kundin** *f* customer, client.
Kundendienst [ˈkundəndiːnst] *m* after-
sales service.
*kundgeben [ˈkuntgeɪbən] *v* make known,
declare. **Kundgebung** *f* demonstration;
(*Kundgeben*) declaration.
kündigen [ˈkyndigən] *v* give notice.
Kündigung *f* notice.
Kundschaft [ˈkuntʃaft] *f* (*unz.*) customers
pl, clientele.
künftig [ˈkynftiç] *adj* future.
Kunst [kunst] *f* (*pl* **Künste**) art; (*Fertigkeit*) skill. **–akademie** *f* art college.
kunstfertig *adj* skilled. **Kunst‖gegenstand**
m objet d'art. **–griff** *m* trick, dodge.
–handwerker *m* craftsman.
Künstler [ˈkynstlər] *m* **Künstlerin** *f* artist.
künstlerisch *adj* artistic.
künstlich [ˈkynstliç] *adj* artificial.
künstliche Atmung *f* artificial respiration.
Kunst‖stück [*neut* stunt, trick. **–werk**
neut work of art.
Kupfer [ˈkupfər] *neut* (*pl* -) copper. **kup-
fer‖farben** *adj* copper(-coloured). **–n** *adj*
copper.
Kuppel [ˈkupəl] *f* (*pl* -n) dome, cupola.
Kuppelei [kupəˈlai] *f* (*unz.*) procuring,
pimping. **kuppeln** *v* unite, couple; (*Mot*)
declutch. **Kuppler** *m* procurer. **Kupplerin**
f procuress. **Kupplung** *f* coupling; (*Mot*)
clutch.
Kur [kuːr] *f* (*pl* -en) (course of) treatment.
–anstalt *f* sanatorium.
Kurbel [ˈkurbəl] *f* (*pl* -n) crank, handle.
–welle *f* crankshaft.
Kürbis [ˈkyrbis] *m* (*pl* -se) pumpkin.
Kurfürst [ˈkuːrfyrst] *m* elector, electoral
prince.

Kurort *m* spa.
Kurs [kurs] *m* (*pl* -e) course; (*Komm*) rate. **–buch** *neut* railway timetable.
kursiv [kur'ziːf] *adv* in italics.
Kurve ['kurvə] *f* (*pl* -n) curve; (*Straße*) bend.
kurz [kurts] *adj* short. **kurze Hose** shorts *pl*. **kurz und gut** in a word, in short. **sich kurz fassen** be brief, make it short. **Kurz‖arbeit** *f* short time (work). **–ausgabe** *f* abridged edition.
Kürze ['kyrtsə] *f* shortness; (*Zeit*) brevity. **kürzen** *v* shorten. **kürzlich** *adv* recently, lately.
Kurz‖meldung *f* news flash. **–schluß** *m* short circuit. **–schrift** *f* shorthand. **kurzsichtig** *adj* nearsighted, shortsighted.
Kürzung ['kyrtsuŋ] *f* (*pl* -en) shortening, reduction.
Kurz‖waren *f pl* haberdashery. **–welle** *f* shortwave.
Kusine [ku'ziːnə] *f* (*pl* -n) (female) cousin.
Kuß [kus] *m* (*pl* **Küsse**) kiss.
küssen ['kysən] *v* kiss.
Küste ['kystə] *f* (*pl* -n) coast, shore. **–nwache** *f* coastguard.
Kutsche ['kutʃə] *f* (*pl* -n) carriage, coach. **–r** *m* (*pl* -) coachman.

L

labil [la'biːl] *adj* unstable; (*oft krank*) delicate, sickly.
Labor [la'boːr] *neut* (*pl* -s) (*umg.*) lab.
Laboratorium [labora'toːrium] *neut* (*pl* **Laboratorien**) laboratory, (*umg.*) lab.
lächeln ['lɛçəln] *v* smile. **Lächeln** *neut* smile.
lachen ['laxən] *v* laugh. **Lachen** *neut* laughter, laugh. **zum Lachen bringen** make laugh. *das ist zum Lachen* that's ridiculous.
lächerlich ['lɛçərliç] *adj* ridiculous.
Lachs [laks] *m* (*pl* -e) salmon.
Lack [lak] *m* (*pl* -e) lacquer; (*mit Farbstoff*) (enamel) paint. **–farbe** *f* (enamel) paint. **–leder** *neut* patent leather.
*****laden**[1] ['laːdən] *v* load.
*****laden**[2] *v* invite; (*Jur*) summon.
Laden ['laːdən] *m* (*pl* **Läden**) shop; (*Fenster*) shutter. **–diebstahl** *m* shoplifting. **–schluß** *m* closing time. **–tisch** *m* counter.

Lade‖platz *m* loading place; (*Schiff*) wharf. **–raum** *m* hold. **Ladung** (*pl* -en) *f* load; (*Schiffe*) cargo.
Lage ['laːgə] *f* (*pl* -n) situation, position. **in der Lage sein zu** be in a position to.
Lager ['laːgər] *neut* (*pl* -) camp; (*Speicher*) store(s); (*Tier*) lair; (*Geol*) stratum, layer; (*Tech*) bearing. **–feuer** *neut* campfire. **–haus** *neut* warehouse. **lagern** *v* (*im Freien rasten*) camp; (*aufbewahren*) store; (*einlegen*) lay down, place; (*aufbewahrt werden*) be stored.
Lagune [la'guːnə] *f* (*pl* -n) lagoon.
lahm [laːm] *adj* crippled; (*müde*) exhausted; (*schwach*) lame, feeble.
lähmen ['lɛːmən] *v* cripple, paralyze; (*fig*) obstruct. **Lähmung** *f* (*pl* -en) paralysis.
Laib [laip] *m* (*pl* -e) loaf.
Laie ['laiə] *m* (*pl* -n) layman. **Laien‖priester** *m* lay preacher. **–stand** *m* laity.
Lakritze [la'kritsə] *f* (*pl* -n) liquorice.
Lamm [lam] *neut* (*pl* **Lämmer**) lamb. **–fleisch** *neut* lamb. **–wolle** *f* lambswool.
Lampe ['lampə] *f* (*pl* -n) lamp.
Land [lant] **1** *neut* (*unz.*) (*Erdboden, Grundstück, Festland*) land; (*Landschaft*) country(side). **2** *neut* (*pl* **Länder**) land, country; (*Provinz*) state, province. **an Land gehen** go ashore, disembark. **Hügeliges Land** hilly country *or* terrain. **auf dem Lande** in the country. **Land‖arbeiter** *m* farmworker. **–besitz** *m* land, property.
landen *v* land; (*umg.*) land up, end up. **Landenge** *f* isthmus.
Landes‖bank *f* national bank; regional bank. **–flagge** *f* national flag. **–verrat** *m* high treason.
Land‖gut *neut* (landed) estate. **–haus** *neut* country house. **–karte** *f* map. **–leute** *pl* country folk.
ländlich ['lɛntliç] *adj* rural.
Land‖mann *m* countryman; (*Bauer*) farmer. **–messer** *m* surveyor. **–mine** *f* landmine. **–schaft** *f* countryside; (*Malerei*) landscape; (*Gebiet*) area, region. **–schule** *f* village school. **–smann** *m* fellow countryman. **–spitze** *f* cape, headland. **–straße** *f* highway, main road. **–streicher** *m* tramp, vagrant.
Landung ['landuŋ] *f* (*pl* -en) landing. **–ssteg** *m* gangway, landing ramp.
Landweg ['lantveːk] *m* land route. **auf dem Landwege** by land.

Landwirt ['lantviːrt] *m* farmer. **landwirt-schaftlich** *adj* agricultural.
lang [laŋ] *adj* long; (*Mensch*) tall. **viele Jahre lang** for many years. **lange** *adv* (for) a long time.
Länge ['lɛŋə] *f* (*pl* -n) length; (*Mensch*) height; (*Größe*) size; (*Geog*) longitude.
langen ['laŋən] *v* suffice. **langen nach** reach for.
länger ['lɛŋər] *adj* longer; taller. **länger machen** lengthen, extend. **auf längere Zeit** for a considerable period.
Langeweile ['laŋəvailə] *f* boredom.
lang||jährig *adj* of long standing. **–lebig** *adj* long-lived.
länglich ['lɛŋliç] *adj* oblong, longish. **–rund** *adj* oval, elliptical.
längs [lɛŋs] *prep* along.
langsam ['laŋzaːm] *adj* slow. **Langsamkeit** *f* slowness.
Langspielplatte ['laŋʃpiːlplatə] *f* long-playing record, LP.
längst [lɛŋst] *adj* longest. *adv* long ago. **–ens** *adv* (*höchstens*) at the most; (*spätestens*) at the latest.
langweilen ['laŋvailən] *v* bore. **sich langweilen** be bored. **langweilig** *adj* boring, tedious.
Lanze ['lantsə] *f* (*pl* -n) lance.
Lappen ['lapən] *m* (*pl* -) rag, (cleaning) cloth; (*Anat, Bot*) lobe. **lappig** *adj* (*umg.*) flabby; (*Anat, Bot*) lobed.
Lärche ['lɛrçə] *f* (*pl* -n) larch.
Lärm [lɛrm] *m* (*unz.*) noise, din. **lärmen** *v* make a noise. **–d** *adj* noisy.
Laser ['leːzər] *m* (*pl* -) laser.
*lassen ['lasən] *v* (*erlauben*) let, allow; (*unterlassen*) leave, stop; (*überlassen*) leave. **außer Acht lassen** disregard. **bleiben lassen** leave alone. **fallen lassen** (let) drop. **kommen lassen** send for. **sich machen lassen** have done *or* made. **lassen von** renounce. **sich nicht beschreiben lassen** be indescribable *or* beyond words. **laß mich gehen!** let me go! **laß mich in Ruhe!** leave me alone. **es läßt sich nicht machen** it can't be done.
lässig ['lɛsiç] *adj* careless, negligent.
Last [last] *f* (*pl* -en) load; (*Bürde*) burden; (*Gewicht*) weight; (*Fracht*) cargo.
Laster¹ ['lastər] *m* (*pl* -) (*umg.*) lorry, truck.
Laster² *neut* (*pl* -) vice. **lasterhaft** *adj* immoral.

lästern ['lɛstərn] slander. **Lästerung** *f* slander.
lästig ['lɛstiç] *adj* irksome, bothersome.
Last||kahn *m* barge, lighter. **–kraftwagen** (**Lkw**) *m* lorry, truck. **–pferd** *neut* packhorse.
Latein [la'tain] *neut* Latin (language). **–amerika** *neut* Latin America. **lateinisch** *adj* Latin.
Laterne [la'tɛrnə] *f* (*pl* -n) lantern. **–npfahl** *m* lamppost.
Latte ['latə] *f* (*pl* -n) lath.
lau [lau] *adj* lukewarm, tepid; (*Wetter*) mild.
Laub [laup] *neut* (*pl* -e) foliage. **–baum** *m* deciduous tree. **–säge** *f* fretsaw. **–wald** *m* deciduous forest. **–werk** *neut* foliage.
Lauch [laux] *m* (*pl* -e) leek.
lauern ['lauərn] *v* lurk, lie in ambush; (*umg.*) hang around, wait impatiently.
Lauf [lauf] *m* (*pl* **Läufe**) run; (*Sport*) race; (*Fluß*) course; (*Gewehr*) barrel; (*Maschine*) career. **laufen** *v* (*Maschine, Wasser, Weg, usw.*) run; (*zu Fuß gehen*) walk. **laufend** *adj* current, running; (*Zahl*) consecutive. **auf dem laufenden** up to date.
Läufer ['lɔyfər] *m* (*pl* -) (*Sport*) runner; (*Schach*) bishop.
läufig ['lɔyfiç] *adj* (*Hündin*) in heat.
Lauf||planke *f* gangway. **–werk** *neut* mechanism, drive.
Lauge ['laugə] *f* (*pl* -n) lye; (*Seifen-*) suds. **laugenartig** *adj* alkaline, (*Chem*) basic.
Laune ['launə] *f* (*pl* -n) mood, temper; (*Grille*) whim. **launenhaft** *adj* capricious, whimsical. **launig** *adj* humorous, funny. **launisch** *adj* moody, capricious.
Laus [laus] *f* (*pl* **Läuse**) louse.
lauschen ['lauʃən] *v* listen (to); (*heimlich*) listen in, eavesdrop.
lausig ['lauziç] *adj* lousy.
laut¹ [laut] *adj* loud. *adv* aloud.
laut² *prep* according to.
Laut [laut] *m* (*pl* -e) sound.
Laute ['lautə] *f* (*pl* -n) lute.
lauten ['lautən] *v* read, say; (*klingen*) sound.
läuten ['lɔytən] *v* ring, sound.
lauter ['lautər] *adj* pure; (*echt*) genuine; (*nichts als*) nothing but, sheer.
Laut||sprecher *m* loudspeaker. **–stärke** *f* volume, loudness.
lauwarm ['lauvarm] *adj* lukewarm.

Lawine [la'viːnə] *f* (*pl* -n) avalanche.
lax [laks] *adj* lax.
leben ['leɪbən] *v* live. **von . . . leben** live on
. . . . **Es lebe die Königin!** Long live the
Queen! **Leben** *neut* (*pl* -) life; (*Geschäf-
tigkeit*) activity, bustle. **am Leben** alive.
ums Leben kommen lose one's life, die.
lebend *adj* living, alive. **-ig** *adj* alive, living; (*munter*) lively.
Lebens‖art *f* lifestyle. **-freude** *f* joy of
life. **-funktion** *f* vital function. **-gefahr** *f*
danger to life. **-haltungskosten** *pl* cost of
living *sing*. **-jahr** *neut* year of one's life.
im 16. Lebensjahr during the sixteenth
year of his/her life.
lebenslänglich ['leɪbənsleŋliç] *adj* life-
long; (*Jur*) for life.
Lebens‖lauf *m* curriculum vitae, c.v.
-mittel *pl* food *sing*. **-standard** *m* standard of living. **-stil** *m* lifestyle.
-unterhalt *m* livelihood. **-versicherung** *f*
life insurance. **-weise** *f* way of life.
Leber ['leɪbər] *f* (*pl* -n) liver. **-fleck** *m*
birthmark. **-wurst** *f* liver sausage.
Lebe‖wesen *neut* living creature, organism. **-wohl** *neut* farewell.
lebhaft ['leɪphaft] *adj* lively. **Lebhaftigkeit**
f liveliness.
leblos ['leɪploːs] *adj* lifeless.
leck [lɛk] *adj* leaky. **Leck** *neut* (*pl* -e)
leak.
lecken ['lɛkən] *v* lick.
lecker ['lɛkər] *adj* delicious. **-bissen** *m*
delicacy, titbit.
Leder ['leɪdər] *neut* (*pl* -) leather. **-hose** *f*
leather shorts *pl*. **ledern** *adj* leather; (*fig*)
dry, boring. **Leder‖riemen** *m* leather
strap. **-waren** *pl* leather goods.
ledig ['leɪdiç] *adj* single, unmarried; (*frei*)
free (of). **lediger Stand** *m* celibacy. **ledig-
lich** *adv* solely.
Lee [leɪ] *f* lee.
leer [leɪr] *adj* empty; (*unbesetzt*) unoccupied; (*Stellung*) open; (*Seite*) blank.
Leere *f* emptiness; (*Physik*) vacuum.
leeren *v* empty. **Leer‖lauf** *m* (*Mot*)
idling, tick-over. **-ung** *f* (*pl* -en) emptying; (*Post*) collection.
legal [le'gaɪl] *adj* legal.
legen ['leɪgən] *v* lay, place, put (down);
(*Eier*) lay; (*installieren*) install, fit. **sich
legen** lie down; (*wind*) abate.
Legende [le'gɛndə] *f* (*pl* -n) legend.
legieren [le'giɪrən] *v* (*Metalle*) alloy;
(*Suppe*) thicken.

legitim [legi'tiːm] *adj* legitimate.
Lehm [leɪm] *m* (*pl* -e) loam.
Lehne ['leɪnə] *f* (*pl* -n) support, prop;
(*Stuhl*) back. **lehnen** *v* lean, rest. **sich
lehnen** lean, rest. **Lehn‖sessel** *or* **-stuhl**
m armchair, easy chair.
Lehrbuch ['leɪrbux] *neut* textbook. **Lehre**
f (*pl* -n) teaching; (*Lehrzeit*) training.
lehren *v* teach. **Lehrer** *m* (*pl* -) teacher,
schoolmaster. **-in** *f* (*pl* -nen) teacher,
schoolmistress. **Lehr‖film** *m* educational
film. **-gang** *m* curriculum, course of
instruction. **-ling** *m* (*pl* -e) apprentice.
lehrreich *adj* instructive. **Lehr‖satz** *m*
rule, proposition. **-zeit** *f* training,
apprenticeship.
Leib [laip] *m* (*pl* -er) body. **Leibes‖frucht**
f foetus. **-übung** *f* physical exercise.
Leiche ['laiçə] *f* (*pl* -n) corpse.
Leichen‖halle *neut* mortuary. **-schau** *f*
postmortem, autopsy. **Leichnam** *m* (*pl*
-e) corpse.
leicht [laiçt] *adj* light; (*einfach*) easy.
leicht zugänglich easily accessible. **es sich
leicht machen** take it easy. **Leichtathletik**
f athletics. **leichtfertig** *adj* superficial;
(*Antwort*) glib. **Leichtgewichtler** *m* light-
weight. **leichtgläubig** *adj* credulous.
Leichtigkeit *f* lightness; (*Mühelosigkeit*)
ease. **leichtlebig** *adj* easy-going. **-sinnig**
adj thoughtless.
leid [lait] *adj* disagreeable, painful. **es ist
(or es tut) mir leid** I am sorry. **Leid** *neut*
(*unz.*) sorrow, grief; (*Schaden*) harm. **leiden** *v* suffer; (*erlauben*) tolerate, allow.
leiden an suffer from. *ich kann ihn nicht
leiden* I can't stand him. **leidend** *adj* suffering; (*kränklich*) sickly.
Leidenschaft ['laidənʃaft] *f* (*pl* -en) passion. **leidenschaft‖lich** *adj* passionate.
-slos *adj* dispassionate.
leider ['laidər] *adv* unfortunately. **leider
muß ich . . .** I am afraid I have to . . . .
leidig [laidiç] *adj* tiresome, disagreeable.
leidlich ['laitliç] *adj* tolerable.
Leier ['laiər] *f* (*pl* -n) lyre. **die alte Leier**
the same old story. **leiern** *v* (*sprechen*)
drawl.
leihen ['laiən] *v* lend; (*borgen*) borrow.
Leihbibliothek *f* lending library.
Leim [laim] *m* (*pl* -e) glue.
Lein [lain] *m* (*pl* -e) flax.
Leine ['lainə] *f* (*pl* -n) line, cord; (*Hund*)
leash.

leinen

294

leinen ['lainən] *adj* linen. **Leinen** *neut* linen.

leise ['laizə] *adj* quiet; (*sanft*) gentle, soft.

Leiste ['laistə] *f* (*pl* -n) (*Anat*) groin.

leisten ['laistən] *v* do; (*schaffen*) accomplish, achieve; (*ausführen*) carry out. **Hilfe leisten** help, assist. **sich leisten** allow oneself. *ich kann mir einen neuen Wagen nicht leisten* I cannot afford a new car. **Leistung** *f* (*pl* -en) achievement, accomplishment; (*Tat*) deed; (*Arbeit*) output. **leistungsfähig** *adj* capable; productive. **Leistungsfähigkeit** *f* ability (to work); productivity.

leiten ['laitən] *v* (*führen*) (*Elek, Musik*) conduct. **-d** *adj* guiding, leading; (*Person*) prominent, senior. **Leiter¹** ['laitər] *m* (*pl* -) leader; manager. **Leiter²** *f* (*pl* -n) ladder. **Leit‖faden** *m* clue; (*Lehrbuch*) guide, textbook. **-satz** *m* guiding principle. **-ung** *f* (*pl* -en) (*Führung*) leadership; (*Verwaltung*) management; (*Elek*) circuit; (*Draht*) wire; (*Wasser*) pipes *pl*, mains *pl*.

Lektüre lɛk'tyːrə] *f* (*pl* -n) reading; (*Lesestoff*) reading material, literature.

Lende ['lɛndə] *f* (*pl* -n) (*Anat*) lumbar region; (*Fleisch*) loin.

lenken ['lɛŋkən] *v* steer; (*führen*) direct. **Lenk‖er** *m* guide; (*Flugzeug*) pilot; (*Leiter*) manager. **-rad** *m* steering wheel. **-ung** *f* (*pl* -en) (*Mot*) steering; (*Leitung*) direction.

Leopard [leo'part] *m* (*pl* -en) leopard.

lepra ['leipra] *f* leprosy. **-kranke(r)** leper.

Lerche ['lɛrçə] *f* (*pl* -n) lark.

lernen ['lɛrnən] *v* learn. **Lernen** *neut* (*unz.*) learning.

lesbar ['leisbair] *adj* readable. **Lese** *f* (*pl* -n) vintage. **Lesebuch** *neut* reading book. **lesen** *v* read; lecture; (*sammeln, ernten*) gather, harvest. **Leser** *m* (*pl* -), **Leserin** *f* (*pl* -en) reader. **leserlich** *adj* legible. **Leserschaft** *f* readership, readers. **Lesesaal** *m* reading room.

letzt [lɛtst] *adj* last; (*spätest*) latest, final. **letzte Nummer** current issue. **letztens** *adv* lately; (*zum Schluß*) lastly.

Leuchte ['lɔyçtə] *f* (*pl* -n) light, lamp. **leuchten** *v* emit light, shine. **-d** *adj* shining, luminous. **Leuchter** *m* (*pl* -) candlestick. **Leuchtturm** *m* lighthouse.

leugnen ['lɔygnən] *v* deny.

Leukämie [lɔykɛ'miː] *f* leukaemia.

Leute ['lɔytə] *pl* people.

Leutnant ['lɔytnant] *m* (*pl* -e) lieutenant.

leutselig ['lɔytzeːliç] *adj* affable, sociable.

Lexikon ['lɛksikɔn] *neut* (*pl* **Lexika**) dictionary.

Libelle [li'bɛlə] *f* (*pl* -n) (*Insekt*) dragonfly; (*Tech*) (spirit) level.

liberal [libe'raːl] *adj* liberal.

licht [liçt] *adj* bright; (*Farbe*) light; (*Wald*) sparse, thin. **Licht** *neut* (*pl* -er) light; (*Kerze*) candle. **-bild** *neut* photograph. **lichtdurchlässig** *adj* translucent. **lichten** ['liçtən] *v* (*Wald*) clear; (*Anker*) weigh. **Licht‖jahr** *neut* lightyear. **-pause** *f* blueprint. **-signal** *neut* light signal. **lichtundurchlässig** *adj* opaque. **Lichtung** ['liçtuŋ] *f* (*pl* -en) glade, clearing.

Lid [liːt] *neut* (*pl* -er) eyelid.

lieb [liːb] *adj* dear; (*nett*) nice; (*angenehm*) agreeable. *ein liebes Kind* a good child. *es wäre ihm lieb* he would appreciate it. *das ist lieb von Ihnen* that is most kind of you. **Liebchen** ['liːpçən] *neut* (*pl* -) darling. **Liebe** ['liːbə] *f* (*pl* -n) love. **Liebelei** *f* (*pl* -en) flirtation. **lieben** *v* love. **liebens‖wert** *adj* lovable. **-würdig** *adj* amiable, helpful, kind. **lieber** ['liːbər] *adj* dearer. *adv* rather; (*besser*) better. **lieber haben** prefer. **lieber als** rather than. *Ich gehe lieber zu Fuß* I prefer to walk. *das hättest Du lieber nicht sagen sollen* you had better not say that. **Liebes‖affäre** *f* (love) affair. **-brief** *m* love letter. **-paar** *neut* lovers *pl*, couple. **liebevoll** ['liːbəfɔl] *adj* affectionate, loving. ***liebhaben** ['liːphaibən] *v* love, like. **Liebhaber** *m* (*pl* -), **Liebhaberin** *f* (*pl* -nen) lover. **lieb‖kosen** *v* caress, fondle. **-lich** *adj* lovely. **Lieb‖ling** *m* darling; (*Günstling*) favourite. **-reiz** *m* charm, attraction. **liebst** [liːpst] *adj* favourite, best-loved. *adv* **am liebsten haben** like best of all. **am liebsten machen** like doing best.

Lied [liːt] *neut* (*pl* -er) song. **-erbuch** *neut* songbook. (*Rel*) hymnbook.

liederlich *adj* slovenly; (*sittenlos*) debauched, dissipated.

Lieferant [liːfə'rant] *m* (*pl* -en) supplier. **liefern** *v* deliver, supply; (*Ertrag*) yield. **Lieferung** *f* (*pl* -en) delivery, supply.

Liege ['liːɡə] f (pl -n) couch. **liegen** v lie. **–bleiben** v remain; (Waren) be unsold; (Arbeit) remain unfinished; (Panne haben) break down. **–lassen** v leave (behind). **Liege‖platz** m berth. **–stuhl** m deckchair.

Liga ['liːɡa] f (pl Ligen) league.

Likör m (pl -e) liqueur.

lila ['liːla] adj lilac, purple. **Lila** neut lilac, purple.

Lilie ['liːliə] f (pl -n) lily.

Limonade [limo'naːdə] f (pl -n) lemonade, soda-pop.

Linde ['lində] f (pl -n) lime tree.

lindern ['lindərn] v alleviate, mitigate.

Lineal [line'aːl] neut (pl -e) ruler, rule.

Linie ['liːniə] f (pl -n) line.

Linke ['liŋkə] f (pl -n) left, left(-hand) side; (Pol) the Left. **linkisch** adj clumsy. **links** adv (on or to the) left. **Linkshänder** m left-hander. **linkshändig** adj left-handed. **Links‖radikale(r)** m (radical) left-winger. **–steuerung** f left-hand drive.

Linse ['linzə] f (pl -n) (Foto, Anat) lens; (Küche) lentil.

Lippe ['lipə] f (pl -n) lip. **–nstift** m lipstick.

lispeln ['lispəln] v lisp.

Lissabon ['lissabon] neut Lisbon.

List [list] f (pl -en) (Schlauheit) cunning; trick, ruse.

Liste ['listə] f (pl -n) list.

listig ['listiç] adj cunning.

Litanei [lita'nai] f (pl -en) litany.

Liter ['liːtər] neut or m (pl -) litre.

literarisch [lite'raːriʃ] adj literary. **Literatur** f literature.

Live-Sendung ['laifzɛnduŋ] f live or direct broadcast.

Lizenz [li'tsɛnts] f (pl -en) licence. **–inhaber** m licensee.

Lob [loːp] neut (pl -e) praise. **loben** v praise. **Lob‖gesang** m song of praise. **–hudelei** f adulation.

Loch [lɔx] neut (pl Löcher) hole; (Reifen) puncture. **lochen** v pierce, punch; (perforieren) perforate.

löcherig ['lœçəriç] adj full of holes.

Lochung ['lɔxuŋ] f (pl -en) perforation.

Locke ['lɔkə] f (pl -n) curl, lock.

locken ['lɔkən] v lure, entice.

locker ['lɔker] adj loose; (Lebensart) lax, slack. **lockern** v loosen (up). **sich lockern** v become loose; (entspannen) relax.

lockig ['lɔkiç] adj curly.

Lock‖speise f bait. **–vogel** m decoy.

lodern ['loːdərn] v blaze (up); (fig) glow, smoulder.

Löffel ['lœfəl] m (pl -) spoon.

Loge ['loːʒə] f (pl -n) (Theater) box; (Freimaurer) lodge.

logieren [lo'ʒiːrən] v lodge.

Logik ['loːɡik] f logic. **logisch** adj logical.

Lohn [loːn] m (pl Löhne) (Gehalt, Bezahlung) wages pl, pay; (Belohnung) reward; (verdiente Strafe) deserts pl. **–arbeiter** m wage-earner, (weekly-paid) worker. **lohnen** v reward. **es lohnt sich (nicht)** it's (not) worth it. **Lohn‖forderung** f wage claim. **–schreiber** m hack (writer). **–stopp** m wage freeze. **–tag** m payday.

lokal [lo'kaːl] adj local. **Lokal** neut (pl -e) pub, tavern.

Lokomotive [lokomo'tiːvə] f (pl -n) locomotive.

Lorbeer ['lɔrbeɪr] m (pl -en) laurel. **–blatt** neut bay leaf. **–kranz** m laurel wreath.

los [loːs] adj free; (nicht fest) loose. adv away, off. **los!** go on! off you go! **was ist los?** what's going on? **was ist mit dir los?** what's the matter (with you)? **etwas/jemanden los sein/werden** be/get rid of something/someone.

Los neut (pl -e) (Schicksal) fate, lot; (Lotterie) lottery ticket. **das Los ziehen** draw lots.

lösbar ['lœːsbaɪr] adj soluble.

*los‖binden v untie. **–brechen** v break loose.

löschen ['lœʃən] v (Feuer) put out, extinguish; (Licht) turn off, switch off; (Schuld) cancel, write off; (Tinte) blot; (Firma) liquidate; (Durst) quench. **Löscher** m (Feuer) extinguisher; (Tinte) blotter.

lose ['loːzə] adj loose.

Lösegeld ['lœːzəɡɛlt] neut ransom.

lösen ['lœːzən] v loosen; (Knoten) unravel (a plot); (Verschluß) unfasten; (Rätsel, Problem) solve; (abtrennen) detach; (Chem) dissolve.

*los‖fahren v drive off. **–gehen** v set out, get going. **–knüpfen** v untie. **–kommen** v get away or free. **–lassen** v let go.

löslich ['lœːzliç] adj soluble.

los‖lösen v free, detach. **–machen** v unfasten, release. **–reißen** v tear away. **–sagen** v **sich lossagen von** renounce.

los‖schießen v fire away/off. **–shrauben** v unscrew. **–sprechen** v acquit, release.

Losung ['lo:zuŋ] f (pl **-en**) password.

Lösung ['lœ:zuŋ] f (pl **-en**) solution; (Lösen) loosening. **–smittel** neut solvent.

los‖werden v get rid of. **–ziehen** v set out.

Lot [lo:t] neut (pl **-e**) plumbline; (zum Löten) solder. **loten** v take soundings.

löten v solder.

lotrecht ['lo:treçt] adj perpendicular, vertical.

Lotse ['lo:tsə] f (pl **-n**) (Schiff) pilot.

Lotterie [lɔte'ri:] f (pl **-n**) lottery.

Löwe ['lœ:və] m (pl **-n**) lion. **–nzahn** m dandelion. **Löwin** f lioness.

Luchs [luks] m (pl **-e**) lynx.

Lücke ['lykə] f (pl **-n**) gap; (Auslassung) omission; (eines Gesetzes) loophole. **–nbüßer** m stopgap. **luckenhaft** adj defective; (fig) patchy, full of gaps.

Luft [luft] f (pl **Lüfte**) air. **–ansicht** f aerial view. **–bild** neut aerial photograph. **–bremse** f air brake. **–brücke** f airlift. **luftdicht** adj airtight.

lüften ['lyftən] v ventilate, air.

Luftfahrt ['luftfa:rt] f aviation. **luftgekühlt** adj air-cooled. **Lufthafen** m airport. **luftig** adj airy, breezy. **Luft‖krankheit** f airsickness. **–krieg** m aerial warfare. **–post** f airmail. **–reifen** m pneumatic tyre, (US tire). **–röhre** f windpipe. **–schiff** neut airship.

Lüftung ['lyftuŋ] f (pl **-en**) ventilation.

Luftverkehr ['luftvɛrke:r] m air traffic. **–sgesellschaft** f airline.

Lüge ['ly:gə] f (pl **-n**) lie. **lügen** v (tell a) lie. **–haft** adj lying. **Lügner** m liar.

Lump [lump] m (pl **-**) rag. **–händler** m rag-and-bone man.

Lunge ['luŋə] f (pl **-n**) lung. **Lungen‖entzündung** f pneumonia. **–krebs** m lung cancer.

Lupe ['lu:pə] f (pl **-n**) magnifying glass. **unter die Lupe nehmen** scrutinize, examine closely.

Lust [lust] f (pl **Lüste**) delight, pleasure; (Verlangen) desire; (Wollust) lust. **Lust haben an** take pleasure in. **Lust haben (zu tun)** feel like (doing). **keine Lust haben (zu tun)** not be in the mood (to do), not feel like (doing).

lüstern ['lystərn] adj (geil) lascivious, lecherous.

Lustfahrt ['lustfa:rt] f pleasure trip. **lustig** adj merry, joyful; (unterhaltend) amusing, funny. **sich lustig machen über** make fun of. **Lustigkeit** f gaiety, merriment. **lustlos** adj dull, inactive. **Lust‖mord** m sex murder. **–spiel** neut comedy.

lutschen ['lutʃən] v suck. **Lutscher** m (baby's) dummy, (US) pacifier.

Luxus ['luksus] m luxury. **–artikel** m luxury item; pl luxuries.

Luzern ['lutsɛrn] neut Lucerne.

lyrisch ['ly:riʃ] adj lyrical.

M

Maat [ma:t] m (pl **-e**) mate; (Kriegsmarine) petty officer.

machen ['maxən] v make; do; (Rechnung) come to. **eine Prüfung machen** sit an exam. **fertig machen** get ready. **Licht machen** switch on a light. **(das) macht nichts**, it doesn't matter, never mind. **mach's gut!** good luck! all the best!

Macht [maxt] f (pl **Mächte**) power. **mächtig** ['mɛçtiç] adj powerful; mighty; (riesig) immense.

Machtkampf m power struggle. **machtlos** adj powerless. **Machtprobe** f trial of strength.

Mädchen ['mɛ:tçən] neut (pl **-**) girl. **mädchenhaft** adj girlish. **Mädchenname** m maiden name.

Made ['ma:də] f (pl **-n**) maggot.

Mädel ['mɛ:dəl] neut (pl **-**) girl.

Magazin [maga'tsi:n] neut (pl **-e**) store(house); (Zeitschrift, auch Gewehr-) magazine.

Magd [ma:kt] f (pl **Mägde**) maid(servant).

Magen ['ma:gən] m (pl **-Mägen**) stomach. **–brennen** neut heartburn. **–schmerzen** pl stomach-ache sing.

mager ['ma:gər] adj thin, lean.

Magie [ma'gi:] f magic. **magisch** adj magic(al).

Magnet [mag'ne:t] m (pl **-en**) magnet. **magnetisch** adj magnetic.

Mahagoni [maha'go:ni] neut (pl **-s**) mahogany.

Mähdrescher ['mɛ:drɛʃər] m combine harvester. **mähen** v mow.

Mahl [ma:l] neut (pl **-e**) meal.

*mahlen ['ma:lən] v mill, grind.

Mahl‖zahn *m* molar. **-zeit** *f* meal; *interj* good appetite!
Mähne ['mɛːnə] *f* (*pl* -n) mane.
mahnen ['maːnən] *v* remind, admonish; warn. **Mahnung** *f* reminder, warning.
Mai [mai] *m* (*pl* -e) May. **-blume** *f* lily of the valley.
Mais [mais] *m* maize, (*US*) corn. **-kolben** *m* cob of corn. **-mehl** *neut* cornflour.
Majestät [majɛsˈtɛːt] *f* (*pl* -en) majesty. **majestätisch** *adj* majestic.
Majoran [majoˈraːn] *m* marjoram.
Makel ['maːkəl] *m* (*pl* -) stain, spot; (*Fehler*) defect, fault. **makellos** *adj* spotless; faultless.
Makler ['maːklər] *m* (*pl* -) broker.
Makrele [maˈkreːlə] *f* (*pl* -n) mackerel.
mal [maːl] *adv* (*Math*) times; (*einmal*) once, just. **drei mal fünf** three times five. **hör' mal!** just listen!
Mal[1] [maːl] *neut* (*pl* -e) time. **zum ersten Mal** for the first time.
Mal[2] *neut* (*pl* -e *or* **Mäler**) mark, sign; (*Denkmal*) monument; (*Grenzstein*) boundary stone.
Malaria [maˈlaːria] *f* malaria.
malen ['maːlən] *v* paint; (*zeichnen*) draw. **Maler** *m* (*pl* -) painter. **Malerei** *f* (*pl* -en) painting. **malerisch** *adj* picturesque.
Malz [malts] *neut* (*pl* -e) malt. **-bier** *neut* malt beer, stout.
Mama [maˈma] *f* (*pl* -s) mamma.
man [man] *pron* one, you; (*die Leute*) people. **man sagt** people say, it is said. **man tut das nicht** that is not done, you shouldn't do that.
Manager ['mɛnidʒər] *m* (*pl* -) manager.
manch [manç] *pron, adj* many a, some. **manche** *pl* several, many. **-mal** *adv* sometimes.
Mandat [manˈdaːt] *neut* (*pl* -e) mandate.
Mandel ['mandəl] *f* (*pl* -n) almond; (*Anat*) tonsil. **-entfernung** *f* tonsillectomy. **-entzündung** *f* tonsillitis.
Mangel[1] ['maŋəl] *f* (*pl* -n) mangle.
Mangel[2] [*m* (*pl* **Mängel**) lack, want; (*Knappheit*) shortage; (*Fehler*) fault.
mangeln ['maŋəln] *v* lack, want. **es mangelt mir an** I lack.
Manie [maˈniː] *f* (*pl* -n) mania.
Manier [maˈniːr] *f* (*pl* -en) manner, way; (*Stil*) style. **Manieren** *pl* manners. **maniert** *adj* affected, mannered. **manierlich** *adj* well-mannered, civil.

Manifest [maniˈfɛst] *neut* (*pl* -e) manifesto.
manisch ['maːniʃ] *adj* manic.
Mann [man] *m* (*pl* **Männer**) man; (*Ehemann*) husband.
Männchen ['mɛnçən] *neut* (*pl* -) little man; (*Tier*) male.
Mannesalter ['manəsaltər] *neut* (age of) manhood. **mannhaft** *adj* manly.
Mannequin [manəˈkɛ̃] *neut* (*pl* -s) mannequin, fashion model.
mannigfaltig ['maniçfaltiç] *adj* varied, manifold.
männlich ['mɛnliç] *adj* male; (*fig, Gramm*) masculine. **Männlichkeit** *f* manhood; masculinity.
Mannschaft ['manʃaft] *f* (*pl* -en) crew; (*Sport*) team; (*Belegschaft*) personnel. **-sführer** *m* (*Sport*) captain.
Manöver [maˈnøːvər] *neut* (*pl* -) manoeuvre. **manövrieren** *v* manoeuvre.
Manschette [manˈʃɛtə] *f* (*pl* -n) cuff.
Mantel ['mantəl] *m* (*pl* -**Mäntel**) coat; (*Umhang*) cloak.
Manuskript [manuˈskript] *neut* (*pl* -e) manuscript.
Mappe ['mapə] *f* (*pl* -n) briefcase; (*Aktenmappe*) folder, portfolio.
Märchen ['mɛːrçən] *neut* (*pl* -) fairytale. **märchenhaft** *adj* fairytale, magical.
Margarine [margaˈriːnə] *f* (*pl* -n) margarine.
Marien‖bild *neut* (picture of the) Madonna. **-käfer** *m* ladybird.
Marine [maˈriːnə] *f* (*pl* -n) (*Kriegsmarine*) navy; (*Handelsmarine*) merchant navy. **-soldat** *m* marine.
marinieren [mariˈniːrən] *v* marinate.
Marionette [marioˈnɛtə] *f* (*pl* -n) marionette.
Mark[1] [mark] *neut* (*unz.*) (bone) marrow. **bis ins Mark** (*fig*) to the core.
Mark[2] *f* (*pl* -) (*Geld*) mark.
Mark[3] *f* (*pl* -en) boundary; (*Grenzgebiet*) marches *pl*, border-country.
Marke ['markə] *f* (*pl* -n) (*Zeichen*) mark, stamp; (*Fabrikat, Sorte*) brand; (*Handelszeichen*) trademark; (*Briefmarke*) (postage) stamp; (*Wertschein*) token. **-nname** *m* tradename, brand-name.
Markt [markt] *m* (*pl* **Märkte**) market. **-halle** *f* covered market, market hall. **-platz** *m* marketplace. **-tag** *m* market day. **-wirtschaft** *f* (free) market economy.

Marmelade [marmə'laɪdə] ƒ (pl -n) jam.
Marmor ['marmɔr] m (pl -e) marble.
Mars [maɪrs] m Mars. **–bewohner** m
Martian.
Marsch[1] [marʃ] m (pl **Märsche**) march.
Marsch[2] [marʃ] ƒ (pl **-en**) marsh.
Marschall ['marʃal] m (pl **Marschälle**)
marshal.
marschieren [maɪr'ʃɪɪrən] v march.
Märtyrer ['mɛrtyrər] m (pl -) martyr.
–tum neut martyrdom.
Märtyrin [mɔɪr'tyrin] ƒ (pl **-nen**) martyr.
Marxismus [mar'ksismus] m (unz.) Marx-
ism.
März [mɛrts] m (pl **-e**) March.
Masche ['maʃə] ƒ (pl **-n**) mesh; (Stricken)
stitch; (Trick) trick.
Maschine [ma'ʃɪɪnə] ƒ (pl **-en**) machine;
(Mot) engine. **Maschinen‖bau** m
mechanical engineering. **–fabrik** ƒ engineering works. **–gewehr** neut machine-
gun. **–schreiben** neut typewriting, typing. **–schreiber(in)** m typist.
Maske ['maskə] ƒ (pl **-n**) mask. **Mas-
ken‖ball** m fancy-dress ball. **–kostüm**
neut fancy dress (costume).
Maß [maɪs] neut (pl **-e**) measure;
(Mäßigung) moderation; (Grenze) limit;
(Umfang) extent. **in hohem Maße** to a
great extent. **Maß halten** be moderate.
Masse ['masə] ƒ (pl **-n**) mass; (Jur) estate,
assets. **die Massen** the masses. **Mas-
sen‖erzeugung** ƒ mass production.
–karambolage ƒ multiple collision,
(umg.) pile-up. **–versammlung** ƒ mass
meeting. **massenweise** adv wholesale, in
large numbers.
Maßgabe ['maɪsgaɪbə] ƒ standard.
maßgeblich adj authoritative.
mäßig ['mɛɪsiç] adj moderate. **mäßigen** v
moderate. **Mäßigung** ƒ modulation.
massiv [ma'siɪf] adj massive.
maßlos ['maɪslos] adj immoderate.
Maßnahme ƒ (pl **-n**) measure, step.
Maßnahmen treffen take steps. **Maßstab**
m measure; (Tech) scale; (fig) yardstick.
Mast [mast] m (pl **-e** or **-en**) mast.
mästen ['mɛstən] v fatten.
Material [materi'aɪl] neut (pl **-ien**) material. **–ismus** m materialism. **materialistisch**
adj materialist(ic).
Materie [ma'teɪriə] ƒ (pl **-n**) matter, stuff,
substance.
Mathematik [matema'tiɪk] ƒ (unz.) mathe-

matics. **-er** m (pl -) mathematician.
mathematisch adj mathematical.
Matratze [ma'tratsə] ƒ (pl **-n**) mattress.
Mätresse [mɛ'trɛsə] ƒ (pl **-n**) mistress.
Matrize [ma'triitsə] ƒ (pl **-n**) (Druck) sten-
cil; (Math) matrix.
Matrose [ma'troɪzə] m (pl **-n**) sailor.
Matsch [matʃ] m mud; (Schnee-) slush.
matschig adj muddy; (breiig) squashy.
matt [mat] adj faint, weary; (glanzlos)
dull, matt; (Licht) dim; (Schach) mate.
Matte ['matə] ƒ (pl **-n**) mat.
Mattheit ['mathait] ƒ weariness; dullness.
mattherzig adj fainthearted.
Mauer ['mauər] ƒ (pl **-n**) wall. **mauern** v
build (a wall). **Mauerwerk** neut masonry.
Maul [maul] neut (pl **Mäuler**) (animals)
mouth, snout, muzzle; (vulgär) (person's)
mouth.
Maurer ['maurər] m (pl -) bricklayer,
building worker.
Maus [maus] ƒ (pl **Mäuse**) mouse.
Mause‖falle ƒ mousetrap. **–loch** neut
mousehole.
maximal [maksi'maɪl] adj maximum.
Maximum neut maximum.
Mechanik [me'çaɪnik] **1** ƒ (unz.) mechanics. **2** (pl **-en**) (Mechanismus) mechanism.
-er m mechanic. **mechanisch** adj
mechanical.
meckern ['mɛkərn] v bleat; (nörgeln)
grumble, moan.
Medaille [me'daijə] ƒ (pl **-n**) medal.
Medikament [medika'mɛnt] neut (pl **-e**)
medicine.
Medizin [medi'tsiɪn] ƒ (pl **-en**) medicine.
-er m doctor, physician; (student) medical student. **medizinisch** adj medical.
Meer [meɪr] neut (pl **-e**) sea. **–enge** ƒ
straits pl. **Meeres‖boden** m sea bed.
–spiegel m sea level.
Mehl [meɪl] neut (pl **-e**) flour. **mehlig** adj
floury, mealy.
mehr [meɪr] adv, adj more. **mehr als** more
than. **nicht mehr** no longer. **immer mehr**
more and more. **noch mehr** still more.
Mehrbetrag m surplus. **mehrdeutig** adj
ambiguous.
mehrere ['meɪrərə] pl pron, adj several.
mehrfach adj multiple.
Mehr‖gepäck neut excess baggage.
–gewicht neut excess weight. **–heit** ƒ
majority.
mehr‖mals adv repeatedly, several times.
–seitig adj many-sided; (Math) polygo-

nal. −sprachig *adj* multilingual. −stöckig *adj* multistoreyed.

Mehr‖wertsteuer (MwSt) *f* value added tax (VAT). −zahl *f* majority; (*Gramm*) plural.

*meiden ['maidən] *v* avoid.

Meierei ['maiərai] *f* (*pl* -en) farm; (*Milchwirtschaft*) dairy farm.

Meile ['mailə] *f* (*pl* -n) mile.

mein [main] *adj, pron* my; mine. meinerseits *adv* for my part. meinesgleichen *pron* people like me, the likes of me. meinethalben, meinetwegen, meinetwillen *adv* for my sake. meinige *pron* (der, die, das meinige) mine.

Meineid ['mainait] *m* (*pl* -e) perjury.

meinen ['mainən] *v* mean; (*denken*) think; (*äußern*) say; (*beabsichtigen*) intend. Meinung *f* opinion. Ich bin der Meinung, daß I am of the opinion that. meiner Meinung nach in my opinion. Meinungs‖forschung *f* opinion research. −umfrage, *f* opinion poll. −verschiedenheit *f* difference of opinion.

Meißel ['maisəl] *m* (*pl* -) chisel. meißeln *v* chisel.

meist [maist] *adj* most. die meisten(Leute) most people. am meisten for the most part. Meistbietende(r) *m* highest bidder. meistens *adv* mostly.

Meister ['maistər] *m* (*pl* -) master; (*Sport*) champion. meisterhaft *adj* masterly. Meisterin *f* (*Sport*) champion. meistern *v* master. Meister‖schaft *f* mastery; (*Sport*) championship. −schaftsspiel *neut* championship match. −stück *or* −werk *neut* masterpiece.

meistgekauft ['maistgəkauft] *adj* best-selling.

Meldeamt ['mɛldəaamt] *neut* registration office. melden *v* inform; (*ankündigen*) announce. sich melden report, present oneself; (*Stelle*) apply. Meldung *f* report; (*ankündigung*) announcement; (*bei der Polizei, usw.*) registration.

*melken ['mɛlkən] *v* milk. Melkmaschine *f* milking machine.

Melodie [melo'diː] *f* (*pl* -n) melody. melodisch *adj* melodious.

Melone [me'loːnə] *f* (*pl* -n) melon.

Membran(e) [mem'brain] *f* (*pl* Membranen) membrane.

Menge ['mɛŋə] *f* (*pl* -n) quantity; (*Menschen*) crowd. eine (ganze) Menge a lot (of), lots (of). mengen *v* mix. sich mengen in meddle.

Mensa ['mɛnsa] *f* (*pl* Mensen) student refectory.

Mensch [mɛnʃ] *m* (*pl* -en) human (being), man, person. Menschenfeind *m* misanthrope. menschenfeindlich *adj* misanthropic. Menschenfreund *m* philanthropist. menschenfreundlich *adj* philanthropic; (*gütig*) affable. Menschen‖kunde *f* anthropology. −leben *neut* human life; (*Lebenszeit*) lifetime. −liebe *f* human kindness. −rechte *pl* human rights. −würde *f* human dignity.

Menschheit ['mɛnʃhait] *f* mankind, human race. menschlich *adj* human; (*human*) humane. Menschlichkeit *f* humanity.

menstrual [mɛnstru'aɪl] *adj* menstrual. Menstruation *f* (*pl* -nen) menstruation. menstruieren *v* menstruate.

Mentalität [mɛntali'tɛɪt] *f* (*pl* -en) mentality.

merkbar ['mɛrkbaɪr] *adj* noticeable. merken *v* notice, note. sich etwas merken make a mental note of something. merklich *adj* evident. Merkmal (*pl* -e) *neut* characteristic, attribute. merkwürdig *adj* remarkable, peculiar.

Meßband ['mɛsbant] *neut* tape measure. meßbar *adj* measurable.

Messe ['mɛsə] *f* (*pl* -n) (*Rel*) mass; (*Ausstellung*) (trade) fair.

*messen ['mɛsən] *v* measure. sich messen mit compete with.

Messer[1] ['mɛsər] *m* (*pl* -) (*Gerät*) gauge, meter.

Messer[2] *neut* (*pl* -) knife.

Messing ['mɛsiŋ] *neut* (*pl* -) brass.

Messung ['mɛsuŋ] *f* (*pl* -en) measurement; (*Messen*) measuring.

Metall [me'tal] *neut* (*pl* -e) metal. metallisch *adj* metallic.

Meteor [mete'oɪr] *neut* (*pl* -e) meteor. −ologe *m* meteorologist. −ologie *f* meteorology. meteorologisch *adj* meteorologist.

Meter ['meɪtər] *neut* (*pl* -) metre.

Methode [me'toɪdə] *f* (*pl* -n) method. methodisch *adj* methodical.

metrisch ['meɪtriʃ] *adj* metric.

Mettwurst ['mɛtvurst] *f* a type of German sausage.

metzen ['mɛtsəln] *v* massacre, slaughter.

Metzger m (pl -) butcher. **-ei** f (pl -en) butcher's shop.
Meuchelmord ['mɔyçəlmɔrt] m assassination.
Meuterei [mɔytə'rai] f (pl -en) mutiny.
meutern v mutiny.
mich [miç] pron me.
Mieder ['miːdər] neut (pl -) bodice.
Miene ['miːnə] f (pl -n) expression, look.
mies [miːs] adj (umg.) nasty, wretched.
Miete ['miːtə] f (pl -n) hire; (für Wohnung) rent. **mieten** v (Haus, Wohnung) rent; (Wagen, usw.) hire.
Mieter m (pl -), **Mieterin** f (pl -nen) tenant, lessee. **Miet‖shaus** neut block of flats, tenement. **-wagen** m hired car. **-wohnung** f rented apartment.
Mikrophon [mikro'foɪn] neut (pl -e) microphone.
Mikroskop [mikro'skoɪp] neut microscope. **mikroskopisch** adj microscopic.
Milbe ['milbə] f (pl -n) mite.
Milch [milç] f milk. **milchig** adj milky. **Milchstraße** f Milky Way.
mild [milt] adj mild; (sanft) soft, gentle. **Milde** f mildness; gentleness. **mildern** v alleviate, moderate. **Milderung** f (pl -en) alleviation. **mildtätig** adj charitable.
Militär [mili'tɛɪr] 1 neut (unz.) army, military. 2 m (pl -s) military man, soldier.
Milliarde [mil'jardə] f (pl -n) thousand million, (US) billion.
Million [mil'joɪn] f (pl -en) million. **-är** m (pl -e) millionaire.
Mimik ['miːmik] f (pl -en) mimicry, miming. **-er** m (pl -) mimic.
minder ['mindər] adj lesser, smaller. adv less.
Minderheit f minority. **Minderjährige(r)** minor. **minderjährig** adj under age. **minderwertig** adj inferior. **Minderwertigkeit** f inferiority.
mindest ['mindəst] adj least; (kleinst) smallest. **-ens** adv at least. **Mindestzahl** f minimum number; (Pol) quorum.
Mine ['miːnə] f (pl -n) mine.
Mineral [mine'raɪl] neut (pl -ien) mineral. **-wasser** neut mineral water.
Miniatur [minia'tuɪr] f (pl -en) miniature.
minimal [mini'maɪl] adj minimum. **Minimum** neut minimum.
Minister [mi'nistər] m (pl -) minister. **-ium** neut ministry. **-präsident** m prime minister.

minus ['miːnus] adv minus, less.
Minute [mi'nuɪtə] f (pl -n) minute.
mir [miɪr] pron (to) me.
mischen ['miʃən] v mix, blend. **sich mischen in** meddle or interfere in. **Misch‖ling** m (Pflanze) hybrid; (Tier) mongrel; (Mensch) half-breed. **-sprache** f pidgin. **-ung** f (pl -en) mixture.
mißach‖ten [mis'axtən] v disregard. **Mißachtung** f disregard.
Mißbildung ['misbilduŋ] f deformity.
mißbilligen ['misbiligən] v disapprove (of), object (to). **Mißbilligung** f disapproval.
Mißbrauch ['misbraux] m misuse, abuse. **mißbrauchen** v misuse, abuse.
mißdeuten [mis'dɔytən] v misinterpret, misunderstand. **Mißdeutung** f misinterpretation.
Mißerfolg ['misɛrfɔlk] m failure.
Missetat ['misətaɪt] f misdeed. **Missetäter** m wrong-doer; (Verbrecher) criminal.
*****mißfallen** [mis'falən] v displease. **Mißfallen** neut displeasure.
Mißgeschick ['misgəʃik] neut misfortune.
mißgestaltet ['misgəʃtaltət] adj misshapen.
mißhandeln [mis'handəln] v maltreat. **Mißhandlung** f maltreatment.
Mission [misi'oɪn] f (pl -en) mission. **-ar** m (pl -e) missionary.
Mißklang ['misklaŋ] m discord.
mißlich ['misliç] adj awkward, embarrassing.
*****mißlingen** v fail. **mißlungen** adj failed, unsuccessful.
mißtrauen [mis'trauən] v distrust. **Mißtrauen** neut distrust. **-svotum** neut vote of no confidence.
Mißverständnis ['misfɛrʃtɛntnis] neut misunderstanding. **mißverstehen** v misunderstand.
Mist [mist] m (pl -e) dung, manure.
Mistel ['mistəl] f (pl -n) mistletoe.
mit [mit] prep with; (mittels) by; (Zeit) at. adv along with; (außerdem) also, as well. kommst du mit? are you coming (with us)? mit 10 Jahren at the age of ten. mit einemmal suddenly. mit dabei sein be concerned or involved.
Mitarbeiter ['mitaɪrbaitər] m colleague, fellow worker; (Zeitschrift) contributor.
Mitbestimmung ['mitbəʃtimuŋ] f worker participation, co-determination.

mitbeteiligt ['mitbətailiçt] *adj* participating, taking part.

***mitbringen** ['mitbriŋən] *v* bring along.

miteinander [mitain'andər] *adv* together, with each other.

miteinbegriffen [mit'ainbəgrifən] *adj* included.

Mitgefühl ['mitgəfyɪl] *neut* sympathy.

Mitglied ['mitglitt] *neut* member. **–schaft** *f* membership.

mithin [mit'hin] *adv* consequently, therefore.

***mitkommen** ['mitkɔmən] *v* come along (with); keep up.

Mitlaut ['mitlaut] *m* consonant.

Mitleid ['mitlait] *neut* pity, sympathy. **mitleid haben mit** have pity on, be sorry for.

mitmachen ['mitmaxən] *v* take part in, join in; (*erleben*) go *or* live through.

Mitmensch ['mitmɛnʃ] *m* fellow man.

***mitnehmen** ['mitneɪmən] *v* take (along); (*im Auto*) give a lift to; (*erschöpfen*) exhaust. **Essen zum Mitnehmen** food to take away.

mitnichten [mit'niçtən] *adv* by no means.

***mitreißen** ['mitraisən] *v* drag along; (*fig*) sweep along, transport.

Mittag ['mitaɪk] *m* noon, midday. **–essen** *neut* lunch, midday meal. **mittags** *adv* at noon. **Mittagspause** *f* lunch hour.

Mitte ['mitə] *f* (*pl* **-n**) middle, centre; (*Math*) mean.

mitteilen ['mittailən] *v* communicate, inform of, tell. **jemandem etwas mitteilen** inform *or* notify someone of something. **Mitteilung** *f* communication, report.

Mittel ['mitəl] *neut* (*pl* -) means, way; (*Ausweg*) remedy; (*Durchschnitt*) average, mean. **–alter** *neut* Middle Ages. **mittelalterlich** *adj* medieval.

Mittel‖amerika *f* Central America. **–gewichtler** *m* middleweight.

mittelgroß ['mitəlɡroɪs] *adj* of medium size.

Mittelläufer ['mitəllɔyfər] *m* (*Fußball*) centre-half.

mittel‖los *adj* destitute. **–mäßig** *adj* mediocre.

Mittel‖meer *neut* Mediterranean (Sea). **–punkt** *m* centre.

mittels ['mitəls] *prep* by (means of).

Mittel‖stand *m* middle classes *pl*. **–stürmer** *m* (*Fußball*) centre-forward.

mitten ['mitən] *adv* in the middle, midway. **mitten in/auf/unter** in the middle of. **mitten drin** in the middle.

Mitternacht ['mitərnaxt] *f* midnight.

mittler ['mitlər] *adj* **in mittlerem Alter** middle-aged. **mittlerweile** *adv* in the meantime.

Mittwoch ['mitvɔx] *m* (*pl* -e) Wednesday.

mitwirken ['mitvirkən] *v* cooperate, take part, participate. **–d** *adj* participating, contributing.

Möbel ['mœɪbəl] *neut* (*pl* -) piece of furniture; (*pl*) furniture *sing*.

mobil [mo'biːl] *adj* movable, mobile; (*flink*) active, lively.

möblieren [mœ'bliːrən] *v* furnish. **möbliert** *adj* furnished.

Mode ['moɪdə] *f* (*pl* **-n**) fashion, vogue. **in Mode sein** be in fashion. **aus der Mode kommen** become unfashionable. **Modeartikel** *pl* fancy goods, fashions.

Modell [mo'dɛl] *neut* (*pl* -e) model; (*Muster*) pattern. **Modellierbogen** *m* cutting-out pattern. **modellieren** *v* model.

Modenschau ['moɪdənʃau] *f* fashion show. **Modezeichner** *m* dress *or* fashion designer.

Moder ['moɪdər] *m* decay, mould. **moderig** *adj* mouldy, putrid. **modern** *v* rot, decay.

modern [mo'dɛrn] *adj* modern. **modernisieren** *v* modernize.

modifizieren [modifi'tsiːrən] *v* modify.

modisch ['moɪdiʃ] *adj* fashionable.

mogeln ['moɪɡəln] *v* cheat.

***mögen** ['mœɪɡən] *v* like; (*wünschen*) wish; (*können*) may, might. **nicht mögen** dislike. *Ich mag ihn* I like him. *das mag sein* that may be so. *Wer mag das sein?* who might that be? *Ich möchte* I would like. *Ich möchte lieber* I would prefer. *Er mag ruhig warten!* let him wait!

möglich ['mœɪɡliç] *adj* possible. **–erweise** *adv* possibly. **Möglichkeit** *f* possibility. **möglichst** *adv* as ... as possible.

Mohammedaner [mohame'daːnər] *m* (*pl* -) Muslim, Mohammedan. **mohammedanisch** *adj* Muslim, Mohammedan.

Mohn [moɪn] *m* (*pl* -e) poppy; (*Samen*) poppyseed.

Mohr [moɪr] *m* (*pl* **-en**) moor, black(man).

Möhre ['mœɪrə] *f* (*pl* **-n**) carrot.

Mohrrübe ['moɪrryɪbə] *f* (*pl* **-n**) carrot.

Molekül [mole' kyɪl] *neut* (*pl* -e) molecule.
molekular *adj* molecular.
Molkerei [mɔlkə'rai] *f* (*pl* -en) dairy.
Moll [mɔl] *neut* (*unz.*) (*Musik*) minor.
Moment[1] [mo'mɛnt] *m* (*pl* -e) moment, instant. **Moment mal!** Just a moment!
Moment[2] *neut* (*unz.*) (*Physik*) moment; (*Anlaß*) motive; (*Umstand*) factor.
Monarch [mo'narç] *m* (*pl* -en) monarch. -**ie** *f* (*pl* -n) monarchy. -**ist** *m* (*pl* -en) monarchist.
Monat ['moɪnat] *m* (*pl* -e) month. **monatelang** *adv* for months. **monatlich** *adj* monthly. **Monats‖blutung** *f* menstruation. -**karte** *f* (monthly) season ticket.
Mönch [mœnç] *m* (*pl* -e) monk.
Mond [moɪnt] *m* (*pl* -e) moon. -**finsternis** *f* lunar eclipse. -**schein** *m* moonlight. -**strahl** *m* moonbeam.
Monogramm [mɔno'gram] *neut* (*pl* -e) monogram, initials.
Monopol [mono'poɪl] *neut* (*pl* -e) monopoly. **monopolisieren** *v* monopolize.
Montag ['moɪntaɪk] *m* Monday. **montags** *adv* (on) Mondays.
Montage [mɔn'taɪʒə] *f* (*pl* -n) assembly; installation. -**band** *neut* assembly line.
Monteur [mɔn'tœɪr] *m* (*pl* -e) mechanic, fitter. **montieren** *v* install, assemble.
Moor [moɪr] *neut* (*pl* -e) marsh, moor.
Moos [moɪs] *neut* (*pl* -e) moss.
Moped ['mopɛt] *neut* (*pl* -s) moped.
Moral [mo'raɪl] *f* (*pl*-en) moral; (*Sittlichkeit*) morality; (*Zuversicht*) morale. **moralisieren** *v* moralize.
Mord [mɔrt] *m* (*pl* -e) murder.
Mörder ['mœɪrdər] *m* (*pl* -) murderer. **mörderisch** *adj* murderous.
morgen ['mɔrgən] *adv* tomorrow. **morgen früh** tomorrow morning. **Morgen** *m* (*pl* -) morning. -**dämmerung** *f* dawn. -**land** *neut* Orient. -**stern** *m* morning star, Venus.
Morphium ['mɔrfium] *neut* morphine.
morsch [mɔrʃ] *adj* rotten.
Morseschrift ['mɔrzəʃrift] *f* Morse code.
Mörtel ['mœɪrtəl] *m* (*pl* -) mortar, cement.
Mosaik [moza'iɪk] *neut* (*pl* -e) mosaic.
Moschee [mɔ'ʃeɪ] *f* (*pl* -n) mosque.
Mosel ['moɪzəl] *f* Moselle.
Moskau ['mɔskau] *neut* Moscow.
Most [mɔst] *m* (*pl* -e) new wine, must.
Motiv [mo'tiɪf] *neut* (*pl* -e) (*Antrieb*)

motive; (*Kunst, Dichtung*) theme, motif.
motivieren *v* motivate.
Motor ['moɪtɔr] *m* (*pl* -en) motor, engine. -**ausfall** *m* engine failure. -**boot** *neut* motorboat. -**haube** *f* bonnet, (*US*) hood. -**rad** *neut* motorcycle. -**roller** *m* (motor) scooter.
Motte ['mɔtə] *f* (*pl* -n) moth.
Möwe ['mœɪvə] *f* (*pl* -n) seagull.
Mücke ['mykə] *f* (*pl* -n) midge, gnat. **Mücken‖netz** *neut* mosquito net. -**stich** *m* midge *or* gnat bite.
müde ['myɪdə] *adj* tired. **Müdigkeit** *f* tiredness, fatigue.
Muff[1] [muf] *m* (*unz.*) musty smell.
Muff[2] *m* (*pl* -e) (*Pelz*) muff.
Muffel ['mufəl] *m* (*pl* -) grumpy person. **muffelig** *adj* grumpy, sullen.
muffig ['mufiç] *adj* (*moderig*) musty.
Mühe ['myɪə] *f* (*pl* -n) trouble, pains *pl*. **sich Mühe geben** take pains. **nicht der Mühe wert** not worth the trouble. **mühelos** *adj* effortless. **sich mühen** trouble oneself, take pains. **mühevoll** *adj* laborious, troublesome.
Mühle ['myɪlə] *m* (*pl* -n) mill.
mühsam ['myɪzaɪm] *adj* also **mühselig** troublesome; (*schwierig*) difficult.
Mulde ['muldə] *f* (*pl* -n) trough; (*Landschaft*) depression, hollow.
Mull [mul] *m* (*pl* -e) muslin.
Müll [myl] *m* refuse, rubbish, (*US*) garbage. -**abfuhr** *f* refuse disposal. -**eimer** *m* dustbin.
Müller ['mylər] *m* (*pl* -) miller.
Multiplikation [multiplikatsi'oɪn] *f* (*pl* -en) multiplication. **multiplizieren** *v* multiply.
Mumie ['mumiə] *f* (*pl* -n) mummy.
Mummenschanz ['mumənʃants] *m* (*pl* -e) masquerade.
München ['mynçən] *neut* Munich. **Münchner** *adj* (of) Munich.
Mund [munt] *m* (*pl* Münder) mouth. -**art** *f* dialect.
münden ['myndən] *v* **münden in** (*Fluß*) flow into; (*Straße*) run into, join.
mund‖faul *adj* taciturn. -**fertig** *adj* glib. -**gerecht** *adj* appetizing. **Mund‖geruch** *m* bad breath, halitosis. -**harmonika** *f* mouth organ, harmonica.
mündig ['myndiç] *adj* of age. **mündig werden** come of age. **Mündigkeit** *f* majority, full legal age.

mündlich ['myntlıç] *adj* oral.
Mundstück ['muntʃtyk] *neut* mouthpiece.
Mündung ['myndʊŋ] *f* (*pl* -en) (*Fluß*) estuary.
Munition [munitsi'oɪn] *f* (*pl* -en) ammunition.
munter ['muntər] *adj* lively, cheerful, merry. **Munterkeit** *f* liveliness, cheer.
Münze ['myntsə] *f* (*pl* -n) coin; (*Anstalt*) mint. **für bare Münze nehmen** take at face value. **Münz‖einwurf** *m* coin-slot.
–**fernsprecher** *m* pay phone, call box.
mürbe ['myrbə] *adj* (*Fleisch*) tender; (*morsch*) rotten, soft; (*brüchig*) brittle; (*Gebäck*) crumbly. **Mürbeteig** *m* short pastry.
murmeln ['murməln] *v* murmur.
murren ['murən] *v* grumble.
mürrisch ['myrıʃ] *adj* morose, grumpy.
Mus [muɪs] *neut* purée.
Muschel ['muʃəl] *f* (*pl* -n) mussel; (*Telef*) (telephone) receiver. –**tier** *neut* mollusc.
Museum [mu'zeɪum] *neut* (*pl* **Museen**) museum.
Musical ['mjuɪzikəl] *neut* (*pl* -s) musical.
Musik [mu'ziɪk] *f* music; (*Kapelle*) band. **musikalisch** *adj* musical.
Musik‖antenknochen *m* (*umg.*) funnybone. –**er** *m* (*pl* -) musician. –**freund** *m* music-lover. –**instrument** *m* musical instrument.
Muskat [mus'kaɪt] *m* (*pl* -e) nutmeg.
–**blüte** *f* mace. –**nuß** *f* nutmeg.
Muskel ['muskəl] *m* (*pl* -n) muscle.
–**kraft** *f* muscular strength. –**krampf** *m* muscle spasm. –**zerrung** *f* pulled muscle.
Muße ['muɪsə] *f* leisure. **müßig** *adj* idle.
***müssen** ['mysən] *v* must, have to. *ich mußgehen* I must go. *ich muß nicht gehen* I don't have to go. *ich muß fort* I must leave. *ich müßte* I ought to.
Muster ['mustər] *net* (*pl* -) model, pattern; (*Stoffverzierung*) pattern, design; (*warenprobe*) sample. –**stück** *neut* sample, specimen. –**zeichnung** *f* design.
Mut [muɪt] *m* courage. **mutig** *adj* brave, courageous. **mutlos** *adj* discouraged, despondent.
mutmaßen ['mutmaɪsən] *v* suppose, surmise. **Mutmaßung** *f* (*pl* -en) conjecture.
Mutter¹ ['mutər] *f* (*pl* **Mütter**) mother.
Mutter² *f* (*pl* -n) (*Tech*) nut.
mütterlich ['mytərlıç] *adj* motherly.

–**erseits** *adv* on one's mother's side, maternal.
Mutter‖liebe *f* mother-love. –**mal** *neut* birthmark. –**schaft** *f* motherhood.
–**sprache** *f* mother tongue, native language.
Mütze ['mytsə] *f* (*pl* -n) cap.
mysteriös [mysteri'œɪs] *adj* mysterious.
Mystik ['mystik] *f* (*unz.*) mysticism. –**er** *m* mystic. **mystisch** *adj* mystical.
Mythe ['mytə] *f* (*pl* -n) myth. **mythisch** *adj* mythical.

N

na [na] *interj* well! (come) now!
Nabe ['naɪbə] *f* (*pl* -n) hub.
Nabel ['naɪbəl] *m* (*pl* -) navel. –**schnur** *f* umbilical cord.
nach [naɪx] *prep* after; (*örtlich*) to, towards; (*gemäß*) according to, by. *adv* after. **nach und nach** gradually. **der Größe nach** by size. **nach außen** externally.
nachahmen ['naɪxaɪmən] *v* imitate. **Nachahmung** *f* imitation.
Nachbar ['naɪxbaɪr] *m* (*pl* -n) neighbour.
–**land** *neut* neighbouring country.
–**schaft** *f* neighbourhood.
Nachbildung ['naɪxbildʊŋ] *f* copy, replica.
nachdem [naɪx'deɪm] *adv* afterwards. *conj* after. **je nachdem** according as.
***nachdenken** ['naɪxdɛŋkən] *v* think (over), reflect. **Nachdenken** *neut* reflection, thinking over. **nachdenklich** *adj* reflective, thoughtful.
Nachdruck ['naɪxdruk] *m* (*Betonung*) emphasis, stress; (*Festigkeit*) vigour. **nachdrücklich** *adj* emphatic; forceful.
nacheifern ['naɪxaifərn] *v* emulate.
nacheinander ['naɪxainandər] *adv* one after another.
Nachfolge ['naɪxfɔlgə] *f* succession. **nachfolgen** *v* succeed, follow. **Nachfolger** *m* successor.
Nachfrage ['naɪxfraɪgə] *f* (*Erkundigung*) inquiry; (*Komm*) demand.
***nachgeben** ['naɪxgeɪbən] *v* give way *or* in.
Nachgeburt ['naɪxgəburt] *f* afterbirth.
***nachgehen** ['naɪxgeɪən] *v* follow; (*untersuchen*) investigate; (*Uhr*) be slow.

nachgemacht ['naɪxgəmaxt] *adj* imitated, false.

Nachgeschmack ['naɪxgəʃmak] *m* aftertaste.

nachgiebig ['naɪxgiːbiç] *adj* pliable, flexible; (*Person*) compliant, yielding.

nachher [naɪx'heɪr] *adv* afterwards.

Nachhilfe ['naɪxhilfə] *f* help, assistance. –**stunden** *pl* coaching *sing*, private tuition *sing*.

nachholen ['naɪxhoɪlən] *v* fetch later; (*fig*) make up for, catch up on.

Nach‖hut ['naɪxhuɪt] *f* rearguard. –**klang** *m* echo, resonance.

Nachkomme ['naɪxkɔmə] *m* (*pl* -**n**) descendant. **nachkommen** *v* follow, come after; (*Verpflichtung*) fulfil. **Nachkommenschaft** *f* posterity, descendants *pl*.

Nachkriegszeit ['naɪxkriːkstsait] *f* postwar era.

Nachlaß ['naɪxlas] *m* (*pl* **Nachlässe**) (*Preis*) reduction, discount; (*Erbschaft*) inheritance, estate. **nachlassen** *v* slacken, abate; (*aufhören*) cease; (*Strafe*) remit; (*Preis*) reduce. **nachlässig** *adj* careless, negligent.

nachmachen ['naɪxmaxən] *v* copy, imitate.

Nachmittag ['naɪxmitaɪk] *m* afternoon. **nachmittags** *adv* in the afternoon(s).

Nachnahme ['naɪxnaɪmə] *f* **gegen** *or* **per Nachnahme** cash on delivery (COD).

Nachname ['naɪxnaɪmə] *m* (*pl* -**n**) surname.

nachprüfen ['naɪxpryɪfən] *v* verify, check again.

Nachricht ['naɪxriçt] *f* (*pl* -**en**) report, (item of) news. **Nachrichten** *pl* news *sing*. **Nachrichten‖büro** *neut* news agency. –**dienst** *m* (*Radio*) news service; (*Mil*) intelligence service.

Nachruf ['naɪxruɪf] *m* (*Zeitung*) obituary; (*Rede*) memorial address.

***nachschlagen** ['naɪxʃlaɪgən] *v* (*Buch*) look up, consult. **Nachschlagebuch** *neut* reference book.

Nach‖schrift ['naɪxʃrift] *f* (*Brief*) postscript; (*eines Vortrages*) transcript. –**schub** *m* (*Mil*) reinforcement(s); (*Material*) supplies *pl*.

***nach‖sehen** ['naɪxzeɪən] *v* (*nachblicken*) watch, follow with one's eyes; (*prüfen*) examine, check; (*nachschlagen*) consult; (*verzeihen*) overlook. –**senden** *v* send on; (*Post*) forward.

Nach‖sicht ['naɪxziçt] *f* leniency. –**sorge** *f* (medical) aftercare. –**spiel** *neut* epilogue, sequel. –**speise** *f* dessert.

nächst [nɛçst] *adj* next; (*Entfernung*) nearest; (*Verwandte*) close, closest; (*umg: kürzest*) shortest. *adv* next. *prep* next to. **am nächsten** next. **nächste Woche** next week. *das nächste Dorf liegt 10 km von hier entfernt* the nearest village is 10 km away. **Nächste(r)** fellowman, neighbour.

***nach‖stehen** ['naɪxʃteɪən] *v* be inferior to. –**stellen** re-adjust; (*Uhr*) put back; (*Frau*) molest, bother.

Nächstenliebe ['nɛçstənliːbə] *f* charity, love of one's fellow men. **nächstens** *adv* shortly.

Nacht [naxt] *f* (*pl* **Nächte**) night. **heute Nacht** tonight. **über Nacht** overnight.

Nachteil ['naɪxtail] *m* disadvantage; (*Schaden*) damage, detriment. **nachteilig** *adj* disadvantageous, unfavourable.

Nachthemd ['naxthɛmt] *neut* nightshirt, nightgown.

Nachtigall ['naxtigal] *f* (*pl* -**en**) nightingale.

Nach‖tisch ['naɪxtiʃ] *m* dessert. –**trag** *m* supplement. **nachträglich** *adj* subsequent, later.

nachts [naxts] *adv* at *or* by night. **Nachtwächter** *m* nightwatchman. **nachtwandeln** *v* sleepwalk.

Nach‖untersuchung ['naɪxuntərzuɪxuŋ] *f* check-up. –**wahl** *f* by-election. –**weis** *m* proof, evidence. **nachweisen** *v* prove, demonstrate.

Nach‖wirkung ['naɪxvirkuŋ] *f* after-effect. –**wort** *neut* epilogue. –**wuchs** *m* new *or* young generation.

***nachziehen** ['naɪxtsiːən] *v* drag, draw along; (*nachzeichnen*) trace; (*folgen*) follow.

Nachzügler ['naɪxtsyːklər] *m* (*pl* -) straggler, late-comer.

Nacken ['nakən] *m* (*pl* -) (nape of the) neck.

nackt [nakt] *adj* naked, bare. **Nacktheit** *f* nakedness.

Nadel ['naɪdəl] *f* (*pl* -**n**) needle; (*Stecknadel*) pin. –**baum** *m* conifer. –**öhr** *neut* eye (of a needle). –**wald** *m* coniferous forest.

Nagel ['naɪgəl] *m* (*pl* **Nägel**) nail. –**feile** *f* nail-file. –**haut** *f* cuticle. –**lack** *m* nail varnish. **nageln** *v* nail. **nagelneu** *adj* brand-new. **Nagelschere** *f* nail scissors *pl*.

nagen ['naːɡən] *v* gnaw.

Nagetier ['naːɡətiːr] *neut* rodent.

nah(e) ['naː(ə)] *adj, adv* near, close. *prep* near to. **einer Person zu nahe treten** offend a person. **nahe dabei** *or* **gelegen** nearby. **nahe Freundschaft** close friendship.

Nahaufnahme ['naːaufnaːmə] *f* (*Foto*) close-up.

Nähe ['nɛːə] *f* nearness; (*Sicht-, Hörweite*) vicinity. **in der Nähe** close by, in the vicinity.

***nahe‖kommen** *v* approach. **–liegend** *adj* obvious; (*örtlich*) close, nearby.

nähen ['nɛːən] *v* sew, stitch.

näher ['nɛːər] *adj* nearer, closer; (*ausführlicher*) more detailed. **nähere Angaben** further details. **nähere Umstände** exact circumstances. **Nähere(s)** *neut* particulars *pl*, details *pl*. **nähern** *v* bring near. **sich nähern** approach, draw near.

nahe‖stehend *adj* close, friendly. **–zu** *adv* nearly, almost.

Näh‖kasten *m* sewing box. **–machine** *f* sewing machine. **–nadel** *f* sewing needle.

nähren ['nɛːrən] *v* nourish; (*unterhalten*) support. **sich nähren von** live on.

nahrhaft ['naːrhaft] *adj* nutritious.

Nährmittel ['nɛːrmitəl] *pl* foodstuffs, food *sing*.

Nahrung ['naːruŋ] *f* (*unz.*) food; (*Unterhalt*) support. **–smittel** *pl* foodstuffs.

Naht ['naːt] *f* (*pl* **Nähte**) seam; (*Med*) suture.

naiv [na'iːf] *adj* naive.

Name ['naːmə] *or* **Namen** *m* (*pl* **Namen**) name. **namens** *adv* named, by the name of.

nämlich ['nɛːmlɪç] *adv* that is (to say), namely.

Napf [napf] *m* (*pl* **Näpfe**) basin, bowl.

Narbe ['narbə] *f* (*pl* **-n**) scar.

Narkose [nar'koːzə] *f* (*pl* **-n**) (*Betäubung*) anaesthesia. **Narkotikum** *neut* (*pl* **Narkotika**) narcotic. **narkotisch** *adj* narcotic.

Narr [nar] *m* (*pl* **-en**) fool. **zum Narren haben** make a fool of. **Narrheit** *f* folly, foolishness.

närrisch ['nɛrɪʃ] *adj* foolish, crazy, silly.

Nase ['naːzə] *f* (*pl* **-n**) nose. **die Nase voll haben von** be fed up with. **Nasen‖loch**

neut nostril. **–höhle** *f* (*anat*) sinus. **–spitze** *f* tip of the nose. **naseweis** *adj* cheeky.

naß [nas] *adj* wet; (*feucht*) moist, damp. **Nässe** ['nɛsə] *f* wet, wetness.

Nation [natsi'oːn] *f* (*pl* **-en**) nation. **national** *adj* national. **National‖flagge** *f* national flag. **–hymne** *f* national anthem.

nationalisieren [natsionaːli'ziːrən] *v* nationalize. **Nationalisierung** *f* nationalization. **Nationalismus** *m* nationalism. **nationalistisch** *adj* nationalist(ic).

National‖mannschaft *f* national team. **–sozialismus** *m* national socialism, Nazism. **–tracht** *f* national costume.

Natter ['natər] *f* (*pl* **-n**) adder.

Natur [na'tuːr] *f* (*pl* **-en**) nature. **–anlage** *f* temperament, disposition. **–forscher** *m* scientist, naturalist. **–kunde** *f* natural history. **natürlich** *adj* natural. **Natur‖schutz** *m* preservation (of nature). **–trieb** *m* instinct. **–wissenschaft** *f* natural science.

Nazi ['naːtsi] *m* (*pl* **-s**) Nazi.

Nebel ['neːbəl] *m* (*pl* **-**) fog; (*dünner*) mist. **–horn** *neut* foghorn. **nebelig** *adj* foggy; misty.

neben ['neːbən] *prep* near (to), beside; (*im Vergleich zu*) compared with, next to. **–an** *adv* next door. **–bei** *adv* by the way; (*außerdem*) besides. **Neben‖beschäftigung** *f* second job, sideline. **–buhler** *m* rival.

nebeneinander ['neːbənainandər] *adv* side by side. **–stellen** *v* juxtapose. **Neben‖fach** *neut* subsidiary subject. **–fluß** *m* tributary. **–gebäude** *neut* annexe. **–kosten** *pl* extras, additional expenses.

nebensächlich ['neːbənsɛçlɪç] *adj* incidental.

necken ['nɛkən] *v* tease.

Neffe ['nɛfə] *m* (*pl* **-n**) nephew.

negativ ['neːɡatiːf] *adj* negative.

Neger ['neːɡər] *m* (*pl* **-**) Negro, Black. **–in** *f* (*pl* **-nen**) Black (woman).

***nehmen** ['neːmən] *v* take.

Neid [nait] *m* envy, jealousy. **neid‖en** *v* envy. **–isch** *adj* envious, jealous.

Neige ['naiɡə] *f* (*pl* **-n**) slope, incline. **neigen** *v* incline. **neigen zu** tend (to), be inclined (to). **sich neigen** incline, slope. **Neigung** *f* slope; (*fig*) inclination.

nein [nain] *adv* no.

Nelke ['nɛlkə] *f* (*pl* -n) carnation; (*Gewürz*) clove.

***nennen** ['nɛnən] *v* call, name. **Nenn‖er** *m* denominator. **–ung** *f* naming; (*Sport*) entry. **–wert** *m* nominal value.

Nerv [nɛrf] *m* (*pl* -en) nerve. **Nerven‖kitzel** *m* thrill. **–krankheit** *f* nervous disease. **nervös** *adj* nervous.

Nessel ['nɛsəl] *f* (*pl* -n) nettle.

Nest [nɛst] *neut* (*pl* -er) nest.

nett [nɛt] *adj* nice; (*gepflegt*) neat.

netto ['netto] *adv* net. **Netto‖gewinn** *m* net profit. **–preis** *m* net price.

Netz [nɛts] *neut* (*pl* -e) net; (*System*) grid, network. **–haut** *f* retina. **–werk** *neut* network.

neu [nɔy] *adj* new; (*modern*) modern. **–artig** *adj* novel.

Neu‖ausgabe *f* new edition. **–bau** *n* new building.

neuerdings ['nɔyərdiŋs] *adv* recently, lately.

Neuerer ['nɔyərər] *m* (*pl* -) innovator.

Neuerscheinung ['nɔyɛɪrʃainuŋ] *f* (*pl* -en) new book.

Neu‖erung ['nɔyəruŋ] *f* (*pl* -en) innovation.

neuestens ['nɔyəstəns] *adv* of late.

neu‖geboren *adj* new-born. **–gestalten** *v* reorganize.

Neugier(de) ['nɔygɪɪr(də)] *f* (*unz.*) curiosity. **neugierig** *adj* curious.

Neu‖heit *f* (*pl* -en) novelty. **–igkeit** *f* (*pl* -en) (item of) news. **–jahr** *neut* New Year. **–jahrstag** *m* New Year's Day.

neulich ['nɔyliç] *adv* recently, lately.

neun [nɔyn] *pron*, *adj* nine. **neunte** *adj* ninth. **neunzehn** *pron*, *adj* nineteen. **neunzig** *pron*, *adj* ninety.

Neu‖ordnung *f* reorganization. **–reiche(r)** nouveau riche, wealthy parvenu.

Neurologe [nɔyro'loɪgə] *m* (*pl* -n) neurologist. **Neurologie** *f* neurology. **neurologisch** *adj* neurological.

Neurose [nɔy'roɪzə] *f* (*pl* -n) neurosis. **neurotisch** *adj* neurotic.

Neuseeland [nɔy'zeɪlant] *neut* New Zealand.

neutral [nɔy'traɪl] *adj* neutral. **neutralisieren** *v* neutralize. **Neutralität** *f* neutrality.

neuzeitlich ['nɔytsaitliç] *adj* modern.

nicht [niçt] *adv* not. **durchaus nicht** not at all. **nicht einmal** not even. **bitte nicht** please don't. **nicht mehr** no longer. **nicht wahr?** isn't it? don't you agree?

Nicht‖achtung *f* disregard. **–annahme** *f* nonacceptance. **–beachtung** *f* nonobservance.

Nichte ['niçtə] *f* (*pl* -n) niece.

Nicht‖einmischung *f* nonintervention. **–erscheinen** *neut* nonappearance.

nichtig ['niçtiç] *adj* futile, empty; (*ungültig*) null, void. **Nichtigkeit** *f* futility; invalidity.

Nicht‖mitglied *neut* non-member. **–raucher** *m* non-smoker. **–raucherabteil** *neut* no-smoking compartment.

nichts [niçts] *pron* nothing. **nichts daraus machen** not take seriously. **(es) macht nichts** it doesn't matter. **nichts dergleichen** nothing of the kind. **Nichts** *neut* nothing(ness).

nichts‖sagend *adj* meaningless. **–würdig** *adj* worthless, base.

Nicht‖vorhandensein *neut* lack, absence. **–zutreffende(s)** *neut* (that which is) nonapplicable.

Nickel ['nikəl] *neut* nickel.

nicken ['nikən] *v* nod, bow; doze, nod off. **Nickerchen** *neut* nap.

nie [niɪ] *adv* never.

nieder ['niɪdər] *adj* low; (*fig*) inferior. *adv* down.

***nieder‖brennen** *v* burn down. **–drücken** *v* depress. **–fallen** *v* fall down.

Nieder‖frequenz *f* low frequency. **–gang** *m* decline, downfall; (*Sonne*) setting.

***nieder‖gehen** *v* go down; (*Aero*) land. **–geschlagen** *adj* depressed.

Niederlage ['niɪdərlaɪgə] *f* defeat.

Niederlande ['niɪdərlandə] *pl* Netherlands. **Niederländer** *m* Dutchman. **–in** *f* Dutchwoman. **niederländisch** *adj* Dutch.

***niederlassen** ['niɪdərlasən] *v* lower. **sich niederlassen** settle down; (*Vogel*) land, settle. **Niederlassung** *f* (*pl* -en) settlement; (*Komm*) branch.

niederlegen ['niɪdərleɪgən] *v* lay down.

Niedersachsen ['niɪdəzaksən] *neut* Lower Saxony.

Niederschlag ['niɪdərʃlaɪk] *m* (*Regen, usw.*) precipitation; (*auf Fensterscheiben*) condensation; (*Chem*) sediment, precipitation; (*Boxen*) knock-down.

***niederschlagen** *v* knock down; (*Augen*) lower; (*Aufstand*) suppress.

nieder‖schmettern *v* strike down.
–schreiben *v* write down. **–setzen** *v* put down. **–werfen** *v* throw down. **sich niederwerfen** prostrate oneself.
niedlich ['niːdliç] *adj* nice, (*umg.*) cute, dainty.
niedrig ['niːdriç] *adj* low. **Niedrigkeit** *f* lowness. **Niedrigwasser** *neut* low water, low tide.
niemals ['niːmaːls] *adv* never.
niemand ['niːmant] *pron* no one, nobody. **Niemandsland** *neut* no-man's-land.
Niere ['niːrə] *f* (*pl* **-n**) kidney.
nieseln ['niːzəln] *v* drizzle.
niesen ['niːzən] *v* sneeze. **Niesen** *neut* sneeze.
Niet [niːt] *neut* (*pl* **-e**) rivet.
Niete ['niːtə] *f* (*pl* **-n**) (*Lotterie*) blank (ticket); (*Person*) nonentity, failure; (*Theater*) flop.
Nikotin [niko'tiːn] *neut* nicotine.
Nilpferd ['niːlpfeɪrt] *neut* hippopotamus.
nimmer ['nimər] *adv* never. **–mehr** *adv* never again.
nippen ['nipən] *v* sip.
nirgends ['nirgənts] *or* **nirgendwo** *adv* nowhere.
Nische ['niːʃə] *f* (*pl* **-n**) niche, alcove.
nisten ['nistən] *v* (build a) nest.
Niveau [niː'voː] *neut* (*pl* **-s**) level; (*fig*) standard; (*geistig*) culture, good education. **Niveau haben** be cultured *or* sophisticated.
noch [nox] *adv* (*außerdem*) in addition. *conj* nor. **noch nicht** not yet. **noch einmal** once again. **noch etwas?** anything else? **noch dazu** in addition. **weder ... noch ... ** neither ... nor .... **nochmals** *adv* once again.
Nockenwelle ['nɔkənvɛlə] *f* camshaft.
Nomade [no'maːdə] *m* (*pl* **-n**) nomad.
Nominativ ['noːminatiːf] *m* (*pl* **-e**) nominative.
nominell [nomi'nɛl] *adj* nominal.
Nonne ['nɔnə] *f* (*pl* **-n**) nun. **–nkloster** *neut* convent, nunnery.
Nord [nɔrt] *m* north. **–amerika** *f* North America. **–en** *m* north. **nordisch** *adj* northern; (*Skandinavisch*) nordic. **Nordländer 1** *m* (*pl* **-**) Northerner. **2** *pl* northern countries.
nördlich ['nœrtliç] *adj* northern. *adv* northwards. **prep** to the north of.
Nordost(en) ['nɔrtɔst(ən)] *m* northeast. **nordöstlich** *adj* northeast(ern).

Nord‖pol *m* North Pole. **–rhein-Westfalen** *neut* North Rhine-Westphalia. **–see** *f* North Sea. **nordwärts** *adv* northwards.
Nordwest(en) ['nɔrtvɛst(ən)] *m* northwest. **nordwestlich** *adj* northwest(ern).
nörgeln ['nœrgəln] *v* grumble, grouse.
Norm [nɔrm] *f* (*pl* **-en**) standard, norm. **normal** *adj* normal. **–erweise** *adv* normally. **normalisieren** *v* normalize. **–maß** *neut* standard measure. **normgerecht** *adj* conforming to a standard.
Norwegen ['nɔrveɪgən] *neut* Norway. **Norweger** *m* (*pl* **-**), **Norwegerin** *f* (*pl* **-nen**) Norwegian. **norwegisch** *adj* Norwegian.
Not [noːt] *f* (*pl* **Nöte**) (*Armut*) need, want; (*Gefahr*) danger; (*Bedrängnis*) distress; (*Knappheit*) lack, shortage.
Notar [no'taːr] *m* (*pl* **-e**) notary.
Not‖ausgang *m* emergency exit. **–bremse** *f* emergency brake. **–durft** *f* call of nature. **–dürftig** *adj* scanty; hard up.
Note ['noːtə] *f* (*pl* **-n**) note; (*Schul-*) mark, grade; banknote, (*US*) bill; (*Musik*) note. **–nständer** *m* music stand.
Not‖fall *m* emergency. **–hilfe** *f* emergency service.
notieren [no'tiːrən] *v* note.
nötig ['nœːtiç] *adj* necessary. **–en** *v* compel, force.
Notiz [no'tiːts] *f* (*pl* **-en**) notice; (*Vermerk*) note. **–buch** *neut* notebook.
Not‖lage *f* distress, predicament. **–landung** *f* emergency landing. **–lüge** *f* white lie. **notleidend** *adj* distressed; (*arm*) needy, destitute.
notorisch [no'tɔriʃ] *adj* notorious.
Not‖ruf *m* distress call; (*Telef*) emergency call. **–stand** *m* emergency.
notwendig ['noːtvɛndiç] *adj* necessary. **Notwendigkeit** *f* necessity.
Notzucht ['noːttsuxt] *f* rape.
Novelle [no'vɛlə] *f* (*pl* **-n**) short story, short novel.
November [no'vɛmbər] *m* (*pl* **-**) November.
Novize [no'viːtsə] *m* (*pl* **-n**) novice.
Nuance [ny'ãsə] *f* (*pl* **-n**) nuance.
Nüchternheit ['nyçtərnhait] *f* sobriety; (*fig*) realism, clear-headedness.
Nudeln ['nuːdəln] *pl* noodles.
null [nul] *adj* nil, zero; (*ungültig*) null. **null und nichtig** null and void. **Null** *f* (*pl* **-en**) nought, zero.

numerieren [numeˈriːrən] v number.
numerisch adj numerical.
Nummer [ˈnumər] f (pl -n) number. **Nummern‖scheibe** f (telephone) dial. **–schild** neut number plate.
nun [nuːn] adv now. interj well! **was nun?** what now? **nun also** why then. **–mehr** adv (by) now.
nur [nuːr] adv only, merely; (eben) just. conj nevertheless, but. **nur noch** only, still. **nicht nur ... sondern auch ...** not only ... but also ... .
Nürnberg [ˈnyrnbɛrk] neut Nuremberg.
Nuß [nus] f (pl Nüsse) nut. **–baum** m walnut tree. **Nuß‖knacker** m nutcracker. **–schale** f nutshell.
nutz [nuts] adj useful. **–bar** adj useful. **–bringend** adj profitable.
nutzen [ˈnutsən] or **nützen** v be of use, be useful; (gebrauchen) make use of, use. **Nutzen** m (pl -) use; (Vorteil) profit, advantage. **Nutzen ziehen aus** derive advantage from, benefit from. **zum Nutzen von** for the benefit of. **Nutzfahrzeug** neut commercial vehicle.
nützlich [ˈnytsliç] adj useful. **Nützlichkeit** f usefulness.
nutzlos [ˈnutsloːs] adj useless. **Nutz‖losigkeit** f uselessness. **–nießer** m beneficiary. **–ung** f use, utilization.
Nylon [ˈnailɔn] neut (pl -s) nylon.

O

Oase [oˈaːzə] f (pl -n) oasis.
ob [ɔp] conj whether. **als ob** as if, as though.
Obdach [ˈɔpdax] neut (unz.) shelter. **obdachlos** adj homeless.
oben [ˈoːbən] adv above, at the top; (Haus) upstairs. **oben auf** on top of. **von oben** from above.
ober [ˈoːbər] adj upper, higher; (fig) superior; (Dienstgrad) senior, principal. **Ober** m (pl -) (head) waiter. **die Oberen** those in authority.
Ober‖arm m upper arm. **–befehlshaber** m commander-in-chief. **–bürgermeister** m (lord) mayor. **–fläche** f surface (area). **oberflächlich** adj superficial.
oberhalb [ˈoːbərhalp] adv, prep above.
Ober‖hand f upper hand, ascendancy. **–haupt** m chief, head. **–hemd** neut shirt.

–in f (pl -nen) (Rel) mother superior; (Krankenschwester) matron.
oberirdisch [ɔbərˈirdiʃ] adj above ground; (Leitung) overhead.
Ober‖kellner m head waiter. **–klasse** f upper class. **–schicht** f ruling class, upper classes pl. **–schule** f secondary school. **–schwester** f (Med) sister. **–seite** f upper side.
oberst [ˈoːbərst] adj highest, uppermost; (fig) supreme. **Oberst** m (pl -en) colonel.
obgleich [ɔpˈglaiç] conj although.
Obhut [ˈɔphuːt] f (unz.) care, protection. **in seine Objut nehmen** take care of, take under one's wing.
obig [ˈoːbiç] adj above-mentioned, foregoing.
Objekt [ɔpˈjɛkt] neut (pl -e) object. **objektiv** adj objective.
*obliegen [ˈɔpliːgən] v (einer Aufgabe) perform, carry out. **es liegt ihm ob, zu** it is his job or duty to. **Obliegenheit** f duty.
obligatorisch [ɔbligaˈtoːriʃ] adj obligatory, compulsory.
Obmann [ˈɔpman] m foreman; (Vorsitzender) chairman; (Sprecher) spokesman.
Oboe [oˈboːə] f (pl -n) oboe. **Oboist** m oboist.
Obrigkeit [ˈoːbriçkait] f (pl -en) authorities pl, government.
obschon [ɔpˈʃoːn] conj although.
Observatorium [ɔpzɛrvaˈtoːrium] neut (pl Observatorien) observatory.
obskur [ɔpsˈkuːr] adj obscure.
Obst [oːpst] neut (unz.) fruit. **–baum** m fruit tree. **–garten** m orchard. **–händler** m fruiterer.
obszön [ɔpsˈtsœːn] adj obscene.
obwohl [ɔpˈvoːl] conj although.
Ochse [ˈɔksə] m (pl -n) ox. **Ochsen‖fleisch** neut beef. **–schwanz** m oxtail.
Ode [ˈoːdə] f (pl -n) ode.
öde [ˈœːdə] adj desolate, bleak; (fig) dull, bleak. **Öde** f (unz.) desert, wasteland; (fig) dullness, tedium.
oder [ˈoːdər] conj or.
Ofen [ˈoːfən] m (pl Öfen) stove; (Back-, Tech) oven.
offen [ˈɔfən] adj open; (freimütig) open, frank; (Stellung) vacant. **–bar** adj obvious. **–baren** v reveal, disclose. **Offenheit** f openness, frankness. **offen‖herzig** adj open-hearted. **–kundig** adj evident. **–sichtlich** adj obvious, evident.

offensiv [ɔfɛn'ziːf] *adj* offensive. **Offensive** *f* (*pl* -n) offensive.

offenstehend ['ɔfənʃteːənt] *adj* open; (*Schuld*) outstanding.

öffentlich ['œfəntliç] *adj* public. **Öffentlichkeit** *f* publicity; (*das Volk*) public.

offiziell [ɔfi'tsjɛl] *adj* official.

Offizier [ɔfi'tsiːr] *m* (*pl* -e) officer. **Offiziers‖messe** *f* officers' mess. –**patent** *neut* (officer's) commission.

offiziös [ɔfitsi'øːs] *adj* semi-official.

öffnen ['œfnən] *v* open. **Öffnung** *f* opening. –**szeiten** *pl* opening hours.

oft [ɔft] *adv* often; frequently. **wie oft?** how many times?

öfter ['œftər] *adj* frequent. *adv* more often *or* frequently. **öfters** *adv* often.

Oheim ['oːhaim] *m* (*pl* -e) uncle.

ohne ['oːnə] *prep, conj* without. **ohne daß ich es wußte** without my knowledge. **ohne‖dies** *or* –**hin** *adv* all the same, besides.

Ohnmacht ['oːnmaxt] *f* unconsciousness, faint. **ohnmächtig** *adj* unconscious. **ohnmächtig werden** *v* faint.

Ohr [oːr] *neut* (*pl* -en) ear. **die Ohren spitzen** prick up one's ears. **ganz Ohr sein** be all ears.

Öhr [œːr] *neut* (*pl* -e) eye (of a needle).

Ohren‖schmalz *neut* ear wax. –**schmerz** *m* earache. **Ohrfeige** *f* slap across the face. **ohrfeigen** *v* slap (across the face). **Ohr‖läppchen** *neut* ear lobe. –**muschel** *f* (external) ear. –**ring** *m* earring.

Ökonom [œko'noːm] *m* (*pl* -en) (*Hausverwalter*) caretaker, steward; (*Wirtschaftswissenschaftler*) economist. –**ie** *f* housekeeping; economics. **ökonomisch** *adj* economic; (*sparsam*) economical.

Oktave [ɔk'taːvə] *f* (*pl* -n) octave.

Oktober [ɔk'toːbər] *m* (*pl* -) October.

Okzident ['ɔktsidɛnt] *m* occident.

Öl [œːl] *neut* (*pl* -e) oil. –**baum** *m* olive tree. **ölen** *v* oil, lubricate. **Ölfarbe** *f* oil paint.

Olive [o'liːvə] *f* (*pl* -n) olive. **olivengrün** *adj* olive-green. **olivenöl** *neut* olive oil.

Öl‖leitung *f* (oil) pipeline. –**meßstab** *m* dipstick.

Olympiade [olympi'aːdə] *f* (*pl* -n) Olympiad, Olympic games. **olympisch** *adj* Olympic.

Ölzweig ['œːltsvaik] *m* olive branch.

Oma ['oːma] *f* (*pl* -s) granny, grandma.

Omelett [ɔmə'lɛt] *neut* (*pl* -e) *or* **Omelette** *f* (*pl* -n) omelette.

Ondulieren [ɔndu'liːrən] *v* wave.

Onkel ['ɔŋkəl] *m* (*pl* -) uncle.

Opa ['oːpa] *m* (*pl* -s) grandad, grandpa.

Opal [o'paːl] *m* (*pl* -e) opal.

Oper ['oːpər] *f* (*pl* -n) opera; (*Opernhaus*) opera house.

Operation [operatsi'oːn] *f* (*pl* -en) operation. –**ssaal** *m* operating theatre. **operieren** *v* operate.

Opfer ['ɔpfər] *neut* (*pl* -) (*Verzicht, Gabe*) sacrifice; (*Geopfertes*) victim. **opfern** *v* sacrifice, offer. **Opferung** *f* sacrifice.

Opium ['oːpium] *neut* opium.

opportun [ɔpɔr'tuːn] *adj* opportune.

Opposition [ɔpozitsi'oːn] *f* (*pl* -n) opposition. –**sführer** *m* leader of the opposition.

Optik ['ɔptik] *f* optics. –**er** *m* optician.

optimal [ɔpti'maːl] *adj* optimum. **Optimismus** *m* optimism. **Optimist** *m* optimist. **optimistisch** *adj* optimistic.

optisch ['ɔptiʃ] *adj* optic(al).

Orange [o'rãːʒə] *f* (*pl* -n) orange. **orange** *adj* orange. **Orangensaft** *m* orange juice.

Orchester [ɔr'kɛstər] *neut* (*pl* -) orchestra.

Orchidee [ɔrçi'deːə] *f* (*pl* -n) orchid.

Orden ['ɔrdən] *m* (*pl* -) (*Gesellschaft*) order; (*Ehrenzeichen*) decoration, order. **Ordens‖bruder** *m* member of an order; (*Rel*) monk, friar. –**schwester** *f* nun.

ordentlich ['ɔrdəntliç] *adj* (*ordnungsgemäß*) orderly; (*ordnungsliebend, geordnet*) tidy; (*anständig, auch umg.*) proper, decent. **Ordentlichkeit** *f* orderliness; decency, respectability.

ordinär [ɔrdi'nɛːr] *adj* common, vulgar.

Ordinarius [ɔrdi'naːrius] *m* (*pl* Ordinarien) professor.

Ordination [ɔrdina'tsioːn] *f* (*pl* -en) ordination. **ordinieren** *v* ordain.

ordnen ['ɔrdnən] *v* put in order, arrange, classify. **Ordner** *m* (*pl* -) organizer; (*Versammlungen*) steward; (*Mappe*) file. **Ordnung** *f* (*pl* -en) order; (*Regel*) regulation. **ordnungs‖gemäß** *or* –**mäßig** *adj* orderly, lawful. *adv* properly, duly. –**widrig** *adj* irregular, illegal.

Organ [ɔr'gaːn] *neut* (*pl* -e) organ. –**isation** *f* organization. **organ‖isch** *adj* organic. –**isieren** *v* organize. **Organismus** *m* (*pl* Organismen) organism.

Orgasmus [ɔr'gazmus] *m* (*pl* **Orgasmen**) orgasm.

Orgel ['ɔrgəl] *f* (*pl* **-n**) organ. **-spieler** *m* (*pl* **-**), **-spielerin** *f* (*pl* **-nen**) organist.

Orgie ['ɔrgiə] *f* (*pl* **-n**) orgy.

Orient ['ɔriɛnt] *m* Orient. **Orientale** *m* (*pl* **-n**), **Orientalin** (*pl* **-nen**) Oriental. **orientalisch** *adj* oriental.

orientieren [oriɛn'tiːrən] *v* locate. **sich orientieren** orientate oneself. **Orientierung** *f* orientation. **Orientierungs‖punkt** *m* reference point. **-vermögen** *neut* sense of direction.

original [origi'naɪl] *adj* original. **Original** *neut* (*pl* **-e**) original.

originell [ɔrigi'nɛl] *adj* original, novel; (*eigenartig*) peculiar.

Orkan [ɔr'kaɪn] *m* (*pl* **-e**) hurricane.

Ornat [ɔr'naɪt] *m* (*pl* **-e**) (official) robes.

Ort [ɔrt] *m* (*pl* **-e**) place; (*Ortschaft*) town; (*Dorf*) village; (*Punkt*) point.

orthodox [ɔrto'dɔks] *adj* orthodox.

Orthopädie [ɔrtopɛ'diː] *f* orthopaedics.

örtlich ['œrtliç] *adj* local.

Orts‖gespräch *neut* local call. **-verkehr** *m* local traffic. **-zeit** *f* local time.

Öse ['œːzə] *f* (*pl* **-n**) eye(let). **Haken und Ösen** hooks and eyes.

Ost(en) ['ɔst(ən)] *m* east. **der Nahe/Ferne Osten** the Middle/Far East. **Ostblock** *m* Eastern bloc, Eastern Europe.

Oster‖ei *neut* Easter egg. **-hase** *m* Easter bunny.

Ostern ['ɔɪstərn] *neut pl* Easter.

Österreich ['œːstərraiç] *neut* Austria. **Österreicher** *m* (*pl* **-**), *f* **Österreicherin** (*pl* **-nen**) Austrian. **österreichisch** *adj* Austrian.

Osteuropa ['ɔstɔyropa] *f* Eastern Europe.

östlich ['œstliç] *adj* east(ern).

Ost‖politik *f* East policy, policy towards the Eastern bloc. **-see** *f* Baltic Sea.

Otter ['ɔtər] *m* (*pl* **-**) or *f* (*pl* **-n**) otter.

Ouvertüre [uvɛr'tyːrə] *f* (*pl* **-n**) overture.

Ovarium [o'vaɪrium] *neut* (*pl* **Ovarien**) ovary.

oval [o'vaɪl] *adj* oval.

Oxyd [ɔ'ksyɪt] *neut* (*pl* **-e**) oxide. **oxydieren** *v* oxidize.

Ozean ['ɔɪtseain] *m* (*pl* **-e**) ocean. **ozeanisch** *adj* oceanic.

P

paar [paɪr] *adj* **ein paar** a few. **Paar** *neut* (*pl* **-e**) pair, couple. **paaren** *v* (*Tiere*) pair, couple; (*vereinigen*) join. **sich paaren** couple, mate. **Paarung** *f* (*pl* **-en**) mating. **paarweise** *adv* in couples.

Pacht [paxt] *f* (*pl* **-en**) lease; (*Entgelt*) rent. **-brief** *m* lease. **pachten** *v* lease.

Pächter ['pɛçtər] *m* (*pl* **-**) leaseholder; (*Bauer*) tenant farmer.

Pack [pak] *m* (*pl* **Päcke**) pack; packet; bundle.

Päckchen ['pɛkçən] *neut* (*pl* **-**) packet, small parcel.

packen ['pakən] *v* grasp, seize; (*einpacken*) pack. **-d** *adj* thrilling, fascinating. **Pack‖kasten** *m* packing case. **-pferd** *neut* pack-horse. **-esel** *m* (*fig*) drudge. **-stoff** *m* packing (material). **Packung** *f* (*pl* **-en**)package.

Pädagogik [pɛda'goɪgik] *f* pedagogy, education. **pädagogisch** *adj* pedagogic. **pädagogische Hochschule** teacher-training college.

Paddel ['padəl] *neut* (*pl* **-**) paddle. **paddeln** *v* paddle.

Page ['paɪʒə] *m* (*pl* **-n**) page(boy).

Paket [pa'keɪt] *neut* (*pl* **-e**) packet, parcel.

Pakt [pakt] *m* (*pl* **-e**) pact, agreement.

Palast [pa'last] *m* (*pl* **Paläste**) palace.

Palästina [palɛ'stiːna] *neut* Palestine.

Palette [pa'lɛtə] *f* (*pl* **-n**) palette.

Palme ['palmə] *f* (*pl* **-n**) palm. **Palmsonntag** *m* Palm Sunday.

Pampelmuse ['pampəlmuːzə] *f* (*pl* **-n**) grapefruit.

Panda ['panda] *m* (*pl* **-**) panda.

Paneel [pa'neɪl] *neut* (*pl* **-e**) panel, panelling.

paniert [pa'niːrt] *adj* coated with breadcrumbs.

Panik ['paɪnik] *f* (*pl* **-en**) panic. **panisch** *adj* panic-stricken, panicky.

Panne ['panə] *f* (*pl* **-n**) breakdown.

Pantoffel [pan'tɔfəl] *m* (*pl* **-n**) slipper.

Pantomime [panto'miːmə] *f* (*pl* **-n**) pantomime.

Panzer ['pantsər] *m* (*pl* **-**) armour; (*Panzerwagen*) tank; (*Tiere*) shell. **-hemd** *neut* coat of mail. **panzern** *v* armour. **Panzer‖ung** *f* (*pl* **-en**) armour-plating. **-wagen** *m* tank, armoured car. **-weste** *f* bullet-proof vest.

Papa [pa'paı, 'papa] *m* (*pl* -s) daddy, papa.
Papagei [papa'gai] *m* (*pl* -en) parrot.
Papier [pa'piɪr] *neut* (*pl* -e) paper.
–**bogen** *m* sheet of paper. –**korb** *m* wastepaper basket. –**tüte** *f* paper bag. –**waren** *pl* stationery *sing*.
Pappe ['papə] *f* (*pl* -n) cardboard.
Pappel ['papəl] *f* (*pl* -n) poplar.
pappen ['papən] *v* paste (together).
Pappschachtel ['papʃaxtəl] *f* cardboard box.
Paprika ['paprika] *m* (*pl* -s) paprika.
–**schote** *f* green *or* red pepper, capsicum.
Papst [paɪpst] *m* (*pl* **Päpste**) pope.
päpstlich ['peɪpstlıç] *adj* papal.
Parabel [pa'raɪbəl] *f* (*pl* -n) parable; (*Math*) parabola.
Parade [pa'raɪdə] *f* (*pl* -n) parade.
paradieren *v* parade; (*fig*) make a show, show off.
Paradies [para'diɪs] *neut* (*pl* -e) paradise.
paradox [para'dɔks] *adj* paradoxical.
Paradoxie *f* paradox.
Paragraph [para'graɪf] *m* (*pl* -en) paragraph, section.
parallel [para'leɪl] *adj* parallel. **Parallele** *f* parallel.
Paralyse [para'lyɪzə] *f* (*pl* -n) paralysis.
paralysieren *v* paralyse. **Paralytiker** *m* paralytic. **paralytisch** *adj* paralytic.
Paranuß ['paranus] *f* Brazil nut.
Parasit [para'ziɪt] *m* (*pl* -en) parasite.
Pärchen ['peɪrçən] *neut* (*pl* -) couple, lovers.
Parenthese [parɛn'teɪzə] *f* (*pl* -n) parenthesis.
Parfüm [par'fyɪm] *neut* (*pl* -e) perfume.
parfümieren *v* perfume, scent.
parieren [pa'riɪrən] *v* (*Angriff*) parry; (*Pferd*) rein (in); (*gehorchen*) obey, toe the line.
Parität [pari'teɪt] *f* (*pl* -en) parity.
Park [park] *m* (*pl* -s) park. –**anlagen** *f pl* park, public gardens. **parken** *v* park.
Parkett [par'kɛt] *neut* (*pl* -e) (*Fußboden*) parquet; (*Theater*) stalls.
Park‖platz *m* car park, (*US*) parking lot. –**uhr** *f* parking meter.
Parlament [parla'mɛnt] *neut* (*pl* -e) parliament. –**arier** *m* (*pl* -) parliamentarian.
parlamentarisch *adj* parliamentary.
Parodie [paro'diɪ] *f* (*pl* -n) parody.
parodieren *v* parody.

Partei [par'tai] *f* (*pl* -en) (*Pol, Jur*) party. –**führer** *m* party leader. **partei‖isch** *or* –**lich** *adj* biased, partial. –**los** *adj* impartial. **Partei‖politik** *f* party politics. –**tag** *m* party conference.
Parterre [par'tɛr] *neut* (*pl* -s) ground floor; (*Theater*) pit. –**wohnung** *f* ground-floor flat.
Partie [par'tiɪ] *f* (*pl* -n) (*Teil, Musik*) part; (*Spiel, Heirat*) match; (*Jagd-*) party.
Partikel [par'tiɪkəl] *f* (*pl* -n) particle.
Partisan [parti'zaɪn] *m* (*pl* -en) partisan.
Partitur [parti'tuɪr] *f* (*pl* -en) (*Musik*) score.
Partizip [parti'tsiɪp] *neut* (*pl* -ien) participle.
Partizipation [paɪrtisipa'tsioɪn] *f* participation. **partizipieren** *v* participate.
Partner ['paɪrtnər] *m* (*pl* -) partner. **Partnerschaft** *f* partnership.
Party ['paɪrti] *f* (*pl* -s) party.
Parzelle [par'tsɛlə] *f* (*pl* -n) plot (of land).
Paß [pas] *m* (*pl* **Pässe**) (*Reisepaß*) passport; (*Durchgang*) pass.
passabel [pa'saɪbəl] *adj* tolerable, passable.
Passage [pa'saɪʒə] *f* (*pl* -n) passage. **Passagier** *m* (*pl* -e) passenger.
Passant [pa'sant] *m* (*pl* -en) passer-by.
Paßbild ['pasbilt] *neut* passport photograph.
passen ['pasən] *v* fit, suit; (*Kartenspiel*) pass. **gut zueinander passen** go well together. **das paßt mir nicht** that doesn't suit me. **passend** *adj* fitting, suitable.
passieren [pa'siɪrən] *v* (*geschehen*) happen; (*vorübergehen*) pass; (*überqueren*) cross. **Passierschein** *m* permit, pass.
Passion [pasi'oɪn] *f* (*pl* -en) passion. **sich passionieren für** be enthusiastic about. **passioniert** enthusiastic, dedicated. **Passions‖spiel** *neut* Passion Play. –**woche** *f* Holy Week.
passiv ['pasiɪf] *adj* passive. **Passiv** *neut* passive.
Paßkontrolle ['paskɔntrɔlə] *f* passport inspection.
Pastellfarbe [pa'stɛlfaɪrbə] *f* pastel colour.
Pastete [pa'steɪtə] *f* (*pl* -n) (savoury) pie, pasty.
pasteurisieren [pastœri'ziɪrən] *v* pasteurize.
Pastille [pa'stilə] *f* (*pl* -n) lozenge.

Pastor ['pastɔr] *m* (*pl* -en) pastor, priest.
Pate ['paːtə] *m* (*pl* -n) godfather. **–nkind** *neut* godchild.
Patent [pa'tɛnt] *neut* (*pl* -e) patent; (*Erlaubnis*) licence; (*Mil*) commission. **patentieren** *v* patent. **Patentinhaber** *m* patentee.
pathetisch [pa'teːtiʃ] *adj* (*feierlich*) solemn, lofty; (*übertrieben*) rhetorical, flowery.
Pathologe [pato'loːgə] *m* (*pl* -n) pathologist. **Pathologie** *f* pathology. **pathologisch** *adj* pathological.
Patient [patsi'ɛnt] *m* (*pl* -en) patient.
Patin ['paːtin] *f* (*pl* -nen) godmother.
Patriot [patri'oːt] *m* (*pl* -en) patriot. **patriotisch** *adj* patriotic. **Patriotismus** *m* patriotism.
Patron [pa'troːn] *m* (*pl* -e) patron; (*umg.*) fellow, customer.
Patrone [pa'troːnə] *f* (*pl* -n) cartridge.
Patrouille [pa'truljə] *f* (*pl* -n) patrol.
Patt [pat] *neut* (*pl* -s) stalemate.
Pauke ['paukə] *f* (*pl* -n) kettledrum. **pauken** *v* (*umg.*) cram, swot. **Pauker** *m* drummer; (*umg.*) crammer.
pausbackig ['pausbakiç] *adj* chubby(-faced).
pauschal [pau'ʃaːl] *adj* all-inclusive. **Pauschalsumme** *f* lump sum.
Pause ['pauzə] *f* (*pl* -n) pause, break; (*Theater*) interval. **Pause machen** take a break. **pausenlos** *adj* uninterrupted, continuous.
Pavian ['paːviaɪn] *m* (*pl* -e) baboon.
Pazifik [pa'tsiːfik] *m* Pacific Ocean. **pazifisch** *adj* Pacific.
Pazifismus [patsi'fismus] *m* pacifism. **Pazifist** *m* (*pl* -en) pacifist.
Pech [pɛç] *neut* (*pl* -e) pitch; (*fig*) bad luck. **Pech haben** be unlucky. **pechdunkel** *adj* pitch dark.
Pedal [pe'daːl] *neut* (*pl* -e) pedal.
Pedant [pe'dant] *m* (*pl* -en) pedant. **pedantisch** *adj* pedantic.
peilen ['pailən] *v* take (one's) bearings; (*loten*) sound; (*umg.*) sound out.
Pein [pain] *f* (*unz.*) pain, torment, agony. **pein‖igen** *v* torment. **–lich** *adj* awkward, embarrassing; (*genau*) (over-)careful, fussy.
Peitsche ['paitʃə] *f* (*pl* -n) whip, lash.
Pelikan ['peːlikaɪn] *m* (*pl* -e) pelican.
Pelle ['pɛlə] *f* (*pl* -n) peel, skin.

Pellkartoffel *pl* potatoes (boiled) in their jackets.
Pelz [pɛlts] *m* (*pl* -e) fur, pelt. **pelzig** *adj* furry. **Pelzmantel** *m* fur coat.
Pendel ['pɛndəl] *neut* (*pl* -) pendulum. **pendeln** *v* swing, oscillate; (*fig*) commute. **Pendler** *m* commuter.
penibel [pe'niːbəl] *adj* meticulous.
pennen ['pɛnən] *v* (*umg.*) doss, kip down. **Penne** *f* (*umg.*) school. **Penner** *m* dosser.
Pension [pã'sjoːn] *f* (*pl* -en) guest house, boarding house; (*Ruhegehalt*) pension. **pensionieren** *v* pension off. **Pensionierte(r)** pensioner.
per [pɛr] *prep* by, per. **per Adresse** care of, c/o.
perfekt [pɛr'fɛkt] *adj* perfect. **einen Vertrag perfekt machen** clinch a deal.
perforieren [pɛrfo'riːrən] *v* perforate. **Perforation** *f* perforation.
Pergament [pɛrga'mɛnt] *neut* (*pl* -e) parchment. **–papier** *neut* greaseproof paper.
Periode [peri'oːdə] *f* (*pl* -n) period. **periodisch** *adj* periodic.
Perle ['pɛrlə] *f* (*pl* -n) pearl; (*Glas-*) bead. **perlen** *v* sparkle. **Perl‖enkette** *f* string of pearls. **–mutter** *f* mother-of-pearl.
permanent [pɛrma'nɛnt] *adj* permanent.
perplex [pɛr'plɛks] *adj* perplexed, confused.
Person [pɛr'zoːn] *f* (*pl* -en) person.
Personal [pɛrzo'naːl] *neut* staff, personnel. **–abteilung** *f* personnel department. **–ausweis** *m* pass, ID card. **–chef** *m* personnel manager.
Personen‖kraftwagen (Pkw) *m* (passenger) car. **–verzeichnis** *neut* (*Theater*) dramatis personae. **–zug** *m* (local) passenger train.
persönlich [pɛr'zœːnliç] *adj* personal. **Persönlichkeit** *f* personality.
Perspektive [pɛrspɛk'tiːvə] *f* (*pl* -n) perspective.
Perücke [pe'rykə] *f* (*pl* -n) wig.
pervers [pɛr'vɛrs] *adj* perverse. **Perversion** *f* perversion.
Pessimismus [pɛsi'mismus] *m* pessimism. **Pessimist** *m* (*pl* -en) pessimist. **pessimistisch** *adj* pessimistic.
Pest [pɛst] *f* (*pl* -en) plague.
Petersilie [petər'ziːliə] *f* (*pl* -n) parsley.
Petroleum [pe'troːleum] *neut* petroleum; (*Kerosin*) paraffin, (*US*) kerosene.

petzen ['pɛtsən] v (umg.) tell tales, sneak.
Pfad [pfaɪt] m (pl -e) path. **–finder** m Boy Scout.
Pfahl [pfaɪl] m (pl Pfähle) post, stake; (Stange) pole. **–werk** neut paling, palisade.
Pfalz [pfalts] f Palatinate.
Pfand [pfant] neut (Pfänder) pledge, security; (Flaschen, usw.) deposit. **–brief** m mortgage (deed). **–leiher** m pawnbroker.
Pfanne ['pfanə] f (pl -n) pan. **Pfannkuchen** m pancake.
Pfarrbezirk ['pfaɪrbətsirk] m parish. **Pfarrer** m parson. **Pfarrhaus** neut parsonage.
Pfau [pfau] m (pl -en) peacock.
Pfeffer ['pfɛfər] m (pl -) pepper. **–kuchen** m gingerbread. **–minz** neut (pl -e) peppermint (sweet). **–minze** f (Bot) peppermint.
Pfeife ['pfaifə] f (pl -n) pipe. **pfeifen** v whistle. **Pfeifer** m whistler; (Pfeife) piper.
Pfeil [pfail] m (pl -e) arrow.
Pfeiler ['pfailər] m (pl -) pillar.
pfeilschnell ['pfailʃnɛl] adj swift as an arrow. **Pfeilschütze** m archer.
Pfennig ['pfɛniç] m (pl -e) pfennig; (fig) penny.
Pferch [pfɛrç] m (pl -e) fold, pen. **pferchen** v pen.
Pferd [pfeɪrt] neut (pl -e) horse. **Pferde‖bremse** f horsefly. **–knecht** m groom. **–rennbahn** f race course. **–rennen** neut horseracing. **–stall** m stable. **–stärke** (Ps) f horsepower (hp).
Pfiff [pfif] m (pl -e) (Ton) whistle; (Kniff) trick.
Pfifferling ['pfifərliŋ] m (pl -e) (Bot) chanterelle (edible mushroom). **das ist keinen Pfifferling wert** that's (worth) nothing.
Pfingsten ['pfiŋstən] neut (pl -) Whitsun(tide).
Pfirsich ['pfirziç] m (pl -e) peach.
Pflanze ['pflantsə] f (pl -n) plant. **pflanzen** v plant. **–fressend** adj herbivorous. **Pflanzen‖fresser** m herbivore. **–öl** neut vegetable oil. **–reich** neut vegetable kingdom.
Pflaster ['pflastər] neut (pl -) (Straße) pavement; (Wunden) plaster. **–stein** m paving stone.
Pflaume ['pflaumə] f (pl -n) plum.

Pflege ['pfleɪgə] f (pl -n) care. **–dienst** m service. **–eltern** pl foster parents. **–kind** neut foster child. **–mutter** f foster mother. **pflegeleicht** adj easy-care.
pflegen ['pfleɪgən] v care for; (Kranken) nurse; (Pflanzen) cultivate; (gewohnt sein) be accustomed to. **er pflegte zu sagen** he used to say. **Pfleger** m male nurse; (vormund) guardian. **Pflegerin** f nurse, sister.
Pflege‖sohn m foster son. **–mutter** f foster mother. **–tochter** f foster daughter. **–vater** m foster father.
pfleglich [pfleɪkliç] adj careful. **pfleglich behandeln** handle with care.
Pflicht [pfliçt] f (pl -en) duty. **pflicht‖bewußt** adj conscientious. **–gemäß** adj dutiful, in accordance with duty. **–getreu** adj dutiful, conscientious.
Pflock [pflɔk] m (pl Pflöcke) peg, pin.
pflücken ['pflykən] v pluck; gather.
Pflug [pfluɪk] m (pl Pflüge) plough.
pflügen ['pflyɪgən] v plough.
Pflüger ['pflyɪgər] m ploughman.
Pforte ['pfɔrtə] f (pl -n) door, gate.
Pförtner ['pfœɪrtnər] m (pl -) doorkeeper, porter.
Pfosten ['pfɔstən] m (pl -) post, stake.
Pfote ['pfoɪtə] f (pl -n) paw.
Pfropf [pfrɔpf] m (pl -e oder Pfröpfe) (Blutgerinsel) blood clot; (Watte) wad (of cotton wool). **pfropfen** v (Flasche) cork, stopper; (Bäume) graft; (stopfen) pack, stuff. **Pfropf‖en** m (pl -) cork, stopper. **–reis** neut graft.
pfui [pfui] interj pooh, ugh.
Pfund [pfunt] neut (pl -e) pound.
pfuschen ['pfuʃən] v botch, bungle, make a mess. **Pfuscher** m botcher, bungler. **–ei** f bungling; (Arbeit) botch-job, botch-up.
Pfütze ['pfytsə] f (pl -n) puddle.
Phänomen [fɛno'meɪn] neut (pl -e) phenomenon.
Phantasie [fanta'ziː] f (pl -n) (Einbildungskraft) imagination; (Trugbild) fantasy. **phantasie‖los** adj unimaginative. **–reich** adj imaginative. **–ren** v fantasize, daydream; (Med) be delirious. **phantastisch** adj fantastic.
Phantom [fan'tɔim] neut (pl -e) phantom.
Phase ['faizə] f (pl -n) phase.
Philister [fi'listər] m (pl -) philistine. **philisterhaft** adj philistine, narrow-minded.

Philosoph [filo'zoːf] *m* (*pl* -en) philosopher. **–ie** *f* philosophy. **philosophisch** *adj* philosophical.

Phonetik [fo'neɪtik] *f* (*unz.*) phonetics. **phonetisch** *adj* phonetic.

Phosphor ['fɔsfɔr] *m* (*unz.*) phosphorus.

Photo ['foːto] *neut* (*pl* -s) photo, photograph. **–album** *neut* photograph album. **–apparat** *m* camera. **photogen** *adj* photogenic. **Photograph** *m* (*pl* -en) photographer. **–ie** *f* photography. **photograph‖ieren** *v* photograph. **–isch** *adj* photographic.

Phrase ['fraɪzə] *f* (*pl* -n) phrase; (*fig*) empty talk, fine phrases.

Physik [fy'ziːk] *f* physics. **–er** *m* physicist.

Physiologie [fyziolo'giː] *f* physiology. **physiologisch** *adj* physiological.

physisch ['fyːziʃ] *adj* physical.

Pianist [pia'nist] *m* (*pl* -en), **Pianistin** *f* (*pl* -nen) pianist.

Pickel[1] ['pikəl] *m* (*pl* -), **Picke** *f* (*pl* -n) pickaxe.

Pickel[2] ['pikəl] *m* (*pl* -) (*Med*) pimple, spot.

piep [piːp] *interj* cheep. **nicht piep sagen** not say a word. **Piep** *m* (*pl* -se) peep, chirp. **piep‖en** *v* chirp. **–sen** *v* (*Maus*) squeak.

Pietät [pie'tɛːt] *f* piety; (*Ehrfurcht*) reverence.

Pik [piːk] *neut* (*pl* -s) spades *pl*.

pikant [pi'kant] *adj* spicy; (*fig*) suggestive, racy.

Pikkoloflöte ['pikoloflœːtə] *f* piccolo.

Pilger ['pilgər] *m* (*pl* -), **Pilgerin** *f* (*pl* -nen) pilgrim. **Pilgerfahrt** *f* pilgrimage.

Pille ['pilə] *f* (*pl* -n) pill. **die Pille** (*umg.*) the (contraceptive) pill.

Pilot [pi'loːt] *m* (*pl* -en) pilot.

Pilz [pilts] *m* (*pl* -e) mushroom.

Pinguin [piŋgu'iːn] *m* (*pl* -e) penguin.

Pinie ['piːniə] *f* (*pl* -n) stone pine. **–nnuß** *f* pine kernel.

Pinne ['pinə] *f* (*pl* -n) pin, peg; (*Ruder-*) tiller.

Pinsel ['pinzəl] *m* (*pl* -) brush; (*Farbe*) paintbrush. **pinseln** *v* paint, daub.

Pionier [pio'niːr] *m* (*pl* -e) pioneer.

Pirat [pi'raːt] *m* (*pl* -en) pirate.

Piste ['pistə] *f* (*pl* -n) track; (*Ski*) ski-run; (*Flugzeug*) runway.

Pistole [pi'stoːlə] *f* (*pl* -n) pistol.

pissen ['pisən] *v* (*vulgär*) piss.

Plackerei [plakə'rai] *f* (*pl* -en) drudgery, toil.

plädieren [plɛ'diːrən] *v* plead. **Plädoyer** *neut* (*pl* -s) (*Jur*) plea.

Plage ['plaːgə] *f* (*pl* -n) nuisance, bother, vexation. **plagen** *v* torment, annoy.

Plagiat [plagi'aɪt] *neut* (*pl* -e) plagiarism. **plagiieren** *v* plagiarize.

Plakat [pla'kaːt] *neut* (*pl* -e) poster, placard.

Plan [plaɪn] *m* (*pl* **Pläne**) (*Absicht*) plan, intention; (*Zeichnung*) plan, diagram; (*Stadt*) map; (*Skizze*) design, scheme.

Plane ['plaːnə] *f* (*pl* -n) awning.

planen ['plaɪnən] *v* plan.

Planet [pla'neɪt] *m* (*pl* -en) planet. **–arium** *neut* (*pl* -arien) planetarium.

planieren [pla'niːrən] *v* plane, level, smooth. **Planierraupe** *f* grader, bulldozer.

Planke ['plaŋkə] *f* (*pl* -n) plank.

Plänkelei [plɛŋkə'lai] *f* (*pl* -en) (*Gefecht*) skirmish; (*Wortstreit*) bantering.

planmäßig ['plaɪnmɛːsiç] *adj* systematic; (*nach einem Plan*) according to plan. *der Zug fährt planmäßig um drei Uhr ab* the train is scheduled to leave at 3 o'clock.

Plantage [plan'taːʒə] *f* (*pl* -n) plantation.

Planung ['plaɪnuŋ] *f* planning. **Planwirtschaft** *f* planned economy.

plappern ['plapərn] *v* chatter.

plärren ['plɛrən] *v* blubber, cry, sob.

Plastik ['plastik] *f* (*pl* -en) (*Kunst*) sculpture; (*Med*) plastic surgery; (*Kunststoff*) plastic. **plastisch** *adj* plastic.

Platin [pla'tiːn] *neut* platinum.

plätschern ['plɛtʃərn] *v* (*Bach*) babble; (*Regen*) splash, patter; (*planschen*) paddle.

platt [plat] *adj* flat, level; (*Redensart*) silly, trite; (*erstaunt*) tongue-tied, flabbergasted. **Plattdeutsch** *neut* Low German.

Platte ['platə] *f* (*pl* -n) plate, dish; (*Stein*) flag; (*Metall, Holz*) sheet, slab; (*Tisch*) leaf; (*Schallplatte*) record, disc. **–nspieler** *m* record-player.

Platz [plats] *m* (*pl* **Plätze**) place; (*Sitz*) seat; (*Raum*) space, room; (*Stadt*) square. **–anweiser** *m* usher. **–anweiserin** *f* usherette.

platzen ['platsən] *v* burst, split; (*explodieren*) explode; (*Scheck*) bounce.

Platz‖karte *f* seat-reservation ticket. **–patrone** *f* blank cartridge. **–regen** *m* downpour, heavy shower.

plaudern ['plaudərn] v chat.
plausibel [plau'ziːbəl] adj plausible.
Plazenta [pla'sɛnta] f (pl -s or **Plazenten**) placenta.
pleite ['plaitə] adj bankrupt; (umg.) broke. **Pleite** f bankruptcy; (fig) flop, wash-out.
plombieren [plɔm'biːrən] v seal; (Zahn) fill.
plötzlich ['plœtsliç] adj sudden.
plump [plump] adj (grob) coarse; (ungeschickt) clumsy. **plumps** Interj bump, thud. **plumpsen** v fall down (with a thud), plump down.
plündern ['plyndərn] v plunder.
Plural ['pluːraːl] m (pl -e) plural.
pneumatisch [pnɔy'maːtiʃ] adj pneumatic.
Pöbel ['pœːbəl] m mob, rabble.
pochen ['pɔxən] v knock, tap; (Herz) beat.
Pocken ['pɔkən] pl smallpox sing.
Pokal [po'kaːl] m (pl -e) (Sport) cup. **–endspiel** neut (Sport) cup final. **–spiel** neut cup tie.
Pökel ['pœːkəl] m (pl -) brine (for pickling). **pökeln** v pickle, salt.
Pol [poːl] m (pl -e) pole. **polar** adj polar. **Polarmeer** neut Arctic Ocean. **südliches Polarmeer** Antarctic Ocean.
Polemik [po'leːmik] f (pl -en) polemic, controversy. **polemisch** adj polemic(al).
Polen ['poːlən] neut Poland. **Pole** m (pl -n), **Polin** f (pl -nen) Pole. **polnisch** adj Polish.
Police [po'liːs, po'liːsə] f (pl -n) (insurance) policy.
polieren [po'liːrən] v polish. **Poliermittel** neut polish.
Politik [poli'tiːk] f (unz.) (Staatskunst) politics; (Verfahren, Programm) policy. **–er** m (pl -) politician. **politisch** adj political.
Politur [poli'tuːr] f (pl -en) polish.
Polizei [poli'tsai] f (pl -en) police. **–hund** m police dog. **–kommisar** or **–kommissär** m police inspector. **polizeilich** adj police. **Polizei‖präsident** m chief constable, commissioner. **–stunde** f closing time. **–wache** f police station. **Polizist** m (pl -en) policeman. **–in** f (pl -nen) policewoman.
Polster ['pɔlstər] neut (pl -) cushion; (Polsterung) upholstery. **polstern** v upholster. **Polsterung** f upholstery.

Poltergeist ['pɔltərgaist] m poltergeist, hobgoblin.
Polyp [po'lyːp] m (pl -en) (umg.) copper.
Polytechnikum [poly'tɛçnikum] neut (pl **Polytechniken**) technical college.
Pommern ['pɔmərn] neut (unz.) Pomerania.
Pommes frites [pɔm'friːt] pl (potato) chips, (US) French fries.
Pomp [pɔmp] m pomp. **pomphaft** adj stately, with pomp.
Pony ['pɔni] neut (pl -s) pony; (Frisur) fringe.
Pop-Musik ['pɔp mu'ziːk] f pop (music).
populär [popu'lɛːr] adj popular. **popularisieren** v popularize.
Pore ['poːrə] f (pl -n) pore.
Pornographie [pɔrnogra'fiː] f pornography. **pornographisch** adj pornographic.
porös [po'røːs] adj porous.
Porree ['pɔre] m (pl -s) leek.
Portion [pɔrtsi'oːn] f (pl -en) portion, helping.
Porto ['pɔrto] neut (pl -s) postage. **portofrei** adv post-free.
Porträt [pɔr'trɛː, pɔr'trɛːt] neut (pl -s) portrait.
Portugal ['pɔrtugal] neut Portugal. **Portugiese** m (pl -n), **Portugiesin** f (pl -nen) Portuguese. **portugiesisch** adj Portuguese.
Porzellan [pɔrtse'laːn] neut (pl -e) porcelain, china.
Posaune [po'zaunə] f (pl -n) trombone.
Pose ['poːzə] f (pl -n) pose, attitude. **Poseur** m poseur. **posieren** v (strike a) pose.
Position [pozitsi'oːn] f (pl -en) position.
positiv ['poːzitiːf] adj positive.
Posse ['pɔsə] f (pl -n) (Theater) farce. **Possen** m (pl -) prank, practical joke, trick. **possenhaft** adj farcical.
possessiv ['pɔsɛsiːf] adj possessive.
Post [pɔst] f (pl -en) post (office), postal service; (Briefe) post, mail. **–amt** neut post office. **–anweisung** f postal order. **–beamte(r)** m post office official. **–bote** m postman.
Posten ['pɔstən] m (pl -) place, post; (Stellung) position, post; (Mil) sentry; (Ware) item; (Streik–) picket.
Post‖fach ['pɔstfax] neut post-office box, PO box. **–gebühr** f postage. **–karte** f postcard.
postlagernd ['pɔstlaːgərnt] adj poste restante, (US) general delivery.

post‖leitzahl f postal code. **–sparkasse** f post-office savings bank. **–stempel** m postmark.
Postulat [pɔstu'laːt] neut (pl -e) postulate.
postulieren v postulate.
postwendend ['pɔstvɛndənt] adj by return (of) post. **Postwertzeichen** neut postage stamp.
potent [po'tɛnt] adj capable; (Med) potent.
potential [potɛntsi'aːl] adj potential. **Potential** neut potential. **potentiell** adj potential, possible.
Potenz [po'tɛnts] f (pl -en) power.
Pottasche ['pɔtaʃə] f potash.
Pracht [praxt] f splendour, magnificence.
prächtig ['prɛçtiç] adj splendid, magnificent.
Prag [praːk] neut Prague.
Präge ['prɛːgə] f (pl -n) mint. **prägen** v stamp; (Münze) mint, coin.
pragmatisch [prag'maːtiʃ] adj pragmatic. **Pragmatiker** m (pl -) pragmatist.
prägnant [prɛg'nant] adj precise, terse.
prahlen ['praːlən] v brag, boast. **Prahler** m (pl -)braggart. **prahlerisch** adj boastful.
Praktikant [prakti'kant] m (pl -en), **Praktikantin** f (pl -nen) trainee, probationer. **Praktik‖er** m experienced person, expert. **–um** neut (pl -a) training course, field course. **praktisch** adj practical; (zweckmäßig) useful; (Person) handy.
prall [pral] adj (rund) plump, chubby; (straff) tight; (sonne) blazing. **Prall** m (pl -e) collision, impact. **prallen** v (Ball) bounce, rebound. **prallen gegen** collide with, bump into.
Prämie ['prɛmiə] f (pl -n) bonus; (Versicherungs-) premium.
Prämisse [prɛɪ'misə] f (pl -n) premise.
Präparat [prɛpa'raːt] neut (pl -e) preparation; (Med) medicament.
präsentieren [prɛɪzen'tiːrən] v present. **Präsenz** f (pl -en) presence.
Präsident [prɛzi'dɛnt] m (pl -en) president. **–enwahl** f presidential election. **–schaft** f presidency. **präsidieren** v preside, act as chairman.
prasseln ['prasəln] v clatter; (Regen) patter, drum; (Feuer) crackle.
präventiv [prɛven'tiːf] adj preventive. **Präventiv‖maßnahme** f preventive measure. **–mittel** neut contraceptive.
Praxis ['praksis] f (pl Praxen) practice.

Präzedenzfall [prɛtse'dɛntsfal] m precedent.
präzis [prɛ'tsiːs] adj precise.
predigen ['prɛɪdigən] v preach. **Prediger** m (pl -) preacher. **Predigt** f (pl -en) sermon.
Preis [prais] m (pl -e) price; (Belohnung) prize; (Lob) praise.
Preißelbeere ['praisəlbeɪrə] f cranberry.
preisgeben ['praisgeɪbən] v give up, abandon; (opfern) sacrifice. **Preisgebung** f surrender; sacrifice.
Preis‖liste f price list. **–senkung** f price reduction. **–steigerung** f price rise. **–stopp** m price freeze. **–sturz** m slump or fall in prices. **preiswert** adj cheap. **Preiszettel** m price tag.
prellen ['prɛlən] v (betrügen) swindle, cheat; (Ball) bounce.
Premiere [prem'jɛɪrə] f (pl -n) première, first night.
Premierminister [prem'jeɪrministər] prime minister, premier.
Presse ['prɛsə] f (pl -n) (Zeitungen) the press; (Druckmaschine) press; (Saft) squeezer. **–agentur** f press agency. **–freiheit** f freedom of the press. **pressen** v press.
Preß‖holz neut chipboard. **–kohle** f briquette. **–luftbohrer** m pneumatic drill.
Preuße ['prɔysə] m (pl -n), **Preußin** f (pl -nen) Prussian. **Preußen** neut Prussia. **preußisch** adj Prussian.
prickeln ['prikəln] v prickle, tingle. **–d** adj tingling.
Priester ['priːstər] m (pl -) priest. **–in** f priestess. **priesterlich** adj priestly.
prima ['priːma] adj (umg.) first-rate, excellent. **Prima** f sixth form.
primär [pri'mɛɪr] adj primary.
Primarschule [pri'maːrʃuːlə] f primary school (in Switzerland).
Primel ['priːməl] f (pl -n) primrose.
primitiv [primi'tiːf] adj primitive.
Prinz [prints] m (pl -en) prince. **-essin** f (pl -nen) princess.
Prinzip [prin'tsiːp] f (pl -ien) principle. **aus Prinzip** on principle. **im Prinzip** in principle, theoretically. **Prinzipal** m principal.
Priorität [priɔri'tɛɪt] f (pl -en) priority.
Prise ['priːzə] f (pl -n) pinch.
Prisma ['prisma] neut (pl Prismen) prism.
privat [pri'vaːt] adj private. **Privat‖adresse**

f home address. **–angelegenheit** *f* personal matter.
Privileg [privi'leɪk] *neut* (*pl* **-ien**) privilege. **privilegiert** *adj* privileged.
Probe ['proɪbə] *f* (*pl* **-n**) (*Versuch*) test, trial; (*Theater*) rehearsal; (*Muster*) sample, specimen. **auf Probe** on approval. **auf die Probe stellen** put to the test. **Probe‖abzug** *m* (*Druck*) proof. **–zeit** *f* probationary period. **probieren** *v* (*versuchen*) try, attempt; (*Speise*) taste, sample.
Problem [pro'bleɪm] *neut* (*pl* **-e**) problem. **problematisch** *adj* problematic.
Produkt [pro'dukt] *neut* (*pl* **-e**) product; (*Landwirtschaft*) produce. **–ion** *f* production. **produktiv** *adj* productive. **Produzent** *m* producer; (*Landwirtschaft*) grower. **produzieren** *v* produce.
Professor [pro'fɛsor] *m* (*pl* **-en**) professor. **professorisch** *adj* professorial. **Professur** *f* (*pl* **-en**) professorship.
Profil [pro'fiɪl] *f* (*pl* **-e**) profile; (*Reifen*) tread. **profilieren** *v* outline, sketch.
Profit [pro'fiɪt] *m* (*pl* **-e**) profit. **profit‖abel** *adj* profitable. **–ieren** *v* profit, gain. **Profitmacher** *m* profiteer.
Prognose [pro'gnoɪzə] *f* (*pl* **-n**) (*Med*) prognosis; (*Wetter*) outlook, forecast.
Programm [pro'gram] *neut* (*pl* **-e**) programme. **programmgemäß** *adj* according to plan. **programmieren** *v* (*Computer*) program. **Programm‖ierer** *m* (*pl* **-**), **–iererin** *f* (*pl* **-nen**) programmer. **–ierung** *f* programming.
Projekt [pro'jɛkt] *neut* (*pl* **-e**) (*Plan*) plan; (*Entwurf*) scheme. **projektieren** *v* plan; scheme. **Projektionsapparat** *m* projector.
projizieren [proji'siɪrən] *v* project.
proklamieren [prokla'miɪrən] *v* proclaim.
Proletariat [proletaɪri'aɪt] *neut* (*pl* **-e**) proletariat. **Proletarier** *m* proletarian. **proletarisch** *adj* proletarian.
Prolog [pro'loɪk] *m* (*pl* **-e**) prologue.
Promenade [promə'naɪdə] *f* (*pl* **-n**) promenade.
Promotion [promotsi'oɪn] *f* (*pl* **-en**) (awarding of a) doctorate; (*Komm*) (sales) promotion. **promovieren** *v* be awarded a doctorate.
prompt [prɔmpt] *adj* prompt.
Propaganda [propa'ganda] *f* propaganda. **Propagandist** *m* (*pl* **-en**) propagandist.
Propeller [pro'pɛlər] *m* (*pl* **-**) propeller.
Prophet [pro'feɪt] *m* (*pl* **-en**) prophet. **–ie**

f prophecy. **prophe‖tisch** *adj* prophetic. **–zeien** *v* prophesy. **Prophezeiung** *f* (*pl* **-en**) prophecy.
Proportion [proportsi'oɪn] *f* (*pl* **-en**) proportion. **proportional** *adj* proportional.
Prosa ['proɪza] *f* prose.
prosit ¡'proɪzit] *interj* cheers! your health! **prosit Neujahr!** a Happy New Year!
Prospekt [pro'spɛkt] *m* (*pl* **-e**) prospectus, leaflet; (*Ansicht*) prospect.
prostituieren [prostitu'iɪrən] *v* prostitute. **Prostituierte** *f* (*pl* **-n**) prostitute. **Prostitution** *f* prostitution.
Protest [pro'tɛst] *m* (*pl* **-e**) protest.
Protestant [protɛ'stant] *m* (*pl* **-en**) Protestant. **protest‖antisch** *adj* protestant. **–ieren** *v* protest.
Prothese [pro'teɪzə] *f* (*pl* **-n**) prosthesis; (*Arm-, Bein-*) artificial limb; (*Zahn-*) denture.
Protokoll [proto'kɔl] *neut* (*pl* **-e**) (*Jur*) record; (*einer Versammlung*) minutes *pl*; (*Diplomatie*) protocol.
Protz [prɔts] *m* (*pl* **-en**) snob. **protzen** *v* put on airs, swagger. **–haft** *adj* snobbish.
Proviant [provi'ant] *m* provisions *pl*, victuals *pl*.
Provinz [pro'vints] *f* (*pl* **-en**) province. **provinzial** *adj* provincial, regional. **provinziell** *adj* provincial, narrow-minded.
Provision [provizi'oɪn] *f* (*pl* **-en**) (*Komm*) commission.
provisorisch [provi'zoɪriʃ] *adj* provisional.
provozieren [provo'tsiɪrən] *v* provoke.
Prozedur [protse'duɪr] *f* (*pl* **-en**) procedure.
Prozent [pro'tsɛnt] *neut* (*pl* **-e**) percent. **–satz** *m* percentage.
Prozeß [pro'tsɛs] *m* (*pl* **Prozesse**) (*Jur*) lawsuit, trial; (*Vorgang*) process.
Prozession [protsɛsi'oɪn] *f* (*pl* **-en**) procession.
prüde ['pryɪdə] *adj* prudish.
prüfen ['pryɪfən] *v* (*Kenntnisse*) examine, test; (*erproben*) try, test; (*untersuchen*) inspect, check. **Prüf‖ling** *m* (*pl* **-e**) (examination) candidate. **–stein** *m* touchstone. **–ung** *f* (*pl* **-en**) examination, test.
Prügel ['pryɪgəl] *m* (*pl* **-**) cudgel, club; *pl* beating. **prügeln** *v* beat, thrash. **Prügelstrafe** *f* corporal punishment.
Prunk [pruŋk] *m* pomp, show, splendour. **prunken** *v* show off. **Prunkstück** *neut*

showpiece. **prunk‖süchtig** *adj* ostentatious. **–voll** *adj* magnificent, gorgeous.
Psalm [psalm] *m* (*pl* -en) psalm.
Pseudonym [psɔydo'nyɪm] *neut* (*pl* -e) pseudonym.
Psychiater [psyki'aɪtər] *m* (*pl* -) psychiatrist. **Psychiatrie** *f* psychiatry. **psychiatrisch** *adj* psychiatric. **psychisch** *adj* psychic.
Psycho‖analyse [psyçoana'lyɪzə] *f* psychoanalysis. **–loge** *m* (*pl* -n) psychologist. **psychologisch** *adj* psychological.
Psycho‖path *m* (*pl* -en) psychopath. **–therapeut** *m* (*pl* -en) psychotherapist. **–therapie** *f* psychotherapy.
Pubertät [pubɛr'tɛɪt] *f* puberty.
Publikum ['puɪblikum] *neut* public; (*Zuhörer*) audience.
publizieren [publi'tsiɪrən] *v* publish. **Publizist** *m* journalist.
Pudding ['pudiŋ] *m* (*pl* -s) pudding.
Pudel ['puɪdəl] *m* (*pl* -) poodle.
Puder ['puɪdər] *m* (*pl* -) powder.
Puff¹ [puf] **1.** *m* (*pl* **Püffe**) push, thump. **2.** *m* (*pl* -e) pouffe.
Puff² *neut* (*Spiel*) backgammon.
puffen ['pufən] *v* shove, thump; (*knallen*) pop. **Puffer** *m* buffer; (*Kartoffel-*) pancake, fritter. **Puff‖mais** *m* popcorn. **–spiel** *neut* backgammon.
Pulli ['puli] *m* (*pl* -s) pullover. **Pullover** *m* (*pl* -) pullover.
Puls [puls] *m* (*pl* -) pulse. **pulsieren** *v* pulsate, throb. **Puls‖schlag** *m* pulse. **–zahl** *f* pulse rate.
Pult [pult] *neut* (*pl* -e) desk. **-dach** *neut* lean-to roof.
Pulver ['pulvər] *neut* (*pl* -) powder. **pulver‖artig** *adj* powdery. **–isieren** *v* pulverize.
Pumpe ['pumpə] *f* (*pl* -n) pump. **pumpen** *v* pump.
Pumpernickel ['pumpərnikəl] *m* black (rye) bread.
Punkt [puŋkt] *m* (*pl* -e) point; (*Ort*) place, spot; (*Gramm*) full stop. **punktieren** *v* punctuate; (*Med*) puncture; (*tüpfeln*) dot. **punktiert** *adj* dotted.
pünktlich ['pyŋktliç] *adj* punctual, on time. **Pünktlichkeit** *f* punctuality.
Pupille [pu'pilə] *f* (*pl* -n) (*Anat*) pupil.
Puppe ['pupə] *f* (*pl* -n) doll; (*Theater*) puppet; (*Insekten*) pupa, chrysalis. **Puppen‖haus** *neut* doll's house. **–theater** *neut* puppet show.

pur [puɪr] *adj* pure, unadulterated; (*Getränk*) neat.
Puritaner [puri'taɪnər] *m* (*pl* -) Puritan. **puritanisch** *adj* puritan.
Purpur ['purpur] *m* purple. **purpurn** *adj* purple.
Purzelbaum *m* somersault. **purzeln** *v* somersault.
Pustel ['pustəl] *f* (*pl* -n) pustule.
Pute ['puɪtə] *f* (*pl* -n) turkey (hen). **Puter** *m* (*pl* -) turkey (cock).
Putsch [putʃ] *m* (*pl* -e) putsch, uprising. **putschen** *v* revolt, rise.
Putz ['puts] *m* (*pl* -e) (*Kleidung*) finery, fine dress; (*Zierat*) ornaments *pl*, trimmings *pl*; (*Bewurf*) plaster. **putzen** *v* clean; (*Schuhe*) polish. **sich putzen** dress up. **sich die Nase putzen** wipe one's nose. **Putzer** *m* (*pl* -), **Putzerin** *f* (*pl* -nen) cleaner. **Putz‖frau** *f* charwoman, cleaner. **–tuch** *f* polishing cloth.
Pyjama [pi'dʒaɪma] *m* (*pl* -s) pyjamas *pl*.
Pyramide [pyra'miɪdə] *f* (*pl* -n) pyramid.

Q

quabbelig ['kvabəliç] *adj* flabby, wobbly. **quabbeln** *v* wobble, quiver.
Quacksalber ['kvakzalbər] *m* (*pl* -) quack, charlatan.
Quadrat [kva'draɪt] *neut* (*pl* -e) square. **–meter** *neut* square metre. **–wurzel** *f* square root. **–zahl** *f* (*Math*) square. **quadrieren** *v* (*Math*) square.
quäken ['kvɛɪkən] *v* squeak.
Qual [kvaɪl] *f* (*pl* -en) torment, pain.
quälen ['kvɛɪlən] *v* torment; (*foltern*) torture. **sich quälen** toil. **quälerisch** *adj* tormenting.
Qualifikation [kvalifikatsi'oɪn] *f* (*pl* -en) qualification; (*Fähigkeit*) ability, fitness. **qualifizieren** *v* qualify. **sich qualifizieren** be fit (for).
Qualität [kvali'tɛɪt] *f* (*pl* -en) quality.
Qualle ['kvalə] *f* (*pl* -n) jellyfish.
Qualm [kvalm] *m* dense smoke; (*Wasser*) vapour, steam. **qualmen** *v* smoke; (*Wasser*) steam.
qualvoll ['kvaɪlfɔl] *adj* painful; agonizing.
Quantität [kvanti'tɛɪt] *f* (*pl* -en) quantity.
Quarantäne [kvaran'tɛɪnə] *f* (*pl* -n) quarantine.

Quark [kvark] *m* curds *pl*, curd cheese; (*fig*) tripe, rubbish. **–käse** *m* curd cheese.
Quartal [kvar'taːl] *neut* (*pl* -e) quarter (of a year).
Quartett [kvar'tɛt] *neut* (*pl* -e) quartet.
Quartier [kvar'tiːr] *neut* (*pl* -e) accommodation; (*Mil*) quarters *pl*; (*Stadt*) quarter, district.
Quarz [kvarts] *m* (*pl* -e) quartz.
quasi ['kvaːzi] *adv* as it were, in a way.
Quatsch [kvatʃ] *m* (*umg.*) rubbish, nonsense. **quatschen** *v* babble, talk nonsense.
Quecksilber ['kvɛkzilbər] *neut* quicksilver, mercury.
Quelle ['kvɛlə] *f* (*pl* -n) (*Wasser*) spring; (*Herkunft*) source, origin; (*Öl*) well. **aus guter Quelle** on good authority. **quellen** *v* spring, gush; arise.
quer [kveːr] *adj* cross, transverse; (*seitlich*) lateral. *adv* across, crosswise. **kreuz und quer** hither and thither. **Quer‖balken** *m* crossbeam. **–baum** *m* crossbar. **querdurch** *adv* (right) across.
quetschen ['kvɛtʃən] *v* squeeze, squash. **Quetschung** *f* (*pl* -en) bruise.
quietschen ['kviːtʃən] *v* (*Person, Bremsen*) squeal; (*Tür*) squeak.
Quintett [kvin'tɛt] *neut* (*pl* -e) quintet.
Quirl [kvirl] *m* (*pl* -e) whisk, beater. **quirlen** *v* whisk, beat.
quitt [kvit] *adj* quits, even.
Quitte [kvitə] *f* (*pl* -n) quince.
quittieren [kvi'tiːrən] *v* (*aufgeben*) abandon; (*Rechnung*) give a receipt for. **Quittung** *f* (*pl* -en) receipt.

R

Rabatt [ra'bat] *m* (*pl* -e) discount, rebate.
Rabbiner [ra'biːnər] *m* (*pl* -) rabbi.
Rabe ['raːbə] *m* (*pl* -n) raven. **rabenschwarz** *adj* jet-black.
rabiat [rabi'aːt] *adj* furious, raging.
Rache ['raxə] *f* revenge, vengeance. **Rache nehmen an** revenge oneself on.
Rachen ['raxən] *m* (*pl* -) throat; (*Maul*) jaws *pl*, mouth.
rächen ['rɛçən] *v* avenge. **sich rächen an** take revenge on.
Rad [raːt] *neut* (*pl* **Räder**) wheel.
Radar ['raːdaːr] *neut or m* radar.
Rädchen ['rɛːtçən] *neut* (*pl* -) caster.

Rädelsführer ['rɛːdəlzfyːrər] *m* ringleader.
***radfahren** ['raːtfaːrən] *v* cycle. **Radfahrer** *m* (*pl* -), **Radfahrerin** *f* (*pl* -nen) cyclist.
radieren [ra'diːrən] *v* erase, rub out; (*Kupfer*) etch. **Radiergummi** *m* rubber, eraser.
Radieschen [ra'diːsçən] *neut* (*pl* -) radish.
radikal [radi'kaːl] *adj* radical. **Radikal‖e(r)** radical. **–ismus** *m* radicalism.
Radio ['raːdio] *neut* (*pl* -s) radio. **radioaktiv** *adj* radioactive. **Radioaktivität** *f* radioactivity.
Radium ['raːdium] *neut* radium. **–therapie** *f* radiotherapy.
raffen ['rafən] *v* snatch (up); (*Stoff*) gather; (*langes Kleid*) take up.
raffinier‖en [rafi'niːrən] *v* refine. **–t** *adj* refined; (*fig*) clever, crafty.
ragen ['raːgən] *v* project, tower up.
Rahm [raːm] *m* cream.
rahmen ['raːmən] *v* frame. **Rahmen** *m* (*pl* -) frame; (*fig*) framework, limit; (*Umgebung*) surroundings *pl*, setting. **im Rahmen von** in the context of.
Rakete [ra'keːtə] *f* (*pl* -n) rocket.
Rakett [ra'kɛt] *neut* (*pl* -s) (*Sport*) racket.
Ramme ['ramə] *f* (*pl* -n) pile-driver.
Rampe ['rampə] *f* (*pl* -n) ramp; (*Bühne*) apron. **–nlicht** *neut* footlight.
'ran [ran] *V* **heran**.
Rand [rant] *m* (*pl* **Ränder**) edge; (*Seite*) margin; (*Gefäß, Hut*) brim; (*Grenze*) border, boundary. **–bemerkung** *f* marginal note.
Rang [raŋ] *m* (*pl* **Ränge**) rank, class; (*Theater*) circle.
rangieren [rãˈʒiːrən] *v* rank; (*Eisenbahnwagen*) shunt.
Ranke ['raŋkə] *f* (*pl* -n) tendril, shoot.
Ränke ['rɛŋkə] *pl* intrigues *pl*, machinations *pl*.
Ranzen ['rantsən] *m* (*pl* -) knapsack; (*Schule*) satchel.
ranzig ['rantsiç] *adj* rancid.
rar [raːr] *adj* rare, scarce. **Rarität** *f* (*pl* -en) rarity.
rasch [raʃ] *adj* rapid, swift.
rascheln ['raʃəln] *v* rustle.
Raschheit ['raʃhait] *f* swiftness.
rasen ['raːzən] *v* rage, storm; (*eilen*) race.
Rasen ['raːzən] *m* (*pl* -) lawn, grass.
rasend ['raːzənt] *adj* furious, raving. **rasend werden** go mad, (*umg.*) blow one's top.

rasieren [ra'ziːrən] v shave. **Rasierapparat** f safety razor. **elektrischer Rasierapparat** electric razor. **sich rasieren** shave (oneself). **Rasier∥klinge** f razor blade. **−krem** f shaving cream. **−messer** neut razor. **−pinsel** m shaving brush.

Raspel ['raspəl] f (pl -n) rasp; (Küche) grater.

Rasse ['rasə] f (pl -n) race; (Tiere) breed. **Rassehund** m pedigree dog.

Rassel ['rasəl] f (pl -n) rattle. **rasseln** v rattle, clatter.

Rassen∥diskriminierung f racial discrimination. **−haß** m racial hatred. **−integration** f racial integration. **−kreuzung** f cross-breeding. **−trennung** f racial segregation.

rassig ['rasiç] adj purebred; (schwungvoll) racy.

rassisch ['rasiʃ] adj racial. **Rassismus** m racialism, (US) racism. **rassistisch** adj racialist, (US) racist.

Rast [rast] f (pl -en) rest; (Pause) halt, break. **rasten** v rest. **rastlos** adj restless; (unermüdlich) unwearying. **Raststätte** f (motorway) service area.

Rasur [razuːr] f (pl -en) (Radieren) erasure; (Rasieren) shave.

Rat [raːt] 1 m (unz.) advice. 2 (pl **Räte**) (Versammlung) council; (Beamter) councillor. **um Rat fragen** ask for advice. **sich Rat holen bei** consult. **Rat wissen** know what has to be done.

Rate [raːtə] f (pl -n) instalment, payment.

***raten** ['raːtən] v advise; (mutmaßen) guess.

Ratenkauf ['raːtənkauf] m hire purchase. **ratenweise** adv by instalments.

Rat∥geber(in) adviser, counsellor. **−haus** neut town hall.

ratifizieren [ratifi'tsiːrən] v ratify. **Ratifizierung** f ratification.

Ration [ra'tsioːn] f (pl -en) ration.

rationalisieren [ratsionali'ziːrən] v rationalize. **Rationalisierung** f rationalization. **rationell** adj rational.

rationieren [ratsio'niːrən] v ration.

rat∥los ['raːtloːs] adj helpless, perplexed. **−sam** adj advisable; (nützlich) useful; (förderlich) expedient. **Ratschlag** m (piece of) advice. **ratschlagen** v deliberate, consult together.

Rätsel ['rɛːtsəl] neut (pl -) puzzle, riddle; (Geheimnis) mystery. **rätselhaft** adj puzzling; mysterious.

Rats∥herr ['raːtshɛːr] m (town) councillor. **−keller** m town-hall restaurant. **−versammlung** f council meeting.

Ratte ['ratə] f (pl -n) rat.

Raub [raup] m robbery; (Beute) loot. **−anfall** m (armed) raid. **rauben** v rob; (Person) abduct; (plündern) plunder.

Räuber ['rɔybər] m (pl -) robber.

raubgierig ['raupgiːriç] adj rapacious. **Raub∥tier** m beast of prey. **−vogel** m bird of prey.

Rauch [raux] m smoke. **−rauchen** v smoke. **Rauchen** neut smoking. **Raucher** m (pl -) smoker.

räuchern ['rɔyçərn] v cure, smoke.

Rauch∥fang m chimney. **−fleisch** neut smoked meat. **rauch∥frei** adj smokeless. **−ig** adj smokey.

'rauf [rauf] V **herauf**.

Raufbold ['raufbɔlt] f (pl -e) ruffian, rowdy. **raufen** v (Haare) tear out. **sich raufen mit** brawl with. **Rauferei** f (pl -en) fight, brawl. **rauflustig** adj quarrelsome.

rauh [rau] adj rough; (grob) coarse; (Klima) inclement. **Rauheit** f roughness; coarseness; harshness.

Raum [raum] 1 m (unz.) room, space. 2 m (pl **Räume**) room; (Gebiet) area. **räumen** ['rɔymən] v evacuate, remove; (Zimmer) vacate. **Raum∥fahrt** f space travel. **−inhalt** m volume, capacity.

räumlich ['rɔymliç] adj spatial, of space.

Raumschiff ['raumʃif] neut space ship.

Räumung ['rɔymuŋ] f (pl -en) evacuation, removal; (Gebiet) cleaning.

Raupe [raupə] f (pl -n) caterpillar. **−nkette** f caterpillar track.

'raus [raus] V **heraus**.

Rausch [rauʃ] m (pl **Räusche**) intoxication.

rauschen ['rauʃən] v (Blätter) rustle; (Bach) babble, murmur.

Rauschgift ['rauʃgift] neut drug, narcotic. **−sucht** f drug addiction. **−süchtige(r)** (drug) addict.

Reagenzglas [rea'gɛntsglaːs] neut test tube.

reagieren [rea'giːrən] v react.

Reaktion [reaktsi'oːn] f (pl -en) reaction. **reaktionär** adj reactionary.

real [re'aːl] adj real. **−isieren** v realize. **Real∥ismus** m realism. **−ist** m (pl -en) realist. **realistisch** adj realistic.

Rebe ['reːbə] *f* (*pl* -n) vine.
Rebell [re'bɛl] *m* (*pl* -en) rebel. **rebellieren** *v* rebel. **Rebellion** *f* (*pl* -en) rebellion. **rebellisch** *adj* rebellious.
Rebhuhn ['rɛphuːn] *neut* partridge.
Rebstock ['reːpʃtɔk] *m* vine.
rechen ['rɛçən] *v* rake. **Rechen** *m* (*pl* -) rake.
Rechen‖fehler *m* miscalculation. **–kunst** *f* arithmetic. **–maschine** *f* calculating machine. **–schaft** *f* (*unz.*) account.
rechnen ['rɛçnən] *v* calculate. **rechnen auf** count on. **rechnen mit** reckon with. **Rechnen** *neut* arithmetic. **Rechner** *m* calculator. **Rechnung** *f* calculation; (*Waren*) invoice; (*Gaststätte*) bill. **Rechnungs‖abschluß** *m* balancing of accounts. **–führer** *m* accountant, bookkeeper. **–prüfer** *m* auditor. **–wesen** *neut* accountancy, accounting.
recht [rɛçt] *adj* right. *adv* (*sehr*) quite, very. *mir ist das recht* that suits me. **recht haben** be (in the) right. **ganz recht!** just so! **Recht** *neut* (*pl* -e) right; (*Gesetze*) law. **–e** *f* right (side), right-hand side; (*Pol*) the Right. **–eck** *neut* rectangle. **Rechtfertigung** *f* justification. **recht‖fertigen** *v* justify. **–gläubig** *adj* orthodox. **Rechthaber** *m* (*pl* -) dogmatic person, (*umg.*) know-all. **recht‖haberisch** *adj* dogmatic, obstinate. **–lich** *adj* legal, of law; (*ehrlich*) honest, just. **–mäßig** *adj* legal, lawful.
rechts [rɛçts] *adv* on *or* to(wards) the right.
Rechtsanwalt *m* lawyer.
Rechtschreibung *f* spelling.
Rechts‖fall *m* law suit, case. **–gleichheit** *f* equality before the law. **–händer** *m* right-handed person, right-hander. **rechts‖händig** *adj* right-handed. **–kräftig** *adj* legally binding, legal.
Rechtsprechung *f* (*pl* -en) judicial decision, verdict; (*Gerichtsbarkeit*) jurisdiction.
rechtsradikal *adj* extreme right-wing. **Rechts‖radikale(r)** *m* right-wing radical. **–spruch** *m* (*Urteil*) verdict, judgment; (*Strafe*) sentence. **–steuerung** *f* right-hand drive. **–streit** *m* law suit. **recht‖swidrig** *adj* illegal.
recht‖winklig *adj* right-angled. **–zeitig** *adj* timely, opportune; *adv* in (good) time.

recken ['rɛkən] *v* stretch.
Redakt‖eur [redak'tœːr] *m* (*pl* -) editor. **–ion** *f* editing; (*Arbeitskräfte*) editorial staff.
Rede ['reːdə] *f* (*pl* -n) speech, talk. **redefertig** *adj* fluent, eloquent. **Rede‖freiheit** *f* freedom of speech. **–kunst** *f* rhetoric.
reden ['reːdən] *v* speak, talk. **offen reden** speak out. **mit sich reden lassen** be open to persuasion, listen to reason. **Reden** *neut* speech, talking. **–sart** *f* expression, idiom. **Redewendung** *f* turn of speech, idiom.
redigieren [redi'giːrən] *v* edit.
redlich ['reːtliç] *adj* honest, upright, just. **Redlichkeit** *f* honesty.
Redner ['reːdnər] *m* (*pl* -) speaker, orator.
reduzieren [redu'tsiːrən] *v* reduce, decrease. **sich reduzieren** diminish, be reduced.
Reeder ['reːdər] *m* (*pl* -) shipowner.
reell [re'ɛl] *adj* respectable, honest, reliable.
Referat [refe'raːt] *neut* (*pl* -e) lecture, talk; (*Gutachten*) report, review. **Referent** *m* lecturer, speaker; (*Fachmann*) expert adviser, reviewer.
reflektieren [reflɛk'tiːrən] *v* reflect.
Reflex [re'flɛks] *m* (*pl* -e) reflex. **–bewegung** *f* reflex action.
Reform [re'fɔrm] *f* (*pl* -en) reform. **–ation** *f* reformation. **–er** *m* (*pl* -) reformer. **–haus** *neut* health-food shop. **reformieren** *v* reform.
Regal [re'gaːl] *neut* (*pl* -e) (book)shelf.
rege ['reːgə] *adj* active, lively.
Regel ['reːgəl] *f* (*pl* -n) rule. **regel‖los** *adj* irregular (*unordentlich*) chaotic. **–mäßig** *adj* regular. **regelmäßigkeit** *f* regularity. **regeln** *v* regulate, arrange. **Regelung** *f* regulation, arrangement. **regelwidrig** *adj* against the rule(s). **Regelwidrigkeit** *f* irregularity; (*Sport*) foul.
Regen ['reːgən] *m* rain. **–bogen** *m* rainbow. **–fall** *m* rainfall. **–mantel** *m* raincoat. **–tropfen** *m* raindrop. **–wetter** *neut* rainy weather. **–wurm** *m* earthworm. **–zeit** *f* rainy season, rains *pl*.
Regie [re'ʒiː] *f* (*pl* -n) (*Theater, Film*) direction; (*Verwaltung*) administration, management.
regieren [re'giːrən] *v* rule, govern. **Regierung** *f* government.

Regiment [regi'mɛnt] *neut* (*pl* -er) regiment.

Regisseur [reʒi'sœːr] *m* (*pl* -e) (theatre *or* film) director.

Register [re'gistər] *neut* (*pl* -) register; (*Buch*) index. **registrieren** *v* register.

Registrierkasse *f* cash register.

Regler ['reiglər] *m* (*pl* -) regulator.

regnen ['reignən] *v* rain. **regnerisch** *adj* rainy.

regulieren [regu'liːrən] *v* regulate.

Regung ['reiguŋ] *f* (*pl* -en) motion; (*Gefühle*) stirring, emotion; (*Antrieb*) impulse.

Reh [reː] *neut* (*pl* -e) roe deer. **–bock** *m* roebuck. **rehfarben** *adj* fawn. **Reh‖fleisch** *neut* venison. **–kalb** *neut* fawn. **–ziege** *f* doe.

*reiben ['raibən] *v* rub; (*Käse, usw.*) grate. **Reibung** *f* rubbing; (*fig, Tech*) friction; (*Käse*) grating.

reich [raiç] *adj* rich.

Reich [raiç] *neut* (*pl* -e) empire; (*fig*) realm; (*Tier-, Pflanzen*) kingdom.

reichen ['raiçən] *v* reach; (*überreichen*) pass, hand; (*anbieten*) offer; (*genügen*) be enough.

reich‖haltig *adj* copious; (*Programm*) full. **–lich** *adj* plentiful, ample.

Reichs‖adler *m* (German) imperial eagle. **–tag** *m* (German) Imperial Parliament (1871–1934).

Reichtum ['raiçtuːm] *m* (*pl* **Reichtümer**) wealth, riches *pl*; (*Fülle*) abundance.

Reichweite ['raiçvaitə] *f* range.

reif [raif] *adj* (*Frucht*) ripe; (*Person*) mature.

Reif [raif] *m* hoarfrost.

Reife ['raifə] *f* (*Frucht*) ripeness; (*Person*) maturity. **reifen** *v* mature.

Reifen ['raifən] *m* (*pl* -) ring, hoop; (*Mot*) tyre. **–druck** *m* tyre pressure.

Reihe ['raiə] *f* (*pl* -n) row; (*Satz*) series, set. **ich bin an der Reihe** it is my turn. **eine ganze Reihe (von)** a lot (of), a whole series (of). **reihen** *v* line up, put in a row; (*Perlen*) string; (*Stoff*) gather; (*heften*) tack. **Reihenfolge** *f* order, sequence.

Reiher ['raiər] *m* (*pl* -) heron.

Reim [raim] *m* (*pl* -e) rhyme. **reimen** *v* rhyme. **sich reimen** make sense.

rein [rain] *adj* pure; (*sauber*) clean; (*vollkommen*) perfect; (*Komm*) net. **ins Reine bringen** clear up, settle. *adv* completely. **die reine Wahrheit** the plain truth.

'rein [rain] *V* herein.

Reinemachen ['rainəmaxən] *neut* cleaning. **Reinheit** *f* purity; cleanness, cleanliness. **reinigen** *v* clean; (*fig*) purify, cleanse. **Reinigung** *f* cleaning; purification. **chemische Reinigung** *f* dry cleaning. **rein‖lich** *adj* clean, neat, tidy. **–rassig** *adj* purebred; (*Pferd*) thoroughbred.

Reis [rais] *m* rice.

Reise ['raizə] *f* (*pl* -n) trip, journey; (*See*) voyage. **–büro** *neut* travel agency. **–leiter(in)** courier. **reisen** *v* travel. **–d** *adj* itinerant, travelling. **Reisende(r)** traveller. **Reise‖paß** *m* passport. **–tasche** *f* travelling bag. **–scheck** *m* traveller's cheque.

Reißbrett ['raisbrɛt] *neut* drawing board. **reißen** *v* tear, rip; (*zerren*) pull. **sich reißen um** fight for. **reißend** *adj* rapid; (*Schmerz*) sharp, shooting. **Reiß‖kohle** *f* charcoal. **–verschluß** *m* zip, zipper.

*reiten ['raitən] *v* ride. **Reit‖en** *neut* riding. **–er** *m* rider, horseman. **–erin** *f* rider, horsewoman. **–kunst** *f* horsemanship, equitation.

Reiz [raits] *m* (*pl* -e) charm, attractiveness; (*Erregung*) stimulation. **reiz‖bar** *adj* irritable. **–en** *v* excite, stimulate; (*anziehen*) attract, charm; (*zornig machen*) irritate. **–end** *adj* charming, enchanting.

Reklame [re'klaimə] *f* (*pl* -n) advertising, publicity; (*einzelne*) advertisement. **Reklame machen für** promote, advertise.

Rekord [re'kɔrt] *m* (*pl* -e) record.

Rekrut [re'kruit] *m* (*pl* -en) recruit. **rekrutieren** *v* recruit.

Rektor ['rɛktor] *m* (*pl* -en) (*Universität*) vice-chancellor; (*andere Schulen*) principal, head.

relativ [rela'tiːf] *adj* relative. **Relativität** *f* relativity.

Relief [rə'ljɛf] *neut* (*pl* -s) (*Kunst*) relief.

Religion [religi'oin] *f* (*pl* -en) religion. **–sbekenntnis** *neut* confession of faith. **religiös** *adj* religious.

Ren [rɛn] *neut* (*pl* -e) reindeer.

Rennbahn ['rɛnbain] *f* racecourse. **rennen** *v* run; (*Sport*) race. **Renn‖en** *neut* running; race. **–pferd** *neut* racehorse. **–wagen** *m* racing car.

renovieren [reno'viːrən] *v* renovate.

rentabel [rɛn'taɪbəl] *adj* profitable. **Rentabilität** *f* profitability. **Rente** *f* (*Alters-*) pension; (*Versicherung*) annuity. **rentieren** *v* sich rentieren be profitable. **Rentner** *m* (*pl* -) **Rentnerin** *f* (*pl* -nen) pensioner.
Reparatur [repara'tuːr] *f* (*pl* -en) repair. **–werkstatt** *f* repair shop. **reparieren** *v* repair.
Report [re'pɔrt] *m* (*pl* -e) report. **–age** *f* (*pl* -n) (eye-witness) report. **–er** *m* (*pl* -) reporter.
Repressalien [repre'saɪliən] *pl* reprisals.
Reproduktion [reproduk'tsioɪn] *f* (*pl* -en) reproduction. **reproduzieren** *v* reproduce.
Reptil [rep'tiːl] *neut* (*pl* -ien) reptile.
Republik [re'publik] *f* (*pl* -en) republic. **–aner** *m* (*pl* -) republican. **republikanisch** *adj* republican.
Reserve [re'zɛrvə] *f* (*pl* -n) reserve. **–rad** *neut* spare wheel. **reservier‖en** *v* reserve, book. **–t** *adj* reserved.
Residenz [rezi'dɛnts] *f* (*pl* -en) residence.
Resonanz [rezo'nants] *f* (*pl* -en) resonance.
Respekt [re'spɛkt] *m* respect. **respekt‖abel** *adj* respectable. **–ieren** *v* respect. **–los** *adj* disrespectful. **–voll** *adj* respectful.
Rest [rɛst] *m* (*pl* -e) remainder, rest.
Restaurant [resto'rã] *neut* (*pl* -s) restaurant.
Restbetrag *m* balance, remainder. **restlich** *adj* remaining.
Resultat [rezul'taɪt] *neut* (*pl* -e) result.
retablieren [reta'bliːrən] *v* re-establish.
Retorte [re'tɔrtə] *f* (*pl* -n) retort.
retten ['rɛtən] *v* save. **Retter** *m* (*pl* -) rescuer; (*Rel*) Saviour. **Rettung** *f* (*pl* -en) rescue, deliverance. **Rettungs‖boot** *neut* lifeboat. **–gürtel** *m* lifebelt.
Reue ['rɔyə] *f* remorse, regret. **reuen** *v* regret. *es reut mich, daß ich es getan habe* I regret doing that, I am sorry I did that.
Revanche [re'vãʃə] *f* (*pl* -n) revenge, vengeance. **sich revanchieren** *v* take one's revenge.
Revers[1] [re'vɛrs] *m* (*pl* -e) (*Rückseite*) reverse, back.
Revers[2] [re'vɛr] *m or neut* (*pl* -) (*Jacke*) lapel.
Revers[3] [re'vɛrs] *m* (*pl* -e) written undertaking, bond.
reversibel [revɛr'siːbəl] *adj* (*Med, Chem*) reversible.

revidieren [revi'diːrən] *v* revise.
Revier [re'viːər] *neut* (*pl* -e) district; (*Polizei*) beat; (*Wache*) station.
Revis‖ion [revizi'oɪn] *f* (*pl* -en) revision, (*Jur*) appeal; (*Komm*) auditing. **–or** *m* auditor.
Revolte [re'vɔltə] *f* (*pl* -n) revolt, insurrection.
Revolution [revolutsi'oɪn] *f* (*pl* -en) revolution. **revolutionär** *adj* revolutionary. **Revolutionär** *m* (*pl* -e) revolutionary. **revolutionieren** *v* revolutionize.
Revolver [re'vɔlvər] *m* (*pl* -) revolver.
rezensieren [retsɛn'ziːrən] *v* review.
Rezept [re'tsɛpt] *neut* (*pl* -e) recipe; (*Med*) prescription.
Rhabarber [ra'baɪrbər] *m* rhubarb.
Rhapsodie [rapso'diː] *f* (*pl* -n) rhapsody.
Rhein [rain] *m* Rhine. **–hessen** *neut* Rhenish Hesse. **rheinisch** *adj* Rhine, Rhenish. **Rheinland** *neut* Rhineland. **––Pfalz** *f* Rhineland-Palatinate. **Rheinwein** *m* hock, Rhine wine.
rhetorisch [re'toɪriʃ] *adj* rhetorical.
Rheumatismus [rɔyma'tizmus] *m* (*pl* Rheumatismen*) rheumatism.
Rhinozeros [ri'noɪtserɔs] *neut* (*pl* -se) rhinoceros.
rhythmisch ['rytmiʃ] *adj* rhythmic(al). **Rhythmus** *m* (*pl* Rhythmen) rhythm.
richten ['riçtən] *v* (*zurechtmachen*) arrange, prepare; (*einstellen*) adjust, set; (*reparieren*) repair; (*Frage, Brief*) address; (*Gewehr*) aim; (*Jur*) judge. **sich richten an** address oneself to. **sich richten nach** follow. **Richter** *m* (*pl* -) judge.
richtig ['riçtiç] *adj* correct, right. *ein richtiger Berliner* a real Berliner. **Richtigkeit** *f* correctness, rightness. **richtigstellen** *v* correct, set right.
Richt‖linie *f* guideline. **–preis** *m* recommended price.
Richtung [riçtuŋ] *f* (*pl* -en) direction; (*Neigung*) trend, tendency.
Richtweg ['riçtveɪk] *m* short cut.
***riechen** ['riːçən] *v* smell. **riechen nach** smell of. **gut/übel riechen** smell good/bad.
Riegel ['riːɡəl] *m* (*pl* -) bolt, bar; (*Seife, Schokolade*) bar. **riegeln** *v* bolt, bar.
Riemen ['riːmən] *m* (*pl* -) strap, belt; (*Gürtel*) belt.
Riese ['riːzə] *m* (*pl* -n) giant. **Riesen-** *adj* colossal, huge. **Riesenerfolg haben** be a great success, (*umg.*) be a smash hit.

riesengroß or **riesig** adj gigantic, huge.
Riesin f (pl **-nen**) giantess.
Riff [rif] neut (pl **-e**) reef.
Rille ['rilə] f (pl **-n**) groove; (Furche) furrow.
Rind [rint] neut (pl **-er**) (Ochse) ox; (Kuh) cow.
Rinde ['rində] f (pl **-n**) (Baum) bark; (Käse) rind; (Brot) crust.
Rind‖erbraten m roast beef. **-fleisch** neut beef. **-vieh** neut cattle.
Ring [riŋ] m (pl **-e**) ring; (Straße) ring road; (Komm) combine, cartel; (Kettenglied) link. **-elchen** neut (pl **-**) ringlet.
***ringen** ['riŋən] v wrestle; (Hände) wring. **ringen um** struggle for. **Ringen** neut struggle, battle.
Ringfinger m ring finger. **ringförmig** adj ring-shaped.
Ringkampf m wrestling (match).
rings [riŋs] adv around. **-herum** adv all around.
Ringstraße f ring road.
Rinne ['rinə] f (pl **-n**) channel, groove; (Dach-) gutter.
Rippchen ['ripçən] neut (pl **-**) cutlet, chop. **Rippe** f (pl **-n**) rib.
Risiko ['riːziko] neut (pl **-s** or **Risiken**) risk. **risk‖ant** adj risky. **-ieren** v risk.
Riß [ris] m (pl **Risse**) (Stoff, Haut) tear; (Mauer) crack; (fig) breach, rift; (Zeichnung) technical drawing, plan.
rissig ['risiç] adj cracked; (Haut) chapped.
Ritt [rit] m (pl **-e**) ride.
Ritter ['ritər] m (pl **-**) knight. **ritterlich** adj chivalrous. **Ritterlichkeit** f chivalry.
rittlings ['ritliŋs] adv astride.
rituell [ritu'el] adj ritual. **Ritus** m (pl **Riten**) rite.
Ritz [rits] m (pl **-e**) or **Ritze** f (pl **-n**) crack; (Schramme) scratch.
Robbe ['rɔbə] f (pl **-n**) seal.
Roboter ['rɔbɔtər] m (pl **-**) robot.
Rock [rɔk] m (pl **Röcke**) (Frauen) skirt; (Obergewand) cloak; (Jacke) jacket, coat.
Rodel ['roːdəl] m (pl **-**) toboggan. **rodeln** v toboggan.
roden ['roːdən] v clear (land). **Rodung** f (pl **-en**) cleared land.
Rogen ['roːgən] m (pl **-**) (fish) roe.
Roggen ['rɔgən] m rye. **-brot** neut ryebread.
roh [roː] adj raw; (grausam) cruel, brutal; (Stein, Person) rough. **rohe Gewalt** brute force. **Roheit** f rawness; brutality; roughness. **Roh‖gewicht** neut gross weight. **-öl** neut crude oil.
Rohr [roːr] neut (pl **-e**) tube, pipe; (Gewehr) barrel; (Bot) seed.
Röhre ['rœːrə] f (pl **-n**) tube, pipe; (Radio) valve; (Leitung) conduit, duct.
Rohr‖leitung f pipeline. **-leitungen** pl pipes, plumbing sing. **-stock** m cane, bamboo. **-stuhl** m cane chair. **-zucker** m cane sugar.
Rohstoff m raw material.
Rolladen ['rɔlaɪdən] m (pl **-** or **Rolläden**) rolling shutter.
Rollbahn f runway.
Rolle ['rɔlə] f (pl **-n**) roll; (Theater, Film) role; (Tech) pulley. **eine Rolle spielen** play a part. **keine Rolle spielen** make no difference, not matter.
rollen ['rɔlən] v roll; (Flugzeug) taxi.
Roll‖mops m pickled herring. **-schuh** m roller skate. **-schuhlaufen** neut roller-skating. **-stuhl** m wheelchair. **-treppe** f escalator. **-tür** f sliding door.
Rom [roːm] neut Rome.
Roman [ro'maɪn] m (pl **-e**) novel.
Romantik [ro'mantik] f Romanticism. **-er** m (pl **-**) romantic. **romantisch** adj romantic.
Römer ['rœɪmər] m (pl **-**) Roman. **römisch** adj Roman. **römisch-katholisch** adj Roman Catholic.
röntgen [rœntgən] v x-ray. **Röntgen‖behandlung** f radiation therapy. **-bild** neut x-ray (photograph) **-strahlen** pl x-rays.
rosa ['roɪza] adj pink, rose.
Rose ['roɪzə] f (pl **-n**) rose. **Rosen‖busch** m rose bush. **-kohl** m Brussels sprouts pl. **-kranz** m rose garland; (Rel) rosary.
Rosine [ro'ziɪnə] f (pl **-n**) raisin.
Rosmarin [rozma'riɪn] m rosemary.
Roß [rɔs] neut (pl **Rosse**) steed, horse. **-kastanie** f horse chestnut.
Rost¹ [rɔst] m (pl **-e**) grate; (Kochen) grill.
Rost² m rust.
rost‖beständig adj rustproof. **-braun** adj rust(-brown).
Röstbrot ['rœstbroɪt] neut toast.
rosten ['rɔstən] v rust.
rösten ['rœstən] v roast; (Brot) toast.
rot [roɪt] adj red. **Rot** neut red.
Röte ['rœɪtə] f red(ness).
Röteln ['rœɪtəln] pl German measles, rubella.

rot‖glühend *adj* red-hot. **–haarig** *adj* red-haired. **Rot‖käppchen** *neut* Little Red Riding Hood. **–kehlchen** *neut* robin.

rötlich ['rœːtliç] *adj* reddish.

Rotte ['rɔtə] *f* (*pl* **-n**) gang, band; (*Tiere*) pack. **sich rotten** *v* band together, gang up.

Roulade [ru'laːdə] *f* (*pl* **-n**) rolled meat; (*Musik*) trill.

Rübe ['ryːbə] *f* (*pl* **-n**) (*Bot*) rape. **weiße/gelbe/rote Rübe** turnip/carrot/beetroot.

Rubin [ru'biːn] *m* (*pl* **-e**) ruby.

Rubrik ['ruːbrik] *f* (*pl* **-en**) (*Titel*) title, heading; (*Spalte*) column; (*fig*) category.

ruchbar ['ruːxbaɪr] *adj* notorious.

Ruck [ruk] *m* (*pl* **-e**) jolt, jerk, start.

Rück‖ansicht *f* rear view. **–blende** *f* flashback. **–blick** *m* glance back; (*fig*) retrospect.

rücken ['rykən] *v* move, shift; (*Platz machen*) move up, shift up.

Rücken ['rykən] *m* (*pl* **-**) back. **–lehne** *f* back (of a chair). **–mark** *neut* spinal cord. **–schmerzen** *pl* backache *sing*. **–schwimmen** *neut* backstroke.

Rück‖erstattung *f* return; (*Geld*) repayment. **–fahrkarte** *f* return ticket. **–fahrt** *f* return journey. **–gabe** *f* return, restoration. **–gang** *m* decline, retrogression. **rückgängig** *adj* retrograde. **rückgängig machen** cancel, annul. **Rück‖grat** *neut* backbone. **–griff** *m* recourse. **–halt** *m* support. **–handschlag** *m* (*Tennis*) backhand (stroke). **–kehr** *f* return. **–licht** *neut* rear light.

Rucksack ['rukzak] *m* rucksack, pack.

Rück‖schlag *m* set-back, reverse. **–schritt** *m* retrogression, relapse. **–seite** *f* reverse (side), back.

Rücksicht *f* consideration, regard. **Rücksicht nehmen auf** take into consideration; (*Person*) show consideration to. **mit Rücksicht auf** with respect to. **Rücksichtnahme** *f* consideration, regard. **rücksichtslos** *adj* inconsiderate (*hart*) ruthless. **Rücksichtslosigkeit** *f* lack of consideration; ruthlessness.

Rück‖sitz *m* back seat. **–spiegel** *m* rearview mirror. **–spiel** *neut* return match.

Rückstand *m* rest, remainder. **im Rückstand** in arrears. **rückständig** *adj* in arrears; (*altmodisch*) old-fashioned, backward.

Rücktritt *m* resignation; (*in den Ruhestand*) retirement.

rückwärts *adv* back(wards). **–gehen** *v* decline, retrogress.

Rück‖wirkung *f* reaction, repercussion. **–zug** *m* retreat. **–zahlung** *f* repayment, reimbursement.

Rudel ['ruːdəl] *neut* (*pl* **-**) (*Schar*) troop; (*Hunde*) pack; (*Rehe, Schafe*) herd.

Ruder ['ruːdər] *neut* (*pl* **-**) oar; (*Steuer*) rudder. **–boot** *neut* rowing boat. **rudern** *v* row. **Rudersport** *m* rowing.

Ruf [ruːf] *m* (*pl* **-e**) call, shout; (*Tier*) cry; (*Vogel*) call; (*Ruhm*) reputation, good name; (*Aufforderung*) summons. **rufen** *v* call, shout, cry. **Rufnummer** *f* telephone number.

Rüge ['ryːgə] *f* (*pl* **-n**) rebuke, reprimand. **rügen** *v* rebuke, reprimand.

Ruhe ['ruːə] *f* quiet, stillness; (*Erholung*) rest; (*Gefaßtsein*) composure, calm. **in Ruhe lassen** leave alone. **zur Ruhe gehen** go to bed. **ruhelos** *adj* restless. **Ruhelosigkeit** *f* restlessness. **ruhen** *v* rest; (*schlafen*) sleep; (*begründet sein*) be based. **–d** *adj* resting; (*Tech*) latent. **Ruhe‖pause** *f* break, rest period. **–platz** *m* resting place. **–stand** *m* retirement. **–stätte** *f* resting place. **–störung** *f* breach of the peace. **–tag** *m* day of rest.

ruhig ['ruːiç] *adj* still, quiet; (*gefaßt*) calm, composed.

Ruhm [ruːm] *m* fame, glory.

rühmen ['ryːmən] *v* praise. **sich rühmen** boast. **rühmlich** *adj* glorious.

Ruhr [ruːr] *f* dysentery.

Rührei ['ryːrai] *neut* scrambled egg(s). **rühren** *v* (*bewegen*) move; (*vermischen*) stir; (*innerlich*) move, affect. **sich rühren** stir, move. **rühr‖end** *adj* (*fig*) touching, moving. **–selig** *adj* sentimental. **Rührung** *f* (*unz.*) feeling, emotion.

Ruine [ru'iːnə] *f* (*pl* **-n**) ruin. **ruinieren** *v* ruin.

Rülps [rylps] *m* (*pl* **-e**) belch. **rülpsen** *v* belch.

Rum [rum] *m* (*pl* **-s**) rum.

Rumäne [ru'mɛːnə] *m* (*pl* **-n**) Rumanian. **Rumänien** *n* Rumania. **Rumänin** *f* (*pl* **-nen**) Rumanian (woman). **rumänisch** *adj* Rumanian.

Rummel ['ruməl] *m* (*unz.*) (*umg.*) bustle, activity; (*Lärm*) hubbub, racket. **–platz** *m* fairground.

Rumpf [rumpf] *m* (*pl* **Rümpfe**) trunk, torso; (*Tier*) carcass; (*Schiff*) hull; (*Flugzeug*) fuselage.

rümpfen [rympfən] *v* turn up (one's nose).

rund [runt] *adj* round. *adv* about. **Rundblick** *m* panorama. **Runde** *f* (*pl* **-n**) circle; (*Boxen*) round; (*Rennen*) lap; (*Sport*) heat; (*Polizist*) beat. **runden** *v* round (off).

Rund‖fahrt *f* (circular) tour. **–frage** *f* questionnaire. **–funk** *m* radio; (*Übertragung*) broadcasting. **–funksendung** *f* radio programme. **–gang** *m* tour (of inspection); (*Spaziergang*) stroll. **–heit** *f* roundness.

rund‖heraus *adv* frankly, flatly. **–lich** *adj* rotund, plump.

Rund‖schau *f* panorama; (*Zeitschrift*) review. **–schreiben** *neut* circular. **–ung** *f* curve.

'runter ['runtər] *V* **herunter**.

Runzel ['runtsəl] *f* (*pl* **-n**) wrinkle. **runzelig** *adj* wrinkled. **runzeln** *v* wrinkle. **die Stirn runzeln** frown.

rupfen ['rupfən] *v* pluck.

Ruß [rus] *m* soot.

Russe ['rusə] *m* (*pl* **-n**) Russian.

rußig ['ruːsiç] *adj* sooty.

Russin ['rusin] *f* (*pl* **-nen**) Russian (woman). **russisch** *adj* Russian.

Rußland ['ruslant] *neut* Russia.

rüsten ['rystən] *v* prepare; (*Mil*) arm, prepare for war. **sich rüsten** (**auf**) get ready (for). **Rüstung** *f* armament; (*Kriegsvorbereitung*) arming; **Rüstungs‖fabrik** *f* armaments factory. **–wettbewerb** *m* arms race.

Rute ['ruːtə] *f* (*pl* **-n**) rod; (*Gerte*) switch; (*Anat*) penis.

Rutsch [rutʃ] *m* (*pl* **-e**) slide; (*Erde*) landslip. **rutsch‖en** *v* slip; (*gleiten*) slide. **–ig** *adj* slippery.

rütteln ['rytəln] *v* shake (up); (*beim Fahren*) jolt.

S

Saal [zaːl] *m* (*pl* **Säle**) hall, large room.

Saat [zaːt] *f* (*pl* **-en**) (*Samen*) seed; (*Säen*) sowing; (*grün*) green corn. **–korn** *neut* seed corn.

Sabbat ['zabat] *m* (*pl* **-e**) Sabbath.

Säbel ['zɛːbəl] *m* (*pl* **-**) sabre.

Sabotage [zabo'taːʒə] *f* sabotage. **sabotieren** *v* sabotage.

Saccharin [zaxa'riːn] *neut* saccharine.

Sachbearbeiter ['zaxbəarbaitər] *m* executive, official in charge. **Sache** *f* thing; (*Angelegenheit*) affair, matter; (*Tat*) fact. **Sachen** *pl* things, belongings; (*Kleider*) things, clothes. **Sach‖kundige(r)** expert. **–lage** *f* situation, state of affairs. **sachlich** *adj* businesslike, matter-of-fact; (*objektiv*) objective.

Sachse ['zaksə] *m* (*pl* **-n**) Saxon. **Sachsen** *neut* Saxony.

Sächsin ['zɛksin] *f* (*pl* **-nen**) Saxon (woman). **sächsisch** *adj* Saxon.

sacht(e) [zaxt(ə)] *adv* softly, gently.

Sack [zak] *m* (*pl* **Säcke**) sack, bag. **–gasse** *f* cul-de-sac, (*US*) dead end.

Sadismus [za'dizmus] *m* sadism. **Sadist** *m* (*pl* **-en**) sadist. **sadistisch** *adj* sadistic.

säen ['zɛːən] *v* sow.

Safari [za'faːri] *f* (*pl* **-s**) safari.

Safe [seɪf] *m* (*pl* **-s**) safe.

Saft [zaft] *m* (*pl* **Säfte**) juice; (*Baum*) sap; (*umg.: Strom, Benzin*) juice. **saftig** *adj* juicy; (*Witz*) spicy.

Sage ['zaːɡə] *f* (*pl* **-n**) legend, fable.

Säge ['zɛːɡə] *f* (*pl* **-n**) saw. **–maschine** *f* mechanical saw. **–mehl** *neut* sawdust.

*sagen ['zaːɡən] *v* say; (*mitteilen*) tell. *was Sie nicht sagen!* you don't say! *sagen wir* let's say, suppose. *wie gesagt* as I said. *das sagt mir etwas* that means something to me.

sägen ['zɛːɡən] *v* saw.

sagenhaft ['zaːɡənhaft] *adj* legendary; (*umg.*) splendid, great.

Sahne ['zaːnə] *f* cream. **–kuchen** *m* cream cake. **sahnig** *adj* creamy.

Saison [zɛ'zɔ̃] *f* (*pl* **-s**) season. **stille Saison** off-season.

Saite ['zaitə] *f* (*pl* **-n**) string. **–ninstrument** *neut* stringed instrument.

Sakrament [zakra'mɛnt] *neut* (*pl* **-e**) sacrament.

Salat [za'lait] *m* (*pl* **-e**) salad; (*Kopfsalat*) lettuce. **–kopf** *m* head of lettuce.

Salbe ['zalbə] *f* (*pl* **-n**) ointment, salve.

Salbei [zal'bai] *f* or *m* (*Bot*) sage.

salben ['zalbən] *v* anoint.

Saldo ['zaldo] *m* (*pl* **Salden**) (*Komm*) balance.

Saumpferd

Salon [za'lɔ̃] *m* (*pl* -e) drawing room.
salonfähig *adj* presentable (in society).
Salut [za'luːt] *m* (*pl* -e) salute. **salutieren** *v*
salute.
Salve ['zalvə] *f* (*pl* -n) volley.
Salz [zalts] *neut* (*pl* -e) salt. **salzen** *v* salt.
Salzfaß *neut* salt cellar. **salzig** *adj* salty.
Salz‖kartoffeln *pl* boiled potatoes.
-wasser *neut* salt water.
Samen ['zaːmən] *m* (*pl* -) seed; (*Tiere*)
sperm. **-erguß** *m* ejaculation. **-händler**
m seed merchant. **-pflanze** *f* seedling.
-staub *m* pollen.
Sämischleder ['zɛːmɪʃleːdər] *neut* chamois
(leather).
sammeln ['zaməln] *v* gather; (*Hobby*) collect. **Samm‖elplatz** *m* assembly point.
-ler *m* collector. **-lung** *f* collection.
Samstag ['zamstaːk] *m* Saturday. **sam-
stags** *adv* on Saturdays.
samt [zamt] *prep* (together) with, including.
Samt [zamt] *m* (*pl* -e) velvet.
sämtlich ['zɛmtlɪç] *adj* complete, entire;
(*alle*) all; (*Werke*) complete.
Sand [zant] *m* (*pl* -e) sand.
Sandale [zan'daːlə] *f* (*pl* -n) sandal.
Sandbank *f* sandbank. **sandfarben** *adj*
sandy(-coloured). **Sand‖papier** *neut*
sandpaper. **-stein** *m* sandstone.
sanft [zanft] *adj* gentle, soft. **Sanftheit** *f*
gentleness, softness. **sanftmütig** *adj* gentle, mild.
Sänger ['zɛŋər] *m* (*pl* -), **Sängerin** *f* (*pl*
-nen) singer.
sanieren [za'niːrən] *v* heal; (*Betrieb*)
rationalize, make viable; (*Stadt, Viertel*)
redevelop. **Sanierung** *f* (*Komm*) reorganization; (*Gebäude*) renovation.
sanitär [zani'tɛːr] *adj* sanitary, hygienic.
sanitäre Anlagen *pl* sanitation *sing*.
Sankt [zaŋkt] *adj* Saint.
Sanktion [zaŋk'tsioːn] *f* (*pl* -en) sanction.
sanktionieren *v* sanction.
Saphir ['zafiːr] *m* (*pl* -e) sapphire.
Sardelle [zar'dɛlə] *f* (*pl* -n) anchovy.
Sardine [zar'diːnə] *f* (*pl* -n) sardine.
Sarg [zark] *m* (*pl* **Särge**) coffin.
sarkastisch [zar'kastɪʃ] *adj* sarcastic.
Satan ['zaːtan] *m* (*pl* -e) Satan; (*böser
Mensch*) devil, demon. **satanisch** *adj*
satanic.
Satellit [zate'liːt] *m* (*pl* -en) satellite.
Satin [za'tɛ̃] *m* (*pl* -s) satin.

Satire [za'tiːrə] *f* (*pl* -n) satire. **Satiriker** *m*
(*pl* -) satirist. **satirisch** *adj* satirical.
satt [zat] *adj* satisfied, satiated; (*Farbe*)
deep, rich. **satt sein** have had enough;
(*nach dem Essen*) be full. **satt haben** have
had enough of, be tired of.
Sattel ['zatəl] *m* (*pl* **Sättel**) saddle. **satteln**
v saddle. **Sattel‖schlepper** *m* (trac or for
an) articulated truck. **-tasche** *f* saddlebag.
Satz [zats] *m* (*pl* **Sätze**) (*Sprung*) leap,
jump; (*Gramm*) sentence; (*Sammlung,
Math*) set; (*Musik*) movement; (*Bodensatz*) sediment; (*Wein*) dregs *pl*; (*Grundsatz*) principle; (*Geld*) price, rate;
(*Druck*) composition, setting. **-lehre** *f*
syntax.
Satzung ['zatsuŋ] *f* (*pl* -en) statute; (*Vorschrift*) rule. **satzungs‖gemäß** *or* **-mäßig**
adj statutory.
Sau [zau] *f* (*pl* **Säue**) sow.
sauber ['zaubər] *adj* clean; (*hübsch*) pretty, nice; (*ordentlich*) tidy. **Sauberkeit** *f*
cleanliness; niceness; tidiness.
säuberlich ['zɔybərlɪç] *adj* clean; (*ordentlich*) tidy; (*anständig*) proper.
saubermachen *v* clean (up).
sauer ['zauər] *adj* (*Geschmack*) sour;
(*säurehältig*) acid. **Sauerbraten** *m* roast
marinated beef.
Sauerei *f* (*pl* -en) (*Unanständigkeit*)
smuttiness; (*Pfuscherei*) mess.
Sauerkraut ['zauərkraut] *neut* pickled
cabbage, sauerkraut.
Sauerstoff *m* oxygen. **sauersüß** *adj* bittersweet; (*Speise*) sweet-and-sour.
*****saufen** ['zaufən] *v* drink; (*umg.*) drink,
booze.
Säufer ['zɔyfər] *m* (*pl* -) heavy drinker,
boozer.
*****saugen** ['zaugən] *v* suck; (*einziehen*)
absorb. **Saugen** *neut* suction, sucking.
säugen ['zɔygən] *v* suckle, nurse. **Säug‖en**
neut suckling, nursing. **-etier** *neut* mammal. **-ling** *m* baby.
Säule ['zɔylə] *f* (*pl* -n) column, pillar.
Saum [zaum] *m* (*pl* **Säume**) seam, hem;
(*Rand*) border, margin.
säumen[1] ['zɔymən] *v* (*Kleid*) hem;
(*allgemein*) edge; (*fig*) skirt, fringe.
säumen[2] *v* (*zögern*) delay, hesitate.
Säumnis ['zɔymnɪs] *f* (*pl* -se) *or neut* (*pl*
-e) delay.
Saumpferd ['zaumpfɛrt] *neut* packhorse.

Sauna ['zauna] *f* (*pl* -s) sauna.
Säure ['zɔyrə] *f* (*pl* -n) acid; sourness.
Sauregurkenzeit [zaurə'gurkəntsait] *f* silly season.
sausen ['zauzən] *v* (*eilen*) rush, dash, zoom; (*Wind*) howl, whistle.
Saxophon [zakso'foɪn] *neut* (*pl* -e) saxophone.
schaben ['ʃaɪbən] *v* scrape; (*Fleisch*) cut into strips.
schäbig ['ʃɛɪbiç] *adj* shabby.
Schablone [ʃa'bloɪnə] *f* (*pl* -n) stencil, pattern, model.
Schach [ʃax] *neut* (*Spiel*) chess; (*Warn-ruf*) check. **in Schach halten** keep in check. **Schachbrett** *neut* chessboard.
Schacherei [ʃaxə'rai] *f* haggling, bargaining.
Schachfigur *f* chessman.
Schacht [ʃaxt] *m* (*pl* -e) shaft.
Schachtel ['ʃaxtəl] *f* (*pl* -n) box.
schade ['ʃaɪdə] *adv* a pity. *es ist schade* it's a pity, it's a shame. *schade, daß Sie ... what a pity that you .... wie schade!* what a pity!
Schädel ['ʃɛɪdəl] *m* (*pl* -) skull.
schaden ['ʃaɪdən] *v* harm, injure, hurt. **Schaden** *m* damage; (*Verlust*) loss; (*körperlich*) injury, harm. **–ersatz** *m* compensation. **–freude** *f* malicious joy, gloating. **schadenfroh** *adj* malicious, gloating. **schadhaft** *adj* damaged.
schädigen ['ʃɛɪdigən] *v* harm, damage; (*körperlich*) injure. **Schädigung** *f* damage; injury. **schädlich** *adj* dangerous, injurious.
Schaf [ʃaɪf] *neut* (*pl* -e) sheep.
Schäfer ['ʃɛɪfər] *m* (*pl* -) shepherd. **–hund** *m* sheepdog; (*deutscher*) Alsatian (dog). **–in** *f* (*pl* -nen) shepherdess.
Schaffell *neut* sheepskin, fleece.
schaffen ['ʃafən] *v* (*hervorbringen, gestalten*) create.
schaffen² *v* (*bringen*) bring, convey; (*fertigbringen*) manage, accomplish; (*arbeiten*) work.
Schaffner ['ʃafnər] *m* (*pl* -) (*Zug*) guard; (*Bus*) conductor. **–in** *f* (*pl* -nen) guard; conductress.
Schaf‖pelz *m* sheepskin. **–stall** *m* sheepfold.
Schaft [ʃaft] *m* (*pl* **Schäfte**) shaft; (*Griff*) handle; (*Gewehr*) stock; (*Baum*) trunk.
Schale ['ʃaɪlə] *f* (*pl* -n) (*Schüssel*) bowl;

basin; (*Ei, Nuß*) shell; (*Frucht, Gemüse*) peel, skin; (*fig*) cover(ing).
schälen ['ʃɛɪlən] *v* shell; peel.
Schalk [ʃalk] *m* (*pl* -e) rogue, knave.
schalkhaft *adj* roguish.
Schall [ʃal] *m* (*pl* -e) sound. **–dämpfer** *m* silencer. **schallen** *v* sound, resound; (*Glocke*) ring, peal. **Schall‖platte** *f* (gramophone) record. **–welle** *f* soundwave.
schalten ['ʃaltən] *v* switch; (*Mot*) change (gear). **Schalt‖er** *m* (*Bank, usw.*) counter, window; (*Elek*) switch. **–hebel** *m* control lever, switch; (*Mot*) gear lever. **–jahr** *neut* leap year. **–plan** *m* circuit diagram. **–ung** *f* wiring; (*Mot*) gear-change.
Scham [ʃaɪm] *f* shame; (*Scheu*) modesty.
schämen ['ʃɛɪmən] *v* **sich schämen** *v* be ashamed.
scham‖haft *adj* bashful, modest. **–los** *adj* shameless, immodest.
Schampoo [ʃam'puɪ] *neut* shampoo.
schampoonieren *v* shampoo.
Schande ['ʃandə] *f* (*pl* -n) disgrace, shame.
schänden ['ʃɛndən] *v* disgrace; (*verderben*) spoil; (*entheiligen*) desecrate; (*Frau*) rape, violate.
Schandfleck ['ʃantflɛk] *m* blemish, stain.
schändlich ['ʃɛntliç] *adj* shameful, disgraceful.
Schandtat ['ʃanttait] *f* misdeed, crime.
Schank ['ʃaŋk] *m* (*pl* **Schänke**) bar.
Schanze ['ʃantsə] *f* (*pl* -n) fortification; (*Erdwall*) earthworks *pl*; (*Skilauf*) skijump.
Schar [ʃaɪr] *f* (*pl* -en) troop, band; (*Gänse*) flock; (*Hunde*) pack. **sich scharen** *v* gather, congregate.
scharf [ʃarf] *adj* sharp; (*Gewürze*) spicy, hot.
Schärfe ['ʃɛrfə] *f* (*pl* -n) sharpness, edge; (*Ätzkraft*) acidity; (*Klarheit*) clarity. **schärfen** *v* sharpen.
Scharfschütze *m* marksman, sharpshooter. **scharfsichtig** *adj* sharpsighted. **Scharfsinn** *m* shrewdness. **scharfsinnig** *adj* shrewd.
Scharlachfieber ['ʃarlaxfiɪbər] *neut* scarlet fever. **scharlachrot** *adj* scarlet.
Scharm [ʃarm] *m* charm. **scharmant** *adj* charming, delightful.
Scharnier [ʃar'niɪr] *neut* (*pl* -e) hinge.
scharren ['ʃarən] *v* scrape, scratch.

Schatten ['ʃatən] *m* (*pl* -) shadow; (*Dunkel*) shade. **in den Schatten stellen** overshadow. **Schattenbild** *neut* silhouette. **schatten‖haft** *adj* shadowy. **–ig** *adj* shaded.

Schatz [ʃats] *m* (*pl* **Schätze**) treasure; (*fig*) darling. **–amt** *neut* treasury.

schätzen ['ʃɛtsən] *v* value; (*ungefähr*) estimate. **–swert** *adj* valuable, estimable.

Schatz‖kammer *f* treasury. **–meister** *m* treasurer.

Schätzung ['ʃɛtsuŋ] *f* (*pl* -en) estimate; (*Hochschätzung*) esteem. **schätzungsweise** *adv* approximately; at a guess.

Schau [ʃau] *f* (*pl* -en) show; (*Ausstellung*) exhibition; (*Überblick*) survey, review. **zur Schau stellen** exhibit.

schaudern ['ʃaudərn] *v* shudder, shiver. **–haft** *adj* horrible.

schauen ['ʃauən] *v* look (at), observe.

Schauer ['ʃauər] *m* (*pl* -) (*Regen*) shower; (*Schrecken*) horror; (*Zittern*) thrill.

Schaufel ['ʃaufəl] *f* (*pl* -n) shovel; (*Tech*) blade.

Schaufenster *neut* shop window.

Schaukel ['ʃaukəl] *f* (*pl* -n) (child's) swing. **–pferd** *neut* rocking horse. **–stuhl** *m* rocking-chair.

Schaum [ʃaum] *m* (*pl* **Schäume**) foam; (*Seife*) lather.

schäumen ['ʃɔymən] *v* foam; (*Wein*) sparkle.

schaumig ['ʃaumiç] *adj* foamy.

Schauspiel *neut* play; drama; (*fig*) spectacle. **–er** *m* (*pl* -) actor. **–erin** *f* (*pl* -nen) actress. **–haus** *neut* theatre.

Scheck [ʃɛk] *m* (*pl* -s) check. **–buch** *neut* check book.

Scheibe ['ʃaibə] *f* (*pl* -n) disc; (*Brot, Wurst*) slice; (*Glas*) pane. **Scheiben‖bremse** *f* disc brake. **–wischer** *m* windshield wiper.

Scheide ['ʃaidə] *f* (*pl* -n) sheath; (*Anat*) vagina; (*Grenze*) limit. **scheiden** *v* separate; (*Ehepartner*) divorce. **sich scheiden** part, separate. **sich scheiden lassen** get a divorce. **Scheideweg** *m* crossroads. **Scheidung** *f* separation; (*Ehe*) divorce.

Schein [ʃain] *m* (*pl* -e) (*Aussehen*) appearance; (*Licht*) light; (*Glanz*) shine; (*Geld*) bill (*US*); banknote; (*Bescheinigung*) certificate. **schein‖bar** *adj* apparent, ostensible. **–en** *v* (*aussehen*) appear, seem; (*leuchten*) shine. **–heilig** *adj* sanctimoni-

ous. **Schein‖heilige(r)** hypocrite. **–krankheit** *f* feigned sickness. **–werfer** *m* (*pl* -) searchlight; (*Reflektor*) reflector; (*Theater*) spotlight; (*Mot*) headlight.

Scheiße ['ʃaisə] *f* (*vulgär*) shit. **scheißen** *v* shit.

Scheitel ['ʃaitəl] *m* (*pl* -) top; (*Kopf*) crown, top of the head; (*Haar*) parting.

scheitern ['ʃaitərn] *v* fail, come to nought; (*Schiff*) be wrecked.

Schelle ['ʃɛlə] *f* (*pl* -n) small bell; (*Hand-*) handcuff.

Schellfisch ['ʃɛlfiʃ] *m* haddock.

Schelm [ʃɛlm] *m* (*pl* -e) rogue.

Schema ['ʃema] *neut* (*pl* -ta *or* **Schemen**) scheme; (*Muster*) pattern; (*Darstellung*) diagram.

Schenkel ['ʃɛŋkəl] *m* (*pl* -) thigh. **–knochen** *m* thigh-bone, femur.

schenken ['ʃɛŋkən] *v* give, present; (*Getränk*) pour (out). **Schenk‖er** *m* (*pl* -) donor, giver. **–ung** *f* donation.

Scherbe ['ʃɛrbə] *f* (*pl* -n) fragment.

Schere ['ʃɛrə] *f* (*pl* -n) scissors *pl*; (*große*) shears *pl*; (*Krebs*) claw. **scheren** *v* (*Wolle*) shear; (*Haare*) cut; (*Hecke*) cut, trim; (*Rasen*) mow.

Scherz [ʃɛrts] *m* (*pl* -e) joke; (*Unterhaltung*) fun. **scherz‖en** *v* joke, have fun. **–haft** *adj* joking.

scheu [ʃɔy] *adj* shy.

Scheuche ['ʃɔyçə] *f* (*pl* -n) scarecrow.

scheuen ['ʃɔyən] *v* shy away from, avoid; (*Pferd*) shy; (*Mühe, usw.*) spare. **sich scheuen vor** be afraid of.

Scheuerbürste ['ʃɔyərbyrstə] *f* scrubbing brush. **scheuern** *v* scrub, scour.

Scheune ['ʃɔynə] *f* (*pl* -n) barn.

Scheusal ['ʃɔyzal] *neut* (*pl* -e) monster.

scheußlich ['ʃɔysliç] *adj* horrible, hideous. **Scheußlichkeit** *f* hideousness.

Schicht [ʃiçt] *f* (*pl* -en) layer; (*Arbeit*) shift; (*Gesellschaft*) class. **–arbeit** *f* shift work. **–holz** *neut* plywood. **–ung** *f* stratification; (*fig*) classification.

schick [ʃik] *adj* elegant, chic, smart.

schicken ['ʃikən] *v* send. **sich schicken** (*sich gehören*) suit, be becoming; (*sich entwickeln*) happen.

schicklich ['ʃikliç] *adj* becoming, fit, proper. **Schicklichkeit** *f* fitness, propriety.

Schicksal ['ʃikzal] *neut* (*pl* -e) fate, destiny. **–sschlag** *m* stroke of fate, blow.

Schiebedach ['ʃiːbədax] *neut* sliding roof; (*Mot*) sun-roof. **schieben** *v* push; (*Schuld*) pass on; (*Arbeit*) put off.
Schiebetür *f* sliding door.
Schieds‖gericht ['ʃiːtsgəriçt] *neut* arbitration court, tribunal. **–richter** *m* arbitrator; (*Sport*) referee, umpire. **–spruch** *m* arbitration, award.
schief [ʃiːf] *adj* slanting, sloping; (*fig*) wrong, amiss.
Schiefer ['ʃiːfər] *m* (*pl* -) slate.
***schiefgehen** *v* go wrong *or* amiss.
schielen ['ʃiːlən] *v* squint. **Schielen** *neut* (*Med*) strabismus, squint.
Schienbein ['ʃiːnbain] *neut* shin(bone).
Schiene ['ʃiːnə] *f* (*pl* -n) rail; (*Med*) splint.
***schießen** ['ʃiːsən] *v* shoot. **Schieß‖en** *neut* shooting. **–erei** *f* gunfight.
Schiff [ʃif] *neut* (*pl* -e) ship; (*Kirche*) nave. **–ahrt** *f* navigation; (*Verkehr*) shipping. **–bau** *m* shipbuilding. **–bruch** *m* shipwreck. **–brüchig** *adj* shipwrecked. **Schiffs‖küche** *f* galley. **–raum** *m* hold; (*Inhalt*) tonnage. **–verkehr** *m* shipping. **–werft** *f* shipyard.
Schikane [ʃiˈkaːnə] *f* (*pl* -n) chicanery. **schikanieren** *v* make trouble for.
Schild¹ [ʃilt] *m* (*pl* -e) shield.
Schild² *neut* (*pl* -er) sign; (*Namen-*) name-plate; (*Flasche*) label; (*Mütze*) peak.
schildern ['ʃildərn] *v* depict, describe. **Schilderung** *f* depiction, description.
Schildkröte *f* turtle; (*Land*) tortoise.
Schilf [ʃilf] *neut* (*pl* -e) reed.
Schilling ['ʃiliŋ] *m* (*pl* -e) (Austrian) Schilling.
Schimmel ['ʃiməl] *m* (*pl* -) mildew, mould. **schimmel‖ig** *adj* mouldy. **–n** *v* become mouldy.
Schimmer ['ʃimər] *m* (*pl* -) glimmer, gleam. **schimmern** *v* gleam, shine.
Schimpanse [ʃimˈpanzə] *m* (*pl* -n) chimpanzee.
Schimpf [ʃimpf] *m* (*pl* -e) abuse, insult. **schimpfen** *v* swear, curse; (*umg.: tadeln*) curse, scold. **Schimpfwort** *neut* swearword.
***schinden** ['ʃindən] *v* (*ausnützen*) exploit. **sich schinden** work hard, slave.
Schinken ['ʃiŋkən] *m* (*pl* -) ham.
Schippe ['ʃipə] *f* (*pl* -n) shovel; (*Karten*) spade(s).
Schirm [ʃirm] *m* (*pl* -e) (*Regen-*) umbrel-

la; (*Lampen-*) shade; (*Bild-*) screen; (*Mütze*) peak; (*fig: Schutz*) protection. **schirmen** *v* protect, screen.
schizophren [ʃitsoˈfreːn] *adj* schizophrenic. **Schizophrenie** *f* schizophrenia.
Schlacht [ʃlaxt] *f* (*pl* -en) battle. **schlachten** *v* slaughter.
Schlächter ['ʃlɛçtər] *m* (*pl* -) butcher.
Schlacht‖feld *neut* battlefield. **–hof** *m* slaughterhouse. **–schiff** *neut* battleship.
Schlaf [ʃlaːf] *m* sleep. **–anzug** *m* pyjamas *pl*. **schlafen** *v* sleep. **–d** *adj* sleeping; (*fig*) dormant. **Schlafenszeit** *f* bedtime.
Schläfer ['ʃlɛːfər] *m* (*pl* -) sleeper.
schlaff [ʃlaf] *adj* slack; (*fig*) lax; (*welk*) limp.
Schlaf‖losigkeit *f* sleeplessness, insomnia. **–mittel** *neut* sleeping pill.
schläfrig ['ʃlɛːfriç] *adj* sleepy.
Schlaf‖wagen *m* sleeping car. **–zimmer** *neut* bedroom.
Schlag [ʃlaːk] *m* (*pl* Schläge) blow, stroke; (*Elek*) shock; (*Med*) stroke; (*Art*) sort, kind. **schlagen** *v* hit, strike; (*besiegen*) beat, defeat; (*mit der Faust*) punch; (*Vögel*) warble, sing; (*Wurzel*) take root. **kurz und klein schlagen** smash to pieces. **Alarm schlagen** sound the alarm. **nach jemandem schlagen** take after someone. **Schlagen** *neut* striking, hitting. **schlagend** *adj* striking; (*fig*) impressive; (*entscheidend*) decisive.
Schlager *m* (*pl* -) (great) success, hit; (*Musik*) hit (song).
Schläger ['ʃlɛːgər] *m* (*pl* -) (*Tennis*) racket; (*Golf*) club; (*Kochen*) beater; (*Raufbold*) rowdy.
schlagfertig ['ʃlaːkfɛrtiç] *adj* quick-witted. **Schlag‖instrument** *neut* percussion instrument. **–sahne** *f* whipped cream. **–wort** *neut* slogan. **–zeile** *f* headline. **–zeug** *neut* percussion (instruments) *pl*.
Schlamm [ʃlam] *m* (*pl* -e) mud. **schlammig** *adj* muddy.
Schlampe ['ʃlampə] *f* (*pl* -n) slut. **schlampig** *adj* slovenly.
Schlange ['ʃlaŋə] *f* (*pl* -n) snake; (*Reihe Menschen*) queue, (*US*) line. **Schlange stehen** *v* queue, (*US*) line up. **Schlangen‖gift** *neut* snake venom. **–leder** *neut* snakeskin.
schlank [ʃlaŋk] *adj* slender, slim. **Schlank‖heit** *f* slenderness, slimness. **–skur** *f* (reducing) diet.

schlapp [ʃlap] *adj* slack, limp.
schlau [ʃlau] *adj* cunning, sly, clever. **Schlauheit** *f* cunning, slyness.
Schlauch [ʃlaux] *m* (*pl* **Schläuche**) hose; (*Reifen*) inner tube.
schlecht [ʃlɛçt] *adj* bad; (*unwohl*) ill; (*Qualität*) poor, inferior; (*Luft*) stale, foul. **mir ist schlecht** I feel ill. **–gelaunt** *adj* bad-tempered. **Schlechtigkeit** *f* wickedness. **Schlechtheit** *f* badness. **schlechthin** *adv* simply, plainly.
Schlegel [ʃleɪɡəl] *m* (*pl* -) (wooden) mallet; (*Trommel*) drumstick.
***schleichen** [ʃlaiçən] *v* creep; (*heimlich*) slink, sneak.
Schleier [ʃlaiər] *m* (*pl* -) veil.
Schleife [ʃlaifə] *f* (*pl* -n) loop, slip-knot; (*Band*) bow.
***schleifen¹** [ʃlaifən] *v* slide, glide, slip.
schleifen² *v* (*schleppen*) drag; (*Messer*) sharpen, grind; (*Edelstein*) cut.
Schleim [ʃlaim] *m* (*pl* -e) slime; (*Med*) mucus. **schleimig** *adj* slimy; mucous.
***schleißen** [ʃlaisən] *v* slit; (*spalten*) split; (*reißen*) rip, tear.
schlendern [ʃlɛndərn] *v* saunter. **Schlendrian** *m* (*pl* -) (*umg.*) old routine.
Schleppboot [ʃlɛpboit] *neut* tug(boat).
schleppen *v* drag, pull; (*tragen*) carry, lug. **sich schleppen** *v* drag oneself along.
Schlesien [ʃleɪziən] *neut* Silesia.
Schleuder [ʃlɔydər] *f* (*pl* -n) sling, catapult; (*Wäsche*) spin-drier, spinner; (*Zentrifuge*) centrifuge. **–preis** *m* cut-price, give-away price. **schleudern** *v* sling, hurl; (*Mot*) skid; (*Wäsche*) spin-dry; (*Komm*) dump, sell off cheap.
schleunig [ʃlɔyniç] *adj* prompt, speedy.
Schleuse [ʃlɔyzə] *f* (*pl* -n) sluice; (*Kanal*) lock.
schlicht [ʃliçt] *adj* simple, plain; (*bescheiden*) modest. **–en** *v* (*glätten*) smooth; (*ebnen*) level; (*Streit*) settle. **Schlichtung** *f* (*pl* -en) settlement.
***schließen** [ʃliisən] *v* close, shut; (*mit dem Schlüssel*) lock; (*zum Schluß bringen*) close, end, conclude; (*folgern*) conclude, infer. **Schließfach** *neut* (*Bank*) safe-deposit box. **schließlich** *adv* finally, (at) last.
schlimm [ʃlim] *adj* bad. **schlimmstenfalls** *adv* at worst.
Schlinge [ʃliŋə] *f* (*pl* -n) noose, loop; (*Jagd, fig*) snare, trap.

***schlingen¹** [ʃliŋən] *v* wind; (*flechten*) twist; (*verknüpfen*) tie, knot.
***schlingen²** *v* (*schlucken*) swallow; (*gierig essen*) devour, wolf.
Schlitten [ʃlitən] *m* (*pl* -) sledge. **Schlittschuh** *m* skate. **Schlittschuh laufen** skate.
Schlitz [ʃlits] *m* (*pl* -e) slit; (*Münzeinwurf*) slot; (*Hosen-*) fly.
Schloß [ʃlɔs] *neut* (*pl* **Schlösser**) lock; (*Burg*) castle.
Schlosser [ʃlɔsər] *m* (*pl* -) fitter, mechanic, locksmith.
Schlot [ʃloit] *m* (*pl* -e) chimney.
schlott(e)rig [ʃɔt(ə)riç] *adj* (*wackelig*) wobbly, shaky; (*schlaff*) loose; (*kleider*) baggy.
Schluck [ʃluk] *m* (*pl* -e) sip, gulp, mouthful. **–auf** *m* hiccup. **schlucken** *v* swallow.
Schlund [ʃlunt] *m* (*pl* **Schlünde**) throat; (*geog*) abyss, gorge; (*fig*) gulf.
schlüpfen [ʃlypfən] *v* slip, slide. **Schlüpfer** *m* knickers *pl*. **schlüpfrig** *adj* slippery; (*fig*) lewd.
Schlupfwinkel [ʃlupfviŋkəl] *m* hiding place.
Schluß [ʃlus] *m* (*pl* **Schlüsse**) end, close; (*Folgerung*) inference, conclusion. **zum Schluß** finally. **Schluß machen** stop, finish.
Schlüssel [ʃlysəl] *m* (*pl* -) key; (*Musik*) clef; (*Tech*) spanner, (*US*) wrench. **–bein** *neut* collarbone. **–bund** *m* bunch of keys. **–loch** *neut* keyhole. **–ring** *m* keyring.
Schluß‖prüfung *f* final examination, finals *pl*. **–runde** *f* (*Sport*) final. **–verkauf** *m* end-of-season sale.
Schmach [ʃmax] *f* disgrace, dishonour.
schmächtig [ʃmɛçtiç] *adj* slim, slender.
schmackhaft [ʃmakhaft] *adj* appetizing, delicious.
schmal [ʃmail] *adj* narrow, thin, slender; (*fig*) scanty, poor.
Schmalz [ʃmalts] *neut* (*pl* -e) fat, grease, dripping; (*fig*) sentimentality.
schmarotzen [ʃmaˈrɔtsən] *v* (*umg.*) sponge, scrounge. **Schmarotzer** *m* (*Tier, Pflanze*) parasite; (*Person*) scrounger, parasite.
schmatzen [ʃmatsən] *v* smack one's lips, eat noisily; (*küssen*) give a smacking kiss.
schmecken [ʃmɛkən] *v* taste; (*gut*) taste good. **schmecken nach** taste of. **(wie)**

schmeckt es? do you like it? **es schmeckt (mir)** I like it, it's good.
Schmeichelei [ʃmaiçə'lai] f (pl -en) flattery. **schmeicheln** v flatter.
Schmeichler m (pl -) flatterer. **schmeichlerisch** adj flattering.
*schmeißen ['ʃmaisən] v throw, cast; (umg.) chuck; (Schlagen) strike, smash.
Schmelz [ʃmɛlts] m (pl -e) (Email) enamel; (Glasur) glaze; (Stimme, Töne) mellowness, sweetness. **schmelzen** v melt; (Erz) smelt.
Schmerz [ʃmɛrts] m (pl -en) pain; (seelisch) grief, pain. **Schmerzen haben** be in pain. **schmerzen** v hurt; (seelisch) grieve, pain. **schmerz‖haft** adj painful. **–lich** adj painful, hurtful. **–los** adj painless.
Schmetterling ['ʃmɛtərliŋ] m (pl -e) butterfly. **–sschwimmen** neut butterfly (stroke).
Schmied [ʃmiːt] m (pl -e) (black)smith. **Schmiede** f (pl -n) forge, smithy. **–eisen** neut wrought iron. **schmieden** v forge; (Pläne) devise.
Schmiere ['ʃmiːrə] f (pl -n) grease; (Theater, umg.) small (touring) company. **schmieren** v (fetten) grease; (ölen) oil, lubricate; (streichen) spread. **Schmierung** f (pl -en) lubrication.
Schminke ['ʃmiŋkə] f (pl -n) make-up. **schminken** v make up. **sich schminken** put on make-up; make oneself up.
Schmorbraten ['ʃmoːrbraitən] m stewed steak, pot roast. **schmoren** v stew, braise.
Schmuck [ʃmuk] m (pl -e) ornament, decoration; (Juwelen) jewellery.
schmücken ['ʃmykən] v adorn, decorate; (Kleider) trim.
schmuggeln ['ʃmugəln] v smuggle. **Schmuggelware** f contraband. **Schmuggler** m (pl -) smuggler.
Schmus [ʃmuːs] m (umg.) (empty) chatter, soft-soap; **schmusen** v chatter, soft-soap.
Schmutz [ʃmuts] m dirt, filth. **schmutzig** adj dirty, filthy. **Schmutzpresse** f gutter press.
Schnabel ['ʃnaːbəl] m (pl Schnäbel) bill, beak.
Schnalle ['ʃnalə] f (pl -n) clasp; (Schuh, Gürtel) buckle; (Tür) latch. **schnallen** v buckle.
schnappen ['ʃnapən] v snap; (erwischen) grab, catch. **nach Luft schnappen** gasp for air.

Schnaps [ʃnaps] m (pl Schnäpse) liqueur, schnaps, brandy.
schnarchen ['ʃnarçən] v snore.
schnattern ['ʃnatərn] v (Geflügel) cackle; (Menschen) prattle.
schnaufen ['ʃnaufən] v pant, puff.
Schnauze ['ʃnautsə] f (pl -n) snout, muzzle; (Kanne) spout. **halt die Schnauze!** (vulgär) shut up! belt up!
Schnecke ['ʃnɛkə] f (pl -n) snail; (nackte) slug.
Schnee [ʃneː] m snow. **–glöckchen** neut snowdrop. **–lawine** f avalanche. **–mann** m snowman. **–schläger** m egg whisk. **–schuh** m ski. **–sturm** m blizzard. **–wehe** f snowdrift.
Schneide ['ʃnaidə] f (pl -n) (cutting) edge. **schneiden** v cut; (Braten) carve. **Schneider** m (pl -) tailor. **–ei** f (pl -en) tailor's shop. **–in** f (pl -nen) dressmaker, seamstress.
schneien ['ʃnaiən] v snow.
schnell [ʃnɛl] adj fast, quick. **mach schnell!** hurry up! get a move on! **Schnellboot** neut speedboat. **schnellen** v jerk, spring. **Schnell‖gaststätte** f fastfood restaurant, cafeteria. **–igkeit** f speed. **–imbiß** m snack. **–zug** m express train.
schnippisch ['ʃnipiʃ] adj pert, saucy.
Schnitt [ʃnit] m (pl -e) cut; (Scheibe) slice; (Art) style; (Math) intersection; (Zeichnung) (cross-)section. **–lauch** m chive(s). **–ling** m (Bot) cutting.
Schnitzel ['ʃnitsəl] neut (pl -) chip, shaving; (Fleisch) cutlet, escalope.
schnitzen ['ʃnitsən] v carve (wood). **Schnitzer** m carver; (Fehler) blunder, bloomer.
Schnörkel ['ʃnœrkəl] m (pl -) flourish; (Kunst, Architektur) scroll.
schnüffeln ['ʃnyfəln] v snuffle, sniff; (fig) snoop, nose around.
Schnuller ['ʃnulər] m (pl -) (baby's) dummy, (US) pacifier.
schnupfen ['ʃnupfən] v take snuff. **Schnupfen** m (pl -) catarrh, (head) cold. **einen Schnupfen bekommen/haben** catch/have a cold. **Schnupftabak** m snuff.
Schnur [ʃnuːr] f (pl Schnüre) string, cord; (Elek) flex, wire.
schnüren ['ʃnyːrən] v tie (up), fasten.

schnurgerade ['ʃnuːrgəraɪdə] *adj, adv* (as) straight (as a die).
Schnurrbart ['ʃnurbaːrt] *m* moustache.
schnurren ['ʃnurən] *v* hum, buzz; (*Katze*) purr.
Schock [ʃɔk] *m* (*pl* -s *or* -e) shock.
schokieren *v* shock, scandalize.
Schokolade [ʃokoˈlaɪdə] *f* (*pl* -n) chocolate.
Scholle ['ʃɔlə] *f* (*pl* -n) (*Erde*) clod, clump; (*Eis*) floe; (*Fisch*) plaice; (*fig*) native soil, home.
schon [ʃoɪn] *adv* already; (*bestimmt*) certainly; (*zwar*) indeed. **schon lange** for a long time. **schon lange her** a long time ago. **ich komme schon!** I'm coming! **schon wieder** yet again. **schon der Name** the mere name, the name alone.
schön [ʃœɪn] *adj* beautiful, pretty; (*Wetter*) fine, fair. **danke schön** thank you. **bitte schön** (if you) please. **schön machen** beautify.
schonen ['ʃoɪnən] *v* spare; treat carefully, go carefully with. **-d** *adj* considerate, careful.
Schönheit ['ʃœɪnhait] *f* (*pl* -en) beauty. **Schönheits‖fehler** *m* blemish, flaw. **-königin** *f* beauty queen. **-pflege** *f* beauty treatment.
Schonkost ['ʃoɪnkɔst] *f* (bland) diet.
Schopf [ʃɔpf] *m* (*pl* Schöpfe) shock, tuft.
schöpfen ['ʃœpfən] *v* scoop, ladle; (*Atem*) take, draw; (*Mut*) take.
Schöpfer[1] ['ʃœpfər] *m* (*pl* -) creator.
Schöpfer[2] *m* (*pl* -) (*zum Schöpfen*) scoop.
schöpferisch ['ʃœpfəriʃ] *adj* creative.
Schöpflöffel ['ʃœpflœfəl] *m* ladle.
Schöpfung ['ʃœpfuŋ] *f* creation.
Schornstein ['ʃɔrnstain] *m* chimney. **-feger** *m* chimney-sweep. **-kappe** *f* chimney-pot.
Schoß[1] [ʃoɪs] *m* (*pl* Schöße) lap; (*fig*) bosom. **-hund** *m* lap-dog.
Schoß[2] [ʃɔs] *m* (*pl* Schosse) (*Bot*) shoot, sprout.
Schote ['ʃoɪtə] *f* (*pl* -n) pod. **Schoten** *pl* (green) peas.
Schotte ['ʃɔtə] *m* (*pl* -n) Scot, Scotsman.
Schottin *f* (*pl* -nen) Scot, Scotswoman.
schottisch *adj* Scottish, Scots. **Schottland** *neut* Scotland.
schräg [ʃrɛːk] *adj* sloping, slanting, oblique.
Schrank [ʃraŋk] *m* (*pl* Schränke) cupboard; (*Kleider*) wardrobe.

Schranke ['ʃraŋkə] *f* (*pl* -n) barrier, bar. **schrankenlos** *adj* limitless, boundless.
Schraube ['ʃraubə] *f* (*pl* -n) screw. **Schraubdeckel** *m* screw-cap. **Schrauben‖schlüssel** *m* spanner, (*US*) wrench. **-zieher** *m* screwdriver.
Schrebergarten ['ʃreibərgartən] *m* allotment (garden).
Schreck [ʃrɛk] *m* (*pl* -e) *or* **Schrecken** *m* (*pl* -) fright, terror. **einen Schreck bekommen/kriegen** receive/get a fright. **schrecken** *v* terrify, frighten. **schrecklich** *adj* terrible, frightful.
Schrei [ʃrai] *m* (*pl* -e) cry, shout, scream.
schreien *v* cry, shout; (*kreischen*) shriek, screech; (*weinen*) cry, weep.
*schreiben ['ʃraibən] *v* write; (*buchstabieren*) spell. **schreibfaul** *adj* lazy about writing (letters). **Schreib‖fehler** *m* spelling error. **-krampf** *m* writer's cramp. **-maschine** *f* typewriter. **-tisch** *m* desk. **-ung** *f* (*pl* -en) spelling. **-waren** *pl* stationery *sing*.
Schrein [ʃrain] *m* (*pl* -e) (*Kasten*) chest, box; (*Reliquien*) shrine. **-er** *m* (*pl* -) joiner, carpenter.
*schreiten ['ʃraitən] *v* stride, step.
Schrift [ʃrift] *f* (*pl* -en) writing; (*Handschrift*) handwriting; (*Geschriebenes*) pamphlet, paper; (*Art*) script, type. **schriftlich** *adj* in writing, written. **Schrift‖steller** *m* (*pl* -), **Schriftstellerin** *f* (*pl* -nen) writer, author. **-stück** *neut* document, paper.
Schritt [ʃrit] *m* (*pl* -e) step, stride; (*Gangart*) gait; (*Tempo*) pace. **Schritt halten mit** keep pace with. **Schrittmacher** *m* (*fig, Med*) pacemaker. **schrittweise** *adv* step-by-step.
schroff [ʃrɔf] *adj* steep, precipitous; (*fig*) gruff, surly.
Schrot [ʃroit] *m or neut* (*pl* -e) (*Getreide*) groats *pl*; (*Bleikügelchen*) (buck)shot. **-brot** *neut* wholemeal bread.
Schrott [ʃrɔt] *m* (*pl* -e) scrap (metal).
schrubben ['ʃrubən] *v* scrub.
schrumpfen ['ʃrumpfən] *v* shrink. **Schrumpfung** *f* shrinking, contraction.
Schub [ʃuip] *m* (*pl* Schübe) shove, push; (*Tech*) thrust. **-fach** *neut* drawer. **-karren** *m* wheelbarrow. **-lade** *f* drawer.
schüchtern ['ʃyçtərn] *adj* shy. **Schüchternheit** *f* shyness.

Schuft [ʃuft] *m* (*pl* -e) rascal, rogue.
schuften *v* (*umg.*) toil, sweat, graft.
Schuh [ʃuː] *m* (*pl* -e) shoe. –**krem** *f* shoe polish. –**macher** *m* shoemaker. –**werk** *neut* footwear.
Schul‖arbeit *f* homework, task. –**buch** *neut* school book.
schuld [ʃult] *adj* guilty. **schuld haben** be guilty. **Schuld** *f* (*pl* -en) (*Geld*, *fig*) debt; (*Rel*, *Jur*) guilt. **schuld sein an** be to blame for. **Schulden haben** be in debt. **die Schuld schieben auf** push the blame onto. **schulden** *v* owe. **Schuldgefühl** *neut* sense of guilt. **schuldig** *adj* guilty; (*Geld*) indebted. **Schuldig‖e(r)** guilty person, culprit. –**keit** *f* (*unz.*) obligation; (*Pflicht*) duty. –**sprechung** *f* conviction, verdict of guilty.
Schuldirektor *m* headmaster. –**in** *f* headmistress.
schuldlos [ˈʃultloːs] *adj* innocent. **Schuld‖ner** *m* (*pl* -), –**nerin** *f* (*pl* -nen) debtor. –**schein** *m* promissory note, IOU.
Schule [ˈʃuːlə] *f* (*pl* -n) school. **schulen** *v* school, train.
Schüler [ˈʃyːlər] *m* (*pl* -) schoolboy; (*bei einem Meister*) pupil; (*Rel*) disciple. –**in** *f* (*pl* -nen) schoolgirl; pupil; disciple.
Schul‖fach *neut* (school) subject. –**ferien** *pl* school holidays. **schulfrei haben** have a holiday. **Schul‖freund** *m* school friend. –**geld** *neut* school fees. –**hof** *m* (school) playground. –**junge** *m* schoolboy. –**lehrer** *m* (*pl* -), –**lehrerin** *f* (*pl* -nen) schoolteacher. –**mädchen** *neut* schoolgirl. –**schluß** *m* end of term, breaking-up.
Schulter [ˈʃultər] *f* (*pl* -en) shoulder. –**blatt** *neut* shoulder blade.
Schulung [ˈʃuːluŋ] *f* (*pl* -en) schooling, training. **Schul‖wesen** *neut* educational system. –**zimmer** *neut* classroom, schoolroom.
Schund [ʃunt] *m* trash, rubbish.
Schuppe [ˈʃupə] *f* (*pl* -n) scale. **Schuppen** *pl* dandruff. **schuppig** *adj* scaly.
schüren [ˈʃyːrən] *v* stir up, incite; (*Feuer*) poke, stoke.
schürfen [ˈʃyrfən] *v* (*Haut*) scratch, graze; (*Metall*) prospect. **Schürfung** *f* (*pl* -en) graze, abrasion; prospecting.
Schurke [ˈʃurkə] *m* (*pl* -n) villain, scoundrel.
Schürze [ˈʃyrtsə] *f* (*pl* -n) apron.

Schuß [ʃus] *m* (*pl* Schüsse) shot. –**loch** *neut* bullet-hole. –**waffe** *f* firearm. –**weite** *f* range. –**wunde** *f* gunshot wound.
Schüssel [ˈʃysəl] *f* (*pl* -n) bowl, dish.
Schuster [ˈʃuːstər] *m* (*pl* -) cobbler, shoemaker.
Schutt [ʃut] *m* (*Trümmer*) debris; (*Abfall*) refuse.
schütteln [ˈʃytəln] *v* shake.
schütten [ˈʃytən] *v* pour (out). **es schüttet** it's pouring (with rain).
schüttern [ˈʃytərn] *v* tremble, shake.
Schutz [ʃuts] *m* (*pl* -e) protection; (*Obdach*) shelter; (*Schirm*) screen. –**anzug** *m* protective clothing. –**brille** *f* goggles *pl*.
Schütze [ˈʃytsə] *m* (*pl* -n) marksman, sharpshooter; (*Bogen*) archer. **schützen** *v* protect, defend; (*behüten*) guard.
Schutz‖farbe *f* camouflage. –**heilige(r)** *m* patron saint.
Schützling [ˈʃytsliŋ] *m* (*pl* -e) protégé(e), charge.
schutzlos [ˈʃutsloːs] *adj* defenceless. **Schutz‖mann** *m* policeman. –**maßnahme** *f* precaution, preventive measure. –**mittel** *neut* preservative. –**umschlag** *m* (Book) jacket, dust cover.
Schwabe [ˈʃvaːbə] *m* (*pl* -n) Swabian (man). –**n** *neut* Swabia.
Schwäbin [ˈʃvɛːbin] *f* (*pl* -nen) Swabian woman. **schwäbisch** *adj* Swabian.
schwach [ʃvax] *adj* weak; (*kränklich*) delicate, sickly; (*klein*) small; (*gering*) scanty, poor.
Schwäche [ˈʃvɛçə] *f* (*pl* -n) weakness. **schwächen** *v* weaken.
Schwachheit [ˈʃvaxhait] *f* (*pl* -en) weakness.
schwächlich [ˈʃvɛçliç] *adj* feeble, sickly, delicate.
Schwachsinn [ˈʃvaxzin] *m* feeblemindedness. **schwachsinnig** *adj* feebleminded.
Schwager [ˈʃvaːgər] *m* (*pl* Schwäger) brother-in-law.
Schwägerin [ˈʃvɛːgərin] *f* (*pl* -nen) sister-in-law.
Schwalbe [ˈʃvalbə] *f* (*pl* -n) (*Vogel*) swallow.
Schwall [ʃval] *m* (*pl* -e) flood, torrent.
Schwamm [ʃvam] *m* (*pl* Schwämme) sponge.
Schwan [ʃvaːn] *m* (*pl* Schwäne) swan.

schwanger ['ʃvaŋər] *adj* pregnant. **Schwangere** *f* (*pl* -n) pregnant woman. **Schwangerschaft** *f* pregnancy. **–vorsorge** *f* ante-natal care.

schwanken ['ʃvaŋkən] *v* sway, swing; (*taumeln*) stagger, reel; (*zögern*) waver; (*Preise*) fluctuate. **–d** *adj* (*Person*) wavering. **Schwankung** *f* (*pl* en) swaying, wavering, fluctuation.

Schwanz [ʃvants] *m* (*pl* **Schwänze**) tail.

Schwarm [ʃvarm] *m* (*pl* **Schwärme**) swarm; (*Vogel*) flock; (*Fische*) shoal; (*Rind, Schaf*) herd; (*Menschen*) crowd; (*fig*) craze.

schwärmen ['ʃvɛrmən] *v* swarm; (*Mil*) deploy. **schwärmen für** rave about, gush over. **schwärmerisch** *adj* wildly enthusiastic.

schwarz [ʃvarts] *adj* black. **Schwarz** *neut* black (colour). **–brot** *neut* black bread. **–e(r)** Black, Negro.

Schwärze ['ʃvɛrtsə] *f* (*pl* -n) blackness; (*Druck*) printer's ink. **schwärz‖en** *v* blacken. **–lich** *adj* blackish, darkish.

Schwarz‖markt *m* black market. **–wald** *m* Black Forest. **schwarzweiß** *adj* black-and-white.

schwatzen ['ʃvatsən] *v* *also* **schwätzen** chatter, prattle; (*Geheimnisse*) gossip.

Schwebe ['ʃveːbə] *f* suspense. **in der Schwebe** *adj* undecided, pending. **schweben** *v* float, hover; (*hängen*) hang, be suspended; (*fig*) remain undecided.

Schwede ['ʃveːdə] *m* (*pl* -n), **Schwedin** *f* (*pl* -nen) Swede. **Schweden** *neut* Sweden. **schwedisch** *adj* Swedish.

Schwefel ['ʃveːfəl] *m* sulphur.

schweifen ['ʃvaifən] *v* roam, wander.

*schweigen ['ʃvaigən] *v* be silent. **ganz zu schweigen von** to say nothing of. **Schweigen** *neut* silence. **schweigsam** *adj* silent; (*fig*) secretive.

Schwein [ʃvain] *neut* (*pl* -e) pig; (*fig*) (good) luck. **Schweine‖braten** *m* roast pork. **–fett** *neut* lard. **–fleisch** *neut* pork. **–hund** *m* (*vulgär*) bastard, swine. **–rei** *f* filthy mess; (*fig*) dirty trick. **–stall** *m* pigsty. **Schweinsrippchen** *neut* pork chop.

Schweiß [ʃvais] *m* (*pl* -e) sweat, perspiration. **schweißen** *v* weld; (*Wild*) bleed.

Schweiz [ʃvaits] *f* **die Schweiz** Switzerland. **Schweizer** *m* (*pl* -), **Schweizerin** *f* (*pl* -nen) Swiss. **schweizerisch** *adj* Swiss.

Schwelle ['ʃvɛlə] *f* (*pl* -n) threshold; (*Eisenbahn*) sleeper.

*schwellen ['ʃvɛlən] *v* swell.

schwemmen ['ʃvɛmən] *v* wash down; (*Vieh*) water.

Schwengel ['ʃvɛŋəl] *m* (*pl* -) (*Glocke*) clapper; (*Pumpe*) pump handle.

schwenken ['ʃvɛŋkən] *v* turn; (*Fahne, Hut*) wave, flourish.

schwer [ʃveːr] *adj* heavy; (*schwierig*) difficult; (*ernst*) serious. **es ist 2 Kilo schwer** it weighs two kilos. **schwere Arbeit** hard work. **–beschädigt** *adj* seriously disabled. **Schwere** *f* weight. **schwerfällig** *adj* clumsy, awkward. **Schwergewichtler** *m* heavyweight. **schwerhörig** *adj* hard of hearing. **Schwer‖industrie** *f* heavy industry. **–kraft** *f* gravity. **schwer‖lich** *adj* with difficulty, hardly. **–mütig** *adj* melancholy, sad.

Schwert [ʃveːrt] *neut* (*pl* -er) sword.

Schwester ['ʃvɛstər] *f* (*pl* -n) sister. **schwesterlich** *adj* sisterly. **Schwesternschaft** *f* sisterhood.

Schwieger‖eltern *pl* parents-in-law; (*umg.*) in-laws. **–mutter** *m* mother-in-law. **–sohn** *m* son-in-law. **–tochter** *f* daughter-in-law. **–vater** *m* father-in-law.

schwierig ['ʃviːriç] *adj* difficult, hard. **Schwierigkeit** *f* (*pl* -en) difficulty.

Schwimmbad ['ʃvimbaːt] *neut* swimming pool. **Schwimmbecken** *neut* swimming pool. **schwimmen** *v* swim; (*Gegenstand*) float. **Schwimmen** *neut* swimming. **schwimmend** *adj* swimming; floating. **Schwimmer** *m* (*pl* -) swimmer; float.

Schwindel ['ʃvindəl] *m* (*pl* -) giddiness; (*Täuschung*) swindle, fraud. **schwindel‖haft** *adj* giddy; fraudulent. **–ig** *adj* giddy, dizzy. **schwindeln** *v* cheat, swindle. **mir schwindelt** I feel giddy. **Schwindler** *m* (*pl* -) swindler, cheat.

*schwingen ['ʃviŋən] *v* swing, (*Fahne, Waffe*) wave, flourish. **Schwingung** *f* (*pl* -en) oscillation, vibration.

schwitzen ['ʃvitsən] *v* sweat.

*schwören ['ʃvœːrən] *v* swear.

schwul [ʃvuːl] *adj* (*vulgär*) queer, homosexual.

schwül [ʃvyːl] *adj* sultry, hot and humid.

Schwulst [ʃvulst] *m* (*pl* **Schwülste**) bombast, pomposity. **schwülstig** *adj* bombastic, pompous.

Schwund [ʃvunt] *m* contraction, shrinkage; (*Med*) atrophy.

Schwung [ʃvʊŋ] m (pl **Schwünge**) impetus, momentum; (fig) drive, vitality,
verve. **–kraft** f centrifugal force; (fig)
verve. **–rad** neut flywheel.
Schwur [ʃvuːr] m (pl **Schwüre**) oath.
–gericht neut court with jury.
sechs [zɛks] pron, adj six. **sechst** adj sixth.
Sechstel neut sixth (part).
sechzehn [ˈzɛçtseːn] pron, adj sixteen.
sechzehntel adj sixteenth.
sechzig [ˈzɛçtsiç] pron, adj sixty. **die
sechziger Jahre** the '60s. **sechzigst** adj
sixtieth.
See [zeː] 1 m (pl **-n**) lake. 2 f (pl **-n**) sea.
–fahrt f voyage. **–jungfer** f mermaid.
seekrank adj seasick.
Seele [ˈzeːlə] f (pl **-n**) soul, spirit. **seelisch**
adj spiritual.
See‖löwe m sealion. **–räuber** m pirate.
–wasser neut sea water.
Segel [ˈzeːɡəl] neut (pl **-**) sail. **–boot** neut
sailing boat. **–flugzeug** neut glider, sailplane. **segeln** v sail. **Segeltuch** neut canvas.
Segen [ˈzeːɡən] m (pl **-**) blessing;
(Tischgebet) grace. **segnen** v bless.
Segnung f (pl **-en**) blessing.
*sehen [ˈzeːən] v see; (anblicken) look;
(beobachten) watch, observe. **sehen lassen** display, show. **Sehen** neut (eye)sight,
vision. **–swürdigkeit** f (tourist) sight.
Seh‖feld neut field of vision. **–kraft** f
eyesight, vision.
Sehne [ˈzeːnə] f (pl **-n**) sinew, tendon;
(Bogen) string.
sehnen [ˈzeːnən] v **sich sehnen nach** long
for.
sehr [zeːr] adv very.
Sehweite [ˈzeːvaɪtə] f range of vision.
seicht [zaɪçt] adj shallow.
Seide [ˈzaɪdə] f (pl **-n**) silk.
Seife [ˈzaɪfə] f (pl **-n**) soap.
Seifen‖schaum m lather. **–wasser** neut
suds pl, soapy water.
Seil [zaɪl] neut (pl **-e**) rope; (Kabel) cable.
–bahn f funicular.
sein¹ [zaɪn] adj, pron his, its. **seinerseits**
adv on or for his part. **seinesgleichen**
pron the likes of him pl, people like him
pl. **seinethalben, seinetwegen,** or
seinetwillen adv for his sake. **seinige** pron
der, die, das seinige his.
*sein² v be. **es sei denn, daß** unless. **kann
sein** perhaps. **sein lassen** leave alone. **mir
ist kalt/warm** I feel cold/warm.

seit [zaɪt] prep since. **–dem** conj since;
adv since then. **seit damals** since then.
seit wann? since when? **seit zwei Jahren**
for two years.
Seite [ˈzaɪtə] f (pl **-n**) side; (Buch) page.
auf die Seite bringen put aside. **von
seiten** on the part (of). **Seiten‖lampe** f
side lamp. **–schiff** neut aisle. **–straße** f
side street. **–wagen** m sidecar.
seither [zaɪtˈheːr] adv since then.
seitlich [ˈzaɪtlɪç] adj lateral, side. **seitwärts**
adv sideways.
Sekretär [zekreˈtɛːr] m (pl **-e**) secretary;
(Schreibschrank) bureau, locking desk.
–in f (pl **-nen**) secretary.
Sekt [zɛkt] m (pl **-e**) sparkling wine.
Sekte [ˈzɛktə] f (pl **-n**) sect. **sektiererisch**
adj sectarian.
sekundär [zekunˈdɛːr] adj secondary.
Sekunde [zeˈkundə] f (pl **-n**) second.
selber [ˈzɛlbər] V selbst.
selbst [zɛlpst] pron self. adv even. **ich
selbst** I myself. **von selbst** on one's own
accord; (Sache) by itself. **sie kann es
selbst machen** she can do it by herself.
selbst wenn even though. **Selbst** neut
self. **–achtung** f self-respect.
selbständig [ˈzɛlpstɛndɪç] adj independent. **Selbständigkeit** f independence.
Selbst‖bedienung f self-service. **–beherrschung** f self-control. **–mitleid** f self-pity.
–bestimmung f self-determination.
selbstbewußt adj self-confident;
(eingebildet) conceited. **Selbstbewußtsein**
neut self-confidence; conceit.
Selbsterkenntnis f self-knowledge.
selbst‖gebacken adj home-made. **–gefällig** adj self-satisfied. **–gerecht** adj self-
righteous.
Selbsthilfe f self-help; (Jur) self-defence.
selbst‖klebend adj adhesive, gummed.
–los adj selfless.
Selbst‖mord m suicide. **–mörder** m suicide. **–schutz** m self-defence.
selbstsicher adj self-confident. **Selbstsicherheit** f self-confidence.
Selbstsucht f selfishness. **selbstsüchtig**
adj selfish.
Selbst‖täuschung f self-deception. **–versorgung** f self-sufficiency.
selbstverständlich adj self-evident. adv
obviously, naturally.
Selbstvertrauen neut self-confidence.

selig ['zeːliç] *adj* blessed; (*verstorben*) late, deceased; (*überglücklich*) blissful, delighted.
Sellerie ['zɛləriː] *f* (*pl* **-n**) *or* *m* (*pl* **-s**) celeriac. **–stangen** *pl* celery *sing.*
selten ['zɛltən] *adj* rare. *adv* rarely, seldom.
seltsam ['zɛltzaɪm] *adj* strange, odd, curious.
Semester [ze'mɛstər] *neut* (*pl* **-**) semester, (half-yearly) session.
Seminar [zemi'naɪr] *neut* (*pl* **-e**) training college; tutorial group.
Semit [ze'miːt] *m* (*pl* **-en**) Semite. **semitisch** *adj* Semitic.
Semmel ['zɛməl] *f* (*pl* **-n**) bread roll.
Senat [ze'naɪt] *m* (*pl* **-e**) senate. **–or** *m* (*pl* **-en**) senator.
*senden ['zɛndən] *v* send; (*Funk*) transmit, broadcast. **Sender** *m* (*pl* **-**) (*Gerät*) transmitter; (*Anstalt*) station. **Sendung** *f* (*pl* **-en**) package; (*Waren*) consignment; (*Funk*) broadcast.
Senf [zɛnf] *m* (*pl* **-e**) mustard.
sengen ['zɛŋən] *V singe.*
Senkblei ['zɛŋkblai] *neut* plumb-line.
Senkel ['zɛŋkəl] *m* (*pl* **-**) (shoe)lace.
senken ['zɛŋkən] *v* lower; (*Kopf*) bow; (*Preise*) reduce. **sich senken** sink. **senkrecht** *adj* vertical, perpendicular. **Senkung** *f* (*pl* **-en**) sinking; (*Preise*) reduction; (*Vertiefung*) depression.
Sensation [zɛnzatsi'oɪn] *f* (*pl* **-en**) sensation. **sensationell** *adj* sensational.
Sense ['zɛnzə] *f* (*pl* **-n**) scythe.
sensibel [zɛn'ziːbəl] *adj* sensitive.
sentimental [zɛntimɛn'taɪl] *adj* sentimental.
separieren [zɛpa'riːrən] *v* separate.
September [zɛp'tɛmbər] *m* (*pl* **-**) September.
septisch ['zɛptɪʃ] *adj* septic.
Serie ['zeːriə] *f* (*pl* **-n**) series. **–nherstellung** *f* mass production.
seriös [zeri'œɪs] *adj* serious, earnest; (*Firma*) reliable, honourable.
Service¹ [zɛr'viːs] *neut* (*pl* **-**) (dinner) service.
Service² *neut or m* (*pl* **-s**) (customer) service.
servieren [zɛr'viːrən] *v* serve. **Servierwagen** *m* trolley. **Serviette** *f* (*pl* **-n**) (table) napkin.
Sesam ['zɛzaɪm] *m* sesame.

Sessel ['zɛsəl] *m* (*pl* **-**) armchair. **–lift** *m* chairlift.
seßhaft ['zɛshaft] *adj* settled, established; (*ansässig*) resident.
setzen ['zɛtsən] *v* set, put, place; (*einpflanzen*) plant; (*Druck*) compose, set; (*Spiel*) wager, bet. **in Bewegung setzen** set in motion. **außer Kraft setzen** invalidate. **in die Welt setzen** give birth to. **sich setzen** sit down. **sich in Verbindung setzen mit** get in contact with.
Seuche ['zɔyçə] *f* (*pl* **-n**) epidemic.
seufzen ['zɔyftsən] *v* sigh. **Seufzer** *m* (*pl* **-**) sigh.
Sex [zɛks] *m* (*pl* **-**) sex. **Sexual‖ität** *f* sexuality. **–aufklärung** *f* sex education. **sexuell** *adj* sexual. **sexy** *adj* sexy.
sezieren [ze'tsiːrən] *v* dissect.
sich [ziç] *pron* himself, herself, itself, yourself, oneself, yourselves; themselves; (*miteinander*) (with) one another, each other. **an (und für) sich** in itself. **bei sich haben** have with one. **sich die Hände waschen** wash one's hands. **sie lieben sich** they love each other.
Sichel ['ziçəl] *f* (*pl* **-n**) sickle; (*Mond-*) crescent.
sicher ['ziçər] *adj* safe, secure; (*gewiß*) sure, certain. *adv* surely, certainly. **Sicherheit** *f* safety; certainty; trustworthiness; (*Pol, Psychol*) security. **Sicherheits‖bestimmungen** *pl* safety regulations. **–gurt** *m* safety belt. **–nadel** *f* safety pin. **sicher‖lich** *adv* surely, certainly. **–n** *v* secure; (*schützen*) protect. **–stellen** *v* secure, guarantee. **Sicherung** *f* (*pl* **-en**) protection; (*Elek*) fuse; (*Tech*) safety device.
Sicht [ziçt] *f* (*unz.*) sight; (*Aussicht*) view; (*Sichtbarkeit*) visibility. **sichtbar** *adj* visible. **Sichtbarkeit** *f* visibility.
sickern ['zikərn] *v* trickle, seep.
sie [ziː] *pron* she, it; her; they; them. **Sie** *pron* you.
Sieb [ziːp] *neut* (*pl* **-e**) sieve; (*Tee*) strainer.
sieben¹ ['ziːbən] *v* sift, sieve.
sieben² *pron, adj* seven. **siebent** *or* **siebt** *adj* seventh.
siebzehn ['ziːptsein] *pron, adj* seventeen. **siebzehnt** *adj* seventeenth.
siebzig ['ziːptsiç] *pron, adj* seventy. **siebzigt** *adj* seventieth.
siedeln ['ziːdəln] *v* settle, colonize.

*sieden ['ziːdən] v boil. **Siedepunkt** m boiling point.

Siedler ['ziːdlər] m (pl -) settler. **Siedlung** f (pl -en) settlement (place); (am Stadtrand) housing estate.

Sieg [ziːk] m (pl -e) victory.

Siegel ['ziːgəl] neut (pl -) seal, signet.

siegen ['ziːgən] v win, triumph, be victorious. **Sieger** m (Mil) conqueror, victor; (Sport) winner. **siegreich** adj victorious.

Signal [zig'naɪl] neut (pl -e) signal. **–feuer** neut beacon. **–rakete** f rocket-flare.

Signatur [zigna'tuːr] f (pl -en) mark, symbol; (Unterschrift) signature.

Silbe ['zilbə] f (pl -n) syllable.

Silber ['zilbər] neut silver. **silbern** adj silver.

Silvesterabend [zil'vɛstəraɪbənt] m New Year's Eve.

simpel ['zimpəl] adj simple.

Sims [zims] neut (pl -e) (Fenster) window-sill.

simulieren [zimu'liːrən] v pretend; (Krankheit) malinger; (Tech) simulate.

Sinfonie [zinfo'niː] f (pl -n) symphony.

*singen ['ziŋən] v sing. **Singvogel** m songbird.

*sinken ['ziŋkən] v sink; (fig) diminish; (Preise) fall. **Sinken** neut fall, drop; (Werte) depreciation; (fig) decline.

Sinn [zin] m (pl -e) sense; (Gedanken) mind, thoughts pl. es hat keinen Sinn it makes no sense. es kam mir in den Sinn, daß ... it crossed my mind that ... . **Sinn für Humor** sense of humour. **Sinn für Literatur** interest in literature. **Sinnbild** neut symbol. **sinn‖bildlich** adj symbolic. **–en** v reflect, think (over). **–lich** adj sensual. **–los** adj senseless. **Sinnspruch** m epigram, maxim.

Sippe ['zipə] f (pl -n) tribe; (Verwandte) kin.

Sirup ['ziːrup] m (pl -e) syrup.

Sitte ['zitə] f (pl -n) custom; (Gewohnheit) habit. **Sitten** pl morals. **Sittenlehre** f ethics. **sittenlos** adj immoral. **sittlich** adj moral. **Sittlichkeit** f morality. **–sverbrechen** neut indecent assault.

Situation [zituatsi'oɪn] f (pl -en) situation.

Sitz [zits] m (pl -e) seat; (Kleidung) fit. **–bank** f bench. **sitzen** v sit; (Kleidung) fit. **–bleiben** v remain seated. **Sitzung** f (pl -en) sitting; (Versammlung) session.

Skala ['skaɪla] f (pl Skalen) scale. **Skalenscheibe** f dial.

Skandal [skan'daɪl] m (pl -e) scandal. **skandalös** adj scandalous.

Skandinavien [skandi'naɪviən] neut Scandinavia. **Skandinavier** m (pl -), **Skandinavierin** f (pl -nen) Scandinavian. **skandinavisch** adj Scandinavian.

Skelett [ske'lɛt] neut (pl -e) skeleton.

Skeptiker ['skɛptikər] m (pl -) sceptic. **skeptisch** adj sceptical.

Ski [ʃiː] m (pl -er)· ski. **–fahrer(in)** skier.

Skizze ['skitsə] f (pl -n) sketch. **skizzieren** v sketch.

Sklave ['sklaɪvə] m (pl -n) slave. **Sklaverei** f slavery. **Sklavin** f (pl -nen) (female) slave, slave girl.

Skorpion ['skɔrpiɔn] m (pl -e) (Tier) scorpion; (Astrol) Scorpio.

Skrupel ['skruːpəl] m (pl -) scruple. **skrupellos** adj unscrupulous. **skrupulös** adj scrupulous.

Skulptur [skulp'tuːr] f (pl -en) sculpture.

Smaragd [sma'rakt] m (pl -e) emerald. **smaragdgrün** adj emerald(-green).

Smoking ['smoːkiŋ] m (pl -s) dinner jacket, (US) tuxedo.

so [zoɪ] adv thus, so, in this way. conj consequently, therefore. **so daß** so that. **so ein** such a. **so sehr** so much. **so ... wie ...** as ... as .... **um so besser** all the better. **–bald** conj as soon as.

Socke ['zɔkə] f (pl -n) sock.

Sockel ['zɔkəl] m (pl -) pedestal, base.

sodann [zo'dan] adv, conj then, in that case.

Sodawasser ['zoɪdavasər] neut soda water.

Sodbrennen ['zoɪtbrɛnən] neut heartburn.

soeben [zo'eɪbən] adv just (now).

Sofa ['zoɪfa] neut (pl -s) sofa.

sofern [zo'fɛrn] conj as or so far as.

sofort [zo'fɔrt] adv at once, immediately. **–ig** adj immediate.

Sog [zoɪk] m (pl -e) suction; (Boot) wake.

sogar [zo'gaɪr] adv even.

sogenannt ['zoɪgənant] adj so-called.

Sohle ['zoɪlə] f (pl -n) (Fuß, usw.) sole. **sohlen** v sole.

Sohn [zoɪn] m (pl **Söhne**) son.

solang(e) [zo'laŋ(ə)] conj as long as; (während) while.

solch [zɔlç] pron, adj such. **solcher‖art** adv of this sort, along these lines. **–lei** adj of such a kind. **–weise** adv in such a way.

Soldat [zɔl'daɪt] *m* (*pl* -en) soldier. **Soldat werden** enlist, join up.
Söldner ['zœldnər] *m* (*pl* -) mercenary.
solid [zo'liːt] *adj also* **solide** (*Person*) reliable, decent; (*Leben*) decent, respectable; (*Gegenstand*) solid, robust. **–arisch** *adj* united, unanimous. **Solidarität** *f* solidarity.
Solist [zo'list] *m* (*pl* -en), **Solistin** *f* (*pl* -nen) soloist.
Soll [zɔl] *neut* (*pl* -s) (*Komm*) debit; (*Produktion*) target. **sollen** *v* ought to, have to, should; (*angeblich*) be supposed to be. **ich sollte** I should. **was soll das?** what is this supposed to be *or* mean? *sie soll reich sein* she is said to be rich. *Kinder sollen gehorchen* children should be obedient. *du sollst nicht töten* thou shalt not kill.
Solo ['zoːlo] *neut* (*pl* -s *or* **Soli**) solo. **–sänger** *m* soloist, solo singer.
Sommer ['zɔmər] *m* (*pl* -) summer. **–ferien** *pl* summer holidays. **–sprosse** *f* freckle.
Sonate [zo'naːtə] *f* (*pl* -n) sonata.
Sonde ['zɔndə] *f* (*pl* -n) (*Tech*) probe.
Sonder‖angebot *neut* special offer. **–ausgabe** *f* special edition. **sonder‖bar** *adj* strange, peculiar. **–lich** *adj* remarkable, special.
sondern[1] ['zɔndərn] *v* separate.
sondern[2] *conj* but. **nicht nur ... sondern auch ...** not only ... but also ... .
Sonder‖preis *m* special price. **–ung** *f* (*pl* -en) separation.
Sonnabend ['zɔnaːbənt] *m* Saturday. **sonnabends** *adv* on Saturdays.
Sonne ['zɔnə] *f* (*pl* -n) sun. **sonnen** *v* air, put out in the sun. **sich sonnen** sun oneself, lie in the sun.
Sonnen‖aufgang *m* sunrise. **–blume** *f* sunflower. **–brand** *m* sunburn. **–bräune** *f* suntan. **–finsternis** *f* solar eclipse. **–schein** *m* sunshine. **–stich** *m* sunstroke. **–system** *neut* solar system. **–untergang** *m* sunset.
sonnig ['zɔniç] *adj* sunny.
Sonntag ['zɔntaːk] *m* Sunday. **sonntags** *adv* on Sundays.
sonst [zɔnst] *adv* otherwise, else. **sonst etwas?** anything else? **sonst nichts** nothing else. **wer sonst?** who else? **wie sonst** as usual. **–ig** *adj* other, miscellaneous. **–wie** *adv* some other way. **–wo** *adv* elsewhere.

Sopran [zo'praɪn] *m* (*pl* -e) soprano. **–istin** *f* (*pl* -nen) soprano (singer).
Sorge ['zɔrgə] *f* (*pl* -n) (*Kummer*) care, worry; (*Pflege*) care. **sich Sorgen machen (um)** worry (about). **sorgen für** take care of. **dafür sorgen, daß** make sure that, see to it that. **sich sorgen** be anxious, worry. **sorgen‖frei** *or* **–los** *adj* carefree. **–voll** *adj* careworn. **sorg‖lich** *adj* careful, caring. **–los** *adj* careless. **–sam** *adj* careful, cautious.
Sorte ['zɔrtə] *f* (*pl* -n) sort, kind; (*Ware*) brand. **sortieren** *v* sort (out). **Sortiment** *neut* (*pl* -e) assortment.
Soße ['zoːsə] *f* (*pl* -n) sauce; (*für Fleisch*) gravy.
Souveränität [suvərɛni'tɛɪt] *f* sovereignty.
soviel ['zofiːl] *conj* as far as. *adv* as *or* so much. **soviel wie** as much as. **soweit** *conj* as *or* so far as; *adv* so far. **sowenig(wie)** *conj* as little (as). **sowie** *conj* as soon as; (*außerdem*) as well as, and also. **sowieso** *adv* in any case.
Sowjet [zɔ'vjɛt] *m* (*pl* -e) Soviet. **sowjetisch** *adj* Soviet. **Sowjetunion** *f* Soviet Union.
sowohl [zo'voːl] *conj* as well as. **sowohl ... als auch ...** both ... and ... .
sozial [zotsi'aɪl] *adj* social. **Sozial‖abgaben** *pl* national insurance contributions. **–demokrat** *m* social democrat. **–einrichtungen** *pl* social services. **–fürsorge** *f* (social) welfare.
Sozialismus [zotsia'lizmus] *m* socialism. **Sozialist** *m* socialist. **sozialistisch** *adj* socialist.
Sozial‖politik *f* social policies *pl*. **–produkt** *neut* (gross) national product. **–unterstützung** *f* social security.
Soziologe [zotsio'loːgə] *m* (*pl* -n) sociologist. **Soziologie** *f* sociology. **soziologisch** *adj* sociological.
sozusagen [zotsu'zaːgən] *adv* so to speak.
spähen ['ʃpɛːən] *v* look out, watch; (*Mil*) scout.
Spalt [ʃpalt] *m* (*pl* -e) crack, slit. **–e** *f* (*Druck*) column; crack, crevice. **spalten** *v* split.
Span [ʃpaɪn] *m* (*pl* **Späne**) chip, shaving; (*Splitter*) splinter.
Spange ['ʃpaŋə] *f* (*pl* -n) clasp; (*Schnalle*) buckle.
Spanien ['ʃpaɪniən] *neut* Spain. **Spanier** *m* (*pl* -), **Spanierin** *f* (*pl* -nen) Spaniard. **spanisch** *adj* Spanish.

Spann [ʃpan] *m* (*pl* -e) instep.
Spanne [ʃpanə] *f* (*pl* -n) span.
spannen [ʃpanən] *v* stretch; (*straff ziehen*) tighten. **-d** *adj* thrilling, exciting. **Spann‖seil** *neut* guy(-rope). **-ung** *f* (*pl* -en) tension.
sparen [ʃpaːrən] *v* save; (*sparsam sein*) economize. **Sparer** *m* (*pl* -) saver.
Spargel [ʃpargəl] *m* (*pl* -) asparagus. **-kohl** *m* broccoli.
Sparkasse [ʃpaːrkasə] *f* savings bank. **-nbuch** *neut* deposit book.
spärlich [ʃpɛːrliç] *adj* scanty, meagre. **Spärlichkeit** *f* scarcity.
Sparmaßnahme [ʃpaːrmaːsnaːmə] *f* economy measure.
Spaß [ʃpaːs] *m* (*pl* **Späße**) fun; (*Scherz*) joke. **Spaß haben an** enjoy. *es macht uns Spaß* it amuses us, it is fun. **spaß‖en** *v* make fun, joke. **-haft** *or* **-ig** *adj* comical. **Spaßvogel** *m* joker, clown.
spät [ʃpɛːt] *adj* late. *wie spät ist es?* what is the time?
Spaten [ʃpaːtən] *m* (*pl* -) spade.
später [ʃpɛːtər] *adj* later. **spätestens** *adv* at the latest.
Spatz [ʃpats] *m* (*pl* -en) sparrow.
spazieren [ʃpaˈtsiːrən] *v* go for a walk, stroll. **-fahren** *v* go for a drive. **-gehen** *v* go for a walk, walk. **Spazier‖fahrt** *f* drive. **-gang** *m* walk, stroll.
Specht [ʃpɛçt] *m* (*pl* -e) woodpecker.
Speck [ʃpɛk] *m* (*pl* -e) bacon; (*Schmalz*) lard, fat. **speckig** *adj* greasy.
spedieren [ʃpeˈdiːrən] *v* forward, transport, ship. **Spediteur** *m* (*pl* -e) shipping agent, haulier, carrier. **Spedition** *f* (*pl* -en) shipping (agency).
Speer [ʃpeːr] *m* (*pl* -e) spear.
Speichel [ʃpaiçəl] *m* spittle, saliva.
Speicher [ʃpaiçər] *m* (*pl* -) warehouse, storehouse; (*Getreide*) granary; (*Computer*) memory. **speichern** *v* store.
Speise [ʃpaizə] *f* (*pl* -n) food; (*Gericht*) dish. **-eis** *neut* ice cream. **-karte** *f* menu. **speisen** *v* dine, eat. **Speise‖röhre** *f* gullet. **-saal** *m* dining room. **-wagen** *m* dining car.
Spektakel [ʃpɛkˈtaːkəl] *m* (*pl* -) spectacle; (*Aufregung*) uproar.
Spekulation [ʃpekulatsiˈoːn] *f* (*pl* -en) speculation. **spekulieren** *v* speculate.
Spende [ʃpɛndə] *f* (*pl* -n) donation. **spenden** *v* contribute, donate. **Spender** *m* (*pl* -), **Spenderin** *f* (*pl* -nen) donor.

Sperre [ʃpɛrə] *f* (*pl* -n) barrier; (*Verbot*) ban. **sperren** *v* close, bar; (*untersagen*) ban; (*Strom*) cut off. **Sperr‖riegel** *m* (door) bolt. **-kette** *f* door chain. **-klinke** *f* safety catch. **-ung** *f* blocking, barring. **-zeit** *f* closing time.
Spesen [ʃpeːzən] *pl* expenses.
Spezialfach [ʃpeitsiˈaːlfax] *neut* speciality. **spezialisieren** *v* specialize. **Spezialist** *m* specialist. **speziell** *adj* special.
spezifisch [ʃpeˈtsiːfiʃ] *adj* specific.
Sphäre [ˈsfɛːrə] *f* (*pl* -n) sphere.
Spiegel [ʃpiːgəl] *m* (*pl* -) mirror; (*Schiff*) stern. **-ei** *neut* fried egg. **-glas** *neut* plate glass. **spiegeln** *v* reflect; (*glänzen*) shine. **Spiegelung** *f* (*pl* -en) reflection.
Spiel [ʃpiːl] *neut* (*pl* -e) game; (*Theater*) play; (*Glücksspiel*) gambling. **aufs Spiel setzen** put at stake. **auf dem Spiel stehen** be at stake. **-automat** *m* slot machine. **-bank** *f* casino. **-brett** *neut* board.
spielen [ʃpiːlən] *v* play; (*Geld*) gamble.
Spieler [ʃpiːlər] *m* (*pl* -), **Spielerin** *f* (*pl* -nen) player; (*Schauspiel*) actor *m*, actress *f*; (*Geld*) gambler. **Spielergebnis** *neut* result, (final) score. **spielerisch** *adj* playful. **Spiel‖feld** *neut* playing field. **-karte** *f* playing card. **-platz** *m* playground. **-zeug** *neut* toy.
Spieß [ʃpiːs] *m* (*pl* -e) spear; (*Bratspieß*) spit. **-bürger** *m* philistine.
Spinat [ʃpiˈnaːt] *m* (*pl* -e) spinach.
Spindel [ʃpindəl] *f* (*pl* -n) spindle, axle.
Spinne [ʃpinə] *f* (*pl* -n) spider. **spinnen** *v* spin; (*umg.*) talk nonsense. *du spinnst ja!* you're crazy!
Spion [ʃpiˈoːn] *m* (*pl* -e) spy. **-age** *f* espionage. **spionieren** *v* spy.
Spirale [ʃpiˈraːlə] *f* (*pl* -n) spiral.
Spirituosen [ʃpirituˈoːzən] *pl* spirits, liquor *sing*.
spitz [ʃpits] *adj* sharp, pointed. **Spitze** *f* (*pl* -n) point, tip. **Spitzen** *pl* (*Gewebe*) lace *sing*. **spitzen** *v* sharpen. **Spitzen‖geschwindigkeit** *f* top speed. **-leistung** *f* maximum performance, record. **Spitzer** *m* (*pl* -) pencil-sharpener. **spitzfindig** *adj* shrewd, ingenious; (*haarspalterisch*) over-critical, hair-splitting. **Spitzname** *m* nickname.
Splitter [ʃplitər] *m* (*pl* -) splinter. **-gruppe** *f* splinter group.
spontan [ʃpɔnˈtaːn] *adj* spontaneous.

Spore ['ʃpɔɪrə] *f* (*pl* **-n**) spore.
Sporn [ʃpɔrn] *m* (*pl* **Sporen**) spur.
spornen *v* spur.
Sport [ʃpɔrt] *m* (*pl* **-e**) sport. **Sport treiben** go in for sport(s). **Sport‖feld** *neut* sports ground. **-ler** *m* (*pl* **-**) sportsman. **-lerin** *f* (*pl* **-nen**) sportswoman. **sportlich** *adj* sporting.
Spott [ʃpɔt] *m* ridicule. **spottbillig** *adj* dirt cheap. **spotten über** ridicule, deride.
spöttisch ['ʃpœtiʃ] *adj* mocking, scornful.
Sprache ['ʃpraːxə] *f* (*pl* **-n**) language, speech. **Sprachfehler** *m* speech defect; (*Gramm*) grammatical error. **sprach‖lich** *adj* linguistic. **-los** *adj* speechless.
***sprechen** ['ʃprɛçən] *v* speak. **sprechen mit** talk to, speak with. **Sprecher** *m* (*pl* **-**), **Sprecherin** *f* (*pl* **-nen**) speaker; (*offiziell*) spokesman.
sprengen ['ʃprɛŋən] *v* explode, blow up; (*aufbrechen*) burst open; (*bespritzen*) sprinkle. **Spreng‖kopf** *m* warhead. **-stoff** *m* explosive.
Sprichwort ['ʃpriçvɔrt] *neut* (*pl* **Sprichwörter**) proverb.
***sprießen** ['ʃpriːsən] *v* sprout.
Spring [ʃpriŋ] *m* (*pl* **-e**) spring. **-brunnen** *m* fountain. **springen** *v* jump, spring; (*Ball*) bounce; (*platzen*) burst, break; (*Schwimmen*) dive. **Springen** *neut* jumping; (*Schwimmen*) diving. **Springer** *m* (*pl* **-**) jumper; (*Schach*) knight. **Spring‖feder** *f* spring. **-seil** *neut* skipping rope.
Sprit [ʃprit] *m* (*pl* **-e**) (*umg.*) gas, juice.
Spritze ['ʃpritsə] *f* (*pl* **-n**) syringe; (*Einspritzung*) injection; (*Tech*) spray. **spritzen** *v* squirt; (*besprengen*) sprinkle; (*Med*) inject.
spröde ['ʃprœːdə] *adj* brittle; (*Person*) reserved, cool.
Sproß [ʃprɔs] *m* (*pl* **Sprosse**) shoot, sprout.
Spruch [ʃprux] *m* (*pl* **Sprüche**) saying, aphorism; (*Jur*) sentence.
Sprudel ['ʃpruːdəl] *m* (*pl* **-**) spring, source (of water); mineral water. **sprudeln** *v* bubble up; (*Mineralwasser, usw.*) sparkle. **-d** *adj* bubbling; sparkling. **Sprudelwasser** *neut* mineral water.
Sprühdose ['ʃpryːdoːzə] *f* spray can, aerosol pack. **sprühen** *v* spray; (*Regen*) drizzle. **Sprühregen** *m* drizzle.
Sprung [ʃpruŋ] *m* (*pl* **Sprünge**) leap, jump; (*Schwimmen*) dive; (*Riß*) crack, split. **-brett** *neut* diving board.

spucken ['ʃpukən] *v* spit.
Spuk [ʃpuːk] *m* (*pl* **-e**) ghost.
Spülbecken ['ʃpyːlbɛkən] *neut* sink.
Spule ['ʃpuːlə] *f* (*pl* **-n**) spool; (*Elek*) coil. **spulen** *v* wind.
spülen ['ʃpyːlən] *v* rinse, wash; (*Geschirr*) wash up; (*WC*) flush. **Spül‖ung** *f* rinsing, washing; flushing. **-wasser** *neut* dishwater.
Spur [ʃpuːr] *f* (*pl* **-en**) track, trail; (*fig*) trace.
spürbar ['ʃpyːrbaɪr] *adj* perceptible, noticeable. **spüren** *v* trace; (*folgen*) track; (*fühlen*) feel. **Spürsinn** *m* shrewdness.
Staat [ʃtaːt] *m* (*pl* **-e**) state. **staatlich** *adj* state. **Staats‖angehörige(r)** *m* citizen, national. **-angehörigkeit** *f* nationality. **-anwalt** *m* public prosecutor. **-bürger** *m* citizen. **-mann** *m* statesman. **-streich** *m* coup d'état.
Stab [ʃtaːp] *m* (*pl* **Stäbe**) staff; (*Metall*) bar; (*Holz*) stick, pole.
stabil [ʃta'biːl] *adj* stable. **-isieren** *v* stabilize. **Stabilität** *f* stability.
Stachel ['ʃtaxəl] *m* (*pl* **-n**) spike, prickle; (*Biene*) sting. **-beere** *f* gooseberry. **-draht** *m* barbed wire. **stachel‖ig** *adj* prickly; stinging. **-n** *v* prick, sting. **Stachelschwein** *neut* porcupine.
Stadion ['ʃtaːdiɔn] *neut* (*pl* **Stadien**) stadium.
Stadt [ʃtat] *f* (*pl* **Städte**) town, city.
städtisch ['ʃtɛtiʃ] *adj* urban; (*Verwaltung*) municipal.
Stadt‖mitte *f* town centre. **-plan** *m* town map. **-rat** *m* town council; (*Person*) councillor.
Staffel ['ʃtafəl] *f* (*pl* **-n**) rung, step; (*Mil*) detachment; (*Lauf*) relay. **-ei** *f* (*pl* **-en**) easel.
Stahl [ʃtaːl] *m* (*pl* **-e**) steel.
Stall [ʃtal] *m* (*pl* **Ställe**) (*Pferde*) stable; (*Hunde*) kennel; (*Schweine*) sty; (*Kuhe*) cowshed.
Stamm [ʃtam] *m* (*pl* **Stämme**) (*Volk*) tribe; (*Baum*) trunk; (*Stengel*) stalk, stem. **-baum** *m* family tree, genealogy; (*Hund*) pedigree. **stammen (von)** *v* (*Ort*) come (from); (*Familie*) be descended (from); (*fig, Gramm*) be derived (from).
stampfen ['ʃtampfən] *v* stamp; (*zerstampfen*) mash, crush.
Stand [ʃtant] *m* (*pl* **Stände**) stand; (*Markt*) stall; (*Höhe*) level, height; (*Stellung*) position, situation.

Standard ['ʃtandart] *m* (*pl* -s) standard.
Standbild ['ʃtantbilt] *neut* statue.
Ständer ['ʃtɛndər] *m* (*pl* -) stand.
Standesamt ['ʃtandəzamt] *neut* registry office.
standhaft ['ʃtandhaft] *adj* steadfast.
Standhaftigkeit *f* steadfastness.
standhalten *v* stand firm.
ständig ['ʃtɛndiç] *adj* permanent; (*laufend*) constant.
Stand‖ort *m* position, station. **–punkt** *m* standpoint.
Stange ['ʃtaŋə] *f* (*pl* -n) pole, bar.
Stanniol [ʃtani'oːl] *neut* (*pl* -e) tinfoil.
Stapel ['ʃtaːpəl] *m* (*pl* -) pile, heap, stack.
stapeln *v* pile up.
Star[1] [ʃtaːr] *m* (*pl* -e) (*Vogel*) starling.
Star[2] *m* (*pl* -s) (*Film*) star.
Star[3] *m* (*pl* -e) (*Med*) cataract.
stark [ʃtark] *adj* strong; (*Zahl*) numerous; (*dick*) thick(set). **starke Erkältung** severe cold. **stark gesucht** in great demand.
Stärke ['ʃtɛrkə] *f* (*pl* -n) strength; (*Dicke*) stoutness; (*Gewalt*) violence; (*Wäsche-, Chem*) starch. **stärken** *v* strengthen.
starr [ʃtar] *adj* rigid; (*Blick*) fixed, staring. **starren** *v* stare. **Starrheit** *f* rigidity; (*Charakter*) obstinacy.
Start [ʃtart] *m* (*pl* -e) start; (*Flugzeug*) take-off. **starten** *v* start; take off. **Starter** *m* (*pl* -) ·(*Mot, Sport*) starter. **–klappe** *f* (*Mot*) choke.
Station [ʃtatsi'oːn] *f* (*pl* -en) station; (*Krankenhaus*) ward.
Statistik [ʃta'tistik] *f* (*pl* -en) statistics. **statistisch** *adj* statistical.
statt [ʃtat] *prep* instead of. **Statt** *f* place, stead.
Stätte ['ʃtɛtə] *f* (*pl* -n) place, spot.
*statt‖finden *v* take place. **–haft** *adj* allowed, permissible. **–lich** *adj* stately; (*Summe*) considerable.
Statut [ʃta'tuːt] *neut* (*pl* -en) statute.
Staub [ʃtaup] *m* dust. **staubig** *adj* dusty. **Staubtuch** *neut* duster.
stauen ['ʃtauən] *v* dam (up); (*Ladung*) stow (away). **sich stauen** accumulate, pile up.
staunen ['ʃtaunən] *v* be astonished. **Staunen** *neut* (*pl* -) astonishment.
Steak [steːk] *neut* (*pl* -s) steak.
*stechen [ʃtɛçən] *v* (*Insekt*) sting; (*Dorn*) prick; (*mit einer Waffe*) stab, jab. **–d** *adj* stinging; (*fig*) piercing. **Stechpalme** *f* holly.

Steck‖brief *m* warrant (for arrest). **–dose** *f* (*Elek*) socket.
stecken ['ʃtɛkən] *v* put, place, insert; (*sich befinden*) be, lie. *etwas in die Tasche stecken* put something in one's pocket. **in Brand stecken** set fire to. *da steckt er!* there he is! that's where he's hiding! *es steckt etwas dahinter* there's more to it than meets the eye. **steckenbleiben** *v* be or get stuck. **Steck‖enpferd** *neut* hobbyhorse; (*fig*) hobby. **–er** *m* (*pl* -) (*Elek*) plug. **–nadel** *f* pin.
Steg [ʃteːk] *m* (*pl* -e) (foot)path; (*Brücke*) (foot)bridge; (*Geige*) bridge.
*stehen ['ʃteːən] *v* stand; (*sein*) be (situated). **in Verdacht stehen** be suspected. **offen stehen** be open. *das Kleid steht dir* (*gut*) the dress suits you. **stehen‖bleiben** *v* (*nicht weitergehen*) come to a standstill, stop; (*nicht umfallen*) remain standing. **–d** *adj* standing; (*ständig*) permanent.
*stehlen ['ʃteːlən] *v* steal. **Stehlen** *neut* (*unz.*) stealing, theft.
steif [ʃtaif] *adj* stiff. **Steifheit** *f* stiffness.
Steig [ʃtaik] *m* (*pl* -e) path. **–bügel** *m* stirrup. **steigen** *v* rise; (*klettern*) climb. **–d** *adj* rising; (*wachsend*) growing.
steigern ['ʃtaigərn] *v* raise, increase. **Steigerung** *f* (*pl* -en) rise, increase.
Steigung ['ʃtaiguŋ] *f* (*pl* -en) rise, incline.
steil [ʃtail] *adj* steep.
Stein [ʃtain] *m* (*pl* -e) stone. **–bock** *m* (*Tier*) ibex; (*Astrol*) Capricorn. **–bruch** *m* quarry. **steinern** *adj* stone. **Steingut** *neut* stoneware, pottery. **steinigen** *v* stone (to death). **Steinzeit** *f* Stone Age.
Stelle ['ʃtɛlə] *f* (*pl* -n) place; (*Arbeit*) job, position; (*in einem Buch*) passage. **an Ort und Stelle** on the spot. **an Stelle von** in place of. **eine Stelle bekleiden** hold a position.
stellen ['ʃtɛlən] *v* put, place; (*Frage*) ask; (*Forderung*) make. **zufriedenstellen** satisfy. *eine Falle stellen* set a trap. **sich stellen** present oneself; (*vortäuschen*) pretend, feign.
Stellen‖angebot *neut* vacancy, vacant position. **–nachweis** *m* employment agency.
Stellung ['ʃtɛluŋ] *f* (*pl* -en) position; (*Arbeit*) post, position; (*Ansicht*) attitude, opinion; (*Körperhaltung*) posture. **–nahme** *f* comment, opinion.

stellvertretend *adj* deputy, delegated. **Stellvertret‖er** *m* deputy, representative. **–ung** *f* representation.
Stelze ['ʃtɛltsə] *f* (*pl* -n) stilt.
Stempel ['ʃtɛmpəl] *m* (*pl* -) stamp. **–geld** *neut* (*umg.*) dole money. **stempeln** *v* stamp. **stempeln gehen** (*umg.*) go on the dole.
Stengel ['ʃtɛŋəl] *m* (*pl* -) stalk.
Stenograph [ʃteno'graːf] *m* (*pl* -en) stenographer. **–ie** *f* shorthand. **Stenotypist(in)** shorthand typist.
Steppe ['ʃtɛpə] *f* (*pl* -n) steppe, prairie.
Sterbe‖bett *neut* deathbed. **–fall** *m* a death.
*sterben ['ʃtɛrbən] *v* die. **Sterben** *neut* death. **sterblich** *adj* mortal. **Sterblichkeit** *f* mortality.
Stereoanlage ['ʃtereoanlaːgə] *f* stereo (system).
steril [ʃte'riːl] *adj* sterile. **–isieren** *v* sterilize.
Stern [ʃtɛrn] *m* (*pl* -e) star. **–bild** *neut* constellation. **–chen** *neut* asterisk. **–kunde** *f* astronomy.
stet [ʃteːt] *or* **stetig** *adj* constant, continual. **stets** *adv* always, constantly.
Steuer ['ʃtɔyər] *f* (*pl* -n) tax.
Steuer‖behörde *f* inland revenue, (*US*) internal revenue. **–berater** *m* tax consultant. **–erklärung** *f* tax return. **–hinterziehung** *f* tax evasion.
steuern ['ʃtɔyərn] *v* steer.
steuerpflichtig ['ʃtɔyərpfliçtiç] *adj* taxable, subject to taxation.
Steuer‖rad *neut* steering wheel. **–säule** *f* steering column.
Steuerung ['ʃtɔyəruŋ] *f* (*pl* -en) steering.
Steuerzahler ['ʃtɔyərtsaːlər] *m* tax-payer.
Stich [ʃtiç] *m* (*pl* -e) prick; (*Insekt*) sting; (*Messer*) stab; (*Nähen*) stitch; (*Kartenspiel*) trick. **im Stich lassen** abandon, leave in the lurch.
sticken ['ʃtikən] *v* embroider. **Stickerei** *f* embroidery.
Stickstoff ['ʃtikʃtɔf] *m* nitrogen.
Stiefbruder ['ʃtiːfbruːdər] *m* stepbrother.
Stiefel ['ʃtiːfəl] *m* (*pl* -) boot.
Stief‖eltern *pl* step-parents. **–kind** *neut* stepchild. **–mutter** *f* stepmother. **–mütterchen** *neut* pansy. **–schwester** *f* stepsister. **–sohn** *m* stepson. **–tochter** *f* stepdaughter. **–vater** *m* stepfather.
Stiel [ʃtiːl] *m* (*pl* -e) handle; (*Bot*) stalk.

Stier [ʃtiːr] *m* (*pl* -e) bull. **–kampf** *m* bullfight.
Stift[1] [ʃtift] *m* (*pl* -e) peg; (*Bleistift*) pencil; (*Pflocke*) pin.
Stift[2] *neut* (*pl* -e *or* -er) (charitable) foundation; (*Kloster*) monastery.
stiften ['ʃtiftən] *v* donate; (*gründen*) found, establish; (*Frieden*) make. **Stifter** *m* founder. **Stiftung** *f* (*pl* -en) (charitable) foundation, institution; (*geschenktes Vermögen*) endowment, bequest.
Stil [ʃtiːl] *m* (*pl* -e) style.
still [ʃtil] *adj* quiet, still; (*schweigend*) silent. **Stille** *f* quiet, stillness, silence. **stillen** *v* allay, stop; (*Schmerz*) soothe; (*Durst*) quench; (*Säugling*) nurse. **stillschweigen** *v* be silent. **–d** *adj* silent; (*fig*) implicit, tacit. **Stillstand** *m* standstill. **stillstehen** *v* stand still; (*aufhören*) stop.
Stimme ['ʃtimə] *f* (*pl* -n) voice; (*Wahl*) vote; (*Musik*) part. **seine Stimme abgeben** cast one's vote. **sich der Stimme enthalten** abstain (from voting). **stimmen** *v* (*richtig sein*) be right *or* true, tally; (*Wahl*) vote; (*Instrument*) tune. **hier stimmt etwas nicht!** something's wrong here! **stimmt schon!** that's all right. **Stimm‖enthaltung** *f* abstention. **–recht** *neut* franchise. **–ung** *f* (*pl* -en) mood, atmosphere; (*Musik*) tuning.
*stinken ['ʃtiŋkən] *v* stink.
Stipendium [ʃti'pɛndium] *neut* (*pl* Stipendien) scholarship, (student) grant.
Stirn [ʃtirn] *f* (*pl* -en) forehead. **die Stirn runzeln** frown.
stöbern ['ʃtøːbərn] *v* rummage (about).
Stock [ʃtɔk] *m* (*pl* Stöcke) stick, rod; (*Musik*) baton; (*Etage*) storey. **stockdunkel** *adj* pitch dark.
stocken ['ʃtɔkən] *v* stoop, come to a standstill; (*Milch*) curdle. **Stockung** *f* (*pl* -en) standstill, stop; (*Verkehr*) congestion, jam.
Stockwerk ['ʃtɔkvɛrk] *neut* floor, storey.
Stoff [ʃtɔf] *m* (*pl* -e) matter; (*Gewebe, fig*) material.
stöhnen ['ʃtøːnən] *v* groan.
Stolle ['ʃtɔlə] *f* (*pl* -n) *or* **Stollen** *m* (*pl* -) (German) Christmas cake.
stolpern ['ʃtɔlpərn] *v* stumble.
stolz [ʃtɔlts] *adj* proud. **Stolz** *m* pride.
stopfen ['ʃtɔpfən] *v* stuff, fill; (*Strümpfe*) darn; (*sättigen*) fill up; (*Med*) constipate.

Stopp [ʃtɔp] *m (unz.)* hitchhiking.
Stoppel ['ʃtɔpəl] *f (pl -n)* stubble.
stoppen ['ʃtɔpən] *v* stop. **Stopplicht** *neut* brake light.
Stöpsel ['ʃtœpsəl] *m (pl -)* stopper; *(Elek)* plug.
Storch [ʃtɔrç] *m (pl Störche)* stork.
stören ['ʃtœɪrən] *v* disturb; *(belästigen)* bother, trouble; *(Radio)* interfere. **–d** *adj* disturbing, troublesome. **Störenfried** *m* troublemaker. **Störung** *f (pl -en)* disturbance; trouble; *(Radio)* interference.
Stoß [ʃtoɪs] *m (pl Stöße)* push, shove; *(Schlag)* blow; *(Tritt)* kick; *(Haufen)* heap. **–dämpfer** *m* shock-absorber.
stoßen *v* push, shove; knock; *(fig)* take offence. **stoßen an** run across. **sich stoßen an** bump into *or* against; *(fig)* take offence at. **Stoß‖stange** *f* bumper. **–zahn** *m* tusk.
stottern ['ʃtɔtərn] *v* stutter, stammer.
Straf‖anstalt *f* prison, penal institution. **–arbeit** *f (Schule)* punishment, lines *pl*.
strafbar *adj* punishable.
Strafe ['ʃtraɪfə] *f (pl -n)* punishment; *(fig)* penalty; *(Jur)* sentence. **strafen** *v* punish.
Straferlaß *m* pardon; *(allgemeiner)* amnesty.
straff [ʃtraf] *adj* tight, taught; *(fig)* strict, stern.
Straf‖geld *neut* fine. **–gericht** *neut* criminal court.
sträflich ['ʃtrɛɪfliç] *adj* punishable. **Sträfling** *m* prisoner.
Straf‖recht *neut* criminal law. **–tat** *f* offence.
Strahl [ʃtraɪl] *m (pl -en)* ray, beam; *(Blitz)* flash; *(Wasser)* jet. **strahlen** *v* radiate; *(fig)* beam. **–d** *adj* beaming. **Strahlmotor** *m* jet engine. **Strahlung** *f* radiation.
Strand [ʃtrant] *m (pl -e)* beach, shore. **stranden** *v* run aground; *(fig)* founder.
strapazieren [ʃtrapa'tsiɪrən] *v* fatigue, tire; *(abnutzen)* wear out.
Straße ['ʃtraɪsə] *f (pl -n)* street. **Straßen‖bahn** *f* tram, *(US)* street car. **–kreuzung** *f* crossing. **–laterne** *f* street lamp. **–sperre** *f* roadblock. **–überführung** *f* overpass. **–unterführung** *f* underpass.
sträuben ['ʃtrɔybən] *v* ruffle (up). **sich sträuben** *(Haare)* stand up on end; *(fig)* struggle (against), resist.
Strauch [ʃtraux] *m (pl Sträucher)* bush.

Strauß¹ [ʃtraus] *m (pl -e) (Vogel)* ostrich.
Strauß² *m (pl Sträuße)* bouquet, bunch (of flowers).
streben ['ʃtreɪbən] *v* strive.
Strecke ['ʃtrɛkə] *f (pl -n)* stretch, distance; *(Math, Sport)* distance; *(Teilschnitt)* section. **strecken** *v* stretch (out), extend.
Streich [ʃtraiç] *m (pl -e)* stroke, blow; *(Peitsche)* lash; *(Possen)* trick, prank.
streicheln ['ʃtraiçəln] *v* stroke, pet.
*streichen ['ʃtraiçən] *v* stroke, rub; *(Farbe)* paint; *(gehen)* wander, ramble. **Streich‖instrument** *neut* string instrument. **–musik** *f* string music. **–quartett** *neut* string quartet.
Streife ['ʃtraifə] *f (pl -n)* patrol; *(Streifzug)* stroll, look around.
Streifen ['ʃtraifən] *m (pl -)* stripe; *(Land)* strip.
streifen ['ʃtraifən] *v* streak, stripe; *(berühren)* brush (against), touch; *(wandern)* wander, roam.
Streik [ʃtraik] *m (pl -s)* strike. **–brecher** *m* strike-breaker; *(umg.)* scab. **streiken** *v* (go on) strike.
Streit [ʃtrait] *m (pl -e)* dispute, quarrel; *(Kampf)* conflict; *(Schlägerei)* fight, brawl. **streiten** *v* dispute, quarrel. **sich streiten um** quarrel about, fight over. **Streitfrage** *f* matter in dispute. **streit‖ig** *adj* contested; *(fraglich)* controversial. **–lustig** *adj* quarrelsome, aggressive.
streng [ʃtrɛŋ] *adj* stern, severe, strict. **Strenge** *f* severity, strictness.
streuen ['ʃtrɔyən] *v* scatter, spread.
Strich [ʃtriç] *m (pl -e)* stroke, line; *(Vogel)* flight; *(Gebiet)* district; *(Kompaß)* compass point. **–punkt** *m* semicolon.
Strick [ʃtrik] *m (pl -e)* cord, string, (thin) rope; *(Kind)* rascal. **–arbeit** *f* knitting; *(Artikel)* knitwear. **stricken** *v* knit. **Strick‖maschine** *f* knitting machine. **–nadel** *f* knitting needle. **–zeug** *neut* knitting.
strittig ['ʃtritiç] *adj* questionable, debatable; *(Angelegenheit)* disputed.
Stroh [ʃtroɪ] *neut* straw. **–dach** *neut* thatched roof.
Strolch [ʃtrɔlç] *m (pl -e)* tramp, vagabond. **strolchen** *v* roam, stroll about.
Strom [ʃtroɪm] *m (pl Ströme) (Fluß)* (large) river; *(Strömung, Elek)* current;

(*fig*) stream. **strom‖abwärts** *adv* downstream. **–aufwärts** *adv* upstream.
strömen [ʃtrœɪmən] *v* stream, flow; (*Regen*) pour.
Strom‖erzeuger *m* generator. **–sperre** *f* power cut.
Strömung ['ʃtrœɪmuŋ] *f* (*pl* -en) current.
Struktur [ʃtruk'tuːr] *f* (*pl* -en) structure.
Strumpf [ʃtrumpf] *m* (*pl* **Strümpfe**) stocking; (*Socke*) sock.
Stube ['ʃtuːbə] *f* (*pl* -n) room, chamber. **stubenrein** *adj* house-trained.
Stück [ʃtyk] *neut* (*pl* -e) piece; (*Theater*) play; (*Vieh*) head. **in Stücke gehen** fall to pieces. **Stückchen** *neut* bit, little piece; (*Papier*) scrap. **stückeln** *v* cut *or* chop into pieces.
Student [ʃtu'dɛnt] *m* (*pl* -en) student. **–enheim** *neut* hall of residence, (*US*) dorm(itory). **Studentin** *f* (*pl* -nen) (woman) student.
Studien‖direktor *m* headmaster, (*US*) principal. **–plan** *m* syllabus.
studieren [ʃtu'diːrən] *v* study. **Studio** *neut* studio. **Studium** *neut* studies *pl*; (*Untersuchung*) study.
Stufe ['ʃtuːfə] *f* (*pl* -n) step; (*Leiter*) rung; (*fig*) stage. **stufen‖los** *adj* infinitely variable. **–weise** *adv* gradually.
Stuhl [ʃtuːl] *m* (*pl* **Stühle**) chair; (*ohne Lehne*) stool. **–gang** *m* bowel movement.
stumm [ʃtum] *adj* mute, dumb; (*schweigend*) silent. **Stumme(r)** *m* mute, dumb person.
Stummel ['ʃtuməl] *m* (*pl* -) stump. **Stumm‖film** *m* silent film. **–heit** *f* dumbness.
stumpf [ʃtumpf] *adj* blunt; (*Mensch*) dull. **Stumpf‖heit** *f* bluntness; dullness. **–sinn** *m* stupidity. **stumpfsinnig** *adj* stupid, dull-witted.
Stunde ['ʃtundə] *f* (*pl* -n) hour; (*Unterricht*) lesson. **Stunden‖plan** *m* timetable. **–satz** *m* hourly rate.
stupid [ʃtu'piːt] *adj* half-witted, idiotic. **stur** [ʃtuːr] *adj* stubborn.
Sturm [ʃturm] *m* (*pl* **Stürme**) storm; (*Angriff*) attack.
stürmen ['ʃtyrmən] *v* storm; (*Wind*) blow. **Stürmer** *m* (*pl* -) assailant; (*Fußball*) forward. **stürmisch** *adj* stormy.
Sturz [ʃturts] *m* (*pl* **Stürze**) fall; (*Zusammenbruch*) collapse.
stürzen ['ʃtyrtsən] *v* (*fallen*) fall (down); (*umkippen*) overturn; (*Regierung*) over-

throw; (*eilen*) dash, rush. **sich stürzen auf** rush at.
Sturzhelm ['ʃturtshɛlm] *m* crash-helmet.
Stute ['ʃtuːtə] *f* (*pl* -n) mare. **–nfüllen** *neut* foal, filly.
Stütze ['ʃtytsə] *f* (*pl* -n) prop, support.
stutzen[1] ['ʃtutsən] *v* stop short, be startled.
stutzen[2] *v* (*schneiden*) clip, trim; (*Schwanz*) dock.
stützen ['ʃtytsən] *v* prop, support. **Stützpunkt** *m* fulcrum; (*Mil*) stronghold.
subjektiv [subjɛk'tiːf] *adj* subjective.
subtil [zup'tiːl] *adj* subtle.
Subvention [zupvɛntsi'oɪn] *f* (*pl* -en) subsidy.
Suche ['zuːxə] *f* (*pl* -n) search. **suchen** *v* look for, search for. **Sucher** *m* (*pl* -) searcher. **Sucht** *f* (*pl* **Süchte**) addiction; (*fig*) craving, passion.
süchtig ['zyçtiç] *adj* addicted. **Süchtige(r)** *m* addict.
Süd(en) [zyːt ('zyːdən)] *m* south. **Süd‖afrika** *neut* South Africa. **–amerika** *neut* South America. **–länder(in)** southerner.
südlich ['zyːtliç] *adj* southern.
Südost(en) [zyːd'ɔst(ən)] *m* southeast. **südöstlich** *adj* southeast(ern); (*Wind, Richtung*) southeasterly.
Südpol ['zyːtpoɪl] *m* South Pole.
südwärts ['zyːtvɛrts] *adv* southwards.
Südwest(en) [zyːd'vɛst(ən)] *m* southwest. **südwestlich** *adj* southwest(ern); (*Wind, Richtung*) southwesterly.
Sühne [zyːnə] *f* (*pl* -n) atonement. **sühnen** *v* atone for.
Sultanine [zulta'niːnə] *f* (*pl* -n) sultana.
Sülze ['zyltsə] *f* (*pl* -n) brawn.
Summe ['zumə] *f* (*pl* -n) sum total; (*Geld*) sum, amount.
summen ['zumən] *v* buzz, hum.
summieren [zu'miːrən] *v* add up. **Summierung** *f* summation.
Sumpf [zumpf] *m* (*pl* **Sümpfe**) swamp, marsh.
Sund [zunt] *m* (*pl* -e) sound, channel.
Sünde ['zyndə] *f* (*pl* -n) sin. **–nbock** *m* scapegoat. **Sünder(in)** sinner. **sündhaft** *adj* sinful.
Suppe ['zupə] *f* (*pl* -n) soup.
süß [zyːs] *adj* sweet. **Süße** *f* sweetness. **süßen** *v* sweeten. **Süßigkeit** *f* sweetness. **Süßigkeiten** *pl* sweets, (*US*) candy *sing*. **süßlich** *adj* sweetish; (*fig*) slushy, senti-

---

Symbol

---

mental. **Süß‖waren** pl sweets, (US) candy sing. **-wasser** neut fresh water.

Symbol [zym'boːl] neut (pl -e) symbol. **symbol‖isch** adj symbolic. **-isieren** v symbolize.

sympathisch [zym'paːtiʃ] adj likeable, congenial.

Symptom [zymp'toːm] neut (pl -e) symptom.

Synagoge [zyna'goːgə] f (pl -n) synagogue.

synchron ['zynkron] adj synchronous. **-isieren** v synchronize.

Synthese [zyn'teːzə] f (pl -n) synthesis.

Syphilis ['zyːfilis] f syphilis.

System [zys'teːm] neut (pl -e) system. **systematisch** adj systematic.

Szene ['stseːnə] f (pl -n) scene.

T

Tabak ['taːbak] m (pl -e) tobacco.

Tabelle [ta'bɛlə] f (pl -n) table, list. **tabellenförmig** adj tabular.

Tablette [ta'bletə] f (pl -n) pill, tablet.

Tadel ['taːdəl] m blame; reproach, reprimand; (Schule) bad mark. **tadellos** adj faultless. **tadeln** v reproach, scold, criticize.

Tafel ['taːfəl] f (pl -n) board; (Schule) blackboard; (Schokolade) bar; (Tabelle) table, chart. **die Tafel decken** lay the table.

Tag [taːk] m (pl -e) day. **am Tag** by day. **Tages‖anbruch** m dawn, daybreak. **-licht** neut daylight. **-zeitung** f daily (newspaper). **täglich** adj daily.

Taille ['taljə] f waist.

Takelwerk ['taːkəlverk] neut rigging.

Takt [takt] m (Musik) time, beat; (Tech) stroke; (Höflichkeit) tact. **Zweitaktmotor** m two-stroke engine.

Taktik ['taktik] f (pl -en) tactics pl. **taktisch** adj tactical.

taktlos ['taktloːs] adj tactless.

Tal [taːl] neut (pl Täler) valley, vale.

Talent [ta'lent] neut (pl -e) talent, gift. **talentiert** adj talented, gifted.

Talk [talk] m talcum.

Tampon [tã'põ] m (pl -s) (Med) swab; (für Frauen) tampon.

tändeln ['tɛndəln] v flirt; (langsam gehen,

usw.) dawdle, dally. **Tändelei** f (pl -en) flirtation.

Tang [taŋ] m (pl -e) seaweed.

Tank [taŋk] m (pl -e) tank. **tanken** v (Mot) refuel, fill up. **Tank‖schiff** neut tanker. **-stelle** f petrol station.

Tanne ['tanə] f fir. **Tannen‖baum** m fir-tree. **-zapfen** m fir-cone.

Tante ['tantə] f (pl -n) aunt.

Tanz [tants] m (pl Tänze) dance; (Tanzen) dancing. **tanzen** v dance. **Tänzer** m (pl -), **Tänzerin** f (pl -nen) dancer. **Tanz‖lokal** neut dancehall. **-platz** m dance-floor.

Tapete [ta'peːtə] f (pl -n) wallpaper. **tapezieren** v paper, decorate.

tapfer ['tapfər] adj brave, courageous. **Tapferkeit** f bravery, courage.

tappen ['tapən] v grope, fumble about.

Tarif [ta'riːf] m (pl -e) price list. **-verhandlungen** pl collective bargaining sing.

tarnen ['tarnən] v camouflage. **Tarnung** f camouflage.

Tasche ['taʃə] f (pl -n) pocket; suitcase; handbag; (Schule) satchel; (Aktentasche) briefcase. **Taschen‖dieb** m pickpocket. **-geld** neut pocket money. **-lampe** f torch. **-messer** neut penknife.

Tasse ['tasə] f (pl -n) cup. **eine Tasse Kaffee** a cup of coffee.

Taste ['tastə] f (pl -n) (Klavier, Schreibmaschine) key; (push)button. **tasten** v feel, touch. **Tastenbrett** (Musik) neut also **Tastatur** keyboard.

Tat [taːt] f (pl -en) deed, act. **in der Tat** in reality, really.

tätig ['tɛːtiç] adj active, busy, employed. **tätig sein als** be employed as, practise. **tätig sein bei** work for. **Tätigkeit** f (pl -en) activity; (Beruf) work, occupation.

tätowieren [tɛto'viːrən] v tattoo. **Tätowierung** f (pl -en) tattoo.

Tatsache ['taːtzaxə] f (pl -n) fact. **tatsächlich** adj real, actual. adv really, actually. interj really? is that so?

Tatze ['tatsə] f (pl -n) paw.

Tau¹ [tau] neut (pl -e) (Seil) rope, cable.

Tau² m (unz.) dew. **Tauwetter** neut thaw.

taub [taup] adj deaf.

Taube ['taubə] f (pl -n) pigeon, dove.

taubstumm ['taupʃtum] adj deaf and dumb. **Taubstumme(r)** deaf mute.

tauchen ['tauxən] v dive, plunge; immerse, dip. **Tauchen** neut diving. **Taucher** m (pl -) diver.

tauen ['tauən] v thaw, melt.
Taufe ['taufə] f (pl -n) baptism, christening. **taufen** v baptize, christen. **Taufname** m Christian name.
taugen ['taugən] v taugen zu be good or fit for. **zu nichts taugen** be useless or worthless. **Taugenichts** m (pl -e) good-for-nothing.
taumeln ['tauməln] v stagger, reel.
Tausch [tauʃ] m (pl -e) exchange. **tausch‖bar** adj exchangeable. **–en** v exchange, swap.
täuschen ['tɔyʃən] v deceive, delude. **–d** adj deceptive.
Tauschhandel ['tauʃhandəl] m barter.
Täuschung ['tɔyʃuŋ] f (pl -en) delusion, illusion; (Schwindel) deception, fraud.
tausend ['tauzənt] adj thousand.
Taxe ['taksə] f (pl -n) charge, fee; (Schätzung) valuation. **taxieren** v value, assess.
Taxi ['taksi] neut or m (pl -s) taxi. **–fahrer** m taxi-driver.
Technik ['tɛçnik] f (pl -n) technique; engineering, technology. **–er** m (pl -) technician. **Technologie** f technology. **technologisch** technological.
Tee [teɪ] m (pl) tea. **–kanne** f teapot. **–löffel** m teaspoon. **–service** neut tea-set.
Teer [teɪr] m (pl -e) tar, pitch.
Teich [taiç] m (pl -e) pond.
Teig [taik] m (pl -e) dough; (flüssig) batter. **–waren** pl noodles pl.
Teil [tail] m or neut (pl -e) part; share, portion. **teilbar** adj divisible. **Teil‖beschäftigung** f part-time work. **–chen** neut particle. **teil‖en** v divide; share out. **–haben** take part (in). **Teilnahme** f participation; interest; (Mitleid) sympathy. **teil‖nehmen** v take part in. **–s** adv partly. **Teilung** f (pl -en) division, partition; sharing out, distribution. **teilweise** adj partial. adv partly.
Telegramm [tele'gram] neut (pl -e) telegram.
Telephon [tele'foɪn] neut (pl -e) telephone. **–buch** neut telephone directory. **telephonieren** v telephone, ring up. **Telephon‖zelle** f call box. **–zentrale** f telephone exchange.
Teleskop [tele'skoɪp] neut (pl -e) telescope.
Teller ['tɛlər] m (pl -) plate; (Tech) disc.
Tempel ['tɛmpəl] m (pl -) temple.

Temperament [tempera'mɛnt] neut (pl -e) temperament, disposition. **temperamentvoll** adj high-spirited, lively.
Temperatur [tempera'tuɪr] f temperature.
Tempo ['tɛmpo] neut (pl -s or -pi) pace, tempo.
temporär [tempo'rɛɪr] adj temporary.
Tendenz [tɛn'dɛnts] f (pl -en) tendency, propensity.
Tennis ['tɛnis] neut tennis. **–platz** m tennis court. **–schläger** m tennis racket.
Tenor [tɛ'nɔr] m (pl -e) tenor.
Teppich ['tɛpiç] m (pl -e) carpet, rug; (Wand) tapestry.
Termin [tɛr'miɪn] m (pl -e) fixed date; closing date, deadline. **–geschäft** neut (Komm) futures pl.
Terpentinöl [tɛrpɛn'tiɪnœɪl] neut turpentine.
Terrasse [tɛ'rasə] f (pl -n) terrace.
Terror ['tɛrɔr] m terror. **–ismus** m terrorism. **–ist(in)** terrorist. **terroristisch** adj terrorist.
Testament [testa'mɛnt] neut (pl -e) will; (Bibel) testament. **Testaments‖bestätigung** f probate. **–vollstrecker** m executor.
testieren [tɛs'tiɪrən] v make one's will; bequeath.
teuer ['tɔyər] adj expensive, dear; (lieb) dear, cherished. adv dearly. **Teuerung** f (pl -en) rising prices pl, increase in the cost of living. **Teuerungszulage** f cost-of-living bonus.
Teufel ['tɔyfəl] m devil, Satan. **Teufels‖beschwörung** f exorcism. **–skreis** m vicious circle. **teuflisch** adj devilish, diabolical.
Text [tɛkst] m (pl -e) text; (Lied) lyrics pl; (Oper) libretto. **–buch** neut libretto.
Textilien [tɛks'tiɪliən] or **Textilwaren** pl textiles.
Theater [te'aɪtər] neut (pl -) theatre; (umg.) fuss, to-do. **theatralisch** adj theatrical.
Thema ['teɪmə] neut (pl Themen) theme, subject.
Theologe [teo'loɪgə] m (pl -n) theologian. **Theologie** f theology. **theologisch** adj theological.
Theoretiker [teo'reɪtikər] m (pl -) theorist. **theoretisch** adj theoretical. **Theorie** f (pl -n) theory.
Therapie [tera'piɪ] f (pl -n) therapy

thermisch ['tɛrmɪʃ] *adj* thermal.
Thermometer [tɛrmo'meɪtər] *neut* (*pl* -) thermometer.
Thermosflasche ['tɛrmɔsflaʃə] *f* vacuum flask, thermos .
Thermostat [tɛrmo'ʃtaɪt] *m* (*pl* -en) thermostat.
These [teɪzə] *f* (*pl* -n) thesis.
Thrombose [trɔm'boɪzə] *f* (*pl* -n) thrombosis.
Thron [troɪn] *m* (*pl* -e) throne. **-erbe** *m* heir to the throne.
Thunfisch ['tuɪnfɪʃ] *m* tuna.
Thüringen ['tyrɪŋən] *neut* Thuringia.
Thymian ['tymian] *m* thyme.
ticken ['tikən] *v* tick.
tief [tiɪf] *adj* deep; (*Musik*) low(-pitched), bass; (*Stimme*) deep; (*Sinn*) profound; extreme. *adv* deep; (*Atmen*) deeply. **aus tiefstem Herzen** from the bottom of one's heart. **tief in der Nacht** at dead of night. **tiefbewegt** *adj* deeply moved. **Tief‖druckgebeit** *neut* low-pressure area. **-e** *f* depth. **-ebene** *f* lowlands *pl*. **tief‖gekühlt** *adj* deep-frozen. **-greifend** *adj* far-reaching. **Tief‖kühltruhe** *f* freezer, deep freeze. **-punkt** *m* low(est) point.
Tiegel ['tiɪgəl] *m* (*pl* -) saucepan.
Tier [tiɪr] *neut* (*pl* -e) animal, beast. **hohes Tier** (*umg.*) big shot. **Tier‖arzt** *m* veterinary surgeon, (*umg.*) vet. **-garten** *m* zoological gardens *pl*. **tierisch** *adj* animal; (*brutal*) bestial, brutal. **Tier‖kreis** *m* zodiac. **-welt** *f* animal kingdom, fauna. **-zucht** *f* livestock breeding.
Tiger ['tiɪgər] *m* (*pl* -) tiger.
tilgen ['tilgən] *v* (*streichen*) delete, erase; (*ausrotten*) exterminate; (*Schuld*) pay off. **Tilgung** *f* (*pl* -en) deletion; extermination; discharge, repayment.
Tinte ['tintə] *f* ink. **-nklecks** *m* ink-stain.
Tip [tip] *m* (*pl* -s) hint; (*Sport*) tip.
tippen ['tipən] *v* tap; (*mit der Schreibmaschine*) type. **Tippfehler** *m* typing error.
Tisch [tiʃ] *m* (*pl* -e) table. **den Tisch decken/abdecken** lay/clear the table. **Tich‖gast** *m* diner, guest (at table). **-gesellschaft** *f* dinner party.
Tischler ['tiʃlər] *m* carpenter, cabinet-maker. **-arbeit** *f* carpentry.
Titel ['tiɪtəl] *m* (*pl* -) title. **-bild** *neut* frontispiece. **-kopf** *m* heading.
Toast [toɪst] *m* (*pl* -e) toast. **toasten** *v* toast. **Toaster** *m* (*pl* -) toaster.

toben ['toɪbən] *v* rage, rave. **tobsüchtig** *adj* raving, frantic.
Tochter ['tɔxtər] *f* (*pl* **Töchter**) daughter.
Tod [toɪt] *m* (*pl* -e) death. **Todes‖anzeige** *f* obituary. **-fall** *m* (a case of) death. **-kampf** *m* death throes *pl*. **-strafe** *f* death penalty. **-wunde** *f* mortal wound.
Todfeind *m* deadly enemy. **tödlich** *adj* deadly, fatal, lethal. **todmüde** *adj* dead tired.
Toilette [toa'lɛtə] *f* (*pl* -n) toilet, lavatory; toilette; dressing-table. **-papier** *neut* toilet paper.
tolerant [tole'rant] *adj* tolerant. **Toleranz** *f* toleration. **tolerieren** *v* tolerate.
toll [tɔl] *adj* raving mad, crazy, wild; (*umg.*) fantastic. **Toll‖heit** *f* (*pl* -en) madness; fury. **-wut** *f* rabies.
Tölpel ['tœlpəl] *m* (*pl* -e) awkward person; oaf, boor.
Tomate [to'maɪtə] *f* (*pl* -n) tomato.
Ton¹ [toɪn] *m* (*pl* -e) clay.
Ton² *m* (*pl* **Töne**) sound; (*Musik*) tone, note; accent, stress; tone, fashion. **-art** *f* (*Musik*) key, pitch. **-band** *neut* magnetic tape. **-bandgerät** *neut* tape-recorder. **-blende** *f* tone control.
tönen ['tœɪnən] *v* ring, resound; (*Foto*) shade, tint.
Ton‖fall *m* intonation; (*Musik*) cadence. **-fülle** *f* volume (of sound). **-leiter** *f* (musical) scale. **-spur** *f* soundtrack.
Tonne ['tɔnə] *f* (*pl* -n) ton; cask, barrel.
Topf [tɔpf] *m* (*pl* **Töpfe**) pot.
Töpfchen ['tœpfçən] *neut* (*pl* -) (child's) potty. **Töpfer** *m* (*pl* -) potter. **-waren** *pl* pottery *sing*.
Tor¹ [toɪr] *m* (*pl* -en) fool.
Tor² *neut* (*pl* -e) gate; (*Sport*) goal. **-schütze** *m* (football) scorer.
Torf [tɔrf] *m* peat.
Torheit ['tɔrhait] *f* (*pl* -en) folly.
töricht ['tœɪriçt] *adj* foolish. **Törin** *f* (*pl* -nen) fool, foolish woman.
torkeln ['tɔrkəln] *v* stagger, reel.
Torpedo [tɔr'peɪdo] *m* (*pl* -s) torpedo. **-boot** *neut* torpedo boat.
Torte ['tɔrtə] *f* (*pl* -n) (fruit) flan, tart, gâteau.
Tor‖waächter *m* (*pl* -) gatekeeper. **-wart** *m* goalkeeper.
tot [toɪt] *adj* dead.
total [to'taɪl] *adj* total, complete.
Tote(r) ['toɪtə(r)] dead person.

töten ['tœɪtən] v kill.
Toten‖bett neut deathbed. **–gräber** m
gravedigger. **–hemd** neut shroud.
–wagen m hearse.
totgeboren ['toɪtgəbɔɪrən] adj stillborn.
sich totlachen v split one's sides laughing. **totschießen** v shoot dead.
Totschlag ['toɪtʃlak] m manslaughter.
tot‖schlagen v slay, kill; (Zeit) waste
(time). **–schweigen** v hush up. **–sicher**
adj absolutely or dead certain.
Tötung ['tœɪtuŋ] f (pl **-en**) killing.
Tour [tuɪr] f (pl **-en**) tour, trip. **–ismus** m
tourism. **–ist** m (pl **-en**) tourist.
Trab [traɪp] m trot. **traben** v trot.
Tracht [traxt] f (pl **-en**) costume, dress.
Tradition [traditsi'oɪn] f (pl **-en**) tradition.
traditionell adj traditional.
träge ['trɛɪgə] adj (faul) lazy; (langsam)
ponderous, slow; (schläfrig) sleepy.
***tragen** ['traɪgən] v carry; (Kleider) wear;
(stützen) support; (ertragen) endure,
bear.
Träger ['trɛɪgər] m (pl **-**) carrier; (Mensch)
porter; (Balken) girder.
Trägheit ['trɛɪkhait] f laziness; (Langsamkeit) slowness.
tragisch ['traɪgiʃ] adj tragic. **Tragödie** f (pl
-n) tragedy.
Trainer ['trɛɪnər] m (pl **-**) (Sport) coach,
trainer. **trainieren** v train. **Training** neut
training. **–sanzug** m track suit.
Traktor ['traktɔr] m (pl **-en**) tractor.
trampeln ['trampəln] v trample, stamp.
trampen ['trɛmpən] v hitchhike.
Tran [traɪn] m (pl **-e**) whale oil.
tranchieren [trãˈʃiɪrən] v carve.
Tranchiermesser neut carving knife.
Träne ['trɛɪnə] f (pl **-n**) tear.
Trank [traŋk] m (pl **Tränke**) drink.
tränken ['trɛŋkən] v water; (durchtränken)
soak.
transatlantisch [transat'lantiʃ] adj transatlantic.
Transmission [transmisi'oɪn] f (pl **-en**)
transmission.
Transport [trans'pɔrt] m (pl **-e**) transportation. **transportieren** v transport. **Transportunternehmen** neut haulage or shipping company.
Tratte ['tratə] f (pl **-n**) bill of exchange,
draft.
Traube ['traubə] f (pl **-n**) grape; bunch of
grapes. **Trauben‖lese** f vintage. **–saft** m
grape juice. **–zucker** m glucose.

trauen ['trauən] v trust; (Ehepaar) marry,
join in wedlock. **sich trauen** dare.
Trauer ['trauər] f sorrow, grief; (für Tote)
mourning. **–anzeige** f death notice.
–gottesdienst m funeral service. **trauern**
v grieve, mourn. **Trauer‖spiel** neut tragedy. **–weide** f weeping willow. **traurig** adj
sad.
Traufe ['traufə] f (pl **-n**) eaves pl. **aus dem
Regen in die Traufe** out of the frying
pan into the fire. **Traufrinne** f gutter.
traulich ['trauliç] adj snug, cosy, comfortable.
Traum [traum] m (pl **Träume**) dream.
–bild neut vision.
träumen ['trɔymən] v dream. **Träumer** m
(pl **-**) dreamer. **–ei** f (pl **-en**) daydream,
reverie. **träumerisch** adj dreamy.
Trau‖ring m wedding ring.
***treffen** ['trɛfən] v (begegnen) meet;
(erreichen) hit; (betreffen) concern;
(Vorkehrungen) make; (Maßnahmen)
take. **sich treffen** meet; (zufällig geschehen) happen. **Treffen** neut meeting.
treffend adj striking; (Antwort) pertinent.
Treffpunkt m meeting place.
***treiben** ['traibən] v drive, move;
(drängen) urge, impel; (Metall) work;
(Pflanzen) force; (tun) do, occupy oneself
with; (Blüte) blossom; (im Wasser) float.
treibend adj driving; (im Wasser) floating. **Treib‖er** m driver; (Vieh) drover.
–haus neut hothouse. **–kraft** f moving
force. **–stoff** m fuel.
trennbar ['trɛnbaɪr] adj separable. **trennen**
v separate; (abtrennen) sever, cut; (Telef)
cut off. **sich trennen** part, separate. **Trennung** f (pl **-en**) separation.
Treppe ['trɛpə] f (pl **-n**) staircase, stairs
pl. **–ngeländer** neut handrail, banister.
***treten** ['treɪtən] v tread, step; (betreten)
step on; (stoßen) kick. **Trethebel** m
treadle.
treu [trɔy] adj loyal, faithful, true; (redlich) honest, sincere. **Treubruch** m disloyalty, breach of faith. **Treue** f loyalty,
faithfulness. **treu‖lich** adj loyal, faithful.
–los adj disloyal, faithless.
Tribüne [tri'byɪnə] f (pl **-n**) platform; (für
Zuschauer) gallery.
Trichter ['triçtər] m (pl **-**) funnel;
(Bombe) crater.
Trick [trik] m (pl **-s**) trick. **–film** m
animated cartoon.

Trieb [triːp] *m* (*pl* -e) force, drive; (*Antrieb*) impulse; (*Bot*) shoot; (*Instinkt*) instinct.
*triefen ['triːfən] *v* trickle, drip. **triefnaß** *adj* dripping wet.
triftig ['triftiç] *adj* convincing, plausible.
Triller ['trilər] *m* (*pl* -) trill. **trillern** *v* trill.
trinkbar ['triŋkbaːr] *adj* drinkable, potable. **trinken** *v* drink. **Trink‖er** *m* (*pl* -) drinker. **–geld** *neut* tip. **–halm** *m* (drinking) straw. **–spruch** *m* toast.
Tripper ['tripər] *m* (*pl* -) gonorrhoea.
Tritt [trit] *m* (*pl* -e) step, tread; (*Stoß*) kick; (*Fußspur*) footprint. **–leiter** *f* stepladder.
Triumph [tri'umf] *m* (*pl* -e) triumph.
trocken ['trɔkən] *adj* dry. **Trockenheit** *f* dryness. **trocknen** *v* dry. **Trockner** *m* (*pl* -) drier.
Trödel ['trœːdəl] *m* junk, rubbish. **trödeln** *v* dawdle; (*handeln*) trade in old junk.
Trommel ['trɔməl] *f* (*pl* -n) drum. **–fell** *neut* drumskin; (*Anat*) eardrum. **trommeln** *v* drum. **Trommler** *m* (*pl* -) drummer.
Trompete [trɔm'peːtə] *f* (*pl* -n) trumpet.
Tropen ['troːpən] *pl* tropics.
tröpfeln ['trœpfəln] *v* trickle, drip.
Tropfen ['trɔpfən] *m* (*pl* -) drop.
tropisch ['troːpiʃ] *adj* tropical.
Trost [troːst] *m* consolation, solace, comfort.
trösten ['trœːstən] *v* console, solace, comfort. **sich trösten mit** take comfort in.
trostlos ['trɔstloːs] *adj* disconsolate.
Tröstung ['trœːstuŋ] *f* (*pl* -en) consolation, comfort.
Trott [trɔt] *m* (*pl* -e) trot.
Trottel ['trɔtəl] *m* (*pl* -) idiot, fool.
trotz [trɔts] *prep* despite, in spite of. **Trotz** *m* defiance; (*Eigensinn*) obstinacy. **trotzdem** *conj, adv* nevertheless. **trotzen** *v* defy; (*widersetzlich sein*) be obstinate. **trotzig** *adj* defiant, obstinate.
trüb(e) ['tryːb(ə)] *adj* cloudy, opaque; (*glanzlos*) dull; (*fig*) gloomy. **trüben** *v* cloud, dim, darken. **Trübsinn** *m* gloom, depression. **trübsinnig** *adj* gloomy, miserable.
Trug [truːk] *m* (*Täuschung*) fraud, deceit; (*Sinnes*) delusion.
*trügen ['tryːgən] *v* be deceptive; (*betrügen*) deceive. **trügerisch** *adj* treacherous, deceitful.

Truhe ['truːə] *f* (*pl* -n) chest, trunk.
Trümmer *pl* ruins, debris *sing*.
Trumpf [trumpf] *m* (*pl* **Trümpfe**) trump. **–karte** *f* trump (card).
Trunk [truŋk] *m* (*pl* **Trünke**) drink. **–enheit** *f* drunkenness, intoxication. **–sucht** *f* alcoholism.
Trupp [trup] *m* (*pl* -s) troop, gang, band. **Truppe** *f* (*pl* -n) (*Theater*) company; (*Mil*) (combat) troops *pl*. **Truppen** *pl* troops.
Truthahn ['truːthaːn] *m* turkey-cock.
Tscheche ['tʃɛçə] *m* (*pl* -n), **Tschechin** *f* (*pl* -nen) Czech. **tschechisch** *adj* Czech. **Tschechoslowakei** *f* Czechoslovakia.
Tuberkulose [tubɛrku'loːzə] *f* tuberculosis, TB.
Tuch [tuːx] **1** *neut* (*pl* -e) cloth, fabric. **2** *neut* (*pl* **Tücher**) (piece of) cloth; (*zum Trocknen*) towel. **–händler** *m* draper.
tüchtig ['tyçtiç] *adj* capable, able; (*leistungsfähig*) efficient; (*fleißig*) hard-working; (*klug*) clever. **Tüchtigkeit** *f* ability; efficiency; cleverness.
Tücke ['tykə] *f* (*pl* -n) spite, malice. **tückisch** *adj* spiteful.
Tugend ['tuːgənt] *f* (*pl* -en) virtue. **tugendhaft** *adj* virtuous.
Tulpe ['tulpə] *f* (*pl* -n) tulip.
*tun [tuːn] *v* do; (*machen*) make. **tun als ob** pretend to. **nur so tun** pretend. **zu tun haben** be busy, have things to do. **groß tun** boast. **etwas in etwas tun** put something into something.
Tünche ['tynçə] *f* (*pl* -n) whitewash, distemper.
Tunke ['tuŋkə] *f* (*pl* -n) sauce. **tunken** *v* dip, dunk.
Tunnel ['tunəl] *m* (*pl* -) tunnel.
Tupfen ['tupfən] *m* (*pl* -) dot, spot. **tupfen** *v* dot.
Tür [tyːr] *f* (*pl* -en) door.
Türkis [tyr'kiːs] *m* (*pl* -e) turquoise.
Türklinke ['tyːrkliŋkə] *f* doorhandle.
Turm [turm] *m* (*pl* **Türme**) tower; (*Schach*) rook, castle; (*Elek*) pylon. **–spitze** *f* spire, steeple.
turnen ['turnən] *v* do gymnastics. **Turnen** *neut* gymnastics. **Turnhalle** *f* gymnasium.
Turnier [tur'niːr] *neut* (*pl* -e) tournament.
Türschwelle ['tyːrʃvelə] *f* threshold.
Tusche ['tuʃə] *f* (*pl* -n) Indian ink, drawing ink.
tuscheln ['tuʃəln] *v* whisper.

Tüte ['tyːtə] *f* (*pl* -n) paperbag.
tuten ['tuːtən] *v* hoot, honk.
Typ [tyːp] *m* (*pl* -en) type. -e *f* (*Druck*) type.
Typhus ['tyːfus] *m* typhoid (fever).
typisch ['tyːpiʃ] *adj* typical.
Tyrann [ty'ran] *m* (*pl* -en) tyrant. -ei *f* tyranny. **tyrann‖isch** *adj* tyrannical. -**isieren** *v* tyrannize.

U

U-Bahn ['uːbaɪn] *f* underground (railway), (*US*) subway.
übel ['yːbəl] *adj* evil, wicked; (*schlecht*) bad; (*unwohl*) sick, ill. *mir wird übel* I feel sick. *übel daran sein* be in a bad way. **Übel** *neut* (*pl* -) evil; (*Mißgeschick*) misfortune; (*Krankheit*) sickness. **übel‖gelaunt** *adj* bad-tempered. -**gesinnt** *adj* evil-minded. -**nehmen** *v* be offended by, take amiss. -**riechen** *v* smell bad.
üben ['yːbən] *v* practise.
über ['yːbər] *prep* over, above; (*quer über*) across; (*während*) during; (*betreffend*) about; (*mehrals*) over; (*weg*) via.
überall [yːbər'al] *adv* everywhere.
überanstrengen [yːbər'anʃtrɛŋən] *v* overwork. **sich überanstrengen** overexert oneself. **Überanstrengung** *f* overexertion.
überarbeiten [yːbər'aɪrbaitən] *v* revise. **sich überarbeiten** *v* overwork, work too hard.
überbelichten ['yːbərbəliçtən] *v* (*Foto*) overexpose.
***überbieten** [yːbər'biːtən] *v* outbid; (*fig*) surpass, beat.
Überbleibsel ['yːbərblaipsəl] *neut* (*pl* -) remainder.
Überblick ['yːbɔrblik] *m* survey, overall view.
***überbringen** [yːbər'briŋən] *v* deliver.
überbrücken [yːbər'brykən] *v* bridge.
überdies [yːbər'diːs] *adv* besides.
überdrüssig ['yːbərdrusiç] *adj* sick (of), disgusted (with).
übereifrig ['yːbəraifriç] *adj* too eager, over-zealous.
übereilen [yːbər'ailən] *v* rush, hurry too much. **übereilt** *adj* hasty; (*Benehmen*) inconsiderate.
übereinander [yːbərain'andər] *adv* one

upon another. -**greifen** *v* overlap. -**legen** *v* lay one upon another.
***übereinkommen** [yːbər'ainkɔmən] *v* agree. **Überein‖kommen** *neut* (*pl* -) *or* **kunft** *f* agreement.
übereinstimmen [yːbər'ainʃtimən] *v* concur, agree; (*zueinander passen*) correspond, tally. **Übereinstimmung** *f* agreement, concord.
überempfindlich ['yːbərɛmpfintliç] *adj* hypersensitive.
***überfahren** ['yːbərfaɪrən] take *or* drive across. (*Mot*) run over. **Überfahrt** *f* crossing.
Überfall ['yːbərfal] *m* (sudden) attack, assault. **überfallen** *v* attack (suddenly). **Überfallkommando** *neut* flying squad.
Überfluß ['yːbərflus] *m* excess, overabundance. **überflüssig** *adj* superfluous.
überführen ['yːbərfyːrən] *v* transport, convey. [-'ryːrən] (*Jur*) convict. **Überführung** *f* transport; (*Brücke*) viaduct, overpass.
Übergabe ['yːbərgaɪbə] *f* surrender, handing-over.
Übergang ['yːbərgaŋ] *m* crossing, passage; (*fig*) transition.
***übergeben** ['yːbərgeɪbən] *v* deliver, hand over; (*Mil*) surrender. **sich übergeben** vomit.
übergehen ['yːbərgeɪən] *v* cross (over); (*werden*) pass into, become. [-'geɪən] omit, overlook.
Übergewicht ['yːbərgeviçt] *neut* overweight.
***übergreifen** ['yːbərgraifən] *v* overlap. **übergreifen auf** encroach on.
***überhandnehmen** [yːbər'hantneɪmən] *v* increase (rapidly).
überhaupt [yːbər'haupt] *adv* in general. **wenn überhaupt** if at all. **überhaupt nicht** not at all. **überhaupt kein ...** no ... whatever.
***überheben** [yːbər'heɪbən] *v* exempt, spare. **einer Mühe überheben** spare the trouble. **überheblich** *adj* presumptuous, arrogant.
überholen [yːbər'hoɪlən] *v* overtake; (*Tech*) overhaul. **überholt** *adj* outmoded.
überhören [yːbər'hœɪrən] *v* not hear; (*ignorieren*) ignore, let pass.
überirdisch ['yːbərirdiʃ] *adj* celestial; (*übernatürlich*) supernatural.
überkochen ['yːbərkɔxən] *v* boil over.

*überlassen [y:bər'lasən] v leave.
überlaufen ['y:bərlaufən] v overflow;
(Mil) defect.
überleben [y:bər'le:bən] v survive.
überlegen [y:bər'le:gən] v consider,
reflect. adj superior. Überlegenheit f
superiority. überlegt adj considered,
deliberate. Überlegung f consideration,
reflection.
überleiten ['y:bərlaitən] v lead on to; (fig)
convert.
überliefern [y:bər'li:fərn] v deliver; (der
Nachwelt) pass on, hand down.
Übermacht ['y:bərmaxt] f superiority.
übermächtig adj overwhelming, too powerful.
Übermaß ['y:bərmais] neut excess.
übermäßig adj excessive.
Übermensch ['y:bərmɛnʃ] m superman.
übermenschlich adj superhuman.
übermitteln [y:bər'mitəln] v convey.
übermorgen ['y:bərmɔrgən] adv the day
after tomorrow.
übermüdet [y:bər'my:dət] adj overtired.
Übermut ['y:bərmu:t] m arrogance; (Aus-
gelassenheit) high spirits pl. übermütig
adj arrogant; high-spirited.
übernächst ['y:bərnɛiçst] adj the next but
one, the one after.
übernachten [y:bər'naxtən] v spend the
night, stay overnight.
übernatürlich ['y:bərnatu:rliç] adj supernatural.
*übernehmen [y:bər'ne:mən] v take over;
(Pflicht) undertake.
überprüfen [y:bər'pry:fən] v verify, check,
examine. Überprüfung f verification,
check.
überqueren [y:bər'kveirən] v cross.
überragen [y:bər'raigən] v rise above,
tower above; (fig) surpass, outdo. –d adj
excellent.
übersinnlich ['y:bərzinliç] adj spiritual,
transcendental.
überspannen [y:bər'ʃpanən] v overstretch,
overtighten; (fig) go too far, exaggerate;
(bedecken) stretch over. überspannt adj
eccentric.
*überspringen [y:bər'ʃpriŋən] v jump
over; (auslassen) omit, skip.
*überstehen [y:bər'ʃteiən] v survive.
*übersteigen [y:bər'ʃtaigən] v climb over,
surmount; (fig) exceed.
Überstunden ['y:bərʃtundən] pl overtime

sing. Überstunden machen v work overtime. überstürzen [y:bər'ʃtyrtsən] v rush,
hurry. sich überstürzen rush, act too
hastily. überstürzt adj hasty.
Übertrag ['y:bərtraik] m (pl Überträge)
balance brought forward. übertragen v
carry over; (Komm) bring forward;
(befördern) transport; (übersetzen) translate; (Radio, Med) transmit. Übertragung
f transfer; (Radio, Med) transmission;
(Übersetzung) translation.
*übertreffen [y:bər'trɛfən] v excel, sur-
pass.
*übertreiben [y:bər'traibən] v exaggerate.
Übertreibung f exaggeration.
*übertreten [y:bər'tre:tən] v overstep.
['y:bər-] (Fluß) overflow; (Sport) step
over.
übertrieben [y:bər'tri:bən] adj exaggerated.
Übervölkerung [y:bər'fœlkəruŋ] f over-
population.
überwachen [y:bər'vaxən] v supervise.
Überwachung f supervision.
überwältigen [y:bər'vɛltigən] v overpower, overwhelm. –d adj overwhelming.
Überwältigung f overpowering, conquest.
*überweisen [y:bər'vaizən] v transfer.
Überweisung f transfer; (Post-) money
order.
überwiegend [y:bər'viigənt] adj preponderant. adv primarily, mainly.
*überwinden [y:bər'vindən] v overcome.
sich überwinden (zu) bring oneself (to).
Überwindung f overcoming, conquest.
überwuchern [y:bər'vuxərn] v overrun,
overgrow.
überzeugen [y:bər'tsɔygən] v convince.
–d adj convincing. überzeugt adj con-
vinced, sure. Überzeugung f conviction.
*überziehen ['y:bərtsii:ən] v pull over, put
on. [-'tsii:ən] cover; (Konto) overdraw;
(Bett) change (the sheets of).
Überziehung f overdraft.
Überzug ['y:bərtsuik] m cover(ing).
üblich ['y:pliç] adj usual.
U-Boot ['uibɔit] neut submarine.
übrig ['y:briç] adj remaining, left(-over).
die Übrigen the rest, the others. übrig
haben have left (over). –bleiben v
remain, be left (over). –ens adv by the
way, incidentally.
Übung ['y:buŋ] f (pl -en) exercise; (Üben)
practice.

Ufer ['uːfər] *neut* (*pl* -) bank, shore.
-damm *m* embankment.
Uhr [uːr] *f* (*pl* -en) clock; (*Armbanduhr*)
watch; (*Gas, usw.*) meter; (*Kraftstoff*)
gauge. **-armband** *neut* watch strap.
-werk *neut* clockwork. **-zeiger** *m*
(clock) hand. **-zeigersinn** *m* clockwise
direction. **im Uhrzeigersinn** *adv* clockwise. **entgegen dem Uhrzeigersinn** *adv*
anticlockwise (*US*) counterclockwise.
Ulk [ulk] *m* (*pl* -e) fun, lark. **ulkig** *adj*
funny.
Ulme ['ulmə] *f* (*pl* -n) elm.
um [um] *prep* (*zeitlich, örtlich*) around,
about; (*wegen*) for; (*Maßangeben*) by;
(*ungefähr*) about. *adv* about. *conj* in
order to. **um zu** (in order) to. **um diese
Zeit** around this time. **um so besser** so
much the better. **bitten um** ask for. **um 2
cm länger** longer by 2 cm.
umändern ['umɛndərn] *v* change, alter.
Umänderung *f* change, alteration.
umarmen [um'armən] *v* embrace.
Umarmung *f* embrace.
Umbau ['umbau] *m* alteration, rebuilding,
conversion. **umbauen** *v* rebuild, alter,
convert.
umbilden ['umbildən] *v* transform,
remodel. **Umbildung** *f* transformation.
***umbinden** ['umbindən] *v* tie (up), tie
around (oneself), put on.
Umblick ['umblik] *m* panorama, survey.
umblicken *v* (*sich umblicken*) look
around.
***umbringen** ['umbriŋən] *v* kill. (*sich
umbringen*) commit suicide.
umdrehen ['umdreɪən] *v* turn over *or*
around. **sich umdrehen** rotate, spin;
(*Person*) turn around. **Umdrehung** *f* turn,
rotation.
***umfahren** ['umfaɪrən] *v* run over, knock
down; [-'faɪrən] drive around.
***umfallen** ['umfalən] *v* fall over.
Umfang ['umfaŋ] *m* (*pl* **Umfänge**) (*Kreis*)
circumference; (*Ausdehnung*) extent;
(*Größe*) size. **umfangreich** *adj* extensive.
umfassen [um'fasən] *v* put one's arm
around, hold, clasp; (*fig*) embrace, cover; (*Mil*) encircle. **-d** *adj* comprehensive.
Umfrage ['umfraɪgə] *f* poll, inquiry.
Umgang ['umgaŋ] *m* circuit, turn;
(*Verkehr*) intercourse, (social) contact.
umgänglich *adj* sociable.
***umgeben** [um'geɪbən] *v* surround.

Umgebung *f* surroundings *pl*, environment.
***umgehen** *v* ['umgeɪən] go around;
(*behandeln*) handle, deal with; (*mit Menschen*) associate (with). [-'geɪən] go
around; (*vermeiden*) avoid.
umgekehrt ['umgəkeɪrt] *adv* the other
way round. *adj* inverted, reverse(d).
umgestalten ['umgəʃtaltən] *v* alter, transform; (*umorganisieren*) reorganize.
Umgestaltung *f* alteration, transformation; reorganization.
Umhang ['umhaŋ] *m* wrap, cape.
umher [um'heɪr] *adv* about, (a)round.
-blicken *v* look around. **-laufen** run
around.
umhüllen [um'hylən] *v* wrap up.
Umkehr ['umkeɪr] *f* turning back, return;
(*fig*) change, conversion. **umkehren** *v* turn
back, return; (*umdrehen*) turn over; (*fig*)
reform.
umkippen ['umkipən] *v* tip over.
umklammern [um'klamərn] *v* clasp.
umkleiden ['umklaidən] *v* **sich umkleiden**
change (one's clothes). **Umkleideraum** *m*
changing room.
***umkommen** ['umkɔmən] *v* die, perish,
be killed; (*verderben*) go bad.
Umkreis ['umkrais] *m* neighbourhood,
vicinity. **umkreisen** *v* (en)circle.
Umlauf ['umlauf] *m* circulation. **im
Umlauf** in circulation.
Umlaut ['umlaut] *m* vowel modification.
umleiten ['umlaitən] *v* divert. **Umleitung** *f*
diversion.
umlernen ['umlɛrnən] *v* learn anew,
relearn.
umliegend ['umliːgənt] *adj* surrounding.
umordnen ['umɔrdnən] *v* rearrange.
umpflanzen ['umpflantsən] *v* transplant.
umrahmen [um'raɪmən] *v* frame.
umrechnen ['umrɛçnən] *v* convert,
(ex)change. **Umrechnung** *f* conversion.
-skurs *m* rate of exchange.
***umreißen** ['umraisən] *v* pull down,
demolish. [-'raisən] sketch, outline.
umringen [um'riŋən] *v* surround.
Umriß ['umris] *m* sketch, outline. **umris-
sen** *adj* defined.
umrühren ['umryɪrən] *v* stir.
ums [ums] *prep* + *art* **um das**.
Umsatz ['umzats] *m* turnover, sales.
umsäumen ['umzɔymən] *v* hem.
[-'zɔymən] enclose, surround.

umschalten ['umʃaltən] v (fig) switch or change over. **Umschaltung** f (fig) changeover, switch.

umschauen ['umʃauən] v **sich umschauen** look around.

umschiffen [um'ʃifən] v circumnavigate; trans-ship. **Umschiffung** f circumnavigation.

Umschlag ['umʃlaik] m cover; (Brief) envelope; (Buch) wrapper, jacket; (Hose) turn-up; (Kleid) hem; (Veränderung) change; (Komm) turnover. **umschlagen** v change (Boot) capsize; (Wind) veer; (umwenden) turn over; (umwerfen) knock down.

***umschließen** [um'ʃliisən] v surround, enclose.

***umschreiben** ['umʃraibən] v rewrite; transcribe. [-'ʃraibən] paraphrase.

umschulen ['umʃuilən] v retrain; (neue Schule) send to a new school. **Umschulung** f retraining.

Umschwung ['umʃvuŋ] m turn; (fig) sudden change, reversal.

***umsehen** ['umzeiən] v **sich umsehen** look around; (rückwärts) look round.

umsetzen ['umzɛtsən] v transpose; (Pflanze) transplant; (verkaufen) sell.

Umsicht ['umziçt] f prudence, circumspection. **umsichtig** adj prudent, circumspect.

umsiedeln ['umziidəln] v resettle. **Umsiedlung** f resettlement.

umsonst [um'zɔnst] adv free (of charge); (vergebens) in vain.

Umstand ['umʃtant] m circumstance. **in anderen Umständen** (umg.) expecting, in the family way. **ohne Umstände** without fuss. **nähere Umstände** further particulars. **unter diesen Umständen** in these circumstances.

***umsteigen** ['umʃtaigən] v change (trains, buses, etc.). **Umsteiger** m through-ticket.

***umstoßen** ['umʃtoisən] v overturn, knock over; (ungültig machen) revoke; (Pläne) upset.

Umsturz ['umʃturts] m overthrow; (Pol) revolution. **umstürzen** v overturn; (Regierung) overthrow; (umfallen) fall over.

Umtausch ['umtauʃ] m exchange. **umtauschen** v exchange, (umg.) swap.

umwälzen ['umvɛltsən] v roll over; (gründlich ändern) revolutionize.

umwandeln ['umwandəln] v change, transform; (Elek) transform, (Komm) convert.

Umweg ['umveik] m detour, long way round.

Umwelt ['umvɛlt] f environment. **umweltfreundlich** adj non-polluting, conservationist. **Umweltverschmutzung** f (environmental) pollution.

***umwenden** ['umvɛndən] v turn over; (Wagen) turn round.

***umwerben** [um'vɛrbən] v court.

***umwerfen** ['umvɛrfən] v upset, overturn; (Kleider) wrap round oneself.

umwickeln [um'vikəln] v wrap round.

umzäunen [um'tsɔynən] v fence in.

***umziehen** ['umtsiiən] v move (house); (Kind) change (clothes). **sich umziehen** change (clothes).

Umzug ['umtsuik] m move, removal; procession.

unabänderlich [unap'ɛndərliç] adj unalterable.

unabhängig ['unapheŋiç] adj independent. **Unabhängig‖e(r)** (Pol) independent. **–keit** f independence.

unabkömmlich ['unapkœmliç] adj indispensable.

unablässig ['unaplɛsiç] adj incessant.

unabsichtlich ['unapziçtliç] adj unintentional.

unachtsam ['unaxtzaim] adj careless.

unähnlich ['unɛinliç] adj unlike, dissimilar (to).

unangemessen ['unangəmɛsən] adj unsuitable; (Forderung) unreasonable.

unangenehm ['unangəneim] adj unpleasant; (peinlich) awkward.

Unannehmlichkeit ['unanneimliçkait] f unpleasantness; (lästige Mühe) inconvenience.

unansehnlich ['unanzeinliç] adj unsightly.

unanständig ['unanʃtɛndiç] adj indecent, improper. **Unanständigkeit** f indecency.

unartig ['unairtiç] adj badly-behaved, rude.

unauffällig ['unauffɛliç] adj inconspicuous.

unaufgefordert ['unaufgəfɔrdət] adj unbidden, unasked.

unaufhörlich ['unaufhœirliç] adj incessant.

unaufmerksam ['unaufmɛrkzaim] adj inattentive.

unaufrichtig ['unaufrɪçtɪç] *adj* insincere.
unausgeglichen ['unausgəglɪçən] *adj* uneven, unbalanced.
unbändig ['unbɛndɪç] *adj* tremendous.
unbeabsichtigt ['unbəapzɪçtɪçt] *adj* unintentional.
unbeachtet ['unbəaxtət] *adj* unnoticed, unheeded.
unbedacht ['unbədaxt] *adj* inconsiderate, thoughtless, rash.
unbedeutend ['unbədɔytənt] *adj* unimportant, insignificant.
unbedingt ['unbədɪŋt] *adj* absolute, unconditional. *adv* by all means.
unbefahrbar ['unbəfaːrbaːr] *adj* impassable.
unbefriedigend ['unbəfriːdɪgənt] *adj* unsatisfactory.
unbefugt ['unbəfukt] *adj* unauthorized.
unbegreiflich ['unbəgraɪflɪç] *adj* incomprehensible, inconceivable.
Unbehagen ['unbəhaɪgən] *neut* uneasiness, discomfort. **unbehaglich** *adj* uneasy, uncomfortable.
unbeholfen ['unbəhɔlfən] *adj* clumsy, awkward.
unbekannt ['unbəkant] *adj* unknown.
unbekümmert [unbə'kymərt] *adj* unconcerned.
unbemerkt ['unbəmɛrkt] *adj* unnoticed, unobserved.
unbemittelt ['unbəmɪtəlt] *adj* poor, without means.
unbequem ['unbəkveːm] *adj* uncomfortable.
umberechenbar ['unbəreçənbaːr] *adj* incalculable.
unberechtigt ['unbəreçtɪçt] *adj* (*ungerechtfertigt*) unjustified; (*unbefugt*) unauthorized. *adv* without authority.
unberührt ['unbəryːrt] *adj* untouched, intact.
unbeschränkt ['unbəʃrɛnkt] *adj* unlimited, unrestricted.
unbeschreiblich ['unbəʃraɪplɪç] *adj* indescribable.
unbesonnen ['unbəzɔnən] *adj* imprudent; (*unüberlegt*) rash, hasty.
unbeständig ['unbəʃtɛndɪç] *adj* unsettled, unstable; (*nicht dauernd*) inconstant.
unbestimmt ['unbəʃtɪmt] *adj* indefinite.
unbestreitbar [unbə'ʃtraitbaːr] *adj* indisputable.
unbestritten ['unbəʃtritən] *adj* undisputed, uncontested.

unbeteiligt ['unbətailɪçt] *adj* unconcerned; (*nicht beteiligt*) uninvolved.
unbeweglich ['unbəveːklɪç] *adj* immovable; (*bewegungslos*) motionless.
unbewußt ['unbəvust] *adj* unconscious.
unbiegsam ['unbiːkzaːm] *adj* unbending.
unbrauchbar ['unbrauxbaːr] *adj* useless.
und [unt] *conj* and.
undankbar ['undaŋkbaːr] *adj* ungrateful; (*Arbeit*) thankless. **Undankbarkeit** *f* ingratitude.
undenkbar [un'dɛŋkbaːr] *adj* unthinkable.
undeutlich ['undɔytlɪç] *adj* unclear, indistinct.
undurchdringlich ['undurçdrɪŋlɪç] *adj* impenetrable.
undurchlässig ['undurçlɛsɪç] *adj* impermeable; (*Wasser-*) water-proof.
undurchsichtig ['undurçzɪçtɪç] *adj* opaque; (*Person*) inscrutable.
uneben ['uneːbən] *adj* uneven, rough.
unecht ['unɛçt] *adj* not genuine, false; (*künstlich*) artificial.
unehelich ['uneəlɪç] *adj* illegitimate.
unehrlich ['uneːrlɪç] *adj* dishonest. **Unehrlichkeit** *f* dishonesty.
unendlich [un'ɛntlɪç] *adj* endless, infinite.
unentbehrlich [unɛnt'beːrlɪç] *adj* indispensable.
unentschieden ['unɛntʃiːdən] *adj* undecided; (*Fussball*) drawn. **Unentschiedenheit** *f* indecision.
unentschlossen ['unɛntʃlɔsən] *adj* undecided, irresolute. **Unentschlossenheit** *f* indecision, irresolution.
unentwickelt ['unɛntvikəlt] *adj* undeveloped.
unentzündbar ['unɛntzyntbaːr] *adj* non-flammable.
unerbittlich [unɛr'bɪtlɪç] *adj* relentless.
unerfahren ['unɛrfaːrən] *adj* inexperienced.
unerhört [unɛr'hœːrt] *adj* unheard-of, outrageous.
unerklärbar ['unɛrkleːrbaːr] *adj* inexplicable.
unerläßlich [unɛr'lɛslɪç] *adj* indispensable.
unerlaubt ['unɛrlaupt] *adj* not permitted; (*ungesetzlich*) forbidden, illegal.
unermeßlich [unɛr'mɛslɪç] *adj* immense, immeasurable.
unermüdlich [unɛr'myːtlɪç] *adj* indefatigable, untiring.

unerreichbar ['unɛraiçbaːr] *adj* unattainable. **unerreicht** *adj* unequalled, unrivalled.
unersättlich ['unɛrzɛtliç] *adj* insatiable.
unerschrocken ['unɛrʃrɔkən] *adj* fearless, undaunted.
unerschütterlich ['unɛrʃytərliç] *adj* imperturbable, unshakeable.
unersetzlich ['unɛrzɛtsliç] *adj* irreplaceable.
unerträglich ['unɛrtrɛːkliç] *adj* unbearable, intolerable.
unerwartet ['unɛrvaːrtət] *adj* unexpected.
unfähig ['unfɛːiç] *adj* incapable; (*nicht instande*) unable. **Unfähigkeit** *f* incapacity; inability.
unfair ['unfɛːr] *adj* unfair.
Unfall ['unfal] *m* accident. **–station** *f* first-aid post. **–verhütung** *f* accident prevention.
unfaßbar ['unfasbaːr] *adj* inconceivable.
unfehlbar [un'feːlbaːr] *adj* infallible.
unflätig ['unflɛːtiç] *adj* filthy, coarse.
unfreundlich ['unfrɔyntliç] *adj* unfriendly; (*barsch*) rude; (*Wetter*) disagreeable, inclement. **Unfreundlichkeit** *f* unfriendliness, unkindness.
Unfug ['unfuːk] *m* misconduct; (*Dummheiten*) mischief.
unfühlbar ['unfyːlbaːr] *adj* intangible, impalpable.
Ungar ['uŋgar] *m* (*pl* **-n**), **Ungarin** *f* (*pl* **-nen**) Hungarian. **ungarisch** *adj* Hungarian. **Ungarn** *neut* Hungary.
ungastlich ['ungastliç] *adj* inhospitable.
ungeachtet ['ungəaxtət] *adj* overlooked, disregarded. *prep* notwithstanding.
ungebeten ['ungəbeitən] *adj* uninvited.
ungebildet ['ungəbildət] *adj* uneducated; (*Benehmen*) ill-mannered.
ungebührend ['ungəbyːrənt] *or* **ungebührlich** *adj* improper, unbecoming.
ungebunden ['ungəbundən] *adj* unbound; (*fig*) unrestrained, free.
Ungeduld ['ungədult] *f* impatience. **ungeduldig** *adj* impatient.
ungeeignet ['ungəaiknət] *adj* unsuitable.
ungefähr ['ungəfɛːr] *adv* approximately, about, roughly. *adj* approximate.
ungefährlich ['ungəfɛːrliç] *adj* not dangerous.
ungeheuer ['ungəhɔyər] *adj* enormous. **Ungeheuer** *neut* (*pl* **-**) monster.
ungehorsam ['ungəhoːrzaim] *adj* disobedient. **Ungehorsam** *m* disobedience.

ungekünstelt ['ungəkyːnstəlt] *adj* unaffected, natural.
ungelegen ['ungəleigən] *adj* inconvenient.
ungelernt ['ungəlɛrnt] *adj* unskilled.
ungemächlich ['ingəmɛçliç] *adj* uncomfortable, unpleasant.
ungemein ['ungəmain] *adj* uncommon, extraordinary.
ungemütlich ['ungəmyːtliç] *adj* uncomfortable; (*grob*) unpleasant, nasty.
ungenannt ['ungənant] *adj* unnamed.
ungeniert ['unʒəniːrt] *adj* free and easy, relaxed and informal.
ungenießbar ['ungəniːsbaːr] *adj* inedible, unenjoyable.
ungenügend ['ungənyːgənt] *adj* insufficient; (*Qualität*) inadequate.
ungeraten ['ungəraitən] *adj* (*Kind*) spoiled.
ungerecht ['ungərɛçt] *adj* unjust.
ungereimt ['ungəraimt] *adj* (*fig*) nonsensical, absurd.
ungern ['ungɛrn] *adv* unwillingly, reluctantly.
Ungeschick ['ungəʃik] *neut* ineptitude, clumsiness. **ungeschickt** *adj* clumsy, awkward.
ungesellig ['ungəzɛliç] *adj* unsociable.
ungesetzlich ['ungəzɛtsliç] *adj* illegal, unlawful.
ungestüm ['ungəʃtyːm] *adj* impetuous.
ungesund ['ungəzunt] *adj* unhealthy, unwell.
ungewiß ['ungəvis] *adj* uncertain. **Ungewißheit** *f* uncertainty.
ungewöhnlich ['ungəvœːnliç] *adj* unusual, uncommon. **ungewohnt** *adj* unaccustomed.
Ungeziefer ['ungətsiːfər] *neut* vermin.
ungezogen ['ungətsoigən] *adj* rude; (*Kind*) naughty.
ungezwungen ['ungətsvuŋən] *adj* free, natural, uninhibited.
ungläubig ['unglɔybiç] *adj* incredulous, disbelieving; (*Rel*) unbelieving. **Ungläubige(r)** *m* sceptic; (*Rel*) unbeliever.
unglaublich ['unglaupliç] *adj* incredible, unbelievable. **unglaubwürdig** *adj* (*Person*) untrustworthy, unreliable; (*Sache*) incredible.
ungleich ['unglaiç] *adj* unequal, uneven; (*verschieden*) different; (*unähnlich*) unlike; (*Zahl*) odd. **Ungleichheit** *f* inequality; difference.

Unglück ['unglyk] *neut* misfortune; (*Katastrophe*) disaster, catastrophe; (*Pech*) bad luck. **unglücklich** *adj* unlucky; (*traurig*) unhappy. **-erweise** *adv* unfortunately. **Unglücksfall** *m* accident.
Ungnade ['ungnaɪdə] *f* disgrace, displeasure. **ungnädig** *adj* ungracious, churlish.
ungünstig ['ungynstiç] *adj* unfavourable.
unhaltbar ['unhaltbaɪr] *adj* untenable.
Unheil ['unhail] *neut* mischief, harm. **unheil‖bar** *adj* incurable. **-bringend** *adj* unlucky, fateful.
unheimlich ['unhaimliç] *adj* weird, sinister, uncanny. *adv* (*umg.*) tremendously.
unhöflich ['unhœɪfliç] *adj* impolite, rude. **Unhöflichkeit** *f* rudeness, incivility.
unhörbar ['unhœɪrbaɪr] *adj* inaudible.
uniform [uni'fɔrm] *adj* uniform. **Uniform** *f* (*pl* -en) uniform.
uninteressant ['unintərɛsant] *adj* uninteresting. **uninteressiert** *adj* disinterested.
universal [univɛr'saɪl] *or* **universell** *adj* universal.
Universität [univɛrzi'tɛɪt] *f* (*pl* -en) university.
Universum [uni'vɛrzum] *neut* universe.
unkenntlich ['unkɛntliç] *adj* unrecognizable. **Unkenntnis** *f* ignorance.
unklar ['unklaɪr] *adj* unclear, obscure; (*trübe*) muddy, cloudy.
unklug ['unkluɪk] *adj* unwise, unintelligent.
Unkosten ['unkɔstən] *pl* expenses, costs; (*Komm*) overheads.
Unkraut ['unkraut] *neut* weed.
unlängst ['unlɛŋst] *adv* recently, lately.
unlauter ['unlautər] *adj* impure; (*nicht ehrlich*) unfair, dishonest. **unlauterer Wettbewerb** unfair competition.
unlesbar ['unlɛɪzbaɪr] *adj* illegible, unreadable.
unlogisch ['unlɔɡiʃ] *adj* illogical.
unlösbar ['unlœɪsbaɪr] *adj* insoluble.
unmäßig ['unmɛɪsiç] *adj* immoderate.
Unmenge ['unmɛŋə] *f* huge quantity.
Unmensch ['unmɛnʃ] *m* brute, monster, barbarian. **unmenschlich** *adj* inhuman, brutal. **Unmenschlichkeit** *f* inhumanity.
unmittelbar ['unmitəlbaɪr] *adj* immediate, direct.
unmodisch ['unmɔɪdiʃ] *adj* unfashionable.
unmöglich ['unmœɪkliç] *adj* impossible. **Unmöglichkeit** *f* impossibility.

unmoralisch ['unmoraɪliʃ] *adj* immoral.
unmündig ['unmyndiç] *adj* under age.
unnachgiebig ['innaxɡiɪbiç] *adj* unyielding, uncompromising.
unnatürlich ['unnatyrliç] *adj* unnatural.
unnötig ['unnœɪtiç] *adj* unnecessary.
unnütz ['unnyts] *adj* useless, unprofitable.
unordentlich ['unɔrdəntliç] *adj* disorderly, untidy. **Unord‖entlichkeit** *f* untidiness, disorderliness. **-nung** *f* disorder.
unorganisch ['unɔrɡaɪniʃ] *adj* inorganic.
unpaar ['unpaɪr] *adj* odd.
unparteiisch ['unpartaiiʃ] *or* **unparteilich** *adj* impartial, unbiased. **Unparteilichkeit** *f* impartiality.
unpassend ['unpasənt] *adj* unsuitable, inappropriate; (*unschicklich*) improper.
unpersönlich ['unpɛrzœɪnliç] *adj* impersonal.
unpolitisch ['unpoliɪtiʃ] *adj* nonpolitical.
Unrat ['unraɪt] *m* refuse, dirt.
unratsam ['unraɪtzaɪm] *adj* inadvisable.
unrecht ['unrɛçt] *adj* wrong; (*ungerecht*) unjust. **Unrecht** *neut* wrong; (*Ungerechtigkeit*) injustice. **unrechtmäßig** *adj* illegal, unlawful, illegitimate.
unregelmäßig ['unreɪɡəlmɛɪʃiç] *adj* irregular. **Unregelmäßigkeit** *f* irregularity.
unreif ['unraif] *adj* unripe; (*Mensch*) immature.
unrein ['unrain] *adj* dirty, unclean; (*fig*) impure.
unrentabel ['unrentaɪbəl] *adj* unprofitable.
unrichtig ['unriçtiç] *adj* incorrect.
Unruhe ['unruɪə] *f* restlessness; (*Aufruhr*) unrest. (*Uhr*) balance(-wheel). **unruhig** *adj* restless.
uns [uns] *pron* (to) us; (*Reflexiv*) (to) ourselves.
unsauber ['unzaubər] *adj* unclean, dirty; (*unfair*) unfair.
unschätzbar ['unʃɛtsbaɪr] *adj* inestimable.
unscheinbar ['unʃainbaɪr] *adj* inconspicuous.
unschicklich ['unʃikliç] *adj* improper, unseemly.
unschlüssig ['unʃlysiç] *adj* irresolute.
unschön ['unʃœɪn] *adj* unlovely, unpleasant.
Unschuld ['unʃult] *f* innocence. **unschuldig** *adj* innocent.
unselbständig ['unzɛlpʃtɛndiç] *adj* dependent.

unselig ['unzeɪlɪç] *adj* unfortunate, fatal.
unser ['unzər] *adj* our. *pron* ours. **unser(er) seits** *adv* for our part, as for us.
unser(es)gleichen *pron* people like us.
pron **der, die, das uns(e)rige** ours.
unserthalben, unsertwegen, unsertwillen for our sakes.
unsicher ['unzɪçər] *adj* unsafe, insecure; (*zweifelhaft*) uncertain. **Unsicherheit** *f* insecurity, uncertainty.
unsichtbar ['unzɪçtbaːr] *adj* invisible.
Unsinn ['unzin] *adj* nonsense. **unsinnig** *adj* nonsensical.
unsittlich ['unzitlɪç] *adj* indecent, immoral. **Unsittlichkeit** *f* immorality.
unsre ['unzrə] *V* unser.
unsrige ['unzrɪgə] *V* unser.
unsterblich ['unʃterplɪç] *adj* immortal. **Unsterblichkeit** *f* immortality.
unstet ['unʃteɪt] *adj* unsteady, inconstant.
Unstimmigkeit ['unʃtimɪçkait] *f* (*pl* **-en**) inconsistency; (*Meinungsverschiedenheit*) disagreement.
unsympathisch ['unzympaːtiʃ] *adj* disagreeable, unpleasant.
Untat ['untaɪt] *f* outrage, crime.
untätig ['untɛɪtɪç] *adj* inactive, idle. **Untätigkeit** *f* inactivity, idleness.
untauglich ['untauklɪç] *adj* unfit; (*Sache*) unusable.
unten ['untən] *adv* below, at the bottom; (*im Hause*) downstairs. **nach unten** downwards. **von oben bis unten** from top to bottom. **von unten an** from the bottom (up).
unter ['untər] *prep* below, under; (*zwischen*) between, among. *adj* lower. **unter allen Umständen** under any circumstances. **unter uns** between you and me. **unter vier Augen** in private. **unter der Hand** secretly.
Unterarm ['untərarm] *m* forearm.
Unterbau ['untərbau] *m* foundations *pl*.
unterbelichten ['untərbəlɪçtən] *v* (*Foto*) underexpose.
unterbevölkert ['untərbəfœlkərt] *adj* underpopulated.
unterbewußt ['untərbəvust] *adj* subconscious. **Unterbewusstsein** *neut* subconsciousness.
*unterbleiben [untər'blaibən] *v* not occur.
*unterbrechen [untər'brɛçən] *v* interrupt; (*Telef*) cut off, disconnect. **Unterbrechung** *f* interruption.

*unterbringen ['untərbriŋən] *v* accommodate, lodge, shelter; (*lagern*) store.
unterdrücken [untər'drykən] *v* suppress. **Unterdrückung** *f* suppression.
untereinander [untərain'andər] *adv* with each other, with one another.
unterentwickelt ['untərɛntvikəlt] *adj* underdeveloped.
Unterführung [untər'fyɪruŋ] *f* underpass.
Untergang ['untərgaŋ] *m* (*Sonne*) setting; (*Schiff*) sinking, wreck; (*fig*) decline, fall.
Untergebene(r) [untər'geɪbənə(r)] *m* subordinate.
*untergehen ['untərgeɪən] *v* sink; (*Sonne*) set; (*fig*) perish, be lost.
untergeordnet ['untərgəɔrdnət] *adj* subordinate.
Untergestell ['untərgəʃtɛl] *neut* undercarriage.
Untergewicht ['untərgəvɪçt] *neut* short weight. **Untergewicht haben** be underweight.
*untergraben [untər'graibən] *v* undermine.
Untergrund ['untərgrunt] *m* subsoil. **–bahn** *f* underground (railway), (*US*) subway.
unterhalb ['untərhalp] *prep* below, under(neath).
Unterhalt ['untərhalt] *m* support, keep; (*Instandhaltung*) maintenance.
unterhalten *v* (*Person*) keep, support; (*Instand halten*) maintain; (*zerstreuen*) entertain. **sich unterhalten** enjoy oneself; (*reden (mit*)) converse (with), talk (to). **unterhaltsam** *adj* entertaining, amusing. **Unterhaltung** *f* entertainment, amusement; (*Instandhaltung*) maintenance. **–skosten** *pl* maintenance costs.
unterhandeln [untər'handəln] *v* negotiate.
Unterhaus ['untərhaus] *neut* lower chamber (of parliament).
Unterhemd ['untərhɛmt] *neut* vest, (*US*) undershirt.
Unterholz ['untərhɔlts] *neut* undergrowth.
Unterhose ['untərhoɪzən] *f* underpants *pl*.
unterirdisch ['untərirdɪʃ] *adj* underground.
*unterkommen ['untərkɔmən] *v* find accommodation *or* shelter; (*Arbeit*) find work.
Unterkunft ['untərkunft] *f* accommodation, lodgings *pl*.

Unterlage ['untərlaːgə] *f* base, basis, foundation; (*Beweisstück*) (documentary) evidence.
Unterlaß ['untərlas] *m* **ohne Unterlaß** incessantly, unceasingly.
***unterlassen** [untər'lasən] *v* neglect, fail (to do), omit. **Unterlassung** *f* omission.
unterlegen [untər'leːgən] *adj* inferior.
Unterleib ['untərlaip] *m* abdomen.
***unterliegen** [untər'liːgən] *v* be defeated. **es unterliegt keinem Zweifel** it is not open to doubt.
Untermieter ['untərmiːtər] *m* lodger.
***unternehmen** [untər'neːmən] *v* undertake, attempt. **Unternehmen** *neut* undertaking, enterprise; (*Firma*) firm. **Unternehmer** *m* entrepreneur, contractor. **unternehmungslustig** *adj* enterprising.
Unteroffizier ['untərɔfitsiːr] *m* noncommissioned officer, NCO.
Unterredung [untər'reːduŋ] *f* (*pl* **-en**) conversation, discussion.
Unterricht ['untərriçt] *m* (*pl* **-e**) instruction, lessons *pl*, teaching. **Unterricht geben** teach, give lessons. **unterrichten** *v* teach, give lessons. **unterrichten** *v* instruct, teach; (*benachrichtigen*) inform.
Unterrock ['untərrɔk] *m* slip, petticoat.
unters ['untərs] *prep + art* **unter das**.
untersagen [untər'zaːgən] *v* forbid, prohibit.
***unterscheiden** [untər'ʃaidən] *v* distinguish. **sich unterscheiden** differ.
***unterschieben** [untər'ʃiːbən] *v* attribute (to); substitute.
Unterschied ['untərʃiːt] *m* (*pl* **-e**) difference. **unterschiedlich** *adj* different.
***unterschlagen** [untər'ʃlaːgən] *v* (*Geld*) embezzle; (*Nachricht*) suppress. **Unterschlagung** *f* embezzlement; suppression.
Unterschlupf ['untərʃlupf] *m* (*pl* **Unterschlüpfe**) refuge, hiding place.
***unterschreiben** [untər'ʃraibən] *v* sign.
Unterschrift ['untərʃrift] *f* signature.
Unterseeboot ['untərzeːboːt] *neut* submarine. **unterseeisch** *adj* submarine.
unterst ['untərst] *adj* lowest, bottom, undermost.
***unterstehen** [untər'ʃteːən] *v* be subordinate (to). **sich unterstehen** dare.
***unterstreichen** [untər'ʃtraiçən] *v* underline.
unterstützen [untər'ʃtytsən] *v* support,

assist. **Unterstützung** *f* (*pl* **-en**) support, assistance.
untersuchen [untər'zuːxən] *v* examine. **Untersuchung** *f* examination. **–shaft** *f* imprisonment on remand.
Untertan ['untərtain] *m* (*pl* **-en**) subject.
Untertasse ['untərtasə] *f* saucer.
untertauchen ['untərtauxən] *v* dive; (*verschwinden*) disappear.
Unterteil ['untərtail] *m* bottom (part).
Untertitel ['untərtiːtəl] *m* (*Film*) subtitle.
unterwärts ['untərvɛrts] *adv* downwards.
Unterwäsche ['untərvɛʃə] *f* underwear.
unterwegs [untər'veːks] *adv* on the way, en route.
***unterweisen** [untər'vaizən] *v* instruct, teach. **Unterweisung** *f* instructions *pl*.
Unterwelt ['untərvɛlt] *f* underworld.
***unterwerfen** [untər'vɛrfən] *v* subject (to); (*besiegen*) subjugate. **sich unterwerfen** submit, surrender. **unterworfen** *adj* subject (to).
unterwürfig [untər'vyrfiç] *adj* obsequious.
unterzeichnen [untər'tsaiçnən] *v* sign. **Unterzeichnung** *f* signature.
***unterziehen** [untər'tsiːən] *v* subject. **sich unterziehen** undergo, submit (to).
untief ['untiːf] *adj* shallow.
untreu ['untrɔy] *adj* unfaithful.
untrüglich [un'tryːkliç] *adj* infallible, certain.
untüchtig ['untyçtiç] *adj* incompetent, incapable.
Untugend ['untuːgənt] *f* vice.
unüberlegt ['unyːbərleıkt] *adj* ill-considered, hasty.
unüberwindlich ['unyːbərvintliç] *adj* impregnable; insurmountable, insuperable.
ununterbrochen ['ununtərbrɔxən] *adj* uninterrupted.
unveränderlich ['unfɛrɛndərliç] *adj* unchangeable.
unverantwortlich [unfɛr'antvɔrtliç] *adj* irresponsible. **Unverantwortlichkeit** *f* irresponsibility.
unverbesserlich [unfɛr'bɛsərliç] *adj* incorrigible.
unverbindlich [unfɛr'bintliç] *adj* not binding; (*Komm*) without obligation.
unverdaulich ['unfɛrdauliç] *adj* indigestible.
unverderblich ['unfɛrdərpliç] *adj* incorruptible.

unverdient ['unfɛrdiːnt] *adj* unearned, undeserved.

unvereinbar [unfɛr'ainbaːr] *adj* incompatible.

unverfroren ['unfɛrfroːrən] *adj* impudent, brazen. **Unverfrorenheit** *f* impudence.

unvergänglich ['unfɛrgɛsliç] *adj* imperishable; immortal.

unvergeßlich [unfɛr'gɛsliç] *adj* unforgettable.

unverhältnismäßig ['unfɛrhɛltnismɛisiç] *adj* disproportionate.

unverheiratet ['unfɛrhairaːtət] *adj* unmarried.

unvermeidlich [unfɛr'maitliç] *adj* unavoidable.

unvermittelt ['unfɛrmitəlt] *adj* sudden, unexpected.

Unvermögen ['unfɛrmœːgən] *neut* inability, powerlessness.

unvermutet ['unfɛrmuːtət] *adj* unexpected.

unvernünftig ['unfɛrnynftiç] *adj* unreasonable.

unverschämt ['unfɛrʃɛːmt] *adj* impudent, impertinent. **Unverschämtheit** *f* impudence, impertinence.

unversehens ['unfɛrzeːəns] *adv* suddenly, unexpectedly.

unversöhnlich ['unfɛrzœːnliç] *adj* irreconcilable.

unverständlich ['unfɛrʃtɛntliç] *adj* unintelligible.

unverträglich ['unfɛrtrɛikliç] *adj* incompatible; unsociable.

unverzagt ['unfɛrtsakt] *adj* undaunted, fearless.

unverzüglich ['unfɛrtsykliç] *adj* immediate, instant.

unvollkommen ['unfɔlkəmən] *adj* imperfect.

unvoreingenommen ['unfɔraingənəmən] *adj* unprejudiced.

unvorsichtig ['unfɔrziçtiç] *adj* careless, incautious; (*unklug*) imprudent.

unvorstellbar ['unfɔrʃtɛlbaːr] *adj* unimaginable.

unvorteilhaft ['unfɔrtailhaft] *adj* unfavourable.

unwahr ['unvaːr] *adj* untrue. **–haft** *adj* untruthful. **Unwahrheit** *f* untruth, falsehood. **unwahrscheinlich** *adj* unlikely, improbably; (*umg.*) fantastic, incredible. *adv* (*umg.*) incredibly.

unweit ['unvait] *prep, adv* near, not far (from).

Unwetter ['unvɛtər] *neut* storm.

unwichtig ['unviçtiç] *adj* unimportant. **Unwichtigkeit** *f* unimportance; (*Sache*) trifle.

unwiderruflich [unviːdər'ruːfliç] *adj* irrevocable.

unwiderstehlich [unviːdər'ʃteːliç] *adj* irresistible.

unwillig ['unviliç] *adj* indignant; (*widerwillig*) unwilling, reluctant.

unwillkürlich ['unvilkyːrliç] *adj* involuntary; instinctive.

unwirksam ['unviːrkzaːm] *adj* ineffective.

unwissend ['unvisənt] *adj* ignorant. **Unwissenheit** *f* ignorance. **unwissentlich** *adv* unconsciously, unwittingly.

unwürdig ['unvyrdiç] *adj* unworthy.

Unzahl ['untsaːl] *f* endless number.

unzählbar ['untsɛːlbaːr] *or* **unzählig** *adj* innumerable.

unzeitgemäß ['untsaitgəmɛis] *adj* inopportune; (*unmodisch*) outdated. **unzeitig** *adj* premature; (*Obst*) unripe.

unzerbrechlich [untsɛr'brɛçliç] *adj* unbreakable.

unzertrennlich [untsɛr'trɛnliç] *adj* inseparable.

unziemlich ['untsiːmliç] *adj* unseemly.

Unzucht ['untsuxt] *f* lechery, fornication; (*Jur*) sexual offence. **unzüchtig** *adj* lewd, lecherous.

unzufrieden ['untsufriːdən] *adj* dissatisfied.

unzugänglich ['untsuːgɛŋliç] *adj* inaccessible.

unzulänglich ['untsuːlɛŋliç] *adj* inadequate, insufficient.

unzulässig ['untsuːlɛsiç] *adj* inadmissible.

unzureichend ['untsuraiçənt] *adj* insufficient, inadequate.

unzuverlässig ['untsufɛrlɛsiç] *adj* unreliable.

unzweifelhaft ['untsfaifəlhaft] *adj* undoubted.

üppig ['ypiç] *adj* abundant, luxuriant; (*blühend*) exuberant; (*wollüstig*) voluptuous.

uralt ['uːralt] *adj* very old, ancient.

Uran [u'raːn] *neut* uranium.

uranfänglich ['uranfɛŋliç] *adj* original, premordial.

Uraufführung ['uːrauffyːruŋ] *f* first performance, première.

urban [ur'baɪn] *adj* urbane.

urbar ['uɪrbaɪr] *adj* arable.

Ureinwohner ['uɪrainvoɪnər] *m* aboriginal.

Ureltern ['uɪrɛltərn] *pl* ancestors.

Urenkel ['uɪrɛŋkəl] *m* (*Kind*) great-grandchild, (*Junge*) great-grandson. **–in** *f* great-granddaughter.

Urgeschichte ['uɪrgəʃɪçtə] *f* prehistory.

Urgroß‖eltern ['uɪrgroɪsɛltərn] *pl* great-grandparents. **–mutter** *f* great-grandmother. **–vater** *m* great-grandfather.

Urheber ['uɪrheɪbər] *m* (*pl* -) author, creator. **–recht** *neut* copyright.

Urin [u'riɪn] *m* urine. **urinieren** *v* urinate.

Urkunde ['uɪrkundə] *f* document, deed; (*Zeugnis*) certificate. **urkundlich** *adj* documentary.

Urlaub ['uɪrlaup] *m* (*pl* -e) leave (of absence); (*Ferien*) holiday, vacation. **im** *or* **auf Urlaub** on holiday, on vacation.

Urmensch ['uɪrmɛnʃ] *m* primitive man.

Urne ['urnə] *f* (*pl* -n) urn.

Ursache ['uɪrzaxə] *f* cause. **keine Ursache!** don't mention it!

Ursprung ['uɪrʃpruŋ] *m* source, origin. **ursprünglich** *adj* original. **Ursprungsland** *neut* country of origin.

Urteil ['urtail] *neut* judgment, verdict; (*Strafmaß*) sentence; (*Urteilskraft*) judgment. **urteilen** *v* judge. **Urteils‖kraft** *f* (power of) judgment, discernment. **–spruch** *m* verdict, sentence.

Urvater ['uɪrfaɪtər] *m* forefather.

Urwelt ['uɪrvɛlt] *f* primeval world.

Urzeit ['uɪrtsait] *f* prehistory, earliest times *pl*. **urzeitlich** *adj* primordial, primeval.

Utopie [uto'piɪ] *f* (*pl* -n) Utopia. **utopisch** *adj* utopian.

V

vag [vaɪk] *adj* vague.

Vagabund [vaga'bunt] *m* (*pl* -en) vagabond, tramp.

vakant [va'kant] *adj* vacant.

Vakuum ['vaɪkuum] *neut* (*pl* **Vakua**) vacuum.

validieren [vali'diɪrən] *v* make valid, validate.

Valuta [va'luɪta] *f* (*pl* **Valuten**) (*Wert*) value; (*Währung*) currency.

Vampir ['vampiɪr] *m* (*pl* -e) vampire.

Vandale [van'daɪlə] *m* (*pl* -n) vandal. **Vandalismus** *m* vandalism.

Vanille [va'niljə] *f* vanilla.

Varietät [varie'tɛɪt] *f* (*pl* -en) variety.

Variation [variatsi'oɪn] *f* (*pl* -en) variation.

Vase ['vaɪzə] *f* (*pl* -en) vase.

Vater ['faɪtər] *m* (*pl* **Väter**) father. **–land** *neut* native land, fatherland. **vaterländisch** *adj* national; patriotic.

väterlich ['fɛɪtərliç] *adj* paternal, fatherly. **väterlicherseits** *adv* on the father's side.

Vaterschaft ['faɪtərʃaft] *f* (*pl* -en) paternity.

Vegetarier [vege'taɪriər] *m* (*pl* -) vegetarian. **vegetarisch** *adj* vegetarian.

Veilchen ['failçən] *neut* (*pl* -) violet. **veilchenblau** *adj* violet.

Vene ['veɪnə] *f* (*pl* -n) vein. **Venenentzündung** *f* (*Med*) phlebitis.

Venedig [ve'neɪdiç] *neut* Venice. **venezianer** *m* (*pl* -), **Venezianerin** *f* (*pl* -nen) Venetian. **venezianisch** *adj* Venetian.

Ventil [ven'tiɪl] *neut* (*pl* -e) valve. **–ator** *m* (*pl* -en) ventilator; (*Mot*) fan; (*Elek*) electric fan.

verabreden [fɛr'apreidən] *v* agree (upon); (*Ort, Zeitpunkt*) fix, appoint. **Verabredung** *f* agreement; appointment.

verabscheuen [fɛr'apʃɔyən] *v* abhor, detest.

verabschieden [fɛr'apʃiɪdən] *v* dismiss; (*Gesetze*) pass. **sich verabschieden von** take one's leave of, say goodbye to.

verachten [fɛr'axtən] *v* despise. **verächtlich** *adj* contemptible. **Verachtung** *f* contempt.

verallgemeinern [fɛralgə'mainərn] *v* generalize. **Verallgemeinerung** *f* generalization.

veralten [fɛr'altən] *v* become outmoded, go out of use. **veraltet** *adj* out-of-date.

veränderlich [fɛr'ɛndərliç] *adj* changeable. **verändern** *v* change, alter. **sich verändern** change, alter. **Veränderung** *f* change, alteration.

Verankern [fɛr'aŋkərn] *v* moor, anchor.

veranlagt [fɛr'anlaıkt] *adj* talented, gifted.

veranlassen [fɛr'anlasən] *v* cause, bring about. **Veranlassung** *f* cause; (*Beweggrund*) motive.

veranschaulichen [fɛr'anʃauliçən] *v* make clear.

veranstalten [fɛr'anʃtaltən] v organize, arrange. **Veranstalt‖er** m (pl -) organizer. **–ung** f (pl -en) event, function; (Veranstalten) organization.
verantworten [fɛr'antvɔrtən] v take responsibility for, answer for. **verantwortlich** adj responsible. **Verantwort‖lichkeit** f responsibility. **–ung** f (pl -en) responsibility; (Rechtfertigung) justification.
verarbeiten [fɛr'aɪbaɪtən] v manufacture, make; (bearbeiten) work, process; (durchdenken) assimilate. **Verarbeitung** f manufacture; working; assimilation.
verargen [fɛr'argən] v blame.
verärgern [fɛr'ɛrgərn] v annoy, vex.
verarmen [fɛr'aɪmən] v become poor. **verarmt** adj impoverished.
Verb [vɛrp] neut (pl -en) verb.
Verband [fɛr'bant] m (pl Verbände) (Med) bandage, dressing; (Verein) association, society.
verbannen [fɛr'banən] v banish. **Verbann‖te(r)** exile. **–ung** f banishment, exile.
*verbergen [fɛr'bɛrgən] v hide.
verbessern [fɛr'bɛsərn] v improve; (berichtigen) correct. **Verbesserung** f (pl -en) improvement; correction.
verbeugen [fɛr'bɔygən] v sich verbeugen bow.
*verbieten [fɛr'biɪtən] v forbid, prohibit.
*verbinden [fɛr'bindən] v connect, join; (Med) bandage, dress; (Teleſ) connect, put through. **sich verbinden mit** join up with, combine with. **verbindlich** adj binding, obligatory; (zuvorkommend) obliging. **Verbindung** f connection; (Med) bandage, dressing; (Teleſ) connection. **in Verbindung mit** in association with. **im Verbindung treten mit** get in touch with. **im Verbindung stehen mit** be in contact with. **in Verbindung setzen mit** put in contact with.
verbissen [fɛr'bisən] adj grim, dogged.
verbittern [fɛr'bitərn] v embitter. **Verbitterung** f bitterness.
verblassen [fɛr'blasən] v turn or grow pale; (Farbe, Erinnerung) fade.
Verbleib [fɛr'blaip] m whereabouts. **verbleiben** v remain.
verblenden [fɛr'blɛndən] v blind, dazzle, delude; (Mauerwerk) face. **Verblendung** f blindness, delusion.
verblüffen [fɛr'blyfən] v dumbfound, nonplus. **verblüfft** adj dumbfounded, non-

plussed. **Verblüffung** f amazement, stupefaction.
verbluten [fɛr'bluɪtən] v bleed to death.
verbohrt [fɛr'boɪrt] adj stubborn.
verborgen [fɛr'bɔrgən] adj hidden. **Verborgenheit** f concealment, secrecy.
Verbot [fɛr'boɪt] neut (pl -e) prohibition, ban. **verboten** adj prohibited, forbidden.
Verbrauch [fɛr'braux] m consumption, use. **verbrauchen** v consume, use up. **Verbraucher** m (pl -) consumer. **Verbrauchsgüter** pl consumer goods pl.
Verbrechen [fɛr'brɛçən] neut crime. **–er** m criminal. **verbrechen** v commit a crime. **verbrecherisch** adj criminal.
verbreiten [fɛr'braitən] v spread. **weit verbreitet** adj widespread.
*verbrennen [fɛr'brɛnən] v burn; (Leichen) cremate. **Verbrennung** f burning; cremation. **–smotor** m internal combustion engine.
*verbringen [fɛr'briɲən] v spend (time).
verbrühen [fɛr'bryɪən] v scald.
Verbum ['vɛrbum] neut (pl Verben) verb.
verbünden [fɛr'byndən] v sich verbünden mit ally oneself with. **Verbündete(r)** m ally.
verchromt [fɛr'krɔɪmt] adj chromium-plated. **Verchromung** f chromium plating.
Verdacht [fɛr'daxt] m (pl -e) suspicion. **in Verdacht kommen** arouse suspicion, be suspected. **verdächtig** adj suspicious. **–er** v suspect.
verdammen [fɛr'damən] v condemn, damn. **verdammt** adj damned. inter, damn! **Verdammung** f damnation.
verdampfen [fɛr'dampfən] v evaporate, vaporize. **Verdampfung** f evaporation, vaporization.
verdanken [fɛr'daŋkən] v owe.
verdauen [fɛr'dauən] v digest. **verdaulich** adj digestible. **Verdauung** f digestion.
Verdeck [fɛr'dɛk] neut (pl -e) canopy, covering; (Mot) roof; (Schiff) deck. **verdecken** v cover, conceal. **verdeckt** adj masked, concealed.
Verderb [fɛr'dɛrp] m ruin, destruction. **verderben** v spoil, ruin; (verführen) corrupt; (Speisen) spoil, go bad; (Menschen) come to grief, perish. **Verderben** neut ruin, destruction. **verderblich** adj destructive, pernicious; (Waren) perishable. **verderbt** adj corrupt(ed).

verdeutlichen [fɛr'dɔytliçən] *v* make clear, elucidate.

verdichten [fɛr'diçtən] *v* compress. **Verdichtung** *f* compression.

verdicken [fɛr'dikən] *v* thicken.

verdienen [fɛr'diːnən] *v* (*Geld*) earn; (*Beachtung, Lob*) deserve. **er hat es verdient** he deserves it; (*negativ*) it serves him right. **Verdienst 1** *m* (*pl* -e) earnings *pl*, gains *pl*. **2** *neut* (*pl* -e) deserts *pl*. **–spanne** *f* margin (of profit).

verdingen [fɛr'diŋən] *v* hire out.

verdoppeln [fɛr'dɔpəln] *v* double. **Verdoppelung** *f* doubling.

verdorben [fɛr'dɔrbən] *adj* spoilt; (*fig*) corrupted.

verdrängen [fɛr'drɛŋən] *v* displace, push out; (*vertreiben*) drive away; (*Psychol*) repress.

verdrehen [fɛr'dreːən] *v* distort, twist.

*****verdrießen** [fɛr'driːsən] *v* vex, annoy. **verdrießlich** *adj* sullen, disgruntled; tiresome irksome.

verdrossen [fɛr'drɔsən] *adj* sullen. **Verdruß** [fɛr'drus] *m* annoyance.

verdummen [fɛr'dumən] *v* stupefy; (*dumm werden*) grow stupid.

verdunkeln [fɛr'duŋkəln] *v* darken.

verdünnen [fɛr'dynən] *v* dilute, thin.

veredeln [fɛr'eːdəln] *v* ennoble; (*fig*) improve, refine.

verehren [fɛr'eːrən] *v* (*Rel*) worship; (*lieben*) adore; (*hochschätzen*) venerate, respect. **Verehr‖er** *m* worshipper; adorer; admirer. **–ung** *f* worship; adoration; veneration.

Verein [fɛr'ain] *m* (*pl* -e) society, association; (*Klub*) club. **vereinbar** *adj* reconcilable, compatible. **vereinbar‖en** *v* agree upon. **–t** *adj* agreed (upon). **Vereinbarung** *f* (*pl* -en) agreement.

vereinfachen [fɛr'ainfaxən] *v* simplify.

vereinheitlichen [fɛr'ainhaitliçən] *v* unify, standardize.

vereinigen [fɛr'ainigən] *v* unite, join. **sich vereinigen** unite. **vereinigt** *adj* united. **die Vereinigten Staaten** *pl* the United States. **Vereinigung** *f* (*pl* -en) union; association, society; (*Zusammenschluß*) combination. **–spunkt** *m* meeting point.

vereint [fɛr'aint] *adj* united.

vereiteln [fɛr'aitəln] *v* frustrate. **Vereitelung** *f* frustration.

vererben [fɛr'ɛrbən] *v* leave, bequeath;

(*Krankheit, Eigenschaft*) transmit. **vererblich** *adj* hereditary. **Vererbung** *f* heredity.

verewigen [fɛr'eːvigən] *v* immortalize.

verfahren [fɛr'faːrən] *v* act, proceed. **sich verfahren** lose one's way. **Verfahren** *neut* procedure; (*Methode*) method; (*Tech*) process.

Verfall [fɛr'fal] *m* ruin; (*allmählich*) decline, decay. **verfallen** *v* decline, decay.

verfälschen [fɛr'fɛlʃən] *v* falsify. **Verfälschung** *f* falsification.

verfassen [fɛr'fasən] *v* compose, write; (*Urkunde*) draw up. **Verfasser** *m* (*pl* -), **Verfasserin** *f* (*pl* -nen) author, writer.

*****verfechten** [fɛr'fɛçtən] *v* fight for, defend.

verfehlen [fɛr'feːlən] *v* miss, not reach; (*versäumen*) fail. **Verfehlung** *f* mistake, lapse.

verfeinern [fɛr'fainərn] *v* refine.

verflechten [fɛr'flɛçtən] *v* interweave; (*fig*) involve.

verfluchen [fɛr'fluːxən] *v* curse. **verflucht** *adj* cursed, damned. *interj* damn (it)!

verfolgen [fɛr'fɔlgən] *v* pursue; (*beobachten*) follow; (*gerichtlich*) prosecute; (*plagen*) persecute. **Verfolger** *m* pursuer; persecutor. **Verfolgung** *f* pursuit; prosecution; persecution.

Verformung [fɛr'fɔrmuŋ] *f* distortion, warping.

verfügbar [fɛr'fyːkbair] *adj* available. **verfügen** *v* order, decree. **verfügen über** have at one's disposal, dispose of. **Verfügung** *f* disposal; (*Anordnung*) order. **zur Verfügung stehen/stellen** be/put at the disposal (of).

verführen [fɛr'fyːrən] *v* seduce; (*verleiten*) lead astray. **Verführ‖er** *m* seducer; tempter. **–ung** *f* seduction; temptation.

vergangen [fɛr'gaŋən] *adj* past. **Vergangenheit** *f* past. **vergänglich** *adj* transitory, impermanent.

Vergaser [fɛr'gaizər] *m* (*pl* -) carburettor.

*****vergeben** [fɛr'geːbən] *v* (*verzeihen*) forgive; (*verschenken*) give away; (*verteilen*) distribute. **vergeb‖ens** *adv* in vain. **–lich** *adj* vain. *adv* in vain. **Vergebung** *f* forgiveness. *interj* pardon me!

vergegenwärtigen [fɛrgeigən'vɛrtigən] *v* represent.

*****vergehen** [fɛr'geːən] *v* pass. **vergehen vor** die of. **sich vergehen** *v* commit an offence, err. **Vergehen** *neut* misdeed.

*vergelten [fɛr'gɛltən] *v* pay back.
Vergeltung *f* reward; retaliation.
*vergessen [fɛr'gɛsən] *v* forget. **Vergessenheit** *f* oblivion. **vergeßlich** *adj* forgetful.
vergeuden [fɛr'gɔydən] *v* waste, squander.
Vergeudung *f* waste, dissipation.
vergewaltigen [fɛrgə'valtigən] *v* rape.
Vergewaltiger *m* rapist. **Vergewaltigung** *f*
rape.
*vergießen [fɛr'giːsən] *v* shed, spill.
vergiften [fɛr'giftən] *v* poison. **Vergiftung**
f poisoning.
Vergißmeinnicht [fɛr'gismainniçt] *neut*
(*pl* **-e**) forget-me-not.
verglasen [fɛr'glaːzən] *v* glaze.
Vergleich [fɛr'glaiç] *m* (*pl* **-e**) comparison; (*Redewendung*) simile; (*Abkommen*)
agreement, settlement. **einen Vergleich
schließen** come to an agreement. **im Vergleich mit/zu** in comparison with/to.
vergleichbar *adj* comparable. **vergleichen**
v compare; settle, agree.
Vergnügen [fɛr'gnyːgən] *neut* enjoyment.
vergnügen *v* amuse. **sich vergnügen**
amuse oneself. **vergnügt** *adj* merry, happy. **Vergnügung** *f* pleasure, enjoyment.
–spark *m* amusement park.
vergoldet [fɛr'gɔldət] *adj* (*Metall*) gold-
plated; (*Holz*) gilt.
vergöttern [fɛr'gœtərn] *v* deify; (*fig*) idolize.
vergraben [fɛr'graːbən] *v* bury.
vergriffen [fɛr'grifən] *adj* sold out; (*Buch*)
out of print.
vergrößern [fɛr'grœːsərn] *v* enlarge, magnify. **Vergrößerung** *f* (*pl* **-en**) enlargement.
Vergünstigung [fɛr'gynstiguŋ] *f* (*pl* **-en**)
privilege; (*Rabatt*) discount.
vergüten [fɛr'gyːtən] *v* compensate (for);
(*Unkosten*) reimburse. **Vergütung** *f* (*pl*
-en) compensation; reimbursement.
verhaften [fɛr'haftən] *v* arrest. **verhaftet**
adj arrested; (*fig*) bound, connected.
Verhaftung *f* (*pl* **-en**) arrest.
*verhalten [fɛr'haltən] *v* hold back. **sich
verhalten** behave, act; (*Sache*) be.
Verhalten *neut* behaviour.
Verhältnis [fɛr'hɛltnis] *neut* (*pl* **-se**) relation, proportion; (*Beziehungen*) relation;
(*Liebesaffäre*) relationship; liaison. **im
Verhältnis zu** in comparison with.
Verhältnisse *pl* circumstances. **Verhältn-**

ismäßig *adj* proportional. *adv* relatively,
comparatively.
verhandeln [fɛr'handəln] *v* negotiate. **Verhandlung** *f* negotiation.
Verhängnis [fɛr'hɛŋnis] *neut* (*pl* **-se**) fate,
destiny. **verhängnisvoll** *adj* fateful.
verhaßt [fɛr'hast] *adj* odious, hated.
verheeren [fɛr'heːrən] *v* devastate, lay
waste.
verheimlichen [fɛr'haimliçən] *v* conceal,
keep secret.
verheiraten [fɛr'hairaitən] *v* marry. **sich
verheiraten** get married, marry.
*verheißen [fɛr'haisən] *v* promise.
*verhelfen [fɛr'hɛlfən] *v* assist, help.
verherrlichen [fɛr'hɛrliçən] *v* glorify.
Verherrlichung *f* glorification.
verhindern [fɛr'hindərn] *v* prevent.
Verhinderung *f* prevention.
verhöhnen [gɛr'høːnən] *v* ridicule, mock.
Verhör [fɛr'høːr] *neut* (*pl* **-e**) interrogation, examination. **verhören** *v* interrogate, examine. **sich verhören** hear wrongly, misunderstand.
verhungern [fɛr'huŋərn] *v* starve (to
death).
verhüten [fɛr'hyːtən] *v* prevent, ward off.
–d *adj* preventive. **Verhütung** *f* prevention. **–smittel** *neut* contraceptive.
verirren [fɛr'irən] *v* **sich verirren** go
astray, get lost.
verjüngen [fɛr'jyŋən] *v* rejuvenate;
(*erneuern*) renew. **Verjüngung** *f* rejuvenation; renewal.
Verkauf [fɛr'kauf] *m* sale. **verkaufen** *v*
sell. **Verkäufer** *m* seller; (*Angestellter*)
salesman; (*im Laden*) sales assistant. **–in**
f saleswoman, sales assistant. **verkäuflich**
adj for sale. **Verkaufs‖abteilung** *f* sales
department. **–automat** *m* vending
machine. **–bedingungen** (*pl*) terms of
sale. **–förderung** *f* sales promotion.
–preis *m* selling price.
Verkehr [fɛr'keːr] *m* traffic; (*Umgang*)
intercourse; (*Handel*) trade. **verkehren** *v*
(*Bus*) run; (*verdrehen*) distort; (*besuchen*)
frequent; (*Menschen*) associate (with).
Verkehrs‖ampeln *f pl* traffic lights.
–ordnung *f* traffic regulation. **–spitze** *f*
rush hour. **–stockung** *f* traffic jam.
–unfall *m* road accident. **verkehrt** *adj*
inverted, wrong way round; (*falsch*)
wrong.
*verkennen [fɛr'kɛnən] *v* mistake, mis-
judge; (*Person*) not recognize.

verklagen [fɛr'klaːgən] v (*Jur*) sue (for); (*umg.*) inform against.
verklären [fɛr'klɛːrən] v transfigure; (*fig*) illumine. **Verklärung** f transfiguration; illumination.
verkleiden [fɛr'klaidən] v cover, mask; (*Wand*) face. **sich verkleiden** disguise oneself. **Verkleidung** f (*pl* -en) disguise; facing, lining.
verkleinern [fɛr'klainərn] v reduce, diminish. **Verkleinerung** f (*pl* -en) reduction, diminution.
verknüpfen [fɛr'knypfən] v knot (together), join; (*fig*) connect. **verknüpft** adj connected.
***verkommen** [fɛr'kɔmən] v (*Person*) degenerate, (*umg.*) go to the dogs; (*speisen*) go bad; (*Gebäude*) decay, be neglected.
verkörpern [fɛr'kœrpərn] v embody. **Verkörperung** f embodiment, incarnation.
verkrümmen [fɛr'krymən] v bend, make crooked. **Verkrümmung** f (*pl* -en) crookedness, distortion; (*Rückgrat*) curvature.
verkrüppeln [fɛr'krypəln] v cripple.
verkünden [fɛr'kyndən] v announce, proclaim; (*Urteil*) pronounce. **verkündigen** v proclaim. **Mariä Verkündigung** Annunciation, Lady Day.
verkürzen [fɛr'kyrtsən] v shorten, abbreviate; (*Buch*) abridge. **sich verkürzen** shrink, diminish. **Verkürzung** f shortening; (*Buch*) abridgment.
***verladen** [fɛr'laːdən] v load; (*verschicken*) dispatch. **Verladung** f loading.
Verlag [fɛr'laːk] m (*pl* -e) publishing house, publisher.
verlangen [fɛr'laŋən] v demand; (*benötigen*) require. **verlangen nach** long for. **Verlangen** neut demand; (*Wunsch*) desire. **auf Verlangen** on demand.
verlängern [fɛr'lɛŋərn] v extend, lengthen; (*Gültigkeit, usw.*) extend. **Verlängerung** f (*pl* -en) extension.
verlangsamen [fɛr'laŋzaimən] v · slow down.
Verlaß [fɛr'las] m trustworthiness, reliability. **verlassen** v leave; (*im Stich lassen*) desert, abandon. adj abandoned, forsaken. **sich verlassen auf** rely on. **verläßlich** adj reliable.
Verlauf [fɛr'lauf] m course. **verlaufen** v (*Zeit*) pass; (*Angelegenheit*) go, turn out; (*Weg*) run, to. **es ist alles gut verlaufen**

everything went very well. **sich verlaufen** lose one's way.
verlautbaren [fɛr'lautbairən] v notify.
verlegen [fɛr'leːgən] v misplace; (*Platz ändern*) transfer, remove; (*Buch*) publish; (*Termin*) postpone. adj embarrassed. **Verleg‖enheit** f embarrassment; (*Schwierigkeit*) difficulty. **–er** m (*pl* -) publisher.
***verleihen** [fɛr'laiən] v lend; (*Preise*) confer, bestow.
verleiten [fɛr'laitən] v lead astray, mislead.
verlernen [fɛr'lɛrnən] v forget.
***verlesen** [fɛr'leizən] v read out; (*auslesen*) pick. **sich verlesen** misread.
verletzen [fɛr'lɛtsən] v injure, wound; (*kränken*) hurt, offend; (*Gesetze*) infringe. **verletzlich** adj vulnerable; (*fig*) sensitive, touchy. **Verletzung** f (*pl* -en) injury; (*Vergehen*) offence.
verleugnen [fɛr'lɔygnən] v deny; (*Kind, Freunde*) disown.
verleumden [fɛr'lɔymdən] v slander. **Verleumder** m (*pl* -) slanderer. **verleumderisch** adj slanderous. **Verleumdung** f (*pl* -en) slander.
verlieben [fɛr'liːbən] v **sich verlieben in** fall in love with.
***verlieren** [fɛr'liːrən] v lose. **sich verlieren** get lost.
verloben [fɛr'loːbən] v **sich verloben mit** get engaged to. **Verlobte** f (*pl* -n) fiancée. **Verlobter** m (*pl* -en) fiancé. **Verlobung** f (*pl* -en) engagement.
verlocken [fɛr'lɔkən] v tempt, entice. **–d** adj tempting. **Verlockung** f (*pl* -en) enticement, temptation.
verlogen [fɛr'loːgən] adj untruthful, lying.
verloren [fɛr'loːrən] adj lost. **–gehen** v be lost.
Verlust [fɛr'lust] m (*pl* -e) loss. **verlustbringend** adj detrimental.
vermachen [fɛr'maxən] v bequeath, leave. **Vermächtnis** neut (*pl* -se) (*Testament*) will; (*Vermachtes*) legacy, bequest.
vermehren [fɛr'meirən] v also **sich vermehren** increase. **Vermehrung** f (*pl* -en) increase.
***vermeiden** [fɛr'maidən] v avoid. **vermeidlich** adj avoidable. **Vermeidung** f avoidance.
vermeintlich [fɛr'maintliç] adj supposed, presumed.

Vermerk 366

Vermerk [fɛr'mɛrk] m (pl -e) note,
remark. **vermerken** v note, remark.
*****vermessen** [fɛr'mɛsən] v measure;
(Land) survey. adj presumptuous.
Vermess‖er m surveyor. **-ung** f measurement; (Land) survey.
vermieten [fɛr'miːtən] v let, rent (out).
Vermiet‖er m landlord. **-ung** f letting.
vermindern [fɛr'mindərn] v reduce,
decrease. **Verminderung** f reduction,
decrease.
vermischen [fɛr'miʃən] v mix, blend.
vermissen [fɛr'misən] v miss. **vermißt** adj
missing.
vermitteln [fɛr'mitəln] v mediate, negotiate; (verschaffen) procure, obtain.
Vermittl‖er m mediator, go-between;
(Komm) agent. **-ung** f (pl -en) mediation, negotiation; (Telef) exchange.
*****vermögen** [fɛr'mœɪgən] v be able (to).
-d adj well-to-do. **Vermögen** neut fortune, wealth, property; (Fähigkeit) ability. **-sverwalter** m trustee (of an estate).
vermuten [fɛr'muːtən] v suppose, suspect.
vermutlich adj supposed. adv probably,
presumably. **Vermutung** f (pl -en) supposition, suspicion.
vernachlässigen [fɛr'naxlɛsigən] v neglect.
vernarren [fɛr'narən] v **sich vernarren in**
become infatuated with; (Kind) dote on.
*****vernehmen** [fɛr'neɪmən] v perceive;
(Gefangene) interrogate. **vernehmlich** adj
perceptible.
verneinen [fɛr'nainən] v deny; (Frage)
say no, answer in the negative.
Verneinung f denial; negation.
vernichten [fɛr'niçtən] v destroy, annihilate. **-d** adj annihilating, crushing.
Vernichtung f destruction, annihilation.
vernieten [fɛr'niːtən] v rivet.
Vernunft [fɛr'nunft] f reason; (Besonnenheit) sense, commonsense. **zur
Vernunft kommen** come to one's senses.
vernünftig adj sensible, reasonable.
veröden [fɛr'œːdən] v become desolate.
veröffentlichen [fɛr'œfəntliçən] v publish.
Veröffentlichung f publication.
verordnen [fɛr'ɔdnən] v order; (Med) prescribe. **Verordnung** f order; prescription.
verpachten [fɛr'paxtən] v lease, let.
verpacken [fɛr'pakən] v pack.
verpassen [fɛr'pasən] v miss.
verpfänden [fɛr'pfɛndən] v pawn, pledge.

verpflegen [fɛr'pfleɪgən] v feed, cater for.
Verpflegung f food, board.
verpflichten [fɛr'pliçtən] v oblige, commit. **sich verpflichten** bind or commit
oneself. **Verpflichtung** f obligation, commitment, duty.
verpfuschen [fɛr'pfuʃən] v bungle, botch,
make a mess of.
verprügeln [fɛr'pryɪgəln] v thrash, beat.
verputzen [fɛr'putsən] v plaster; (umg.)
scoff, put away.
Verrat [fɛr'raɪt] m (unz.) treachery; (Pol)
treason; (eines Geheimnisses) betrayal.
verraten v betray. **Verräter** m (pl -) traitor. **verräterisch** adj treacherous.
verrechnen [fɛr'rɛçnən] v reckon up. **sich
verrechnen** miscalculate. **Verrechnung** f
miscalculation.
verreisen [fɛr'raizən] v go away (on a
journey).
verrenken [fɛr'rɛŋkən] v dislocate, sprain.
Verrenkung f (pl -en) dislocation, sprain.
verrichten [fɛr'riçtən] v perform, do, execute.
verriegeln [fɛr'riɪgəln] v bolt, bar.
verringern [fɛr'riŋərn] v reduce, lessen.
verrotten [fɛr'rɔtən] v rot. **verrottet** adj
rotten.
verrücken [fɛr'rykən] v shift, displace.
verrückt adj crazy.
Verruf [fɛr'ruɪf] m ill repute, disrepute. **in
Verruf bringen/kommen** bring/fall into
disrepute.
Vers [fɛrs] m (pl -e) line; (Strophe) verse.
versagen [fɛr'zaɪgən] v fail; (verweigern)
refuse. **Versager** m (pl -) failure.
versammeln [fɛr'zaməln] v assemble,
gather. **sich versammeln** meet. **Versammlung** f (pl -en) meeting, assembly, convention.
Versand [fɛr'zant] m dispatch, shipment,
forwarding. **-handel** m mail-order (trad-
ing).
versäumen [fɛr'zɔymən] v neglect, fail;
(verpassen) miss. **Versäumnis** f neglect,
omission.
verschaffen [fɛr'ʃafən] v obtain, procure.
verschämt [fɛr'ʃɛɪmt] adj bashful,
ashamed.
Verschanzung [fɛr'ʃantsuŋ] f (pl -en) fortification, entrenchment.
verschärfen [fɛr'ʃɛrfən] v sharpen, intensify.
*****verscheiden** v die. **verschieden** adj dead.

verschicken [fɛr'ʃikən] v send off, dispatch.
*****verschieben** [fɛr'ʃiːbən] v move, shift; (*Termin*) postpone. **Verschiebung** f displacement; postponement.
verschieden [fɛr'ʃiːdən] adj different. –**artig** adj various. **Verschiedenheit** f difference.
verschiffen [fɛr'ʃifən] v ship.
verschimmeln [fɛr'ʃiməln] v moulder, grow mouldy.
*****verschlafen** [fɛr'ʃlaːfən] v oversleep; (*Sorgen*) sleep off. adj sleepy.
Verschlag [fɛr'ʃlaːk] m shed.
verschlechtern [fɛr'ʃlɛçtərn] v make worse, aggravate. **sich verschlechtern** deteriorate, get worse. **Verschlechterung** f deterioration.
verschleiern [fɛr'ʃlaiərn] v veil; (*fig*) camouflage, conceal.
Verschleiß [fɛr'ʃlais] m (*pl* -e) wear and tear. **verschleißen** v wear out.
verschleudern [fɛr'ʃlɔydərn] v waste, squander.
verschließbar [fɛr'ʃliːsbair] adj lockable. **verschließen** v lock; (*Sachen*) lock up or away.
verschlimmern [fɛr'ʃlimərn] v make worse, aggravate. **sich verschlimmern** become worse, deteriorate. **Verschlimmerung** f deterioration.
*****verschlingen** [fɛr'ʃliŋən] v devour, gorge; (*verflechten*) twist, intertwine.
verschlossen [fɛr'ʃlɔsən] adj locked; (*Person*) reserved, withdrawn.
verschlucken [fɛr'ʃlukən] v swallow.
Verschluß [fɛr'ʃlus] m fastening; (*Propfen*) stopper, plug; (*Phot*) shutter.
verschmähen [fɛr'ʃmɛiən] v disdain, scorn.
*****verschmelzen** [fɛr'ʃmɛltsən] v melt, fuse; (*ineinander*) merge.
*****verschneiden** [fɛr'ʃnaidən] v trim, prune; (*Wein*) mix, adulterate; (*kastrieren*) castrate.
verschollen [fɛr'ʃɔlən] adj missing.
verschonen [fɛr'ʃoinən] v spare.
verschönern [fɛr'ʃøːnərn] v beautify.
verschränken [fɛr'ʃrɛŋkən] v fold, cross.
verschulden [fɛr'ʃuldən] v fall into or be in debt; (*Übel*) be to blame for. **Verschulden** neut guilt, fault. **verschuldet** adj in debt.
*****verschweigen** [fɛr'ʃvaigən] v keep secret, hide. **Verschweigung** f concealment.

verschwenden [fɛr'ʃvɛndən] v waste, squander. **verschwenderisch** adj wasteful. **Verschwendung** f waste.
verschwiegen [fɛr'ʃviːgən] adj discreet; (*Platz*) secluded, quiet. **Verschwiegenheit** f discretion.
*****verschwinden** [fɛr'ʃvindən] v disappear.
verschwommen [fɛr'ʃvɔmən] adj blurred, hazy.
verschwören [fɛr'ʃvøːrən] v renounce, abjure. **sich verschwören** conspire, plot. **Verschwör‖er** m conspirator, plotter. –**ung** f conspiracy.
*****versehen** [fɛr'zeiən] v (*versorgan*) provide, supply; (*Dienst*) discharge; (*Haus, usw.*) look after. **sich versehen** make a mistake. **Versehen** neut mistake; (*Übersehen*) oversight. **versehentlich** adv by mistake.
*****versenden** [fɛr'zɛndən] v send, dispatch.
versengen [fɛr'zɛŋən] v singe, scorch.
versenken [fɛr'zɛŋkən] v lower; (*unter Wasser*) submerge; (*Schiff*) sink. **sich versenken in** become absorbed in.
versessen [fɛr'zɛsən] adj **versessen auf** mad about or on.
versetzen [fɛr'zɛtsən] v move, transfer; (*verpfänden*) pawn; (*umg.*) leave in the lurch, jilt. **Versetzung** f removal, transfer.
verseuchen [fɛr'zɔyçən] v contaminate.
versichern [fɛr'ziçərn] v insure; (*überzeugen*) assure. **sich versichern** make certain. **Seien Sie versichert, daß** you may rest assured that. **Versicherung** f insurance. –**spolice** f insurance policy.
versiegeln [fɛr'ziːgəln] v seal.
versöhnen [fɛr'zøːnən] v reconcile. **sich versöhnen mit** become reconciled with. **versöhnlich** adj conciliatory. **Versöhnung** f reconciliation.
versorgen [fɛr'zɔrgən] v (*Kind, usw.*) provide for. **versorgen mit** provide or supply with. **Versorgung** f care, provision; (*staatlich*) maintenance, (public) assistance.
verspäten [fɛr'ʃpɛitən] v delay. **verspätet** adj late, delayed. **Verspätung** f (*pl* -en) delay. **10 Minuten Verspätung haben** be running 10 minutes late.
versperren [fɛr'ʃpɛrən] v bar; obstruct.
verspielen [fɛr'ʃpiːlən] v gamble away, lose.

verspotten [fɛr'ʃpɔtən] v scoff at, ridicule. **Verspottung** f ridicule.

***versprechen** [fɛr'ʃprɛçən] v promise. **sich versprechen** make a (verbal) mistake. **Versprechen** neut (pl -) promise.

versprengen [fɛr'ʃprɛŋən] v (Mil) scatter, disperse.

versprochen [fɛr'ʃprɔxən] adj promised.

verstaatlichen [fɛr'ʃtaːtliçən] v nationalize. **Verstaatlichung** f nationalization.

Verstand [fɛr'ʃtant] m understanding; (Geist) mind, intelligence. **den Verstand verlieren** lose one's reason, go out of one's mind. **verständig** adj intelligent; sensible. **verständigen** v inform. **sich verständigen mit (über)** come to an understanding with (about). **Verständigung** f understanding, arrangement. **verständlich** adj intelligible. **Verständnis** neut understanding, comprehension. **verständnis‖los** adj uncomprehending, unappreciative. **–voll** adj understanding, sympathetic.

verstärken [fɛr'ʃtɛrkən] v strengthen; (Ton) amplify; (Farbe, Spannung) intensify. **Verstärk‖er** m amplifier. **–ung** f strengthening; (Ton) amplification; (Mil) reinforcements pl.

Versteck [fɛr'ʃtɛk] neut (pl -e) hiding place. **verstecken** v hide. **sich verstecken** hide. **versteckt** adj hidden; (Anspielung) veiled, implied.

***verstehen** [fɛr'ʃteːən] v understand. **zu verstehen geben** give to understand. **sich verstehen mit** come to an understanding with.

Versteigerer [fɛr'ʃtaigərər] m (pl -) auctioneer. **versteigern** v (sell by) auction. **Versteigerung** f (pl -en) auction.

versteinern [fɛr'ʃtainərn] v petrify. **versteinert** adj petrified.

verstellbar [fɛr'ʃtɛlbaːr] adj adjustable, movable. **verstellen** v adjust; (versperren) block, bar; (unkenntlich machen) disguise. **sich verstellen** feign, dissemble. **Verstellung** f (pl -en) adjustment; (fig) pretence.

verstimmt [fɛr'ʃtimt] adj (Musik) out of tune; (Person) bad-tempered; (Magen) upset.

verstockt [fɛr'ʃtɔkt] adj stubborn.

verstohlen [fɛr'ʃtoːlən] adj furtive, stealthy.

verstopfen [fɛr'ʃtɔpfən] v plug, stop up;

(Med) constipate. **Verstopfung** f obstruction; (Med) constipation.

verstorben [fɛr'ʃtɔrbən] adj deceased, late. **Verstorbene(r)** the deceased.

Verstoß [fɛr'ʃtoːs] m offence. **verstoßen** v offend; (von sich stoßen) reject.

verstricken [fɛr'ʃtrikən] v entangle, ensnare.

verstümmeln [fɛr'ʃtyməln] v mutilate, maim.

Versuch [fɛr'zuːx] m (pl -e) attempt; (Probe) test, trial; (Experiment) experiment. **versuchen** v attempt, try; (kosten) taste, try. **Versuchs‖fahrt** f trial run. **–kaninchen** neut (fig) guinea pig.

vertagen [fɛr'taːgən] v adjourn.

vertauschen [fɛr'tauʃən] v exchange.

verteidigen [fɛr'taidigən] v defend. **Verteidig‖er** m (pl -) defender; (Jur) defence counsel. **–ung** f (pl -en) defence.

verteilen [fɛr'tailən] v distribute; (zerteilen) divide. **Verteil‖er** m (pl -) distributor. **–ung** f (pl -en) distribution.

vertiefen [fɛr'tiːfən] v deepen. **sich vertiefen in** be absorbed in. **vertieft** adj sunk; (fig) absorbed. **Vertiefung** f depression, hollow; (fig) absorption.

vertikal [vɛrti'kaːl] adj vertical.

vertilgen [fɛr'tilgən] v exterminate; (vernichten) destroy. **Vertilgung** f extermination; destruction.

Vertrag [fɛr'traːk] m (pl Verträge) contract; (Pol) treaty. **vertragen** v bear, endure. **sich vertragen mit** get on well with. **vertraglich** adj stipulated, agreed.

verträglich [fɛr'trɛːkliç] adj (Person) good-natured, obliging; (Speise) light, digestible.

Vertrags‖bruch m breach of contract. **–nehmer** m contractor.

vertrauen [fɛr'trauən] v trust. **vertrauen auf** trust in, have confidence in. **Vertrauen** neut trust, confidence. **Vertrauens‖sache** f confidential affair. **–votum** neut vote of confidence. **vertrauens‖voll** adj trustful, trusting. **–würdig** adj trustworthy. **vertraulich** adj confidential. **vertraut** adj familiar.

***vertreiben** [fɛr'traibən] v expel, drive away; (verkaufen) sell. **Vertreibung** f (pl -en) expulsion.

***vertreten** [fɛr'treːtən] v represent; (vorübergehend) replace, stand in for; (eintreten für) advocate. **Vertret‖er** m (pl

-) representative; (*Komm*) sales representative; **–ung** *f* (*pl* **-en**) representation.

Vertrieb [fɛr'triːp] *m* (retail) sale.

***vertun** [fɛr'tuːn] *v* squander, spend.

vertuschen [fɛr'tuʃən] *v* hush up.

verunglimpfen [fɛr'unglimpfən] *v* defame, revile.

verunglücken [fɛr'unglykən] *v* be involved in an accident; (*Angelegenheit*) fail.

verunreinigen [fɛr'untainigən] *v* pollute, soil.

verunstalten [fɛr'unʃtaltən] *v* disfigure.

veruntreuen [fɛr'untrɔyən] *v* embezzle.

verursachen [fɛr'uːrzaxən] *v* cause, bring about.

verurteilen [fɛr'uːrtailən] *v* condemn; (*Jur*) sentence. **Verurteilung** *f* condemnation; conviction.

vervielfältigen [fɛr'fiːlfɛltigən] *v* duplicate, copy. **Vervielfältigung** *f* reproduction, duplication.

vervollkommnen [fɛr'fɔlkɔmnən] *v* perfect.

vervollständigen [fɛr'fɔlʃtɛndigən] *v* complete.

***verwachsen** [fɛr'vaksən] *v* grow together; (*Wunde*) heal up; (*bucklig werden*) become deformed; (**sich verbinden**) be tied to. *adj* deformed.

verwahren [fɛr'vairən] *v* keep; (*schützen*) protect, preserve.

verwahrlosen [fɛr'vailozən] *v* neglect. **verwahrlost** *adj* neglected; (*Kind*) scruffy, unkempt.

verwalten [fɛr'valtən] *v* administer, manage. **Verwalter** *m* administrator; (*Fabrik, Büro*) manager; (*Gut, Haus*) steward. **Verwaltung** *f* administration; management.

verwandeln [fɛr'vandəln] *v* transform; (*ändern*) change. **Verwandlung** *f* transformation; change.

verwandt [fɛr'vant] *adj* related. **Verwandt‖e(r)** relative, relation. **–schaft** *f* relationship; (*Verwandte*) relatives *pl*.

verwechseln [fɛr'vɛksəln] *v* confuse. **verwechseln mit** mistake for, confuse with. **Verwechslung** *f* confusion.

verwegen [fɛr'veigən] *adj* bold, audacious.

verweichlicht [fɛr'vaiçliçt] *adj* effeminate.

verweigern [fɛr'vaigərn] *v* refuse. **Verweigerung** *f* refusal.

verweilen [fɛr'vailən] *v* linger, stay.

Verweis [fɛr'vais] *m* (*pl* **-e**) reprimand,

rebuke; (*Hinweis*) reference. **verweisen** *v* reprimand, rebuke; (*verbannen*) exile, banish. **verweisen auf** refer to.

***verwenden** [fɛr'vɛndən] *v* use, employ; apply; (*Zeit*) spend. **Verwendung** *f* use; application.

***verwerfen** [fɛr'vɛrfən] *v* throw away; (*zurückweisen*) reject.

verwesen[1] [fɛr'veisən] *v* (*verwalten*) administer.

verwesen[2] *v* (*verfaulen*) decay.

verwickeln [fɛr'vikəln] *n* entangle. **sich verwickeln in** become involved in. **verwickelt** *adj* complicated. **Verwicklung** *f* (*pl* **-en**) entanglement, complication.

verwirken [fɛr'virkən] *v* forfeit.

verwirklichen [fɛr'virkliçən] *v* realize. **sich verwirklichen** come true, materialize. **Verwirklichung** *f* realization.

***verwirren** [fɛr'virən] *v* confuse, bewilder. **verwirrt** *adj* confused. **Verwirrung** *f* confusion.

verwischen [fɛr'viʃən] *v* blur, smear; (*fig*) cover up, wipe out.

verwitwet [fɛr'vitvət] *adj* widowed.

verwöhnen [fɛr'vœnən] *v* spoil. **verwöhnt** *adj* pampered, spoiled.

verworfen [fɛr'vɔrfən] *adj* depraved.

verworren [fɛr'vɔrən] *adj* confused.

verwundbar [fɛr'vuntbaɪr] *adj* vulnerable. **verwunden** *v* wound, hurt. **verwundet** *adj* wounded. **Verwundete(r)** injured person; (*Mil*) casualty. **Verwundung** *f* wound, injury.

verwunderlich [fɛr'vundəarliç] *adj* surprising. **verwundern** *v* surprise, astonish. **sich verwundern über** be astonished by, wonder about. **Verwunderung** *f* astonishment.

verwünschen [fɛr'vynʃən] *v* curse. **verwünscht** *adj* cursed, bewitched.

verwüsten [fɛr'vyistən] *v* devastate. **Verwüstung** *f* devastation.

verzagt [fɛr'tsaikt] *adj* downcast, despondent.

verzaubern [fɛr'tsaubərn] *v* enchant, charm. **verzaubert** *adj* enchanted, magic.

Verzehr [fɛr'tseir] *m* consumption (of food and drink). **verzehren** *v* consume, take, eat.

verzeichnen [fɛr'tsaiçnən] *v* note, enter, write down. **Verzeichnis** *neut* (*pl* **-se**) list, catalogue; (*Buch*) index; (*Register*) register.

*verzeihen [fɛr'tsaiən] *v* pardon, forgive. **verzeihen Sie!** pardon (me)! I'm sorry! **Verzeihung** *f* pardon, forgiveness. *interj* I beg your pardon! excuse me!
verzerren [fɛr'tsɛrən] *v* distort.
Verzicht [fɛr'tsiçt] *m* (*pl* -e) renunciation. **verzichten auf** renounce, do without.
verziehen [fɛr'tsiːən] *v* distort; (*Kinder*) spoil.
verzieren [fɛr'tsiːrən] *v* decorate, adorn.
verzögern [fɛr'tsœːgərn] *v* delay. **Verzögerung** *f* (*pl* -en) delay.
verzollen [fɛr'tsɔlən] *v* pay duty on.
verzücken [fɛr'tsukən] *v* enrapture. **verzückt** *adj* enraptured, ecstatic. **Verzückung** *f* (*pl* -en) rapture, ecstasy.
verzuckern [fɛr'tsukərn] *v* sugar.
Verzug [fɛr'tsuk] *m* (*unz.*) delay.
verzweifeln [fɛr'tsvaifəln] *v* despair. **verzweifelt** *adj* desperate. **Verzweiflung** *f* despair.
verzwickt [fɛr'tsvikt] *adj* complicated, difficult.
veterinär [veteri'nɛr] *adj* veterinary. **Veterinär** *m* (*pl* -e) veterinary surgeon.
Vetter ['fɛtər] *m* (*pl* -n) (male) cousin.
Vibration [vibratsi'oɪn] *f* (*pl* -en) vibration. **vibrieren** *v* vibrate.
Vieh [fiː] **1** *neut* (*unz.*) cattle *pl*. **2** *neut* (*pl* Viecher) beast. **viehisch** *adj* bestial, brutal. **Vieh‖stall** *m* cowshed. **–treiber** *m* drover. **–zucht** *f* cattle-breeding.
viel [fiːl] *adj* much. **viele** *pl adj* many. **so viel** so much. **viel besser** much better. **viel mehr als** far more than. **recht viel** a great deal. **viel halten von** think much *or* highly of. **viel‖fach** *adj* multiple. *adv* frequently, many times. **–fältig** *adj* various, manifold.
vielleicht [fi'laiçt] *adv* perhaps.
viel‖mal(s) *adv* often, many times. **–mehr** *adv*, *conj* rather. **–seitig** *adj* many-sided. **–versprechend** *adj* (very) promising.
vier [fiːr] *pron*, *adj* four. **Viereck** *neut* square, rectangle. **viereckig** *adj* square, rectangular. **viermal(s)** *adv* four times. **viert** *adj* fourth. **Viertaktmotor** *m* four-stroke engine. **Viertel** *neut* quarter. **–stunde** *f* quarter (of an) hour. **viertens** *adv* fourthly.
vierzehn ['fiːrtsein] *pron*, *adj* fourteen. **vierzehn Tage** fortnight. **vierzehnt** *adj* fourteenth.

vierzig ['fiːrtsiç] *pron*, *adj* forty. **vierzigst** *adj* fortieth.
Villa ['vila] *f* (*pl* Villen) villa.
Viola [vi'oːla] *f* (*pl* Violen) viola. **Viol‖ine** *f* violin. **–inist** *m* (*pl* -), **–inistin** *f* (*pl* -nen) violinist. **–oncello** *neut* violoncello, cello.
Virtuose [virtu'oɪzə] *m* (*pl* -n) virtuoso.
Visite [vi'ziːtə] *f* (*pl* -n) visit. **–nkarte** *f* visiting card.
Visum ['viːzum] *neut* (*pl* Visa) visa.
Vitamin [vita'miːn] *neut* (*pl* -e) vitamin.
Vlies [fliːs] *neut* (*pl* -e) fleece.
Vogel ['foːgəl] *m* (*pl* Vögel) bird. **–gesang** *m* bird-song. **–haus** *neut* aviary. **–kunde** *f* ornithology. **–perpektive** *f or* **–schau** *f* bird's-eye view.
vokal [vo'kaɪl] *adj* vocal. **Vokal** *m* vowel.
Volk [fɔlk] *neut* (*pl* Völker) people, folk; nation.
Völker‖kunde *f* ethnology. **–schaft** people, tribe. **völkisch** *adj* national.
Volks‖eigentum *neut* public property. **–entscheid** *m* plebiscite, referendum. **–gruppe** *f* ethnic group. **–lied** *neut* (traditional) folksong. **–menge** *f* crowd. **–schule** *f* primary school. **–staat** *m* republic. **–tanz** *m* folk dance. **–tracht** *f* national costume.
volkstümlich ['fɔlkstyːmliç] *adj* popular.
Volkswirt ['fɔlksvirt] *m* economist. **–schaft** *f* (political) economy. **volkswirtschaftlich** *adj* economic.
voll [fɔl] *adj* full. *adv* fully. *der Topf ist voll Wasser* the pot is full of water. *ein Glas voll Milch* a glassful of milk. *in voller Blüte* in full bloom. *volles Gesicht* round face. **voll‖auf** *adv* in abundance. **–automatisch** *adj* fully automatic. **–berechtigt** *adj* fully authorized. **–beschäftigt** *adj* fully employed. **–blütig** *adj* full-blooded.
*vollbringen [fɔ'briŋən] *v* accomplish. **Vollbringung** *f* accomplishment.
vollenden [fɔl'ɛndən] *v* finish, end, complete. **vollendet** *adj* completed; (*vervollkomnet*) perfect. **Vollendung** *f* completion; perfection.
voller ['fɔlər] *adj or* **voll von** full (of).
völlig ['fœliç] *adj* complete, entire, whole.
vollkommen ['fɔlkɔmən] *adj* perfect, finished. **Vollkommenheit** *f* perfection.
Voll‖kornbrot *neut* wholemeal bread. **–macht** *f* power of attorney, authority. **–milch** *f* whole milk.

voll‖ständig adj complete. **–stopfen** v stuff.
vollstrecken [fɔl'ʃtrɛkən] v execute, carry out. **Vollstreck‖er** m (pl -), **–erin** f (pl -nen) executor. **–ung** f (pl -en) execution.
*vollziehen [fɔl'tsiːən] v carry out, execute.
Volontär [volɔn'tɛːr] m (pl -e) volunteer (worker), unpaid helper.
vom [fɔm] prep + art von dem.
von [fɔn] prep from; (einer Person gehörig) of; (einer Person stammend) by. das Buch von Peter Peter's book. ein Buch von Greene a book by Greene. ein Freund von ihm a friend of his. **von ... an** starting, from. **von nun an** from now on. **von mir aus** as far as I am concerned. **von selbst** by itself, automatically.
vor [foːr] prep in front of; (zeitlich) before. vor acht Tagen a week ago. vor allem above all. nach wie vor as ever. nicht vor not until. Viertel vor 12 (a) quarter to twelve. vor Zeiten formerly.
Vorabend [foːraɪbənt] m eve.
Vorahnung [foːraːnuŋ] f presentiment.
voran [fo'ran] adv at the head, in front, first. **–gehen** v go ahead, precede. **–kommen** v make progress.
Voranschlag [foːr'anʃlaɪk] m rough estimate.
Vorarbeiter [foːr'arbaɪtər] m foreman, supervisor.
voraus [fo'raus] adv ahead, in front. im voraus in advance. **vorausbestimmen** v predetermine. **vorausgesetzt daß** provided that. **Voraussage** f prediction. **voraus‖sagen** v predict, forecast. **–sehen** v foresee. **Voraus‖setzung** f assumption; (Vorbedingung) prerequisite. **–sicht** f foresight. **voraussichtlich** adv probably. **Vorauszahlung** f advance payment.
vorbedacht [foːrbədaxt] adj premeditated. **Vorbedacht** m forethought. **mit Vorbedacht** on purpose, advisedly.
Vorbedingung [foːrbədiŋuŋ] f precondition, prerequisite.
Vorbehalt [foːrbəhalt] m (pl -e) reservation, proviso. **vorbehalten** v hold in reserve, withhold.
vorbei [fɔr'bai] adv (örtlich) past, by; (zeitlich) past, over. **vorbei sein** be all over. **vorbei‖gehen** v go past, pass. **–kommen** v pass by. **–marschieren** v march past.

vorbereiten [foːrbəraitən] v prepare. **Vorbereitungen** pl preparations.
vorbestellen [fɔːrbəʃtɛlən] v book in advance.
Vorbestrafte(r) [foːrbəʃtraːftə(r)] m person with previous conviction.
vorbeugen [foːrbɔygən] v prevent. **Vorbeugung** f prevention.
Vorbild [foːrbilt] neut model, example. **vorbildlich** adj model, exemplary.
*vorbringen [foːrbriŋən] v bring up, put forward.
vorder [foːrdər] adj fore(most), front. **Vorder‖bein** neut foreleg. **–grund** m foreground. **–radantrieb** m front-wheel drive. **–seite** f façade; obverse; face (of coin). **–teil** m front (part). **–tür** f front door.
*vordringen [foːrdriŋən] v advance, press forward. **vordringlich** adj urgent, pressing.
voreilig [foːrailiç] adj premature, hasty, precipitate.
voreingenommen [foːraingənɔmən] adj prejudiced. **voreingenommen gegen** prejudiced against. **voreingenommen für** biased in favour of. **Voreigenommenheit** f prejudice.
*vorenthalten [foːrɛnthaltən] v hold back, withhold.
vorerst [foːreːrst] adv for the time being.
vorerwähnt [foːrɛrvɛɪnt] adj above-mentioned, already mentioned, aforesaid.
Vorfahr [foːrfaɪr] m (pl -en) ancestor.
Vorfahrt [foːrfaɪrt] f right-of-way.
Vorfall [foːrfal] m incident.
vorführen [foːrfyɪrən] v bring forward, present; (zeigen) show; (Film) project. **Vorführung** f presentation, demonstration; (Film) showing.
Vorgang [foːrgaŋ] m event, incident; (Tech) process; (Komm) file, record. **Vorgänger** m predecessor.
*vorgeben [foːrgeɪbən] v pretend.
Vorgebirge [foːrgəbirgə] neut foothills pl; (Kap) promontory.
vorgeblich [foːrgeɪpliç] adj alleged, ostensible.
vorgefaßt [foːrgəfast] adj preconceived.
Vorgefühl [foːrgəfyɪl] neut presentiment.
*vorgehen [foːrgeɪən] v go forward; (handeln) act, proceed; (geschehen) occur; (Uhr) be fast; (wichtiger sein) take precedence; (führen) lead (on). **Vorgehen** neut advance; proceedings pl.

vorgenannt ['foːrgənant] *adj* above-mentioned.

Vorgeschichte ['foːrgəʃiçtə] *f* previous history; (*Urgeschichte*) prehistory.

Vorgeschmack ['foːrgəʃmak] *m* foretaste.

Vorgesetzte(r) ['foːrgəzɛtstə] superior.

vorgestern ['foːrgɛstərn] *adv* the day before yesterday.

***vorhaben** ['foːrhaːbən] *v* intend, plan. *haben Sie heute etwas vor?* have you anything arranged for today?

Vorhalle ['foːrhalə] *f* vestibule, entrance (hall).

vorhanden ['foːrhandən] *adj* existing, available. **Vorhandensein** *neut* existence, availability.

Vorhang ['foːrhaŋ] *m* (*pl* **Vorhänge**) curtain.

vorher [foːr'heɪr] *adv* before(hand), previously. **Vorhersage** *f* prediction. **vorher‖sagen** *v* predict. **–sehen** *v* foresee.

vorherrschend ['foːrhɛrʃənt] *adj* predominant.

vorhin ['foːrhin] *adv* a short while ago, just now.

Vorhut ['foːrhuːt] *f* (*pl* **-en**) vanguard.

vorig ['foːriç] *adj* previous.

Vorjahr ['foːrjaɪr] *neut* last year. **vorjährig** *adj* last year's.

vorjammern ['foːrjamərn] *v* lament, complain.

Vorkämpfer ['foːrkɛmpfər] *m* (*pl* **-**) advocate, champion.

Vorkehrung ['foːrkeɪruŋ] *f* (*pl* **-en**) precaution.

Vorkenntnis ['foːrkɛntnis] *f* previous knowledge. **Vorkenntnisse** *pl* rudiments, basic knowledge *sing*.

***vorkommen** ['foːrkɔmən] *v* (*geschehen*) happen, take place; (*sich finden*) occur, be found; (*nach vorn kommen*) come forward; (*scheinen*) seem, appear.

***vorladen** ['foːrlaɪdən] *v* summon. **Vorladung** *f* summons.

Vorlage ['foːrlaɪgə] *f* submission, presentation; (*Muster*) model; (*Gesetz*) bill.

Vorläufer ['foːrlɔyfər] *m* forerunner. **vorläufig** *adv* provisional, temporary.

vorlaut ['foːrlaut] *adj* forward, nosy.

vorlegen ['foːrleɪgən] *v* present; (*Essen*) serve.

***vorlesen** ['foːrleɪzən] *v* read out, read aloud. **Vorlesung** *f* (*pl* **-en**) lecture.

vorletzt ['foːrlɛtst] *adj* last but one, penultimate.

Vorliebe ['foːrliːbə] *f* preference, liking.

***vorliegen** ['foːrliːgən] *v* be, exist; (*Arbeit*) be in hand. **der vorliegende Fall** the case in point, the case in question.

Vormachtstellung ['foːrmaxtʃtɛluŋ] *f* hegemony.

vormals ['foːrmaɪls] *adv* formerly.

Vormittag ['foːrmitaɪk] *m* morning. **vormittags** *adv* in the morning.

Vormund ['foːrmunt] *m* guardian.

vorn [fɔrn] *adv* in front, ahead. **nach vorn** forward. **von vorn** from the start.

Vorname ['foːrnaɪmə] *m* first name, Christian name.

vornehm ['foːrneɪm] *adj* (*von höherem Stand*) distinguished; (*edel*) noble; elegant, (*umg.*) posh.

vornherein ['fɔrnherain] *adv* **von vornherein** from the start.

Vorort ['foːrɔrt] *m* outpost.

Vorrang ['foːrraŋ] *m* precedence, priority.

Vorrat ['foːrraɪt] *m* supply, stock. **vorrätig** *adj* in stock.

Vorrecht ['foːrrɛçt] *neut* privilege.

Vorrede ['foːrreidə] *f* introduction; (*Buch*) preface.

Vorrichtung ['fɔrriçtuŋ] *f* (*pl* **-en**) device.

vorrücken ['foːrrykən] *v* move forward, advance.

Vorsatz ['foːrzats] *m* intention, purpose. **vorsätzlich** *adj* intentional.

Vorschau ['foːrʃau] *f* preview; (*Film*) trailer.

***vorschieben** ['foːrʃiːbən] *v* push forward; (*Entschuldigung*) plead (as an excuse).

vorschiessen ['foːrʃiːsən] *v* advance (money).

Vorschlag ['foːrʃlaɪk] *m* suggestion, proposal. **vorschlagen** *v* suggest, propose.

Vorschlußrunde ['fɔːrʃlusrundə] *f* semifinal.

vorschneiden ['fɔːrʃnaidən] *v* carve.

vorschreiben ['foːrʃraibən] *v* prescribe, order.

Vorschrift ['foːrʃrift] *f* rule, regulation; (*Befehl*) order; (*Med*) prescription. **vorschrifts‖gemäß** *adj, adv* in accordance with regulations. **–widrig** *adj, adv* contrary to regulations.

Vorschub ['foːrʃuːp] *m* assistance, support. **Vorschub leisten** assist, support.

Vorschule ['foːrʃuːlə] *f* prep school.

Vorschuß ['foːrʃus] *m* (cash) advance.

vorschützen ['foɪrʃytsən] *v* pretend. Unwissenheit vorschützen plead ignorance.
vorsehen ['fɔɪrzeɪən] *v* assign, earmark. sich vorsehen take care, mind. **Vorsehung** *f* providence.
vorsetzen ['foɪrzɛtsən] *v* put (forward); (*anbieten*) offer, put before.
Vorsicht ['foɪrziçt] *f* caution, care. *interj* be careful! take care! **vorsichtig** *adj* careful, cautious. **Vorsichtsmaßnahme** *f* precaution.
Vorsitz ['foɪrzits] *m* chair(manship). den Vorsitz führen be in the chair, preside. **Vorsitzende(r)** chairman.
Vorsorge ['foɪrzɔrgə] *f* (*unz.*) provision, precaution, advance measure. **versorglich** *adj* provident. *adv* as a precaution.
Vorspeise ['foɪrʃpaizə] *f* hors d'oeuvre, starter.
vorspiegeln ['foɪrʃpiːgəln] *v* **jemandem etwas vorspiegeln** delude someone with something. **Vorspiegelung** *f* misrepresentation.
Vorspiel ['foɪrʃpiːl] *neut* prelude.
*vorspringen ['foɪrʃpriŋən] *v* leap forward; (*hervorragen*) project.
Vorsprung ['foɪrʃpruŋ] *m* (*Vorteil*) lead, advantage; (*Arch*) projection.
Vorstadt ['foɪrʃtat] *f* suburb.
Vorstand ['foɪrʃtant] *m* board of directors, management.
*vorstehen ['foɪrʃteɪən] *v* protrude; (*leiten*) manage, be head of. **-d** *adj* protruding; (*vorangehend*) preceding. **Vorsteher** *m* chief, superintendant, manager. **-in** *f* manageress.
vorstellbar ['foɪrʃtɛlbaɪr] *adj* imaginable. **vorstellen** *v* put forward; (*Person*) introduce; (*bedeuten*) mean. sich vorstellen introduce oneself. sich etwas vorstellen imagine something. **Vorstellung** *f* introduction; (*Begriff*) idea; (*Theater*) performance. **-skraft** *f* (power of) imagination.
vorstrecken ['foɪrʃtrɛkən] *v* stretch out.
Vorstufe ['foɪrʃtuːfə] *f* first stage.
Vorteil ['fɔrtail] *m* advantage. **vorteilhaft** *adj* advantageous, favourable.
Vortrag ['foɪrtraɪk] *m* (*pl* **Vorträge**) (*Vorlesung*) talk, lecture; (*Komm*) balance carried forward. **vortragen** *v* lecture; (*Gedicht*) recite; (*Meinung*) express;

(*Rede*) deliver. **Vortragssaal** *m* lecture hall.
vortrefflich [fɔr'trɛfliç] *adj* excellent.
*vortreten ['fɔrtreɪtən] *v* step forward; (*hervorragen*) protrude.
Vortritt ['fɔrtrit] *m* precedence.
vorüber [fo'ryɪbər] *adv* past; (*Zeit*) over, past. **-gehen** *v* pass. **-gehend** *adj* passing, temporary.
Vorurteil ['foɪrurtail] *neut* prejudice. **vorurteilsfrei** *adj* unprejudiced.
Vorverkauf ['foɪrfɛrkauf] *m* advance sale; (*Theater*) advance booking.
Vorwahl ['foɪrvail] *f* preliminary election, (*US*) primary. **Vorwahlnummer** *f* (*Telef*) area code.
Vorwand ['foɪrvant] *f* pretence, pretext, excuse.
vorwärts ['foɪrvɛrts] *adv* forward(s), onward(s). **-bringen** *v* promote, further. **-gehen** *v* go ahead. **-kommen** *v* make progress.
vorweg [for'vɛk] *adv* in advance. **-nehmen** *v* anticipate, forestall.
*vorwerfen ['foɪrvɛrfən] *v* reproach with.
vorwiegend ['foɪrviːsən] *adj* preponderant. *adv* chiefly, mostly.
Vorwissen ['foɪrviːsən] *neut* foreknowledge, prescience.
Vorwort ['foɪrvɔrt] *neut* (*pl* -e) preface, foreword.
Vorwurf ['foɪrvurf] *m* reproach.
Vorzeichen ['foɪrtsaiçən] *neut* omen; (*Math*) sign.
*vorzeigen ['foɪrtsaigən] *v* produce, display.
Vorzeit ['foɪrtsait] *f* antiquity. **vorzeitig** *adj* premature, too early.
*vorziehen ['foɪrtsiːən] *v* (*bevorzugen*) prefer; (*hervorziehen*) pull forward.
Vorzug ['foɪrtsuɪk] *m* preference; (*Vorteil*) advantage; (*Eigenschaft*) merit, good quality. **vorzüglich** *adj* excellent, superb. **Vorzugsrecht** *neut* priority.
vulgär [vul'gɛɪr] *adj* vulgar.
Vulkan [vul'kaɪn] *m* (*pl* -e) volcano. **vulkanisch** *adj* volcanic.

W

Waage ['vaɪgə] f (pl -n) scales pl. **waagerecht** adj horizontal.
wabbelig ['vabəliç] adj wobbly, flabby.
Wabe ['vaɪbə] f (pl -n) honeycomb.
wach [vax] adj awake. **Wache** f (pl -n) watch, guard; (Polizei) station. **wachen** v be awake; (Wache halten) keep watch. **wachen über** watch over.
Wachs [vaks] neut (pl -e) wax.
wachsam ['vaxzaɪm] adj watchful, alert. **Wachsamkeit** f watchfulness, vigilance.
***wachsen** ['vaksən] v grow. **-d** adj increasing, growing. **Wachstum** neut growth.
Wacht [vaxt] f (pl -en) watch, guard.
Wachtel ['vaxtəl] f (pl -n) quail.
Wächter [veçtər] m (pl -) watchman, guard. **Wacht‖hund** neut watchdog. **-meister** m sergeant-major; (Polizist) constable. **-turm** m watchtower.
wackelig ['vakəliç] adj wobbly, shaky. **wackeln** v wobble, shake.
wacker ['vakər] adj brave, stout; (anständig) worthy.
Wade ['vaɪdə] f (pl -n) (Anat) calf.
Waffe ['vafə] f (pl -n) weapon.
Waffel ['vafəl] f (pl -n) waffle; (Eis) wafer.
waffenlos ['vafənlois] adj unarmed. **waffnen** v arm. **Waffenstillstand** m armistice.
wagehalsig ['vaɪgəhalsiç] adj reckless, daring. **Wagemut** m daring. **wagen** v dare, risk, venture. **sich wagen** venture.
Wagen ['vaɪgən] m (pl -) (Mot) car; (Kutsche) coach; (Karren) wagon, cart; (Eisenbahn) carriage.
***wägen** ['veɪgən] v weigh.
Wagen‖führer m driver. **-heber** m (Mot) jack.
Waggon [va'gõ] m (pl -s) (railway) wagon.
Wagnis ['vaɪknis] neut (pl -se) (Mut) daring; (Unternehmen) venture; (Risiko) risk.
wahl [vaɪl] f (pl -en) choice; (Pol) election. **wahlberechtigt** adj enfranchised, entitled to vote. **Wahl‖bezirk** m constituency, electoral district. **-bude** f polling booth.
wählen ['veɪlən] v choose; (Pol) elect; (Telef) dial.
wählerisch ['veɪləriʃ] adj particular, fussy, choosy. **Wählerschaft** f electorate, voters pl.
Wahl‖feldzug m (election) campaign.

-gang m ballot. **wahllos** adj indiscriminate. **Wahlrecht** neut franchise, suffrage.
Wählscheibe ['veɪlʃaibə] f (telephone) dial.
Wahl‖tag m election day. **-zettel** m ballot (paper).
Wahn [vaɪn] m (unz.) delusion; madness. **-sinn** m insanity, madness. **wahnsinnig** adj insane, mad. **Wahnsinnige(r)** madman, madwoman.
wahr [vaɪr] adj true; (wirklich) real; (echt) genuine.
wahren ['vaɪrən] v take care of; (schützen) protect; (erhalten) maintain.
währen ['veɪrən] v last.
während ['veɪrənt] prep during. conj while.
wahrhaft ['vaɪrhaft] adj true, genuine. adv really, truly. **-ig** adj sincere, truthful. adv really, indeed. **Wahr‖haftigkeit** f truthfulness. **-heit** f (pl -en) truth. **wahr‖nehmen** v perceive; (Interessen) protect; (Gelegenheit) seize, take. **-sagen** v foretell (the future). **-scheinlich** adj likely, probable. **Wahrscheinlichkeit** f probability.
Wahrung ['vaɪruŋ] f preservation, maintenance.
Währung ['veɪruŋ] f (pl -en) currency.
Waise ['vaizə] (pl -n) orphan. **-nknabe** m orphan boy.
Wal [vaɪl] m (pl -e) whale.
Wald [valt] m (pl Wälder) wood, forest. **-beere** f cranberry. **-brand** m forest fire. **waldig** adj wooded. **Wald‖ung** f (pl -en) woodland. **-wirtschaft** f forestry.
Walfang ['vaɪlfaŋ] m whaling.
Wall [val] m (pl Wälle) earthworks pl, embankment.
wallen ['valən] v boil.
***wallfahren** ['valfaɪrən] v go on a pilgrimage. **Wall‖fahrer** m pilgrim. **-fahrt** f pilgrimage.
Walnuß ['valnus] f walnut.
Wal‖öl neut whale-oil. **-roß** neut walrus.
Walze ['valtsə] f (pl -n) roller. **walzen** v roll; (tanzen) waltz.
wälzen ['veltsən] v roll.
Walzer ['valtsər] m (pl -) waltz.
Wand [vant] f (pl Wände) wall.
Wandel ['vandəl] m change. **wandelbar** adj variable; (Person) changeable, fickle. **wandeln** v change. **sich wandeln in** change or turn into.

Wanderer ['vandərər] *m* (*pl* -) wanderer; (*auf dem Lande*) hiker, rambler. **Wander-lust** *f* wanderlust. **wandern** *v* wander; ramble, hike. **-d** *adj* wandering; (*Volk, Tiere*) migratory. **Wanderung** *f* (*pl* -en) (*zu Fuß*) walking-tour, hike; (*Volk, Tiere*) migration.

Wandgemälde ['vantgəmɛldə] *neut* mural.

Wandlung ['vandluŋ] *f* (*pl* -en) change; (*total*) transformation; (*Rel*) transubstan-tiation.

Wange ['vaŋə] *f* (*pl* -n) cheek.

Wankelmut ['vaŋkəlmuːt] *m* fickleness, inconstancy. **wankelmütig** *adj* fickle, inconstant.

wanken ['vaŋkən] *v* rock, sway; (*Person*) totter, reel; (*fig*) waver, vacillate. **-d** *adj* wavering.

wann [van] *adv* when.

Wanne ['vanə] *f* (*pl* -n) tub; (*Badewanne*) bath(tub). **-nbad** *neut* bath.

Wanze ['vantsə] *f* (*pl* -n) bug.

Wappen ['vapən] *neut* (*pl* -) (coat of) arms. **-kunde** *f* heraldry.

Ware ['vaːrə] *f* (*pl* -n) article, commodity. **Waren** *pl* goods, wares, merchandise *sing.* **Waren‖haus** *neut* department store. **-markt** *m* commodity market.

warm [varm] *adj* warm; (*Getränk, Essen*) hot. **warmer Bruder** (*umg.*) homosexual.

Wärme ['vɛrmə] *f* warmth; temperature; (*Physik*) heat. **wärmen** *v* warm (up), heat. **Wärmflasche** *f* hot-water bottle.

warnen ['varnən] *v* warn. **Warnung** *f* (*pl* -en) warning.

Warschau ['varʃau] *neut* Warsaw.

warten ['vartən] *v* wait; (*pflegen*) care for; (*Maschine*) service, maintain. **warten auf** wait for.

Wärter ['vɛrtər] *m* (*pl* -), **Wärterin** *f* (*pl* -nen) attendant; (*Kranken*) nurse; (*Gefängnis*) warder.

Warte‖saal *m* waiting room. **-zimmer** *neut* waiting room. **Wartung** *f* mainte-nance, upkeep.

warum [va'rum] *adv* why.

Warze ['vaːrtsə] *f* (*pl* -n) wart; (*Brust*) nipple.

was [vas] *pron* what; (*umg.*) something. **ach was!** nonsense! **was ist mit ...** how about .... **was für ...** what sort of .... *alles was ich sehe* everything that I see.

Waschbecken ['vaʃbekən] *neut* wash basin.

Wäsche ['vɛʃə] *f* (*pl* -n) washing, laundry.

waschecht [vaʃeçt] *adj* (*Farbe*) (colour-) fast; (*fig*) thorough, dyed-in-the-wool.

Wäsche‖klammer *f* clothes-peg, (*US*) clothes-pin. **-korb** *m* laundry basket. **-leine** *f* clothes-line.

***waschen** [vaʃən] *v* wash.

Wäscherei ['vɛʃaˈrai] *f* (*pl* -en) laundry.

Wasch‖lappen *m* facecloth. **-maschine** *f* washing machine. **-mittel** *neut* deter-gent, washing powder. **-tag** *m* wash(ing) day.

Wasser ['vasər] *neut* (*pl* -) water. **-abfluß** *m* drain. **-abfuhr** *f* drainage. **-behälter** *m* tank, reservoir. **-dampf** *m* steam, water vapour.

wasser‖dicht *adj* waterproof; (*Gefäß*) watertight. **-fest** *adj* waterproof.

wässerig ['vɛsəriç] *adj* watery.

Wasser‖kraftwerk *neut* hydroelectric plant. **-leitung** *f* water mains *pl.* **-mann** *m* (*Astrol*) Aquarius.

wässern ['vɛsərn] *v* water; (*bewassern*) irrigate; (*Erbsen, usw.*) soak.

Wasser‖pflanze *f* aquatic plant. **-rad** *neut* water wheel. **-stoff** *m* hydrogen. **-tier** *neut* aquatic animal.

Wässerung ['vɛsəruŋ] *f* watering; (*Bewäs-sern*) irrigation.

Wasser‖versorgung *f* water supply. **-weg** *m* waterway. **-werk** *neut* water-works *pl.*

Watte ['vatə] *f* (*pl* -n) wadding, cotton wool. **-bausch** *m* swab.

weben ['veːbən] *v* weave. **Web‖er** *m* (*pl* -), **Weberin** *f* (*pl* -nen) weaver. **-stoff** *m* tex-tile. **-stuhl** *m* loom.

Wechsel ['vɛksəl] *m* (*pl* -) change; (*Aus-tausch*) exchange; (*Komm*) bill (of exchange). **-folge** *f* alternation. **-geld** *neut* change. **-jahre** *pl* menopause *sing,* change of life *sing.* **wechseln** *v* (ex)change; (*variieren*) vary. **wechselsei-tig** *adj* alternating; (*gegenseitig*) mutual, reciprocal. **Wechsel‖strom** *m* alternating current. **-zahn** *f* milk tooth.

wecken ['vɛkən] *v* awaken, wake up. **Wecker** *m* (*pl* -) alarm clock.

wedeln ['veːdəln] *v* (*Schwanz*) wag.

weder ['veːdər] *conj* neither. **weder ... noch ...** neither ... nor ....

weg [vɛk] *adv* away, off, gone. *Hände weg!* hands off! *er ist schon weg* he has already left. *meine Uhr ist weg* my watch has gone. **weit weg** far off. **Weg** *m* (*pl* -e) way; (*Straße*) road; (*Pfad*) path.

weg‖bleiben v stay away. **–blicken** v look away. **–bringen** v take away, remove.
wegen ['veɪgən] *prep* because of, on account of.
weg‖fahren v drive away; (*abfahren*) leave. **–fallen** v fall away; (*aufhören*) stop; (*ausgelassen werden*) be omitted. **–führen** v lead away. **–gehen** v go away. **–kommen** v get away. **–lassen** v omit. **–müssen** v must go, have to leave.
Wegnahme [vɛknaɪmə] f (pl -n) confiscation, seizure. **wegnehmen** v take away; (*beschlagnahmen*) confiscate, seize; (*Zeit, Raum*) occupy. **weg‖räumen** v clear away. **–schaffen** v get rid of. **–schikken** v send away. **–schließen** v lock away. **–treiben** v drive off.
Wegweiser [veɪkvaizər] m (pl -) signpost; (*Buch, Mensch*) guide.
weg‖wenden v turn aside. **–werfen** v throw away, discard. **–werfend** adj disdainful. **–ziehen** v pull aside; (*Wohnsitz wechseln*) move away.
weh [veɪ] *adj* sore, painful; (*seelisch*) sad. *interj* alas. *mein Hals tut mir weh* my throat hurts. *sich weh tun* hurt oneself. *jemandem weh tun* hurt someone, cause someone pain. **Weh** *neut* (pl -e) pain; sorrow.
Wehe ['veɪə] f (pl -n) drift (of snow or sand). **wehen** v blow; (*Fahne*) flutter.
Wehr[1] [veɪr] f (pl -en) weapon; (*Schutz*) defence; (*Rüstung*) armament; (*Widerstand*) resistance.
Wehr[2] *neut* (pl -e) weir, dam.
Wehrdienst ['veɪrdiːnst] m military service. **–verweigerer** m conscientious objector. **wehren** v restrain. *sich wehren gegen* defend oneself against. **wehrlos** adj (*waffenlos*) unarmed; (*schutzlos*) defenceless.
Wehr‖macht f armed forces pl. **–pflicht** f compulsory military service. **–pflichtige(r)** person liable for military service.
Weib [vaip] *neut* (pl -er) woman; (*Gattin*) wife. **–chen** *neut* (*Tier*) female. **weiblich** adj female; (*Gramm*) feminine.
weich [vaiç] *adj* soft; (*sanft*) gentle.
Weiche ['vaiçə] f (pl -n) (*Anat*) side, flank.
weichen[1] ['vaiçən] v soften; (*einweichen*) soak.
weichen[2] v give way; (*nachgeben*) yield; (*Preise*) fall.

Weichheit ['vaiçhait] f softness. **weichherzig** adj tender-hearted, gentle. **Weichkäse** m soft cheese. **weichlich** adj soft, weak, effeminate.
Weide[1] ['vaidə] f (pl -n) (*Baum*) willow.
Weide[2] f (pl -n) (*Wiese*) pasture.
***weiden** ['vaidən] v graze. *sich weiden an* feast one's eyes on.
weigern ['vaigərn] v *sich weigern* refuse. **Weigerung** f (pl -en) refusal.
Weihe ['vaiə] f (pl -n) consecration; (*Einweihung*) initiation. **weihen** v consecrate.
Weihnachten ['vainaxtən] *neut* (pl -) Christmas. **Weihnachts‖abend** m Christmas Eve. **–baum** m Christmas tree. **–geschenk** *neut* Christmas present. **–lied** *neut* Christmas carol. **–mann** m Father Christmas, (*US*) Santa Claus.
weil [vail] *conj* because, since.
Weile ['vailə] f while, short time.
Wein [vain] m (pl -e) wine; (*Pflanze*) vine. **–berg** m vineyard. **–brand** m brandy.
weinen ['vainən] v cry, weep. **Weinen** *neut* crying, weeping, tears pl.
Wein‖lese f (pl -n) vintage. **–stock** m vine. **–stube** f wine bar. **–traube** f bunch of grapes.
weise ['vaizə] *adj* wise.
Weise ['vaizə] f (pl -n) manner, way; (*Melodie*) melody. *Art und Weise* manner, way. *auf diese/jede/kleine Weise* in this way/in any case/by no means.
weisen ['vaizən] v show; (*Finger, Zeiger*) point. *weisen auf* point to. *weisen nach* direct to.
Weisheit ['vaishait] f (pl -en) wisdom. **–szahn** m wisdom tooth.
weiß [vais] *adj* white. **Weißbrot** *neut* white bread. **Weiße** f whiteness. **Weiße(r)** White (man/woman). **weiß‖en** v whitewash. **–glühend** adj white-hot. **Weiß‖kohl** m (white) cabbage. **–waren** pl linens. **–wein** m white wine.
weit [vait] *adj* wide; (*breit*) broad; (*geräumig*) vast, spacious; (*lang*) long; (*entfernt*) far (off). *bei weitem* by far. *von weitem* from a distance. *weit entfernt (von)* far away (from). **weit‖ab** adv far away. **–aus** adv by far. **Weite** f (pl -n) width; (*Ausdehnung*) extent; (*Größe*) size. **weiten** v widen; (*vergrößern*) enlarge.

weiter ['vaitǝr] *adj* wider; *(Entfernung)* farther; *(zusätlich)* further. *adv (Entfernung)* farther; *(fig)* further; *(sonst)* else; *(weiterhin)* furthermore. **ohne weiteres** directly, immediately. **bis auf weiteres** for the present. **weiter nichts?** nothing else? **und so weiter** and so forth. **es geht weiter** it goes on. **weiter‖bringen** *v* harp on. **–geben** *v* pass (to). **–gehen** *v* move on. **–hin** *adv* moreover, furthermore. **–kommen** *v* make progress, get on. **–machen** *v* carry on. **weit‖gehend** *adj* far-reaching. **–her** *adv* from afar. **–hergeholt** *adj* far-fetched. **–herzig** *adj* broad-minded. **–reichend** *adj* far-reaching. **–sichtig** *adj* far-sighted. **–verbreitet** *adj* widespread.
Weizen ['vaitsǝn] *m* wheat. **–brot** *neut* white bread. **–kleie** *f* bran.
welch [vɛlç] *adj, pron* which, what, who. **welche** *pl* some, any. **welch ein Glück!** what luck! **welches Kind?** which child? **welche schöne Blumen** what beautiful flowers. **möchtest du welche?** would you like some?
welk [vɛlk] *adj* withered. **welken** *v* wither.
Welle ['vɛlǝ] *f (pl -n)* wave; *(Tech)* shaft, axle. **wellen** *v* wave; *(rollen)* roll. **Wellen‖länge** *f* wavelength. **–sittich** *m* budgerigar.
Welt [vɛlt] *f (pl -en)* world. **–all** *neut* universe. **–anschauung** *f (pl -en)* philosophical outlook. **welt‖berühmt** *adj* world-famous. **–bügerlich** *adj* cosmopolitan. **–erschütternd** *adj* world-shaking. **–lich** *adj* worldly, mundane. **Welt‖macht** *f* world power. **–raum** *m* (outer) space. **–rekord** *m* world record.
wem [veim] *pron* to whom.
wen [vein] *pron* whom.
Wende ['vɛndǝ] *f (pl -n)* turn; *(Änderung)* change. **–l** *f (pl -n)* coil, spiral. **wenden** *v* turn. **Wendepunkt** *m* turning point. **wendig** *adj* manoeuvrable; *(Person)* agile. **Wendung** *f (pl -en)* turn; *(Änderung)* change.
wenig ['veiniç] *adj* little. *adv* not much, slightly. **ein wenig** a little. **wenige** *pl* a few. **–er** *adj* less, fewer. **wenigst** *adj* least. **am wenigsten** *adv* least (of all). **wenigstens** *adv* at least.
wenn [vɛn] *conj (falls)* if; *(sobald)* when. **auch wenn** even if. **wenn nicht** unless. **wenn nur** if only.

wer [veir] *pron* who; *(derjenige, der)* whoever.
Werbe‖büro *neut* advertising agency. **–feldzug** *m* advertising campaign.
werben ['vɛrbǝn] *v* advertise, publicize; *(Rekruten)* enlist. **Werb‖esendung** *f* commercial. **–ung** *f* advertising.
*werden ['vɛrdǝn] *v* become; *(allmählich)* grow; *(Futurum)* will, shall; *(Passiv)* be. **es wird dunkel** it is growing *or* getting dark. **er wird kommen** he will come. **er will Arzt werden** he wants to be a doctor. **der Baum wurde gefällt** the tree was felled. **würden Sie so freundlich sein?** would you be so kind? **Werden** *neut* development, growth. **werdend** *adj* developing, growing; *(Mutter)* expectant.
*werfen ['vɛrfǝn] *v* throw.
Werft [vɛrft] *f (pl -en)* shipyard, dockyard.
Werk [vɛrk] *neut (pl -e)* work; *(Fabrik)* factory, works *pl*; *(Getriebe)* mechanism. **–statt** *or* **statte** *f* workshop. **–tag** *m* working day. **–zeug** *neut* tool.
Wermut ['veirmuit] *m* wormwood; *(Wein)* vermouth.
wert [vɛrt] *adj* worth; *(würdig)* worthy; *(lieb)* dear. **für wert halten** consider worthwhile. **nicht der Mühe wert** not worth the bother. **fünf Mark wert** worth five Marks. **Wert** *m* value, worth. **wert‖en** *v* value. **–los** *adj* worthless. **Wert‖sachen** *pl* valuables. **–ung** *f (pl -en)* (e)valuation.
Wesen ['veizǝn] *neut (pl -)* being; *(Kern)* essence; *(Natur)* nature; *(Benehmen)* conduct. **–sart** *f* nature, character. **wesentlich** *adj* essential.
weshalb [vɛs'halp] *adv, conj* why.
Wespe ['vɛspǝ] *f (pl -n)* wasp.
wessen ['vɛsǝn] *pron (Person)* whose; *(Sache)* of which.
West [vɛst] *m* west.
Weste ['vɛstǝ] *f (pl -n)* waistcoat.
Westen ['vɛstǝn] *m* west. **West‖europa** *f* western Europe. **–falen** *neut* Westphalia. **–indien** *neut* West Indies *pl*. **westlich** *adj* western; *(Wind, Richtung)* westerly.
Westmark *f* West German mark.
wett [vɛt] *adj* equal, even.
Wettbewerb ['vɛtbǝverp] *m* competition. **–er** *m* competitor. **wettbewerbsfähig** *adj* competitive.
Wette ['vɛtǝ] *f (pl -n)* bet. **Wetteifer** *m*

rivalry. **wetteifern mit** vie with, compete with. **wetten** v bet.
Wetter ['vɛtər] *neut* (*pl* -) weather. **–bericht** *m* weather report. **–kunde** *f* meteorology. **–vorhersage** *f* weather forecast.
Wett‖kampf *m* contest, match. **–kämpfer** *m* contestant. **–lauf** *m* race. **–streit** *m* contest.
wichtig ['viçtiç] *adj* important. **Wichtig‖keit** *f* importance. **–tuer** *m* busybody; pompous person.
Widder ['vidər] *m* (*pl* -) ram; (*Astrol*) Aries.
wider ['viːdər] *prep* against, contrary to. **–fahren** v happen to, befall.
Wider‖haken *m* barbed hook. **–hall** *m* response; (*Echo*) echo. **widerhallen** v echo.
wider‖legen v refute. **–lich** *adj* repulsive; (*ekelhaft*) disgusting. **–natürlich** *adj* unnatural. **–rechtlich** *adj* unlawful, illegal.
Widerruf ['viːdərruːf] *m* (*Befehl*) revocation, countermand; (*Nachricht*) denial. **widerrufen** v revoke, countermand; deny.
widersetzen [viːdər'zɛtsən] v **sich widersetzen** oppose. **widersetzlich** *adj* obstructive.
wider‖spenstig *adj* contrary, difficult, stubborn. **–spiegeln** v reflect. **–sprechen** v contradict. **Widerspruch** *m* contradiction.
Widerstand ['viːdərʃtant] *m* resistance, opposition.
***widerstehen** [viːdər'ʃteːən] v resist.
Widerstreit ['viːdərʃtrait] *m* (*Kampf*) conflict; (*Widersprüche*) opposition.
widerwärtig ['viːdərvɛrtiç] *adj* disgusting, repulsive.
Widerwille ['viːdərvilə] *m* aversion, intense dislike. **widerwillig** *adj* reluctant, unwilling.
widmen ['vitmən] v devote, dedicate; (*Buch*) dedicate. **Widmung** *f* (*pl* **-en**) dedication.
widrig ['viːdriç] *adj* adverse, unfavourable.
wie [viː] *adv* how. *conj* as.
wieder ['viːdər] *adv* again; (*zurück*) back. **immer wieder** again and again.
Wiederaufbau ['viːdəraufbau] *m* reconstruction, rebuilding. **wiederaufbauen** v reconstruct, rebuild. **Wiederauf‖erstehung** *f* resurrection. **–nahme** *f* resumption. **wiederauf‖nehmen** v resume.

–tauchen v come to light again, resurface.
***wieder‖bringen** v bring back, return. **–erkennen** v recognize.
Wiedergabe ['viːdərgaibə] *f* reproduction. **wiedergeben** v give back, return; (*darbieten*) render.
wiedergeboren ['viːdərgəboːrən] *adj* reborn, regenerated. **Wiedergeburt** *f* rebirth, regeneration.
***wieder‖gewinnen** v recover, retrieve. **–gutmachen** v make up for, compensate for.
wiederholen [viːdər'hoːlən] v repeat. **wiederholt** *adj* repeated. **Wiederholung** *f* (*pl* **-en**) repetition.
Wiederhören ['viːdərhœːrən] *n* **auf Wiederhören!** (*Telef*) goodbye!
wieder‖kehren v return. **–kommen** v come back, return.
***wiedersehen** ['viːdərzeːən] v see *or* meet again. **Wiedersehen** *neut* reunion. **auf Wiedersehen!** goodbye!
wiederum ['viːdərum] *adv* (*nochmals*) again, afresh; (*andererseits*) on the other hand.
wieder‖vereinigen v reunite; (*versöhnen*) reconcile. **–verheiraten** v remarry.
Wiege ['viːgə] *f* (*pl* **-n**) cradle.
wiegen[1] ['viːgən] v (*Gewicht*) weigh.
wiegen[2] v (*sanft schaukeln*) rock.
Wiegenlied ['viːgənliːt] *neut* lullaby.
wiehern ['viːərn] v neigh; (*Mensch*) guffaw.
Wien [viːn] *neut* Vienna.
Wiese ['viːzə] *f* (*pl* **-n**) meadow.
Wiesel ['viːzəl] *neut* (*pl* -) weasel.
wieso [vi'zoː] *adv* why.
wieviel [vi'fiːl] *adj*, *adv* how much. **wieviele** *pl* how many.
wild [vilt] *adj* wild; (*unzivilisiert, ungestüm*) savage. **Wild** *neut* game. **–dieb** *m* poacher. **–heit** *f* wildness; savageness. **–leder** *neut* deerskin. **–nis** *f* wilderness.
Wille ['vilə] *m* (*pl* -**n**) *or* **Willen** *m* (*pl* -) will. **um . . . willen** for the sake of. **willens‖schwach** *adj* weak-willed. **–stark** *adj* strong-willed. **willig** *adj* willing.
willkommen ['vilkɔmən] *adj* welcome. **willkommen heißen** v welcome, greet. **Willkommen** *neut* welcome.
Willkür ['vilkyːr] *f* arbitrariness, whim. **willkürlich** *adj* arbitrary.
wimmeln ['viməln] v **wimmeln von** swarm *or* teem with.

Wimper ['vimpər] f (pl -n) eyelash. **ohne mit der Wimper zu zucken** without batting an eyelid.

Wind [vint] m (pl -e) wind.

Winde ['vində] f (pl -n) windlass; (Bot) bindweed.

Windel ['vindəl] f (pl -n) nappy, (US) diaper.

***winden** ['vindən] v wind, twist. **sich winden** wind.

Wind||**hund** m greyhound. **–mühle** f windmill. **–pokken** pl chickenpox sing. **–schutzscheibe** f windscreen, (US) windshield. **–stoß** m gust, blast of wind.

Windung ['vinduŋ] f (pl -en) winding, turn.

Wink [viŋk] m (pl -e) sign; (Hand) wave; (Kopf) nod; (Augen) wink; (fig) hint.

Winkel ['viŋkəl] m (pl -) (Ecke) corner; (Math) angle. **winkelig** adj angular. **winkelrecht** adj rectangular.

Winter ['vintər] m (pl -) winter. **winterlich** adj wintry. **Winter**||**schlaf** m hibernation. **–sport** m winter sports pl.

winzig ['vintsiç] adj tiny.

Wipfel ['vipfəl] m (pl -) treetop.

Wippe ['vipə] f (pl -n) seesaw, balance.

wir [viːr] pron we.

Wirbel ['virbəl] m (pl -) whirl; (Wasser) whirlpool; (Luft) whirlwind; (Trommeln) roll; (Rücken) vertebra; (Scheitel) crown (of head). **wirbel**||**los** adj spineless; (Tiere) invertebrate. **–n** v whirl, swirl; (Trommeln) roll. **Wirbel**||**säule** f spine. **–tier** neut vertebrate. **–wind** m whirlwind.

wirken ['virkən] v work (on), act (on). **–d** adj active; (erfolgreich) effective. **wirklich** adj real, actual; (echt) genuine. **Wirklichkeit** f reality. **wirksam** adj effective. **Wirkung** f (pl -en) effect.

wirr [vir] adj tangled, disorderly; (Haare) dishevelled. **Wirrwarr** m chaos, jumble, disorder.

Wirt [virt] m (pl -e) innkeeper, landlord; (Gastgeber) host; (Zimmervermieter) landlord. **–in** f (pl -nen) innkeeper, landlady; hostess; landlady. **wirtlich** adj hospitable.

Wirtschaft ['virtʃaft] f (pl -en) economy; (Haushaltung) housekeeping; (Gaststätte) inn, public house. **wirtschaft**||**en** v manage; (Haushalt) keep house. **–lich** adj economic; (sparsam) economical. **Wirtschafts**||**krise** f economic crisis. **–politik** f economic policy. **–wunder** neut economic miracle.

Wirtshaus ['virtshaus] neut inn, public house.

wischen ['viʃən] v wipe. **Wischlappen** m cloth, duster.

wispeln ['vispəln] or **wispern** v whisper.

Wißbegier(de) ['visbəgiːr(də)] f intellectual curiosity, thirst for learning. **wißbegierig** adj inquisitive, eager to learn.

***wissen** ['visən] v know. **etwas tun wissen** know how to do something. **Wissen** neut knowledge.

Wissenschaft ['visənʃaft] f (pl -en) science, knowledge. **–ler** m (pl -), **-lerin** f (pl -nen) scientist. **wissenschaftlich** adj scientific.

wissentlich ['visəntliç] adj conscious, deliberate. adv knowingly, wittingly.

Witterung ['vitəruŋ] f (pl -en) weather (conditions).

Witwe ['vitvə] f (pl -n) widow. **Witwer** m (pl -) widower.

Witz [vits] m (pl -e) (Gabe) wit; (Spaß) joke. **–bold** m witty fellow, clown. **–blatt** neut comic (paper). **witzig** adj witty; (spaßhaft) humorous, funny. **witzeln über** joke about.

wo [voː] adv where. conj when. **ach wo!** what nonsense! **wo**||**anders** adv elsewhere. **–bei** adv whereby, by which.

Woche ['vɔxə] f (pl -n) week. **Wochen**||**blatt** neut weekly (paper). **–ende** neut weekend.

wöchentlich ['vœçtliç] adj weekly.

Wodka ['vɔdkə] m (pl -s) vodka.

wo||**durch** adv whereby, by which; (Frage) how? by what means? **–für** adv for which; (Frage) for what? what ... for? **–gegen** adv against which. conj whereas. **–her** adv from where, whence. **–hin** adv (to) where, whither.

wohl [voːl] adv well; (vermutend) probably, I suppose. **Wohl** neut well-being, welfare.

wohlauf ['voːl'auf] adv well. interj come on! cheer up!

Wohl||**befinden** neut well-being, (good) health. **–behagen** neut comfort.

wohl||**bekannt** adj well-known. **–erzogen** adj well brought up.

Wohlfahrt ['voːlfaːrt] f welfare. **–sstaat** m welfare state.

wohl‖gemeint *adj* well-intentioned.
-geraten *adj* well done; (*Kind*) well-behaved.
Wohl‖geruch *m* perfume, fragrance.
-geschmack *m* pleasant *or* agreeable taste.
wohlhabend ['voːlhaːbənt] *adj* well-to-do, well-off.
Wohlklang ['voːlklaŋ] *m* harmony.
Wohlstand ['voːlʃtant] *m* prosperity, affluence. **-sgesellschaft** *f* affluent society.
Wohl‖tat *f* kindness, kind deed; (*Annehmlichkeit*) boon, benefit. **-täter** *m* benefactor. **-täterin** *f* benefactress. **wohltätig** *adj* charitable. **Wohltätigkeit** *f* charity. **-sverein** *m* charitable association.
***wohltun** ['voːltuːn] *v* do good.
Wohlwollen ['voːlvɔlən] *neut* good will, benevolence. **wohlwollend** *adj* benevolent.
wohnen ['voːnən] *v* live, dwell, reside.
wohnhaft *adj* resident. **Wohn‖ort** *m* place of residence. **--Schlafzimmer** *neut* bed-sitting room, (*umg.*) bedsit. **-ung** *f* (*pl* -en) flat, (*US*) apartment. **-wagen** *m* caravan, (*US*) trailer. **-zimmer** *neut* living-room, sitting-room.
Wölbung ['vœlbuŋ] *f* (*pl* -en) vault, arch, dome.
Wolf [vɔlf] *m* (*pl* **Wölfe**) wolf.
Wölfin ['vœlfin] *f* (*pl* -nen) she-wolf.
Wolke ['vɔlkə] *f* (*pl* -n) cloud. **-nkratzer** *m* skyscraper.
Wolle ['vɔlə] *f* (*pl* -n) wool.
***wollen**[1] ['vɔlən] *v* want, wish. *ich will gehen* I want to go, I intend to go. *ich will nicht gehen* I don't want to go, I will not go. *wollen Sie bitte ...* would you please .... *tun Sie, was Sie wollen* do as you please.
wollen[2] *adj* woollen, (*US*) woolen.
wollig ['vɔliç] *adj* woolly.
Wollust ['vɔlust] *f* lust, voluptuousness.
wollüstig ['vɔlʏstiç] *adj* lustful, voluptuous, sensual.
wo‖mit *adv* with which; (*Frage*) with what? **-nach** *adv* after which, whereupon.
Wonne ['vɔnə] *f* (*pl* -n) bliss; (*Freude*) joy; (*Entzücken*) rapture.
woran [vo'ran] *adv* on which. **woran denkst du?** what are you thinking about? **woran liegt es, daß ... ?** how is it that ... ? **wo‖rauf** *adv* upon which, whereup-on. **-raus** *adv* from which, whence. **-rin** *adv* in(to) which.

Wort [vɔrt] **1** *neut* (*pl* **Wörter**) word. **2** *neut* (*pl* **Worte**) (spoken) word.
Wörterbuch ['vœrtərbux] *neut* dictionary.
wörtlich *adj* literal.
Wort‖schatz *m* vocabulary. **-spiel** *neut* pun.
wovon [vo'fɔn] of *or* from which; (*Frage*) from what? *wovon lebt er?* what does he live on? *wovon spricht er?* what is he talking about? **wozu** *adv* to which; (*warum*) what ... for, why.
Wrack [vrak] *neut* (*pl* -s) wreck.
***wringen** ['vriŋən] *v* wring.
Wucher ['vuːxər] *m* profiteering. **wuchern** *v* profiteer; (*Pflanze*) proliferate, be rampant. **Wucherpreis** *m* exorbitant price.
Wuchs [*m* (*pl* **Wüchse**) growth; (*Körperbau*) physique, build.
Wucht [vuxt] *f* (*pl* -en) weight, impetus, force. **wuchtig** *adj* heavy, weighty.
wülen ['vyːlən] *v* root, dig; (*durchstöbern*) rummage; (*Gefühle*) well up. **sich wühlen in** burrow into. **wühlerisch** *adj* subversive.
Wulst [vulst] *m* (*pl* **Wülste**) swelling, bulge. **wulstig** *adj* swollen.
wund [vunt] *adj* sore. **Wunde** *f* (*pl* -n) wound.
Wunder ['vundər] *neut* (*pl* -) miracle, wonder. **wunderbar** *adj* wonderful, marvellous. **Wunder‖kind** *neut* child prodigy. **-land** *neut* fairy-land. **wunder‖lich** *adj* odd, strange, peculiar. **-n** *v* surprise, astonish. **sich wundern über** be astonished by, wonder at. **wunderschön** *adj* (very) beautiful. **Wundertat** *f* miracle, miraculous feat.
Wunsch [vunʃ] *m* (*pl* **Wünsche**) wish, desire.
wünschen ['vynʃən] *v* wish, desire. **-swert** *adj* desirable.
Würde ['vyrdə] *f* (*pl* -n) dignity; (*Ehre*) honour. **würde‖los** *adj* undignified. **-voll** *adj* dignified. **würdig** *adj* worthy. **-en** *v* appreciate. **Würdigung** *f* (*pl* -en) appreciation.
Wurf [vurf] *m* (*pl* **Würfe**) throw, cast; (*Tiere*) litter, brood.
Würfel ['vyrfəl] *m* (*pl* -) cube; (*Spielstein*) die.
würgen ['vyrgən] *v* choke; (*erwürgen*) strangle, throttle.

Wurm [vurm] *m* (*pl* **Würmer**) worm.
wurmig *adj* worm-eaten.
Wurst [vurst] *f* (*pl* **Würste**) sausage.
Würstchen ['vyrstçən] *neut* (*pl* -) (small)
sausage; (*Mensch*) little man, insignificant person.
Würze ['vyrtsə] *f* (*pl* -n) seasoning, spice.
Wurzel ['vyrtsəl] *f* (*pl* -n) root. **wurzeln** *v*
take root; (*fig*) be rooted in.
würzen ['vyrtsən] *v* season, spice. **würzig**
adj seasoned, spiced.
wüst [vyːst] *adj* desert, desolate; (*wirr*)
disorderly; (*Person*) coarse, vile. **Würste**
f (*pl* -n) desert, waste.
wut [vuːt] *f* rage, fury.
wüten ['vyːtən] *v* rage, be furious. **–d** *adj*
furious.

X

X-Beine ['iksbainə] *pl* knock-knees. **X-
beinig** *adj* knock-kneed.
x-mal ['iksmaːl] *adj* (*umg.*) many times, *n*
times.
X-Strahlen ['iksʃtraːlən] *pl* x-rays.

Z

Zacke ['tsakə] *f* (*pl* -n) *or* **Zacken** *m* (*pl* -)
point, jag; (*Gabel*) prong; (*Kamm*) tooth.
zackig *adj* pointed, jagged; pronged;
toothed.
zaghaft ['tsaːkhaft] *adj* timid.
zäh [tsɛː] *adj* tough; (*Flüssigkeit*) thick;
(*Person*) stubborn.
Zahl [tsaːl] *f* (*pl* -en) number; (*Ziffer*)
figure, numeral. **zahlbar** *adj* payable.
zahlen *v* pay.
zählbar ['tsɛːlbaːr] *adj* countable. **zählen** *v*
count; (*Sport*) keep the score. **zählen auf**
count *or* rely on.
Zahler ['tsaːlər] *m* (*pl* -) payer.
Zähler ['tsɛːlər] *m* (*pl* -) counter; (*Bank*)
teller; (*Gerät*) meter, recorder.
zahl‖los *adj* countless. **–reich** *adj* numerous. **Zahl‖tag** *m* payday. **–ung** *f* (*pl* -en)
payment.
Zählung ['tsɛːluŋ] *f* (*pl* -en) counting;
(*Volkszählung*) census.
zahlungs‖fähig [*adj* (*Komm*) solvent.
–unfähig *adj* insolvent.

zahm [tsaːm] *adj* tame.
zähmen ['tsɛːmən] *v* tame.
Zahn [tsaːn] *m* (*pl* **Zähne**) tooth. **–arzt** *m*
dentist. **–bürste** *f* toothbrush. **–fleisch**
neut gum, gums *pl*. **–paste** *f* toothpaste.
–rad *neut* cogwheel, gearwheel.
–schmerz *m* toothache.
Zange ['tsaŋə] *f* (*pl* -n) pliers *pl*, tongs *pl*;
(*Pinzette*) tweezers *pl*.
Zank [tsaŋk] *m* (*pl* **Zänke**) quarrel.
zanken *v* scold. **sich zanken** quarrel.
Zapfen ['tsapfən] *m* (*pl* -) plug, bung;
(*Bot*) cone.
zappelig ['tsapəliç] *adj* fidgety. **zappeln** *v*
fidget.
Zar [tsaːr] *m* (*pl* -en) tsar, czar. **–in** *f* (*pl*
-nen) tsarina.
zart [tsaːrt] *adj* (*Fleisch, Gemüt*) tender;
(*sanft*) gentle, soft; (*zerbrechlich*) delicate. **–heit** *f* tenderness; gentleness.
zärtlich ['tsɛːrtliç] *adj* tender, loving,
affectionate. **Zärtlichkeit** *f* tenderness,
affection.
Zauber ['tsaubər] *m* (*pl* -) magic. **–bann**
m spell, charm. **–ei** *f* magic, sorcery.
–er *m* (*pl* -) magician, sorcerer. **–erin** *f*
(*pl* -nen) magician, sorceress. **zauberhaft**
adj magical. **Zauber‖kunst** *f* sorcery;
(*Sinnestäuschung*) conjuring. **–künstler**
m conjurer. **–kunststück** *neut* conjuring
tricks *pl*. **zaubern** *v* practise magic;
(*Zauberkunst*) conjure. **Zauberspruch** *m*
magic spell.
zaudern ['tsaudərn] *v* hesitate, waver.
Zaum [tsaum] *m* (*pl* **Zäume**) rein, bridle.
zäumen ['tsɔymən] *v* (*Pferd*) bridle; (*fig*)
curb, restrain.
Zaun [tsaun] *m* (*pl* **Zäune**) fence; (*Hecke*)
hedge.
Zebra ['tseːbra] *neut* (*pl* -s) zebra.
Zeche ['tsɛçə] *f* (*pl* -n) (*Gasthaus*) bill;
(*Bergwerk*) mine, pit.
Zehe ['tseːə] *f* (*pl* -n) toe. **–nspitze** *f* tip
of the toe.
zehn [tseːn] *pron, adj* ten. **zehnte** *adj*
tenth. **Zehntel** *neut* tenth (part).
zehren ['tseːrən] *v* **zehren an** (*fig*) gnaw
at. **zehren von** live *or* feed on.
Zeichen ['tsaiçən] *neut* (*pl* -) sign;
(*Merkmal*) mark; (*Signal*) signal;
(*Hinweis*) indication. **–brett** *neut* drawing board. **–(trick)film** *m* animated cartoon. **zeichnen** *v* draw; (*kennzeichnen*)
mark; (*unterschreiben*) sign; (*Muster*)

design. **Zeichnung** *f* drawing; marking; (*Muster*) design.
Zeigefinger ['tsaigəfiŋər] *m* forefinger, index finger. **zeigen** *v* point out, show; (*zur Schau stellen*) show, display; (*beweisen*) demonstrate, show. **Zeiger** *m* pointer, indicator; (*Uhr*) hand.
Zeile ['tsailə] *f* (*pl* -n) line.
Zeit [tsait] *f* (*pl* -en) time. **auf Zeit** on credit. **freie Zeit** spare *or* free time. **für alle Zeiten** for all time. **in kurzer Zeit** shortly, soon. **Zeit‖alter** *neut* age, era. −**folge** *f* chronological order. −**geist** *m* spirit of the age.
Zeitgenosse ['tsaitgənɔsə] *m* (*pl* -n), **Zeitgenossin** *f* (*pl* -nen) contemporary. **zeitgenössisch** *adj* contemporary.
zeitig ['tsaitiç] *adj* early.
Zeit‖karte *f* season ticket. −**lang** *f* while. **ein Zeitlang** for some time, for a while. **Zeitlauf** *m* course of time.
zeitlich ['tsaitliç] *adj* temporal.
Zeit‖punkt *m* (point in) time, moment. −**raum** *m* period. −**schrift** *f* magazine, periodical.
Zeitung ['tsaituŋ] *f* (*pl* -en) newspaper. **Zeitungs‖anzeigt** *f* newspaper advertisement. −**ausschnitt** *m* press cutting. −**händler** *m* newsagent. −**stand** *m* newsstand, kiosk. −**wesen** *neut* the press, journalism.
Zeit‖verschwendung *f* waste of time. −**vertrieb** *m* pastime, diversion. **zeitweilig** *adj* temporary.
Zeitwort ['tsaitvɔrt] *neut* verb.
Zelle ['tsɛlə] *f* (*pl* -n) cell.
Zelt [tsɛlt] *neut* (*pl* -e) tent. −**decke** *f* awning, canopy. **zelten** *v* camp. **Zeltplatz** *m* camp.
Zement [tse'mɛnt] *m* (*pl* -e) cement.
Zensur [tsɛn'zuːr] *f* (*pl* -en) censorship; (*Schule*) mark.
Zentimeter [tsɛnti'meːtər] *m or neut* centimetre.
Zentner ['tsɛntnər] *m* (*pl* -) hundredweight, 50 kilos.
zentral [tsɛn'traːl] *adj* central. **Zentrale** *f* (*pl* -n) central office; (*Telef*) telephone exchange. **Zentral‖heizung** *f* central heating. −**isierung** *f* centralization. **Zentrum** *neut* (*pl* **Zentren**) centre.
zerbrechen [tsɛr'brɛçən] *v* break (in pieces), shatter. **zerbrechlich** *adj* fragile, breakable.

zerdrücken [tsɛr'drykən] *v* crush; (*Kleider*) crumple, crease.
Zeremonie [tseremo'niː] *f* (*pl* -n) ceremony. **zeremoniell** *adj* ceremonial.
Zerfall [tsɛr'fal] *m* decay, disintegration; (*Chem*) decomposition. **zerfallen** *v* disintegrate, fall to pieces; (*auflösen*) dissolve. **zer fallen mit** fall out with.
zerfetzen [tsɛr'fɛtsən] *v* shred, tear up.
***zerfressen** [tsɛr'frɛsən] *v* gnaw; (*Chem*) corrode.
***zergehen** [tsɛr'geːən] *v* melt.
zergliedern [tsɛr'gliːdərn] *v* dismember; (*fig*) analyse.
zerhacken [tsɛr'hakən] *v* chop up, chop into pieces.
zerkleinern [tsɛr'klainərn] *v* cut up, chop up.
zerlegen [tsɛr'leːgən] *v* take apart, separate; (*Fleisch*) carve; (*fig*) analyse. **Zerlegung** *f* (*pl* -en) taking apart; carving; analysis.
zerlumpt [tsɛr'lumpt] *adj* ragged.
zermahlen [tsɛr'maːlən] *v* grind.
zermürben [tsɛr'myrbən] *v* wear down. **Zermürbung** *f* attrition. −**skrieg** *m* war of attrition.
zerplatzen [tsɛr'platsən] *v* explode, burst.
zerquetschen [tsɛr'kvɛtʃən] *v* squash, crush.
Zerrbild ['tsɛrbilt] *neut* distortion, caricature.
***zerreißen** [tsɛr'raisən] *v* tear up/to pieces; (*entzweigehen*) rip, tear, break.
zerren [tsɛrən] *v* tug, pull; (*Med*) strain, pull. **Zerrung** *f* (*pl* -en) (*Med*) strain.
zerschellen [tsɛr'ʃɛlən] *v* be dashed to pieces.
***zerschlagen** [tsɛr'ʃlaːgən] *v* knock *or* smash to pieces.
zerschlissen [tsɛr'ʃlisən] *adj* tattered, shredded.
***zerschneiden** [tsɛr'ʃnaidən] *v* cut up.
zersetzen [tsɛr'zɛtsən] *v* disintegrate; (*untergraben*) undermine, demoralize. **sich zersetzen** disintegrate; (*Chem*) decompose. **Zersetzung** *f* disintegration.
zersplittern [tsɛr'ʃplitərn] *v* splinter, shatter; (*fig*) split up. **Zersplitterung** *f* splintering; splitting-up.
zersprengen [tsɛr'ʃprɛŋən] *v* blow up, burst (open).
zerstäuben *v* pulverize; (*Flüssigkeit*) spray, atomize. **Zerstäuber** *m* spray atomizer.

zerstören [tsɛr'ʃtœɪrən] v destroy. **-d** adj destructive. **Zerstör‖er** m destroyer. **-ung** f destruction.

zerstreuen [tsɛr'ʃtrɔyən] v disperse, scatter; (unterhalten) amuse, entertain. **zerstreut** adj scattered; (geistig) distracted, absent-minded. **Zerstreuung** f dispersion; distraction; (Unterhaltung) amusement.

zerteilen [tsɛr'tailən] v divide, separate; (zerstückeln) cut up.

*zertreten [tsɛr'treɪtən] v tread on, trample on.

zertrümmern [tsɛr'trymərn] v smash, wreck; (vernichten) destroy.

zerzausen [tsɛr'tsauzən] v rumple, tousle. **zerzaust** adj tousled, dishevelled.

zetern ['tseɪtərn] v cry out, shout (for help).

Zettel ['tsɛtəl] m (pl -) slip (of paper); (Merkzettel) note; (Preis) ticket.

Zeug [tsɔyk] neut (pl -e) material, stuff; (Arbeitsgeräte) tools pl; (allerlei Dinge) stuff, things pl.

Zeuge ['tsɔygə] m (pl -n) witness.

zeugen¹ ['tsɔygən] v testify, give evidence. **von etwas zeugen** be evidence of something.

zeugen² v (Kind) procreate, beget; (fig) generate, produce.

Zeugen‖bank f witness box. **-beweis** m evidence. **Zeugin** (pl -nen) f (female) witness. **Zeugnis** neut evidence, testimony; (Bescheinigung) certificate; (Schule) report.

Zeugung ['tsɔyguŋ] f (pl -en) generation, procreation.

Zickzack ['tsiktsak] m (pl -e) zigzag.

Ziege ['tsiɪgə] f (pl -n) goat.

Ziegel ['tsiɪgəl] m (pl -) (Backstein) brick; (Dachziegel) (roof-)tile. **-stein** m brick.

Ziegen‖bock m billy goat. **-leder** neut kid (leather), goatskin. **-milch** f goat's milk.

*ziehen ['tsiɪən] v pull, draw; (Zeichnen) draw; (strecken) stretch; (wandern) wander; (marschieren) march; (Tee) infuse; (Zigarre) draw or pull (on); (umziehen) move. **es zieht** (Luft) there is a draught. **sich in die Länge ziehen** drag on.

Ziel [tsiɪl] neut (pl -e) aim, goal; (Geschoß) target; (Wettlauf) finish. **ziel‖en** v aim (at). **-los** adj aimless. **Zielscheibe** f target.

ziemlich ['tsiːmliç] adj considerable. adv rather, moderately.

Zier [tsiːr] f (pl -en) decoration. **zier‖en** v decorate. **sich zieren** be affected, behave with affectation. **-lich** adj dainty; (elegant) elegant.

Ziffer ['tsifər] f (pl -n) cipher, numeral. **-blatt** neut clock-face.

Zigarette [tsiga'rɛtə] f (pl -n) cigarette. **Zigaretten‖etui** neut cigarette case. **-stümmel** m cigarette end. **Zigarre** f (pl -n) cigar.

Zigeuner [tsi'gɔynər] m (pl -), **Zigeunerin** f (pl -nen) Gipsy.

Zimmer ['tsimər] neut (pl -) room. **-arbeit** f carpentry. **-mann** m carpenter. **-spiel** neut (parlour) game.

zimperlich ['tsimpərliç] adj prim.

Zimt [tsimt] m (pl -e) cinnamon.

Zink [tsiŋk] neut zinc.

Zinke ['tsiŋkə] f (pl -n) prong; (Kamm) tooth.

Zinn [tsin] neut tin. **zinnern** adj tin. **Zinnfolie** f tinfoil.

Zins [tsins] m (pl -en) (Miete) rent; (Abgabe) tax, duty. **Zinsen** pl interest. **Zinsfuß** m rate of interest.

Zipfel ['tsipfəl] m (pl -) tip; (Ecke) corner.

Zirkel ['tsiɪrkəl] m (pl -) (Kreis) circle; (Gerät) (pair of) compasses pl.

Zirkus ['tsirkus] m (pl -se) circus.

zirpen ['tsirpən] v chirp.

zischen ['tsiʃən] v kiss.

Zitat [tsi'taɪt] neut (pl -e) quotation, quote. **zitieren** v quote, cite; (vorladen) summon.

Zitrone [tsi'troɪnə] f (pl -n) lemon.

zittern ['tsitərn] v tremble, shake.

Zitze ['tsitsə] f (pl -n) nipple, teat.

zivil [tsi'viɪl] adj civil. **Zivilisation** f (unz.) civilization. **zivil‖isieren** v civilize. **-isiert** adj civilized, cultured. **Zivil‖ist** m (pl -en) civilian. **-kleidung** f civilian clothes pl.

zögern ['tsœɪgərn] v hesitate.

Zoll¹ [tsɔl] m (pl -e) (Längenmaß) inch.

Zoll² m (pl Zölle) (customs) duty; (umg.: Zollabfertigungsstelle) customs pl.

Zoll‖abfertigung f customs clearance. **-beamte(r)** m customs official.

Zone ['tsoɪnə] f (pl -n) zone.

Zoo [tsoɪ] m (pl -s) zoo. **-loge** m (pl -n) zoologist. **-logie** f zoology. **zoologisch** adj zoological.

Zopf [tsɔpf] m (pl **Zöpfe**) plait, pigtail.
Zorn [tsɔrn] m anger. **zornig** adj angry.
zu [tsuː] prep (Richtung) to, toward(s);
(Ziet, Ort) at, in; (neben) beside. adv too;
(geschlossen) closed, shut. **zu Hause** at
home. **zu verkaufen** for sale. **zu Mittag** at
noon. **zu Fuß** on foot. **ab und zu** now
and then. **um zu** in order to.
Zubehör ['tsuːbəhœɪr] neut (pl -e) fittings
pl; (Tech) accessories pl. **-teil** neut
attachment, accessory.
zubereiten ['tsuːbəraitən] v prepare.
***zubringen** ['tsuːbriŋən] v bring or take
(to); (Zeit) spend.
Zucht [tsuxt] 1 f (unz.) discipline;
(Pflanzen) cultivation, breeding; (Vieh)
rearing, breeding. 2 f (pl -en) breed.
züchten ['tsyçtən] v breed. **Züchter** m
breeder; (Bienen) beekeeper; (Pflanzen)
grower.
züchtigen ['tsyçtigen] v punish, discipline.
Züchtigung f (pl -en) punishment.
zuchtlos ['tsuxtloɪs] adj undisciplined.
Zuck [tsuk] m (pl -e) jerk. **zucken** v start,
jerk.
Zucker ['tsukər] m sugar. **zuckerkrank** adj
diabetic. **Zucker‖kranke(r)** m diabetic.
-krankheit f diabetes. **-rohr** m sugar-
cane.
zudecken ['tsuːdɛkən] v cover (up).
zudem [tsu'deɪm] adv moreover, besides.
zudrehen ['tsuːdreɪən] v turn off.
zudringlich ['tsuːdriŋliç] adj importunate,
pushing.
zueinander [tsuain'andər] adv to each
other.
zuerst [tsu'eɪrst] adv (at) first.
Zufahrt ['tsuːfaɪrt] f approach, driving in.
-straße f access road; (Haus) driveway.
Zufall ['tsuːfal] m chance, accident. **glück-
licher Zufall** happy coincidence. **zufällig**
adj accidental, chance; adv by chance,
accidentally.
Zuflucht ['tsuːfluxt] f refuge, shelter.
Zufluß ['tsuːfluss] m influx; (Fluß) tributary; (Waren) supply.
zufolge [tsu'fɔlgə] prep owing to, in consequence of.
zufrieden [tsu'friːdən] adj contented.
Zufriedenheit f content(ment). **zufriedenstellen** v satisfy.
zufügen ['tsuːfyɪgən] v add (to); (Böses)
inflict (on).
Zufuhr ['tsuːfuɪr] f (pl -en) supply.
zuführen v supply; (zuleiten) lead to.

Zug [tsuɪk] m (pl **Züge**) pull; (Eisenbahn)
train; (Charakter) trait; (Gesicht) feature; (Luft) draught; (Schub) thrust;
(Brettspiel) move; (Einatmen) inhalation;
(Rauchen) puff, pull; (Festzug) procession; (Zeichnen) stroke, dash; (Umriß)
outline; (Vögel) migration.
Zugabe ['tsuɪgaɪbə] f addition; (Zuschlag)
extra.
Zugang ['tsuɪgaŋ] m entry, access; (Eingang) entrance; accession. **zugänglich** adj
accessible; (Mensch) approachable.
Zugbrücke ['tsuɪgbrykə] f drawbridge.
***zugeben** ['tsuɪgeɪbən] v add; (einräumen)
admit; (gestatten) permit.
zugegen [tsu'geɪgən] adj present.
***zugehen** ['tsuɪgeɪən] v close, be closed;
(weitergehen) go on; (geschehen) happen.
zugehören ['tsuɪgəhœɪrən] v belong (to).
Zügel ['tsyɪgəl] m (pl -) rein(s); (fig) curb.
zügel‖los adj unrestrained, unbridled.
-n v rein; (beherrschen) control, curb.
Zugeständnis ['tsuɪgəʃtɛntnis] neut concession.
***zugestehen** ['tsuɪgəʃteɪən] v admit, con-
cede.
Zugführer ['tsuɪkfyɪrər] m (Eisenbahn)
guard, (US) conductor.
***zugießen** ['tsugiɪsən] v pour (in).
zugig ['tsuɪgiç] adj draughty.
Zugluft ['tsuɪgluft] f draught.
***zugreifen** ['tsuɪgraifən] v grasp, grab;
(helfen) lend a hand; (bei Tisch) help
oneself.
zugrunde [tsu'grundə] adv **zugrunde
gehen** v perish, be ruined.
zugunsten [tsu'gunstən] prep in favour of.
zugute [tsu'guɪtə] adv to one's advantage.
zugute halten v take into consideration,
allow for.
***zuhalten** ['tsuɪhaltən] v keep shut.
zuhalten auf head for. **Zuhälter** m pimp.
zuhanden [tsu'handən] adj (ready) at
hand, ready.
Zuhause [tsuhauzə] f (unz.) home.
zuhören ['tsuːhœɪrən] v listen. **Zuhörer** m
(pl -), **Zuhörerin** f (pl -nen) listener.
Zuhörer pl audience sing; (Radio) listen-
ers.
zuklappen ['tsuɪklapən] v slam, clap shut.
zuknöpfen ['tsuɪknœpfən] v button up.
***zukommen** ['tsuɪkɔmən] v (gebühren)
befit. **zukommen lassen** send, supply.
zukommen auf come up to.

Zukunft ['tsuːkunft] *f* future. **zukünftig** *adj* future; *adv* in (the) future.

Zulage ['tsuːlaɪgə] *f* extra pay, bonus.

zulänglich ['tsuːlɛŋlɪç] *adj* sufficient.

*zulassen ['tsuːlasən] *v* permit, admit; (*hereinlassen*) let in, admit. **zulässig** *adj* permissible. **Zulassung** *f* permission; admission; (*Mot*) registration. **–sschein** *m* permit, licence.

zuleiten ['tsuːlaitən] *v* lead to.

zuletzt [tsuˈlɛtst] *adv* finally, last.

zuliebe [tsuˈliːbə] *adv* **jemandem zuliebe** to please someone.

Zulieferer ['tsuːliːfərər] *m* (*pl* -) subcontractor.

zum [tsum] *prep + art* **zu dem.**

zumachen ['tsuːmaxən] *v* shut, close.

zumeist [tsuˈmaist] *adv* mostly.

zumindest [tsuˈmindəst] *adv* at least.

zumute [tsuˈmuːtə] *adv* **gut/schlecht zumute sein** be in high/low spirits.

zumuten ['tsuːmuːtən] *v* expect, demand. **Zumutung** *f* presumption, unreasonable expectation.

zunächst [tsuˈnɛːçst] *adv* first (of all). *prep* near, close to.

Zunahme ['tsuːnaːmə] *f* (*pl* -n) increase.

Zuname ['tsuːnaːmə] *m* surname.

zünden ['tsyndən] *v* catch fire,. light; (*Mot, Tech*) ignite.

Zunder ['tsundər] *m* (*pl* -) tinder.

Zünder ['tsyndər] *m* (*pl* -) fuse, detonator. **Zünd‖kerze** *f* sparking plug. **–schlüssel** *m* ignition key. **–ung** *f* ignition; (*Sprengladung*) detonation.

*zunehmen ['tsuːneimən] *v* increase; (*wachsen*) grow; (*dicker werden*) put on weight. **–d** *adj* increasing, accelerating.

zuneigen ['tsuːnaigən] *v* incline, lean; (*fig*) incline, tend. **Zuneigung** *f* inclination; (*Sympathie*) affection.

Zunft [tsunft] *f* (*pl* **Zünfte**) guild.

Zunge ['tsuŋə] *f* (*pl* -n) tongue. **zungenfertig** *adj* glib, fluent.

zunichte [tsuˈnɪçtə] *adv* **zunichte machen** (*Hoffnungen*) destroy, shatter; (*Pläne*) frustrate.

zunicken ['tsuːnikən] *v* nod to.

zunutze [tsuˈnutsə] *adv* **sich etwas zunutze machen** utilize something, put something to use.

zuoberst [tsuˈoːbərst] *adv* at the top.

zupfen ['tsupfən] *v* pluck; (*Fasern*) pick.

zur [tsuːr] *prep + art* **zu der.**

zurechnen ['tsuːrɛçnən] *v* (*zuschreiben*) ascribe, attribute. **Zurechnung** *f* attribution.

zurecht [tsuˈrɛçt] *adv* right, correctly, in order. **sich zurechtfinden** *v* find one's way. **zurechtkommen** *v* arrive in time. **zurechtkommen mit** get along with. **zurecht‖machen** *v* prepare. **–weisen** *v* reprimand.

zureden ['tsuːreidən] *v* urge, coax.

zureichen ['tsuːraiçən] *v* (*ausreichen*) do, be enough; (*hinreichen*) hand, pass. **–d** *adj* sufficient.

zurichten ['tsuːriçtən] *v* prepare, get ready; (*umg.*) mess up, make a mess of.

zürnen ['tsyrnən] *v* be angry.

zurück [tsuˈryk] *adv* back(wards); (*hinten*) behind. **–behalten** *v* keep back, detain. **–bekommen** *v* get back, recover. **–bezahlen** *v* refund, pay back. **–bleiben** *v* remain behind. **–blicken** *v* look back. **–bringen** *v* bring back. **–datieren** *v* backdate; (*stammen aus*) date back. **–erstatten** *v* return, restore; (*ausgelegtes Geld*) reimburse. **–fahren** *v* drive back; (*vor Schreck*) recoil, start.

Zurückgabe [tsuˈrykgaibə] *f* restitution, restoration. **zurückgeben** *v* give back, restore.

zurück‖gehen *v* go back, return; (*nachlassen*) decrease, fall off. **zurückgehen auf** originate in, go back to. **–gezogen** *adj* retiring, withdrawn.

zurückhalten [tsuˈrykhaltən] *v* (*Person*) keep, detain; (*Sache*) retain, withhold. **–d** *adj* reserved; (*vorsichtig*) cautious. **Zurückhaltung** *f* reserve.

zurück‖kehren *v* return. **–kommen** *v* come back; (*wieder aufgreifen*) revert (to). **–legen** *v* put aside; (*Geld*) put by. **–melden** *v* report back.

Zurücknahme [tsuˈryknaimə] *f* (*pl* -n) withdrawal, taking back. **zurücknehmen** *v* take back; (*Worte*) withdraw; (*Anordnung, Auftrag*) cancel.

zurück‖scheuen *v* shrink back (from), shy (at). **–schicken** *v* send back. **–setzen** *v* put *or* place back; (*herabsetzen*) reduce; (*Person*) neglect, slight. **–strahlen** *v* reflect. **–reten** *v* step back; (*vom Posten*) resign, retire. **–weisen** *v* refuse, reject. **–zahlen** *v* pay back, repay. **–ziehen** *v* draw back, withdraw. **sich zurückziehen** withdraw, retire.

Zuruf ['tsuːruːf] *m* shout. **zurufen** *v* shout, call.

Zusage ['tsuːzaːgə] *f* promise; (*Bejahung*) assent, consent. **zusagen** *v* (*versprechen*) promise; (*Einladung*) accept, agree to come; (*gefallen*) suit, please.

zusammen [tsu'zamən] *adv* together; (*insgesamt*) all told, all together.

Zusammenarbeit *f* cooperation. **zusammenarbeiten** *v* cooperate.

zusammenballen *v* roll up; (*Faust*) clench. **sich zusammenballen** gather.

*****zusammenbrechen** *v* collapse, break down. **Zusammenbruch** *m* collapse.

zusammendrängen *v* **sich zusammendrängen** crowd together.

*****zusammen‖fahren** *v* travel together; (*aufeinanderstoßen*) collide; (*zusammenschrecken*) wince, start. **–fallen** *v* fall down, collapse; coincide.

zusammenfassen *v* summarize. **–d** *adj* comprehensive. **Zusammenfassung** *f* summary.

zusammengesetzt *adj* composed, compounded.

Zusammenhang *m* (*Verbindung*) connection; (*Text*) context. **zusammenhängen** *v* (*verbunden sein*) be connected. **–d** *adj* coherent.

zusammenklappen *v* fold up.

Zusammenkunft *f* (*pl* **Zusammenkünfte**) meeting.

zusammen‖legen *v* put together; (*falten*) fold (up); (*vereinigen*) combine; (*Geld*) pool. **–passen** *v* go (well) together, match; (*Menschen*) get on well.

Zusammenprall *m* collision. **zusammenprallen** *v* collide.

*****zusammenschließen** *v* join together. **sich zusammenschließen** unite. **Zusammenschluß** *m* union, merger.

zusammensetzen *v* put together, construct. **sich zusammensetzen** sit down with one another; (*bestehen*) consist (of). **Zusammensetz‖spiel** *neut* jigsaw puzzle. **–ung** *f* composition.

zusammenstellen *v* (*vereinigen*) join; (*vergleichen*) compare.

Zusammenstoß *m* collision; (*Streit*) clash, conflict. **zusammenstoßen** *v* collide; clash, conflict.

Zusammentreffen *neut* coincidence; (*Begegnung*) encounter, meeting.

*****zusammenziehen** *v* close, draw together; (*verkürzen*) shorten, contract;

(*verbinden*) join together; (*sammeln*) gather. **sich zusammenziehen** (*Stoff*) shrink. **Zusammenziehung** *f* shrinking; contraction.

Zusatz ['tsuːzats] *m* addition; (*Ergänzung*) supplement; (*Anhang*) appendix. **zusätzlich** *adj* additional, extra.

zuschauen ['tsuːʃauən] *v* watch, look on, observe. **Zuschauer** *m* (*pl* -), **Zuschauerin** *f* (*pl* -nen) spectator, onlooker.

Zuschlag ['tsuːʃlaːk] *m* surcharge, extra charge. **zuschlagen** *v* hit (out); (*Tür*) slam (shut).

*****zuschließen** ['tsuːʃliːsən] *v* lock (up).

*****zuschneiden** ['tsuːʃnaidən] *v* cut out. **Zuschnitt** *m* cut, style.

*****zuschreiben** ['tsuːʃraibən] *v* attribute, ascribe; (*übertragen*) transfer to. *das hast du dir selbst zuzuschreiben* you have yourself to blame for that.

Zuschuß ['tsuːʃus] *m* subsidy, allowance.

*****zusehen** ['tsuːzeːən] *v* look on, watch. **zusehen, daß** see to it that.

*****zusenden** ['tsuːzɛndən] *v* send on, forward.

zusetzen ['tsuːzɛtsən] *v* (*hinzufügen*) add; (*verlieren*) lose; (*bedrängen*) press, importune.

Zuspruch ['tsuːʃprux] *m* encouragement, approval.

Zustand ['tsuːʃtant] *m* condition, state.

zustande [tsu'ʃtandə] *adv* **zustande bringen** achieve, bring about. **zustande kommen** come about, materialize.

zuständig ['tsuːʃtɛndiç] *adj* appropriate; competent; responsible.

zustellen ['tsuːʃtɛlən] *v* deliver; (*Klage*) serve on. **Zustellung** *f* (*pl* -en) delivery.

zustimmen ['tsuːʃtimən] *v* consent, agree. **Zustimmung** *f* consent, agreement.

zustopfen ['tsuːʃtopfən] *v* plug (up), stop (up); (*flicken*) darn.

*****zustoßen** ['tsuːʃtoisən] *v* (*Tür*) push to; (*geschehen*) happen (to), befall.

zutage [tsu'taːgə] *adv* **zutage bringen** bring to light.

Zutaten ['tsuːtaːtən] *f pl* ingredients; (*Beiwerk*) trimmings.

zuteilen ['tsuːtailən] *v* assign, allocate; issue. **Zuteilung** *f* allocation.

zutiefst [tsu'tiːfst] *adv* deeply.

*****zutragen** ['tsuːtraːgən] *v* carry to. **sich zutragen** happen, take place. **zuträglich** *adj* beneficial.

zutrauen ['tsuːtrauən] *v* credit (with), believe (of). **Zutrauen** *neut* confidence, trust, faith.

***zutreffen** ['tsuːtrɛfən] *v* be right, be *or* hold true. **-d** *adj* right, accurate.

Zutritt ['tsuːtrɪt] *m* access. **Zutritt verboten!** keep out! no admission!

***zutun** ['tsuːtuːn] *v* (*hinzutun*) add; (*schließen*) shut.

zuverlässig ['tsuːfɛrlɛsɪç] *adj* reliable. **Zuverlässigkeit** *f* reliability.

Zuversicht ['tsuːfɛrzɪçt] *f* confidence, trust. **zuversichtlich** *adj* confident.

zuviel [tsu'fiːl] *adv* too much.

zuvor [tsu'foːr] *adv* before, previously. **-kommen** *v* anticipate.

Zuwachs ['tsuːvaks] *m* growth; (*Vermehrung*) increase.

zuwege [tsu'veːgə] *adv* **zuwege bringen** bring about, cause.

zuweilen [tsu'vailən] *adv* sometimes, at times.

***zuweisen** ['tsuːvaizən] *v* assign, allot.

***zuwenden** ['tsuːvɛndən] *v* turn (towards); (*geben*) present, let have. **sich zuwenden** apply oneself (to).

zuwider [tsu'viːdər] *prep* (*entgegen*) contrary to. *adj* (*widerwärtig*) repugnant.

zuwinken ['tsuːvɪŋkən] *v* wave (to).

***zuziehen** ['tsuːtsiːən] *v* draw together; (*Vorhänge*) draw; (*Wohnung*) move in. **sich zuziehen** incur; (*Med*) contract, catch.

Zwang [tsvaŋ] *m* (*pl* **Zwänge**) compulsion; (*Gewalt*) force; (*Hemmung*) restraint.

zwängen ['tsvɛŋən] *v* force, press.

zwanglos ['tsvaŋloːs] *adj* unconstrained; (*ohne Förmlichkeit*) informal. **Zwangs‖arbeit** *f* hard labour. **-kauf** *m* compulsory purchase. **zwangsläufig** *adj* inevitable.

zwanzig ['tsvantsɪç] *pron, adj* twenty. **zwanzigst** *adj* twentieth.

zwar [tsvaːr] *adv* indeed, certainly. **und zwar** namely, in fact.

Zweck [tsvɛk] *m* (*pl* **-e**) purpose, object; (*Ziel*) goal. *es hat keinen Zweck* it's pointless, it is of no use.

Zwecke ['tsvɛkə] *m* (*pl* **-n**) tack; (*Reißnagel*) drawing pin, (*US*) thumbtack.

zweck‖los *adj* pointless. **-mäßig** *adj* expedient, appropriate. **-s** *prep* for the purpose of.

zwei [tsvai] *pron, adj* two. **zwei‖deutig** *adj* ambiguous. **-erlei** *adj* of two kinds *or* sorts.

Zweifel ['tsvaifəl] *m* (*pl* **-**) doubt. **zweifel‖haft** *adj* doubtful. **-los** *adj* doubtless. **-n** *v* doubt.

Zweig [tsvaik] *m* (*pl* **-e**) branch, twig; (*fig*) branch. **-stelle** *f* branch (office).

zwei‖jährig *adj* two-year-old; (*Bot*) biennial. **-jährlich** *adj* biennial. **-mal** *adv* twice. **-seitig** *adj* two-sided; (*fig*) bilateral. **-sprachig** *adj* bilingual.

zweit [tsvait] *adj* second. **-ens** *adv* secondly. **-klassig** *adj* second-rate.

zweiwöchentlich ['tsvaivœçəntlɪç] *adj* fortnightly.

Zwerchfell ['tsvɛrçfɛl] *neut* diaphragm.

Zwerg [tsvɛrk] *m* (*pl* **-e**) dwarf. **zwergenhaft** *adj* dwarf.

Zwetsche ['tsvɛtʃə] *or* **Zwetschge** *f* (*pl* **-n**) plum.

Zwick [tsvik] *m* (*pl* **-e**) pinch. **zwicken** *v* pinch; (*Fahrschein*) punch, clip.

Zwieback ['tsviːbak] *m* (*pl* **-e**) rusk, biscuit.

Zwiebel ['tsviːbəl] *f* (*pl* **-n**) onion; (*Blumen*) bulb.

Zwiegespräch ['tsviːgərʃprɛç] *neut* dialogue.

Zwielicht ['tsviːlɪçt] *neut* twilight.

Zwiespalt ['tsviːʃpalt] *m* (inner) conflict; (*Uneinigkeit*) dissension, discord.

Zwietracht ['tsviːtraxt] *f* conflict, dissension.

Zwilling ['tsvilɪŋ] *m* (*pl* **-e**) twin. **Zwillinge** *pl* (*Astrol*) Gemini. **Zwillings‖bruder** *m* twin brother. **-schwester** *f* twin sister.

Zwinge ['tsviŋə] *f* (*pl* **-n**) vice.

***zwingen** ['tsviŋən] force, compel; (*leisten können*) manage, cope with.

zwischen ['tsviʃən] *prep* between; (*mitten unter*) among. **Zwischen‖bemerkung** *f* remark, aside. **-händler** *m* middleman. **-raum** *m* (intervening) space, interval. **-satz** *m* insertion. **-stunde** *f* free period, break, interval. **-zeit** *f* interim, interval. **in der Zwischenzeit** (in the) meantime.

zwitschern ['tsvitʃərn] *v* chirp, twitter.

zwo [tsvoː] *V* **zwei**.

zwölf [tsvœlf] *pron, adj* twelve. **zwölft** *adj* twelfth.

zyklisch ['tsyːklɪʃ] *adj* cyclic.

Zyklone [tsy'kloːnə] *f* (*pl* **-n**) low-pressure area, depression.

Zyklus ['tsyːklus] *m* (*pl* **Zyklen**) cycle.
Zylinder [tsi'lindər] *m* (*pl* -) cylinder;
(*Hut*) top hat. **–kopf** *m* cylinder head.
Zyniker ['tsyːnikər] *m* (*pl* -) cynic. **zynisch**
adj cynical.
Zypern ['tsyːpərn] *neut* Cyprus. **Zyprer** *m*
(*pl* -), **Zyprerin** *f* (*pl* -nen) Cypriot.
zyprisch *adj* Cypriot.

THE HIPPOCRENE MASTERING SERIES

MASTERING ARABIC
320 pages, 5 1/2 x 8 1/2
0-87052-922-6 $14.95pb
2 Cassettes
 0-87052-984-6 $12.95
Book and Cassettes Package
0-87052-140-3 $27.90

MASTERING FINNISH
278 pages, 5 1/2 x 8 1/2
0-7818-0233-4 $14.95pb
2 Cassettes
0-7818-0265-2 $12.95
Book and Cassettes Package
0-7818-0266-0 $27.90

MASTERING FRENCH
288 pages, 5 1/2 x 8 1/2
0-87052-055-5 $11.95pb
2 Cassettes
0-87052-060-1 $12.95
Book and Cassettes Package
0-87052-136-5 $24.90

MASTERING GERMAN
340 pages, 5 1/2 x 8 1/2
0-87052-056-3 $11.95pb
2 Cassettes
0-87052-061-X $12.95
Book and Cassettes Package
0-87052-137-3 $24.90

MASTERING ITALIAN
360 pages, 5 1/2 x 8 1/2
0-87052-057-1 $11.95pb
2 Cassettes
0-87052-066-0 $12.95
Book and Cassettes Package
0-87052-138-1 $24.90

MASTERING JAPANESE
368 pages, 5 1/2 x 8 1/2
0-87052-923-4 $14.95pb
2 Cassettes
0-87052-938-8 $12.95
Book and Cassettes Package
0-87052-141-1 $27.90

MASTERING POLISH
288 pages, 5 1/2 x 8 1/2
0-7818-0015-3 $14.95pb
2 Cassettes
0-7818-0016-3 $12.95
Book and Cassettes Package
0-7818-0017-X $27.90

MASTERING RUSSIAN
278 pages, 5 1/2 x 8 1/2
0-7818-0270-9 $14.95
2 Cassettes
0-7818-0270-9 $12.95
Book and Cassettes Package
0-7818-0272-5 $27.90

MASTERING SPANISH
338 pages, 5 1/2 x 8 1/2
0-87052-059-8 $11.95pb
2 Cassettes
0-87052-067-9 $12.95
Book and Cassettes Package
0-87052-139-X $24.90

MASTERING ADVANCED SPANISH
300 pages, 5 1/2 x 8 1/2
0-7818-0081-1   11.95pb
2 Cassettes
0-7818-0089-7 $12.95
Book and Cassettes Package
0-7818-0090-0 $24.90